Professional Oracle® Programming

Professional Oracle® Programming

Rick Greenwald, Robert Stackowiak, Gary Dodge, David Klein, Ben Shapiro,
Christopher G. Chelliah

WILEY
Wiley Publishing, Inc.

Published by Wiley Publishing, Inc., Indianapolis, Indiana

Published simultaneously in Canada

For general information on our other products and services please contact our Customer Care Department within the United States at (800) 762-2974, outside the United States at (317) 572-3993 or fax (317) 572-4002.

Wiley also publishes its books in a variety of electronic formats. Some content that appears in print may not be available in electronic books.

Library of Congress Cataloging-in-Publication Data:

Professional Oracle programming / Rick Greenwald ... [et al.].

p. cm.

Includes indexes.

ISBN-13: 978-0-7645-7482-5 (paper/website)

ISBN-10: 0-7645-7482-5 (paper/website)

1. Oracle (Computer file) 2. Relational databases. I. Greenwald, Rick.

QA76.9.D3P76646 2005

005.75'85--dc22

2005010511

ISBN 13: 978-076-457482-5

ISBN 10: 0-7645-7482-5

Printed in the United States of America

10 9 8 7 6 5 4 3 2 1

1B/QS/QW/QV/IN

About the Authors

Rick Greenwald has been in the technology industry for over 20 years and is the author of 12 previous books, most of them on Oracle. He has been involved with development and databases for his entire career, including stops at Data General, Cognos, Gupta Technologies, and his current employer, Oracle. Computers and computing are a sideline for Rick — his real job is father to his three wonderful girls, with a primary hobby of music appreciation.

Robert Stackowiak is Senior Director of Business Intelligence (BI) in Oracle's Technology Business Unit. He is recognized worldwide for his expertise in business intelligence and data warehousing in leading the North American BI team at Oracle. His background includes over 20 years in IT related roles at Oracle, IBM, Harris Computer Systems, and the U.S. Army Corps of Engineers including management of technical teams, software development, sales and sales consulting, systems engineering, and business development.

Gary Dodge has been focused on database technology since his first COBOL programming job with IMS DB/DC in 1976. He joined Oracle Corporation in 1987 and has served in various management and technical positions within both the sales and consulting divisions. He has been a frequent speaker on database topics at many local and national information technology conferences. In addition to several magazine articles, he is co-author (with Tim Gorman) of *Oracle8 Data Warehousing* and *Essential Oracle8i Data Warehousing*, both published by John Wiley & Sons.

David Klein has been in the technology industry for over 20 years with a variety of companies, including Data General, Wang Laboratories, Gupta Technologies, Oracle, and a few consulting services companies. He has had many roles, including management of application development and database design teams, sales and sales consulting, systems engineering and marketing. Recently, he has focused on developing classroom and online training courses. An active wife and two boys and a 200-year-old house take up any free time.

Ben Shapiro is the president of ObjectArts Inc., a New York City-based technology consulting company, and has been designing database systems with Oracle since 1997. ObjectArts has worked with many large corporate clients developing XML-based publishing tools and web-based applications. Before ObjectArts, Ben worked with several NYC-based startup companies as a technical lead building content management software.

Christopher G. Chelliah joined Oracle as a Consultant in 1995. He brings with him project management, architecture, and development experience from a number of large, multinational sites in the mining, oil and gas, and telecom industries. Chris has been involved with emerging and database technologies for his entire career and is an accomplished software architect with a flair for business development. His expertise has been actively sought by a number of major Oracle clients in Australia, Europe, and the United States. Chris, his wife and two kids are currently in Singapore, where he leads a team defining and executing on innovative E-Government strategies for Oracle's Public Sector industry in Asia Pacific.

Credits

Vice President and Executive Group Publisher
Richard Swadley

Vice President and Publisher
Joseph B. Wikert

Executive Editor
Robert Elliott

Editorial Manager
Mary Beth Wakefield

Senior Production Editor
Geraldine Fahey

Development Editor
Sharon Nash

Production Editor
Felicia Robinson

Technical Editors
Michael Ault, Tim Gorman,
Wiley-Dreamtech India Pvt Ltd

Text Design & Composition
Wiley Composition Services

Acknowledgments

Although there are a number of names listed on the title page of this book, there are many other people involved in the creation of the work you are currently reading.

First and foremost, all of the authors would like to thank Bob Elliott and Sharon Nash for their steady hands on the throttle of this project. Although the birthing of this baby had more than the normal share of labor pains, the worth and beauty of this offspring owes an enormous amount to them.

Rick Greenwald, in particular, would like to thank two people. First of all, the process of writing three (is it three already) titles and several revisions of books with Bob Stackowiak has been a wonderful experience, both professionally and personally. I am delighted to count Bob as a friend, and, thanks to him, I still don't know what BI stands for.

Secondly, throughout my writing career, Steven Feurstein has been a mentor as well as a sterling example of what an author and person should be like. I hope to someday reach his level in terms of writing and, even more importantly, humanity.

And, of course, I would like to thank my family — LuAnn for helping me have a life that supports writing and working, and Elinor Vera, Josephine, and Robin Greenwald for giving me all the inspiration anyone would ever need.

In addition, Rick would like to acknowledge all those people who came through with suggestions and knowledge at crucial times, including Richard Foote, Raj Mattamal and Tyler Muth.

Contents

Introduction

Introduction

Professional Oracle Programming is intended for application developers who use Oracle as their database. As such, this book does not devote much space to topics which are primarily of interest to database administrators, such as backup and recovery. Most importantly, this book is designed to help a programmer understand the database issues that can have a direct impact on the operation and performance of their applications.

What Does This Book Cover?

Although it is impossible to cover all the topics that a professional developer could use to the level of depth required in a single book, this volume attempts to provide a foundation for these developers, as well as guidance and examples of some of the key areas of interest and necessity. These areas include accessing data using SQL, handling issues such as multi-user concurrency and data integrity and security, the basics of programming with Java, PL/SQL and XML, and data warehousing. For a more complete list of topics, please refer to the section called "How Is This Book Structured?" later in this introduction.

Who Is This Book For?

The entire topic of Oracle databases is certainly not a new one. Oracle has been one of, if not the, leading databases in the world for almost two decades now. The standard Oracle documentation runs over 13,000 pages, and leaves out a lot of the good stuff. Determining the proper audience for this book, and writing at a level appropriate for that audience, was the biggest conceptual challenge for all of the authors.

Through discussions early in this project, the authors and publishers of this book came up with a fairly distinct profile of our presumed reader. This book is intended for people whose primary job is to create application systems. They are developers, rather than database administrators.

Following through on this profile, we believe that you, the professional developer, are well informed and skilled in the creation of these application systems. In our experience, even professional developers may think of the database they use as nothing more than a place to store data.

This description of you, the target reader, has guided the selection of topics as well as the actual content of this book.

What You Need to Use This Book

Although you do not necessarily need to have a working instance of an Oracle database to benefit from this book, the book includes many examples that can be run against your Oracle database.

All of the examples have been created against Oracle Database 10g, although, with a few noted exceptions, you could run the examples against Oracle*9i*. Since Oracle is a cross-platform database, the actual operating system that your version of Oracle runs on is unimportant.

All of the examples can be run in either the standard Oracle utilities, such as iSQL*Plus, that come with the product, or a standard development environment, including tools such as TOAD. Directions on how to run the examples are included in Chapter 7 of this book on installing an Oracle database, or in the chapter in which the examples are given.

Most of the screen shots in this book have used a Windows client platform, but that platform is simply a standard used for consistency, not a requirement.

How Is This Book Structured?

In a broad sense, this book is divided up into three main areas — information you need to know about how the Oracle database works, information that can help you to use the capabilities of the Oracle database in creating your application systems, and information to help you achieve optimal performance with your application systems. Although these three areas are covered in the order listed in the book, you will find relevant information for each of these areas throughout all of the chapters, along with tips, techniques, and code samples.

Part I: Oracle Essentials

Although the Oracle database is a standards-compliant SQL database, the architecture of the Oracle database and the way it operates include some unique features that are crucial to your effective use of Oracle. The first part of Oracle for Professional Developers covers topics that every developer must understand in order to use the Oracle database effectively. Please don't think of these chapters as simply introductory material, since some of the information in these chapters can have an enormous effect on the eventual operation of your applications.

The topics covered in this section include:

- A brief introduction to the architecture and components of the Oracle database
- A detailed look at how Oracle processes your SQL requests and the impact this can have on your application code
- A description of how Oracle handles data access by multiple users, and how this impacts your application design
- A primer on effective database design
- A discussion on how Oracle administers security and how you can use this for your applications

- An overview of the Oracle data dictionary, which contains information about the objects and operations of a specific Oracle database
- A brief tutorial on installing an Oracle database

Part II: Data Topics

The second section of this book focuses on how to access and manipulate the data in the Oracle database. The topics in this section are relevant to all developers, regardless of the language they are using to implement their applications.

The topics covered in this section include:

- An introdution to both basic SQL and some of the more sophisticated uses of this powerful data access language
- Indexes, which help to speed the performance of data retrieval
- Constraints, which are used to both validate and limit the data added to your Oracle database
- A discussion of a variety of other database objects, such as sequences
- The use of functions, both built-ins that come with the Oracle database and your own custom defined functions
- A discussion of data manipulation as a distributed database environment

Part III: Database Programming Languages

The Oracle database allows you to include logic that runs in the database itself.Traditionally, the language used for this work is PL/SQL — a set of procedural extensions based on the SQL language. Oracle8*i* introduced a Java engine into the database, which allowed you to use this language for implementing procedural logic in the database.

Part III of this book includes three chapters on PL/SQL and one on Java. The PL/SQL chapters are divided into one on the basics of PL/SQL, one on using PL/SQL in conjunction with SQL, and one of PL/SQL packages, which are a way of organizing and exposing the logic you create with PL/SQL.

Part IV: Programming Techniques

Part IV of this book dives into the wide and varied area of implementing logic with various programming techniques to use in the database and your applications.

The topics covered include:

- The use of triggers, which contain logic that is automatically executed whenever certain types of data access and manipulation are performed
- Regular expressions, which are a powerful syntax for implementing matching conditions, and the expression filter — both of these features are new with Oracle Database 10*g*

- The use of your Oracle database with object types, both for storage and for interactions with objects in your applications
- The use of Oracle with XML
- HTML-DB, a development environment that comes as part of Oracle Database 10*g*

Part V: Business Intelligence Techniques

Business intelligence describes the process of using raw data in a database as the raw material for analysis that can affect the direction of business operations. Business intelligence in the Oracle database encompasses the use of several specific features and techniques, which are covered in this section.

The topics covered include:

- Moving data between different databases, which is often used to take data from an OLTP system to a system used for business intelligence
- Data loading and management, which covers the manipulations that are sometimes required to prepare data for use in business intelligence operations
- And specific query features used for business intelligence, such as analytic functions

Part VI: Optimization

Creating an application is the first part of any programming project. But no application will be acceptable to your constituents if it does not run efficiently.

This final section of the book introduces you to the concepts behind optimization in the Oracle database. The chapter includes a discussion of how Oracle determines the optimal access paths to your data, how to see what Oracle has determined, and how to shape the behavior of your Oracle database in this area. Although database optimization is a subject worthy of many excellent volumes, this chapter is intended to give you all the information you need to start to make your applications perform well.

The Bigger Picture

As mentioned at the start of this introduction, no one book is complete enough to cover everything you will need to know to use Oracle as an effective database for your applications. We have tried to give you a map that can be used over the course of many years of working with an Oracle database. If you believe that there are destinations we have left off of this map, or descriptions that could be more useful or informative, we welcome your comments.

Conventions

To help you get the most from the text and keep track of what's happening, we've used a number of conventions throughout the book.

Boxes like this one hold important, not-to-be forgotten information that is directly relevant to the surrounding text.

Tips, hints, tricks, and asides to the current discussion are offset and placed in italics like this.

As for styles in the text:

- We *highlight* important words when we introduce them
- We show keyboard strokes like this: Ctrl+A
- We show file names, URLs, and code within the text like so: `persistence.properties`
- We present code in two different ways:

```
In code examples we highlight new and important code with a gray
background.
```

```
The gray highlighting is not used for code that's less important in
the present context, or has been shown before.
```

Source Code

As you work through the examples in this book, you may choose either to type in all the code manually or to use the source code files that accompany the book. All of the source code used in this book is available for download at `http://www.wrox.com`. Once at the site, simply locate the book's title (either by using the Search box or by using one of the title lists) and click the Download Code link on the book's detail page to obtain all the source code for the book.

Because many books have similar titles, you may find it easiest to search by ISBN; for this book the ISBN is 0-7645-7482-5.

Once you download the code, just decompress it with your favorite compression tool. Alternately, you can go to the main Wrox code download page at `http://www.wrox.com/dynamic/books/download.aspx` to see the code available for this book and all other Wrox books.

Errata

We make every effort to ensure that there are no errors in the text or in the code. However, no one is perfect, and mistakes do occur. If you find an error in one of our books, like a spelling mistake or faulty piece of code, we would be very grateful for your feedback. By sending in errata you may save another reader hours of frustration and at the same time you will be helping us provide even higher quality information.

To find the errata page for this book, go to `http://www.wrox.com` and locate the title using the Search box or one of the title lists. Then, on the book details page, click the Book Errata link. On this page you can view all errata that has been submitted for this book and posted by Wrox editors. A complete book list including links to each book's errata is also available at `www.wrox.com/misc-pages/booklist.shtml`.

If you don't spot "your" error on the Book Errata page, go to `www.wrox.com/contact/techsupport.shtml` and complete the form there to send us the error you have found. We'll check the information and, if appropriate, post a message to the book's errata page and fix the problem in subsequent editions of the book.

p2p.wrox.com

For author and peer discussion, join the P2P forums at `p2p.wrox.com`. The forums are a Web-based system for you to post messages relating to Wrox books and related technologies and interact with other readers and technology users. The forums offer a subscription feature to e-mail you topics of interest of your choosing when new posts are made to the forums. Wrox authors, editors, other industry experts, and your fellow readers are present on these forums.

At `http://p2p.wrox.com` you will find a number of different forums that will help you not only as you read this book, but also as you develop your own applications. To join the forums, just follow these steps:

1. Go to `p2p.wrox.com` and click the Register link.
2. Read the terms of use and click Agree.
3. Complete the required information to join as well as any optional information you wish to provide and click Submit.
4. You will receive an e-mail with information describing how to verify your account and complete the joining process.

You can read messages in the forums without joining P2P but in order to post your own messages, you must join.

Once you join, you can post new messages and respond to messages other users post. You can read messages at any time on the Web. If you would like to have new messages from a particular forum e-mailed to you, click the Subscribe to this Forum icon by the forum name in the forum listing.

For more information about how to use the Wrox P2P, be sure to read the P2P FAQs for answers to questions about how the forum software works as well as many common questions specific to P2P and Wrox books. To read the FAQs, click the FAQ link on any P2P page.

1

Oracle Architecture and Storage

The core theoretical purpose of a relational database is to separate logical interaction with data within the database from the physical storage of that data. As a user or developer, you shouldn't really have to know how an Oracle database works internally, or stores its data, in order to use it properly. At a high level, this is certainly true. You don't need to know anything about the Oracle database to write SQL, the access language used to interact with the database, or to create programs that use SQL.

The Oracle database automatically takes care of translating your logical requests to access the data within its control. But, like all applications, the way your Oracle database is actually implemented can have an impact on what you do and do not do in the creation and maintenance of your application systems. Having a basic understanding of how Oracle does its jobs provides a foundation for the rest of this book. And understanding the ways that Oracle stores your data, which is also covered in this chapter, can have a direct impact on the way you write your applications that use that data.

This first chapter introduces you to a lot of the behind-the-scenes underpinnings of the Oracle database — the architecture of the database and how the data is stored within it. You very well may not ever have to use this information in your day-to-day tasks, but the substance of this chapter is necessary for the more detailed information about programming.

This chapter covers the architecture of the Oracle database as well as the storage options for your data. Depending on how the responsibilities are divided in your particular environment, there may be database administrators (DBAs) who do most of the work of translating your logical requirements into physical storage, or you may be called upon to perform some of these tasks yourself. In either case, this chapter gives you some familiarity with the way your Oracle database handles your data.

Architecture

The Oracle database is a relational database. The theory of relational databases was first put forward by Dr. E. F. Codd, a research scientist working for IBM, in the mid-1970s. Codd proposed a number of rules for a database to follow to be considered a relational database. For the first decade or so after these rules were proposed, early relational databases fought to show that they were the most compliant with Codd's rules. Those early days are far behind us now, and the basic features of a relational database, such as guaranteeing transactional integrity and allowing ad hoc access to data, are well established in all major relational databases.

The Oracle database consists of two main parts: the instance, which is the software service that acts as an intermediary between application requests and its data, and the actual data files, which are where the data is kept. The instance is a dynamic process and uses a variety of tasks and memory to support its operations. The data files are stored on disk, so the data itself will survive most service interruptions, except for catastrophic media failure.

The Instance

The Oracle instance is the collection of processes that handle requests from a client for a data. Some of these processes are shown in Figure 1-1. Figure 1-1 also includes some of the main areas of memory that an instance uses.

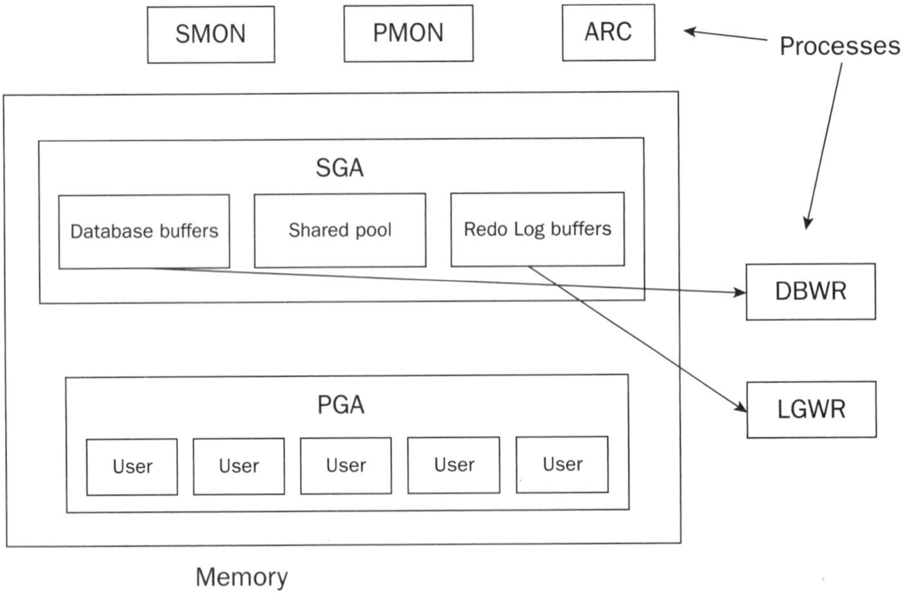

Figure 1-1: Oracle instance architecture.

An Oracle instance is either started as part of the process of booting a server or can be started explicitly with commands. Although you start an instance with a single command, there are actually three distinct steps in the startup process:

- Starting the instance process itself

- Mounting the database, which consists of opening the control files for the instance
- Opening the database, which makes the database available for user requests

An instance can be stopped with another command or via the system console, which follows the same sequence of events in reverse. You can stop an instance gracefully by stopping users from logging on to the database and only shutting down when the last active user has logged off, or you can simply stop the instance, which may result in incomplete transactions (described in detail in Chapter 3, "Handling Multiple Users").

Processes Supporting an Instance

A number of processes are associated with an instance and perform specific tasks for the instance.

Listener

The Listener is a process that listens on the network for requests coming in to an Oracle instance. A Listener process can support one or more Oracle instances. The Listener acts as the intermediary between user requests from remote machines and the instance. The failure of the Listener will mean that the instance it supports is not accessible by a remote client—such as any application that accesses the instance.

Background Processes

A whole set of processes run in the background on an Oracle server, supporting the actions of the Oracle instance. The main processes are listed here, with the standard acronyms of the processes in parentheses:

- **Database Writer (DBWR).** Writes data blocks from the database buffers, as described in the following section.
- **Log Writer (LGWR).** Writes redo log information from the redo log buffer in memory to the redo log on disk.
- **System Monitor (SMON).** Monitors the health of all components of an Oracle instance, and helps to recovery the database when it is restarted after a crash.
- **Process Monitor (PMON).** Watches individual user processes that access the Oracle instance and cleans up any resources left behind by an abnormal termination of a user process.
- **Archiver (ARC).** Writes a copy of a filled redo log file to an archive location. An Oracle instance can have up to 10 Archiver processes.

Files Supporting an Instance

There are a number of files that are used by an instance. The basic files for storing data are discussed in the next section on data organization. An Oracle instance has its own set of files that do not store user data but are used to monitor and manage the Oracle instance itself.

Initialization Files

Many parameters exist that affect the way that your Oracle instance operates. These parameters are typically set and maintained by a database administrator and, as such, are beyond the scope of this book. The initial values for these parameters are kept in initialization files.

Prior to Oracle9*i*, each instance had its own specific initialization file called INIT.ORA, as well as an optional file with additional configuration information called CONFIG.ORA. Starting with Oracle9*i*, you could have a virtual initialization file called the SPFILE, which could be shared with multiple instances. SPFILE was especially handy for two reasons: You could change a configuration parameter for a running instance and not have to save the change to the SPFILE, which means that the value of the parameter would be reset to the stored value on the next startup. You can also use the SPFILE with Real Application Clusters, discussed later in this chapter, where multiple instances worked together in a cluster and shared the same initialization procedures.

Control File

The control file is used to store key information about an instance, such as the name of the instance, the time the database was created, and the state of backup and log files for the database. An Oracle instance requires a control file in order to operate. Although a control can be rebuilt, most Oracle installations use multiple copies of the control file to avoid this possibility.

Redo Log Files

One of key features of a relational database is its ability to recover to a logically consistent state, even in the event of a failure. Every relational database, including Oracle, uses a set of redo log files. These files keep track of every interaction with the database. In the event of a database failure, an administrator can recover the database by restoring the last backup and then applying the redo log files to replay user interactions with the database.

Redo log files eventually fill up and roll over to start a new volume. You can set up Oracle to avoid writing over existing logfiles by creating the database to automatically archive log files in ARCHIVELOG mode, which is discussed in detail in the Oracle documentation.

Since redo logs are crucial for restoring a database in the event of a failure, many Oracle shops set up an instance to keep multiple copies of a redo log file.

Rollback Segments

Unlike all other major databases, Oracle also uses rollback segments to store previous versions of data in the database. The use of rollback segments makes it possible for the Oracle database to avoid the use of read locks, which can significantly reduce performance degradation based on multiuser access as well as providing a consistent view of data at any particular point in time. For more on rollback segments and how they support multiuser concurrency, see Chapter 3, "Handling Multiple Users," which covers this important topic in detail.

Because rollback segments track every change to data, the rollback segments are updated as soon as a change is made. This real-time update lets the Oracle database delay writing its redo log files until a time when these writes can be done efficiently.

Oracle 10*g* includes the ability to designate an automatic UNDO tablespace, which assigns the responsibility for managing rollback segments to the Oracle database itself.

Memory Used by an Instance

Figure 1-1, shown previously, includes several areas of memory that are used by an individual Oracle instance.

System Global Area

The System Global Area (SGA) is an area of memory that is accessible to all user processes of an Oracle instance. Three main areas are used by the SGA:

- The redo log buffer holds information used for recovery until the information can be written to the redo log.
- The shared pool holds information that can be shared across user processes, such as execution plans for SQL statements, compiled stored procedures, and information retrieved from the Oracle data dictionary.
- The database buffer pools are a group of memory areas that are used to hold data blocks. A data block held in a buffer pool can be accessed much more rapidly than going to disk to retrieve the block, so efficient use of these memory pools is essential for achieving optimal performance. Following are the three basic database buffer pools:
    - The DEFAULT pool holds all database objects, unless otherwise specified.
    - The KEEP pool is used to hold objects in memory if specified for a table or index.
    - The RECYCLE pool is used for objects that are not likely to be reused again.

  Keep the following two points in mind:

    - For all of these pools, the Oracle instance uses a Least Recently Used (LRU) algorithm to determine what data blocks to swap out.
    - In addition to these main pools, the Oracle instance can also use a large pool, which is used for shared server, backup and recovery, and I/O operations. You can either configure a large pool or Oracle can create it automatically, if you configure adaptive parallelism, which is described further in Chapter 2.

Program Global Area

The Program Global Area (PGA) is an area of memory that is just available to a single server process. The PGA contains items like user variables and cursor information for an individual user's SQL statement, such as the number of rows that have been retrieved so far. The PGA is also used for sorting data for an individual user process.

Each time a new SQL statement is received for a user, a new space in the PGA has to be initialized. To avoid this overhead, transaction-intensive applications, such an online transaction processing (OLTP) applications, typically use a small set of SQL statements that are continually reused by a user process, reducing this potential source of overhead.

You can have a single server process handle more than one user process by configuring shared servers, which are described in Chapter 2, "Using SQL."

The database administrator typically does the memory allocations for these areas, but setting these values inappropriately can have a dramatic affect on the performance of your applications. Oracle 10*g* makes it easier to manage these portions of memory, since it eliminates the need to specify an allocation for the individual components of each of these pools. With Oracle 10*g*, you can simply set a maximum size for the SGA and the PGA, and Oracle will take care of the allocation for the individual components of these areas.

Real Application Clusters

As you know, a single server can have one or more CPUs within it. You can also use a technique called *clustering* to combine more than one server into a larger computing entity. The Oracle database has supported the ability to cluster more than one instance into an single logical database for over 15 years. Oracle combines multiple instances into a cluster, shown in Figure 1-2, which uses underlying hardware and software to create a single database image from multiple separate servers.

Since Oracle9*i*, Oracle has called these clusters Real Application Clusters, commonly referred to as RAC. As Figure 1-2 shows, RAC instances share a common source of data, which allows RAC to provide greater database horsepower for scalability while also providing higher levels of availability.

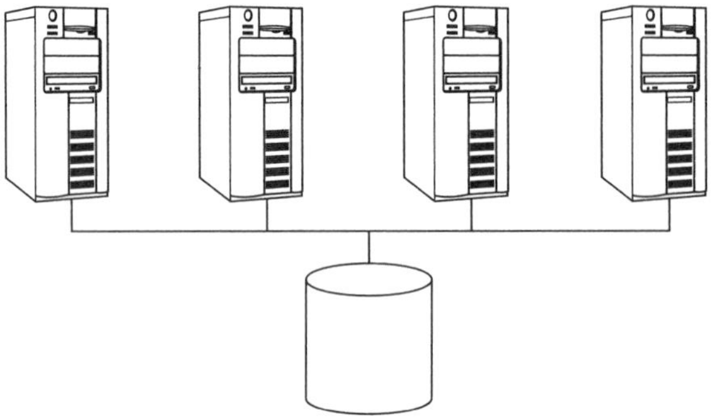

Figure 1-2: A Real Application Cluster deployment.

One of the best features of RAC is that you, as an application developer, don't even have to think about it, since a RAC implementation uses the same API and SQL that a single instance uses. You also don't have to worry about whether your Oracle application will be deployed to a single instance or a cluster when you are designing and creating your application, since there are virtually no specific performance considerations that only affect a RAC installation. As a developer, you don't really have to know anything more about Real Application Clusters.

Data Organization

The previous section focused on the organization of the Oracle instance. As an application developer, you might find this type of material interesting (and it lays the foundation for a deeper understanding of the Oracle database that will come in handy later), but what you really care about is your data.

Data in a relational database is organized on two different levels — a logical level and a physical level. On a logical level, Oracle organizes your data into tables, rows, and columns, like other relational databases. A *table* is a collection of information about a specific entity, such as an employee or a department. In non-relational systems, the equivalent of a table is a file. A *row* is an individual occurrence of a set of data, such as information about an individual employee or department. A *column* is one piece of data within a row, such as an employee's name or the identifier for a department.

One of the key qualities of a relational database is to separate the logical organization of data, such as tables and rows, from the physical storage of data. Although you will be accessing data through the logical structures of tables, rows, and columns, this section introduces you to additional storage structures, both physical and logical, used by Oracle to organize your data. Since the care and feeding of storage is normally the responsibility of the database administrator, this section does not provide detailed descriptions on how to implement and optimize these storage structures. If you will be acting as the DBA for any of your databases, we would suggest that you also get an Oracle book that is oriented towards DBAs, such as *Oracle Administration And Management* by Michael R. Ault (Wiley, 0-471-21886-3).

The hierarchy of logical and physical storage units is shown in Figure 1-3.

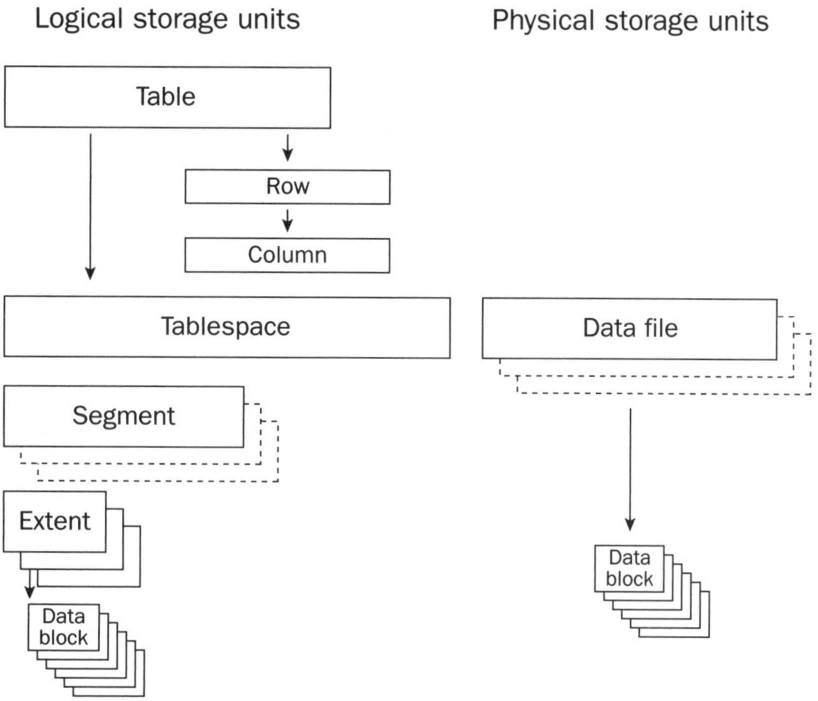

Figure 1-3: Data organization.

Tablespaces

The *tablespace* is another logical organizational unit used by the Oracle database, which acts as the intermediary between logical tables and physical storage. Every table or index, when created, is placed into a tablespace. A tablespace can contain more than one table or index, or the table or index can be partitioned across multiple tablespaces, as described later in the section on partitions. A tablespace maps to one or more files, which are the physical entities used to store the data in the tablespace. A file can only belong to one tablespace. A tablespace can contain row data or index data, and a table and an index for a table can be in different tablespaces.

A tablespace has a number of attributes, such as the block size used by the tablespace. This block size is the smallest amount of data retrieved by a single I/O (input/output) operation by the Oracle database. Your database administrator (hopefully) selected an appropriate block size for a tablespace, which depends on a wide range of factors, including the characteristics of the data and the block size of the underlying operating system.

Prior to Oracle9i, you could only have a single block size for an entire database. With Oracle9i, multiple block sizes are supported within a single database, although each block size must have its own data buffers in the SGA.

A tablespace is the basic administrative unit in an Oracle database. You can take a tablespace online or offline (that is, make it available or unavailable through the Oracle database instance) or back up and recover a tablespace. You can make a tablespace read-only to prevent write activity to the tablespace.

You can also use a feature called transportable tablespaces as a fast way to move data from one database to another. The normal way to take data out of one Oracle database and move it to another Oracle database is to export the data and then import the data. These processes operate by reading or writing each row. A transportable tablespace allows you to move the entire tablespace by simply exporting descriptive information about the tablespace from the data dictionary. Once you have exported this information, you can move the files that contain the tablespace and import the descriptive information into the data dictionary of the destination database (this is described in detail in Chapter 6, "The Oracle Data Dictionary." This method of moving data is significantly faster than importing and exporting data. Data movement is discussed in more detail in Chapter 24, "High-Speed Data Movement."

The 10g release of the Oracle database includes the ability to use transportable tablespaces between Oracle databases on different operating system platforms.

Segments and Extents

Individual objects in the database are stored in *segments*, which are collections of extents. Data blocks are stored in an extent. An *extent* is a contiguous piece of disk storage. When Oracle writes data to its data files, it writes each row to a data block that has space available for the data. When you update information, Oracle tries to write the new data to the same data block. If there is not enough space in that block, the updated data will be written to a different block, which may be in a different extent.

If there are no extents that have enough space for new information, the Oracle database will allocate a new extent. You can configure the number and size of extents initially and subsequently allocated for a tablespace.

Partitions

As mentioned previously, you can use partitions to spread data across more than one tablespace. A *partition* is a way to physically segregate the data in a table or index based on a value in the table or index. There are four ways you can partition data in an Oracle database:

- Range partitioning, which divides data based on a range of values, such as putting customers with a last name starting with the letters A–G in one partition, the customers with last names starting with the letters H–M in another partition, and so on.
- Hash partitioning, which divides data based on the result of a hashing algorithm. Hash partitioning is used when range partitioning would result in unbalanced partitions. For instance, if you are partitioning a table based on a serial transaction identifier, the first partition will completely fill before the second partition is used. A hash algorithm can spread data around more evenly, which will provide greater benefits from partitioning.
- Composite partitioning, which uses a hash algorithm within each specific range partion.
- List partitioning, which partitions based on a list of values. This type of partitioning is useful when a logical group, such as a list of states in a region, cannot be easily specified with a range description.

Partitions are defined when you create a table or an index. Since each partition of a table can be placed in a different tablespace, you can perform maintenance on a single partition, such as backup and recovery or moving tablespaces.

Partitions can also contribute to the overall performance of your Oracle database. The Oracle query optimizer is aware of the use of partitions, so when it creates a plan to execute a query, the plan will skip partitions that have been eliminated from the query with selection criteria. In addition, partitions can be in different tablespaces, which can be in different parts of your disk storage, which can reduce disk head contention during retrievals. Query optimization and parallel execution are covered in more detail in Chapter 28, "Optimization."

Data Types

One aspect of data storage that does significantly affect application development is data types. Each column in an Oracle database (or variable in a PL/SQL program, as described in Chapter 16, "PL/SQL and SQL," is designated as a particular data type. The data type dictates some of the characteristics of the data. At the most basic level, the data type specifies how data will be stored and, more importantly, interpreted by the Oracle database. If you define a column as a number, Oracle interprets all data entered into that column as a number. Oracle stores that data as a number and returns the values as numbers.

Obviously, this type of gross distinction is crucial in defining data. But there are other differences between data types that can affect how you use them in your data design and applications. The remainder of this section covers the data types supported in the Oracle database.

You specify the data type for a column when you define the column, such as:

```
CREATE TABLE (ID NUMBER, EMP_NAME VARCHAR2(256));
```

Some data types can have a length indicated after the data type name, while others either do not take a length or have a default value for length, which makes the length specification optional. You can query the data dictionary, which is covered in Chapter 6, to retrieve the data type for any particular column.

Character Data Types

The Oracle database supports a number of different data types for storing character data. All of these data types interpret data entered and retrieved as character values, but each of the data types has additional characteristics as well.

CHAR

`CHAR` columns can have a length specification after the data type or are assigned the default length of 1. A `CHAR` column will always use the assigned space in the database. If a column is defined as `CHAR(25)`, every instance of that column will occupy 25 bytes in the database. If the value entered for that column does not contain 25 bytes, it will be padded with spaces for storage and retrieval.

VARCHAR2 and VARCHAR

`VARCHAR2` columns also can have a length specification, but this data type only stores the number of characters entered by the user. If you define a column as `VARCHAR2(25)` and the user only enters 3 characters, the database will only store those three characters. Because of this distinction, there may be some issues with comparison between a `CHAR` column and a `VARCHAR2` column.

The following SQL code snippet adds the same value, `'ABC'`, to two columns: `ABCCHAR`, which is described as a `CHAR` column with 20 characters, and `ABCVARCHAR`, which is described as a `VARCHAR2` column with 20 characters.

```
INSERT INTO TEST_TABLE COLUMNS(ABCCHAR, ABCVARCHAR) ('ABC', 'ABC');
IF ABCCHAR = ABCVARCHAR
```

This final test will fail, since it is comparing ABCCHAR, which has a value of "ABC   " with ABCVARCHAR, which has a value of "ABC". These comparison problems could be resolved by truncating the ABCCHAR column, but it is much easier to just avoid them by using VARCHAR2 for normal character columns. The VARCHAR2 data type will also save storage space, which improves overall performance.

The VARCHAR data type is synonymous with the VARCHAR2 data type, but Oracle recommends using VARCHAR2 to protect against possible future changes in the behavior of the VARCHAR data type.

NCHAR and NVARCHAR2

The Oracle database can store character data from many different languages, including Chinese or Japanese, which require 2 bytes of storage for each character. These double-byte languages use the NCHAR and NVARCHAR2 data types, which allow for the extended storage needed for the characters in these languages.

Prior to Oracle9*i*, using these data types would automatically indicate that each character required 2 bytes of storage. With Oracle9*i*, you can specify the storage for a column either in bytes or as a number of characters. If you define a column with characters, Oracle automatically allocates the appropriate number of bytes for storage of the data.

LONG

The CHAR and NCHAR data types have a limit of 2,000 characters, while the VARCHAR, VARCHAR2, and NVARCHAR data types have a limit of 4,000 characters. The LONG data type allows you to enter up to 2 GBs of data in a single column. The use of the LONG data type has been superceded by the CLOB and NCLOB data types described next, since they have fewer restrictions on their use than the older LONG data type.

BLOB, CLOB, and NCLOB

Like the LONG data type, these three data types, collectively referred to a LOB data types, are designed to hold more that 4,000 characters. The BLOB data type holds binary data, the CLOB data type holds character data, and the NCLOB data type holds double-byte information, just as the NVARCHAR2 data type does. With Oracle10*g*, a single CLOB or NCLOB data type can hold up to 128 TBs (!) of data; prior to that release, the same data types could hold up to 4 GBs of data.

The data for a column of this data type is not stored in an actual row; instead, the column holds a pointer to the location of the data. LOB columns can participate in transactions, but if you want to manipulate the data in one of these columns, you have to use specific calls in the PL/SQL built-in package DBMS_LOB. The use of this package is beyond the scope of this book, since many readers may not be using these long data types in their applications, but it is covered in the Oracle documentation set.

BFILE

The BFILE data type allows you to have a column that points to a storage location outside of the Oracle database's internal storage. You can also attain some of this functionality by using external tables, which were introduced in Oracle9*i*. Both BFILEs and external tables can only be used for reading data, and BFILEs cannot be used in transactions.

Numeric Data Types

There are several numeric data types for the Oracle database. These data types, which are listed next, specify the attributes of the values stored in their corresponding columns. However, with the exception of the `BINARY` data types listed later on, the Oracle database stores all numbers in the same internal format. As a developer, you may define numeric values in your applications with all sorts of numeric characteristics, such as `DECIMAL`, `INT`, or `SMALLINT`, but the storage of those values is limited by the data types of the columns in the database.

You can also define columns as standard ANSI or DB2 numeric data types, including `NUMERIC`, `DECIMAL`, `INTEGER`, `INT`, or `SMALLINT`, but these data types will be created using the underlying Oracle `NUMBER` data type.

NUMBER

The `NUMBER` data type is the basic numeric data type used in the Oracle database. Data with this data type is stored with up to 38 digits of precision. You can specify the precision and the scale of a `NUMBER` column with the syntax:

```
NUMBER(p,s)
```

where *p* is the precision of the column and *s* is the scale of the column. *p* can be any number up to 38. The *s* variable can be either positive, which indicates the number of digits to the right of the decimal point that will be stored, or negative, which will round the number up by the number of places to the left of the decimal point. If you do not define a scale, the scale is assumed to be 0. The following table shows the effect of precision and scale on a value.

Value	Data Type	Result
12345.678	`NUMBER`	12345.678
12345.678	`NUMBER(9)`	12345
12345.678	`NUMBER(9,3)`	12345.678
12345.678	`NUMBER(9,2)`	12345.68
12345.678	`NUMBER(9,-2)`	12300

BINARY

You can also use either the `BINARY_FLOAT` or `BINARY_DOUBLE` data type for numbers in an Oracle database. These types store numbers in a binary format. There is no restriction on the scale of these numbers, and pure arithmetic may run a little faster with these binary representations. Keep in mind, however, that because not all decimals can be stored accurately as binary numbers, you may lose some accuracy.

The Oracle database also supports the `FLOAT` and `FLOAT(n)` data type for ANSI compliance.

Date Data Types

The third major category of data types is the `DATE` data type. As with numeric data types, Oracle stores all dates in a single internal representation. However, the format used for entering and returning dates is determined by the `NLS_DATE_FORMAT` value for the instance. You can set this value in the initialization file for the instance, or you can change it with an `ALTER SESSION` command for an individual database session.

The default format used by into Oracle for dates is DD-MMM-YY HH:MI:SS, where DD is a two-digit representation of the day number, MMM is a three-character representation of the month name, and YY is a two-digit representation of the year. HH, MI, and SS are two-digit representations of hours, minutes, and seconds, respectively. If you do not specify a time portion of a date, these values default to 0.

Oracle does store dates with four-digit centuries, although you have to use a date format other than the default format to enter and display four-digit centuries.

The three date data types are as follows:

- `DATE`—Includes the day, month, year, hour, minute and second specification.
- `TIMESTAMP(`*n*`)` —Can extend the standard DATE data type with fractional seconds. The number of decimal places for the fractional seconds component is indicated with the *n* variable.
- `TIMESTAMP(`*n*`) WITH [LOCAL] TIMEZONE`—Includes the time zone of either the database server or the client (when using the `LOCAL` keyword).

You can perform simple arithmetic on date values, where integers represent whole days and fractions represent portions of days. If `COLTIME` contains a value of December 31, 2003, at 6 P.M., `COLTIME + 1` would equal January 1, 2004, at 6 P.M., and `COLTIME + .5` would equal January 1, 2004, at 6 A.M.

Oracle9*i* introduced two new date data types used for date arithmetic.

- `INTERVAL YEAR TO MONTH` – Can store an interval of years and months
- `INTERVAL DAY TO SECOND` – Can store an interval of days, hours and seconds

You can use the `TO_DATE` function to covert character values into dates. Oracle includes a set of extended date functions that allow you to manipulate dates, such as creating a date value from character representations of days, months, and years. These functions are discussed in detail in Chapter 13, "Functions."

RAW and LONG RAW

Normally, the Oracle database converts a value to an internal representation for storage, and reconverts that value upon retrieval. The `RAW` and `LONG RAW` data types circumvent this interpretation, and require Oracle to simply store the bits sent to it without any type of conversion. Since these data types are used for special situations, they will not be referred to in the remainder of this book.

Other Data Types

Oracle allows you to define your own object data types, which you can use for creating objects, discussed in detail in Chapter 21, "Object Relational Interactions with Oracle." Oracle also includes specialized data types for working with XML, spatial data, and media data, as well as ways to access type descriptions when the data type is not known. Since these data types are only used in specialized situations, and since you will probably want detailed information about these data types if you are going to be using them, you should consult the Oracle documentation if you feel you need the capabilities they provide.

Summary

Understanding the architecture of the Oracle database is important in order to interact with the database in the most appropriate manner. An Oracle database is made up of an instance, which is the service that interacts with the underlying data, and the database, which is the storage of data on disk. Each instance includes a number of processes and different memory areas.

The Oracle database has a hierarchy of logical organizational levels, including tables and rows, tablespaces, segments, extents, and data blocks, as well as physical storage, which includes data files and operating system data blocks.

When you create a column in an Oracle database, you assign a data type to the column, which controls the basic representation and storage of the data in the column. Oracle supports a number of different character, numeric, and date data types. It can also define your own data types for objects and other types of nonstandard data.

2

Using SQL

The end users of the applications you develop are almost never aware of the code used to retrieve their data for them, or insert and update changes to the data back into the database. Your application acts as a black box, handling all the interactions with the underlying database.

In some ways, we developers have our own black box, although the box is much smaller. We send SQL statements off to the database and the database does its magic. The aim of this chapter is to take a close look at what the Oracle database does in response to those SQL statements. Although you may have some understanding of what takes place on the Oracle server, this chapter also provides some practical explanations that will help you to avoid some of the most common pitfalls facing developers accessing an Oracle database.

This chapter concentrates on what is going on in the Oracle server, rather than on the code you use to trigger those actions from your application. These actions are the Oracle database responding to your requests, regardless of what programming language you use. Most languages use some form of application programming interface (API) calls to use SQL against the Oracle database, and those calls and code will be introduced later in this book.

The Processing Cycle for SQL Statements

To process an SQL statement you submit to your Oracle database, the database goes through several phases as part of the execution of the statement:

- Connect to the database, to establish communication between your client application and the Oracle database server.
- Create a cursor, to hold the context for an SQL statement.
- Submit an SQL statement to the Oracle database for processing, which includes checking the validity of the statement and potentially creating an optimized execution plan for it.
- Receive data back from the Oracle database in response to the submission of a query.

This cycle of events is shown in Figure 2-1, with mandatory events shown in white and potentially optional events shown as shaded. Each of these phases is discussed in more detail later in the chapter.

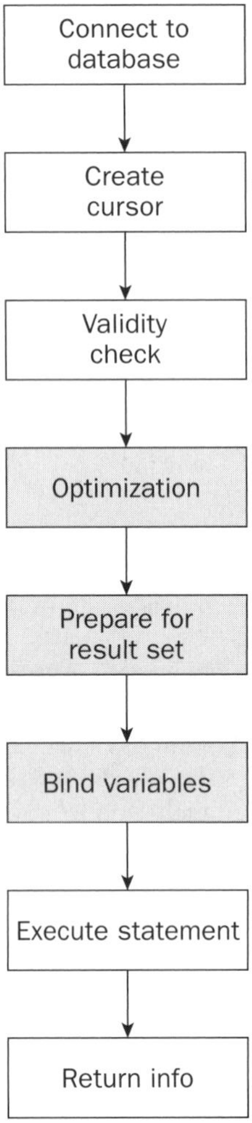

Figure 2-1: The processing cycle for an SQL statement.

Connecting to a Database

The first step in accessing an Oracle database from your application is to establish a connection to the database. This connection is the path that acts as the path from your client application to a shadow process in the Oracle database that handles the SQL requests from your application.

Normally, a connection goes from a client machine over a network to a server machine. The connection is implemented on top of a network protocol, such as TCP/IP. The connection request is actually received by the Oracle Listener, which listens on a port for connection traffic. Once the connection is established, the Listener passes requests to the shadow process associated with the connection, as shown in Figure 2-2.

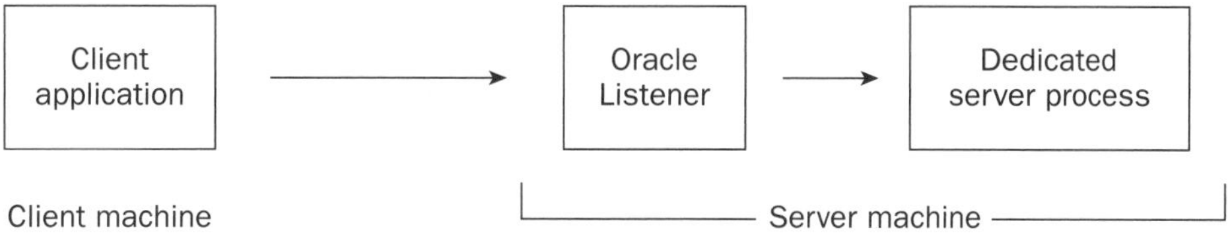

Figure 2-2: Establisihng a connection to an Oracle database from a client application.

If you are using Java as your program language, the connection will be executed with a driver, which is software designed to handle the complexities of communication over the network. The various types of Java drivers are described in Chapter 7, "Installing Oracle."

A connection to an Oracle database is always created on behalf of a user. Consequently, establishing a connection requires identifying and authenticating that user with a username and password. The details of authentication are described in Chapter 5, "Oracle Security."

A connection to an Oracle database is referred to as a *session*. The session is the overriding context for all SQL interactions that take place. When a connection is either terminated or is lost for any other reason, the context for that session, including any information in any uncommitted transactions within that session, is lost. Chapter 3, "Handling Multiple Users," describes in detail the use of transaction in an Oracle database.

Every session is supported by a shadow process on the Oracle server. Normally, this means that every session has its own process. But, as you can imagine, each shadow process uses some server memory resources, so the scalability of an individual Oracle instance might be limited by the number of sessions it can support. To address this issue, Oracle has a feature known as *shared servers*, which was referred to as multithreaded servers, or MTS, before Oracle9*i*.

Shared servers add another layer to the connection architecture, as shown in Figure 2-3. When a connection comes into the Listener, it passes the request to a dispatcher. The dispatcher assigns the request to a session that can be shared. Once the request is completed, the session becomes available to service other requests.

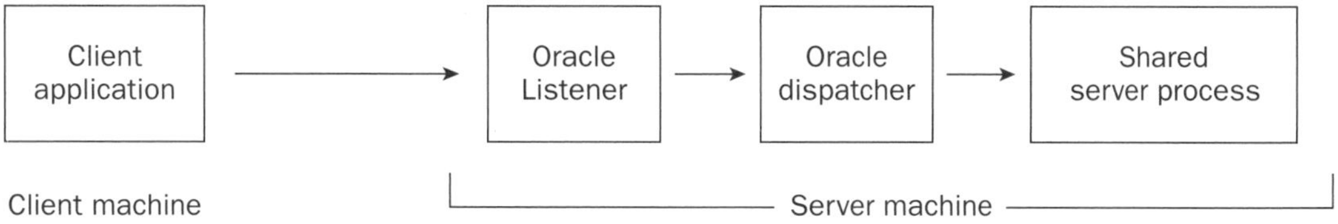

Figure 2-3: Shared servers.

Use of shared servers is completely transparent to your application. A single Oracle instance can use a combination of shared servers and dedicated servers — the instance has different connection identifiers for a dedicated session or a shared session.

When should you use a shared server? As with most issues involving performance, the answer depends on the particulars of your particular implementation.

If you are running out of memory because of a large number of connections, shared servers can help to address the problem by lowering the overall amount of memory required for sessions. Obviously, some overhead is also involved with the use of a dispatcher and the functions it performs. This overhead can be balanced against the more limited use of resources required by the shared server architecture.

Typically, a shared server can do the most good for applications that require periodic access to the database, since the connections used by these applications will not be performing work much of the time, and as such they are candidates to be shared with other sessions. A browsing application would fit this description, while a heads-down transaction processing application would not. The good news is that you can switch between using shared sessions and dedicated sessions by simply changing the connection parameters, so it is fairly easy to test the effect of shared sessions on your overall application performance.

You have to establish a connection to your Oracle database instance before you can send any SQL to the instance, but you do not necessarily have to create a connection each time you want to use one. You can reuse connections inside of an application, or a portion of an application, or you can use connection pooling to maintain a set of connections that a user can grab when he or she needs it. Using a connection manager with Java is covered in Chapter 18, "Introduction to Java Database Programming."

Establishing a Cursor

Once a connection is established, the next step is to open a *cursor* for your SQL statements. A cursor is a connection to a specific area in the Program Global Area (PGA) that contains information about a specific SQL statement.

For a description of the PGA, please refer to Chapter 1, "Oracle Architecture and Storage."

The cursor acts as the intermediary between the SQL statements your application submits and the actions of the Oracle database as a result of those statements. The cursor holds information about the current state of the SQL statement, such as the parsed version of the SQL statement. For statements that return multiple rows of data, the cursor keeps track of where you are in terms of returning rows from the result set. This important piece of information is also called a cursor, in that the cursor for a particular result set is the pointer to the current row. But the cursor exists before any rows have been returned for a query, which is why advancing the cursor to the next row at the start of retrieving data places the cursor on the first row in the result set.

You don't necessarily have to explicitly open a cursor to execute an SQL statement, because the Oracle database can automatically take care of this for you. As with most aspects of application programming, explicit control over cursor creation and use will give you more options for implementing your logic efficiently. You may want to open more than one cursor to improve the operation of your application. For instance, if you have an SQL statement that is repeatedly used, you might want to open a cursor for the statement so that Oracle will not have to re-parse the statement. Of course, the Oracle database uses its own internal caches to hold parsed versions of SQL statements also, so creation of individual cursors may not be necessary for optimal performance in many cases.

Submitting SQL Statements

At this point in the processing cycle, your application has established a connection to the database and allocated a cursor to hold the context for your SQL operations. The next step is to submit an SQL statement to the Oracle database.

Submitting a statement is a single line of application code, but the Oracle database performs a series of actions in response to this submission before it responds to the request. The individual actions performed depend on the type of SQL statement submitted—a data definition language (DDL) statement for creating or modifying database objects, a write operation (`INSERT`, `UPDATE`, or `DELETE`), or a query using the `SELECT` verb. The actions taken for each of these are detailed in the following table.

Action	DDL	Write operation	Query
Validate	X	X	X
Optimize		X	X
Prepare for results			X
Bind variables	X	X	X
Execute statement	X	X	X
Return success code	X	X	X
Return result count		X	
Return rowset			X

Each of these actions is described in the following.

Check Validity of Statement

Parsing is the process of checking an SQL statement to ensure that it is valid, as well as creating an optimal execution plan for the statement. Validity checks are used to ensure that an SQL statement will be able to be executed by the Oracle database.

The first step in the process is to check the syntax of the SQL statement. This syntax check includes checking the validity of the actual keywords used in the statement as well as whether the table and column names refer to valid entities that the submitting user can access properly. If you misspell a verb (`SELECT`), a column, or a table name, or try to access a database object you do not have privileges to access, Oracle will return an error at this phase.

For DDL and write operations, the statement is now loaded into the shared SQL area, since the statement is ready to run. For queries, the statement has to go through an additional step of optimization.

After an SQL statement has been checked, the Oracle database computes a hash algorithm to check whether a version of the statement exists in the shared SQL area. As mentioned in Chapter 1, the Oracle instance includes an area for shared SQL statements in the System Global Area memory (SGA) area. Since the next step in the processing cycle, optimization, can be a relatively expensive operation in terms of resource usage, Oracle can save a lot of work if it can avoid that step. If the statement is located, Oracle just uses the execution plan for the found statement.

If Oracle cannot find the statement in the shared pool, the instance proceeds to the next step of optimization. This type of parse is called a *hard parse*. If Oracle can find the statement in the shared pool, it simply retrieves the execution plan for the statement in what is called a *soft parse*. Later in this chapter, we explain how the use of bind variables can improve performance by increasing the chances that shared SQL will be reused.

Oracle will not bother to check for execution plans for DDL statements in the shared SQL pool, since these plans are not placed into the pool. The advantages of soft parses come into play when SQL statements are repeatedly executed, and since DDL statements are, in almost all cases, done only once, Oracle properly assumes that this portion of the process would be useless overhead for DDL.

Optimize

One of the great advances made by relational database technology was to give users the ability to request data without having to specify how the data was to be retrieved. Rather than telling a database exactly what structures to use to get to the data, you can simply send an SQL statement to the database and let Oracle figure out the most efficient way to retrieve the data.

In a complex production database, there may be many, many possible retrieval paths that could be used to retrieve the data for a query. The Oracle query optimizer analyzes the various paths and evaluates them in terms of how efficient they should be. This analysis takes into account data structures, such as indexes; selection criteria and how they might affect finding the requested rows' as well as environmental conditions, such as the amount of CPU and memory available.

The end result of the optimization process is an execution plan, which details exactly how your Oracle instance retrieves the data requested by the submitted SQL statement. Optimization is a nontrivial topic, covered at length in Chapter 28, "Optimization." At this point, you only have to know that optimization is both crucial to the efficient performance of your Oracle database and often fairly time-consuming. Because of this, the reuse of already optimized statements retrieved from the shared SQL pool can, in many cases, significantly improve the performance of your Oracle database.

Queries will always require optimization. Write operations may also require optimizations, since the first part of many write operations involves retrieving the rows that will be used in the write operation. DDL statements are not optimized.

Prepare for Results

If an SQL statement is a query, the Oracle database has to do some additional work to prepare for the return of the result set. This work involves describing the results of the query in terms of data type, data length, and data names for the query and associating each returning item with a variable for return.

Bind Variables

Once Oracle has prepared the SQL statement, it binds any variables into the SQL statement. A *bind variable* is a value in an SQL statement that is not known until the statement is run. In an SQL statement, the bind variable acts as a placeholder for this subsequent data. In Oracle SQL syntax, a bind variable is indicated by a colon (:) before the variable name.

For instance, the following SQL statement is used to insert data into the EMP table.

```
INSERT INTO EMP(ENAME, DEPT, SAL) VALUES(:sEname, ;sDept, :nSal);
```

The values listed in the `VALUES` clause are bind variables — the actual data used is sent later. You can use bind variables for values, selection criteria in the `WHERE` clause, and many other places in an SQL statement. You cannot use bind variables for SQL keywords.

When Oracle checks the syntax of your submitted statement, the validity of the value of bind variables cannot be checked. Because of this, a statement with bind variables could compile properly and still give you runtime errors. In the previous example, the value submitted for the `:nSal` bind variable could end up being invalid for the data type defined for the `SAL` column.

Bind variables are useful from both the logical and execution standpoint. In terms of logic, you can create a small set of SQL statements that can be used repeatedly to perform the same function for different data, and less SQL syntax means a smaller number of possible errors. In terms of performance, bind variables can increase the use of shared SQL — an important topic that is covered in detail at the end of this chapter.

Execute

Once the Oracle database has performed all of the steps detailed previously, the instance can execute the SQL statement using the execution plan that has been prepared. This execute phase is where Oracle actually performs the operation indicated by the submitted SQL statement.

Returns

Oracle returns information about each SQL statement it processes. All SQL statements return a simple boolean value to indicate whether the statement was successfully executed. For a write operation, Oracle also returns an integer that indicates how many rows were affected by the operation.

Queries return result sets — groups of rows that have been retrieved to satisfy the query. Retrieving those rows is the subject of the next section.

Receiving Data

A query is a request for data. In response to a query, the Oracle database prepares a result set that satisfies the conditions of the query. An application retrieves the rows of the result set by performing a series of fetch operations to return rows.

When you are using Java to access Oracle data, the Java API implements a pre-fetch. A pre-fetch returns a designated number of rows with a fetch command, when needed. By default, the pre-fetch returns 10 rows, but you can change the default for an individual connection programmatically.

When a fetch is first executed for a result set, the return includes 10 rows from the result set. For the next nine fetch operations, the data is already residing at the client. In this scenario, the 11th fetch result would retrieve another 10 rows.

Performance Considerations

The previous description of the execution cycle for SQL statements provides a brief description of how SQL statements are processed. But this factual description does not really help you understand the things you can do to create applications that will run effectively and perform optimally.

Understanding the SQL processing cycle is a prerequisite to understanding how to get the most out of your Oracle database. The rest of this book is essentially commentary on this topic. Performance tuning is an enormous subject in itself. This book devotes a chapter exclusively to the topic (Chapter 28), and many books have been devoted to achieving optimal performance with your Oracle database. Optimal performance comes from optimal design, optimal implementation, and optimal use of resources in terms of your particular logical and physical environment. In this introductory chapter, we cannot give you comprehensive advice on performance tuning, but there are three areas that have a broad effect on performance for all applications — how data is retrieved, the effect of bind variables on the processing cycle for SQL in an Oracle database, and the use of parallelism to improve performance.

Retrieval Performance

The final, and in many ways the most important, event in the SQL processing cycle is the return of data to the application that requested it. On one level, the speed of this final step is determined by your network, since the amount of bits that can move from the server to the client is ultimately limited by the amount of network bandwidth. The effects of this potential limitation cannot be overcome. But you can affect how much work the Oracle database performs before it starts returning data to the user.

Well, how much work does Oracle have to do before it returns data? You would think the answer to this question would be self-evident — "As much as it needs to do to get the data." But how much data does Oracle need to get before it *starts* to send data back to the application?

As developers, we tend to think of the end results of an action. A user requests data, so he or she obviously must want all of that data to do what he or she has to do. But users tend to be more, shall we say, immediate in their outlook. For us, performance is the time it takes to complete an SQL operation, such as a query. For a user, performance is how long they wait before something comes back to them.

You can take advantage of this dichotomy by setting the way that Oracle returns data. You can specify that Oracle should start returning rows to the user as soon as it gets the rows, or you can specify that Oracle will only start returning rows to the user once it has collected all the rows for the query.

You instruct your Oracle database as to which approach to take by setting a parameter called `OPTIMIZER_MODE`. The two settings for `OPTIMIZER_MODE` that are relevant to this example are `ALL_ROWS` and `FIRST_ROWS`, which tell Oracle to only return data once all rows have been fetched or as soon as it can, respectively. You can also use either one of these values as a hint for a particular query.

For more on optimization and hints, please refer to Chapter 28, which is dedicated entirely to the subject.

The best choice for this parameter obviously depends on your application. If a user is unable to do any work until he or she receives all the data, or if you don't want the user to do any work until he or she receives all the data, the `ALL_ROWS` parameter is the right choice. In applications that typically fetch data for the user to peruse and possible use, `FIRST_ROWS` may deliver better perceived performance without much logical downside. If your application is not retrieving large amounts of data, this particular optimizer choice shouldn't really affect performance.

Regardless of the setting of this parameter, there are some times when Oracle will properly wait until it has retrieved all rows until it returns any rows. One case is when a query includes aggregate values. Oracle knows that it has to get all the rows before it can calculate aggregate values, so no rows will be returned until all rows have been retrieved and the calculations performed.

Another case is when you ask for the rows to be returned in sorted order. Normally, Oracle cannot return the first rows until the sort has been performed, since the sort determines what the first row is, not the order that the rows are retrieved from the database. The exception to this rule is when the query has requested a sort order that is already implemented in an index. For instance, a user may request employee names in alphabetical order based on the last name, and there is an index that sorts the rows on that criterion. The Oracle database knows that the index has already sorted the rows, so it does not have to sort them and the first rows can be returned as soon as they are retrieved.

Using Bind Variables

The previous performance tip centered around how the Oracle database returns data to the user. This next tip has to do with the exact way that the Oracle database processes SQL statements. Unlike the previous tip, which did not affect your application code, this area requires that you implement your code in a particular way to reduce the use of resources and improve the performance of your Oracle database.

Earlier in this chapter, we discussed how Oracle stores SQL statements in the shared pool area of memory. When the Oracle database receives an SQL statement, it checks the shared pool to see if an optimized execution plan already exists for the statement. If the plan exists in the pool, the plan is simply retrieved from memory, which is much more efficient than reoptimizing the statement. Use of the shared pool helps Oracle to scale for large numbers of users and perform well with any load.

If you have to reoptimize every statement, each statement adds to the overall workload of the target Oracle database. This means that the overhead on your system increases with the number of statements and that, eventually, you will run into resource limitations that will decrease performance. If every statement has to go through the complete cycle of execution, your scalability will be limited.

Fortunately, a real-world application is not a series of unique SQL requests. In fact, most applications use the same SQL statements over and over again. Theoretically, this would mean that the repeated SQL will be picked up from the shared pool, which is much less expensive from a resource standpoint. Since Oracle needs exclusive access to some resources when optimizing an SQL statement, optimizing SQL statements cannot be done in parallel, so the more optimizations Oracle has to do, the greater the elapsed time for a query to be processed.

The way to reduce this potential bottleneck is to help your Oracle database to avoid performing hard parses as much as possible. You can help this to occur by using bind variables to help re-use SQL statements.

Remember that the method used to identify a statement is a comparison of the hash algorithm created from the statement. The value of this hash is derived from the characters in the statement.

Consider the following two statements:

```
SELECT ENAME FROM EMP WHERE EMP_ID = 7

SELECT ENAME FROM EMP WHERE EMP_ID = 5
```

You can quickly tell that these two statements should use identical optimizer plans. If the execution plan for the first statement is still in the shared pool, Oracle should use it, right? Unfortunately, Oracle may not be able to find the plan, since the hash value created by the second statement will very likely be different from the hash value created by the first statement, based on the different characters.

At this point, bind variables come to the rescue. A bind variable is a placeholder in an SQL statement. Oracle can process a statement containing a bind variable but can only execute the statement when it receives the value of the variable.

You identify a bind variable by preceding it with a colon in the SQL statement. The previous SQL statements could both be represented by the single SQL statement following, which uses a bind variable.

```
SELECT ENAME FROM EMP WHERE EMP_ID = :n_EmpID
```

If you use this syntax twice, instead of using the two different SQL statements shown previously, Oracle will be able to retrieve the execution plan from the shared pool, saving lots of resources.

The statements used to illustrate the use of bind variables previously are not that complex, so you may doubt how much the use of bind variables could help. But remember that your own SQL statements are considerably more complex, where the creation of an execution plan could likely be the biggest resource hog in the entire sequence of SQL processing. Also, remember that not only will your application likely repeat the same SQL statement over and over again but that this effect is multiplied by the use of your application by many different users.

Those of you who think of yourself as primarily as programmers and don't give no never mind about databases may be rising up in protest at this point. There is some common wisdom that says the code required to use bind variables, a `PreparedStatement` call in Java, executes slower than the code to execute a hard-coded statement, a `Statement` call in Java. We certainly can't argue this simple fact (although others have), but remember that there is more to performance than simply the time required to execute a call.

The use of bind variables can have an enormous impact on the time Oracle needs to return data to the user. Since performance is an aggregate, it doesn't make sense to save time in the execution of a single call if those savings are going to be outweighed by slower performance from the database.

The bottom line is that you should train yourself to use bind variables whenever you have SQL statements that only differ in the value of a particular item in the statement and that are repeatedly executed in your application.

The use of bind variables is so important that Oracle introduced a setting called `CURSOR_SHARING`. You can set the value of this parameter to specify what type of SQL statement should be forced to share cursors — for instance, if the SQL statements are exactly alike except for literal values. You can set the value for this parameter in either the initialization file for your Oracle database (`INIT.ORA` or the shared parameter file `SPFILE`) or with the `ALTER SESSION` command for your session; Oracle will automatically search out places where a literal could be substituted with a bind variable and perform the translation for you. This setting is handy, but it works across all literals, including some that are truly serving the function of literals in that they represent a value that does not change. Substituting these true literals with bind variables could cause Oracle to make an inappropriate optimizer decision. Training yourself to properly use bind variables is a better route to creating applications that perform and scale well.

Parallel Operations

Have you moved recently? If you moved yourself, you probably found that having more people working together resulted in reducing the overall time that it took to complete the job. Of course, there was no doubt some overhead involved in getting everyone to work together, and there may have been a point where getting even more people involved actually increased the time to complete the job.

Oracle implements a similar type of work sharing called parallelism. Parallelism makes it possible for Oracle to split up the work of a specific SQL statement among multiple worker tasks to reduce the elapsed time to complete the SQL operation.

Oracle has had the capability since version 7, although the scope of this functionality has been continuously improved. Oracle now supports parallel operations for queries, updates, and inserts, as well as for backup, recovery, and other operations. Parallelism for batch-type jobs like loading data is also supported. Parallel operations are only available with the Enterprise Edition of Oracle 10*g* Database.

Oracle implements parallelism on the server, without requiring any particular code to work. This final section will look at how Oracle implements parallel operations to improve performance.

How it Works

Parallel execution in Oracle divides a single task into smaller units and co-ordinates the execution of these smaller units. The server process for a user becomes a parallel coordinator, rather than simply executing the SQL statement.

The Oracle database provides parallel operations for each step in the processing of a query. Oracle can provide parallelism for data retrieval, joins, sorting, and other operations to provide performance improvements across the whole spectrum of SQL processing.

You have to use the `ALTER SESSION ENABLE PARALLEL` call, followed by the keyword `DML` or `DDL` to turn on parallel operations. The corresponding command `ALTER SESSION DISABLE PARALLEL` will turn off parallel operations for the session. You can specify a degree of parallelism with these statements.

Managing Parallel Server Processes

The Oracle database has a pool of parallel server processes available for execution. Oracle automatically manages the creation and termination of these processes. The minimum number of parallel processes is specified in the initialization parameter `PARALLEL_MIN_SERVERS`. As more parallel execution processes are requested, Oracle starts more parallel execution processes as they are needed, up to the value specified in the `PARALLEL_MAX_SERVERS` initialization parameters. The default for this parameter is 5, unless the `PARALLEL_AUTOMATIC_TUNING` parameter is set to TRUE, in which case the default is set to the value of the `CPU_COUNT` parameter times 10.

Caveats

The discussion of parallel processing above is extremely short and is meant as a mere introduction to the capabilities of parallel processing You should be aware that not every situation can benefit from parallel processing. For instance, a particular operation might be I/O bound, where the performance bottleneck is the interaction with the data on disk. This type of operation will not benefit from parallel processing, which can only reduce the overall CPU time spent by dividing the work up between multiple processes. In fact, this type of operation may actually get slower, as the process of coordination of different parallel processes can add to the already overburdened I/O workload.

In addition, if your SQL statement is already running optimally, adding parallelism may not help the performance, and may harm it.

The saving grace with parallelism is that you can easily run SQL operations with parallelism on or off, and with varying degrees of parallelism. Although you should be aware of the potential provided by parallel operations, you should not see them as a panacea for all performance problems—you should test the potential effect of parallelism if you have any doubts as to whether this option can help in a particular scenario.

Summary

This chapter covered the steps that your Oracle database performs when it receives an SQL statement from your application. Although these steps are not visible to either the user or yourself, understanding how Oracle works internally can help you to design and implement applications effectively.

For SQL queries, Oracle receives the query, either parses and optimizes it or retrieves an already prepared version of the query, executes the statement, retrieves the desired rows, and then returns those rows to the user. Write statements and data definition language do not perform all of these steps.

Once you understand that an SQL query can either be parsed and optimized, or its prepared version simply retrieved, you can understand why the proper use of bind variables can have an important impact on the performance of your applications.

Finally, this chapter gave an overview of parallel operations and how, in some circumstances, they can provide better response time for your SQL operations.

3

Handling Multiple Users

If the only purpose of a database was to store data, an enormous amount of the inner workings of the Oracle database, as well as years of development, could have been avoided. But the real magic of a modern relational database like Oracle is not that it simply stores data. The tricky part comes in when more than one user wants to use the same piece of data.

Handling multiple concurrent requests for data is one of the most devilish tasks a database has to accomplish. There are three main reasons for this complexity. The most basic reason is that each user wants to think that he or she is the *only* user for that data. Every user has to be isolated from all other activity in the database, whether it is taking place on completely unrelated data structures or on the exact same table, row, and columns that a user is working on.

The second reason is that the database has to be able to handle these multiple potentially conflicting requests without adversely affecting performance. In other words, you don't want to see the response time for data retrieval or update fall off the table as the number of users increases.

The third reason is that both of these qualities must continue to exist as the demand on the application increases. This is true even as the load on the database increases into the hundreds and thousands of requests.

Creating applications that will work for multiple users is also one of the most devilish tasks facing developers. You have to create applications that will run properly and efficiently for potentially large numbers of users, even though your test harness will almost inevitably not be able to simulate the wide variety of potential interactions by these users.

So a modern, enterprise database must be able to handle simultaneous requests for hundreds of users without unduly increasing overhead. Sounds a bit like wanting an application created fast, cheap, and good — at best, you can get two of them.

Fortunately, the Oracle database has a terrific built-in strategy for dealing with these exact issues. As a developer, you can pretty much let Oracle take care of handling concurrent requests for data — certainly to a greater extent than for any other major relational database.

Although it may seem somewhat contradictory to devote an entire chapter to a functionality that works by default, many of you may have experience with other databases that do not handle large numbers of users as well. This may have led you into the habit of coding to avoid their potential problems. It is crucial that you understand both the potential problems that concurrent multiuser access can create and how Oracle addresses them.

Most importantly, properly understanding and implementing the features that ensure accurate and well-performing multiuser data access is absolutely essential to creating viable applications. Frankly, your ability to create applications that can handle many, many users is really at the core of this book. As a developer, you are responsible for creating applications for entire communities of users that use the data in an Oracle database. You create the interface between those user communities and their data. The more the built-in features of the Oracle database can help you accomplish this task, the better. A complete understanding of the issues surrounding multiuser access, as well as how Oracle deals with these issues, is essential for all Oracle developers.

So, even if you feel you are completely familiar with how to deal with these issues, you will probably want to at least skim through the first part of this chapter for review.

Multiuser concurrency issues are one area that really separates Oracle DBAs from Oracle developers. A DBA is concerned with keeping the database running, but not necessarily with how the database is supporting applications. You, as a developer, take things like backup and maintenance for granted, but care deeply about the eventual functionality and performance delivered to end users.

Goals

The previous section discussed some specific issues related to multiple users and a database. But before you can start to understand those issues in more detail, it is worthwhile to step back and think about the overall goals that the database must achieve as it supports multiple users.

Data Integrity

Even though you write application code, the concept of data integrity is hopefully one that you have already taken to heart. *Data integrity* refers to the overall quality of your data. You, and, more importantly, your users, should be able to depend on the data in the Oracle database being both accurate and consistent.

Data integrity implies many things. In terms of multiple users, data integrity implies that any changes in the data do not overwrite other users' changes unknowingly. In its most complete sense, data integrity also implies that data returned to a user will represent a consistent set of data at any one point in time. This consistent view of data is sometimes referred to as a snapshot.

This consistency is provided by Oracle for multiple users, but not necessarily as easily or completely by other databases. Your users would probably not be happy with inconsistent data, so developers using other databases sometimes have to implement other types of solutions, such as reporting databases, to address this issue. But not with Oracle.

Data integrity covers a lot more than just multiuser issues. In a well-designed database, internal capabilities in the database, such as constraints, help to ensure that the data is also logically consistent. Chapter 11, "Constraints," focuses on how you can use constraints to implement logical data integrity.

Isolation

The key sticking point in handling multiple users is not just that you have a lot of users. Each user wants to think and believe that he or she is the only user for the entire database. From a user's self-centered view, this isolation may primarily manifest itself as a demand for optimal performance, at all times, for the user. In this sense, each user wants ideal performance for his or her applications, without a whole lot of concern for other users or other applications that may be using the same data.

You, who are responsible for all users, rather than any particular user at any particular time, have to extend this self-absorption to the realm of data. If a user is making changes in his or her data, whether these changes are adding new data, changing existing data, or deleting data, you have to make sure that these changes do not affect the work of other users.

The Oracle database must allow users to be isolated from all other users, at all times.

Serialization

With even these two simple requirements — data integrity and isolation — you can probably begin to imagine the overall complexity of the problems raised by multiple users. One way to place some kind of boundaries on this complexity is to divide the overall work of any user into smaller pieces, known as transactions and described in more detail in the next section. Transactions are the basic unit of work for relational databases. Each transaction must provide data integrity for all the work done in the transaction, and as well as from the work of other transactions.

A database must be able to guarantee that transactions occur in a logical order, as if they were being submitted to the database serially. The database as a whole must implement serialization for all of its transactions.

Serialization also helps to sort out some of the multiuser data integrity issues discussed later in the chapter. The database handles the data affected by each transaction based on the order that the transaction affecting the data was received and completed.

Transactions

The transaction is the key tool used to deal with both the issue of data integrity and to address the problems created by multiple simultaneous requests for the same data. A *transaction* is defined as a unit of work. Within a transaction, all of the SQL activity aimed at a database is guaranteed to be completed, and at the same time. You can begin a transaction either explicitly, with the `BEGIN TRANSACTION` syntax, or implicitly, by issuing an SQL statement. You end a transaction by either writing the changes to the database and making them visible to other users, with the keyword `COMMIT`, or by erasing all the work in the transaction, with the keyword `ROLLBACK`. The code for a simple transaction is shown in the following example, with the optional keywords `BEGIN TRANSACTION` included:

```
BEGIN TRANSACTION;
UPDATE USER_ACCT SET BALANCE = BALANCE + :nAmount WHERE ACCT_ID = :nDestAcct;
UPDATE USER_ACCT SET BALANCE = BALANCE - :nAmount WHERE ACCT_ID = :nSourceAcct;
COMMIT;
```

This code illustrates the classic use of a transaction. The transaction is taking money from one account and moving it to another account. You would not want one part of this transaction to succeed and the other part to fail. Although the SQL that adds an amount to the destination account actually comes before the SQL that subtracts the same amount from a source account, the order of statements in the transaction doesn't matter. In a transaction, either the results of all the statements are applied permanently to the database or all the transactions are rolled back with the syntax `ROLLBACK`.

Within transactions, a `ROLLBACK` rolls back all the changes made by the transaction. There may be times when you do not want to roll back all the changes, just some of them. To handle these situations, you can use the `SAVEPOINT` syntax. A `ROLLBACK` either rolls back all the work for the entire transaction or just to the point of the last checkpoint. In the following example, the first piece of SQL shown is adding a line to an overall order. The application allows a user to delete just that line of an order without destroying the entire order. The `SAVEPOINT` statement sets a point for the end of a rollback in this scenario.

```
.
.
INSERT INTO ORDER_HEADERS (CUSTOMER_NAME, ORDER_HEADER_ID) VALUES (:sCustomerName,
     :sOrderHeaderID);
SAVEPOINT first_insert;
INSERT INTO ORDER_LINES (ORDER_HEADER_ID, ITEM_ID, QUANTITY) VALUES
     (:sOrderHeaderID, :sItemID, :nQuantity);
IF ORDER_LINE_DELETED
    ROLLBACK TO first_insert;
ENDIF;
.
.
```

The transaction provides not only the mechanism to ensure logical data integrity but also the container for implementing user isolation. Until a transaction is committed, the changes made by the transaction are not visible to any other users in the database. But multiple users, accessing the same sets of data, can create problems of data integrity.

Also, please remember, as we discuss in Chapter 8 on the basics of SQL, an implicit `COMMIT` occurs with any data definition language statement. In addition, this implicit `COMMIT` takes places at the end of a PL/SQL block with the END statement.

Concurrent User Integrity Problems

There are three basic types of integrity problems that can be created by users accessing the same type of data. The first, and most problematic, of these problems is called the lost update. Figure 3-1 illustrates a lost update scenario.

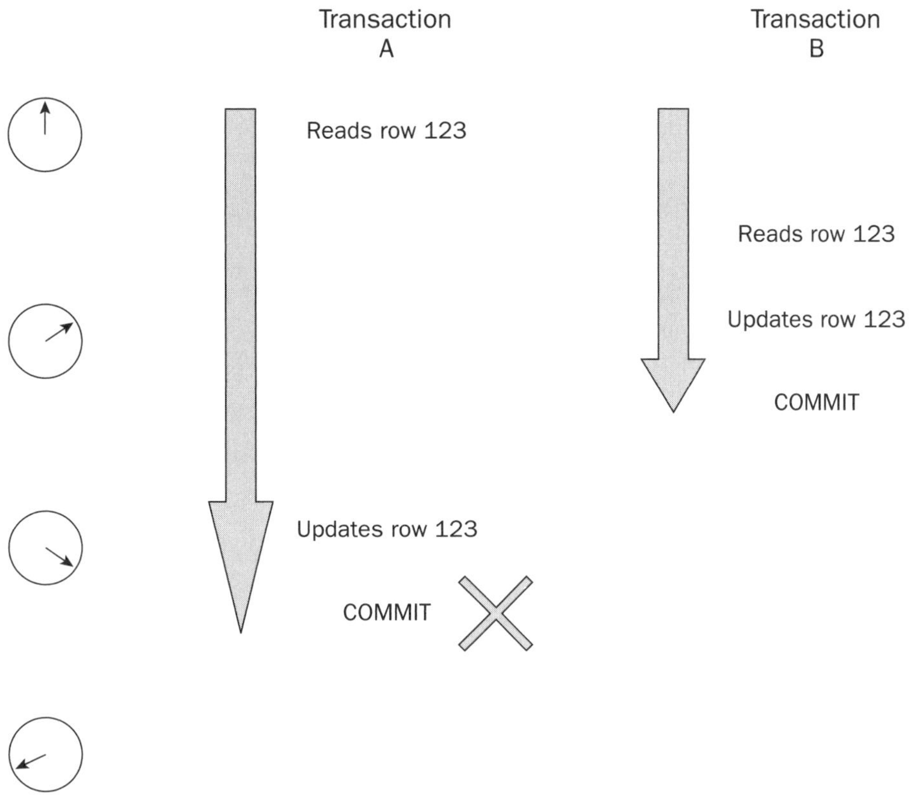

Figure 3-1: A lost update.

In this picture, you can see that transaction A began before transaction B, but transaction B is completed before transaction A. The changes made by transaction B were overwritten by the changes made by transaction A. When you take this scenario and include hundreds of potential transactions, data integrity can be severely compromised.

The second scenario is called a nonrepeatable read. In this case, a user retrieves data on the basis of a `SELECT` statement that includes a `WHERE` clause that specifies the data retrieved. For instance, the `WHERE` clause might limit the rows returned to only those order items where the quantity was over 50. The user works on the rows returned by the query, and then repeats the query within the context of the transaction. While the user has been reading the rows, another user has changed the quantity of one of the rows from 60 to 40, as shown in Figure 3-2.

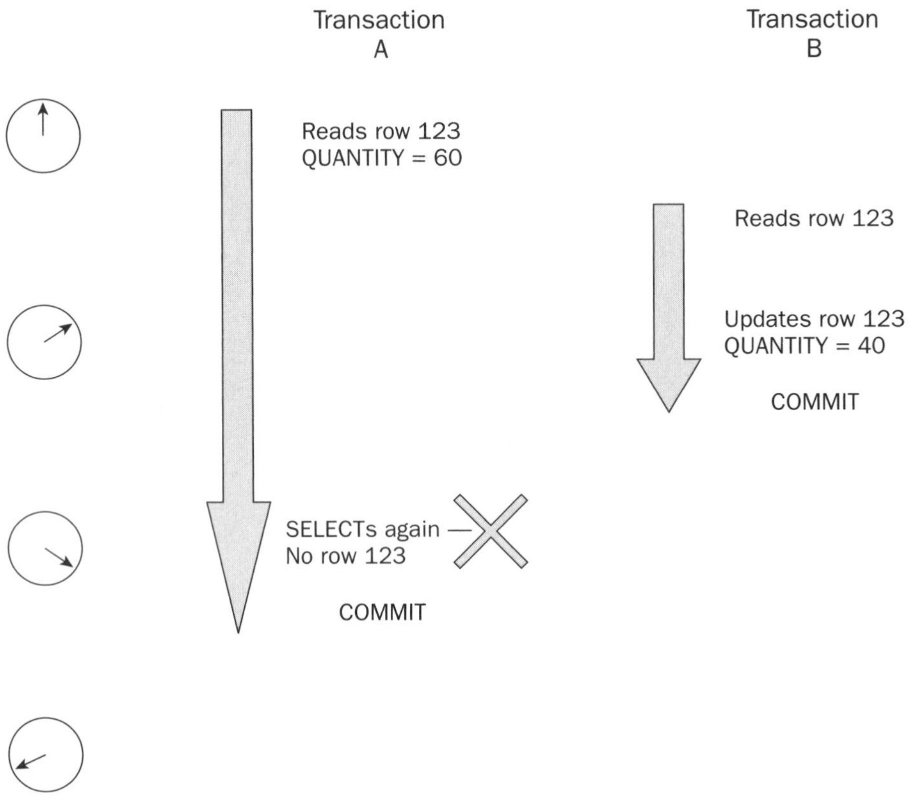

Figure 3-2: Nonrepeatable read.

If the initial user tries to repeat the query, a different set of rows will be returned. The user must be able to count on data remaining consistent throughout the transaction.

The third scenario is called a phantom read. A phantom read can occur when a user selects data with a limiting `WHERE` clause. In this case, another user adds data to the database during the transaction. This new data would have been part of the initial read if it had been present during the query from the initial user, as shown in Figure 3-3.

This situation may not seem so troublesome at first glance, but consider the case where the initial query is returning an aggregate value, such as a total or an average. Phantom rows would result in the value of the aggregate changing during the course of the transaction, which would alter the integrity of the data. The same effect would come from the nonrepeatable read described previously.

To avoid these problems, a database uses a system of locks.

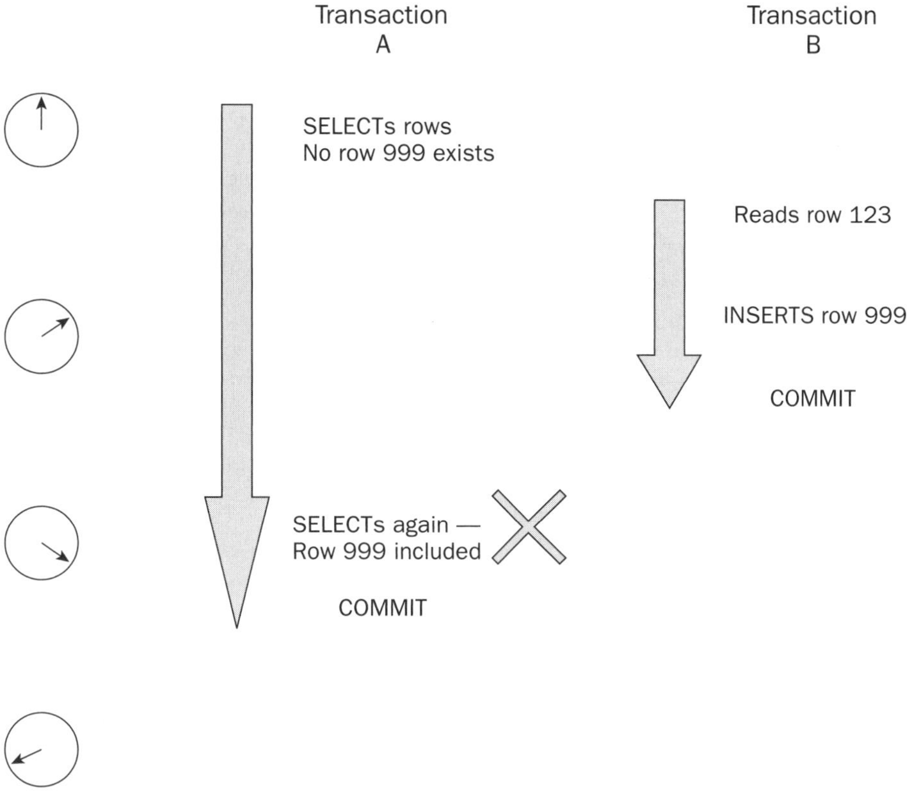

Figure 3-3: Phantom read.

Locks

A lock in a database performs a similar function to a lock on a door — it prevents access, but to data instead of a room. Locks are used to isolate activity during a transaction and are automatically released when a transaction is concluded through a `COMMIT` or a `ROLLBACK`.

There are two basic types of interactions with data, which call for two different types of locks. When you read a piece of data, you don't care if other people also read it. This type of data sharing is the core of a multiuser database. This requirement calls for a *shared* lock, sometimes known as a read lock. Many different people can read the same data, and many shared locks can be placed on an individual row. Shared locks prevent the problems of non-repeatable reads.

But since there is only one physical copy of a row in a database, you cannot have more than one user writing to a row at a time. To enforce this limitation, and to avoid problems like lost updates, the database uses *exclusive* locks, sometimes known as write locks. An exclusive lock prevents more than one user from accessing a piece of data.

> *You may have noticed our strict use of the phrase "piece of data" rather than "row." Locks are a physical entity placed on a physical entity. A lock can be placed on a row, or the page that row resides in. As you will quickly realize in the discussion of contention that follows, page locks can cause a lot more performance degradation than a row lock. Oracle was one of the first databases to support row locking, but other databases have gradually implemented this level of lock granularity.*

Since an exclusive lock only allows a single user for a piece of data, the database cannot issue an exclusive lock for a piece of data that already has a shared lock on it. This limitation makes sense from the point of the user who is writing data, as well as the user who is reading the data. If the database allowed another user to change the data in the middle of your transaction, the result could be either a lost update, a nonrepeatable read, or some phantom data.

Contention

The good news is that most databases use a system of locks to protect data integrity and implement locking automatically. When you request data to read, a shared lock is used; when you write data, an exclusive lock is used.

Unfortunately, there is some bad news. Locks act like traffic cops at a busy intersection, allowing some access to data and preventing other types of access. If a user is reading a row, no one else can update that row. If a user is updating a row, no one else can update or read that row. And when you consider that you may have hundreds of individual transactions interacting with hundreds of rows at a time, you can see a marvelous opportunity for gridlock.

Just as in a real traffic jam, no amount of horsepower can get you past this type of gridlock. You can have the fastest car on the planet, but in a tunnel full of backed-up traffic, you won't go faster than anyone else. If a row is exclusively locked, no amount of CPU, memory, or disk space can provide access to it that overrides the lock.

Worst of all, this type of problem is difficult to account for in the testing process. Even if you are running your applications against production data, you almost never have a test scenario that duplicates your full user community working with the application at the same time. An application that performs perfectly in your test environment could grind to a standstill once your real user community gets their hands on it.

Fortunately, Oracle has a great solution for reducing contention while supporting large use communities.

The Oracle Solution

So, there you have it. A system of locks that are absolutely necessary to provide critical data integrity can also cause performance problems as contention increases with use of the database. This looks like a situation where you have to compromise on one or both of these essential qualities in your overall system.

For most databases, you do have to find some sort of compromise. For instance, many databases allow you to perform a dirty read. A *dirty read* simply reads the current data in the database, regardless of whether it has been committed or not, and does not use a read lock. The advantage of the dirty read is that it avoids the contention caused by exclusive write locks. The disadvantage of the dirty read is that you are reading data that may very well be rolled back, producing inaccurate results and losing data integrity — not a great choice.

But Oracle has solved this aspect of contention with a unique system called *multiversion read consistency*. Although this isn't the snappiest feature name in the world, the feature itself is revolutionary and has been one of the primary distinguishing features of the Oracle database since it was introduced in the late 1980s. And, best of all, it completely eliminates the need for you to worry about some types of contention.

Multiversion Read Consistency

The somewhat cumbersome name multiversion read consistency, henceforth referred to as MVRC, does describe how the Oracle database works to provide its unique consistency. Whenever any transaction changes data in the database, Oracle creates a new version of the changed row. Oracle uses its rollback buffer to store earlier versions of rows. Simple enough, but the value it provides is impressive.

Each row version is marked with the system change number, or SCN, of the transaction that changed the values. Every transaction gets a global SCN number assigned in the order that the transaction was started. The SCN provides an absolute record of the serial order of the transaction.

When a transaction is retrieving rows to satisfy a query, it checks the SCN of the latest version of the row. If the SCN is smaller than the SCN associated with the transaction, the row version is retrieved. If the SCN of the row is larger than the transaction SCN, Oracle automatically knows that it cannot use that version of the row. Oracle reaches back into the rollback buffers to retrieve an earlier version of the row with an appropriate SCN. This process is shown in Figure 3-4.

> *If, for some reason, Oracle cannot find an appropriate version of the row in the rollback buffers, the database will return an ORA-01555 error, which reads as "Snapshot too old." You should size your rollback buffers to be large enough to avoid this type of error. Starting with Oracle9i, you can choose to allow the database to automatically handle UNDO, which should eliminate these errors.*

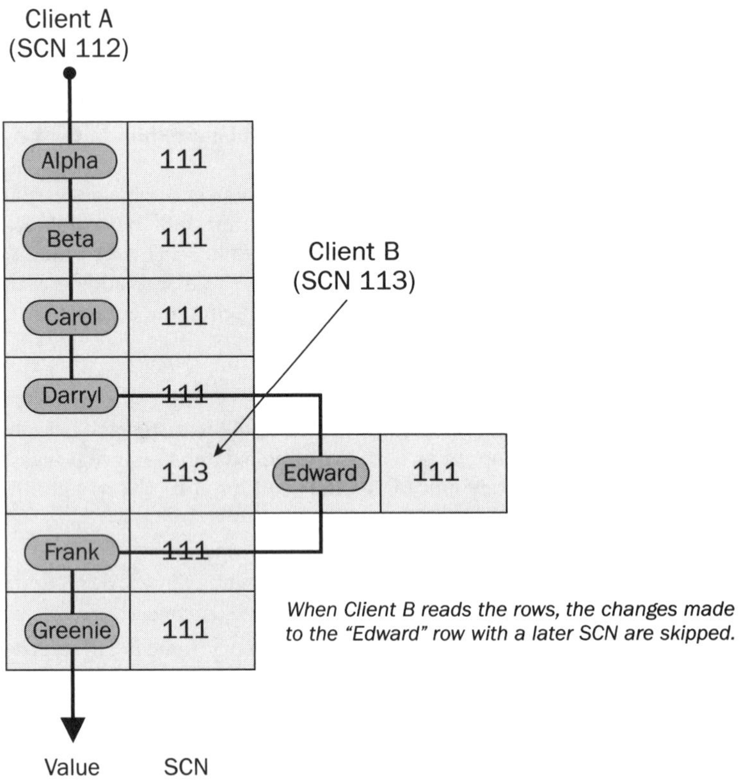

Figure 3-4: Multiversion read consistency at work.

MRVC gives each user a specific view of their data, at the point in time that their transaction began. Because of this, there is no need for Oracle to use read locks in their locking system. No read locks means less contention in two ways.

First, write operations do not block read operations. If another user changes data during the course of a transaction, there is no need to protect the data, since the version of the data that has been read will be stored as a version in the database.

Even more importantly, read operations do not block write operations. Since no read locks are used, a transaction can grab an exclusive write lock whenever it needs to, regardless of whether anyone is reading the data at the time or not.

For both of these reasons, you typically have less contention with an Oracle database, which not only means better overall performance at run time but less time spent developing applications that run against Oracle, since you don't have to add logic to deal with either the possibility of contention or the repercussions of that contention.

The Oracle database keeps track of the SCN of the oldest active transaction. When it needs to reclaim space in the rollback buffer, it cleans out versions of data that are no longer required by any active transactions— in other words, data rows that have an SCN number smaller than the SCN of the oldest active transaction.

Integrity Implications

MVRC can significantly reduce contention, but it also provides a level of data integrity that most other databases can only dream about. With Oracle, you are always getting a *snapshot* view of the database—the exact state of the database at one particular point in time.

If you start a query at 12:00:00, the data returned is the data, as it was committed to the database, for that exact millisecond. Other databases cannot offer this type of integrity, so you sometimes have to do things like create reporting databases just to provide a consistent view of data. With Oracle, this type of workaround is entirely unnecessary. The consistent snapshot view of data also prevents phantom reads.

If you are used to working with other databases, this concept may take a while to integrate into your overall view of databases and their use. We have actually had developers tell us that they prefer to have dirty reads—hmm, so they prefer potentially inaccurate data to accurate data? But MVRC works, and has worked well with Oracle for over 15 years.

Performance Implications

All this use of rollback buffers sounds like it might take up a lot of resources, which would impact performance. Granted, the Oracle database is a complex piece of software, but rollback buffers have been built into the core of the Oracle database for over 15 years. Oracle uses a variety of techniques to reduce the overhead of using this unique architecture. Although we hesitate to make performance claims for any software, since so much of performance depends on good design and implementation, industry standard benchmarks have shown the Oracle database to certainly be one of the fastest and most scalable databases in the world.

There is another side performance benefit of the way that the Oracle database implements locking that is not directly related to MVRC but does have to do with locks. Most other databases manage locks in memory. Since these databases typically use more locks than Oracle, they keep track of these locks in memory for faster performance. Memory is typically one of the more constrained resources, so the overhead of managing locks can take away from the memory used by the database. In addition, database administrators have to make sure that there is sufficient memory to manage all the locks in the database, since a problem with the lock manager can impact the entire database.

Oracle does not store locks in memory. Instead, the Oracle database keeps track of row locks in the header of the physical page that contains the row. This header also stores the location of a previous version of its rows in the rollback segments. If a row is going to be accessed for an SQL operation, the page it resides on has to be retrieved, so the lock information will be present in the page header. Because of this, there is no need for a separate lock manager. In addition, there is no increased overhead for an increased number of rows with locks. So Oracle not only eliminates the number of locks used to handle large numbers of users but also eliminates one of the ways that larger numbers of users demand greater resource usage.

Of course, the performance benefits delivered by reduced contention can be extremely significant. It doesn't matter how fast your database can go if you are waiting on locked rows. Add to this the fact that you, as a developer, don't have to spend any time writing code to achieve this level of concurrency and data integrity, and you have a significant advantage overall.

Isolation Levels

MVRC avoids contention by eliminating the use of read locks. But there is still a need to support two different levels of transaction isolation in the Oracle database, depending on the level of integrity demanded by your users and applications.

The first isolation level is called `READ COMMITTED`. The `READ COMMITTED` isolation level provides serialization at the level of a single SQL statement. The second isolation level is called `SERIALIZABLE`. This isolation level guaratees transactional integrity across an entire transaction, regardless of the number of statements in the transaction.

The `READ COMMITTED` transaction level cannot prevent nonrepeatable reads or phantom reads within a transaction, since the complete integrity of the data is only guaranteed for the statement, not the transaction. Another user's transaction could change data between the execution of a particular SQL statement and the next time that statement is executed in the transaction.

However, the `SERIALIZABLE` isolation level comes with its own potential issue. Think about what happens when a transaction encounters a lock on a row of data. With the `READ COMMITTED` isolation level, the statement is just guaranteed to return consistent data for the statement, not for the entire transaction. With the `SERIALIZABLE` isolation level, there is no sense in waiting for a lock to be released, since data integrity is guaranteed for the entire session. Even if the other lock is released, you still probably won't be able to update the row, because the row will probably have been updated by the other transaction. Since leaving the session will destroy all transactions anyway, the Oracle database returns an error as soon as it hits a locked row and the isolation level is set to `SERIALIZABLE`, rather than waiting for the lock to be released as it would be for `READ COMMITTED`.

Which isolation level should you use? Like most questions related to design and performance, this question has an easy, but less than helpful, answer: "It depends." If you want a guarantee of the highest level of integrity, you have to go with `SERIALIZABLE`, but in a heavily updated database, this level may result in lots of errors returned for your application to handle. If you have lots of updates, but the updates are short-lived, a brief wait for a lock to be removed might be an appropriate compromise.

> *Did you spot a potential problem in the description of `READ COMMITTED`? How long will a transaction wait for a lock to be released? As long as it takes. If you have a database where you expect a lot of contention, you can work around this problem by using the `SELECT . . . FOR UPDATE NOWAIT` statement, which reads rows of data but places exclusive locks on the rows, in anticipation of an update. The `NOWAIT` keyword indicates that Oracle should return an error immediately if it finds a row has been locked by another transaction. You will have to include logic to deal with this error in your code. If you keep your transactions short, as we recommend later on, you will probably be able to avoid implementing this type of workaround with Oracle.*

The `READ COMMITTED` isolation level is the default isolation level for Oracle, and also the one used by most developers. You may consider your particular scenario and decide that `SERIALIZABLE` is required for your situation. In fact, you should always consider your particular usage patterns, even if you end up using the default isolation level, since you will still have other logical problems to deal with, as described in the next section.

You can set the isolation level for a session with the `ALTER SESSION` statement, or for an individual transaction, with the `SET TRANSACTION` statement, so you could potentially use the more restrictive `SERIALIZABLE` isolation level only on transactions that require the highest levels of data integrity.

In the interests of completeness, we should mention that there is another isolation level supported by Oracle, `READ ONLY`. This level prevents any type of write operations on the database, as well as providing the standard snapshot view of data. Preventing write access reduces contention but also has a large impact on database operations, so this isolation level is in a class of its own.

Oracle uses rollback buffers to implement MVRC, which are unique to Oracle architecture. The rollback segments are also used to implement other Oracle features, such as flashback technology that lets you roll back the database to an earlier time.

Implementation Issues

Oracle's MVRC is a great help for developers, but it doesn't solve all the problems posed by multiuser access. You still have to deal with limiting contention caused by exclusive locks and protecting data integrity despite changes made by other users. These problems are universal, so the planning and effort you make to address these issues is not unique to Oracle, but something that all developers have to face.

Write Contention

The lack of read locks eliminates the need to do anything to avoid contention between readers and writers. But you could still end up with contention between competing writers. There is no way around this problem, since you cannot allow two processes to write to the same piece of data at the same time without losing all control over data integrity.

Since you can't eliminate the potential affect of competing writers, your best approach is to limit the window of time where this contention can occur. Because of this, we recommend doing your write operations at the end of your transactions. In other words, you should perform a `COMMIT` as soon after a write operation as possible, to reduce the time that the database holds write locks. This approach is appropriate for all databases, since all databases can suffer from write contention.

Oracle does have a feature called `AUTOCOMMIT`, which can be turned on at the session level. `AUTOCOMMIT` automatically executes a `COMMIT` statement after each SQL statement. Some programmers like to use the `AUTOCOMMIT` option for two reasons. When you have `AUTOCOMMIT` turned on, your application does not have to send specific `COMMIT` statements to the database, which saves you a round-trip between the application and the database server. In addition, `AUTOCOMMIT` works automatically, so you don't have to remember to code the `COMMIT` statement every time.

We don't really like the use of this option. First, transactions really become useful when you have to treat multiple write operations as a single unit of work, as with the credit/debit example in the beginning of this chapter. `AUTOCOMMIT` will completely destroy this capability, since the feature would do a separate `COMMIT` for the debit and then again for the credit. Second, we strongly believe it is good programming practice to actually have code for the crucial functionality you are implementing. In the real world, leaving things like `COMMIT`s to be done automatically can lead to a world of pain if later problems should occur. Imagine trying to find the source of a killer integrity problem in someone else's code, without remembering to check whether `AUTOCOMMIT` has been turned on.

Call us "glass half empty" guys, but this type of scenario happens all too frequently in the real world. For every minute of programming time you save with `AUTOCOMMIT`, you may cause hours of debugging later in the life cycle of the application.

Avoiding Changed Data

All of the discussion in this chapter has centered around the use of transactions to protect data integrity. Take the case of multiple writers. Exclusive locks protect two writers from writing at the same time. But what about the case of serial writers, where one transaction reads data, another transaction writes to the data and changes it, and the initial transaction then tries to change the same data? This scenario was illustrated in Figure 3-1 on lost updates.

Other databases protect against this by the use of shared locks, but dirty reads are often used to avoid the potential contention caused by these read locks. Oracle, as has been illustrated previously, does not have the contention problem, but with the `READ COMMITTED` isolation level, another user could overwrite those changes.

For either one of these scenarios, there could still be more contention than is logically necessary. Remember that Oracle, and many other databases, lock at the level of a row. What happens if one transaction updates one column in a row and another transaction updates another column in a row, as shown in Figure 3-5? In this scenario, there is no potential integrity problem in letting both transactions do their thing.

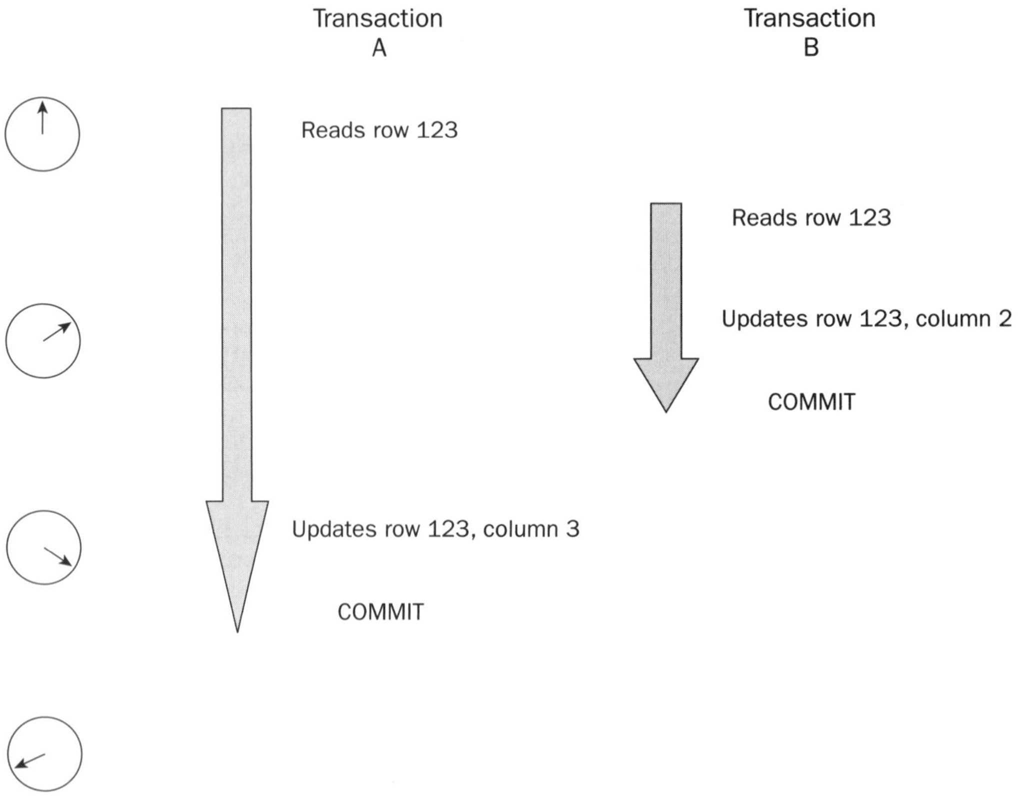

Figure 3-5: A lost update?

There is a pretty straightforward way of dealing with this issue in all situations. You just write an `UPDATE` statement that uses the previous values for all changed columns, as well as the primary key used to uniquely identify the column, in the `WHERE` clause. If this statement succeeds, you can rest assured that no one else has modified the data. If the statement fails, you can be sure that some other transaction has made a change.

The code following illustrates the use of this method:

```
. . .
SELECT PRIMARY_KEY, QUANTITY FROM ORDER_LINE INTO :nPrimaryKey, :nQuantity
.


.
UPDATE ORDER LINE SET QUANTITY = :nNewQuantity WHERE PRIMARY_KEY = :nPrimaryKey AND
        QUANTITY = :nQuantity;
COMMIT;
```

This code is perhaps more than you were thinking about writing for every single update of the data. But the code is not only foolproof in protecting against lost updates, it is also simple, straightforward, and pretty much self-documenting. Once again, imagine that you are not the brilliant original developer, writing elegant and complex code to solve a problem, but rather the poor slug that has to try and track down problems in the code left behind. Unfortunately, everyone has to take on the role of slug on occasion, so be kind to your future selves with clearly documented and functional code.

Summary

As soon as you have multiple users trying to access the same data, you can have issues of data integrity and contention. Databases use the concept of transaction to ensure that a single set of changes is consistent, but the need to guarantee this consistency also leads to the need for locks.

Other databases typically use both read locks, to protect data being read from being changed, and write locks, to protect the absolute integrity of the transaction. Oracle has a feature called multiuser read consistency that eliminates the need for read locks.

This feature gives a consistent view of data at the point in time when a transaction begins, regardless of how much read or write activity has gone on since that time. MVRC can help provide improved scalability in applications, especially those that do a fair amount of writing. In addition, MVRC gives you a consistent view of data at a single point in time.

4

Database Design Basics

There is a common belief that database design is done by the database administrator (DBA), while program design is done by programmers. This may seem like a natural division of labor, but it is actually quite unfortunate. Applications are made up of two equal and interrelated parts: data and processes. Neither has any purpose without the other and weaknesses in the design of either (or their intimate relationship) will be reflected in the entire system.

Design of the database and design of the total application require parallel efforts with frequent validations of each against the other. An elegant database design that requires awkward programming will be a maintenance nightmare. A tightly integrated and effective delineation of program modules can be rendered useless if the data needed by those modules is not structured for convenient access. Even worse is the discovery, as an application nears its final integration, that some data needed for a particular function isn't available or that some portion of the database has no means of being populated or maintained. It happens.

The solution is for the entire development team, analysts, programmers, and DBAs to work together with the system's eventual users to mutually discover both functional and data requirements and coordinate their implementation. DBAs need to gain an appreciation for modern programming constructs, while programmers need to understand the tenets of good database design.

This chapter isn't intended to teach object-oriented programming concepts to DBAs, but it does provide developers with the basics of relational database design and knowledge of the additional data management facilities of the Oracle database.

Some parts of application development (systems engineering) are methodical and almost scientific. There are straightforward ways of performing certain common tasks that can be readily adopted to solve specific problems. Database design tends to have more guidelines and ideas than absolute rules. What rules do exist are always presented in the context of when they should be broken. This chapter looks at the rules for normalized design and then turns immediately to the reasons and techniques for denormalization — intentional (and well-considered) violation of the normalization rules.

So consider database design to be more art than science. Don't ever attempt to argue that your chosen layout is the one correct design; further, be extremely suspicious of anyone else (DBA, consultant, manager, or Peruvian llama farmer) who insists that his or her approach is the only right solution.

The only absolute rule of database design is that there are always alternatives. That is not to say that some alternatives are not better than others; clearly there are wrong designs. The point is that the relative merits of design alternatives are only evaluated in the context of how the database will be used. These "how" issues are the province of the process designers and programmers. No DBA can develop an optimal database design without intimate knowledge of the way all of the programs will need to access the data.

Even with knowledge of the programs' data needs, it is still necessary to evaluate alternatives in light of multiple often-conflicting priorities. Performance is generally one of the priorities, but then it is necessary to determine which of the programs' performance needs are most critical. Modifying the database design to optimize a particular access will inevitably make some other accesses less efficient.

For an order entry system that takes in thousands of small, online orders each day, it may be most critical to optimize the database to accommodate that specific process, even though reporting, inventory management, shipping, and other related functions are either made slower or more complex. Another order entry system that receives only a few orders per hour for thousands of line items that have stringent availability requirements might be better designed around the needs of demand forecasting and analytics.

Let me offer one war story. I was the lead database designer for an order entry and customer service database for a large retailer in the early 1990s. The eventual system, when it went into production, included the largest known Oracle database on Unix in the world. I had an idea for a rather radical physical design change that would dramatically increase the availability of data in the event of a disk failure. (With the size of the total database using the 2 GB disks of the day, with no available disk mirroring, we calculated that we could expect an average of one disk failure per month.) This change would reduce recovery time by at least 50 percent and allow continued access, during most failures, to 90 percent of the customers' data while the 10 percent was being recovered.

The denormalization idea that I was considering would place some additional programming requirements on most of the common modules that had interfaces to the database. The design choice would also make certain types of access impractical, if not impossible. I spent two full months coordinating with each analyst from every subsystem team to make sure that there were no requirements to access customer order history data except within the context of a particular customer. Finally, everyone agreed that they had no such requirement. I made the database design change, and all database access modules in the system were modified to access the redesigned table structures.

All was well until about a month before we were ready to begin stress testing with an almost fully loaded database. A developer had been experimenting (without requirements or specifications) on a really interesting set of reports that would allow management to see the popularity of products across all customers. Nobody knew about this "skunkworks" operation until he brought me the SQL queries and asked to have access to the stress test database that was then about half loaded. I looked at his queries and told him they couldn't run. He was indignant and insisted that I was just a consultant and only his management could decide what was allowed to run. I tried to explain that I was not discussing permission, but practical reality. He wouldn't take no for an answer, so I let him start one of the reports before I left on Friday. When I returned on Monday morning, he understood my distinction between "can not run" and "may not run." I killed the still incomplete query.

So who was to blame? Not him—his idea would have been a great tool for management and just predated an analytical warehouse in that shop by about three years. Not me—I built a database designed to meet all of the application requirements and provide extremely high availability given the technology of the day. The blame (if that concept even applies) was only in the project management that allowed the mismatch between program/functional design and database design; neither took the other fully into account.

Only by understanding the many conflicting requirements of a system, evaluating their relative importance and then understanding the implications of the trade-offs can the design team achieve a final, optimized design.

Database Design Phases

Database design is not a single effort. Typically the design of the database goes through multiple high-level phases. At each step it is necessary to review the current state of the database design and compare it to the current state of the processing design. At each phase the comparison becomes more detailed and exacting.

Conceptual Database Design

There is no significant reason to separate conceptual design from logical design. Some designers or methodologies move some preliminary activities into this phase, such as identifying key business drivers and high-level purposes of an application (and its database). The output of such a preliminary phase would typically be a few paragraphs (or, at most, pages) that describe the opportunity for improving a business process or to provide a new service with an estimate of potential benefits and a statement of the scope of the effort. This can provide a useful perspective to set boundaries on the rest of the design processes to prevent expanding beyond what can be reasonably accomplished.

Logical Database Design

From a list of requirements (as they are discovered and documented), the team initially identifies a long list of data elements that they know must be included in the database. They additionally sort the data elements into groupings, informally at first and then with more rigor, around the entities of importance to the organization.

Logical design is performed without concern to the specific database management system that will eventually host the application's data. The logical database design for a system will look identical whether the eventual system will be hosted on DB2 on the mainframe or on SQL Server on a Windows workstation. That isn't to say that the eventual systems will be identical — it's just to say that those differences don't appear during logical design.

During the logical design phase the development team determines what data needs to be acquired, stored, and used by a particular application. Simultaneously, the team identifies what functional processes need to be performed by the application. As each model is refined, it is compared to the other to ensure that needed data for each process is included in the data model and that each element of data included in the data model has some identified processes that will create, use, and (usually) modify or purge the data.

Various methodologies, some very rigorous, others very casual, may be used by an organization for gathering requirements and identifying data elements that may be of importance to an application. Two complementary techniques (Entity-Relationship Diagramming and Unified Modeling Language) are discussed later in this chapter.

For all of the data elements collected in this phase, it is necessary to begin documenting some basic characteristics of the data. You need to know where the data comes from (if it isn't being created by the new application), and you will want to gather some preliminary estimates of the type of data:

- Is it strictly numeric? Will it always be integers or allow decimal values?
- Is the data item a date? If so, what granularity is required . . . to the day? to the minute? to the millisecond?
- Will the data be alphanumeric or will it need to include other characters?
- What if a needed element isn't character data but an image or some other unstructured object? If so, how large do you expect each instance to be?
- Is there a defined domain (range or list of allowable values) associated with the data? Does the domain relate to other data expected to be in your system? Does the domain have an external definition rule (such as spatial coordinates limited to valid latitude and longitude pairs)?
- What is the expected lifetime of this particular data element? Is it transitory or does it continue to exist for a predictable period of time?

Gathering an initial shopping list of data elements is a necessary but relatively casual process during the early parts of logical system design. Some discipline, however, is soon needed. The primary means of organizing this rapidly growing list of data elements is *normalization* and is traditionally documented using *Entity-Relationship Diagram* (ERD) techniques. Both ERDs and the process of normalization are covered in more detail in a later section of this chapter.

When developers and DBAs are working effectively together, the ERDs may be supplemented with use case diagrams as well. Examples of both of these techniques are shown in the discussion of database design tools later in this section.

Physical Design

The logical database design phase delivered a consistent structure of the data without regard to the eventual deployment within a specific database environment. It is possible to directly translate the logical design into a set of tables and build a database. It is usually appropriate, though, to take advantage of the specific capabilities (and limitations) of the selected relational database management system (RDBMS).

We have encountered some shops that have declared that they want to maintain RDBMS neutrality and therefore will not utilize any of the extended capabilities offered by any single RDBMS. This argument is naïve in at least three aspects.

- First is the assumption that the "least common denominator" capabilities of all RDBMSs will be sufficient to satisfy the application's needs. The standard SQL language is the basis of all current relational database systems, but SQL does not include specifications for much of the necessary infrastructure of an actual database. Additionally, there have been several revisions of the SQL standard as well as different levels of compliance by commercial products for each revision. Two RDBMSs may both be SQL-compliant but incompatible because of the different subsets of functionality that they implement. Discovering what the true "lowest common denominator" between every SQL database would be more work than just choosing one and exploiting it.

- Second is the assumption that by avoiding special features, the resulting design will actually be portable across RDBMSs without changes. There are so many operational and administrative differences between different databases that the SQL commonality isn't enough to facilitate simple transfer of data and application from one RDBMS to another.
- The argument for this decision is commonly expressed as, "We decided to purchase Oracle because our study indicates that it is the best product on the market today. However, if another product is better three years from now, we want to be able to move our application to that new platform." Do you see the fundamental flaw in this logic? What led this organization to determine that Oracle was the best product available today? Inevitably it was the extended set of features differentiating it from competitors that influenced this decision and justified the expense of licensing Oracle. Ignoring all of those additional capabilities means the organization pretty much wasted the months of evaluation time as well as the licensing costs.

In any event, if your organization wants to build a system that will run unchanged on either Oracle or MySQL, you should just choose MySQL and save some money rather than lobotomize Oracle so that it will behave like MySQL.

So, logically, the next step must be to translate the generic logical design into something that is specific to the implementation using a particular RDBMS. For this book's purpose, that RDBMS will obviously be Oracle. How do you represent the logical table structure into the most reliable, best performing, most scalable, and highest concurrency database that can be built? Many of the specific features and structures provided by Oracle, beyond the basics already covered, will be described in chapters throughout this book.

We won't try to preview Oracle's many features here. We will move on from this topic with the understanding that it is during this physical design phase that you should select the appropriate technology options available from Oracle that will best meet your application needs. You will need to determine access paths to the data and decide on appropriate indexing and partitioning schemes. You will have to look at your tables' needs for unique key values and build corresponding sequence generators. You'll consider the groups of users that will need similar privileges and will incorporate them into roles. You'll consider the need for alternative and potentially conflicting access patterns and possibly define views or materialized views to meet those needs. You'll consider your transactions' needs for storing intermediate result sets and define appropriate global temporary tables. If you find that you have user groups with the need for segregating their data, you will evaluate the alternatives of creating separate databases, and separate schemas or using virtual private database policies or adding label columns in the data tables to support Oracle Label Security.

It is during this phase that knowledge of available RDBMS features and experience with the requirements, usage, and limits of each comes into play. Physical database design is primarily an evaluation of trade-offs. For any given logical design, we guarantee that there are at least a hundred possible physical designs to implement it. We'll further guarantee that there will be significant differences in how those alternative physical designs behave, operate, and perform. There is usually not one absolutely correct alternative in that list, but some will fit the total set of requirements better than the others. Sorting through the alternatives by evaluating the compromises imposed by the conflicting requirements is the heart of the art of database design.

Practical Design

Okay, if you read the many good books devoted to the topic of database design, you probably won't see practical design listed as one of the standard phases of design. But in real systems development projects, there is a final phase in which the physical design is actually tested and various accommodations, minor or otherwise, are made in response to the discoveries made during testing. Even the most experienced database designers will not be able to fully anticipate the effects of the actual programs running with actual data volumes.

If your team did a good job with physical design, then the database that you create and load is likely to meet the design requirements well. However, many of the requirements that are obtained early in the process may get revised as programs are built and users are able to do their first hands-on testing of the application. Sometimes the estimates of how many users, how many rows, how many transactions, and so on turn out to be inaccurate. As this new knowledge is acquired, it is important to revisit the physical design and potentially reconsider some of the alternatives set aside earlier.

In many cases, this ongoing practical design process can be transparent to the application programs. The Oracle DBA can generally change indexing, partitioning, and virtual private database policies; add views and materialized views; and move a LOB (large object, either of character or binary data) to out-of-line storage without having to modify actual SQL. However, learning late in the development cycle that what you thought was a one-to-one relationship is actually one-to-many can have significant ripples throughout the design.

The key point of considering this as an ongoing part of the development cycle is that the earlier you recognize the need for adapting your database design, the easier it will be to fully investigate alternatives, make the necessary changes, and fully test the results. Discovering these needed changes the day after you put the database and application into production will be several orders of magnitude more painful.

Database Design Tools

Using a tool to support the documentation, diagramming, and iterative evolution of data models is strongly advised. Simple databases with only a few entities may not require a modeling tool, but "real" systems with dozens of entities, hundreds of data elements, and large development teams will need the capabilities of such a tool.

One good book on database design, not directed toward DBAs, *Database Design for Mere Mortals*, 2nd Edition by Michael J. Hernandez (Addison-Wesley, 2003), provides a thorough description of one approach to the logical (but not physical) database design process. It provides a system for doing design supported by paper forms rather than an automated tool. Such an approach is possible and is actually a good general way to learn the subject. The paper forms to gather and organize information about tables, fields, physical and logical characteristics, relationships, business rules, and so on work well for a college course case study's level of complexity. The book is recommended to a developer who wants more depth on the process of logical database design — but with the two caveats that any significant project will require automation of the overwhelming amount of data gathered and organized and that the book does not cover physical design topics specific to Oracle.

Over the past 20 years or so, data modeling using entity-relationship diagrams, as originally proposed by Peter Chen, has become a standardized methodology with excellent support from several vendors' modeling tools. The most common of these tools (although not necessarily the most powerful) is ERwin Data Modeler, now provided by Computer Associates. Oracle Corporation's tool in this space, Oracle Designer, has unfortunately been somewhat lost in the shadow of its newer sister product, JDeveloper. Both are bundled into the Oracle Developer Suite along with Oracle's other development tools. If your shop acquires JDeveloper for building, debugging, and deploying Java and PL/SQL modules, be aware that you have also already acquired an excellent data modeling tool (along with Oracle Warehouse Builder for designing data warehouses and their requisite data extraction and transformation processes).

Most of these tools do a reasonable job of aiding the team during logical design, since, by definition, this is a generic process that isn't tied to a specific database management system's particular capabilities and extensions. It is during the later stages of physical (and practical) design that it is important to have a tool that is capable of fully exploiting all of the capabilities of the RDBMS. In the case of designing a database specifically for Oracle, you'll want a tool that can let you define and build partitioned tables, index-organized tables, sequence number generators, global temporary tables, bitmap indexes, materialized views, and so on. (These Oracle structures are introduced in later chapters.)

With a tool that isn't aware of the full capabilities of the specific RDBMS, the development team must manually modify and maintain the database definitions generated by the tool. In the long run, this manual effort will present a lot of additional work and risk.

Object-Oriented Design Tools

At least a small entry needs to be added to discuss a class of program development tools that have the capability of generating database structures. Developer frameworks, such as J2EE Entity Beans, can automatically generate a database object (and the necessary access routines) that will meet the narrow needs of the particular bean to persist its state. It is dangerous to depend upon such default database objects, however. In many cases the generated object will not properly exploit the underlying database's features for performance and scalability. Further, the administration of a database with such unmodeled objects will be unnecessarily difficult and potentially lead to problems in production.

This is not to say that developers shouldn't use the capability when prototyping their program modules. Just consider the generated objects as an input to the actual database design process and not a substitute for it. Several narrowly defined objects may be better modeled as part of a larger picture, tied to more general business requirements, and thereby become more resilient to future application enhancements.

Database Design Techniques

In the preceding section on design tools, we mentioned entity-relationship modeling as a key technique used in the development and discussion of database designs. Unified Modeling Language is another set of popular techniques that can also aid in this process.

Entity-Relationship Modeling

Entity-Relationship Diagrams (ERDs) attempt to accomplish two things early in the design of a database. First they document the entities of interest to the enterprise. Entities may represent things (such as a customer, an employee, or a product) or an event (like a registration, a shipment, or an order). Entities have identifying characteristics and additional descriptive characteristics. For instance, an employee has an employee number, a name, a home address, a work location, a supervisor, a hire date, a pay rate, and so on. One of the challenges during design will be sorting through all of the available data "thingies" to figure out which are entities, which are identifiers of entity instances, and which are descriptive of particular instances of an entity.

In addition to documenting entities, an ERD documents the relationship between entities. From the list of example entities in the previous paragraph, you might conclude that there is a relationship between a customer and a product. It might be direct (a `CUSTOMER` owns a `PRODUCT`) or it might be more complex set of relationships:

- each `CUSTOMER` may place one or more `ORDER`s
- each `ORDER` must include one or more `PRODUCT`s
- each `SHIPMENT` must include at least one `PRODUCT` to one and only one `CUSTOMER`
- each `ORDER` may be fulfilled with one or more `SHIPMENT`s
- a `SHIPMENT` may include parts of one or more `ORDER`s for one and only `CUSTOMER`
- and so on

This list is an example of the relationship rules that might exist for a company. Another company with the same entities may have very different relationships and rules. For instance, an alternative relationship might be that "a SHIPMENT fulfills one and only one ORDER". Sorting through these relationships and the business rules that define them is the essence of designing a database that will meet the requirements of a specific business. Getting one rule wrong during logical design can lead to a database that will not be able to support necessary business processes.

Setting aside the order entry discussion, see Figure 4-1 for a quick illustration of the ERD modeling technique for documenting a logical database design that might be part of a (highly simplified) insurance billing system. Each box designates an entity . . . an object of importance to the enterprise. The ERD doesn't attempt to show all of the low-level data elements (attributes) associated with each entity. At most, identifying elements (keys) are shown. A total of seven entities have been shown in this example.

Relationships between entities are indicated by lines connecting them. Figure 4-1 illustrates an ERD with eight entities and nine relationships.

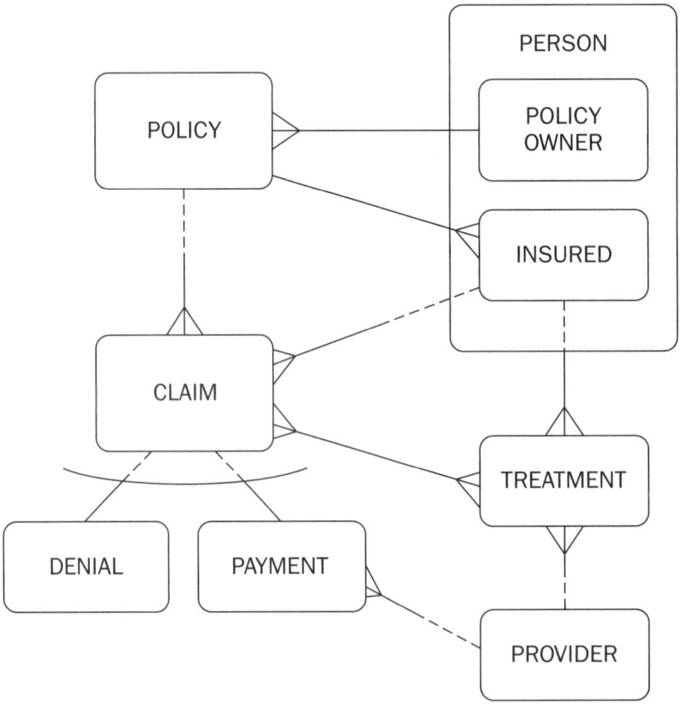

Figure 4-1: A simplified example of an ERD for the medical insurance claims.

While we might have shown INSURED and POLICY_OWNER as completely distinct entities, this model assumes that there are many characteristics of the two that overlap, so they have been shown as two subtypes of the PERSON entity.

As we said, the second aspect of an ERD is to document the relationships between entities, as shown by the connecting lines. One line is drawn for each relationship; every entity should be expected to have at least one relationship to some other entity, but not all entities are necessarily related to every other entity. It is possible for two entities to have more than one relationship.

Further, it should be recognized that every relationship exists in two directions. If entity A has a relationship to entity B, then entity B has a relationship to entity A. A single line defines this bidirectional relationship, but it is useful to define the relationship in both directions. Many methodologies and tools are not strict in this regard, but it helps when reading an ERD to be able to traverse the relationships without having to translate on the fly. In Figure 4-1, the relationship between `POLICY` and `CLAIM` entities can be stated in two ways: (1) A `POLICY` may have one or more `CLAIM`s submitted and (2) A `CLAIM` must be submitted against exactly one `POLICY`.

The nature of each relationship may be optional or mandatory in one direction or both. In this statement of the bi-directional relationship between the `POLICY` and `CLAIM` entities, the term "MUST" indicates that the relationship is mandatory in that direction (a `CLAIM` cannot exist without an associated `POLICY`.) A solid line in the ERD indicates that the relationship, in that direction, is mandatory.

An optional relationship exists in the other direction — the term "MAY" informs us that a `POLICY` is allowed to exist without any associated `CLAIM`s. In the ERD, a broken line indicates that end of the line to indicate that the relationship from that direction is optional.

The degree of each relationship, additionally, may be a one-to-one correspondence between the entities or, more commonly, a one-to-many relationship. Where many occurrences of an entity may exist for a relationship, a "crow's foot" is used to designate the many end of the one-to-many relationship, such as the fact that multiple `CLAIM`s are allowed for a `POLICY`. The written description of the relationship uses the "one or more" phrase to designate this.

Where only one occurrence of an entity may participate in the particular relationship, no crow's foot is used and we'll describe the relationship using "one and only one" or "exactly one" terminology.

Many-to-many relationships do occur in the real world, and during this logical design phase, they may appear in our ERD. Figure 4-1 showed such a relationship between `CLAIM` and `TREATMENT`. Many-to-many relationships, however, present difficulties in creating a physical database. Remember that a relational database makes its connection between tables using data values themselves rather than pointers. We will eventually, during physical design, implement a one-to-many relationship by carrying the key value of the "one" side as a data value stored within each row on the "many" side table. Many-to-many relationships can't be stored that way, so data modelers will resolve the many-to-many relationship into two one-to-many relationships and by creating a new connecting entity to help define the relationship. This issue was ignored in the preliminary example, but Figure 4-2 shows that specific portion of our total ERD with this relationship resolved.

Figure 4-2: Resolving a many-to-many relationship using a connecting entity.

A note on diagramming conventions: The example ERD uses one convention for showing characteristics of a relationship. Different methodologies (such as the original methodology of Peter Chen) and tools will possibly use a different diagramming technique to represent that a relationship is mandatory or the degree of the relationship. Learn and use the conventions of your chosen tool and don't get hung up on the differences from the example.

Another common construct included within an ERD are "Type of" subentities exemplified by INSURED and POLICY_OWNER that have been shown as subtypes of the PERSON entity. At a later revision of this ERD, some differences in types of PROVIDERs might have been discovered that would lead to a similar subtyping for doctors, hospitals, physical therapists, and pharmacies.

One other ERD diagramming convention shows "one of" choices among multiple relationships. This option is shown by the arc crossing the relationship lines connecting the CLAIM entity to DENIAL and PAYMENT with an arc. According to our simple ERD, either (but not both) of these may exist for any given CLAIM.

The primary advantage of ERD diagramming is that ERDs are easily explained to nontechnical users and sponsors of a proposed system. Most business people can easily validate the important entities, their identifying attributes, and the rules that define the relationships between the entities in their real world. A second advantage is that ERDs are very easily translated from their logical representation to a preliminary physical design of a relational database. It is, after all, a relational technique. The third advantage of ERD modeling is that ERDs can scale to show the total information model of an entire enterprise or a restricted view can present just the subset of entities of interest to a particular system. (Pulling a small part of the entire ERD, as in Figure 4-2, is an example of this capability.) This allows enterprise data architects a wonderful way to "zoom" in and out to examine global relationships or detailed implications of a proposed change in one particular program.

The disadvantage of ERD modeling is that it is primarily a data-focused methodology and doesn't attempt to model the processing needs of the application. Processing will have to be designed to support each relationship, but the ERD doesn't suggest how that processing will be handled. ERDs, as valuable as they are, require a complementary design and documentation technique to handle processing needs and module decomposition.

Unified Modeling Language

Application designers have been modeling systems for the 50 years that computerized systems have been developed. Flowcharts (some of us actually used the plastic diagram templates to draw them) were an early means of documenting the processing requirements and how data and, more specifically, control passed from module to module. During the 1970s new structured programming methods improved our ability to model the behavior of COBOL programs.

Along with the adoption of object-oriented design and development techniques in the early 1990s, a new set of similar (but distinct) design methodologies arose. OO developers learned and adopted the Booch, Jacobson (OOSE) and/or Rumbaugh (OMT) methodologies. Each of these methodologies had its strengths and its proponents. While they shared many concepts and goals, there were enough differences to make it challenging to pull together a development team that could agree on a common approach to the design of a new system.

The current solution to this dilemma is the Unified Modeling Language (UML), formally adopted as a standard by the Object Management Group in 1997. Today UML is almost universally accepted as the methodology and documentation techniques for nearly all object-oriented application design.

We spent a great portion of this chapter providing a somewhat detailed introduction to entity-relationship diagrams and normalization as database design practices. We will not attempt, however, to provide as much coverage of the use of UML for several reasons. First, many of the developers reading this book to learn about how to utilize Oracle may already have extensive experience with UML. Second, UML is a very comprehensive modeling "language" beyond the scope of this book. The third, and most important, reason arises from the origins and emphasis of UML.

Before any reader interprets this section as a criticism of UML, let us immediately put that concern to rest. When we introduced the ERD concept for logical modeling of relational databases, we immediately admitted that ERD techniques are extremely data-centric — their weakness is that they don't provide any assistance to the documentation of processes. Neither data nor process can be adequately modeled alone. Each complements the other and the two aspects of a system must be consistently reviewed within the context of the other.

UML can do a far better job of balancing the focus of design on both process and data than an ERD. UML is, however, very process-oriented in its orientation. This is not a criticism; in fact, it is what makes UML the perfect complement to data-oriented design techniques. Many UML practitioners focus on use case diagrams to document interactions between users (Actors) and processes (Tasks) and the relationships (Composition, Association, Triggers) between tasks. Secondary emphasis is given to documenting Scenarios, Sequence Diagrams, and Narrative Descriptions. (Note that at this point the UML process begins to identify entities and attributes, the building blocks of the database design techniques discussed previously.) All of these aspects of UML are primarily focused on process, with only a secondary acknowledgement of data.

Working through the UML facilities, we finally get to UML class diagrams. We recognize that they closely mimic the diagramming techniques of ERD modeling. It is, however, tempting for many designers to consider their class and object modeling from a limited perspective of the particular use case on which they are focused. Nothing in UML prevents or restricts data definition from being performed from a more global perspective, and in fact, it has to be. Design of database objects requires all of the rigor and emphasis that is given to any particular user interface problem — in fact, more. The effects of an inappropriate database design will have ramifications throughout the entire system, and correction of any data design deficiencies are likely to force major changes within many program modules as well.

The danger of UML modeling is not a weakness of the UML techniques themselves. It is an unfortunate tendency within development teams to focus their attention on the process design techniques and ignore class diagrams.

What this chapter hopes to encourage is an increased emphasis on the part of UML practitioners for the data aspects of the process/data dichotomy. Data used by only a single process or limited sequence of tasks may not have global effects, but the very nature of centralizing data storage within a relational database provides both benefits and potential risks — failure to properly model the shared data objects is one of the greater risks. By gaining additional understanding of the data modeling process (no pun intended), application designers can produce more resilient systems that better satisfy the needs of all their user communities.

Database Design Case Study Example

As you go through the various steps of designing a simple database, you will need some example application data. Rather than use one of the sample schemas, such as OE, HR, or SH used in most chapters, you will start here from scratch so the end design isn't already known. The example of a (highly!) simplified medical insurance system continues with a list of some data elements that were uncovered as part of gathering requirements:

POLICY_ID	POLICY_TYPE	CLAIM_DATE	CLAIM_AMT
DIAGNOSIS_CD	EXPIRATION_DATE	EFFECTIVE_DATE	INSURED_GENDER
TREATMENT_DATE	PAYMENT_DATE	POLICY_OWNER	DEDUCTIBLE_AMT
CLAIM_STATUS	COPAY_AMT	PROVIDER_NAME	MONTHLY_PREMIUM
POLICY_STATUS	CHECK_NUMBER	EFFECTIVE_DATE	INSURED_NAME
ASSIGN_AMT	COVERAGE_TYPE	TREATMENT_CD	DATE_OF_BIRTH
RX_NAME	ANNUAL_MAX_OUT_ OF_POCKET_EXP	BILLED_AMT	COVERAGE_LIMIT
BENEFIT_AMT	DENIAL_REASON_CD	PAYMENT_AMT	ASSIGN_STATUS
AGENT_NAME	ADDRESS	CLAIM_TYPE	DIAGNOSTIC_CODE
BENEFICIARY_ID	BENEFICIARY_NAME	EXCESS_PAY_AMT	DRUG_CLASS

It may turn out as you go through this design process that some of these data elements will need to be further defined or more accurately named. You will find that some of these data elements may not fit into the scope of the design and still other elements may have to be added in order to complete the exercise. You will also likely find that some of the elements that are initially uncovered turn out to be synonyms—different names, probably used by different business units, that describe the same thing.

For those readers who actually work in the insurance industry, it will be readily apparent that this example violates numerous specific business rules and avoids lots of real-world complexity. (Just think of the issues if this same example were carried forward into Chapter 5, "Oracle Security.") We will go ahead and use the example since we can expect most readers to have some basic understanding of the data and processes involved in providing and using medical insurance in the United States, as bizarre as they may seem to readers in many other countries.

Normalization

Relational databases are based on the theoretical (and subsequent practical) work in the 1960s of Dr. Edgar (Ted) Codd, a research scientist for IBM. Relational databases are inherently based upon the data values stored within the database. This seems intuitive today, but the hierarchical and network database management systems in use during the 1970s (when Dr. Codd proposed this mathematically derived alternative database organization) made no such assumptions.

Pre-relational DBMSs were highly dependent on the physical structure that defined the database. The designer defined explicit relationships, and records in one part of the database were linked to records in other parts via pointers stored directly with the data records. The only way to navigate through the database was to follow those explicitly defined pathways. Alternative access paths that had not been predefined were not possible.

The initial enthusiasm for relational databases was based on the flexibility of being able to restrict, project, and join (and perform other mathematical set operations) data based on just the content of data. It is hard to recognize now how revolutionary this was at the time. A simple relational projection and restriction such as "show me all the names of employees in the accounting department" could be expressed in a single statement of less than 20 words. The equivalent access to an IMS (Information Management System) database would require at least a few hundred lines of COBOL code with a `DATA` division to describe the department and employee structures along with several internal variables and output record definitions and a `PROCEDURE` division that would successively process each employee record with `GET NEXT` or possibly `GET NEXT WITHIN PARENT` commands (depending on how the DBA had defined the database structure and its pointers.)

Of course, the idea that big pieces of procedural code could be replaced by a single nonprocedural statement that could act on a set of data rows (tuples) was both exciting and threatening. The vast majority of mainframe COBOL programmers, along with IMS and IDMS (Integrated Database Management System) administrators, declared this new relational stuff to be a complete joke and totally without value in handling real database applications. Initially, relational databases could not provide performance to threaten the dominance of these hierarchical and network DBMSs.

Relational databases made their first inroads into organizations for decision support and ad hoc reporting that required flexibility of access and easy-to-develop query languages. In the early 1980s first ORACLE (back then the product name was in all caps to distinguish it from the company name, "Oracle"), followed by Ingres, Nomad, SQL/DS, and eventually DB2, were introduced. Over time, performance, reliability, and recoverability improvements were constructed underneath the relational model to go beyond the "flexibility" advantage and to move up the food chain of systems that were once strictly the realm of the older pointer-based database systems.

Since relational database management was based on mathematical rules, it is understandable that effective relational database design must also follow simple rules as well. Dr. Codd (and others) laid down the rules that define the logical (relational) design of a database, along with the mathematical operations that allowed well-formed databases to operate with predictable results.

This set of rules was defined as the process of normalizing the data. Initially, three successive levels, or forms, of normalization were defined. Further development of relational theory evolved several additional levels of relational purity through supplemental normalization rules. Three decades later the same normalization rules define database designs that will operate as expected. Since this isn't a book designed for relational theorists, the discussion will be limited to the original three basic normalization forms and the concepts will be described without mathematical proofs.

Additionally, we will be somewhat lax in our usage of terminology within this chapter. Some terms, such as entity or attribute, are properly used during logical design, while the terms table or column should technically be used only during the physical design of an actual database. We will sometimes use them somewhat interchangeably—not to confuse the concepts, but to make the description more readable, recognizing that even during logical design, we all tend to begin thinking of potential physical representations. This might offend a relational design purist, but we are attempting to be practical rather than pedantic.

One related naming convention deserves to be mentioned. It is customary for entities to be named as singular nouns during logical design. Once the corresponding physical tables are being named, it is customary to use plural nouns.

Normalization should also be considered in the context of a common computing paradigm of the pre-database days (and, to some extent, today), that of the sequential ("flat") master file. If we don't have an easy or efficient way to join data from multiple data stores, the temptation is to put everything into a single two-dimensional data structure. Users may be creating and modifying spreadsheets today to meet the business requirements that your database system will take over. Did you ever look at the common spreadsheet layout?

Consider, for instance, a marketing manager's spreadsheet designed to track people who have registered to attend a seminar. There will be a column (or two) to store their names, another for their company names, and others for their phone numbers, e-mail addresses, confirmation status, and so on. What happens when two people from the same company register for the seminar? The marking manger probably duplicates the company name values and perhaps the address information.

This kind of redundancy raises a few issues. First, this redundancy means that we have to store identical information multiple times. That wastes space and means that a change will require updating many records. It also allows for discrepancies.

For the marketing seminar it may not be critical that we have accidentally recorded registrations from ACME, Inc., ACME Corp. and ACME Incorporated. As the marketing manager reads the spreadsheet these may be easily determined to be the same organization. When a computer program reads the information, however, it will assume that these are three separate companies. Also, what if there are three participants from BigCorp, Inc but you show three different addresses? Does that mean that BigCorp has (at least) three locations? Or that some registrants used their home addresses? Or that you have a data entry error? It's hard to tell from the spreadsheet.

By normalizing data in your database design, you minimize redundancy in the database. Your goal will be to store data only once but in the proper place. All related data should be able to reference the one correct entry. If all three participants from ACME are indeed employed by the same company, storing company information once and then referencing it from the individual registrations improves data quality. If some of the registrants have provided a home address and others have provided a work address, it would be good to recognize that and even accommodate keeping individual data values associated with the individual and similar organizational data associated with the organization.

None of these issues of redundancy are too bad for the spreadsheet of 50 people coming to a seminar but extremely critical when applied to a larger data store like the billing records for a telephone company. This normalized design avoids the duplication of storage and maintenance as well as prevents many of the integrity issues caused by repeatedly entering what should be the same data.

First Normal Form

In the mathematical works that underpin relational theory, the fundamental logical grouping of data elements is known as a *relation*. A particular instance of a relation is known as a *tuple*. Now that we've tossed that bone to those relational purists, we'll move along. Anyone using the term tuple outside of a classroom is going to receive either a blank stare or a condescending sneer, so we'll go ahead and use the corresponding physical terms *row* of a *table* even in this logical design phase discussion. (If you want to be a purist, go ahead and drop the term tuple in a design meeting or at a dinner party—just don't say you weren't warned about the consequences.)

All of the columns (attributes, data elements) that form a table should have something in common. It is not likely that any relational data structure is going to simultaneously store the species names of my favorite marine fishes and the name of the only jazz vocalist to win three consecutive Grammy awards. Both are very important to me, but beyond that, they have no relationship.

The goal of normalization isn't actually that the proposed elements (table columns) should have any relationship between them. Instead the relationship of each element that properly belongs in the table should be between the element and the key of the table.

This leads to a critical side discussion of what a key means in this context. There must be some way of identifying each individual row (tuple) from all of the others in the same table (relation). Pre-relational databases connected data through the use of physical pointers. A record in the `ORDERS` segment was defined with a pointer to the first of its `ORDER_LINES`, which in turn had a physical pointer to the next `ORDER_LINES` record for that specific order. Since all of the related records could be found by following the pointers, there was no need for each `ORDER_LINES` record to also store the `ORDER_NUMBER`. There was no need to be able to independently identify `ORDER_LINES` records, since they were linked together by the database's pointers.

Because the relational database (as least logically) links data only through data values, there must be something in the data that lets you find a specific row when you want it. This identifying key may be one column (perhaps `ORDER_ID` in an `ORDERS` table), or it may require multiple columns (such as the combination of `ORDER_ID` and `ORDER_LINE_NUMBER` within an `ORDER_LINES` table.)

> *We'll be using this concept of keys throughout the discussion of normalization in the following sections. There are several forms of keys (primary keys, candidate keys, foreign keys) that we'll address more precisely when we get to the physical design stage. For now, we'll be using the general term" key" to loosely refer to the primary key of a physical table.*

So, for first normal form, each column must be related to the key of the table, but more than just related—each should be dependent upon the key for its identity. Another way of stating this is that for a table in first normal form, if you know the value of a row's key, then you can determine, without ambiguity, the value for each column in the table. Once you find a row in that table using a key value you have also found the single value for each of the other columns of that row.

This need to have a row identifier also implies another critical rule of normalized tables—the key must be unique. No two rows may have the same values of the key column(s). (If you somehow had two identical `EMPLOYEE_ID`s in your database, it would be impossible to determine the name and phone number for the specific employee—which row should you trust if they differ? This is a major reason why `EMPLOYEE_ID`s are used instead of just using the employees' names.)

Less obviously, unique row identifiers also imply that a value must be provided for each part of the key. As you will see later, in general, a column in a table may be allowed to not contain any value. (An unmarried employee's `SPOUSE` column would not be populated.) Missing or unknown data for which there is no value is referred to as "NULL" data. Handling of null values has several mathematical ramifications on certain operations on the data. We won't go into detail at this point but will just state that key values may not be null even though other non-key columns may be allowed to be empty.

Sometimes it is easiest to see a rule through an example and by demonstrating an exception to the rule. By going back to the list of medical insurance data elements that was presented earlier in this chapter, you can see which ones can be grouped into the `POLICY` entity. Figure 4-3 shows a first pass at grouping attributes into this entity.

Given a table of medical insurance policies, it should be possible to look up zero or one (but never more) policies using a value of the policy number key. From that one policy it should then determine anything directly related to that key value, such as the type of policy, the owner of the policy, the expiration date of the policy, and so on. Note that in our diagramming technique, key attributes are designated by a '#' in front of the attribute name.

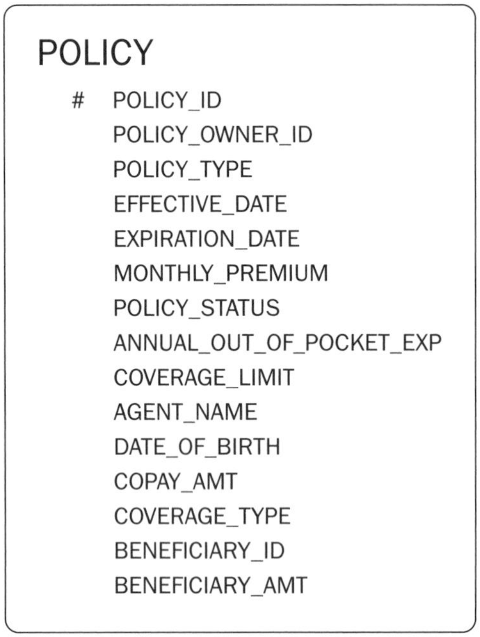

Figure 4-3: Proposed `POLICY` entity with attributes.

As you study Figure 4-3, though, you might notice a couple of things that may not be correct. First, note a proposed attribute for `DATE_OF_BIRTH`. Does this really belong here? Can it be determined by knowing the `POLICY_ID`? No, since one policy may cover an entire family and each member will have a date of birth, this column belongs elsewhere (somewhere in our `PERSON` super-entity).

If you ever discover that multiple values might exist for a candidate column, then you can be sure that that column needs to be in another entity that has a one-to-many relationship with the entity/table you are working with. Does that entity exist already in the ERD? The `INSURED` subentity does and is connected already by a one-to-many relationship.

If an appropriate entity doesn't already exist, you now have to go back and update the ERD to create it and the one-to-many relationship. By moving the multivalued column to another table, you can represent each value as a single row. This may require you to search for (or even invent) an additional key column for that new table. In Figure 4-3 you might need to do more research on `COPAY_AMT` as well. Is its value determined only by the `POLICY_ID`, or are there possibly multiple `COPAY_AMT`s depending upon the type of service, provider, or claim?

What about `COVERAGE_TYPE`? If the policy is for only one type of coverage, then there is some reason to wonder if this might be the same thing as `POLICY_TYPE`. Or are there are multiple types of coverage associated with the `POLICY`? If there is more than one value of `COPAY_AMT` or `COVERAGE_TYPE`, then you can't uniquely identify a single value for each just by knowing the `POLICY_ID` and they should be moved to another entity (connected to `POLICY` in a one-to-many relationship).

Continuing on that line of inquiry, you might also suspect that `BENEFICIARY_ID` and `BENEFICIARY_AMT` don't fit with the stated scope of a medical insurance system. These sound more like attributes of a life insurance system, don't they? Such a discovery might cause you, as a designer, to remove these attributes (because they are not in the scope), or it might lead you to turn POLICY into a super-entity (like PERSON) that has subentities. All of the attributes that apply to any type of policy would remain at the POLICY level and those attributes that are specific to a particular type of policy would then be moved into the subentities (HEALTH_POLICY or LIFE_POLICY) as appropriate. For this simple example, we won't make that decision but will only raise it as an example of some of the normal examination, questioning, and sorting of entities and attributes that must happen during normalization.

You might notice another concern as well. In the list of candidate attributes, there are two entries named "EFFECTIVE_DATE". You need to decide whether there are two separate effective dates in the system that apply to two separate entities or whether this is a simple duplication that needs to be cleaned up. If it is the former case, you might want to give them distinctive names (such as "POLICY_EFFECTIVE_DATE" and "CLAIM_EFFECTIVE_DATE") to avoid later confusion.

There are several other data elements that, at first impression, might appear to be related to a POLICY, but that do not belong with the POLICY entity. Several items in the candidate column list are dependent upon the specifics of a particular claim, for instance. You know that a POLICY may have multiple CLAIMs, so just knowing a policy number can't definitively identify a CLAIM_AMT. CLAIM_AMT, therefore, clearly belongs in our CLAIM entity. So, even though at first glance they are "related" to POLICY, they are not dependent upon the POLICY_ID.

So, the rule of first normal form (1NF) is that all data attributes in the table must be dependent upon the key of that table to provide their context and thereby derive their meaning. Multivalued attributes must be moved to another entity connected by a one-to-many relationship. Key values must be unique and must not be null (unknown).

Second Normal Form

Sometimes a table requires a multiple part key. If so, then every attribute (column) must be dependent upon the entire multiple part key and not just part of the key. There is one example in the insurance data model (created by resolving the many-to-many relationship). Each CLAIM must have at least one CLAIM_TREATMENT.

To build the key to this new entity, you will have to include the CLAIM_ID (key to the CLAIM entity) and another key that will relate each row to a particular TREATMENT entity key. Deciding which attributes belong with CLAIM and which belong with CLAIM_TREATMENT is done by assessing whether the attribute can be uniquely identified by just the CLAIM_ID or whether you will have to know which specific TREATMENT of that CLAIM. Therefore, in Figure 4-4, you see that TREATMENT_ID has been included in this entity. CLAIM_DATE has been left in the CLAIM entity because it applies to the entire claim. Further analysis may lead to additional attributes that are dependent upon this entity's composite key, but frequently intersection entities like this carry just the key values that related it to the two primary entities in order to resolve the many-to-many relationship.

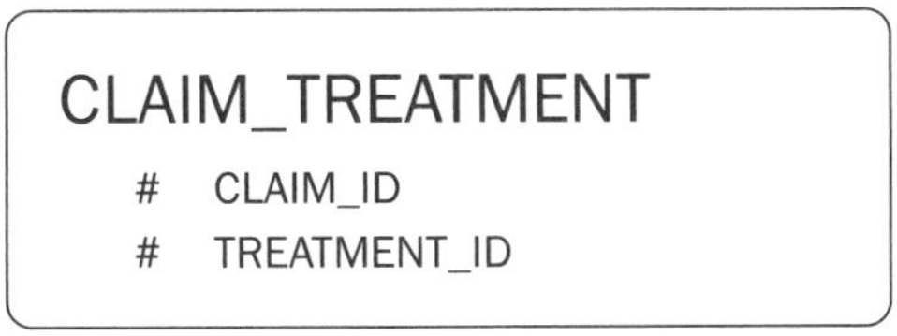

Figure 4-4: CLAIM_TREATMENT entity with attributes.

So, the rule of second normal form (2NF) is that, for any entity that has a multiple-column key, all data attributes in that entity must be dependent upon the full key, not just part of that key. If the value of a column could be determined strictly through knowing part of the key, then that column doesn't belong in this entity (or else you have not correctly defined the key structure.).

When you find that you need multiple columns to identify an instance of an entity, our rule not allowing keys to be null now applies to each of the columns in the multipart key.

Third Normal Form

Once an entity is in 2NF, the final test of purity of design that is performed looks for transient dependencies among the entity's attributes. In this third normal form (abbreviated as 3NF), you verify that each attribute is really dependent upon the key as opposed to being dependent upon some other attribute that is dependent upon the key. Did that make sense? Let's look at a violation of 3NF as a way to better understand it.

Look back at Figure 4-3. There's another questionable attribute in the first-pass `POLICY` entity attribute list. Does `ANNUAL_MAX_OUT_OF_POCKET_EXP` really belong here? Is this dependent upon the key, `POLICY_ID`? Perhaps. But it may be true that this value changes each year as the policy is renewed. If so, the value of `ANNUAL_MAX_OUT_OF_POCKET_EXP` is dependent upon the `POLICY_ID` and the year. Since you may need to process `CLAIMs` from one year during the next year, it might be necessary to keep both the current year and some previous years' values in the database. This attribute, and perhaps some others, really should be put into a new entity, `POLICY_YEAR`. Further discussion of requirements will be needed to know for sure.

Let's continue our examination of Figure 4-3's proposed list of attributes just a little longer. What about `AGENT_NAME`? It can be argued that the agent for any given policy should be known once you identify the specific policy, so there isn't a clear violation of first normal form. However, as you continue to flesh out the design, you are likely to find that you need an `AGENT` entity to which the `POLICY` entity will be related. When that happens you will want to carry the key (such as `AGENT_ID`) within the `POLICY` entity and use `AGENT_NAME` as a non-key attribute within the `AGENT` entity. This would be a better 3NF design if you are going to track any other information about agents besides their name.

Other Keys

Earlier we said that there were different types of keys but that we'd postpone discussion of the alternatives for a bit. Well, it is now time to introduce the key types other than primary keys. First, once you have decided on a primary key that uniquely identifies each row in a table, you may find that you have some other columns that might also be able to uniquely identify rows as well. You may have already chosen `EMPLOYEE_ID` as the primary key for the `EMPLOYEE` entity, but you see that `SOCIAL_SECURITY_NUMBER` (in the United States) is also unique and never null. It could also be used as a key (SSN was once commonly used as the employee number in most corporations, but, for privacy reasons, companies shouldn't be doing that today). You might even decide that the combination of `LAST_NAME`, `FIRST_NAME`, `MIDDLE_INITIAL` would uniquely define an individual. (While it might do so today, a new hire next week could easily mess up that plan.) Adding `BIRTH_DATE` to the name combination makes it more likely to be unique.

The point of the last discussion is that you may identify several *candidate keys*. Any column (or combination of columns) that will never be null and that can uniquely identify each individual row is a candidate for use as a primary key. Sometimes one of those will be clearly better than the others. Other times none of them will be particularly good; in these situations, you may elect to create a new ID column strictly for use within the database. Order numbers fall in this category. Once upon a time, when you went to the general store and bought what you needed and paid cash, there was no need to have an order number. If the general store had to order something special, the customer and owner could discuss the order in terms of what was ordered, when it was ordered, and so on and still understand the business. Only as we began to computerize the ordering process did the artificial construct of putting a unique number on each order begin to have value.

Alternate Keys

Once a primary key has been selected, the remaining candidate keys can be examined. If one or more of them still seems to meet all of our criteria (uniqueness, not null, privacy issues, etc.), you might elect to designate the candidate as an alternate key. As an example, we'll move away from the United States and consider vehicle registrations in the United Kingdom. An automobile is issued a license plate in the United Kingdom that will remain with the vehicle as long as the vehicle continues to operate, even after it is sold to a new owner. A factory-issued vehicle identification number might still be the best primary key, but for as long as the vehicle remains within the United Kingdom, its license plate number is also a unique identifier and could be designated as an alternate key.

Alternate keys are never required as part of your design. They are strictly for convenience. If one is evident and there is an identified use for it, then feel free to document it.

Foreign Keys

Foreign keys as a physical construct are discussed in much more depth in Chapter 11, "Constraints." Within this chapter it is important to introduce the concept of foreign keys from a logical design perspective.

Every relationship in our ERD (and some that are created to some new tables in a page or two) may be defined to the database and implemented as a foreign key. Logically, a foreign key is the data column (or columns) within one table that allows that table to be related to the corresponding column(s) that serve as the primary key (or, less frequently, an alternate key) in another table.

From the earlier insurance company example, each `CLAIM` record has to somehow be related to the `POLICY` under which the claim is made. This is done by including a `POLICY_ID` column in the `CLAIM` entity that will provide the navigational linkage from an individual claim record to its parent policy record. The `POLICY_ID` column in the `POLICIES` table is its primary key. The `POLICY_ID` column in the `CLAIM` entity is a foreign key.

Notice that by adding the foreign key column into the "child" entity, a certain level of data redundancy to the data model has been introduced. While the goal of normalization, as stated previously, was to minimize redundant storage of data, we were careful not to say "eliminate" redundancy. This is a case in which introducing controlled redundancy is both appropriate and necessary to ensure the integrity of the relational database. This is, however, a good argument for choosing simple primary keys. A six-digit `EMPLOYEE_ID` is a better primary key than the alternative of using full name and date of birth. If you must have a level of redundancy, then you want to make it as manageable and efficient as possible.

For the new connecting (sometimes called an "association" or "intersection") entity of `CLAIM_TREATMENT` you saw that the primary key would have to be the combination of `CLAIM_ID` and `TREATMENT_ID`. These attributes are also individually foreign keys to the `CLAIM` and `TREATMENT` entities.

You document foreign keys as part of the logical design of tables and their relationships. When you implement the physical foreign key integrity constraint in Oracle, the database ensures that only valid values are ever allowed into the foreign key column(s) of any data row.

Normalization Summary

Two generations of database designers have remembered these three rules of data normalization by means of the phrase, "my data is dependent upon the key, the whole key and nothing but the key, so help me Codd." As corny as it has become over the years, it is still a good reminder of the basic relational design requirements.

Every relation (table) must have a unique identifying key that may consist of one or more data attributes (columns), none of which may be null. Each non-key attribute (column) must be either null or have a single value that can be determined directly from knowing the value of the key. If a multiple-part key is defined, then each non-key attribute must be determined only by knowing the values of the entire key. Attributes in the relation should be identifiable by their relationship to the relation's key rather than a relationship to some other attribute.

For those who choose to go beyond third normal form, there are additional rules that can further purify a logical design (for instance, eliminating any data attributes that can be functionally derived from existing attributes in the same entity), but for our purposes, third normal form is generally sufficient. While theoretically interesting, Boyce-Codd normal form, fourth normal form, fifth normal form, and so on have little practical value. Almost inevitably, the need to perform physical design and denormalization for performance reasons will override any additional purity added by these higher forms of normalization.

If your relational design during the logical design phase satisfies all of these normalization rules (that is to say, your data is strictly in 3NF), you have documented the keys (primary, alternate, and foreign) and you can cross-check the data model with your processing model and requirements documents, then you are ready to go on to the physical design phase.

Defining Additional Entities (Tables)

Logical design provided a list of the data entities that will be translated into tables to hold the data required for the application. That will provide the majority of the data in the database. However, as you also evaluate the various data integrity requirements and business rules, you are likely to find that you will want some additional tables to hold reference data—not the data about the `POLICY` and `CLAIM` entities themselves, but lists of allowable values for columns in those tables.

For instance, if the fictional insurance company provides not only medical insurance but also life insurance, disability insurance, personal liability insurance, and so on, it is likely that the physical `POLICIES` table will have a column for storing `POLICY_TYPE`. To ensure that only valid values are entered into that column, you can either code all of the allowable values into every program that ever enters or modifies data in that table or you can create a reference table that holds the valid values. The first option requires us to maintain code anytime the business changes, whereas the second just requires us to change data in a table. Which is easier? Which is more reliable? Going the second route, the database can automatically perform the integrity check whenever data is changed. Further, this reference table can still allow the program to have the same intelligence without coding changes; the program just has to read the reference table to give the user a current and accurate list of available options.

If the logical design included any many-to-many relationships, we would have translated them into intersection entities with one-to-many relationships to the original entities as was done back in Figures 4-2 and 4-4. In addition to the reference tables, these new intersection entities will be added to the design as tables.

We mentioned during the discussion of normalization that we sometimes discover multivalued columns. We said that normalized data also doesn't allow multiple values (they are not uniquely identified by the primary key), but we didn't decide how to handle them. The solution is to add a new entity. The example of having different values for ANNUAL_MAX_OUT_OF_POCKET_EXP may lead us to create a new entity, POLICY_YEAR, as shown in Figure 4-5.

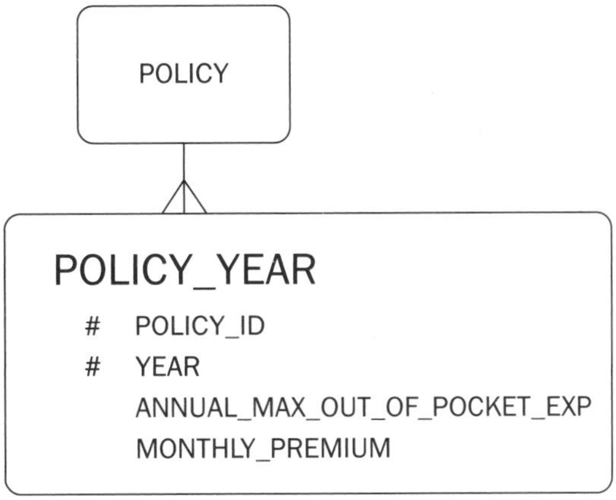

Figure 4-5: Creating a new POLICY_YEAR entity to store policy information that changes annually.

Further analysis of the proposed POLICY attributes identified the need to move MONTHLY_PREMIUM into this new entity as well.

Denormalization

During the logical design phase, you normalized data to minimize redundancy and validate the correct assignment of data columns to the "correct" tables. This fully normalized design makes it easy to confirm that the design is consistent and relationally pure. While having a pure, consistent, and validated design is certainly a worthwhile goal, another goal has to be a design that will perform adequately when actually implemented.

Remember that when you reach the physical design phase, your primary objective is to translate the logical model into the physical objects of Oracle. You have many options (partitioning, indexing, etc.) to consider for your physical design. There are times, however, when the direct translation of logical entities into physical tables will not meet your application goals. It is frequently necessary to consider options that will slightly corrupt your pure design by reintroducing some of the data redundancy and even some multiple valued fields that you worked so hard to eliminate.

Denormalization is not an excuse for failing to properly normalize data in the first place. Denormalization should be a conscious decision rather than mere laziness.

One of the common forms of denormalization is to take multiply occurring values out of one-per-row storage in a separate table and storing them as separate values within the "parent" table. This can be done using individual columns or with an Oracle VARRAY object. (Note that the use of a VARRAY or nested table appears to be a denormalization from the viewpoint of the programmer even though the database can most efficiently use a separate table at a physical level. Defining the storage of an apparent denormalization may still be done using a normalized physical table structure.)

Another common denormalization is to store data redundantly. Even though avoiding redundant storage is a primary advantage of the relational model, there are times when controlled redundancy may be worthwhile for the overall performance of a system. Someone once described flying an airplane as an ongoing controlled fall. Redundancy, if introduced, follows the same model — it takes extra maintenance energy to control the data redundancy just as it takes extra thrust to maintain lift and overcome the forces of gravity and drag on an airplane.

So what would lead us into consciously violating the supposedly inviolable rules of database design? Usually an anticipated performance issue. Consider the following examples:

- The application may have reporting needs that will require multiple-table joins with aggregations that are expected to take longer to execute than the users will tolerate. Possible solution: Introduce redundancy by storing a prejoined, aggregated version of the data using a materialized view. Doing so will speed those queries, but it also means that the materialized view will have to be maintained to reflect changes in the base data tables.
- The normalized design example from this chapter that split `POLICY_YEAR` out as a separate entity is relationally pure. However, if you determine that millions of transactions per year are going to require an additional lookup into that table every time they add or maintain any claims data, you might be concerned about the performance impact. A possible denormalization would be to carry the current year and past year values in two separate columns of the `POLICIES` table. That would reduce your need to read the extra table as part of every transaction, but it also means that once a year you're going to have to execute a large update of the `POLICIES` to update these values. It also means that you would give up the flexibility of keeping more than one year of history.
- Another denormalization option for this same problem would be to keep the `POLICY_YEARS` table but redundantly store the current year's `ANNUAL_MAX_OUT_OF_POCKET_EXP` in both tables. This would save you the extra I/O on most (current year) transactions and maintain the multiyear history but would mean than any changes to the current value will have to be applied to two physical tables.

Note that we are not going to recommend one of these options in this example because we don't know the specific performance reasons that, for a real application, would justify "corrupting" our pure normalized design. Notice that every denormalization suggestion has both a positive and negative effect. Usually the positive effect is a performance boost for one or more functional parts of the system. The negative effects may be a performance degradation for other parts of the system, a limitation on the flexibility of the system, or an increased maintenance requirement. Before deciding on any denormalization the development team must thoroughly evaluate the trade-offs and be comfortable that the costs are justified by the expected gains.

Other Physical Design Options

Features of Oracle (or any RDBMS, for that matter) provide capabilities to make the physical database perform or behave in desirable ways that are ignored by theoretical logical design. Some of the additions to the Oracle physical database design include indexes, partitioning, views, materialized views, sequences, and so on. Further, someone has to create the physical database including application tablespaces to house all of our objects, the physical data files to hold the tablespaces, log files to provide database recovery . . . the list of critical things unknown to logical database design is extensive.

All of these Oracle-specific physical objects are described in depth throughout the rest of this book and will not be addressed here. As one example, we'll touch on one of the most frequent physical object types — indexes — here but will save the details until Chapter 10, "Indexes." Many other physical design options are addressed in Chapter 12, "Other Database Structures."

There is no mathematical basis for indexes within the underlying set theory of relational databases. Relational theory has the luxury of not having to meet performance expectations of users. Realistically, there have to be physical capabilities within the software of a relational database management system to efficiently execute the theoretical relational operations.

- Each table is designed to have a primary key that uniquely identifies each individual row in the table. Finding a specific row with a particular key value generally requires something more efficient than reading the entire table until you find the row you want.
- Primary keys of tables are required to be unique, but some mechanism must be provided to actually ensure uniqueness across millions of rows in a table.
- Even though rows are uniquely identified by their primary key values, it is often necessary to find a set of rows based on other criteria. Finding all customers in Virginia does not use the primary key but generally must be performed more quickly than a complete search through the entire customer table.
- The data within two tables allow rows from one to be joined to those of another. To do so efficiently, you often must look up matching rows in the second table quickly.

Relational theory ensures that you can perform these actions. To do so, however, requires more than theory. One of the most common tasks during physical design of a database is the addition of indexes to particular columns of tables. Some of these indexes can be added automatically (for primary keys, for instance). Others will be added because of knowledge of how Oracle performs specific operations (an index on the foreign key of a child table affects the locking model when rows are deleted in a parent table). Others will be added to support specific query access.

DBAs are frequently seen as being in charge of the physical database design process. While it is reasonable that they should take the lead, they cannot do the job completely independently. This example of indexing is a perfect illustration of why developers must be involved in the physical database design process. Unless the DBA knows that a particular set of queries will need to access a table in a particular way, he or she will not have a reason to create an index on a particular set of columns.

Every option that enhances one particular access has some side effects that may adversely affect other accesses to the table. Working in a vacuum, DBAs sometimes create indexes on dozens of columns just in case some search is going to be done on one of those columns. Every additional index increases the workload for Oracle whenever a new table row is inserted or deleted or the value in one of those columns is changed within an existing row. We have seen several tuning engagements where one of the first performance improvements is to drop unused indexes.

Every choice made during physical database design is a balancing of potentially conflicting needs, a trade-off between various beneficial and adverse effects. There are very few, if any, "free lunch" choices in physical design. It is almost inevitable that enhancing one form of database access will have some effect on another form of access. The trick is to determine the frequency and criticality of each of those alternative accesses and then make an intelligent decision on how to balance them for the overall good of the user-owners of the database and application. No DBA can successfully perform that trick without the critical information that only the application developers can provide as they design the programs that will access the database.

Object-Oriented Design Options of Oracle

Object-oriented design and development sometimes seems to be at odds with the concepts of relational database storage. The definition of an object/class violates several of the rules we've just said are required for a normalized relational database, such as the need to store items with multiple values. Reconciling the object model with the relational storage model used to be a very tedious and painful task.

Fortunately, this process is made simpler by the object-relational enhancements provided by the Oracle database. Chapter 21, "Object Relational Interactions with Oracle," covers these object capabilities in depth. Two points need to be made prior to the discussion in that chapter, though.

First, all of the object-oriented data definition options in Oracle are actually implemented, under the covers, using relational tables and indexes. The ability to define and use a variable-length array (VARRAY), for instance, is convenient for access from an OOP environment, but its actual physical implementation will include a multirowed table that will store the multiple-valued object. The developer and DBA will need to communicate well to ensure that the physical implementation of objects will perform adequately.

Second, the ability to define objects in Oracle does not eliminate the need for performing thorough data analysis, normalization, and physical design. It is still critical to completely understand, document, and integrate the various accesses to all database objects within the entire scope of the application.

Summary

Database design is an integral part of designing effective and efficient applications. Without a conscious effort to produce an integrated database design, application programs are likely to fail to achieve the benefits provided by a powerful RDBMS such as Oracle. Data design and process design need to be equal partners in the total application development effort.

Database design is done in phases. A conceptual design forms the basis for a logical database design, which, in turn, evolves into a physical design. The physical design is then reviewed and possibly modified to accommodate practical considerations.

Logical database design is somewhat a creative exercise, but well-defined techniques, such as entity-relationship modeling and normalization, allow the art to be constrained by something of a science.

Physical design is partly a translation of logical entities into physical tables, but it also includes the creation of a number of additional physical objects such as views, indexes, partitions, sequence generators, and object-relational features of Oracle. It also consciously incorporates very specific denormalizations to the normalized logical design in order to provide adequate performance characteristics for the application. Each denormalization decision must evaluate the expected performance benefit against the other impacts to performance, flexibility and maintainability of the total application.

All of the Oracle features described throughout the rest of this book will either influence the database design or be impacted by it.

5

Oracle Security

Security within most applications is a critical and increasingly complex subject. Database applications have more stringent security requirements because of the centralized storage of information. Modern multi-tier application architectures present additional security challenges because each level and each network connection provides additional opportunities for data to be inappropriately viewed, modified, or corrupted. When an application is exposed to the public Internet, all of these concerns are magnified by the potential millions of users, at least some of whom are intensely interested in bypassing the security measures to either see or manipulate data inappropriately.

This chapter focuses primarily on the security capabilities of the Oracle database. Application developers will be connecting to the database from a variety of different application servers, and each of these has its own set of both security issues and features. Even though we cannot attempt to cover the specifics of each application server, we will provide an overview of the issues and concerns that an application developer must consider when building an application that will connect to Oracle from a multi-tiered environment.

Security Concepts

This book focuses on Oracle development, and this chapter, correspondingly, focuses on the security capabilities provided by Oracle. Database security is a key concern because of the nature of the data stored within corporate databases. However, it is critical that security is considered throughout the entire application architecture including network transport, network access, and physical protection of servers, as well as access points to the application and network.

This chapter first examines some of the issues and needs regarding security and explores the reasons for applying security measures at the database level.

Confidentiality and Privacy

Databases hold data of all kinds. Some have no particular confidentiality concerns, such as a table of all valid zip codes in the United States that are publicly available. Other data, though, may identify personal information about individual employees, customers, patients, and so on and be subject to both stringent legal as well as ethical constraints on who may see it. Still other data is of financial concern such as credit card or banking account information, company customer lists, product costing, or trade secrets (such as the source code for your software product!). The costs of failures in this arena can literally be bankruptcy and prison time.

Preserving confidentiality and privacy would be relatively easy if nobody were allowed to see or modify the data. The applications that you build, however, are only created because there is a need to provide access to this and other data in the database. Your challenge, then, is to ensure that only those individuals, who have a legitimate reason to see, create, and maintain that data are allowed to do so. Even that requirement is overly simplistic; frequently one individual may have restricted rights to see only portions of the available data (just his or her own personal information, for instance).

Your application systems must provide controlled access by properly identified users to perform specifically authorized actions with appropriately restricted data.

Integrity

In addition to controlling who is allowed to do what to subsets of our data, you also need to ensure that the integrity of data is preserved throughout all of the processing. Integrity can be violated by intent (such as fraud), by accident (e.g., batch purge job run with an incorrect parameter value), or by simple corruption because of a network or disk failure.

You can do much to control the integrity of your data through access controls to ensure that only valid actions are performed by authorized users through defined and tested programs. You can also document various business rules that govern the integrity of the data and implement them within the logic of your programs and directly in the database. Finally, you can transmit and store data using protocols that verify that the data received is the data that was sent and provide mechanisms for recovery from any corruptions.

Why Database-Level Security?

For many developers who have not worked in a database environment, it seems intuitive that controls on access and data modification should be part of the logic of their program. "If," asks the programmer, "my order entry program guarantees that only valid amounts are entered into a particular field, then that should be the end of the issue, no?"

Unfortunately, this is rarely the case. That specific program is probably only one of several that needs to be developed to work with a particular table in the database. In addition to your online form for customers to use, there will need to be additional online programs for customer service staff and still others for corrections by supervisors or accounting personnel. There may be various batch programs created to move data from one database to another, change order status for back orders and shipments, post the data to accounts receivable, and so on. The same logic will have to be incorporated into each of those and maintained in each. "Well," the programmer may say, "I'll create a method that performs the validation that can be called from each of those." This is a good step forward as long as the developer of each of those other programs is aware of the method and remembers to incorporate it.

But even if all of the authorized programs contain the same validation logic, you still have an exposure. What about the *unauthorized* program? How do you prevent people from connecting to the database from their own program (or even SQL*Plus!) and changing the value in that particular field? How do you ensure that the same transfer of funds transaction that your program initiated wasn't captured and then executed a few hundred extra times?

Imagine the royal family of the Duchy of Datastein. The walls, fences, gates, and guards keep most casual intruders from ever reaching the ancestral family castle. But various delivery vans, household service staff, repairmen, guards, and invited visitors enter the castle grounds each day. So the royal family installs a security system in the castle that electronically monitors all of the doors and windows and even motion within the chambers. Are they fully protected? Well, some of those guests, repairmen, and service staff — like their maid, chauffeur, and gardener — may not be as trustworthy as others. If the valuable Datastein crown jewels and royal treasury are left sitting around the castle, then they are still not secure. At this point it might be wise to put the valuables into a safe with a combination known only to the duke, duchess, and trusted lord chamberlain. Now the maid may dust the Waterford crystal and the chauffeur can wash the Bentley (as their jobs require), but they can't count the carets or tap the treasury.

This is an artificial example, of course, but the point is that security, to be most effective, has to be extended from the periphery to as close to the item being secured as possible. As long as there are authorized accesses through a particular level of security, there will continue to be some exposure. Each application program is like one of the secured gates, doors, or windows into the castle. What you don't know is whether the ancestral castle has any secret tunnels, hidden passageways, or trapdoors. (In the movies they all do, don't they?)

No security plan is totally without exposure. Our royal family is still subject to embezzlement by that lord chamberlain, but they now have a controlled environment in which very specific individuals can be vetted and proper procedures put in place to observe and record accesses to the royal family vault.

In short, security measures established within the database cannot be bypassed by finding an alternative access to the database. This provides greater protection than equivalent security measures established only in each (known) program accessing the database. Besides, they are less work for the application development team to implement and maintain!

Authentication

Okay, you've now considered the need for controlling who will be allowed to access your database. How do you know that the person asking for Joe Smith's account balance is really Joe Smith? This is the first step in a security system. You must authenticate users before allowing them access to any controlled information.

Users and Passwords

The traditional approach to authentication is to assign each user a unique username and a password. By providing the correct password for his or her username, the individual demonstrates that he or she is that particular user. While the most common method of authentication, passwords are far from totally secure. Some users may choose easily guessed passwords such as their phone number or spouse's first name. Others may use the same password on multiple systems so that if an attacker can get them to create an account on his or her Internet shopping portal, the attacker may be able to discover their password for their e-mail, banking, and retirement accounts. Then there are the users who write down all of their user IDs and passwords in their daily planner, in their PDA, or on sticky notes firmly posted on their monitor. Finally, there are the users who share their user ID and password with someone else as a friendly gesture to bypass the red tape of setting up a new account.

Back in 1981, in a modern tribute to Ambrose Bierce, Stan Kelly-Bootle in The Devil's DP Dictionary, provided the following definition: "password, n. 1 The user's first name, or the first four characters of the user's first name . . . 4 A device aimed at encouraging free and open cooperation among the staff."

So, user IDs and passwords are not infallible. Oracle does provide mechanisms for ensuring that passwords are chosen that meet certain complexity rules such as minimum length, required mixture of alphabetic and numeric characters, avoidance of obvious values (such as duplicating the user ID itself, "password," etc.), or other criteria that the DBA or security administrator may dictate. Oracle can also expire passwords after a designated period of time, forcing users to select new ones. Oracle passwords are always disguised when requested by Oracle, entered by a user, passed across Oracle Network Services connections and then when they are stored in the data dictionary.

One concern about passwords worth noting is that if users connect to the database with their userid and password on the Unix command line (such as `sqlplus scott/tiger`), this full command will be visible to anyone issuing a `ps` command. Encourage all developers and users to respond to the prompts for userid and password rather than issuing them as part of a program invocation command.

Prior to Oracle release 10*g*, there were several special accounts that had default passwords. Lazy (or unaware) administrators quite commonly left some of these passwords at their default values, opening a huge security hole. Now when creating a 10*g* database, Oracle prompts for passwords for each of these accounts (SYS, SYSTEM, DBSNMP, SYSMAN). This won't solve the laziness problem, but at least the administrator is aware of the special accounts!

Oracle accounts can (and should) be locked if they are not intended for login use. No user should be expected to directly log in to the schema that owns the tables of an application, for instance.

The most important means of securing user IDs and passwords, however, is always education of the users. This is particularly true for users who have been granted extended privileges in the database.

Smart Cards and Biometric Identification

Although not used widely, Oracle supports the use of various alternative technologies for identifying users. Smart cards or other physical devices that identify a user, when combined with a password or personal identification number (PIN), can be incorporated into an application architecture using the Oracle Advanced Security Option. ASO is discussed later in this chapter.

Oracle Syntax

Users and authentication rules are defined in the database using the `CREATE USER` and `ALTER USER` SQL statements. There is some difference in the available syntax for these two commands, but we will attempt to cover all of the syntax options. Following is a demonstration of some of the basic capabilities for defining users to the database:

```
create user joe identified by newpass1;
create user cam identified by origpass password expire;
create user ops$mary identified externally;
create user chris identified globally as 'CN=chris,O=xyzcorp';
create user app_proxy_user identified by app_serv_pw;

alter user joe password expire;
alter user cam identified by newpass3 replace origpass;
alter user ops$mary account lock;
alter user chris grant connect through app_proxy_user
           authentication required;
```

In this series of commands, you see the creation of five new database user accounts. The first, "joe," is created with a password that will be used for authentication. The second, "cam," is given a password also, but it is set to expire so that it will have to be reset by the administrator or "cam" before the account can be used to connect to the database. The "ops$mary" account will be authenticated using an external mechanism (the operating system) rather than by supplying a password; the O/S user "mary" will be able to connect directly to the "ops$mary" database account. User "chris" will be authenticated through the use of an Lightweight Directory Access Protocol (LDAP) directory, the topic of another section later in this chapter. The final account being created is going to be a proxy account used by an application server to be able to maintain a connection and share it among various application users. This is different than simply having the application server use a single account for multiple end user transactions in that the database will be able to track the individual users who are proxied. This is useful for maintaining different authorizations for individual users, for applying virtual private database policies, or for proxy auditing, discussed later in this chapter. The fundamental purpose of using proxy users is the ability to preserve the actual user identity even though the actual connection is made through a "generic" user connection.

(The `ops$` prefix is a default used for external authorization through the operating system but it can be modified by setting the `OS_AUTHENT_PREFIX` initialization parameter.)

The code example continues by showing five examples of altering existing user accounts to change authentication rules. First the password for the "joe" account is explicitly expired by the DBA (although you'll see later how to force periodic password expiration automatically.) Next, the "cam" password is explicitly changed. This can be done by the DBA or by cam directly if cam has the alter user privilege. (The extra clause shown here of `REPLACE current_password` is only needed when a user is changing his or her own password and a password complexity routine has been specified by the administrator.)

The third change shown locks the "ops$mary" account so no logins will be allowed.

The final example alters the "chris" account to allow connections for this account to be made using the shared "app_proxy_user" account that was created for this purpose. (This example shows the syntax from Oracle 10*g*; slightly different syntax for proxy authentication was available in release 9*i*.) You will see how such proxy accounts are used later in the chapter.

We mentioned that password complexity routines can be defined by the DBA to ensure that users specify passwords that meet certain minimum standards for complexity to reduce the chance of someone guessing their password or discovering it through repeated trial and error. A password complexity routine is assigned as part of a profile that is assigned to a user. Typically, an organization will define one or more standard profiles, and every user account will be assigned one of these when the user is created. Profile assignments can also be changed:

```
alter user joe profile corp_security_profile;
```

Profiles must first be created by the DBA using the `CREATE PROFILE` command. Profiles are used for two purposes, as a means of controlling resources used by an account and for enforcing password and other authentication rules. Here is an example of password and login control:

```
CREATE PROFILE corp_security_profile
    LIMIT
       failed_login_attempts       5
       password_lock_time          1
       password_life_time         90
       password_grace_time         3
       password_reuse_max          5
       password_reuse_time       365
       password_verify_function  f_corp_pwd_vfy;
```

Most organizations will not necessarily implement all of the available password rules as shown in this exhaustive example. This command says that any user who has been assigned the corp_security_profile will have his or her account locked after five successive failed attempts to log in and that the account will remain locked for 24 hours (one day) unless explicitly unlocked by the DBA. Any password can be used for no more than 90 days, but the user will receive advance warnings for three days before the actual password expiration. A user's password cannot be reused until five other password changes have been made, and a password can't be reused within 365 days.

Finally, the profile specifies that all passwords will be validated using a verification function, named f_corp_pwd_vfy. This function can perform any tests on the actual proposed password string and will either accept or reject the password. If rejected, the user will have to select another password. Before this profile can be created this function will have to be written using PL/SQL using techniques discussed later in Chapter 13, "Functions." Since many readers don't have extensive PL/SQL experience yet, we'll show an overly simple example of how this function might be coded just to ensure that a user doesn't use his or her username as a password. (This function must be created by the privileged user SYS in order for it to be used in a profile.)

```
CREATE OR REPLACE FUNCTION f_corp_pwd_vfy
      (in_username       IN VARCHAR,
       in_new_password   IN VARCHAR,
       in_old_password   IN VARCHAR)
    RETURN BOOLEAN
    AS
        pwd_okay BOOLEAN;
    BEGIN
        IF in_new_password = in_username THEN
           raise_application_error(-20001, 'Password may not be username');
        END IF;
        RETURN TRUE;
END f_corp_pwd_vfy;
/
```

Remember this simple example only makes one test of password validity. Oracle provides a script (utlpwdmg.sql, found within the rdbms/admin subdirectory under the ORACLE_HOME directory) to create a more useful password verification routine or to use as a template for your own routine. Figure 5.1 shows what happens when a user who has been assigned this profile attempts to change his password in violation of the rule.

This user is prevented from changing his password to dbu since it is his username. A more complete password complexity routine would have several rules (and corresponding error messages) defined to help ensure that passwords are not easily broken. It might also be appropriate, for instance, to keep a maintain a table of disallowed passwords (such as "password," "secret," "welcome," your application or company name, and so on). Your password verification function can then reference this table. A quick Internet search will yield many listings of common (and therefore inappropriate) passwords.

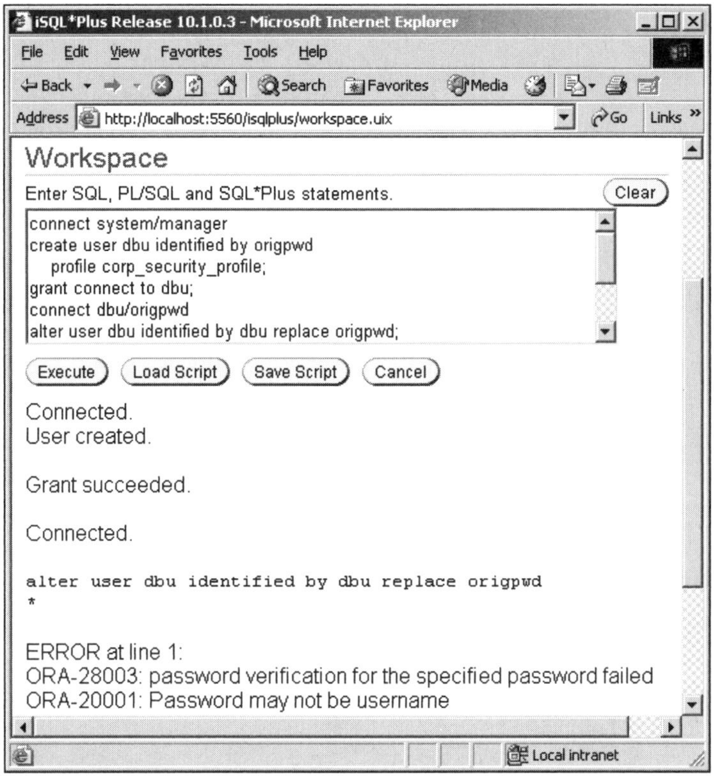

Figure 5-1: Effects of violating rules of a password complexity function.

Authorization

Once a user has been authenticated to the database, the user is allowed to perform actions using data in the database. But what actions? Which data? These questions are determined by what the user is authorized to do. Users receive authorizations directly by being granted certain privileges or indirectly by being granted roles that are defined as a set of privileges. Other database privileges are granted by invocation of supplied packaged procedures. Without any privileges, the user will not be able to do anything (including establish a connection) with the database.

Half of the job (actually the easier half) of maintaining user authorizations is granting privileges to users necessary to run their applications. The second half of the job is revoking those privileges when they are no longer needed. Failure to perform the second half of the job exposes the data in the database to inappropriate access by an employee or other user who should no longer be allowed this ability. You will see how roles and, a little later, how centralized administration through LDAP can simplify these tasks and improve your ability to enforce authorization rules within the database.

System Privileges

System privileges allow a user to do certain types of things. System privileges can be very narrow (the `CREATE SESSION` privilege allows a user to connect to the database but nothing more) or very broad (the `DROP USER` system privilege allows the recipient to drop any user schema and its contents from the database). The list of available system privileges in version 6 was limited to only three (`CONNECT`, `RESOURCE`, and `DBA`). Version 7 included about 80 possibilities, and with Oracle 10*g* that number is over 130. As new features and database object types are introduced, corresponding privileges for creating, altering, and dropping these objects are added.

System privileges are not usually granted directly to users because of the complexity of tracking dozens of privileges and potentially thousands of users. In general, users are categorized into groups that require the same set of privileges. The set of privileges are defined as a *role*, and the role can be granted to each user in the group.

System privileges can be granted `WITH ADMIN OPTION`. This option allows the recipient of the privilege to then grant or revoke that privilege to or from other users. The use of `WITH ADMIN OPTION` is rarely justified for system privileges.

Object Privileges

The number of object privilege types is much more limited than the number of system privileges. A total of 16 possible object privileges can be granted, and some of these apply to only specific object types. A table, for instance, has 11 privileges (`ALTER`, `DELETE`, `DEBUG`, `FLASHBACK`, `INDEX`, `INSERT`, `ON COMMIT REFRESH`, `QUERY REWRITE`, `REFERENCES`, `SELECT`, and `UPDATE`) that can be granted to another user by the owner. Sequences, for a simpler example, can only have `ALTER` and `SELECT` granted on them.

After a user has been granted a specific privilege on a specific object, that user can then perform that one action. For instance, if you've been granted `SELECT` privilege on the `SH.SALES` table, you may read any of the data in that table. You may not `INSERT` new rows or `DELETE` or `UPDATE` existing rows. You may not create a new index on that table or build a foreign key from one of your tables to it. Each of these actions requires another object privilege.

Further granularity of access can be imposed via object privileges. In this example we allow user "joe" to query any data from the `HR.EMPLOYEES` table, but he is restricted to just making updates to four columns:

```
GRANT SELECT, UPDATE (email, phone_number, job_id, manager_id)
   ON hr.employees
   TO joe;
```

Even though Joe may be able to see everyone's salary, he is not able to give himself or his buddy a raise. It may be desirable to further restrict Joe's access by either row or column within this table. You will see how to do so when we discuss access control a little later in this chapter.

Object privileges may be granted `WITH GRANT OPTION`. Somewhat similar to the `WITH ADMIN OPTION` of system privileges (and roles), the `WITH GRANT OPTION` clause allows you to extend your granted privilege to other users. You may not, though, revoke the privilege from other users who were granted it by someone else. Also, if your privilege is later revoked, all of the users to whom you have granted the privilege will also lose it.

Direct granting of object privileges to users is again not recommended for production environments. It may be useful in development and testing, but the set of necessary object privileges required to execute the application should be bundled together as a role and the role granted to the eventual end users.

Roles

As mentioned, a role in Oracle is a named set of privileges. A role is granted various system or object privileges and possibly other roles. The total set of privileges given the role can be quickly and easily provided to an end user by simply granting that one role. Rather than granting 100 privileges to each of 1,000 users (100,000 grants), a role can allow you to make 100 grants to the role and then 1,000 grants of the role to the users (a total of only 1,100 grants).

This approach also simplifies the security administration when a user leaves the company or changes job functions. Rather than having to revoke each of those 100 privileges individually, a single revocation of the role performs the entire task.

One restriction on roles is important for developers to understand. You cannot create any objects based on privliges received via a role. The required privileges must have been directly granted. The concept of roles was created to help manage hundreds or thousands of users, not just a handful of developers.

Users may have multiple roles granted to them but not all of them are necessarily active at any given time. Roles can be default roles, in which case they will automatically be enabled upon login. The user (or the application) may disable or enable granted roles at any time. In this manner an application may turn on a set of privileges for a user of that application that will not be available when the user is not connected to the database from that application.

The roles facility, as initially implemented in Oracle version 7, was a great conceptual leap forward for managing large numbers of users. The same concepts have since been expanded from just the database realm to full enterprise-wide management of all user security controls with the advent and widespread adoption of LDAP services.

Database Roles

Roles are created in the database with the `CREATE ROLE rolename` command. Optionally, the role may be protected by a password or an external authorization mechanism. A password-protected role can only be explicitly enabled with the password. Here's an example of creating a role and assigning it to a user, "joe":

```
connect system/manager

create role sales_analyst identified by xyt33;
grant select on sh.times to sales_analyst;
grant select on sh.costs to sales_analyst;
grant select on sh.products to sales_analyst;
grant select on sh.channels to sales_analyst;
grant select on sh.promotions to sales_analyst;
grant select on sh.customers to sales_analyst;
grant select on sh.sales to sales_analyst;

alter user joe identified by bullfrog;
grant connect to joe;
grant sales_analyst to joe;
alter user joe default role all except sales_analyst;
```

Note that the final step ensures that Joe does not have this role automatically enabled when he connects to the database. With the role created and a set of privileges assigned to it, you can see how Joe uses the role to perform his sales analyst job. Figure 5-2 demonstrates how Joe uses the password protected `SALES_ANALYST` role.

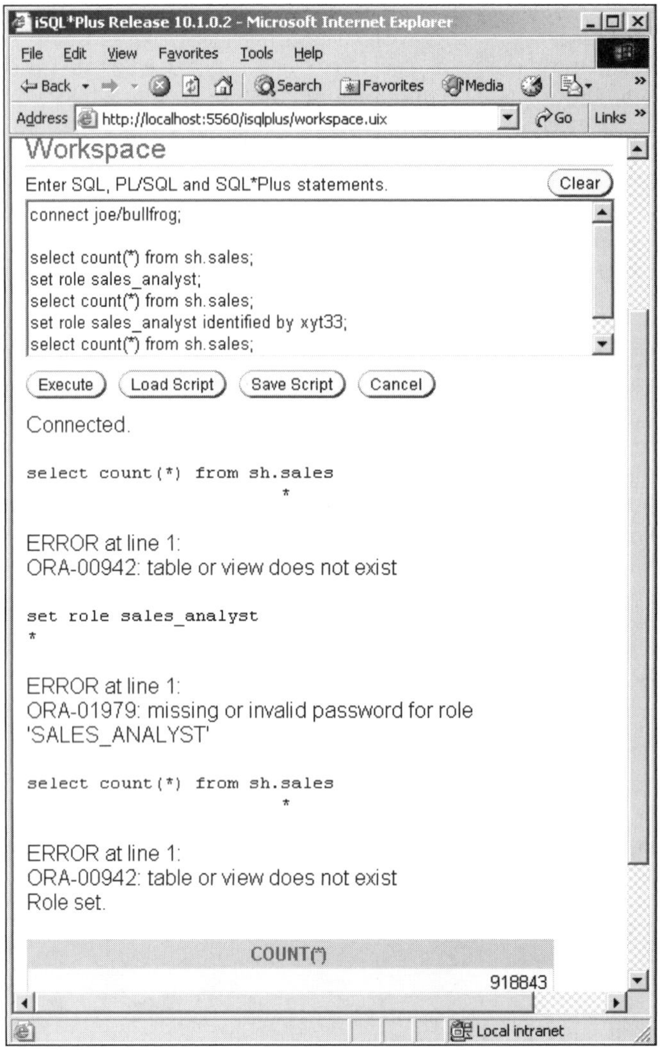

Figure 5-2: Enabling a password-protected role.

When Joe first connects, he is unable to see the SH.SALES table that has been granted to the role. He realizes that he has not enabled the SALES_ANALYST role and attempts to do so but neglects to provide the password. Recognizing his error, he sets the role again, including the correct password. Now he is able to see the data in the SALES table. If he were, however, to try to modify any of that data, he would receive an error because the role only provided SELECT privileges.

Predefined Database Roles

Earlier in the chapter in the discussion of system privileges, we mentioned that prior to Oracle 7, there were only three system privileges (CONNECT, RESOURCE, and DBA). For compatibility, Oracle 7 provided three roles of these same names that included roughly the same privileges. One of these roles (CONNECT) was used in setting up user Joe prior to Figure 5-2. It is important to review these predefined roles to verify that they accurately reflect the set of system privileges by examining the data dictionary view, `ROLE_SYS_PRIVS`. The `CONNECT` role, for instance, actually provides many system privileges (such as `CREATE TABLE`) that may not be appropriate for all users. The `DBA` and `RESOURCE` roles also include the `UNLIMITED TABLESPACE` privilege that could allow someone to (accidentally or maliciously) create objects that consume all of the available free space that is needed for legitimate application objects.

In many cases, DBAs have continued to use `CONNECT`, `RESOURCE`, and `DBA` out of habit (or laziness) where it might be more appropriate to create new roles that include just the set of system privileges needed by a group of users. Joe (and his peers) may have only needed the `CREATE SESSION` and `ALTER SESSION` privileges, and creating and granting a role with just those two privileges would be more secure.

External Roles

When a role is created (or altered), it need not have a password assigned to it. Some shops may choose to do as much of their security administration outside of the database. They may still want to control which users are able to set the role and receive its privileges. External roles provide that capability. Originally in Oracle 7, these were called OS roles because they were assigned to users by operating system group assignments. If a user were a member of the sales_analyst Unix group, then he or she could be automatically given the corresponding role within the database. This made sense in a day when many or most users connected to the database while directly logged on to the server that hosted the database service.

In the dozen or so years since this feature was added, there have been several developments. First, most users are never logging in to their company's database servers. First client/server and now application server architectures have made that option less useful except for certain administrative and batch programs. However, the capability has been extended to take advantage of other external security services, such as a RADIUS authorization service. External roles are defined within Oracle as:

```
CREATE ROLE role_name IDENTIFIED EXTERNALLY;
```

Two special external roles have been pre-created by Oracle for specific administration purposes. `OS_DBA` provides full DBA privileges to the DBA group. This is intended to allow DBAs and their privileged batch jobs to directly connect to the database as the SYS account without providing a database userid and password. The second provided external role, `OS_OPER`, provides a more restricted set of privileges appropriate to a member of the operations staff who needs to start, stop, backup or recover the database but who does not require the other capabilities of a DBA. Because of the extensive privileges included, it is essential to ensure that membership in these two operating system groups be carefully controlled.

Secure Application Roles

Another means of enabling roles has been added to specifically control the role from within an application. In earlier Oracle releases this might have been done by including the password of a normal database role in the application code. This approach met the need but wasn't terribly secure, since the application code or even the compiled program could potentially be inspected to find the string of the role name and then find the password. (Plus security policies for changing passwords were complicated by this approach.)

Since then, another means of setting roles has been added in which the application calls a stored package within the database. That package can verify the application context from which it is called before allowing the role to be set. This allows the package to verify that the correct application is making the connection before enabling the role. Application roles are defined as:

```
CREATE ROLE role_name IDENTIFIED USING packagename;
```

Global Roles

Global roles are created with just slightly different syntax:

```
CREATE ROLE role_name IDENTIFIED GLOBALLY;
```

Global roles are used differently, however. Authorization to use a global role is provided from entries made within the enterprise LDAP directory. Global roles apply only within the context of the database in which they are defined; however they are not directly granted to users of that database. Instead they are granted to enterprise roles within the security structure of the LDAP directory service. When a user attempts to set a global role, the LDAP directory is queried to determine whether the user has an enterprise role that includes the requested global role for this database.

Enterprise Roles

Enterprise roles are LDAP directory structures consisting of one or more global roles for databases within the enterprise. LDAP directory services, extended with the enterprise role facility, allow all security administration to be managed from within an enterprise-wide facility. For larger organizations and those with multiple resources (various databases, e-mail service, portal accesses, and applications), such an approach simplifies the entire job of controlling users and their actions.

Stored Procedures

It is common to use stored procedures to control user authorization. By encapsulating all of the necessary logic into the stored procedure, the DBA can grant `EXECUTE` privilege on just the procedure without having to give the user direct privileges for the objects referenced by the procedure. The procedure executes, by default, using the privileges of the procedure's owner. This prevents the user from bypassing the procedural controls of the application code (as implemented in the procedure) and directly interacting with the tables, views, and other objects of the application.

Sometimes, however, it is desirable to have a generic procedure that will be able to access specific data and objects based upon the security authorizations of the user of the procedure as opposed to the owner. This can be accomplished by adding the `AUTHID CURRENT_USER` clause to the definition of the procedure. This procedure will then use the current user's set of privileges, and any unqualified object names within the procedure will be interpreted as objects within the executing user's schema as opposed to those in the schema of the procedure's owner.

Access Control

System and object privileges provide increasing levels of granularity to control which objects in a database may be viewed or used by a user. Roles make the administration of privileges easier. Remember the example earlier in this chapter where Joe was given full `SELECT` authority on the `HR.EMPLOYEES` table, even though you were able to restrict him to just making changes to four of the total columns? You may want to take a little more control of Joe's actions. Being able to see everyone's salary and commission, for instance, could be a risk. Further, you might want to restrict Joe's ability to update phone numbers, e-mail addresses, and so on to just the people within Joe's own department.

Oracle provides several facilities for further restricting access to data within objects.

Views

The oldest and still simplest means of limiting access to specific rows or columns of a table is to create a view with any necessary restrictions in the SELECT column list and WHERE clause. (If you are not yet familiar with the concept of views, they are explained in more detail in Chapter 12, "Other Database Structures.")

If you want to limit Joe to seeing only employees in his own department and from seeing anyone's salary or commission rate, you might create a simple view:

```
connect hr/hr
create or replace view joes_employees
    as select employee_id, first_name, last_name, email, phone_number,
              hire_date, job_id, manager_id, department_id
         from hr.employees
        where department_id = 100;
revoke all on employees from joe;
grant select, update on joes_employees to joe;
```

What happens now when Joe accesses the table? Let's have Joe set up a private synonym (also discussed in Chapter 12) and then query this new view, as shown in Figure 5-3.

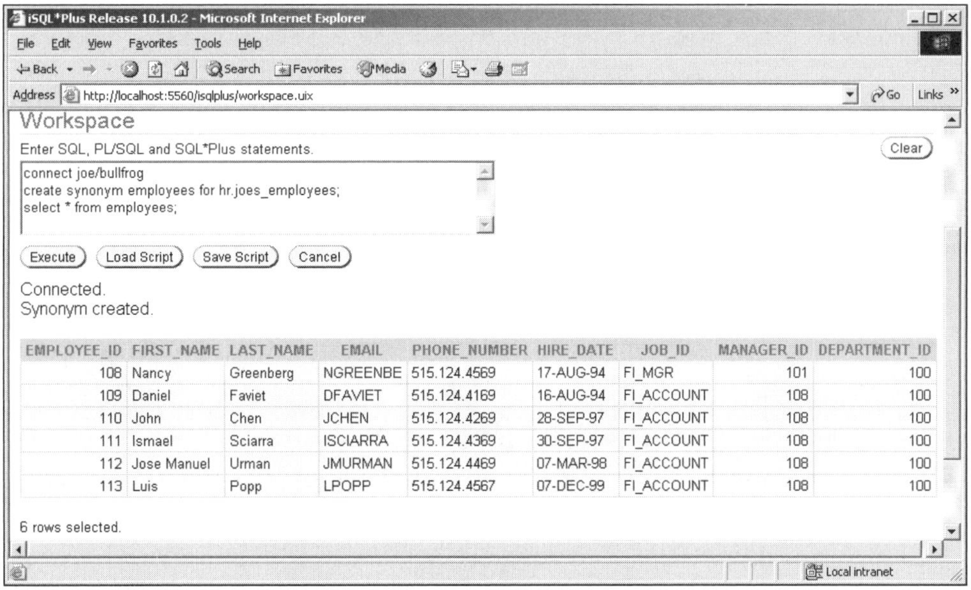

Figure 5-3: Querying a view using a private synonym.

Figure 5-3 shows that the task has been accomplished. However, by focusing on the specific situation of Joe, a more general need may have been ignored. Do other users have a similar need in their departments? You could have created a more general case by changing the fixed WHERE clause condition department_id=100 to a subquery that would retrieve the user's own department ID from the database and then include only other employees in the same department. (We won't actually demonstrate that here since we don't have a direct way of finding Joe's department in the HR.EMPLOYEES table. If you had a business rule that said each user's database user ID was the same as his or her e-mail name, which is part of the EMPLOYEES table, then you could use that to relate the user to his or her department.)

This view was not created WITH CHECK OPTION, so Joe is actually able to modify data in some nonintuitive ways. Figure 5-4 shows that Joe can move people from his department but then can no longer see them!

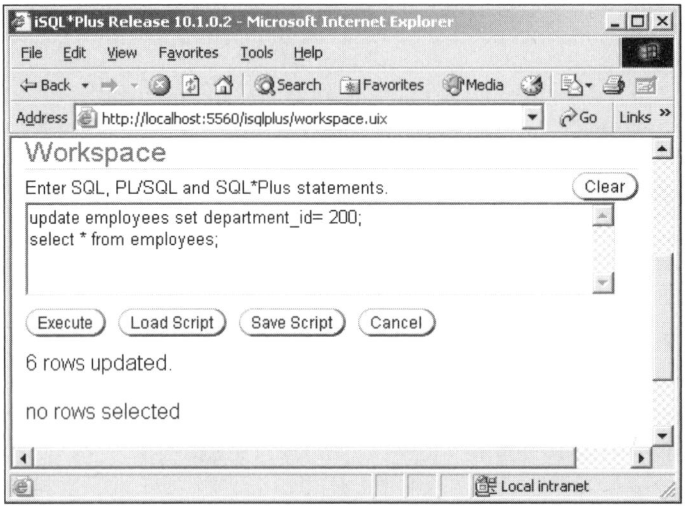

Figure 5-4: Changing data in a view defined without the WITH CHECK OPTION.

To prevent this behavior, the WITH CHECK OPTION clause in the view's definition will only allow updates that will still allow the rows to be visible through the view.

Simple views such as this or more complex view including joins between tables and aggregations and dynamic conditions within the WHERE and HAVING clauses can provide a means of restricting which rows and columns a user is able to see or modify.

Encryption

As an alternative to screening out columns containing sensitive data using a view, you might want to consider encrypting that sensitive data in the database. This would allow users to retrieve it only if they have the encryption key. It also prevents other prying eyes (anyone who has been granted the SELECT ANY TABLE privilege, for instance) from covertly viewing your employee data.

An encryption feature is provided by Oracle that will perform data encryption for data stored in the database. Before examining how this is performed, we must provide a little bit of background on encryption in general. Encryption is a means of scrambling data, using one of several defined standard algorithms such as DES (Data Encryption Standard) or triple DES (3DES) and an encryption key. Keys can be randomly generated or provided, but the security of the encrypted data is determined primarily by the difficulty involved in discovering the key. Just as some passwords are easy to guess, a predictable key will be easier to break.

Key management (generation, passing, storing of keys) is much more challenging than the actual encryption and decryption. If the key is stored in the database, then it, too, must be secured and retrieved by the application before decrypting data. The key value (or values) can be stored in a secured table that is accessed only by a function that is also secured and can be invoked only through a secure application role. This approach, although workable, is hampered by the need to create multiple layers of security, each protecting the one below it. Any breach at any of these layers can compromise the rest of the layers.

Wrapping a PL/SQL routine (so the actual source text is not visible) that performs key operations is another possible approach to improving key management between application and database. While wrapping prevents examination of the PL/SQL code, it unfortunately does not securely hide any embedded string data so actually retaining the encryption keys in the PL/SQL procedure or function would not be adequate protection. Having your PL/SQL code wrappered aids in hiding details of the application's logic but doesn't solve the key management problem by itself.

Storing the encryption key in an operating system file is another alternative whose security is similarly limited by the operating system's ability to store and pass the key securely. A fourth alternative is to have the users retain the key and provide it when needed. This has the same downside as typical password management by users (writing them down, forgetting them, sharing them, etc.), coupled with the need to securely transmit it between user, application, and database. This also requires network encryption of each network segment.

Finally, a more recent and rapidly growing trend is to use Public Key Infrastructure (PKI) security certificates complying with x.509 standards to store keys within a secure LDAP directory. Oracle provides the Oracle Wallet Manager as a utility for managing certificates.

> *Oracle database 10g release 2 has been announced but not delivered as of the writing of this section. It is always a little risky to mention future enhancements that may take on different characteristics before actual production release, but a quick mention of expected new encryption capabilities in 10g release 2 is warranted here. Transparent data encryption in release 2 is expected to allow data in a sensitive column to be encrypted quickly and easily with a new variation on the* `ALTER TABLE` *command. Encryption and decryption of data will then be performed transparently as part of normal* `SQL DML` *commands. Key management, the toughest challenge, will be managed internally by Oracle rather than requiring external storage and management.*

We can't investigate all of the ramifications of key management within this one chapter, but you are advised to thoroughly investigate available alternatives when deciding to utilize encryption in the database. The only thing less secure than unsecured data is probably a false sense of security.

On to the specifics of Oracle's database encryption capabilities. Up through the first release of Oracle 10*g*, encryption and decryption of data is performed by a supplied PL/SQL package called the `DBMS_OBFUSCATION_TOOLKIT`. Procedures within the package will generate keys, encrypt data with either DES or 3DES algorithms, and optionally provide basic checksum processing to ensure that data is properly transmitted. Well over 20 pages of the Oracle 10*g* *PL/SQL Packages and Types Reference* manual are devoted to this one package.

New in Oracle 10*g* release 1, however, is another package, `DBMS_CRYPTO`, that should be used instead of the older `DBMS_OBFUSCATION_TOOLKIT` unless compatibility with previous releases is required. `DBMS_CRYPTO` provides additional advanced encryption algorithms, including AES, RC4 and 3DES_2KEY. It also provides new options for cryptographic checksums, padding, keyed hash algorithms, secure random number generation, and support of the CLOB and BLOB data types. Again, extensive documentation on this package is included in the Oracle 10*g* *PL/SQL Packages and Types Reference* manual.

Virtual Private Database

Introduced in Oracle8*i* as fine-grained access control, Virtual Private Database (VPD) is a feature of the Enterprise Edition of the Oracle database that allows a single table to physically store data for multiple organizations or customers while each user sees what appears to be a private table with only his or her own data. This feature can be used to provide another means of isolating data similar to the JOES_EMPLOYEES view earlier in the chapter. But VPD can be much more powerful than even complex dynamic views.

For the restricted view definition example, we were limited to conditions that could be expressed within the WHERE clause of the view's defining query. Virtual Private Database uses Oracle's query rewrite facility to generate additional WHERE clause criteria that are dynamically appended to the user's SQL statement by the VPD *policy* (a set of extended security filter rules) attached to a table.

When a user connects to the database, Oracle does several additional steps as part of the basic authentication process. It must determine, for instance, what roles that user has available and which of them to enable automatically as default roles. Additionally, it populates a number of other session attributes that can be used later by VPD to determine how to filter data from each object that has a defined VPD policy. VPD can also utilize *application context* to allow it to filter data based on the criteria of importance as established by the application.

If, for instance, you simply wanted to limit user "joe" to seeing rows from the EMPLOYEES table that were for department 100, you might write a policy that would take Joe's input:

```
select * from hr.employees;
```

and turn it automatically into:

```
select * from hr.employees
 where department_id = 100;
```

Such a transformation is simple to do with VPD since "joe" is a known database user. (VPD can also perform its security magic when users are proxied by a single database user from an application server.) Note two things about this example. First, Joe is actually going directly against the HR.EMPLOYEES table—no extra view or copy of the data was made. Notice also that, at least in this example, Joe is given access to all of the columns in the table, unlike the JOES_EMPLOYEES view created previously that prevented Joe from seeing pay information. VPD prior to Oracle 10*g* was just able to do row filtering.

Oracle 10*g* has enhancements for VPD to work at the column level as well. By default, column-level VPD will not display rows for which sensitive data is included in a particular column. Another variation is to do column masking in which the rows will be returned with the particular sensitive data passed as null rather than as their actual values. Before deciding to use the new column level VPD capabilities, consider how it will impact your programs.

With VPD, you can create policies (procedural code using PL/SQL) that will be invoked each time the table (or view or synonym) is accessed. This code can be as complex as necessary to fully implement the required business rule. Policies are created and maintained on tables, views, or synonyms using the supplied DBMS_RLS package or through the graphical Oracle Policy Manager within Oracle Enterprise Manager.

It is possible to create either static (evaluated once per session) or context-sensitive (may be reevaluated whenever application context changes) policies. Static policies are more efficient, but for multi-tier applications with many different applications (and possible changes of context), it is generally necessary to use one of the context-sensitive forms.

Since we haven't covered any details of the PL/SQL language, at this point we'll use a very simple example. First, you need to create a function that will evaluate the current user context and then generate a predicate that you'll use as part of your security policy. This function looks at the current user and compares that to the `EMAIL` column in the `HR.EMPLOYEES` table in order to find the user's `DEPARTMENT_ID`.

```
create or replace function hr.f_jobhist_vpd
   (object_schema     in varchar2,
    object_name       in varchar2)
  RETURN varchar2
  AS
     curr_user          varchar2(30);
     query_dept         number        := 0;
     return_predicate   varchar2(100) := '1=2';
  BEGIN
        select upper(user) into curr_user from dual;
        if upper(object_schema) = curr_user
            then return_predicate := null;
        else
            select department_id
              into query_dept
             from hr.employees
             where email=curr_user;
            return_predicate := 'department_id = '||query_dept;
        end if;
        RETURN return_predicate;
    EXCEPTION WHEN NO_DATA_FOUND THEN RETURN '1=2';
  END f_jobhist_vpd;
/
```

This routine provides us a new predicate that you can use to limit access to another table, in this case the `HR.JOB_HISTORY` table. Next, you will add a policy to the `JOB_HISTORY` table that will invoke the function just written:

```
begin
   DBMS_RLS.ADD_POLICY (
      object_schema   => 'HR',
      object_name     => 'JOB_HISTORY',
      policy_name     => 'POL_JOBHIST',
      function_schema => 'HR',
      policy_function => 'F_JOBHIST_VPD',
      statement_types => 'SELECT',
      enable          => TRUE);
end;
/
```

Now for this example to work, you have to have user IDs that match up with e-mail IDs as recorded in the `EMPLOYEES` table. So you'll have to create a few users and give them some privileges:

```
create user akhoo identified by test;
create user daustin identified by test;
create user sking identified by test;
grant connect to akhoo, daustin, sking;
grant select on hr.job_history to akhoo, daustin, sking;
```

Now you can see the effects as these users issue queries against the `JOB_HISTORY` table in Figure 5-5.

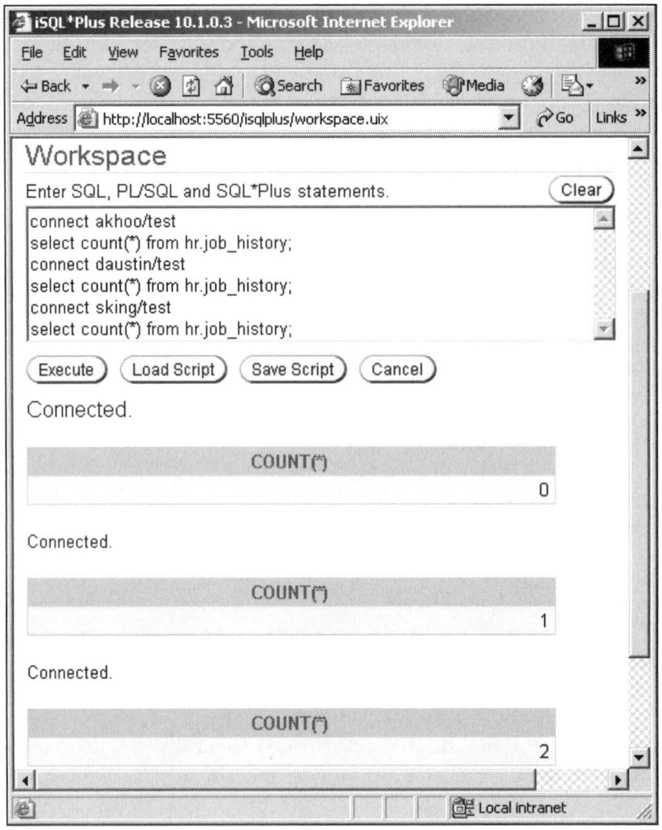

Figure 5-5: Different users may see different data from a view with a dynamic `WHERE` clause.

Since users "akhoo," "daustin," and "sking" all have e-mail addresses in `EMPLOYEES` and are in different departments, they each see a different subset of the `JOB_HISTORY` table even though they issue the same query.

Issuing the same query while connected to the `HR` schema would return all 16 rows, whereas another user (who hadn't been configured to have the same user ID as an e-mail address in `EMPLOYEES`) would have no rows returned at all.

Oracle Label Security Option

Virtual Private Database is a built-in feature to the Oracle Enterprise Edition. It provides a lot of functional freedom, but a developer will have to be assigned to build the necessary security policy functions for each table to be protected. No changes to the data structures are required for VPD.

The Oracle Label Security Option uses the VPD technology to deliver an out-of-the-box security model for situations where tables have an extra column that can be used to determine each row's security needs. In a simple hierarchical case, each row might be labeled as "Unrestricted," "Confidential," "Secret," or "Top Secret." Users with one of these security levels will be allowed to see data rows at their level or below. A user with a "Confidential" clearance will be able to see unrestricted and confidential data but will have no way of determining that any secret or top secret data exists in that table.

The advantage of using the Label Security Option rather than using the native VPD facilities is that no coding is required with label security. Instead, all of the programming is provided along with an extended set of data dictionary objects and graphical administration tools used to develop labels and assign label authorizations (including hierarchies) to users and their sessions, and to the data tables, views, and other database objects.

Accountability

Once you have dealt with ways to authenticate users as being who they claim to be, authorized them to do certain operations (and not others) and limited their access to particular parts of the database, you have formed a pretty solid foundation for ensuring only valid queries and modifications of your valuable and confidential data. You still have another level of responsibility, however. With increasing regulatory and legal restrictions in the United States, the European Union, and elsewhere, it isn't enough just to limit access to particular information to a group of 20 known clerks and managers. It is frequently necessary to determine which of those 20 authorized individuals may have actually made a specific change or even looked at a particular individual's computerized records.

Just like video cameras in a convenience store, monitoring users' interactions with the database has two primary effects. It allows you to detect or investigate possibly improper behavior, but it can also deter individuals from that behavior if they are aware that their actions are being recorded. Additional benefits may accrue because the record of activity can be analyzed for purposes unrelated to security, such as determining usage patterns for particular tables that can help with design or tuning efforts.

Auditing

Oracle provides built-in auditing functions that allow the database to automatically keep track of the actions of users. Some actions can be tracked at a high level, such as failed connection attempts, while others are recorded on a very detailed level, such as which employees' rows were looked at (but only if salary information was included in the query).

The fundamental tool for enabling auditing in the database is the `AUDIT` command. `AUDIT` can be applied at the level of types of SQL statements or system privilege usage. It can also be specified at the individual database object level. In general, auditing rules are specified for each type of auditing desired but then must also be enabled at the Oracle instance level to actually take effect.

Certain privileged operations by users connected using the special `SYSDBA` or `SYSOPER` roles can be audited by setting the `AUDIT_SYS_OPERATIONS` initialization parameter. This is generally advised so that users with these special privileges are not able to completely bypass auditing rules.

Statement Auditing

Statement auditing generates an audit entry each time a specific SQL statement (or any of a class of statements) is issued for any user or for selected users. Also, statement auditing may be further restricted to just recording successful or unsuccessful statement operations. As a common example, it is suggested to enable auditing of failed attempts to connect to the database as a means of discovering possible hacking attempts (or users who may need assistance) as:

```
audit connect whenever not successful;
```

Privilege Auditing

Privilege auditing records each time a particular system privilege is utilized to perform an action. This, again, may be applied to all users or a specific list of users.

To reduce the volume of the audit log, you can just audit the use of certain statements or privileges once per session rather than on every occurrence:

```
audit create any table by access;
audit drop user by session;
```

The first of these will record every time a table is created in another schema through the use of the CREATE ANY TABLE system privilege. The second will enter a single audit record the first time in a user's session that a user is dropped.

Another option available for both statement and privilege auditing is to specify certain users who will have the particular action audited. This example sets users "joe" and "mary" to have an audit record created if they try unsuccessfully to modify data:

```
audit insert table, update table, delete table
      by joe, mary
      whenever not successful;
```

Schema Object Auditing

Schema object auditing is more even granular and records specific types of actions (such as UPDATEs or SELECTs) performed on a particular database object. Common schema objects that can be audited include tables, views, materialized views, sequences, standalone stored procedures (and functions), or packages. Unlike statement- or privilege-level auditing, object-level auditing applies to all database users and may not be specified to record actions of individual users. The following will record each time any user modifies or reads data in the EMPLOYEES table:

```
audit insert, delete, update, select
      on hr.employees;
```

Auditing of schema objects may also specify either the WHENEVER SUCCESSFUL or WHENEVER NOT SUCCESSFUL clauses. This may be useful, for instance, to determine whether someone is trying to access a table in a way that he or she is not permitted.

Fine-Grained Auditing

Finally, a newer feature, fine-grained auditing, allows you to be very specific in the details of what actions on an object will be recorded. This lets you limit your audit records based on columns accessed or even the values of those columns. Before the introduction of fine-grained auditing, the developer or DBA would either have to audit all accesses of a particular type and then later sort through to find worrisome specifics or use a trigger (as discussed in the next session), which is relatively expensive, since procedural logic of the trigger has to be executed in every case in order to determine whether the data values warrant recording.

Fine-grained auditing is configured using the DBMS_FGA supplied package to establish a security policy. A policy can be applied to any table or view and monitors SELECT and DML actions. Up to 256 separate policies may be defined on any given object. If any of the data used or modified by a statement causes the policy to evaluate to TRUE, then an audit record is written to the standard audit trail. Because the policy is developed in PL/SQL code, the policy may also include a special audit event handler to perform other actions such as e-mailing or paging a security officer.

Efficiency of fine-grained auditing is enhanced by being able to declare that only relevant columns in the object should be evaluated. For instance, an FGA policy on the EMPLOYEES table might limit actions to just the SALARY and COMMISSION_PCT columns. A user's SELECT that retrieves only names and phone numbers would not invoke the policy code.

Once the policy is activated, it may decide to log only accesses to particular rows based on the values stored in them. For instance, you might want to check all accesses to salary or commission information and record the access if the any employee included in the query or DML statement has a SALARY in excess of $10,000 or works in department 90 (Executive):

```
begin
  DBMS_FGA.ADD_POLICY (object_schema => 'hr',
    object_name=> 'employees',
    policy_name => 'emp_policy',
    audit_condition => 'salary > 10000 or department_id = 90',
    audit_column => 'salary, commission_pct',
    enable => TRUE,
    statement_types => 'SELECT, INSERT, UPDATE, DELETE');
end;
/
```

Since we haven't covered PL/SQL language conventions yet, this is an anonymous block of PL/SQL code. It calls a procedure called ADD_POLICY that is part of a package called DBMS_FGA. This procedure has many input parameters of which we've named and assigned values to seven. This procedure call will create a policy called EMP_POLICY on the HR.EMPLOYEES table that implements the desired auditing of accesses to the pay records of executive or other highly paid individuals.

As shown, this procedure will work in Oracle 10g, but it would error in release 9i because it includes the `statement_types` *argument that was added in 10g. (Enhancements such as this are not uncommon, so it is important to review each new release for opportunities to improve your application and its administration.)*

Using selective auditing in this way has two benefits. It makes it easier to find important information in the audit trail because there is less unimportant "noise" to sift through. It also helps limit the size of the audit trail, making its management less painful.

Audit Trails

It is worth noting a few things about where all of these audit records are recorded. Oracle can audit either into a special table (SYS.AUD$) within the data dictionary or to an operating system file. The audit trail destination is set with initialization parameter AUDIT_TRAIL. Setting this parameter equal to DB (or, for backward compatibility, TRUE) will use the database audit trail. Using the database audit trail provides the ability to include more information than the operating system audit trail and also provides the additional security, integrity and recoverability of the database environment. In release 10*g* a new option (AUDIT_TRAIL = DB_EXTENDED) has been added that captures additional information about the specific SQL statements being issued.

The database audit trail works identically for all Oracle installations, but capabilities and locations for using the operating system audit trail vary by platform. Operating system auditing is enabled by setting AUDIT_TRAIL = OS and then supplemented with the parameter AUDIT_FILE_DEST.

Whether using database or operating system auditing, the security administrator must monitor the audit trail destination and ensure adequate space for recording audit records.

Auditing by Proxy

Earlier in this chapter we showed how to create a proxy user that will allow an application server to make a single connection to the database and work on behalf of various other users using the proxy user connection. To provide for reliable auditing in this configuration, the `AUDIT` command includes special syntax, `BY PROXY`, to record either activities directly by the proxy user or statements issued on behalf of other users through the proxy connection.

You are also able to specifically audit actions performed on behalf of proxy users. Here's a simple example based on the users created and altered earlier in the chapter.

```
AUDIT SELECT TABLE BY app_proxy_user ON BEHALF OF chris;
```

The application server is able to set the actual user's identity as part of the session characteristics, so direct auditing of that user's activities would occur as if unproxied. Even though the actual connection to the database uses the "app_proxy_user" account, the database will be able to track activity performed on behalf of user "chris".

Triggers

Triggers will be covered in Chapter 19, "Triggers." Triggers are extended procedural actions that are added to the default behavior of certain operations on a table or view. Triggers can perform many valuable functions in the database. They can—as you'll see in Chapter 11, "Constraints"—be used to enforce complex integrity rules on tables.

They can also be used to develop a customized auditing facility. Triggers can have visibility, for instance, to the before and after column values of a row being changed by a statement. The trigger can then write to a user-defined audit table and retain both of these values along with the identity of the user who made the change and the timestamp of when it occurred.

The performance impact of triggers is generally more expensive than simple schema object or even fine-grained auditing. Also, by default, a trigger's actions (such as an `INSERT` statement to the audit table) will be committed or rolled back in synch with the DML statement that caused the trigger to fire. (Starting in Oracle8*i*, this behavior can be overridden by declaring the trigger with `PRAGMA AUTONOMOUS_TRANSACTION`). The `AUDIT` facility, on the other hand, records its information into the audit log outside the scope of the transaction's own boundaries. `AUDIT` can therefore record unsuccessful or abandoned operations that a trigger would not be able to record. For these two reasons, triggers should only be used to perform customized auditing that cannot be accomplished with Oracle's native `AUDIT` facility. Prior to the introduction of fine-grained auditing, this was relatively common but now is rarely required.

Enterprise Security

This chapter has explored many facilities provided by Oracle to secure the database and to control and monitor accesses to it. Database security is just one part of an enterprise security environment, however. Most organizations today have dozens or hundreds of databases. The days when DBAs could be expected to independently administer their security (as well as other characteristics) is rapidly disappearing.

The objective of an enterprise should be to elevate their security focus to recognize each user (whether an employee, a customer, a supplier, or even an anonymous guest to a Web site) as an entity within the enterprise that has a set of responsibilities and privileges. The next step should be to begin managing all of those privileges from a central security directory and forcing every secured resource to reference that directory to authenticate and authorize users.

Administrators benefit from an enterprise security environment by having fewer places that require constant monitoring and administration of security information. Users, too, see a great benefit once an organization has implemented an enterprise security framework because the single sign-on or single password authentication approach lessens their need to remember and periodically change multiple passwords for all of their databases and applications. By simplifying the users' responsibilities, overall security is enhanced.

Providing enterprise security involves several Oracle concepts and components.

LDAP

Such a centralized security directory service is commonly implemented using products that comply with the standards of *Lightweight Directory Access Protocol*. Describing LDAP services in detail is beyond the scope of this chapter, but you should be aware that Oracle can use LDAP services to replace or supplement the security features of the database.

When an organization commits to using LDAP for centralizing its security, it must also recognize the need for the directory to be secure itself. Further, all communication with the directory that exchanges security information must likewise be secured. Finally, the directory service must be engineered to be both scalable enough to handle all of the requests from secured resources throughout the organization and highly available. If a centralized security service becomes unavailable, all systems throughout the enterprise that depend upon it will be impacted.

Many vendors supply LDAP directory products. Oracle's LDAP product is called Oracle Internet Directory (OID), part of the Oracle Identity Management solution. LDAP directories, including OID, must comply with standards for access and interoperability. Many of these products, however, extend certain capabilities beyond those specified in the standard.

Like so many topics, the details of configuring and using OID and LDAP could easily fill an entire book rather than a small section of a chapter. Additional information on OID can be found in the *Oracle 10g Database Security Guide*, as well as several papers available from the Oracle Technology Network, `http://otn.oracle.com`.

Enterprise Users

Enterprise users are defined within the centralized LDAP directory service, and all of their privileges to use enterprise resources are assigned to them within this repository. Enterprise roles, discussed earlier, allow enterprise users to receive appropriate privileges when they interact with a database.

Shared Schemas

Even though Oracle has traditionally equated a user with a schema, this is not always appropriate in an enterprise security framework. Oracle now supports the ability to have schema-less users who are then mapped to a shared schema when they connect to a particular database. This saves the overhead of maintaining meaningless schema information for hundreds of users who will never need to create or own any objects of their own. Each schema-independent user is known to and identified by the LDAP directory, which, in turn, maps them to the appropriate schema when the user connects to an application and database.

Database Security

In addition to all of the earlier material in this chapter on database security, a couple of additional points should be made. Developers, administrators, and operators all need to be aware of database exposures that can occur outside of the database itself.

An export or a backup of a secure database must be controlled and tracked just as carefully as the database itself. This applies equally to a backup copy created to instantiate a test database or for off-site storage as part of a disaster recovery plan. Sensitive data should always be removed from the copy or somehow "desensitized" before it is moved to an insecure test environment or handed over to a partner for use in an uncontrolled manner.

It is also necessary (although perhaps obvious) that the storage devices that hold the secure database must be equally secure. Most individuals do not have the knowledge, skill, or patience to decipher the block structure of an Oracle database, but it can be done.

Network Security

We've already touched on Oracle's capability to support proxy authentication in which a single proxy user's connection to the database is shared by multiple end users of the application. This can be a secure feature that saves overhead of creating/dropping database connections. It can also potentially be abused. The proxy user should never be given blanket privileges within the database beyond those actually needed for the application. Further, secure application roles protected by passwords and application context-sensitive uses of native Oracle security features (such as Virtual Private Database) are necessary steps to avoid misuse of this efficiency tool.

Encryption

We examined the ability of Oracle to encrypt information as it is stored in the database and then decrypt it when later requested by someone with the appropriate key. We also mentioned that Oracle users' passwords are automatically encrypted as they are passed through Oracle Net Services. These are important points for data encryption but are a small part of the total need.

Most of the native data communication protocols that are used within and between organizations are inherently insecure. TCP/IP, the most common, passes packets along shared network segments that can be read by any other machine on that network. Freeware "sniffers" can be installed in minutes that will capture the clear text communication of any other computer sharing the network. So having an encryption toolkit within the database is great, but if the data traversing the network between the database, the application server, and the end user are not encrypted, then there is still a great exposure.

Network traffic between Web servers and browsers is typically encrypted using Secure Sockets Layer (SSL), a protocol developed and popularized by Netscape. However, in too many organizations, traffic behind the Web server or over older client/server connections is not encrypted. These other network connections can be encrypted using hardware or software products. All Oracle Network Services traffic (beyond the natively encrypted password passing) can be encrypted using Oracle's Advanced Security Option. This product performs other security functions as well and is discussed a little later in this chapter.

Just like the chain in the proverb, an enterprise network is only as secure as the weakest point through which sensitive data passes.

Firewalls

Firewalls are software and/or hardware features for separating networks or converting protocols. They should be used to separate any network zones of different security needs. We commonly think of them as dividing an organization's internal network from the great Internet beyond. This is certainly a necessary use, but there are valid reasons for separating different parts of the internal network. Limit the number of openings in any firewall to just the minimum number of protocols and ports necessary for each valid connection type. Use proxies where possible to further reduce exposure.

Securing Oracle Net Services

In addition to privileged database accounts being left with default passwords, one of the most common exposures in many Oracle installations is the failure to use the security configuration options included with Oracle Net Services (formerly named and still frequently referred to as SQL*Net). A key component in Oracle Net Services is the Listener that accepts incoming connection requests and directs them to the appropriate database instance.

For starters the listener should have a secure password assigned by the administrator, since, by default, no password is necessary to query or reconfigure the listener! Even this basic precaution is frequently overlooked.

Additionally, the listener can (and should) be configured using the `protocol.ora` file to limit the IP address ranges that are allowed to make connections. By default, the listener accepts requests from all IP addresses. If you have a network subnet of production application servers that need to connect to a database, then the database listener should be restricted to accepting connection requests from only that range of IP addresses.

Oracle provides the Oracle Connection Manager (CMAN) as a tool for multiplexing multiple client sessions through a single physical connection. CMAN serves as a proxy server for connections. It can also filter connections by source and destination and by hostnames to supplement IP filtering (IP addresses can easily be faked) to ensure that database connections are made only from trusted application servers.

CMAN is installed and configured on each Web server. Programs (typically Java programs using JDBC) can then make lightweight connections to CMAN as if it were a local database. CMAN then takes the responsibility for rerouting traffic to the proper database services as defined during its configuration. In addition to enhanced security, CMAN can simplify the overall management of the JDBC environment.

Oracle Advanced Security Option

Originally introduced in Oracle8 (known then as the Advanced Networking Option) ASO is one of the least known but most useful options to the Oracle Enterprise Edition database. The most widely publicized feature of this product is the ability to encrypt all Oracle Network Services transmissions. This is absolutely essential to the security of client/server-type applications where sensitive data is passed along networks between the database and desktops throughout the organization. Even in applications on application servers, the normal connection between the application server and database server is not encrypted. Anyone with access to that network segment could potentially be reading data from that packet stream.

ASO provides strong data encryption beyond SSL and DES encryption, including various degrees of RC4 encryption and either two or three-key 3DES algorithms and complies with the U.S. Federal Information Processing Advanced (FIPS) Encryption Standard. An even more strict algorithm, Advanced Encryption Standard (AES), is also supported by ASO.

ASO, however, includes many other Enterprise User Security capabilities that we've discussed in this chapter, such as support for x.509 certificate proxy authentication and LDAP distinguished names. It also provides interfaces to external security services from RADIUS, Kerberos, and others, including hardware SSL accelerators. ASO also allows authentication of users of the database using PKI with private keys and certificates stored in a three-key Triple-DES-secured Oracle Wallet, administered with Oracle Wallet Manager.

ASO uses Oracle Internet Directory for Enterprise User Security but can interoperate with other LDAP-compliant directory services using the OID Integration Platform.

Security Practices

All of the security features provided by Oracle can be used to create a highly secure database environment. They can also be used to create a false sense of security if they are implemented improperly or if the organization's security practices are lax.

It is important to never become complacent regarding security. Policies, procedures, and actual practices must be reviewed and even tested frequently. It is all too common for a security hole to be opened "temporarily" in order to expedite a particular task and then forgotten, thereby remaining a vulnerability.

Summary

This chapter covered some general security considerations but concentrated on specific Oracle database security features. You've seen how Oracle provides means for authenticating users of the database and how they are then authorized to do specific actions within the database.

Oracle's collection of system privileges, object privileges, and roles can be used to customize the authorizations necessary for a class of users to execute application functions. Stored procedures can be used to encapsulate and control functionality so that users do not require any direct privileges on the actual tables, views, and other objects of the database. You have seen how proxy users can be used to maintain application server connections in order to perform work on behalf of other users.

We reviewed the many options for auditing users' activities against specific objects or by the command or system privilege used. We introduced the use of triggers as another mechanism for creating custom audit capabilities within an application.

We also introduced three optional Oracle security products that work with the Enterprise Edition, Oracle Label Security, the Advanced Security Option, and Oracle Identity Management. We closed with a brief warning that all of the security tools in the database (or the rest of the world) can only be as effective as the policies and procedures used to implement and enforce them within an organization.

6

The Oracle Data Dictionary

Virtually everything you could ever want to know about an Oracle database is available by consulting the data dictionary. In this chapter we first consider the data dictionary from a conceptual perspective and then we dive into its structure and contents. We conclude with a discussion of whether you can utilize the data dictionary while programming in the Oracle environment.

If you have used another relational database management system, you'll find that the conceptual description of a data dictionary is probably already familiar to you. If, on the other hand, your programming experience has been with file systems, you may find that the conceptual discussion is new and, we hope, eye-opening.

What Is the Data Dictionary?

Every programming environment has two basic components: program logic — the instructions of what the program needs to do — and data. Data can be held temporarily in variables within the program or persistently in an external store, such as a file or a database. Traditional file structures require the programmer to understand and then to describe the structure of the file so that the program can properly access and manipulate the fields and records of the file. Within the Oracle relational database, however, the structure of the entire database (including its tables, views, indexes, users, security rules, etc.) is stored within a special set of tables and views known as the data dictionary.

The Oracle data dictionary is owned by a special user account known as `SYS`. The `SYS` account is equivalent to the root superuser of a Unix system. Generally, programmers will never need to connect to a shared database as this privileged account. Even database administrators are discouraged from using the `SYS` account for any but the few actions that require this level of power. If you are serving as both developer and DBA, perhaps on your personal copy of the Oracle database, you need to understand the potential risks of doing interactive work while connected as SYS.

Another general item of interest about the Oracle data dictionary is that its tables are stored within a few special tablespaces (such as `SYSTEM` and `SYSAUX`). No other application database objects should ever be created in these special tablespaces.

The key to the Oracle data dictionary is that it can be accessed using the same SQL language used to access the application's data structures within the database. Generally, direct access to the dictionary is limited to `SELECT` statements (you will never issue `INSERT`, `UPDATE`, or `DELETE` statements against dictionary objects). The data dictionary is instead modified indirectly through special SQL statements, known generally as data manipulation language (DML) commands. DML statements, such as `CREATE TABLE`, `DROP INDEX`, `GRANT`, and so on, require special permissions. They are generally performed by a DBA in development organizations that divide responsibilities between DBAs and developers. Student or developers working independently will have to learn the SQL DML commands in order to build and maintain their database environment.

Structure of the Oracle Data Dictionary

The Oracle data dictionary has multiple levels. The level that you will interact with is a series of views (owned by the `SYS` account) that are designed to be easy to use. (Some might question that statement, but it is apparent once these views are compared to the underlying tables of the dictionary!) These dictionary views and their columns are all clearly named to represent their contents. Almost all of our direct interactions with the data dictionary will use these views.

> *Historically all of the data dictionary views and their underlying tables were owned by the SYS account. This is still generally true, but as new functionality has been added to the Oracle RDBMS, some dictionary objects have been created in some other special schemas, such as* `CTXSYS`.

These dictionary views are defined on a series of underlying tables that can be, to say the least, cryptic. These tables were designed only for use by the developers at Oracle who maintain the database management system. Before banishing these from our consciousness forever, we'll look at one example. The upcoming queries demonstrate several ways of retrieving information about tables in the database. To do so, you need to query dictionary views such as `USER_TABLES`. Here's how `USER_VIEWS` is defined within the data dictionary:

```
select o.name, v.textlength, v.text, t.typetextlength, t.typetext,
       t.oidtextlength, t.oidtext, t.typeowner, t.typename,
       decode(bitand(v.property, 134217728), 134217728,
              (select sv.name from superobj$ h, obj$ sv
              where h.subobj# = o.obj# and h.superobj# = sv.obj#), null)
from sys.obj$ o, sys.view$ v, sys.typed_view$ t
where o.obj# = v.obj#
  and o.obj# = t.obj#(+)
  and o.owner# = userenv('SCHEMAID')
```

For this example we looked at `USER_VIEWS`, rather than `USER_TABLES`, because this view definition is only nine lines long—`USER_TABLES` is nearly 80 lines of equally unintelligible references to the data dictionary's underlying tables. From this one example, it is easy to see why the more friendly views are provided! Let's put that unpleasantness aside and return to learning about the more useful dictionary views. When a query is issued against `USER_TABLES`, it gets translated via the complex, 80-line view definition and then presented in a form that you can easily interpret.

Although it isn't a firm rule, the dictionary views can be considered to fall into five categories:

1. The first is the set of views that describe the objects directly owned by the user issuing the query. The names of these views are prefixed by USER_. There are a few USER_ views that don't show owned objects because they reference objects that relate to the entire database rather than a single user's schema. USER_USERS, for example, gives you some basic information about other users of the database.

2. Views in the second set are prefixed by ALL_ and display information about all of the objects included in the USER_ views as well as those accessible to the user based on permissions granted from other user accounts.

3. Another set of views provide a way of seeing information about all of the objects in the database, regardless of owner. These views are intended for use by the database administrators and are therefore prefixes with DBA_.

4. The fourth set of dictionary views are provided for compatibility with ANSI standardized dictionary access. Most Oracle developers and administrators use the first three sets of views and ignore this fourth grouping, which provides less information. You should be aware of them, however, if you are working with multiple RDBMSs and need a consistent access to their dictionaries.

5. The final set of data dictionary objects are not intended for direct access by most users or common programs. Over 1,000 of these views (called fixed views) have names beginning with V$ or GV$. (The V$ views provide information about the instance you are connected to while the GV$ views provide a global view of all instances within a Real Application Clusters database environment.) Monitoring and tuning tools as well as SQL scripts developed by system DBAs will commonly select from these V$ and GV$ views. Developers without access to these tools may find useful tuning information in some of these views such as V$SQLAREA and V$SYSSTAT. (Access to these views is, by default, restricted so developers will generally have to be granted the SELECT ANY DICTIONARY system privilege by a DBA before they will be able to view this information.) Another set of a few hundred special dictionary views, with names that start with V_$, are even more rarely used directly, even by the DBAs. Rather than being defined over physical tables within the data dictionary, these views are constructed on top of various dynamic "tables" that are not actually tables at all. These structures are named with an X$ prefix and are mappings of memory structures within the Oracle SGA. They are exposed as X$ tables in order to allow access vian SQL SELECT statements. This allows SQL to be used as a single, consistent interface to all structures, both user-constructed and system-defined, within the Oracle database.

Before you look at how a developer might take advantage of the information contained within the data dictionary, here's a quick look at an example from each of these view categories. A simple SELECT will be issued against each to see the differences in the rows returned and descriptive information available. For simplicity, we won't show all of the columns available in these views, just a few key columns to show that each of the views gives a different subset of the total information available.

USER_TABLES

Since USER_ dictionary views display information about just the objects owned by the connected user, we must first connect to a user schema that owns some objects; in this example we'll use the SCOTT schema. And rather than display all 47 columns of information about each table, we'll just return two, the name of the table and the tablespace in which it is stored. Figure 6-1 shows that the SCOTT schema owns four tables.

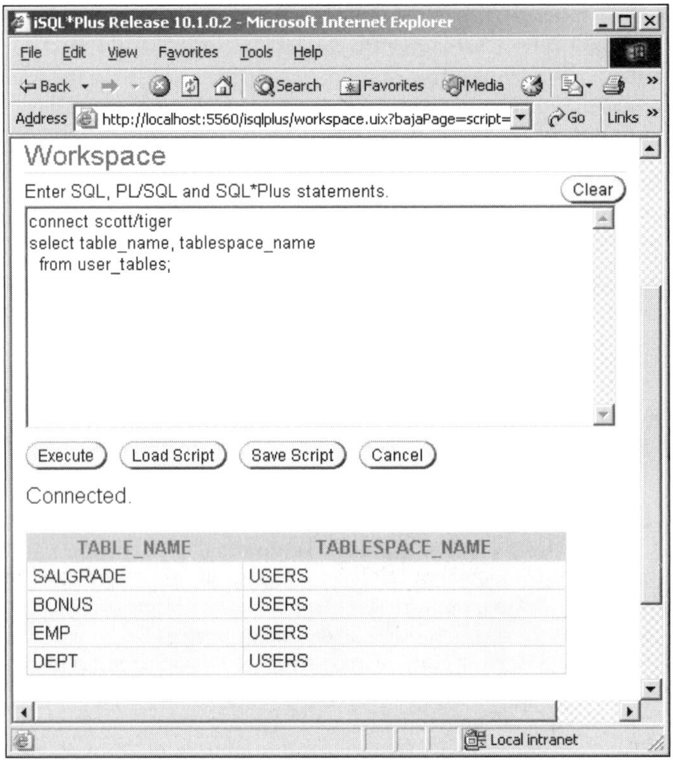

Figure 6-1: Tables owned by the `SCOTT` schema.

ALL_TABLES

The `ALL_TABLES` view shows all of the tables that the current user is allowed to access. To demonstrate the difference from `USER_TABLES`, it was necessary to first connect to the `HR` user and grant `SCOTT` one or more privileges on some HR tables. Now, in addition to the four tables that `SCOTT` owns, Figure 6-2 shows an additional four tables owned by HR that `SCOTT` is allowed to access. Note that even though the query asked about any tables in four schemas, `SCOTT` is not allowed to access any of the tables owned by `OE` or `SH` so none appear in the output.

Not shown in this particular view, however, are the specific privileges `SCOTT` has actually been given. To see the specific privileges, `SCOTT` could query the `USER_TAB_PRIVS` view.

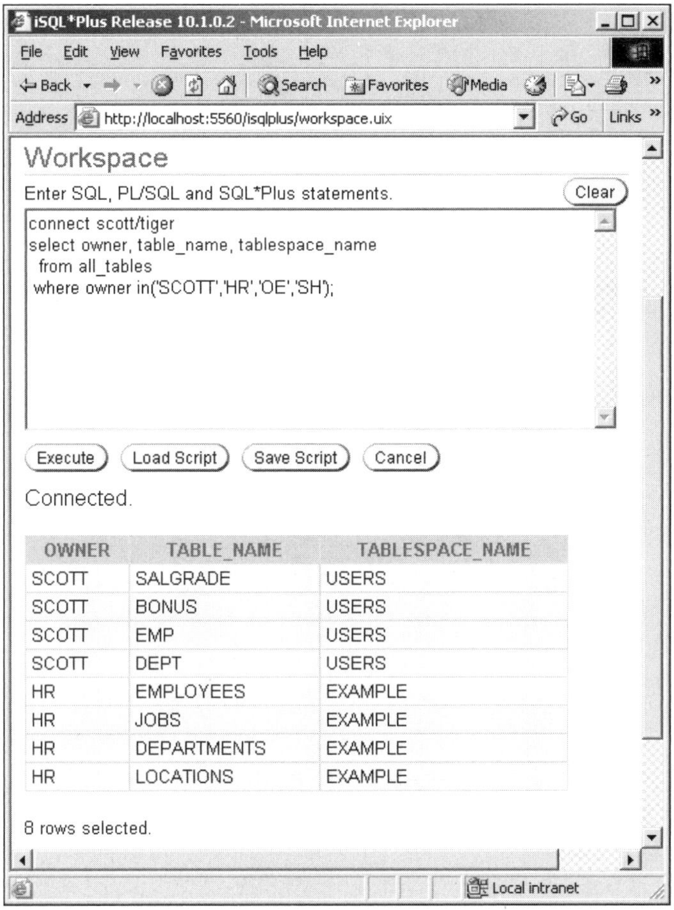

Figure 6-2: Additional tables owned by `HR` that are visible to `SCOTT`.

DBA_TABLES

To illustrate the third category of dictionary views, those prefixed with `DBA_`, it will be necessary to switch to another user. Since `SCOTT` has not been given the necessary DBA privileges, the view will appear not to exist if queried by `SCOTT`. We will connect to a DBA-privileged account, `SYSTEM`, instead to execute a related query. Because the `DBA_TABLES` view will show all of the tables in the entire database, the query in Figure 6-3 will use a `GROUP BY` clause to show the owner schema and a count of the tables in that schema.

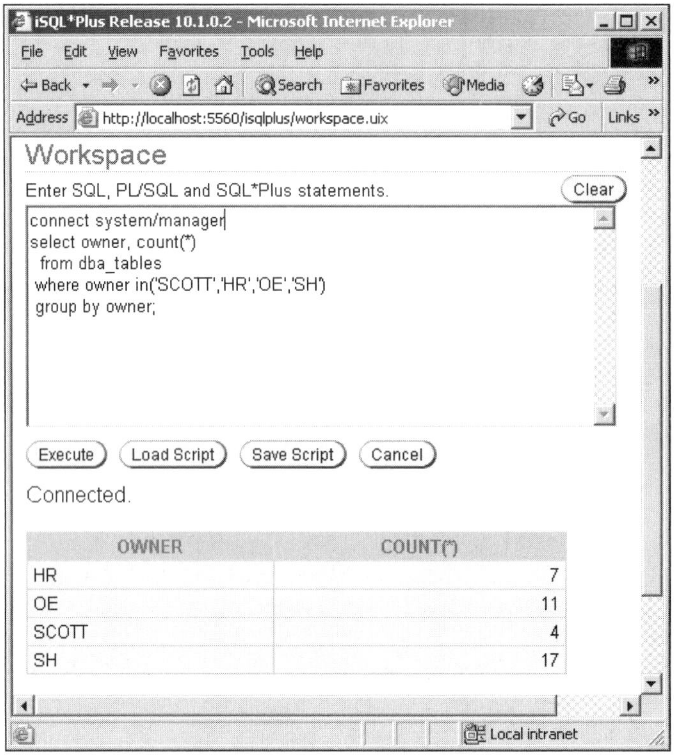

Figure 6-3: **DBA_TABLES** shows tables in all schemas.

This view, queried from this user, is able to see all of the tables from all four of the specified schemas. Because of SYSTEM's privileged status, it does not have to have explicit GRANTs of privileges on the individual objects to be able to see and even modify these tables. This is potentially dangerous since a simple slip of the fingers could end up damaging the integrity of the database. For this reason, DBAs will generally not give DBA-level privileges to developers but will, instead, grant them the specific privileges necessary to do their work.

TAB

The fourth example uses one of the "generic" dictionary views that are not unique to Oracle. These views tend to have less information — specifically they avoid the details of physical implementation — than the related Oracle-specific views. They can be useful, however, if you need to develop an application that will access multiple databases managed by Oracle and another RDBMS. Because the TAB view only has three columns, Figure 6-4 will simply select all columns and all rows.

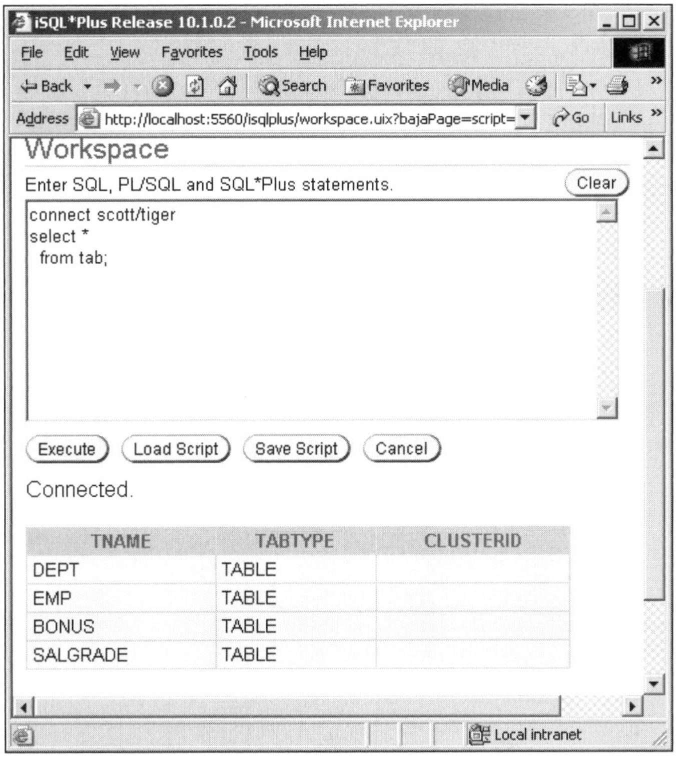

Figure 6-4: Selecting from the `TAB` view.

Note that the specific rows returned from the `TAB` view are identical to the Oracle `USER_TABLES` view. The amount of information available for those rows is much more limited.

V_$FIXED_TABLE

Normally developers rarely have to access any of the special dictionary views and tables represented in this final category. To illustrate the concept, however, we'll need to connect back in as the privileged `SYSTEM` user. There is no view in this category that directly corresponds to the same information that you have been examining, so Figure 6-5 looks at the view that lists the various fixed tables (those with the `X$` prefix that allow you to use SQL to see the contents of various in-memory structures of the database).

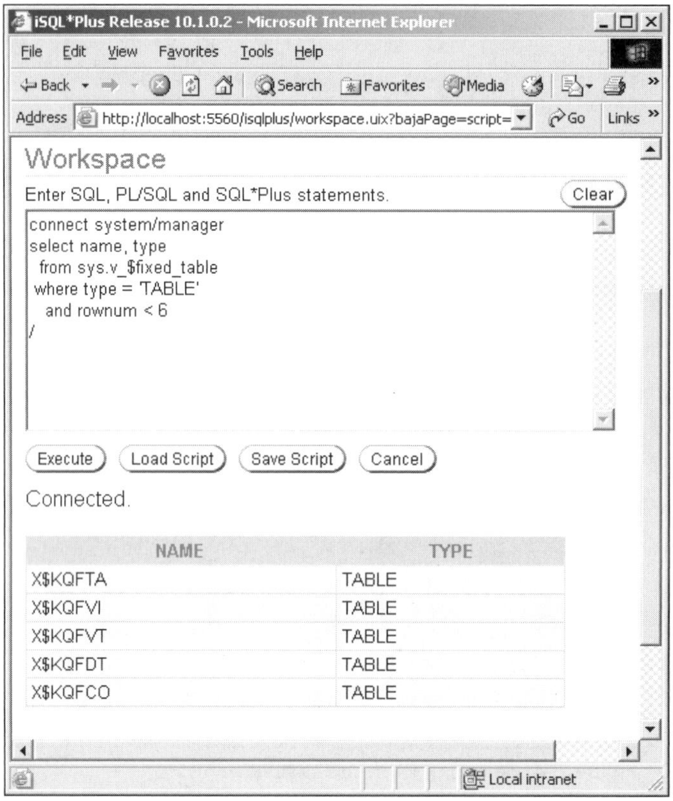

Figure 6-5: Querying `V_$FIXED_TABLE` shows internal data dictionary structures.

To avoid having hundreds of rows returned this query is limited to no more than five rows of output by using Oracle's `ROWNUM` pseudo-column.

These five queries just provide a flavor of the different types of dictionary views available. There are hundreds of others that provide information on every aspect of your database. We'll reference several others in the rest of this chapter, but we can only scratch the surface. Most of the dictionary views that you will need are named meaningfully (even if not intuitively.) For a complete listing of the data dictionary views you will need to look in the Oracle Reference manual (not the SQL Reference manual!) for the release of the Oracle Server that you are using, available online from the Oracle Technology Network at `http://otn.oracle.com`.

In general, you will probably be working within an environment that will interact with the Oracle data dictionary on your behalf. Now that you have an idea of the structure of the data dictionary, you can consider how this resource can aid you during the development process.

The Oracle Data Dictionary During Development

The basic job of a developer is to produce procedural code that will implement a business function using some data structures. When the developer is working with "flat" files, it is common for the developer to define the structure of those files. A database, however, is generally used by several programs and serves data to many business processes. The data requirements of all of those processes and programs need to be accommodated by the design of the database, as you saw in Chapter 4, "Database Design Basics." Once the final structure of the database is determined, several developers will need to access it as they build their programs.

Of course, it is possible to distribute reports of the database structure to each developer (just like we published COBOL copybooks 30 years ago), but the project will benefit from a more interactive approach where the current table structure is available immediately when needed.

Modern application development typically is done from within a development environment such as the Oracle JDeveloper product that allows the developer to interactively work with the database structures, database stored procedures, and the actual code being developed. Of course, many development environments of this type exist, and each programmer (or each development shop) chooses a favorite. It is impossible to cover every development environment that might be used to build an Oracle application within the scope of this book, but it is possible to look at what each of those development environments does in order to expose the structures and contents of the database.

Although your development environment will probably do most or all of the dictionary accesses for you, we will approach this topic as if you are going to code at the "bare metal" level. If your chosen environment does all of this for you, this section will help you understand how it is working. If some of the following capabilities are, for some reason, not provided by your development environment, you will be able to directly access the Oracle data dictionary to get the information you need.

Development proceeds with two types of access to the data dictionary. First, as briefly examined in the previous section, you need to be able to query the dictionary to see the existing data structures, stored procedures, and so on. Second, you will sometimes need to create new objects in the database and will then need to issue various data manipulation statements. For these accesses the dictionary is updated automatically when needed as the user issues data definition language (DDL) SQL statements or data manipulation language (DML) SQL statements.

Locating and Describing Data Dictionary Views

Okay, so there are hundreds of data dictionary views. How do you know what information is available? What view should you be looking at and what information does it contain? Of course, there is always the Oracle Reference manual, but it isn't always necessary to reach for the manual. The Oracle data dictionary is self-describing, once you know just a few key entry points. To find the names of the views that might be applicable to a task, you can query on the `ALL_VIEWS` dictionary view. Perhaps you want to know all of the dictionary views that are related to stored procedures (PL/SQL and stored procedures are covered in Chapters 15, "PL/SQL Basics," and 16, "PL/SQL and SQL.") Figure 6-6 shows such a query.

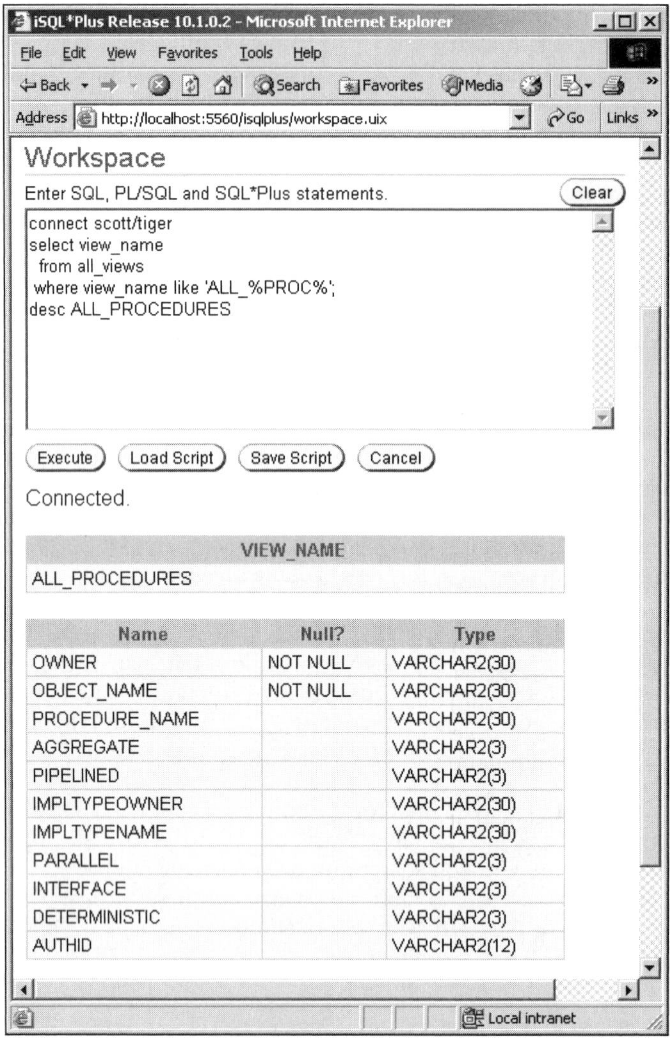

Figure 6-6: Using the data dictionary to locate other entries in the data dictionary.

Once you know that the `ALL_PROCEDURES` view is likely to be of interest, you need to know the columns presented for that view. SQL*Plus and iSQL*Plus make this easy with the `DESCRIBE` command (which is frequently abbreviated to just `DESC`.)

The description of `ALL_PROCEDURES` shows that there are 11 columns in this view. Most of them probably won't mean much before reading the PL/SQL chapters in Part III and gaining a little experience, so we won't go into details yet. For now, just notice three columns: `OWNER`, `OBJECT_NAME`, and `PROCEDURE_NAME`. The `OWNER` column tells you which schema the particular procedure is owned by. The `PROCEDURE_NAME` column is pretty self-evident. Or is it? You'll find that the `PROCEDURE_NAME` column will be populated only when the procedure is part of a package. In this case the package name will be provided in the `OBJECT_NAME` column. A standalone procedure will have its name presented in the `OBJECT_NAME` column and the `PROCEDURE_NAME` column will be empty.

So, as mentioned earlier, the data dictionary isn't always intuitive. Part of this is just due to the complexity of the dictionary. Most of it, though, is because this complexity has developed over many years. For compatibility, each new release has kept the same dictionary view names and columns as the previous release whenever possible. Lots of enhancements over the years have caused the interpretation of some views to be enhanced as well and many new views to be added.

While we're on the topic of describing data dictionary views, it is worth noting that the SQL*Plus `DESCRIBE` command that was used to see the structure of a dictionary view can also be used to get the column structure of any database table or view. `DESCRIBE` is also able to give you the calling structure of packages, stored procedures and functions. When you `DESCRIBE` one of these PL/SQL stored program units, you will get a listing of the arguments used to invoke the object.

Which Set of Views?

In almost all cases, you will probably want to use the `ALL_` views rather than the `USER_`, as was done in the previous section. Typically the schema that is used to store database objects for an application is not the one that the team of developers will use for their development work. This is true for a couple of reasons.

Building on the discussions in Chapter 5, "Oracle Security," keep in mind that users of the application (or specific modules) will need to have the necessary privileges to perform necessary application functions but no unnecessary privileges. Every privilege granted has some risk of allowing inappropriate or accidental damage to the database. One of the ways of protecting the integrity of the database is to isolate accesses to the database objects from the objects themselves. The schema that owns an object has full authority to modify (or even drop) that object — this is generally more authority than needed by the application. Specific privileges (or roles of privileges) will be granted to users or programs to allow them to perform necessary data manipulation while protecting against inappropriate modifications.

As the application is being designed, it is appropriate to identify the necessary database accesses and include the corresponding privileges into a role. It is easier and safer to do development within this security model rather than working directly in the schema that has ownership and all privileges.

That argument plays well with DBAs but may not appeal to the developer who would rather not be restricted, so let's consider another argument for why the developers would actually prefer to be working in individual schemas.

Another reason for separating the schema that owns the database objects from the developers' is that it allows multiple developers to work simultaneously without interfering with each other's work. If all of the developers are doing their work connecting to a single schema, then each developer will be constantly recreating/recompiling objects such as stored procedures and functions that may be needed by other developers. Separating schemas allows for a more stable environment even in the midst of change.

Figures 6-7 and 6-8 illustrate this for a small development team (with only two members) working on their assigned modules. Each is developing some stored procedures or functions that may be needed by the other developers. Tim is responsible for a stored procedure called `SP_CALC_TOTAL` that will need to call another module, a function called `F_CALC_TAX`, being built by Sarah.

If Sarah and Tim are both working in the same schema, as in Figure 6-7, then Tim is going to be frustrated because the `F_CALC_TAX` function is being changed simultaneously and possibly giving back different results as Sarah continues to refine and recompile it. Sometimes a change may include an error that even prevents the `F_CALC_TAX` function from compiling, which then prevents Tim from even running a `SP_CALC_TOTAL` test! There is only one version of the `F_CALC_TAX` function available — while Sarah is enhancing and testing it, Tim is trying to test his procedure using a moving target.

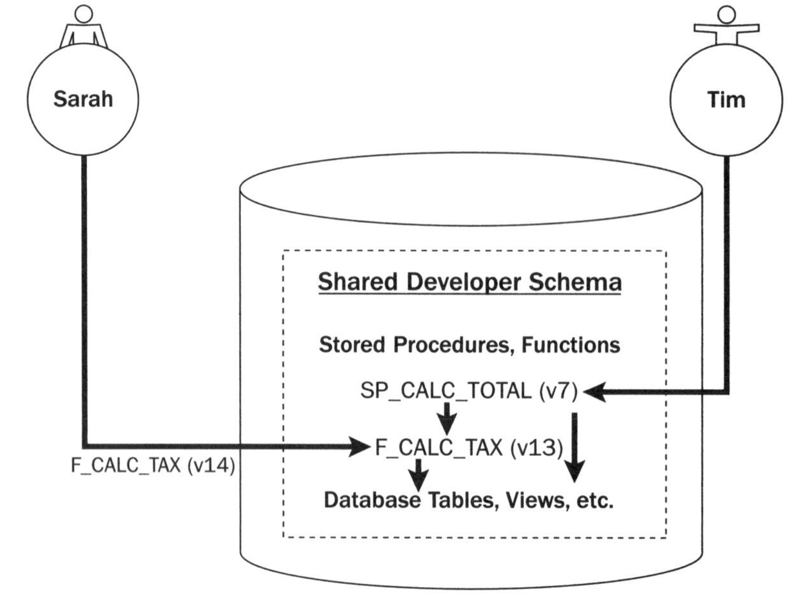

Figure 6-7: Developers sharing a single development schema.

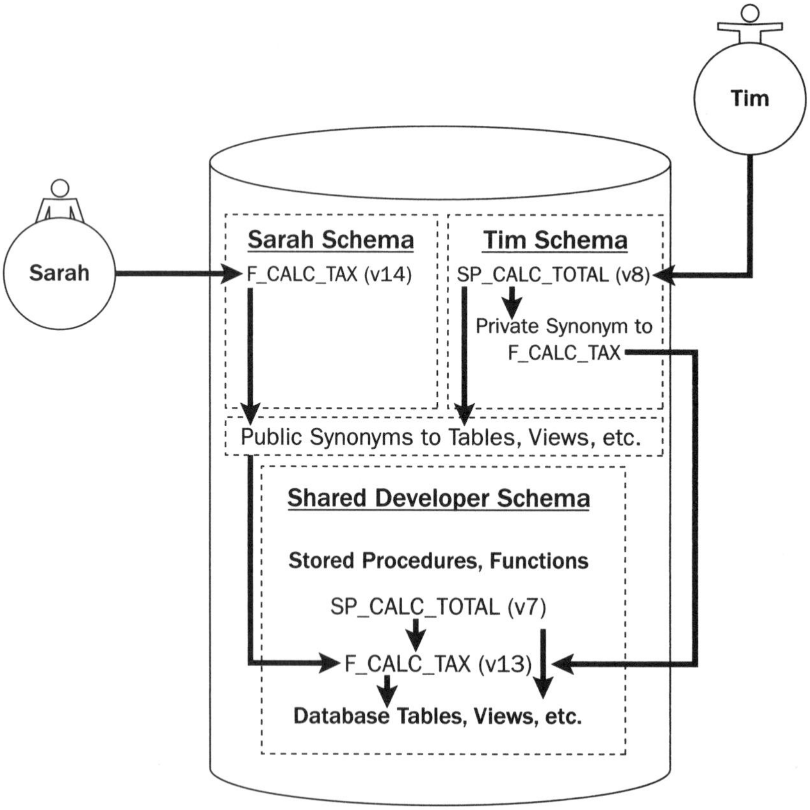

Figure 6-8: Developers using their own schemas and referencing a shared schema.

The configuration shown in Figure 6-8, by contrast, allows each to work independently with occasional coordinated handoffs of a new stable version of the function. Here you see that a version of F_CALC_TAX is contained within the shared schema. Initially, it may be a simple stub of a function that always returns $1. While far from the final code, this allows Tim to continue development and testing of SF_CALC_TOTAL with predictable behavior of the called function.

In addition to the stable version (v13) of F_CALC_TAX in the shared schema, Sarah can have another version (v14) in her private schema. Any changes made to SARAH.F_CALC_TAX will not impact other developers like Tim who continue to access the shared development schema's version of F_CALC_TAX as defined through a synonym. When Sarah has completed a new and stable version of F_CALC_TAX, she lets Tim know that it is available. Tim can then (if desired) verify the stability by calling SARAH.F_CALC_TAX. Rather than changing his code, he can point to the new version by re-creating his private synonym. Once Sarah and Tim agree that the new version is stable, she can deploy her new version into the shared development schema.

Both developers are still referencing the tables, views, and possibly other stored procedures within the shared development schema through public synonyms. Their code can be written without having to prefix object names with the actual schema name so that when the code is ready, it can be copied into that shared schema without having to change references.

Since there is no corresponding schema or an F_CALC_TAX function in the standard example schemas provided by Oracle, we'll illustrate the point using the SCOTT schema and a table rather than a function. Remember earlier that SELECT was granted on some of the HR tables to SCOTT. To avoid having to always reference the JOBS table as HR.JOBS, the DBA has initially created a public synonym to allow everyone (who has an appropriate privilege) to reach HR.JOBS just by querying against JOBS.

Figure 6-9 shows the results of using synonyms. First you create a public synonym. Then, as SCOTT, you issue a simple query against JOBS (which now points to HR.JOBS). Next SCOTT creates a variation of the JOBS table (called MY_JOBS, with only four rows) and creates a private synonym to point at it. Now, the same query returns just four rows rather than 19. From this you can see how the code in a program (in this case a single, simple query) can point to different objects without changing the code.

This very technique allows SCOTT, as a developer, to keep a private version of a table (or other object such as Sarah's function) within his schema in order to begin testing with a new object definition that other developers aren't ready to see. Whenever the new version is ready for public consumption, the DBA can migrate it from SCOTT's schema to the shared application schema referenced by everyone.

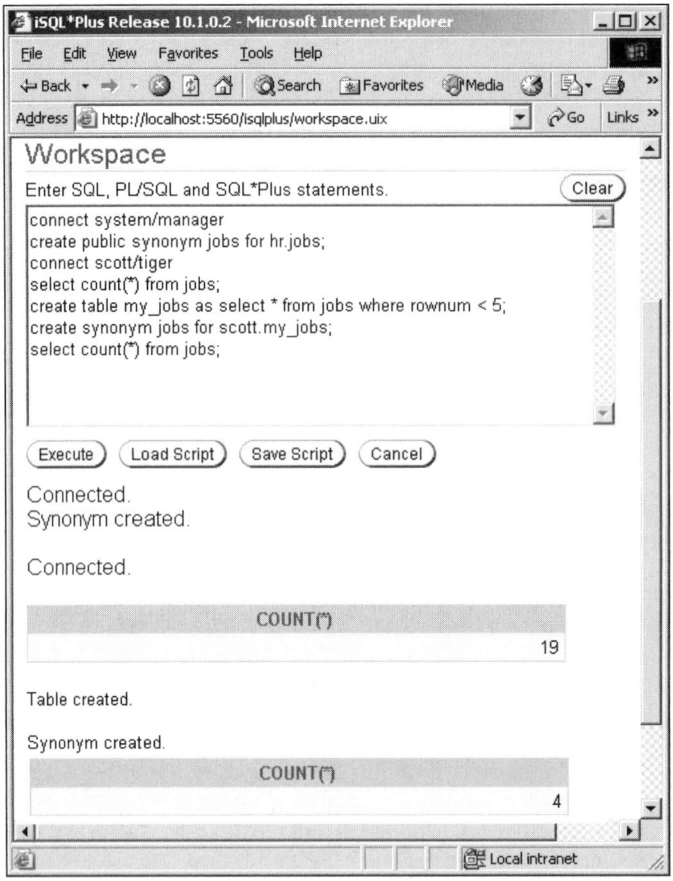

Figure 6-9: Using public and private synonyms to redirect access.

Of course, with the possibility of different versions of objects being in multiple schemas or under different names, but referenced with synonyms there is a chance that SCOTT or our developer Tim might forget which version is currently being referenced. If the redirection is being done with synonyms, Tim can always determine which copy of F_CALC_TAX is actually being used by examining the ALL_SYNONYMS view.

Figure 6-10 issues such a query that shows that there are two applicable synonyms. The private synonym owned by SCOTT will override the public synonym. If SCOTT wished to redirect his code back to the general version of the JOBS table pointed to by the public synonym, he would simply need to drop the private synonym that he created back in Figure 6-9.

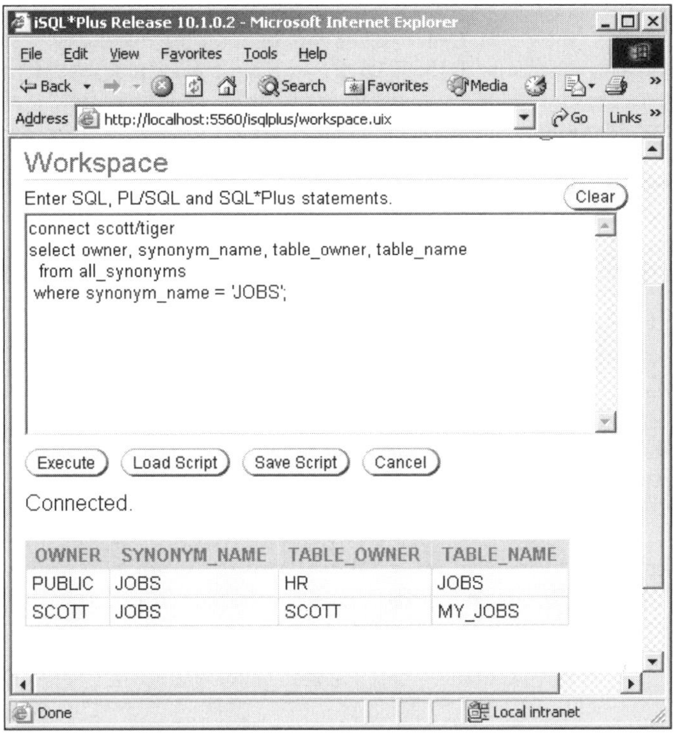

Figure 6-10: Viewing synonyms and what they reference.

Updating the Data Dictionary

As you've seen, it is necessary to directly inquire about information in the data dictionary. Such inquiries are done using the SQL `SELECT` command or through shortcuts (such as the SQL*Plus `DESCRIBE` command).

Updates to the data dictionary are never done using standard SQL DML commands such as `INSERT`, `UPDATE`, and `DELETE`. As you've seen, the dictionary views that are for inquiry are complex views based, in most cases, on joins of multiple underlying dictionary tables. Adding a table to your schema in the database requires far more than just inserting a row into `USER_TABLES`. Dozens of base tables may have to be modified to add the definition of the table, definition of the columns, and definition of any defined constraints; to build any referenced indexes, to allocate some free space; and to record the fact that the space used for the table and indexes is no longer available. Whew! The complexity is extreme and the risk of database corruption is so great that nobody should even think about attempting to do this manually even if it were permitted. Thankfully, it isn't.

The data dictionary is updated on your behalf when you issue DDL commands such as CREATE TABLE, ALTER VIEW, DROP INDEX, and so on. Oracle takes care of all of the necessary details to protect the integrity of the dictionary when one of these DDL commands is issued. Just as you need specific object privileges to access an object, the DBA will also have to grant an appropriate system privilege (such as the CREATE TABLE privilege) for you to execute DDL commands.

Other changes to the data dictionary are performed as a result of some special DBA commands (such as the now obsolete ANALYZE TABLE) or packaged procedures (such as its replacement, DBMS_STATS.GATHER_TABLE_STATS). Incidentally, the dictionary may also be updated when users of the application execute DML statements that change application data in certain ways.

One Oracle quirk, related to this topic, is of interest to developers. Whenever a DDL command is issued, Oracle performs an implicit COMMIT *of any current transaction. If your application's design includes any DDL activity (such as to create an intermediate result table), make sure that it is done outside the boundaries of a transaction. Otherwise, the first part of the transaction will be automatically committed even if the program later issues a* ROLLBACK*. Incidentally, Oracle also provides a useful feature to avoid the expensive operations of creating and dropping temporary tables — see the discussion on Global Temporary Tables in Chapter 12, "Other Database Structures."*

Developers may need to do some creation of data objects such as tables or indexes, but more commonly, they will create or modify procedural objects such as stored procedures, functions, and packages. Again, the dirty work of actually updating the data dictionary is performed for you when you issue a command such as CREATE OR REPLACE PROCEDURE.

The Oracle Data Dictionary at Execution Time

In most cases an application is developed with knowledge of what data structures each query will need to access. It might have to retrieve a subset of rows from a given table, and so you use bind variables to tie specific values to known columns in the WHERE clause. In these typical situations, the developer of the code uses the data dictionary to build the query, and no other dictionary inquiries are needed when the program executes.

Sometimes, however, a program must be built that operates in a more dynamic manner. It may be necessary to build an SQL statement on the fly as the program runs and then execute it immediately. Facilities for performing dynamic SQL operations such as these vary somewhat depending upon the programming language and environment being used. For general examples of the technique, we will use SQL and PL/SQL, since these languages are available to all Oracle developers regardless of whether the main body of the application is written in Java, C++ or other language. From the examples you should be able to perform similar operations in the native programming language of choice.

SQL to Generate SQL

From a scripting environment such as shell or Perl, it is sometimes easiest to issue a query that will generate another file of SQL statements that can then be executed from the same script. For the sake of an example, let's consider a need to produce a simple report that tells the user how many rows are in each table in a schema. If you knew in advance exactly what tables would exist (and that the list wouldn't change), it would be possible to just build a list of `SELECT COUNT(*) FROM tablename` commands in your script, such as:

```
SELECT COUNT(*) FROM TABLE1;
SELECT COUNT(*) FROM TABLE2;
SELECT COUNT(*) FROM TABLE3;
```

But if the purpose of the script is to help the application user manage the space used by the tables that the user has personally created, you would have no way of knowing the names of those tables at the time you developed the report. In this case, though, you would remember that the data dictionary has such a list of table names ready for you to use. The developer's challenge is to take that raw list of tables and turn it into the necessary list of `SELECT` statements.

You will need to combine some data from the `USER_TABLES` dictionary view with some constant strings. Here's a simple SQL*Plus query that, when run in the `SCOTT` schema, returns four rows:

```
SQL> select 'SELECT COUNT(*) FROM ' || table_name ||';'
  2    from user_tables
  3   order by table_name
  4  /

'SELECTCOUNT(*)FROM'||TABLE_NAME||';'
----------------------------------------------------
SELECT COUNT(*) FROM BONUS;
SELECT COUNT(*) FROM DEPT;
SELECT COUNT(*) FROM EMP;
SELECT COUNT(*) FROM SALGRADE;

4 rows selected.
```

That quickly gives you the basic contents of the dynamic script you'd like to run. If this were run in any other schema, it would return a `SELECT` statement for each table in that schema. To automate this, however, you need to do a couple of things. You'll want to adjust the query so that it will display the name of each table in addition to just the number of rows. You'll need to store the query in an SQL script. You'll need to turn off the header and footer information. Finally, you'll need to save the output of the query into another script file and then invoke it. SQL*Plus offers the necessary controls to do these things. Here's what a `GEN_ROW_COUNTS.SQL` script should look like after adding these simple changes:

```
set echo off pagesize 0 heading off feedback off termout off
spool row_counts.sql
select 'SELECT '''||rpad(table_name||':',31)||''', COUNT(*) FROM ' || table_name
||';'
  from user_tables
 order by table_name;
spool off
set termout on
@row_counts
```

The goal here isn't necessarily to learn all of the details of the SQL*Plus environment—although it is the standard means of executing SQL scripts for an Oracle database. Let's take just a moment to see what each of the changes to our script was for. The `SET` command on the first line set up the environment so that commands in the script are not echoed, no page breaks occur, no headings are printed, and no row count feedback appears as a query footer. The `SET` command finally uses the `TERMOUT OFF` option to temporarily turn off output from the script to the screen. The SPOOL command directs the output of the script to a new SQL file. In the SQL statement itself, the table_name column is combined twice, once as part of a literal and then as a column in the SELECT list. To get the first occurrence to appear as a literal, including single quotes was necessary. Since this part of the original query was bounded by single quotes, a series of three quote marks were used to produce each one on output. The SQL RPAD function was used to ensure that the output lines were all aligned properly, and a colon was included in the string after the table name. Finally, the spooling to the second file was turned off, the terminal output was turned back on, and then the generated file was executed. Here is what was spooled into the ROW_COUNTS.SQL file:

```
SELECT 'BONUS:                              ', COUNT(*) FROM BONUS;
SELECT 'DEPT:                               ', COUNT(*) FROM DEPT;
SELECT 'EMP:                                ', COUNT(*) FROM EMP;
SELECT 'SALGRADE:                           ', COUNT(*) FROM SALGRADE;
```

Finally, here's what was output when executed GEN_ROW_COUNTS.SQL in SQL*Plus was executed:

```
SQL> @gen_row_counts
BONUS:                                  0
DEPT:                                   4
EMP:                                   14
SALGRADE:                               5
```

The result is a simple dynamic report in only eight lines of code! We could have done more, if we chose, to spool the output of the generated query to another text file or even generate the output from the database in HTML or XML formats.

Dynamic SQL

Scripting such as this is very useful, but it certainly doesn't solve all of the potential needs for dynamic SQL processing. PL/SQL provides another facility for producing and executing dynamic SQL from within an application. PL/SQL is the procedural language environment first introduced with Oracle version 6. Its primary purpose is to provide a procedural language environment closely integrated with both the SQL language and the internal workings of the Oracle database. PL/SQL is the primary language used for building stored procedures, functions, and packages as part of an application. Additionally, many of the built-in utility functions of the database are implemented in PL/SQL packages that can be called from your application. Because you haven't yet learned the basics of PL/SQL (you will start in Chapter 15, "PL/SQL Basics"), we will keep the examples in this chapter very simple just to demonstrate how the output of a data dictionary query can be used as input to dynamic SQL.

An entire chapter of the PL/SQL User's Guide and Reference manual is dedicated to the topic of dynamic SQL. In addition to SQL statements, the dynamic SQL feature of PL/SQL can also dynamically define and execute blocks of PL/SQL code for even more power.

Within PL/SQL it is necessary to construct the SQL statement by concatenating various strings with data returned from the data dictionary. You could use PL/SQL's EXECUTE IMMEDIATE statement that parses the string that was built and then executes it. You can either store the string containing the SQL statement into a PL/SQL VARCHAR2 variable and pass it as an argument to EXECUTE IMMEDIATE or build it directly as part of the statement.

Prior to the introduction of the `EXECUTE IMMEDIATE` PL/SQL command dynamic SQL was performed using the `DBMS_SQL` package. This package is still available as an alternative to `EXECUTE IMMEDIATE`.

It is possible, for instance, to create a stored procedure that takes the name of a schema as an input and then returns a list of all the tables contained within that schema back to the calling application program. That program could then use that list to dynamically create a drop-down list for the user to choose a particular table that would be passed in as an argument to another stored procedure that would look up the columns of that table to dynamically produce a cursor with the correct column specifications. That cursor could then be passed back to the application to fetch data rows from the cursor and display them on the user's screen in the appropriate format.

Our simple example won't do anything quite that exotic. The following PL/SQL block bypasses the use of the `EXECUTE IMMEDIATE` statement through the use of a shortcut of simply opening a cursor that is dynamically defined by the string of SQL statement text.

```
DECLARE
TYPE Dyn_Sql_Cursor_Type    IS ref cursor;
Dyn_Sql_Cursor              Dyn_Sql_Cursor_type;
Dyn_Sql_Cursor_Text         varchar2(2000);
type return_rec_type        is record(
     column_name            varchar2(30),
     column_datatype        varchar2(30),
     column_length          number);
return_rec                  return_rec_type;
my_table_name               varchar2(30)    := 'EMP';
BEGIN
     Dyn_Sql_Cursor_Text := 'select rpad(column_name,20), rpad(data_type,12), ' ||
                            'data_length '||
                            ' from user_tab_columns '||
                            'where table_name = :tn '||
                            'order by column_id';
     OPEN Dyn_Sql_Cursor FOR Dyn_Sql_Cursor_Text USING my_table_name;
     Loop
          FETCH Dyn_Sql_Cursor into return_rec;
          EXIT WHEN Dyn_Sql_Cursor%NOTFOUND;
          dbms_output.put_line('Column Name: '||return_rec.column_name||
                               ' Datatype: '  ||return_rec.column_datatype||
                               ' Length: '    ||return_rec.column_length
                              );
     END LOOP;
     CLOSE Dyn_Sql_Cursor;
END;
/
```

This PL/SQL example uses syntax and structures that will seem strange to someone being exposed to the language for the first time. In short, it declares some data types and then some variables of those types. It defines the text string of an SQL statement using a bind variable that was pre-defined with a value of `'EMP'`. (Note that this value would probably be passed in as an argument value in a less artificial situation.) You open the cursor using your SQL text string and then loop through each of the rows returned by the query. The `DBMS_OUTPUT` utility allows you to display the output onto your screen. Finally, you close the cursor and end the PL/SQL block.

Executing this PL/SQL block (saved as a script named `dyn_SQL_example.sql`) in SQL*Plus from the `SCOTT` schema returns the following results:

```
SQL> set serveroutput on
SQL> @dyn_SQL_example
Column Name: EMPNO                  Datatype: NUMBER       Length: 22
Column Name: ENAME                  Datatype: VARCHAR2     Length: 10
Column Name: JOB                    Datatype: VARCHAR2     Length: 9
Column Name: MGR                    Datatype: NUMBER       Length: 22
Column Name: HIREDATE               Datatype: DATE         Length: 7
Column Name: SAL                    Datatype: NUMBER       Length: 22
Column Name: COMM                   Datatype: NUMBER       Length: 22
Column Name: DEPTNO                 Datatype: NUMBER       Length: 22
```

This simple example provides a hint of the power of dynamic SQL and demonstrates how it can use data dictionary information to present information that is unique to the user and status of the database at a particular point in time.

Summary

The Oracle data dictionary is composed of hundreds of tables and views owned by a special account, named `SYS`. Developers, DBAs, and end users who need to inquire on the structure of the database can issue SQL `SELECT` queries against the dictionary views. The views are grouped into five general categories. The ones of greatest use to the developer are named with prefixes of either `USER_` or `ALL_`.

During the development process, you will need to reference the data dictionary to determine the structure of tables, views, stored procedures, privileges, and so on. Modern application development environments, such as Oracle JDeveloper, will do most of the queries on the developer's behalf and display the structure of the database objects back in a graphical presentation.

Updates to the data dictionary are never performed directly by `INSERT`, `UPDATE`, or `DELETE` statements. Dictionary updates are performed by Oracle on the behalf of the developer or user when an allowed DDL command is executed.

Some applications need to perform dynamic operations that cannot be known in specific detail at the time the application is developed. It is possible for the program to dynamically build SQL statements using information retrieved at run time from the data dictionary as well as other database application data.

7

Installing Oracle

If you have been reading this book sequentially, you have now learned quite a bit about the basic concepts of the Oracle database, along with a few tips and techniques you can use as a developer accessing the Oracle database. Now it's time to install the Oracle software so you can do the hands-on work in the rest of the book.

This chapter covers the installation of Oracle 10*g* Database. The installation procedure was one of the areas that was significantly improved in the Oracle 10*g* release from earlier releases, so the following description will also help to display some of the advantages that the 10*g* release brought to the Oracle arena.

If you already have a running Oracle database, you may not need to read the remainder of this chapter. However, it may be worthwhile, since you may have to install a version of Oracle 10*g* for testing purposes.

Getting Oracle Software

For the purpose of completeness, this chapter will assume you don't even have Oracle software. You can download a copy of Oracle 10*g* Database standard edition from the Oracle Technology Network at `http://otn.oracle.com`.

> *Oracle Technology Network, commonly referred to as OTN, is an incredibly useful site for anyone using Oracle technology, full of articles, official and extended documentation, and discussion boards. It doesn't cost anything to register for OTN, although you may want to purchase a TechTrack for $199. A TechTrack, as of this writing, provides a suite of software for development use as well as access to online technical support information.*

The version of the Oracle database you will download is free, but you can only use if internally for development, as detailed in the OTN License Agreement that is presented during the download process. If you wish to deploy the software, you have to obtain a license from Oracle for the particular deployment scenario.

The home page of OTN (at the time that this process was being documented) is shown in Figure 7-1. The content of the home page changes regularly, but the basic areas typically remain the same.

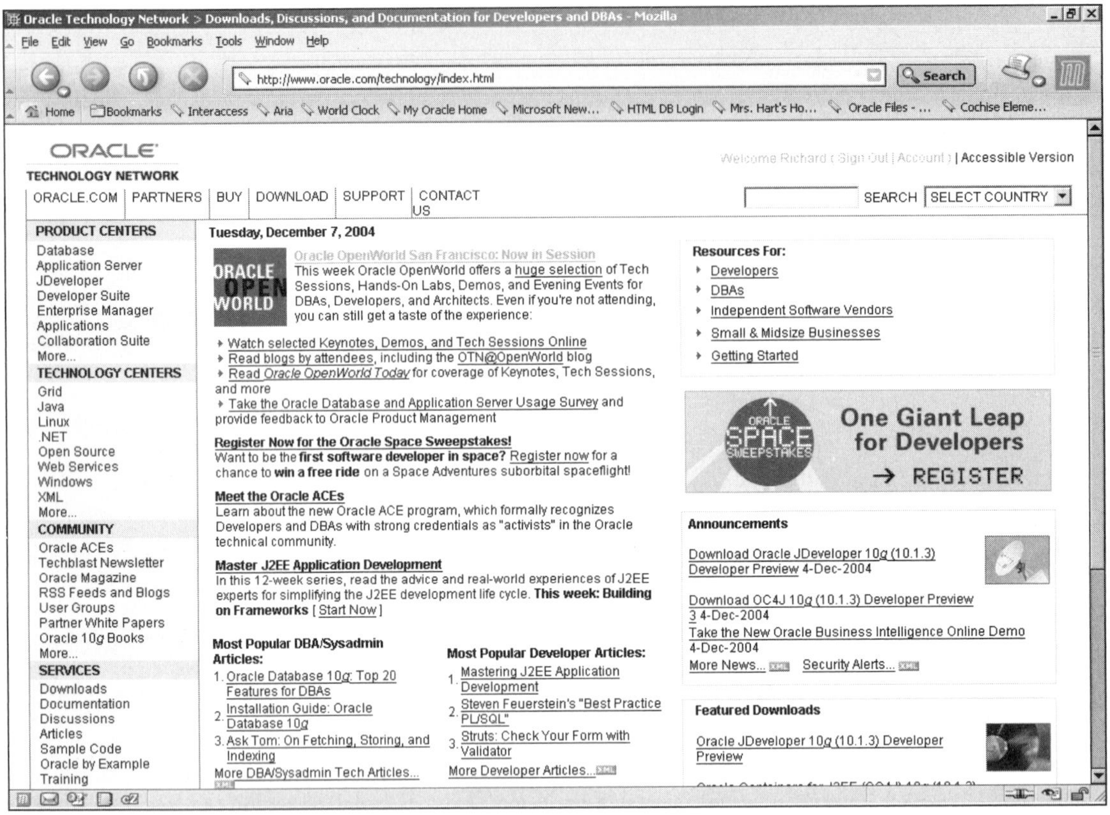

Figure 7-1: The Oracle Technology Network home page.

The fastest way to get to the download area for an OTN product is to scroll to the bottom of the page and click on the product center, which is on the far left. The home page for the database product center is shown in Figure 7-2.

The left-hand navigation area contains an entry for downloads. Click on this entry to get a list of downloads, and then select Database from the list. This action brings up a page with downloads for Oracle Database 10*g* for a number of platforms, including Windows and Linux.

Once you select one of the downloads, you will be asked to sign in, either give or verify some of your contact information, answer some survey questions, and certify that you will not use the software for forbidden foreign export — a small price to pay for downloading Oracle Database 10*g*. You will also see the particulars of the OTN License Agreement here, which you must agree to by clicking on the button labeled *I Accept* before you can begin a download. Of course, this free download will not allow you to use Oracle technical support.

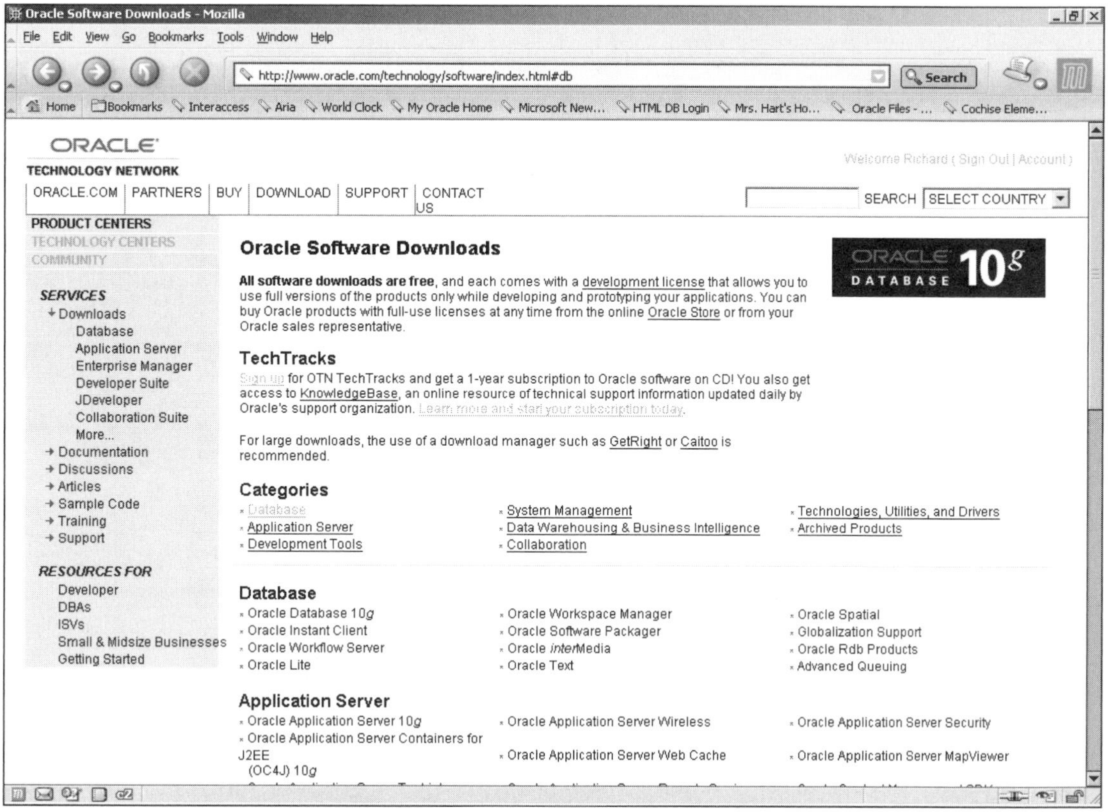

Figure 7-2: The home page for Oracle Database 10g on OTN.

The page shown in Figure 7-3 is the home page for downloading Oracle 10*g* Database for a Windows 32-bit platform. The remainder of this chapter illustrates downloading and installing Oracle 10*g* Database on a 32-bit Windows platform. Since Oracle is a portable database, your download and installation process may differ slightly for other platforms but will essentially remain the same.

On this page, click on the link under the title *Download the Complete Files* to get an installable image of Oracle 10*g* Database. The complete download for Windows 32-bit is 576 MBs, at the time of this documented download. I use a cable modem for my Internet connection, and the download took just under 38 minutes on my server machine, which was dedicated to the download for the duration.

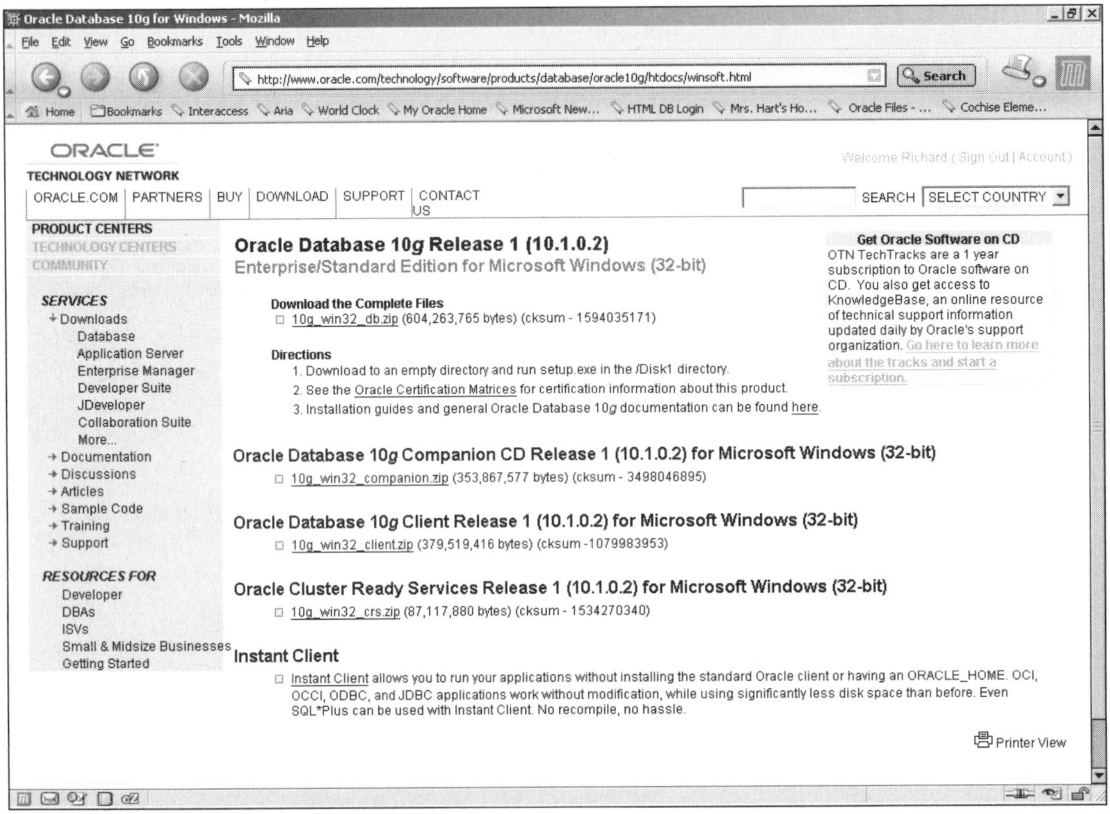

Figure 7-3: Home page on OTN for downloading Oracle 10g Database for 32-bit Windows.

Installing Oracle Server Software

Once you have downloaded the server software from OTN, your next step is to install the Oracle database server software. This process is highly automated and wizard-driven, and it includes the creation of a sample database, which you can use for the examples in this book.

System Requirements

Before you start installing the Oracle database software, you should check to make sure that the system you are using as the target has the appropriate resources available. For Windows 32-bit, the minimum recommended system resources include 100 MB of temporary disk space and 1.5 GBs of available hard disk space. In addition, the installation guide recommends 512 MB of RAM, although the minimum amount of required RAM is 256 MB. You can take Oracle's word that this will work, but we have found that a more optimal minimum amount of memory is 1 GB for the 32-bit Windows platform.

You can consult the installation guide for your platform to determine the minimum system requirements for your particular platform.

Installing the Software

The first step is to uncompress the files contained in the ZIP file you just downloaded. Your machine may have software installed that will prompt you to do this automatically once you have downloaded the master ZIP file.

> *If you are installing Oracle Database 10g from a CD, you can simply insert the CD into the server drive and the* `AUTOEXEC.INF` *file will start the installation. This autorun file essentially starts the same Setup program that the next step will start.*

To start the installation process, you must be logged on to the Windows server as an Administrator. To begin, simply click on the `SETUP.EXE` file in File Explorer. This file should be located in the Disk 1 subdirectory of the directory holding the unzipped files. This action calls up the first page of the Oracle Database 10*g* Installer, as shown in Figure 7-4.

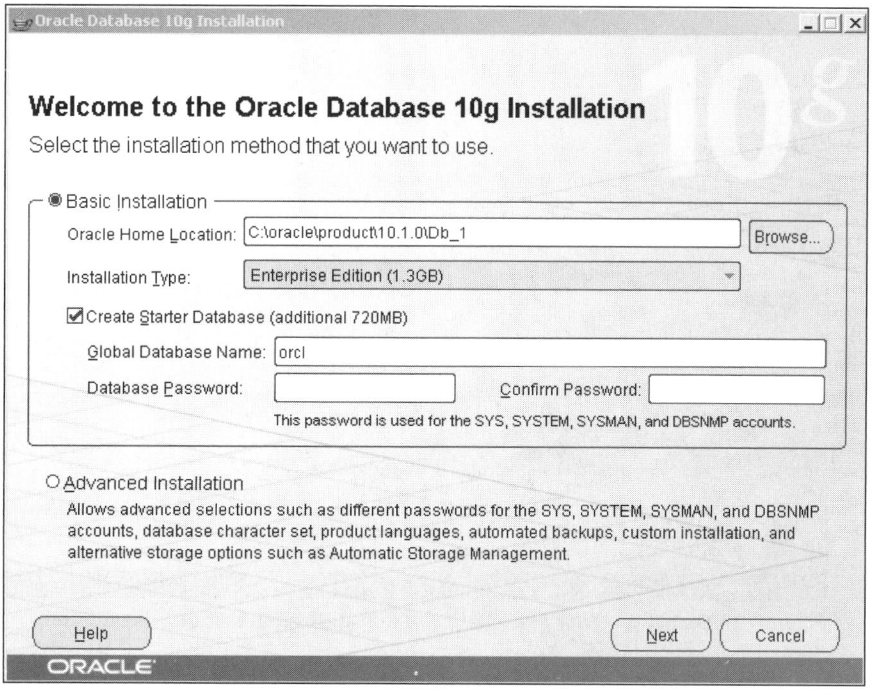

Figure 7-4: The Oracle Database 10*g* Universal Installer initial page.

The page lists some basic choices: the directory where you want to install the software, the version of Oracle you want to install (Enterprise Edition, Standard Edition, or Personal Oracle), and whether you want to create a starter database. This chapter, and the rest of the book, will use the default location for files and the default global database name for the starter database (orcl).

The one option you must enter on this page is the password for the system accounts `SYS`, `SYSTEM`, `SYSMAN`, and `DBSNMP`. These accounts have very powerful privileges, so assign a highly secure password for these accounts. You have to both enter the password and then confirm it in the text box to the right before you can go on.

If you wanted to assign different passwords for these accounts, or adjust other installation options, like setting up automated backups, you would select the Advanced Installation option toward the bottom of the page. For the purposes of this book, the basic installation will be appropriate.

Once you have entered a password for the system accounts, click on the Next button. The Oracle Installer then goes through a preparation stage, where it assembles a summary of the installation options.

The next step is to click on the Install button at the bottom of the page. Once you begin the install, a status page is shown that keeps you informed of the progress of the install. A screen shot of this page is shown in Figure 7-5. On the right-hand side of this page, a light blue box will cycle through the key features of Oracle 10*g* Database as the installation proceeds.

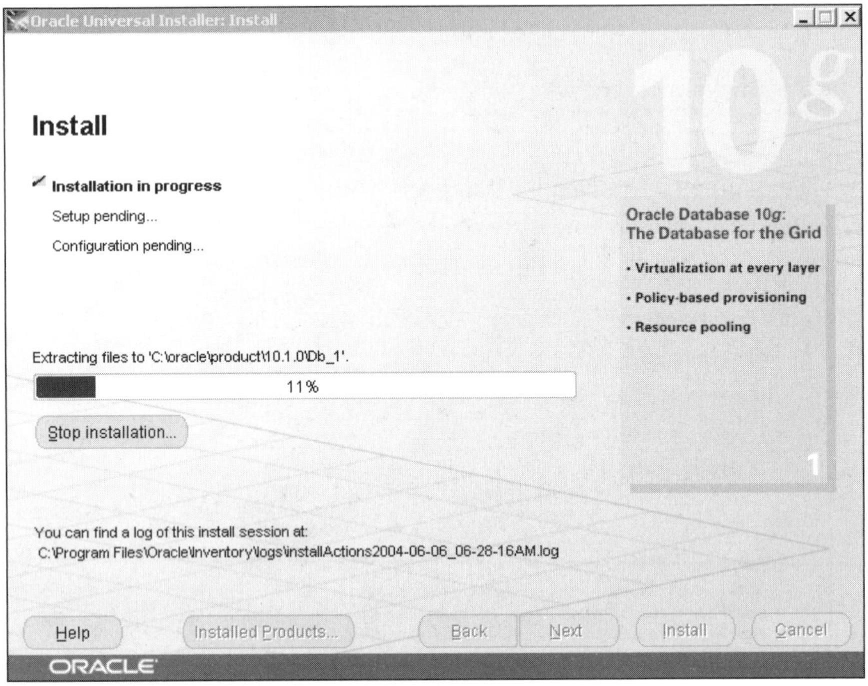

Figure 7-5: Status page for install of Oracle 10*g* Database Enterprise Edition.

After the initial files are installed, the Oracle Installer runs a number of Configuration Assistants. For this default installation, the Oracle Net Configuration Assistant, *i*SQL*Plus Configuration Assistant, and the Oracle Database Configuration Assistant were run. These Configuration Assistants create the default configuration files needed to run your Oracle database and its accompanying products or, in the case of the Database Assistant, create the sample database you specified on the initial page of the installer. The progress of the Database Configuration Assistant is shown in Figure 7-6.

On the installation on my server, the Configuration Assistants started around nine minutes into the installation process. The Configuration Assistants completed their work 19 minutes into the installation process.

Once the Database Configuration Assistant completes its work, it presents the page shown in Figure 7-7, which contains relevant information about your sample database, including its name, the location of the parameter file for the database instance, and the URL to access Enterprise Manager for the instance.

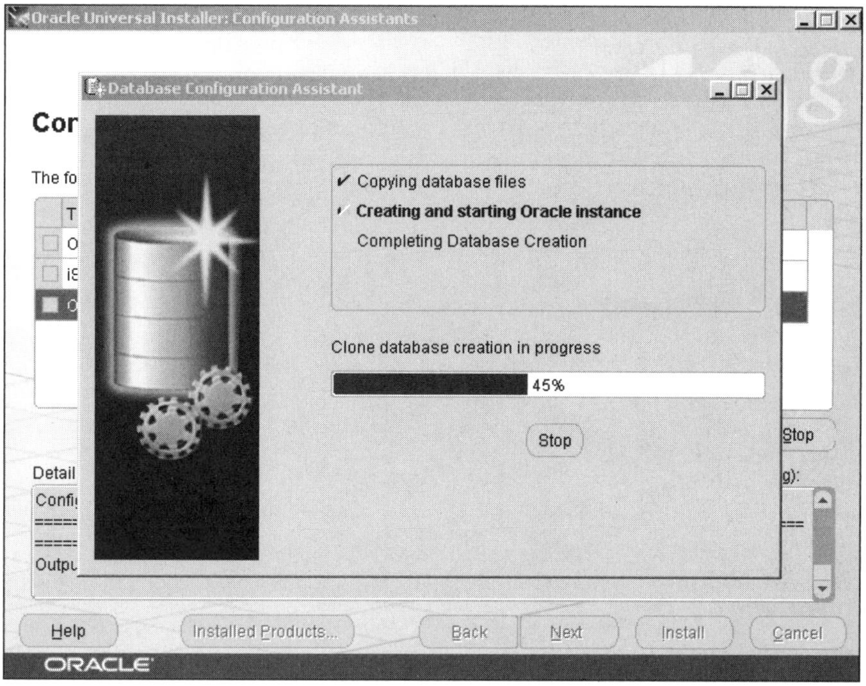

Figure 7-6: Progress page for Database Configuration Assistant.

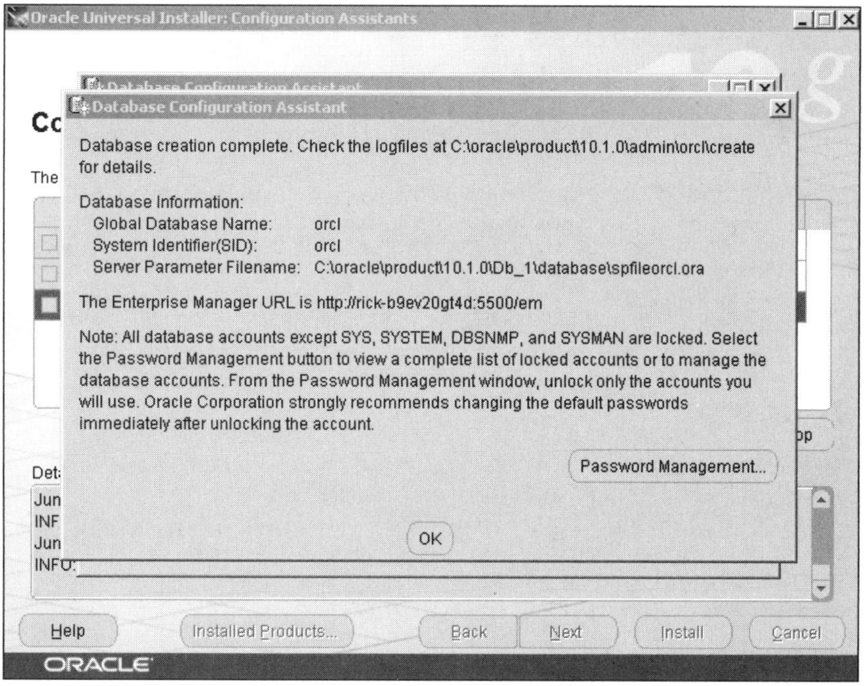

Figure 7-7: Completion of Database Configuration Assistant.

Once you click OK on this page, you get a page indicating that the Oracle 10*g* Database installation is complete, as shown in Figure 7-8. This page includes URLs to access *i*SQL*Plus, a basic tool for interacting with your Oracle database, as well as a URL for accessing UltraSearch, a search tool that is part of Oracle 10*g* Database Enterprise Edition, and the Enterprise Manager URL. Note that each of these uses the domain name for your server (in this case, rick-b9ev20gt4d) followed by a colon and the port number for the component.

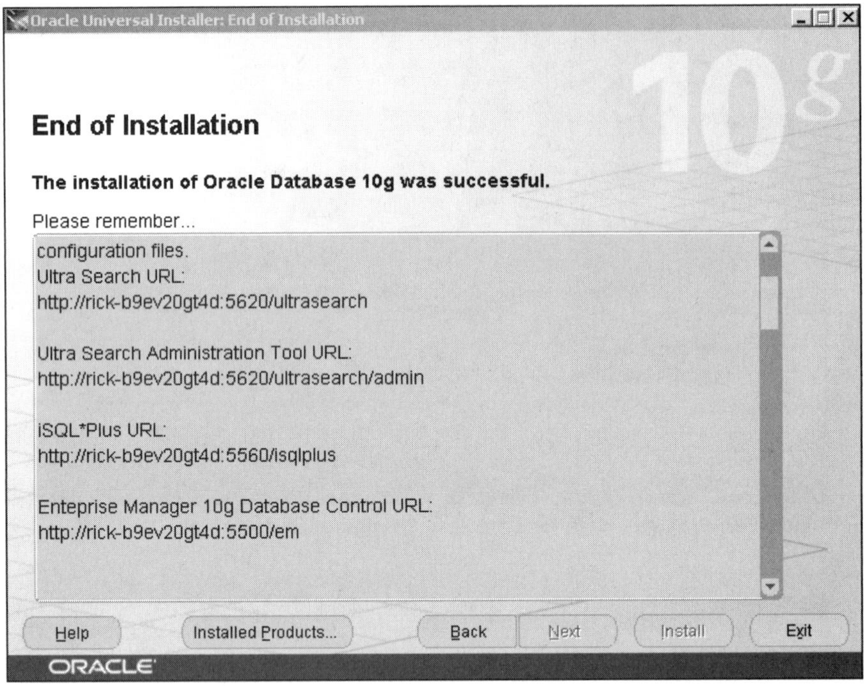

Figure 7-8: Completion page for Oracle Installer for Oracle 10*g* Database Enterprise Edition.

Click on the Exit button and let the installer know that yes, you really do want to exit. The installer opens up a browser window and put you into the logon page for Enterprise Manager, as shown in Figure 7-9.

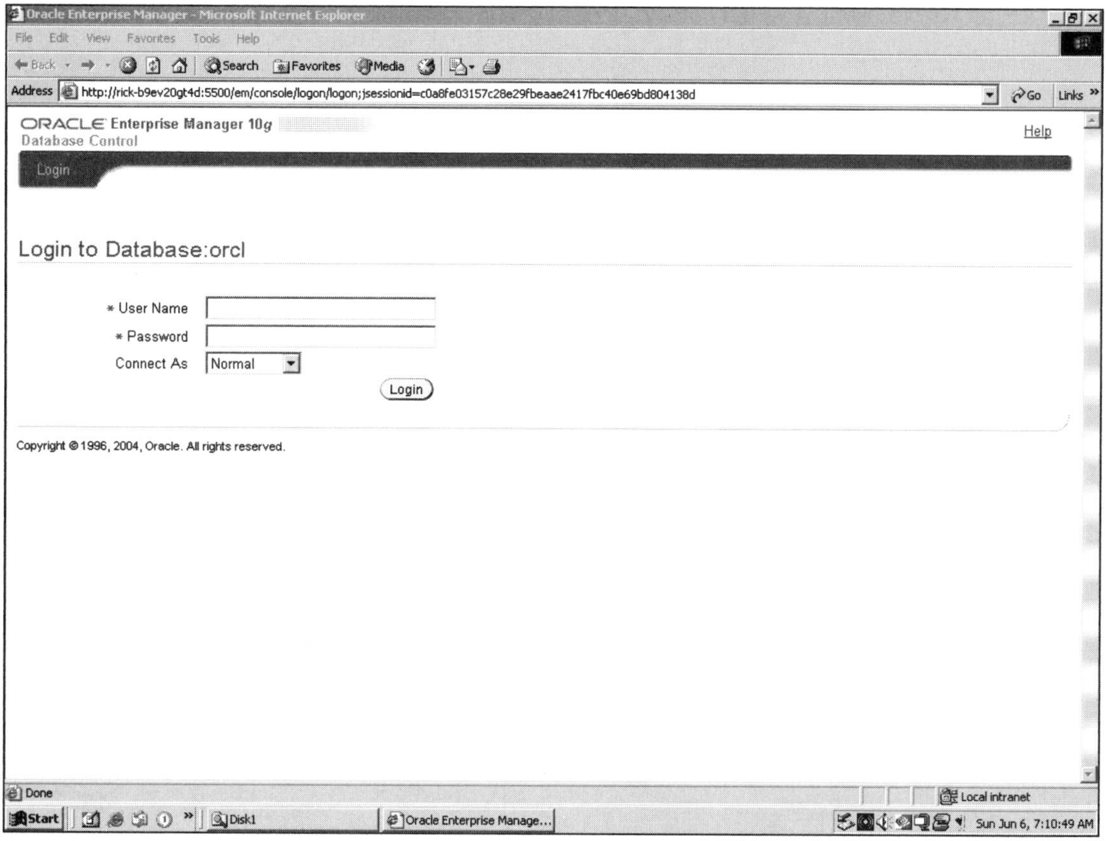

Figure 7-9: Login page for Enterprise Manager.

Log in with the username SYSMAN and the password you assigned at the start of the installation process. A page appears that tells you that the functionality you are about to use requires a license for the Oracle database as well as a separate license for the add-on packs for Enterprise Manager. When you click on the I Agree button, you are taken to the home page for your instance, as shown in Figure 7-10.

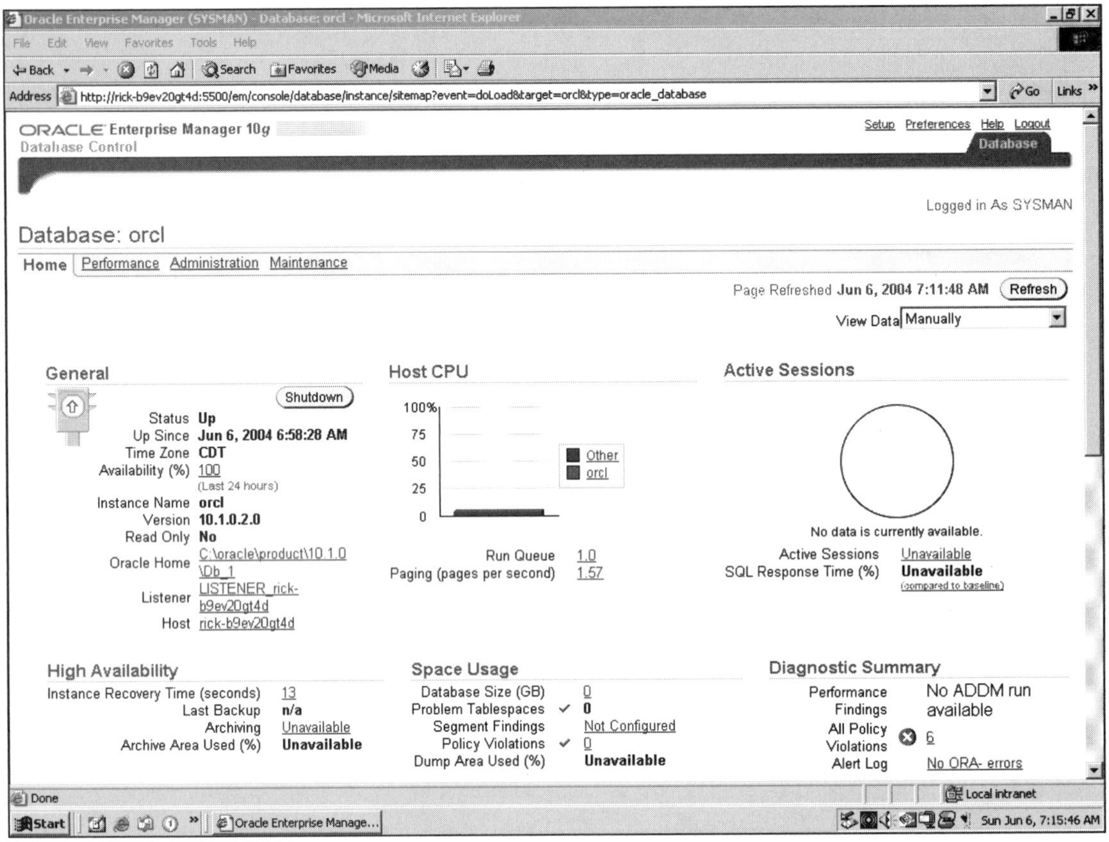

Figure 7-10: Enterprise Manager home page.

There is a wealth of information on this page. For now, you can be satisfied that your Oracle database is up and running, as shown by the traffic signal on the left of the page.

Accessing Your Oracle Database

To further test that your Oracle database is up and running, you can access it directly through the browser-based *i*SQL*Plus tool. This basic tool gives you the ability to execute SQL statements from a text window in your browser and have any pertinent results returned to you.

Access your installation of *i*SQL*Plus by opening up a browser window and entering the following URL:

```
http://domain:5560/isqlplus
```

where *domain* is the domain name of your server. You can use this URL to access *i*SQL*Plus either from the server machine itself or any computer that can access the server through your network.

This URL brings up a login screen for *i*SQL*Plus. For this exercise, use the username of `SYSMAN` and the password you assign to it in the installation process. Once you enter the username and password, you get the basic *i*SQL*Plus page.

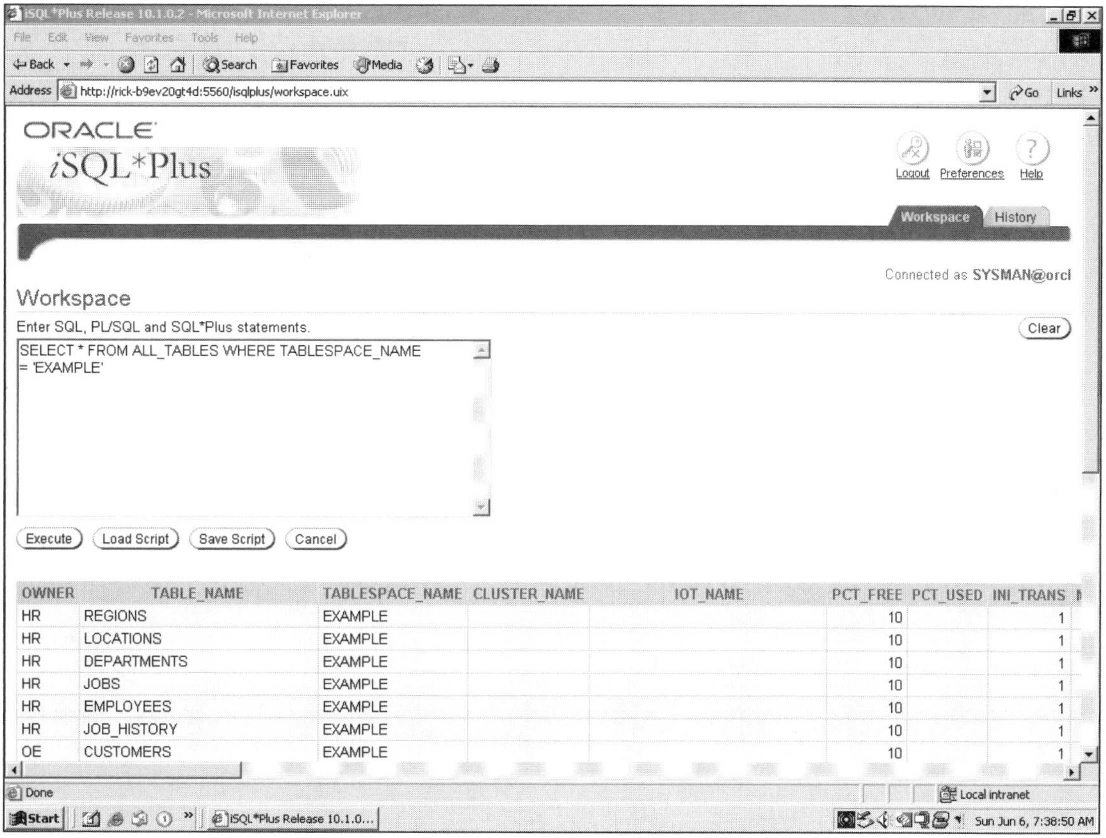

Figure 7-11: iSQL*Plus with query and results.

Enter the following SQL just to

```
SELECT * FROM ALL_TABLES WHERE TABLESPACE_NAME = 'EXAMPLE'
```

and click on the Execute button to see how iSQL*Plus works. Your Oracle database returns all the information about the tables in the tablespace `EXAMPLE` from the system table `ALL_TABLES`. The results from this query are shown in Figure 7-11.

Installing Oracle Client Software

At this point, you have successfully installed the Oracle software that is used by your Oracle server. You have even been able to communicate with that server from the *i*SQL*Plus client. Since *i*SQL*Plus is browser-based, it uses HTTP to communicate to the Oracle Listener, which in turn passes the communication on to the Oracle server instance. We use *i*SQL*Plus to demonstrate many of the examples in this book.

When you are using *i*SQL*Plus, the client software that communicates with the Oracle database is the browser itself. However, in most circumstances, you will use an application to talk to the Oracle server. For this application to work properly, you will have to have some type of software on each client machine that is accessing the Oracle database. For Java, which is the application development language of choice for this book, you will have to use some type of driver.

Java Drivers

A Java driver acts as the interface between the application and communication to the database. There are two basic types of drivers available for Oracle — a Type 2 driver, or mixed mode driver, and a Type 4 driver, or pure Java driver.

To understand the difference, you will have to know that the basic application programming interface, or API, used to access Oracle is called the Oracle Call Interface, or OCI. This interface is written in C. The Type 2 driver uses a Java library to access the OCI calls — hence the name "mixed," since it uses both C and Java in the driver software.

The Type 4 driver does not call the OCI directly. Instead, it uses Java calls to emulate the functionality in the OCI layer. This driver is written entirely in Java, so it is just another library that you have to call and distribute with your application.

Which driver should you use? There are arguments for using each of them, with both facts and faith coming into play. To understand all the differences, you need to understand the process of installing client software, the subject of the next section. This topic is revisited after this next section.

Oracle Client Software

There are two types of Oracle client software you can install. The traditional client for Oracle installs the OCI API, messages used by the client for information, demo applications and sample code, warnings and error reporting, documentation, and SQL*Plus, a character-based utility for accessing the Oracle database.

With the Oracle 10*g* Database release, Oracle now also supports a lightweight client called Instant Client. This version of the client supplies the necessary files for applications written using OCI and other APIs to operate properly, but not much else.

Oracle client software is released with each version of the database. However, you typically do not have to upgrade every client software installation when you upgrade your server. In almost every case, previous versions of the Oracle client work against an upgraded server version. Of course, the OCI contained in the earlier version of the client software will not have any way to access new features in a more recent release, but all the functionality of the previous version remains intact. This support gives you more flexible options for deploying new versions of Oracle across your organization.

Both of these client options are available from OTN for download and installation. For the purposes of this book, you will install the Instant Client.

Installing the Instant Client

You can get the Oracle 10*g* Instant Client from the same area of OTN that you used to download the server software you installed earlier in this chapter. The home page for downloading the different versions of the Instant Client is shown in Figure 7-12.

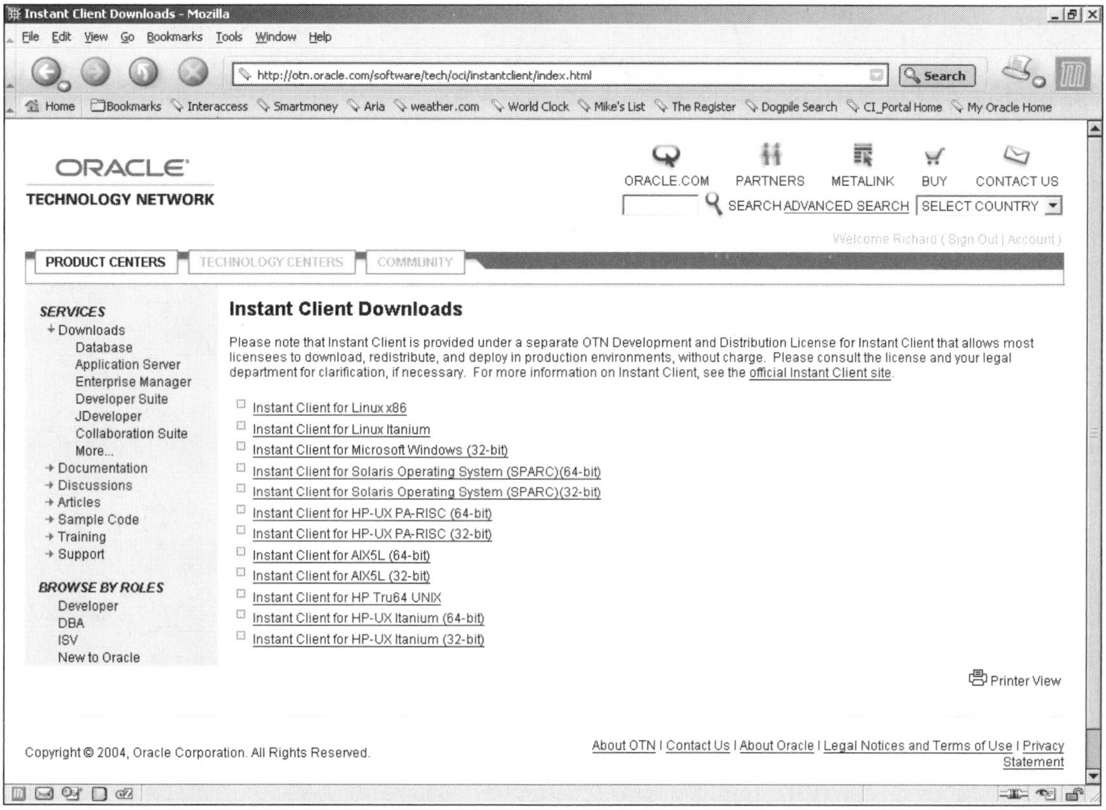

Figure 7-12: Instant Client software home page.

Once you select the correct version of Instant Client for your platform, you are prompted again to answer questions to ensure that your use of the software does not violate any export laws.

The next page of the download process, shown in Figure 7-13, allows you to choose which type of Instant Client you want. As you can see, you can select the most basic form of the Instant Client or supplemental files to add some functionality.

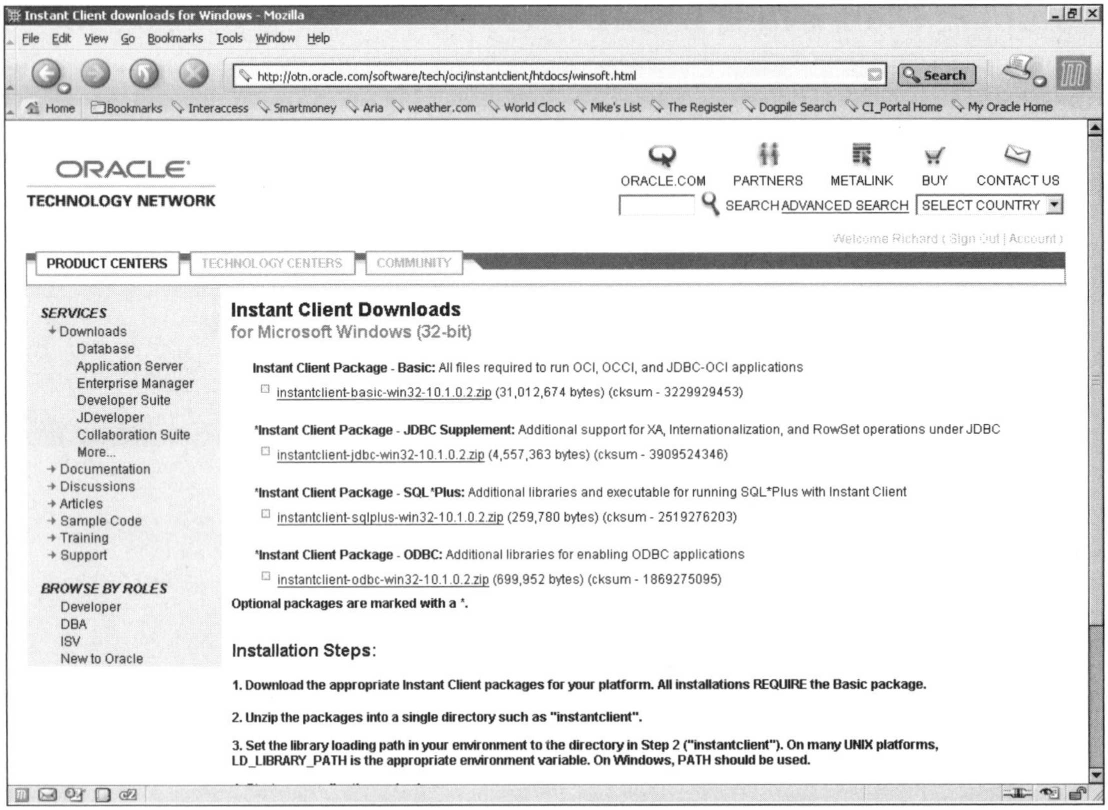

Figure 7-13: Instant Client selection page.

To understand the virtue of the Instant Client, keep in mind that the ZIP file for the basic Instant Client is around 30 MB, while the complete Oracle client is over 600 MB. Click on the file for the basic Instant Client to download the ZIP file to your client machine.

Once you have downloaded the ZIP file, simply unzip the DLL and JAR files into a directory and adjust the library loading path of your machine to include that directory.

Which Driver?

Now that you have seen how to install the Instant Client, we can revisit the question of which driver you should use.

The following table represents the differences between using the Type 2 and the Type 4 JDBC drivers.

Feature	Type 2 driver	Type 4 driver
Complete support of all OCI features	Yes	No
Separate installation procedure	Yes	No
Best performance	?	?

The table contains some clear answers, but the requirements of your particular environment can affect how these pluses and minuses play out for you. For instance, the Type 2 driver uses the current version of the OCI, and therefore provides complete support for all features in the version. The Type 4 driver is usually missing support for some of the features of the release, but these are typically features that are less widely used, such as some advanced security features.

The need for a separate installation for the Oracle client would appear to be a significant maintenance issue in favor of the Type 4 driver. But many environments include the Oracle client as part of the standard set of client software, so you will not have to do any additional work to support this in your environment. The Type 4 driver can be rolled out as just another library with your application.

The final row in the table has question marks for answers. Frankly, Oracle claims that the Type 2 driver gives better performance, while independent testing has shown that this is not always true. We have found that the two previously discussed differences between the two drivers can frequently dictate the choice of a driver, regardless of the particular performance impact. If you truly have a choice, we advise you to test some of your Oracle access with each driver, which will allow you to make an informed choice appropriate for your own environment.

Finally, there is one other driver that can be used. A Type 1 driver provides a bridge from JDBC to the more common ODBC access protocol. Sun provides JDBC-ODBC bridge software that can be used with standard Oracle ODBC drivers, which are part of the standard client installation. This driver might be appropriate for your environment if there are organizational requirements that force all database access to use ODBC.

Summary

This chapter showed you how to obtain and install an Oracle database and the client software you will need to use the database. With this software installed, you can move forward fearlessly through the examples in the rest of the book.

8

Introduction to SQL

Up until now, this book has focused on giving you an essential understanding of some of the most important issues involved in using an Oracle database. The material from the earlier chapters gives you the foundation of what Oracle is and how it is structured, as well as an understanding of the larger issues facing you in your work with the Oracle database. You need this background before you can do anything with the database. But now it's time to start interacting with data in your Oracle database.

This chapter introduces you to the basics of Structured Query Language, more commonly known as SQL. Most of what is covered in this chapter can be used with any number of relational databases, so if you are familiar with SQL from other relational databases, you can probably give this chapter a light skimming. More complex SQL syntax is covered in the following chapter, and some of the syntax covered in the next chapter is not available with all relational databases.

This chapter covers a set of statements that you can use to create data structures and access data within an Oracle database. There is more to SQL than the contents of this chapter alone, but the goal of the chapter is to give you the necessary essentials of this powerful access language.

A Bit of History

To discover the real roots of SQL, you can refer to Dr. E. F. Codd's paper, "A Relational Model of Data for Large Shared Data Banks," which can currently be found at `www.acm.org/classics/nov95/toc.html`. This paper led to the creation of a language—Structured English Query Language—by IBM Corporation and its release of System R. Oracle, which was originally called Software Development Laboratories and renamed Relational Software, Inc. (RSI) in 1979, released the first commercially available implementation of SQL in 1979 as Oracle Release 2. RSI was renamed Oracle Corporation in 1983.

In its early days, some relational databases used a less-than-standard version of the SQL language. This caused a lot of problems moving applications from one database to another, and also made programmers have to relearn the language when they used a different system. The standards committees, noted in the section that follows, helped resolve this incompatibility by creating a base-level syntax that all database vendors followed. At the current time, most every database vendor will support a version of the current SQL standards. You will find odd syntax at times because of committed support of older versions of a particular database, as well as syntax that implements features beyond the range of an existing specification.

Standards

One of the great virtues of SQL is that it is a standardized data language for use with relational databases. Whenever you have a standard, you have standards bodies that create official versions of the standard.

There are two organizations that publish SQL standards:

- The American National Standards Institute (ANSI), whose latest standard is called ANSI X3.135-1999
- The International Standards Organization (ISO) & International Electrotechnical Commission (IEC), whose latest standard is called ISO/IEC 9075:1999, which will be replaced by ISO/IEC 9075:2003 in 2005

Companies claiming conformance to the ANSI and ISO standards must state the type of conformance and the components that map to this conformance. The minimal conformance is called CORE SQL:2003. You will find various Oracle documents, such as SQL Reference, Part No. B10759-01, which explain which parts of the SQL standard Oracle supports fully, which parts of the SQL standard have partial support, and the parts where Oracle provides equivalent functionality.

You should be aware that there are features of the Oracle Database that differ from the published standards. This is true for most every relational database — there will be features that provide faster response, special capabilities, and alternative implementation of statements or historical conventions that do not conform to the standards.

Of course, many of these additions are also key differentiators between different relational databases, or places where Oracle has gone beyond the dry specification of the standard to provide additional functionality. If you are thinking about writing code that could run against more than one relational database, you will have to check for compliance of all target databases with the standards and the functionality you want to implement, or code only to the lowest common SQL functionality provided by all database vendors.

SQL Statement Groupings

There are two distinct grouping within the SQL language:

- **Data manipulation language (DML).** The chapter covers the basic keywords and clauses used by DML — `SELECT`, `INSERT`, `UPDATE`, `DELETE`, the `WHERE` clause, joins, `GROUP BY`, `ORDER BY`, and subqueries. This set of statements are the main pieces of the SQL language that you will use in your applications.
- **Data definition language (DDL).** As the name implies, these statements are used to create and modify objects stored in the database. You may not find yourself using these statements very often, for a few reasons. First, initial creation of database objects is often the responsibility of the database administrator, rather than the developer. Second, some of the important clauses in DDL statements have to do with more administrative attributes of objects, which are beyond the scope of this book. Third, plenty of tools are available to create database objects. Even HTML-DB, covered in Chapter 23, has HTML-based tools to help you create database objects.

Although you will probably use DDL less than DML, you may have to create database objects before you can populate them with data your application will use. For that reason, the next section describes basic DDL syntax.

For any SQL statement, you can specify a qualified name for the basic database object, such as a table or a view. The qualified name uses the schema name, followed by a dot (.), and then the table name. The schema name with the dot is optional, but if you do not specify them, Oracle will assume that the database object is in the current schema.

Data Definition Language (DDL)

Oracle DDL statements can be organized in five groups of statements.

- **Schema Object Manipulation.** These statements allow you to create, alter, or drop schema objects (tables, views, keys, and the like).
- **Privileges.** These statements allow you to grant or revoke privileges or rights and roles.
- **Analysis.** These statements allow you to analyze information about your tables, indexes, and clusters.
- **Auditing.** These statements allow you to initiate auditing options.
- **Commenting.** These statements allow you to manage comments/information in the data dictionary.

For the purposes of this basic introduction, you will need to understand three basic types of DDL statements: `CREATE`, `ALTER`, and `DROP`.

CREATE

The `CREATE` statement can be used to create many different types of database objects, including a database, package, procedure, role, profile, tables, triggers, users, views, and more. Many other types of schema objects are described in Chapter 12, "Other Database Structures." In this section, you will learn the essential variations of the `CREATE` statement to create tables and views.

CREATE TABLE

The format for using DDL to create a standard user data table is as follows:

```
CREATE TABLE <schema.tablename> [<table_properties>
  <relational_properties>
  <physical_properties>]
```

Technically, everything after the *`tablename`* is optional, although you almost always use the <*`table_properties`*> clause to specify columns for a table when you create it. The <*`table_properties`*> clauses further define the attributes of the table — such as columns. The <*`relational_properties`*> clauses relate to the creation of relational tables. The <*`physical_properties`*> clauses identify the physical storage characteristics of your tables. The simplest statement could be as follows:

```
CREATE TABLE BOB;
```

A more realistic create operation would be to create a table called HIGH_COMM, which is included as CH08_TABLE_DDL.SQL. The code to create this table is as follows:

```
CREATE TABLE SCOTT.HIGH_COMM
   (EMPNO NUMBER(4) PRIMARY KEY,
    ENAME VARCHAR2(10),
    COMM NUMBER(7,2),
    HIREDATE DATE DEFAULT SYSDATE,
    EMAIL VARCHAR(50)
     CONSTRAINT EMAIL01
       NOT NULL,
    NACOUNTRY VARCHAR2(20),
      CONSTRAINT COUNTRY01
        CHECK (NACOUNTRY IN ('USA', 'CANADA', 'MEXICO' ))
TABLESPACE TESTSPACE
STORAGE (INITIAL 2048
      NEXT 2048
      MINEXTENTS 1
            MAXEXTENTS 2);
```

In this example, you can see a list of columns, each with its data type. Two of the columns have constraints attached, which are the subject of Chapter 11, "Constraints. " For the EMAIL column, the constraint forces entry of a value. For the NACOUNTRY constraint, the constraint only allows the value for the column to be USA, CANADA, or MEXICO. The HIREDATE column includes a default value, the system variable SYSDATE, which will be used if there is no value specified for the column.

The TABLESPACE clause identifies a tablespace called TESTSPACE as the physical location of the table. You will not necessarily be able to run this SQL against your database, unless you have a tablespace already created called TESTSPACE, but you can alter the script to target a tablespace in your database.

Finally, the SQL statement includes some storage parameters, which tell Oracle how to initially allocate space for the table, and conditions for allocating additional space for the table if needed.

CREATE VIEW

Another version of the CREATE statement is used to create views. A view is a logical table that is based on one or more tables or views. It contains no actual data itself but rather selectively displays columns from the tables it was created from — the base tables. Views allow you to limit the visibility of data; you can give some users access to a view to hide data that they should not be able to access.

An example of this might be to give all managers access to employee information but to hide employee salary information from managers in other departments. You could also have a limited view of the Human Resources employee tables to allow everyone in the company to access the month and day of everyone's birth date, but not the year.

As a simple example, you can create a view that gives you access to some of the columns in the EMP table and the DEPT table that come as examples in the SCOTT schema in your Oracle database. To create this view, you would use the following syntax, which is included as CH08_CREATE_VIEW.SQL:

```
CREATE VIEW SCOTT.EMPVIEW AS
    (SELECT EMPNO, ENAME, DNAME, LOC
    FROM SCOTT.EMP, SCOTT.DEPT
    WHERE EMP.DEPTNO = DEPT.DEPTNO);
```

Once the view is created, you could use the simple SQL of

```
SELECT * FROM SCOTT.EMPVIEW;
```

to get the results shown in Figure 8-1:

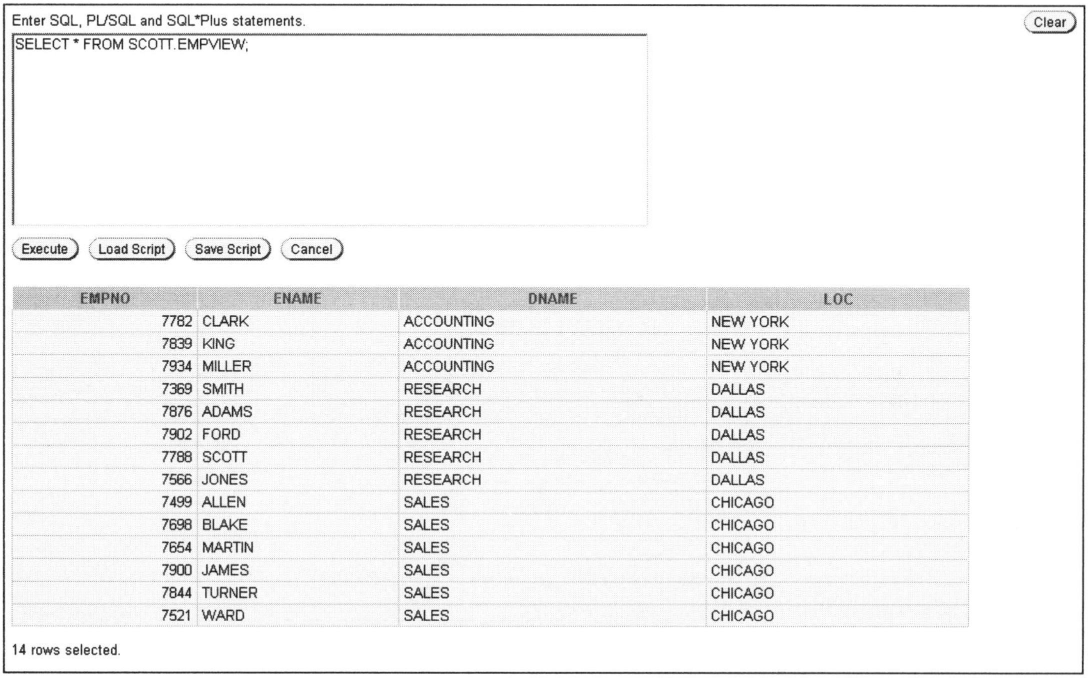

EMPNO	ENAME	DNAME	LOC
7782	CLARK	ACCOUNTING	NEW YORK
7839	KING	ACCOUNTING	NEW YORK
7934	MILLER	ACCOUNTING	NEW YORK
7369	SMITH	RESEARCH	DALLAS
7876	ADAMS	RESEARCH	DALLAS
7902	FORD	RESEARCH	DALLAS
7788	SCOTT	RESEARCH	DALLAS
7566	JONES	RESEARCH	DALLAS
7499	ALLEN	SALES	CHICAGO
7698	BLAKE	SALES	CHICAGO
7654	MARTIN	SALES	CHICAGO
7900	JAMES	SALES	CHICAGO
7844	TURNER	SALES	CHICAGO
7521	WARD	SALES	CHICAGO

Figure 8-1: The results of a query on a view.

Remember that views only provide access to data; they do not actually contain data, which is kept in the underlying tables. A user can update or add data in a view, but only if he or she has proper privileges on the underlying tables—which frequently runs counter to entire reason for creating the view in the first place.

You can use `INSTEAD OF` triggers to provide write capabilities for views, which are covered in Chapter 19, "Triggers."

ALTER

Once an SQL object has been created, you can change its composition or attributes with the `ALTER` statement. To change a table, the basic syntax is as follows:

```
ALTER TABLE tablename <column_clauses> <alter_table_clauses> <constraint_clauses
```

Additional types of alteration can be handled with additional clauses, as well as the ability to enable and disable some features of the table, but these clauses are the most commonly used.

The *column_clause* is used to change the number or attributes of a column within a table. To add a column to the HIGH_COMM table mentioned previously, you would use the following syntax:

```
ALTER TABLE SCOTT.HIGH_COMM ADD (phone_no VARCHAR2(20));
```

To drop the column from the same table, you would use the following syntax:

```
ALTER TABLE SCOTT.HIGH_COMM DROP COLUMN phone_no;
```

Keep in mind that there is no ALTER COLUMN statement; you must use the *column_clause* of the ALTER TABLE statement to change columns within a table. You can also use different column clauses to rename a column and change other properties specific to columns of particular data types.

The *alter_table_clause* can change the way the table as a whole operates — its storage characteristics, logging attributes, compression, and parallelism.

The *constraint_clause*, as you can probably guess, can be used to add, modify, rename, or drop the constraints for a particular table.

The ALTER statement can be used to modify all types of database objects, as well as shape entities like your database session or user characteristics. Refer to the Oracle documentation for complete descriptions of the capabilities of the ALTER statement.

DROP

The DROP statement is used to delete an object from a database schema. This statement has a very simple syntax:

```
DROP object_type object_name;
```

where *object_type* specifies the type of the object, such as TABLE or VIEW, and *object_name* gives the name of the object. Dropping an object deletes the object and any data that it contains from the database.

Caveat!

This particular caveat is so important that it deserves the exclamation mark.

In Oracle SQL, each DDL statement performs an invisible COMMIT, which ends the current transaction and commits all changes to the database. This small aspect of Oracle DDL has a couple of very important repercussions. First, you cannot roll back any DDL statements. For a CREATE, this limitation is not that important, since you can just drop the object. For an ALTER, it may be a bit harder to get the object back to its original state. But for a DROP, the consequences are fairly disastrous. If you get rid of a table, it's gone for good except with Oracle Database 10*g*, which gives you the FLASHBACK DROP command to recover the table from a recycle bin.

The second repercussion is that any statements prior to the DDL are also commited. So if you execute a DDL statement after some DML that makes changes to the database, those changes will also be committed.

You should be aware of this important repercussion of using DDL statements with Oracle. In practice, you will not be using DDL statements very frequently in your application code, but it is better that you understand this limitation now than be bit by it down the road.

Data Manipulation Language (DML)

As mentioned earlier, most of your work as a programmer will use SQL to read and write data from an Oracle database. This section explores the basic SQL DML statements — `SELECT`, to retrieve data; `INSERT`, to write new data to a table; `UPDATE`, to modify existing data; and `DELETE`, to drop data — as well as reviews some basic concepts about manipulating data with SQL.

SQL: Set-Orientated and Nonprocedural

As described in Chapter 1, "Oracle Architecture and Storage, " data is stored in relational databases in tables with rows and columns of data. SQL statements work on these tables. When you retrieve data from your Oracle database, the result is returned as a set of rows.

In this section, you will be working with the `EMP` table in the `SCOTT` schema. The `EMP` table is pretty simple, containing a handful of rows and the following columns: `EMPNO`, `ENAME`, `JOB`, `MGR`, `HIREDATE`, `SAL`, `COMM`, and `DEPTNO`.

You could access this data in a number of ways with the same basic SQL syntax. For instance, you could ask for the `EMPNO`, `ENAME`, and `SAL` columns for all the employees whose salary (`SAL`) was greater than 1000. What would be returned is a set of rows, called a result set, with 12 rows and with three columns in each row. The number of rows returned would be determined by the number of rows that matched the selection criterion; it could be any number from 0 to the whole table, and the basic SQL statement would be the same. The key point here is that SQL retrieves a set of rows — not just a fixed number of rows. This capability makes SQL a very powerful language and simplifies the syntax you need for data manipulation.

In the same way, a single SQL statement could be used to change all the rows that matched this criterion, for instance, increasing the `SAL` to 3000. Once again, you do not need to know how many rows might meet this criterion. SQL takes care of the whole set of appropriate rows.

Of course, the set-oriented nature of SQL also poses some challenges, since you frequently will want to process data one row at a time. The chapters on PL/SQL and Java will explain how to perform this type of processing in your application.

SELECT Statement

The `SELECT` statement is the most frequently used SQL statement, simply because data is read more frequently than it is written. A `SELECT` statement tells the Oracle database that the SQL statement will be reading data rather than modifying data. Everything that follows the `SELECT` verb helps the engine determine exactly what will be returned in the result set based on the defined rules of Oracle SQL syntax. On receiving a `SELECT` statement, the Oracle database accesses the low-level data structures and then returns the result set to you.

Basic SELECT

A `SELECT` statement returns data from one or more tables in your Oracle database. The most basic form of `SELECT` can be used against the `EMP` table with the result shown in Figure 8-2.

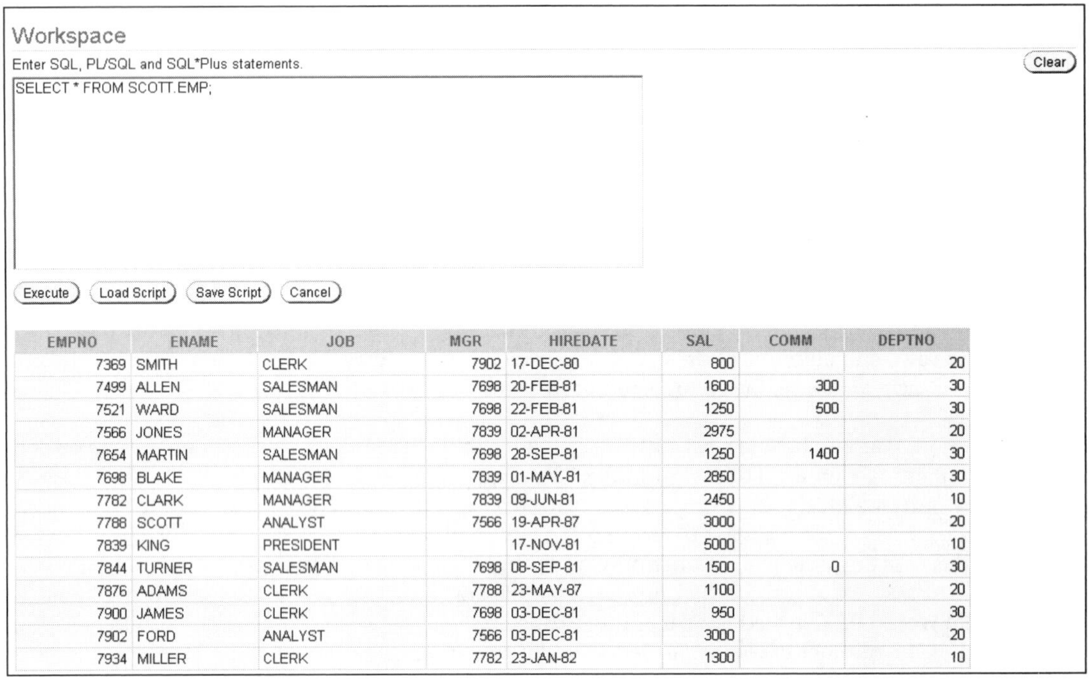

EMPNO	ENAME	JOB	MGR	HIREDATE	SAL	COMM	DEPTNO
7369	SMITH	CLERK	7902	17-DEC-80	800		20
7499	ALLEN	SALESMAN	7698	20-FEB-81	1600	300	30
7521	WARD	SALESMAN	7698	22-FEB-81	1250	500	30
7566	JONES	MANAGER	7839	02-APR-81	2975		20
7654	MARTIN	SALESMAN	7698	28-SEP-81	1250	1400	30
7698	BLAKE	MANAGER	7839	01-MAY-81	2850		30
7782	CLARK	MANAGER	7839	09-JUN-81	2450		10
7788	SCOTT	ANALYST	7566	19-APR-87	3000		20
7839	KING	PRESIDENT		17-NOV-81	5000		10
7844	TURNER	SALESMAN	7698	08-SEP-81	1500	0	30
7876	ADAMS	CLERK	7788	23-MAY-87	1100		20
7900	JAMES	CLERK	7698	03-DEC-81	950		30
7902	FORD	ANALYST	7566	03-DEC-81	3000		20
7934	MILLER	CLERK	7782	23-JAN-82	1300		10

Figure 8-2: A basic `SELECT`.

You can see that the `*` character is used to indicate that the statement should return all the data from the table. This is a quick and dirty way of finding out what columns are in the table. However, this method could result in getting back a large amount of data, if the table has many columns, or even a single column with a large amount of data, such as a large object. Another way to get column information is to use the `DESC` verb, as shown in Figure 8-3.

You can also specify the columns that you want to be returned, in a comma-separated list. A column can be listed with or without the table name as a prefix — in other words, you could ask for the `ENAME` column or the `EMP.ENAME` column. This option is only available if you are not accessing tables with duplicate column names. For instance, if you were accessing both the `EMP` and `DEPT` tables and included `DEPTNO` as a column, Oracle would return an error, since the `DEPTNO` column occurs in both tables. You will learn how to `SELECT` from multiple tables shortly.

The Oracle database does not care about the case of any SQL keywords — you can use `SELECT` or `select` or `SeLeCt`. (but, of course, you must spell it right). However, for readability, it helps to follow a consistent capitalization scheme.

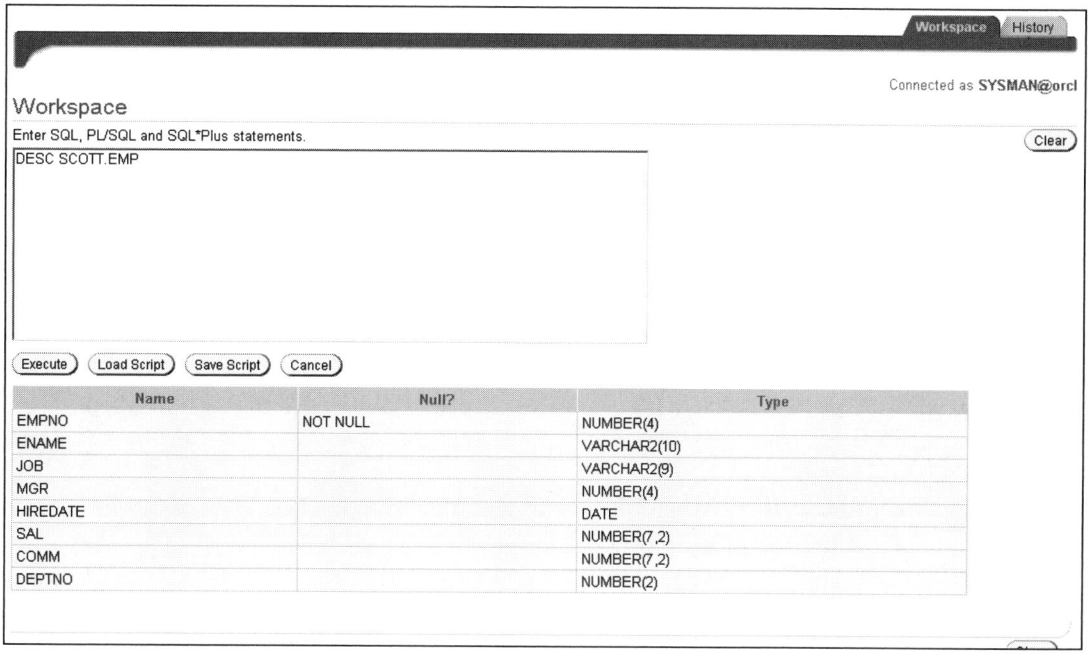

Figure 8-3: Using DESC.

Aliases

There are two types of aliases you can use in an SQL statement. One type is a table alias. You specify a table alias by including the alias after the table name, separated by a space. Once you specify a table alias, you can use it instead of the table name as a qualifier, as in the following:

```
SELECT E.EMPNAME FROM SCOTT.EMP E;
```

In some situations, such as when using hints, which are covered in Chapter 28, "Optimization," you have to use a table alias.

You can also specify a column alias, which will be used as the heading for the column in the data returned in iSQL*Plus. Figure 8-4 shows the use of a column alias and its effect on the data returned.

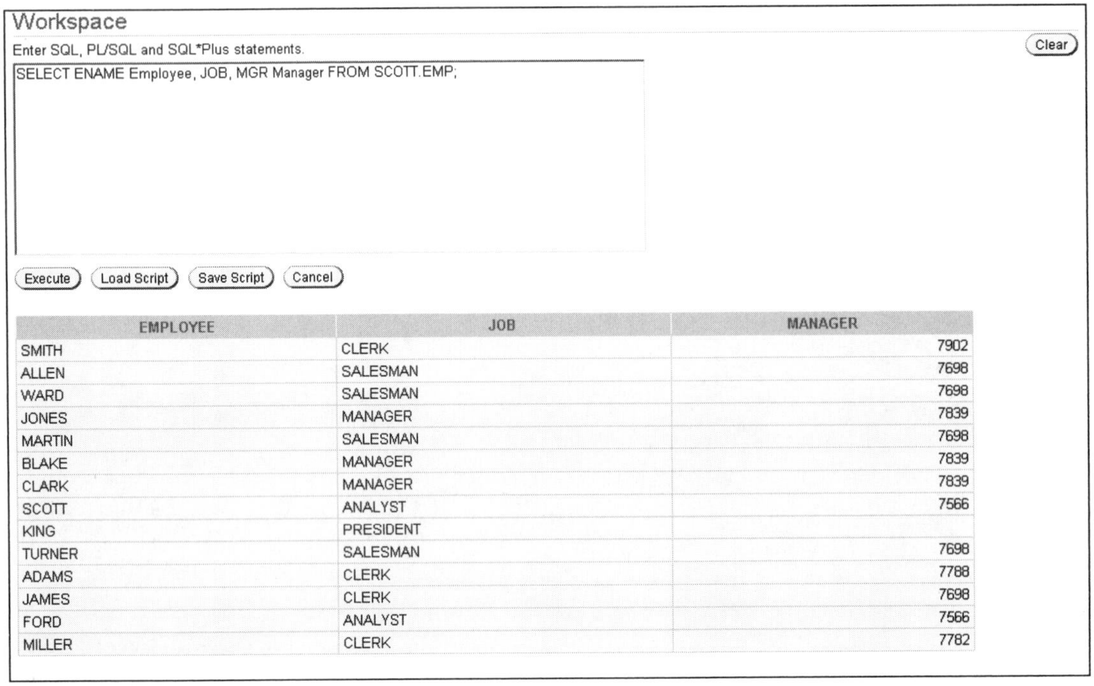

EMPLOYEE	JOB	MANAGER
SMITH	CLERK	7902
ALLEN	SALESMAN	7698
WARD	SALESMAN	7698
JONES	MANAGER	7839
MARTIN	SALESMAN	7698
BLAKE	MANAGER	7839
CLARK	MANAGER	7839
SCOTT	ANALYST	7566
KING	PRESIDENT	
TURNER	SALESMAN	7698
ADAMS	CLERK	7788
JAMES	CLERK	7698
FORD	ANALYST	7566
MILLER	CLERK	7782

Figure 8-4: The use of a column alias.

You can have column aliases with more than one word, separated by a space, but you must enclose these types of aliases in double quotes so that the Oracle parser does not misinterpret the spaces in the alias.

WHERE Clause

The `WHERE` clause of the `SELECT` statement restricts the number of rows that are returned in the result set. The expressions in this clause must evaluate to either `TRUE` or `FALSE`. If all expressions evaluate as `TRUE`, the row is added to the result set.

Figure 8-5 shows a `SELECT` statement and its results using a simple `WHERE` clause

Rather than the 14 rows that were returned in the unqualified `SELECT` statement, the only rows that were returned were those where the `SAL` is greater than 1500.

A `WHERE` clause can use any operator where the result evaluates to `TRUE` or `FALSE`. The following table contains a list of the common comparison operators.

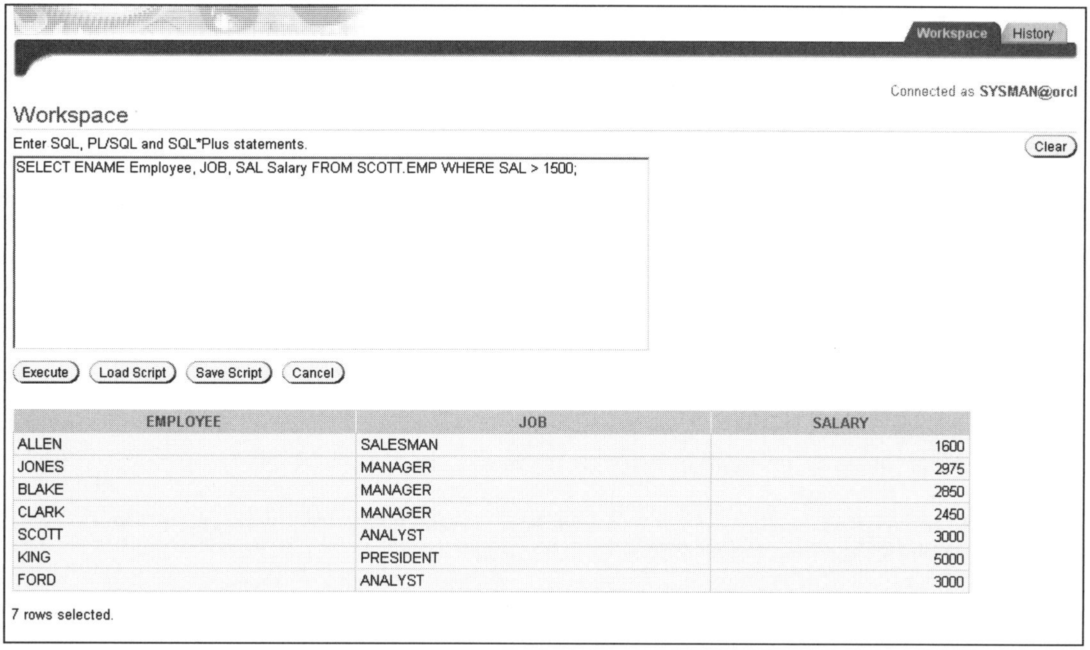

Figure 8-5: Using a simple `WHERE` clause.

Comparison Operator	Function
=	Equal to
>	Greater than
<	Less than
>=	Greater than or equal to
<=	Less than or equal to
<> or !=	Not equal to
IS NULL	Contains a NULL value. Note that a NULL value will evaluate as FALSE for both = and !=
IS NOT NULL	Contains a value
IN	In the included list, which follows this operator, enclosed in parentheses and separated by commas
NOT IN	Not in the included list

Multiple Selection Conditions

You can have multiple expressions within a WHERE clause that are linked with an AND or an OR. Using OR allows a result to be added in the result set if either of the two conditions on either side of the OR evaluate to TRUE. Because of this, Oracle will not evaluate the second condition in an OR clause if the first condition evaluates to TRUE.

Using an AND requires that the conditions before and after the AND evaluate to TRUE before the result can be added to a result set. Both conditions always have to be evaluated with an AND clause.

When you start to combine AND and OR conditions to your WHERE clause, it can become very complicated to determine what result is expected. You can use both spacing and parentheses to make these type of complex WHERE clauses more comprehensible.

For instance, examine the following fairly simple WHERE clauses:

```
WHERE DEPTNO = 20 OR DEPTNO = 30 AND SALARY > 1000
```

It may be somewhat difficult to understand exactly what data is required by this statement. In fact, as Figure 8-6 shows, Oracle will evaluate the AND clause first.

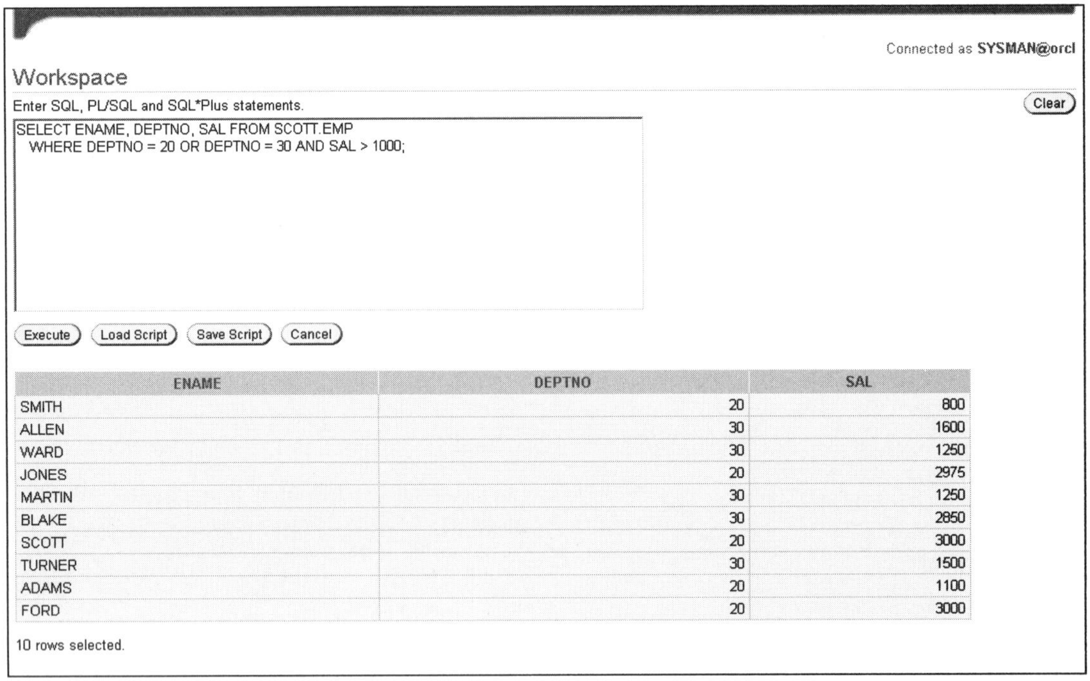

ENAME	DEPTNO	SAL
SMITH	20	800
ALLEN	30	1600
WARD	30	1250
JONES	20	2975
MARTIN	30	1250
BLAKE	30	2850
SCOTT	20	3000
TURNER	30	1500
ADAMS	20	1100
FORD	20	3000

Figure 8-6: Evaluating a WHERE clause.

This result is probably not what you wanted — you wanted rows for anyone in either Department 20 or 30 with a salary of more than 1000. To let Oracle know how to evaluate the conditions to get this result, use the following code for the WHERE clause

```
WHERE (DEPTNO = 20 OR DEPTNO = 30) AND SALARY > 1000
```

and you will get the proper result shown in Figure 8-7:

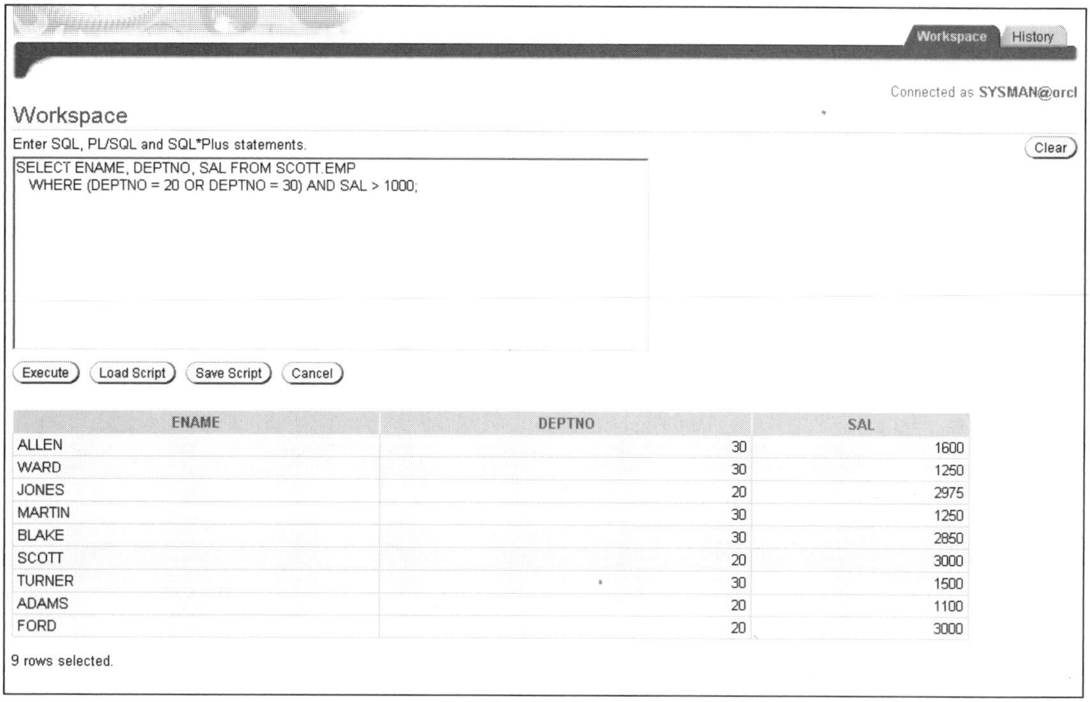

Figure 8-7: Using parentheses for `WHERE` conditions.

Using parentheses with compound `WHERE` conditions not only ensures that Oracle will interpret the conditions properly but also helps to make your code more understandable on subsequent examinations. For more complex conditions, it helps to separate individual `WHERE` components onto their own lines.

ORDER BY Clause

When you issue a `SELECT` statement, the rows that are returned do not come back in any particular logical order. You must explicitly specify an order if you want the rows to be sorted. You indicate sort order by using the `ORDER BY` clause.

You can order your rows by one or more columns or expressions. A column or expression does not have to be in the list of columns or expressions that are being returned for the query. You can specify ascending (`ASC`, the default) or descending (`DESC`) sort order. The `NULL` value is considered to be the largest value, so rows with a `NULL` in the sort column(s) would be first in a descending sort or last in an ascending sort. The `ORDER BY` goes after all other clauses in your `SELECT` statement.

Figures 8-8 and 8-9 show using the default `ASC` and specifying `DESC` for the sort condition on the `SAL` column in the same query used to illustrate the preceding compound `WHERE` clause.

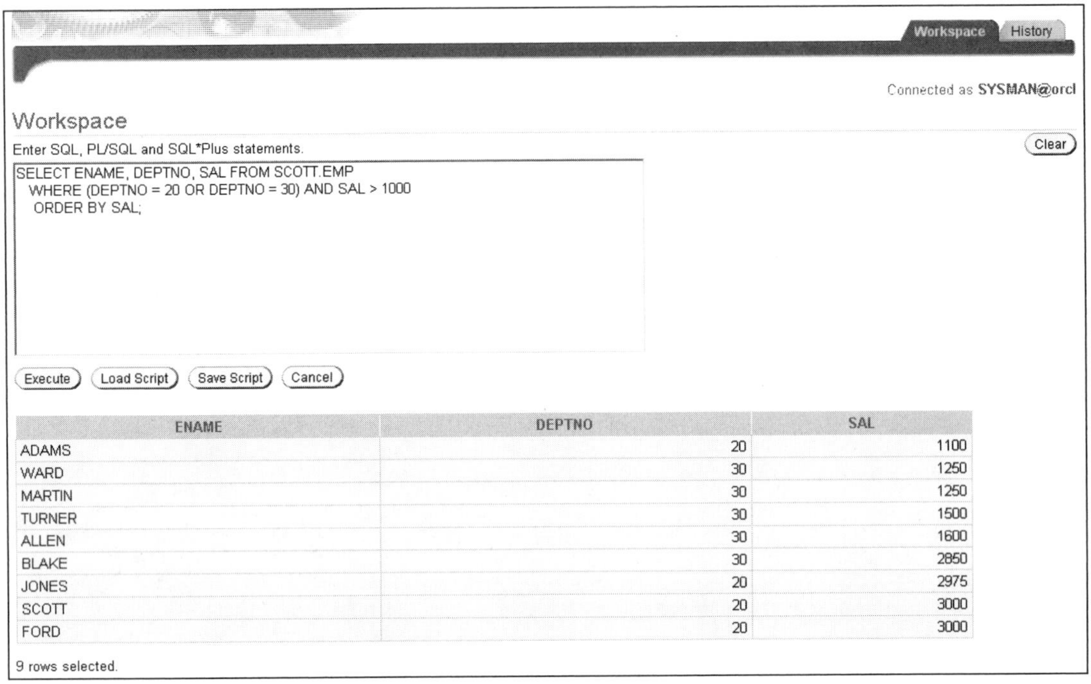

Figure 8-8: ORDER BY using a default ASC.

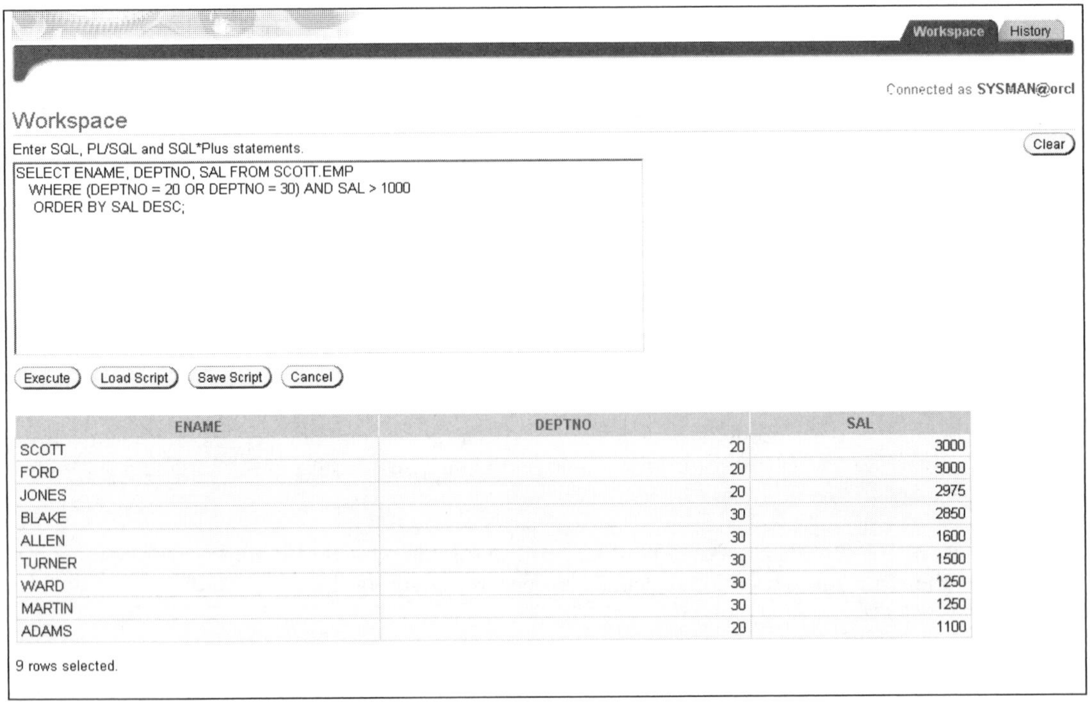

Figure 8-9: ORDER BY using DESC.

The first SELECT statement returns all the rows sorting by the SAL column in ascending order. The second SELECT statement returns the same result set sorting by the SAL column in descending order.

You can specify more than one column or expression in the ORDER BY clause. Each entry must be separated by a comma. Oracle takes the first entry in a list as the primary sort key and sorts the rows for that value by subsequent values in the list, as shown in Figure 8-10.

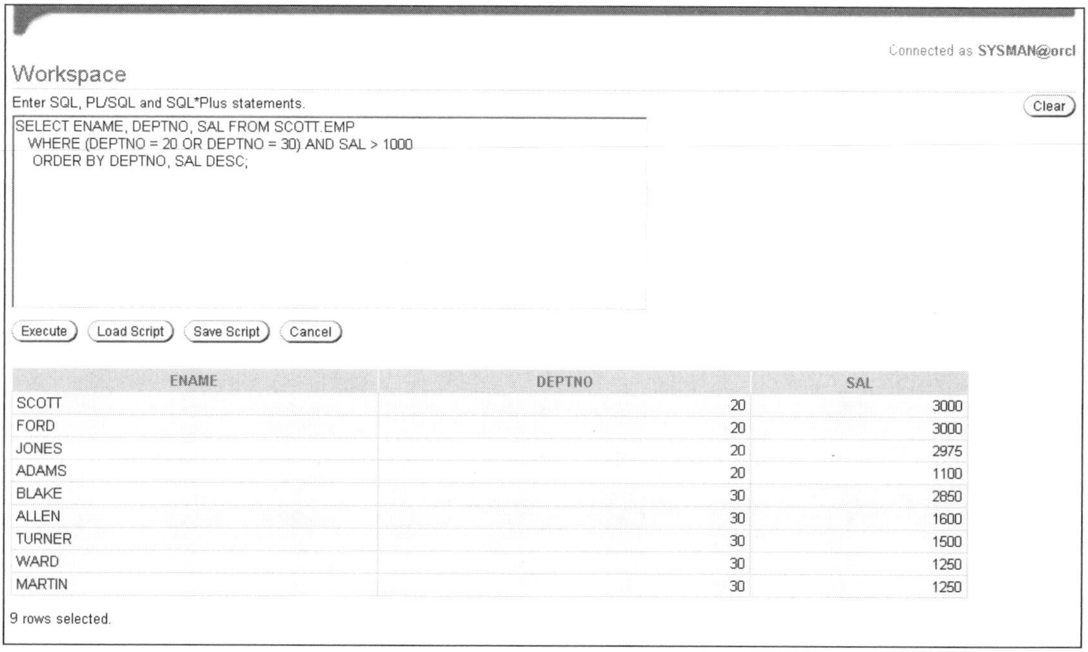

Figure 8-10: Multiple columns for ORDER BY.

Note that each entry in the list of ORDER BY values can either be ascending or descending.

You can use numbers in an ORDER BY clause that reflect the position of an entry in the column list of the SELECT statement. You might want to use this syntax if you are specifying an expression in the column list and want to use the same expression, without reentering it, in the ORDER BY list. A simplistic version of this approach is shown in Figure 8-11.

This approach has the advantage of avoiding mistakes brought on by entering in a slightly different expression, or having to keep a value in two parts of the same SQL statement in synch. However, this approach also makes the results of the SQL statement change, based on the order of the column list.

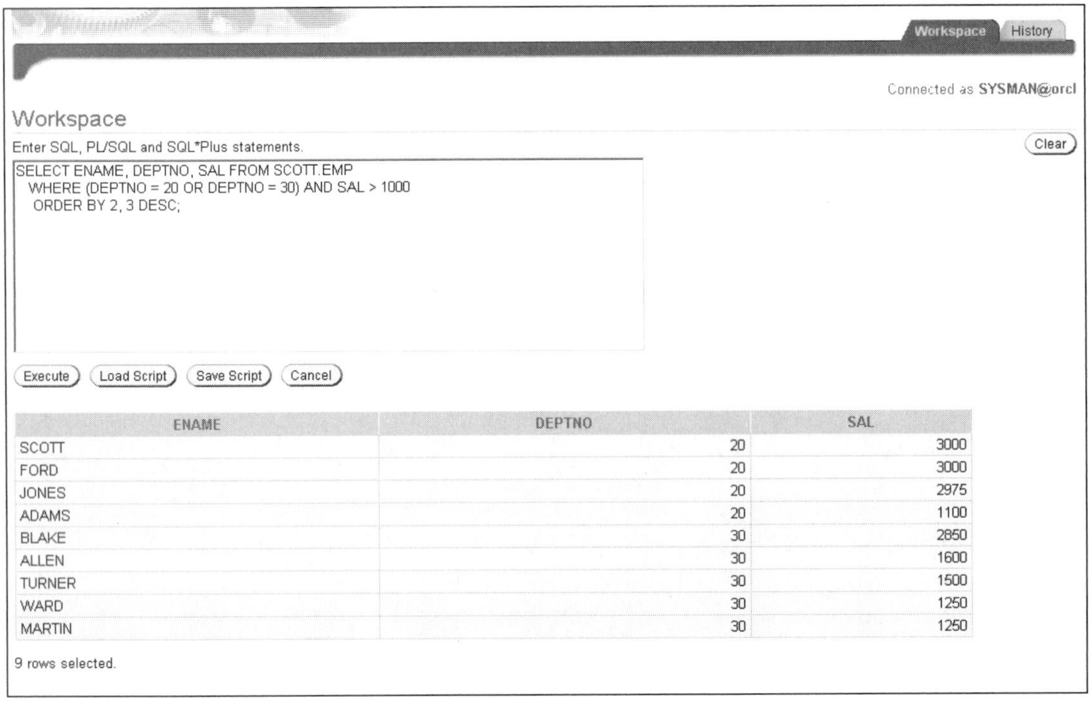

Figure 8-11: Specifying columns in `ORDER BY` by position.

GROUP BY Clause

The `GROUP BY` clause is used to aggregate information. Within the `SELECT` statement, you can include functions that operate on multiple values — such as `SUM`, `AVG`, `MIN`, `MAX`, or `COUNT`.

Aggregate, and other, functions are covered in detail in Chapter 13, "Functions."

To illustrate this, you might want to determine the gross salary for each department. To get this aggregate, you would use the `SUM` function, as in the following:

```
SELECT DEPTNO, SUM(SAL) FROM SCOTT.EMP;
```

This SQL would not produce the result that you wanted. Remember, the rows would not be returned in sorted order with this statement. When using an aggregate function, you have to use the `GROUP BY` clause to let Oracle know how to handle the aggregate. In fact, the SQL shown previously would not run. Oracle would return an error (pointing out that `DEPTNO` is not a single group function).

The proper way to use this aggregate is to list all columns that are not the targets of aggregate functions in the `GROUP BY` clause, as shown in Figure 8-12.

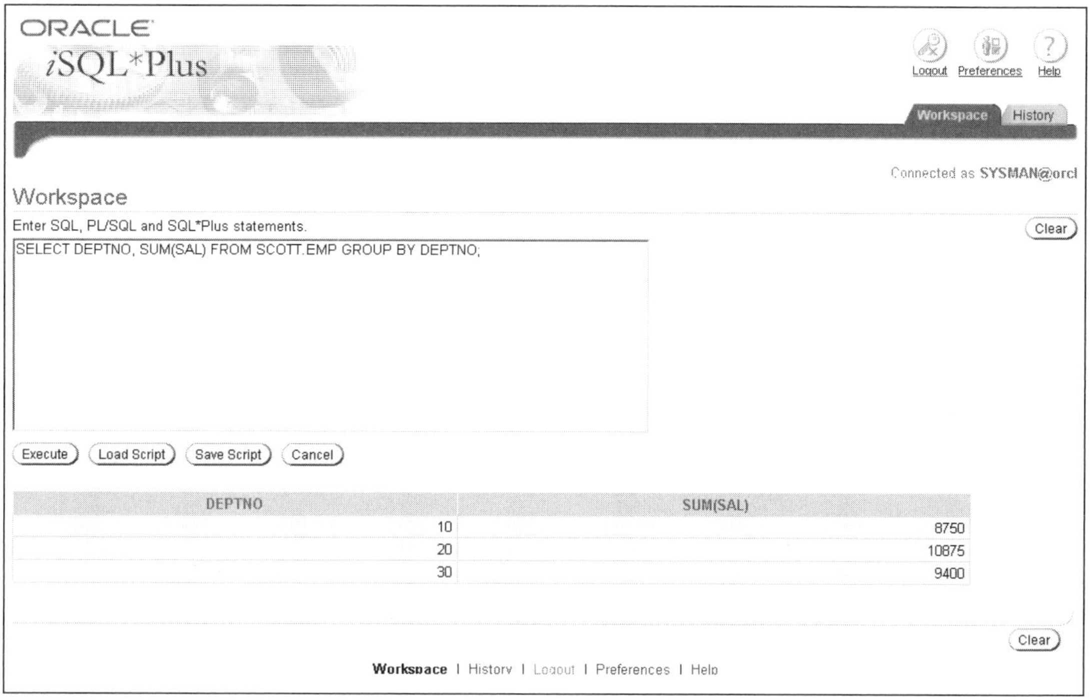

Figure 8-12: An aggregate function and the `GROUP BY` clause.

The `SUM` function adds up all the non-`NULL` values in the `SAL` column for each row in our result set and returns one value for each `DEPTNO`.

As mentioned previously, you have to list all the nonaggregate columns in the `GROUP BY` clause. The following SQL statement would return an error

```
SELECT DEPTNO, JOB, SUM(SAL) FROM SCOTT.EMP
    GROUP BY DEPTNO;
```

because you have not included `JOB` in the `GROUP BY` list. Of course, the statement would not make a lot of sense without listing `JOB` in the `GROUP BY`, since the rows would not be grouped by `JOB` within each `DEPTNO`. The correct SQL, and its results, are shown in Figure 8-13.

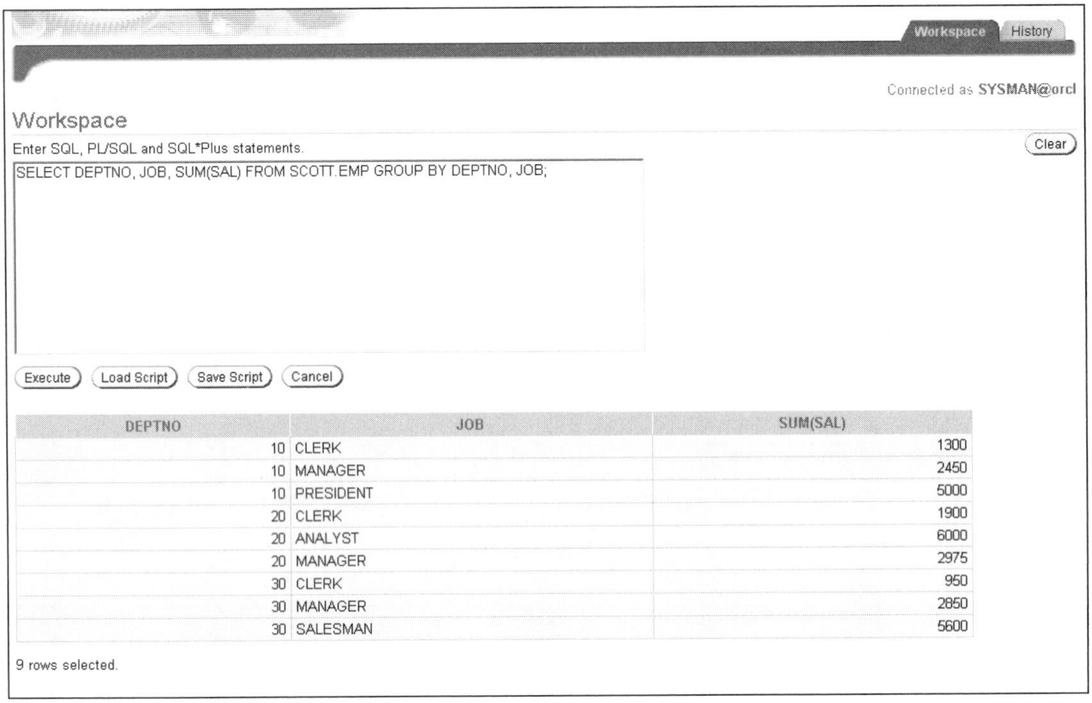

DEPTNO	JOB	SUM(SAL)
10	CLERK	1300
10	MANAGER	2450
10	PRESIDENT	5000
20	CLERK	1900
20	ANALYST	6000
20	MANAGER	2975
30	CLERK	950
30	MANAGER	2850
30	SALESMAN	5600

Figure 8-13: `GROUP BY` with two columns.

HAVING Clause

The `HAVING` clause can only be used when there is a `GROUP BY` clause. The `HAVING` clause works on the results of a `GROUP BY` in the same way that the `WHERE` clause limits the rows for a `SELECT`. This is similar to a `SELECT` reading all the rows of a table and the `WHERE` clause weeding out certain rows based on your conditions. Think of the `GROUP BY` as generating rows of results based on the aggregation conditions and the `HAVING` clause selecting groups based on certain conditions.

For example, you can add a `HAVING` clause to the previous `GROUP BY` example to come up with the results shown in Figure 8-14.

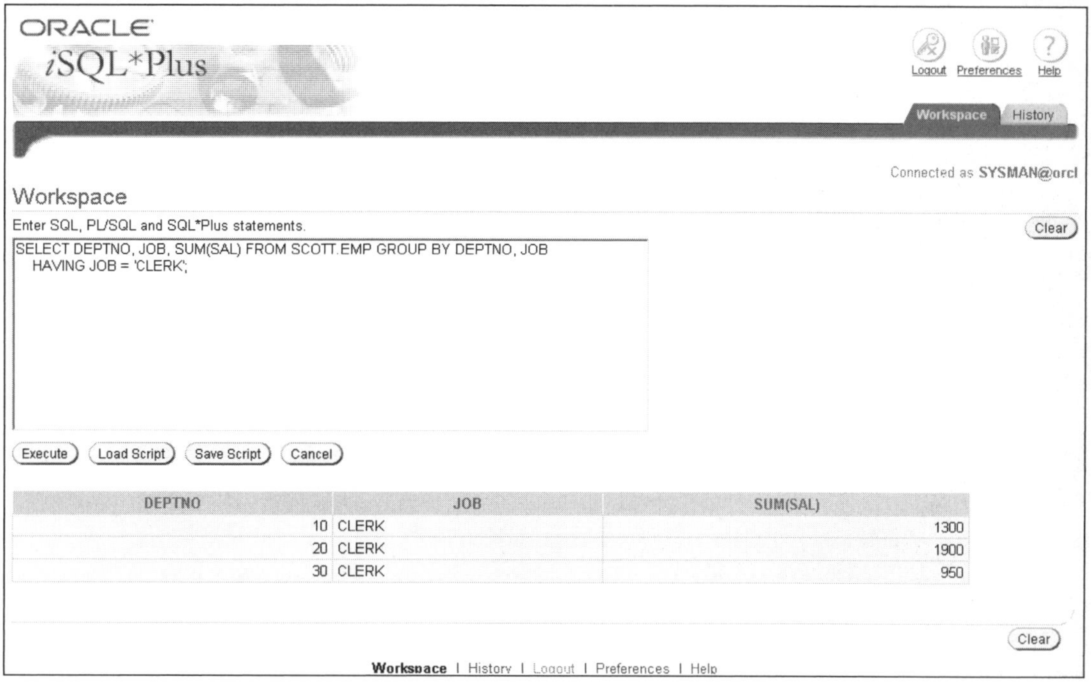

Figure 8-14: **GROUP BY** with **HAVING** clause.

Multi-Table Access

Relational database design calls for normalized table structures, as described in Chapter 4 on database design. One of the results of this design approach is that you frequently have to access data from multiple tables in a single `SELECT` statement. You can use SQL to access information in multiple tables, as with the example whose last page is shown in Figure 8-15, which displays the first set of data returned in iSQL*Plus:

This is an example of selecting multiple columns from two tables. When you execute this statement, you will notice that there are 56 rows. The engine has taken all 14 rows from the `EMP` table and mapped them to each individual row from the `DEPT` table. So 14*4 is 56, the result displayed from our query.

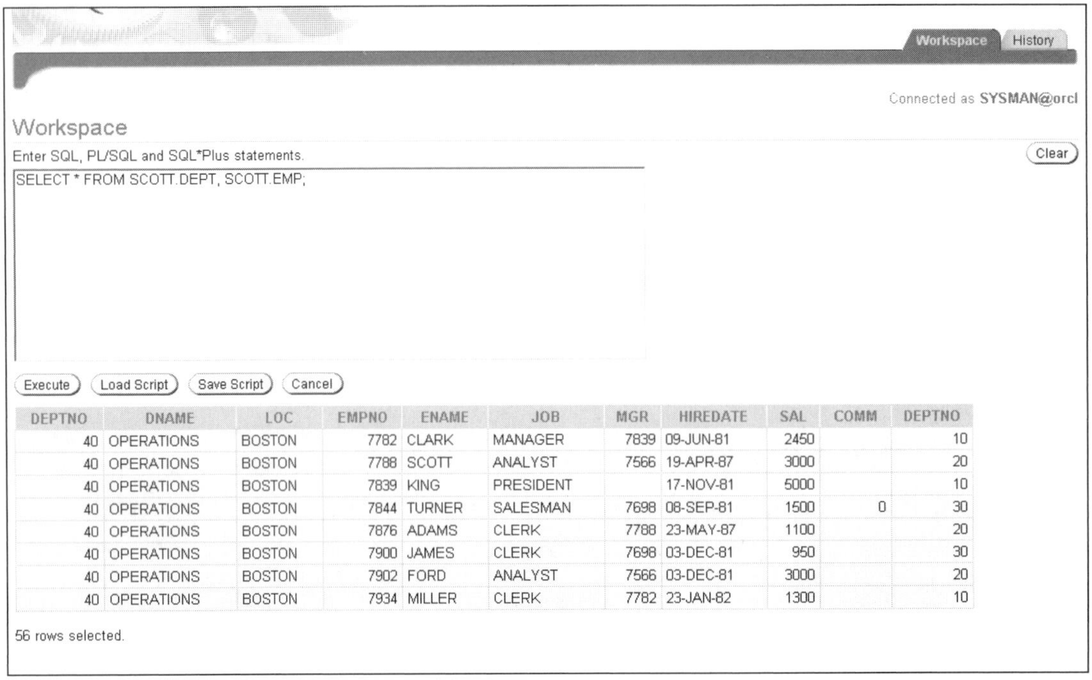

DEPTNO	DNAME	LOC	EMPNO	ENAME	JOB	MGR	HIREDATE	SAL	COMM	DEPTNO
40	OPERATIONS	BOSTON	7782	CLARK	MANAGER	7839	09-JUN-81	2450		10
40	OPERATIONS	BOSTON	7788	SCOTT	ANALYST	7566	19-APR-87	3000		20
40	OPERATIONS	BOSTON	7839	KING	PRESIDENT		17-NOV-81	5000		10
40	OPERATIONS	BOSTON	7844	TURNER	SALESMAN	7698	08-SEP-81	1500	0	30
40	OPERATIONS	BOSTON	7876	ADAMS	CLERK	7788	23-MAY-87	1100		20
40	OPERATIONS	BOSTON	7900	JAMES	CLERK	7698	03-DEC-81	950		30
40	OPERATIONS	BOSTON	7902	FORD	ANALYST	7566	03-DEC-81	3000		20
40	OPERATIONS	BOSTON	7934	MILLER	CLERK	7782	23-JAN-82	1300		10

Figure 8-15: Example of joining two tables without join criteria.

This result is called a Cartesian product, the simple product of joining every row from one table with every row from another table. This product is typically not what you really need. You want to get the `LOC` value for each row in the `EMP` table, based on the value of the `DEPTNO` column in both the `EMP` and `DEPT` tables.

Bringing data together from multiple tables is called a *join*. There are two basic types of joins — an inner join and an outer join, which are described in the next two sections.

Inner Joins

An inner join is the standard way of joining tables together. To use an inner join, you set a condition in the `WHERE` clause that specifies that the value in a column in one table must be equal to the value in a column in another table. The basis syntax for this type of join is as follows:

```
tableA.column = tableB.column
```

In a normal case, the reference `tableA.column` would be the primary key in `tableA` and `tableB.column` would be the foreign key in the second table that refers to `tableA.column`.

Foreign keys are covered in more detail in Chaper 11, "Constraints."

In the `EMP/DEPT` example, `tableA.column` would be `deptno` in the `dept` table and `tableB.column` would be `deptno` in the `EMP` table, so that the `SELECT` statement would be as follows:

```
SELECT DEPT.DEPTNO, DNAME, EMPNO, ENAME
    FROM SCOTT.DEPT, SCOTT.EMP
    WHERE DEPT.DEPTNO = EMP.DEPTNO;
```

Figure 8-16 shows the SQL statement and its result.

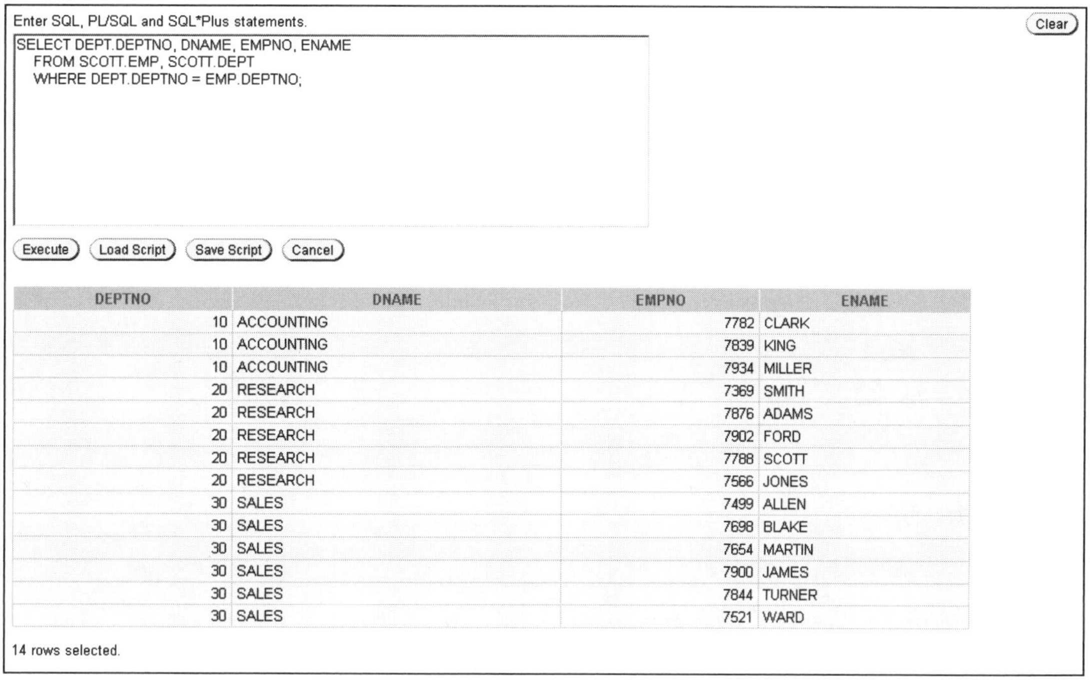


```
SELECT DEPT.DEPTNO, DNAME, EMPNO, ENAME
  FROM SCOTT.EMP, SCOTT.DEPT
  WHERE DEPT.DEPTNO = EMP.DEPTNO;
```

DEPTNO	DNAME	EMPNO	ENAME
10	ACCOUNTING	7782	CLARK
10	ACCOUNTING	7839	KING
10	ACCOUNTING	7934	MILLER
20	RESEARCH	7369	SMITH
20	RESEARCH	7876	ADAMS
20	RESEARCH	7902	FORD
20	RESEARCH	7788	SCOTT
20	RESEARCH	7566	JONES
30	SALES	7499	ALLEN
30	SALES	7698	BLAKE
30	SALES	7654	MARTIN
30	SALES	7900	JAMES
30	SALES	7844	TURNER
30	SALES	7521	WARD

14 rows selected.

Figure 8-16: A basic inner join.

Oracle9*i* introduced the ability to perform what is called a *natural join* in SQL statements. A natural join automatically uses columns in each table which have the same name as the basis for the join and eliminates the need to place these comparison conditions in the `WHERE` clause. The above query could have been rewritten as

```
SELECT DEPT.DEPTNO, DNAME, EMPNO, ENAME
    FROM SCOTT.DEPT, SCOTT.EMP;
```

This feature is especially useful when you are also using complex `WHERE` clauses, and, of course, where you have named the columns in the joined tables appropriately.

Outer Joins

One of the natural outcomes of an inner join is the elimination of the return of some of the rows in the `EMP` table. If a row in the `EMP` table has a value in the `DEPTNO` column that does not exist in the `DEPTNO` column of a row in the `DEPT` table, the row in the `EMP` table will not be shown.

In the previous example, one row in `DEPT` table contains a value of 40 for the `DEPTNO` column. There is no corresponding value of 40 in the `DEPTNO` column in `EMP`. So when the `DEPT` and `EMP` tables were joined, the result set did not include a row with the value of 40.

You may not want this elimination to be put into effect. For instance, you could have a `CUSTOMER` table and a related `ORDER` table, and you might want a result set that included all customers, regardless of whether they had any orders. For this scenario, you can use an *outer join*.

An outer join selects all rows of one of the tables in the join, regardless of whether that row has a match in the other join table. With an outer join, missing values from the second table are filled in with `NULL`s.

The operator `(+)` is used to indicate an outer join. The `(+)` follows the table name, which should include all rows, and is only used in the portion of the `WHERE` clause that joins two tables.

To use this with the previous example, you would use the syntax

```
SELECT DEPT.DEPTNO, DNAME, EMPNO, ENAME
    FROM SCOTT.DEPT, SCOTT.EMP
    WHERE dept.deptno = emp.deptno (+);
```

The result of this query is shown in Figure 8-17.

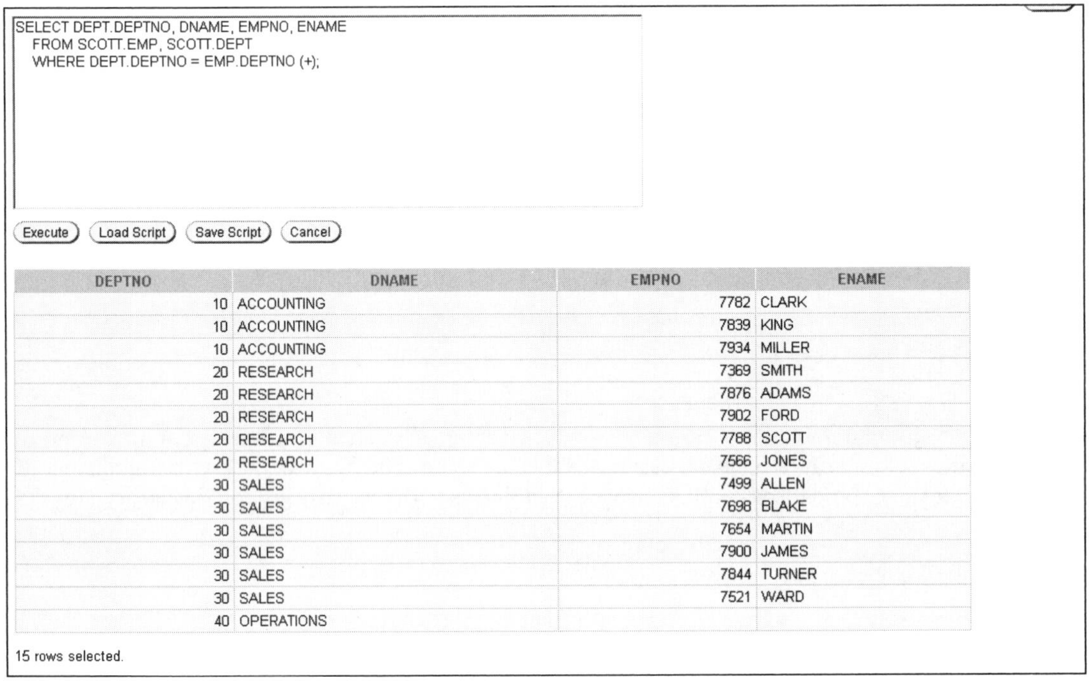

DEPTNO	DNAME	EMPNO	ENAME
10	ACCOUNTING	7782	CLARK
10	ACCOUNTING	7839	KING
10	ACCOUNTING	7934	MILLER
20	RESEARCH	7369	SMITH
20	RESEARCH	7876	ADAMS
20	RESEARCH	7902	FORD
20	RESEARCH	7788	SCOTT
20	RESEARCH	7566	JONES
30	SALES	7499	ALLEN
30	SALES	7698	BLAKE
30	SALES	7654	MARTIN
30	SALES	7900	JAMES
30	SALES	7844	TURNER
30	SALES	7521	WARD
40	OPERATIONS		

Figure 8-17: Using an outer join `joinSubqueries`.

Oracle9*i* introduced ANSI standard notation for joins. This notation allows you to use the keywords of `INNER JOIN`, `OUTER LEFT JOIN` or `OUTER RIGHT JOIN` between the two tables that are to be joined, rather than a comma.

Subqueries

Up to this point, all the `WHERE` conditions in the examples have compared two columns. You can also have a query whose results are used to limit the content of the result set. This query within an SQL statement is called a subquery.

You will often find subqueries in WHERE and HAVING clauses to qualify the results that are returned in your result set. For example, if you want to return all the people who worked in one of the departments represented in the DALLAS office, you could construct a query like:

```
SELECT DEPTNO, EMPNO, ENAME
    FROM SCOTT.EMP
    WHERE EMP.DEPTNO =
      (SELECT DEPT.DEPTNO
         FROM SCOTT.DEPT
         WHERE loc='DALLAS');
```

This example of a subquery seems a bit like overkill. You could get to the same result by simply joining together the EMP and DEPT tables, and selecting on the value of 'DALLAS' for the LOC column in the DEPT table, as in the following:

```
SELECT DEPT.DEPTNO, EMPNO, ENAME
    FROM SCOTT.DEPT, SCOTT.EMP
    WHERE DEPT.DEPTNO = EMP.DEPTNO AND
      DEPT.LOC = 'DALLAS';
```

But one of the really powerful aspects of subqueries comes with the use of what are called correlated subqueries. A *correlated subquery* is one where the subquery uses values passed from the driver query in its own execution. The easiest way to understand this capability is to demonstrate it with an example.

The example is a fairly common type of logical request. Using the EMP table, you want to be able to find out which employees have a salary that is higher than the average salary for their department. The first part of the SQL is simple:

```
SELECT ENAME, SAL, DEPTNO FROM SCOTT.EMP
    WHERE SAL > ???
    ORDER BY DEPTNO, SAL
```

The WHERE clause is the tricky part. You want to compare the SAL of each employee with the average salary for his or her department. You can compute that average with a simple SQL query, which will be a subquery in this updated example.

```
SELECT ENAME, SAL, DEPTNO FROM SCOTT.EMP E
    WHERE SAL >
      (SELECT AVG(SAL) FROM SCOTT.EMP E1
        WHERE E1.DEPTNO = E.DEPTNO)
    ORDER BY DEPTNO, SAL;
```

Notice two differences in this code. First of all, you used an alias for the EMP table in the main query. You had to do this in order to reference the value in that query in the subquery. The subquery references the value of DEPTNO from the E table — the table in the outer query.

Figure 8-18 shows the results of this query, included in the code for this book as CH08_CORRELATED_SUBQUERY.SQL, which gives you exactly the information you wanted to retrieve.

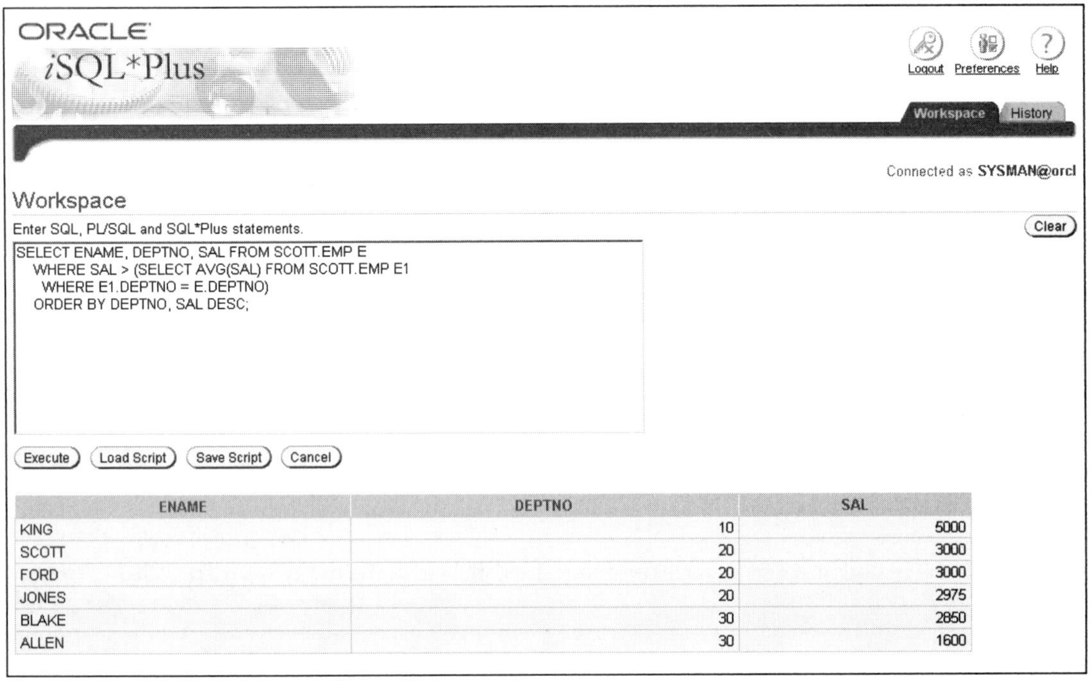

Figure 8-18: A correlated subquery and its results.

Before leaving the topic of subqueries, you should also understand that you can use a subquery anywhere that you could use a single value — for instance, in a list of values to be retrieved. The query that follows illustrates the use of this option.

In this query, you want to find out how many columns and indexes are associated with a particular table in the database. You can find out either one of these pieces of information by joining the relevant view, `ALL_TAB_COLUMNS` and `ALL_INDEXES`, respectively, to the data dictionary view `ALL_TABLES`. But the following code, included as `CH08_SUBQUERY_VALUE.SQL`, lets you see this count from two different tables in the same query.

```
SELECT TABLE_NAME,
      (SELECT COUNT(*) FROM ALL_TAB_COLUMNS C WHERE C.TABLE_NAME =
        T.TABLE_NAME) Columns,
      (SELECT COUNT(*) FROM ALL_INDEXES I WHERE I.TABLE_NAME = T.TABLE_NAME)
        Indexes
    FROM ALL_TABLES T WHERE OWNER = 'SH';
```

The results of this code are shown in Figure 8-19.

```
SELECT TABLE_NAME,
   (SELECT COUNT(*) FROM ALL_TAB_COLUMNS C WHERE C.TABLE_NAME =
      T.TABLE_NAME) Columns,
   (SELECT COUNT(*) FROM ALL_INDEXES I WHERE I.TABLE_NAME = T.TABLE_NAME) Indexes
  FROM ALL_TABLES T WHERE OWNER = 'SH';
```

Execute   Load Script   Save Script   Cancel

TABLE_NAME	COLUMNS	INDEXES
SALES	7	6
COSTS	6	2
TIMES	38	1
PRODUCTS	34	4
CHANNELS	6	1
PROMOTIONS	13	2
CUSTOMERS	38	10
COUNTRIES	13	2
SUPPLEMENTARY_DEMOGRAPHICS	14	1
MVIEW$_EXCEPTIONS	5	0
CAL_MONTH_SALES_MV	2	0
FWEEK_PSCAT_SALES_MV	5	4
DRSUP_TEXT_IDXI	6	1
DRSUP_TEXT_IDXK	2	1
DRSUP_TEXT_IDXR	2	0
DRSUP_TEXT_IDXN	2	1
SALES_TRANSACTIONS_EXT	9	0

Figure 8-19: A subquery in a `SELECT` value list.

Insert

So far, the examples have been using data that someone else has been kind enough to load — actually the default `scott` schema that comes on the Oracle installation disk. But your applications will have to add data to your Oracle database as well as read it. You add data to a table with the `INSERT` statement.

The `INSERT` statement is used to add one or more rows into one or more tables (though generally one table). To be able to insert rows into a table, you must either own the table in your schema or you must have `INSERT` privilege on the table. The format for a typical insert would be as follows:

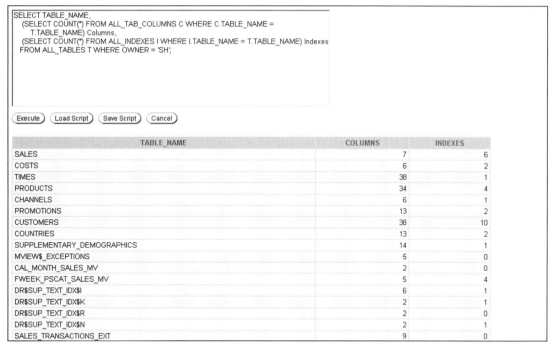

```
INSERT INTO <table-expression> <column-list>
    VALUES (<values>);
```

What does this mean? First, *`<table-expression>`* is a table name like `EMP`. You can specify using the syntax *`schema.table name`* if you don't own the table but can read data from the table.

The *`<column-list>`* clause is optional. You can use the column-list to specify the exact columns that you want populated; this way you do not have to care about the order of the columns in the table nor do you need to fill in every column with a value.

Of course, using a column list does not subvert any of the requirements on the columns. If you have a column that does not allow `NULL` values, it must either receive a value in the `INSERT` or have a default value specified.

If you do not specify a column-list, you must be very careful. The first entry in the values section maps into the first column in the table, the second value to the second column in the table, and so on until all the values are exhausted. For purposes of documentation alone, it can help to explicitly specify the list of columns.

The next step is to supply the values that get inserted into the table. You have the option to insert one row or multiple rows. The easiest is to insert a single row. After the `VALUES` keyword, you will supply a comma-separated list of values enclosed in parentheses. The data type of each of these values must match or can be implicitly convertible to the data type of the column.

The following simple example illustrates the syntax for a specific `INSERT` statement:

```
INSERT INTO SCOTT.EMP (empno, ename, sal)
    VALUES (900, 'David', 123.99);
```

This statement enters one row into the `EMP` table and sets the columns `EMPNO` to `900`, `ename` to `'David'` and `SAL` to `123.99`. The columns in the list happen to be in order, but the statement could just as easily supplied `ENAME`, `SAL`, and `EMPNO`—with the values lined up appropriately. The statement has also not passed values back into every column of `EMP`. Remember, when doing a description of `EMP`, the only required field in this table is `EMPNO`, which was defined to be `NOT NULL`.

You can also use a `SELECT` statement to populate one table from the content of another table. In this next bit of SQL, you can assume that you have a table called `NO_COMM` in the `SCOTT` schema that contains three columns: `EMPNO`, `ENAME`, and `COMM`. To populate the `NO_COMM` table with some of the rows in the `EMP` table, you would use the following syntax:

```
INSERT INTO SCOTT.NO_COMM (EMPNO, ENAME, COMM)
     SELECT EMPNO, ENAME, COMM
       FROM SCOTT.EMP
       WHERE EMPNO IN (800, 900);
```

You can also use the `INSERT` verb to insert rows into multiple tables. Remember, the `EMP` table has a column called `COMM`. For the example, you might want to create three new tables: the first will be high commission employees (`HIGH_COMM`), the second all other commission employees (`OTHER_COMM`), and the third will be employees where the commission is `NULL` (`NO_COMM`).

To perform a multi-table insert, you would use the following syntax:

```
INSERT FIRST
    WHEN COMM >= 1000 THEN
        INTO HIGH_COMM
    WHEN COMM < 1000 THEN
        INTO OTHER_COMM
    ELSE
        INTO NO_COMM
  SELECT EMPNO, ENAME, COMM
    FROM EMP;
```

This `INSERT` statement will send each row to one of the three tables specified. Notice that the `ELSE` clause will put all rows into the `NO_COMM` table that do not fit into the other tables.

Also, the keyword `FIRST` specifies that the `INSERT` statement should only insert rows into the first destination table whose `WHEN` clause evaluates to `TRUE`. This syntax is appropriate since none of the rows in the original

EMP table will be inserted into two different destination tables. If you wanted to have a row from the source table potentially be inserted into multiple destination tables, you would use the keyword ALL instead, which would force the evaluation of every condition in the list.

UPDATE

The INSERT statement is used to add new data to a table. To change data that already exists in a row, you use the UPDATE verb. The syntax for an UPDATE looks like this:

```
UPDATE  table_name
    SET column=value [,column=value]
   [WHERE <restrictive-condition>]
```

The UPDATE statement is also fairly straightforward. The *table_name* is the name of the table that will be updated. The SET keyword precedes a list of columns in that table that will be updated. The value can either be a specific value, either declared or passed as a bind variable, or the result of a SELECT statement that returns a single row. Following is an example of this usage:

```
UPDATE SCOTT.EMP E
    SET SAL = (SELECT AVG(SAL) FROM SCOTT.EMP D
      WHERE D.DEPT_NO = E.DEPTNO);
```

In this example, you are using a correlated subquery to even out the salaries across each department. The subquery figures the average of the SAL column, and the UPDATE sets the SAL column for each row to that value.

You can use a subquery to set more than one column in an UPDATE statement, with the only additional requirements being that the multiple column names must be enclosed in parentheses and the subquery must have the same number of columns as listed within the parentheses.

The WHERE clause on an UPDATE statement, as you would expect, limits the rows in the target table that will be updated. Remember, the WHERE clause is optional, from a syntax point of view. You will not get an error if you do not include it, but the results could dramatically alter your data. If you wanted to give the employees in department 10 a 15 percent raise for excellent performance, you would use this statement:

```
UPDATE SCOTT.EMP
    SET SAL = SAL*1.15
    WHERE DEPTNO = 10;
```

If you left off the crucial WHERE clause, you might make the other employees very happy, but your balance sheet would certainly suffer. As explained in the last section of this chapter, any mistakes like this do not become final until you explicitly commit them.

DELETE

The DELETE statement removes from a table all the rows that match the selection criteria. This statement is pretty simple — the only variable pieces of syntax are the table name and selection attributes. The syntax for a DELETE statement is as follows:

```
DELETE FROM table-name
    WHERE <restriction-clause>
```

COMMIT/ROLLBACK/SAVEPOINT

The COMMIT and ROLLBACK keywords do not really manipulate data like other DML, but they are used with DML statements to mark the boundaries of a transaction as well implement or cancel the changes made by a transaction.

The COMMIT keyword makes all changes to the database made during this transaction permanent. The ROLLBACK keyword removes all changes that were made during this transaction.

The syntax for these two statements is simple—just the keyword itself. For adherence to the SQL standard, you can include the keyword WORK after each of these statements, as in the following:

```
COMMIT WORK;
```

There is one additional option that you can use with the ROLLBACK keyword. By itself, the ROLLBACK keyword rolls back an entire transaction. But there may be times when you only want to roll back part of the changes implemented in a transaction. You can think of this as the difference between the clear key and the clear error key on a calculator. The clear key wipes out the entire transaction, like a standalone ROLLBACK. The clear error key erases the last entry, but maintains the rest of the transaction, which would work like a ROLLBACK TO SAVEPOINT command.

The syntax for using a savepoint with the ROLLBACK keyword is

```
ROLLBACK TO [SAVEPOINT] savepoint_name;
```

where *savepoint_name* is the name of the savepoint previously set. To set a savepoint at any place in a transaction, you have to use the syntax

```
SAVEPOINT savepoint_name;
```

with a unique name for the *savepoint_name* variable.

You should make it a practice to issue a COMMIT or ROLLBACK after every transaction. If you end an application with an open transaction, Oracle will automatically roll back that transaction. Similarly, if your application crashes in the middle of a transaction, the Oracle database will roll back the transaction when it senses that the application is no longer connected—the proper thing to do for the sake of data integrity.

Transactions are a nontrivial part of your overall application logic. You should consider them carefully and understand Oracle's somewhat unique way of handling transaction locks, as explained in Chapter 3, "Handling Multiple Users."

Summary

SQL is a powerful, set-oriented language. SQL syntax includes verbs to retrieve data from the database (SELECT), add data to the database (INSERT), modify data in the database (UPDATE), and remove data from the database (DELETE).

The SQL language includes a clause that can limit the number of rows affected by these operations: the `WHERE` clause. Since transactions are an integral part of modern relational databases, SQL includes keywords for controlling the scope and affect of transactions with `COMMIT` and `ROLLBACK`.

You can add more capability into these basic SQL statements by adjusting the way rows are returned from a query with `ORDER BY` and `GROUP BY`, as well as use data from more than one table through the use of joins or in a subquery.

Although this chapter covered a lot of admittedly very basic ground, you, as a professional developer, may be asking yourself Peggy Lee's musical question, "Is that all there is?" This chapter has only introduced you to the bare essentials of the key SQL statements — although hopefully it has shown you some of its power, too. There are more SQL syntax and structures that can help you to use Oracle effectively, and these extended pieces of syntax are covered in the next chapter.

9

Extended SQL

The previous chapter introduced you to the basics of using SQL to access the Oracle database. There is, of course, much more to using SQL against Oracle than was covered in the previous chapter.

This chapter takes you further into using SQL against Oracle. The chapter covers a variety of topics, including more detail on additional syntax, database objects, and the use of one of Oracle's unique features with your SQL.

Although this chapter offers you more information on the type of SQL used with Oracle, it cannot give you and complete and exhaustive examination of all the facets of SQL and Oracle. There have been entire books written on using SQL effectively against Oracle, so even two chapters will not be able to deliver everything you might use in the course of a development career. But we, the authors, hope that the material in this chapter will help you to become more accomplished in using SQL against your Oracle database.

Extended Conditions

This section covers some of the conditional expressions that can be used with Oracle that were outside the scope of the previous chapter.

LIKE and REGEXP_LIKE

Oracle, like most modern databases, divides data into a few basic types — numbers, text and dates, with some other more peripheral types as well as the possibility of user-defined types. Numbers use a standard set of mathematical comparison operators, including `+`, `-`, `>`, and `<`. Number comparisons are fairly black-and-white, in that they are either absolutely true or absolutely false.

Text, on the other hand, is more nuanced. The words "rich," "ricochet," and "rice" have some commonality — their first three letters are the same, even though their meanings are completely different. The comparison operator `LIKE` is designed to help you to identify these similarities.

The use of LIKE goes hand in hand with the use of wildcards. The only way to identify all three of the previous words as similar is to tell Oracle to only pay attention to the first three letters of the words. The syntax to enable this comparison uses the LIKE operator and the standard Oracle wildcard '%', such as

```
WHERE WORD_VALUE LIKE 'ric%'
```

This selection criteria would retrieve all three words when they were contained in the WORD_VALUE column in this example.

There are other wildcards you can use in Oracle, but with strings, the target of the LIKE condition, the most relevant one is the _ (underscore) character. The underscore is used to substitute for a single character, as opposed to the % wildcard, which can be replaced by any number of characters.

These wildcards can be used for more exact specifications. For instance, the names of the figures used in this book have to be in the format of the number of the book, followed by a space, followed by the letters "FG," followed by the two-digit representation of the chapter. If the figures could have a variable number of alphanumeric characters following this initial set of identifiers, the selection criterion to retrieve the figures for this book from a column in an Oracle database could be as follows:

```
WHERE FIGURE_ID LIKE '564825 FG__%'
```

In this example, wildcards were used at the end of a string. This arrangement is typically how wildcards are used effectively. Trailing wildcards make it faster for Oracle to determine if a value matches the expression. Trailing wildcards also can use indexes, if available, for rapid identification of rows that will pass the condition. If you use a wildcard at the start of a comparison, Oracle will usually have to go through all the rows or index values in the target to evaluate the condition.

The LIKE condition provides some capabilities for identifying particular character strings. Oracle Database 10*g* supports the use of regular expressions, which are covered in detail in Chapter 20, "Regular Expressions and Expression Filter." If you want to use a regular expression to match character strings, you will have to use the new REGEXP_LIKE, which allows you to replace the character pattern on the right of the expression with a regular expression. You can use this capability to implement functionality like case-insensitive searches.

Finally, if you believe that extensive text search might be an essential part of your data usage, you should investigate the use of Oracle Text, which gives you much more control over search and retrieval of data based on text content. Although this feature of Oracle is beyond the scope of this book, it provides fairly sophisticated functionality, such as the ability to find text strings in large objects based on the string appearing anywhere in the object, one string occurring a set number of words away from another string,

IN and EXISTS

The two conditions IN and EXISTS both are used to determine if a value from one result set is in another result set. The basic syntax for the IN condition in a WHERE clause is as follows:

```
WHERE column_name IN (value_list | subquery)
```

The *value_list* is a comma-separated list of actual values or expressions that are used for comparison with the named in *column_name*. If you have a small and known number of values you want to use for inclusion, using a value list works.

But frequently, you may want to use a subquery to retrieve either a larger list of values or a list of dynamic values. In the following simple example, included as `CH09_IN.SQL` and shown in Figure 9-1, you use a simple subquery to return a list of departments where the department number is greater than 20, and then show the names of the employees in those departments.

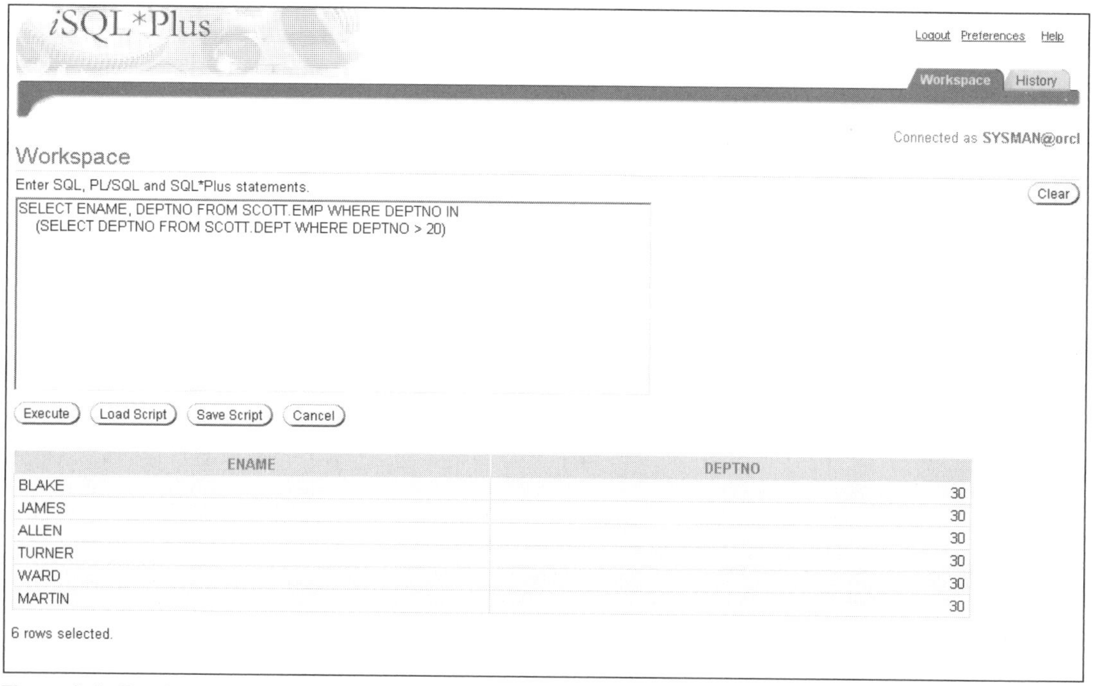

Figure 9-1: Employees selected with an `IN` clause.

Although there are two departments with department numbers over 20, only one of them has employees. The `IN` clause dictates that Oracle will first assemble the list of values following the `IN` clause and then perform a join using the values returned from the subquery with the tables mentioned in the main, or outer, query.

The `EXISTS` clause is similar to the `IN` clause, in that it compares the existence of values with the tables in the main part of the query, but it differs in both syntax and operation. The syntax for the use of the `EXISTS` clause is as follows:

```
SELECT . . . . WHERE EXISTS sub-query
```

You can see that you no longer are comparing a column to the results of the `EXISTS` clause. This syntactical difference points to the difference in operation of the `EXISTS` clause. The `EXISTS` clause does not call for a join with the table in the main part of the query. This clause is only used to determine if any results are returned from the subquery portion of the clause.

You can see the difference in the SQL statement included as `CH09_EXISTS1.SQL`, which is shown in Figure 9-2 .

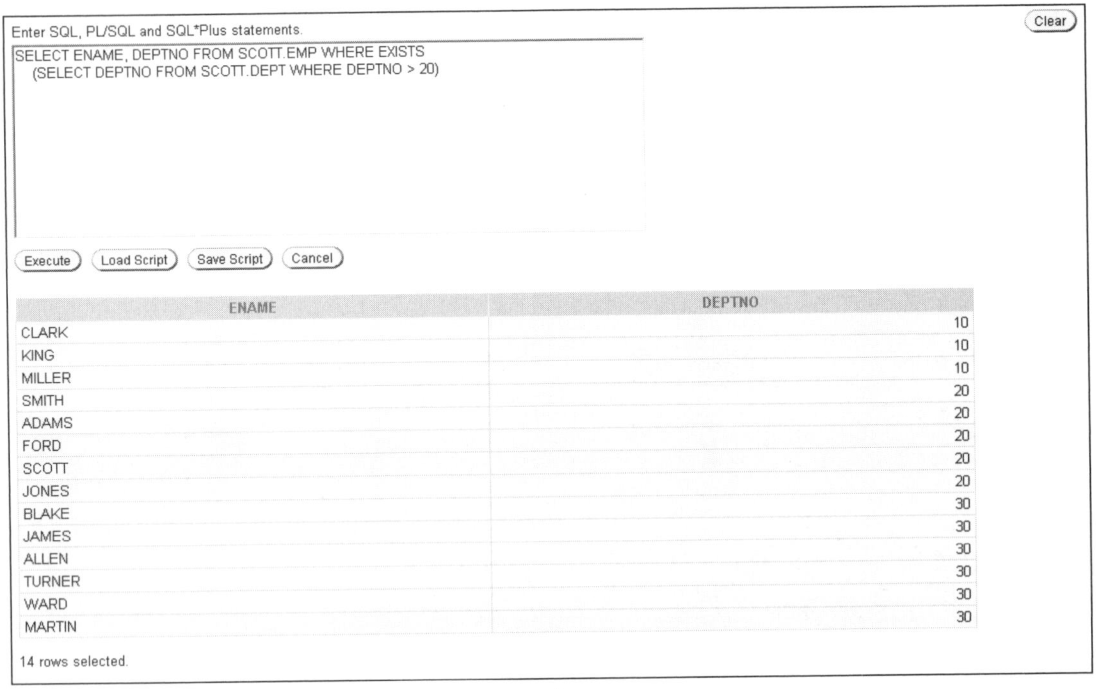

Figure 9-2: Replacing an `IN` clause with an `EXISTS` clause.

Since the subquery returned some rows, all the rows in the main query are returned. The way to make this `EXISTS` query equivalent to the `IN` query in Figure 9-2 is to add another condition to the subquery, one that imposes the same type of join implied by the `IN` query, as included in `CH09_EXISTS2.SQL` and shown in Figure 9-3.

This added condition makes the `EXISTS` query return the same results as the query that was used the `IN` clause.

But remember that the `IN` query does a join, while the `EXISTS` query only requires a row to be returned. This can cause logical problems in situation where a `NULL` is returned as the only part of the result set.

Consider the following query:

```
SELECT MGR FROM SCOTT.EMP WHERE JOB = 'PRESIDENT';
```

This statement will return a single row where the value of `MGR` is `NULL`, since the president has no manager. When this is used as the subquery in an SQL statement with an `IN` clause, as included as `CH09_IN_NULL.SQL`, it produces the results shown in Figure 9-4.

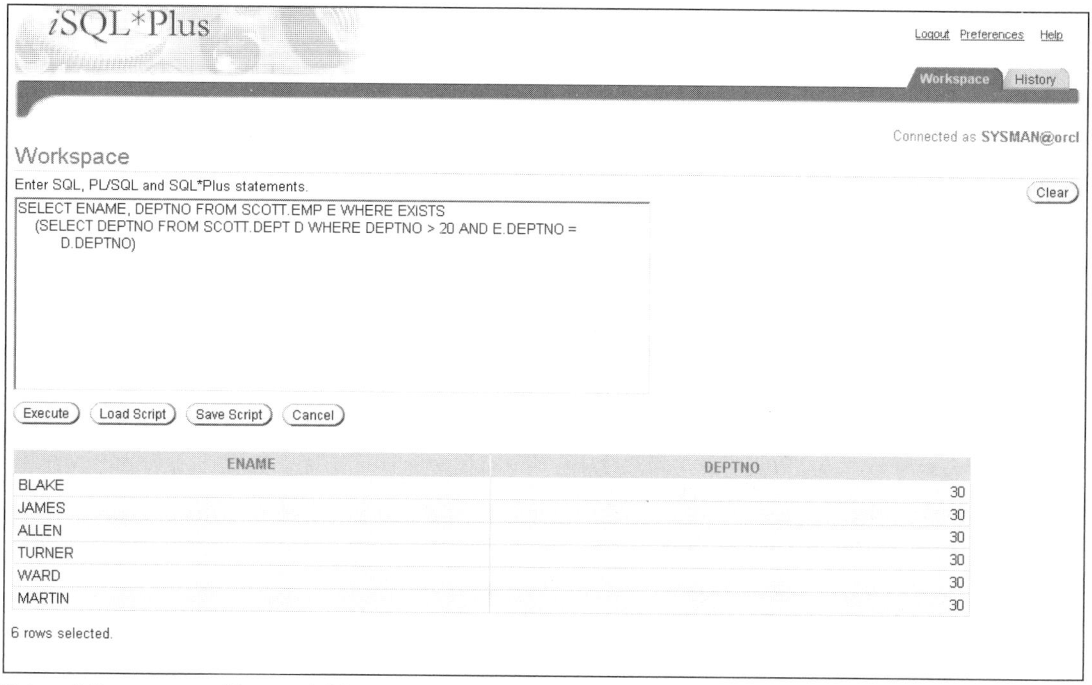

Figure 9-3: **`EXISTS`** with an additional condition.

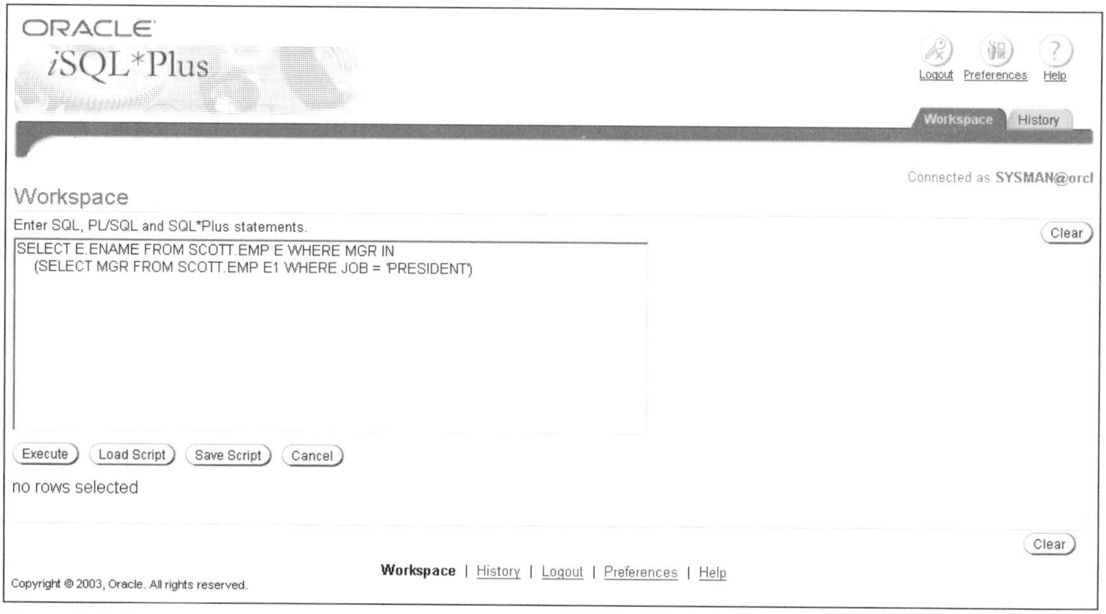

Figure 9-4: A query where the **`IN`** clause returns a **`NULL`**.

You did not get any rows back, because the main query could not link to the NULL value. Remember, NULL does not equal any other value.

But using the same subquery, with the added equivalence condition, as demonstrated previously and listed in CH09_EXISTS_NULL.SQL, will produce the result, as shown in Figure 9-5.

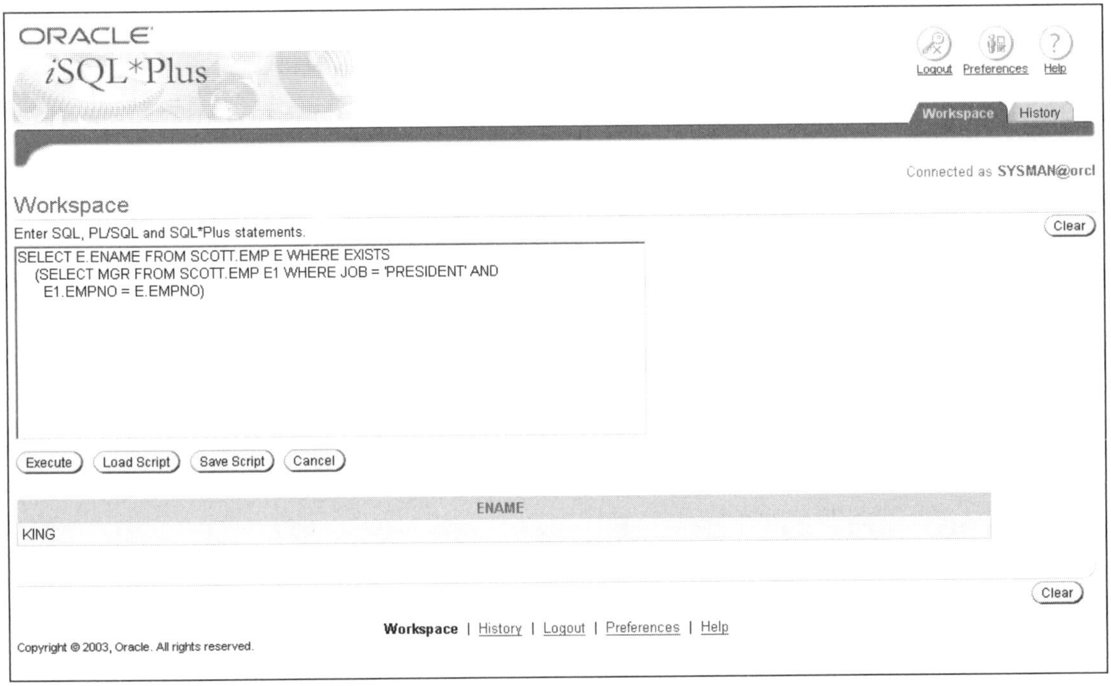

Figure 9-5: A query where the EXISTS clause returns a NULL.

Even though the subquery only returned a NULL value, a row was still selected, which means that the main table could still use the collated subquery to return the proper value of KING.

ALL, SOME, and ANY

The two conditions covered in the preceding section are used to compare a row to a set of rows. There is another set of conditions that perform a similar function to the IN and EXISTS conditions. These conditions check for the existence of a row in another query set, but unlike IN and EXISTS, they can be used in conjunction with relational operators such as greater than (>) and less than (<).

These three conditions are as follows:

- ANY, which checks to see if the expression on the left side of the condition exists in any of the rows on the right side of the condition
- SOME, which performs the same comparison as ANY
- ALL, which checks to see that the expression on the left of the condition is true for all rows in the result set on the right of the condition

All of these conditions use the same syntax:

```
expression relational_operator ALL | SOME | ANY sub-query | expression
```

where the `relational_operator` is >, <, =, or any combination of these conditions. Typically, these conditions are used to compare one or more rows against values in another set of rows.

As an example, you can stick with the familiar `EMP` table in the `SCOTT` schema. Your boss has the not unusual suspicion that there are salespeople in the company who are making more than him, or more than other contributing members of the organization. You want to start by finding out what employees have a larger compensation than any of the salesmen, whose compensation includes both salary and commission. The SQL statement to determine this, which is included as `CH09_ANY.SQL`, and its results are shown in Figure 9-6.

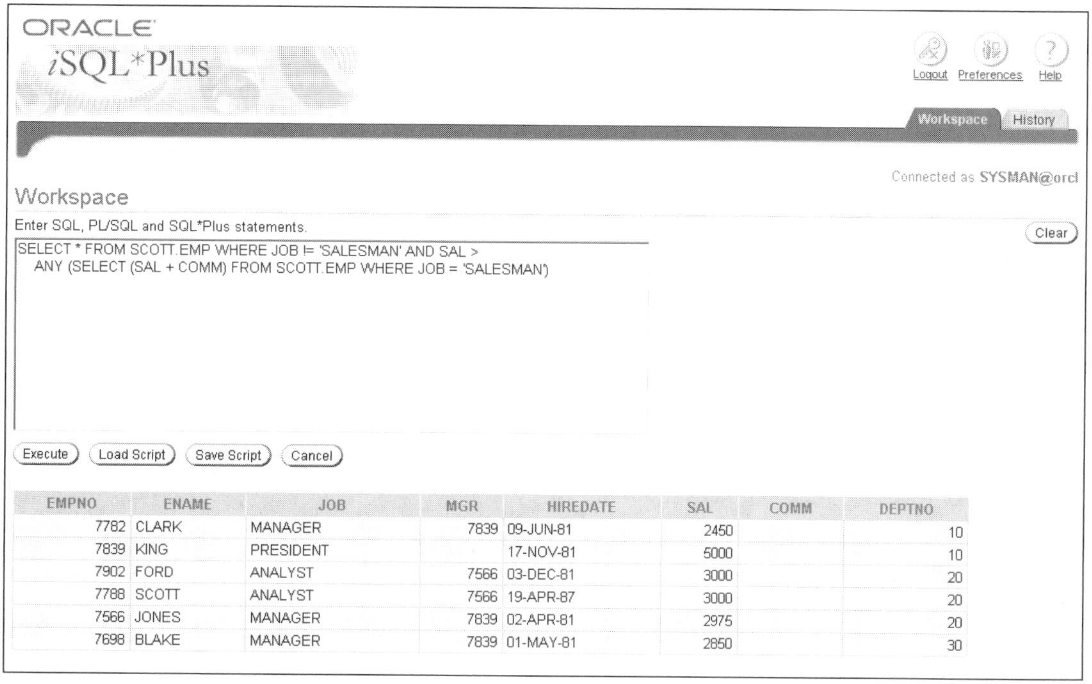

Figure 9-6: Using the ANY comparison.

As you can see, six members of the company have a `SAL` larger than the combined `SAL` and `COMM` of any of the salesmen.

Whew, that was a relief—especially since all the analysts are making more than some of the salesmen. (But, really, when you think about it, any analyst is worth more than any salesman.) The query shown in Figure 9-7, and included as `CH09_ALL.SQL`, shows that most of these same people are making more than any of the salesmen.

These two queries use the same subquery, but the first query is just looking to see if the salary of the person in the `EMP` table is larger than the salary of any of the salesmen—similar to using a comparison with the `MIN` function for the salemen's compensation. The second query is used to determine which employees have a larger salary than any of the salesmen—similar to using the `MAX` function with the salemen's compensation. The difference between each of these queries is that using the `MIN` or `MAX` function requires the result set in the subquery to be sorted. For a small set of rows like this, using the `MAX` and `MIN` comparison is slightly less costly, but, like all performance issues, the results in your scenario depend on many factors, such as whether there is an index on the target of the `MAX` and `MIN` function, the size of the result set, and environmental considerations.

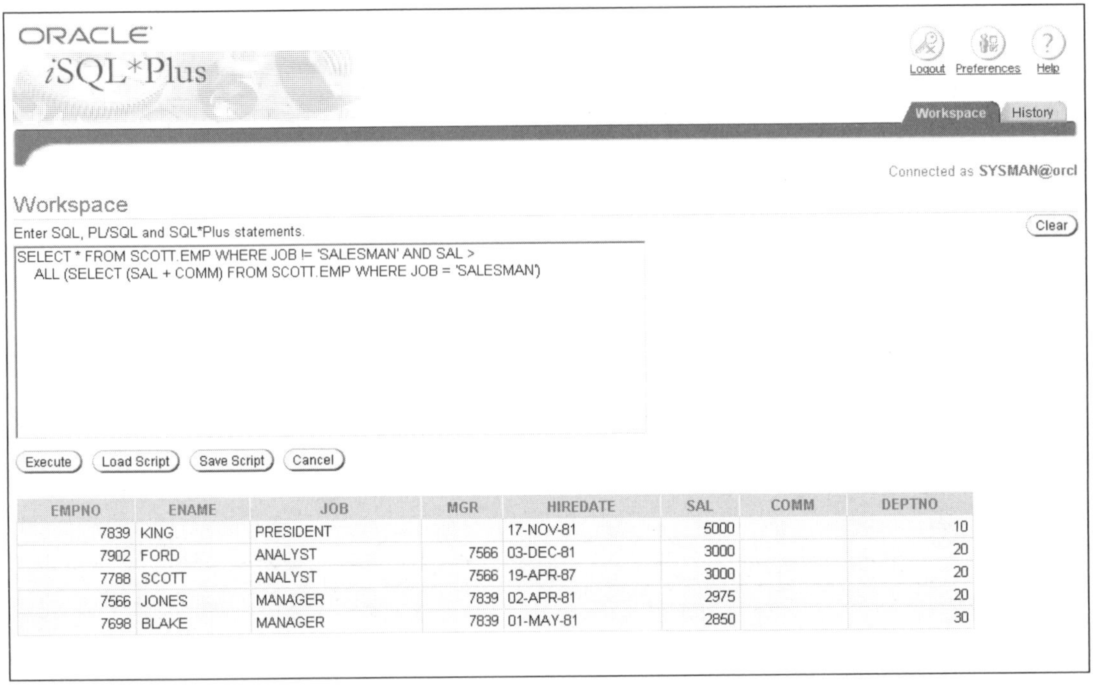

Figure 9-7: Using the `ALL` comparison.

Extended Set Operations

SQL is a set-oriented language. Even the simplest SQL query returns a set of results. Oracle SQL includes some operations that work on complete sets of data, which can multiply the power of using sets.

All of these set operators have a similar set of restrictions. They cannot be used with large objects, such as `LONG`, `BLOB`, or `CLOB` data types, and they cannot be used with nested tables or `VARRAY`s. You can use more than one type of set operator in a single SQL statement, but we recommend that you group the operators with parentheses, as you would use in a compound `WHERE` clause, both for readability and because Oracle may change the order in which different set operators are evaluated.

UNION

You can use the `UNION` operator to bring together tables that are normally separated. The syntax for using this operator consists of two SQL statements separated by the `UNION` keyword, as in the following:

```
sql_statement
UNION
sql_statement
```

This statement will produce the combination of the results of both SQL statements. The `UNION` operator can also be used for more than one result set. The same syntax is used for each of the set operators by using either the `INTERSECT` or `MINUS` operator in place of the `UNION` operator.

Both of the SQL statements must have the same number of values returned, and those values must have the same data types. You can use the `ORDER BY` clause with the `UNION` keyword, but it must follow the final SQL statement. This operator is not used that frequently, since many of the potential benefits it can deliver have to do with separating data for performance and ease of management—benefits that Oracle delivers with partitioning.

To see these set operators in action, you can use two tables in the HR schema: `EMPLOYEES`, which contains a list of all current employees, and `JOB_HISTORY`, which tracks jobs that employees used to have.

If you wanted to get a list of all jobs ever held by all employees, you would use the SQL shown in the following code snippet, which is included as `CH09_UNION.SQL` and is also shown Figure 9-8.

```
SELECT EMPLOYEE_ID, DEPARTMENT_ID, JOB_ID FROM HR.EMPLOYEES
UNION
SELECT EMPLOYEE_ID, DEPARTMENT_ID, JOB_ID FROM HR.JOB_HISTORY;
```

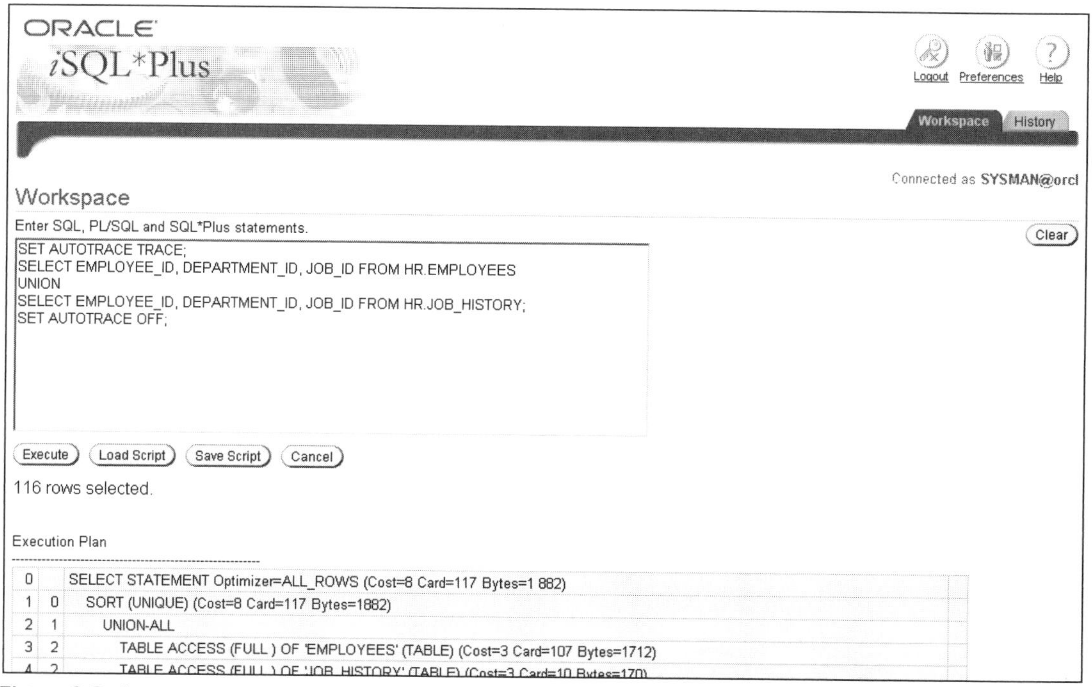

Figure 9-8: A `UNION` statement.

To show the results of the `UNION` statement clearly, the `CH09_UNION.SQL` file turns off the display of the result set and shows only the statistics and the execution plan for the statement. You can compare the number of rows returned for this statement with the number of rows in the `EMPLOYEES` table by using the following:

```
SELECT COUNT(*) FROM HR.EMPLOYEES
```

The requirement for a matching set of columns is enforced by checking on the data type of each column in order. Because of this, you could have a UNION statement like this:

```
SELECT EMPLOYEE_ID, LAST_NAME, DEPARTMENT_ID, JOB_ID FROM HR.EMPLOYEES
UNION
SELECT EMPLOYEE_ID, JOB_ID, DEPARTMENT_ID, JOB_ID FROM HR.JOB_HISTORY;
```

This statement has two columns, LAST_NAME from EMPLOYEES and JOB_ID from JOB_HISTORY, in the same position. The UNION operator works because both of these columns are VARCHAR2, even though they logically contain different types of data.

By default, the UNION operator only returns distinct rows from the combined result sets. If a row in the first result set is exactly the same as a row in the second result set, it is only included once in the final result set. To force the return of duplicate rows, you can use the UNION ALL operator.

Other databases sometimes use the UNION operator for a specific purpose, which is not needed with Oracle. For reasons of performance or maintenance, a database designer may split up a single table into multiple smaller tables. The purpose for this design is to allow the smaller tables to be queried and backed up independently. If you want to accomplish the same result with Oracle, you simply partition the table. The Oracle optimizer is smart enough to know to skip partitions if they are not needed in a query, and each partition can be in its own tablespace, which can be backed up and recovered independently. For more on partitioning, see Chapter 12, "Other Database Structures."

INTERSECT

The INTERSECT operator returns the rows that occur in every result set named in the compound SQL statement. The best way to illustrate how an INTERSECT operator works is with a Venn diagram, used to show set interaction, as shown in Figure 9-9.

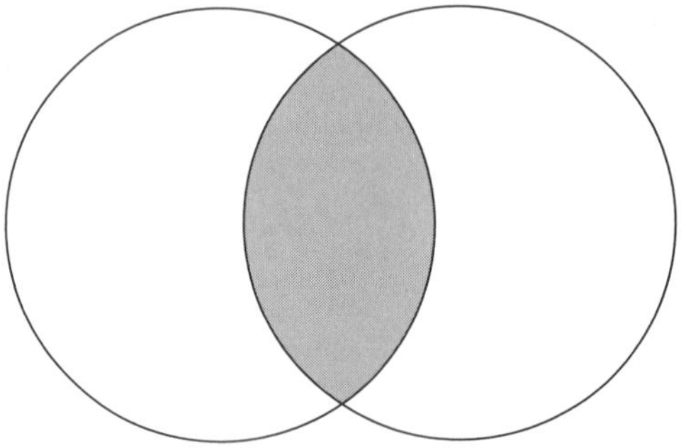

Figure 9-9: A Venn diagram to illustrate the INTERSECT set operator.

The INTERSECT operator returns the rows that are in both result sets in the overall SQL statement. To illustrate the use of the INTERSECT operator, you can use the EMPLOYEES and JOB_HISTORY tables again. This time, you want to get a result set that contains the employees that have had more than one job. The SQL statement used to produce this result is included as CH09_INTERSECT.SQL and is shown in Figure 9-10.

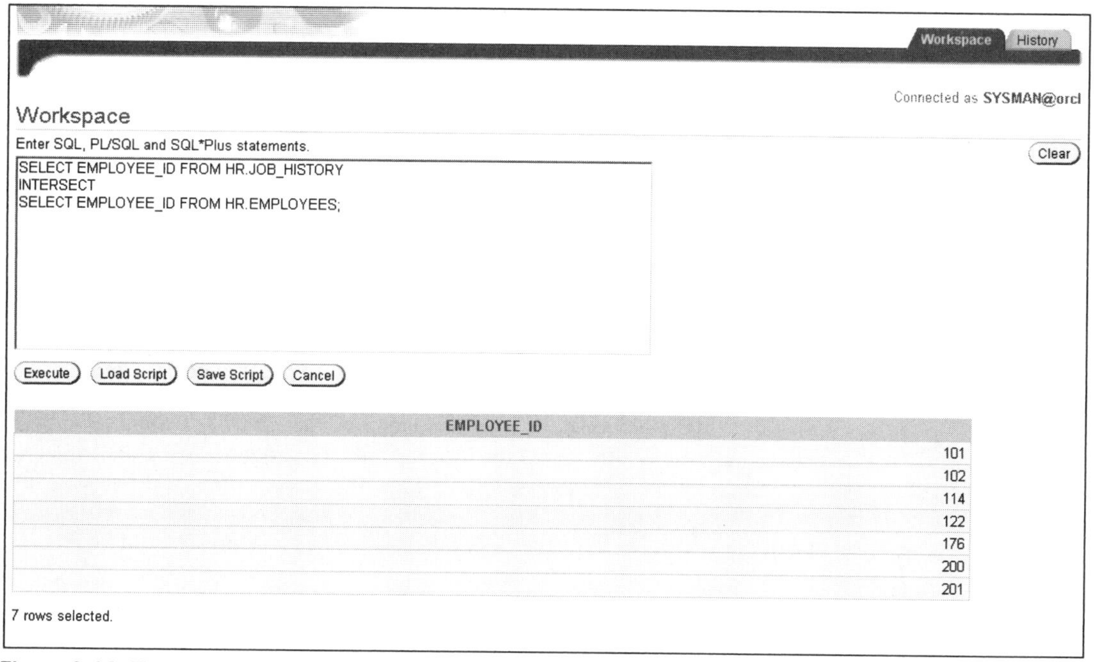

Figure 9-10: The result of an `INTERSECT` operator.

If you wanted to get a list of all employees who have had more than one job in the same department, you would use the following SQL code:

```
SELECT EMPLOYEE_ID, DEPARTMENT_ID FROM HR.JOB_HISTORY
INTERSECT
SELECT EMPLOYEE_ID, DEPARTMENT_ID FROM HR.EMPLOYEES;
```

This SQL includes the additional requirement that rows in each result set must have the same department number. This code is included as `CH09_INTERSECT_2.SQL`, so you can run it yourself to see the results it produces.

MINUS

The `MINUS` set operator uses two result sets, but only returns the rows in the first result set that are not in the second result set. The Venn diagram shown in Figure 9-11 illustrates the logic of the `MINUS` operator.

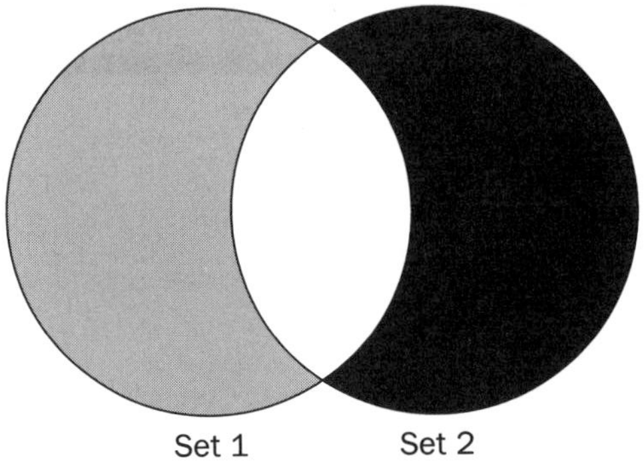

Figure 9-11: A Venn diagram to illustrate the `MINUS` set operator.

You can clearly see that the data in the white part of the diagram will not be returned. But, unlike the `UNION` and `INTERSECT` operators, the order of the component result sets does make a difference. If your SQL statement had a query returning Set 1 listed first, the data in the gray area would be returned. If your SQL statement had a query that returned Set 2 first, the data in the black area would be returned.

The following SQL query, included as `CH09_MINUS.SQL` and shown in Figure 9-12, returns the employee information for employees who have had more than one job, but not the same job they currently have:

```
SELECT EMPLOYEE_ID, JOB_ID FROM HR.JOB_HISTORY
MINUS
SELECT EMPLOYEE_ID, JOB_HISTORY FROM HR.EMPLOYEES;
```

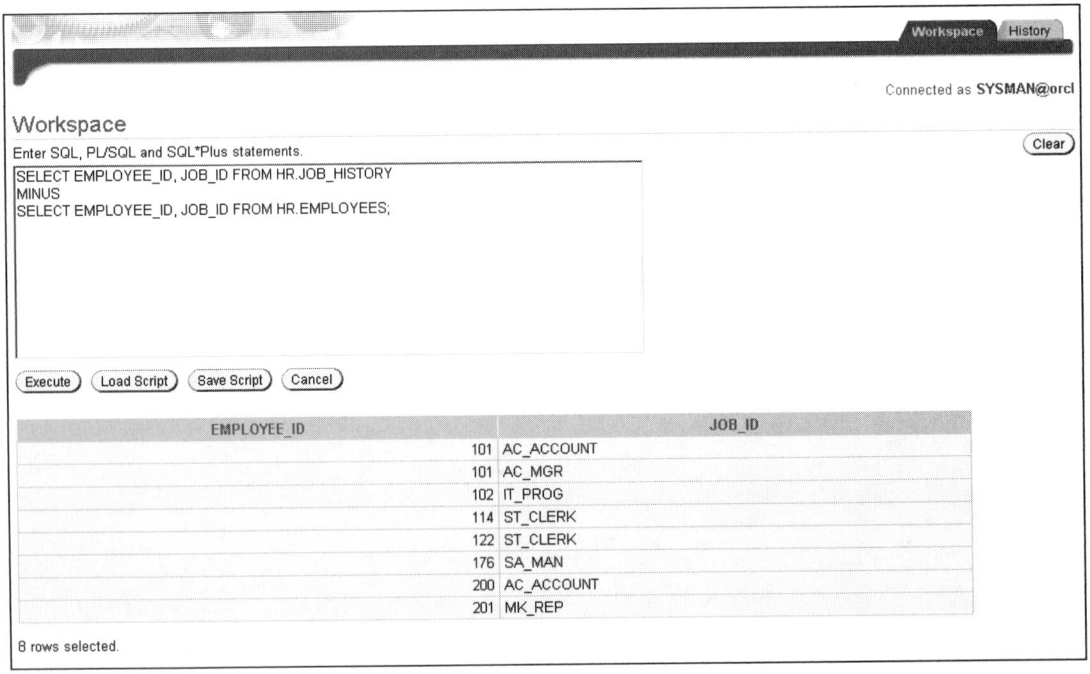

Figure 9-12: The result of a `MINUS` operator.

The query shown in the code snippet shows employees who have had two different jobs. If you wanted to also show employees who have had the same job, but in two different departments, you would simply add the `DEPARTMENT_ID` to the column list in both statements. This SQL statement is included as `CH09_MINUS_2.SQL`, so you can run it yourself.

MERGE

The `MERGE` verb was introduced for Oracle in Oracle9*i*. The `MERGE` verb is designed for combining two tables. As you would expect, this verb can perform several write operations at the same time, combining `UPDATE`s, `INSERT`s, and even `DELETE`s together, all based on specific conditions and comparisons between the two tables.

The basic syntax for the `MERGE` statement is as follows:

```
MERGE INTO target_table
    USING source_table
    ON merge_condition
    update_clause
    insert_clause
```

In this syntax, *`target_table`* is the destination table for the `MERGE` activity. The *`source_table`* can be a table, view, or subquery that will supply the rows that will be merged with the target table. This clause assembles the values that will be used for the `INSERT` and `UPDATE` activities. This clause is usually a subquery, and so must be followed by an alias so its columns can be referenced later in the statement.

The *`merge_condition`* is an expression that acts as a switch between `UPDATE` and `INSERT` activity — if the condition is `TRUE`, then the target table row is updated; if the condition is `FALSE`, then the row from the source table is `INSERT`ed into the target table. This condition typically checks to see if the primary key of the target table exists.

Finally, the *`update_clause`* and *`insert_clause`* specify how to perform the specific `UPDATE` or `INSERT` for the operation.

There is also a *`delete_clause`* that is used in conjunction with the *`update_clause`*. This clause deletes a row that meets the conditions specified in the clause. The evaluation of the delete condition takes place after the row is updated and is only applied to rows that have been updated. The delete clause is used to insure that rows are not updated to an inappropriate value. The delete clause can either be part of the update clause or as its own part of the `MERGE` statement, but since it only affects rows that have been updated, it makes sense to include it as part of the update clause.

The `MERGE` statement can perform better than using separate `INSERT` and `UPDATE` statements, since the target table only has to be accessed once for both operations. In addition, the `MERGE` statement is a part of the latest SQL standard — Oracle is one of the few vendors who have implemented it at this time.

The `MERGE` verb is a powerful statement, and the best way to understand how it works is to see it in action with two small tables.

An Example

You will be using data from the old familiar EMP table in the SCOTT schema, along with the BONUS table. The BONUS table can be used to store additional compensation for any particular employee. Your boss wants to help those employees who are in the bottom half of their paygrade—those whose SALs (salaries) are below the midpoint between the HISAL and LOSAL listed for their grades in the SALGRADE table. To locate these employees, you would use the following SQL statement, which will be part of the USING clause in the eventual MERGE statement:

```
SELECT ENAME FROM SCOTT.EMP E, SCOTT.SALGRADE S
       WHERE
         (E.SAL > S.LOSAL AND E.SAL < S.HISAL)
         AND E.SAL < ((S.LOSAL + S.HISAL) / 2);
```

There is one problem with this particular query. The query will return eight employees, including four salesmen, whose compensation plans are driven by commissions. Since these folks can increase their income by increasing their commissions, they should not be considered for this one-time bonus. To eliminate the salesmen from this query, simply check to make sure that the COMM value in the EMP table is null, which will produce the following query:

```
SELECT ENAME FROM SCOTT.EMP E, SCOTT.SALGRADE S
       WHERE
         (E.SAL > S.LOSAL AND E.SAL < S.HISAL)
         AND E.SAL < ((S.LOSAL + S.HISAL) / 2)
         AND COMM IS NULL
```

This query will form the source_table clause for your MERGE statement. To build the complete MERGE statement, start by adding the beginning of the MERGE statement to the subquery of the USING clause, as in the following:

```
MERGE INTO SCOTT.BONUS B
    USING (SELECT ENAME FROM SCOTT.EMP E, SCOTT.SALGRADE S
      WHERE
        (E.SAL > S.LOSAL AND E.SAL < S.HISAL)
        AND E.SAL < ((S.LOSAL + S.HISAL) / 2)
        AND COMM IS NULL) E1
```

Your next piece of syntax is to put in the ON clause, which will determine if a row is updated or inserted. This clause is straightforward:

```
ON (B.ENAME = E1.ENAME)
```

The last step in this process is to add in the update and insert clauses. The complete MERGE statement is shown below and included as CH09_MERGE.SQL.

```
MERGE INTO SCOTT.BONUS B
    USING (SELECT ENAME FROM SCOTT.EMP E, SCOTT.SALGRADE S
      WHERE
        (E.SAL > S.LOSAL AND E.SAL < S.HISAL)
        AND E.SAL < ((S.LOSAL + S.HISAL) / 2)
        AND COMM IS NULL) E1
    ON (B.ENAME = E1.ENAME)
```

```
WHEN MATCHED THEN UPDATE SET B.SAL = B.SAL+ 2000
WHEN NOT MATCHED THEN INSERT (ENAME, SAL)
   VALUES(E1.ENAME, 2000);
```

Notice that you do not name the table in the INSERT or UPDATE clause; there is no need for that, since the MERGE clause already identifies the target table.

The MERGE statement is ready to go, but to run it now would be fairly disappointing. The reason is simple: By default, there are no rows in the BONUS table, so all the selected rows would simply receive a new row. To see the MERGE statement at its finest, run the CH09_POPULATE_BONUS.SQL script, which will add a row to the BONUS table for SMITH, with a value of 1,000 for the SAL column, and for CLARK, with a value of 3,000 for the SAL column.

Now you can run the MERGE statement to see some rows updated and some rows inserted. Figure 9-13 shows the result of the statement.

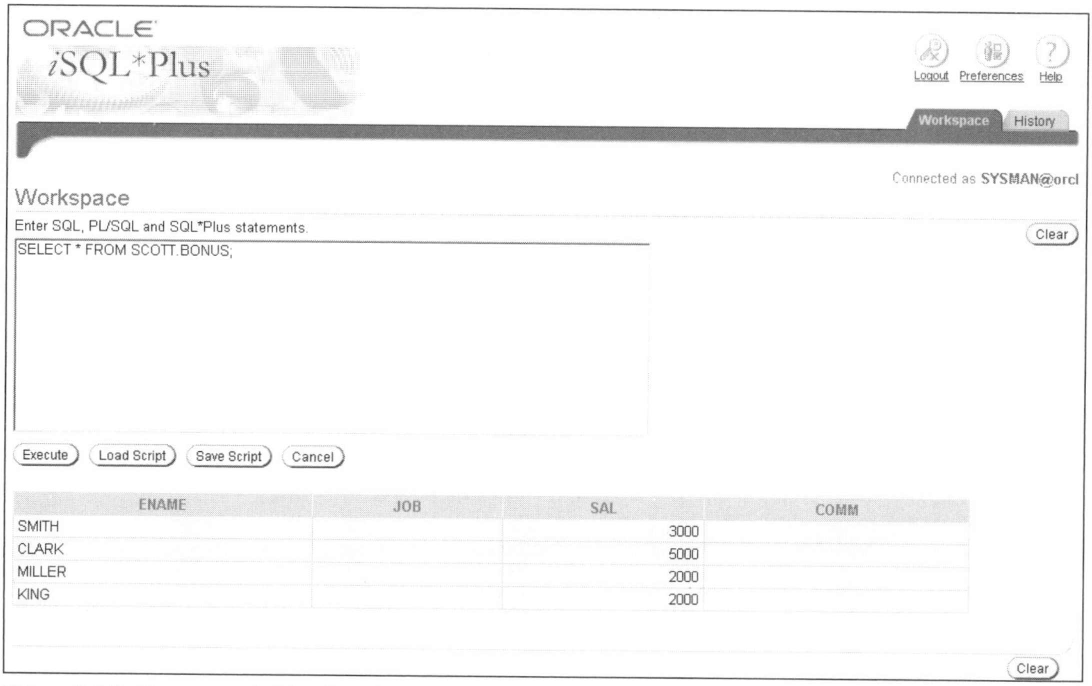

Figure 9-13: The BONUS table after the MERGE.

At this point, the rows in the SCOTT.BONUS table have been inserted, with the first script, and then further modified with the MERGE statement. To return the BONUS table to its original state, you can simply issue a ROLLBACK command to undo the changes. The BONUS table, in its original form, has no rows, so you could also enter

```
DELETE FROM SCOTT.BONUS;
```

to get rid of the new rows, if you wish.

Caveats

The example shown did not do a whole lot, mainly because of the small table that was used to clearly illustrate the effect of the MERGE statement. Typically, you would use MERGE for an import of a large amount of data, as with a data warehouse. In this scenario, the ability to insert, update, and even delete on a large target table in a single pass can improve performance noticeably.

The MERGE cannot be used to circumvent Oracle security, as the user running the statement must have the appropriate UPDATE, INSERT, or DELETE privileges to run the statement. In Oracle Database 10*g*, the MERGE statement does not need to have an INSERT section, in case you wanted to simply update and delete in a single pass.

Finally, the MERGE can only be used when a single row is available in the target table for the selection condition used in the ON clause. In most cases, this means the source table for the MERGE will be linked to the unique primary key of the target table.

TRUNCATE

TRUNCATE is a special piece of SQL syntax. The TRUNCATE keyword performs the same action as the DELETE keyword, with one key difference. When you perform any type of write activity with the other appropriate keywords — INSERT, UPDATE, or DELETE — Oracle logs the changes, as it should, just in case you want to roll back the changes rather than commit them.

With TRUNCATE, the Oracle database does not bother to log the deletion of rows. This elimination can make TRUNCATE much faster than using DELETE to get rid of data. Of course, eliminating log writes means that you can't roll back the action of the SQL statement. In effect, using TRUNCATE is logically like doing a DELETE with an immediate COMMIT statement. Because of this lack of potential forgiveness, you should not use TRUNCATE unless you have determined that you can improve performance with its use, and unless you are really, really, really sure you want those rows gone.

ROWNUM and Ranking

Any SQL statement will return a set of rows from a database, but by default, there is no guarantee of the order the rows will be returned in. You can, of course, specify the way that rows are returned with the ORDER BY clause. You will sometimes want to combine this ordering or rows with the ability to limit the retrieval of rows — in other words, to create a query that will return only a certain number of top values for an expression, such as the top five highest paid people in a company.

There are two ways to produce this result. One way, which uses the ROWNUM pseudocolumn, can be done with any version of Oracle. The other way uses the newer capability provided by analytics.

Using ROWNUM

The first way to produce a result set with a fixed number of ranked rows is to use the pseudocolumn ROWNUM. The ROWNUM pseudocolumn is an "invisible" column that Oracle adds to any result set. You can see the value for this pseudocolumn by including it in the column list of a SELECT.

The ROWNUM pseudocolumn is calculated and assigned as rows are added to the final result set. To use the ROWNUM column to limit the number of rows returned, you use its value as a part of the WHERE clause, as shown in Figure 9-14.

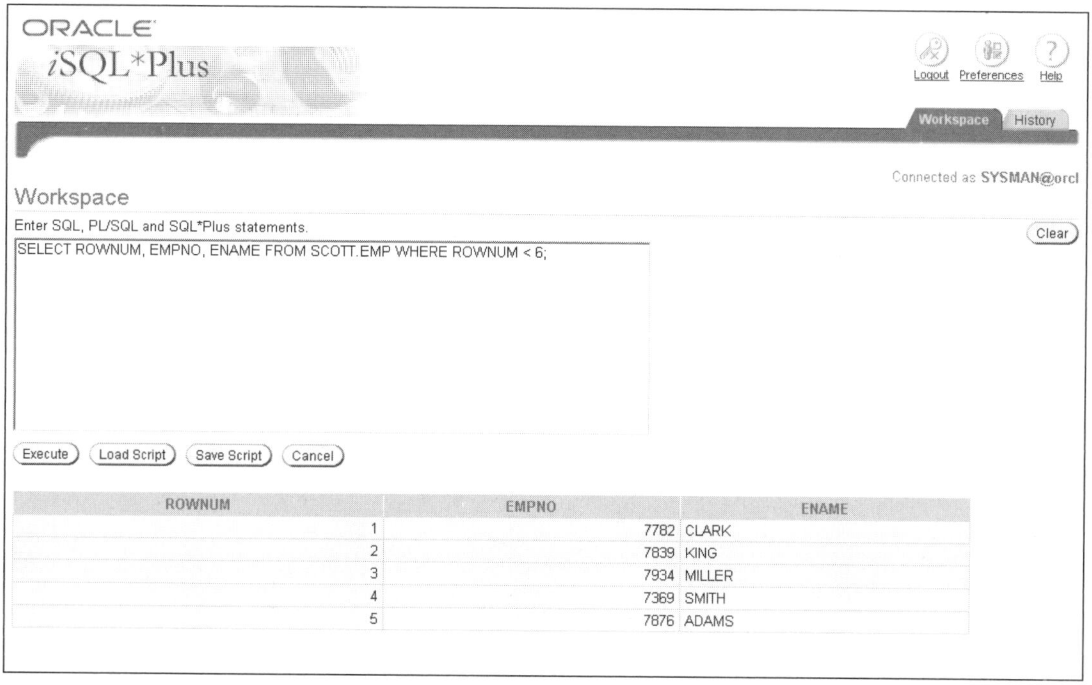

Figure 9-14: Limiting retrieval of rows with ROWNUM.

This simple example, included as CH09_ROWNUM.SQL, illustrates how to use ROWNUM to return the first rows from a result set. But what if you wanted to get the "top" rows from an ordered result set? You would think the following query would work:

```
SELECT ROWNUM, ENAME, SAL FROM SCOTT.EMP WHERE ROWNUM < 6 ORDER BY SAL DESC;
```

but look at the result shown in Figure 9-15.

The result may not be what you expected. The rows are sorted by SAL, but these rows are not the top five salaries in the table. The result is correct once you understand that Oracle assigns ROWNUMs when a row is first added to the result set. The ORDER BY clause is applied *after* the result set is collected, for obvious reasons. So the ROWNUM is, in this case, like an artifact of the original retrieval.

You can still get the desired result by using ROWNUM and a subquery. The subquery returns the complete result set in the proper order, and then you can use ROWNUM in the outer query to limit its result set. The following statement, included as CH09_ROWNUM_SUBQUERY.SQL and shown in Figure 9-16, does work, since the result set created in the subquery is returned to the outer query in the properly sorted order. The ROWNUM in the outer query is used to limit the number of rows returned.

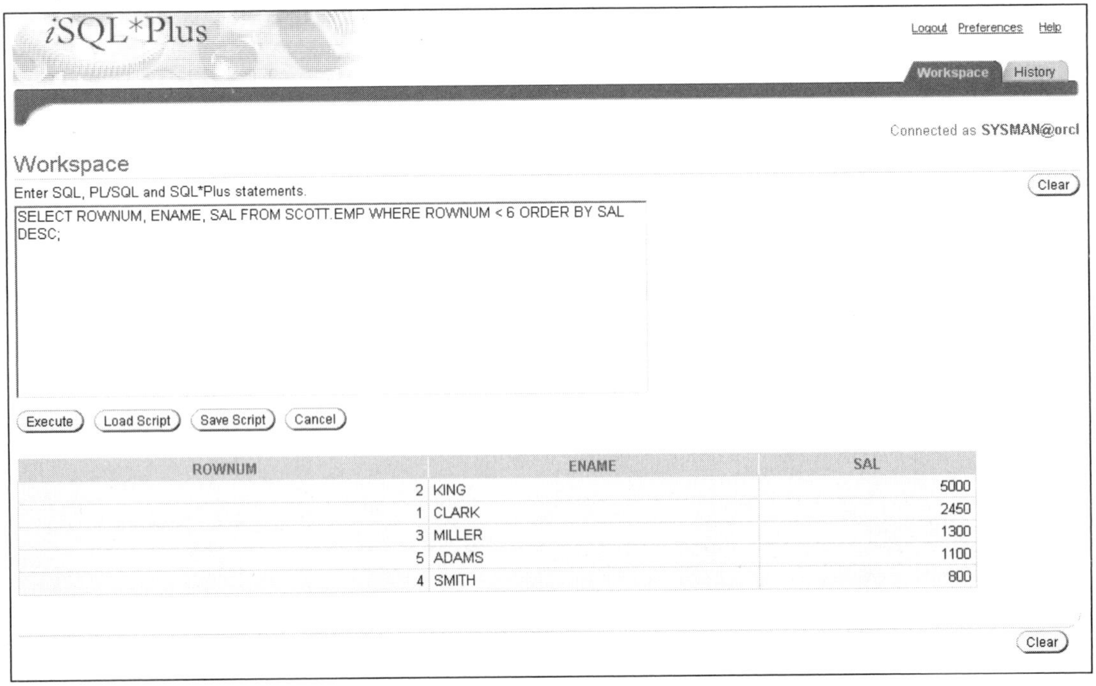

Figure 9-15: An unexpected result.

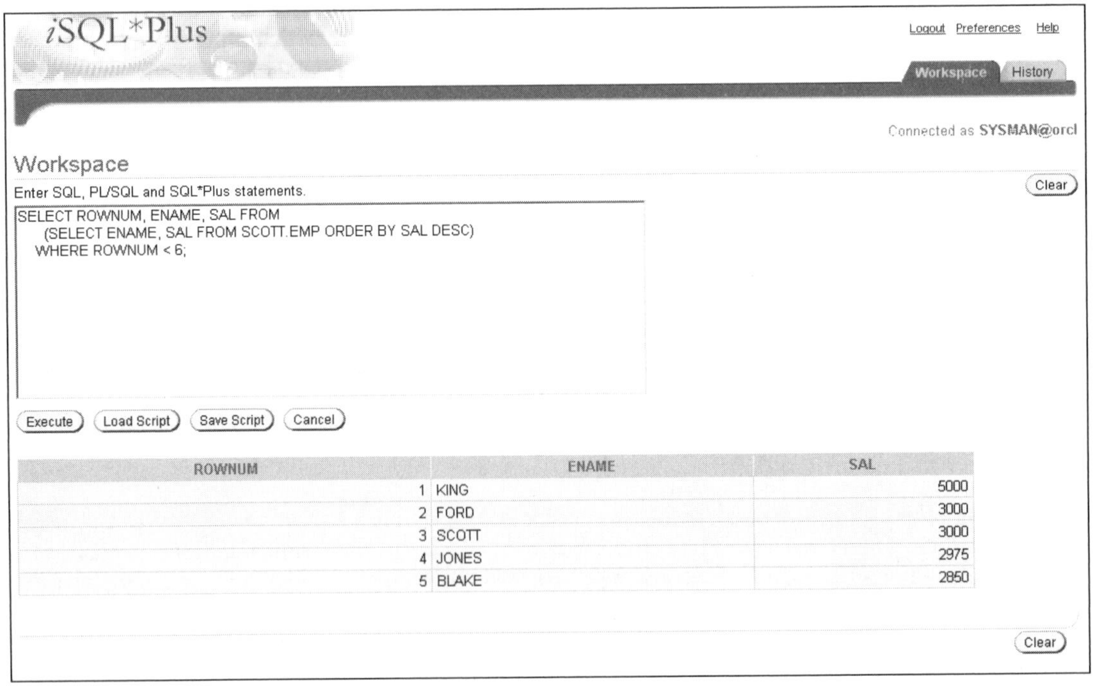

Figure 9-16: Using `ROWNUM` and a subquery to get the right result.

This same approach is needed if you want to get any set of rows other than the "top" set. To get rows from the middle of a result set, using the ROWNUM pseudocolumn, you might think that you could use the following:

```
SELECT ENAME, SAL FROM SCOTT.EMP
    WHERE (ROWNUM > 3 AND ROWNUM < 7)
    ORDER BY SAL
```

This statement would not work, because ROWNUM is assigned as rows are returned to the initial result set. If a row does not remain in the result set because of the WHERE clause, it is discarded. This query retrieves a row, assigns it ROWNUM 1, discards it because that ROWNUM does not fit the selection criteria, and then retrieves another row, which it reassigns the value of 1 for ROWNUM.

You can get the desired result by using the same type of subquery to retrieve the result set and then imposing the selection criteria, as with the following:

```
SELECT ENAME, SAL FROM
      (SELECT ENAME, SAL, ROWNUM R FROM SCOTT.EMP
      ORDER BY R)
    WHERE (R > 3 AND R < 7);
```

Using Analytics

Oracle9*i* offered a whole new set of SQL functions called analytics. The Oracle 10*g* Database release expanded the number of available analytic functions. Analytic functions compute values based on groups of rows and can be used to achieve the same results the ROWNUM pseudocolumn delivered in the previous example.

There is an analytic function called ROW_NUMBER() used to calculate row numbers, but this function can include an ordering clause, as in the following SQL statement, included as CH09_ANALYTIC_ROWNUM1.SQL and shown in Figure 9-17.

```
SELECT ENAME, SAL,
    ROW_NUMBER() OVER (ORDER BY SAL DESC) AS SAL_ORDER FROM SCOTT.EMP;
```

In this single SQL statement, you are able to get row numbers assigned on an ordered set of rows. The analytic function knew to use the ORDER BY clause before assigning a row number.

This is pretty cool, but analytics are much more powerful than this simple example shows. The ROW_NUMBER() analytic function can not only assign row numbers to a single ordered set of rows, but it can be used to assign row numbers to rows while starting the numbering process over for specific groups of row within the result set. Consider this SQL statement, included as CH09_ANALYTIC_ROWNUM2.SQL:

```
SELECT ENAME, SAL,
    ROW_NUMBER() OVER (PARTITION BY DEPTNO ORDER BY SAL DESC) AS SAL_ORDER
    FROM SCOTT.EMP;
```

The results are shown in Figure 9-18.

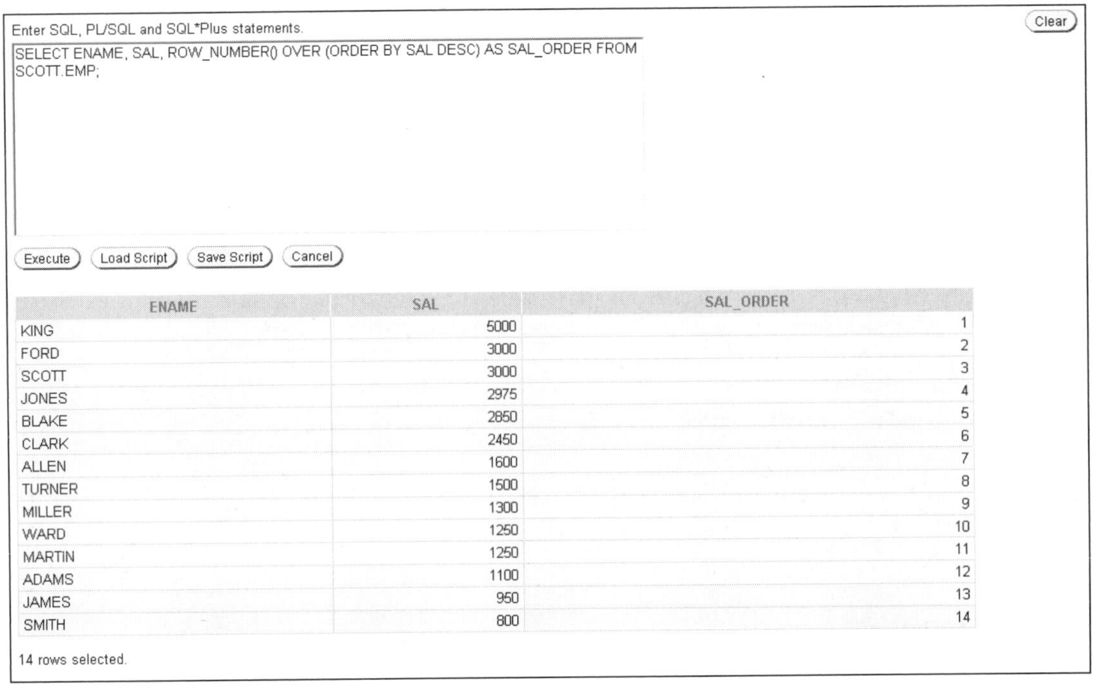

Figure 9-17: The most basic form of an analytic function.

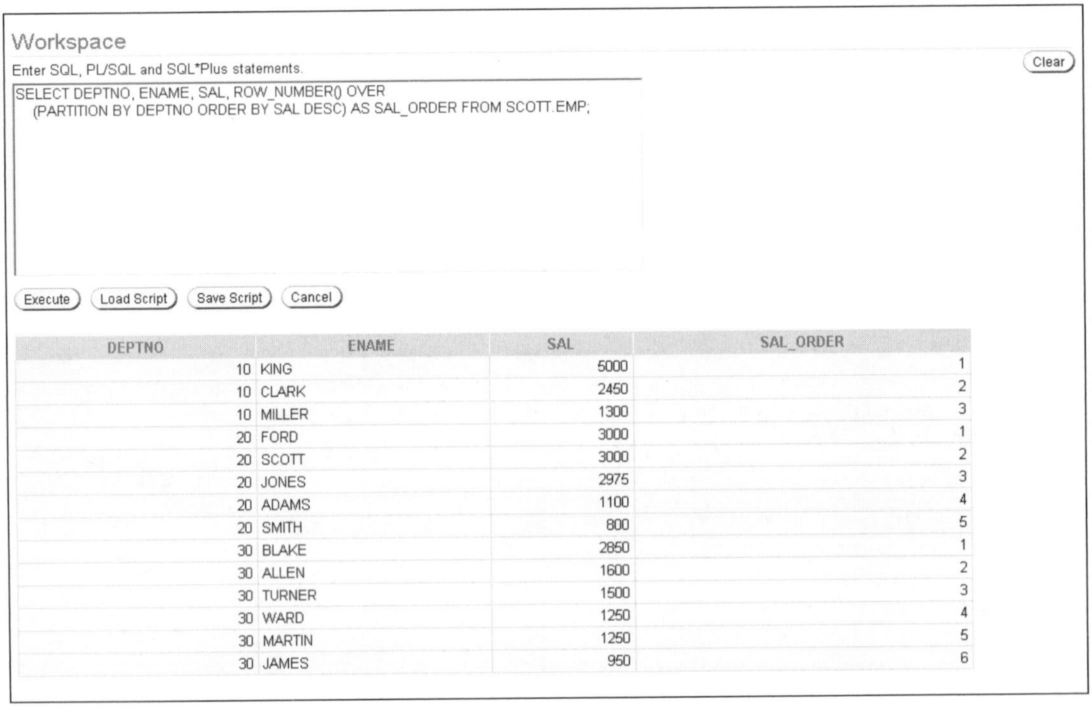

Figure 9-18: An analytic function working over partitions.

Even cooler, right? Finally, you could combine this functionality in a subquery and use the outer query to limit the retrieval of rows, as illustrated with the code in `CH09_ANALYTIC_ROWNUM3.SQL` and shown in Figure 9-19 to only retrieve the employee in each department with the highest salary.

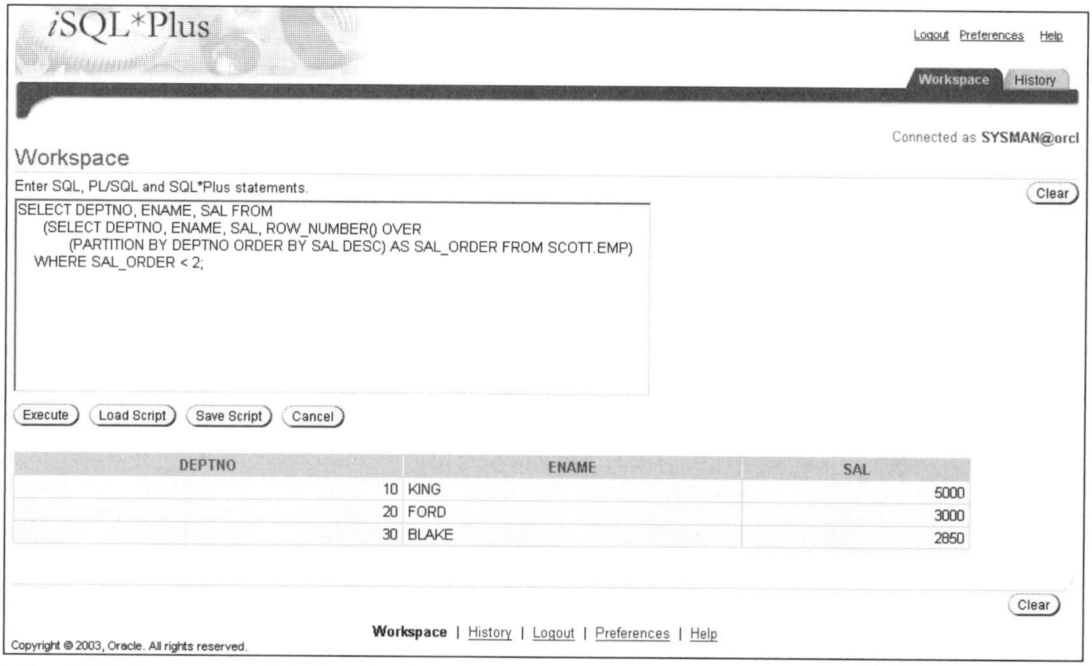

Figure 9-19: Using an analytic function in a subquery.

There is a whole world of functionality encompassed in the use of analytic functions. Analytic functions are discussed in relation to data warehouses, where they are commonly used, and in more detail in Chapter 27, "Business Intelligence Analysis."

Flashback Query

Up to this point, we have been mainly talking about standard SQL, the sort of syntax you can use with Oracle or any other modern relational database. With this topic, however, we are touching on a topic that is uniquely available for the Oracle database.

Flashback query lets you actually go back in time to obtain the results of a query as they would have been returned at some earlier point. Flashback query is supported by the same unique architecture that is used to implement Oracle's multiversion read consistency model, as discussed in Chapter 3, "Handling Multiple Users." That nifty capability has provided Oracle with some significant scalability advantages over the years. Starting with Oracle9*i*, the same architecture delivers the new world of flashback query.

How It Works

Oracle marketing describes flashback query as a time machine. With flashback query, you can get the results of a query as it would have been returned at an earlier point in time. This capability is great for handling those "oops" moments—you know, "oops, I just deleted *and committed* a bunch of rows that I shouldn't have.

The key to flashback query is the rollback segments, which were described in Chapter 3 on multiversion read consistency. As you recall, these segments hold previous images of changed rows, which allows Oracle to present a consistent view of data while not having to use read locks. Since the rollback buffers contain previous versions of data, flashback query lets you go back and retrieve those images.

Syntax

You can use flashback query with any standard SQL statement with the following syntax:

```
SELECT .... FROM table AS OF SCN scn_number | TIMESTAMP timestamp
```

where `scn_number` is a system change number and `timestamp` is a timestamp. The system change number (SCN) is the unique number that Oracle uses to keep track of changed data across the database. It is an arbitrary number, but it comes with the guarantee that a transaction with a larger SCN came later than a smaller SCN. The timestamp is represented as a time value, but be aware that the timestamp approximates an SCN—the SCN is more exact. This small potential inconsistency should not really be a problem, except in very, very high transactional environments, since the timestamp can only vary by a few milliseconds.

An Example of Flashback Query

Although implementing the underlying architecture that supports flashback queries is nontrivial, using flashback query is pretty straightforward. For the purposes of this test case, you start by retrieving the current SCN. You use the following code, which is included as `CH09_GET_SCN.SQL` to retrieve the current number:

```
SELECT DBMS_FLASHBACK.GET_SYSTEM_CHANGE_NUMBER() FROM DUAL;
```

This SQL statement has a couple of new aspects to it. First, you can see that the value returned is the result of a function—the `GET_SYSTEM_CHANGE_NUMBER` function that is included with the PL/SQL package called `DBMS_FLASHBACK`. This package comes with the Oracle database and is used to support a number of features related to flashback capabilities.

The range of built-in packages is enormous—far beyond the scope of this book. The manual for these packages is over 3,700 pages! Even a concise reference like Oracle in a Nutshell *(Authors – Rick Greenwald and Dave Kreines, O'Reilly and Associates) requires over 200 pages to completely document the packages, procedures, and functions, as well as their syntax. But there is a wealth of functionality in these packages, so you might want to spend some time getting familiar with them.*

The second new part of the SQL statement is the target table `DUAL`. This table has been a part of the Oracle database for many revisions. The `DUAL` table has a single column (`DUMMY`) and a single row. The purpose of the `DUAL` table is to use as a placeholder when you want to get information back from Oracle without returning any data—like the SQL statement above that gets the current SCN.

Once you have used the preceding statement to get the SCN number, either copy it to the clipboard or some file, since you will be using it later to demonstrate flashback.

Thus prepared, you are ready for anything the world can throw at you. The world, in the form of your boss, decides that those salesmen are not adding much value to company. He is thinking about getting rid of them, but first he wants to see their compensation. So you run a simple SQL statement that returns the results shown in Figure 9-20.

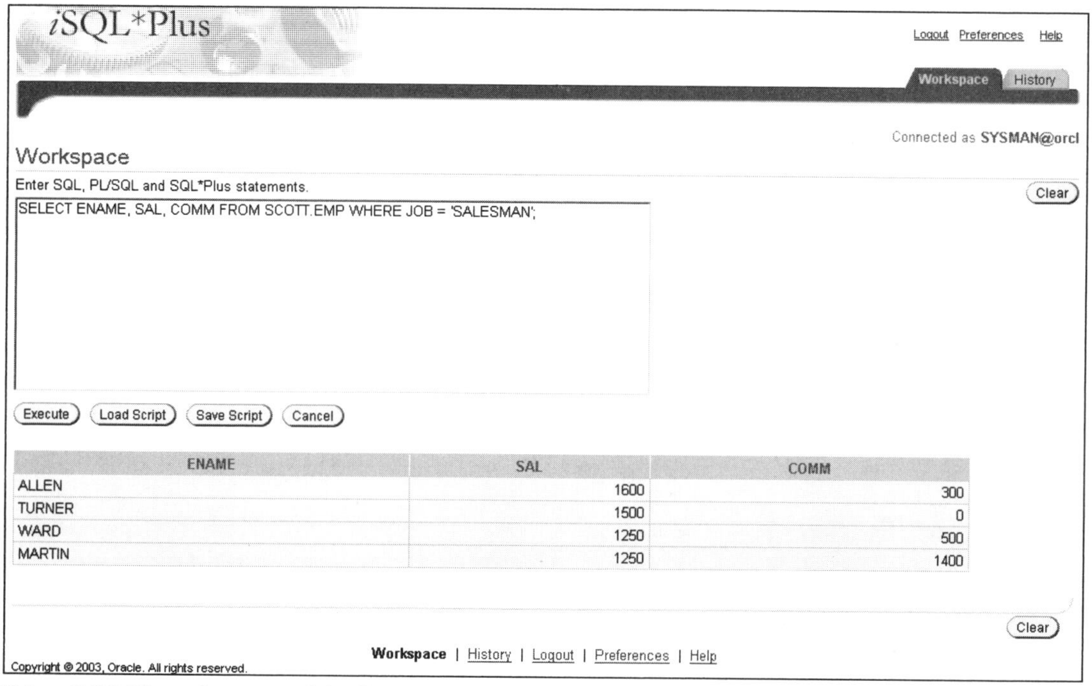

Figure 9-20: The salesmen, originally.

On reviewing the data, your boss decides he would be better off without the sales reps, so he tells you to delete their rows — the IT equivalent of being fired. You execute the following statement:

```
DELETE FROM SCOTT.EMP WHERE JOB = 'SALESMAN';
```

but you ask your boss again if he is sure he wants to get rid of the reps. He vehemently restates his intention, so you execute a `COMMIT` statement to make the changes permanent. After this deletion, you run the SQL statement again to show that the salesmen are truly gone, as shown in Figure 9-21.

Your boss leaves, satisfied.

But he returns shortly thereafter. It seems he was a bit hasty to relieve himself of the salesmen, with employment rules and all. How can you find out the salesmen and their information?

Flashback query to the rescue. As you can see in Figure 9-22, using the flashback syntax along with the SCN gives you back the rows in the table as they existed before any of your deleting started.

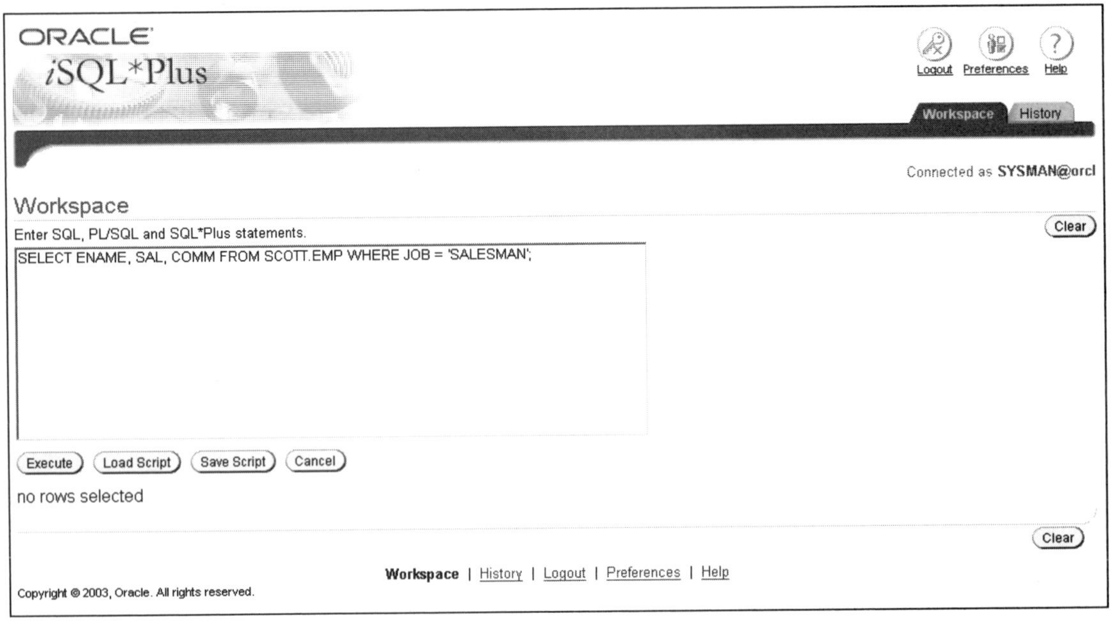

Figure 9-21: The salesmen, gone.

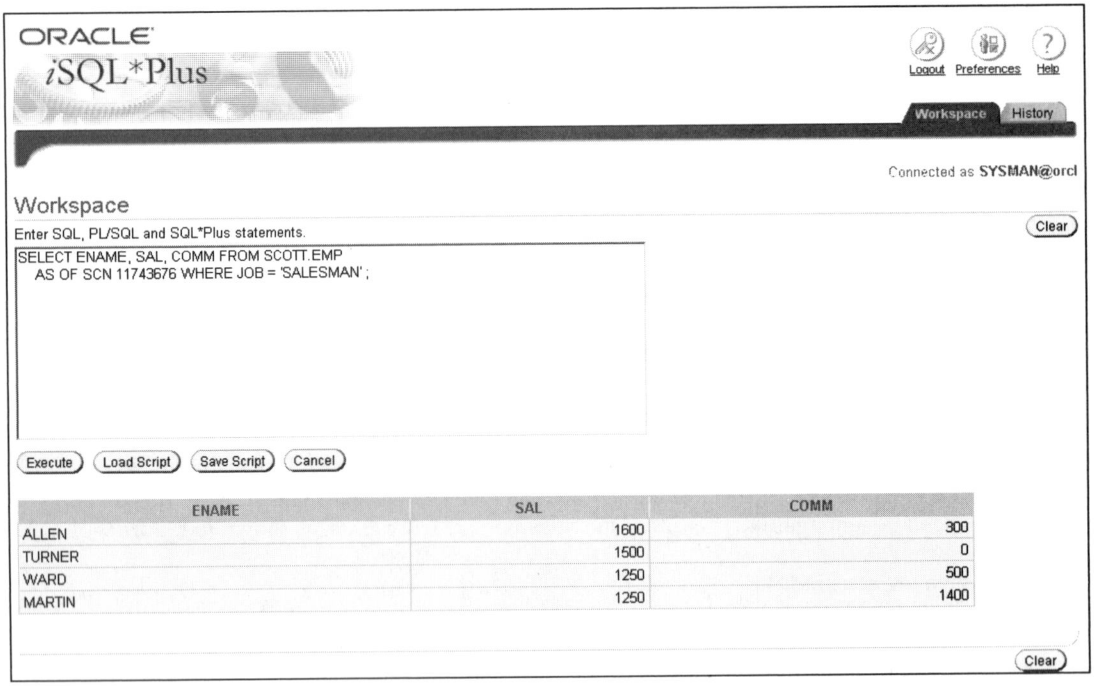

Figure 9-22: Flashback in time.

This handy capability is only available in the Oracle database, starting with Oracle9*i*.

If you performed the deletion and commit described in this section, you can use the `CH09_RESTORE_SALESMEN.SQL` script to add the rows back into the `SCOTT.EMP` table.

Caveats

Flashback query really works, as the preceding example demonstrates, but flashback capability is, by nature, limited in its range.

The flashback information comes from the rollback segments, which are finite. This limitation means you can only roll back so far in time. If you attempt to roll back beyond the range of the rollback segments, you will get an Oracle error ORA-01555, which tells you that there was not enough information in the rollback segments to retrieve the proper version of the data.

How far back can you go? The timeframe depends on the overall activity in the database and the size of the rollback buffers. Keep in mind that the rollback buffers log every change to the database, including internal tables that Oracle updates itself. Because of this limitation, you probably don't want to use flashback query to go back in time very far. As with the above example, using flashback to gather data for error correction is probably appropriate. Using flashback for data warehouse type drill down is probably not.

Extended Flashback Capabilities

Flashback query was introduced as part of the Oracle9*i* database. With the 10*g* release, Oracle has added a whole host of additional flashback capabilities, including the following:

- Flashback database, which allows you to rewind the entire database to a previous point in time. This option is much less intrusive than having to perform a point-in-time recovery
- Flashback table, which rolls back an entire table to a particular point in time.
- Flashback version query, which lets you see the versions a row has gone through over time
- Flashback transaction query, which lets you view the changes made by a transaction. This information can help diagnose problems in transactions.
- Flashback drop, which helps to address the ultimate "oops" moment—just after you drop a table.

All of these capabilities work in a similar manner to flashback query. Some of these flashback option require you to set up some additional files for use by Oracle. For more information on their usage and syntax, refer to the Oracle documentation.

Returning Data from Write Operations

Performing write operations— `INSERT`, `UPDATE`, and `DELETE`—affects your Oracle database. Once you commit these write changes, they are permanent. Although flashback operations, as described previously, can help you find out the prior state of your data in some cases, it might be nice to see how data was affected by a write operation before you committed the changes. There may also be times when you want to use the values affected by a write operation in your programming logic.

You can use the RETURNING clause with any of these write operations to return data affected by the operations. The code for this option is as follows:

```
sql_write_statement RETURNING expression_list INTO variable_list
```

For any of these statements, the values returned are those in the expression list for the rows that have been affected. You can use aggregate functions, such as COUNT, in the expression list, but you cannot combine aggregate expressions and individual row values.

For an UPDATE or DELETE statement, an array of expression results will be returned when more than one row has been affected. If you are using this clause with PL/SQL, the variable list could be a PL/SQL record or table of PL/SQL records, which are described in Chapter 16, "PL/SQL and SQL."

Chapter 16 also describes the use of FORALL to insert multiple rows into the database with one operation. For these scenarios, the RETURNING clause could return an array for an INSERT.

Additional Extensions

As mentioned in the beginning of this chapter, there are more particular clauses and capabilities of using SQL with Oracle than can be covered in a mere two chapters. Further discussions of specific areas of SQL appear later in this book, including the following:

- Chapter 13, "Functions"
- Chapter 20, "Regular Expressions and Expression Filter"
- Chapter 27, "Business Intelligence Analysis"

Although even these extended discussions will still not cover the complete power and functionality delivered by Oracle's SQL, you should have enough to implement most functionality and, most importantly, have a firm basis to investigate all the facets of SQL and Oracle in more detail.

Summary

SQL, a powerful set-oriented language, has a wealth of functionality and features. This chapter covered some of the most used and useful of these capabilities.

The chapter covered extended conditions, such as LIKE and EXISTS, to provide more logical capabilities to shape your SQL statement results. The chapter also covered both set comparisons, like ALL and SOME, and set operations, such as UNION.

The MERGE statement is a new feature of the SQL language that combines the functionality of an INSERT and an UPDATE to allow you to handle complex logical write operations with a single pass through the database. The chapter also included an introduction to the use of analytics, one of the most powerful features to enter the SQL language. In addition, flashback query was discussed, which uses an extension from standard SQL to take advantage of some unique Oracle functionality and can let you go back in time to view the state of the database at an earlier moment.

10

Indexes

Prior to the advent of the relational database, database users would have to specifically know how to get at a particular piece of data. The navigation path to that data had to be included as a part of the request for the data. One of the biggest advances relational databases made was to eliminate the need for this extra information, which was usually meaningless to the end user, and a source of complexity and errors.

Oracle, like all true relational databases, does not require any navigation information in an SQL query. Instead, Oracle maps the logical data request to the underlying physical structures. This feat makes things easier for developers and users — but it doesn't eliminate the need to get data quickly and efficiently.

In response to a query, the Oracle database could simply retrieve all possible rows that could answer a query and then eliminate the rows that don't match the selection criteria. But this could be inordinately inefficient. What if a user wanted to get a handful of rows out of a pool of millions? Worse yet, what if a user wanted to get rows from a combination of tables, which would cause Oracle to compare all the rows from all the tables in an enormous Cartesian product?

Indexes are a way to reduce the overhead of these common data operations. In true relational fashion, the existence of indexes is transparent to the user. But an index, properly used, can dramatically speed up retrieval operations. Even more importantly, an index can provide consistent performance for random data access when data is fairly evenly distributed). When a query requests a row, it doesn't matter whether the row is located in the overall table; an index will perform the same number of I/O operations to get the row. In the field of performance, expectation is everything, so this consistent performance is, in some ways, at least as important as optimal performance.

This chapter covers all of the index types supported by Oracle Database 10*g*, including B-tree indexes, reverse indexes, bitmap indexes, function-based indexes, and domain indexes. In addition, this chapter looks at index-organized tables as well as clustered tables. Finally, the chapter concludes with some broad advice on the design and use of indexes.

Index Basics

The Oracle database supports a number of different types of indexes, but all or most of these index types share a number of basic characteristics. All indexes are used to speed access to data. All indexes use some kind of internal structure to either reduce the amount of data required to read to determine which rows to retrieve, or deliver to those rows faster than scanning through the table that contains the rows. And all indexes are transparent to users, which means you can add, change, or drop indexes without changing any application code.

How an Index Works

The power of an index to speed data retrieval comes from one of the most basic facts of modern computing architecture — the slowest function in the overall system is retrieving data from disk. When this simple physical fact is coupled with usage patterns of users, the power of an index becomes clear.

The example at the start of the chapter pointed out how going through all the rows in a table to select a small percentage of them for a query could require a lot of resources. An index is designed to let the Oracle database find and retrieve specific rows with less overall I/O.

The central way an index accomplishes this is by storing a subset of the information in the complete row in a more compact and searchable organization. These attributes mean that there is less I/O involved to use an index to locate a particular piece of data, improving performance.

In addition, an index, which is much smaller than the table it operates on, is more likely to be cached than the table itself. Using an index that is completely cached in memory can be an extremely fast way to access data.

An index can be used to determine which rows should be returned for a query. An index entry includes a pointer to the actual data row, which is the fastest way to retrieve a data row. Once the Oracle database has used the index to identify target rows, the pointer is used to retrieve the row.

Usage patterns come into play when you are deciding what indexes to create for a particular table. Your users may want different columns in a table at different times, but they will typically use a small number of columns to select and sort data in queries. These columns are ideal candidates for indexes.

An Index in Action

In this chapter, we will use *i*SQL*Plus to show the effects of indexes on typical queries. We will use some of the sample tables that come with the Oracle 10*g* Database for these examples. To show the effects of index usage cleanly, we have always flushed the shared SQL pool and data buffers before running the queries to eliminate the effect that caching has on the performance of queries, using the SQL script `CH10_CLEAR.SQL`.

> *Note that this technique of clearing the buffers is only to demonstrate the absolute effect of indexes for this book. In the real world, you would want to test under production conditions, so if an SQL statement was to be frequently cached, you would want to replicate that in your test scenario.*

In addition, we turned `AUTOTRACE` on in *i*SQL*Plus so that the execution plan would be displayed to prove that Oracle used or did not use an index. Finally, we turned timing on, so that the total elapsed time for the query would be displayed.

To show the overall effect of the index, we used a query to return a count of the rows in the `PRODUCT_DESCRIPTIONS` table. In Figure 10-1, you can see the results of that query, included as `CH10_INDEX.SQL`—an index was used, and the query took about 0.17 seconds.

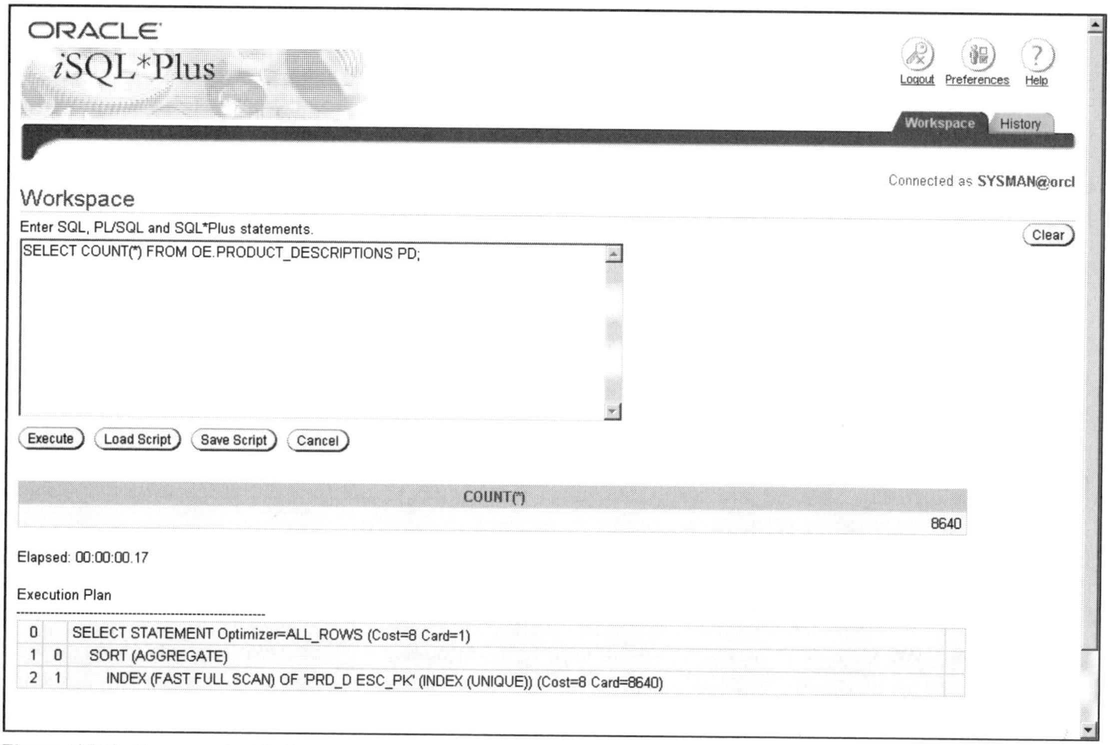

Figure 10-1: Query using index.

To demonstrate the same query without an index, we used a hint to force a complete table scan of the table.

> *We don't like using hints, for a number of reasons, which are explained in Chapter 28, "Optimization," but they serve a useful function here for demonstration purposes.*

As Figure 10-2 shows, the same query run with a hint that disallows index usage, `CH10_NO_INDEX.SQL`, took over 50 percent longer.

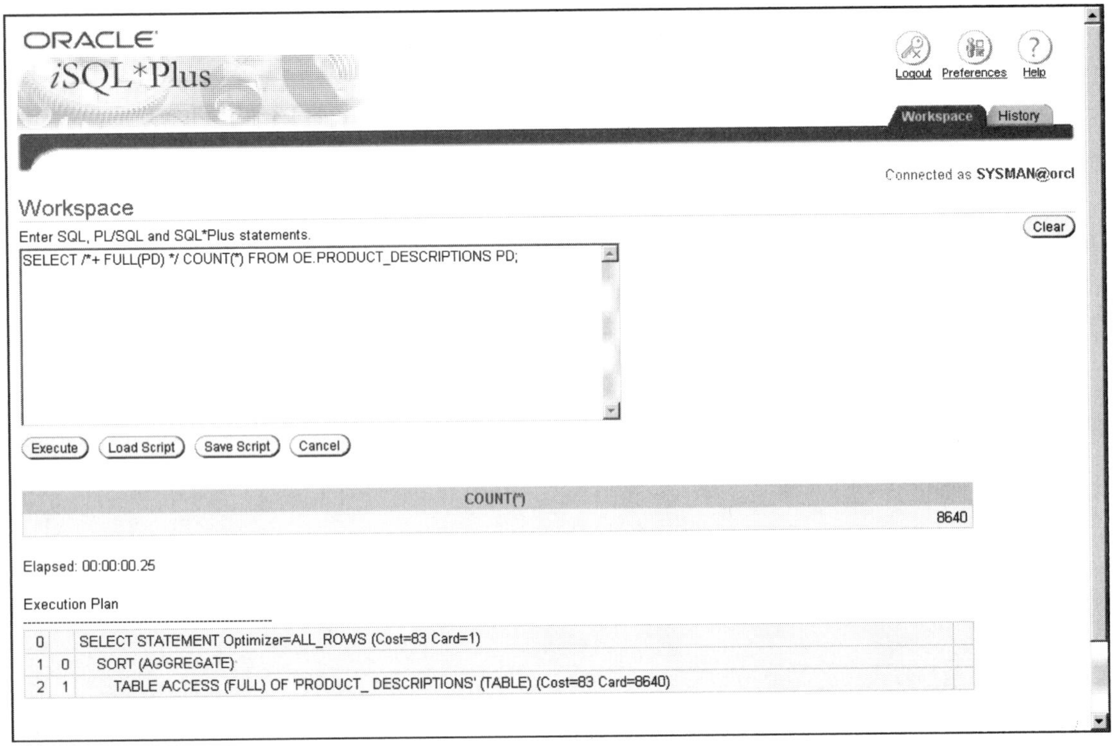

Figure 10-2: Query not using index.

Is an Index Always Used?

At this point, you may be thinking that there is something wrong with this explanation. If the slowest part of the query process is retrieving data from disk, and if using an index requires retrieving the index and then retrieving data, isn't that causing more I/O instead of less I/O? You do have a point.

Just because an index exists that can be used in a query does not mean that it will be used in a query. For instance, if you were going to select 80 percent of the rows in a table, it would most likely be faster to simply scan through the entire table to eliminate the undesired 20 percent of the rows. In fact, the Oracle database can read database blocks very fast, so if a query is going to select a significant number of rows in a table, Oracle will chose not to use the index for faster performance.

The following example in *i*SQL*Plus illustrates this clearly. The queries used are almost exactly the same—both select from the `PRODUCT_DESCRIPTIONS` table, based on a selection criteria. The first query, `CH10_USE_TABLESCAN.SQL`, returns 90 rows, and Oracle determined that it would be faster to do a table scan for the results, as shown in Figure 10-3. For the display shown in this figure, we included commands in the script to only show the execution plan and suppress the display of the results of the query.

1749	HU	DIMM - 256MB	Memória-DIMM: RAM - 256 MB (100 MHz-es regisztrált SDRAM)
1749	ESA	DIMM - 256MB	Memoria DIMM: 256 MB de RAM. (SDRAM Registrada de 100 MHz)
1749	ZHT	DIMM - 256MB	□□□ DIMM□RAM 256 MB□(100-MHz □□□ SDRAM)
1749	TR	DIMM - 256MB	Bellek DIMM: RAM 256 MB. (100-MHz Kayıtlı SDRAM)
1749	SF	DIMM - 256 Mt	DIMM-muisti: RAM 256 Mt. (100 MHz Registered SDRAM)
1749	PTB	DIMM - 256MB	DIMM de Memória: 256 MB RAM. (SDRAM Registrada de 100-MHz)
1749	RO	DIMM - 256MB	DIMM de memorie: RAM 256 MO. (SDRAM înregistrat 100MHz)
1749	RU	DIMM - 256MB	Модуль памяти DIMM: ОЗУ 256 Мб. (SDRAM с номинальной частотой 100 МГц, зарегистрир.)
1749	S	DIMM - 256MB	DIMM-minne: RAM 256 MB. (100 MHz registrerat SDRAM)
1749	EL	DIMM - 256MB	Μνήμη DIMM: RAM 256 MB. (καταχωρημένη SDRAM 100-MHz)

PRODUCT_ID	LANGUAGE_	TRANSLATED_NAME	TRANSLATED_DESCRIPTION
1749	E	DIMM - 256MB	Memoria DIMM: 256 MB de RAM. (SDRAM Registrada de 100 MHz)
1749	DK	DIMM - 256MB	DIMM-hukommelse: RAM 256 MB. (100-MHz registreret SDRAM)
1749	D	DIMM - 256MB	Memory DIMM: RAM 256 MB. (100-MHz registrierter SDRAM)
1749	AR	DIMM - 256MB	DIMM للذاكرة: RAM ميجا بايت 256 سعة. (SDRAM 100 ميجا هيرتز مسجل)
1749	CS	DIMM - 256MB	Paměť DIMM: RAM 256 MB. (100-MHz SDRAM s registrem)
1749	CA	DIMM - 256MB	Memòria DIMM: RAM de 256 MB. (SDRAM registrada a 100 MHz)

390 rows selected.

Elapsed: 00:00:02.89

Execution Plan

0		SELECT STATEMENT Optimizer=ALL_ROWS (Cost=84 Card=116 Bytes= 32828)
1	0	SORT (ORDER BY) (Cost=84 Card=116 Bytes=32828)
2	1	TABLE ACCESS (FULL) OF 'PRODUCT_ DESCRIPTIONS' (TABLE) (Cost=83 Card=116 Bytes=32828)

Clear

Workspace | History | Logout | Preferences | Help

Figure 10-3: Choosing to scan the table.

The second query, `CH10_USE_INDEX.SQL`, delivers 30 rows, at which point Oracle determined that using the index would be faster, as shown in Figure 10-4.

The job of the Oracle optimizer is to select the fastest way to retrieve data — a job that it performed well in both cases shown. With its awareness of how the Oracle database works, the optimizer selected a different execution plan for two similar queries, based on the number of rows to be retrieved and the efficiency of the different retrieval methods.

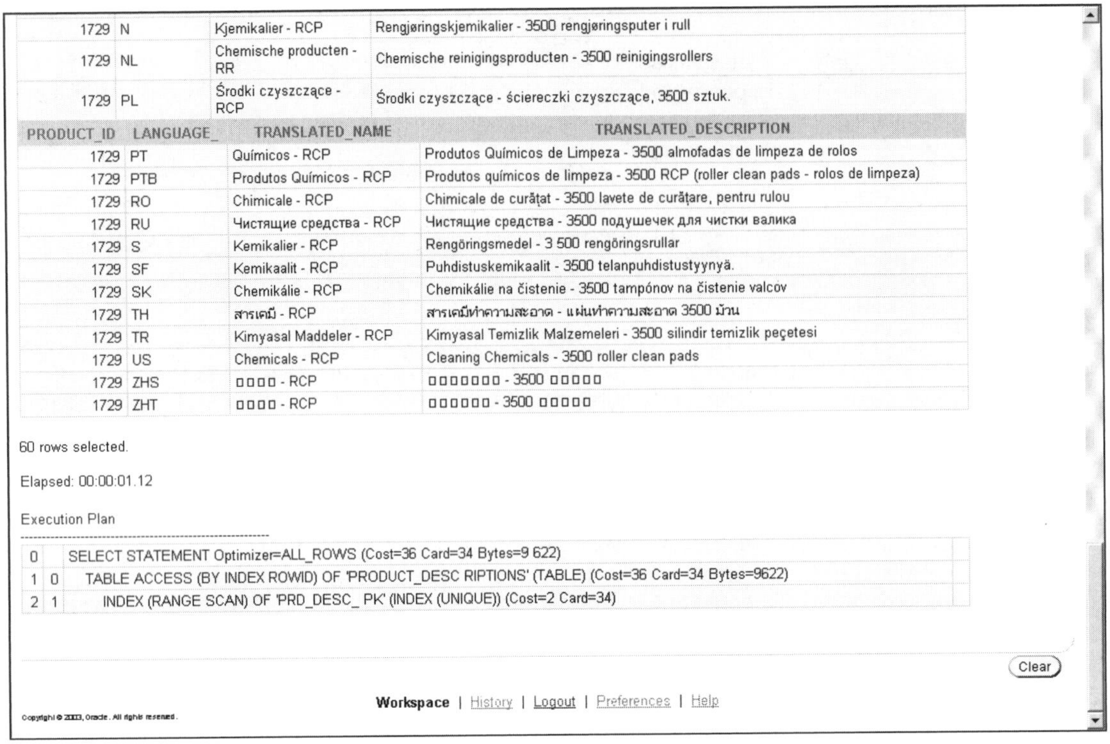

1729	N	Kjemikalier - RCP	Rengjøringskjemikalier - 3500 rengjøringsputer i rull
1729	NL	Chemische producten - RR	Chemische reinigingsproducten - 3500 reinigingsrollers
1729	PL	Środki czyszczące - RCP	Środki czyszczące - ściereczki czyszczące, 3500 sztuk.
PRODUCT_ID	LANGUAGE_	TRANSLATED_NAME	TRANSLATED_DESCRIPTION
1729	PT	Químicos - RCP	Produtos Químicos de Limpeza - 3500 almofadas de limpeza de rolos
1729	PTB	Produtos Químicos - RCP	Produtos químicos de limpeza - 3500 RCP (roller clean pads - rolos de limpeza)
1729	RO	Chimicale - RCP	Chimicale de curățat - 3500 lavete de curățare, pentru rulou
1729	RU	Чистящие средства - RCP	Чистящие средства - 3500 подушечек для чистки валика
1729	S	Kemikalier - RCP	Rengöringsmedel - 3 500 rengöringsrullar
1729	SF	Kemikaalit - RCP	Puhdistuskemikaalit - 3500 telanpuhdistustyynyä.
1729	SK	Chemikálie - RCP	Chemikálie na čistenie - 3500 tampónov na čistenie valcov
1729	TH	สารเคมี - RCP	สารเคมีทำความสะอาด - แผ่นทำความสะอาด 3500 ม้วน
1729	TR	Kimyasal Maddeler - RCP	Kimyasal Temizlik Malzemeleri - 3500 silindir temizlik peçetesi
1729	US	Chemicals - RCP	Cleaning Chemicals - 3500 roller clean pads
1729	ZHS	□□□□ - RCP	□□□□□□□ - 3500 □□□□□
1729	ZHT	□□□□ - RCP	□□□□□□ - 3500 □□□□□

60 rows selected.

Elapsed: 00:00:01.12

Execution Plan

```
----------------------------------------------------------
0     SELECT STATEMENT Optimizer=ALL_ROWS (Cost=36 Card=34 Bytes=9 622)
1  0    TABLE ACCESS (BY INDEX ROWID) OF 'PRODUCT_DESC RIPTIONS' (TABLE) (Cost=36 Card=34 Bytes=9622)
2  1      INDEX (RANGE SCAN) OF 'PRD_DESC_ PK' (INDEX (UNIQUE)) (Cost=2 Card=34)
```


Figure 10-4: Choosing to use an index.

Keys

The information that makes up the content of an index is known as a key. You can think of a key as a logical entity that identifies a particular index entry.

A key can consist of one or more columns in a database table. You can also have a key that is based on a function, as described later in the section on function-based indexes. Each column in a key can have its own sort order (ascending or descending). The entire key is used to determine uniqueness, if specified as an attribute for the index.

If a key consists of more than one column, a query can use the leading columns to improve performance without using all of the columns. For instance, if an index key is made up of `COLUMN_A`, `COLUMN_B`, and `COLUMN_C`, Oracle could use the index for selection criteria based on `COLUMN_A` alone, on `COLUMN_A` and `COLUMN_B`, on `COLUMN_A` and `COLUMN_C`, or on all three columns. Oracle, from version 9*i* on, includes the ability to use an index for selection criteria that does not include leading columns, such as `COLUMN_C` alone, but this use of the index does not necessarily provide the same performance efficiency as the use of the entire index or the leading columns.

Index Attributes

Most of the index types described later in this chapter can have a number of different attributes. These attributes contribute to the functionality and performance of an index.

Transparency

Any discussion of index attributes should start with a restatement of the obvious: The existence and use of an index is completely transparent to users and applications. You can add or drop indexes without changing anything in your SQL. You saw this effect in action in the first example — the same query would run with or without an index and return the same results.

This attribute makes it much easier to investigate whether an index can help the overall performance of your applications, since you can add and drop indexes without having to adjust the SQL access code in your application.

Consistent Performance

Data is almost inevitably accumulated over time, which means that the overall amount of data stored increases over time. If all data access were simply dependent on the amount of I/O necessary to find and retrieve data, increasing volumes of data would lead to increasing response times.

A key characteristic of indexes is that they provide relatively consistent performance, regardless of the size of the underlying table, given an even distribution of values. Because of this, indexes are invaluable in virtually all enterprise databases.

Sort Order

Indexes, by default, store values in a sorted order — either ascending, which is the default, or descending. This powerful attribute can help to improve performance in three ways.

First, the sorted nature of an index allows the Oracle database to select data based on simple comparisons. If an index is sorted in ascending order, and a particular index entry is greater than the target value, Oracle knows that there are no matching values past this index entry. The B-tree index, described later in this chapter, makes use of this fact in its internal structure.

Second, the sorted nature of an index makes it easy for Oracle to select ranges of data. If the index entries are in ascending sorted order, all Oracle has to do is to find the beginning of the range as a starting point and simply walk through the index entries until it reaches a value that is greater than the end of the range.

Last, and certainly not least, is the reduction in post-selection sorting that is required when an index is used. If a user wants data sorted in a particular way, and the index entries are already sorted in this way, the Oracle database will not have to perform any additional sorting once the rows have been selected through the index.

Keep in mind that using a descending sort order can end up with your index blocks being less populated than using an ascending sort order. If you are using an index with ascending order, and the Oracle database notices that you are continually adding higher values to the right of the index, the database will adjust the way it does index block splits. Normally, when Oracle attempts to add a value to an index block that is full, the existing values for the block are split evenly between the existing block and a new block, as shown in Figure 10-5.

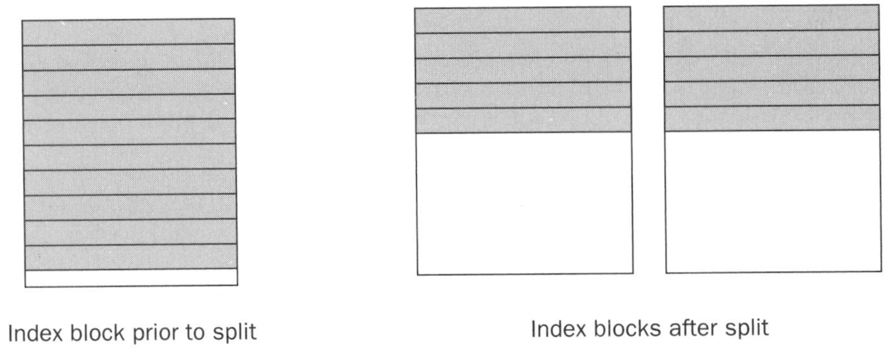

Figure 10-5: Normal index block split.

If you are continually adding values to an index, Oracle leaves all the data in the existing block and just begins to add data to the new block, as shown in Figure 10-6. This type of split is referred to as a "90/10" leaf split, although Oracle retains 100 percent of the existing data in the existing block.

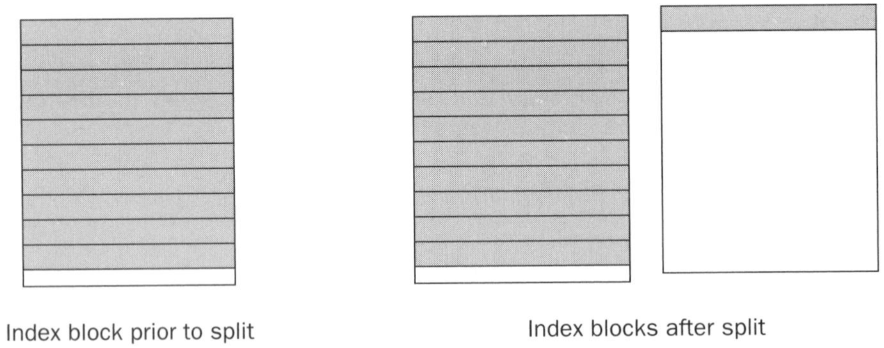

Figure 10-6: "90/10" leaf split.

This "90/10" split will leave the existing block more heavily populated and give the new block more room to grow. Performing a series of "90/10" splits will end up with a set of blocks are completely populated, with one block at the end that is partially populated. With a series of normal block splits, all the blocks will be populated at around 50 percent. This extra space can lead to more I/O, which can affect overall performance.

Uniqueness

An index is often used to speed the retrieval of randomly accessed rows in a data table. An index can be very useful for rapidly accessing a single row if the values in the index are unique.

You can specify that an index only has unique values when you create the index. The index will enforce the uniqueness of the key values as rows are added or modified.

As described in Chapter 11, "Constraints," a constraint can also be used to force a value to be unique. Oracle creates an index to enforce this constraint-based uniqueness.

NULL Values

NULL values, as discussed in Chapter 3, "Handling Multiple Users," are an important part of a relational database. A NULL value indicates the absence of value, so both A = B and A != B are false if either A or B are NULL values.

An Oracle index does not have an index entry if the key for the associated table is NULL, with the exception of the bitmap index type. Because of this, even an index with a uniqueness constraint, as described in the previous section, can exist on a table with multiple NULL keys.

B-Tree Indexes

The default type of index used in an Oracle database is the B-tree index. A B-tree index is designed to provide both rapid access to individual rows and quick access to groups of rows within a range. The B-tree index does this by performing a succession of value comparisons. Each comparison eliminates many of the rows in the potential result set from consideration, which can significantly improve query performance.

How It Works

A B-tree index has three basic components, as shown in Figure 10-7: a root page, which is the entry point to the index structure, one or more levels of branch pages, and leaf pages, the lowest level of the tree.

This description is valid for B-tree indexes with more than one level. A single-level index will only have a root page and no levels of branch pages.

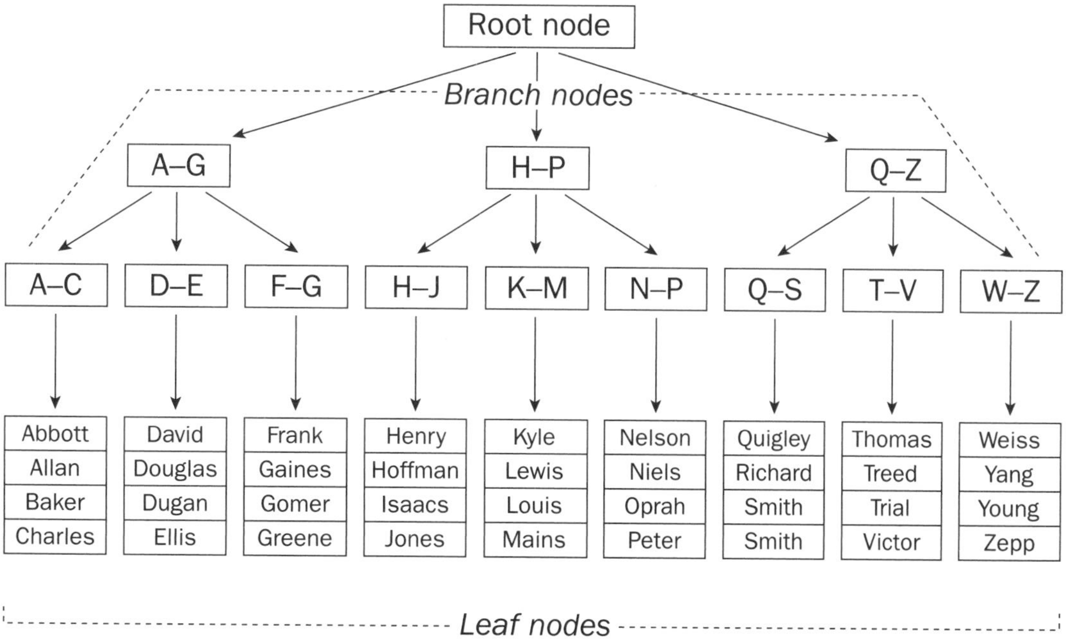

Figure 10-7: Structure of a B-tree index.

Each branch page contains a number of entries, each of which points to either another level of branch pages or a leaf page. Each entry has the maximum value for the next level of pages. For instance, if a request to the index shown in Figure 10-7 were to ask for a value of "aaron," the search would branch to the left at the root page, to the left again at the first level of branch pages, and, using the second level of branch pages, to the leftmost leaf page.

The leaf pages contain the actual values for the index and a `ROWID` that points to the row the index entry represents. An index leaf page also has a pointer to the next and previous index leaf pages, which makes it easy to walk through the index to get a series of rows in a range of values.

As leaf pages fill up, they will split into two leaf pages and the branch pages will be modified accordingly. Occasionally, a branch page may also have to be split.

As you can see, the idea behind the B-tree index is to allow the Oracle database to make a series of decisions about the location of a potential index entry. Each decision effectively eliminates half of the remaining potential index entries, which makes finding individual rows quick and efficient. When this performance improvement is added to the virtues of pre-sorting the entries, you can see how a B-tree index can help reduce I/O operations and improve performance.

B-Tree Index Myths

The subject of database administration and maintenance are too broad to be effectively dealt with in this, a book aimed primarily at developers. However, there are some common myths about how to feed and care for B-tree indexes that we should take some time to debunk in this space. Many thanks to Richard Foote and others who contribute to the comp.databases.oracle.server newsgroup (an excellent resource) for their help in understanding these issues.

A B-Tree Index Can Become Unbalanced

One of the needless worries about B-tree indexes is that, over time, they will become unbalanced. The classic case that creates this problem is the order entry scenario that uses a sequential key. Orders are entered with an escalating order number, which is the index key. As the order number continually gets bigger, new index entries are added to the right of the B-tree index.

In addition to this rightward growth, the business operations of the company call for older orders to be moved from this table to another, causing the rows indexed on the left-hand side to be deleted. Theoretically, this could result in an index structure shown in Figure 10-8, where some rows have more levels of branch pages than others. This organization would add a performance penalty of more index levels for those rows that are probably more frequently accessed.

The structure shown in Figure 10-8 could not occur in an Oracle B-tree index, for a number of reasons. First, no Oracle B-tree index can have an unequal number of branch pages to get to the leaf pages. It is not possible; a branch page level is always complete.

Second, the structure shown in Figure 10-6 implies that there are branch pages that no longer have leaf pages associated with them just hanging around on the left. This situation is also not possible. As a leaf page is emptied, it is placed back into a pool for reuse by Oracle.

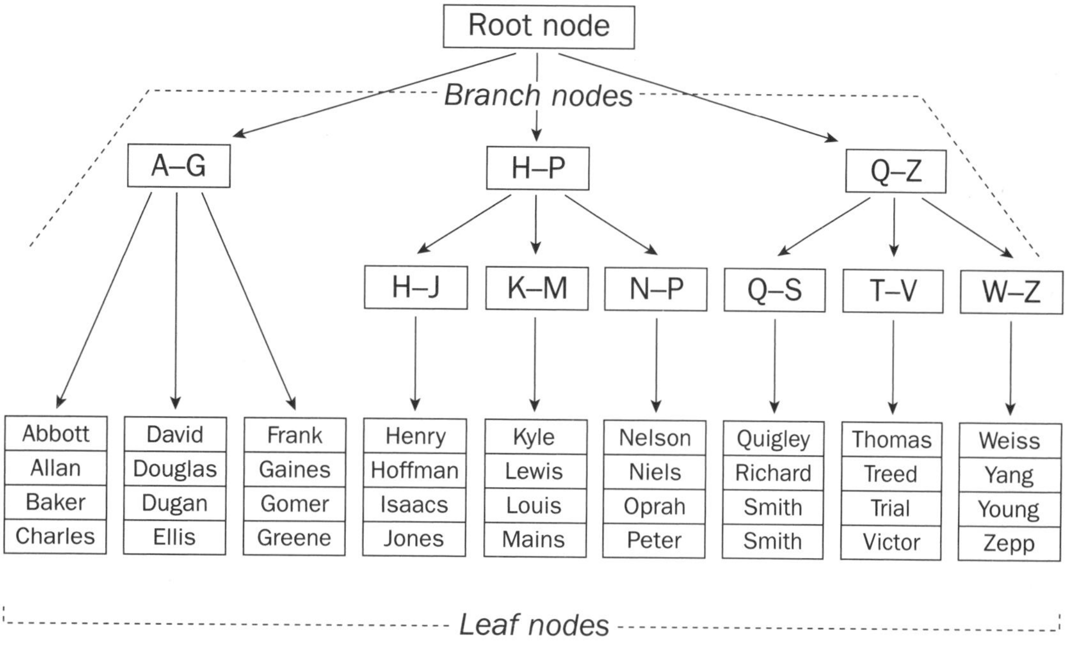

Figure 10-8: An unbalanced B-tree index?

It is possible that this scenario could cause the leaf pages on the left-hand side of the index could be more sparsely populated than the pages on the right, but this typically does not have a large impact on performance.

Reorganizing a B-Tree Index Improves Performance

This myth follows closely on the heels of the previous myth. If your indexes are in danger of becoming unbalanced, you should periodically reorganize them to compress the space, reduce the number of leaf page levels, eliminate the effects that an unbalanced index can cause, and improve performance overall.

We have already explained that unbalanced indexes don't exist with Oracle B-tree indexes. What about the other effects of reorganizing? In most cases, reorganizing an index will not reduce the number of leaf levels in an index. Oracle assigns leaf levels pretty efficiently, and only rarely could the removal of some empty index entries cause a complete elimination of a leaf level. If an index is subject to a lot of data entry and deletion, as a target index in this example would be, the branch page level will rapidly be added back in with subsequent activity, causing a significant amount of page split activity, so you wouldn't even want this to happen.

Compressing space can lead to some performance benefits, but since Oracle maintains balanced B-tree indexes and includes pointers to the next and previous index pages in a table, this effect will not necessarily have a pronounced effect for most indexes.

There is one more aspect to this myth having to do with something called the *clustering factor* between an index and a table. Remember that all indexes are stored in sorted order; tables are not. The rows in a table are basically added to database pages in the order the rows are added to the database. The clustering factor is the ratio between the data blocks used in the leaf pages of an index and the data blocks used to store the referenced rows in the table.

A poorly clustered table will have a higher clustering factor, since each "next" index entry could point to a completely separate data block containing the row than the current index entry. A well-clustered table will have a lower clustering factor, since the sorted entries in an index leaf page will point to database blocks that contain more than one target row. This arrangement can lead to reduced I/O for things like range scans, since the Oracle database will not have to retrieve as many database blocks for each complete index leaf page used. The Oracle database uses the clustering factor to determine if the optimal retrieval path will use the index or a table scan. If there is a high clustering factor, more data blocks in the table itself will have to be read, so Oracle will lean towards a full table scan with a larger selectivity factor.

There is some repeated wisdom that claims that reorganizing an index will reduce the clustering factor and consequently improve performance. The first part of this statement and the last part do not go together. The clustering factor is based on the *order* of the table rows in relation to the index values — reorganizing the index blocks will not have an effect on the overall ratio.

However, you can affect the clustering factor by reorganizing the data in a table to ensure that order of the rows of the table are more closely aligned with the order of the index entries. In fact, if you have tables that are more or less static, it makes sense to pack them as soon as they contain the appropriate data, since this will help to improve performance.

The ability to reorganize an index while leaving the index available was introduced in Oracle 9*i*, which allowed index reorganization to have less of an impact to online operations. But you still should not necessarily reorganize all indexes, hoping to see performance improvements.

We are preaching part of our uniform message here. It's a natural tendency for any developer to think that he or she knows his or her own situation and how to handle it better than a general-purpose piece of software. But we believe that the Oracle database is a pretty smart piece of software— smarter than most of us poor developers. Because of this, we always suggest that you should let the Oracle database do its thing before you go messing around changing your design, implementation, or maintenance plans to anticipate and prevent problems you think it might have. We go over this in depth in Chapter 28, "Optimization."

Reverse Key Indexes

A reverse key index is designed to address a very specific situation. The situation begins with an index based on an ascending value, such as a sequence. With this key, all new rows will be inserted into the rightmost index leaf block, since each new value is the highest value. If there are a lot of inserts going on at the same time, with all of them reaching to write to the same index leaf, you could end up with performance degradation caused by contention issues. These issues could be made even more apparent in an environment like the old version of clustering, Oracle Parallel Server, which extracted a penalty for concurrent writes to the same data block.

To avoid this situation, Oracle introduced the reverse key index. This index automatically takes the values in a key and reverses their order. The effect, as shown in Figure 10-9, would spread sequential key values around, which would, in turn, end up placing them in different index leaf blocks and potentially avoiding some of the contention problem.

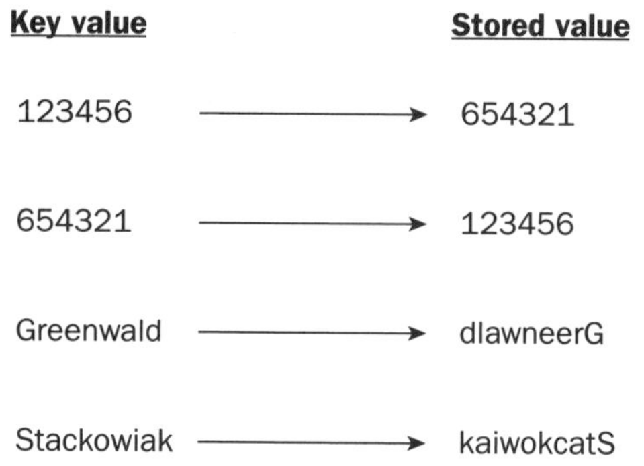

Figure 10-9: The effect of a reverse key index.

Reverse key indexes have a couple of distinct downsides, though. A standard B-tree index will help to make range scans faster. If a user wants to select all rows that have an index between value A and value B, a B-tree index can simply locate the first row of value A and keep walking the index until it gets past value B. Since a reverse index does not store values in sorted order, range scans cannot be done with a reverse index.

In addition, a reverse key index can cause index blocks to be less compact than standard B-tree indexes, for the same reason discussed under the "Sort Order" section earlier in the chapter.

Function-Based Indexes

Function-based indexes, which were introduced in Oracle 8*i*, provide powerful logical and performance benefits. This type of index can use a standard B-tree or bitmap index structure, but instead of using a column as the value for the key, the function-based index uses the results of a function as the value.

This small change opens up a world of possibility, from the mundane to the exotic, in two ways. First, by using the results of a function as the value in an index, you can avoid an alternative that could use up a whole lot of resources by having to perform the function on each potential row.

To understand the implications of function-based indexes, you can look at a classic example. You want to allow users to return information from the `EMP` table sorted without having to worry about the case of the letters. Without a function-based index, your basic `SELECT` code would look like this:

```
SELECT UPPER(ENAME) FROM EMP WHERE . . . ORDER BY UPPER(ENAME)
```

To return the values from this query, the Oracle database would have to perform the selection and then convert every `ENAME` column with the `UPPER()` function. This operation could consume quite a bit of resources, depending on the number of rows returned.

But wait—it could be much worse. Look at this slightly modified version of the query:

```
SELECT UPPER(ENAME) FROM EMP WHERE UPPER(ENAME) = . . . .
```

This version is probably more likely; you want the user to be able to select an employee without caring about the case of the stored value. For this query, Oracle would have to perform the `UPPER()` function for each and every row in the table, just to see if the row passed the selection criteria.

With a function-based index, the result of the `UPPER()` function is already stored in the index, so there is no need to perform the `UPPER()` function on the `ENAME` column. The function-based index stores the result of the function, eliminating the need to perform the function many, many times.

The reduction in resources shown in the preceding example is a huge advantage, but not the only one provided by function-based indexes. As Chapter 13, "Functions," illustrates, you can create your own functions with Oracle. This capability, coupled with function-based indexes, means that you can create some fairly sophisticated logic that can be utilized by the Oracle database without much query overhead.

Function-Based Indexes at Work

The example tables included with Oracle 10*g* include one example of a function-based index. The index is on the `CUSTOMERS` table in the `OE` schema, and the function is an `UPPER()` function on the `CUST_LAST_NAME` column, similar to the scenario we have been discussing.

You can see Oracle choose this index when appropriate with a query in *i*SQL*Plus, as shown in Figure 10-10, which runs the `CH10_FBI_ON.SQL` script.

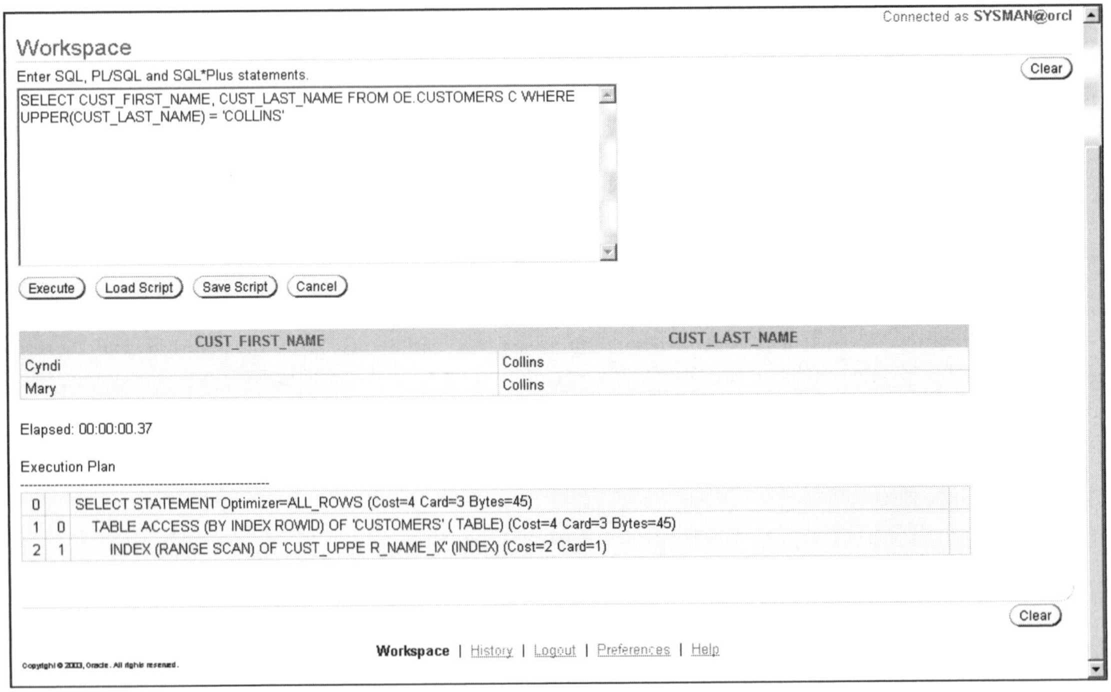

Figure 10-10: Using a function-based index.

Figure 10-11 shows what happens when you force Oracle to ignore the function-based index with the `FULL` table scan hint, as used in the `CH10_FBI_OFF.SQL` script.

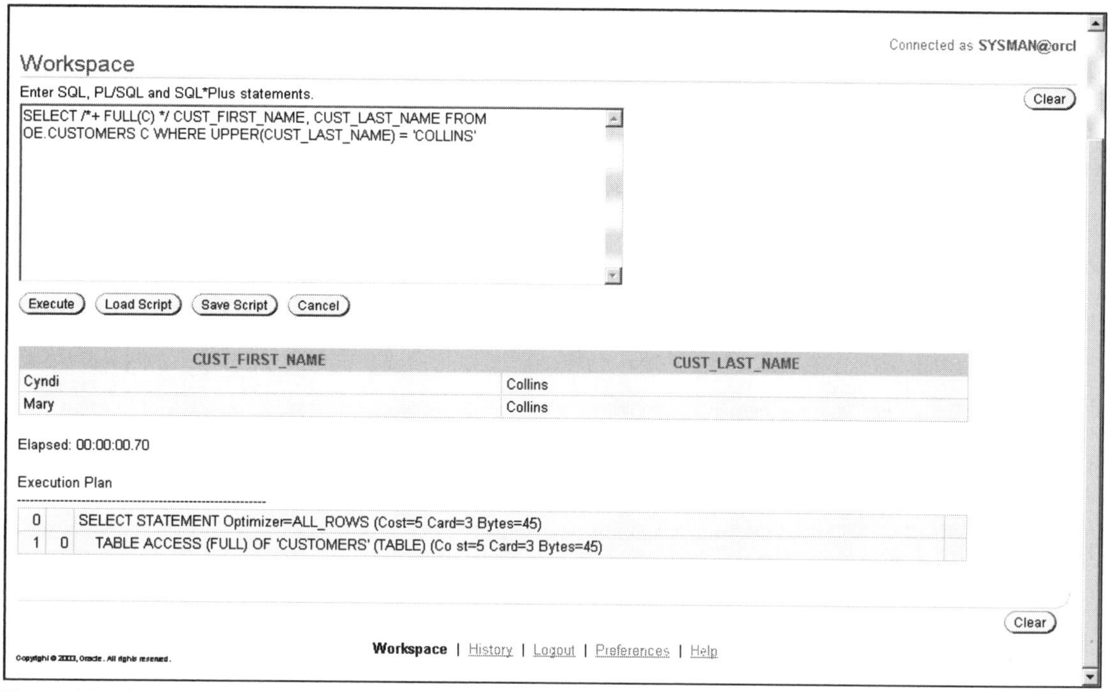

Figure 10-11: Ignoring a function-based index.

You can see that the cost of the query is slightly higher when the function-based index is not used. The cost is only slightly higher, based on the fact that this is a rather small table and simple function, but Oracle still makes the decision to use the function-based index when it can.

This example just showed the cost of the query with and without using a function-based index. The table that this index is on is too small for the use of the index to make a significant difference in actual performance. To see an example of the type of performance improvement that function-based indexes can create with a larger table, you can create a similar function-based index on the `CUSTOMERS` table in the `SH` schema with the script labeled `CH10_CREATE_FBI_VIEW.SQL`.

```
CREATE OR REPLACE VIEW SH.FBI_VIEW
 AS
   SELECT cust_id, UPPER(cust_last_name) upper_last_name, cust_first_name,
   cust_last_name, cust_street_address FROM SH.CUSTOMERS;
```

Once you have created this view, you can compare running a query against the table that uses the function-based index, as shown in Figure 10-12 running script `CH10_LARGE_FBI_ON.SQL`, against running the same query with a hint intentionally preventing the use of the index, as shown in Figure 10-13 running script `CH10_LARGE_FBI_OFF.SQL`.

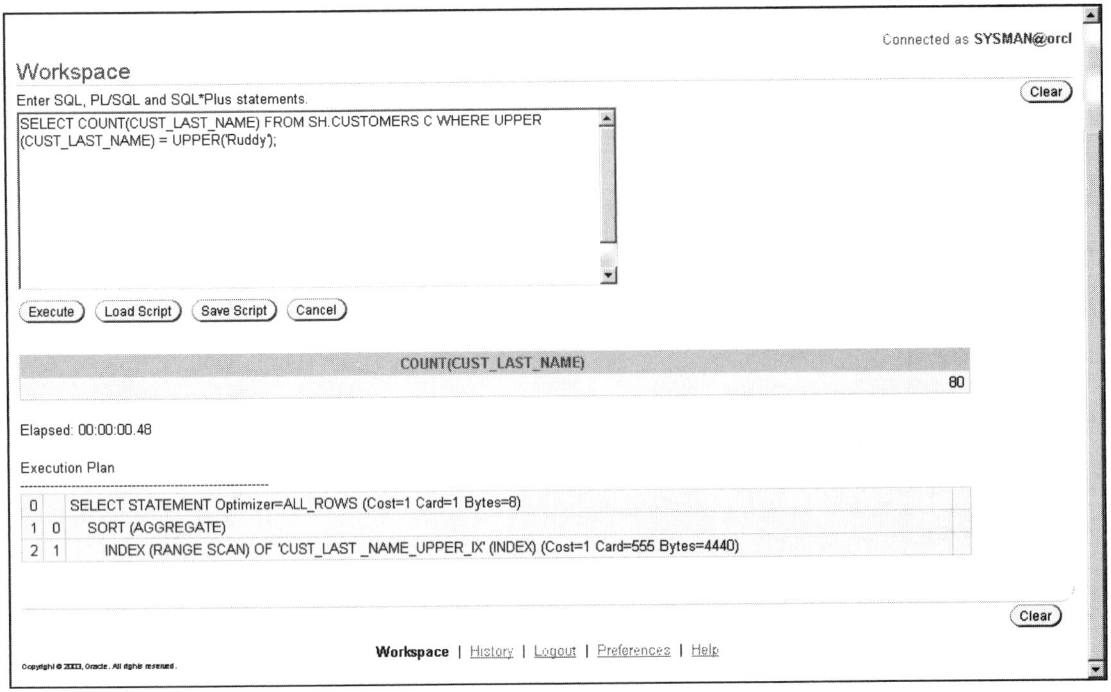

Figure 10-12: Using a function-based index on a large table.

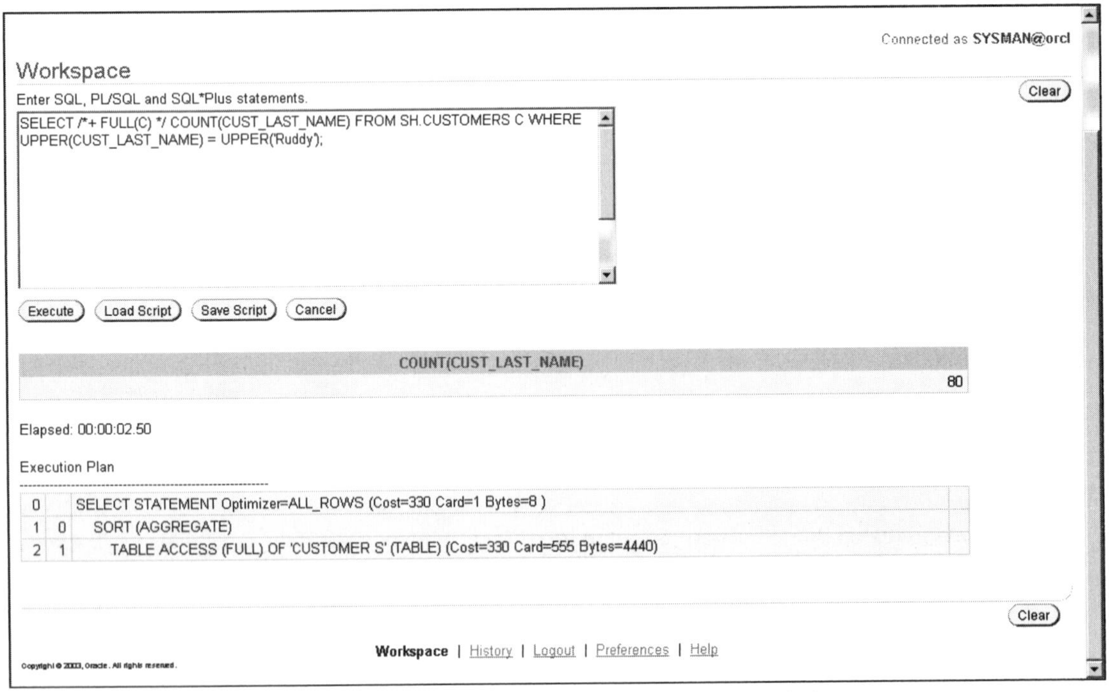

Figure 10-13: Performance of a query that does not use the function-based index.

Even though there are still not that many individual entries in the function-based index, you can see that the index can have a very significant effect on the performance of queries that require the function used in the index.

Caveats

Oracle is a very good database, but it cannot read your mind. Therefore, if you want Oracle to use a function-based index for a query, you must use the exact same text for the function in the query as you do in your function-based index. For instance, the following query, although similar to the one shown in Figure 10-11, will not use the function-based index:

```
SELECT * FROM SH.CUSTOMERS S WHERE CUST_LAST_NAME = UPPER('Ruddy')
```

Although the selection criteria logically dictates that CUST_LAST_NAME should be the result of an UPPER() function, you cannot expect Oracle to deduce this on its own. This simple example makes sense, but for more complex function-based indexes, you will have to remember to use the same implementation in your SQL statements as you did when you defined the function-based index.

You can avoid this potential caveat by creating a view based on a function-based index. The view will create a column that uses the same function as the function-based index, in effect adding the invisible function-based index column to the table.

To implement this for the function-based index we have been working with, you could run the following code, included as script CH10_CREATE_FBI_VIEW.SQL:

```
CREATE OR REPLACE VIEW SH.FBI_VIEW
 AS
   SELECT cust_id, UPPER(cust_last_name) upper_last_name, cust_first_name,
   cust_last_name, cust_street_address FROM SH.CUSTOMERS;
```

With this view, you can now run the query shown in Figure 10-14. In this query, you have replaced the column name that links to the underlying CUST_FIRST_NAME column to the column name that links to the function in the view definition, UPPER_LAST_NAME. Oracle knows to substitute the column name for the defined function, which in turn uses the function-based index, as shown in Figure 10-14. Notice that this query does not explicitly use the same function but still picks the proper function-based index.

As you can see from Figure 10-14, the view eliminates the need to exactly duplicate the function in the SELECT statement. Wrapping a view around a function-based index can eliminate the need for other developers or end users to know the functions used in the index, but you will still have to make sure that usage patterns call for the implementation of any particular index, function-based or otherwise.

There is also one caveat on using user-defined functions in a function-based index: The function must be *deterministic*, which means that the function must return the same values whenever it is called with the same parameters. This restriction means the function cannot access other information, such as data in the database, in a way that could affect the value returned.

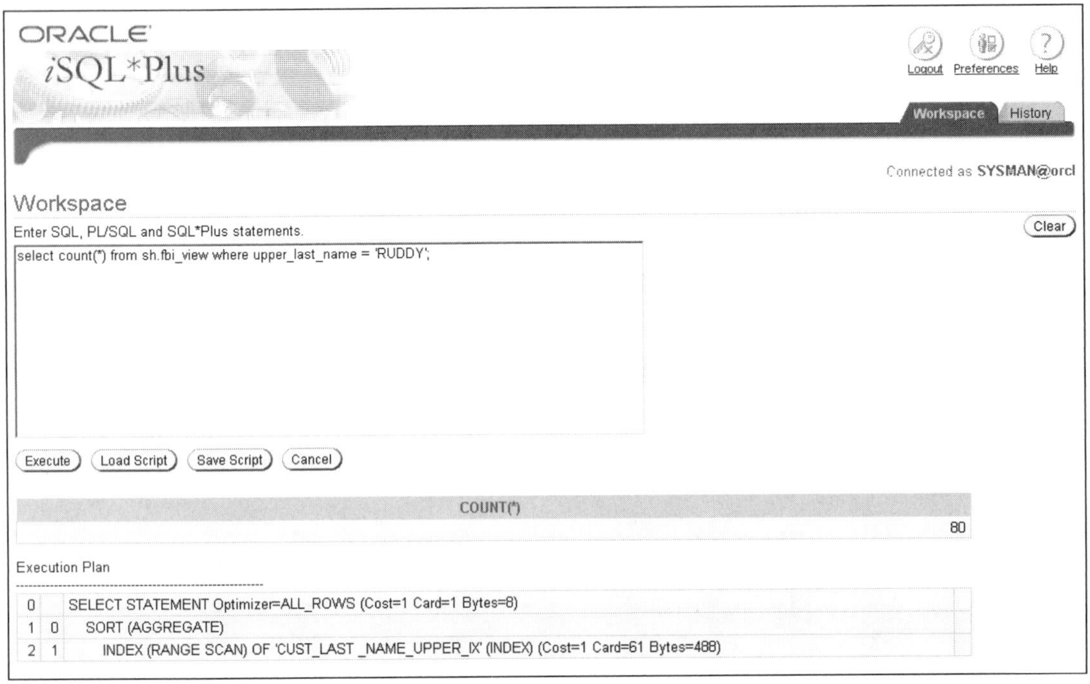

Figure 10-14: Using a view to hide a function-based index.

Domain Indexes

Domain indexes extend the indexing capabilities of the Oracle database even further than function-based indexes. You can create your own operators to perform specific logical functions and create new index types based on these operators. Domain indexes require a number of steps to create. Since domain indexes are used for nonstandard scenarios, we will not cover them in this book. Refer to Oracle documentation for more detailed information on domain indexes.

Bitmap Indexes

We have saved the explanation of bitmap indexes for last, since this type of index is designed for a specific purpose — to use in a data warehouse.

In a typical data warehouse, there is a central *fact table*, which contains information typically required by users, surrounded by a number of *dimension tables*, which are used to limit the selection of information from the fact table. Figure 10-15 shows a typical star schema for a data warehouse, with the central fact table surrounded by dimension tables.

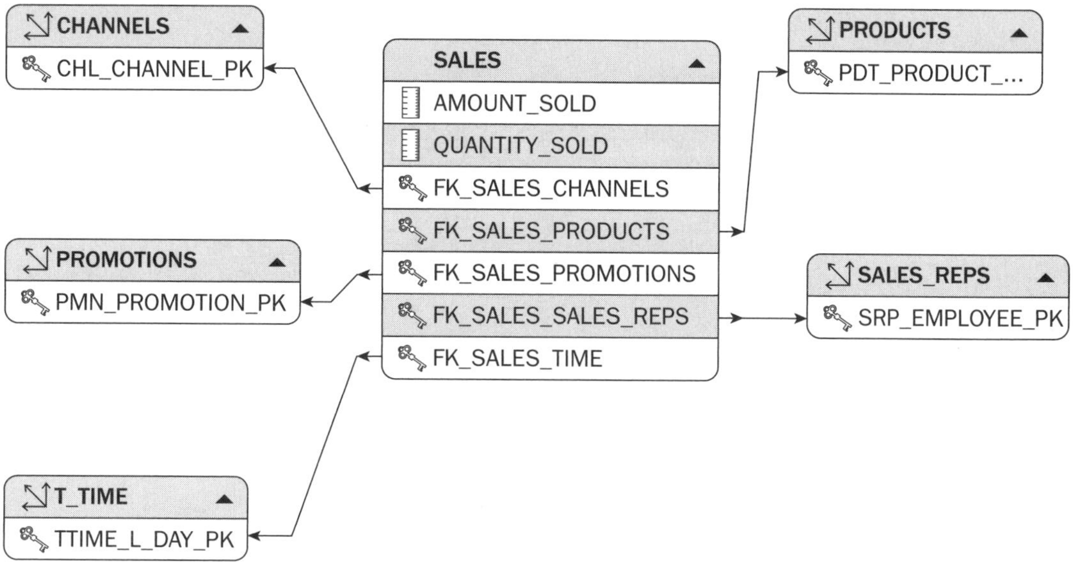

Figure 10-15: A typical star schema.

Star schemas are covered in much more detail in Chapter 26, "Business Intelligence Query."

With this schema, a user might want to see the sales of a particular project, through a particular channel, for a particular time period. All of these dimensions are part of this star schema.

A data warehouse typically has a large amount of rows in the fact table and a relatively small number of values in each dimension table. The primary keys in the dimension table are referenced by foreign keys in the fact table, which are ideal candidates for bitmap indexes.

Bitmap indexes are only included in Oracle 10*g* Enterprise Edition.

The Structure of a Bitmap Index

A bitmap index is different from other indexes, which have an entry for each non-`NULL` row in the table. In a bitmap index, each value has a bitmap, with each bit in the bitmap pointing to each row that contains that value, as shown in Figure 10-16.

The power of the bitmap index comes when a query requires selection on several different dimensions. The Oracle database server can perform bitwise `AND` or `OR` operations on each bitmap index, which are extremely fast. You can imagine how quickly this can work by visualizing each bitmap index as a punch card. To find a join on several different values, you can simply see where a knitting needle could penetrate multiple punch cards at once. Compare this with the alternative of locating each value on multiple dimension indexes, and then doing a complex join.

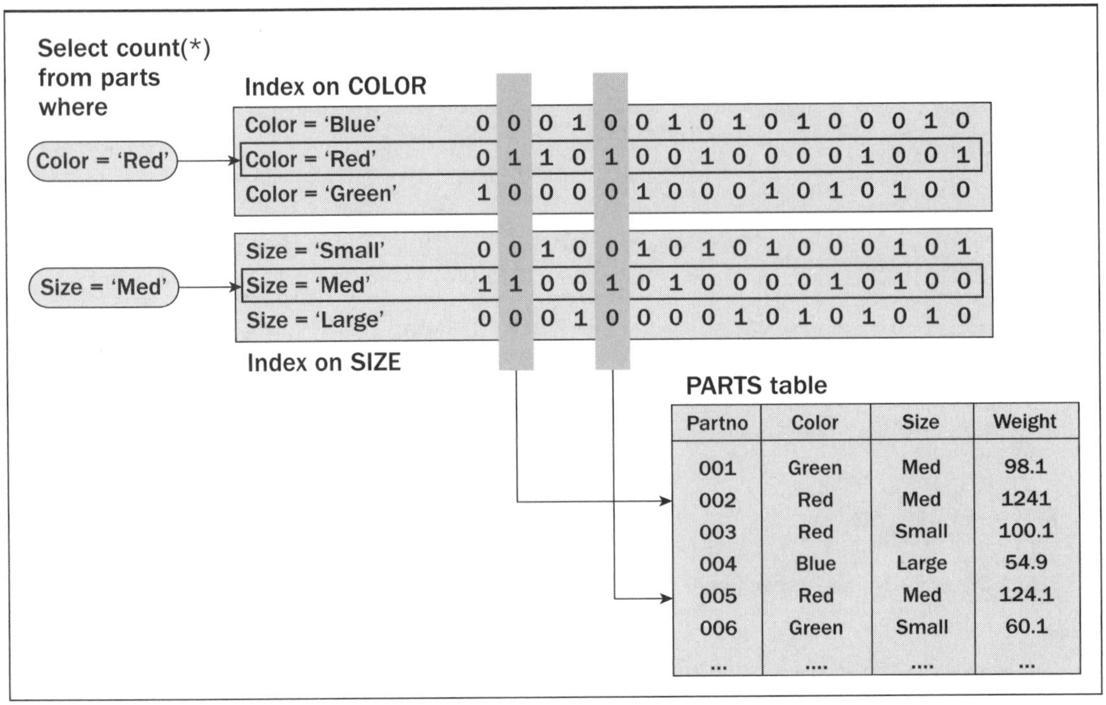

Figure 10-16: A logical view of a bitmap index.

Although a bitmap index could also be used with any column or set of columns with a low number of distinct values, or *cardinality*, in practice bitmap indexes are used almost exclusively with data warehouses.

There is also a good reason *not* to use a bitmap index with a table used for online transaction processing (OLTP). Whenever inserts are done into a table, any index blocks affected have to be locked for the duration of the transaction, just as a data block affected would have to be. In order to use a bitmap index, Oracle has to decompress the values, which takes some time and makes them inappropriate for OLTP scenarios, which can have thousands of small transactions simultaneously.

The Impact of a Bitmap Index

As with the other types of indexes, you can see the powerful affect of a bitmap index on performance with a few simple queries against a sample table with this type of index. We will use tables in the SH example schema that comes with the Oracle 10*g* database.

First, you can run a query to determine the sales of a single product using a bit-mapped index, with script `CH10_BMI_1.SQL`, and without using a bitmap index, with script `CH10_NO_BMI_1.SQL`. You can see the results in Figures 10-17 and 10-18.

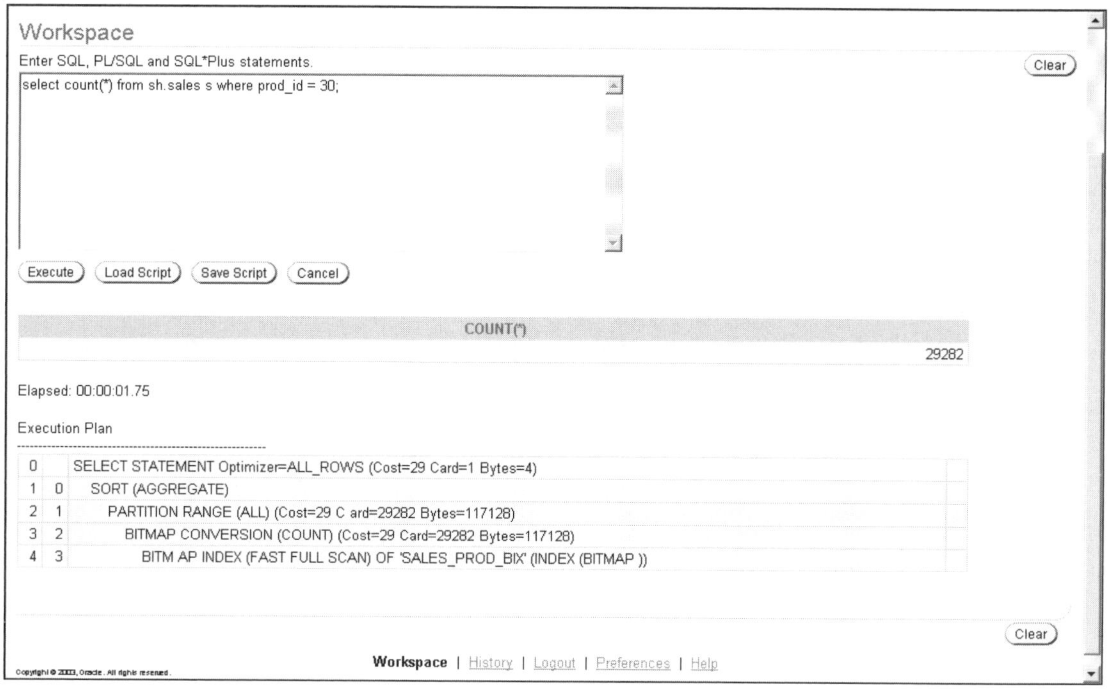

Figure 10-17: Single selection criterion using a bitmap index.

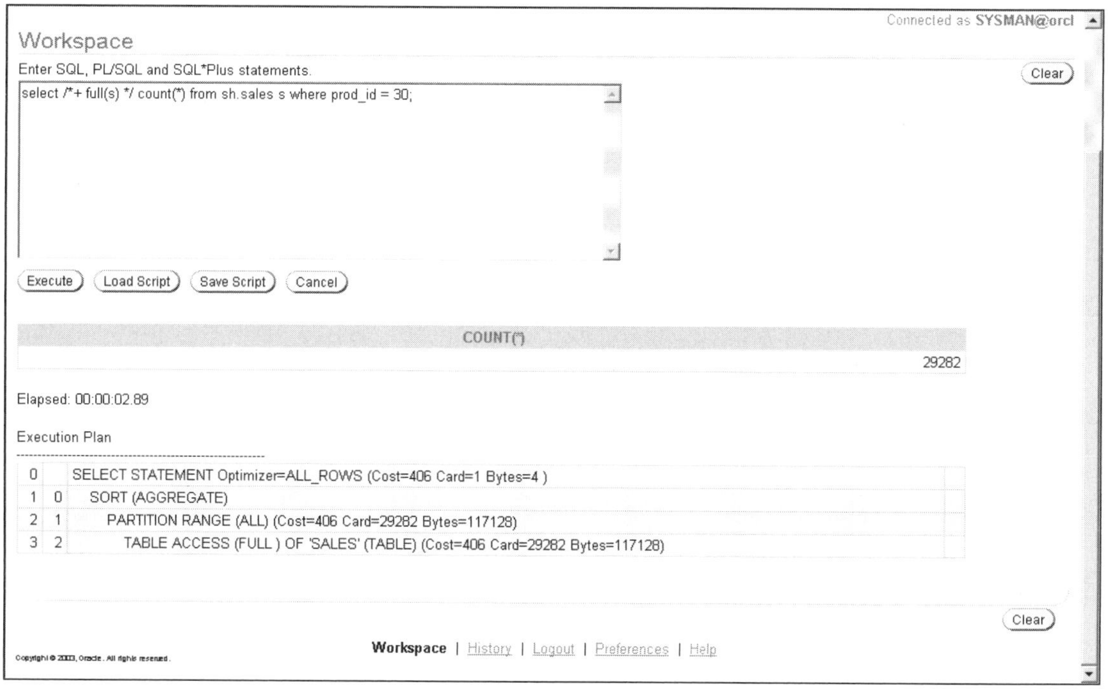

Figure 10-18: Single selection criterion without using a bitmap index.

The bitmap index caused a pretty significant performance difference — on average, the simple query with the bitmap index took 4.98 seconds, while the same query on average took 11.93 seconds without using the bitmap index. This difference becomes even more pronounced when you run a more typical data warehouse query, which will look for the number of products sold to a particular customer for a particular promotion. This query, using three bitmap indexes with the script CH10_BMI_2.SQL and shown in Figure 10-19, runs, on average, in 5.19 seconds. The same query, which does not use bitmap indexes with the script CH10_NO_BMI_2.SQL and shown in Figure 10-20, takes almost three times as long on average, 14.34 seconds.

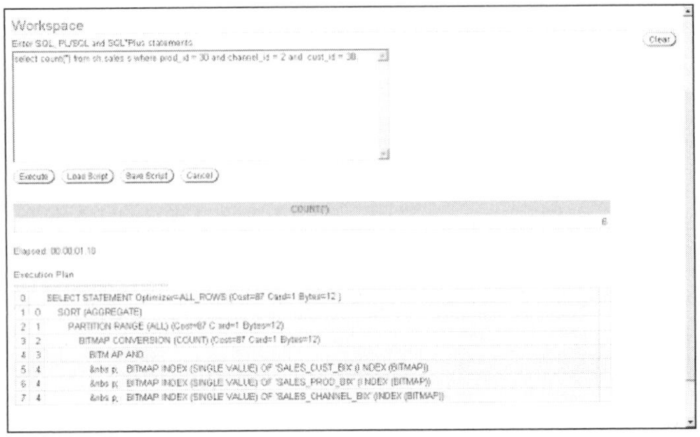

Figure 10-19: More complex data warehouse query with bitmap indexes.

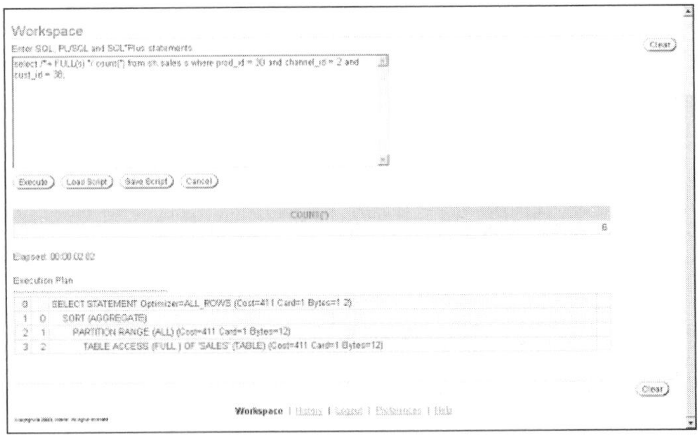

Figure 10-20: More complex data warehouse query without bitmap indexes.

Bitmap Join Index

A bitmap join index can improve performance in a data warehouse even more than a bitmap index. The bitmap join index uses the same storage scheme as the bitmap index, but the bits in the index indicate how one table, generally the fact table, is joined to another table.

A query can use a bitmap index instead of having to perform a join between two tables, which can in turn improve performance for a commonly performed join — sometimes dramatically. Bitmap indexes and bitmap join indexes are discussed in their normal context of business intelligence in Chapter 26, "Business Intelligence Query".

Index-Organized Tables

At the start of this chapter, we described the basic virtues of indexes. Essentially, they allow users to get at data with less I/O than performing a complete table scan in many cases. Typically, your queries will require information beyond that found in the index, so once the Oracle database has selected the appropriate index entry, the database still has to use the pointer in the index entry to retrieve the extra information in the row. Although access through the pointer in an index entry is the fastest way to access a row in a table, the retrieval still requires some overhead. Eliminating this overhead could speed up a query even more. Enter the index-organized table.

This aptly named structure allows Oracle to keep the entire table in an index structure, so the same efficiencies offered by an index are used to retrieve all of the data in the row. An IOT stores both key values and non-key values within its pages. Oracle provides an overflow option that allows you to indicate that some non-key values are stored outside of the index structure, based on storage room available in the actual index block.

Because an IOT is organized around a primary key value, you must have a primary key defined for an IOT. Because the IOT does not normally use an index value pointing to the same value in a data row, the storage requirements for the table and index are reduced.

You can have additional indexes on an IOT. These indexes can be either standard B-tree-based indexes or bitmap indexes and work in the same way as an index on a normal table structure. These additional indexes use a logical row ID, rather than a physical row ID like other index types, to access the data rows in the table. If an IOT row uses the overflow option described previously, the physical row ID to the overflow area is part of the IOT index entry.

There are a number of restrictions on the use of IOTs, such as the fact that an IOT cannot contain columns with `LONG` or any of the varieties of LOB data types, for obvious reasons. In addition, an IOT cannot be stored in a cluster, which is described in the following section.

And, of course, as with all potentially performance-enhancing changes, you should make sure that using IOTs actually will give you a gain in performance by testing your application against standard tables and IOTs. Since your application code will be the same, regardless of which database structure you use, switching between these two options is possible with some administrative work.

Index Clusters

The final types of organization in this chapter address the same issue as an index, but in a different way. Oracle normally stores the rows added to a table in the order that rows are added to the table, rather than in any particular logical order. A cluster is a way of storing table rows so that their actual storage is related to the logical values in some of the columns.

A cluster can hold either rows from a single table or related rows from more than one table. Figure 10-21 shows a block from a clustered table that contains rows from the DEPT table and the EMP table. The cluster is organized using the cluster key, a value that is shared by both tables. In this example, the DEPT_NO column is the cluster key, so the same data block contains the EMP rows that have the same DEPT_NO as a row of the DEPT table.

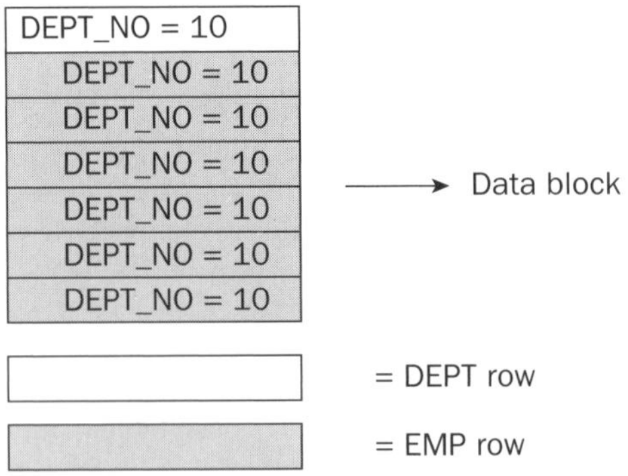

Figure 10-21: Storage of a cluster with multiple tables.

This type of organization makes sense if you are frequently accessing the same data together. When Oracle fetches a data block for the DEPT value, the related EMP rows have also been retrieved. A cluster also reduces storage requirements, since the value of the cluster key is only stored once, rather than in both the DEPT and EMP table.

Why not just combine the rows into a single logical row? The example illustrates one way that the data is accessed, but the normalization process, described in Chapter 4, "Database Design Basics," may call for distinct tables for logical purposes and the overall performance of the application system.

To implement a cluster, you have to first create a cluster and then add tables to the cluster. There are limitations to using a cluster, such as the fact that you cannot have partitions in a cluster or do direct-path loads into a cluster.

Since each data block holds the rows for tables with the same cluster key, using a cluster that leaves a lot of empty space in the block can waste space and decrease performance. By default, Oracle will only store the rows for one cluster key value in each data block, although you can change this behavior with a parameter when you create the table. You should also only use a cluster when the values for the cluster key are varied — using a key with an extremely low cardinality can negate the value of the cluster, since Oracle will be able to find the first block of the cluster, but then have to go through the same random retrieval for the rest of the blocks for the value. In addition, clusters are only appropriate when the number of rows for the different values for the cluster key are similar in size. If the number of rows for some values are much greater than the number for others, the cluster will be skewed, which will decrease the effectiveness of the cluster by adding a lot of "empty" space on the less populated values and reducing the efficiency of full table scans.

Hash Cluster

A cluster groups data from one or more tables together in the same data blocks, organized by a cluster key. Retrieving the data is faster because the Oracle database does not have to re-fetch data blocks to get data from related cluster key values. A request for a cluster still goes through the process of locating a value for the cluster key and then fetching blocks. But what if this index retrieval could be eliminated also?

Oracle supports another table organization called a hash cluster. This type of table uses the result of a hash function on the cluster key to determine where to store and retrieve the row data in the cluster. A hash cluster lets Oracle find the blocks that contain the rows in the cluster by performing a logical function rather than I/O operations. Oracle can calculate a value and go straight to data blocks containing rows for that value. This capability substitutes some CPU activity for some I/O, which is frequently a good trade-off in terms of overall performance. For a hash cluster to provide optimal value, you should be able to estimate the total number of hash values when you create the cluster, so Oracle can pre-allocate all the space required for each of the values for the hash key in an efficient way. If the size of the hash key entries grows beyond the initial estimate, the performance benefit of the organization is decreased as additional blocks are added to the cluster.

You can have a hash cluster that only contains a single table. This type of cluster lets Oracle access rows in the table directly once the hash value is calculated, which reduces I/O and can help performance in appropriate situations, such as a table used for lookups.

Oracle Database 10*g* also supports a sorted hash cluster. This organization stores data based on a hash value, but also in the order that the data was entered. Some types of data, such log records from a phone system, are very appropriate for a sorted hash cluster. In this example, the user would typically want to access rows by customer ID, the cluster key, which could be rapidly retrieved with a hash value, but then want to access the data for that customer based on when it was entered. A sorted hash cluster is not appropriate for all scenarios, but the right situation can produce large performance benefits.

Design and Performance Tips

You are now familiar with the types of indexes supported by the Oracle Database 10*g*. We have conspicuously avoided talking about the specific impact that a proper index can have on performance, for a very simple reason. As with all performance-related questions, the answer to the question "How much can an index speed up data access" is "It depends." It depends on the design of your overall database, and on the current and future usage patterns within your database.

Given that ever-present warning, the following topics are ones that you generally should consider when deciding on indexes for any particular schema.

Start Small

At this point, we have spent over 20 pages discussing the benefits that indexes can provide. You may be tempted to just start adding indexes all over the place, willy-nilly. Since indexes improve performance, the more the better, right?

When talking about performance in this chapter, we have only focused on the performance of queries, where data is retrieved. In these cases, an index will frequently help to improve response time. But adding or updating data to a table will also add or update data to all of the index structures associated with a table. In the case of database writes, more indexes mean slower performance.

Of course, almost every database gets a lot more read activity than write activity. So how do you balance the benefits of indexes for reads with the downside of indexes for writes?

In some ways, database design and performance tuning are arts, not sciences, in that it is difficult to make blanket recommendations about these topics, since the effect of design and tuning always depends on your particular environment.

Your environment consists of both the resources available at any one time and the overall use of the database. Most Oracle databases support many different application modules, so the Oracle instance must be smart in allocating resources for use among the users of different modules.

The Oracle optimizer, discussed in Chapter 28, "Optimization," is pretty clever at taking all of these things into account — which is why that chapter emphasizes leaving the optimizer alone to do its thing.

In terms of creating indexes for a table, we highly recommend starting small and then adding indexes and you test your application. Starting small in this case means only creating indexes that you know you will need — an index on the primary key and any foreign keys for a table. Creating a constraint, as discussed in Chapter 11, "Constraints," will create an underlying index for these situations, but it is probably better design to create the indexes explicitly when you create a table, since you can then apply your own naming conventions and storage attributes to the index and since you should be consciously aware of the need for these indexes at creation time.

As you run your application in test mode, you can see if there are any particular areas where query performance could be improved. As you detect these areas, you can add indexes to help address the issues raised. Remember, in almost all cases, you will be able to add an index to a table without having to modify the application code that accesses the table.

You should also track performance regularly as you deploy your application. Oracle's Enterprise Manager tool will greatly aid you in determining if there are any SQL statements that are performing poorly. As you discover these performance bottlenecks, you can sort out whether adding an index is an appropriate way to address the situation.

Keep It Simple — a good guideline for all sorts of areas of life, including your initial database design. This practice can make development a more incremental and easier process. And remember, there is a decent chance that someone else will end up maintaining your applications and database structures. It's never fun to have to sort out why someone else did something, and the more complex that something is, the more time-consuming and frustrating the sorting-out process is.

Key Compression

As we wrote in the beginning of the chapter, one of the ways that an index improves performance is to reduce the amount of I/O that the Oracle database must perform to perform a variety of tasks, including imposing selection criteria and joining tables together. Another way to reduce I/O even more is with the use of key compression.

Before	**After**
1234511	12345
1234512	11
1234513	12
1234514	13
1234515	14
1234516	15
1234517	16
	17

Figure 10-22: Index without and with key compression.

The end result of key compression looks like a report formed with headers on grouping columns, as shown in Figure 10-22, and the overall result is to reduce the amount of storage space needed for the index. With this reduction, Oracle can use an index without having to retrieve and examine as much data.

You specify key compression on the leading columns of a key. If the overall key is not unique, you can specify all the columns in the key. If the overall key is unique, you cannot compress the last column, which is used to preserve uniqueness. Because of this restriction, key compression cannot be used for all indexes, and may require some modification of your database design to be optimally implemented.

SQL Access Advisor

The Oracle database has been around for more than 25 years. In this time, the database has grown, becoming feature-rich and, more recently, easier to operate and maintain. One of the fruits of this improvement cycle is the SQL Access Advisor.

The challenges of database design have been around for the entire history of databases. Oracle's SQL Access Advisor is a tool to help you create and maintain an optimal set of indexes for your database. The SQL Access Advisor (part of an add-on pack for Enterprise Manager) gives you suggestions on indexes and materialized views to create to improve performance, or on indexes and materialized views you should consider dropping.

Summary

Indexes can provide significant improvements in query performance. Indexes are completely transparent to users, so you can add and adjust indexes without having to touch application code — a key benefit of relational data access.

The standard Oracle index is a B-tree index, which uses a number of levels to speed access to index values. A B-tree index can also be a reverse index to handle those situations where data values tend to "clump" in normal order.

The Oracle 10g Database also supports several other types of indexes. Function-based indexes can be used to "precalculate" the outcomes of commonly used functions. Bitmap indexes can dramatically improve performance of tables with a limited number of index values, as in a data warehouse. Index-organized tables, index clusters, and hash clusters are index types that can improve performance for specific application scenarios.

Since indexes are transparent to applications, you can, and should, start small as far as creating indexes is concerned. You can use a variety of performance tools to spot performance problems and then determine if any of Oracle's index types could help to address the problems.

11

Constraints

For some reason application developers and DBAs often seem to be on opposite sides of the table. It may be because the personality types of those who are successful in one of these jobs is different from those who do well at the other. Perhaps it is a lack of understanding of the other job. Sometimes it is because they tend to work with different tools and languages (or perhaps different subsets of the same language) and therefore have a hard time finding a common basis for communication. And in some cases, unfortunately, it is because they wrestle for control of parts of the application development process.

One of the places that this dichotomy, an attitude of "us versus them," seems to arise is in a decision of where certain business rules should be established and enforced. Application developers and DBAs generally agree on the need for business rules to protect the integrity of the application's critical data. The DBA will frequently want to move business rules into the database where the DBA can see them documented, while the application developer may feel more comfortable coding the rules directly within the application code.

In general, integrity checks should be made in the database whenever possible. This ensures that data entering the database from any program (or ad hoc tool) will conform to the desired rules. It may also be appropriate to define some validation rules within application programs to facilitate immediate feedback to the user. The challenge is to ensure that rules defined in two places always agree with each other. At the very end of this chapter, we'll come back to this challenge and suggest a way to exploit database-defined rules and minimize the program maintenance required when a rule has to be changed.

Database Integrity Features

One of the primary advantages provided by a database management system is a set of capabilities for ensuring the integrity of the data it stores. Some of these capabilities are basic, while some are much more advanced. This chapter explores some of the ways that Oracle can assist the developer in providing automatic validation of data when it is entered into the database, as well as ensure that the data integrity rules are maintained throughout the life of the data within the database.

Data Typing

Data typing is not generally considered as a database integrity feature. However, starting a discussion about this topic may help bridge the common gap between developers and DBAs. Every developer is aware of the capability of data typing to help limit data errors within their programs. By declaring a particular variable as a numeric data type, they will immediately be able to raise an error if a user tries to enter a nonnumeric string into the field.

Just like the programming language, the database can enforce such fundamental limitations on the data that is entered. When the database column definition is of a `DATE` data type, Oracle will not allow inappropriate data to be entered into that column. By taking his or her record and field declarations from the data dictionary's declared data typing, the developer is able to closely coordinate the acceptance and subsequent storage of the data. Similarly, the defined length of program variables, screen display lengths, and database column lengths allow for smooth movement of data throughout the system.

Imagine the additional work that would be required in developing a program if all of the data were allowed to be entered as unrestricted character strings but had to be individually edited, character by character, at each step in every program so that it won't error out at the last step when it is actually submitted to the database for storage. What a nightmare that would be!

The more sophisticated capabilities of ensuring data integrity also should be considered as tools (just like data typing) that benefit both the developer and the DBA. Both should work together to determine the appropriate business rules and define them. By being proactive in defining business rules in ways that allow the database to enforce them, the application developer can avoid surrendering control and, as you will see, make his or her subsequent programming efforts easier and more manageable.

There are several primary reasons for implementing business rules in the database where possible. First, the centralized rule ensures that violating data can't "sneak in" a back door. This becomes a practical matter for the application developer when multiple entry and edit programs have to be created. Perhaps a batch program needs to bulk load data; a Web-based data entry form needs to insert individual rows; finally an edit and correction routine needs to be provided for customer service to modify existing data. These three entry points may, in some cases, be developed in three different languages (for instance, C, Visual Basic, and Java). Every business rule needs to be replicated to all three environments. If the rule ever has to be modified in the future, the maintenance staff (who may not be the original authors) will have to be sure to make the change in three places. Any missed entry point to the system or any differences in logic (especially in complex logic) may allow corruption of the database and be very difficult to diagnose and correct. Any new system input (perhaps a periodic transfer of data from another database) will need to have the same logic implemented yet another time, perhaps in another programming language, such as PL/SQL.

In addition to reducing the maintenance overhead, implementing business rules inside the database can also be more efficient. If your program has to call the database to verify that submitted data agrees with data values already existing in several reference tables, each round-trip query to the database is time your program has to wait. If, on the other hand, your program just has to insert the row and the database can evaluate and validate the data values your program will be more efficient. In the rare (we hope!) cases that an error is encountered, the database will pass you back the transaction and specific details of the error so that you can provide that feedback to the user. Even in this worst case, the number of trips to the database is the same as in the first case; but in the expected case of no errors, you will have saved multiple validation queries to the database.

This is not to imply that a data entry program should not do any validation of the entered data — quite the contrary. Some tests, such as validating month values, will never change and will not be a maintenance issue with your program. Verifying a zip code, on the other hand is much more dynamic and would always need to make a database call. There is no valid reason for assuming that business rules can (or should) be evaluated at just the application level or the database level. For immediate user feedback, it is frequently necessary to perform validation or place limits on input at the application level. For database integrity reasons, it is also appropriate to perform the same check within the database.

As you'll see later in this chapter, your program can even use the database-defined constraints to dynamically validate data at time of data entry through edits or dynamic drop-down lists without the need to modify the program code to accommodate data changes.

Constraints

This chapter is devoted to the ability of the database to declare a large variety of business rules as part of the definition of the data. Just like data typing's ability to restrict which characters are allowed in a numeric field, these constraints can restrict the allowable values of data entered into the database. The key concept of this facility is that these are declarative constraints, which means they are nonprocedural. For simple business rules, this declarative form is easier to "code," easier to understand, and easier to maintain.

Additionally, declarative constraints are self-documenting. The concise syntax of defining these constraints requires no additional commentary to interpret. Procedural code to perform the same validation might require both additional documentation and subsequent maintenance. Storing the constraint in the database as part of the data definition means that you can see the business rule by issuing an SQL query against the data dictionary, as introduced in Chapter 6, "The Oracle Data Dictionary."

One additional advantage of using declarative constraints is related to performance. Constraint checking is often more efficient than performing the same validation within the application. By evaluating declarative constraints within the database the Oracle optimizer has been tuned, whenever possible, to perform these checks efficiently. The communication with the database necessary to insert, update, or delete a row is the only network communication necessary. If a validation in the program needs to check data from the database, that will generally require an additional call and network round-trip or context switch.

After quickly comparing another option for implementing integrity rules in the database, you'll explore the topic of declarative constraints in more depth.

Triggers and Stored Procedures

Not all business rules can be represented in the declarative language of constraints. More complex logic to validate data can be expressed in database triggers. As you will see in Chapter 19, "Triggers, " database triggers can be set on a table to "fire" when particular types of SQL statements are issued. Trigger logic, in addition to validating input data, can also extend the operation of those basic statements. As an example, inserting a row into a table can be extended to populate additional columns in a table and to also insert a new row into a user-defined audit table.

Stored procedures further extend the procedural capability of the database in similar ways. A stored procedure can be invoked as part of a trigger's logic, or you can use a stored procedure to encapsulate complex procedural logic so that a single call to the stored procedure can do the work of several SQL statements and the logic surrounding them. To use a stored procedure in this way, no application calls to perform `INSERT/UPDATE/DELETE` statements directly should be permitted by the security model of the application. To be effective as an integrity enforcement mechanism, stored procedures must be guaranteed to be the only means of modifying data in the table. This method is more prone to error than either triggers or declarative constraints.

More information on these capabilities is presented in the PL/SQL chapters of Part III, "Database Programming Languages."

Types of Constraints

From the available syntax there appear to be six types of relational declarative constraints (as you'll see, there are actually only three basic types plus one related concept) that you can use with Oracle. Some are very straightforward and others have multiple options. For each of the six topics, we will describe the constraint, provide its general syntax, provide one or more examples of its use, and then provide an example of what response will be returned in case of a violation of the constraint. In addition to the relational constraints, there is one extension, the `REF` constraint, for constraining object types that we will describe as a seventh topic in this section.

This section and all of its examples will show the actual constraint type names in all capital letters and will use lowercase when describing the concept of the constraint type. This is just for ease in reading this section; case is not significant in actually entering any of this syntax.

> *There are many acceptable variations on the syntax of defining constraints. This chapter provides several working examples for defining constraints but does not attempt to illustrate every possible alternative. The Oracle SQL Reference manual provides the definitive reference for all syntax.*

Constraints may be declared at the time a table is built with the `CREATE TABLE` command, or they may be added, dropped, or changed in an existing table's definition later by using the `ALTER TABLE` command. Both forms will be illustrated in the examples. Additionally, it is possible to add most constraints "in line" as part of defining the specific column to which the constraint applies. If a constraint includes more than one column (such as a multiple-column `PRIMARY KEY` constraint), then the constraint must be declared "out of line" as part of the table's definition that follows the specification of individual columns. Some developers choose to always use the out-of-line form for all constraints for consistency at the expense of brevity. This is purely a matter of personal choice or workgroup standards; to Oracle they are equivalent syntax.

The actual constraint definition will be visible in the `USER_`, `DBA_` , or `ALL_CONSTRAINTS` dictionary views as either :

- part of the `SEARCH_CONDITION` for `NOT NULL` and `CHECK` constraints
- by reference to an `INDEX_NAME` for `UNIQUE` and `PRIMARY KEY` constraints

or

- by reference to another constraint name for `FOREIGN KEY` constraints.

When you look at one of the *_CONSTRAINTS dictionary views, however, you will not see any COLUMN_NAME attribute. Instead the column(s) of the constraint are visible by looking in the corresponding *_CONS_COLUMNS view. When a constraint applies to more than one column, such as in a multicolumn primary key, there will be multiple rows in the view and the order of columns in the constraint will be determined by the POSITION column in *_CONS_COLUMNS.

All constraints have a name in the data dictionary. The developer or DBA who defines a table or adds a constraint has the ability to name it at that time. If a name is not supplied for a constraint, however, Oracle will assign a system-generated name that will uniquely identify the constraint within its schema but may be a bit cryptic for your uses. System-generated names are prefixed with SYS_C (for "system constraint") followed by a seven-digit integer. If you want to easily identify constraints, perhaps to disable and reenable them, it will be more convenient to provide a more predictable name. Also, if you drop a constraint with a system-generated name and then later add the constraint back to the table, the new system-generated name will have an incremented integer portion in its name. This may limit your ability to easily code routines that manage constraints. In general, name your constraints if you think you may later need to reference them by name.

As mentioned in the introductory section of this chapter, one of the main advantages of declarative constraints is that they are stored in the data dictionary and are therefore easily accessible with SQL queries. Some of the examples in this section will either illustrate this capability or reference an appropriate column (such as CONSTRAINT_TYPE) in the dictionary views (ALL_CONSTRAINTS, USER_CONSTRAINTS, etc.).

NOT NULL

Null is defined in SQL as the absence of any data value for a particular column in a row of a table. Null is distinguished from any possible actual value such as zero (for numeric column) or a space (for a character type column) and is sometimes described as "unknown." In some situations it is important for an application to be able to distinguish the absence of data; in such cases you would want to allow null entry for that column. In other cases the application may need to ensure that some value is always provided. This is where the NOT NULL constraint is used to refine the definition of that column.

The NOT NULL constraint is the oldest constraint supported in the Oracle database. In fact, NOT NULL syntax was supported for many releases before the concept of database constraints was introduced to the ANSI SQL language.

> *Incidentally, the opposite of NOT NULL is NULL, which is also valid syntax. NULL is the default condition for all columns (other than those named in a PRIMARY KEY constraint) that virtually nobody ever enters into their table definitions. NULL is a bit of a misnomer — it actually means "NULLS ALLOWED" and is, therefore, kind of an anticonstraint.*

NOT NULL applies only to the individual column for which it is declared. It prevents a row in that table from ever being entered or updated to have no value in that column.

Earlier in this section we indicated that the six types of constraints were technically only four types. This first constraint type is one of the two exceptions. Even though you declare NOT NULL as its own constraint type, it is actually implemented in the database as a check constraint. Figure 11-1 demonstrates this by retrieving the CHECK constraints (CONSTRAINT_TYPE='C') on the SH.SALES table.

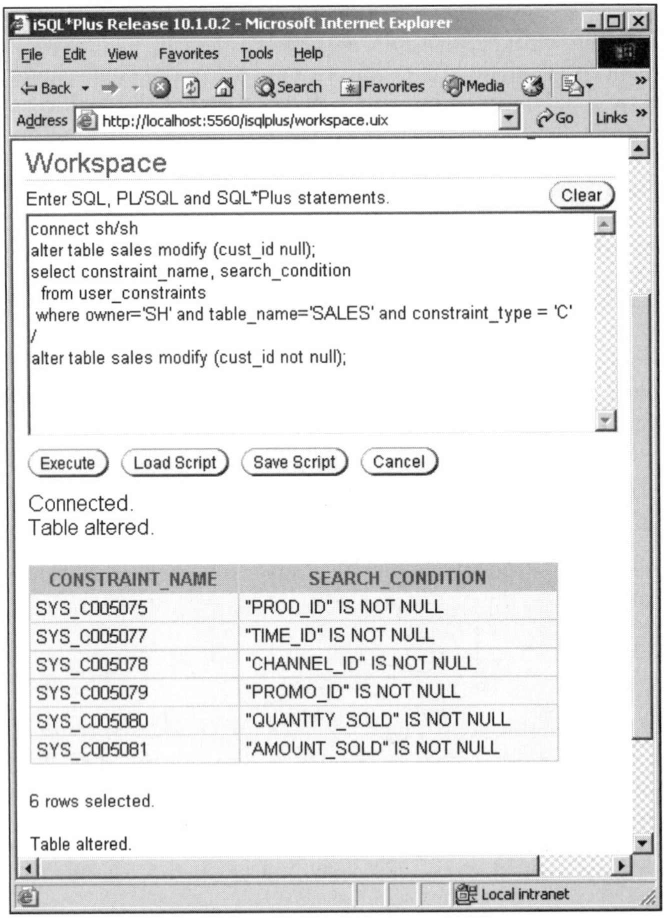

Figure 11-1: Query showing the database CHECK constraints on a table.

In this figure we first show the special syntax for dropping a NOT NULL constraint (thereby allowing nulls) from one of the seven columns that were originally defined with NOT NULL constraint syntax. Then we select all of the check constraints and see the remaining six NOT NULL constraints. Note that each of these constraints was given a system-generated name. Using the normal NOT NULL syntax does not provide a means of naming the constraint. You may, of course, use the more general CHECK constraint syntax (discussed later in the chapter) to create a named constraint. Before leaving the example in Figure 11-1, we demonstrate the syntax necessary to replace the constraint that was dropped at the start.

Figure 11-2 shows the effect of attempting to insert a row that includes null data for a column defined as NOT NULL. Note that Oracle returns a special error (ORA-01400) for this special legacy constraint type that is different than other CHECK constraints.

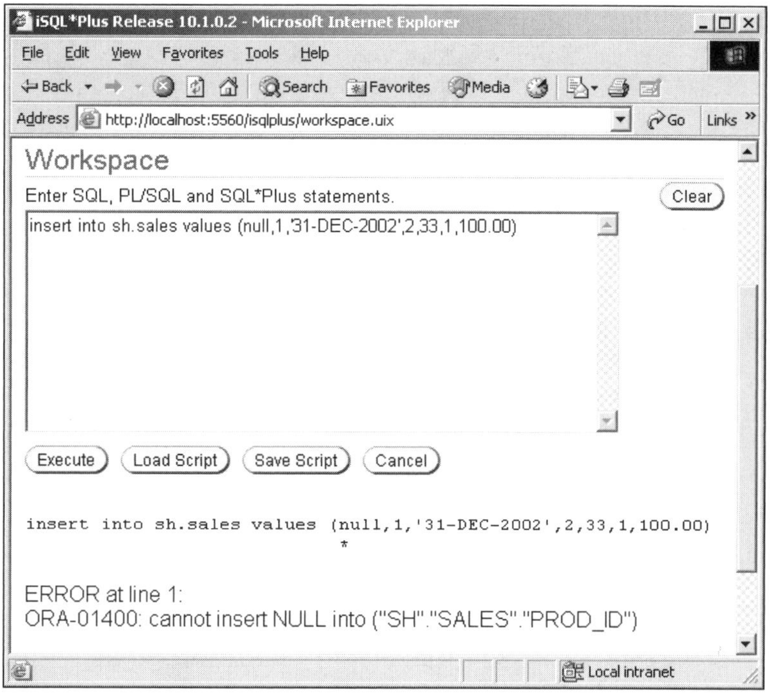

Figure 11-2: Attempting to insert a row that violates a database constraint.

PRIMARY KEY

Any Oracle table may have one (and only one!) `PRIMARY KEY` constraint. The primary key may be one column or combination of columns that applications and users can always depend on to uniquely identify any given row in a table.

Relational database practitioners use the term "key" in several ways. More discussion of the various types of keys was presented in Chapter 4, "Database Design Basics."

It is possible to create a table without a primary key, but this is an exception to conventional relational design principles. The `SH.SALES` example table, for one, has not been defined with a primary key. The designers have decided that there may be multiple rows in the `SALES` table with identical values in all columns and therefore no way to use the data to differentiate them. In most situations, however, you will want to apply some identification rules to prevent duplication or anonymity of rows. The `PRIMARY KEY` constraint does both. It forces uniqueness on the column (or column list) of the `PRIMARY KEY` constraint, preventing two rows from having the identical values. It also ensures that some value is always present. That is, it also implies `NOT NULL`.

Primary keys are generally included in the initial definition of a table. Single-column primary keys are typically included in the column's definition. Figure 11-3 shows the creation of a simple table with this simple inline syntax for the `PRIMARY KEY`.

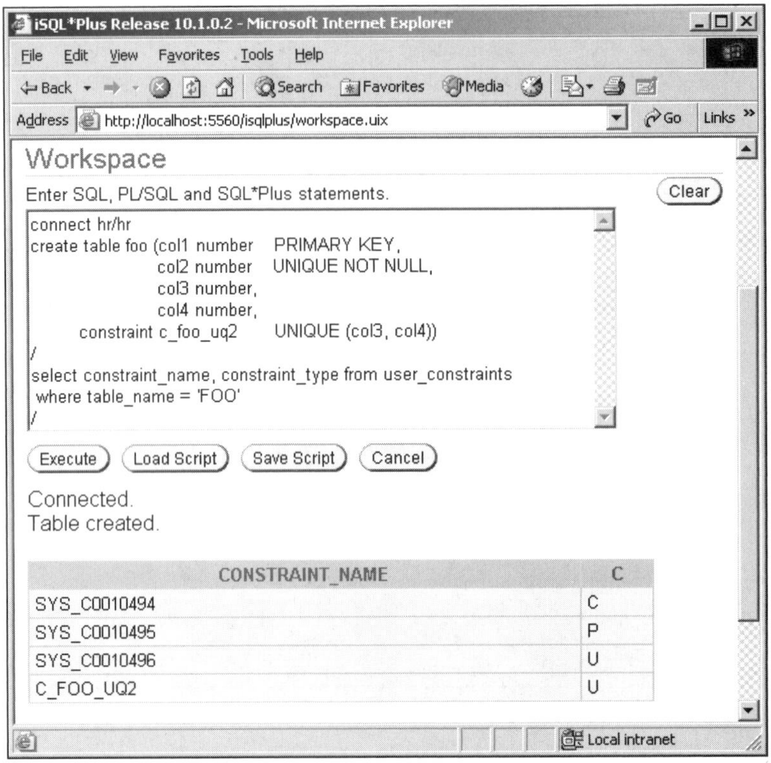

Figure 11-3: Creating a table with implicitly and explicitly named constraints.

Note that in the data dictionary the constraint has been given the name SYS_C0010491, but you know which one you are looking for because you see thatthe CONSTRAINT_TYPE is equal to 'P'. This example also created two UNIQUE constraints (that you will look at in a moment), but the syntax used to create the out-of-line constraint named C_FOO_UQ2 is similar to what you would use for a multicolumn PRIMARY KEY constraint.

Once a primary key is in place, it will constrain the data that users attempt to add or modify within the table. Figure 11-4 shows the two possible errors caused by violating a PRIMARY KEY constraint.

Attempts to insert NULL into a primary key column will still raise the ORA-01400 error just as with the NOT NULL constraint. Trying to insert a value that duplicates an existing row's primary key raises the ORA-0001 error of a UNIQUE constraint violation.

So, just as you saw that NOT NULL is really just a special case of a CHECK constraint with an alternative way to declare it, you now see that the PRIMARY KEY constraint is actually enforced as just the combination of NOT NULL (or CHECK) and UNIQUE constraints even though a query of the data dictionary will show it as a PRIMARY KEY.

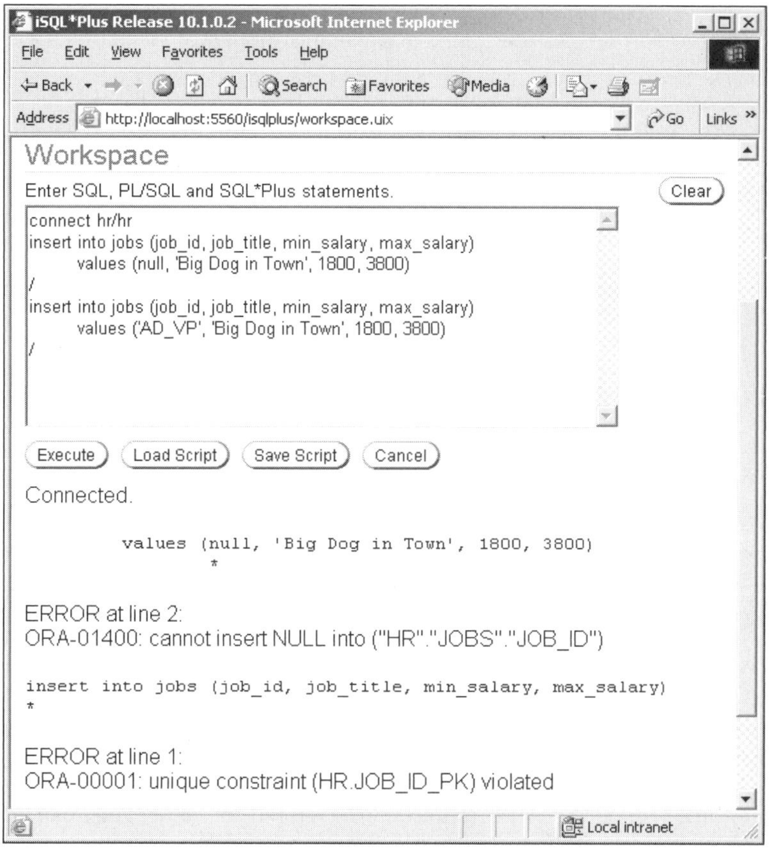

Figure 11-4: Inserts that violate the two rules enforced by a `PRIMARY KEY` constraint.

UNIQUE

You saw in the last section that even though the data dictionary tells you about `PRIMARY KEY` being a special type of constraint, it is actually enforced as two constraints, `NOT NULL` and `UNIQUE`, that together provide the primary means to identify individual rows. Even though a table may only have one designated `PRIMARY KEY`, it is certainly possible to have other ways of uniquely identifying rows in the table. Consider your automobile. Each production vehicle that rolls off a manufacturer's assembly line is given a unique vehicle identification number (or VIN) that fits the criteria of a `PRIMARY KEY` constraint: Each value is unique and none are null (excluding antique vehicles, homemade utility trailers, bicycles, etc. that are not in our domain!). However, if you intend to operate that vehicle on the public highways, you will have to register it and obtain license plates. For residents of the United States, your state generally issues the registration with a unique serial number. Your license plate letters and numbers (when combined with the state and perhaps registration year) are also supposed to be unique. SQL syntax lets you identify and constrain such alternate keys using a `UNIQUE` constraint.

Figure 11-3 also included definition of two UNIQUE constraints, one inline and another that had to be expressed out-of-line because (like the state-license-year combination) it spanned multiple columns.

Note that UNIQUE constraints have no requirement for the data to be NOT NULL as PRIMARY KEY constraints do. For instance, you might own a production vehicle that is only used on a farm or at the racetrack and is therefore not registered with the state even though it had a VIN issued by the manufacturer. With no state registration or license plates, these descriptive attributes of your car would be null. Hence, if the data that you want to designate as an alternative UNIQUE key should never be null, then you will also need to specify the NOT NULL constraint in the table's definition. Figure 11-3 showed this for the constraints on column COL2.

Even though Figure 11-2 was demonstrating violation of a PRIMARY KEY constraint by trying to duplicate an existing row's key, you saw that the violation returned the ORA-00001 error related to UNIQUE constraints, so we won't repeat an example here.

FOREIGN KEY

One of the most frequent integrity needs within a database requires data in one table to be validated by comparing it to data in other tables. When you add a new order, you want to be sure that the product being ordered is a valid product and that you have all of the necessary information about a customer before entering the order. This type of validation is sometimes referred to as *referential integrity*—that is, an integrity rule validated by referencing another table. This same type of integrity check is also known as a foreign key, indicating that you are validating against a key defined in a different (i.e., foreign) table. Both terms are equivalent, and variations in the SQL syntax use both terminologies. We will use the term FOREIGN KEY constraint throughout this section because of the reminder that we are defining the constraint based on key constraints (either PRIMARY KEY or UNIQUE) in the referenced table.

The table that has the foreign key defined is called the referencing table. The table that is used to validate it is called the referenced table. Alternatively, referential integrity rules are sometimes called a parent-child relationship, where the child table is the referencing table and the parent table is the one being referenced. This terminology makes sense in purely hierarchical relationships, such as the one between an ORDERS (parent) table and an ORDER_LINES (child) table, but is less clear when the referencing table has multiple foreign keys referencing a variety of tables. In these more general cases, the parent-child terminology should usually be avoided.

A FOREIGN KEY constraint compares the data values being entered into the table on which they are defined to existing values within the referenced table. Not all data columns in the referenced table are candidates, however. Only the columns that make up a defined key (either a PRIMARY KEY or UNIQUE constraints) in that other table can be used. The definition of the FOREIGN KEY names the local columns that need to be validated but only optionally names columns in the other table. If columns are not named on the referenced table, then Oracle will assume that the reference will be to the primary key columns of that table. Oracle will, of course, verify that the column list of the FOREIGN KEY constraint matches the column list of the referenced PRIMARY KEY or UNIQUE constraint in both number of columns and their data types.

Oracle limits foreign key declarations to be in the same database although they may reference a table in another schema. If you need to validate data against a table in a remote database, the check will have to be made via a trigger. Be aware, however, that if the remote verification can't be performed because of an outage of the other database or the network connection, the trigger won't be able to execute properly. This will either (depending on the logic) prevent the local data modification from being completed or allow unvalidated data to be entered.

Creating FOREIGN KEY Constraints

Like all of the constraints you've looked at, FOREIGN KEY constraints can be created as part of the initial creation of a table or added after the fact. Whenever you build the FOREIGN KEY, the table being referenced must already exist with the referenced PRIMARY KEY or UNIQUE constraint defined. Here is an example (using the OE schema) of the general syntax used for creating these constraints out of line:

```
create table foo
   (foo_key          number primary key,
    foo_custno       number,
    CONSTRAINT FOO_CUST_FK FOREIGN KEY (FOO_CUSTNO)
                           REFERENCES OE.CUSTOMERS (CUSTOMER_ID) );
```

In this simple example, the FOO table will have two constraints, a PRIMARY KEY on the FOO_KEY column and a FOREIGN KEY named FOO_CUST_FK that will constrain the FOO_CUSTNO column to contain only values that are currently stored in the CUSTOMER_ID column of the CUSTOMERS table. Had the primary key of CUSTOMERS been composed of multiple columns, then you would have to name those columns in the correct order in the REFERENCES clause and also name the corresponding columns in the FOO table as part of the FOREIGN KEY column list.

Several shorthand methods for creating FOREIGN KEY constraints are available. This next example creates the same table with the same constraint but allows Oracle to assume you are referencing the PRIMARY KEY of CUSTOMERS rather than explicitly naming the CUSTOMER_ID column:

```
create table foo
   (foo_key          number primary key,
    foo_custno       number,
    CONSTRAINT FOO_CUST_FK FOREIGN KEY (FOO_CUSTNO)
               REFERENCES OE.CUSTOMERS );
```

This syntax will work for either single-column or multiple-column keys. Another form of shorthand, an inline declaration, is available for those situations when the key structure involves only a single column:

```
create table foo
   (foo_key          number primary key,
    foo_custno       number CONSTRAINT FOO_CUST_FK REFERENCES OE.CUSTOMERS );
```

Since the inline declaration is part of the definition of the FOO_CUSTNO column, in this example the FOREIGN KEY (column list) syntax does not need to be included. The REFERENCES (table name) is sufficient for Oracle to determine the meaning and create the same constraint. Further shorthand, that we won't bother to show, would allow you to leave out the CONSTRAINT constraint_name clause, but this would force Oracle to name the constraint for you using its cryptic naming standard. Figure 11-3 showed some constraints with system-generated names.

In general, we recommend explicitly naming all constraints with the exception of NOT NULL constraints.

These three CREATE TABLE statements all build identical foreign keys referencing the CUSTOMERS table's primary key. Remember that a foreign key can also reference a UNIQUE constraint on the reference table. The syntax will be identical to either of the first two examples, except that the two column lists will refer to the alternative key's columns rather than the primary key's column list. To see an example of referencing a UNIQUE constraint instead of a PRIMARY KEY, you'll look at an example in the HR schema. The

EMPLOYEES table has a PRIMARY KEY based on the EMPLOYEE_ID. The EMAIL column in this table has a UNIQUE constraint defined as well. If you wish to enter e-mail addresses into another table, you can verify that you have properly entered the valid e-mail address of a current employee by building a FOREIGN KEY constraint that references the EMAIL column. Here is an example:

```
create table foo_notifications
   (foo_nfy_key       number primary key,
    foo_nfy_email     varchar2(25) CONSTRAINT FOO_EMAIL_FK
                                   REFERENCES HR.EMPLOYEES (EMAIL) );
```

This example uses the inline constraint syntax but requires the specification of column lists.

Setting FOREIGN KEY Constraint Actions

So far you have created FOREIGN KEY constraints using the default action that is to prevent invalid data from being introduced to the referencing table and also to prevent deletion of rows from the referenced tables where the value is actually in use by one or more rows in the referencing table. Invalid changes (from either INSERT or UPDATE statements) to the referencing table only have one possible action — prevent the action and return an error. Changes to the referenced table, however, have other possible actions. For instance, you could actually perform the modification if you also

- Deleted the invalidated rows from the referencing table (ON DELETE CASCADE)
- Set the referencing column values to null for any rows that would be invalidated (ON DELETE SET NULL)
- Updated the column values in the referencing table to match a change made to the value in referenced table (ON UPDATE CASCADE)

Of these three possibilities, Oracle supports the first two. If you find that your application needs the third option, you may have to insert a new row in the referenced table, perform the updates on the referencing table, and then delete the old row from the referenced table. This can't be performed within a declarative constraint and can also not be performed within a trigger, as you will see in the discussion of mutating tables in Chapter 19, "Triggers."

Remember that the syntax to specify ON DELETE CASCADE or ON DELETE SET NULL is defined as part of the constraint on the referencing table even though these clauses control the actions of DELETE statements on the referenced table; the action clauses are, however, controlling what extended actions will be made to the referencing table where the rule is defined, so it all makes sense. Here are some quick examples of the necessary syntax to specify nonstandard actions:

```
create table foo_1
   (foo_key          number primary key,
    foo_custno       number,
    CONSTRAINT FOO1_CUST_FK FOREIGN KEY (FOO_CUSTNO)
               REFERENCES OE.CUSTOMERS (CUSTOMER_ID) ON DELETE CASCADE );

create table foo_2
   (foo_key          number primary key,
    foo_custno       number,
    CONSTRAINT FOO2_CUST_FK FOREIGN KEY (FOO_CUSTNO)
               REFERENCES OE.CUSTOMERS (CUSTOMER_ID) ON DELETE SET NULL );
```

Violations of FOREIGN KEY Constraints

As you saw in the last section, `FOREIGN KEY` constraints have the option to have special options for correcting violations caused by deleting rows from a referenced table. Other violations, however, will generate an error that will be returned to the application program. Figure 11-5 demonstrates some typical errors.

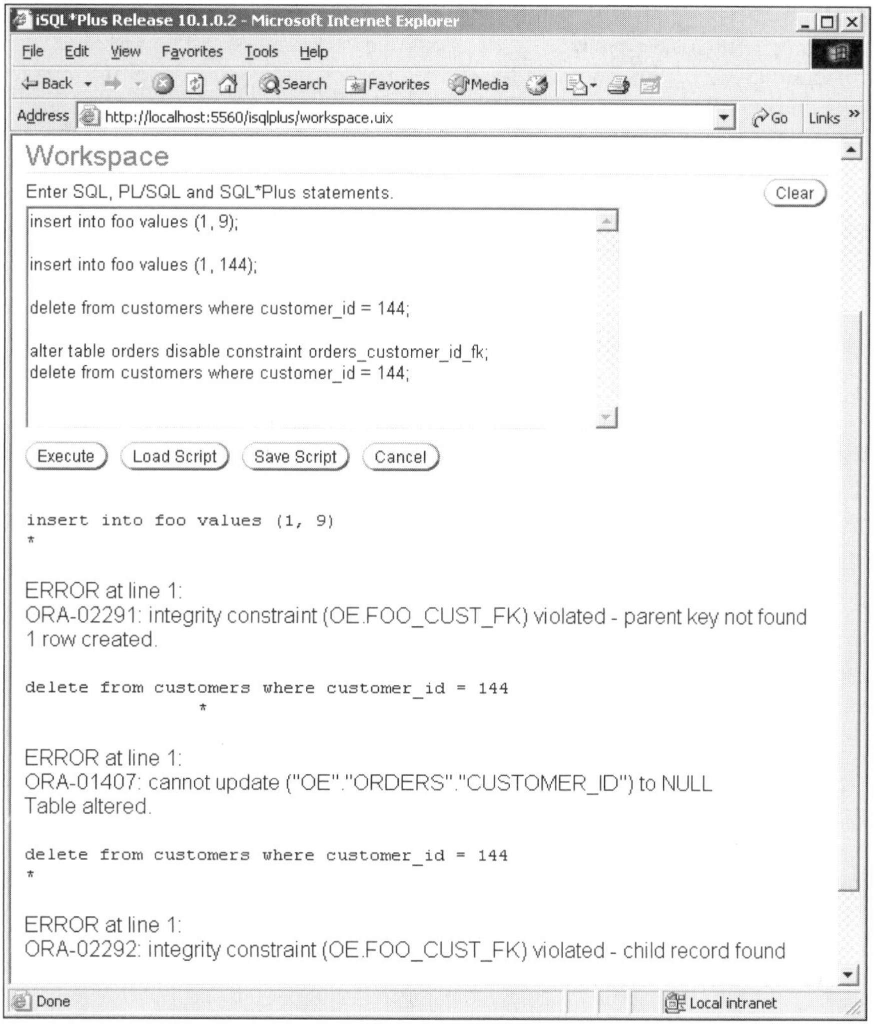

Figure 11-5: Errors returned when violating foreign key constraints.

In this figure we first attempt to insert a row into the `FOO` table (as created above) that uses an invalid `CUSTOMER_ID`, which results in error `ORA-02291`. We then successfully insert a row into `FOO` for customer 144. Attempting to delete that customer should not succeed. When we try this deletion we receive an error, but not the one we were expecting. It turns out that there was already a `FOREIGN KEY` constraint from the `ORDERS` table that specifies `ON DELETE SET NULL`. This returns error `ORA-01407` because the database was unable to set the `ORDERS.CUSTOMER_ID` column to null. This demonstrates the potential problem of having inconsistent constraints in the database. The original developers of this test schema have specified that they want to set these values to null when their parent is deleted, but they have also specified the column to be NOT NULL! Temporarily disabling the original FOREIGN KEY constraint shows the more normal error (ORA-02292) returned by an attempt to delete a parent key value.

FOREIGN KEY Constraints and Nulls

Before moving on to the next constraint type, we should comment on the handling of nulls within the columns of a foreign key. Remember that the PRIMARY KEY constraint also requires that the data in the primary key must not be null. No such restriction applies to FOREIGN KEY columns. Null values in any of the FOREIGN KEY columns will allow the row to be inserted without violation of the constraint. If you wish to ensure that data is always entered, you have to explicitly add a NOT NULL constraint to each column in your declaration of the FOREIGN KEY constraint.

A particularly interesting condition occurs when a multiple-column FOREIGN KEY constraint has at least one but not all of the columns populated. In such a case Oracle will allow the partial data to be entered into the database with no attempt to validate the partial values. Sometimes this is difficult to grasp, but it makes sense if you consider that the PRIMARY KEY or UNIQUE constraint that is being referenced applies to the entire column list. There is no constraint based on any subset of the referenced constraint, so it would be meaningless to attempt to validate just part of the foreign key's data. Once again, you can always define each column included in the FOREIGN KEY to be NOT NULL. In some cases you may wish to ensure that multicolumn constrained data is fully supplied (and validated) or that no data is provided at all. Doing so requires a custom-built CHECK constraint that verifies one of the two conditions (all columns populated or no columns populated) is true.

CHECK

CHECK constraints are the most flexible of the declarative constraint types. CHECK constraints can use (with only a few restrictions) one or more conditions to be checked for the data row in much the same way a WHERE clause can specify the search conditions to find a row. In addition to being able to use compound conditions within a single CHECK constraint, you can apply multiple CHECK constraints on the same column.

If you do specify multiple CHECK constraints, you must validate the combined logic to verify that they are not in conflict. It is entirely possible (but not generally advisable) to have a constraint that says a column must be equal to 2 and another constraint that requires it to be equal to 5. Combine those two with a NOT NULL and you could get a table that is unable to accept any possible data rows!

The CHECK constraint, no matter how simple or complex, must eventually be evaluated as a boolean test with a value of either TRUE or FALSE. If true, the constraint is passed and the row may be inserted or updated as requested. If false, the row will be rejected and an error returned. Your conditions are able to refer to any of the column values in the current row as well as constants, and you may use any combination of built-in functions including logical, mathematical, string, date functions and so on.

What you may not do, however, is reference anything that will not remain constant for the life of this row. Such forbidden references include other rows in the table or a query to another table. You also may not reference the special SQL functions (such as USER, USERENV, SYSDATE, etc.), user-defined PL/SQL functions, or SQL pseudocolumns (e.g., LEVEL or ROWNUM), because these all have transient values that will not have the same context or meaning once the transaction is completed.

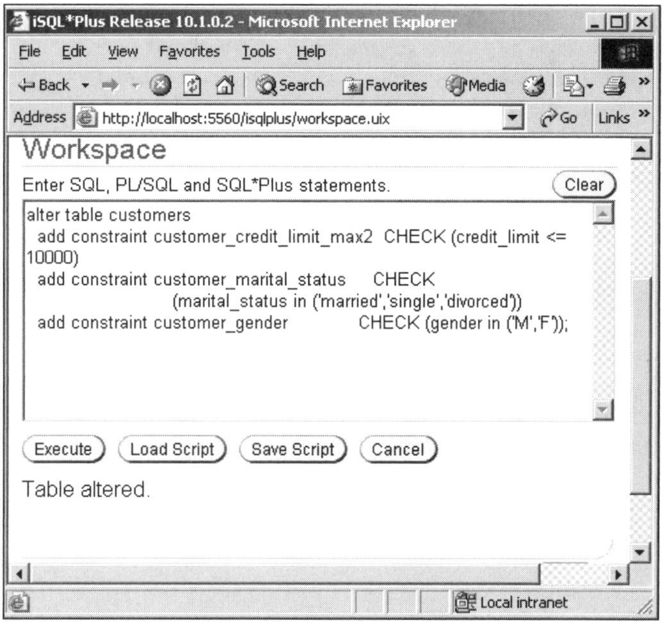

Figure 11-6: Adding constraints to an existing table.

In Figure 11-6 you see a single `ALTER TABLE` command that adds three additional constraints to the `OE.CUSTOMERS` table. The first of these constraints ensures that no rows will ever have a `CREDIT_LIMIT` greater than $10,000 (more on that one a little later). The next two constrain the data to specific allowable values for `GENDER` and `MARITAL_STATUS`. The command completed successfully, so you know that the existing data in the table meets the new data standards that were defined.

But what happens if you attempt to apply a constraint to which the data does not conform? This is demonstrated in Figure 11-7. Here a constraint is defined that will require customers to have been born after January 1, 1900, but before January 1, 2000. As of 2004, this would mean that the customers are not expected to be older than 104 years or younger than 5 years. Reasonable, no?

Well, apparently not, at least for the data as currently loaded in the `OE.CUSTOMERS` table! At least one row in the table has a customer whose recorded birth date is outside the defined range. A simple query (one that reformats the date to include a four-digit year) shows that the maximum date of birth is in 2049! It is doubtful that anyone would actually have such a customer (the table has several of these), who won't be born for nearly half a century. Very likely the Oracle developers who created the application that loaded these rows failed to use a four-digit year on input and no constraint was in place to prevent "49" from being automatically interpreted as the current century, thereby being stored as 2049 instead of the intended 1949! (The curse of Y2K lives on!)

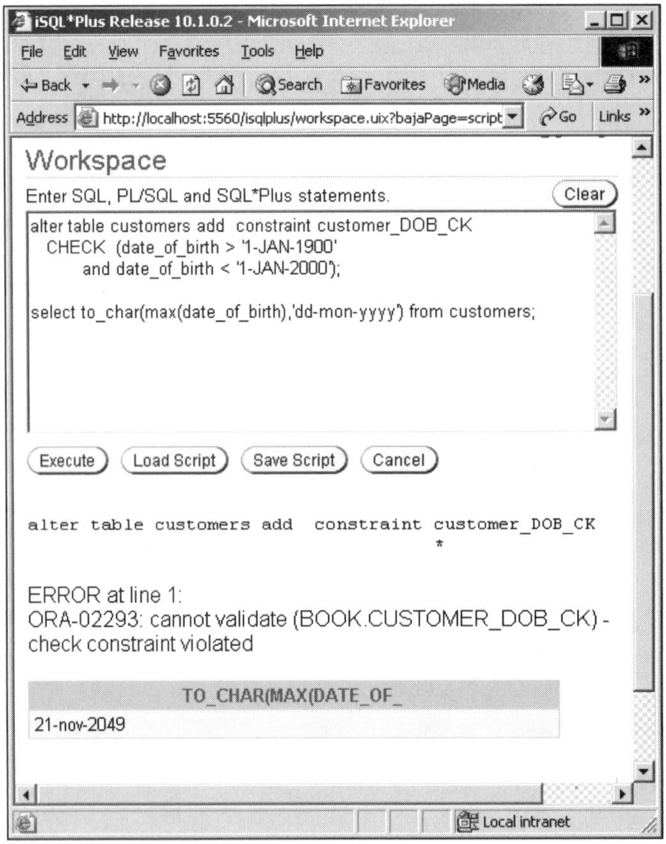

Figure 11-7: Adding a constraint that is violated by existing data in the table.

This example, directly from the Oracle-supplied test schemas, perfectly demonstrates the value of using declarative constraints. Even the Oracle development team makes mistakes on data entry that could have been prevented through intelligent use of database constraints.

Before leaving this example, though, it is probably worthwhile to also discuss the merits of such a constraint. By putting these absolute date values into the table definition, you must be prepared to change them over time. This check of the date of birth isn't terribly granular, and you could change it every couple of years. Other validation, such as verifying that a new `ORDER_DATE` is no more than a week in the past, would not be appropriate for a `CHECK` constraint. Since you can't reference `SYSDATE` in the constraint and constraints have to remain true for existing rows, you would have a problem. A simple `INSERT` trigger, although procedural, could handle a situation like this much more gracefully.

Back in Figure 11-1 we created three new constraints, one of which set a maximum credit limit of $10,000. In Figure 11-8 we attempt to update a row to have a credit limit of $8, 000, but it fails. Yet $8,000 is less than the limit of $10,000, so what's wrong?

Even though we added a $10,000 limit via the `CUSTOMER_LIMIT_MAX2` constraint, we failed to take notice that another constraint (`CUSTOMER_LIMIT_MAX`) is already in place on the customer table that limits the credit limit to $5,000. The two constraints are not actually in conflict with each other, but the new one that we added is not having any effect because it is less stringent than the one that was already in place. If we really want to allow credit limits to be up to $10,000, we must remove the older, less strict constraint before the new limit will take effect. The lesson here is that you must always be careful to review the constraints in place on a table to be sure that they are consistent.

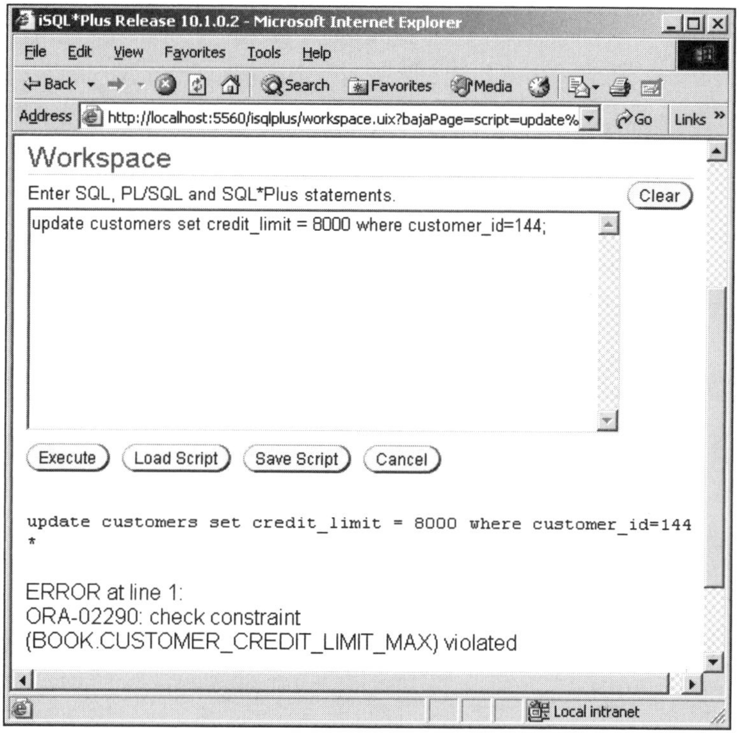

Figure 11-8: An example of multiple constraints with different rules.

Check constraints, as you have seen, are commonly defined on columns of a relational table. They may also be defined to constrain attributes within a column defined using a user-defined data type with only a slight change in syntax. This example first creates a simple object data type with two attributes and then uses that data type within the definition of a table. To constrain the allowable values for an attribute, the constraint will reference the specific attribute within the object column as:

```
create type person_type as object
   (first_name       varchar2(25),
    last_name        varchar2(30),
    birthdate        date,
    work_phone       number(10));
/

create table contact_list
   (contact person_type,
    CHECK (contact.first_name is not null and contact.last_name is not null));
```

More information on the use object features of the Oracle database is presented in Chapter 21, "Object Relational Interactions with Oracle."

DEFAULT

In the introduction to this section, we mentioned that the usual six constraint types could actually be considered as only four actual constraints plus one related concept. Well, `DEFAULT` is the related concept. `DEFAULT` does not actually constrain data during `INSERT` or `UPDATE` operations at all, but it is usually discussed in the same section because its syntax is so similar to the actual declarative constraints. In actual usage, `DEFAULT` can be considered as a substitute behavior for the `NOT NULL` constraint when applied to new rows being entered into the table.

When you define a column with the `DEFAULT` keyword followed by a value, you're actually telling the database that, on `INSERT`, if a row was not assigned a value for this column, go ahead and use the default value that you have specified. Figure 11-9 demonstrates the sometimes perplexing behavior of `DEFAULT`.

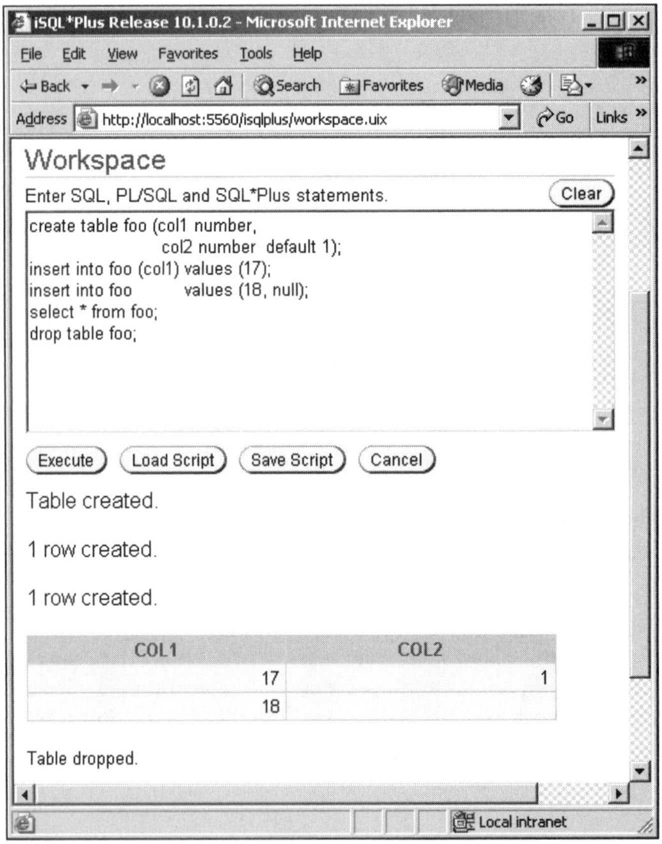

Figure 11-9: Behavior of `INSERT` on a column declared with a `DEFAULT` clause.

In this example we create a simple table that has two columns. The second of these has a default value of 1 specified. The first `INSERT` statement only populates the first column, and Oracle implicitly applies the default value for the unspecified column. The second `INSERT` statement, by contrast, does include a specification for the second column, but it is explicitly assigned null as its value. In this case the default value is not used and the database actually accepts and stores the value of null.

Although not shown in this example, if col2 had been defined with a `NOT NULL` constraint, Oracle would allow you to specify a `DEFAULT` clause as well. The `DEFAULT` would supply a value as it did in the first `INSERT` statement but would return an error in the second case where an explicit null is specified. The `DEFAULT` "constraint" will provide a value for an unspecified column but will not override an explicitly supplied null.

This interaction between the two constraints sometimes confuses developers, because two statements (one with an implicit null and another with an explicitly provided null) that have the same effect in most situations suddenly behave differently.

Also keep in mind that `DEFAULT` is only applied during insertion of new rows. Updating a column value to null will work as long as nulls are allowed in the column and the default value will not be substituted. This is another way in which `DEFAULT` does not behave like the true constraints that ensure that all data in the table remains in compliance whenever the constraint is in effect, as we'll discuss more in the next section.

REF Constraints

As object capabilities were added to the Oracle database beginning in Oracle8*i*, it became clear that the concept of declarative constraints for relational data would also be useful for ensuring the integrity of data stored using the object model. When you are defining an object data type, you may declare a `REF` column that relates data in that object to other data within the database.

Working with Oracle's object model is covered in Chapter 21, which will provide the context to understand this brief introduction to the concepts of `REF` constraints. In quick summary, a `REF` column allows the designer/developer to specify a reference to an existing row in a reference table rather than having to enter all of the same data into the new object directly.

Like the traditional relational constraints, `REF` constraints can be declared either inline or out-of-line but using slightly different syntax. `REF` constraints may define the constraint based on a scope table, a `ROWID` constraint, or a referential integrity constraint.

In general, `REF` columns within an object may have instances that reference rows in multiple object tables. Specifying a scope table as part of the `REF` definition allows the designer to precisely declare which of those object tables should be used for validating new instances of the constrained object. Only one scope table may be named for each `REF` column. Unlike relational constraints that can be added to a populated table and will then validate existing data, scope table `REF` constraints can only be added to an unpopulated table.

Specifying `WITH ROWID` on a `REF` constraint tells Oracle to actually store the `ROWID` (the physical address of a row) as part of the object. This will allow the `DEREF` operation to directly access the referenced data rather than having to perform the lookup using less efficient lookup methods. Once a `REF WITH ROWID` constraint has been built, it cannot later be dropped.

A referential integrity constraint on an object definition is similar to a relational `FOREIGN KEY` constraint. It implicitly restricts the scope to the referenced table. The main difference with object referential integrity constraints is that rather than referencing the `PRIMARY KEY` (or `UNIQUE`) constraint on the referenced table, `REF` constraints defined with the `REFERENCES` clause will actually reference the OID (object identifier) of the referenced object. Within the object model of Oracle, the OID serves the same purpose as a relational primary key by uniquely identifying a particular instance of that object.

Although similar to a relational `FOREIGN KEY` constraint, it is important to recognize that scoped `REF`s do not protect the relationship to the same degree. REF constraints verify that the referenced object table, but not necessarily the specific row object, exists so that deleting a referenced row object is not prevented and, if performed, will leave a dangling REF from the entry in the referencing table.

As brief examples, you'll work with the simple `PERSON_TYPE` type that was introduced earlier in the chapter, then build a `CONTACT_LIST` table of the `PERSON_TYPE` type and a `CLUBS` table that will reference `CONTACT_LIST`. The first example scopes the reference to validate that each club president will be a current entry in the `CONTACT_LIST` table.

```
create type person_type as object
   (first_name       varchar2(25),
    last_name        varchar2(30),
    birthdate        date,
    work_phone       number(10));
/

create table contact_list
    of person_type;

create table clubs
   (club_name        varchar2(30),
    president        REF person_type  scope is contact_list);
```

As an alternative, you can use an OID reference to the `CONTACT_LIST` table in a named referential integrity constraint:

```
create table clubs
   (club_name        varchar2(30),
    president        REF person_type
                     constraint club_pres_contacts_fk references contact_list);
```

Rather than using the OID to find a referenced `CONTACT_LIST` entry, the `REF` column can be defined using a `ROWID` that will be stored with each `CLUBS` row as:

```
create table clubs
   (club_name        varchar2(30),
    president        REF person_type  with rowid);
```

In this final example, the location of a person_type object has not been constrained, but we have decided to increase the storage requirement in order to speed up `DEREF` (lookup) operations. Had the definition of `PRESIDENT` been scoped, Oracle would have ignored the `WITH ROWID` declaration.

Working with Constraints

In addition to specifying constraints during the initial creation of database tables, you often must add, drop, or rename constraints later. Sometimes it is appropriate to modify the way that constraints behave. This section provides an overview of the various ways to modify constraints and their behavior.

Alter Table

The examples in the previous section gave a good overview of the inline and out-of-line syntax for including declarative constraints as part of a CREATE TABLE command. The ALTER TABLE command also allows you to add constraints, but it gives you other capabilities as well.

To add a constraint, you must use the out-of-line constraint syntax (shown in Figure 11-6) unless you are adding a new column and including a constraint declaration as part of that column's definition.

You may also use ALTER TABLE to drop a constraint:

```
alter table customers drop constraint customer_credit_limit_max2;
```

This example shows why it is handy to name your constraints rather than have Oracle generate a SYS_Cnnnnnnn name!

If you attempt to drop a PRIMARY KEY or UNIQUE constraint that is referenced by a FOREIGN KEY constraint, you will receive an error. If you do really intend to drop the referenced constraint, you will have to first drop the FOREIGN KEY constraints that depend upon it or use the CASCADE clause that will drop all dependent FOREIGN KEY constraints along with the PRIMARY KEY or UNIQUE constraint. As always, be careful in using CASCADE. In every command that offers CASCADE, it will do some extra, perhaps unintended, actions to your database! Figure 11-10 shows the effect of attempting (using two syntax options) to drop a PRIMARY KEY constraint that is currently referenced by one or more FOREIGN KEY constraints.

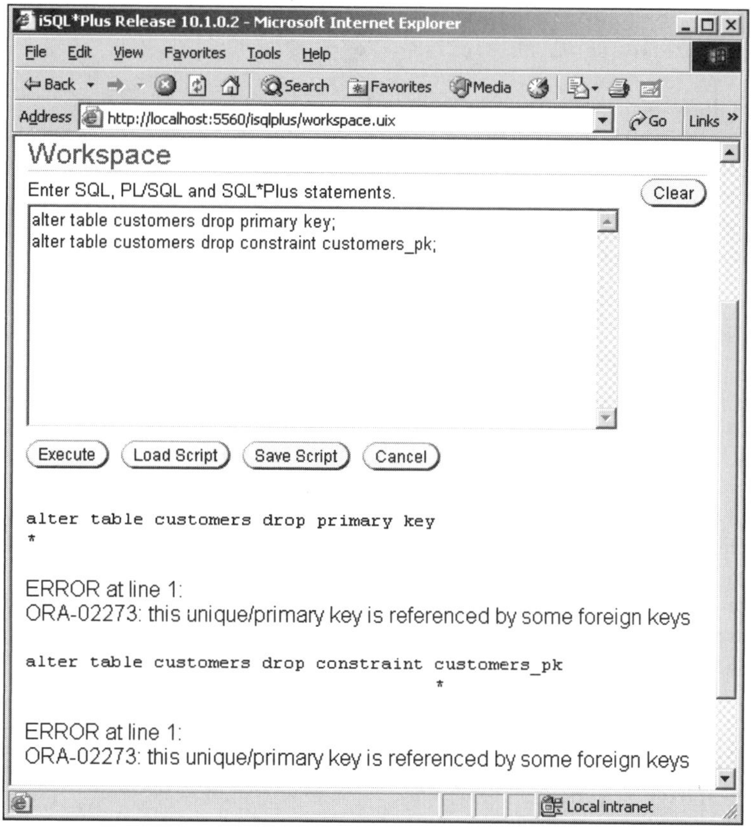

Figure 11-10: Dropping a PRIMARY KEY that is referenced by FOREIGN KEY constraints.

Adding CASCADE to either of the ALTER TABLE commands in Figure 11-10 would drop the CUSTOMERS_PK constraint along with the FOREIGN KEY constraints on the various FOO tables that were created earlier in this chapter. It would also drop the FOREIGN KEY that is protecting the ORDERS table!

Additionally, ALTER TABLE allows you to change the name of an existing constraint (perhaps because you forgot to explicitly name it originally?). In this example you'll go back and rename one of the constraints built earlier so that the constraint type is easily determined from the name:

```
alter table customers rename constraint customer_gender to customer_gender_ck;
```

We also have ALTER TABLE...MODIFY syntax available to change an existing constraint. The only modifications allowed to an existing constraint are ones that change the constraint state (discussed in the next section). To change the actual tested condition or column list of a constraint, you need to first drop the constraint and then re-create it with the new rule.

Constraint States

Constraints can, at any time, be either enabled or disabled. Disabling a constraint allows the definition to remain in the data dictionary during a period in which you choose not to have the constraint active. There are several alternative ways to disable a constraint:

```
alter table customers modify constraint customers_pk disable;
alter table customers modify primary key disable;
alter table customers disable constraint customers_pk;
alter table customers disable primary key;
```

The first two of these examples show the preferred syntax that is the most general. The ability to reference the PRIMARY KEY by type rather than name is special syntax that only applies because there can be at most one PRIMARY KEY constraint on a table. (Similar special syntax also exists for disabling or enabling UNIQUE (column list).)

Enabling a disabled constraint can be done with similar syntax:

```
alter table customers modify constraint customers_pk enable;
```

When you create, enable, or disable a constraint, you may specify some other information regarding how the constraint behaves and how it should be treated. An enabled constraint may be set to validate existing data in the table or not by use of the VALIDATE (the default) or NOVALIDATE options. With ENABLE NOVALIDATE Oracle will not recheck all of the existing data in the table.

Using NOVALIDATE has some risk associated with it. If, during the time that the constraint was disabled, any invalid data was introduced, it will not be found when you ENABLE the constraint with NOVALIDATE. Revalidating all of the data in a very large table may take a long time. If you are absolutely sure that only valid data was added while the constraint was disabled, the NOVALIDATE syntax allows you to save this time when re-enabling the constraint. This approach is sometimes used in an application that has an online window (when user input must be validated) and a separate batch load, during which new data is carefully checked before it is loaded. After the load has completed, the constraint might be re-enabled with the NOVALIDATE option. The risk associated with this approach has to be compared to the savings in time by running the load without redundant checking.

You may also DISABLE VALIDATE a constraint. This is usually done in a data warehousing environment when you want to avoid index maintenance for a large bulk load. When in this state, the only operations that are allowed are SQL*Loader and partition exchange loading. Normal INSERT/UPDATE/DELETE commands are prohibited.

Independent of how existing data is treated, when enabling a constraint, you may also specify how much trust should be put in the constraint. This is done with the RELY or NORELY (default) options. These can only be defined as part of modifying an existing constraint. RELY is used to tell the Oracle optimizer that it can trust the integrity of this constraint, even when disabled or in the NOVALIDATE state, for the purposes of query rewrite and the possible consideration of a materialized view. It is also possible for ad hoc query tools to look at the RELY state to determine whether it is possible to depend upon a constraint even if the constraint is disabled.

When you attempt to ENABLE VALIDATE a constraint, there is a possibility that some of the existing data rows may not meet the requirements of the constraint. It is frustrating to issue a command that takes several minutes or even hours, just to receive an error that tells you that some data violates the constraint. How do you know which rows need to be fixed? You could write an SQL SELECT statement that implements logic opposite to the constraint in order to create a list of violating rows. Fortunately, you don't have to because ability to generate such a list is provided as part of the ENABLE process. The EXCEPTIONS INTO clause forces Oracle to continue the attempt to VALIDATE the data, but for any rows that violate the constraint, the rows' ROWIDs are saved into an exceptions table. Oracle can record either physical or universal ROWIDs. Unless you are working with index organized tables (IOTs), you can use physical ROWIDs.

You will need to prebuild an exceptions table to hold the ROWIDs, table name, and the specific constraint that the row violates. Scripts are provided in the $ORACLE_HOME/rdbms/admin directory to create this table for you. UTLEXCPT will build a table called EXCEPTIONS in your schema to hold physical ROWIDs, and UTLEXPT1 will build a table to hold universal ROWIDs. Figure 11-11 demonstrates the use of an EXCEPTIONS table. In this example, two invalid rows have been added to the FOO table while the FOO_CUST_FK constraint was disabled. By including the EXCEPTIONS INTO clause, you can rapidly find the offending rows using their ROWIDs and either delete them or correct them. Once the exception rows are corrected, you would reissue the ALTER TABLE...ENABLE VALIDATE to reestablish the FOREIGN KEY relationship to the CUSTOMERS table.

If you change a disabled constraint directly to ENABLE VALIDATE as shown in Figure 11-11, you should be aware that Oracle will need to take out a table-level lock on the table. If you are enabling the constraint at a time when you have exclusive access to the table, this won't be a problem. If, however, you need to do the enabling while other users are accessing and possibly modifying data in the table, there is a little trick you should know. If you perform the operation in two steps, first performing a ENABLE NOVALIDATE and then doing the ENABLE VALIDATE, you can avoid the need to lock the table.

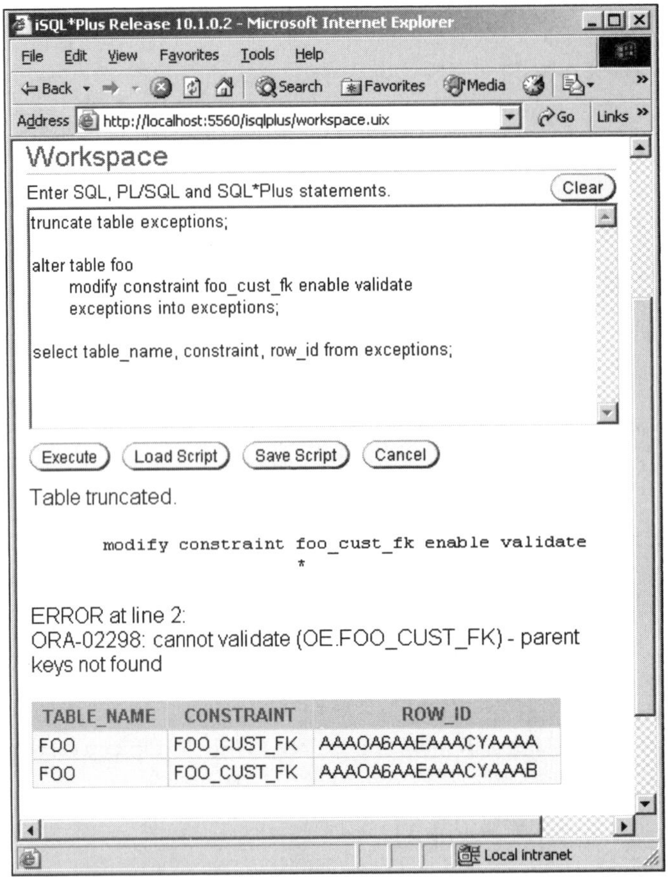

Figure 11-11: Using an `EXCEPTIONS` table while validating a constraint.

Constraints and Indexes

When you create or enable a `PRIMARY KEY` or `UNIQUE` constraint, Oracle will typically need to create a unique index on the column(s) of that constraint. Originally this was the only way to enforce uniqueness, and it remains the default method.

If an appropriate index already exists on the necessary columns, Oracle will use the existing index. If Oracle does have to create a new index, it will be named the same as the constraint.

PRIMARY KEY and UNIQUE Constraints and Indexes

You may take explicit control of the index as part of defining the constraint state by including the `USING INDEX` clause. The following two examples are equivalent. One creates the constraint and index as part of the table definition. The other adds the index and then the constraint using it in separate steps. Both, however, take explicit control of the index and its placement. It is recommended that you take explicit control of index creation (and other index attributes such as storage and tablespace placement) in one of these two ways rather than letting Oracle create an index by default.

```
create table clubs
    (club_name          varchar2(30),
```

```
       meeting_room        number(3),
       meeting_day         varchar2(9),
       constraint club_room_reserve UNIQUE (meeting_room, meeting_day)
                  using index (create unique index club_room_reserve_idx
                        on clubs(meeting_room, meeting_day) tablespace users));

create table clubs
      (club_name           varchar2(30),
       meeting_room        number(3),
       meeting_day         varchar2(9));
create unique index club_room_reserve_idx
    on clubs (meeting_room, meeting_day) tablespace users;
alter table clubs add constraint club_room_reserve UNIQUE (meeting_room,
meeting_day)
      using index club_room_reserve_idx;
```

Both of these examples use a unique index. Unique indexes are the most straightforward way of enforcing uniqueness under either a `PRIMARY KEY` or `UNIQUE` constraint. Oracle is also able to enforce uniqueness with a nonunique index. Figure 11-12 demonstrates this using the same `CLUBS` table from the previous code sample. In this case a nonunique index is created and then used to enforce the `UNIQUE` constraint. Attempting to book the same room on the same day generates the desired error.

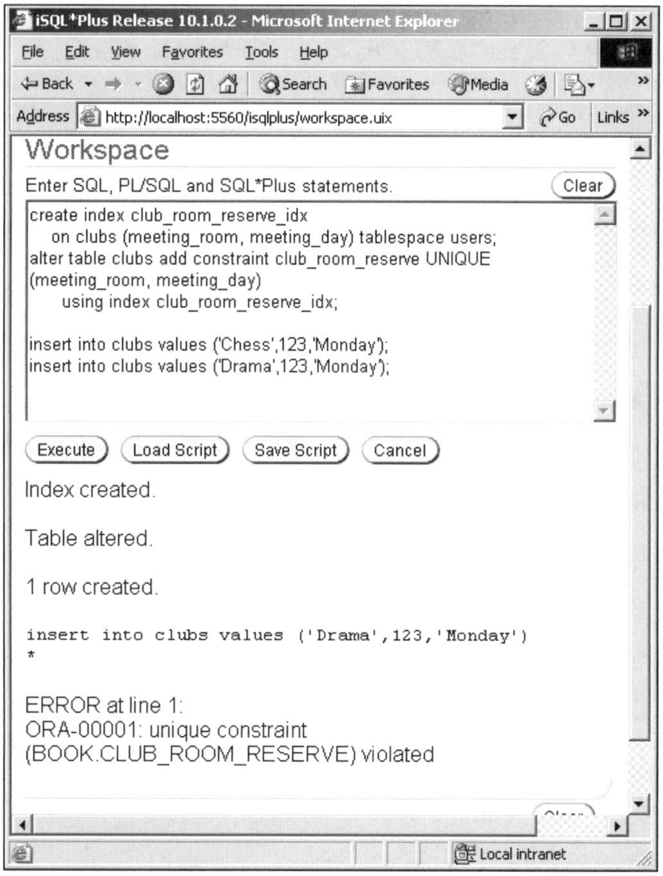

Figure 11-12: Nonunique indexes can be used to enforce uniqueness.

FOREIGN KEY Constraints and Indexes

FOREIGN KEY constraints do not have an index automatically created for enforcement. However, because of the way Oracle must perform locking, it is frequently worthwhile to build an index on the column(s) of each FOREIGN KEY constraint. This is because deleting a row in the parent table has to ensure that there are no matching rows in the child table. Without an index on the corresponding column(s) in the child table, Oracle is forced to take out a table lock on the child while it performs the DELETE on the parent. If an index does exist, Oracle uses it to identify and lock just the necessary rows (if any) in the child table while the parent row is deleted. If you anticipate doing deletes of rows in the table referenced in a FOREIGN KEY constraint while transactions are also needing to access rows in the referencing table, you can avoid concurrency problems by indexing the columns of the FOREIGN KEY constraint.

Deferrable Constraints

All of the examples in this chapter have used the default behavior of constraints — namely, that the constraint is evaluated at the end of each DML (INSERT/UPDATE/DELETE) statement. If a constraint violation occurs, then the single DML statement is rolled back and an appropriate error is returned to the program. This is IMMEDIATE evaluation.

Sometimes the design of a transaction requires there to be temporary violations of a constraint that will be corrected by subsequent steps in the same transaction. To handle conditions like this, Oracle allows constraint validation to be deferred to the end of the transaction. For a transaction to be able to defer validation, the constraint must be DEFERRABLE. This can be specified only when the constraint is defined. Additionally, for a constraint that was defined initially as DEFERRABLE, you may change the constraint from IMMEDIATE validation to DEFERRED validation and back again using ALTER TABLE...MODIFY syntax.

If a constraint has been built with the DEFERRABLE option, then you may use the SET CONSTRAINTS command as part of your transaction to make the constraint validation either IMMEDIATE or DEFERRED for the scope of your transaction. Deferred constraints are automatically validated at the point of transaction commit, but any violations found at that time will cause a complete transaction rollback. You may wish to use SET CONSTRAINTS ALL IMMEDIATE as a final command before the COMMIT so that you are able to trap any errors without losing the entire transaction.

Direct Path Operations

Integrity constraints will be checked (as governed by the constraint state) for any conventional SQL accesses using INSERT, UPDATE, or DELETE statements. Additionally, FOREIGN KEY constraints can control the commands that would DROP or TRUNCATE a table.

The SQL*Loader utility, however, presents some special concerns. As discussed in more depth in Chapter 25, "Data Loading and Management," SQL*Loader has both a conventional path and a direct path. Direct path is designed to speed bulk data loads by bypassing much of the normal SQL processing. When you perform a direct path load, Oracle will continue to enforce NOT NULL constraints. By default, it disables any CHECK and FOREIGN KEY constraints. Special syntax (EVALUATE CHECK CONSTRAINTS) can be specified to retain this type of validation during the direct path load. As an alternative to evaluating new rows during the bulk load, you may specify the REENABLE option, which evaluates all disabled constraints against the new data after the load has completed. Any constraints that are found to have been violated during the load will be left in the ENABLED NOVALIDATE state.

If you don't tell SQL*Loader to REENABLE constraints, it will leave them DISABLED. You can then enable them manually (as demonstrated earlier), but this will require all rows (not just newly added rows) to be evaluated.

FOREIGN KEY constraints always require complete reevaluation after being disabled, since there is no guarantee that parent rows weren't deleted during the time when the constraint was not active. For very large unpartitioned tables, the time required to reevaluate constraints may be longer than the savings derived from using direct path. In these cases it may be appropriate to acquire and implement the partitioning option or else perform conventional path loads.

SQL*Loader, in direct path mode, will also attempt to maintain both UNIQUE and PRIMARY KEY constraints. It indexes newly added data as a second step (after the actual load) and will only detect uniqueness violations at that time. If invalid (duplicate) data was added to the table during the load step, Oracle will be unable to complete the rebuilding of the index supporting the constraint and will leave the index in an unusable state.

It is important that every invocation of direct path SQL*Loader be followed by a step that will determine whether any constraints have been left disabled (or left in the ENABLED NOVALIDATE state) or whether any indexes have been marked as unusable. If so, appropriate corrections should be taken immediately to correct the problem before it impacts other aspects of the application.

Constraints and Export/Import

By default, both the traditional export and import utilities will include constraints. You may turn off either the exporting of constraint information, or if included in the export, the importing of them by setting the parameter CONSTRAINTS to N.

Effect on Mutating Table Triggers

As mentioned in passing earlier in the chapter, FOREIGN KEY constraints can have an impact on the operation of some triggers. This will be discussed in more detail in Chapter 19, "Triggers," but a trigger is not allowed to make changes in the table on which it is defined or other tables related by a FOREIGN KEY constraint. Such tables are described as mutating tables. If a trigger must perform operations on a related table, it will be necessary to remove the FOREIGN KEY constraint and enforce the referential integrity by placing triggers on both tables.

Constraints on Views

Throughout this chapter, we have looked at various constraints on tables. If a view is created on top of a table that has constraints, those constraints will remain valid and be enforced as the table is accessed via the view. A limited subset of these same constraints can also be defined directly on views. By documenting the relationships between views as well as tables, you can let the optimizer know some valuable information.

You can declare PRIMARY KEY, UNIQUE, or FOREIGN KEY constraints on views. These view constraints are not actually enforced, so they must be declared in DISABLE NOVALIDATE state and may not be defined as DEFERRABLE. Other invalid syntax for view constraints include EXCEPTIONS INTO, USING INDEX, and ON DELETE clauses.

The RELY option, however, is available and is required if you wish the optimizer to recognize and use the constraint for query rewrite.

The CREATE VIEW statement does have some older syntax, WITH CHECK OPTION, that can have the same effect as a CHECK constraint.

Using Database Constraints for Application-Side Rule Checking

As you saw earlier in this chapter, there are lots of advantages of defining business rules within the database using declarative constraints. However, there are other advantages in an application aware of the same rules. Primarily, this allows the user interface to provide a more immediate opportunity to present an error (before actually calling the database) or to provide a list of values to aid the user in selecting rather than typing a valid entry for a field.

This latter need is easily integrated with FOREIGN KEY designations in the database. The same table that will be used to validate data on submission to the database can, for instance, be queried by the application to present the list of allowed values. This can either be coded directly into the application or it is possible to determine the table and column list for the FOREIGN KEY constraint using techniques introduced in Chapter 6, "The Oracle Data Dictionary." Selecting the count of rows in the referenced tables first will allow you to produce a list of values for small result sets.

The definition of a CHECK constraint should, as a general rule, be less likely to change, but when it does, it would be helpful to avoid having to locate and change all programs that reference the column protected by the revised CHECK constraint. If the application has coded the same rule into multiple programs, this is exactly what will be necessary. Consider coding the application to retrieve the SEARCH_CONDITION from the data dictionary and parse it to dynamically discover the rules contained within CHECK constraints. This requires additional coding initially, but later changes to the rule defined in the database will automatically be included in the application's validation of input data.

Summary

In this chapter you have seen how data integrity rules can be declared as part of the definition of tables, objects, and even views within the database. By centralizing these business rules, multiple application programs can be freed from repetitive maintenance efforts when a rule needs to be changed. Further, we are able to ensure that data always meets the requirements of the business rule regardless of the path by which the data is modified.

Six types of constraints and the related DEFAULT clause are available in Oracle, along with several options to control specific behavior of the constraints. You have seen how constraints interact with several other Oracle features, such as indexes, the Direct Path mode of SQL*Loader, the Export and Import utilities, and triggers.

Constraints defined in the database can be queried within an application program to dynamically enhance the user interface with current list of values displays or to provide immediate feedback of incorrect data prior to the eventual insertion of data into the database.

12

Other Database Structures

So far, you've seen that the basic building block for Oracle database systems is the table. Most database applications will have dozens, even hundreds, of tables used to store user data. You've also looked at several database building blocks besides tables. Chapter 1, "Oracle Architecture and Storage," introduced several database structures, such as tablespaces, that you'll consider a little more deeply here. Chapter 5, "Oracle Security," introduced the security facilities that protect the database and ensure that only authorized individuals are able to change appropriate parts of the database. In Chapter 6, "The Oracle Data Dictionary," we introduced the Oracle data dictionary that uses hundreds of system tables, indexes, and other structures to manage security, users, application data tables, and everything else within the database. Chapter 10, "Indexes," described various indexing structures available to the database designer to speed access to specific table data and prevent duplicate rows in our tables. Chapter 11, "Constraints," showed the ability of the database to hold declarative business rules and enforce them to ensure integrity of table data.

In this chapter, you'll examine many other components of the Oracle database that designers, developers, and administrators may need to use to achieve application design requirements. Some of these components are merely introduced here and then covered in depth in another chapter. Others are treated in more depth directly.

Tablespaces

Tablespaces, as a logical grouping of physical files that provide a place for storing objects such as tables and indexes, were introduced in Chapter 1, "Oracle Architecture and Storage." At that point we mentioned that tablespaces can be either online or offline (for maintenance) and that a tablespace can be made read-only. Read-only tablespaces protect the data in the tablespace from modification but also eliminate the need for repeatedly backing up the data files of that tablespace. A single backup after making a tablespace read-only will be good for as long as the tablespace is left in the read-only state. We also introduced the concept of a transportable tablespace as a means of moving or copying all of the data in a tablespace to another Oracle database.

In this chapter we'll extend the discussion of tablespaces by introducing two additional types of tablespaces that can be important for the developer to understand — temporary tablespaces and undo tablespaces.

Temporary Tablespaces

A developer will not generally need to create or even specify temporary tablespaces, but their configuration can have performance impacts on some aspects of the application. By understanding how and when temporary tablespaces are used by Oracle, you will be better able to diagnose some performance problems or, better still, design and build the application to avoid them.

Some SQL statements require data to be sorted. `SELECT` statements with `ORDER BY` or `GROUP BY` clauses frequently require sorts. The optimizer may choose to perform joins between multiple tables via a sort operation. Index builds are another case where the column data from the table has to be put into sorted order for the index.

When an SQL statement requires a small sort, Oracle will attempt to perform that sort within memory. Remember in Chapter 1 that we discussed the PGA memory allocation that is used for private use by a process. Prior to Oracle9*i*, database administrators had to predefine a maximum amount of memory to be used by processes for sort or hash operations. Any sort larger than that defined maximum could not be completed in memory and therefore had to be sorted with the assistance of some temporary disk storage. With Oracle9*i* and Oracle 10*g* the concept doesn't change but the specification becomes both easier and more dynamic. Rather than specifying the maximum memory available to each user process, the DBA can specify the maximum available to all users and let Oracle sort it out among them.

In either scenario there will be times when the amount of data that needs to be sorted is larger than the memory Oracle is able to allocate to the sorting process. When this occurs Oracle will assign the process one or more extents (disk allocations) from the user's assigned temporary tablespace. As data is sorted and the amount of sort memory is reached, the intermediate sort results are written to the temporary tablespace and the process begins sorting the next set of data. When all of the data has been sorted and stored into temporary extents, the sort process must retrieve it with a simple ordered merge of values from the extents to create the final sorted result set.

Each user, among other attributes, is assigned a temporary tablespace to be used for any required disk sort operations. The temporary tablespace is shared by all of the users who have been assigned it. The database may have more than one temporary tablespace created, and users can be balanced across the available temporary tablespaces to even the workload.

> *Oracle 10g simplifies this potential allocation problem greatly by allowing the DBA to assign various temporary tablespaces to a new construct, the* `TABLESPACE GROUP`*. Users may then be assigned the* `TABLESPACE GROUP` *as their sort location. This will better distribute sort operations across all available temporary tablespaces.*

The implications of this process to the programmer are twofold. Whenever possible, try to avoid performing large sort operations within the application. Any operation that needs to work with a large amount of data is going to require more extensive resources than a smaller amount of data. Sort operations can sometimes be avoided through the use of indexes (see Chapter 10, "Indexes"), partitioning (examined in the following section), materialized views (introduced in this chapter and explored more completely in Chapter 26, "Business Intelligence Query"), global temporary tables (discussed later in this chapter), and alternative SQL coding techniques.

But sometimes large sort operations cannot be avoided. In these cases it is important to verify that users will have adequate temporary tablespace space available for their sorts to complete. If certain users are more likely to perform large, disk-based sorts, then it will be wise to assign users temporary space with this in mind. If a particular report is going to require much more temporary space than average, it may be advisable to perform that report from a specific user account that has been assigned a large temporary tablespace.

Typically this assignment will be the DBA's responsibility, but a developer can help avoid eventual problems by identifying necessary large sorts early in the development and testing phases and consulting with the DBA to structure assignments accordingly.

Undo Tablespaces

When Oracle makes a change to data as part of a DML statement, an image of the way the data looked before the change has to be saved in case the statement has to be rolled back, or undone. Prior to Oracle9*i* the DBA had to build one or more rollback segments to house these before images. Tuning the number and size of the rollback segments was an extra burden on the DBA's already busy job. Oracle9*i* provided a new way of managing this undo information. Instead of working with individual rollback segments, the DBA can now create another special type of tablespace, an `UNDO` tablespace, to hold the undo information. All users of the database will share one or more (one for each instance if using Oracle Real Application Clusters) undo tablespaces.

In addition to being needed to roll back a statement or transaction, undo information is used by Oracle to provide read consistency. When a query attempts to look at data that is currently being modified by another transaction, Oracle avoids the possible problem of showing inconsistent data by dynamically building a temporary copy of the data block as it would look if that other transaction weren't active. Thus, a query is only seeing a read-consistent view of data — it will never see part of an incomplete transaction.

This is excellent news for the developer who doesn't have to contend with the question of possibly displaying incorrect data to a user or of having a query blocked by an update, a choice that other RDBMSs do require. There is one possible downside to this mechanism of using before images to reconstruct queried blocks. If there isn't enough undo space available (as controlled by the DBA's setting of initialization parameters,) a program may encounter the "ORA-0155 snapshot too old" error.

Developers can help avoid this error by structuring their transactions so they don't hold locks for excessively long periods. Where possible, doing any long series of query activity before initiating the start of a transaction with the first DML statement is one aid. Also, if a large batch operation will have to process an extremely large number of rows, it is sometimes possible to divide the workload into multiple smaller transactions — just be sure to build in a means for tracking progress to make the job restartable!

Compression

Data compression was added as a feature of Oracle9*i* Release 2. Compression of data blocks is actually applied to a table, materialized views, or partition during specific *direct path* operations such as the direct-path mode of the SQL*Loader utility, direct path `INSERT`, or `CREATE/ALTER TABLE` statements that create or move a table or partition in a compressed state.

Compression may also be set at the tablespace level to define the default behavior for storage of data segments in that tablespace.

Figure 12-1 demonstrates the dramatic reduction in storage space that is possible with table compression. For this example, two tablespaces were created. One of them, called `COMPRESS_TS`, was created using the `DEFAULT COMPRESS` clause. Then two identical copies of the `SH.SALES` table were created. Note that both contain the same number of rows, but the copy of the table in the `NOCOMPRESS_TS` uses almost three times as many blocks to store the same data.

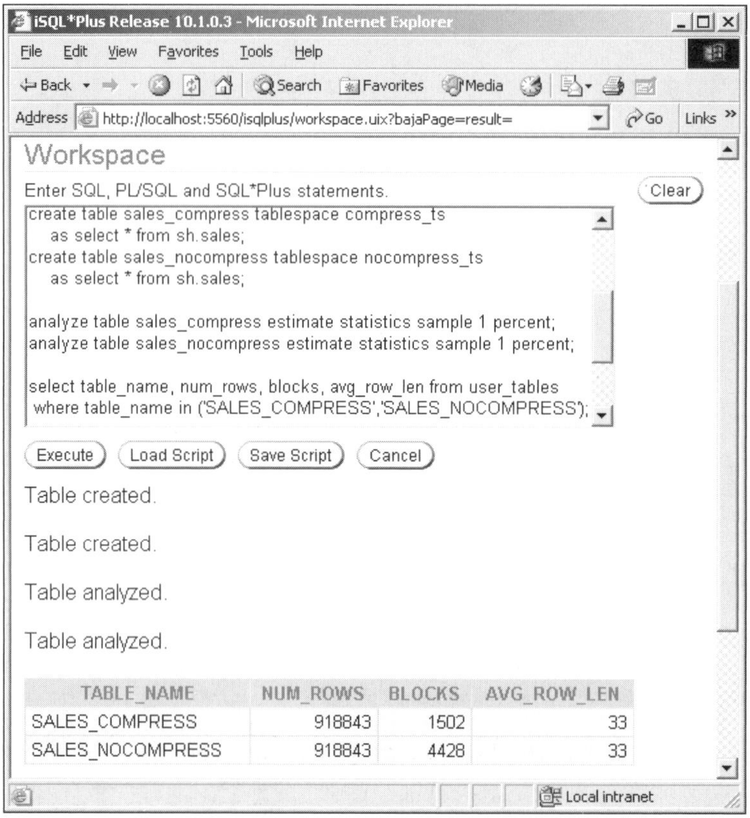

Figure 12-1: Compressed copy of a table uses much less space than uncompressed copy.

That seems like a good thing, right? Well, in some ways it is and in others it may not be. Like everything else in database design, there are trade-offs with compressing a table or partition. The obvious benefit, of course, is that less space is consumed on disk. That also leads to a performance boost when data in the segment is retrieved with a full scan because fewer blocks have to be read from disk. The disadvantage, however, is that compressing and uncompressing the data is somewhat CPU-intensive — it takes a little extra work to initially compress and later decompress the data. But a more dramatic effect may occur if you then perform `UPDATE` statements against the compressed data. The extra CPU workload applies, but this also increases the chances that the changed row will no longer fit within the same space in the block and lead to row chaining.

Deciding to compress a table or a partition or to set the default for new data segments in a tablespace should be made carefully. If you have data that is not going to change (historical data), is of significant volume (thousands of blocks), and that will frequently be accessed with full scans, then compression can be a very useful tool. If you are building a table that will accumulate data slowly but then keep it in a historical context, then it may be useful to combine compression with partitioning to compress only the older partitions once the need to modify data is past.

Partitioning

Oracle's Partitioning Option, introduced in Oracle8 and greatly enhanced with the Oracle8*i* and Oracle9*i* releases, provides a mechanism for storing large database structures (tables, indexes, materialized views, even binary or character large objects that are defined as columns of tables) in multiple segments. For the vast majority of SQL statements, there is no change necessary to access a partitioned table versus a nonpartitioned one. Programmers, though, need to understand the basics of partitioning because of additional options it provides to the optimizer. When the partitioning scheme is well designed in concert with the application's access needs, the result can be better performance and scalability for the application. It is important for developers and DBAs to work together to determine the optimal partitioning scheme for large objects within the database.

Each row is assigned to a specific partition based on the row's values within the columns designated as the partitioning key. This rule is applied as rows are entered into the database or when modifications are made to an existing row. Later, when an SQL query needs to find a row based on values in the partitioning key, it will know the partitions it must search. For a table that might have hundreds of partitions, this advance knowledge of row location can dramatically reduce the amount of data that needs to be searched. This capability of the optimizer to ignore inappropriate partitions is known as partition pruning (or sometimes partition elimination).

Two simple example queries illustrate how partition pruning can benefit a query if the SQL is written properly. In Figure 12-2 two queries are issued that retrieve the same data. The `SH` schema has a table called `SALES` that is partitioned by the `TIME_ID` column. The first example queries are based directly on the value of `TIME_ID` so that Oracle is able to determine that all of the needed rows are in a single partition. The second example eventually finds the same rows and returns the same result. However, because the `WHERE` clause has been based on a `TO_CHAR` function applied to the `TIME_ID`, it requires a full table scan rather than a scan of only one partition.

Note the difference in performance between these two queries. The first `SELECT` that uses partition pruning completes in 2/100 of a second. The second that forces a full table scan takes almost 5 seconds. For this particular million-row table, this represents a better than 200-fold difference in performance!

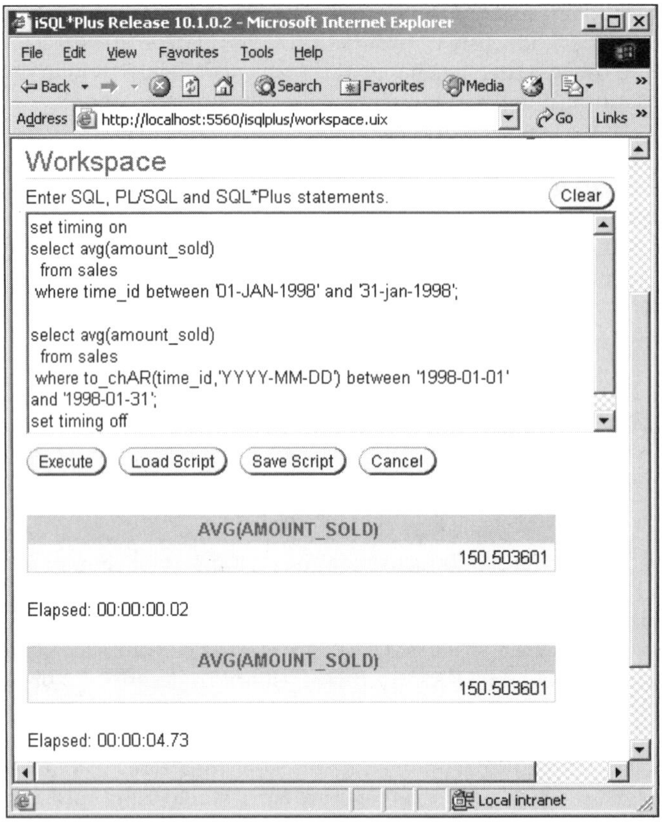

Figure 12-2: Example of query speedup through partition pruning.

In addition to potential performance benefits such as in this example, partitioning can also reduce the administrative load of a database. Individual partitions can be managed independently so administrative tasks such as backups, index rebuilds, data compression, and so on may be performed on individual partitions rather than entire tables.

Views

Views are logical definitions of alternative ways to look at data in the database. You can build a view that only shows 5 out of 10 columns in a table; you can build a view that only displays rows for customers in a particular country. You can build a view that includes joined data from multiple tables. You can build a view that is defined upon another view.

With very few restrictions, any valid `SELECT` statement can be used as a view definition. When a query is executed against a view, the conditions of the issued query are combined with the conditions (including `WHERE` clause, aggregations, `GROUP BY`, etc.) to produce a result set.

Views are created using the `CREATE VIEW` command. If you ever need to redefine the view, you may do so with the extra syntax of `CREATE OR REPLACE VIEW`, which leaves the grants and other references to the view intact while changing the defining query. Some complex views are inherently not updatable (there's no way for Oracle to understand where to store a change to an aggregated `SUM(amount)` column, for instance; hundreds of rows might have been aggregated to provide that one value. But views that can logically be updated are, by default, updatable. (Even some join views can be updated.) To prevent updates through a view, you may create the view with the `WITH READ ONLY` clause. Further, if you do choose to allow modifications through the view, you may ensure that any inserted or updated data will still meet the view's definition by specifying the `WITH CHECK OPTION`. This would, for instance, not allow a row for a German customer to be inserted through the view that was defined to be just the French subset of the entire customer table.

To create a view, you must have the `CREATE VIEW` or `CREATE ANY VIEW` privilege and must either own the underlying base objects in the view definition or have been directly granted the object privileges on those objects. The functionality of the view for reading, updating, deleting, and so on is limited by the privileges of the view owner. Further, once you have created a view, you may grant one or more privileges to use the view to another user without that user needing any privileges on the underlying tables. Figure 12-3 illustrates this security feature.

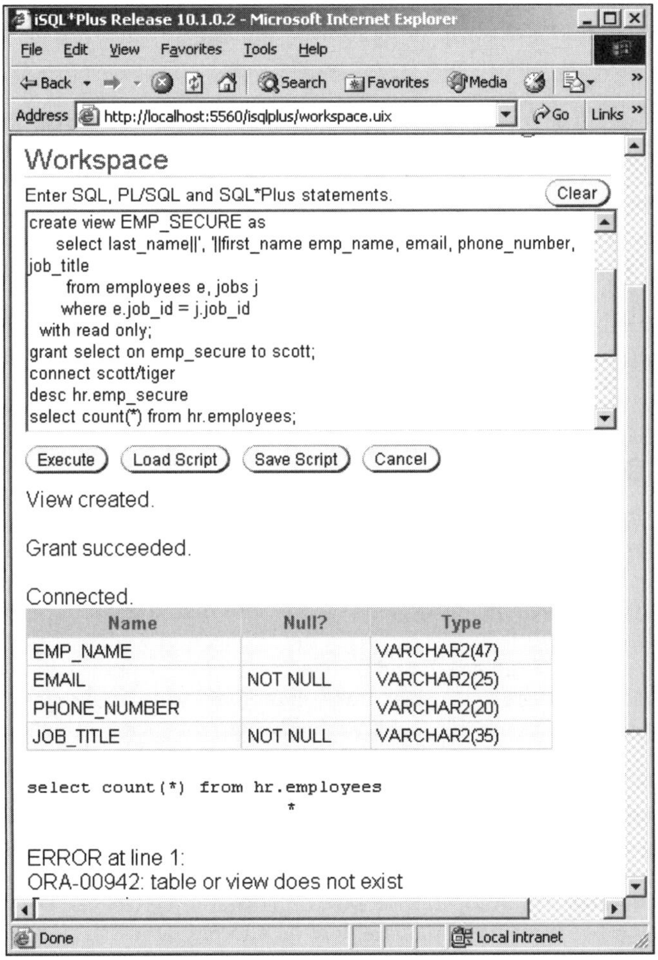

Figure 12-3: Using a view to restrict users from seeing sensitive data.

Here the HR user has created a read-only view of the EMPLOYEES table that conceals sensitive personal information, reformats the name, and does a join with the JOBS table to show the employee's full title. HR then grants SELECT privilege on the view to SCOTT (who has no other privileges on the EMPLOYEES table directly. When SCOTT accesses the view (here with a DESCRIBE), he is able to access the limited data presented by the view but is unable to see anything directly in the HR.EMPLOYEES table upon which the view is based.

Views are a powerful tool that can be used to present customized perspectives of data to selected users, hide complex SQL, include query hints for performance, and even enhance application security.

Materialized Views

As powerful as views can be, they don't solve every problem. If the view performs an aggregation of millions of rows of sales information, query performance of the view may not be what you desire. If hundreds of individual store managers access that view many times every day, Oracle may have to repeatedly access the millions of rows and repeat the aggregation. This is a perfect opportunity to use a materialized view.

A *materialized view* is defined just as a regular view, but the results of the defining query are stored, or materialized, as a persistent database object. Oracle can automatically maintain the data in a materialized view as changes occur in the underlying tables. Now those hundreds of store managers who need to see just their stores' sales totals can retrieve a few hundred summarized rows rather than having to repeatedly summarize millions of rows. The net performance gains for some applications or data warehouses can be several orders of magnitude.

We will postpone further discussion of until Chapter 26, "Business Intelligence Query," where you will see some other fancy tricks that materialized views can perform.

Sequences

One of the common bottlenecks to application scalability used to be the need to generate unique key values for things like order numbers. The common approach over a decade ago was to create a table with one numeric column and one row. Each time a new key value was needed, the application would select that row for update, increment the value by one, and then write it back to the database. This approach worked flawlessly during testing. Then the application went into production and the number of orders processed per day doubled . . . and the system couldn't keep up even though the CPU, I/O, and memory statistics all looked great. Each transaction that locked that one row caused the next transaction to wait. Assuming that each transaction actually held the lock for one second before committing its changes, the maximum throughput of this system design would be 60 transactions per minute.

So, in Oracle version 6, a new object was introduced that would perform the same function without the need for serializing all transactions. The sequence number generator (now just referred to as a sequence) serves up unique integers to an in-memory cache where they can be retrieved by a transaction with no locking required. Even better, the application program doesn't have to call the database to get a number and then use that number for an INSERT statement on another database call. The application can do just the INSERT and have the next unique value automatically included in the key column. Figure 12-4 shows a sequence generator in action.

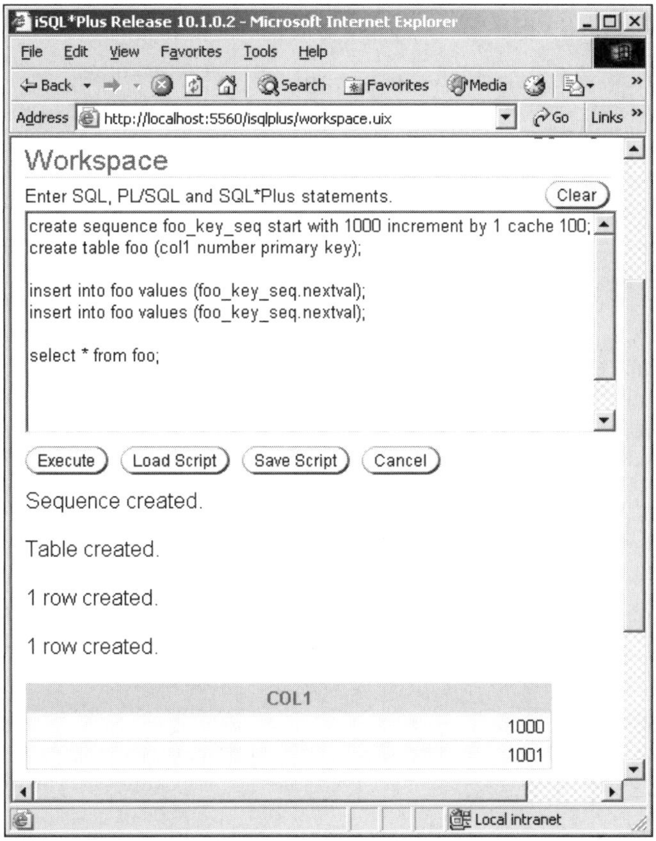

Figure 12-4: Automatically including unique sequence numbers during an INSERT.

In this example a sequence called `FOO_KEY_SEQ` is created with a starting value of 1,000 (that will increment by one) and will generate and cache 100 values at a time. An `INSERT` statement must just specify the name of the sequence and that it wants the `NEXTVAL`. If it were necessary to insert child rows (such as order detail lines) that have to be linked to their parent that just received a `NEXTVAL`, the subsequent `INSERT` statements can use `sequence_name.CURRVAL` to get the same value assigned again.

Hundreds or even thousands of concurrent transactions can be requesting `NEXTVAL`s and reusing their respective `CURRVAL`s without interfering with each other. The only time there is any wait is when the cache of generated numbers needs to be refreshed. If that is happening too often, a simple `ALTER SEQUENCE` command can increase the cache size.

The only "limitation" on sequences is that even though the numbers are guaranteed to be unique, they are not necessarily consecutive. Once the `FOO_KEY_SEQ` was accessed, 100 values were cached into memory. If the database instance were restarted while some of those remained in memory, they would be lost and the next batch of 100 numbers would be generated upon restarting the instance.

Global Temporary Tables

Just as sequences removed a major bottleneck to scalability when they were introduced in Oracle version 6, another feature has been incorporated to remove another bottleneck. Many developers with experience with SQL Server are probably used to creating a table to hold intermediate results from one operation and then using that table as input to the next step. Conceptually this technique can be useful in reducing the number of rows needed in subsequent steps and thereby improve efficiency. However, this approach of creating (and later dropping) tables as part of a transaction or complex query incurs a substantial cost required for allocating new tables and registering them in the data dictionary and then immediately undoing the same work.

Oracle provides a facility for achieving the same conceptual goal without the overhead. Oracle allows you to predefine your temporary tables and then share them among all of the users of your application. For many applications, dozens, hundreds, or even thousands of user sessions will execute a particular transaction type every hour. Each time that transaction type executes, it will need temporary storage of intermediate results in exactly the same format. Why would you want to create and drop thousands of identical tables in an hour? Oracle's global temporary table feature allows you to do the creation just once for all of those transactions.

Even though this special predefined type of table is shared and reused constantly, each transaction gets what appears to be a private temporary table for its use. Oracle isolates each session with an individual allocation of part of the global temporary table. No transaction will see the rows that belong to other transactions or be interfered with by other users.

Use of the global temporary table from within the application is identical to using any other table. The program inserts data rows, reads them back, and may update or delete rows as needed. There are a few restrictions on the definition of global temporary tables — they cannot be partitioned, clustered, or index organized; they can't include foreign key constraints; and they cannot contain nested tables or participate in any distributed transactions. Finally, you may not perform any parallel operations against a global temporary table.

When the session is done with the space, it is released for use by another transaction. A session may use its part of a global temporary table for the length of one transaction (releasing it upon `COMMIT` or `ROLLBACK`), or it may retain the temporary results across subsequent transactions of the same session. This is defined as part of creating the global temporary table by including either the `ON COMMIT DELETE ROWS` or `ON COMMIT PRESERVE ROWS` clause. In session-specific mode, the temporary table allocation is released either by issuing a `TRUNCATE TABLE` against the global temporary table or by ending the session.

As you are building an application program for which temporary table storage will be needed, consider how often that program is going to be executed and how much savings you can achieve by using a predefined global temporary table rather than creating a new table for each execution.

Recycle Bin

Most users of personal computers (Windows or Macintosh operating systems) are familiar with the concept of a recycle bin where deleted files seem to be moved rather than being physically erased from the system. This gives the user a chance to easily recover from an accidental deletion. (It also forces most users into having to manually empty their recycle bin when they realize their hard disk is getting full!) Oracle 10*g* introduced a similar capability for dropped tables.

This new feature is specifically of advantage to developers who may be frequently creating and dropping tables in their own schemas as they develop and test program modules. By default in 10*g*, when you issue a `DROP TABLE` command for one of the tables in your schema, Oracle will not actually remove the table (and its indexes) from the tablespace where it resides. Instead, Oracle renames each of these objects with a system-generated name in case you realize that you actually need the object or until the item is purged.

To see the contents of your recycle bin, you may query the dictionary view `USER_RECYCLEBIN` (or, more simply, the synonym `RECYCLEBIN`). If you are working within SQL*Plus, you may shorten your query even more by issuing the command `SHOW RECYCLEBIN`. Figure 12-5 demonstrates some basic operations of the recycle bin. Here you see a user create a table with a primary key, drop the table, query the contents of the recycle bin, and then purge the dropped table.

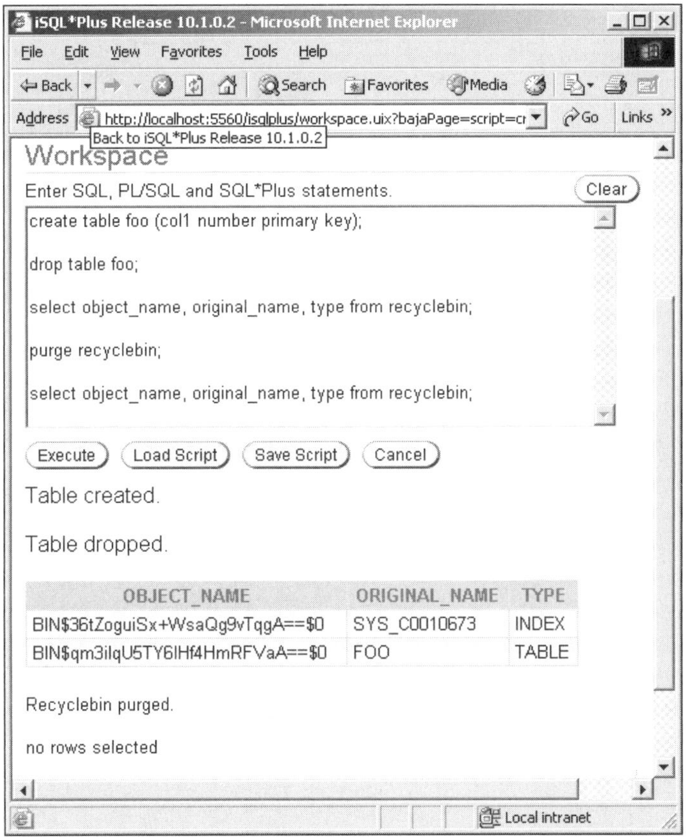

Figure 12-5: A dropped table is preserved in the recycle bin until purged.

Notice that the recycle bin has two items in it: the table, `FOO`, as well as the index that was generated by Oracle automatically to enforce uniqueness for the `PRIMARY KEY` constraint. After the purge, there are no items remaining in the recycle bin. There are several other options to the new `PURGE` command. Rather than purging all items, you may purge individual items by either the long `OBJECT_NAME` or the `ORIGINAL_NAME`. You may purge all objects by tablespace as well.

The system-generated `BIN$` *table name of the dropped table will also show up in the normal dictionary views such as* `USER_TABLES` *until the item has been purged from the recycle bin.*

You may be thinking, "All of this recycle bin stuff is interesting, but it is only useful if it allows me to restore an item that I accidentally dropped." Fear not, that capability is provided through a new 10*g* command, `FLASHBACK TABLE`. Flashback technology, first introduced with Oracle9*i*, allows you to see the state of the Oracle database at a previous point in time (by using the undo management capabilities first introduced in version 6). Figure 12-6 demonstrates the ability to retrieve the dropped table, even if another table of the same name has been created since the drop.

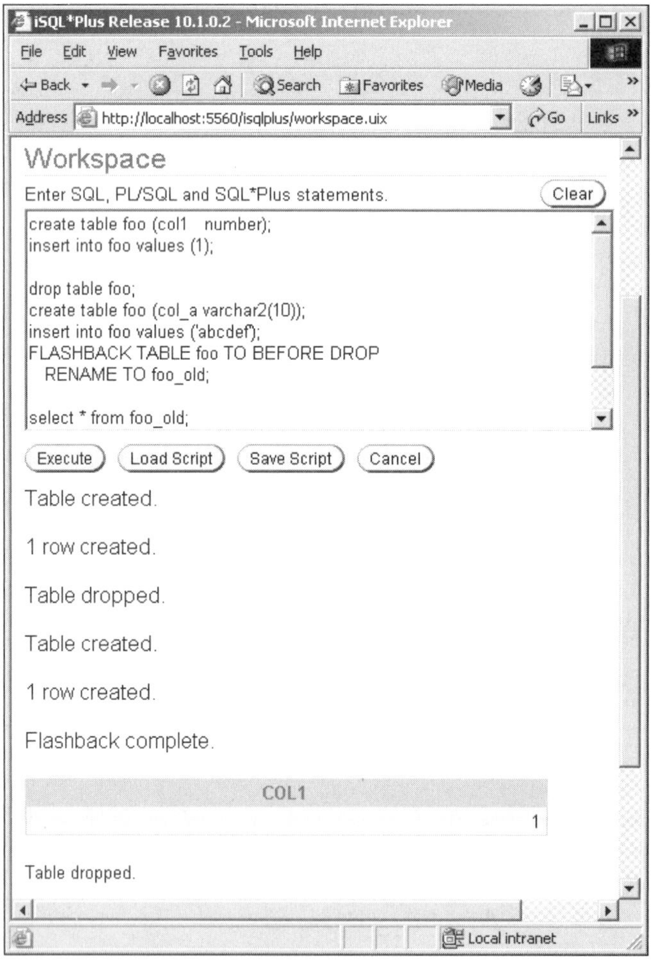

Figure 12-6: Using `FLASHBACK TABLE` to recover a table from the recycle bin.

Synonyms

Synonyms, a means of aliasing object names, should be simple for most developers to understand and use. We already mentioned the use of these aliases in Chapter 6, "The Oracle Data Dictionary," when discussing the data dictionary. It is worth a few paragraphs, however, to clarify both the syntax and scoping of synonyms within the Oracle database environment.

Why Use Synonyms?

Synonyms are used to provide alternative names for database objects such as tables, views, sequences, procedures—even other synonyms! The alternative name may be used as shorthand to allow the SQL code simpler access to an object from another schema without having to qualify the object name with the schema name prefix. All of the dictionary views that were referenced in Chapter 6 are actually accessed via public synonyms. By creating a public synonym named `ALL_TABLES` that refers to `SYS.ALL_TABLES`, you can access that view without always having to specify `SYS`, and you reach it by just referencing `ALL_TABLES`.

This same simplification of names can be extended to remote objects that reside in other databases. Chapter 14, "Distributed Queries, Transactions, and Databases," covers distributed queries in more depth, but we'll give a brief example here. Suppose you're working in a database called `MYDB` but you need to reference the `HR.EMPLOYEES` table in the `HRDB` on another server, perhaps in another data center. Oracle allows you to do so, but the basic syntax is a little awkward. That table reference, fully qualified, would be `HR.EMPLOYEES@HRDB`. (This looks more like an e-mail address, but it has been the Oracle distributed reference format for nearly 20 years.) You can make your code (or your interactive testing) simpler by creating a synonym that removes both the schema prefix and the remote location suffix.

Synonyms allow you to switch references without changing code. If you need to reference the current production version of an object and then later reference the test version of the same object, you can just re-create a synonym to point at the new reference and your SQL statement remains unchanged. Reverting back is just as simple. This is particularly useful when you are working with a code module for which you can't modify source code. A packaged application, for instance, can be tested with a substituted object reference (assuming the module didn't have its `schemaname.objectname` references hard-coded).

Public synonyms give you another opportunity for flexibility. In resolving object name references, Oracle first evaluates any explicit schema or location definitions in the reference. If the name has none, it will then look in the current schema for either an object of the appropriate type or a private synonym. If it doesn't find the object or synonym in the local schema, it will then look for a public synonym of that name that can be resolved to the actual object. By creating public synonyms, you can avoid all hard-coding of schema names in your SQL. Every user who has permission to access the object will be able to do so without specifying a schema name. Later, if a particular user or developer wants to redirect his or her own reference, he or she can create a private synonym that will take precedence over the public synonym.

Working with Synonyms

Synonyms are created with the `CREATE SYNONYM synonym_name FOR referenced_object_name` syntax. To drop a synonym, you would enter `DROP SYNONYM synonym_name`. Creating or dropping public synonyms requires special system-level privilege, but the only change in syntax is to add the word `PUBLIC` before `SYNONYM` in either command. Public synonyms will appear in the data dictionary as if they were owned by a user named `PUBLIC`. This means that they are defined globally and may be used by any user.

Permission for the user to actually access the referenced object is still maintained entirely through the privileges and roles granted to that user on the object itself (or the type of object). A synonym, private or public, does not affect the ability to access an otherwise restricted object.

One point of confusion comes from accessing the data dictionary view related to sequences. The `OE` schema already has five synonyms defined that point to tables within the `HR` schema. In Figure 12-7 another synonym is created, this time to two of `OE`'s own objects, a sequence generator and the synonym just created.

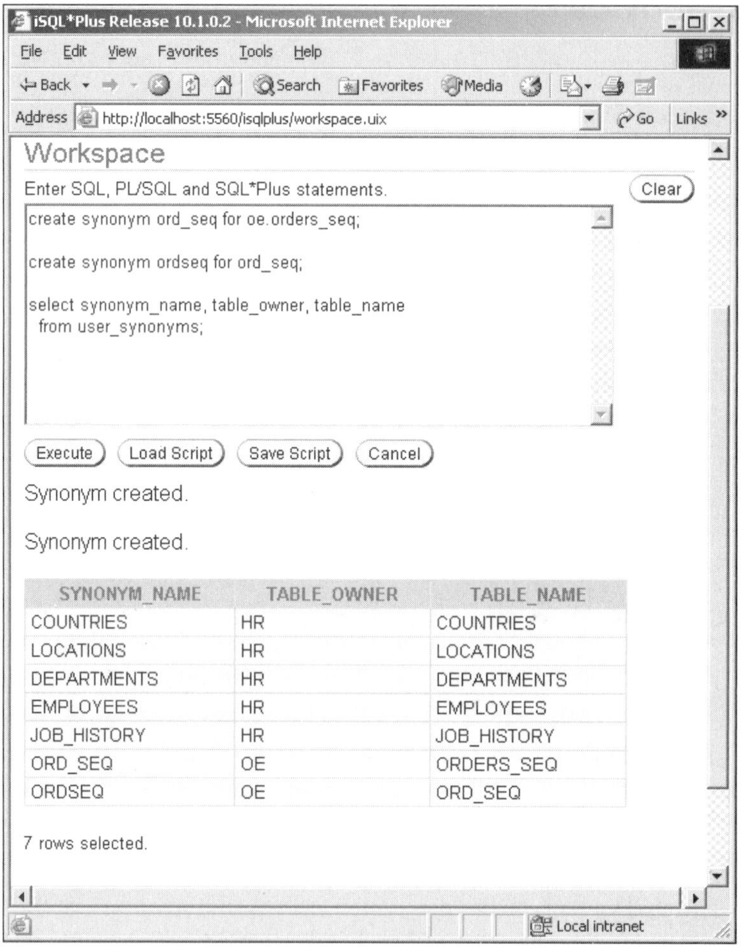

Figure 12-7: Creating synonyms for database objects other than tables or views.

Creating the two synonyms was straightforward, but when you look at the columns of the `ALL_SYNONYMS` view, you see `SYNONYM_NAME`, `TABLE_OWNER`, and `TABLE_NAME`. The definition of this view dates back to much earlier days when tables and views were about the only things that could be referenced in SQL. So, just understand that `TABLE_NAME` in this view is really the referenced object name, no matter what type of object it is.

Database Links

In the previous section, we mentioned that synonyms could be used to remove the reference to the remote database name in a distributed database environment. Actually, the `@HRDB` definition of the remote location is not directly referring to the remote database name. This location identifier is actually referencing a database link (sometimes called a "dblink"). A database link assigns a single word name to what can sometimes be a complex specification. Much of the complexity has been removed since the introduction of early distributed operations with SQL*Net in the mid-1980s. Today, more sophisticated network specifications are possible using the Transparent Network Substrate (TNS) features of what is now called Oracle Net Services. From this SQL session, however, you still need to make use of a database link that will define our connection to the remote database. Database links, like synonyms, can be local to one specific schema or global (PUBLIC), but unlike synonyms, they can have various security options included in their definition. Distributed queries and the use of database links are covered more completely in Chapter 14, "Distributed Queries, Transactions, and Databases."

Advanced Queuing and Streams

Advanced Queuing (AQ) was originally introduced in Oracle8 to provide a facility for two (or more) Oracle processes to exchange messages. The structure of the queues was fundamentally re-architected in Oracle8*i*. With the introduction of the Streams feature in Oracle9*i*, AQ has been renamed to Oracle Streams AQ. Conceptually, though, Streams AQ is still a means for an Oracle program (a "producer") to write (enqueue) a message into a queue. Messages are then dequeued (read) by one or more Oracle programs ("consumers").

Streams AQ

Oracle Streams AQ is a means of exchanging messages among independent Oracle processes. It also interfaces to other proprietary messaging systems such as IBM MQSeries and TIBCO TIB/Rendezvous, as well as the standards-based Java Message Service (JMS). The key point of all of these messaging environments is that the messages are propagated asynchronously—rather than requiring two process to maintain a direct communication and potentially lock one while the other is busy, asynchronous messages allow the producer and consumer processes to work at their own pace. (Think of it metaphorically as the difference between e-mail and instant messaging.)

Queues are database objects (based on tables) but are created using packaged procedure calls rather than a `CREATE` statement. Because the messages are actually stored in physical database tables rather than in memory, it is possible for AQ messages to survive a crash or reboot of the server. Basing queues on table storage also brings all of the other availability and scalability advantages of the Oracle database to the messaging environment.

Messages, consisting of a *payload* and supplementary meta data, are also enqueued and dequeued using packaged procedures (either PL/SQL procedure calls, Oracle Objects for OLE from Visual Basic applications, Java for JMS messages, or even the HTTP protocol for Internet messaging) rather than direct SQL statements.

Even though SQL is not used to create or manipulate queues, it is possible to use `SELECT` statements to see and monitor queue contents and status.

In a simple case a producer process will enqueue a message onto a specific queue and a designated consumer process will dequeue that message and act upon it. AQ does, however, allow for much more complex interactions. For instance, a single message may be

- Enqueued into a single queue by any of several producers
- Dequeued from a single queue by several subscriber processes
- Directed to a specific list of recipients to override the default subscriber list of the queue
- Automatically forwarded from one queue to one or more queues, either in the same database or other databases
- Enqueued with a defined delay before being available for dequeuing
- Defined with an expiration time and automatically deleted if not dequeued before that time

Queues and subscribers can be managed through Oracle Enterprise Manager (OEM) and can be integrated with Oracle Internet Directory. Information about messages (such as sender, one or more recipients, transaction IDs, and timestamps) can be retained for audit and other tracking purposes after messages are dequeued.

Streams AQ is extremely flexible, so the list of possible variations is long — longer than we can possibly describe in this introductory section of one chapter. The *Oracle 10g Streams Advanced Queuing User's Guide and Reference* manual includes many examples of how to use AQ. For this introductory section, we'll just recommend that you keep the facility in mind whenever you find a need for two or more Oracle programs to communicate and coordinate activities asynchronously.

Streams

Introduced in Oracle9*i*, the streams facility encompasses several features (Advanced Queuing, Advanced Replication) from previous releases and adds many new capabilities. Streams can automatically capture events that occur in one database then filter, transform, and propagate those events to apply them into another database.

Beyond the explicit management of messages via queues discussed in the last section, Oracle Streams is designed as a generalized means of sharing information among systems, programs, and databases. Because of the variations in what information you may want to share, Streams provides extreme flexibility in configuration. The general model, however, consists of three steps: capture, staging, and consumption.

Capture

In the discussion of Advanced Queuing, you saw one means of capture — explicitly enqueuing a message into a defined queue. Captured events may also be implicitly defined based on specified rules. Rules may be scoped to recognize only certain operations (such as an `INSERT`) on a single table or all changes for any tables within a specified schema or even the entire database. The latter situation, for instance, would provide a means for replicating an entire database for remote reporting or for one part of a disaster recovery plan.

Having to explicitly enqueue every change in a database would be both a lot of work as well as error-prone, so Oracle Streams provides a means of capturing changes from the database's log files. All changes (unless for some bulk operations that can be explicitly executed with the `NOLOGGING` option) are recorded into the log files to provide local database recovery. Streams can be configured to monitor the log files as they are generated (or optionally from archived log files) and identify and process changes into Logical Change Records (LCRs) that are enqueued for subsequent processing.

Once captured, an identified event is staged into one or more staging areas for either local processing or propagation to other databases as needed. Certain events may be routed to particular destinations based on data values; other events may be broadcast to multiple sites. User-defined functions may be invoked at any step in the propagation process to customize the format or content of the data. Thus, two databases may receive the same change but may have different database structures and therefore apply the change in different ways.

Transformations may be applied by the capturing process that will enqueue a message or by the process that dequeues the message later. Transformations, implemented as PL/SQL functions, may alter the data format (such as object structure, column names, or data types) or the data itself.

Staging

Logical Change Records are staged into queues like those described previously for AQ messages. Subscribers (applications, another queue, or a remote apply process) register their interest in activity in a particular queue. The subscriber monitors activity (or can be notified of activity) on the queue and then may examine each LCR or message to determine whether it needs to act upon it.

Applications (Oracle programs) will explicitly dequeue items of interest and then process them. Subscriber queues will have the message propagated and enqueued for consumption by that queue's set of subscribers.

In defining your Streams environment, you have the capability to define the network paths used by various messages. An event in your corporate database in New York may need to be routed to multiple databases in London, Paris, Milan, and Istanbul. Depending upon your network configuration, you may decide to have New York send four messages to those destinations or you may elect to have a single message sent to London, where rules will cause three additional messages to be directed to the other three European data centers. All of this routing is done by defining the queues that subscribe to other queues.

Propagation of events can be in a single direction (master to one or more replicas) or bidirectional. In multi-master replication environments, a change made to a table in any one of the participating databases will be routed to each of the corresponding tables in the other databases. A change made in database A will be propagated to databases B and C, just as a change made in database B will be replicated in A and C. Of course, this leads to the possibility of conflicting changes being made in both A and B—Streams provides the ability to define conflict resolution rules to handle such situations. You may elect to always have A's changes have priority (corporate rules over branches), or you may choose to mediate conflicts based on whichever change occurred first or last. These rules can be as complex as the business needs dictate, since they can be coded procedurally in PL/SQL.

Oracle Streams automatically tracks additional meta data about each message, such as the source database, so that consumption can be controlled. (To follow the earlier example, a change in database A gets routed to B and a corresponding change is made there; you would not want this subsequent change in B to initiate another change message back to A and start an endless loop!)

Consumption

We already introduced consumption of messages when we discussed the subscribers to a queue, or staging area. An application program may explicitly dequeue messages from a queue and then act upon them in whatever way necessary. This was discussed in the earlier discussion of AQ messages.

Oracle Streams also provides an *apply engine* facility for automatic consumption of recorded DML and DDL SQL changes, as well as user-defined LCRs. The apply engine is an additional set of Oracle instance background processes assigned to just this task. The apply processing can be handled by a default apply engine, or the developer may take control by writing custom apply procedures to define the necessary rules for deciding how to handle each type (and source) of change. The example of multi-master replication not echoing changes back to the original site is one example.

Rules

The capture, staging, and consumption of events are all controlled by rules. Since the number and complexity of rules for an integrated environment of many databases and many queues can quickly become overwhelming, it is recommended that related rules be organized into *rule sets* and are administered through a provided package, `DBMS_RULES_ADM`. Separate rule sets are defined for negative rules (messages and events to be ignored) and then for positive rules of how to handle messages and rules not already excluded by the negative rule set. Only messages that first pass through the negative rule set without rejection and then are included by the positive rule set will be processed by the apply process.

Streams Summary

Oracle Streams is a very robust tool for coordinating asynchronous activities within one database, across databases, or even with foreign data sources. One section of one chapter of one book can only scratch the surface of its capabilities. Entire books could be written (actually there are four in the official Oracle 10*g* documentation set) about all of the possibilities. Our goal from this overview is that the developer recognize situations where decoupling processing into several steps will improve the overall operation of a system.

The usual argument against such an architecture is the challenge of providing a flexible but reliable means of sending messages among the various processes with minimal performance impact on the total system. Oracle Streams provides such a messaging infrastructure, protected by all of the database's recoverability features, that can be used to reliably deliver complex messages between Oracle processes, as well as interface to other messaging systems, such as JMS.

Objects

While Oracle has always been a relational database management system, many extensions have been added since Oracle8 that provide object database management functionality. While all of the actual storage of objects' classes and methods use Oracle's relational and procedural technology, the object model is exposed for direct use from object-oriented development environments.

Oracle's object-oriented extensions to the relational model allow for the definition of custom data types and subtyping, variable length arrays (*varrays*), nested tables, object views (that can expose normal relational data in object form to help integrate traditional programming models with object accesses), and default constructor methods, as well as custom methods, and so on. The list is long and Chapter 21, "Object Relational Interactions with Oracle," is dedicated to explaining this functionality.

The key value of combining these object interfaces with the Oracle database is that all of the underlying Oracle technology such as query optimization, indexing, security model, transaction management, row-level concurrency model, parallelism, and so forth are all available to provide a secure, robust, and performant environment for working with objects just as they are for relational interactions.

These object features are used extensively to support Oracle's XML database facility. Oracle offers many options for working with native XML within the database. XML processing and storage are the topic of Chapter 22, "Oracle XML DB."

Stored Procedures, Functions, and Triggers

Beginning in the next chapter and then continuing on through Part III, we will examine these procedural capabilities of the database in much more depth. At this point we'll only introduce each topic at a very high level.

Stored procedures are program modules that are stored in the database. They are generally written in PL/SQL, Oracle's procedural language extensions to SQL, or they may be written in Java. A stored procedure is invoked by explicitly calling it and passing any necessary input parameters. Upon completion, the procedure will return any specified output parameters. Stored procedures are an efficient way to implement logic that requires repeated database interaction, since they avoid an application program's need to make many separate calls to the database to achieve the same result.

Functions are also stored in the database just as stored procedures are, but they are invoked differently. Just as you would invoke an Oracle built-in function, you may include custom-developed functions directly within SQL statements, or you may call the function from another PL/SQL program unit (such as a stored procedure) and receive the `RETURN` value back. `RETURN` values may be of any PL/SQL data type, including scalar variables, arrays, user-defined record types, or even cursors.

Procedures and functions may be grouped together, along with common error-handling routines, global variables, and so on, into packages. Packages actually consist of two database objects — the package (the interface specification for invoking procedures and functions) and the package body. This allows the developer to make modifications to the actual logic within the package body without disturbing the connections to the external interface in the package body.

Stored procedures, functions, and packages are secured in the same manner as other Oracle objects — a user must have specific authority (the `EXECUTE` privilege) to invoke the object. The developer may also designate the program unit to operate under the security privileges of the schema that contains the object or under the security privileges of the calling schema (user).

Triggers are not invoked explicitly and have no independent security model. A trigger's logic is added to the definition of the table or view to which it applies. Triggers are activated ("fired") when specific actions (such as an `INSERT` of a row) occur to the table. Triggers can be used for additional security, auditing, or to extend the action of a particular statement to include additional procedural logic.

More specific information on how to integrate these stored program units into an application is provided in subsequent chapters.

Accessing Flat Files

The Oracle relational database management system is designed, obviously, to manage the data within the database. There are times, however, when it is convenient to be able to integrate access to database data with data stored in non-database files. Of course, this integration can be done within the application by reading/writing files and then issuing SQL statements to the database.

Other times, however, it may be more efficient to have Oracle directly access the files than to have a large number of records/rows passed through the application program. Features have been added to Oracle allowing Oracle to read and write file system files directly.

External Tables

Chapter 25, "Data Loading and Management," is dedicated to mechanisms of loading large volumes of data into an Oracle database efficiently. One of those methods is to use the SQL*Loader utility that takes data from a file and loads it into one or more tables in the database.

A newer capability, added in Oracle9*i*, is the ability to define the file as an "external file," which provides read-only access vian SQL `SELECT` statements. The goal of external tables is typically not to make permanent connections to the files but to quickly stage the data for additional processing via PL/SQL routines.

UTL_FILE

We haven't yet gotten to the details of Oracle's PL/SQL language, but earlier in this chapter, we provided a high-level introduction to stored procedures, functions, and packages. A lot of Oracle's extended functionality is provided by means of packaged procedures delivered as part of the database. It is beyond the scope of this book to describe the hundreds of packaged procedures provided for your use, but you can find a full definition of them all in the Oracle 10*g* *PL/SQL Packages and Types Reference* manual (in Oracle9*i*, this manual was called the *Supplied PL/SQL Packages and Types Reference*).

The one that we do want to mention in this section is a package called `UTL_FILE` that includes over 20 procedures that allows you to open, read, write, close, and rename files, along with other necessary file functions.

There are a couple of things you should know before using `UTL_FILE` procedures. If you create a new file using `UTL_FILE`, it will be owned by whatever operating system account (usually "oracle") your administrators have chosen to execute the Oracle database software. Other system accounts may not be able to access these files without special intervention by the system administrator. You should also be aware that aliases, shell settings, or environment variables known to your system session will not apply to your file operations using `UTL_FILE`.

SGA Buffer Pool Assignments

Chapter 1, "Oracle Architecture and Storage," briefly described the System Global Area and the portion of the SGA used to buffer database blocks in memory. As mentioned then, the database buffer pool can be divided into three subpools. The `DEFAULT` buffer pool is always available for Oracle to work with data blocks in memory. If desired, the administrator may also specify a special buffer pool, called `KEEP`, in which Oracle will attempt to retain blocks of specific objects indefinitely. Another special allocation of buffers, called the RECYCLE pool, can be set aside for objects whose blocks are not expected to be needed again and therefore no effort should be made to retain in memory.

In general, Oracle manages blocks within the default buffer pool just fine using a "least recently used" algorithm. Blocks that are used frequently tend to stay in memory; those that are brought into memory for a single usage age along the LRU chain and are then released so the buffer can be used for a block that is needed.

In very infrequent cases it may be useful to override part of the default LRU processing. The KEEP pool, once created, can have specific objects assigned to it. If you do elect to allocate a KEEP pool, be sure not to assign too many (or too large) objects; that is, if you decide to put "10 pounds of flour into a 5-pound bag," you will defeat the entire purpose of the KEEP pool. Oracle will be overlaying blocks in the buffers just as it does with the DEFAULT pool. To be effective, the KEEP pool should be used for small reference tables and indexes in which every block needs to be accessed as quickly as possible. The KEEP pool, if used, will provide less efficient memory utilization overall than simply using the DEFAULT pool. (That is, if the blocks were really being used frequently, they'd stay in memory in the DEFAULT pool anyway. The only reason to place an object in the KEEP pool is to keep some blocks in memory that would be aged out because they aren't used frequently enough!) The DBA will create the KEEP cache by specifying the DB_KEEP_CACHE_SIZE initialization parameter.

The RECYCLE pool is even less frequently used than the KEEP pool. Generally, the overhead of managing blocks as they age through the LRU mechanism is minimal. However, if you are certain that the blocks of an extremely large object, once brought into memory as part of a scan operations, will not be used again before they are aged out, you can lighten the LRU chain management by placing the object's blocks into the RECYCLE pool. The size of the RECYCLE pool is controlled by the optional DB_RECYCLE_CACHE_SIZE initialization parameter.

So, given the understanding that the KEEP and RECYCLE pools very rarely provide an overall increase in memory efficiency, how do database objects get placed there? Actually it is quite simple. As part of the CREATE or ALTER TABLE, CREATE/ALTER INDEX, and CREATE/ALTER MATERIALIZE VIEW statements, you may specify the BUFFER_POOL option of the STORAGE clause of the object. The following simple command

```
alter table customers storage (buffer_pool keep);
```

places any newly accessed blocks (not already in the previously assigned buffer pool) of the CUSTOMERS table into the KEEP cache.

Workflows

A common application need is to implement business processes that require many steps, each of which may be separated by hours or even days from its predecessor step. Sometimes these processes aren't strictly sequential but involve alternative paths (for error correction, perhaps) or multiple parallel steps, decision branches, and approval points.

As an example, consider the steps necessary to process an employee's expense report. First, the employee must be able to enter the report, with proper edits for project codes, expense types, and so on. Then the report must be routed to the employee's manager, so it is placed into a hold status and the manager is notified by e-mail that there is something waiting in approval queue. Sometimes the expense report may exceed the manager's approval authority or may involve charges to another cost center and must be routed either to the manager's director or split for review and approval by the other cost center's manager. At any point in the process, an error may be flagged that has to be routed back to the original employee for correction or additional justification. (In some cases the expense report may be rejected entirely and the employee will need to be notified of that fact and the reasons for the rejection.) Eventually, when all approvals are obtained, the expense report must be routed to the accounts payable department for the creation of a reimbursement check.

Most organizations have dozens of applications that involve multistep processes and approval queues similar to this example. Luckily, many of these applications are purchased and somebody else did the coding. However, sometimes the application need is unique to the organization and it has to be custom-built. (And, of course, somebody has to be the programmer at the vendor of the purchased application who implements the process for the packaged application!)

The good news is that most of the difficult tasks of routing, queuing, approval, and notification in this scenario don't have to be written. All of these capabilities (and many more) are built in to the Oracle database as part of a facility known as Oracle Workflow. Workflow was originally developed as part of the Oracle Applications suite of products but has since been made available to assist all of us in developing applications of this type.

Workflow is not installed automatically when a database is created. It is provided on a separate installation CD but is available for no extra charge — the DBA or system administrator will just need to know that it should be installed.

Workflows are designed using a provided graphical tool. Instances of a defined workflow are then executed entirely within the database.

This short section does not have the space to fully explore the many capabilities of Oracle Workflow, but if you find yourself with an application specification that requires any of the characteristics of multistep processes, or even just simple notifications, then consider using the built-in capabilities provided by this powerful utility.

Workspace Manager

Oracle provides a mechanism for users to have what appears to be their own private copy of the database. The user of each workspace is able to make changes to his or her "copy" of the data without impacting other users. They may even make new copies with alternative changes. They can make tentative changes and corrections, and eventually finalize their version of the database without other user's seeing those changes.

Consider the possibilities as each departmental manager makes his or her budget plans for the upcoming year. Rather than doing their planning in a spreadsheet, they can be working within a structured application, with their changes protected against loss by the native recovery features of the Oracle database. As each manager completes a version of the planning cycle, he or she may freeze that state of the data and then make another iteration of changes. When one alternative doesn't work out, the user can return to any of those frozen "snapshots" and try a different approach. Different scenarios can be tried, compared, and even merged together. When the local department's projection is ready to be reviewed, it can be shared with the divisional director or merged with other departments' workspaces to become the division's record. Finally, when all alternatives have been considered and a final approved version is ready, it can be merged back into the mainstream database and become the final reality.

Of course, keeping multiple copies of the entire database to support such "alternative universes" would be terribly expensive and a nightmare for the DBA to manage. The beauty of Oracle Workspace Manager is that it does all of this within the single database. When necessary, it makes a different version of a row that is only visible within the workspace in which the change is made (or any child workspaces created from that workspace) and allows the workspace user to see the remaining rows from the "main" database. Only modified rows within a workspace need to be duplicated.

Oracle Workspace Manager tracks all of these changes, allowing workspaces to be shared for collaborative development, and it provides a mechanism for merging and reconciling the alternative universes into a single reality when the users are ready.

Once again, this short section is not able to provide the details of how to do all of these operations; an entire manual, the *Application Developers Guide—Workspace Manager* is part of the Oracle 10*g* documentation set and presents this facility in greater depth. The goal of this section is to make you aware of this generally unknown and underutilized feature that can be a powerful tool for developing applications that go beyond the traditional concepts what-you-see-is-what-you-get transaction management.

Summary

Even though the majority of your SQL statements will reference database tables, there are many other structures that make up the Oracle database environment that impact your programming capabilities. This chapter provided an introduction to several of these:

- Alternative types of tablespaces
- Options for storing data: compression and partitioning
- Views and materialized views for convenience and performance
- Sequences, global temporary tables
- Recycle bin, part of Oracle's flashback technology
- Synonyms to provide aliases for other database objects
- Database links to define linkages to remote databases
- Advanced Queuing, which provides an asynchronous mechanism for passing information between processes
- Object extensions to the Oracle relational database
- Stored procedures, functions, and packages
- Ways of accessing operating system files
- Controlling how Oracle buffers data and index blocks in memory
- Workflows to keep track of multistep processes
- Workspace Manager

Most of these structures are typically created and controlled by database administrators but will be used by application developers. Better understanding of these capabilities will lead to more effective usage and an enhanced ability to work with the DBA to coordinate the design of the application and the database.

13

Functions

Oracle provides a rich set of functions to extend the power of the database. Functions add to standard SQL and provide a rich toolset for manipulating and massaging data in SQL queries. Oracle provides functions for math operations, string operations, analytic functions, and XML processing, among others. Oracle also allows you to create your own functions in much the same way as you would create custom procedures. After reading this chapter, you will be comfortable using the Oracle-defined functions in your SQL statements, be able to create your own custom functions, and be familiar with the range of functions that Oracle provides in 10*g*.

What Is a Function?

Functions are blocks of code that perform an action and that are referenced by an identifier and can be passed arguments. Functions in Oracle are very similar to object methods in languages like Java or functions or procedures in languages like Visual Basic and C. Functions are different than procedures, as they return a result after they execute and can return multiple results through the use of `OUT` parameters. Functions can be created as standalone objects or included in a package with other objects.

Oracle provides a rich set of functions with the database, but if you need something special, you can create your own. Before you create a new function, it's good practice to review what Oracle provides for you out of the box, as Oracle's functions are highly optimized.

Defining Your Own Functions

If Oracle doesn't come with what you need, you can always define your own functions. Functions are defined just like other items in the database. You create functions in PL/SQL or Java to extend the functionality of the database.

The general form of a function declaration is as follows:

```
CREATE [OR REPLACE] FUNCTION function_name
    [([arg [{IN | OUT}] datatype, .....]
RETURN datatype {IS | AS} function_body_here
```

Functions are declared in a very similar way to procedures. You can specify CREATE OR REPLACE, you can name the function, and you can specify several arguments that can be either IN or OUT. With a function, the arguments are optional, but you must specify a RETURN type, as functions must return a value.

The following example creates a function that converts Fahrenheit to Celsius. You pass a FLOAT into the function as an input parameter, and the function returns a FLOAT representing the temperature in Celsius.

```
CREATE OR REPLACE FUNCTION FtoC(F FLOAT)
RETURN FLOAT IS

BEGIN
 RETURN (5/9)*(F-32);
END FtoC;
```

Functions can also operate on table data, as shown in the following example. You should create this function in the SCOTT schema if you want to execute it.

```
CREATE OR REPLACE FUNCTION moneyMaker(eid emp.EMPNO%type)
RETURN VARCHAR2 IS
 salary NUMBER;
BEGIN
 SELECT SAL into salary FROM emp WHERE empno = eid;
 IF salary >= 3000 THEN
     RETURN 'THIS PERSON MAKES $$!';
 ELSE
     RETURN 'THIS PERSON NEEDS A RAISE'
 END IF;
END moneyMaker;
```

This function takes an employee ID as input and determines his or her current salary status. This function uses the %type type attribute to get the data type from the field directly.

When you create a function, Oracle compiles it and stores the result in the database. That way, when you go to use it, execution is fast, since the code is precompiled. Oracle also checks for any dependencies and recompiles any dependent objects when needed.

Permissions to Create Functions

You must have CREATE PROCEDURE permission to be able to create functions in your schema. You need the EXECUTE permission granted to you to run functions in another user's schema.

Where Can Functions Be Used?

Functions can be used anywhere you can have an expression. They can be used in a SELECT statement, a WHERE clause, the CONNECT BY, START WITH, ORDER BY, and GROUP BY clauses of a SELECT, the VALUES clause of an INSERT, and the SET clause of an UPDATE.

Defining a Java Function

In recent versions of Oracle, you can also create functions in Java. To do this, you must follow four steps:

- Create your Java program exposing public static methods for your functions
- Compile your class file
- Upload the class file into Oracle using the LoadJava utility
- Create a PL/SQL wrapper for the Java function

The following example shows how to implement the temperature conversion function to Java.

First, create a class exposing a public static method:

```
public class f
 public static double f2c(double f){
     double c = (5.0 / 9.0) * (f - 32.0);
     return c
 }
}
```

Second, compile the class using `javac`:

```
javac FtoCjava.java
```

Next, upload the java class to the `SCOTT` schema in Oracle using `LoadJava`. You may have to first grant the `JAVAUSERPRIV` privilege to `SCOTT`:

```
LoadJava -verbose -schema scott -thin -user scott/tiger@localhost:1521:orcl
FtoCjava.class (this should be on one line).
```

Finally, create a PL/SQL wrapper to call the function:

```
CREATE OR REPLACE FUNCTION FtoCJ(F NUMBER) RETURN NUMBER
AS LANGUAGE JAVA NAME 'FtoCjava.f2c(double) return double';
```

Then calling the function would return the following:

```
SQL> select FtoCJ(212) from dual;

FTOCJ(212)
----------
       100
```

Viewing Information about Your Functions

Functions are stored in the data dictionary just like other program types. You can view information about them by running `SELECT` statements against the `user_objects` view. The `user_objects` view contains the following information about the object you have installed in a schema. Executing this in the `SCOTT` schema would yield the following:

```
SQL> desc user_objects;
 Name                                      Null?    Type
```

```
---------------------------------------- -------- ----------------------------
OBJECT_NAME                                       VARCHAR2(128)
SUBOBJECT_NAME                                    VARCHAR2(30)
OBJECT_ID                                         NUMBER
DATA_OBJECT_ID                                    NUMBER
OBJECT_TYPE                                       VARCHAR2(19)
CREATED                                           DATE
LAST_DDL_TIME                                     DATE
TIMESTAMP                                         VARCHAR2(19)
STATUS                                            VARCHAR2(7)
TEMPORARY                                         VARCHAR2(1)
GENERATED                                         VARCHAR2(1)
SECONDARY                                         VARCHAR2(1)
```

You can get specifics about the MONEYMAKER function by issuing the following statement:

```
SELECT OBJECT_TYPE, CREATED, STATUS, TIMESTAMP FROM user_objects WHERE object_name
= 'MONEYMAKER';

OBJECT_TYPE     CREATED                 STATUS     TIMESTAMP
 --------------  ---------------------  ---------  -------------------
 FUNCTION        2004-10-03 22:04:57.0  VALID      2004-10-03:22:09:25
```

OBJECT_TYPE tells you that MONEYMAKER is a function; the STATUS field shows that the function has been successfully compiled, CREATED shows the date that the function was created, and TIMESTAMP shows the last time the function was updated. Oracle uses the TIMESTAMP field to determine dependencies in the database.

Deleting a Function

You can delete a function from a schema by using the DROP FUNCTION statement. The syntax is as follows:

```
DROP FUNCTION function_name;
```

The function will be deleted without any further warnings.

Oracle's Built-In SQL Functions

Oracle provides a rich library of built-in functions for you to use in applications. Before you build your own functions, check the Oracle library to make sure something doesn't already exist that meets your needs. Oracle provides functions to perform math operations, string manipulation, date manipulation, and data conversions, among others. The following section presents some of the most useful functions Oracle provides.

Aggregate Functions

Aggregate functions aggregate multiple results from a column in a SELECT statement into a single value. For example, you can use the AVG function to average all the values in a returned column of a SELECT query. Aggregate functions are often used in conjunction with a GROUP BY clause in a SELECT statement. Most of the aggregate functions can also be used in analytic functions as well. More advanced functions like linear regression and statistical functions are not covered here. Please see the Oracle SQL reference for these.

The following examples use the HR sample schema included with Oracle.

AVG(col_name)

AVG returns the average of a column.

```
SELECT AVG(SALARY) FROM EMPLOYEES;

AVG(SALARY)
-----------
 6461.68224
```

CORR(exp1, exp2)

CORR returns the coefficient of correlation of a pair of numbers. The exp1 and exp2 arguments can be NUMBER values or any value that can be converted to a NUMBER. The following example uses the OE sample schema provided with Oracle:

```
    SELECT supplier_id, CORR(list_price, min_price) as RESULT
    FROM product_information
    GROUP BY supplier_id;

SUPPLIER_ID RESULT
----------- --------------------------
     102050                          1
     102051                 .999201348
     102052                 .999666957
     102053                 .997672754
     102054                 .999968014
     102055                 .999856981
     102056
     102057                 .999820354
     102058                          1
     102059                          1
     102060                 .999291302
```

There are other variations of the CORR function that use different algorithms for calculating the result. See the Oracle SQL reference for more information on these.

COUNT([DISTINCT] exp)

COUNT returns the number of rows returned by the query where exp is not NULL. If you pass the * wildcard to COUNT, then it will return the count of all rows, including ones with NULL values. You can optionally use the DISTINCT keyword to count only unique instances of data.

This example shows that there are 19 rows in the JOBS table:

```
SELECT COUNT(*) FROM JOBS;

  COUNT(*)
----------
        19
```

This example shows that there are 19 unique jobs in the employees table:

```
SELECT COUNT(DISTINCT JOB_ID) FROM EMPLOYEES;

COUNT(DISTINCTJOB_ID)
---------------------
                   19
```

COVAR_POP(exp1, exp2)

COVAR_POP returns the population covariance of a pair of numbers.

```
SELECT supplier_id, COVAR_POP(list_price, min_price) as RESULT
FROM product_information
GROUP BY supplier_id;

SUPPLIER_ID     RESULT
----------- ----------
     102050      65945
     102051     104728
     102052 37484.8889
     102053 24486.1429
     102054 1924.88889
     102055 8500.91667
     102056          0
     102057    65116.8
     102058       5643
     102059       2212
     102060 928678.888
```

COVAR_SAMP(exp1, exp2)

COVAR_SAMP returns the sample covariance of a pair of numbers.

```
SELECT supplier_id, COVAR_SAMP(list_price, min_price) as RESULT
FROM product_information
GROUP BY supplier_id;

SUPPLIER_ID     RESULT
----------- ----------
     102050     131890
     102051     157092
     102052 44981.8667
     102053 28567.1667
     102054 2887.33333
     102055 9273.72727
     102056
     102057      81396
     102058      11286
     102059       4424
     102060 1006068.79
```

CUME_DIST(exp1,....) WITHIN GROUP(ORDER BY)

CUME_DIST returns the relative position of a row within a group meeting certain criteria. You can specify one or more expressions to pass as arguments to the function.

```
SELECT CUME_DIST(5000,103) WITHIN GROUP(ORDER BY SALARY, MANAGER_ID) as RESULT FROM
EMPLOYEES;

    RESULT
----------
.462962963
```

DENSE_RANK(exp1,....) WITHIN GROUP (ORDER BY)

DENSE_RANK returns a NUMBER representing the rank of a row within a group of rows.

```
SELECT DENSE_RANK(5000,103) WITHIN GROUP(ORDER BY SALARY, MANAGER_ID) as RESULT
FROM EMPLOYEES;

    RESULT
----------
        43
```

GROUP_ID()

GROUP_ID assigns a number to each group defined in a GROUP BY clause. GROUP_ID can be used to easily identify duplicate groups in a query.

The following example shows that the specified query has no duplicate groups. The example uses the HR sample schema.

```
select avg(salary), manager_id, group_id() gid from employees group by manager_id;

AVG(SALARY)                                MANAGER_ID     GID
 ----------------------------------------  -------------  ------
 11100                                      100            0
 8980                                       101            0
 9000                                       102            0
 4950                                       103            0
 7920                                       108            0
 2780                                       114            0
 2762.5                                     120            0
 3175                                       121            0
 2950                                       122            0
 3237.5                                     123            0
 2875                                       124            0
 8500                                       145            0
 8500                                       146            0
 7766.666666666666666666666666666666666667  147            0
 8650                                       148            0
 8333.333333333333333333333333333333333333  149            0
 6000                                       201            0
 8300                                       205            0
 24000                                      (null)         0
```

MAX(exp)

MAX returns the maximum value of the exp argument.

This function returns the maximum salary paid for a job:

```
SELECT MAX(max_salary) as max FROM JOBS;

       MAX
----------
     40000
```

MEDIAN(exp)

MEDIAN returns the median value of the exp argument.

The following example returns the median max-salary paid for a job:

```
SELECT MEDIAN(max_salary) as med FROM JOBS;

       MED
----------
     10000
```

MIN(exp)

MIN returns the minimum value of the exp argument.

This function returns the minimum salary paid for a job:

```
SELECT MIN(min_salary) as min FROM JOBS;

       MIN
----------
      2000
```

PERCENTILE_CONT(exp ...) WITHIN GROUP (ORDER BY exp)

PERCENTILE_CONT is an inverse distribution function that assumes a continuous distribution model. It takes a percentile value as an input parameter and returns an interpolated value that would fall into that percentile with respect to the ORDER BY specification. The following example uses the HR schema:

```
SELECT department_id, PERCENTILE_CONT(0.5) WITHIN GROUP (ORDER BY salary DESC) as
RESULT FROM employees GROUP BY DEPARTMENT_ID;

DEPARTMENT_ID     RESULT
 ---------------  ---------
 10               4400
 20               9500
 30               2850
 40               6500
 50               3100
 60               4800
 70               10000
 80               8900
 90               17000
 100              8000
 110              10150
 (null)           7000
```

PERCENTILE_DISC(exp ...) WITHIN GROUP (ORDER BY exp)

PERCENTILE_DISC is an inverse distribution function that assumes a discrete distribution model. It takes a percentile value as an input parameter and returns an interpolated value that would fall into that percentile with respect to the ORDER BY specification. The following example uses the HR schema:

```
SELECT department_id, PERCENTILE_DISC(0.5) WITHIN GROUP (ORDER BY salary DESC) as
RESULT FROM employees GROUP BY DEPARTMENT_ID;

DEPARTMENT_ID      RESULT
 ----------------   ---------
 10                 4400
 20                 13000
 30                 2900
 40                 6500
 50                 3100
 60                 4800
 70                 10000
 80                 9000
 90                 17000
 100                8200
 110                12000
 (null)             7000
```

PERCENT_RANK(exp...) WITHIN GROUP(ORDER BY exp)

PERCENT_RANK is similar to the CUME_DIST function. It takes one or more expressions as input, and returns the percent rank of the selected row within the group, as in the following:

```
SELECT PERCENT_RANK(10000, .05) WITHIN GROUP(ORDER BY salary, commission_pct) as
RESULT FROM EMPLOYEES;

RESULT
 ------------------------------------------
 0.8224299065420560747663551401869158878505
```

RANK(exp ...) WITHIN GROUP (ORDER BY exp)

RANK determines the rank of one or more of the expression exp within a result set.

```
SELECT RANK(10000) WITHIN GROUP(ORDER BY salary DESC) as RESULT FROM EMPLOYEES;

 RESULT
 ---------
 16
```

STDDEV(exp)

STDDEV returns the sample standard deviation of exp. STDDEV returns zero when it has only one row of input data.

```
SELECT STDDEV(COMMISSION_PCT) FROM EMPLOYEES;

STDDEV(COMMISSION_PCT)
----------------------
            .085183933
```

STDDEV_POP(exp)

STDDEV_POP returns the square root of the cumulative population standard deviation of the population variance.

```
SELECT STDDEV_POP(COMMISSION_PCT) FROM EMPLOYEES;

STDDEV_POP(COMMISSION_PCT)
--------------------------
                .083958201
```

STDDEV_SAMP(exp)

STDDEV_SAMP returns the square root of the cumulative sample standard deviation of the sample variance.

```
SELECT STDDEV_SAMP(COMMISSION_PCT) FROM EMPLOYEES;

STDDEV_SAMP(COMMISSION_PCT)
---------------------------
                .085183933
```

SUM(exp)

SUM sums the returned values of the exp argument.

The following example sums the minimum and maximum salary columns in the JOBS table:

```
SELECT SUM(min_salary) as min, SUM(max_salary) as max FROM JOBS;

       MIN        MAX
---------- ----------
    124800     251000
```

VAR_POP(exp)

VAR_POP returns the population variance of a group of numbers after throwing out NULL values.

```
SELECT VAR_POP(COMMISSION_PCT) FROM EMPLOYEES;

VAR_POP(COMMISSION_PCT)
-----------------------
             .00704898
```

VAR_SAMP(exp)

VAR_SAMP returns the sample variance of a group of numbers after throwing out NULL values.

```
SELECT VAR_SAMP(COMMISSION_PCT) FROM EMPLOYEES;

VAR_SAMP(COMMISSION_PCT)
------------------------
             .007256303
```

VARIANCE(exp)

`VARIANCE` returns the variance of the values in `exp`.

```
SELECT VARIANCE(COMMISSION_PCT) FROM EMPLOYEES;

VARIANCE(COMMISSION_PCT)
------------------------
              .007256303
```

Numeric Functions

These functions operate on numeric values and return numeric results. Oracle provides functions to perform numeric conversions as well as standard math operations.

ABS(n)

`ABS` returns the absolute value of a numeric argument. It takes a numeric value, or any value that can be implicitly converted to a numeric value, as its argument and returns the absolute value as a numeric value. The return value is the same type as the numeric type of the argument.

```
Select abs(-255) as absolute_value from dual;

ABSOLUTE_VALUE
--------------
           255
```

ACOS(n)

`ACOS` returns the arc tangent of a numeric argument or an argument that can be implicitly converted to a numeric value in the range of -1 to 1. The returned value is expressed in radians. The returned value is the same type as the numeric type of the argument unless the argument is a `BINARY_FLOAT`. In this case the function returns a `BINARY_DOUBLE`.

```
Select acos(.0324) as acos_value from dual;

ACOS_VALUE
----------
1.53839066
```

ASIN(n)

`ASIN` returns the arc sine of a numeric argument or an argument that can be implicitly converted to a numeric value in the range of -1 to 1. The returned value is expressed in radians. The returned value is the same type as the numeric type of the argument unless the argument is a `BINARY_FLOAT`. In this case the function returns a `BINARY_DOUBLE`.

```
Select asin(.234) as asin_value from dual;

ASIN_VALUE
----------
.236189884
```

ATAN(n)

ATAN returns the arc tangent of a numeric argument or an argument that can be implicitly converted to a numeric value. The returned value is expressed in radians. The returned value is the same type as the numeric type of the argument unless the argument is a BINARY_FLOAT. In this case the function returns a BINARY_DOUBLE.

```
Select atan(.4) as atan_value from dual;

ATAN_VALUE
----------
.380506377
```

ATAN2(n, m)

ATAN2 returns the arc tangent of two numeric arguments or two arguments that can be implicitly converted to a numeric value. The returned value is expressed in radians. The returned value is the same type as the numeric type of the argument unless the argument is a BINARY_FLOAT. In this case the function returns a BINARY_DOUBLE.

```
Select atan2(.4, .2) as atan_value from dual;

ATAN_VALUE
----------
1.10714872
```

CEIL(n)

Ceil returns the next greatest integer nearest the argument. The argument can be a numeric value or any type that can be implicitly converted to a numeric value. The function returns a value that is the same type as the numeric argument type.

```
Select ceil(4.5) as next_int from dual;

  NEXT_INT
----------
         5
```

COS(n)

COS returns the cosine of the argument. The argument can be a numeric value or any type that can be implicitly converted to a numeric value. The argument should be an angle expressed in radians. The function returns a value that is the same type as the numeric argument type unless the argument is a BINARY_FLOAT. In this case the function returns a BINARY_DOUBLE.

```
Select cos(180 * 3.14159265359/180) as cos_value from dual;

COS_VALUE
----------
        -1
```

COSH(n)

COSH returns the hyperbolic cosine of the argument. The argument can be a numeric value or any type that can be implicitly converted to a numeric value. The argument should be an angle expressed in radians.

The function returns a value that is the same type as the numeric argument type unless the argument is a `BINARY_FLOAT`. In this case the function returns a `BINARY_DOUBLE`.

```
Select cosh(0) as cosh_value from dual;

COSH_VALUE
----------
         1
```

EXP(exp)

`EXP` returns 2.71828183 raised to the `exp` power.

```
SELECT EXP(2) as Squared from DUAL;

SQUARED
 ----------------------------------------
 7.38905609893065022723042746057500781320
```

FLOOR(n)

`FLOOR` returns the next integer less than or equal to the argument. The argument can be a numeric value or any type that can be implicitly converted to a numeric value. The function returns a value that is the same type as the numeric argument type.

```
Select floor(4.5) as next_int from dual;

  NEXT_INT
----------
         4
```

LN(n)

`LN` returns the natural log of the argument. The argument can be a numeric value or any type that can be implicitly converted to a numeric value. The function returns a value that is the same type as the numeric argument type unless the argument is a `BINARY_FLOAT`. In this case the function returns a `BINARY_DOUBLE`.

```
Select ln(20) as log_value from dual;

LOG_VALUE
----------
2.99573227
```

LOG(n, n2)

`LOG` returns the log of the second argument with base of argument 1. The base can be any positive number except 0 or 1, and the second argument can be any positive integer. The arguments can be a numeric value or any type that can be implicitly converted to a numeric value. The function returns a `NUMBER` value unless the argument is a `BINARY_FLOAT`. In this case the function returns a `BINARY_DOUBLE`.

```
Select log(10,20) as log_value from dual;

LOG_VALUE
----------
   1.30103
```

MOD(n, n2)

MOD returns the remainder of the first argument divided by the second argument. The arguments can be a numeric value or any type that can be implicitly converted to a numeric value. Oracle will determine the argument with the highest numeric precision and convert all the calculations and result to that level.

```
Select mod(10,3) as mod_result from dual;

MOD_RESULT
----------
         1
```

NANVL(n, n2)

NANVL is used to return an alternate value for a BINARY_FLOAT or BINARY_NUMBER that has a NaN (Not a Number) value. The number to check is the first argument, and the second argument is the replacement value if the first argument is NaN. The best use of this function is to convert NaN values into NULLs or 0. The following example is using the Oracle function to_binary_float to create a NaN value for demonstration, but the NANVL function would most likely be used to operate on a table column in a SELECT statement.

```
select NANVL(to_binary_float('NaN'),0) as nanvl_value from dual;

NANVL_VALUE
-----------
          0
```

POWER(n, n2)

POWER returns the first argument raised to the power of the second. The arguments can be a numeric value or any type that can be implicitly converted to a numeric value. The function returns a NUMBER value unless the argument is a BINARY_FLOAT. In this case the function returns a BINARY_DOUBLE.

```
select power(2,2) as power_value from dual;

POWER_VALUE
-----------
          4
```

REMAINDER(n, n2)

REMAINDER returns the remainder of the first argument divided by the second argument. The arguments can be a numeric value or any type that can be implicitly converted to a numeric value. Oracle will determine the argument with the highest numeric precision and convert all the calculations and result to that level. REMAINDER is similar to MOD, except that REMAINDER uses ROUND in its calculations, whereas MOD uses FLOOR.

```
select remainder(10,3) as remainder_value from dual;

REMAINDER_VALUE
---------------
              1
```

ROUND (n, n2)

ROUND returns the first argument rounded by the number of digits specified by the second argument. The arguments can be a numeric value or any type that can be implicitly converted to a numeric value. The second argument must be an integer value, and if you don't specify it, Oracle will default the rounding precision to 0. The second argument can be a negative number to round the numbers to the left of the decimal point. If the second argument is specified, ROUND will return a NUMBER; otherwise, it will return a value that is the same type as the first argument.

```
select ROUND(10.121,1) as rounded_value from dual;

ROUNDED_VALUE
-------------
         10.1

SELECT ROUND(12.661,-1) as rounded_value from dual;

ROUNDED_VALUE
-------------
           10
```

SIGN(n)

SIGN returns a NUMBER that specifies the sign of the first argument. The argument can be a numeric value or any type that can be implicitly converted by Oracle to a numeric type. The possible return values are as follows:

- -1 if the number is < 0
- 0 if the number is 0
- 1 if the number is > 0
- -1 if the number is a BINARY_FLOAT or BINARY_DOUBLE and is < 0
- 1 if the number is a BINARY_FLOAT or BINARY_DOUBLE and is >=0 or is NaN

```
Select SIGN(-100) as sign_value from dual;

SIGN_VALUE
----------
        -1
```

SIN(n)

SIN returns the sine of the argument expressed in radians. The argument can be a numeric value or a type that Oracle can implicitly convert to a numeric value. The argument must be specified in radians. To get the sin of a 45-degree angle in radians, use the following example:

```
Select SIN(45 * 3.14159265359/180) as sine_value from dual;

SINE_VALUE
----------
.707106781
```

SINH(n)

SINH returns the hyperbolic sine of the argument. The argument can be a numeric value or a type that Oracle can implicitly convert to a numeric value.

```
Select SINH(0) as sine_value from dual;

SINE_VALUE
----------
         0
```

SQRT(n)

SQRT returns the square root of the argument. The argument can be a numeric value or a type that Oracle can implicitly convert to a numeric value. SQRT returns a value that is the same type as the supplied argument.

```
Select SQRT(16) as square_root from dual;

SQUARE_ROOT
-----------
          4
```

TAN(n)

TAN returns the tangent of a numeric argument or an argument that can be implicitly converted to a numeric value. The returned value is expressed in radians. The returned value is the same type as the numeric type of the argument unless the argument is a BINARY_FLOAT. In this case the function returns a BINARY_DOUBLE.

```
Select tan(.4) as tan_value from dual;

TAN_VALUE
----------
.422793219
```

TANH(n)

TANH returns the hyperbolic tangent of the argument. The argument can be a numeric value, or a type that Oracle can implicitly convert to a numeric value.

```
Select TANH(1) as tan_value from dual;

TAN_VALUE
----------
.761594156
```

TRUNC(n, n2)

TRUNC returns the first argument truncated by the number of decimal places specified in the second argument. The arguments can be a numeric value or a type that Oracle can implicitly convert to a numeric value. The second argument can be either a positive integer to specify the right of the decimal point or a negative number to specify the left of the decimal point. If you are truncating to the left of the decimal point, the truncated digit will become 0.

```
Select TRUNC(12.43,1) as truncate from dual;

  truncate
```

```
----------
      12.4

Select TRUNC(12.43,-1) as truncate from dual;

  truncate
----------
        10
```

Character Functions

Oracle provides a rich set of functions for manipulating string data.

ASCII(arg1)

ASCII returns the decimal representation of the character supplied in the arg1 argument. If your database is set to ASCII, this will be the ASCII code for the character. If your database is set to EBCDIC, then it will be the EBCDIC code. The arg1 argument can be a CHAR, VARCHAR2, NCHAR, or NVARCHAR2 data type.

```
SELECT ASCII('Z') from DUAL;

ASCII('Z')
----------
        90
```

CHR(arg1 [using nchar_cs])

CHR returns the character specified by the code passed in the first argument. The returned character depends on the underlying code set that Oracle is using for character data. The argument must either be a numeric value or a type that Oracle can implicitly convert to a numeric value. You can optionally pass CHR using nchar_cs with the first argument to tell Oracle to use the national code set. CHR returns a VARCHAR2 data type.

On an ASCII machine using database character set WE8ISO8859P1, the following example will execute correctly:

```
SELECT CHR(79)||CHR(114)||CHR(97)||CHR(99)||CHR(108)||CHR(101) as DB FROM DUAL;

DB
------
Oracle
```

To use UTF8, you specify using nchar_cs in the argument list.

```
SELECT CHR(49382 USING NCHAR_CS) FROM DUAL;

C
-
¿
```

CONCAT(arg1, arg2)

CONCAT returns arg1 concatenated with arg2. The arguments can be CHAR, VARCHAR2, NCHAR, NVARCHAR2, CLOB, or NCLOB. If the two arguments are the same data type, then CONCAT returns a string of that type. If they are different types, then CONCAT returns a string in data type that would be lossless. For example, if arg1 is a NCLOB and arg2 is a CLOB, then CONCAT would return a string as a NCLOB. CONCAT can be used in place of the concatenation operator ||.

```
SELECT CONCAT('Today''s date is ',(SELECT SYSDATE FROM DUAL)) as THE_DATE FROM
DUAL;
THE_DATE
-------------------------
Today's date is 22-OCT-04
```

INITCAP returns a string that is the same as arg1 with the initial letter of each word capitalized. The argument passed to INITCAP can be a CHAR, VARCHAR2, NCHAR, or NVARCHAR2 data type.

```
SELECT INITCAP('oracle is the best') as RESULT FROM DUAL;
RESULT
------------------
Oracle Is The Best
```

INSTR(arg1, to_find, pos, occurrence)

INSTR returns an integer specifying if a given substring is found in the string argument arg1. The function returns the integer position where the substring is found. The pos argument is a NUMBER that specifies where in the string to start searching. If pos is a positive, then Oracle starts searching from the beginning of the string at that position. If pos is negative, Oracle starts at the specified number of characters from the end of the string and searches backward. The occurrence parameter specifies which occurrence of the string to search for.

```
SELECT INSTR('Search for the second the','the',1,2) as RESULT FROM DUAL;

    RESULT
----------
        23
```

LENGTH(arg1)

LENGTH returns an integer that is the length of the argument arg1. Arg1 can be a CHAR, VARCHAR2, NCHAR, NVARCHAR2, CLOB, or NCLOB data type.

```
SELECT LENGTH('How long am I?') as RESULT FROM DUAL;

    RESULT
----------
        14
```

LOWER(arg1)

LOWER returns a string that is the same as arg1 with all the characters in lowercase. The argument to LOWER can be a CHAR, VARCHAR2, NCHAR, NVARCHAR2, CLOB, or NCLOB data type.

```
SELECT LOWER('ORACLE IS THE BEST') as RESULT FROM DUAL;

RESULT
------------------
oracle is the best
```

LPAD (arg3)

LPAD returns a VARCHAR2 string that is arg1 left padded with arg3 for a length of n. Arg1 and arg3 can be a CHAR, VARCHAR2, NCHAR, NVARCHAR2, CLOB, or NCLOB data type, while n must be numeric or be able to be evaluated to a numeric value. If arg3 is not provided, then Oracle will pad with blank spaces.

```
SELECT LPAD('20 spaces', 20, '-') as RESULT FROM DUAL;

RESULT
--------------------
-----------20 spaces
```

LTRIM(arg1, arg2)

LTRIM returns a VARCHAR2 string that is the same as arg1 with the characters in arg2 removed. LTRIM starts scanning from the leftmost character and keeps removing characters until none match arg2. The arguments to LTRIM can be of data type CHAR, VARCHAR2, NCHAR, NVARCHAR2, CLOB, or NCLOB.

```
SELECT LTRIM('xxxxxxxx-AA-','x') as RESULT FROM DUAL;

RESU
----
-AA-
```

NLS_INITCAP(arg1, ['NLS_SORT=x'])

NLS_INITCAP is the same as INITCAP but can handle multibyte encoded characters. NLS_INITCAP returns a VARCHAR2 string that is the same as arg1 with the initial letters of each word capitalized. NLS_INITCAP takes an optional argument, 'NLS_SORT=', that can specify additional specific linguistic requirements for letter case selection. NLS_INITCAP arguments can be of CHAR, VARCHAR2, NCHAR, or NVARCHAR2 data type. Refer to Chapter 5 of the *Oracle Globalization Guide* included in your product documentation for more information regarding NLS_SORT.

```
SELECT NLS_INITCAP('richard wagner', 'NLS_SORT=XGerman') as RESULT FROM DUAL;

RESULT
--------------
Richard Wagner
```

NLS_LOWER(arg1, ['NLS_SORT=x'])

NLS_LOWER returns a VARCHAR2 string that is the same as arg1 with all characters in lowercase. NLS_LOWER is the same as the LOWER function, but it can handle multibyte characters for international languages. The arguments to NLS_LOWER can be a CHAR, VARCHAR2, NCHAR, NVARCHAR2, CLOB, or NCLOB data type. NLS_LOWER takes an optional argument, 'NLS_SORT=', that can specify additional specific linguistic requirements for letter case selection. Refer to Chapter 5 of the *Oracle Globalization Guide* included in your product documentation for more information regarding NLS_SORT.

```
SELECT NLS_LOWER('RICHARD WAGNER', 'NLS_SORT=XGerman') as RESULT FROM DUAL;
RESULT

--------------
richard wagner
```

NLSSORT(arg1, ['NLS_SORT=x'])

NLSSORT allows you to sort data results based on the specific linguistic requirements of the language you are using in your database. Argument 1 is the field or text to sort, and the second argument specifies the linguistic sort order. The arguments to NLSSORT can be CHAR, VARCHAR2, NCHAR, or NVARCHAR2 data types. NLSSORT returns raw bytes and is used in the ORDER BY clause of your SQL statement, or in comparison operations. NLSSORT is useful when you need to correctly sort results stored in a different language in your database. Refer to Chapter 5 of the *Oracle Globalization Guide* included in your product documentation for more information regarding NLSSORT. You can also set the NLSSORT parameter globally for your session by using session ALTER commands. For example:

```
ALTER SESSION SET NLS_COMP = 'ANSI';
ALTER SESSION SET NLS_SORT = 'XGerman';
```

will set the sort order for the whole session.

NLS_UPPER(arg1, ['NLS_SORT=x'])

NLS_UPPER returns arg1 with all characters in uppercase as a VARCHAR2 string. NLS_UPPER performs the same function as UPPER but allows for multibyte characters. The first argument to NLS_UPPER can be a CHAR, VARCHAR2, NCHAR, NVARCHAR2, CLOB, or NCLOB data type. NLS_UPPER can also take an optional parameter, 'NLS_SORT=x', that can specify additional specific linguistic requirements for letter case selection. Refer to Chapter 5 of the *Oracle Globalization Guide* included in your product documentation for more information regarding NLS_SORT.

```
SELECT NLS_UPPER('â') as RESULT FROM DUAL;

R
-
Â
```

REGEXP_INSTR(source, regex, [pos], [occurrence], [return_option], [match])

REGEXP_INSTR is an advanced version of the INSTR function. REGEXP_INSTR allows you to search the source string with POSIX-compliant regular expressions (POSIX stands for Portable Operating System Interface for UNIX). The function returns an integer specifying the location in the string of the matched pattern. If the source argument is a LOB, then the function will return a CLOB. The source argument can be a CHAR, VARCHAR2, NCHAR, NVARCHAR2, CLOB, or NCLOB data type, while the regex argument can be a CHAR, VARCHAR2, NCHAR, or NVARCHAR2 containing up to 512 bytes of data. This function is only available in Oracle 10*g*.

The arguments for this function are as follows:

- source — The source string to be searched.
- regex — The POSIX-compliant regular expression to use.
- pos (optional) — An integer describing where in the string to start searching. The default value is 1, signifying the beginning of the string.
- occurrence (optional) — An integer describing how many replacements to make. The default is 0, signifying that Oracle should replace all occurrences of the match. If you specify another value, Oracle will replace that number match.

- `return_options` (optional) — An integer describing the location of the matched string. The default is 0, which tells Oracle to return the position of the first character of the matched string. You can also specify 1 to tell Oracle to return the position of the first character after the matched string.
- `match` (optional) — A string that lets you change the default matching behavior of the regular expression engine. Valid options are `i`, specifying case-insensitive matching; `c`, specifying case-sensitive matching; `n`, which allows the period (`.`) operator to match the newline character; and `m`, which treats the source string as multiple lines.

See Appendix C-1 in the *Oracle SQL Reference Appendices* provided in the product documentation for the specifics on regular expression syntax for Oracle.

REGEXP_REPLACE(source, regex, replace, [pos], [occurrence], [match])

`REGEXP_REPLACE` is an advanced version of the `REPLACE` function. `REGEXP_REPLACE` allows you to search the source string with POSIX-compliant regular expressions. The function returns a `VARCHAR2` string with every match of `regex` replaced with the `replace` argument. If the `source` argument is a `LOB`, then the function will return a `CLOB`. The `source` and `replace` arguments can be a `CHAR`, `VARCHAR2`, `NCHAR`, `NVARCHAR2`, `CLOB`, or `NCLOB` data type, while the `regex` argument can be a `CHAR`, `VARCHAR2`, `NCHAR`, or `NVARCHAR2` , containing up to 512 bytes of data. This function is only available in Oracle 10*g*.

The arguments for this function are as follows:

- `source` — The source string to be searched.
- `regex` — The POSIX-compliant regular expression to use.
- `replace` — The replacement string to use when the regular expression matches.
- `pos` (optional) — An integer describing where in the string to start searching. The default value is 1, signifying the beginning of the string.
- `occurrence` (optional) — An integer describing how many replacements to make. The default is 0, signifying that Oracle should replace all occurrences of the match. If you specify another value, Oracle will replace that number match.
- `match` (optional) — A string that lets you change the default matching behavior of the regular expression engine. Valid options are `i`, specifying case-insensitive matching; `c`, specifying case-sensitive matching; *n*, which allows the period (`.`) operator to match the newline character; and `m`, which treats the source string as multiple lines.

See Appendix C-1 in the Oracle SQL Reference Appendices provided in the product documentation for the specifics on regular expression syntax for Oracle.

```
SELECT REGEXP_REPLACE('replace all spaces with dashes','[[:blank:]]','-') as RESULT
FROM DUAL;

RESULT
------------------------------
replace-all-spaces-with-dashes
```

REGEXP_SUBSTR(source, regex, [pos], [occurrence], [match])

`REGEXP_SUBSTR` is an advanced version of the `SUBSTR` function. `REGEXP_SUBSTR` allows you to search the source string with POSIX-compliant regular expressions. The function returns a `VARCHAR2` string, with the substring found in the `source` argument. If the `source` argument is a `LOB`, then the function will return a `CLOB`. The `source` argument can be a `CHAR`, `VARCHAR2`, `NCHAR`, `NVARCHAR2`, `CLOB`, or `NCLOB` data type, while the `regex` argument can be a `CHAR`, `VARCHAR2`, `NCHAR`, or `NVARCHAR2`, containing up to 512 bytes of data. This function is only available in Oracle 10*g*.

The arguments for this function are as follows:

- `source` — The source string to be searched.
- `regex` — The POSIX-compliant regular expression to use.
- `pos` (optional) — An integer describing where in the string to start searching. The default value is 1, signifying the beginning of the string.
- `occurrence` (optional) — An integer describing how many replacements to make. The default is 0, signifying that Oracle should replace all occurrences of the match. If you specify another value, Oracle will replace that number match.
- `match` (optional) — A string that lets you change the default matching behavior of the regular expression engine. Valid options are `i`, specifying case-insensitive matching; `c`, specifying case-sensitive matching; `n`, which allows the period (`.`) operator to match the newline character; and `m`, which treats the source string as multiple lines.

See Appendix C-1 in the Oracle SQL Reference Appendices provided in the product documentation for the specifics on regular expression syntax for Oracle.

The following example will extract a phone number from a string that is formatted xxx-xxx-xxxx:

```
 SELECT REGEXP_SUBSTR('my phone number is 212-555-4444', '([[:digit:]]{3})-
([[:digit:]]{3})-([[:digit:]]{4})') FROM DUAL;

REGEXP_SUBST
------------
212-555-4444
```

REPLACE(arg1, search, replace)

`REPLACE` replaces all occurrences of the `search` argument with the `replace` argument in `arg1`. The arguments can be `CHAR`, `VARCHAR2`, `NCHAR`, `NVARCHAR2`, `CLOB`, or `NCLOB` data types. The function returns a `VARCHAR2` string if `arg1` is a not a `LOB`; otherwise, it returns a `CLOB`. If you don't pass a value for the `replace` argument, then all occurrences of the `search` argument are removed from the result.

```
SELECT REPLACE('Oracle is the worst', 'worst', 'best!') as RESULT FROM DUAL;

RESULT
-------------------
Oracle is the best!
```

RPAD(arg1, n, arg3)

`RPAD` returns a `VARCHAR2` string that is `arg1` right padded with `arg3` for a length of `n`. `Arg1` and `arg3` can be a `CHAR`, `VARCHAR2`, `NCHAR`, `NVARCHAR2`, `CLOB`, or `NCLOB` data type, while `n` must be numeric or be able to be evaluated to a numeric value. If `arg3` is not provided, then Oracle will pad with blank spaces.

```
SELECT RPAD('20 spaces', 20, '-') as RESULT FROM DUAL;

RESULT
--------------------
20 spaces-----------
```

RTRIM(arg1, arg2)

RTRIM returns a VARCHAR2 string that is the result of removing the characters in arg2 from arg1. RTRIM starts scanning from the leftmost character and keeps removing characters until none match arg2. The arguments to RTRIM can be of data type CHAR, VARCHAR2, NCHAR, NVARCHAR2, CLOB, or NCLOB.

```
SELECT RTRIM('-AA-xxxxxxxx','x') as RESULT FROM DUAL;

RESU
----
-AA-
```

SOUNDEX(arg1)

SOUNDEX returns the phonetic representation of arg1. It is often used to do searching in a table to find words that sound the same as each other but are spelled differently. The argument arg1 can be a CHAR, VARCHAR2, NCHAR, or NVARCHAR2 data type.

The following example uses the sample HR schema:

```
SELECT FIRST_NAME from employees WHERE SOUNDEX(FIRST_NAME) = SOUNDEX('DAN');

 FIRST_NAME
 -------------
 Diana
 Den
```

SUBSTR(arg1, pos, len)

SUBSTR returns a substring from arg1 starting at position pos and length len. Arg1 can be a CHAR, VARCHAR2, NCHAR, NVARCHAR2, CLOB, or NCLOB data type, and pos and len must be a number or be able to evaluate to a number expression. Pos can be either positive or negative. If it is positive, Oracle starts counting from the beginning of the string. If it is negative, Oracle starts counting from the end of the string. If len is not passed, Oracle returns the substring up to the end of the string.

```
SELECT SUBSTR('abcdeoraclefghij',6,6) as RESULT FROM DUAL;

RESULT
------
oracle
```

TRANSLATE(arg1, match, replace)

TRANSLATE is similar to the REPLACE function. It differs in that it allows you to make several character replacements in one pass. TRANSLATE returns a VARCHAR2 string that is arg1 with all instances of characters in the match argument replaced with the corresponding characters in the replace argument. The match argument can contain several different characters to replace. If you pass an empty string in the replace argument, the function will return NULL.

The following example will replace all - characters with a *, and all * characters with a *

```
SELECT TRANSLATE('Convert-dashes-and*star','-*', '*-') as RESULT FROM DUAL;

RESULT
-----------------------
Convert*dashes*and-star
```

TREAT(expr AS [REF] schema.type)

`TREAT` allows you to change the declared type of the `expr` argument. This function comes in handy when you have a subtype that is more specific to your data and you want to convert the parent type to the more specific one. The optional `REF` keyword can only be used if the type you are referencing is a `REF` type.

The following example shows how you could treat a generic type as a specific subtype:

```
SELECT name, TREAT(VALUE(content) AS legaldocument).lawfirm_name FROM CONTENT;
```

The example assumes that you have created a type `content_t`, a type `legaldocument` that inherits from `content_t`, and a table `content` of `content_t` types. The example selects from the generic table and casts the results to a specific type.

TRIM([LEADING] [TRAILING] [BOTH] char FROM source)

`TRIM` returns a `VARCHAR2` string with either the leading, trailing, or both the leading and trailing characters `char` trimmed from `source` If you specify `LEADING`, then the leading characters that match `char` will be trimmed. If you specify `TRAILING` then the trailing characters that match `char` will be trimmed. Specifying `BOTH` will trim from both ends of the string. If you do not provide a trim character, Oracle defaults to a blank space. If you only specify the `source` argument, Oracle will remove the trailing and leading blank spaces from the `source` argument.

```
SELECT TRIM('     Too many spaces     ') as RESULT FROM DUAL;

RESULT
---------------
Too many spaces
```

UPPER(arg1)

`UPPER` returns a `VARCHAR2` string that contains all the characters of `arg1` in uppercase. The `arg1` argument can be a `CHAR`, `VARCHAR2`, `NCHAR`, `NVARCHAR2`, `CLOB`, or `NCLOB` data type.

```
SELECT UPPER('oracle is the best!') as RESULT FROM DUAL;

RESULT
-------------------
ORACLE IS THE BEST!
```

Date and Time Functions

ADD_MONTHS(arg1, num)

`ADD_MONTHS` returns a `DATE` that is `arg1` plus `num`, or number of months. The `arg1` argument can be a `DATE` or any type that can implicitly be converted to a `DATE`. The `num` argument can be a `NUMBER` or any type that can be implicitly converted to a NUMBER. Specifying a negative number for the num argument will move the date backwards in time.

```
SELECT TO_CHAR(ADD_MONTHS('12-OCT-04',2)) as RESULT FROM DUAL;

RESULT
---------
12-DEC-04
```

CURRENT_DATE

CURRENT_DATE returns the current date.

```
SELECT CURRENT_DATE as RESULT FROM DUAL;
RESULT
---------
10-SEP-04
```

CURRENT_TIMESTAMP([precision])

CURRENT_TIMESTAMP returns the current system timestamp. You can also specify an optional precision argument to control the precision of the seconds in the time.

```
SELECT CURRENT_TIMESTAMP AS RESULT FROM DUAL;

RESULT
---------------------------------------------------------------------------
13-SEP-04 01.24.11.968000 PM -04:00
```

DBTIMEZONE

DBTIMEZONE returns the current database time zone.

```
SELECT DBTIMEZONE FROM DUAL;

DBTIME
------
+00:00
```

EXTRACT (datepart FROM expr)

EXTRACT allows you to extract parts of a date expression. For example, you may want to extract the year from a date string, or minute value in a date-time expression. Valid extractions include YEAR, MONTH, DAY, HOUR, MINUTE, SECOND, TIMEZONE_HOUR, TIMEZONE_MINUTE, TIMEZONE_REGION, and TIMEZONE_ABBR.

```
SELECT EXTRACT(YEAR FROM DATE '2004-10-12') as RESULT FROM DUAL;

    RESULT
----------
      2004
```

FROM_TZ(timestamp, timezone)

FROM_TZ converts a timestamp and time zone value into a TIMESTAMP WITH TIMEZONE value.

```
SELECT FROM_TZ(TIMESTAMP '2004-10-24 06:00:00', '2:00') as RESULT FROM DUAL;

RESULT
----------------------------
24-OCT-04 06.00.00 AM +02:00
```

LAST_DAY(arg1)

LAST_DAY returns the last day of the month specified in arg1. Arg1 can be a DATE value or a string that can resolve to a DATE data type.

```
SELECT LAST_DAY('12-OCT-04') as RESULT FROM DUAL;

RESULT
---------
31-OCT-04
```

LOCALTIMESTAMP([precision])

LOCALTIMESTAMP returns a TIMESTAMP value. You can also specify an optional integer argument to specify the precision of the seconds field.

```
SELECT LOCALTIMESTAMP FROM DUAL;

LOCALTIMESTAMP
---------------------------------------------------------------------------
13-SEP-04 03.02.49.407000 PM
```

MONTHS_BETWEEN(date1, date2)

MONTHS_BETWEEN returns an integer specifying the number of months between two dates. The result can be either positive or negative depending on which date is greater.

```
SELECT MONTHS_BETWEEN('10-JAN-2036', '10-JAN-2004') as RESULT FROM DUAL;

    RESULT
----------
       384
```

NEW_TIME(the_date, tz1, tz2)

NEW_TIME returns the date and time in time zone tz2 based on the time zone tz1 and the date argument the_date. You must set the NLS_DATE_FORMAT parameter to a 24-hour format before you execute the NEW_TIME function.

The time zone arguments can be any of the following strings:

- AST, ADT: Atlantic Standard or Daylight Time
- BST, BDT: Bering Standard or Daylight Time
- CST, CDT: Central Standard or Daylight Time
- EST, EDT: Eastern Standard or Daylight Time
- GMT: Greenwich Mean Time

- HST, HDT: Alaska-Hawaii Standard Time or Daylight Time
- MST, MDT: Mountain Standard or Daylight Time
- NST: Newfoundland Standard Time
- PST, PDT: Pacific Standard or Daylight Time
- YST, YDT: Yukon Standard or Daylight Time

```
ALTER SESSION SET NLS_DATE_FORMAT = 'DD-MON-YYYY HH24:MI:SS';

SELECT NEW_TIME(TO_DATE('10-23-04 16:00:00', 'MM-DD-YY HH24:MI:SS'),
   'EST', 'PST') as RESULT FROM DUAL;

RESULT
--------------------
23-OCT-2004 13:00:00
```

NEXT_DAY(date, day_to_find)

NEXT_DAY returns the next day specified in the day_to_find argument from the date argument. The day_to_find argument must be a string denoting a valid day of the week.

```
SELECT NEXT_DAY('23-OCT-2004','FRIDAY') as RESULT FROM DUAL;

RESULT
--------------------
29-OCT-2004 00:00:00
```

NUMTODSINTERVAL(n, interval_name)

NUMTODSINTERVAL converts n to an INTERVAL DAY TO SECOND. The interval can be specified as a string in the interval_name argument. This argument can be either DAY, HOUR, MINUTE, or SECOND. The n argument must be a NUMBER or be able to be resolved to a NUMBER.

```
SELECT NUMTODSINTERVAL(50,'HOUR') as RESULT FROM DUAL;

RESULT
---------------------------------------------------------------------------
+000000002 02:00:00.000000000
```

In the previous example, NUMTODSINTERVAL was used to convert 50 hours into the INTERVAL DAY TO SECOND format showing 2 days and 2 hours. This function can be helpful when using the RANGE operator.

NUMTOYMINTERVAL(n, interval_name)

NUMTOYMININTERVAL converts n to an INTERVAL YEAR TO MONTH. The interval can be specified as a string in the interval_name argument. This argument can be either YEAR or MONTH. The n argument must be a NUMBER or be able to be resolved to a NUMBER.

```
SELECT NUMTOYMINTERVAL(34,'MONTH') as RESULT FROM DUAL;

RESULT
---------------------------------------------------------------------------
+000000002-10
```

In this example, the function was used to convert 34 months to the `INTERVAL YEAR TO MONTH` format showing 2 years and 10 months.

ROUND (date, format)

`ROUND` rounds the `date` argument to the next date specified by the format string. If you do not pass a format to `ROUND`, Oracle will round the date to the next day. The `format` argument can be composed of any combination of the following format strings.

Oracle Date Formats from the Oracle SQL Reference	
CC	
SCC	One greater than the first two digits of a four-digit year
SYYYY	
YYYY	
YEAR	
SYEAR	
YYY	
YY	
Y	Year (rounds up on July 1)
IYYY	
IY	
IY	
I	ISO Year
Q	Quarter (rounds up on the sixteenth day of the second month of the quarter)
MONTH	
MON	
MM	
RM	Month (rounds up on the sixteenth day)
WW	Same day of the week as the first day of the year
IW	Same day of the week as the first day of the ISO year
W	Same day of the week as the first day of the month
DDD	
DD	
J	Day
DAY	

Oracle Date Formats from the Oracle SQL Reference	
DY	
D	Starting day of the week
HH	
HH12	
HH24	Hour
MI	Minute

```
SELECT ROUND(TO_DATE('23-OCT-04'),'MONTH') as RESULT FROM DUAL;

RESULT
--------------------
01-NOV-0004 00:00:00
```

SESSIONTIMEZONE

SESSIONTIMEZONE returns the time zone of the current session.

```
SELECT SESSIONTIMEZONE as RESULT FROM DUAL;

RESULT
---------------------------------------------------------------------------
-04:00
```

SYS_EXTRACT_UTC(datetime_with_timezone)

SYS_EXTRACT_UTC returns the Coordinated Universal Time from a datetime string including a time zone code or offset.

```
SELECT SYS_EXTRACT_UTC(TIMESTAMP '2004-10-23 10:25:00.00 EST') as RESULT FROM DUAL;

RESULT
---------------------------------------------
23-OCT-04 02.25.00.000000000 PM
```

SYSDATE

SYSDATE returns a DATE that represents the date and time set on the operating system of the machine Oracle is installed on. The format of SYSDATE is controlled by the NLS_DATE_FORMAT session parameter.

```
SELECT SYSDATE FROM DUAL;

SYSDATE
--------------------
13-SEP-2004 22:38:25
```

SYSTIMESTAMP

SYSTIMESTAMP returns a TIMESTAMP WITH TIME ZONE result from the underlying operating system date, timestamp, fractional seconds, and time zone.

```
SELECT SYSTIMESTAMP FROM DUAL;

SYSTIMESTAMP
-----------------------------------
13-SEP-04 10.40.32.818000 PM -04:00
```

TO_CHAR (datetime, format, ['NLS_DATE_LANGUAGE = language'])

TO_CHAR converts a datetime or interval argument to a VARCHAR2 string. The datetime argument can be a DATE, TIMESTAMP, TIMESTAMP WITH TIME ZONE, or TIMESTAMP WITH LOCAL TIME ZONE data type. The optional NLS_DATE_LANGUAGE parameter can be specified to change the language of the day and month abbreviations.

```
SELECT TO_CHAR(to_date('23-OCT-04'), 'DD-Mon-RR HH24:MI:SS') as RESULT FROM DUAL;

RESULT
------------------
23-Oct-04 00:00:00
```

TO_TIMESTAMP(string, [format], [NLS_TIMESTAMP_FORMAT=])

TO_TIMESTAMP converts a string into a TIMESTAMP value. The string can be a CHAR, VARCHAR2, NCHAR, or NVARCHAR2 data type. The format parameter is a string that can be any valid TIMESTAMP format. If you do not provide a format argument, then the string to convert must be in the default TIMESTAMP format. You can also change the TIMESTAMP default format by including the NLS_TIMESTAMP_FORMAT argument.

```
SELECT TO_TIMESTAMP('23-OCT-04 12:12:12', 'DD-Mon-RR HH24:MI:SS') as RESULT FROM
DUAL;

RESULT
---------------------------------------------------------------------------
23-OCT-04 12.12.12.000000000 PM
```

TO_TIMESTAMP_TZ(string, format, [NLS_TIMESTAMP_FORMAT])

TO_TIMESTAMP_TZ converts a string into a TIMESTAMP WITH TIMEZONE value. The string argument can be a CHAR, VARCHAR2, NCHAR, or NVARCHAR2 data type. The format parameter is a string that can be any valid TIMESTAMP WITH TIMEZONE format. If you do not provide a format argument, then the string to convert must be in the default TIMESTAMP WITH TIMEZONE format. You can also change the TIMESTAMP default format by including the NLS_TIMESTAMP_FORMAT argument.

```
SELECT TO_TIMESTAMP_TZ('23-OCT-04 12:12:12 -5:00', 'DD-Mon-RR HH24:MI:SS TZH:TZM')
as RESULT FROM DUAL;

RESULT
---------------------------------------------------------------------------
23-OCT-04 12.12.12.000000000 PM -05:00
```

TO_DSINTERVAL(arg1, [NLS_NUMERIC_CHARACTERS = "dg"])

TO_DSINTERVAL returns an INTERVAL DAY TO SECOND value from the string argument arg1. The arg1 argument can be a CHAR, VARCHAR2, NCHAR, or NVARCHAR2 data type. The optional parameter NLS_NUMERIC_CHARACTERS can be specified to change the decimal and grouping characters.

```
SELECT TO_DSINTERVAL('50 13:00:00') as RESULT FROM DUAL;

RESULT
--------------------------------------------------------------
+000000050 13:00:00.000000000
```

TO_YMINTERVAL(arg1)

TO_YMINTERVAL returns a INTERVAL YEAR TO MONTH type based on the string passed in argument arg1. The arg1 argument can be a CHAR, VARCHAR2, NCHAR, or NVARCHAR2.

```
SELECT SYSDATE + TO_YMINTERVAL('04-10') as Fouryrs10months FROM DUAL;

FOURYRS10MONTHS
--------------------
13-JUL-2009 23:08:16
```

TRUNC (date, [format])

TRUNC returns a DATE truncated to the format specified in the format argument. See the date format codes under ROUND for options. If you do not specify a format, Oracle defaults to the nearest day.

```
SELECT TRUNC(TO_DATE('23-OCT-04'), 'MONTH') as RESULT FROM DUAL;

RESULT
--------------------
01-OCT-0004 00:00:00
```

TZ_OFFSET(timezone_param)

TZ_OFFSET returns the time zone offset based on the timezone_param. The timezone_param argument can be either the keyword SESSIONTIMEZONE or DBTIMEZONE, a string formatted as + or - HH:SS, or a string time zone name.

```
SELECT TZ_OFFSET('PST') as RESULT FROM DUAL;

RESULT
-------
-07:00
```

Conversion Functions

Oracle provides a rich set of functions that allow you to translate data from one format to another.

ASCIISTR(string)

ASCIISTR takes a string argument and returns the ASCII equivalent. If any of the characters in the string are non ASCII, they are converted to the UTF-16 \xxxx format.

```
SELECT ASCIISTR('a non-ascii char ç') as RESULT FROM DUAL;

RESULT
----------------------
a non-ascii char \00E7
```

BIN_TO_NUM(bit_vector)

BIN_TO_NUM converts its bit_vector argument to its representative decimal number. The bit_vector argument must be a numeric value or be able to be converted to a NUMBER value. Each bit vector item is separated by a comma, and must be either a one or a zero.

```
SELECT BIN_TO_NUM(0,1,1,0) as RESULT FROM DUAL;

    RESULT
----------
         6
```

CAST(arg1 or MULTISET(expression) AS typename)

CAST allows you to convert one type to another.

CHARTOROWID(string)

CHARTOROWID converts a string representation of a ROWID to a ROWID value. The string argument can be a CHAR, VARCHAR2, NCHAR, or NVARCHAR2 data type to ROWID data type.

```
SELECT ID FROM some_table WHERE ROWID = CHARTOROWID('AAAMTmAAEAAAAFmAAA');

        ID
----------
        22
```

This example selects some information from a table based on its ROWID. The ROWID is passed in as a string and converted to a ROWID value.

COMPOSE(char)

COMPOSE allows you to compose a UNICODE string by passing in one or more code points. COMPOSE will add them all together and return the result. The char argument can be a CHAR, VARCHAR2, NCHAR, NVARCHAR2, CLOB, or NCLOB data type.

```
SELECT COMPOSE(UNISTR('Let''s go to the cafe\0301 to get some coffee.')) as RESULT
FROM DUAL;

RESULT
---------------------------------------
Let's go to the café to get some coffee.
```

This example uses the UNISTR function to create a UNICODE string and COMPOSE puts together the accent code point and the e code point in the word café to render it correctly.

CONVERT(string, destination_set, source_set)

CONVERT converts the string argument from one character set to another one. The string argument can be a CHAR, VARCHAR2, NCHAR, NVARCHAR2, CLOB, or NCLOB data type. The source_set argument specifies the character set of the stored data in the database if string is a column name, or the character set of string if it is an argument to the function. Destination_set is the character set you want to convert to.

```
SELECT CONVERT('go to UTF8 from ascii','UTF8','US7ASCII') as RESULT FROM DUAL;

RESULT
---------------------
go to UTF8 from ascii
```

DECOMPOSE(string, [CANONICAL or COMPATIBILITY])

DECOMPOSE performs the opposite operations of the COMPOSE function. DECOMPOSE can only operate on a Unicode string and will decompose each composed character it finds. You can specify CANONICAL or COMPATIBILITY mode for the function. CANONICAL mode creates a string that can be recomposed using the COMPOSE function, and COMPATIBILITY mode creates a string that cannot be recomposed. COMPATIBILITY mode is often used when you want to limit recomposition without extra style or formatting information. The string argument can be a CHAR, VARCHAR2, NCHAR, NVARCHAR2, CLOB, or NCLOB data type.

```
SELECT DECOMPOSE(UNISTR('Let''s go to the café to get some coffee')) as RESULT FROM
DUAL;

RESULT
----------------------------------------
Let's go to the café to get some coffee
```

HEXTORAW(char)

HEXTORAW converts a string representing a hexadecimal number to a RAW value. The char argument can be a CHAR, VARCHAR2, NCHAR, or NVARCHAR2 data type.

```
SELECT HEXTORAW('0E') FROM DUAL;
```

NUMTODSINTERVAL(arg1, interval)

See this function under *Date and Time Functions* earlier in the chapter.

NUMTOYMINTERVAL(arg1, interval)

See this function under *Date and Time Functions* earlier in the chapter.

RAWTOHEX(char)

RAWTOHEX converts a RAW value to the hexadecimal representation of a character. The char argument must be a RAW value.

```
SELECT RAWTOHEX(HEXTORAW('8A')) as RESULT FROM DUAL;
RE
--
8A
```

RAWTONHEX(char)

RAWTONHEX converts a RAW value to the hexadecimal representation of an NVARCHAR2 value. The char argument must be a RAW value.

ROWIDTOCHAR(rowid)

ROWIDTOCHAR converts a ROWID to a string.

```
SELECT ID FROM WEBCONTENT where ROWIDTOCHAR(rowid) = 'AAAMTmAAEAAAAFmAAA';

        ID
----------
        22
```

The preceding example selects the ID values from a table based on its ROWID.

ROWIDTONCHAR(rowid)

ROWIDTONCHAR converts a ROWID value to an NVARCHAR2 value.

SCN_TO_TIMESTAMP(scn)

SCN_TO_TIMESTAMP returns a TIMESTAMP value associated with the system change number given in the scn argument. It is useful to use this function with the ORA_ROWSCN pseudocolumn when you want to get the timestamp of the last time Oracle changed data.

TIMESTAMP_TO_SCN(timestamp)

TIMESTAMP_TO_SCN converts a TIMESTAMP value to a system change number.

```
SELECT TIMESTAMP_TO_SCN(SYSTIMESTAMP) as RESULT FROM DUAL;

    RESULT
----------
   1065364
```

TO_BINARY_DOUBLE(expression, format, params)

TO_BINARY_DOUBLE converts the expression argument to a BINARY DOUBLE value. The expression argument can be a STRING, NUMBER, BINARY_FLOAT, or BINARY_DOUBLE data type. The format argument lets you specify a numeric format for the conversion, and the params argument lets you pass additional information to the function for formatting. The format and params arguments are only valid if you pass a string in the expression argument.

Valid options for the params argument are as follows:

- NLS_NUMERIC_CHARACTERS = To specify the decimal and group characters
- NLS_CURRENCY = To specify the local currency symbol
- NLS_ISO_CURRENCY = To specify the international currency symbol

```
SELECT TO_BINARY_DOUBLE(100) FROM DUAL;

TO_BINARY_DOUBLE(100)
---------------------
             1.0E+002
```

TO_BINARY_FLOAT(expression, format, params)

TO_BINARY_FLOAT converts the expression argument to a BINARY FLOAT value. The expression argument can be a STRING, NUMBER, BINARY_DOUBLE, or BINARY_FLOAT data type. The format argument lets you specify a numeric format for the conversion, and the params argument lets you pass additional information to the function for formatting. The `format` and `params` arguments are only valid if you pass a string in the `expression` argument.

Valid options for the `params` argument are as follows:

- `NLS_NUMERIC_CHARACTERS` = To specify the decimal and group characters
- `NLS_CURRENCY` = To specify the local currency symbol
- `NLS_ISO_CURRENCY` = To specify the international currency symbol

```
SELECT TO_BINARY_FLOAT(100.32) FROM DUAL;

TO_BINARY_FLOAT(100.32)
-----------------------
             1.003E+002
```

TO_CHAR (string)

`TO_CHAR` converts the string argument to the national character set. The string argument can be a `STRING`, `CLOB`, or `NCLOB` data type.

```
SELECT TO_CHAR('change to NCHAR') as RESULT FROM DUAL;

RESULT
---------------
change to NCHAR
```

TO_CHAR (datetime or interval, format, params)

`TO_CHAR` converts the `datetime or interval` argument to the national character set. The `datetime` argument can be a string `DATE`, `TIMESTAMP`, `TIMESTAMP WITH TIME ZONE`, `TIMESTAMP WITH LOCAL TIME ZONE`, `INTERVAL MONTH TO YEAR`, or `INTERVAL DAY TO SECOND` data type. The `format` argument can be any valid date format string. You can pass '`NLS_DATE_LANGUAGE = language`' in the `params` argument to change the language for month and day names.

```
SELECT TO_CHAR(TO_DATE('23-OCT-04')) as RESULT FROM DUAL;

RESULT
------------------------------
23-OCT-04
```

TO_CHAR (number, format, params)

`TO_CHAR` converts the number argument to the national character set. The number argument can be a `NUMBER`, `BINARY_FLOAT`, or `BINARY_DOUBLE` data type. The `format` argument can be any valid format string.

Valid options for the `params` argument are as follows:

- `NLS_NUMERIC_CHARACTERS` = To specify the decimal and group characters
- `NLS_CURRENCY` = To specify the local currency symbol
- `NLS_ISO_CURRENCY` = To specify the international currency symbol

```
SELECT TO_CHAR(200) as RESULT FROM DUAL;

RES
---
200
```

TO_CLOB(string)

TO_CLOB converts character data to a CLOB. The string argument can be a CHAR, VARCHAR2, NCHAR, NVARCHAR2, CLOB, or NCLOB data type.

```
SELECT TO_CLOB('SOME DATA') as RESULT FROM DUAL;

RESULT
--------------------------------------------------------------------------------
SOME DATA
```

TO_DATE(string, format, ['NLS_DATE_LANGUAGE = language'])

TO_DATE converts a string to a DATE. The string argument can be a CHAR, VARCHAR2, NCHAR, or NVARCHAR2 data type. The format argument can be any valid date format. (See the ROUND function under *Date and Time Functions* for the values.) You can also specify the NLS_DATE_LANGUAGE parameter to change the language for month and day names.

```
SELECT TO_DATE('23-OCT-04') as RESULT FROM DUAL;

RESULT
---------
23-OCT-04
```

TO_DSINTERVAL(string, [NLS_NUMERIC_CHARACTERS = "dg"])

TO_DSINTERVAL converts a string to an INTERVAL DAY TO SECOND. See TO_DSINTERVAL under *Date and Time Functions* for details.

TO_LOB(column_name)

TO_LOB converts LONG RAW or LONG columns to LOBs. You can only use this function in a SELECT sub-clause in an INSERT INTO clause. If you are converting LONG columns, the receiving column should be a CLOB, and to convert LONG RAW columns, the receiving column should be a BLOB. The following example inserts a LONG from an old table to a new table with a NUMBER ID column and a CLOB column:

```
INSERT INTO NEW_TABLE(1, SELECT TO_LOB(LOB_COLUMN) FROM OLD_TABLE);
```

TO_MULTI_BYTE(string)

TO_MULTI_BYTE returns the string argument with all its single-byte characters converted to multibyte characters. The string argument can be a CHAR, VARCHAR2, NCHAR, or NVARCHAR2 data type.

TO_NCHAR (string, format, params)

TO_NCHAR converts the string argument to the national character set. The string argument can be a STRING, CLOB, or NCLOB data type. The format argument can be any valid format string. The params argument can be any valid NLS option.

```
SELECT TO_NCHAR('change to NCHAR') as RESULT FROM DUAL;

RESULT
---------------
change to NCHAR
```

TO_NCHAR (datetime or interval, format, params)

`TO_NCHAR` converts the `datetime` or `interval` argument to the national character set. The `datetime` argument can be a `STRING`, `DATE`, `TIMESTAMP`, `TIMESTAMP WITH TIME ZONE`, `TIMESTAMP WITH LOCAL TIME ZONE`, `INTERVAL MONTH TO YEAR`, or `INTERVAL DAY TO SECOND` data type. The `format` argument can be any valid date format string. The `params` argument can be any valid `NLS` option.

```
SELECT TO_NCHAR(TO_DATE('23-OCT-04')) as RESULT FROM DUAL;

RESULT
------------------------------
23-OCT-04
```

TO_NCHAR (number, format, params)

`TO_NCHAR` converts the `number` argument to the national character set. The `number` argument can be a `NUMBER`, `BINARY_FLOAT`, or `BINARY_DOUBLE` data type. The `format` argument can be any valid format string. The `params` argument can be any valid `NLS` option.

```
SELECT TO_NCHAR(200) as RESULT FROM DUAL;

RES
---
200
```

TO_NCLOB(string or lob_column)

`TO_NCLOB` converts a `string` or `LOB` stored in a database column to a `NCLOB`. If you pass a string value, the string can be a `CHAR`, `VARCHAR2`, `NCHAR`, `NVARCHAR2`, `CLOB`, or `NCLOB` data type.

```
SELECT TO_NCLOB('A string') as RESULT FROM DUAL;

RESULT
--------------------------------------------------------------------------------
A string
```

TO_NUMBER(arg1, format, params)

`TO_NUMBER` converts argument `arg1` to a `NUMBER` value. The `arg1` argument can be a `BINARY_FLOAT`, `BINARY_DOUBLE`, `CHAR`, `VARCHAR2`, `NCHAR`, or `NVARCHAR2` data type. The `format` parameter can be any valid date format. See the `ROUND` function under *Date and Time Functions* for valid formats.

Valid options for the `params` argument are as follows:

- `NLS_NUMERIC_CHARACTERS` = To specify the decimal and group characters
- `NLS_CURRENCY` = To specify the local currency symbol
- `NLS_ISO_CURRENCY` = To specify the international currency symbol

```
SELECT TO_NUMBER('15') as RESULT FROM DUAL;

    RESULT
----------
        15
```

TO_SINGLE_BYTE(string)

TO_SINGLE_BYTE returns the string argument with all the multibyte characters converted to single-byte ASCII characters. The string argument can be a CHAR, VARCHAR2, NCHAR, or NVARCHAR2 data type.

```
SELECT TO_SINGLE_BYTE(CHR(15711300)) as RESULT FROM DUAL;

R
-
D
```

TO_TIMESTAMP

TO_TIMESTAMP converts a string value to a TIMESTAMP value. See TO_TIMESTAMP under *Date and Time Functions* for details.

TO_TIMESTAMP_TZ

TO_TIMESTAMP_TZ converts a string value to a TIMESTAMP WITH TIMEZONE value. See TO_TIMESTAMP_TZ under *Date and Time Functions* for details.

TO_YMINTERVAL

TO_YMINTERVAL converts a string value to an INTERVAL YEAR TO MONTH type. See TO_YMINTERVAL under *Date and Time Functions* for details.

TRANSLATE(string USING [NCHAR_CS or CHAR_CS])

TRANSLATE converts a string into either the database character set using the CHAR_CS parameter, or the national character set using the NCHAR_CS parameter.

```
SELECT TRANSLATE('a test string to translate' USING NCHAR_CS) as RESULT FROM DUAL;

RESULT
--------------------------
a test string to translate
```

UNISTR(string)

UNISTR converts a string argument to the national character set. The string argument can also have embedded Unicode literals that the function will convert.

```
SELECT UNISTR('some unicode -> \00ee - \00ff') as RESULT FROM DUAL;

RESULT
---------------------
some unicode -> î - ÿ
```

Collection Functions

CARDINALITY(table_name)

CARDINALITY returns the number of records in a nested table. The function returns a NUMBER result.

```
SELECT ID, NAME, CARDINALITY(some_nested_table) FROM TABLE_NAME;
```

COLLECT(column_name)

COLLECT is used with the CAST function to create a nested table of the specified column name and cast it to the type specified in the CAST function.

```
SELECT CAST(COLLECT(some_column) AS some_type) FROM table_name;
```

SET(table_name)

SET converts the nested table passed as an argument to a SET by removing any duplicate records from the table.

```
SELECT ID, NAME, SET(some_nested_table) FROM TABLE_NAME;
```

Other Oracle Functions

This section lists additional lesser-used Oracle functions that you may run into from time to time.

BFILENAME(dir, file)

BFILENAME returns a BFILE record composed of a DIRECTORY path and FILENAME that represents a BLOB on the system file system. You must first create a DIRECTORY record and use that as the dir argument to the function. The dir argument is the name of the DIRECTORY record, and the file argument is the name of the BLOB on the file system.

```
   CREATE DIRECTORY myDIR AS 'c:\';

INSERT INTO music_table (id, mfile) VALUES (100, bfilename('myDIR',
'audiofile.wav'));
```

COALESCE(arg1, ...)

COALESCE takes a list of expressions as arguments and returns the first not null value. This function is useful in situations where you want to choose a value from a table with many related columns. Take for example, a table of employee salaries. You could have a field with a default salary amount, and a field with an overridden salary amount. If the database ensures that only one can be not NULL, and when one is selected, then the other is marked NULL, you could use COALESCE to automatically select the right value.

```
SELECT COALESCE(reg_salary, special_salary) as PAY FROM employee_data;
```

DECODE(arg1, search, result, search2, result2 ... , default)

DECODE compares the value or expression given in the arg1 argument with each search term. If arg1 matches a search term, its corresponding result is returned. If no match is found, then the default value is returned. The `arg1` and `search` arguments can be a value or expression. You can provide multiple search and result pairs.

```
SELECT DECODE ('a', 'a', 'Letter A',
                    'b', 'Letter B',
                    'c', 'Letter C',
                    'd', 'Letter D',
                    'No letter I know') as RESULT
FROM DUAL;

RESULT
--------
Letter A
```

DUMP(arg1, format, [start], [length])

`DUMP` returns the data type code, length in bytes, and internal representation of the `arg1` argument. The return value of the function is `VARCHAR2`. If you do not specify the `start` and `length` parameters, then `DUMP` will return the entire internal representation. The `format` parameter can have the following values:

- `8` — For octal values
- `10` — For decimal values
- `16` — For hex values
- `17` — For character values

You can also add 1,000 to the format value to add character set data to the format values.

```
SELECT DUMP('abcdef',1017) FROM DUAL;

DUMP('ABCDEF',1017)
---------------------------------------------------
Typ=96 Len=6 CharacterSet=WE8MSWIN1252: a,b,c,d,e,f
```

EMPTY_BLOB, EMPTY_CLOB()

`EMPTY_BLOB` and `EMPTY_CLOB` set a `BLOB` or `CLOB` column to an empty value.

```
UPDATE TABLE_NAME SET CLOB_COLUMN TO EMPTY_CLOB();
```

GREATEST(arg1, arg2, ...)

`GREATEST` returns the greatest value in the list of arguments. The arguments can be a value or expression. The arguments can be string values or numeric.

```
SELECT GREATEST('not so great', 'greater than the first', 'the greatest value since
sliced bread') as RESULT FROM DUAL;
RESULT
-------------------------------------
the greatest value since sliced bread
```

LEAST(arg1, arg2, ...)

LEAST returns the smallest value in the list of arguments. The arguments can be a value or expression. The arguments can be string or numeric values.

```
SELECT LEAST(0,1,2,3) FROM DUAL;

LEAST(0,1,2,3)
--------------
             0
```

LNNVL(conditon)

LNNVL is used in the WHERE clause of a statement and evaluates the condition passed in the condition argument, returning true if it is true and false if it is not. LNNVL can handle NULL conditions where a simple conditional test may not. For example, you may want to retrieve a list of students from a school enrollment table whose graduation year is less than 2010 and you want to include records where the graduation year has not been assigned yet and is NULL.

```
SELECT student_name, ID, grad_year FROM STUDENTS WHERE LNNVL(grad_year < 2010);
```

NLS_CHARSET_DECL_LEN(byte_length, charsetID)

NLS_CHARSET_DECL_LEN returns the declaration length in characters of an NCHAR column. The byte_length argument specifies the length in bytes of the column, and the charsetID argument specifies the ID of the character set used in the column. This function can be useful to determine how many characters you can store in an NCHAR field of a certain byte size.

```
SELECT NLS_CHARSET_DECL_LEN(100, NLS_CHARSET_ID('AL16UTF16')) as RESULT FROM DUAL;

    RESULT
----------
        50
```

NLS_CHARSET_ID(charset)

NLS_CHARSET_ID returns the ID associated with a specific character set.

```
SELECT NLS_CHARSET_ID('AL16UTF16') as RESULT FROM DUAL;

    RESULT
----------
      2000
```

NLS_CHARSET_NAME(ID)

NLS_CHARSET_NAME returns the name of a character set as a VARCHAR2 string given its ID number.

```
SELECT NLS_CHARSET_NAME(2000) as RESULT FROM DUAL;

RESULT
---------
AL16UTF16
```

NULLIF(exp1, exp2)

NULLIF compares its two arguments and returns NULL if they are equal; otherwise, it returns the result of the first argument.

```
SELECT NULLIF('a','b') as RESULT FROM DUAL;

R
-
a
```

NVL(exp1, exp2)

NVL returns exp2 if exp1 is NULL; otherwise, it returns exp1. This function can be useful to replace expressions that result in a NULL value with a default value. You would usually use this function with a table column as the first argument.

```
SELECT NVL(NULL, 'A NULL WAS PASSED') as RESULT FROM DUAL;

RESULT
-----------------
A NULL WAS PASSED
```

NVL2(exp1, exp2, exp3)

NVL2 is similar to NVL except you can specify the return values for a NULL condition and a NOT NULL condition. If exp1 is NULL, then the function returns exp3; if it is not NULL, then the function returns exp2.

```
SELECT NVL2('NOT NULL', 'RETURN #2', 'DO NOT RETURN #3') as RESULT FROM DUAL;

RESULT
---------
RETURN #2
```

ORA_HASH(exp, [max_bucket], [seed])

ORA_HASH returns a hash of the exp argument. The optional max_bucket argument defines a maximum bucket value for the hash , and the optional seed argument allows you to specify a seed value for the hash. The max_bucket and seed values can have a maximum value of 4294967295. This function is only available in Oracle 10*g*.

```
SELECT ORA_HASH(SYSDATE) as RESULT FROM DUAL;

    RESULT
----------
1915521363
```

PRESENTNNV(cell_ref, exp1, exp2)

PRESENTNNV is used on the right side of a MODEL rule within the model_clause of a SELECT statement. If cell_ref exists and is not null before the execution of the model_clause, the function returns exp1; otherwise, it returns exp2.

PRESENTV(cell_ref, exp1, exp2)

PRESENTV is used on the right side of a MODEL rule within the model_clause of a SELECT statement. If cell_ref exists before the execution of the model_clause, the function returns exp1; otherwise, it returns exp2.

SYS_CONNECT_BY_PATH(col, char)

SYS_CONNECT_BY_PATH is used in hierarchical queries to create a path-separated list of data. The col argument specifies the column to operate on in the query, and the char argument is the character string to use to separate the entries. SYS_CONNECT_BY_PATH is used in conjunction with the CONNECT BY clause in an SQL statement.

The following example uses the employees table in the HR sample schema that comes with Oracle:

```
SELECT SYS_CONNECT_BY_PATH(last_name, '->') as RESULT
FROM employees
START WITH last_name = 'Greenberg'
CONNECT BY PRIOR employee_id = manager_id;
```

```
RESULT
--------------------------------------------------------------------
->Greenberg
->Greenberg->Faviet
->Greenberg->Chen
->Greenberg->Sciarra
->Greenberg->Urman
->Greenberg->Popp
```

SYS_CONTEXT(namespace, param, [length])

SYS_CONTEXT returns the information stored in the context specified by the namespace argument. The param argument is the key value, and you can specify a length for the returned data if it is greater than 256 bytes. The maximum value for the length argument is 4,000 bytes. Oracle provides a default namespace named USERENV that stores information about the current user session.

Refer to Table 7-11 in the *Oracle SQL Guide* for the full list of parameters defined in the default USERENV namespace. Some common ones include the following:

- SESSION_USER — The username of the current session
- SESSIONID — The ID of the current session
- TERMINAL — The terminal ID of the computer in the current session
- LANGUAGE — The language and character set of the current session

```
SELECT SYS_CONTEXT('USERENV','LANGUAGE') as RESULT FROM DUAL;

RESULT
--------------------------------------------------------------------
AMERICAN_AMERICA.WE8MSWIN1252
```

SYS_EXTRACT_UTC(Datetime_With_TZ)

SYS_EXTRACT_UTC returns the UTC parsed from a DATETIME WITH TIMEZONE value.

```
SELECT SYS_EXTRACT_UTC(TIMESTAMP '2004-10-28 12:30:00.00 -05:00') as RESULT FROM
DUAL;

RESULT
---------------------------------------------------------------------------
28-OCT-04 05.30.00.000000000 PM
```

SYS_GUID()

SYS_GUID returns a 16-byte GUID (globally unique identifier). GUIDs are guaranteed to be unique across space and time, and are often used as IDs.

```
SELECT SYS_GUID() FROM DUAL;

SYS_GUID()
--------------------------------
EF8BC821E745F48505107BB7B44F24
```

SYS_TYPEID(object_type)

SYS_TYPEID returns the most specific type stored in the object_type column.

UID

UID returns the UID of the user logged into the current session.

```
SELECT UID FROM DUAL;

       UID
----------
        65
```

USER

USER returns the username of the currently logged on session.

```
SELECT USER FROM DUAL;

USER
------------------------------
ORACLEBOOK
```

USERENV('param')

USERENV returns information from the current user's session. The following parameters can be supplied to the function:

- CLIENT_INFO — Returns 64 bytes of session data that can be stored by another application
- ENTRYID — Returns the current audit entry ID
- ISDBA — Returns TRUE if the current user is a DBA

- LANG — returns the ISO abbreviation for the session's language name
- LANGUAGE — Returns the session's language, territory, and character set
- SESSIONID — Returns the session ID
- TERMINAL — Returns the terminal name of the current session

```
SELECT USERENV('LANGUAGE') FROM DUAL;

USERENV('LANGUAGE')
----------------------------------------------------
AMERICAN_AMERICA.WE8MSWIN1252
```

This function is only provided for backward compatibility. You should use the newer SYS_CONTEXT function.

VSIZE(arg1)

VSIZE returns the size of the arg1 argument in bytes. The arg1 argument can be a value or an expression that resolves to a value.

```
SELECT SYSDATE, VSIZE(SYSDATE) FROM DUAL;

SYSDATE   VSIZE(SYSDATE)
--------- --------------
25-SEP-04              7
```

XML Functions

Oracle now provides a rich set of built-in functions for manipulating XML stored in database tables. Using these functions, you can get most of your XML processing done in Oracle. These functions can be used in triggers to update XML documents stored in a table based on row data changes.

EXISTSNODE(XML_type, XPath, [namespace])

EXISTSNODE determines if the nodes specified in the XPath exist in the XML_type argument. The function returns a 0 if no nodes are found and a 1 if nodes are found. The XML_type argument is an XMLType data type, and the XPath argument is a VARCHAR2. You can also specify an optional namespace.

The following example uses the OE sample schema:

```
SELECT EXISTSNODE(warehouse_spec, '/Warehouse/Building') as RESULT FROM WAREHOUSES
WHERE warehouse_id = 1;

    RESULT
----------
         1
```

EXTRACT (XML, XPath, [namespace])

EXTRACT returns an XMLType containing an XML fragment that matches the results of applying the XPath statement passed in the XPath argument. The XPath statement is evaluated against the XMLType passed in the XML argument. The XML argument is an XMLType data type, and the XPath argument is a VARCHAR2. You can also specify an optional namespace.

The following example uses the OE sample schema:

```
SELECT EXTRACT(warehouse_spec, '/Warehouse/Building') as RESULT FROM WAREHOUSES
WHERE warehouse_id = 1;

RESULT
--------------------------------------------------------------------------------
<Building>Owned</Building>
```

EXTRACTVALUE(XMLType, XPath, [namespace])

EXTRACTVALUE is similar to the EXTRACT function, but it returns the value of the XML elements rather than an XML fragment. EXTRACTVALUE applies the XPath statement passed as a VARCHAR2 argument against the XMLType passed in the XML argument. If the XML document in the XMLType value is based on an XML Schema, then the function will return its results as the data type specified in the XML Schema. If there is no XML Schema or Oracle can't figure out what kind of data type the element is, then the function returns its results as VARCHAR2. The XPath you pass to this function must resolve to a single node containing a text node, element, or attribute. The XPath can also resolve to an element with a single text node as its child.

The following example uses the OE sample schema:

```
SELECT EXTRACTVALUE(warehouse_spec, '/Warehouse/Building') as RESULT FROM
WAREHOUSES WHERE warehouse_id = 1;

RESULT
--------------------------------------------------------------------------------
Owned
```

SYS_XMLAGG(exp, [format])

SYS_XMLAGG aggregates several XML documents or fragments specified in the exp argument to a single XML document. The function wraps the new XML document in <ROWSET></ROWSET>. If you want to format the XML document, you can pass an XMLFormat object in the format argument.

The following example uses the HR sample schema provided with Oracle. It also uses the SYS_XMLGEN function to generate XML elements for each record in the select.

```
Select SYS_XMLAGG(SYS_XMLGEN(job_title)) FROM jobs;

SYS_XMLAGG(SYS_XMLGEN(JOB_TITLE))
-----------------------------------------------------------------
<?xml version="1.0"?>
<ROWSET>
<JOB_TITLE>President</JOB_TITLE>
<JOB_TITLE>Administration Vice President</JOB_TITLE>
<JOB_TITLE>Administration Assistant</JOB_TITLE>
<JOB_TITLE>Finance Manager</JOB_TITLE>
<JOB_TITLE>Accountant</JOB_TITLE>
<JOB_TITLE>Accounting Manager</JOB_TITLE>
<JOB_TITLE>Public Accountant</JOB_TITLE>
<JOB_TITLE>Sales Manager</JOB_TITLE>
<JOB_TITLE>Sales Representative</JOB_TITLE>
<JOB_TITLE>Purchasing Manager</JOB_TITLE>
```

```
<JOB_TITLE>Purchasing Clerk</JOB_TITLE>
<JOB_TITLE>Stock Manager</JOB_TITLE>
<JOB_TITLE>Stock Clerk</JOB_TITLE>
<JOB_TITLE>Shipping Clerk</JOB_TITLE>
<JOB_TITLE>Programmer</JOB_TITLE>
<JOB_TITLE>Marketing Manager</JOB_TITLE>
<JOB_TITLE>Marketing Representative</JOB_TITLE>
<JOB_TITLE>Human Resources Representative</JOB_TITLE>
<JOB_TITLE>Public Relations Representative</JOB_TITLE>
</ROWSET>
```

SYS_XMLGEN(exp, [format])

SYS_XMLGEN converts the expression passed in the exp argument to an XML document. You can also specify an XMLFormat type in the format argument to format the XML. If exp is a scalar, then the function returns an element containing that value. If exp is a type, then the function maps the type fields to XML nodes, and if exp is an XMLType, then the function will surround the entire XML document with a <ROW></ROW> element.

The following example uses the OE sample schema provided with Oracle:

```
SELECT SYS_XMLGEN(CUST_ADDRESS) as RESULT FROM CUSTOMERS WHERE CUSTOMER_ID = 927;

RESULT
--------------------------------------------------------------------------------
<?xml version="1.0"?>
<CUST_ADDRESS>
 <STREET_ADDRESS>1614 Crackers Rd</STREET_ADDRESS>
 <POSTAL_CODE>361168</POSTAL_CODE>
 <CITY>Bangalore - India</CITY>
 <STATE_PROVINCE>Kar</STATE_PROVINCE>
 <COUNTRY_ID>IN</COUNTRY_ID>
</CUST_ADDRESS>
```

UPDATEXML(XMLType, XPath, new_val, [namespace])

UPDATEXML allows you to update values stored in an XML file stored in an Oracle table. The XMLType argument is the XMLType to update, the XPath argument is a valid XPath statement, and the new_val argument is the new value for the element. You can also optionally specify a namespace.

The following example uses the OE sample schema supplied with Oracle:

```
UPDATE warehouses SET warehouse_spec = UPDATEXML(warehouse_spec,
'/Warehouse/Building/text()','Leased') WHERE warehouse_id = 1
```

XMLAGG(XMLType, order_by_clause)

XMLAGG is the same as SYS_XMLAGG except it does not allow for formatting, and you can specify an order by clause to sort the results. XMLAGG does not enclose the returned collection with the <ROWSET></ROWSET> element.

XMLCOLATTVAL(exp AS alias_name, ...)

`XMLCOLATTVAL` returns an XML fragment made up of the values of the `exp` parameters passed to the function. You can pass one or more `exp` parameters. You can use the `alias_name` parameter to change the name of each node if you do not want to use the column name.

The following example uses the `HR` sample schema supplied with Oracle:

```
SELECT XMLCOLATTVAL(JOB_TITLE, MIN_SALARY, MAX_SALARY) as RESULT FROM JOBS WHERE
JOB_TITLE = 'President';

RESULT
------------------------------------------------------------------------------
<column name="JOB_TITLE">President</column>
<column name="MIN_SALARY">20000</column>
<column name="MAX_SALARY">40000</column>
```

XMLCONCAT(XMLType, ...)

`XMLCONCAT` concatenates a series of `XMLType` values passed in as arguments to the function. `XMLCONCAT` returns a single `XMLType` that is the result of the concatenation.

The following example uses the `HR` sample schema supplied with Oracle:

```
SELECT XMLCONCAT(XMLELEMENT("Title",JOB_TITLE), XMLELEMENT("low
salary",MIN_SALARY)) FROM JOBS;

XMLCONCAT(XMLELEMENT("TITLE",JOB_TITLE),XMLELEMENT("LOWSALARY",MIN_SALARY))
------------------------------------------------------------------------------
<Title>President</Title>
<low_x0020_salary>20000</low_x0020_salary>

<Title>Administration Vice President</Title>
<low_x0020_salary>15000</low_x0020_salary>

<Title>Administration Assistant</Title>
<low_x0020_salary>3000</low_x0020_salary>

<Title>Finance Manager</Title>
<low_x0020_salary>8200</low_x0020_salary>
```

XMLFOREST(exp AS alias_name, ...)

`XMLFOREST` concatenates all its arguments into an XML fragment. You can change the XML node name for each expression by passing an `alias_name` for each one.

```
SELECT XMLFOREST(job_title,min_salary) as RESULT FROM JOBS WHERE JOB_TITLE =
'President';

RESULT
------------------------------------------------------------------------------
<JOB_TITLE>President</JOB_TITLE>
<MIN_SALARY>20000</MIN_SALARY>
```

XMLSEQUENCE(Cursor, XMLFormat) XMLSEQUENCE(XMLType)

`XMLSEQUENCE` splits an XML document into a `VARRAY` of its top-level nodes. There are two versions: One that receives a cursor and an `XMLFormat` as parameters and another that takes an `XMLType` as an input. The cursor version converts each row in the cursor to an element of the `VARRAY`.

```
SELECT XMLSEQUENCE(EXTRACT(warehouse_spec, '/Warehouse/*')) FROM warehouses
WHERE warehouse_id = 1;
```

```
XMLSEQUENCE(EXTRACT(WAREHOUSE_SPEC,'/WAREHOUSE/*'))
--------------------------------------------------------------------------------
XMLSEQUENCETYPE(XMLTYPE(<Building>Owned</Building>
), XMLTYPE(<Area>25000</Area>
), XMLTYPE(<Docks>2</Docks>
), XMLTYPE(<DockType>Rear load</DockType>
), XMLTYPE(<WaterAccess>Y</WaterAccess>
), XMLTYPE(<RailAccess>N</RailAccess>
), XMLTYPE(<Parking>Street</Parking>
), XMLTYPE(<VClearance>10 ft</VClearance>
))
```

XMLTRANSFORM(XMLType, XSL_XMLType)

`XMLTRANSFORM` transforms an XML document using an XSL style sheet. The function takes two `XMLType` arguments: one that specifies the XML data for the function and one that contains the XSL style sheet to use on the XML document.

Summary

In this chapter, you were introduced to the vast repository of functions that Oracle 10*g* provides to help you get the most from your data. You have seen how to call functions in Oracle and been exposed to functions that format data, perform statistical operations on data, process XML, and convert data from one form to another. Armed with this new knowledge, you should be fully prepared to strike out on your own and make Oracle serve up your data exactly as you want it.

You have also learned how to create your own functions when Oracle doesn't provide one that does exactly what you want. User functions in Oracle can be created in PL/SQL or Java. Remember when working with data in Oracle, you should always first check and see if Oracle provides a function you need before you write your own. Oracle has spent tons of money developing these functions and can probably ensure the highest possible performance. Also, as Oracle is upgraded, the functions are as well, which can make any porting you need to in future releases much easier.

14

Distributed Queries, Transactions, and Databases

In organizations where ownership of data is distributed, data can reside in several different databases and on different systems or nodes. These distributed databases might be built on database products from a single vendor or from multiple vendors. Where data must be obtained from multiple database sources to make business decisions, distributed queries are used. When updates of data in multiple databases are needed, distributed transactions can be implemented.

In this chapter, we cover some of the key technologies used to link together distributed data and databases. For example, distributed Oracle databases can be tied together by establishing a database link from one database to another. As a programmer, you can make access to these distributed sources of data appear to be location-transparent by incorporating views, procedures, and synonyms. Where distributed updates occur across multiple Oracle databases as transactions, there are additional considerations that we cover. We also cover the linkage to distributed databases that are non-Oracle through the use of Heterogeneous Services, Open Database Connectivity (ODBC), or gateways.

Management of distributed databases can be handled in an autonomous manner such that each database is managed through its own management interface. In fact, as of Oracle Database 10*g*, each Oracle database installation includes an installation of Enterprise Manager Database Control on that server. To simplify management of multiple Oracle instances, distributed Oracle databases can be managed through a single interface called Enterprise Manager Grid Control. Since this is a programmers' book, we touch on Enterprise Manager in various portions of this chapter, as it relates to enabling distributed databases, but we suggest you consult administrators' documentation and other sources for more details regarding managing distributed Oracle databases.

An alternative to deploying distributed databases used by many organizations is to instead consolidate the data to a single database. Companies often build operational data stores and enterprise data warehouses as consolidation databases to guarantee data consistency and to create a repository representing a single version of the truth. Other advantages to this approach include tuning simplification, since optimizer performance can be more predictable for a single consolidated database. Of course, the transaction management is also entirely handled by the single database engine. We cover methods for data movement used in loading such repositories elsewhere (Chapters 24 and 25) in this book. In those chapters, we describe high-speed data movement using the Data Pump, Transportable Tablespaces, and Streams, and more traditional data loading and management techniques that are useful in moving data to a single database, including the use of SQL*Loader, External Tables, and Change Data Capture.

We'll begin by exploring how to link distributed Oracle databases and some programming considerations in using these links.

Linking Distributed Oracle Databases

Distributed Oracle databases are linked for queries by establishing and leveraging database links. A database link is most often created by a database administrator responsible for managing access to the distributed sources of data.

Creation of the database link uses the name of the database to be linked to and the name of the server or domain it resides on. This combination of database name and server name is represented in the global database name. The global name better ensures uniqueness, since in many organizations it is very possible to have common database names on more than one node (e.g., a database named sales could be deployed in two different departments for two different purposes). The naming parameters can be initialized through Oracle Enterprise Manager's Database Control and are found in the Initialization Parameters under the Administration Tab. Figure 14-1 shows the SPFile interface where a database domain name is being added. Domain names must follow standard Internet naming conventions. In the example, a `db_domain` name is provided for a database at the Stack company.

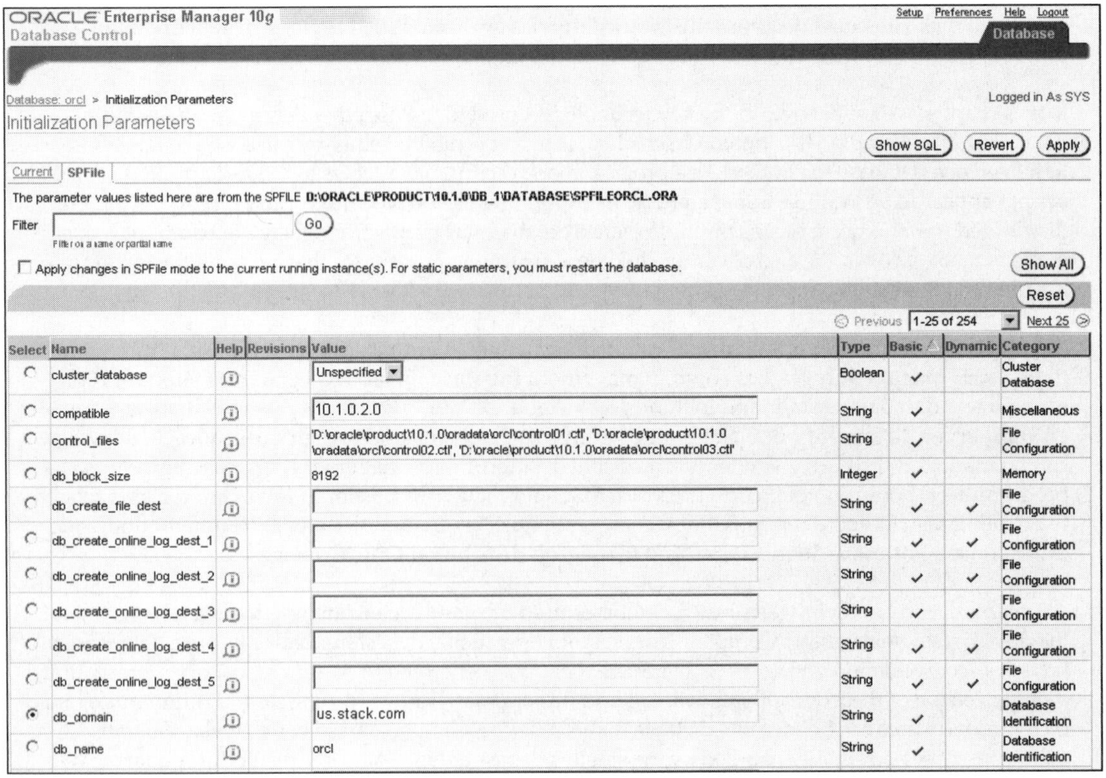

Figure 14-1: Setting up a database domain name.

Once a domain name enabling global names has been established, the next step is to create the database link from one database to another. Links are typically created as private or public links depending on the privileges assigned to create such links and the access that is to be granted to the users. By default, link users and their passwords will be the same as at the originating database. Users are restricted where private links are available, whereas any user can access a public link.

Links can also be created with specified usernames and passwords. This is called an *authenticated link* and can be used for private or public connections.

A private link would be created vian SQL using the global database name for the database named orcl on the `us.stack.com` domain as follows:

```
CREATE DATABASE LINK orcl.us.stack.com;
```

A public link could be created vian SQL using a similar syntax, but specifying public:

```
CREATE PUBLIC DATABASE LINK orcl.us.stack.com;
```

A database link can also be created using Oracle Enterprise Manager. Figure 14-2 shows the interface through which a DBA could create a link (found under the Administration tab in Enterprise Manager Database Control) by providing a database link name, Oracle*Net service name, connection type, username, and password information.

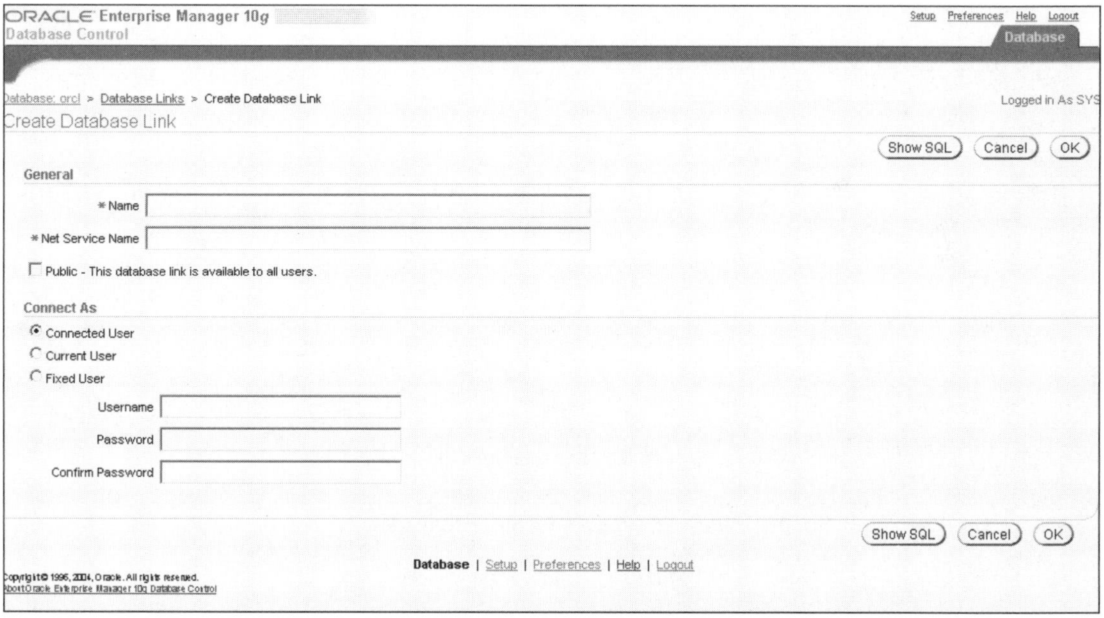

Figure 14-2: Database link creation screen in Oracle Enterprise Manager.

Once the link is created, you can connect through the link by specifying the global database name. For example, a query might be formulated as follows:

```
SELECT * FROM sh.products@orcl.us.stack.com;
```

Views, synonyms, and procedures are useful in distributed database programs, since they can create the appearance of location transparency hiding the global naming that is used. In the following example, a view named `supply` would be formed and provide location transparency by specifying the global database name in a `SELECT` from a remote products table while also performing a `SELECT` from a local inventory table:

```
CREATE VIEW supply AS
SELECT i.product_id, i.warehouse_id, i.quantity_on_hand, p.prod_name, p.prod_status
FROM oe.inventories i, sh.products@orcl.us.stack.com p
WHERE i.product_id = p.prod_id;
```

Synonyms are references to objects that can be created for tables, types, views, materialized views, sequences, procedures, functions, and packages. A synonym might be created for the previous products table in the `orcl.us.stack.com` database using the following syntax:

```
CREATE SYNONYM products FOR sh.products@orcl.us.stack.com;
```

Alternatively, a DBA could also create a synonym using Enterprise Manager Database Control (under the Administration tab) as shown in Figure 14-3:

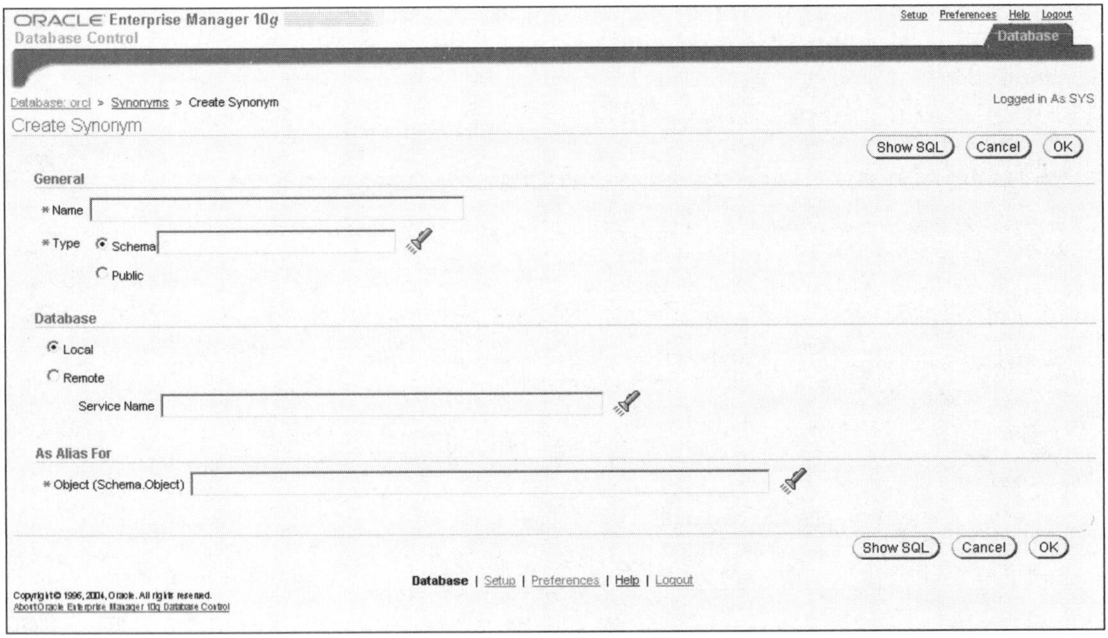

Figure 14-3: Synonym creation screen in Oracle Enterprise Manager.

Procedures can provide transparency by referencing linked data and embedding the global name in the reference or by leveraging synonyms. As a programmer, you will likely work with your DBAs to understand the alternatives available to you for building access to distributed data into your applications.

Distributed applications using database links do require some considerations. Since you may be retrieving large quantities of data across your network, you should also design your applications such that only necessary data should be transferred. For best optimization, you should use the cost-based optimizer regardless of Oracle database version. (Note that for Oracle Database 10*g* and subsequent versions, the cost-based optimizer is the only optimizer supported by Oracle.)

The cost-based optimizer will rewrite a distributed query using collocated inline views where possible. A collocated inline view enables selection of data from multiple tables in a single local database, thus reducing remote database access. The optimization includes merging all mergeable views, creating the collocated inline view, performing a collocated query block test, and rewriting the query using the collocated inline views. Of course, the optimization is completely transparent to the person or the application that submits the query. Such optimization is generally not as effective in situations where there are aggregates, subqueries, or complex SQL present.

In addition to leveraging the optimizer, a method sometimes employed to improve performance and help optimization is by building views. For example, you might build a view over multiple remote tables. Building procedural code is always a possibility, though not often needed for distributed queries.

In situations where updates occur across distributed databases composed of multiple separate databases, failure of part of a distributed statement could trigger an integrity constraint violation. We'll next discuss two-phase commit, since your applications will leverage this capability but should also handle unusual occurrences when transactions are updated.

Distributed Transactions and Two-Phase Commit

Distributed transactions occur when one or more statements update data in two or more databases. Distributed operations may include data manipulation language (DML) or data definition language (DDL) transactions or transaction control statements. DML and DDL operations supported as distributed transactions by Oracle include `CREATE TABLE AS SELECT`, `DELETE`, `INSERT`, `LOCK TABLE`, `SELECT`, and `SELECT FOR UPDATE`. Transaction control statements supported include `COMMIT`, `ROLLBACK`, and `SAVEPOINT`.

Data integrity when change occurs across distributed databases is ensured by Oracle through a two-phase commit. The first phase of a two-phase commit where transactions are distributed is called the prepare phase. In the prepare phase, an initiating system or node (called a global coordinator) notifies and prepares all sites involved in the transaction to be ready to commit or roll back. Nodes that are forced to reference data on other nodes to complete part of the transaction are sometimes called local coordinators. Preparation includes recording information in online redo logs for future commit or rollback, and placing a distributed lock on modified tables to prevent reads of uncommitted data.

In the second phase of the two-phase commit, the transactions are either committed or rolled back. An automatic rollback occurs if a transaction commit is not possible on any of the nodes. A commit point site initiates the commit phase when instructed by the global coordinator. The commit point site is designated as the most reliable site by having the highest value in a `COMMIT_POINT_STRENGTH` initialization parameter (usually set by the DBA). When a transaction is committed, each node releases its locks, records the commit in its local redo log, and notifies the global coordinator.

Under normal situations, Oracle's handling of distributed transactions appears seamless. If there is the unusual situation of failure of a server, network, or software at any point in this process, Oracle has a RECO (recoverer) process designed to resolve the transaction. However, a better solution is to design your distributed application to account for such unusual situations and automate the process transparently.

Let's look at what happens your application does not account for failures and an in-doubt transaction is created that needs manual resolution.

When such failure occurs and the application is unaware, the data is blocked for reads and writes. The transactions in this state are called in-doubt transactions. A DBA can intervene to solve this situation, since such in-doubt transactions can be seen in the `DBA_2PC_PENDING` view. The DBA can view the `LOCAL_TRAN_ID` (local transaction identifier), `GLOBAL_TRAN_ID` (global transaction identifier), `STATE` (collecting, prepared, committed, forced commit, or forced termination/rollback), `MIXED` (e.g., whether committed on one node and rolled back on another), `TRAN_COMMENT` (transaction naming), `HOST` (host machine name), and `COMMIT#` (global commit number).

The session is traced by the DBA using the `DBA_2PC_NEIGHBORS` view. Here, a DBA can see the `LOCAL_TRAN_ID`, `IN_OUT` (incoming or outgoing transactions), `DATABASE` (client requestor or database link), `DBUSER_OWNER` (local user or database link owner), and `INTERFACE` (status). The DBA can then take actions upon the states of the transactions.

Heterogeneous Services

The Oracle database provides Heterogeneous Services used in accessing non-Oracle database systems. Programmers can develop SQL statements or procedures to access non-Oracle environments and then deploy them by leveraging the connectivity supported by Heterogeneous Services. Heterogeneous Services provide generic connectivity through Open Database Connectivity (ODBC) or OLE DB (used for relational and nonrelational sources). The services can also enable Oracle's Transparent Gateways to access specific non-Oracle database sources at a higher level of performance than generic connectivity can provide.

A dedicated Heterogeneous Services agent is set up for each connection using either generic connectivity or the Transparent Gateways. Agents for generic connectivity (ODBC or OLEDB) use drivers that are installed in the Oracle Database. Transparent Gateway agents differ in that they can be installed on any system that is supported. The agents provide SQL mappings and data type conversions. Figure 14-4 shows a typical topology.

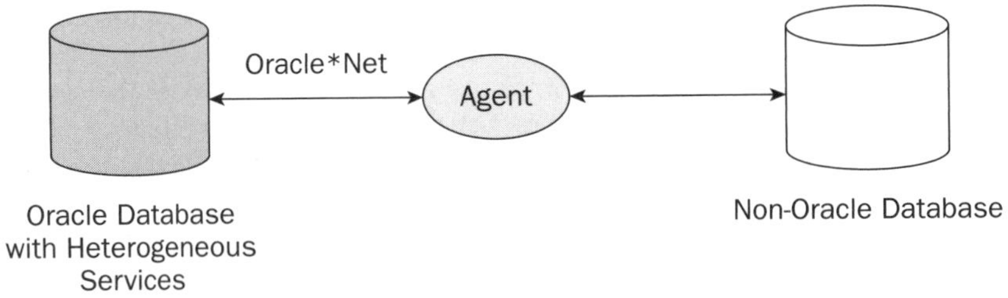

Figure 14-4: Communications between an Oracle database with Heterogeneous Services and a non-Oracle database.

Where Transparent Gateways are used and a large number of connections exist, the DBA can choose to set up multithreaded agents. Multithreaded agents can be configured to provide single monitoring threads and multiple dispatcher threads and task threads to minimize system resource utilization. Performance can also be improved by using Transparent Gateway, since they provide access to non-Oracle systems using the target database's native interface instead of a generic interface.

To better understand configuring Heterogeneous Services for connectivity, take a look at ODBC as an example.

ODBC

ODBC support is provided in various database products to enable the use of generic SQL to access them. The ODBC interface for Oracle provides an ODBC application programming interface (API) and includes support for all core ODBC defined functionality, as well as support for the SQL-99 specification syntax.

A variety of Oracle and non-Oracle drivers are supported through Oracle's ODBC. For example, for Oracle database releases since Oracle9*i* Release 2, support has been provided for .NET through Microsoft's ODBC .NET provider. Oracle provides other extended Microsoft support through ODBC, including the ability to use the Microsoft Transaction Server and support of SQL Server EXEC syntax. Extended Oracle support that is provided includes support of Transparent Application Failover with Oracle Failsafe and support for Oracle Real Application Clusters (RAC).

Heterogeneous Services generic connectivity uses initialization files that are located in the Oracle home directory under the `hs` and then `admin` subdirectories. For example, in a typical Windows installation of the Oracle Database 10*g*, you will find two files, inithsodbc.ora and inithsoledb.ora, under the `oracle\product\10.1.0\Db_1\hs\admin` subdirectory. The `inithsodbc.ora` and `inithsoledb.ora` files are initially installed as sample agent init files that contain the HS parameters that are needed for an ODBC and OLEDB agent, respectively. Over 20 parameters might be defined and are described in the *Oracle Database Heterogeneous Connectivity Administrator's Guide*. Sample `listener.ora` and `tnsnames.ora` files are also found in this subdirectory.

Configuring ODBC to access non-Oracle data sources is a multistep process typically performed by a DBA. Heterogeneous Services ODBC is set up by first adding a `SID_DESC` to `the listener.ora` file for the hsodbc program. In tnsnames.ora, the new SID description is added with `HS=OK` as a parameter in `connect_data`. At this point, the init file for the SID (typically modified from the sample `inithsodbc.ora` file) is also set up.

Next, the client side is configured. For example, if deployed on a Windows platform, the Configuration and Migration Tools installed as Oracle programs are selected and then the Microsoft ODBC Administrator is selected. Selecting the System DSN tab in the ODBC Administrator, a Microsoft Access Driver is added (see Figure 14-5), and then configured as a machine data source to match the ODBC description previously created. A database link is next created and then tested by accessing the remote database.

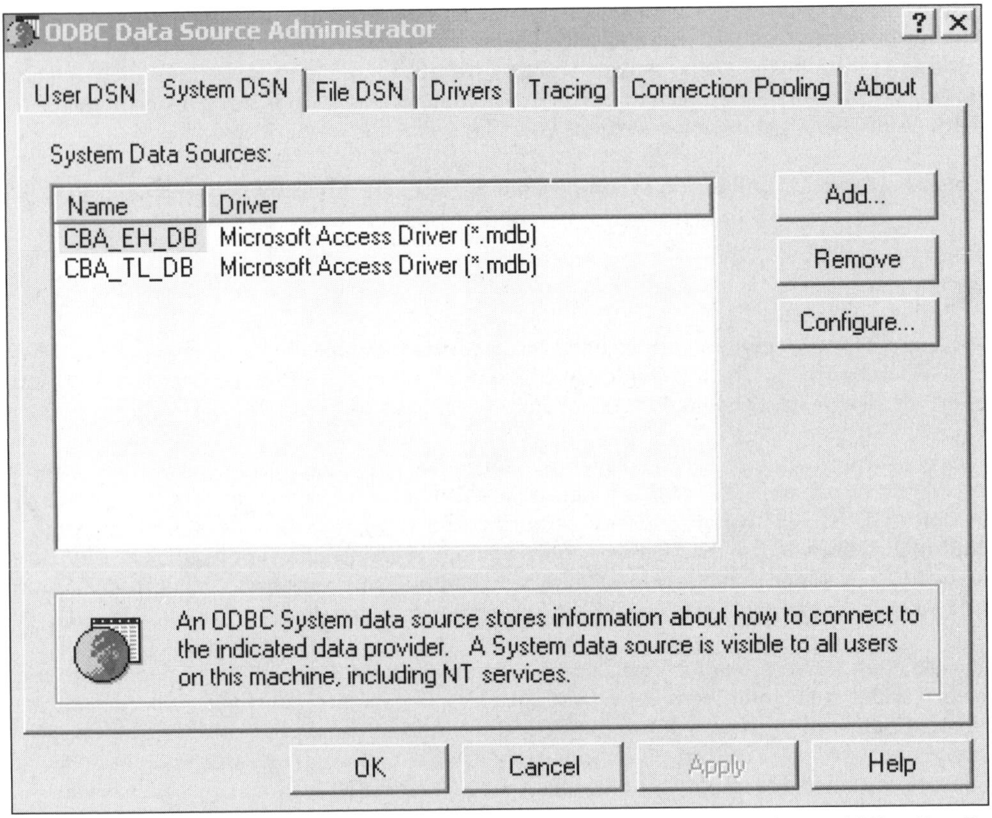

Figure 14-5: Microsoft ODBC Administrator interface in Oracle's Configuration and Migration Tools on WIndows.

Where ODBC is used to connect to an Oracle data source from another computer, the Oracle ODBC driver requires the Oracle OCI client be installed on that computer. A corresponding listener must be set up on the Oracle server. The application created will need to transmit a Transparent Network Substrate (TNS) Service name and Oracle username and password.

In developing applications that use ODBC, several common sense rules apply in order to maximize performance. Whenever possible, the use of bind variables is advised to make statements reusable and better able to leverage the Oracle cache. Do not include columns in a `SELECT` that will not be used. If frequent connects and disconnects occur in your application, the use of connection pooling is advised.

Transparent Gateways

Transparent Gateways enable non-Oracle databases to be accessed as if they were Oracle databases by supporting usage of the same Oracle SQL syntax. As noted previously, Gateways can provide a higher level of performance through the use of multithreaded agents. Transparent Gateways are also useful where stored procedures or distributed transactions are required, since generic connectivity does not support them.

Oracle offers a variety of gateways available on a variety of operating systems. You'll need to investigate availability and capabilities of each target gateway carefully for the specific hardware platforms you are interested in deploying upon as only certain gateways are available for certain platforms.

Gateways available are classified as follows:

- **Open Systems Gateways.** These are for Microsoft SQL Server, Sybase, Rdb, Ingres, Informix, Teradata, and RMS.
- **Enterprise Integration Gateways.** Access Manager for the AS/400, Procedural Gateways for MQSeries and APPC, and Transparent Gateways for DB2/400 and IBM DRDA.
- **Mainframe Integration Gateways.** These are for DB2.
- **EDA/SQL Gateways.** These are for other mainframe data sources such as VSAM, IMS, ISAM, and others.

Each gateway has a specific administration guide for the platforms on which it is available with a description of supported syntax and functions.

At connect time, a Transparent Gateway for a specific non-Oracle target will tell Oracle what functions are supported. If your application uses an Oracle specific function in that is not supported by the target in an `INSERT`, `UPDATE`, or `DELETE`, you will receive an ORA-02070 error that states `database db_link_name does not support function in this context`. For other nonsupported functions (e.g., during a `SELECT` statement), data will be transferred to the local Oracle instance for processing. Therefore, when designing and tuning your application, you should to pay attention to the functions that are supported at the target through the gateway to avoid potential errors and to optimize performance.

Summary

Where possible, many organizations will consolidate data into single databases to better optimize performance and simplify programming. But where such consolidation is not possible, Oracle provides a number of ways to build distributed databases in all-Oracle and heterogeneous database configurations.

Distributed databases are generally defined by DBAs through links. Querying distributed databases is relatively simple in an all-Oracle configuration and simply requires knowledge of any limitations in the services or gateways used in heterogeneous configurations. For distributed transactions, Oracle's support of two-phase commit also simplifies the implementation, though programmers may want to account for unusual infrastructure failures within their applications.

Distributed databases do introduce some added performance tuning considerations. The goal for applications developers and programmers should always be to reduce the amount of traffic between databases wherever possible.

This chapter concludes the Data Topics portion of this book. Now that we have provided a broad background on this topic, you are ready to move into the portion of the book that focuses on PL/SQL and Java programming techniques.

15

PL/SQL Basics

Programmers have long struggled with the power and limitations of SQL. Although SQL is very appropriate for manipulating data, there is more to an application than simply using data. Oracle introduced PL/SQL as a procedural language you can use to implement logic that goes beyond the reach of SQL.

PL/SQL executes in the Oracle database engine and is tightly tied to the database. Oracle PL/SQL has been in use for years, and entire enterprise strength applications (such as much of Oracle's own application suite) have been written in it.

PL/SQL is one of two languages used to implement logic in the database. Since Oracle 8*i*, Java has also been available for implementing logic in the database, including database triggers.

This chapter introduces the basic features of the PL/SQL language.

This chapter is broken down into three main sections:

1. PL/SQL architecture
2. The language of PL/SQL
3. Controlling program flow

Over the next several chapters, you will learn how to use PL/SQL to implement application and database logic. As a programmer, many of the capabilities of PL/SQL will be familiar to you and you will be able to reuse techniques and tricks that you have learned from your language of choice.

Code Architecture

Any programming language presents itself in two guises — the syntax that is used to create the application logic with the code and the actual execution of that code as a running application. This section introduces the basic block structure of the PL/SQL language. A section at the end of this chapter reviews how PL/SQL program units are executed at run time.

PL/SQL uses a block structure for organizing PL/SQL code. The block structure is shown in Figure 15-1.

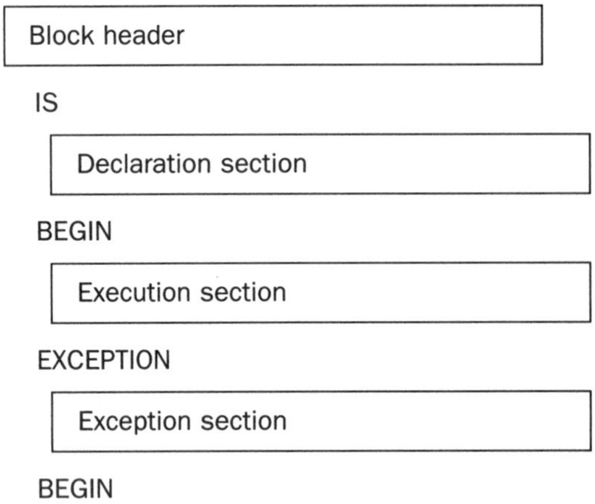

Figure 15-1: PL/SQL block structure.

There are four distinct areas within a PL/SQL block: the block header, the declaration section, the execution section, and the exception section. Each of these is described in the sections that follow.

The Block Header

The header section of a PL/SQL program unit contains the type of unit, the name of the unit, and any parameters that are used to call the unit. The syntax for this section of the PL/SQL block is as follows:

```
PROGRAM_TYPE name ([parameter IN/OUT/IN OUT parm_type specs,] . . .)
   [RETURN datatype]
```

`PROGRAM_TYPE` can be either `FUNCTION`, `PROCEDURE`, or `PACKAGE`. A PL/SQL function returns a value, which is specified with the `RETURN` data type clause. The *`datatype`* variable describes the data type of the returned value. Any PL/SQL function can be used in any standard SQL statement, which gives you a lot of power and flexibility in your development efforts.

A PL/SQL function can use the `RETURN` keyword at any point in the execution section, followed by a value. Once the runtime PL/SQL engine encounters a `RETURN`, it immediately ends the execution of the function and returns the value.

A PL/SQL procedure does not use the RETURN keyword to return a value directly, but a PL/SQL procedure can exchange information with the calling program through parameters. A PL/SQL package is a collection of program units, which are covered in detail in Chapter 16, "PL/SQL and SQL."

All of these program units can have parameters. A parameter is used to pass information to the PL/SQL unit and get information back from the unit. Each parameter has an assigned data type (*`parm_type`*) and is designated as an `IN` parameter, which is passed to the program unit, an `OUT` parameter, which is sent back to the calling program, or an `IN OUT` parameter, which travels both ways. The *`specs`* portion of the parameter can include the keyword `NOT NULL`, which forces this program unit to be called with a value for the parameter, or `DEFAULT`, followed by a value, which assigns a default value for the parameter if a value is not passed by the calling program.

The block header is actually an optional portion of a PL/SQL program unit. If you create a PL/SQL program unit that does not have a block header, it is called an *anonymous block*. The limitation of an anonymous block is that you cannot call it from another section of code. You may choose to use this type of block as a nested block — one that only operates in the context of a block that contains the nested block. Typically, though, this expedient solution is roughly equivalent to writing code without documentation, a practice that tends to haunt either you or the poor soul who is assigned to maintain the undocumented code that you wrote. However, there may be times when you want to use a nested anonymous block for more control over error handling, as described in an upcoming section.

Parameter Notation

When calling a PL/SQL program unit with parameters, you can include the values for the parameters in one of two ways:

- Positional notation, where each parameter value is listed in the order the parameters are included in the header. If you do not want to pass a value for one or more of the parameters, you simply include a comma to hold its position.
- Named notation, where you list the name of the parameter, followed by => and the value, as in the following:

```
anyParam => 'value of parm',
```

When using named notation, you must include a value for all NOT NULL parameters that do not specify a default value. It is good practice to include any parameters that require a value — which are NOT NULL and do not have a default value — at the beginning of a list of parameters, to avoid forcing people to use named notation or to specify all values until the required parameter.

Overloading

You may be able to increase the simplicity of your code and your efficiency by using a technique called *overloading* with PL/SQL program units. Overloading takes advantage of the fact that a PL/SQL program unit is identified by a unique combination of its name and the variables that it accepts.

You can have the same procedure or function called with different sets of parameters, as long as the signature of those parameters is unique. The parameter signature is made up of the parameter position and data type.

As an example, suppose that you wanted a PL/SQL function to return a number with the geographic territory a customers resides in. You could overload a function to accept either a state abbreviation, a city name and state abbreviation, or a zip code. Depending on the parameters passed, the appropriate version of the function would be called and executed.

The code for the header section of each of these three procedures would look like the three examples following:

```
FUNCTION returnTerritory (state_abbreviation IN VARCHAR2) RETURN NUMBER

FUNCTION returnTerritory (city_name IN VARCHAR2, state_abbreviation IN VARCHAR2)
RETURN NUMBER

FUNCTION returnTerritory (zp_code IN NUMBER) RETURN NUMBER
```

The Declaration Section

The *name* of the variable is a unique identifier (within the scope of the block), and the *datatype* is a standard Oracle data type. A *constraint* is a limit on the variable, such as the length of the VARCHAR2 data type or the number of places overall and to the right of the decimal point for a NUMBER data type. You could use NOT NULL as a constraint, which would require the variable or constant to hold a value at all times. You must assign a value to a NOT NULL variable or constant when it is created. If at any time you attempt to make the value of a NOT NULL variable or constant NULL, PL/SQL will return an error.

The CONSTANT keyword is used to identify a variable whose value will not change during the execution of the PL/SQL program unit.

The final portion of the variable declaration allows you to assign a value to the variable when you declare it. Instead of using the assignment operator, :=, you could declare a default value for the variable or constant with the DEFAULT keyword, followed by a value, as in the following:

```
myvariable INTEGER DEFAULT 1;
```

Each variable or constant in the declaration section must be declared on its own line. Although variables are usually declared in the declaration section of a PL/SQL program unit, you can declare variables or constants at any point in a PL/SQL program unit with the following syntax:

```
DECLARE
   name [CONSTANT] datatype [(constraint)] [:= value];
```

The declaration portion of a PL/SQL program unit comes after the header section. You can also declare one or more variables or constants anywhere within a program unit with the following syntax:

```
DECLARE
    name [CONSTANT] datatype [(constraint)] [:= value];
    .
    .
    .
```

The Execution Section

The execution section of a PL/SQL block is where all the action takes place. This section begins with the keyword BEGIN and ends with the keyword END, followed by a semi-colon (;). This section of a PL/SQL program unit is the only mandatory section of the unit. The substance of the PL/SQL program unit is the implementation of application logic, so you will be working with this part of the PL/SQL unit later in this chapter.

The execution section must have at least one executable statement, although that statement could be the NULL keyword, which is described later in this chapter.

The Exception Section

The exception section of a PL/SQL block is the final section of the block. The exception section is optional, but if it is present, this section comes before the END keyword that ends the block.

This section is used to handle any errors that occur during the execution of the logic in the block. The syntax for this section is as follows:

```
EXCEPTION
    WHEN exception_name
    THEN
        error handling statements; . . .
      [WHEN OTHERS
        default exception handling;]
```

There are many exception names that are a part of the PL/SQL runtime environment, such as NO_DATA_FOUND.

The Oracle PL/SQL User's Guide contains a list of all defined PL/SQL exceptions.

This section can have as many WHEN statements as you like to handle specific exceptions; all other exceptions are handled by the WHEN OTHERS section, if present.

You can declare your own exceptions in the declaration section by with the following syntax:

```
exception_name EXCEPTION;
```

where *exception_name* is a unique identifier, as with any other declared variable. The code to initiate a custom-defined exception is as follows:

```
RAISE exception_name;
```

How Exceptions Are Handled

When the PL/SQL engine encounters an error, the execution of the code in the current execution section is immediately stopped and control of the block is passed to the exception section of the block. Once the execution of the appropriate logic in this section is completed, control is returned to the calling program.

You can use nested blocks to catch and handle exception conditions while still continuing to execute logic. Consider the following meta code:

```
BEGIN
    statement1;
    statement2;
    BEGIN
        statement3;
        EXCEPTION
          WHEN OTHERS
            exception1;
    END;
    statement4;
    EXCEPTION
        WHEN OTHERS
          exception2;
END
```

If an exception occurred on *statement1*, *statement2*, or *statement4*, control of the execution of the block would be passed to the final exception section, which would perform the *exception2* logic and then exit the block. If an exception occurred on *statement3*, control of the execution of the block would pass to the exception section contained within the anonymous block. Once this processing was complete, control would be returned to the outer program and continued with *statement4*.

Error-Related Functions

The `WHEN OTHERS` syntax may have raised some concern in those of you who are conscientious coders. Simply dropping out of an exception handler knowing "Why not" rather than "Why" is not good programming practice. On the other hand, there are so many possible errors, it is hard to account for all of them.

You can use two functions that will provide some information on SQL errors that raise exceptions in your PL/SQL code. The `SQLCODE` function returns the error code for an error, while the `SQLERRM` returns the error message for the error.

Scoping and Notation

You can have one PL/SQL block inside of another PL/SQL block. This technique of nesting blocks can be used for many purposes, such as making error handling more granular. Each block or program has its own scope, which affects how you identify objects within and outside of the block.

The scope of any particular identifier is within the block that it is declared within, and any subblocks contained in that block. Identifiers, as mentioned previously, have to be unique, but they only have to be unique within their own scope. If an identifier is defined in an inner block with the same name as an identifier in an outer block, a nonqualified reference to the identifier uses the local identifier.

To access the identifier in the outer block, you would use this notation:

```
block_label.identifer
```

where *block_label* is the name or label associated with the outer procedure.

To understand how this works, consider the following code:

```
<<main>>
DECLARE
    myName VARCHAR2;
    BEGIN
      DECLARE
        myName VARCHAR2;
      myName := main.myName;
      END;
.
.
.
```

In this example, the variable `myName` in the inner block is assumed to be the local version of this variable. The qualified reference to `main.myName` refers to the `myName` variable in the block labeled `main`.

PL/SQL Language

As with any programming language, PL/SQL has its own set of syntax rules, punctuation, specifications, and reserved words.

Character Set

The characters allowed for use in PL/SQL are as follows:

<table>
<tr><td>Letters</td><td>A. . .Z and a. . .z</td></tr>
<tr><td>Numbers</td><td>0..9</td></tr>
<tr><td>Symbols</td><td>~ ! @ # $ % ^ & * ( ) _ - + = { [}] | : ; " ' < , > . ? /</td></tr>
<tr><td>Formatting</td><td>Tabs, spaces, carriage return</td></tr>
</table>

PL/SQL keywords, which are described later, are not case-sensitive, so you can use lowercase letters or uppercase letters—by convention, we will capitalize PL/SQL keywords. For non-keywords, such as string and character literals, case matters.

Special Symbols

There are special symbols or combinations of symbols that have special meaning within PL/SQL. The following symbols are used throughout PL/SQL code:

<table>
<tr><td>Arithmetic operations</td><td>+ - * /</td></tr>
<tr><td>Delimiters</td><td>' ( ) " /* */ --</td></tr>
<tr><td>Relational operators</td><td>= < > <> != ~= ^= <= >=</td></tr>
<tr><td>Indicators</td><td>% : @</td></tr>
<tr><td>Component selector</td><td>.</td></tr>
<tr><td>Item separator</td><td>,</td></tr>
<tr><td>Statement terminator</td><td>;</td></tr>
<tr><td>Special operators</td><td>:= => | | ** ..</td></tr>
</table>

In addition to these special symbols, the following symbols have particular meanings in PL/SQL:

- `:=` —This is the equivalence operator. When you use this, you are setting the value of the variable on the left of the symbol to the value of the expression on the right of the operator.
- `=>` —This symbol equates a parameter, on the left of the symbol, with a value on the right of the symbol. You use this symbol when you want to assign values to a parameter without having to list each parameter for the called program unit in order.
- `||` —This is the concatenation symbol.
- `**` —These are used to identify exponents.

- . . —These two dots are used to separate portions of a range declaration, as with the `FOR` construct, which is defined later in this chapter.
- -- —These are used to start a single line comment in PL/SQL code.
- /* and */ —These are used to begin and end multiline comments in PL/SQL code.

Identifiers

Identifiers are used to name things within a PL/SQL unit, including constants, variables, cursors, subprograms, packages, and exceptions. Every identifier must start with a letter and can then include most of the allowed characters and symbols noted previously. An identifier cannot include hyphens, slashes, ampersands, or spaces.

The following identifiers would not be allowed in PL/SQL:

```
Sign-on          Can't use hyphens
Etc/password     Can't use slash
GreenHEggs&Ham   Can't use ampersand
One world        Can't use space
```

If you absolutely positively needed an identifier that would be considered illegal, PL/SQL will allow you to use quoted identifiers. So a Dr. Seuss package could include GreenEggs&Ham as "GreenEggs&Ham." Quoted identifiers are most unusual and rarely used, since identifiers, as opposed to literals or the values of variables, are only meaningful within the context of their PL/SQL program unit.

Identifiers, like keywords, are case-insensitive. If two identifiers are the same except for the case of the letters, the identifiers are considered to be the same. The following identifiers are all the same:

```
IdEnTiFier#
Identifier#
IDENTIFIER#
```

It is good practice to make your identifiers descriptive, to ease the burden of comprehension and subsequent program maintenance. It also makes sense to establish and adhere to a set of standard naming conventions for identifiers.

Reserved Words

Reserved words are identifiers that have a very specific meaning within PL/SQL. For instance, all PL/SQL keywords and data types are reserved. Because of the way these words are used as a part of PL/SQL's syntax, you cannot use reserved words as your own identifiers.

The following is a partial list of the most common reserved words. You can find a complete and up-to-date list of reserved words in the *PL/SQL User's Guide and Manual* for your version of Oracle.

ALL	AS	BEGIN	BULK	CHECK
ALTER	ASC	BETWEEN	BY	CLOSE
AND	AT	BINARY_INTEGER	CASE	CLUSTER
ANY	AUTHID	BODY	CHAR	COALESCE
ARAY	AVG	BOOLEAN	CHAR_BASE	COLLECT

Literals

Literals are representations of specific numeric, character, string, boolean, or date/time values. There are five main types of literals: numeric, string, boolean, datetime, and interval. These are described in the sections that follow.

Numeric Literals

There are two types of numeric literals — integer and real. Integers do not contain a decimal point; real literals do and may be represented in scientific notation. Numeric literals cannot contain a dollar sign ($) or commas to separate the digits. Leading zeros are allowed. Numeric literals must fall between the range 1E-130 and 10e126-1.

Integer Literals

Integer literals consist of numbers with no decimal point notation. A leading + sign is used to indicate positive numbers. A leading - sign is used to indicate negative numbers. Following are examples of numeric integer literals:

```
100,  +100,  -100,  0100
```

Real Literals

Real literals are whole or fractional numbers that contain a decimal point. They can be represented using scientific notation. Scientific notation is represented by including an `E` or `e` at the end of the number followed by an optional signed integer. The use of `E` indicates the power of 10 used to scale the number. Real literals can also be represented as `BINARY_FLOAT` and `BINARY_DOUBLE` by using trailing characters `f` or `d`. Examples of real literals follow:

```
3.14     0.0     -3.14     +3.14     03.14    6.     6.0
```

The numbers `6.` and `6.0` are considered to be real because they include a decimal point, though you may think of them as integers.

```
3E14       3.14E0       3.14e-14       -6.e01       -6.e-01    3.14E210
```

These are all real numbers. However, the last example, `3.14E210`, can't be represented and would be considered invalid, causing a numeric overflow or underflow error.

```
3.14f      3.14d
```

String Literals

String literals are zero or more characters enclosed by single quotes. You can use any of the printable PL/SQL characters. String literals have the data type `CHAR`, except for the null string '' (two single quotes), which represents null, and null is not a `CHAR`. If you need to include an imbedded single quote, use two single quotes — this can be confusing, but check the following examples:

```
'greeneggs&ham'
'1~gReen ^*egg & HAM'
'green as of 1-Jan-200'
'HAM @ $1,000/lb'
'Egg'
'egg'
```

PL/SQL is case-sensitive with string literals, so the two previous literals are not evaluated as equivalent.

You can use single quotes inside of string literals by using two single quotes, as in the following:

```
'It''s just not right'
```

PL/SQL will interpret this as

```
It's just not right
```

Boolean Literals

Boolean literals are `TRUE`, `FALSE`, or `NULL` only. You cannot use other representations that other databases may allow, such as 1 and 0. Following are examples of the use of boolean literals:

```
IF  25 = TRUE THEN
     .... Do something
ELSE
  ...do nothing    --since 25 does not equal TRUE we will do nothing

IF status_val = TRUE
     Do something   --if status_val is a Boolean and set to TRUE do it
```

Boolean literals can only be used with logical operations — you can't add a number to a boolean, can't concatenate a boolean to a string literal, and can't insert a boolean into a database table.

Datetime and Interval Literals

Datetime and interval literals can be represented in various formats depending on the precision of time. They can be used to represent dates — such as the date of 2004-03-30 — or as specific times with fractional seconds — such as the time of day as 09:10:30.15 — or a combination of both. If the date portion of a datetime value is not included, the default date of the first of the current month is assumed. If the time is not included, the default time of midnight on the specified day is included.

When you assign a value to a datetime literal, you enclose the value in single quotes, as in the following example, which uses the default data format:

```
Day1 DATE := DATE '2004-03-30';
Time1 TIMESTAMP := TIMESTAMP '2004-03-30 09:10:30.15';
```

An interval is used to hold a range of time — such as the time to drive from New York City to San Francisco as 3 days 6 hours 12 minutes 37 seconds. Following are examples representing the previously mentioned datetime and interval literals:

```
Interval1 INTERVAL DAY TO SECOND := INTERVAL '3 06:12:37' DAY TO SECOND;
```

Intervals can be used flexibly in date arithmetic. For instance, if you wanted to find the arrival time for the trip whose duration was defined previously, you could use this code:

```
EstimatedTimeOfArrival := TimeOfDeparture + Interval1
```

where `EstimatedTimeOfArrival` and `TimeOfDeparture` were defined as datetime variables.

For more information on intervals, see the section in Chapter 1, "Oracle Architecture and Storage," on date data types.

Implementing Logic

Up until now, you have been learning the ground rules for using PL/SQL. This section introduces you to the basic ways of implementing logic in PL/SQL, using conditional logic, branching, and iterative logic.

Conditional Logic

The most basic type of logical decision that your program can make is one that is based on a particular condition being true or false. PL/SQL has two basic ways to test for conditions: the `IF...THEN....ELSE` construct and the `CASE` construct.

IF...THEN...ELSE

The `IF...THEN...ELSE` construct is the basic conditional switch used in PL/SQL programs. The syntax for the simplest form of this construct is as follows:

```
IF condition
    THEN
      logic;
END IF;
```

If the `condition` evaluates to `TRUE`, the `logic` is executed. This construct can also use an `ELSE` clause, as in the following:

```
IF condition
    THEN
      logic1;
    ELSE
      logic2;
END IF;
```

In this version, if `condition` evaluates to `TRUE`, `logic1` is executed. If `condition` evaluates to anything other than `TRUE`, `logic2` is executed.

A more complex version of this construct uses `ELSIF` for an additional logical test, as in the following:

```
IF condition1
    THEN
      logic1;
    ELSIF condition2
      logic2;
ELSE
    logic3;
END IF;
```

In this example, if `condition1` evaluates to `TRUE`, `logic1` is implemented. If not, the program evaluates `condition2`. If this condition is `TRUE`, `logic2` executes and the program continues with the first line of code after the `END IF`. If the code in `condition2` is also not `TRUE`, the code in `logic3` executes. In this way, the logic following the `ELSE` keyword acts as a default set of code — if neither the initial condition nor any of the conditions following the `ELSIF`s are not `TRUE`, the `ELSE` logic is run.

You can have as many `ELSIF`s as you need in this construct. However, if you have multiple `ELSIF`s all evaluating the same conditional expression, you might want to consider using the `CASE` construct.

The following is an example of the `IF ELSE` construct with actual code, where a value `nEmpID` is passed to the PL/SQL program unit that contains this code:

```
DECLARE
  mySal   REAL(6,2);
  myComm REAL(6,2);
BEGIN
  SELECT sal, comm INTO mysal, mycomm FROM emp
    WHERE empid = :nEmpID
    FOR UPDATE OF comm;
  IF mysal + mycomm <= 100000. THEN
    UPDATE emp SET comm = 100000. - sal
      WHERE empid = :nEmpID;
  ELSE
    UPDATE emp SET sal = 9999.99
      WHERE empid= :nEmpID;
  END IF;
COMMIT;
END;
```

The `IF` condition is processed and will resolve to be either `TRUE` or `FALSE`. If the condition is `TRUE`, the block of statements following `THEN` will be evaluated. If `FALSE`, the block of statements following `ELSE` will be evaluated. The `END IF` is used to terminate the `IF...THEN...ELSE block`. You can nest `IF` statements, but we recommend that you indent each successive `IF...THEN...ELSE` block a few spaces to make your code easier to read.

CASE Statement

There are two forms of the `CASE` statement. The most commonly used form implements different logic based on the value of a single expression. Unlike the `IF...THEN...ELSE` construct, the expression in a `CASE` construct can have a value other than `TRUE` or `FALSE`. A `CASE` construct works like a traffic cop, directing the flow of the program to different sections of code based on a value.

The syntax for a `CASE` construct is as follows:

```
CASE selector
    WHEN condition1
      THEN logic1
    WHEN condition2
      THEN logic2
.
.
.
    ELSE
      else_logic
END CASE;
```

In this construct, *selector* is a single expression, which is checked by the values in the various *WHEN* statements. You can have as many WHENs as you need. The logic under each WHEN can either be a single line of code or multiple lines of code. If you have multiple lines of code, you must use the BEGIN and END block separators.

Once the construct finds a TRUE, the rest of the conditions are not evaluated and the first line of code following the END CASE is executed. The ELSE condition at the end of the statement is optional, but if it is present, it acts as a default choice — any time none of the WHEN conditions are met, the *else_logic* is executed. The following code is an example of this form of the CASE construct:

```
CASE myoffice
    WHEN 'Boston'
      THEN mycomm := mycomm * 2;
    WHEN 'New York' THEN
      BEGIN
       SELECT RND(10) into randomcomm from DUAL;
       mycomm := mycomm * randomcomm;
      END;
    WHEN 'Atlanta'
      THEN mycomm:= mycomm + 100.;
    ELSE
      BEGIN
        mycomm := mycomm;
      END;
END CASE;
```

Notice that we check myoffice against the list of possible offices where we may want to make adjustments to the commission that the sales representative is paid. Based on the evaluation, the subprogram can execute one of many possible blocks of PL/SQL code. When myoffice is equal to New York, a block of statements for New York will be executed. The subblocks must follow standard PL/SQL block formatting — that is, begin with BEGIN and end with END. The default condition, where myoffice does not evaluate to one of the three options, follows the ELSE clause.

If you do not include an ELSE clause, and the CASE construct cannot find a match, the code raises the CASE_NOT_FOUND exception, which transfers control to the exception section of the block.

There is another form of the CASE construct, called a searched CASE statement, that does not use a selector. This form of the CASE construct can have a separate logical condition for each WHEN in the CASE. The searched CASE construct works just like a set of IF...ELSIF statements.

CASE Expression

The CASE expression fulfills the same function as the CASE statement, except that it is evaluated as a single expression within another statement. Because of this, the syntax is slightly different. You don't use a semicolon after each WHERE clause, the ELSE clause, or the end of the expression; and you end the expression with END, rather than END CASE. And since this version of CASE is an expression, you do not assign a value to a variable in the code; you simply return the value that takes the place of the expression.

An example of a CASE expression is as follows:

```
CASE
    WHEN ENAME = 'JONES' THEN
      'Jonesy'
```

```
        WHEN ENAME = 'SMITH' THEN
          'Smithy'
        ELSE
          ENAME
    END;
```

Branching

The conditional constructs described previously result in the ability to have the same program statements executed in different sequences. For instance, if the first CASE condition is satisfied, the logic within that condition is executed and the remainder of the CASE statement logic is skipped.

You can also redirect the logical flow of you program to another place in the program code by using the GOTO statement. The syntax for this statement is as follows:

```
GOTO label;
```

where *label* is an undeclared identifier is enclosed by double angle brackets. The label must also precede an executable statement or a PL/SQL block. Here is an example of the GOTO statement:

```
IF grade = 'A' THEN
  GOTO honorroll; -- branch to label honorroll
ELSE
... -- Student not 'A' do something else
END IF;
...
<<honorroll>>
IF honorstatus = 'N' THEN
  INSERT INTO honorroll VALUES (name, grade, 1);
  COMMIT;
ELSE
   UPDATE honorroll SET
    Count = count + 1
   WHERE student = name;
   COMMIT;
END IF;
```

Another type of unconditional branching can be achieved with the use of the keyword RETURN. This keyword causes the execution of the current block of PL/SQL code to end and to return control to the calling program. If the PL/SQL program unit is a function, you can follow this keyword with a value of the data type declared in the function header, as in the following:

```
RETURN myinteger;
```

Of course, both GOTO and RETURN result in an unconditional branching — they send you somewhere with no map home. Modern programming practice calls for avoiding this type of unconditional branching except where necessary.

Iterative

You will no doubt end up using iterative, or repeated, logic many times, if for no other reason than the conflict between SQL, a set-oriented data access language, and the need to examine each individual row in a set, one at a time. Three constructs are used to implement iterative logic in Oracle: `LOOP`, `FOR`, and `WHILE`.

LOOP

All of these iterative constructs server the same purpose: to allow a set of statements to be executed repeatedly. The LOOP construct is the most basic of the three constructs and can take two different forms of syntax.

The first form of the `LOOP` construct is the simplest:

```
LOOP
    logic
    EXIT;
END LOOP;
```

This simplest form of the `LOOP` construct uses the keyword `EXIT` to leave the loop. Once this keyword is encountered, the `LOOP` is exited and the next line of code following the `END LOOP` is executed. The `EXIT` is invariably contained in some type of conditional logic — if not, the loop would only be executed once.

The opposite of this last situation is when the `EXIT` is not included, or never encountered. This situation is the famous endless loop, useful for consuming enormous amounts of CPU time while accomplishing little else.

The second form of the `LOOP` includes the conditional test for the `EXIT` as part of the statement:

```
LOOP
    logic
    EXIT WHEN condition;
END LOOP;
```

This form combines the use of a conditional evaluation and the `EXIT` command. The `EXIT WHEN` condition is evaluated when it is encountered in the sequential execution of the code. You can have more than one `EXIT` or `EXIT WHEN` statement in a loop, but as soon as the PL/SQL engine performs an `EXIT`, any subsequent code in the loop is ignored.

FOR . . .LOOP

The `FOR . . . LOOP` construct lets you specify the number of iterations of a `LOOP`. The basic syntax for the FOR construct is as follows:

```
FOR counter [REVERSE] low . . . high
LOOP
    logic
END LOOP;
```

where *`counter`* is a variable that is incremented, *`low`* is the starting value of the counter, and *`high`* is the ending value of the counter. Each time the loop is executed, the value of the counter is incremented by 1.

If you include the `REVERSE` keyword, the counter starts with this high value and counts down to the low value.

The values of *low* and *high* can be variables, but they are only evaluated once when the `LOOP` is initially entered.

`FOR...LOOP` is useful if you can determine the number of iterations of a set of statements in advance. There is another version of the `FOR...LOOP` construct that can be used when you don't exactly know the number of iterations in advance, but that number is based on the number of rows returned by an SQL `SELECT` statement. The syntax for this form of the `FOR...LOOP` construct is as follows:

```
FOR row_index IN [cursor | SELECT statement]
LOOP
    logic
END LOOP;
```

This version of the construct can use a cursor, which, as you will learn in the next chapter on PL/SQL and SQL, acts as a pointer to the current row in a set of rows, or can simply include the `SELECT` statement as part of the construct.

WHILE...LOOP

The `WHILE...LOOP` construct uses the following syntax:

```
WHILE condition
LOOP
    logic
END LOOP;
```

The `WHILE...LOOP` differs from the `FOR...LOOP` construct in two ways:

- In all non-SQL-based versions of `FOR...LOOP`, you could determine the number of iterations in advance by subtracting the low value from the high value.
- A `FOR...LOOP` always executes at least once, whereas a `WHILE...LOOP` may not. Since the execution of the `WHILE...LOOP` is based on the logical condition expressed in the `WHILE` clause, that evaluation could be `FALSE` the first time the clause is evaluated.

Doing Nothing

The control structures discussed earlier in this section all assumed that you wanted to do something, based on some sort of logical condition. There may be times when you want to do nothing, such as a particular condition in a `CASE` statement where no action is appropriate.

For these times, PL/SQL includes the keyword `NULL`. This word can be used to indicate that nothing is done — what is called a no-op in some other languages. It only makes sense to have the `NULL` keyword in a conditional construct alone, since any other code would eliminate the need for the `NULL`.

Creating a PL/SQL Program

Now, at last, you can begin to create a PL/SQL procedure. This section walks you through the process of creating the different sections of the code. You can create PL/SQL code in a number of ways:

- With a standard text editor, after which you would simply run the text file in *i*SQL*Plus or SQL*Plus
- Directly in an Oracle tool, like SQL*Plus or *i*SQL*Plus
- With a third-party utility, like TOAD, from Quest Software (www.quest.com)

For the purposes of this example, we will simply display the code as it is created and then compile it by loading it into TOAD and running it. The completed code is included as `CH15_BASIC_EXAMPLE.SQL` which has been formatted using the TOAD formatter.

The Purpose of the Sample Procedure

The sample PL/SQL procedure that you will be creating is used to perform a small part of the overall functionality needed to register a student for a class. This procedure is used to add a student to a class. The procedure checks to see if the enrolment in the class has reached the limit for the class. If there is still room in the class, the overall student count for the class is increased by 1. If the class is already full, the procedure raises an error to let the calling program know there is a problem.

This procedure only implements a part of the overall processing needed for a registration application, but creating smaller modules to handle specific pieces of functionality is a good design practice.

For the procedure to run properly, you will have to create and populate the table, ROOMS, so that it will operate on in the SCOTT schema. You can accomplish this by running the script `CH15_CREATE_ROOMS_TABLE.SQL` in *i*SQL*Plus.

Starting the Code

The first step in creating a PL/SQL program unit is to create the header portion of the block. Although the actual code for the header will start with either the keywords `PROCEDURE` or `FUNCTION` to identify the program type, the code for creating the procedure must start with instructions to the PL/SQL compiler. The keywords required are either `CREATE`, which will create a PL/SQL program unit, or `CREATE OR REPLACE`, which will replace an existing program unit with the same name with the new code. If you use `CREATE` alone and a PL/SQL program unit with the same name already exists in the compiling schema, the PL/SQL compiler will return an error.

It's not that you are not a flawless programmer; it's just that others may cause you to modify the code later. So in this example, you should start with the more inclusive keywords:

```
CREATE OR REPLACE PROCEDURE addstudent (roomin IN INTEGER) IS
```

This code fragment identifies the program as a procedure, gives the procedure a name (`addstudent`), and indicates that the procedure will be called with an integer parameter, which will be called `roomin` within the scope of the procedure.

Adding Variables

Your next step is to add the variable declarations with the next set of code:

```
CREATE OR REPLACE PROCEDURE addstudent (roomin IN INTEGER)
IS
   roomname       VARCHAR2 (20);
   studentcount   PLS_INTEGER;
   capacity       PLS_INTEGER;
   noroom         EXCEPTION;
```

The first three variables will be used to hold data that will be retrieved from the database with an SQL query. The `NoRoom` exception will be used to flag the error condition that occurs if there is no room left in a classroom for another student.

Adding Logic

Your procedure is properly set up, so you can add the fairly straightforward logic shown in the next section of code:

```
CREATE OR REPLACE PROCEDURE addstudent (roomin IN INTEGER)
IS
   roomname       VARCHAR2 (20);
   studentcount   PLS_INTEGER;
   capacity       PLS_INTEGER;
   noroom         EXCEPTION;
BEGIN
   SELECT scount, cap, rname
     INTO studentcount, capacity, roomname
     FROM scott.rooms
    WHERE room_id = roomin;

   IF studentcount > capacity - 1
   THEN
      RAISE noroom;
   ELSE
      UPDATE scott.rooms
         SET scount = studentcount + 1
       WHERE room_id = roomin;

      COMMIT;
      DBMS_OUTPUT.put_line (   'Student count now '
                            || studentcount
                            || ' in '
                            || roomname
                           );
   END IF;
```

The logic starts out with an SQL query that retrieves the room name (`rname`), the current count of students in the room (`scount`), and the capacity of the room (`cap`) from the database table called Rooms. These values are placed into the variables declared at the start of the procedure.

Once the data is in these variables, a simple `IF` test is used to see if the current count of students is greater than the capacity of the room. If the room is full, the procedure raises the `NoRoom` exception defined in the declaration section, which causes program control to pass to the exception section, described here. If the room is not full, the `ELSE` condition updates the count of students in the room and commits the transaction and sends information about the current student count in the room to the output device with a procedure from the `DBMS_OUTPUT` built-in package.

Of course, this is code is a sample, rather than production-ready. The purpose of the procedure is to show how to create PL/SQL code, rather than implementing the complete logic for a logical module. In a production version of this code, you probably would not write status messages back to the output device.

Adding Exception Handling

You have defined an exception to identify an error condition. When that exception is raised, control passes to the exception section of the procedure, which is shown in the following completed procedure code:

```
CREATE OR REPLACE PROCEDURE addstudent (roomin IN INTEGER)
IS
   roomname       VARCHAR2 (20);
   studentcount   PLS_INTEGER;
   capacity       PLS_INTEGER;
   noroom         EXCEPTION;
BEGIN
   SELECT scount, cap, rname
     INTO studentcount, capacity, roomname
     FROM scott.rooms
    WHERE room_id = roomin;

   IF studentcount > capacity - 1
   THEN
      RAISE noroom;
   ELSE
      UPDATE scott.rooms
         SET scount = studentcount + 1
       WHERE room_id = roomin;

      COMMIT;
      DBMS_OUTPUT.put_line (   'Student count now '
                            || studentcount
                            || ' in '
                            || roomname
                           );
   END IF;
EXCEPTION
   WHEN noroom
   THEN
      DBMS_OUTPUT.put_line ('There is no room in ' || roomname);
   WHEN OTHERS
   THEN
      DBMS_OUTPUT.put_line ('Error ' || SQLERRM || ' occurred.');
END;
```

This final piece of code uses the PUT_LINE procedure to write a message to the defined output device, such as a terminal or a page.

The PUT_LINE procedure concatenates some descriptive text with the name of the room and outputs it to the output device. The code in the exception condition only catches the one logic exception you have defined. If other exceptions occur, the program unit sends a different line to the output device that contains the SQL error message received.

The final step in completing the procedure is to add the END statement, which in this case includes the name of the procedure for documentation purposes.

Using PL/SQL Code

Once you have created a PL/SQL program unit, you have to compile the code to make it accessible at run time. We will use the TOAD tool to compile the code, to make sure that the code contains no syntactical errors, and then call the code to see how it works.

There is a lot of functionality in TOAD, far beyond the scope of this chapter. For the rest of this section, the TOAD Procedure Editor will be used, without any explanation of its capabilities other than those that are directly used. For more information about TOAD, refer to the Quest Software site.

Preparing for Compilation

The previous example was used to illustrate the basic syntax of PL/SQL. But for the code to work, you have to create the table used in the code, ROOMS.

To do this, run the included script CH15_CREATE_ROOMS.SQL This script will not only create the table in the SCOTT schema but also add some data to the table. Once this table is in place and populated, you can begin to compile the PL/SQL code

Compiling PL/SQL Code

The first step to using your PL/SQL code is to compile it. Compiling PL/SQL consists of running the code, which submits it to the Oracle PL/SQL compiler. With TOAD, you use the Procedure Editor to accomplish this by loading the code and clicking on the Run button, which looks like a VCR Play button.

To use TOAD for this step, you should log in as the user SCOTT with the password of TIGER, since you will want the compiled procedure to reside in the SCOTT schema.

If you do this with the code for this basic example, you can see the results in Figure 15-2.

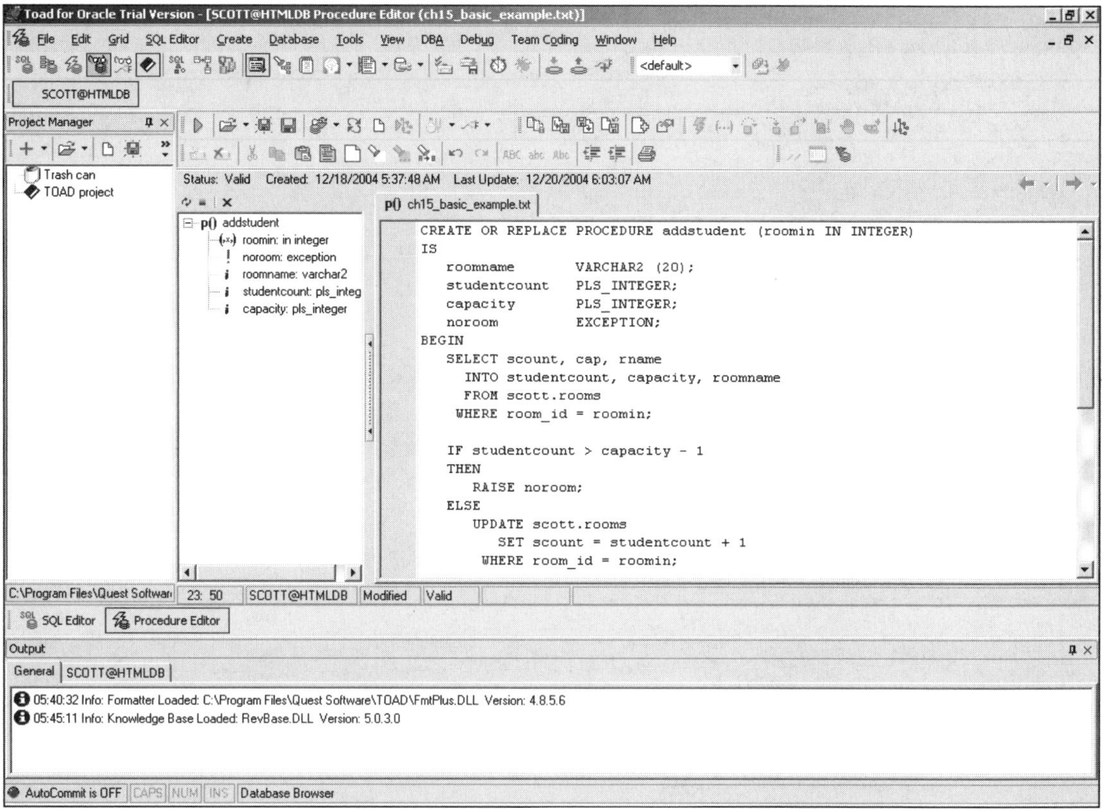

Figure 15-2: Successful compilation of the basic example in TOAD.

Running PL/SQL Code

As mentioned previously, this PL/SQL procedure is meant to be just a small piece of the overall logic of a registration application. You can still test this procedure as it is, using the SQL Editor in TOAD.

Open an SQL Editor window in TOAD. The SQL Editor allows you to see the output produced by the `DBMS_OUTPUT` package if you select the tab with the same name and make sure the little circle on the far left is green. If the circle is red, simply click on it to make it green.

Once you have enabled the display of `DBMS_OUTPUT`, enter the following code:

```
CALL addstudent(102);
```

Click on the Run button to execute the statement. You should see a status message back in the DBMS Output window. Click on the Run button again to run the procedure again. This time, you get back the message from the exception section of the code telling you that the classroom is full.

The results of running this procedure twice in the TOAD SQL Editor are shown in Figure 15-3.

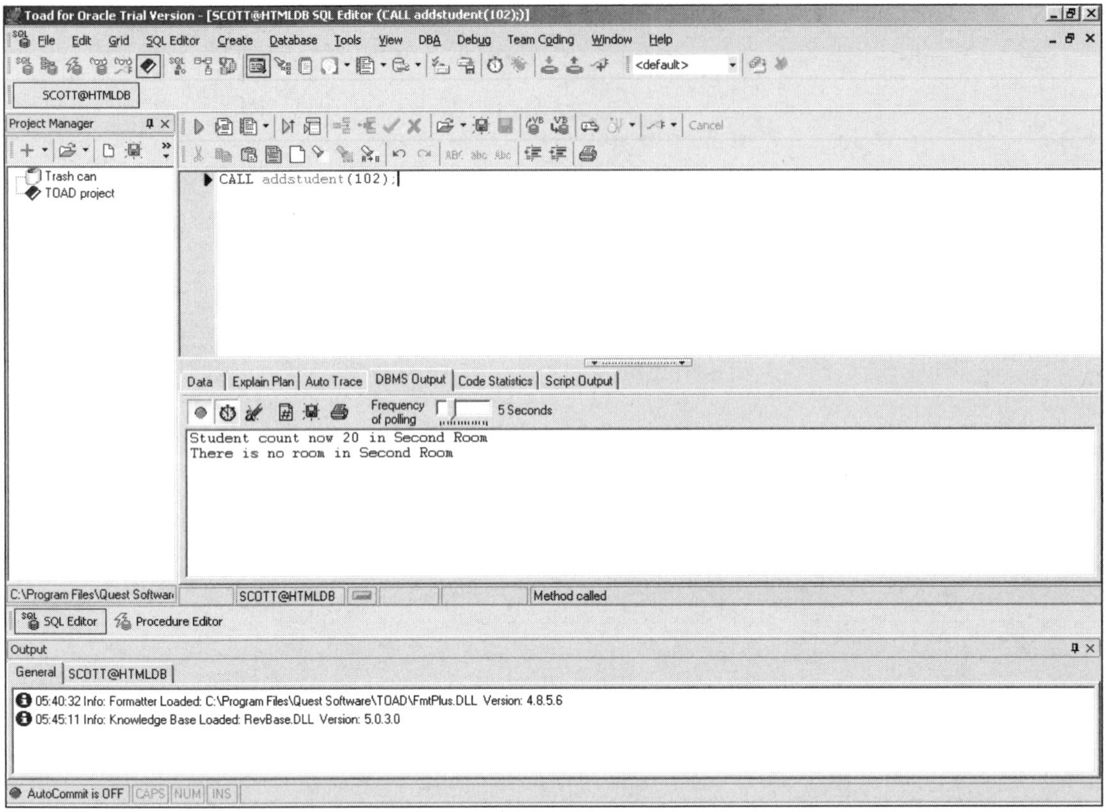

Figure 15-3: Two successful runs of the sample procedure.

Compilation, Source Code, and Dependencies

In the previous steps, you simply compiled the PL/SQL code. The code compiled, so it could be run, but what exactly happened, and when will it have to happen again?

When a PL/SQL program unit is compiled, the PL/SQL engine in the Oracle database does several things, including storing the code for the unit in the database; storing the pcode, which is the runtime version of the code, in the database; and making a list of all objects referenced in the unit — SQL objects as well as any other PL/SQL objects. Once the unit has been successfully compiled, the status of the unit is set to `VALID`.

You can view the source code that is stored for a PL/SQL unit with the following SQL statement:

```
SELECT * FROM ALL_SOURCE WHERE NAME = unit_name AND OWNER = schema_name
```

where *`unit_name`* is the name of the PL/SQL unit and *`schema_name`* is the name that the unit is stored in. If you compiled the previous unit in the `SCOTT` schema, Figure 15-4 shows the result of this query:

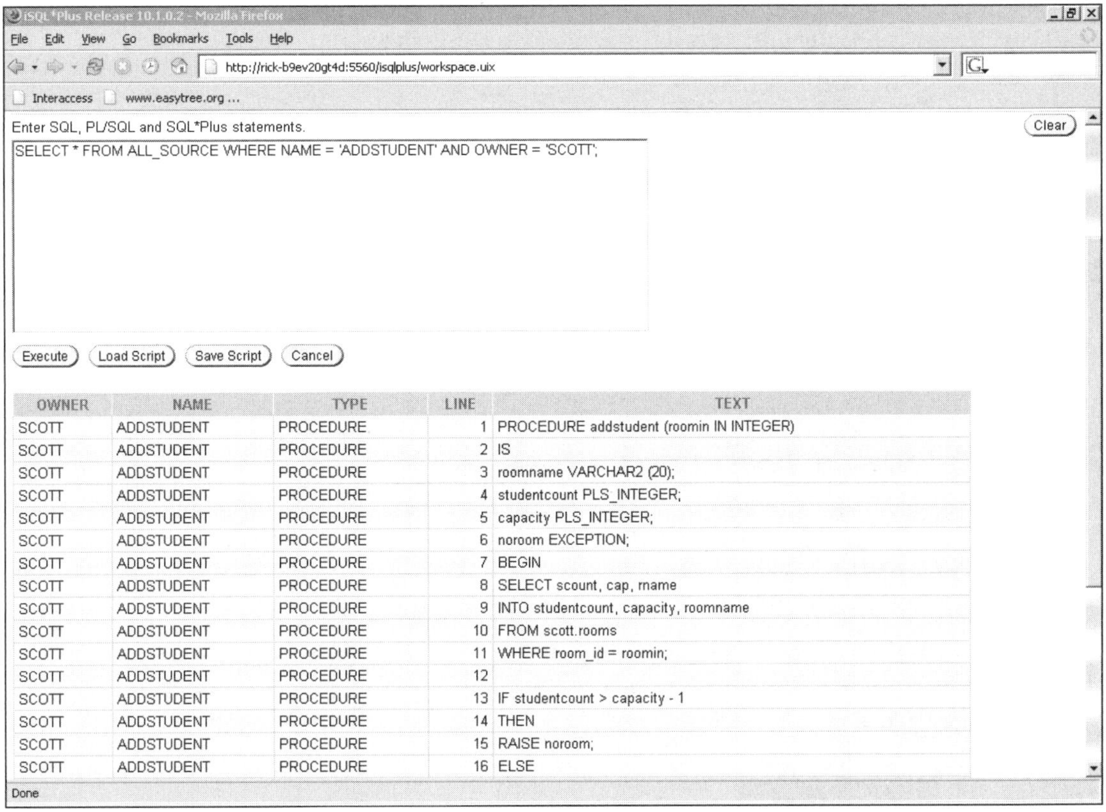

OWNER	NAME	TYPE	LINE	TEXT
SCOTT	ADDSTUDENT	PROCEDURE	1	PROCEDURE addstudent (roomin IN INTEGER)
SCOTT	ADDSTUDENT	PROCEDURE	2	IS
SCOTT	ADDSTUDENT	PROCEDURE	3	roomname VARCHAR2 (20);
SCOTT	ADDSTUDENT	PROCEDURE	4	studentcount PLS_INTEGER;
SCOTT	ADDSTUDENT	PROCEDURE	5	capacity PLS_INTEGER;
SCOTT	ADDSTUDENT	PROCEDURE	6	noroom EXCEPTION;
SCOTT	ADDSTUDENT	PROCEDURE	7	BEGIN
SCOTT	ADDSTUDENT	PROCEDURE	8	SELECT scount, cap, rname
SCOTT	ADDSTUDENT	PROCEDURE	9	INTO studentcount, capacity, roomname
SCOTT	ADDSTUDENT	PROCEDURE	10	FROM scott.rooms
SCOTT	ADDSTUDENT	PROCEDURE	11	WHERE room_id = roomin;
SCOTT	ADDSTUDENT	PROCEDURE	12	
SCOTT	ADDSTUDENT	PROCEDURE	13	IF studentcount > capacity - 1
SCOTT	ADDSTUDENT	PROCEDURE	14	THEN
SCOTT	ADDSTUDENT	PROCEDURE	15	RAISE noroom;
SCOTT	ADDSTUDENT	PROCEDURE	16	ELSE

Figure 15-4: Displaying PL/SQL code.

If any of the objects that the unit depend on are changed in any way, the status of the unit is set to `INVALID`. At run time, if an application detects an invalid PL/SQL unit, the unit is recompiled on the fly. This is necessary to ensure consistency in the units, but it can impose a penalty at run time.

You can find out the dependencies for any object in the database, including PL/SQL objects, by running the following query:

```
SELECT * FROM ALL_DEPENDENCIES WHERE OWNER = owner_name AND NAME = object_name
```

where *`owner_name`* is the name of the schema that contains the object and *`object_name`* is the name of the object. The `ALL_DEPENDENCIES` view contains information about the owner and type of the referenced object.

Both `ALL_SOURCE` and `ALL_DEPENDENCIES` have corresponding views that only list objects for the current schema, `USER_SOURCE` and `USER_DEPENDENCIES`.

There are two ways to avoid paying the price of on-the-fly recompilation. The first way is to use packages, which are described in Chapter 17, "PL/SQL Packages," along with the way that they help to prevent "dependency chains" between different PL/SQL program units.

The second way is to use a procedure in a built-in package to recompile all the objects in a particular schema. The syntax to run this procedure in iSQL*Plus is as follows:

```
EXEC DBMS_UTILITY. COMPILE_SCHEMA(schema_name);
```

where `schema_name` is the name of the schema where you want to recompile all the PL/SQL program units.

Security

PL/SQL program units are subject to security limitations, like everything else in an Oracle database. There are two aspects to PL/SQL program unit security: how users get access to a particular unit and the security privileges that the unit itself possesses.

Granting Access to PL/SQL units

A PL/SQL program unit is a database object, so a user has to have access to the unit in order to run it. For PL/SQL units, an additional level of security defined as `execute`, which, as the name implies, allows a user to execute the unit. You would give execute privileges to a user or role in the same way as you would grant any other right, such as in the following:

```
GRANT EXECUTE ON sample_proc TO PUBLIC;
```

For more on security in your Oracle database, refer to Chapter 5, "Oracle Security."

Program Unit Rights

A PL/SQL program unit can access data in an Oracle database. Since a PL/SQL unit is stored in a schema, by default, the unit has the privileges that have been granted to the schema. You can use this capability to implement two levels of security within the database. For instance, a user might not have access to a particular table but does have execute access to a PL/SQL procedure that, in turn, has access rights to the table. This particular architecture means that the only way this user could get to the data in the table is through the PL/SQL procedure.

This protection is one good reason why some wise people advocate only granting access to data through PL/SQL. The other reason is the transparency provided by this method. If you wanted to move a column from one table to another, you could simple modify the PL/SQL procedures used to access the table, rather than hunt down every reference to the column and table in every program.

There are reasons why this type of security might not be appropriate. You might want to provide the functionality based in a PL/SQL program to a wide range of users who already have different security defined. A perfect example of this is HTML-DB, discussed in Chapter 23. HTML-DB generates PL/SQL code for application components that are used by many different users.

In order to address this scenario, PL/SQL offers a feature know as *invoker's rights*. When you define invokers rights for a PL/SQL program unit, the unit executes with the security rights granted to the user who is currently running, or invoking, the unit. With invoker's rights, all references to database objects are resolved at run time, so an unqualified reference to a table like `EMPLOYEES` would resolve to the table named `EMPLOYEES` as it would for the runtime user.

To create a procedure, function, package, or type in PL/SQL with invoker's rights, use the keywords `AUTHID CURRENT_USER` as part of the header, as in the following:

```
CREATE OR REPLACE PROCEDURE flexible_proc
    AUTHID CURRENT_USER IS
```

The `AUTHID` keyword can be followed with the keyword `DEFINER`, which gives the unit the privileges of the user who compiles the unit, but since this is the default, there is no need to include it in your code.

Keep in mind that invoker's rights are evaluated at run time, as they must be, while the standard rights and privileges are included when a PL/SQL unit is compiled. There may be some impact on performance using invoker's rights, so you should not necessarily use this option if you have critical OLTP routines that will be run very frequently.

Native Compilation

As mentioned previously, the compilation process for PL/SQL code generates pcode, which runs something like interpreted code at run time. Starting with Oracle 9*i*, you have the option of compiling your PL/SQL code into true native code, which is then called by the PL/SQL engine at run time.

The process of compiling PL/SQL code into native code involves four basic steps:

1. Edit the `makefile` `spnc_makefile.mk` which should be in the PLSQL subdirectory under the home directory for your Oracle database.
2. Set the initialization parameter `PLSQL_COMPILER_FLAGS` to `NATIVE`. You should also check the settings on the `PLSQL_NATIVE_C_COMPILER`, `PLSQL_NATIVE_C_LINKER`, `PLSQL_NATIVE_LIBRARY_DIR`, `PLSQL_NATIVE_MAKE_UTILITY`, and `PLSQL_NATIVE_MAKE_FILE_NAME`.
3. Do the normal compile of the PL/SQL program units you want in native code.
4. Check the `USER_STORED_SETTINGS` data dictionary view to make sure that the objects compiled properly. You should also be able to find the shared library of DLL on the file system of the database server.

For more information on native compilation of PL/SQL code, refer to the Oracle documentation.

The amount of performance you can gain from using native PL/SQL compiled code versus standard code varies, depending on the amount of calculation that takes place within the code. If your PL/SQL code is mainly interacting with the database, as described in more depth in the next chapter, native compilation will not improve performance at all, since most of the time spent on database activities is spent in the database, rather than the code. But if you are performing a lot of repeated calculations, you may see some significant improvement in your runtime performance with native compilation — potentially up to double the speed.

Uses of PL/SQL Units

Now that you have learned the basics of writing and using PL/SQL units, it is a good time to review the places that PL/SQL is used within Oracle. PL/SQL is used in procedures and functions, which have been described in this chapter, as well as in packages, which are groups of PL/SQL program units and will be covered in Chapter 17, "PL/SQL Packages." PL/SQL packages use the same standard PL/SQL syntax, but they add another level of organization that can be used very effectively.

PL/SQL is also used to create user-defined functions, which are covered in Chapter 13, "Functions," and triggers, which are covered in Chapter 19, "Triggers."

Summary

PL/SQL was the first procedural language used in the Oracle database, and it is still the most popular way of extending the capabilities of SQL.

PL/SQL uses a block structure with four sections: the block header, declaration, execution, and exception sections. Only the execution section is required, although it is good coding practice to include headers and exception sections. You can create procedures, functions, or packages with PL/SQL. Packages are covered in Chapter 17.

PL/SQL has a standard set of logical operations, as well as a set of standard syntax and restrictions. PL/SQL code can be compiled into native code for faster runtime performance of some types of operations.

PL/SQL is also used to create user-defined functions and triggers in the database, which are covered in Chapters 13 and 19, respectively.

This chapter focused on the basics of PL/SQL in a logical sense. The next chapter takes a more detailed look at how PL/SQL is used with SQL to interact with data in your Oracle database.

16

PL/SQL and SQL

The last three letters in the name of the Oracle programming language are SQL. Since PL/SQL is designed to extend the scope of SQL, it also integrates well with the SQL language itself.

This chapter covers the details of using SQL in your PL/SQL program units. In the last chapter, you used a little SQL in the sample PL/SQL procedure. There is quite a bit more to working with data that is accessed with SQL, including the use of cursors, special data types designed for cooperation with the data types in your Oracle database, and some special types of program structures that can be used to work with sets of data.

Basic SQL in PL/SQL

As shown in the last chapter, you use the `INTO` SQL keyword to retrieve values from the Oracle database into variables in a PL/SQL program unit, such as the following:

```
SELECT COUNT(*) INTO empno FROM SCOTT.EMP;
```

In this example, the count of rows from this query would be placed into the `empno` variable, which would have been declared prior to the execution of this statement. As described in the last chapter, you could have declared the `empno` variable in the declaration section of the PL/SQL block or after the keyword `DECLARE`.

This example will give you everything you need to access a single row result set for an SQL query. Since SQL is a set-oriented language, however, you will frequently be working with more than one row in a result set. The next section introduces you to the PL/SQL object that can help you work with these sets of date.

Cursors

SQL is a set-oriented language. That's part of the power of SQL — you can not only return a set of rows as a response to an SQL SELECT statement, but the number of rows that are returned can vary, depending on the time the query is sent and the values included for conditional comparisons. (Think bind variables — please!)

But frequently you will also want to work with each row in the result set one at a time. To accomplish this, you will usually use one of the LOOP constructs described previously and an entity known as a cursor.

A cursor acts logically as a pointer into a result set. You can move the cursor through the result set, processing each row, until you determine you are at the end of the result set. There are three types of syntax associated with cursors: creating the cursor, fetching with the cursor, and closing the cursor. In addition, there are a number of attributes of a cursor you can use in your logical comparisons.

Creating a Cursor

You declare a cursor just like you would any other variable, with the following syntax in a declaration section, or after the DECLARE keyword:

```
CURSOR cursor_name IS sql_statement;
```

cursor_name is the name of the cursor, and *sql_statement* is the SQL statement associated with the cursor. When you declare a cursor, you are simply allocating memory for the cursor and associating it with an SQL statement.

Keep in mind that a cursor is a special type of variable. You cannot assign values to it in your PL/SQL code.

> *There is a type of variable that can act as a cursor for different SQL statements, which is called a REF CURSOR. This type of cursor is discussed later in this section.*

Opening a Cursor

When a cursor is associated with an SQL SELECT statement, you cause the execution of the SQL in the Oracle database by executing the cursor with the following syntax:

```
OPEN cursor [argument[, argument . . .]];
```

cursor is the name of the declared cursor, while the *argument*s that follow are any values that need to be passed to the statement established for the cursor, such as bind variables.

Fetching Data

Once a cursor has been opened, you can retrieve the rows from the executed query with the following syntax:

```
FETCH cursor INTO variable[, variable];
```

The *variables* listed following the INTO keyword must match the columns returned from the query. There is also a way to declare a variable that will automatically accept the values described in the query using the %ROWTYPE data type, which is described later in this chapter.

Closing the Cursor

Like all variables, cursors take up memory, so for that reason, as well as logical consistency, you probably want to close the cursor once you are done using it.

The syntax to close a cursor is as follows:

```
CLOSE cursor;
```

You must close a cursor before you can reopen it to run a query again. You might want to reopen a cursor to rerun the query with different selection criteria passed to it.

Cursor Attributes

A cursor does more than simply act as a pointer to retrieve a single row at a time. Each cursor also has a number of attributes that you can use to examine and understand the state of the cursor at any point. These attributes are:

- %ISOPEN—Contains TRUE if the cursor is currently open, or FALSE if the cursor is not currently open.
- %FOUND—can contain several values: NULL before a FETCH has been performed on the cursor, TRUE if a row was fetched successfully, and FALSE if a row was not fetched successfully. Returns an INVALID_CURSOR error if used on a cursor that is not open.
- %NOTFOUND—The opposite of %FOUND, although it also returns a NULL if a FETCH has not been performed.
- %ROWCOUNT—Contains the number of rows fetched so far with the cursor. This value is not equal to the total number of rows that may be fetched by the cursor.

To access any of accessing these attributes, you use the following syntax:

```
cursor_name.attribute_name
```

Using a Single Cursor

Now that you have all the essential cursor syntax, you can see an example of how you would use a cursor to retrieve and process data. The following steps walk you through the process of using a cursor in your PL/SQL code.

Declare Variables

The first step in creating your procedure is to add the header and declaration section for the PL/SQL procedure. The procedure will be called `promotion_review_1`, and you will declare variables to hold four columns from the database with the following code:

```
CREATE OR REPLACE PROCEDURE promotion_review_1
IS
   nemployeeid   NUMBER;
   dstartdate    DATE;
   denddate      DATE;
   sjobid        VARCHAR2 (20);
```

Declare Cursor

The next step is to declare the cursor that you will use. The cursor declaration can be put in the declaration section of the PL/SQL procedure as follows:

```
CREATE OR REPLACE PROCEDURE promotion_review_1
IS
   nemployeeid   NUMBER;
   dstartdate    DATE;
   denddate      DATE;
   sjobid        VARCHAR2 (20);

   CURSOR cselectjob
   IS
      SELECT employee_id, start_date, end_date, job_id
        FROM hr.job_history;
```

You can see that the cursor defines the SQL statement that will be used by the cursor. You will direct the output from that cursor into the variables when you open the cursor in the next step.

For the screen shots from TOAD for this example, we will be using the demo username of SCOTT (password TIGER). By default, this user does not have access to the HR *schema, based on security. You can simply log on as a privileged user and GRANT SELECT access to the HR.JOB_HISTORY, HR.JOBS, and HR.EMPLOYEES tables to use the SCOTT user for the examples in this chapter, or simply use a privileged user like SYSMAN to run the examples.*

Open a Cursor

The next step is to open the cursor. This step requires a single line of code that creates the cursor and parses and executes the SQL statement associated with the cursor.

```
CREATE OR REPLACE PROCEDURE promotion_review_1
IS
   nemployeeid   NUMBER;
   dstartdate    DATE;
   denddate      DATE;
   sjobid        VARCHAR2 (20);

   CURSOR cselectjob
```

```
   IS
      SELECT employee_id, start_date, end_date, job_id
        FROM hr.job_history;
BEGIN
   OPEN cselectjob;
END;
```

Fetch

Fetching is an iterative process, so you will use the `FOR` construct to handle the iterations of the loop, as shown in the code following:

```
CREATE OR REPLACE PROCEDURE promotion_review_1
IS
   nemployeeid   NUMBER;
   dstartdate    DATE;
   denddate      DATE;
   sjobid        VARCHAR2 (20);

   CURSOR cselectjob
   IS
      SELECT employee_id, start_date, end_date, job_id
        FROM hr.job_history;
BEGIN
   OPEN cselectjob;

   LOOP
      FETCH cselectjob
       INTO nemployeeid, dstartdate, denddate, sjobid;

      EXIT WHEN cselectjob%NOTFOUND;
      DBMS_OUTPUT.put_line (    'Employee '
                             || nemployeeid
                             || ' had job '
                             || sjobid
                             || ' for '
                             || (denddate - dstartdate)
                             || ' days.'
                           );
   END LOOP;
END;
```

You assign the values being returned with each fetch with the `INTO` clause of the `FETCH` statement.

The actual action of this loop is to write a line to the output device. The output includes a simple piece of date arithmetic to produce the number of days that the employee had the previous job.

The particular line output includes a date calculation. This reportlike functionality is temporary; later in this chapter, you will write this data to a table.

You should take special notice of the `EXIT WHEN` statement. This particular form of the `LOOP` construct, as described in the previous chapter, will keep executing until it finds a reason to stop. The cursor attribute used in this statement ends the loop once a fetch operation does not return any rows — in other words, at the end of the result set. If you forget to include an exit condition, you will not encounter an error, but your loop will simply run forever.

Later in this chapter, you will learn about a different version of the `FOR` *construct. This construct not only allows you to forget about explicitly ending the loop but also uses significantly less code.*

Clean Up

No job is complete until the cleanup is done. With a cursor, this means closing the `cselectjob` cursor, which is done with the last line of code.

```
CREATE OR REPLACE PROCEDURE promotion_review_1
IS
   nemployeeid    NUMBER;
   dstartdate     DATE;
   denddate       DATE;
   sjobid         VARCHAR2 (20);

   CURSOR cselectjob
   IS
      SELECT employee_id, start_date, end_date, job_id
        FROM hr.job_history;
BEGIN
   OPEN cselectjob;

   LOOP
      FETCH cselectjob
       INTO nemployeeid, dstartdate, denddate, sjobid;

      EXIT WHEN cselectjob%NOTFOUND;
      DBMS_OUTPUT.put_line (    'Employee '
                            || nemployeeid
                            || ' had job '
                            || sjobid
                            || ' for '
                            || (denddate - dstartdate)
                            || ' days.'
                           );
   END LOOP;

   CLOSE cselectjob;
END;
```

Running the Procedure

The last step is to make sure the procedure works as expected. To demonstrate this, you can run the procedure in the TOAD SQL editor as the only procedure in an anonymous PL/SQL block with the following code:

```
BEGIN
promotion_review_1;
END;
```

Figure 16-1 shows the result of an execution of this procedure. The screen shot shows the DBMS output window from TOAD, with output enabled.

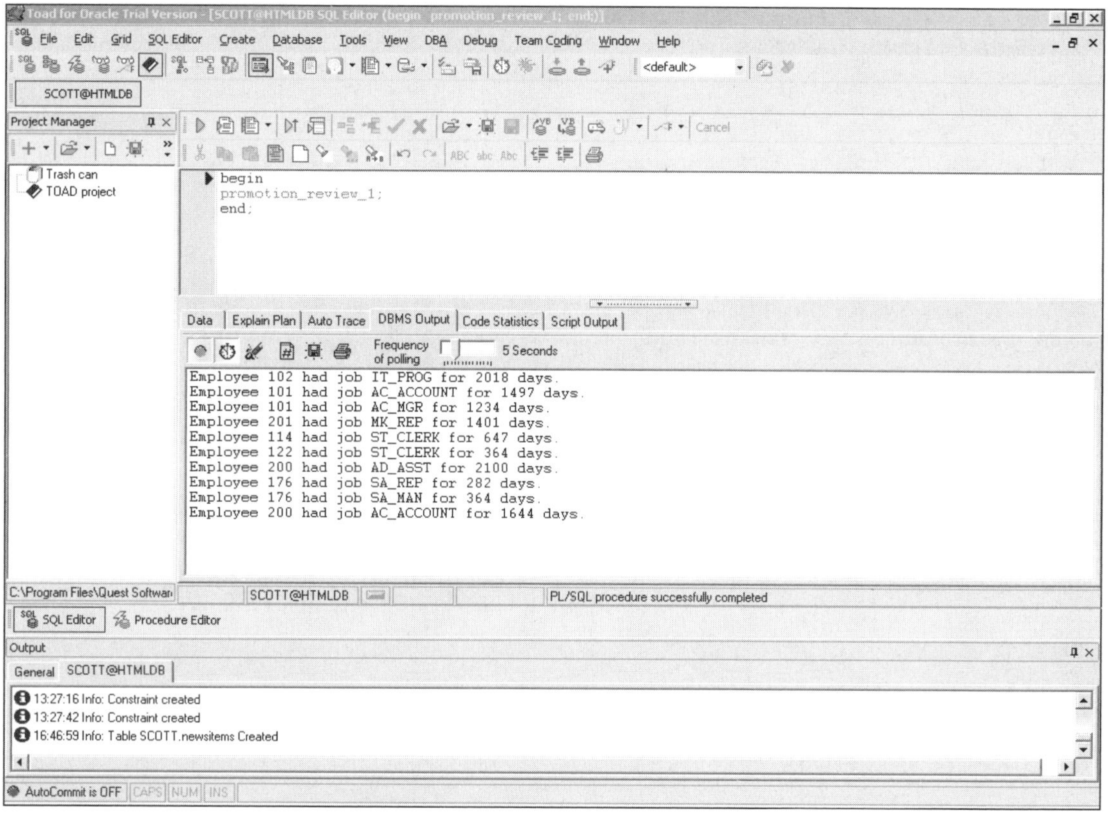

Figure 16-1: The results of the `promotion_review_1` procedure.

Special Data Types

In the previous chapter, you learned about defining variables with a data type. The variables you used in that chapter's example were associated with columns in a table, which had their own data type. Since you will be doing a lot of SQL access of data into variables, wouldn't it be nice if you could simply tell PL/SQL to use a matching data type for these variables?

There are two special data types that allow you to do exactly this: `%TYPE` and `%ROWTYPE`. These data types are known as *anchored declarations.*

%TYPE

The `%TYPE` anchored declaration allows you to dynamically associate the data type of a column in the database with a variable in your PL/SQL program. The syntax for the use of this anchored declaration is as follows:

```
variable_name table.column%TYPE
```

where *table* and *column* are valid entities in the database, and *table* could include a schema name specification, as in the following:

```
nempno scott.emp.empno%TYPE
```

You can assign an initial value to a variable with a %TYPE anchored declaration, but the variable will not inherit any NOT NULL constraints from the corresponding table in the database. If you defined a variable based on a column in the database that had been defined as NOT NULL, the variable could still have a NULL value.

The %TYPE removes the need to discover the data type for each and every variable that is associated with a database column, which saves time and potential errors in the development process. Since %TYPE is a dynamic type declaration, this anchored declaration can also prevent errors in maintenance. If the data type of the database column changes, you will not have to track down each variable that interacts with that column and change the declaration. Of course, changing a data type from a number to a string, for instance, may require other changes in your code, but at least the declarations will not have to be touched.

%ROWTYPE

The %ROWTYPE anchored declaration takes the dynamic declaration of data types a bit farther. This anchored declaration allows you to define a single variable that will include variables for each column in a database table.

The syntax for the %ROWTYPE anchored declaration is as follows:

```
variable_name table%ROWTYPE
```

Once you have defined this record variable, you access the individual columns with the following notation:

```
row_variable.column_name
```

where *column_name* is the name of the column in the database.

Like the %TYPE anchored declaration, any NOT NULL specification for a column in a table is not carried over to the variable declared for it. Unlike the %TYPE data type, you cannot initialize a variable with the %ROWTYPE data type.

You can use a variable that has been declared as %ROWTYPE to insert or update entire records into a database table with a single variable, as in the following code segment:

```
EmpRec scott.emp%ROWTYPE
.
.
.
INSERT INTO SCOTT.EMP VALUES EmpRec;
```

The %ROWTYPE anchored declaration is even more powerful than %TYPE—it saves more code, avoids more errors, and allows the definition of the table to change without necessarily affecting your application code. The concept of this anchored declaration can be used with a form of the FOR construct to reduce the amount of code you need to retrieve and use the result set from an SQL query.

FOR Cursor

The %ROWTYPE anchored declaration can be used with a form of the FOR construct to reduce the amount of code (and possibility of errors) for one of the most common interactions between and application and the database: retrieving the results of an SQL query.

In the PL/SQL procedure used earlier in this chapter, you had to go through a number of steps to retrieve data from the database — define a set of variables, define a cursor, open the cursor, fetch data in a loop, exit the loop when the retrieval was complete, and close the cursor. With this version of the FOR construct, all you have to do is to define the cursor.

Syntax

The syntax for the FOR cursor loop is as follows:

```
FOR record_variable IN cursor
LOOP
        logic . .
END LOOP;
```

The *record_variable* is automatically defined as a variable with the %ROWTYPE anchored declaration. The loop will open the cursor, perform the logic within the loop once for each row, end the execution of the loop when there are no more rows, and close the cursor.

Modifying the Example

To understand both how to use this loop and to see how much less code you can use, the previous procedure has been rewritten using the loop. The procedure is included as PROMOTION_REVIEW_2.SQL and is shown here:

```
CREATE OR REPLACE PROCEDURE promotion_review_2
IS
   CURSOR cselectjob
   IS
      SELECT employee_id, start_date, end_date, job_id
        FROM hr.job_history;
BEGIN
   FOR jh_rec IN cselectjob

   LOOP
      DBMS_OUTPUT.put_line (    'Employee '
                            || jh_rec.employee_id
                            || ' had job '
                            || jh_rec.job_id
                            || ' for '
                            || (jh_rec.end_date - jh_rec.start_date
                                   || ' days.'
                           );
   END LOOP;
END;
```

As you can see, the code is not only shorter but cleaner. For situations where you simply have to iterate through the rows in a result set and take a logical action for each, this type of loop will suit your purposes very well.

Implicit Cursors

All of the syntax and examples shown in the previous part of this section have dealt with *explicit* cursors, cursors that you declare and use. PL/SQL allows you to include SQL statements, including SELECT statements, as a part of your code without declaring a cursor. In this case, PL/SQL uses what is called an *implicit* cursor, one that operates behind the scenes like a declared cursor.

To use an implicit cursor, you simply add the SQL code into your PL/SQL code. The following code is a slight modification of the previous version of the promotion review procedure, which uses an implicit cursor to select a count of rows before writing information about each line to the output device.

```
CREATE OR REPLACE PROCEDURE promotion_review_3
IS
   nempno   NUMBER;

   CURSOR cselectjob
   IS
      SELECT employee_id, start_date, end_date, job_id
        FROM hr.job_history;
BEGIN
   SELECT COUNT (*)
     INTO nempno
     FROM hr.job_history;

   DBMS_OUTPUT.put_line ('There are ' || nempno
                         || ' employee history records.'
                        );

   FOR jh_rec IN cselectjob
   LOOP
      DBMS_OUTPUT.put_line (   'Employee '
                            || jh_rec.employee_id
                            || ' had job '
                            || jh_rec.job_id
                            || ' for '
                            || (jh_rec.end_date - jh_rec.start_date)
                            || ' days.'
                           );
   END LOOP;
END;
```

The procedure shown previously will run and produce the result shown in Figure 16-2.

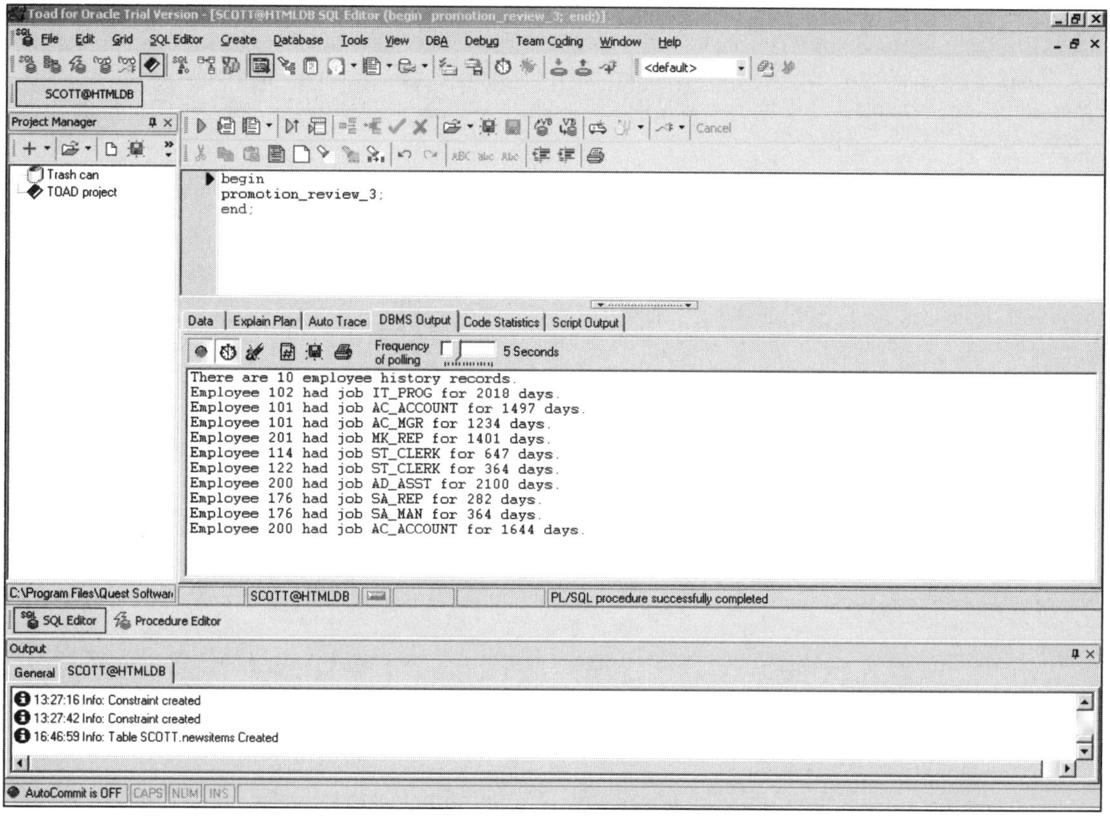

Figure 16-2: The results of the `promotion_review_3` procedure.

You could have used an implicit cursor in the previous `FOR` cursor example by substituting the name of the cursor with the SQL used for the cursor, as in the following code fragment:

```
    FOR jh_rec IN
  SELECT employee_id, start_date, end_date, job_id
      FROM hr.job_history;
```

Because there is less code involved, implicit cursors can perform better, especially when the overhead of interpreting multiple lines of PL/SQL code is weighed against a small amount of data transferred between the client and server. Implicit cursors have their own set of attributes, and a special piece of syntax for the SQL statement that can be used in your application logic.

Implicit cursors have attributes, like those for explicit cursors discussed previously, but one of those attributes has a slightly different meaning. The `%ISOPEN` always returns `FALSE`, since there is no explicit cursor open.

To access an attributed of an implicit cursor, you use this syntax:

```
SQL%attribute
```

The SQL in the previous syntax refers to the last implicit cursor executed.

REF CURSORs

A cursor references a result set. The REF CURSOR allows you to pass a cursor reference from one PL/SQL program unit to another. In other words, it allows you to create a variable that will receive a cursor and enable access to its result set.

To use a REF CURSOR, you have to first declare it as a TYPE and then create an instance of that type. The syntax for declaring a REF CURSOR is as follows:

```
TYPE ref_cursor_name IS REF CURSOR [return_type]
```

The *return_type* clause is optional; you can specify the data types that will be returned from the REF CURSOR or not. If you do not define the return from a REF CURSOR, the cursor is referred to as a weak cursor, since it is weakly typed. Defining the return for a REF CURSOR results in a strong REF CURSOR. PL/SQL comes with a predefined weak REF CURSOR called SYS_REFCURSOR; so the following is a valid declaration:

```
rc SYS_REFCURSOR;
```

Weak REF CURSORs are more prone to programming problems, since it is easy to end up with a type mismatch between the data returned by the REF CURSOR and the variables used in the application.

When creating a strongly typed REF CURSOR, you can either use the anchored declaration %ROWTYPE, as in

```
TYPE rc_employees HR.EMPLOYEES%ROWTYPE;
TYPE rc_emp IS REF CURSOR rc_employees%TYPE;
```

or you can use a PL/SQL record with the anchored declaration of %TYPE, as in

```
TYPE jr_rec
    IS RECORD(
      employee_id JOB_HISTORY.EMPLOYEE_ID%TYPE,
      job_id JOB_HISTORY.JOB_ID%TYPE,
      speed_of_promotion VARCAHR2(4));
TYPE rc_jr IS REF CURSOR jr_rec%TYPE;
```

PL/SQL records are described in the next section.

Although this book will not explore the use of a REF CURSOR with a code example, you can frequently use a REF CURSOR where you want to pass a result set between different code modules. This capability is especially relevant when you want to leave all SQL operations encapsulated in PL/SQL modules on the server. You can call a PL/SQL program from another language and have a cursor returned to the calling program. The calling program can then work directly with the cursor into the database.

In addition, you can use a REF CURSOR to remove SQL from other code modules. Rather than having an application module contain actual SQL, you could simply call another module using a REF CURSOR to pass the result set back. This form of encapsulation can help simplify maintenance over the long term, since you can change the underlying SQL statement without having to touch the calling program.

PL/SQL Records and Collections

So far, so good. If you are a database-type person, using cursors to access data on the back end is the way you think of doing things. After all, you should let the database be what the database is — a way to store data and retrieve sets of results.

But you may be thinking that you want to fetch an entire set of results into an array-like structure in your application program. PL/SQL has a class of variables that will let you accomplish this called collections. A *collection* is a structure that contains multiple instances of a single piece of data or of composite data made up of individual variables. You can compare individual instances within a collection for equivalence, or compare a complete collection with another for equivalence. You can also assign the values of a complete collection to another collection. You can even use a collection as a parameter to pass information to and receive information from another PL/SQL program unit.

Although a collection is essentially a single dimensional array, you can simulate a multidimensional array by creating a collection with a data type that is another collection.

There are three types of collections: associative arrays, nested tables, and variable arrays. Before you can learn about these collections, you have to be formally introduced to the PL/SQL record data type.

PL/SQL Records

You have already been introduced to PL/SQL records in the previous discussion of the `FOR` cursor loop. This loop uses a PL/SQL record to hold the data retrieved with the loop. A PL/SQL record is a composite data type — a single record can have more than one component. The classic use of a PL/SQL record is in conjunction with the `%ROWTYPE` declaration, as in:

```
record_name database_table%ROWTYPE
```

where the *`record_name`* is the name of the record. If you were to do this for the `JOB_HISTORY` table used in the previous example, you would use this code:

```
jh_rec JOB_HISTORY%ROWTYPE;
```

After this declaration, you could access individual columns as you did in the previous example, with the following syntax:

```
record_name.column_name
```

You could also define a PL/SQL record explicitly, so that you could include columns of your own definition. To accomplish this, you would use the following syntax:

```
TYPE record_name IS RECORD (column_name datatype[,...])
```

As an example, if you wanted to have a record with some of the columns from the `JOB_HISTORY` table and a column that you would set yourself, you could define it as the following:

```
TYPE jr_rec
    IS RECORD(
      employee_id JOB_HISTORY.EMPLOYEE_ID%TYPE,
      job_id JOB_HISTORY.JOB_ID%TYPE,
      speed_of_promotion VARCAHR2(4));
```

PL/SQL Records and SQL

You can use PL/SQL records to receive the results of a SELECT statement, as in the following code:

```
SELECT employee_id, start_date, end_date FROM HR.JOB_HISTORY INTO jr;
```

where jr is a PL/SQL record with a structure matching that of the rows being returned from the query.

Starting with Oracle9*i* Release 2, you can use PL/SQL records in an SQL statement to write to an Oracle database. You can use a collection to INSERT values into a database table, as in the following code:

```
INSERT INTO HR.JOB_HISTORY VALUES jr;
```

Notice that you do not include the name of the PL/SQL record in parentheses, as you would a normal VALUES list.

You can use a PL/SQL to update a row in a table, as with the following code:

```
UPDATE HR.JOB_HISTORY SET ROW jr WHERE EMPLOYEE_ID = jr(1).employee_id;
```

The syntax for this UPDATE is slightly different from the standard UPDATE syntax, since it uses the keywords SET ROW.

Finally, you can use a collection to receive a group of rows as the result of the RETURNING clause in an SQL statement, as shown in the following code:

```
DELETE FROM HR.JOB_HISTORY WHERE DEPARTMENT = 1
    RETURNING EMPLOYEE_ID, START_DATE, END_DATE, JOB_ID INTO jr;
```

For more information on the RETURNING clause, refer to Chapter 9, "Extended SQL."

Associative Arrays

Associative arrays are collections of data that are indexed by a value, which is similar to hash tables in some other programming languages. Prior to Oracle9*i* Release 2, associative arrays could only be indexed by a number and were referred to as index-by tables. The reason for the name change came with the ability to index an associative array by a string value as well as by a number.

An associative array is a set of data pairs, with one value in the array and the other value acting as the index for the array. The syntax for declaring an associative array is as follows:

```
TYPE array_name IS TABLE OF datatype
    INDEX BY value;
```

Prior to Oracle9*i* Release 2, the final clause in this syntax had to be INDEX BY BINARY_INTEGER. This syntax made this type of collection an array that was indexed by an integer. Although this collection was useful, in some scenarios, you had to accept an arbitrary value for the index and write code to do things like iterate through the array to find a string value.

With Oracle9*i* Release 2, you can now have an index that can be any of the following data types:

```
BINARY_INTEGER
PLS_INTEGER
POSITIVE
NATURAL
VARCHAR2
```

or even use the `%TYPE` declaration to associate the data type with the type of a column in the database.

The added capability of using a `VARCHAR2` to index an associative array means you can do things like storing a lookup table within an associative array. The following code fragment loads a lookup table for state abbreviations and names into an associative array:

```
DECLARE
  TYPE state_array IS TABLE OF STATES.STATE_NAME%TYPE
    INDEX BY STATES.STATE_AB%TYPE;
  state_aa state_array;
BEGIN
    FOR states IN SELECT STATE_NAME, STATE_ABB FROM STATES
    LOOP
      state_aa(state_rec.STATE_AB) := state_rec.STATE_NAME
END LOOP;
END;
```

In this code, you first declare a type of associative array, `state_array`, which contains the columns `STATE_NAME`, based on the type in the corresponding column in the `STATES` table in the database, which is indexed by the `STATE_ABB` column. The `STATE_ABB` column is also based on the corresponding column in the `STATES` table. Once the type is defined, you then create an instance of the type, `state_aa`.

After the collection is defined, you use the `FOR` cursor loop with an implicit cursor to load the values into the collection. The code may look a little strange, but remember that the index on the table is the string value contained in the `STATE_AB` column of the `STATES` table. All you are doing is adding a row into the associative array that contains the state name indexed by the state abbreviation.

To use the associative array to retrieve the state name for the variable `sStateAbbrev`, you would use this code:

```
sStateName := state_aa(sStateAbbrev);
```

Depending on the size of the lookup table, this approach can lead to significant runtime performance enhancements — sometimes up to one or two orders of magnitude.

You cannot store an associative array directly in the database, so you have to use logic to store and retrieve the values in this type of collection with the database.

Nested Tables

Nested tables use sequential integers as the index to the collection. Although arrays also use integers to index the contents of the array, the integers used to index and array are sequential and consecutive. A nested table can have nonconsecutive numbers as an index, creating what is known as a sparse index. A nested table does not have an upper bound defined for the collection.

The syntax for declaring a nested table is as follows:

```
TYPE collection_name IS TABLE OF datatype [NOT NULL];
```

The *datatype* can be any valid PL/SQL data type, with the exception of REF CURSOR, which was described earlier in this chapter. The NOT NULL keywords indicate that you cannot have an element in the collection with a NULL value.

You can store a nested table in a database column using an object type, and you can access individual elements of the stored table.

Variable Arrays

Variable arrays are also known as VARRAYs. These collections also use integers to index the collection, and can also be stored in a database column. A VARRAY is defined with a specific upper boundary for the index.

The syntax for defining a VARRAY is as follows:

```
TYPE collection_name IS VARRAY (size) OF datatype [NOT NULL];
```

where *size* is the upper limit on the size of the VARRAY. The data type can be any PL/SQL data type except REF CURSOR. The NOT NULL keywords indicate that you cannot have an element in the collection with a NULL value.

You can store a VARRAY in a database column, but the entire contents of this type of collection have to be accessed at the same time. With nested tables, you can access individual elements in the collection.

Working with Collections

You can add values to collections in one of two ways. For nested tables and VARRAYs, assign all the values in a single statement, as in the following:

```
number_collection := (1,4,8,16,32,64);
```

You could assign values when you declare this collection with the following code:

```
TYPE number_array IS TABLE OF NUMBER;
number_collection number_array := (1,4,8,16,32,64);
```

You could assign values one at a time, using the following index value:

```
number_collection(1) := 1;
number_collection(2) := 4;
```

You can also assign the values from one collection to another collection, as long as the two collections have the same data types.

A collection can be used in two types of logical comparisons. You can test if one collection is equal to another collection with the following syntax:

```
collection1 = collection2
```

The comparison is true if both collections have the same data type, as in the following code snippet:

```
TYPE sample1 IS TABLE OF VARCHAR(2);
TYPE sample2 IS TABLE OF VARCHAR(2);
collection1 sample1 := ('A', 'B', 'C');
collection2 sample1 := ('A', 'B', 'C');
IF collection1 = collection2
```

An equivalence comparison will not work is the two collections have the same element type but not the same data type, as in the next code snippet:

```
TYPE sample1 IS TABLE OF VARCHAR(2);
TYPE sample2 IS TABLE OF VARCHAR(2);
collection1 sample1 := ('A', 'B', 'C');
collection2 sample2 := ('A', 'B', 'C');
IF collection1 = collection2
```

You can check to see if a collection contains any elements with this syntax:

```
IF collection1 IS NULL
```

You cannot use collections with other comparison operators, such as greater than or less than.

Collection Operations

All three collection types support a set of methods that operate on individual collections. These methods are summarized in the following table.

Operation	Purpose and Syntax	Syntax
EXISTS	Check to see if an element in a collection exists.	*collection*.EXISTS(*index*)
COUNT	Returns the number of elements in a collection.	*collection*.COUNT
LIMIT	Returns the maximum number of entries in a VARRAY. (Associative arrays and nested tables always return NULL for this method.)	*collection*.LIMIT.
FIRST	Returns first element in collection.	*collection*.FIRST
LAST	Returns last element in collection.	*collection*.LAST

Table continued on following page

Operation	Purpose and Syntax	Syntax
NEXT	Returns next element in collection, or NULL if there is no next element.	*collection*.NEXT
PRIOR	Returns previous element in collection, or NULL if there is no previous element.	*collection*.PRIOR
EXTEND	Extends the number of elements in a collection. Cannot be used on associative arrays or other collections that have not been initialized.	*collection*.EXTEND; (extends collection by a single element) *collection*.EXTEND(*n*);. (extends collection by *n* elements) *collection*.EXTEND(*n*, *I*); (extends collection by *n* elements by copying value in element indexed by *I*)
TRIM	Removes elements from the end of a collection.	*collection*.TRIM;. removes a single element from end of collection *collection*.TRIM(*n*);. removes *n* elements from end of collection
DELETE	Removes elements from collection.	*collection*.DELETE;. removes all elements from collection *collection*.DELETE(*n*);. removes element indexed by *n* *collection*.DELETE(*m*,*n*); removes elements between *m* and *n* index values

There are a few caveats with regard to collection methods:

- All of the collection operations are functions, which return a value, except for EXTEND, TRIM and DELETE.
- Associative arrays with a VARCHAR2 index are sorted in alphabetical order, based on the national language set defined for the environment.
- FIRST and LAST return NULL if a collection is NULL — that is, if it contains no elements.
- NEXT and PRIOR return NULL if there is no next or previous element in the collection.
- EXTEND and TRIM cannot be used with associative arrays.
- LIMIT can be used to limit the number of values being added into a collection, typically with a SELECT . . . INTO a collection.

Which Collection Type?

Okay, collections are all like arrays, but which type should you use? We are firm believers that each one of you knows your own development and deployment scenarios better than we ever could, so you should make that decision based on your own circumstances.

There are a few key differences between the collection types, as summarized in the following table.

	Associative Array	Nested Table	VARRAY
Index type	Number or string	Number	Number
Fixed size declared	No	No	Yes
Sparse index allowed	Yes	Yes	No
Store in the database?	No	Yes	Yes
Access individual elements in stored collection	N/A	Yes	No

BULK COLLECT

We haven't forgotten the need that led to the previous discussion of collections. You want to be able to retrieve a group of rows from a result set in one fell swoop, which can deliver runtime performance benefits as well as logical flexibility.

The reason for the performance improvement is the ability of SQL*Net, the underlying protocol for communication with an Oracle database, to retrieve multiple rows of data in a single fetch operation. Multiple rows of data in a single fetch reduce the number of network round-trips and improve performance.

Another reason why using `BULK COLLECT` delivers better performance is the issue of the context switch. At run time, the Oracle database has to change contexts when executing PL/SQL or SQL — there are two different engines in the database to handle these two different sets of code. If you are in a loop where you get data with SQL, then use PL/SQL to perform logical operations on the data; there will be two context switches for each row retrieved. By using `BULK COLLECT` to load data into a collection, you greatly reduce the number of these context switches.

However, we would like to once again emphasize the virtue of one of the Oracle database's most important features — multiversion read consistency — and how it relates to working with groups of rows.

There may be many reasons why you want a set of data stored in your application, such as the need to work with multiple rows of data concurrently. However, there is one reason for storing results on the client that does not apply to Oracle. Other databases may have locking issues that force you to get all the data in a result set in order to release read locks. This workaround is not necessary with Oracle, whose multiversion read consistency eliminates the use of virtually all read locks.

If you are not familiar with this concept, you obviously skipped Chapter 3 of this book, "Handling Multiple Users." Since multiversion read consistency is one of the most powerful features of the Oracle database, you should take this opportunity to learn about this right now!

Once you get all the data into a collection, you can work with it as you would with an array in any other programming language, as the example in this section will illustrate. You can achieve these benefits by using the BULK COLLECT feature.

Using BULK COLLECT

You can use BULK COLLECT to add to the example discussed previously. You want to be able to print out a line that not only says what the job listed in the JOB_HISTORY table was — the job the employee had — but also the job the employee went to after the job listed in the JOB_HISTORY table.

The next job held by the employee could either be his or her current job, which is in the EMPLOYEES table, or the next row in the JOB_HISTORY table. It is easier to navigate around in a program-based PL/SQL table than to use multiple cursors in this case, so you will start by modifying the previous example to declare a PL/SQL table and load the results of the query into the table with a BULK COLLECT.

The complete code example is included as CH16_REVIEW_PROMOTION_4.SQL The code for the table declaration is shown in the following:

```
CREATE OR REPLACE PROCEDURE promotion_review_4
IS
   old_job          hr.job_history.job_id%TYPE;
   new_job          hr.job_history.job_id%TYPE;

   CURSOR cselectjob
   IS
      SELECT   employee_id, start_date, end_date, job_id
          FROM hr.job_history
      ORDER BY employee_id, start_date;

   TYPE jh_rec IS RECORD (
      employee_id   hr.job_history.employee_id%TYPE,
      start_date    hr.job_history.start_date%TYPE,
      end_date      hr.job_history.end_date%TYPE,
      job_id        hr.job_history.job_id%TYPE
   );

   TYPE jh_table IS TABLE OF jh_rec
      INDEX BY PLS_INTEGER;

   jh_table_array   jh_table;
```

Note that you now have sorted the rows by employee ID and start date, which will be necessary to perform the logic in the next step with the associative array. You have also created two variables with anchored declarations to the JOB_ID column in the JOB_HISTORY table to hold values for the old job and the new job.

The next step is to show the use of the BULK COLLECT syntax to populate the table, which is added to the following code:

```
BEGIN
   OPEN cselectjob;

   FETCH cselectjob
   BULK COLLECT INTO jh_table_array;

   CLOSE cselectjob;
```

You can see that this part of the code hasn't changed very much at all—just the addition of the keywords for the BULK COLLECT operation. Now that the array is ready, you can use it with a LOOP to see if an employee has another record in the JOB_HISTORY table following this job.

If this condition is true, the next job the employee held would be the job listed in the next row of the associative array, so you would use the simple assignment in the code following the IF:

```
FOR counter IN jh_table_array.FIRST .. jh_table_array.LAST
LOOP
   old_job := jh_table_array (counter).job_id;

   IF jh_table_array (counter).employee_id =
                              jh_table_array (counter + 1).employee_id
   THEN
      new_job := jh_table_array (counter + 1).job_id;
```

If the next element in the associative array is not for this employee, then you should get the next job for the employee from the EMPLOYEES table, with the following code:

```
ELSE
   SELECT job_id
     INTO new_job
     FROM hr.employees
    WHERE hr.employees.employee_id =
                                  jh_table_array (counter).employee_id;
END IF;
```

The final step in this particular code module is to use the DBMS_OUTPUT.PUT_LINE() again to print the results of the module to the output device, as shown in this final piece of code:

```
DBMS_OUTPUT.put_line (    'Employee '
                       || jh_table_array (counter).employee_id
                       || ' had job '
                       || old_job
                       || ' for '
                       || (  jh_table_array (counter).end_date
                           - jh_table_array (counter).start_date
```

```
                    )
                || ' days and moved to job '
                || new_job
                || '.'
            );
```

The results of this procedure are shown in Figure 16-3.

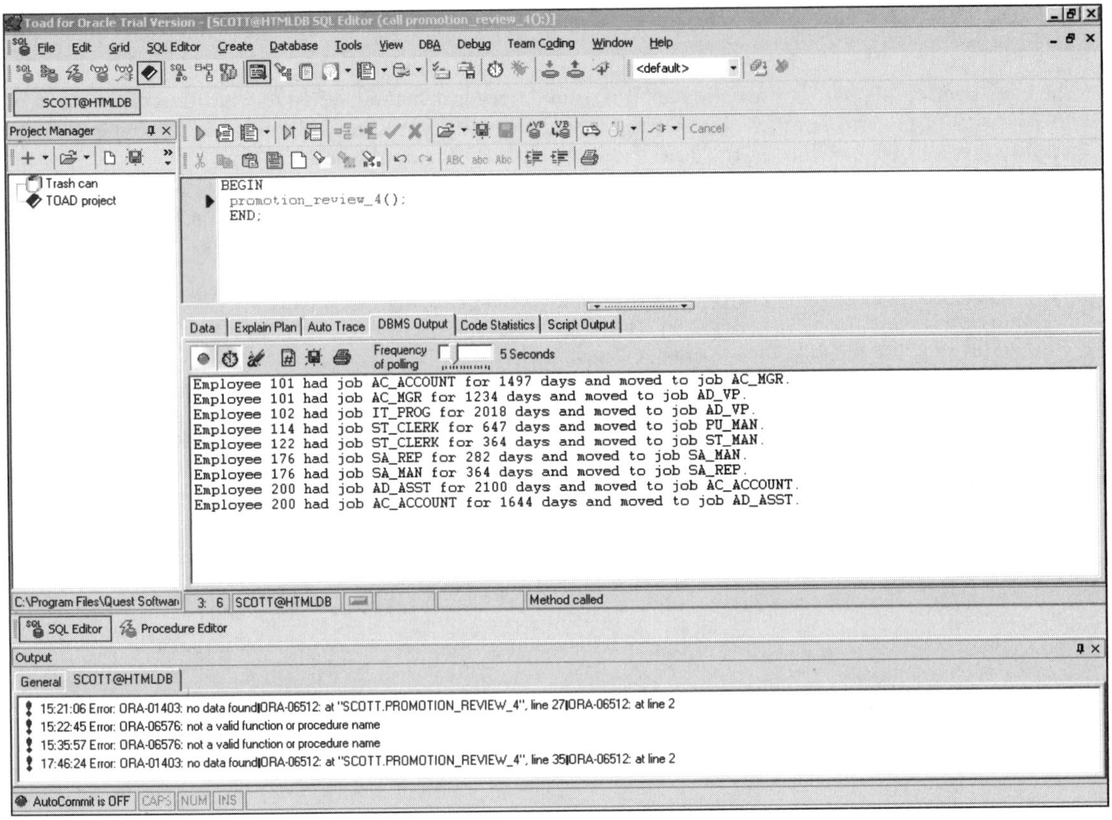

Figure 16-3: Output of new version of PL/SQL procedure.

Can you spot a problem with this output? There are only 9 lines in the report, when there are 10 rows of data in the `JOB_HISTORY` table. The problem lies in this line of code:

```
IF jh_table_array(counter).employee_id =
    jh_table_array(counter + 1).employee_id
```

The reference to `counter + 1` produces an out-of-range error in the loop. There are other potential issues in the code, but you will rewrite this module with packages in the next chapter, when you break the logic into smaller chunks.

FORALL

The `FORALL` construct allows you to gain the same type of efficiency offered by `BULK COLLECT` when you are doing write operations. This construct packages up multiple write statements and sends them off to your Oracle database in a single message, increasing the overall performance of the operation.

Syntax

The syntax for the `FORALL` construct is as follows:

```
FORALL index_name IN lower_bound . . upper_bound
   sql_statement
```

The *`index_name`* is a variable that is implicitly declared for use in the `FORALL` loop. The *`lower_bound`* and *`upper_bound`* limit the range of the collection that was the source of the loop. For example, if you wanted to use `FORALL` to insert all the rows in the `jh` collection, you would use the following code:

```
FORALL jh_index IN jh.FIRST . . jh.LAST
   INSERT INTO HR.JOB_HISTORY VALUES jh(jh_index);
```

Although the amount of code used in this example is about the same as the amount of code used for a simple `FOR` loop with an `INSERT`, the runtime performance will be better for any significant number of independent `INSERT`s.

Exception Cases

You may have noticed a potential problem in the use of the `FORALL` construct as described previously. What happens if Oracle is processing a batch of `INSERT` statements and one of them fails? Normally, this situation would result in the end of the entire `FORALL` job. This functionality would argue against the use of `FORALL` as opposed to a `FOR` loop. With a `FOR` loop, you could place the `INSERT` in a separate block, catch the exception for the block and handle it there, and return to the outer block when you have finished your exception handling.

You can accomplish the same goal by using the `SAVE EXCEPTIONS` keywords, which were introduced in Oracle9*i*. The syntax for using these keywords is as follows:

```
FORALL index_name IN lower_bound . . upper_bound SAVE EXCEPTIONS
        sql_statement
```

These keywords tell the `FORALL` construct to save two pieces of information for each error and then continue to process the rows in the collection. The information is stored in an internal collection called `SQL%BULK_EXCEPTIONS` that is made up of the items `ERROR_INDEX`, which contains the index number of the row in the original collection that caused the error, and `ERROR_CODE`, which contains the actual error code for the offending statement.

When you include the `SAVE EXCEPTIONS` keywords for a `FORALL` loop, the loop does not raise exceptions for errors in individual SQL statements. Instead, the `FORALL` loop raises a single exception, with the error code of –24381, at the end of its processing if any exceptions were raised during the course of that processing.

FORALL Enhancements

Oracle Database 10*g* includes a couple of enhancements that can be used to make the FORALL construct applicable to more programming scenarios.

INDICES OF

One enhancement covers those times when you are working with what is called a sparse collection. Prior to Oracle 10*g*, the FORALL construct would simply iterate through a collection, incrementing the index by 1 for each iteration. If the construct came to an index value that did not have an associated row in the collection, the execution would stop with an error.

A sparse collection is a collection that would cause this type of error. The rows in the collection are not all present — they are sparely distributed within the overall bounds of the collection. Oracle 10*g* includes a new clause for the FORALL construct, INDICES OF, which is used in the following way:

```
FORALL INDICES OF collection_name [BETWEEN lower_bound . . upper_bound ]
   sql_statement
```

This clause instructs the FORALL to read the next index value, rather than the next consecutive value. Using the INDICES OF clause lets you use a sparse collection and the FORALL construct.

The INDICES OF clause also lets you select just a portion of the overall collection by specifying the upper and lower bounds of a range of the collection.

VALUES OF

The INDICES OF clause lets you limit the rows in a collection that are used with the FORALL clause. But the limitations are fairly simple — one to let you get around a previous limitation of FORALL and another that lets you drop the beginning or ending rows from the operation of the construct.

Oracle Database 10*g* includes another enhancement for the FORALL clause that gives you even more flexibility in the use of this clause. The VALUES OF clause lets you use another collection to drive which rows will be the targets of the FORALL clause.

For instance, look at the two collections in Figure 16-4. The collection on the right is the target of the FORALL construct. The collection on the left contains the values of the index for the right-hand collection that you want to use in the FORALL construct.

The syntax for implementing this operation would start with the following:

```
FORALL index_value VALUES OF driver_collection
```

This syntax would instruct the FORALL construct to take the values from the collection called *driver_collection* and use them as the index values for the *update_collection*. The only limitation on the use of this clause is that the drivingcollection must be either a nested table or an associative array. An associative array used in this construct must have both the index and elements be either BINARY_INTEGER or PLS_INTEGER.

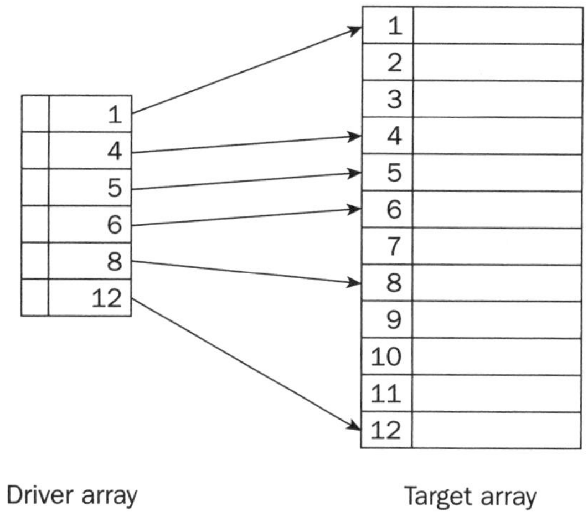

Figure 16-4: Using the `INDICES OF` clause.

Dynamic SQL

Very early on in this book — Chapter 2, "Using SQL" — you learned about using a single SQL statement that could return different result sets. You implement this type of flexibility using bind variables, which allow you to substitute specific values for selection conditions. Using bind variables is a great idea with an Oracle database, since it can dramatically reduce the number of hard parses done by the database and improve performance.

If this last statement is not perfectly clear to you, do yourself a favor and go back and read Chapter 2. Using bind variables is one of the best performance practices you can follow.

There are other times when you have to have even more flexibility with an SQL statement. For instance, you may want to retrieve the same data for a query, but you might want to direct the query to different tables in the database, depending on logical conditions. For these situations, you can use dynamic SQL.

As the name implies, dynamic SQL is SQL that is created at run time. You can use dynamic SQL to create any type of SQL statement. Prior to Oracle8*i*, you had to use a built-in package (`DBMS_SQL`) to form and execute SQL statements dynamically. In later versions, you can use the `EXECUTE IMMEDIATE` syntax. Although the use of the `DBMS_SQL` package is a bit more verbose and complicated than the simple `EXECUTE IMMEDIATE`, the `DBMS_SQL` package still offers some advantages, such as the ability to reuse previously parsed SQL statements.

The difference between `DBMS_SQL` and `EXECUTE IMMEDIATE` highlights why static SQL — which can not only be reused but is also checked at compile time, thereby avoiding possible runtime errors — is better to use than dynamic SQL. Always consider if you could use a static SQL statement with bind variables before jumping into dynamic SQL. For more on the advantages of using bind variables, refer to Chapter 2 on executing SQL.

EXECUTE IMMEDIATE

The syntax for EXECUTE IMMEDIATE is straightforward:

```
EXECUTE IMMEDIATE sql_statement
```

The *sql_statement* is a string that is used as the SQL statement. You put this string together with standard concatenation, such as in the following:

```
EXECUTE IMMEDIATE
   'DELETE FROM ' || table_spec ||
    ' WHERE DEPT_ID = :dept_iD'
    USING dept_in;
```

Dynamic SQL can contain bind variables, as shown in the previous example. You use the USING clause to provide the values for the bind variable or variables.

You can use the keyword INTO to direct the results of an SQL query into a variable or collection. You can also use the RETURNING keyword to direct the return from a write operation to a variable or collection. Note that all three of these keywords (USING, INTO, and RETURNING) follow the SQL statement string and are not within quote marks.

The EXECUTE IMMEDIATE syntax can also be used for executing an anonymous PL/SQL block.

Bulk Operations with Dynamic SQL

You can use BULK COLLECT with dynamic SQL statements. You simply use the keywords at the end of the created string, as in the following:

```
EXECUTE IMMEDIATE
   'SELECT EMPLOYEE_ID, JOB_ID FROM ' ||
    job_table_name
    BULK COLLECT INTO jh_collection
```

More on Dynamic SQL

This final section has been light on examples, because you are going to be using dynamic SQL in the next chapter of this book, where you will learn about packages. One of the PL/SQL program units in one of the packages you create will use dynamic SQL in its code, which will give you an example of both the use of dynamic SQL and how to implement it.

Summary

This chapter delved into the use of PL/SQL in conjunction with SQL. You first learned the basics of working with cursors to retrieve multiple rows in a result set, and also explored implicit cursors as well as REF CURSORs, which can be used to increase the flexibility of your application code.

Anchored declarations can help to reduce data type mismatches between your applications and their data. The chapter went on to cover the important area of collections, which are like arrays in PL/SQL. Collections can be used with two PL/SQL features, `BULK COLLECT` and `FORALL`, to improve the performance of your data operations. Finally, you learned a little bit about using dynamic SQL statements in your code.

The next chapter gives you one more big area of interest in PL/SQL code, the use of packages to help in creating modular and reusable code.

17

PL/SQL Packages

In the previous two chapters, you learned the basics of creating individual PL/SQL program units. As you might imagine, a complete application could be composed of many, many program units. There may be program units that you want to use in more than one application. And you might want to find a way to define program units so that the implementation details are separate from the way the units are called.

You can accomplish all of this with PL/SQL packages.

What Is a Package?

A PL/SQL package is a way to group sets of program units together. With the exception of a few additional keywords, the syntax for creating PL/SQL packages is identical to using PL/SQL to create program units.

The basic difference between packages and standard program units is that a package is divided into two separate modules: a package header, or specification, which lists the interface to a set of program units and contains any variables or constants that are visible to the world outside of the package, and a package body, which contains the implementation of the program units listed in the header, as well as any variables or constants that are only visible to the programs in the package. A package body can also contain program units that are not listed in the header.

The syntax for creating the package header is as follows:

```
CREATE [ OR REPLACE ] PACKAGE package_name
IS
    declaration_section
    program_units
END package_name;
```

The declaration section has the same syntax as the declaration section for a PL/SQL procedure or function. The *program_units* section lists the procedures and functions defined in the package body that are visible to users of the package.

The syntax for creating the package body is as follows:

```
CREATE [ OR REPLACE PACKAGE ] BODY package_name
IS
    declaration_section

    PROCECUDRE/FUNCTION program_name
    .
    .
    .
END package_name;
```

As with the package specification, the declaration section of the package body is just like the declaration section for a PL/SQL procedure or function. The difference between the variables, constants, exceptions, and cursors declared in the package body is that these objects are not visible or accessible to users of the package.

The code for the procedures and functions within the package is the same code you would use for a standalone version of the program.

You can declare PL/SQL program units in the package body that are not listed in the package specification, but, as with the declarations, these units will not be visible to users of the packages.

The definitions of the procedures and functions in the package body must exactly match the definitions of the matching units in the package specification. If there is a mismatch in terms of the number or data type of parameters, the PL/SQL compiler will interpret the specification and the implementation in the body as two separate units, resulting in a resolution error if you call the unit by name.

You could combine both of these in a single text file, but typically you would keep them in separate files. For reasons discussed in the next section, you will probably be changing the information in the package body more frequently than the specification in the package header.

Impact of Packages

From a consumer's point of view, having a standalone procedure or a procedure that is a part of a package is not that different. You would call either one in a very similar manner — the only difference would be that you would have to preface a call to the procedure in a package with the package name, as in

```
promo_package.initialize()
```

for the packaged procedure versus:

```
initialize()
```

for the standalone procedure.

However, there are several significant differences for you, the developer, in using packages rather than individual program units.

Organization

As a developer, you seek to be as efficient as possible. One of the ways you can improve your efficiency is to reuse existing code. The more discrete and modular a particular program unit is, the more flexibly is can be reused. For instance, which of the sets of procedures in Figure 17-1 is more like to be reused?

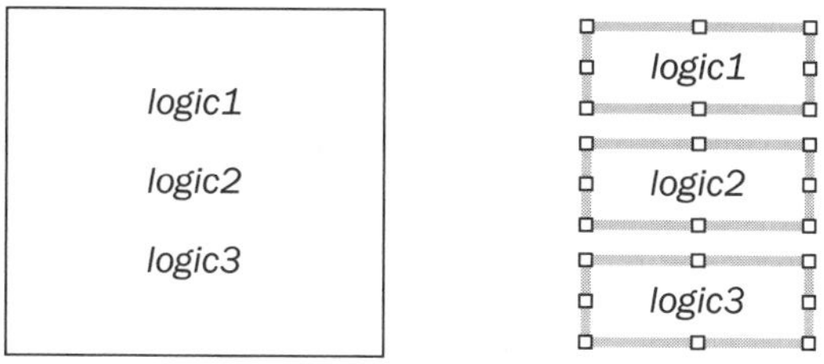

Figure 17-1: Two options for logic.

The option on the right will probably be reused more frequently, since the logic is more modular. Another application does not have to require logical steps 1, 2, and 3—any step can be called independently, which makes the logic more flexible.

The downside of this type of modularization is that it leads to large numbers of individual program units, which can be hard to track. With a PL/SQL package, you get the benefits of the fine-grained functionality of smaller program units and the ease of discovery of larger units.

Visibility

Perhaps even more important, packages give you a way to only expose interfaces and information that you want to make visible. A user can only access the information in the package header specification. Any details of implementation and variables used to implement functionality within the package body can be invisible outside the package body, so you can also define variables and constants within a package body to hide them from external consumers.

The ability to have publicly exposed methods and variables and privately protected methods and variables gives you two advantages. The separation between interface and implementation means you can maintain the way procedures and functions are actually performed, with the code in the package body, without worrying about how those changes will affect their use by other programs. In addition, you can protect data and program units from the outside world. No one outside of a package can get to the data and program units inside the package, which can help in implementing security in your applications.

Scope

The separation between a package specification and the package body introduces another level of scope into your design scheme. With standalone PL/SQL programs, you can use parameters to pass information to and from the program unit from the outside world, or declare them within the body of the program unit, which kept them private. With packages, you have three levels of scope:

- Package declared procedures, variables and constants, which are available to everyone — inside and outside of the package
- Package body declared procedures, variables and constants, which are only available to program units in the package
- PL/SQL program unit declared variables and constants, which are only available within the program unit

Having more options gives you greater flexibility to declare objects where their scope will be both appropriate and logically meaningful. Your declarations are protected from outside access, depending on where you define them.

Dependencies

As mentioned back in Chapter 15, "PL/SQL Basics," a PL/SQL program unit can have a number of dependencies. If one program references another program unit or database entity, the program is dependent on that definition. If the definition of a referenced entity changes, the PL/SQL program unit's status is set to `INVALID` and the unit will have to be recompiled when it is called.

There is, of course, a good logical reason for this recompilation. If a referenced item changes in a way that makes the program unit incorrect, the unit should not execute, and the only way to determine this is to recompile the unit.

Unfortunately, many changes in referenced entities will not cause a program to stop working properly. (In fact, none of them should!) For instance, if internal code in a referenced procedure changed but the interface to the procedure did not, any procedure that referenced the changed procedure would still be marked invalid. When you are creating a rich application system with many, many program units, this scenario can lead to lots and lots of recompilation on the fly. Recompilation introduces performance delays, at seemingly incongruous times to a user.

Without packages, you have the choice of either tracking down the program units that are invalid through system views or simply forcing a recompile of all program units in a particular schema that is home to the application. With packages, this chain of dependency is broken. A procedure in a package is still dependent on a referenced program unit in another package, but the dependency is based on the package header, not the package body. This change means that changing any code in a package body will not force a recompilation of program units that reference the program units in the body. The reference is to the package header, not the body.

This difference alone can be significant enough to suggest the use of packages for all production PL/SQL program units.

Runtime Memory Usage

Oracle Corporation contends that there is no difference in the memory use of PL/SQL packages versus the independent use of the components of the package. There is a difference in the way the memory is used, though. When a PL/SQL program unit is called for the first time, the code for the unit is loaded into the System Global Area (SGA) for the Oracle database. When a PL/SQL package is loaded, the code for all the contents of the package are loaded into the SGA.

Although this may be a wash in the end, the difference means that the initial load of a package may take slightly more time while saving on load times later. To ensure that SGA memory is not wasted, you should make sure that you group only related program units in a PL/SQL package.

Oracle's Endorsement

The usefulness of PL/SQL packages is demonstrated by the simple fact that Oracle itself uses use packages to add functionality to the Oracle database. Oracle 10*g* comes with over 150 packages, which contain thousands of individual procedures and functions. PL/SQL packages provide both an organizational structure that allows users to comprehend this vast scope of functionality and modularization of code, which allows for more rapid development and testing and makes the code much easier to manage, as the examples in this chapter will show.

An Example

Since you have already learned the basics of PL/SQL and how PL/SQL interacts with data in your Oracle database, you can jump right into creating packages. To learn more about packages, you can take the procedure you were building in the previous chapter and re-create it using packages. Although this technique may result in more "decomposition" of functionality than you would prefer to use in the real world, the example for this chapter will help to illustrate the features and functionality of packages.

As you recall, the goal of the PL/SQL procedure created in the previous chapter was to deliver information about an employee's previous job history. The procedure used the information in the table `HR.JOB_HISTORY` as the driving force behind this functionality, although the procedure was starting to bring in information from other tables as well.

As noted in the previous chapter, the examples in this chapter will use the `JOB_HISTORY`, `JOBS` and `EMPLOYEES` tables in the HR schema. The examples shown in the screen shots will be done with the user `SCOTT`, who by default does not have access to the HR schema, based on security. You can log on as a privileged user and `GRANT SELECT` access to the `HR.JOB_HISTORY`, `HR.JOBS` and `HR.EMPLOYEES` tables to use the `SCOTT` user for the examples in this chapter, or simply use a privileged user like `SYSMAN` to run the examples.

In fact, you have to specifically grant access to the user who will be creating these packages. As you no doubt know, you can get access through a direct grant of privileges from the owner of a schema, or by assuming a role that has those privileges. One of the 'gotchas' of PL/SQL is that you have to be granted security privileges *directly* in order to be able to access objects in a different schema. Some highly privileged user accounts, like `SYSMAN`, get their powers from roles. Consequently, although you could easily perform SQL operations on objects in the `HR` schema as `SYSMAN`, you could not reference objects in that schema, since the SQL operation privileges were not directly granted to that user.

To demonstrate how to use packages, you will take the functionality from the complete example in the last chapter and break it down into smaller components. Each of those components will become a procedure or function in the package. You will expose some parts of the functionality and variables to the world, while other parts will remain private within the package body.

The Package Specification

The first decision you have to make when creating a package is what parts of the overall code will be included in the package specification and therefore be available to users. The package specification for this package is shown here, and included as CH17_CALC_PROMOTIONS.PKS. Note the different suffix for the package specification, which will also be used for the package body.

```
CREATE OR REPLACE PACKAGE calc_promotions
IS
   TYPE results IS TABLE OF VARCHAR2 (300)
      INDEX BY PLS_INTEGER;

   promotion_results_array   results;

   PROCEDURE populate_promotions;

   PROCEDURE find_next_job (
      employee_id   IN   hr.job_history.employee_id%TYPE,
      end_date     IN   hr.job_history.end_date%TYPE
   );

   PROCEDURE parse_promotion_results;

END calc_promotions;
```

This package specification is pretty straightforward. You can see that the only data variable is an array of VARCHAR2. This array will be the place when the results of the assembly process will be placed. The array is intentionally left fairly "unformatted." The reason is that the loose nature of the data typing gives you the flexibility to change the format of the results within the package body without having to adjust the package specification—which in turn removes the need to recompile all other programs that reference the package, as you will see later.

Two of the procedures declared in the package specification make sense. The populate_promotions and parse_promotion_results procedures are used to initialize the internal structures and then use the data in these structures to create the desired results. But what about the find_next_job procedure? This is a procedure that could have remained hidden in the package body. But there is a chance that someone might want to use this type of functionality outside the scope of the package. There might be other reasons why someone would want to find out what job an employee had after a particular date. Because of this, the decision was made to expose the procedure to the public by including it in the package specifications.

The Package Body

The real work of the package takes place in the package body. This piece of code includes variable declarations that can only be seen from within the package body, the procedures listed in the package specification, and any other procedures or functions needed for the package body to work properly.

The code for this package body is included as CH17_CALC_PROMOTIONS_BODY_1.PKS and listed here. The remainder of this section examines the contents of this package body in smaller chunks.

```
CREATE OR REPLACE PACKAGE BODY calc_promotions
IS
   TYPE promotion_records IS TABLE OF hr.job_history%ROWTYPE
      INDEX BY PLS_INTEGER;

   promotion_array    promotion_records;
   old_job            hr.job_history.job_id%TYPE;
```

```
new_job           hr.job_history.job_id%TYPE;
new_job_result    VARCHAR2 (100);

PROCEDURE populate_promotions
/* populate internal array */
IS
   CURSOR getjobhistory
   IS
      SELECT   *
          FROM hr.job_history
      ORDER BY employee_id, start_date;
BEGIN
   OPEN getjobhistory;

   FETCH getjobhistory
   BULK COLLECT INTO promotion_array;

   CLOSE getjobhistory;
END;

FUNCTION lookup_next_job (
   table_location     IN   VARCHAR2,
   search_condition   IN   VARCHAR2
)
   RETURN VARCHAR2
/* get new job with dynamic SQL */
IS
   job_history_lookup   VARCHAR2 (200);
   return_job           VARCHAR2 (100);
BEGIN
   job_history_lookup :=
            'SELECT JOB_ID FROM ' || table_location || search_condition;

   EXECUTE IMMEDIATE job_history_lookup
             INTO return_job;

   RETURN return_job;
EXCEPTION
   WHEN NO_DATA_FOUND
   THEN
           return_job := NULL;
           RETURN return_job;
      END;

PROCEDURE find_next_job (
   employee_id   IN   hr.job_history.employee_id%TYPE,
   end_date      IN   hr.job_history.end_date%TYPE
)
/* set value of new_job, calling lookup procedure */
IS
   lookup_table       VARCHAR2 (20);
   search_condition   VARCHAR2 (100);
BEGIN
 search_condition :=
           ' WHERE hr.job_history.employee_id = '
           || employee_id
           || ' AND hr.job_history.start_date = '''
```

```
              || TO_CHAR(end_date + 1)
              || ''''
      new_job :=
            lookup_next_job ('HR.JOB_HISTORY', search_condition);

      IF new_job IS NULL
      THEN
         search_condition :=
               ' WHERE hr.employees.employee_id = '
            || employee_id;
         new_job :=
                  lookup_next_job ('HR.EMPLOYEES', search_condition);
      END IF;
   END;

   PROCEDURE parse_promotion_results
   /* assemble results array in package specification*/
   IS
   BEGIN
      FOR indx IN promotion_array.FIRST .. promotion_array.LAST
      LOOP
         find_next_job (promotion_array (indx).employee_id,
                        promotion_array (indx).end_date
                       );

         IF new_job IS NULL
         THEN
            new_job_result := ' leaving the company';
         ELSE
            new_job_result := ' moving to job ' || new_job;
         END IF;

         promotion_results_array (indx) :=
               'Employee '
            || promotion_array (indx).employee_id
            || ' had job '
            || promotion_array (indx).job_id
            || ' for '
            || (   promotion_array (indx).end_date
                 - promotion_array (indx).start_date
                || ' days before'
                || new_job_result
                || '.'
               );
      END LOOP;
   END;
END calc_promotions;
```

The remainder of this section will look at each part of this package body.

Declarations

The declaration section creates the internal objects that will be used by the package body. This section is shown here:

```
TYPE promotion_records IS TABLE OF hr.job_history%ROWTYPE
   INDEX BY PLS_INTEGER;

promotion_array   promotion_records;
old_job           hr.job_history.job_id%TYPE;
new_job           hr.job_history.job_id%TYPE;
new_job_result    VARCHAR2 (100);
```

The old_job and new_job variables are used to hold the job from the JOB_HISTORY record as the old job and whatever is found for a new job. The new_job_results is a character string that can differ according to what the employee moved on to after the job listed in the JOB_HISTORY table.

The promotion_array inside that package body is more strongly typed than the array in the package specification. This array follows the data types in the actual JOB_HISTORY table. Why have a strongly typed array here and not in the package specification? Although this is just an example, it still made sense to hide the actual content of the JOB_HISTORY table inside the package body. This way you could give anyone access to the fruits of this package without letting the person see the underlying data. If there were parts of the underlying data that any old user should not see, you would not have to worry about granting them access. Because of this ability, some people use packages to give access to all tables.

Procedures and Functions

There are three procedures and one function included in the package body. This section shows you each individual program unit and offers some commentary on the code for each one.

populate_promotions

The populate_promotions procedure, as shown here, initializes the array used for logically processing all the employees who are listed in the JOB_HISTORY table. These are the employees who are the target of the promotions information this package is responsible for producing.

```
PROCEDURE populate_promotions
   /* populate internal array */
   IS
      CURSOR getjobhistory
      IS
         SELECT *
           FROM hr.job_history;
   BEGIN
      OPEN getjobhistory;

      FETCH getjobhistory
      BULK COLLECT INTO promotion_array;

      CLOSE getjobhistory;
   END;
```

The procedure uses a BULK COLLECT to populate the entire array more rapidly. The array itself uses the %ROWTYPE anchored declaration to create the appropriate data types. Although you don't use all the columns in the table in the processing of this package, the table is fairly small, and the needs and requirements of the package might change in the future to require the new data. And it's faster and more error-free to use in code.

lookup_next_job

This function, whose code is shown here, is the only one that is not included in the package specification. This placement means that a user cannot call the function, which is appropriate, since it is used as part of the internal logic of the package. The end result of the functionality provided by this package can be accessed by the `find_next_job` procedure, which is in the package specification and is discussed next.

```
FUNCTION lookup_next_job (
      table_location      IN    VARCHAR2,
      search_condition    IN    VARCHAR2
   )
      RETURN VARCHAR2
   /* get new job with dynamic SQL */
   IS
      job_history_lookup    VARCHAR2 (200);
      return_job            VARCHAR2 (100);
   BEGIN
      job_history_lookup :=
                  'SELECT JOB_ID FROM ' || table_location || search_condition;

      EXECUTE IMMEDIATE job_history_lookup
                   INTO return_job;

      RETURN return_job;
   EXCEPTION
      WHEN NO_DATA_FOUND
      THEN
         return_job := NULL;
         RETURN return_job;
   END;
```

This function uses the `EXECUTE IMMEDIATE` call, which allows you to parse the actual SQL at run time. This code is used primarily to give you an example of using `EXECUTE IMMEDIATE`– the circumstances, as they stand based on today's requirements, don't call for using this syntax. Notice that this function requires an exception section. The reason for this requirement is that the `EXECUTE IMMEDIATE` call is designed to return a single row of data for a `SELECT`. If no row is returned — which is one of the acceptable logical outcomes of this particular `SELECT` statement — you don't want runtime exceptions to interrupt the operation of the application. To avoid this problem, you add the exception section. The `NO_DATA_FOUND` constant identifies a particular error code. By using this constant, you allow the default error handling built into the PL/SQL engine to take care of any other errors, while still returning a proper value for this condition, a `NULL` value.

There are only two variations on this call, so you would probably not use `EXECUTE IMMEDIATE` if this were a production system with only two options, unless you believed there was a good chance that there would be even more options down the road. The reason to hard-code the choices is that `EXECUTE IMMEDIATE` always calls a soft parse, and sometimes a hard parse. For more information on the impact of soft and hard parses, see Chapter 2, "Using SQL," which describes how Oracle executes SQL statements.

find_next_job

This procedure performs a critical piece of functionality in this package. The code for the `find_next_job` procedure is shown here:

```
PROCEDURE find_next_job (
   employee_id    IN    hr.job_history.employee_id%TYPE,
   end_date       IN    hr.job_history.end_date%TYPE
)
/* set value of new_job, calling lookup procedure */
IS
   lookup_table        VARCHAR2 (20);
   search_condition    VARCHAR2 (100);
BEGIN
 search_condition :=
       ' WHERE hr.job_history.employee_id = '
       || employee_id
       || ' AND hr.job_history.start_date = '''
       || TO_CHAR(end_date + 1)
       || ''''
   new_job :=
         lookup_next_job ('HR.JOB_HISTORY', search_condition);

   IF new_job IS NULL
   THEN
      search_condition :=
         ' WHERE hr.employees.employee_id = '
         || employee_id;
   new_job :=
                lookup_next_job ('HR.EMPLOYEES', search_condition);
   END IF;
END;
```

The IF constructs go through the logic required to find the new job. You first look to see if an employee has a second row in the JOB_HISTORY table, one with a job that begins on the day after the previous job ended.

This type of logical test is one that can be a bit shaky, since it is based on an assumption about the data that may not be true. In fact, this logic is slightly flawed, because one employee left the company and then returned. For this scenario, the employee is listed as being with the company twice—employee 200, Jennifer Whalen. Ms. Whalen apparently left the company for over a year, as the rows in the JOB_HISTORY table for her indicate. Unfortunately, the HIRE_DATE in the EMPLOYEES table only shows her original hire date. Whether this problem is because Jennifer left the company and came back or whether a job was left out of the JOB_HISTORY table, this promotions report will point out this data anomaly.

If there isn't a second row for the employee in the JOB_HISTORY table, the next step is to see if the employee is still employed with the company by looking in the EMPLOYEES table. This table only includes a HIRE_DATE, not a START_DATE, so there is no need for the logical matching used in the previous example.

If there is not a row in the EMPLOYEES table for this employee, the employee is no longer with the company. The next procedure will deal with this possibility, which will be signaled by the new_job variable containing a NULL value.

parse_promotion_results

This final procedure in the package body takes the data gathered by the previous procedures and creates a text string. The code for the procedure is listed here:

```
PROCEDURE parse_promotion_results
/* assemble results array in package specification*/
IS
```

```
    BEGIN
       FOR indx IN promotion_array.FIRST .. promotion_array.LAST
       LOOP
          find_next_job (promotion_array (indx).employee_id,
                         promotion_array (indx).end_date
                        );

          IF new_job IS NULL
          THEN
             new_job_result := ' leaving the company';
          ELSE
             new_job_result := ' moving to job ' || new_job;
          END IF;

          promotion_results_array (indx) :=
                'Employee '
                 || promotion_array (indx).employee_id
                 || ' had job '
                 || promotion_array (indx).job_id
                 || ' for '
                 || (   promotion_array (indx).end_date
                      - promotion_array (indx).start_date
                 || ' days before'
                 || new_job_result
                 || '.'
                );
       END LOOP;
    END;
 END calc_promotions;
```

The IF statement in this code handles the possibility that an employee is no longer with the company. This situation is evidenced by the fact that the new_job variable was not set by either trying to select another row from the JOB_HISTORY table or the EMPLOYEES table—that employee is not longer around. To get cleaner syntax in the final text string, these two situations call for two different explanations, which are put into the new_job_result variable.

Running the Example

Your coding work is done. Now it is time to see the results of your labor.

You can run the various procedures exposed in the package declaration with an anonymous PL/SQL block, which is included as the file CH17_RUN_PROMO_REPORT.SQL, as well as listed here:

```
BEGIN
 calc_promotions.populate_promotions;
 calc_promotions.parse_promotion_results;
 FOR indx IN calc_promotions.promotion_results_array.first ..
    calc_promotions.promotion_results_array.last
 LOOP
    DBMS_OUTPUT.PUT_LINE( calc_promotions.promotion_results_array(indx));
 END LOOP;
END;
```

You can see that this simple code calls the visible procedures from the `CALC_PROMOTIONS` package and then takes the result and displays it to the output device. Notice that you can access the `promotion_results` array directly by simply preceding it with the proper package name as a qualifier. Anything in the package specification can be used in this way.

Figure 17-2 following shows the code running in TOAD, as well as the first set of results.

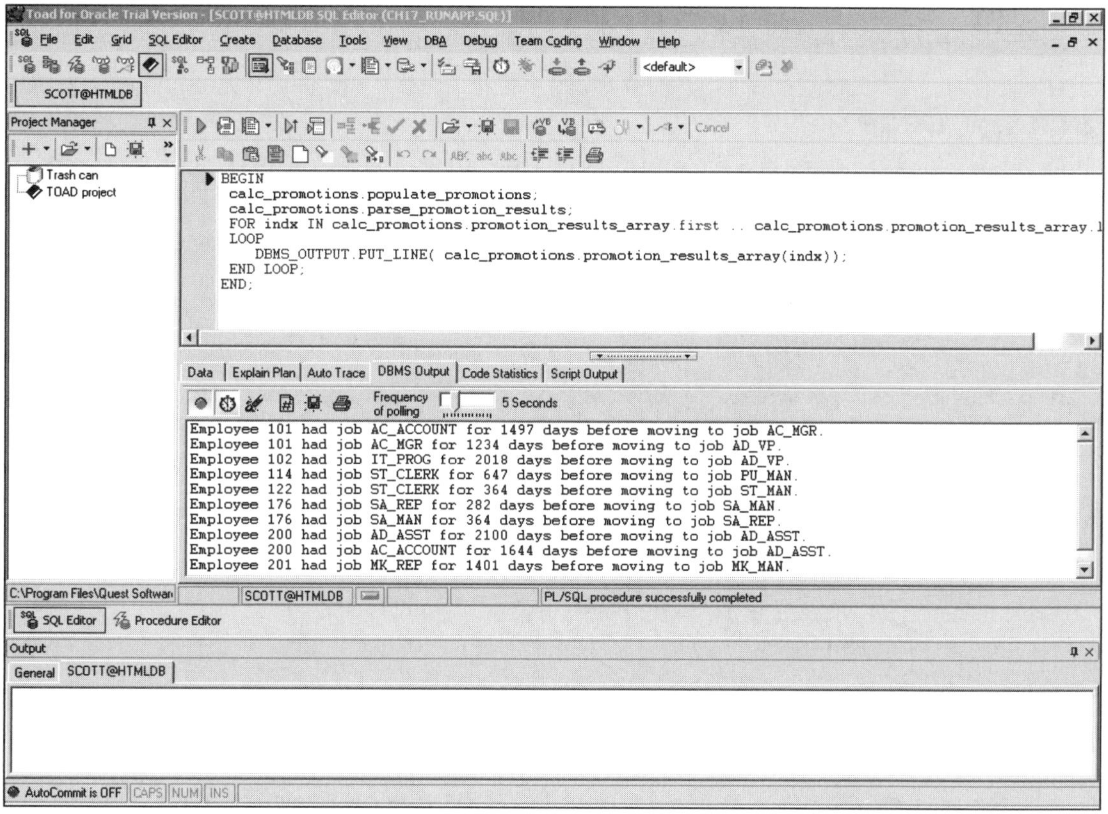

Figure 17-2: The results of your package work.

Using Packages Together

At the start of this chapter, you learned about the advantage of using packages. The previous example showed you how to implement a package, but you used it from an interactive SQL prompt. In most scenarios, you will be using multiple packages together. To understand the implications of using multiple packages, you can take the functionality that was in the command-line code and add it to a second package.

Your Second Package

Gee, that was so much fun, let's do it again! Actually, you are probably already thinking that calling the procedures in the CALC_PROMOTIONS package might be done more effectively from another package, rather than from the command line.

This second package, which is included as CH17_USE_CALC_PROMOTIONS.PKS, will do just that. In addition, using this second package will let you see how packages can reduce the impact that a change to a specific piece of functionality can have on your overall application.

Package Code

This second package doesn't do much, so the code for the package is fairly small. The package specification, shown here and included as CH17_USE_CALC_PROMOTIONS.PKS, contains a single function.

```
CREATE OR REPLACE PACKAGE use_calc_promotions
IS
   PROCEDURE produce_results;
END use_calc_promotions;
```

The package body, shown here and included as CH17_USE_CALC_PROMOTIONS.PKS, simply replicates the code that was in the script file you used to run the CALC_PROMOTIONS package you created earlier.

```
CREATE OR REPLACE PACKAGE BODY use_calc_promotions
IS
   PROCEDURE produce_results
   IS
   BEGIN
      calc_promotions.populate_promotions;
      calc_promotions.parse_promotion_results;

      FOR indx IN
         calc_promotions.promotion_results_array.FIRST ..
calc_promotions.promotion_results_array.LAST
      LOOP
         DBMS_OUTPUT.put_line (calc_promotions.promotion_results_array (indx));
      END LOOP;
   END;
END use_calc_promotions;
```

Figure 17-3 proves that calling the produce_results procedure from the use_calc_promotions package produces the same results as the script used to call your first package earlier in this chapter.

But, of course, your work is not done. The functionality implemented in the calc_promotions package needs to be updated.

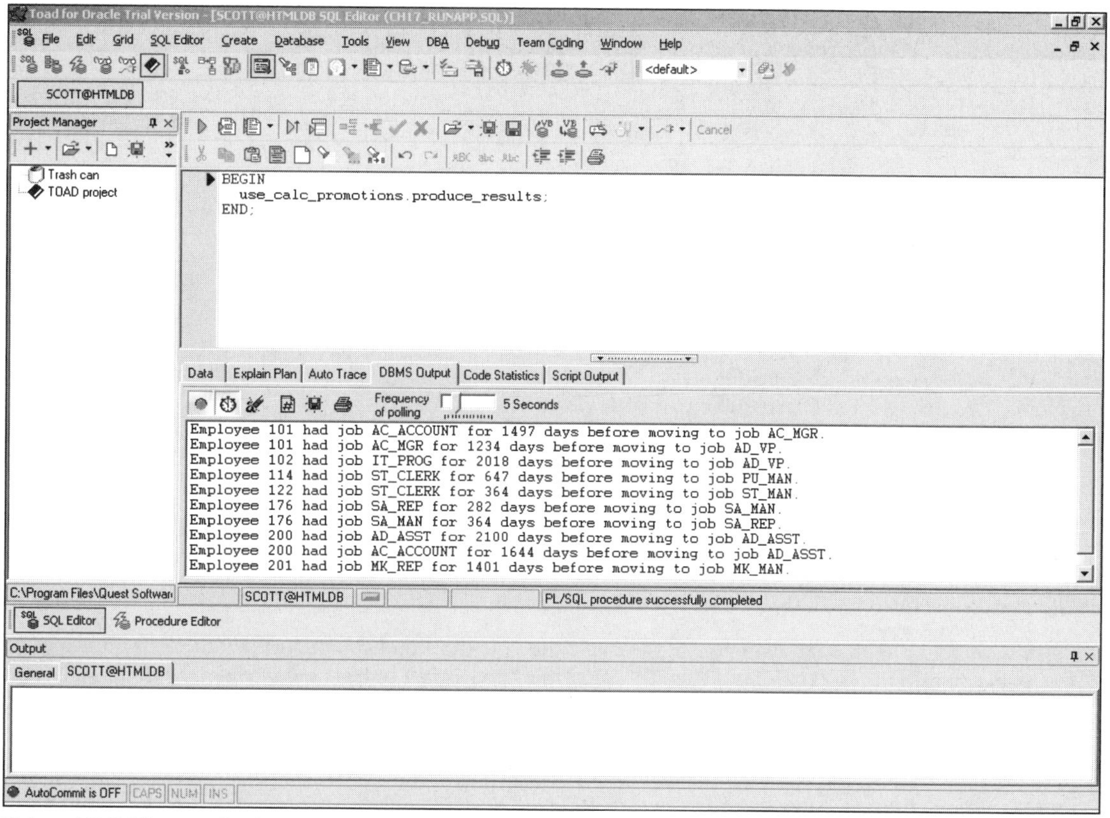

Figure 17-3: The results from calling your second package.

Changing the First Package

Let's pretend that, for some odd reason, your user has changed their mind about the functionality they want from your application. (Of course, in the real world, this would never happen. <g>) The specific change in this case is that the user is a mite confused by the references to employees by their employee number. They want the same report, but they want the employee's name used instead of their number.

This data is readily available from the HR schema, although it is in the `EMPLOYEES` table rather than the `JOB_HISTORY` table. But no matter, the modular nature of packages makes the change easy to implement.

To accomplish this, you can insert another function into the package body for the `CALC_PROMOTIONS .` package. The function will be called `get_employee_name`, and the code is listed here and included as part of the `CH17_CALC_PROMOTIONS_BODY_2.PKS` file.

```
FUNCTION get_employee_name (employee_selected NUMBER)
   RETURN VARCHAR2
IS
   full_name   VARCHAR2 (100);
BEGIN
   SELECT (first_name || ' ' || last_name)
     INTO full_name
```

```
        FROM hr.employees
       WHERE employees.employee_id = employee_selected;

      RETURN full_name;
      NULL;
   END;
```

You can simply modify the statement in the parse_promotion_results to call this function instead of looking in the array for the employee ID, as shown in the modified code following:

```
            promotion_results_array (indx) :=
                  'Employee '
                   || get_employee_name(promotion_array(indx).employee_id)
                   || ' had job '
                   || promotion_array (indx).job_id
                   || ' for '
                   || (   promotion_array (indx).end_date
                        - promotion_array (indx).start_date
                   || ' days before '
                   || new_job_result
                   || '.'
                  );
```

Before you compile this new version of the package, you should check out some of the attributes of both this package and the package that calls it to illustrate the impact of the new version on dependent code.

Impact on the Second Package

To understand the impact of these changes in the first package on the second package, you will have to understand what normally happens when one procedure calls another procedure and the called procedure changes. There are two standalone program units included with this chapter, CH17_STANDALONE_FUNCTION_A.PKS and CH17_STANDALONE_PROCEDURE_B.PKS. The code for the function is shown here:

```
CREATE OR REPLACE FUNCTION standalone_function_a
   RETURN NUMBER
IS
   retrieved_count   NUMBER;
BEGIN
   SELECT COUNT (*)
     INTO retrieved_count
     FROM hr.job_history;

   RETURN retrieved_count;
END;
```

The code for the procedure that calls the function is shown next:

```
CREATE OR REPLACE PROCEDURE standalone_proc_b
IS
BEGIN
   DBMS_OUTPUT.put_line (    'The number of job changes is '
                          || scott.standalone_function_a
                         );

END;
```

Both of these program units compile without errors. When you call `standalone_proc_b`, the compiled code is retrieved from the database.

But what happens if you change `standalone_function_a`? To illustrate, we have changed the SQL statement that retrieves the count of the rows in the `JOB_HISTORY` table to take a `WHERE` clause. This new version compiles without error either. But when you look at the status of these two program units in the `ALL_OBJECTS` view with the query included as `CH17_TEST_VALID.SQL`, you get the result shown in Figure 17-4.

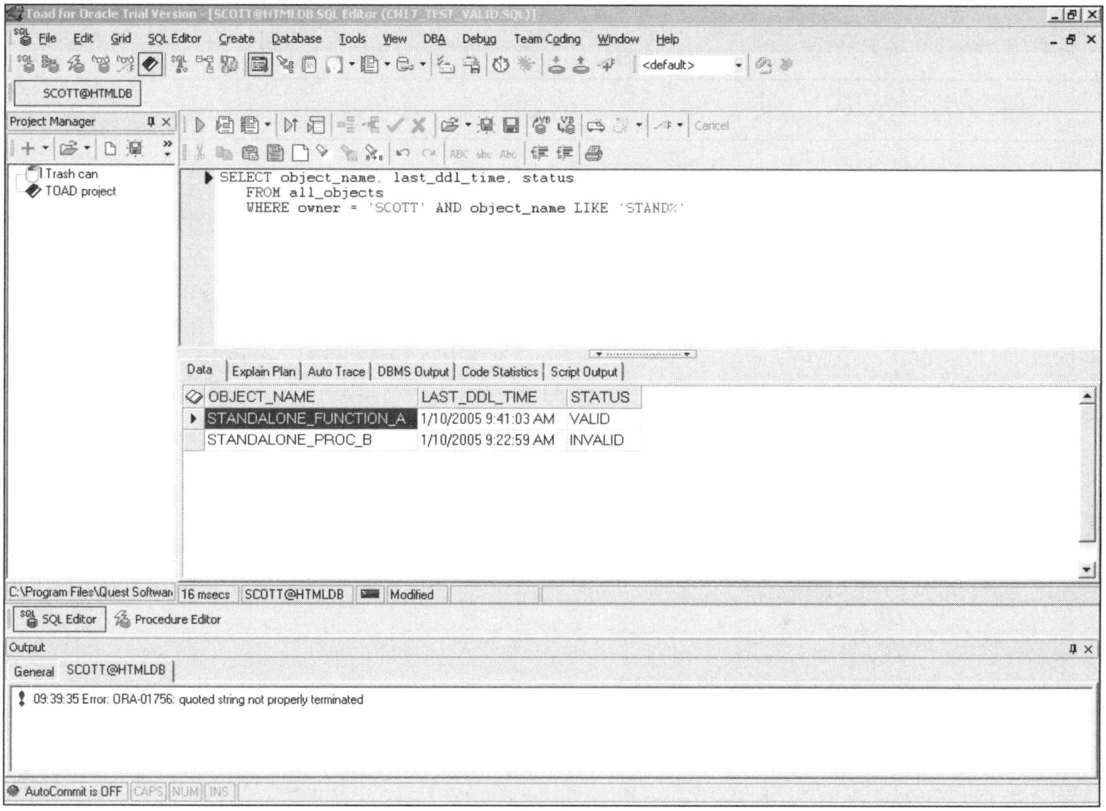

Figure 17-4: Evidence of dependency.

As you can see, the procedure that calls the function is now marked as invalid. When your Oracle database loads an invalid procedure into the SGA, the first thing that happens is that the code is recompiled. This process, of course, takes resources.

When you use packages to encapsulate your functionality, you break this dependency. The SQL query `CH17_TEST_VALID_PACKAGES.SQL` shows what happens after you have changed the package body of the first package you created, as shown in Figure 17-5.

What happens with the status of the second package? Nothing. The second package only looks to the package specification of the first package. Since this interface has not changed, the second package is not marked invalid. In addition, you don't have to be picky about the order in which you define or compile the procedures within packages. The PL/SQL compiler simply checks the package specification as to whether a program unit will be defined in the package body.

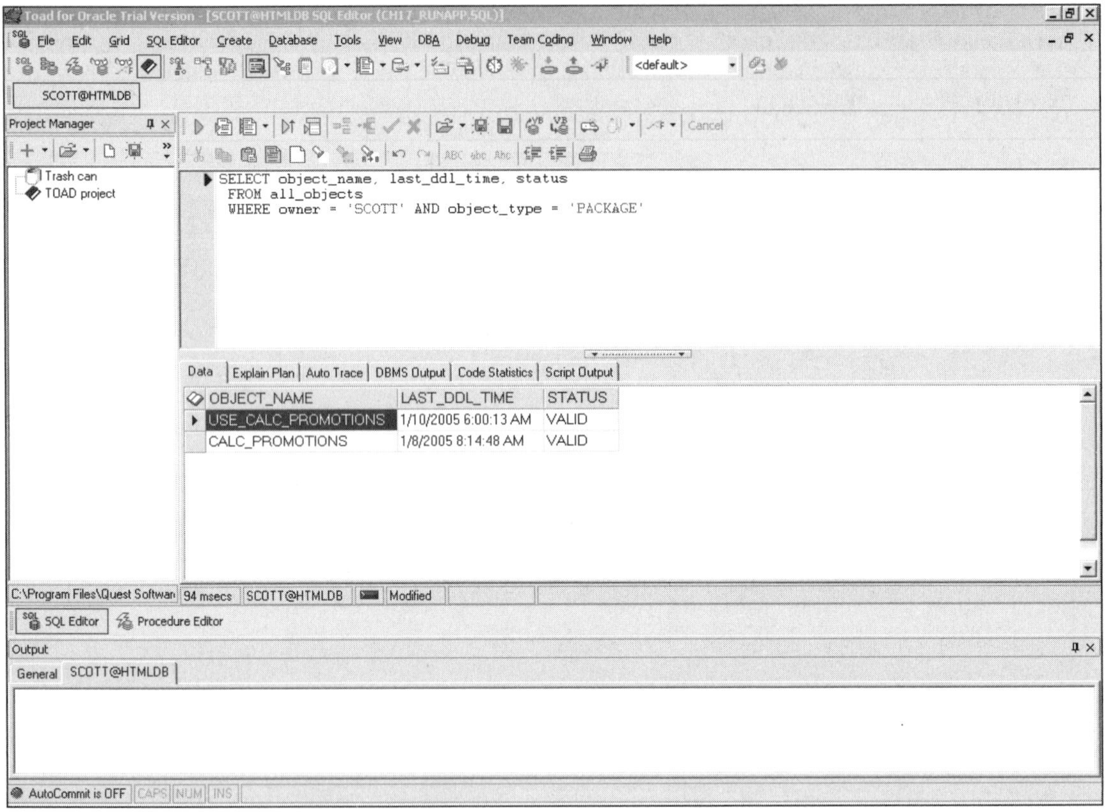

Figure 17-5: Breaking the cycle of dependency.

Although this example is somewhat trivial in terms of overall performance, if you are reusing functionality in program units a lot, the reduction in compilation can have an impact on overall performance. And eliminating the need to carefully recompile program units in a specific order makes it much easier to be more productive at your primary task: implementing logic.

Summary

PL/SQL packages extend the capabilities of the PL/SQL language. A PL/SQL package gives you the ability to define group program units together, both for organization purposes and to reduce the dependency of any particular program unit on any other one.

PL/SQL packages let you separate the interface for functionality from the implementation of that functionality, which not only makes it easier to maintain your code but also prevents users from getting unlimited access to data by keeping the data safe inside the package body.

18

Introduction to Java Database Programming

Earlier chapters have discussed the merits of the Oracle architecture and its ability to effectively store, protect, and manipulate data for a large number of users. While Oracle provides many tools to help populate and extract data from this store, a key requirement for developers is support of flexible, programmatic access to this data.

Oracle already supports many programming languages through its precompiler technology and other language interfaces (for example, COBOL, C, perl), so one could question why Java deserves special treatment. While discussions about the merits of one programming language versus another often degenerate into a fruitless debate, it is fair to open this discussion with two broad reasons in favor of Java:

- Java finally opens the door to standards-based, portable applications that can be written once and easily deployed on multiple databases or platforms. Open standards encourage innovation as vendors compete to differentiate in their implementation of the standards.
- Java is beyond just being a programming language — it is supplemented with the J2EE framework to provide a reusable component-based architecture.

Oracle has an impressive track record supporting open standards, and Java is a shining example. This chapter introduces some of the fundamentals of the Java architecture and benefits of Oracle's wide support for it in different development scenarios.

The first section runs through Java architecture basics. It briefly explains some of the language constructs, terminology, and common issues associated with Java and database programming. It is followed by a section describing Oracle's support for Java in a multi-tier architecture, which describes Oracle's JDBC support and models of Java programming against the database. The last section walks you through some concrete examples of Java database programming in an Oracle environment.

Java Architecture

Java has become a programming language of choice, as indicated by its rapid adoption by developer communities, educational institutions, and software vendors. More than just a programming language, Java is a platform that offers all the pieces needed to build complete applications, from the user interface to server-side business logic to data manipulation. This section provides a basic understanding of Java's architecture and some of the underlying terminology in context of database programming. It should be a familiar refresher to experienced Java programmers and is not intended to be a primer for object-oriented programming or basic Java language syntax.

Java: The Language

A programming language by itself is not the most significant factor in the building of efficient, error-free, reusable software systems. Java is no exception, but it does have some strong characteristics that contribute toward these goals.

First, Java is an object-oriented language, so the language naturally supports the following:

- **Encapsulation.** The ability to keep an object's data and methods that use the data together as part of the object
- **Inheritance.** The ability to take existing object-oriented code and easily extend its capability without code modification
- **Polymorphism.** The ability for all objects within an inheritance hierarchy to respond to a single request but with different implementation methods (or business rules)

Java borrows from the language syntax of C and C++ but reduces the complexity associated with these languages by providing a strong type-based system as well as managing storage and garbage collection for the developer. In essence, Java provides the power of object-oriented programming yet makes it easier, safer, and more productive to use than C or C++.

Java Virtual Machine and Bytecode

Java source code must be compiled before execution. Compiling the code converts it from text into binary bytecode, which is the instruction set that is understood by a Java Virtual Machine (JVM). Bytecode is portable across platforms, so it is not even necessary to recompile Java code when deploying on a different operating system, as illustrated in Figure 18-1.

At the heart of Java is the Virtual Machine. It is an abstract computer implemented in software that executes the bytecode. Defining the specification of a virtual machine and then implementing it on multiple platforms gives Java its cross-platform portability and many of its security and safety capabilities. Today there are JVM implementations on Win32, Mac OS, zOS (mainframe), Unix, and Linux flavors.

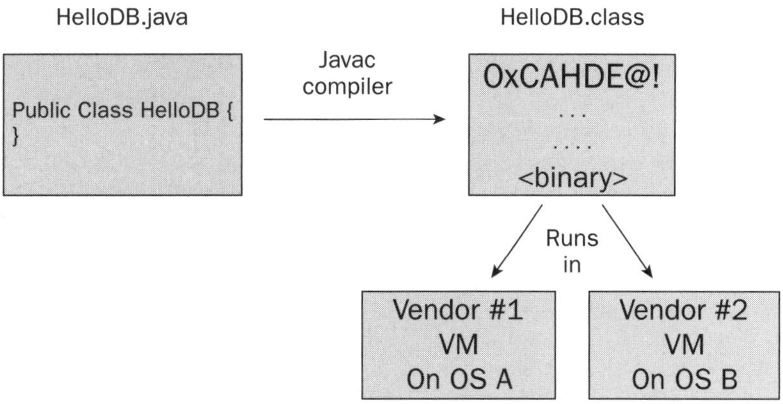

Figure 18-1: Relationship between Java source code, Java bytecode, and the Java Virtual Machine.

In addition to portability, the virtual machine simplifies the storage and creation of objects during runtime. This includes creating and allocating memory structures for arrays and new instances of objects. When the objects are no longer used, they are periodically cleaned up by a garbage collector within the VM. The VM approach provides a well bounded "sandbox" within which applications can safely execute. Over (a long enough period of) time, the VM ensures that there are no memory leaks and the sandbox is in a state of equilibrium. A sandboxed VM is ideal for server-side applications in a multithreaded environment, since it reduces the impact and occurrence of common programming errors (for example, accessing an array out of bounds or referencing a pointer in another application's memory space).

What about Performance?

Efficient memory management, garbage collection, and platform-independent interpreted bytecode are all positive attributes of Java. They are also the same reasons for claims about poor performance with the language. It's true this was an issue with early versions of the JVM. However, thanks to industry momentum, Java has made tremendous gains in improving relative performance over natively compiled languages.

A *just-in-time (JIT)* compiler is the default in most JVM implementations today. Depending on its implementation, most JITs would compile a method or class at a time into native code, as required, for faster execution. As of Java 1.2 and above, the reference implementation has included *Hot Spot*—a combination of JIT with a dynamic profiler to identity exactly when (point in time) and what (usage or code pattern) makes it most appropriate for the VM to bear the cost of compiling just in time. Vendors such as Oracle have also gone the extra step of providing *native compilers* for Java on their platform. A native compiler optionally compiles bytecode down to machine code for a particular platform—a one-time, predeployment operation that can provide a significant boost in runtime performance.

Given these improvements, there are numerous large-scale production Java sites and benchmarks that would show that Java is well established in mission-critical applications and performs equally to if not better than C/C++ in most conditions.

J2SE and J2EE

A byproduct of Java's rapid momentum has been a constant evolution and barrage of products, APIs, JVMs, vendors, and versions to contend with (all of which start with the letter J). To help understand the overall platform, you need to consider the different roles of Java usage—either as a programming language or as a part of the J2EE framework built with the Java programming language (shown in Figure 18-2). This means that all J2EE applications are Java applications, but not all Java applications are J2EE applications.

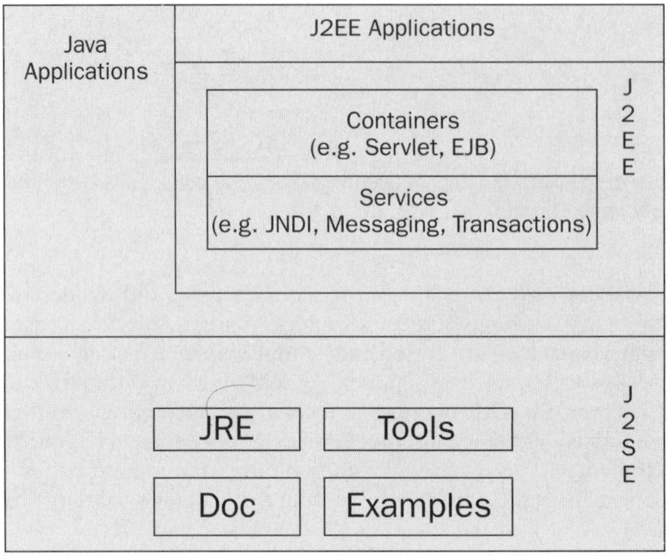

Figure 18-2: Relationship between J2SE and J2EE applications.

Java as a programming language consists of two key components:

- **A runtime environment.** The Java Runtime Environment (JRE) is an implementation of a JVM for a specific platform. A JRE is the minimum requirement to run any Java code, because it interprets the bytecode into native code for that platform.
- **A development environment.** Java 2 Standard Edition (J2SE) is a software development kit for Java. It consists of all tools (albeit command-line, not necessarily a full-blown, graphical, integrated development environment required to develop and deploy Java applications for a particular implementation platform. A J2SE distribution, at minimum, contains a JRE, a compiler, documentation, and optionally tools for code generation. The current production version of J2SE (and hence JRE) is 1.4. The next version will be J2SE 5.0, reflecting the new version numbers to be adopted.

Consider the development effort to build a nontrivial enterprise application. It would require code to connect to the database, manage transactions, manage security roles, and so on. While it is entirely feasible to build this infrastructure from scratch with the Java programming language, there will be limited portability, standardization, and reuse of that code outside of this particular development project.

Enter Java 2 Enterprise Edition (J2EE)—based on the Java language, which defines the key technologies required to build component-based, multi-tier enterprise applications. It is a framework that addresses typical enterprise application requirements, such as connecting to databases, transaction management, application security and roles, and distributed communication through standard APIs.

At the heart of J2EE are API specifications for creating platform-independent, reusable *components*. These components are deployed into J2EE *containers*. A container provides a comprehensive set of services to J2EE components, such as managing the life cycle of the component (for example, create, destroy, activate, passivate), managing concurrent access to the components, and ensuring load balancing and high availability. Leveraging the services provided by the container allows J2EE developers to concentrate on implementing application-specific business logic rather than low-level infrastructure or plumbing. The current production spec is J2EE 1.4.

The following J2EE technologies are most commonly used in the context of database programming:

- **Servlets.** Servlets are a standard way to build server side applications. Servlets have access to all the Java and J2EE APIs and support all Java logic. They are deployed in a J2EE servlet container, which provides runtimes services such as session handling and connection life cycle management.
- **Java Server Pages (JSPs).** Java Server Pages are a productive way for presentation-layer developers (for example, HTML, WML, or XML) to dynamically invoke components or business logic through embedded scripting tags. They separate the user interface from content generation, enabling developers to lay out or alter a page without impact on the underlying dynamic content. JSPs become compiled servlets and run in a J2EE servlet container.
- **Enterprise Java Beans (EJBs).** Enterprise Java Beans define the interface (what it does) and implementation (the logic) of a business component. They are bundled with declarative properties (XML configuration files) on how concurrent access, security, transactions, state management, and database persistence should be handled. EJBs are deployed into an EJB container, which provides the runtime services as configured.
- **Java Messaging Service (JMS).** JMS is a standard API for enterprise messaging. Messaging provides a reliable way for asynchronous exchange of business events across components, applications, and databases.
- **Java Database Connectivity (JDBC).** A standard interface for connecting Java applications to data sources. JDBC is based on the X/Open SQL Call Level Interface and was originally intended as a way to standardize connectivity to relational data sources. The standard allows individual providers to implement the API as a JDBC driver for a particular data source. Because of the popularity of the interface, there are now many implementations of JDBC to nonrelational data sources as well, such as CSV files, Excel spreadsheets, XML, ADABAS, and C-ISAM. By providing a JDBC driver, a vendor makes access to their data source appear like a relational data source and provides a standard means of accessing that data source.

Because of the ubiquity of database applications, the JDBC API is supported in both J2SE and J2EE environments.

Understanding Java Classes

Object-oriented programming languages are based on a *class*. A class defines the representation of some concept or things that share common characteristics. An instance of a class is commonly referred to as an *object*. A class definition can contain the following:

- **Attributes.** Variables (or data elements) that define the class
- **Methods.** Behavior associated with the class
- **Relationships with other objects.** An embedded aggregation or reference to another object
- **Identity.** A unique identifier for each instance of the class (or each object)

To provide some context for this discussion, consider a typical purchase order application. This example uses the existing relational tables (`order_items`, `orders`, and `product_information`) and constraints (primary and foreign keys) as defined in the sample OE schema. A subset of the relevant attributes from the table definitions is shown here.

```
Table ORDERS
 Name                                   Null?    Type
 ------------------------------------ -------- ----------------------------
 ORDER_ID                               NOT NULL NUMBER(12)
 ORDER_DATE                             NOT NULL TIMESTAMP(6) WITH LOCAL TIME ZONE
 ORDER_MODE                                      VARCHAR2(8)
 ORDER_TOTAL                                     NUMBER(8,

Table ORDER_ITEMS
 Name                                        Null?    Type
 ----------------------------------------- -------- ----------------------------
 ORDER_ID                                    NOT NULL NUMBER(12)
 LINE_ITEM_ID                                NOT NULL NUMBER(3)
 PRODUCT_ID                                  NOT NULL NUMBER(6)
 UNIT_PRICE                                           NUMBER(8,2)
 QUANTITY                                             NUMBER(8)

Table PRODUCT_INFORMATION
 Name                                        Null?    Type
 ----------------------------------------- -------- ----------------------------
 PRODUCT_ID                                  NOT NULL NUMBER(6)
 PRODUCT_NAME                                         VARCHAR2(50)
 LIST_PRICE                                           NUMBER(8,2)
 MIN_PRICE                                            NUMBER(8,2)
```

Figure 18-3 represents a possible class diagram to represent this example. A `Product` class is defined with attributes for the product name and price. It is good encapsulation practice to make the attributes themselves private and provide public *accessor* methods to read and write each attribute value (for example, `setProductName()` and `getProductName()`).

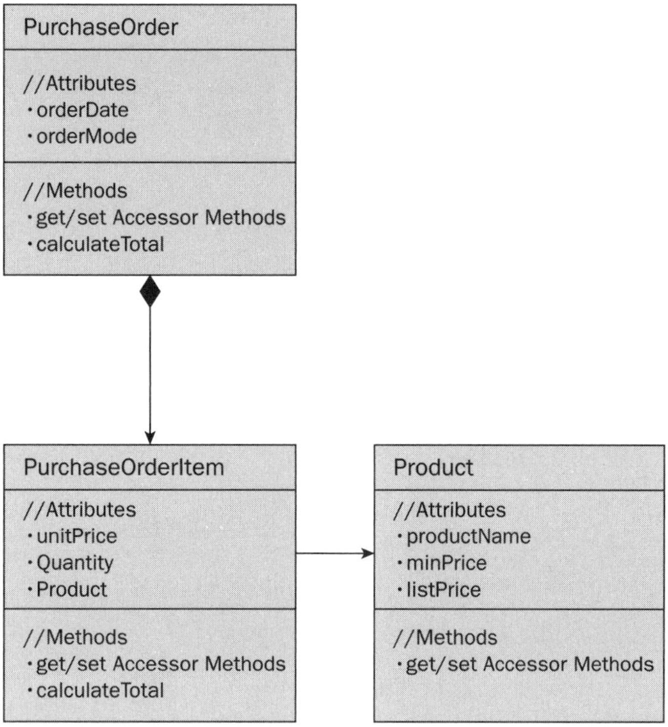

Figure 18-3: A set of Java classes to represent the Purchase Order application.

```
package ch18;

public class Product {

  // Attributes
  private int productId;
  private String productName;
  private float listPrice ;
  private float minPrice ;

  // Constructor
  public Product () {
  }

  public Product (int productId, String productName, float listPrice, float
minPrice)
  {
    setProductId (productId);
    setProductName (productName);
    setListPrice (listPrice);
    setMinPrice (minPrice);
  }

  // Accessor Methods
```

```
  public void setProductName (String productName) {
    this.productName = productName;
  }
  public String getProductName () {
    return productName;
  }

  // Other accessor methods not shown

}
```

Similarly, the `PurchaseOrderItem` class has attributes for `unitPrice/quantity` and an association (reference) to a particular `Product`. It contains a method for `calculateTotal()`, which would return the cost multiplied by quantity for a particular instance.

```
package ch18;
public class PurchaseOrderItem {

  // Attributes
  private Product product; // A reference to an existing Product object
  private float unitPrice;
  private int quantity;

  // Constructor and Accessor methods not shown.

  // Methods
  public float calculateTotal() {
    return (unitPrice * quantity);
  }
}
```

The `PurchaseOrder` class has attributes for order date and order mode (direct or online), as well as a method to `calculateTotal()` for the order. In addition, `PurchaseOrder` has a composition reference to one or more instances of a `PurchaseOrderLines`.

Note that the accessor methods for `PurchaseOrder` and `PurchaseOrderItem` have been removed from the following samples but are part of the complete listing accompanying the text.

```
package ch18;

import java.util.Iterator;
import java.util.Collection;
import java.sql.Timestamp;

public class PurchaseOrder {

  // Attributes
  Timestamp orderDate;
  String orderMode;      // "Direct" or "Online"
  Collection orderItems; // A nested collection of PurchaseOrderItems

  // Constructor and Accessor methods not shown.

  // Methods
```

```
    public float calculateTotal() {
      float total = 0;
      Iterator i = orderItems.iterator();
      while (i.hasNext()) {
        PurchaseOrderItem poItem = (PurchaseOrderItem) i.next(); // fetch next item
        total += poItem.calculateTotal();  // calculate cumulative sum of order total
      }
      return (total);
    }

}
```

Addressing Impedance Mismatch and Persistence Frameworks

The previous class diagram and Java code provide a simplistic but good start to represent the Purchase Order application. What's not shown is the detail of how the accessor methods read, write, and manage the relationships between the Java classes and how they are represented in the database. There is complexity in doing this, because of the underlying differences between the object paradigm (classes, business rules, complex relationships, and inheritance) and relational paradigm (tables, rows, columns, and primary and foreign keys). Beyond just the mapping of class attributes to database fields, there is significant complexity to manage sessions, transaction coordination across objects, and object cache synchronization with the relational database. These issues and differences in paradigms are collectively referred to as *persistence* issues, or the *object-relational impedance mismatch*. In this section, we discuss three possible ways to address the issue, summarized in Figure 18-4.

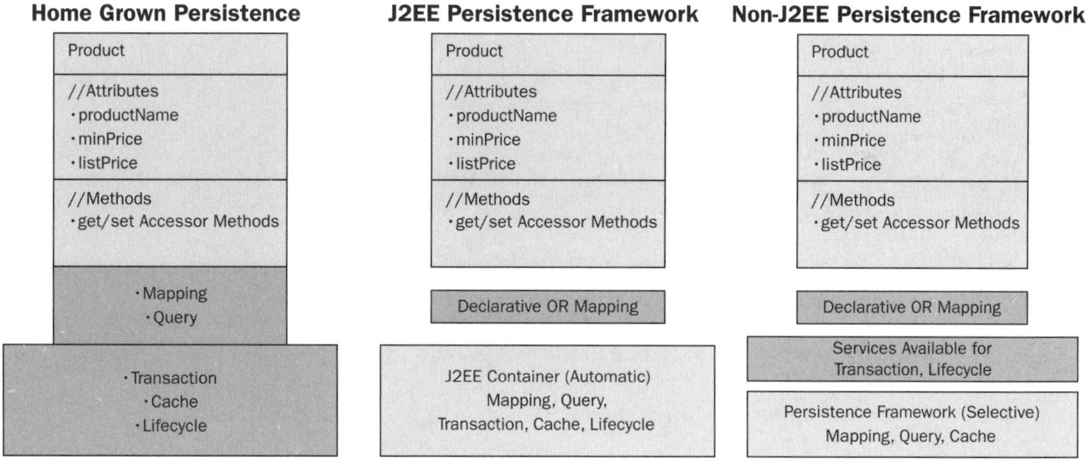

Figure 18-4: Three different approaches to resolving object-relational impedance mismatch.

A common approach to this problem is to use a home-grown persistence framework using Java Database Connectivity and Structured Query Language to support the necessary plumbing between Java classes and relational tables. For example, this would involve embedding JDBC and SQL code in each of the three classes defined previously to manage the mapping and query/update interactions with the database. Additional custom code will be required to manage transaction capability, object caching, and life cycle (when to read from database and write to database) aspects of the application. While this approach provides the maximum flexibility, the effort required to do this is often underestimated and the process will divert a developer's focus from the functional requirements of an application. It is only recommended for the simplest of requirements and even then to be used in conjunction with the Fast Lane Reader Java pattern (`http://java.sun.com/blueprints/patterns/FastLaneReader.html`).

The second approach — J2EE — addresses the persistence issue through Entity Enterprise JavaBeans (Entity Beans). Entity Beans represent a persistent business object that is deployed into an EJB J2EE container, together with declarative configuration details for transaction, query, and mapping properties. For the Purchase Order example, this equates to taking the three previous classes, supplementing them with some XML declarative configuration files, and deploying into a J2EE container. The container then manages all runtime aspects of the object. Entity Beans provide the benefit of handling all the plumbing requirements without any additional code and are (at least theoretically) portable across different vendors' container implementations. A drawback of Entity Beans is the extra overhead attached to the Java object by the container at run time (hence affecting runtime performance). Depending on the container implementation, there may also be very little room to control runtime behavior of the beans. Entity beans are not the answer for every persistent class, and it's recommended to use them in conjunction with the Session Facade Java pattern (`http://java.sun.com/blueprints/patterns/SessionFacade.html`).

A third approach to impedance mismatch is through a hybrid of the previous two. It involves the use of a persistence framework outside of a full-scale Entity Bean deployment (hence avoiding some of the added baggage). For the Purchase Order example, this would first require mapping the Java classes to the relational tables. These mappings are packaged and deployed as descriptor files together with the Java classes and the persistence framework library. At run time, the framework automatically handles the mapping, query/update, and caching of objects based on the descriptor contents. The Java classes can request additional services from the framework for transaction support and life cycle services. Two key benefits of this approach are as follows:

- ❑ The Java classes can remain pure business entities and do not require JDBC/SQL plumbing code embedded within them.
- ❑ A developer can selectively choose the services required from the framework, thus minimizing the overhead imposed by the framework.

This approach is only as good as the mapping flexibility and implementation provided by the persistence framework.

Impedance mismatch is a real issue, and all of the previous solutions have their places. There is no single right approach to the problem. Later in this chapter you will see how Oracle supports all three solution areas, depending on an application's requirements. There are also examples of using these methods to interact with a database. In Chapter 21, "Object-Relational Interactions with Oracle," we further address the issue using the database server's object-relational capabilities.

Oracle's Java Architecture

To put context around Oracle's support for Java and J2EE, it is useful to consider the set of BluePrints and best practices as defined by the J2EE Community (`http://java.sun.com/blueprints/enterprise/index.html`). The BluePrint defines an application model consisting of four tiers (see Figure 18-5): Client-Side Presentation, Server-Side Presentation, Server-Side Business Components, and

Enterprise Information Systems. It depicts Java and J2EE solutions at the first three tiers of the architecture, merely accessing databases in the fourth (Enterprise Systems) tier.

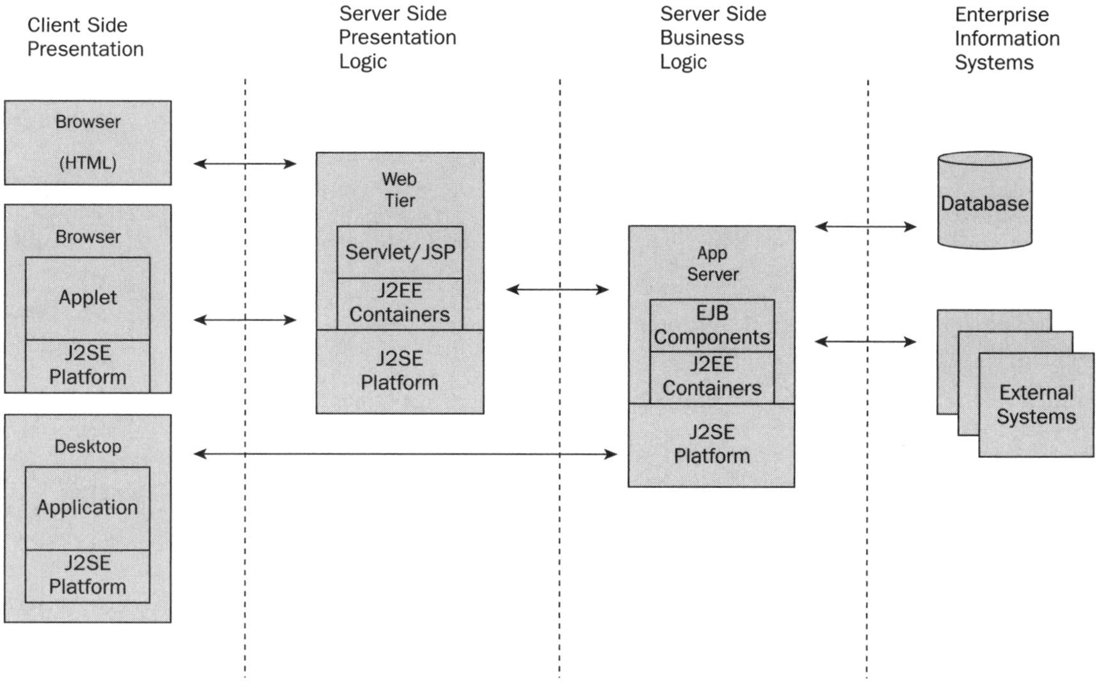

Figure 18-5: BluePrint application model as defined by the J2EE Community.

Oracle supports this application model with the following product components (Figure 18-6):

- **Oracle JDBC Drivers.** A range of drivers for different tiers, providing database connectivity through a standard API.
- **Oracle Application Server**. Specifically:
    - *Oracle Containers for J2EE (OC4J)*—A fully compliant set of J2EE 1.4 containers (servlet container, EJB container) and services (JNDI). The containers support both server-side presentation logic and server-side business logic tiers.
    - *OracleAS TopLink*—An object-relational mapping and database persistence framework.
- **Oracle Database (specifically the Java Option).** An embedded J2SE 1.4 platform and JDBC driver within the database. This feature is also referred to as OracleJVM or Oracle JServer.

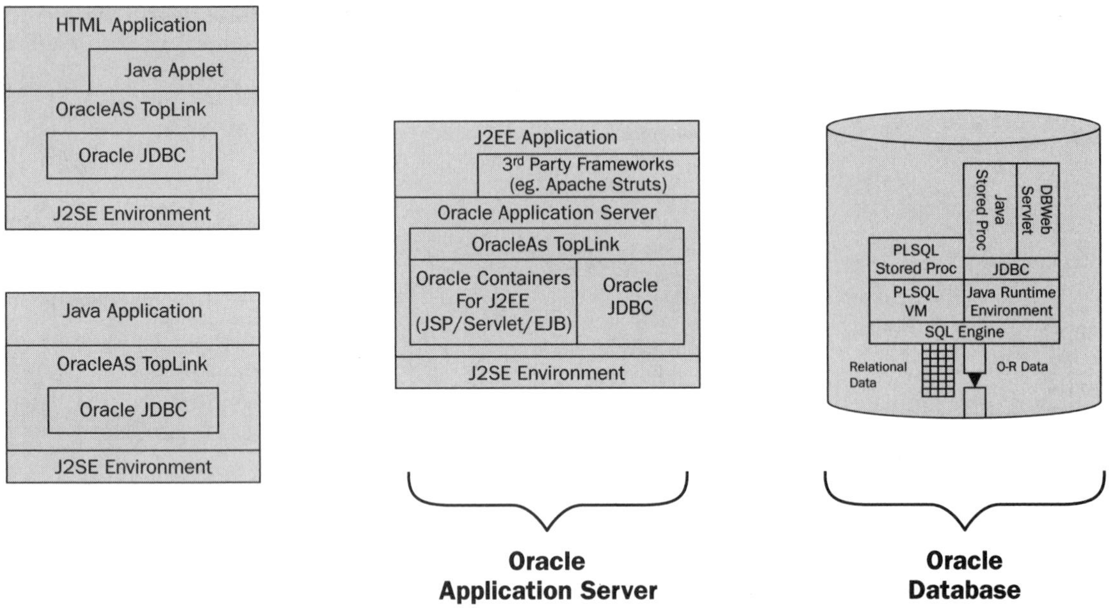

Figure 18-6: Oracle's Java architecture.

Oracle is unique in that it provides an end-to-end Java solution beyond the typical BluePrint application model, by supporting Java in all four tiers. Oracle's support extends beyond just accessing databases, by providing a full J2SE environment within the database as well.

The rest of this section addresses the two primary models of Java programming in an Oracle environment. The first model is for traditional applications that execute outside the Oracle database. These applications use JDBC or other Java frameworks that leverage JDBC (J2EE, OracleAS TopLink) to interact with the database. The second model addresses applications that execute inside the Oracle database, as Java Stored Procedures. Since both models rely on JDBC as a conduit to relational data, we first look at Oracle's support for JDBC and persistence frameworks.

JDBC and Persistence Frameworks

JDBC support is a mandatory requirement for Java database programming. The specification is designed to allow vendors to supply drivers that offer the necessary implementation for a particular database. Oracle supports four JDBC drivers (as shown in Figure 18-7), each suited for different applications and connectivity requirements. Not all drivers are available in all tiers of the BluePrint architecture.

- **Thin Driver.** Also referred to as Type IV driver per the JDBC specification, this is a 100 percent Java implementation of the Oracle TTC protocol using native sockets to converse with the database. The Thin Driver only supports the TCP/IP protocol and not other protocols of Oracle Net Services. This driver does not require any Oracle client-side libraries and is available in all tiers. However, the driver supports only a limited set of connection failover and high-availability features available to Oracle. It is recommended for use by applets and applications in the Client-Side Presentation tier.

- **OCI Driver.** Also referred to as Thick or Type II driver per the JDBC specification, this driver wraps the Oracle OCI C library. This driver requires the Oracle client installation and therefore is Oracle platform specific. It provides extensions to standard JDBC such as connection pooling and application failover by leveraging the OCI C library. This driver is recommended for use by components and services running in the application-server tier.
- **Server-Side Driver.** Sometimes referred to as KPRB driver in Oracle documentation, this driver supports Java code that runs inside an Oracle database and must access the same database — for example, a Java Stored Procedure or Java trigger. It allows the JVM to communicate directly with the SQL engine, all running within the same address space, so that network round-trips are not an issue.
- **Server-Side Thin Driver.** This driver offers the same functionality as the client-side Thin Driver, but it runs inside an Oracle database. It is used by server-side code — for example, a Java Stored Procedure or server-side Web service — to provide access to a remote database or a different session running on the same database.

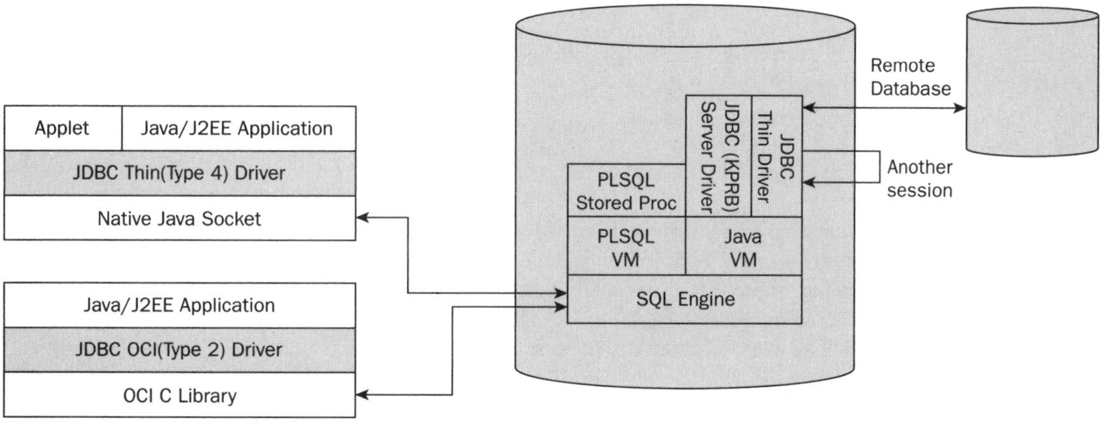

Figure 18-7: Oracle's JDBC driver support.

Because all the JDBC drivers are compliant to the same specification, there are few (if any) code differences when switching drivers. The key differences are in the following:

- The database URL specification. Details are provided in the "Connect to the Database" section later in this chapter.
- Support of extension features not explicitly defined by the JDBC spec (for example, high availability, connection failover).

Having multiple JDBC drivers provides flexibility for developers to build reusable Java applications that can be deployed across any tier of the architecture, with minimal code changes. PL/SQL programmers should be familiar with this cross-tier support.

Although it is the bread and butter of database applications, a pure JDBC approach to persistence can be verbose and involve a lot of mundane, repeated lines of code. For example, consider a Java class with 20 attributes mapped to a relational table. Reading this class from the database would require code to establish a connection and execute a query, followed by at least a call to each of the 20 accessor methods (`setAttribute()`) in the class. This is not effective in a large-scale project with many objects and database tables. A JDBC-only approach is rarely used in those situations. Complex applications will use a persistence framework such as Entity Beans or OracleAS TopLink to abstract database access code and minimize mundane API calls.

Entity Enterprise Java Beans (Entity Beans)

Oracle supports Entity Beans through Oracle Containers for J2EE. An entity bean is made up of four components:

- **Home interface.** A Java interface that defines the methods for retrieving a bean object (how to `create()` a new instance or `find()` an existing instance).
- **Component (or remote) interface.** A Java interface that defines the business methods that clients see and invoke (`calculateTax()` in the Purchase Order example).
- **Implementation (or Bean) class.** For entity beans, most of these methods are automatically generated by the container, except for the business methods defined previously.
- **Deployment descriptors.** Specific properties for the bean to identify data to be managed by the container.

The first three of these are standard across J2EE containers. The flexibility of mappings provided through deployment descriptors is the key differentiator across vendors.

Oracle can generate default mappings to existing or new database tables that automatically take into account referential integrity and cascading constraints. Oracle also supports one-to-one, one-to-many, many-to-one, and many-to-many relationships, where each relationship can be unidirectional or bidirectional. Mapping and deployment descriptors are XML files and can be edited manually. However, Oracle JDeveloper provides wizards to simplify the process.

It is beyond the scope of this chapter to explain all the features of Oracle's Entity Bean support — and probably not necessary, since OracleAS TopLink will become the default persistence manager for entity beans in the upcoming 10.1.*x* release of the application server. An example of how to use OracleAS TopLink follows in the next section.

OracleAS TopLink

OracleAS TopLink is based on the JDBC API and enables developers to persist Java classes in a relational database. It is an alternative way to interact with a database without writing JDBC code. OracleAS TopLink uses a graphical Workbench to read Java classes and one or more relational schemas and apply a set of mapping rules against them to generate mapping descriptors, as shown in the top half of Figure 18-8.

At run time, OracleAS TopLink provides services for persistence behavior, as shown in the bottom half of Figure 18-8. In other words, it generates the underlying JDBC code to read/write object instances from/to the database. OracleAS TopLink incorporates an object cache to improve performance by minimizing database access. This function allows for transactional and thread-safe access to shared database connections and cached objects across the application.

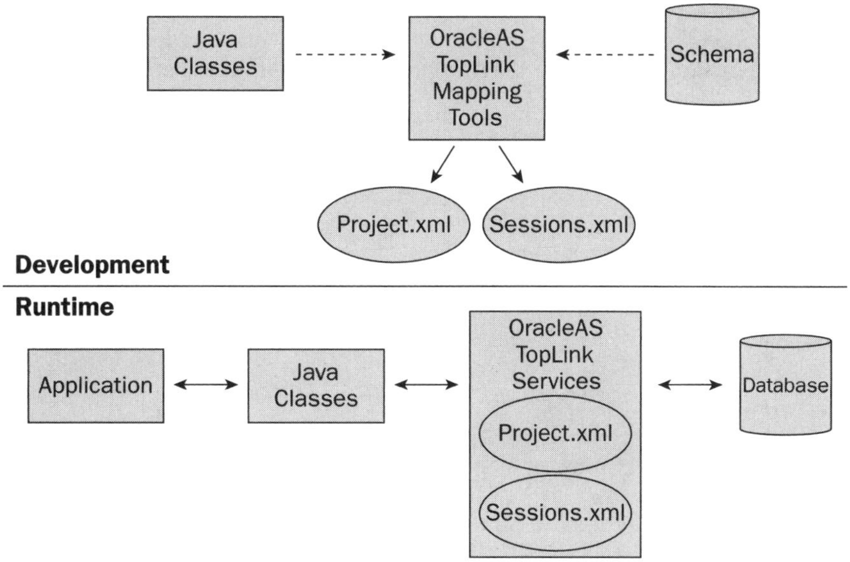

Figure 18-8: Using OracleAS TopLink.

Note that an added benefit of using a persistence framework is that the relationship between table and class is abstracted from each other through the descriptors. Keeping them separate makes it easier to manage schema evolution or business object changes over the life of the application. For example, if a schema changes, it can be remapped through the descriptors with no changes to the Java classes.

An example of how to use OracleAS TopLink to interact with a database is provided in the next section.

Java outside the Database

Given Oracle's support of Java across all tiers of a multi-tiered architecture, there are a myriad of ways to interact with the database, depending on an application's characteristics and requirements. Following are some of the common deployment architectures:

- **Java applet with JDBC (Thin only).** An applet running in a browser's VM making direct JDBC calls to the database. Useful in scenarios with small volumes of data exchange between client and server but with requirements for a richer (than HTML) user interface. It is suitable for use across a firewall.
- **Standalone Java application with JDBC.** A standalone Java application (invoked from `main()` method) making direct JDBC calls to the database. This is useful for intranet applications with requirements for a richer (than HTML) user interface. Since applications are physically deployed on client machines, this approach requires a configuration management strategy to roll out new versions of the application as it evolves.
- **Standalone Java application with OracleAS TopLink.** As before, except the application uses OracleAS TopLink instead of JDBC calls.

- **Web Browser with a servlet using JDBC.** A Web application deployed on an application server. The application server uses JDBC to interact with the database and renders HTML (or other markup language) presentation to the browser. A typical architecture for J2EE Internet applications.
- **Web browser with a servlet using Enterprise Java Beans.** As before, except the servlet uses Enterprise Beans instead of JDBC calls.
- **Web browser with a servlet using TopLink.** As before, except the application uses TopLink instead of JDBC calls.

All of these deployment architectures share an important characteristic: They use the JDBC API (directly or indirectly via a persistence framework) to access the database. Code examples are provided later in this chapter to illustrate these different approaches of accessing Oracle from outside the database.

Java inside the Database

The architecture of bytecode running on a virtual machine, providing portability and security, should be familiar to Oracle veterans. Oracle's support for virtual machines goes back even before Java existed. PL/SQL code is compiled into bytecode (referred to as pcode) and runs in a PL/SQL VM. The database manages independent sessions of these virtual machines and ensures that one failed session does not corrupt other sessions. Oracle has extended the PL/SQL innovation to Java and provides the benefits of an object-oriented language binding in the database.

Since Oracle 8*i*, the database engine has provided a runtime environment for Java objects by implementing a Java Virtual Machine in the same model as the PL/SQL Virtual Machine. The OracleJVM (previously JServer) runs in the same process space and address space as the RDBMS kernel, sharing its memory heaps and directly accessing the underlying data. Each database session appears to have its *own* virtual machine to execute Java code. In reality, however, all sessions share the same JVM but are allocated an individual and isolated session space within that VM. Oracle's session architecture means a smaller incremental memory footprint per session and that the OracleJVM inherits the linear scalability characteristics of the database.

The OracleJVM fully supports the entire core Java class libraries and data structures. Its programming environment consists of the following:

- Java Stored Procedures as a first cousin of PL/SQL stored procedures. Java Stored Procedures can be invoked from SQL or PL/SQL, or as triggers in the database.
- SQL access through server-side JDBC drivers.
- Tools and scripts to help develop, load, and manage classes in the database.

With J2SE support in the database, Oracle has added a new dimension to building standards-based applications. An enterprise can now reap the benefits of stored procedures (increased reuse, performance due to pre-compiled server code, security, and scalability) without having to implement them in a database-dependent language (e.g., PL/SQL, Transact-SQL). There can be standardization on Java and skill sharing between the DBA and application development side of the house. Oracle also supports native compilation of Java Stored Procedures, providing a performance boost at run time.

With each progressive database version, the OracleJVM has incrementally supported later releases of the J2SE specification. Oracle Database 10*g* 10.*x* supports J2SE 1.4—which means Java Stored Procedures can use any of the capability included in this version of the J2SE.

An example of how to develop and deploy a Java Stored Procedure in the database is provided later in the chapter.

Java and PL/SQL — Complementing Technologies

Since Oracle supports both languages as first-class citizens in the database, it begs the question, "When is Java more applicable over PL/SQL (or vice versa)"? Both PL/SQL (procedural) and Java (object-oriented) share some powerful concepts as programming languages but also contain some striking differences. Understanding the likeness between these languages is an important first step to understanding their respective positions and how Java fits in with database programming.

Impedance mismatch is not an issue for PL/SQL. By sharing a type system with the database, PL/SQL avoids the performance overhead associated with converting SQL data types to Java types. The language also supports database-oriented constructs (`cursors`, `records`) natively. These factors mean that PL/SQL can provide better performance and productivity for data-intensive programs.

Java is a good fit when writing complex business logic, especially if it is computationally intensive, instead of data-intensive. It is also very productive for bridging the data world with other technologies such as file IO, networking APIs, XML processing, J2EE, and Web service applications — for example, consider the logic required to bring in the XML results of a Web service interaction, parse the XML DOM tree, perform complex mathematical computation for each node in the tree using some relational data, and then update a table with the results.

Both Java and PL/SQL are suitable for database programming, each with its strengths and limitations. Oracle supports both languages seamlessly and has empowered a developer with the flexibility to choose the right language for each application or even module's requirements.

Building Sample Applications

Now that you have a firm understanding of Java technology and Oracle's support for it, this section walks you through some sample applications of using the different programming models discussed. The examples were developed on Windows XP, JDK 1.4.2_03, and OracleAS TopLink 10*g* (v 9.0.4.2) against Oracle Database 10*g* Enterprise Edition 10.1.0.2 (Win32)

Setting the CLASSPATH

The `CLASSPATH` is an environment variable or container setting that points to the list of libraries, components, and other applications required by the compiler. At the very least, database applications must point to the JDBC driver implementation to connect to the server. The driver version must coincide with the version of JVM used by the application. It must also be compatible with the version of the database server. It is recommended to use the JDBC drivers that ship with the same version of the database, located in <OH>/jdbc/lib. For the 1.4 JVM, the archive to include is ojdbc14.jar

The following command configures the `CLASSPATH` requirements in a Win32 environment for the examples in this chapter. It assumes <OH> is the database ORACLE_HOME and <TH> is the OracleAS TopLink installation directory.

```
SET
CLASSPATH=.;<OH>\jdbc\lib\ojdbc14.jar;<OH>\lib\mail.jar;<OH>\lib\activation.jar;<TH
>\toplink\jlib\toplink.jar;<OH>\lib\xmlparserv2.jar;%CLASSPATH%
```

In a Unix/Linux bourne shell environment, the equivalent command would be:

```
set
CLASSPATH=.:<OH>/jdbc/lib/ojdbc14.jar:<OH>/lib/mail.jar:<OH>/lib/activation.jar:<TH
>/toplink/jlib/toplink.jar:<OH>/lib/xmlparserv2.jar:$CLASSPATH
```

Java Application Using JDBC — Basic Ingredients

In this section you build the equivalent of a Hello World database application. It covers all the steps necessary to use JDBC to connect to the database, execute SQL, and process the results, namely:

- Import the relevant packages and classes
- Connect to the database
- Execute an SQL Statement
- Process the result set
- Release resources

While it is simplistic, this is a good starting point for understanding interactions with a database through the JDBC APIs.

Import Packages

At a minimum, a JDBC application must import `java.sql` to reference the standard APIs. It must also include the implementation classes provided by Oracle or a third-party JDBC vendor. The Oracle driver (ojdbc14.jar) provides its implementation in the `oracle.sql` and `oracle.jdbc.pool` packages. These packages also provide helper classes specific for access to an Oracle database.

```
import java.sql.*;
import javax.sql.*;
import oracle.sql.*;
import oracle.jdbc.pool.*;
```

Connect to the Database

A JDBC resource and a `Connection` handle is first required to interact with the database. In earlier versions (JDBC 1.0), this was achieved through registering and loading a JDBC driver with a `DriverManager`. JDBC 2.0 introduced a (`javax.sql`) `DataSource` to generically specify a database resource. Unlike `DriverManager`, `DataSources` can be bound to a Java Naming and Directory Interface (JNDI) so that once defined, the databases can be referenced by logical names for convenience and portability.

Oracle supports JDBC 2.0 in the 9.*x* and 10.*x* JDBC drivers. The 10.1 JDBC drivers support most of JDBC 3.0 spec as well. In the interest of forward compatibility, examples in the text will use `DataSource`, since `DriverManager` will be deprecated in JDBC 3.0.

A database URL is used to identify the JDBC driver type and properties to use in a connection. The database URL format is as follows:

```
jdbc:oracle:driver_type:[username/password]@database_specifier
```

The first part of the URL indicates the driver type to use. Supported choices are `thin`, `oci`, or `kprb` (server side only). A database specifier follows the URL, to uniquely identify the target database for the interaction. It can be specified a number of ways, depending on the driver. The table following lists the different ways to use `database_specifier`, depending on the JDBC driver.

Database Specifier	Supported Drivers	Example
Oracle Net connection descriptor	Thin, OCI	Same syntax as a tnsnames.ora alias entry. For example, `jdbc:oracle:thin:@(DESCRIPTION = (ADDRESS = (PROTOCOL = TCP)(HOST = cchellia-lap)(PORT = 1521))(CONNECT_DATA = (SERVER = DEDICATED)(SERVICE_NAME = O10G)))`
TNSNames alias	OCI	This syntax references an existing tnsnames.ora file entry. For example, `jdbc:oracle:oci:@O10G`
Bequeath	OCI	A blank `database_specifier` is used to request a bequeath connection using the OCI driver. For instance, `jdbc:oracle:oci`
Thin-style service name	Thin	Older JDBC driver versions used the Host:Port:SID syntax to a specific database. For example, `jdbc:oracle:thin:@cchellia_lap:1521:O10G`. While this is still supported, it is recommended to use the new syntax that is associated with a DB service name: Host:Port/Database_Service_Name, or `jdbc:oracle:thin:@cchellia_lap:1521/O10G`.
LDAP syntax	Thin	This syntax is applicable when an LDAP directory is used as a central store for net service names. The thin driver uses the LDAP protocol to query the directory and access the details required to make the connection. For example, `jdbc:oracle:thin:@ldap://ldap.us.oracle.com:7777/sales,cn=OracleContext,dc=com`.
Server side	KPRB	This is the syntax to fetch a connection from the server-side JDBC driver. Access to this connection is immediate, since the server-side driver is already connected and running within a database connection. Either of the following URLs are possible: `jdbc:oracle:kprb:` or `jdbc:default:connection:`.

This example uses `OracleDataSource`, which implements the `java.sql.DataSource` interface. In this case, the thin driver and connection syntax is used to access a connection within the `DataSource`.

```
// OracleDataSource implements java.sql.DataSource;
OracleDataSource ods = new OracleDataSource();
ods.setURL("jdbc:oracle:thin:@//cchellia-lap:1521/O10G");
ods.setUser("oe");
ods.setPassword("oe");

// Get connection from DataSource
Connection conn = ods.getConnection();
```

There is a subtle difference and benefit in using a `DataSource` and `DriverManager`, even though they both return `Connection` objects. The `DriverManager` returns a Connection object representing a physical connection to the database. `DataSource`, on the other hand, may return a connection from a pool of connections, providing seamless performance and HA capabilities.

In the 10*g* JDBC drivers, Oracle provides an *implicit connection cache*, with the ability to do the following:

- Cache multiple authenticated connections in the pool
- Refresh or recycle stale connections from the cache
- Associate user-defined attributes with connections and then retrieve connections from the pool based on these attributes or weights based on these attributes.

With these features, the implicit connection cache provides great flexibility on how connection pools are managed and cached—both key ingredients for scalability in a high-volume, high-throughput application.

Execute SQL

The `java.sql.Statement` interface is used to execute SQL against the database. Statements are created by calling `createStatement()` on the connection object.

```
Statement stmt = conn.createStatement();
```

Given a statement object, there are three ways to execute SQL, depending on the type of action requested:

- **`executeUpdate()` method.** Executes a given SQL statement, which may be an `insert`, `update`, or `delete` statement or an SQL statement that returns nothing, such as an SQL DDL statement. This method returns an integer: 0 for SQL statements that return nothing; >0 to indicate the number of rows affected by the SQL statement. For example, it would return `9` if the SQL statement was a `delete` statement that removed nine rows in the database.
- **`executeQuery()` method.** Executes a given SQL query, which returns a single `ResultSet` object. This is typically used for `select` statements.
- **`execute()` method.** This is not commonly used, but handy for situations where an SQL statement returns multiple results, for example, executing an unknown SQL string and not knowing if it is a query or update. If used, it must be followed by calls to `getResultSet()` or `getUpdateCount()` to access and process the results accordingly.

The code following shows an example of how to execute DML with a `Statement` object and print the result of number of rows affected by the SQL. When applied against the default table in OE schema, it should return that 21 rows were updated.

```
int result = 0;
result = stmt.executeUpdate("UPDATE product_information SET category_id = 99 WHERE
category_id=17");

// 21 rows should be affected.
System.out.println("Number of rows affected: " + result);
```

Here is another example, this time executing a query:

```
ResultSet rset = null;
// The query string below should be on a single line.
// It has been split across two lines for clarity.
rset = stmt.executeQuery("SELECT product_id,product_name,product_description
                          FROM product_information WHERE category_id=16");
```

An SQL statement that is executed more than once in an application is most efficient as a stored procedure in the database. This provides for best utilization of server caching and efficient execution of that statement in the server. JDBC specifies two other subinterfaces of a statement to cater for precompiled and stored procedures:

- `PreparedStatement` — An interface that represents a pre-compiled SQL statement on the client side. This is useful when invoking an SQL statement repeatedly from a client application and no stored procedure exists on the database server.
- `CallableStatement` — An interface used to execute stored procedures in the database.

The code following shows an example of using a `PreparedStatement`. This example could be accomplished using two slightly different SQL strings with `Statement.executeQuery()`, as shown previously. Instead, with a `PreparedStatement` it requires fewer lines of code. It is also more efficient, since the query is only parsed once and memory structures are only created once. The `PreparedStatement` is then executed twice with different values (as bind parameters).

```
PreparedStatement pstmt = null;
pstmt = createPreparedStmt(conn,"UPDATE product_information SET category_id = ?
WHERE category_id=?");

// 21 rows should be affected
pstmt.setInt(1, 99);
pstmt.setInt(2, 17);
System.out.println("Number of rows affected: " + pstmt.executeUpdate());

// 10 rows should be affected
pstmt.setInt(1, 98);
pstmt.setInt(2, 16);
System.out.println("Number of rows affected: " + pstmt.executeUpdate());
```

An alternative (ideal) solution would be to create a database stored procedure that accepts both the parameters and then use a `CallableStatement` to invoke the procedure. This may not be possible if the developer does not have access to the underlying database schema. The syntax for a `CallableStatement` is very similar to that of a `PreparedStatement`.

An important consideration when using either `PreparedStatement` or `CallableStatement` is the use of bind parameters. A bind parameter is a placeholder for a literal string within an SQL statement. Consider for example, the following query:

```
select * from product_information where product_name = 'something'
```

If this statement will be used repeatedly, substituting 'something' with other values, then each query will be considered a different SQL statement – incurring a server-side performance overhead. However if the literal string is substituted with a bind parameter as shown below, then the server will cache the access path for the query in the Oracle Shared Pool and use the same path repeatedly for each invocation, substituting the bind parameter as necessary.

```
select * from product_information where product_name = '?'
```

It is a best practice to use bind parameters for all literals, especially when there is a large number of possible values for the literal string.

Most method calls on a JDBC statement involves a trip across the network to the database. To minimize the network round-trips, JDBC supports *statement batching*. This requires explicitly adding statements to a batch and at some point executing the batch. In the example following, all three insert statements will be batched into a single database round-trip.

```
Statement stmt = conn.createStatement();
stmt.addBatch("INSERT INTO product_information (product_id) VALUES (50); ");
stmt.addBatch("INSERT INTO product_information (product_id) VALUES (51); ");
stmt.addBatch("INSERT INTO product_information (product_id) VALUES (52); ");
stmt.executeBatch();
```

Batch updates are an effective way to improve the performance of a database application, but its adoption has been limited by a number of factors. First, the API requires a developer to explicitly manage the aggregation of requests into batches and then to optimize the size of the batches. Both factors add complexity to the code. And even with the added complexity, drivers are not required to implement this feature, so the effort may not result in any benefits!

Oracle addresses these concerns in its JDBC drivers. It supports (explicit) batch updates per the specification and the example shown previously. In addition, Oracle has extended its support by also providing implicit batch processing. In this model, the JDBC connection automatically accumulates the operations and will execute the batch based on a (configurable) threshold. The result is a solution that is very simple for developers to use (it is implicit and requires no code changes!) and flexible based on an application's requirements.

Statement batching and Oracle update batching provide minimal benefit with the KPRB JDBC driver, since the driver already runs in the database VM and does not incur network round-trips.

Process Results

Results from executing a database statement are returned in the form of a (`java.sql`) `ResultSet` — a two-dimensional structure of the rows and columns from the query response. A `ResultSet` maintains a cursor pointing to current row of data, initially the first row of the results. The `next()` method moves the cursor to the next row and can be used in a loop until it returns false. Only one `ResultSet` object per `Statement` object can be open at the same time.

```
while (rset.next()) {
  System.out.print(rset.getInt(1) + ", ");                        // product_id
  System.out.print(rset.getString("PRODUCT_NAME") + ", ");  // product_name
  System.out.println(rset.getString(3));                      // product_description
}
```

The interface provides getter methods (`getInt()`, `getString()`, etc.) for retrieving column values from the current row. Values can be retrieved using either the index number (starting from 1) of the column or the name of the column (case-insensitive). In general, using the column index is more efficient. The previous code shows examples of using both methods:

- `getInt(1)` accesses the first result column of the query (`product_id`), which is an integer.
- `getString("product_name")` accesses the result column called "`product_name`" (or column 2) from the query as a string.

Release Resources

Finally, it is just good programming practice to release resources when done with them. Failure to do so increases the potential for memory leaks in the client application. It also has an impact on the server, since processes are not released and may prevent other users from login when a threshold is reached.

Result sets, statements, and connections all have a `close()` method, which should be called to release the resources.

```
// Release Resources
rset.close();
stmt.close();

pstmt.close();
conn.close();
```

Java Application Using OracleAS TopLink

This example shows how to map a Java class to a relational table using OracleAS TopLink. It uses the `Product` class defined in the previous section and the `product_information` table from the OE sample schema. It follows with a number of ways to access and manipulate object instances (database rows) using the persistence services of OracleAS TopLink. The goal is to focus on the Java programming aspects of using OracleAS TopLink, rather than the mapping types supported by the framework. The Java code is similar regardless of the mapping types employed, which is the beauty of using a framework to hide the complexity.

The following steps are required to build this example:

- Create OracleAS TopLink mappings
- Create OracleAS TopLink session information
- Build the controller application
- Package and deploy

Create OracleAS TopLink Mappings

OracleAS TopLink provides a Mapping Workbench GUI to map Java class attributes to database table columns. The Workbench provides a number of intuitive automatic mapping tools to simplify the process of matching the class to the table:

1. Import existing Java classes and generate a set of tables to match the class structure.
2. Reverse engineer an existing database schema and generate Java classes that match the schema.
3. Import existing Java classes and reverse engineer an existing schema and match them based on the underlying attribute/column names and database constraints.

In each case, the developer can modify the results of the automatic mapping to suit the exact requirements of the application. In this example, the third approach is used, since there is an existing Java class and database schema.

To start, click on File→New Project. At the prompt enter a database name ("O10G") and select Oracle as the platform. When prompted, select a location and filename for the project (c:\src\tl\CH18.mwp).

Click on the O10G database icon in the Navigator window (see Figure 18-9). Click the Add button to add a defined login (LocalO10G). This configures JDBC details to connect to the database. Modify the URL, username, and password fields to match your database.

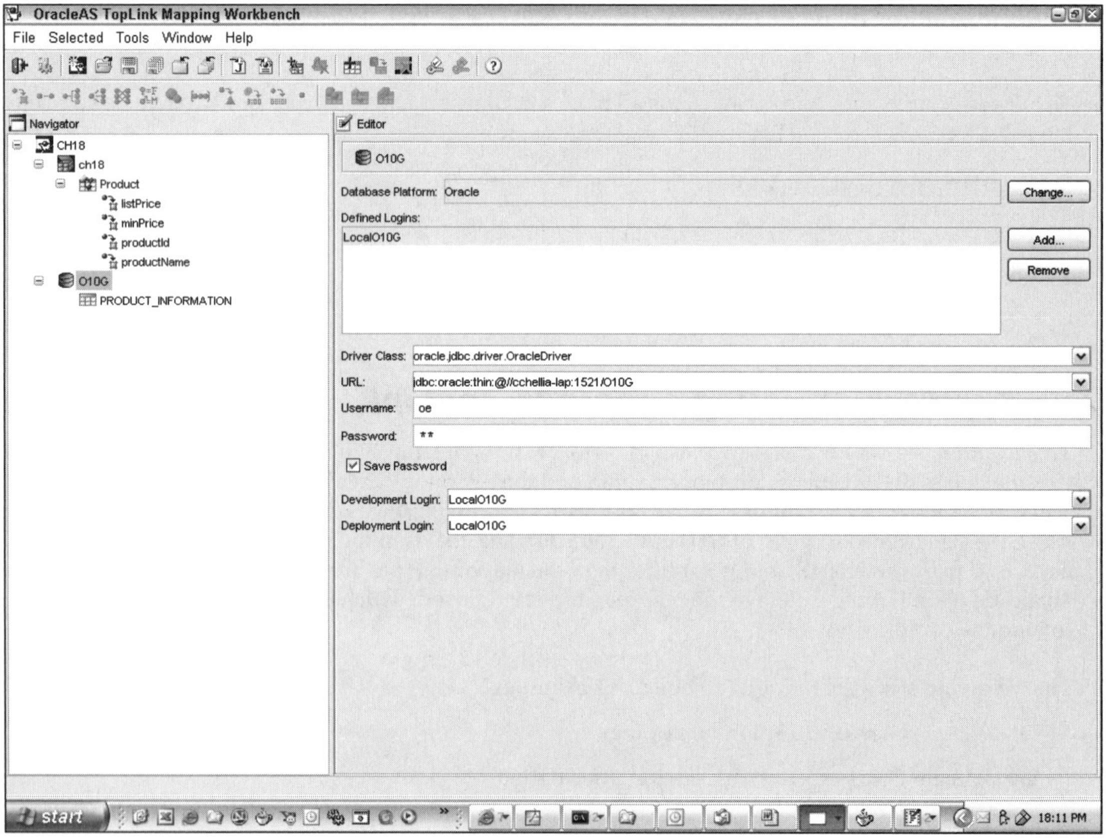

Figure 18-9: Creating a database connection in OracleAS TopLink.

Right-click on the O10G database icon in the Navigator window and select Log In to Database. Right-click on it again and select Add or Update Existing Table from Database. Enter a pattern name of "`%PRODUCT` and click on Get Table Names. Select the `product_information` table and click OK to close the dialog.

Select the `product_information` table in the Navigator and notice that OracleAS TopLink has reverse engineered the table structure, including constraints, from the database (see Figure 18-10).

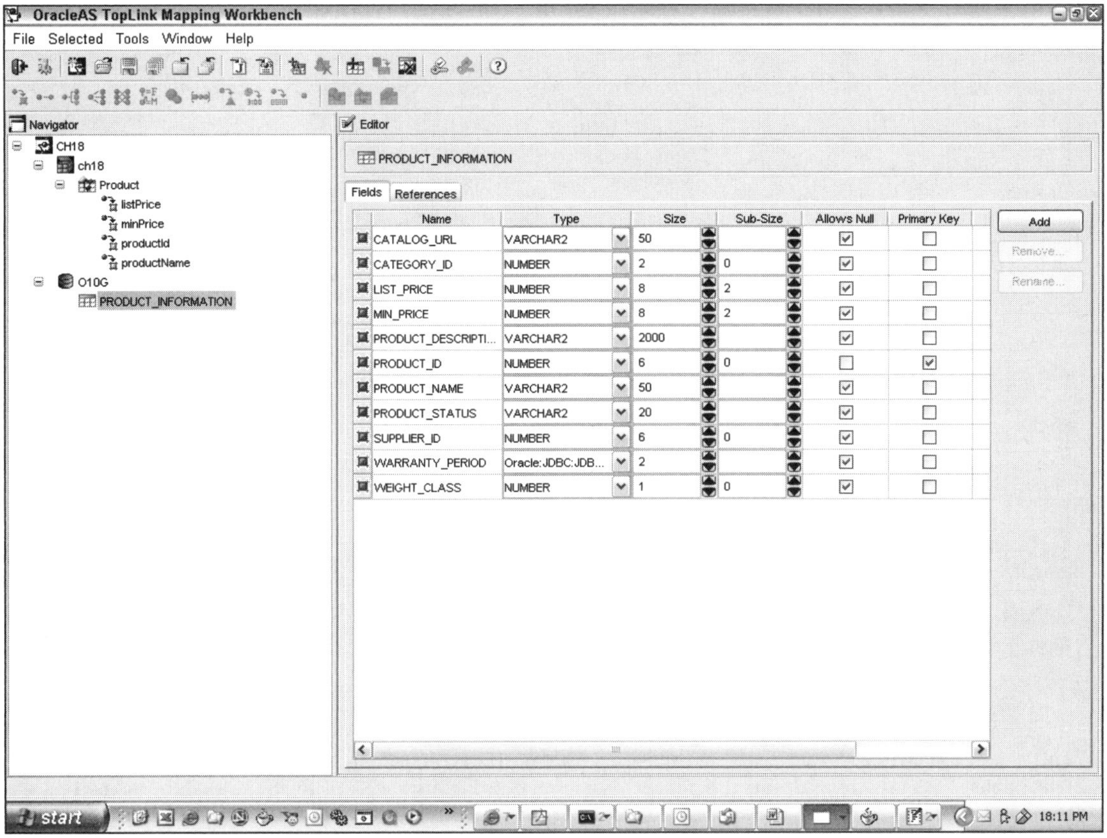

Figure 18-10: Browsing a (reverse engineered) table in OracleAS TopLink.

Select the project in the Navigator window and click the General tab. Click on Add Entries and add two `CLASSPATH` entries (see Figure 18-11) — the Oracle JDBC drivers (for example, `<OH>/jdbc/lib/ojdbc14.jar`) and the location of the compiled Java classes for this project (for example, the location of the `ch18.Product.class`).

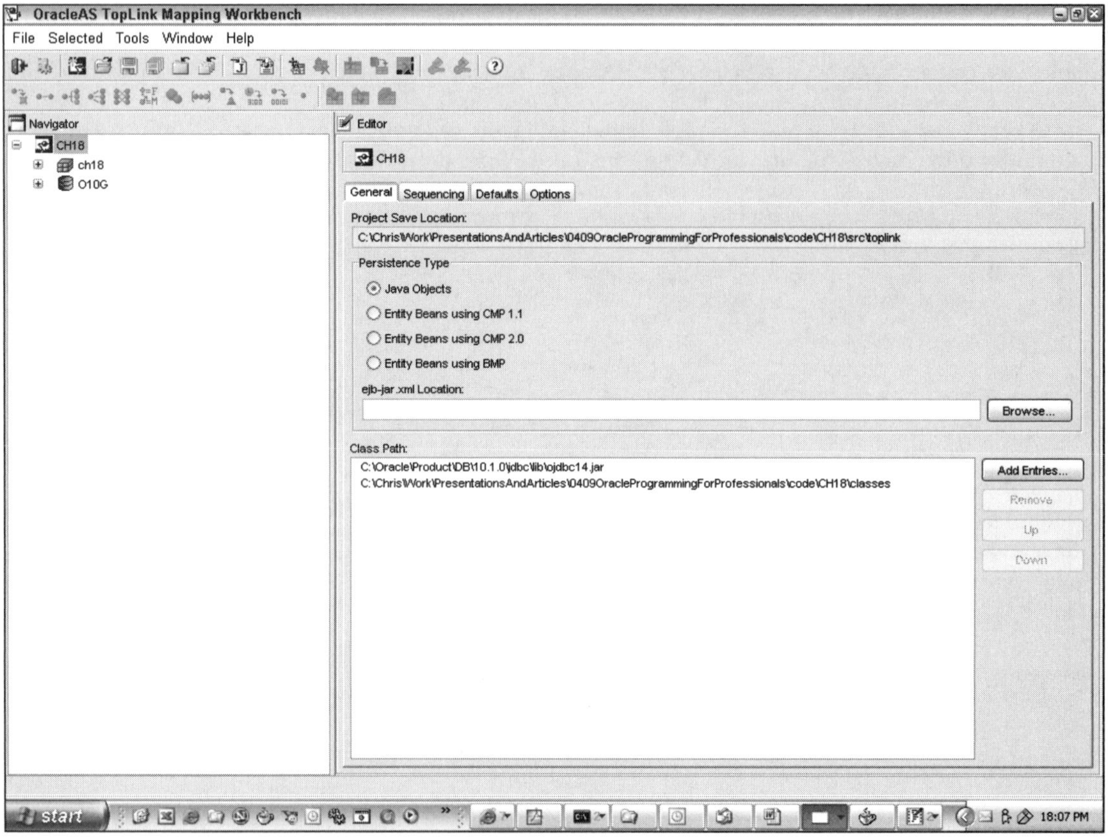

Figure 18-11: Adding CLASSPATH entries in OracleAS TopLink.

Right-click on the project in the Navigator and select Add or Refresh Classes. Browse to the ch18 package and select the ch18.Product class. In the Navigator window, select the newly added Java class. In the Descriptor Info tab, drop down the list for Associated Table and select PRODUCT_INFORMATION (see Figure 18-12).

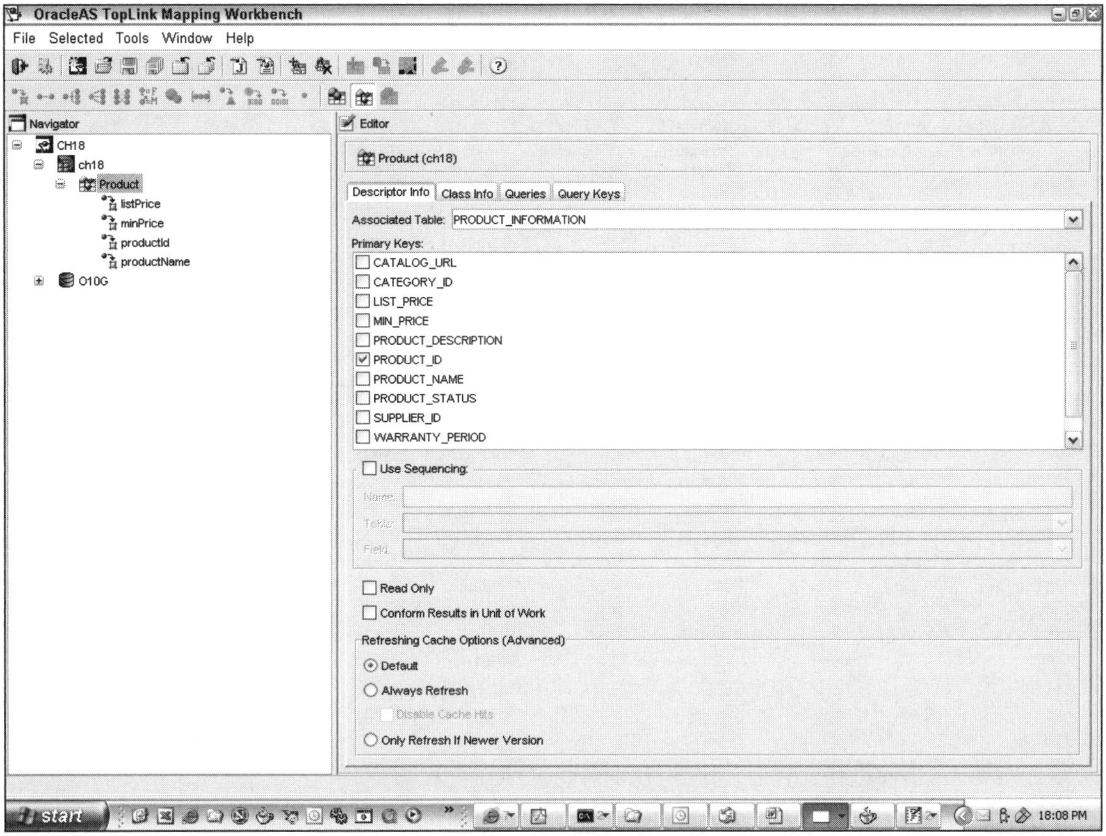

Figure 18-12: Associating a Java class to a table in OracleAS TopLink.

Right-click on the Product class in the Navigator and select Auto Map. Given the simplicity of the class and table structure, the default mapping is 100 percent correct. If it wasn't correct, a developer can continue to refine the model.

Mapping is now complete. To export the Project Deployment XML, right-click on the project and select Export | Project Deployment XML (see Figure 18-13).

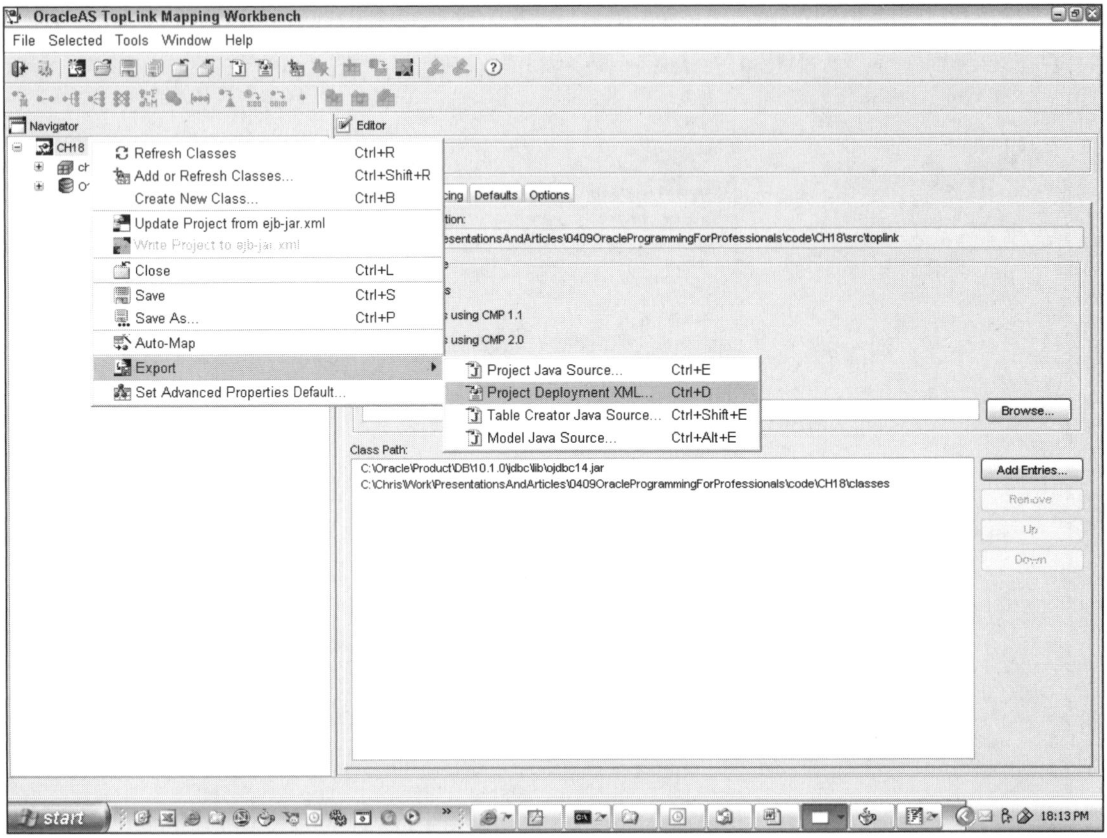

Figure 18-13: Exporting an OracleAS TopLink project for deployment.

Create OracleAS TopLink Session Information

A session represents the connection between an application and the database. OracleAS TopLink provides different session classes, optimized for use in different tiers of the architecture. Session types range from a simple database session providing one user with one connection to the database, to the session broker that provides access to several databases for multiple clients. Session configuration info is stored in the sessions.xml file. This file can be manually edited or managed through the OracleAS TopLink Sessions Editor as shown in Figure 18-14.

Click on File | New to launch a new Sessions Editor. Leave the default name (sessions.xml for the new file. Edit the Session Name field to be something descriptive of the database in use (localO10G).

Select the new session name (localO10G) in the navigator. Select the General tab and Click on the Login icon. Modify database connection URL and settings to access the database in use. Save the sessions file (File | Save).

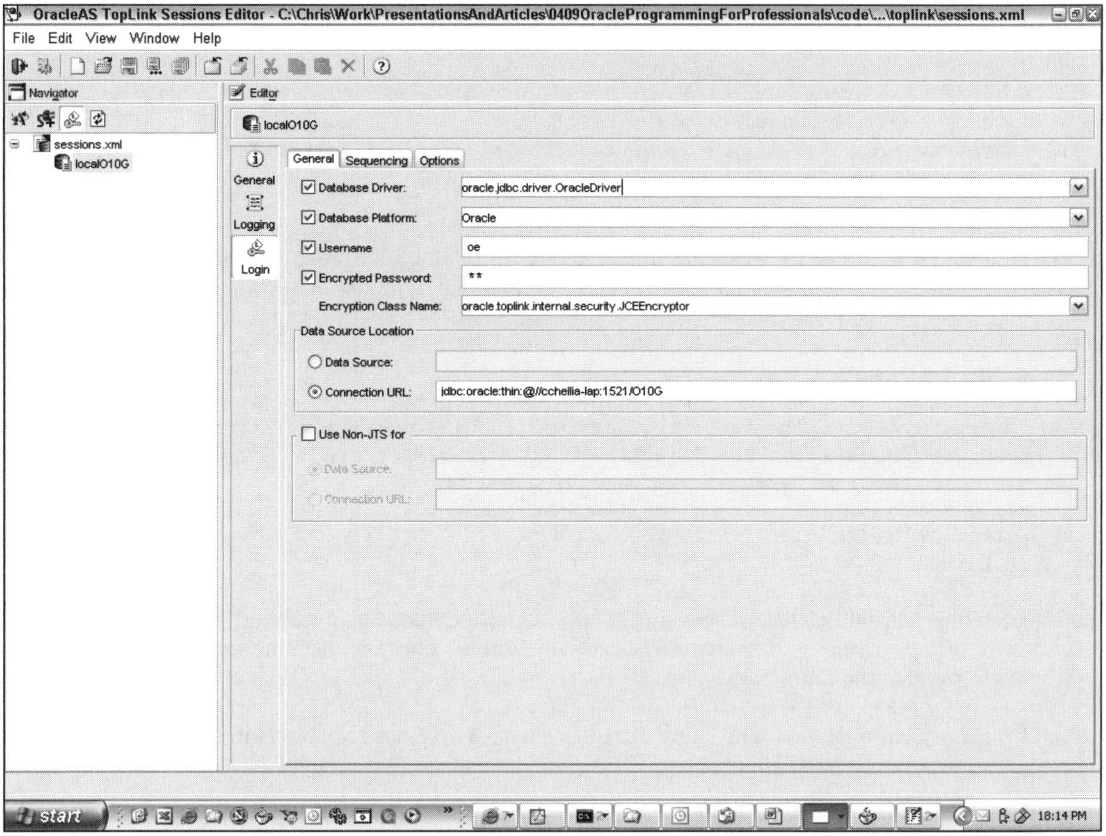

Figure 18-14: OracleAS TopLink Sessions Editor.

Build the Controller Application

The previous two sections completed the application mapping. The next step is to write a Java application that uses the mappings. This section walks you through a standalone Java controller application (TopLinkProductBrowser.java) to use the mappings and session files created previously and access the objects from the database. This code is just as applicable if the controller is a servlet in a multi-tier application architecture.

The program first creates an OracleAS TopLink session to the database. This is the same session name as created in the Sessions Editor shown previously in Figure 18-14 ("localO10G").

```
Session session = SessionManager.getManager().getSession("localO10G");
```

The `Session` object encapsulates a JDBC connection and provides helper methods to read instances from the database. For example, with a single line of code, this helper method reads all rows from the `product` table. For each row, it instantiates a `Product` object with the row values and places that object into a list (collection). As it reads the information from the database, OracleAS TopLink is also populating its local cache, so that this information is accessible to other sessions running in the same Java VM. That's a lot of free plumbing with one line of code!

```
List allProducts = session.readAllObjects(ch18.Product.class);
```

It is now a simple matter of iterating through the list of object instances to print their attributes.

```
Iterator iterator = allProducts.iterator();
while (iterator.hasNext()) {
  Product p = (Product) iterator.next();
  System.out.println("[" + p.getProductName() + "] [" + p.getMinPrice() + "] [" +
p.getListPrice() + "]");
}
```

The next step is to use an `Expression` to selectively find a single instance of an object based on a search criterion. This is the database equivalent of a doing a `select` with a `where` clause specifying predicates. OracleAS TopLink provides an `ExpressionBuilder` class for this construct.

```
Product p = null;
ExpressionBuilder builder = new ExpressionBuilder();
Expression e = builder.get("productName").equalsIgnoreCase("Sharpener - Pencil");
p = (Product) session.readObject(ch18.Product.class, e);
// The command below should be on a single line.
// It has been split across two lines for clarity.
System.out.println("[" + p.getProductName() + "] [" + p.getMinPrice() + "] [" +
 p.getListPrice() +
```

Given an object instance this last step shows how to update that object within the scope of a transaction and committing changes to the database. OracleAS TopLink encapsulates transactions in a Unit of Work (UOW) to provide the following:

- **Transaction context.** The UOW executes changes on clones of objects in its own internal cache until commit is called.
- **Transaction demarcation.** The UOW supports client (explicit) demarcation or demarcation within a J2EE container.
- **Isolation.** UOW supports optimistic locking, read locking and pessimistic locking within the scope of the object clones it works with.

A UOW is acquired from the session, to demarcate the start of a transaction.

```
UnitOfWork uow = session.acquireUnitOfWork();
```

Each object that will change in this transaction should be registered with the UOW. Registering the object returns a clone that is isolated to this transaction.

```
Product pClone = (Product) uow.registerObject(p);
```

Changes should be made to the clone instance of the object.

```
pClone.setMinPrice(minPrice);
pClone.setListPrice(listPrice);
```

When the UOW is committed, OracleAS TopLink will flush the changed attributes from the clones back to the database table and update its cache accordingly.

```
uow.commit(); // or rollback() if necessary
```

Package and Deploy

To package the application, group the following files into a Java archive (JAR):

- **Business entities.** The pure business Java classes (for example, the `Product` class).
- **The Controller application.** In this case, it is TopLinkProductBrower.java.
- **Project deployment XML file.** The output XML from the Mapping Workbench as shown previously in Figure 18-13.
- **Sessions XML file.** The output XML from the Sessions Editor as generated previously in Figure 18-14.

Append the JAR to the `CLASSPATH` configured earlier in this section, and the application is ready for execution from the command line:

```
java ch18.TopLinkProductBrowser
```

Java Stored Procedures

This section walks you through examples of how to write and deploy a Java Stored Procedure in the database. Two stored procedures are defined in the OE schema:

- `sendMail` — The JavaMail API to send mail from a stored procedure in the database. While there are other ways to send mail from an Oracle database (PL/SQL utl_mail, cgi callouts, etc.), this example illustrates the ease of using standard Java APIs from within the database.
- `alertListPriceChange` — An example of a trigger, based on a Java Stored Procedure, which uses the internal JDBC driver to interact with SQL data.

Verify the OracleJVM installation

Before working with Java in the database, you have to ensure that the OracleJVM is installed and configured. To verify this, you can start SQL*Plus and ensure the banner includes the OracleJVM (or JServer) option information, as shown here:

```
SQL*Plus: Release 10.1.0.2.0 - Production on Sun Dec 19 18:24:17 2004
Copyright (c) 1982, 2004, Oracle.  All rights reserved

Connected to:
Oracle Database 10g Enterprise Edition Release 10.1.0.2.0 - Production
With the Partitioning, OLAP and Data Mining options

JServer Release 10.1.0.2.0 - Production
```

If it does not show, then you can initialize the OracleJVM by using the Oracle Database Configuration Assistant (DBCA) or manually with the following steps. This is a one-time execution to install and configure the J2SE instance within an Oracle database. A large amount of resources is required for the configuration, because it loads and resolves more than 8,000 Java classes that make up a JRE instance.

1. Set the `java_pool_size` to be 50 MB (or more) and `shared_pool_size` to be 70 MB (or more). After the installation, these parameters can be dropped to a minimum of 20 MB and 50 MB, respectively.
2. Ensure the SYSTEM tablespace has at least 50 MB of free space.

3. Shut down and restart the database instance to reflect the parameter changes.
4. Connect as SYS AS SYSDBA in a new SQL*Plus session.
5. Run `<OH>\javavm\install\initjvm.sql`.

Depending on the version of Oracle in use, it may not be necessary to restart the database instance in step 3 above if the `ALTER SYSTEM SET` *command is used.*

Methodology and Concepts

Although the OracleJVM is 100 percent compatible with the Java VM and language specifications, it runs within a database session and therefore introduces a number of different concepts and deployment methodologies. We begin with a comparison.

A traditional J2SE environment will access Java sources, classes, and resources (for example, JAR files and properties files) from a set of locations on the file system defined by the `CLASSPATH` environment variable. When a class is executed (for example, `java <my_class_name>`), the VM interpreter will invoke the `static void main()` method in that class as a process on the operating system.

In an OracleJVM environment, the Java source, classes, and resources must first be loaded as schema objects into the database. With everything as schema objects, the role of `CLASSPATH` is replaced by a *resolver spec* to specify one or more schemas to search for source. Resolver specs are granular down to each class, unlike `CLASSPATH`, which is global to all classes. The entry point for a class is no longer assumed to be the `main()` method—any static method within the loaded class can be *published* as an entry point. Published entry points can then be *invoked* directly from the call level.

So the development methodology is this: load, resolve, publish, and invoke.

While OracleJVM calls for a slightly different deployment methodology, it is for good reason. The architecture provides granular control (resolver spec per class) and flexibility (multiple static entry points)—themes that are consistent for other aspects of the OracleJVM as well, for example, authentication and security definitions. And, of course, it is still standard Java code!

The Code

The first class, `JavaMail.java`, defines a `sendMail` method with the usual suspects as parameters. Note that the code should be modified before use to point to an accessible SMTP gateway in your organization. The rest of the implementation is trivial JavaMail code.

```
package ch18;

import javax.mail.*;
import javax.mail.internet.*;
import java.util.*;

public class JavaMail {

  public static String sendMail(String from, String to, String cc,
                                String subject, String message) {

    String returnMsg = "OK!";

    Properties props = System.getProperties();
    // SMTP hostname.  Substitute this with local Host Name/SMTP Server Name
```

```
    String hostSMTP = "your.smtp_gateway.com";
    props.put("mail.smtp.host", hostSMTP);

    // Initiate an SMTP session
    Session sessionSMTP = Session.getDefaultInstance(props, null);

    sessionSMTP.setDebug(false); // Enable the debug mode

    try {
      // Create a New message and set properties
      MimeMessage msg = new MimeMessage(sessionSMTP);

      msg.setFrom(new InternetAddress(from));

      if (null != to) msg.setRecipients(Message.RecipientType.TO,
InternetAddress.parse(to, false));
      if (null != cc) msg.setRecipients(Message.RecipientType.CC,
InternetAddress.parse(cc, false));
      if (null != subject) msg.setSubject(subject);

      // Create and fill the message into a MIME body Part
      MimeBodyPart mbp = new MimeBodyPart();
      mbp.setText(message);

      // Assemble a MIME multipart message
      Multipart mp = new MimeMultipart();
      mp.addBodyPart(mbp);

      // Set the message's content and date
      msg.setContent(mp);
      msg.setSentDate(new Date());

      // Send the message
      Transport.send(msg);

    } catch (MessagingException mex) {
      mex.printStackTrace();
      returnMsg = new String("Error : "+mex.toString());
    }

    return returnMsg;
  }
}
```

Note that OracleJVM uses the Java 2 security model to protect operating system resources. The previous code uses sockets (for SMTP traffic) and accesses the System Properties. Both permissions should be explicitly granted to the OE user by the SYS user:

call dbms_java.grant_permission('OE', 'SYS:java.util.PropertyPermission', '', 'read,write')*

call dbms_java.grant_permission('OE', 'SYS:java.net.SocketPermission', 'your.smtp_gateway.com', 'resolve,connect')

The second class, `JavaTrigger.java`, has a method that accepts a product ID and other parameters. It uses the internal JDBC driver to execute an SQL count of existing order items that include this product ID (an example of calling SQL from Java). This method is used as a trigger to provide an impact analysis alert when the price of a product changes. It uses the previous `sendMail` to send an e-mail alert (an example of calling Java from Java).

```
package ch18;

import java.sql.*;
import javax.sql.*;
import oracle.sql.*;
import oracle.jdbc.pool.*;

public class JavaTrigger {

  public static void alertListPriceChange(int productId, String productName,
                                          float oldPrice, float newPrice) {

    int orderCount = 0;
    try {

      // Get the default (internal) connection from DataSource
      OracleDataSource ods = new OracleDataSource();
      ods.setURL("jdbc:oracle:kprb:");
      Connection conn = ods.getConnection();

      // SQL to find the count of orders that include this particular product
      String sql = "SELECT COUNT(DISTINCT order_id) FROM order_items WHERE
product_id = ?";

      // Prepare SQL query
      PreparedStatement pstmt = conn.prepareStatement(sql);

      // Apply bind parameter based on input parameter
      pstmt.setInt(1, productId);

      // Execute query and process result
      ResultSet rset = pstmt.executeQuery();
      while (rset.next()) {
        orderCount = rset.getInt(1);
      }

      // Release resources
      rset.close();
      pstmt.close();

    } catch (SQLException se) {
       se.printStackTrace();
    }

    // Build Subject and Message body for alert
    String subject = "price change - " + productName;
    String msg = "There has been a price change for product " + productId + " (" +
productName + "), from $" + oldPrice + " to $" + newPrice + ". It will affect " +
orderCount + " orders!";

    // Invoke Java Stored Procedure to send alert via email
    JavaMail.sendMail("alert@database.com", "you@youdomain.com", "", subject, msg);

  }
}
```

Note that it is not our intention to focus on the Java code itself for each of these examples but rather the process of using them within OracleJVM.

Load and Resolve

Loadjava (and its complementary dropjava are scripts in $ORACLE_HOME/bin. It is used to load Java source, classes, and resources into the database schema. The key options associated with loadjava are as follows:

- `-user` — Specifies database user and connect string. Objects are loaded into this schema by default.
- `-resolve` — Compiles and resolves external references in classes after all classes have been loaded. Without this option, files are only compiled by OracleJVM when they are invoked.
- `-resolver` — The resolver spec (database equivalent of `CLASSPATH`) is used by the `-resolve` (compile) option. The default spec is to search the current schema followed by any `public` objects. This option is required to reference classes loaded in a different schema.
- `-synonym` — Creates a `public` synonym for each class loaded.

The classes are loaded into the database with the following command:

```
loadjava -user oe/oe -resolve ch18\JavaMail.java ch18\JavaTrigger.java
```

Publish

Java classes that are loaded must be published with a call spec — a process that maps Java method names and parameter types to their SQL counterparts. A call spec publishes the Java method into the data dictionary and makes it accessible through the SQL engine. Once published, the Java method is accessible from SQL and PL/SQL calls.

The following two commands show the syntax to marry the Java method signatures to PL/SQL method signatures:

```
CREATE OR REPLACE FUNCTION sendMail (
  p_from    VARCHAR2,
  p_to      VARCHAR2,
  p_cc      VARCHAR2,
  p_message VARCHAR2,
  p_subject VARCHAR2)
RETURN VARCHAR2
AS LANGUAGE JAVA
NAME 'ch18.JavaMail.sendMail(java.lang.String, java.lang.String, java.lang.String,
java.lang.String, java.lang.String) return java.lang.String';
/

CREATE OR REPLACE PROCEDURE alertListPriceChange  (
  p_productId       NUMBER,
  p_productName     VARCHAR2,
  p_oldPrice        NUMBER,
  p_newPrice        NUMBER)
AS LANGUAGE JAVA
NAME 'ch18.JavaTrigger.alertListPriceChange(int, java.lang.String, float, float)';
/
```

Later, Chapter 21, "Object-Relational Interactions with Oracle," presents two other methods (Native Java Interface and the Client API) to directly access Java classes in an OracleJVM without requiring a call spec.

Invoke

The JavaMail example is compiled and loaded and has a call spec — it is ready to be invoked! First you access this Java Stored Procedure from a PL/SQL interface (an example of calling Java from SQL). If all goes well it will send an e-mail from `alert@database.com` to `you@yourdomain.com` with the subject "test subject" and message "test message". It will display "OK" upon successful completion (see Figure 18-15).

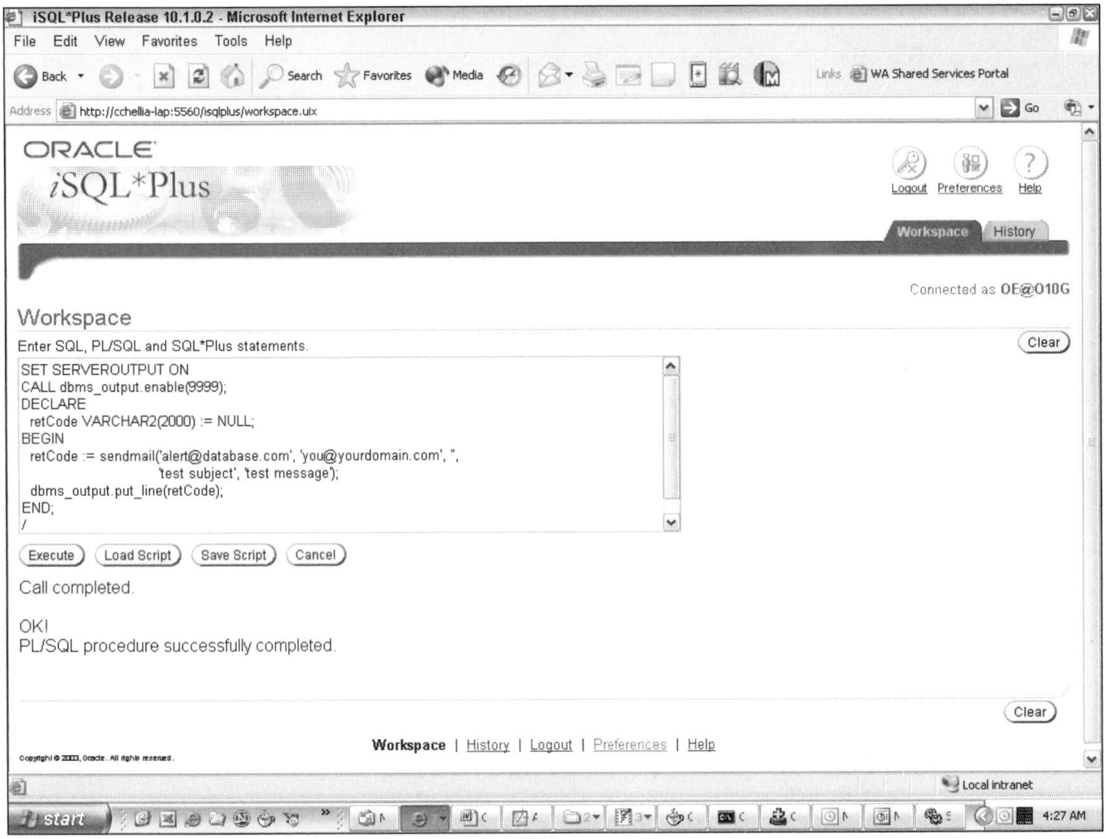

Figure 18-15: Invoking a Java Stored Procedure.

An alternative role for Java Stored Procedures is with trigger implementations. In this case we have defined a trigger on the PRODUCT_INFORMATION table to fire when `list_price` is updated. It will send an impact analysis alert via e-mail.

```
CREATE OR REPLACE TRIGGER alert_list_price_change
AFTER UPDATE OF list_price ON product_information
FOR EACH ROW
-- The command below should be on a single line.
-- It has been split across two lines for clarity.
CALL alertListPriceChange (:old.product_id, :old.product_name, :old.list_price,
  :new.list_price)
```

To test the implementation an SQL call is issued to change the list_price of a product (Figure 18-16) and it results in an e-mail alert to that effect (see Figure 18-17).

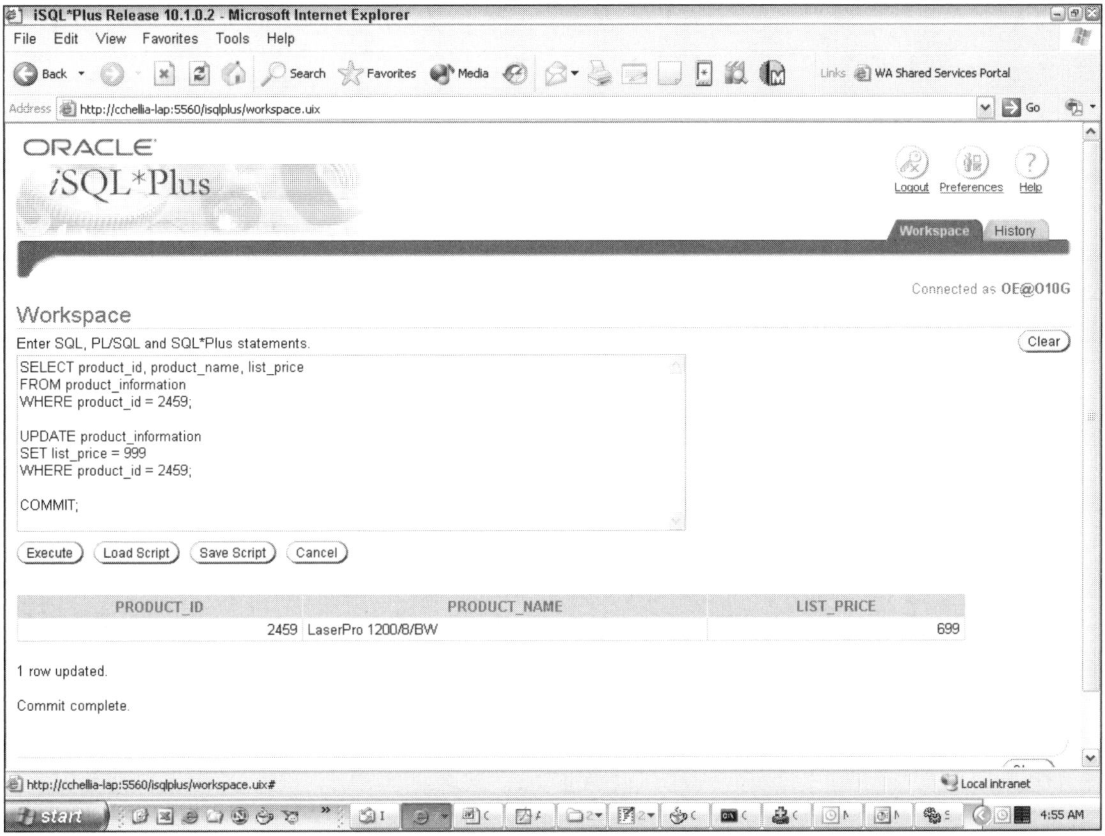

Figure 18-16: Update on the PRODUCT_INFORMATION table.

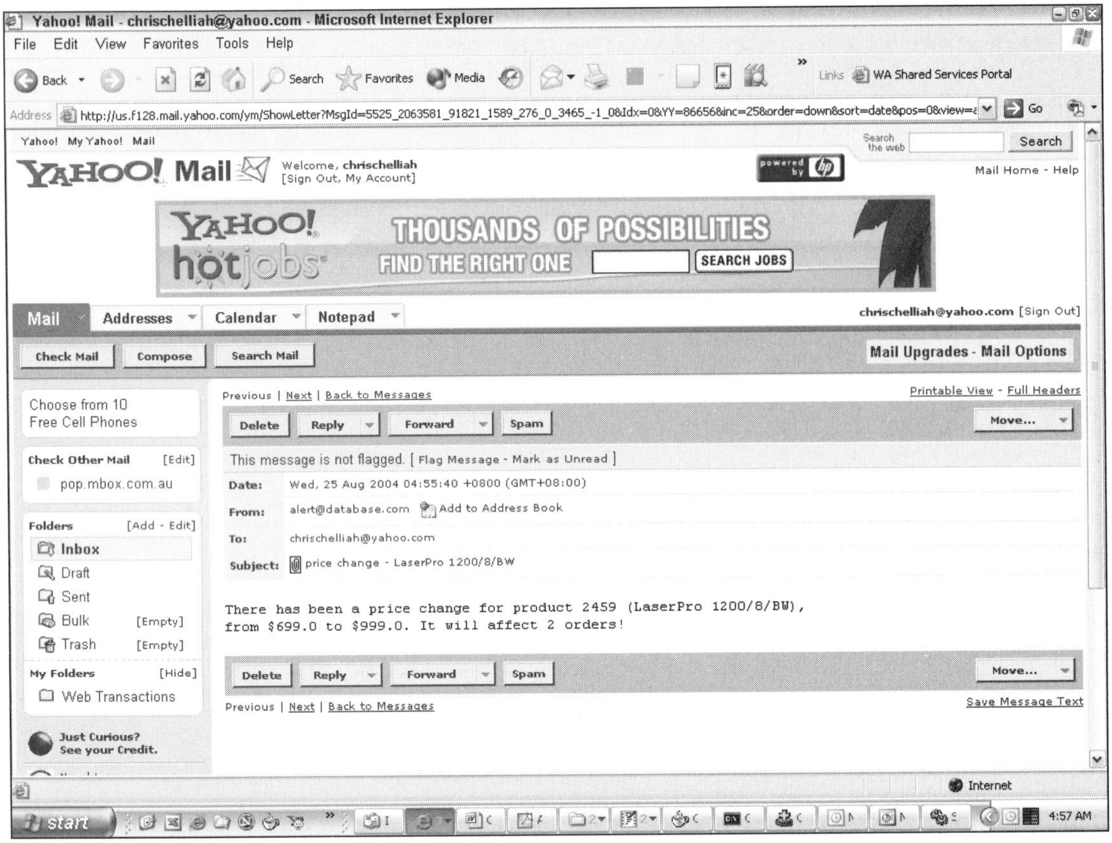

Figure 18-17: E-mail triggered from a Java Stored Procedure.

Summary

Java is here to stay, and Oracle's support for Java is comprehensive and indeed unique in the market today. Sure, most enterprise software vendors claim to support Java in one way or form. In most cases this is limited to providing a JDBC-based entry point into the database. Oracle's solution, on the other hand, truly embraces the open and standards-based nature of Java at all tiers of an application architecture. It does so with the following:

- Comprehensive JDBC support for database connectivity.
- A fully J2EE-compliant application server to support the JSP, servlet, JMS, EJB, and the rest of the J2EE specifications in the middle tier.
- A fully J2SE-compliant JVM running within the Oracle database shared memory — a feat unmatched by other database vendors.
- A comprehensive persistence framework — OracleAS TopLink — to better leverage Java's object-oriented capability against a relational database structure.

This means that application developers can have complete flexibility in deciding how to build an application to meet different user requirements, performance characteristics, and deployment constraints. There is no need to compromise on open standards versus proprietary code at any tier (even database stored procedures can be written as portable Java code), nor is there a need to compromise on open standards versus performance at any tier (Oracle supports native compilation, persistent object caches, and implicit statement batching) in your application design.

Finally, in Chapter 21, "Object-Relational Interactions with Oracle," you will see how Java is weaved even tighter into Oracle's stack with the ability to extend the database and define a new data type specific for your application's requirements.

19

Triggers

Database triggers allow Oracle to manipulate your tables and data based on set criteria and database events. This chapter describes what triggers are and what triggers can do. It shows you the kinds of triggers you can create in Oracle, as well as some examples of common triggers programmers tend to use in day-to-day work. After reading this chapter, you should be able to incorporate triggers in your database design to solve common database issues.

What Are Triggers?

Triggers are simply blocks of code Oracle will execute for you automatically based on some action or event on a database table. Triggers can be used to auto-generate data to insert in a new table row, to create an auditing trail for table data, or to enforce referential integrity on a set of data stored across multiple tables. Like stored procedures or user-defined functions, triggers are stored in the database and are compiled the first time they are called.

Types of Triggers

Oracle provides several types of triggers for you to use based on when the data in the table should be updated. Triggers can operate on an `INSERT`, `UPDATE`, or `DELETE` on a table, and can perform their work either `BEFORE` or `AFTER` those operations. Triggers can also operate on the statement level, or on each row of data being modified by including a `FOR EACH ROW` directive in the trigger definition.

You can also write `INSTEAD OF` triggers that allow you to perform operations on a view that are not normally allowed, such as deleting from a view that joins many tables. Starting with Oracle 8*i*, you can write globally scoped triggers that fire on events for all users at the `DATABASE` level, or events that fire for each user at the `SCHEMA` level. You can have as many triggers as you want on a table, and Oracle will execute them in the proper order based on the trigger definition.

Schema- and database-level triggers can fire on the DDL events CREATE, ALTER, and DROP, as well as database-level events like SERVERERROR, LOGON, LOGOFF, STARTUP, and SHUTDOWN. You should try to avoid creating these types of triggers, as they can add overhead to the execution of your SQL. These triggers should be left for DBAs to create if needed.

> **Triggers are generally defined by three variables: the operation that should activate the trigger (INSERT, UPDATE, DELETE), the timing of the trigger's activation (BEFORE, AFTER), and if the trigger should operate on the statement as a whole or on each row of data (FOR EACH ROW).**

Order of Execution

Triggers execute based on trigger type. Oracle will execute all BEFORE statement-level triggers, then all BEFORE triggers operating on each row, then all AFTER triggers operating on each row, and finally all AFTER statement-level triggers. While the execution order is set by trigger type, Oracle does not guarantee the order in which the triggers of any given type will be executed. You should not write triggers that assume other triggers have been fired before its operations can complete successfully. If you want fine-grained control over the order of operations performed in a trigger, you should create a single trigger and perform those operations by calling functions or procedures from within the trigger body.

The order of execution is as follows:

- All BEFORE statement-level triggers
- All BEFORE triggers with a FOR EACH ROW designation
- All AFTER triggers with a FOR EACH ROW designation
- All AFTER statement-level triggers

Working with Triggers

Now that you've been introduced to triggers, the following sections show you how to create and use them. You will see how to create different types of triggers, modify them, delete them, and perform some advanced operations. You will also learn how to create triggers in Java.

Naming Triggers

Trigger names must be unique within a schema, but two triggers in different schemas can have the same names. Triggers can also be named the same as other objects in the schema, but for clarity, a naming convention that includes the object name and function should be employed to easily locate the object in your schema. All of the following are valid trigger names:

- updateContentID
- delete_related_content
- insertUpdateWebContent_trigger

Permissions for Creating Triggers

To create triggers on tables in your schema, you must have the CREATE TRIGGER permission. To create triggers in other schemas, you must have the CREATE ANY TRIGGER system permission. To create triggers on DATABASE, you must have the ADMINISTER DATABASE TRIGGER system permission.

Creating Triggers

The generic form for creating a basic trigger is as follows:

```
CREATE [OR REPLACE] TRIGGER triggerName [BEFORE | AFTER] [INSERT | UPDATE | DELETE]
ON tableName [FOR EACH ROW [WHEN condition]] triggerBody;
```

If you add the OR REPLACE option, the trigger will be dropped and re-created if it already exists. You can specify if the trigger will execute BEFORE or AFTER the triggering event is fired, as well as what the triggering event should be. By using the FOR EACH ROW option, you can also specify if the trigger should fire for each row that is being updated, or if it should fire only once per operation. Additionally, a WHEN clause can be included to add even more granularity to the triggering condition. You can specify multiple triggering events for a trigger by connecting them with an OR. For example, you can create a trigger that will fire after an INSERT, UPDATE, or DELETE on a table by stating the following:

```
CREATE OR REPLACE TRIGGER triggerName AFTER INSERT OR UPDATE OR DELETE
on tablename
triggerBody;
```

One of the most common uses of triggers is to implement an auto-number primary key for a table. This is done using a sequence to generate the integer for the primary key column and using a trigger to update the primary key field in the table. In this example, you will be creating a table to hold content for a Web site, and creating a sequence and trigger to set the ID column.

First, you need to create the table and sequence. The code to create a sequence that starts with 1 and increments by 1 and caches 10 numbers each execution is as follows:

```
create sequence contentSeq start with 1 increment by 1 cache 10;
```

a table to hold the Web site content by issuing the following SQL statement. The table uses the new Oracle XMLTYPE to store XML data:

```
create table WEBCONTENT
(
  ID                   NUMBER(16) not null,
  NAME                 VARCHAR2(50) not null,
  LASTMODIFIEDBY       VARCHAR2(50) not null,
  CONTENT              XMLTYPE,
  RELATEDCONTENTITEM NUMBER(16),
  APPROVED             NUMBER(1) default 0 not null,
  APPROVEDBY           VARCHAR2(50),
  AUTHORID             NUMBER(8),
  TEMPLATEID           NUMBER(8) default 0
);
```

And then you create the trigger to update the ID column of the table by getting the next value of the sequence:

```
create or replace trigger contentID
  before insert on webcontent
  for each row
begin
  Select contentseq.nextval into :new.ID from dual;
end contentID;
```

This trigger will fire before any insert on the `WEBCONTENT` table, select the next integer value from the `CONTENTSEQ` sequence, and update the new row's ID column.

Figure 19-1 shows what happens after you insert a new row in the `WEBCONTENT` table. Notice that even though the `ID` column is specified as `NOT NULL`, you do not have to supply a value for the column, as the trigger takes care of it.

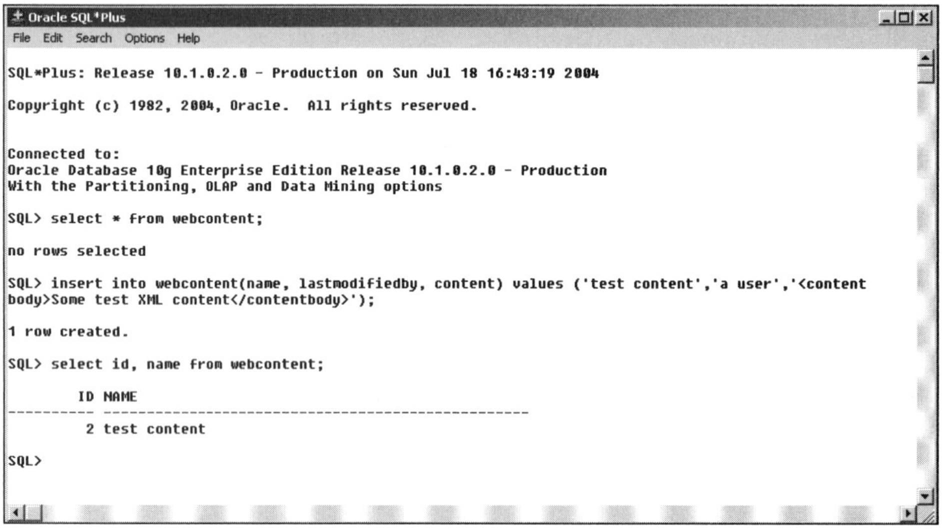

Figure 19-1: Simple trigger execution.

:new and :old

When you create a trigger that operates on each row using the `FOR EACH ROW` statement, Oracle provides two temporary tables for you to access the new and previous values of columns in the row: `:new` and `:old`. On an `INSERT` or `UPDATE` command, you can use `:new` to write new column values to the table, and in an `UPDATE` command, you can copy or compare values from `:old` and `:new`. Because of the nature of `:new` and `:old`, `:old` is defined as `NULL` in an `INSERT` statement, and `:new` is defined as `NULL` in a `DELETE` statement. In Oracle, `:new` and `:old` allow access only to column values; you cannot assign data to them.

Update Triggers

Triggers are also commonly used to write auditing information in a table on update. For example, when someone updates content in the database, you may want to capture that person's username for quality control purposes. You can easily accomplish that with an updated trigger:

```
create or replace trigger contentupdate
  before update or insert on webcontent
  for each row

begin

Select user into :new.lastmodifiedby from dual;

end contentupdate;
```

of the person currently logged in to Oracle will be inserted in the `LASTMODIFEDBY` field and the row will look something like Figure 19-2.

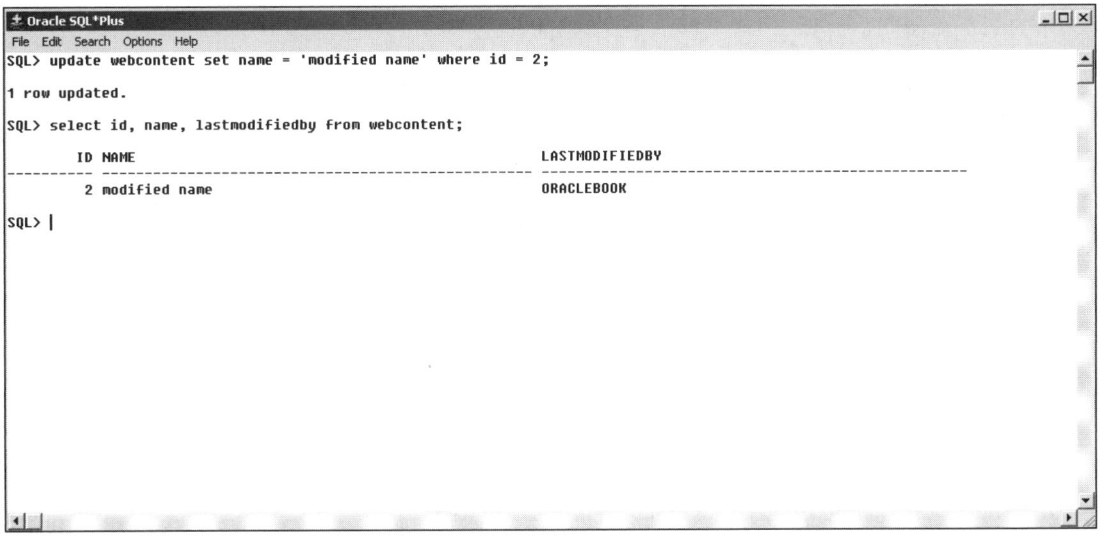

Figure 19-2: `UPDATE` trigger.

Be careful when designing `UPDATE` triggers that you do not create a recursive trigger. This can happen when the `UPDATE` trigger executes an `UPDATE` statement in the trigger body on the table it is currently operating on. This will cause a recursive condition and the trigger will execute until the database runs out of memory.

Delete Triggers

Triggers can also be used to archive content before it is deleted permanently from production tables. Generally you would create a mirrored table of the production data and use a `BEFORE DELETE` trigger on the production table to copy the data to the archive.

First, create the archive table:

```
create  table WEBCONTENTARCHIVE
(
  ID                   NUMBER(16),
  NAME                 VARCHAR2(50),
  LASTMODIFIEDBY       VARCHAR2(50),
  CONTENT              XMLTYPE,
  RELATEDCONTENTITEM NUMBER(16),
  APPROVED             NUMBER(1) default 0,
  APPROVEDBY           VARCHAR2(50),
  AUTHORID             NUMBER(8),
  TEMPLATEID           NUMBER(8) default 0
);
```

Then create the trigger:

```
create or replace trigger archiveContent
  before delete on webcontent
  for each row
begin

     insert into webcontentarchive(ID, NAME, LASTMODIFIEDBY, CONTENT,
RELATEDCONTENTITEM,
     APPROVED, APPROVEDBY, AUTHORID, TEMPLATEID) VALUES (
     :old.ID, :old.NAME, :old.LASTMODIFIEDBY, :old.CONTENT,
:old.RELATEDCONTENTITEM,
     :old.APPROVED, :old.APPROVEDBY, :old.AUTHORID, :old.TEMPLATEID
     );

end archiveContent;
```

Controlling When the Trigger Fires

You may want to have finer-grained control of when the trigger you create will fire than only `INSERT`, `UDPATE`, and `DELETE` events on a table. You may want a trigger to fire only when a certain column is modified or fire based on the value of a column. This can be accomplished by either specifying a column list when you create the trigger, or by using a `WHEN` statement.

When you define a trigger, simply specifying a column name in the definition will limit the trigger to firing only when the column you specified is updated. The trigger definition looks like the following:

```
create or replace trigger contentupdate
  before update or insert of content on webcontent
  for each row

begin

Select user into :new.lastmodifiedby from dual;

end contentupdate;
```

This will modify the auditing trigger to only update the LASTMODIFIEDBY column if the content field is changed. That way, a database administrator could update other fields in the table without overwriting the author's name in the LASTMODIFIEDBY column.

You can set your trigger to fire based on a conditional evaluation in a row-level trigger by using a `WHEN` clause in the trigger definition. A `WHEN` clause in a trigger must have a statement enclosed in parentheses that can evaluate to an SQL boolean `TRUE` or `FALSE`. You can use the `WHEN` clause to check for a specific value in a column, or to compare the values of columns. Unfortunately, you can't use any user-defined or Oracle-supplied functions in the `WHEN` clause, and you cannot use a `WHEN` clause in statement-level triggers or in `INSTEAD OF` triggers that operate on a view.

```
create or replace trigger contentUpdateApprover
  before update on webcontent
  for each row
  when (new.approved = 1)

begin

Select user into :new.approvedby from dual;

end contentupdate;
```

This trigger will only fire when the value of the new approved column is 1 (true). When the content item is approved, the trigger will automatically set the approvedby column to the username of the current database user. Notice that the `WHEN` clause uses the new identifier without a colon. New and old are not preceded by a colon in a trigger `WHEN` clause.

Inserting or Updating?

Sometimes you may want to create a trigger that is fired by multiple events, and you would like the trigger to do different things depending on what event fired the trigger. For example, you may want a trigger that fires on an `INSERT` or `UPDATE` on a table to update different columns. To do this you can use the `INSERTING`, `UPDATING`, and `DELETING` boolean expressions. The general form of these is as follows:

```
IF [INSERTING | UPDATING | DELETING] THEN
    Statements inserted here
END IF;
```

Special Circumstances

Using triggers, you can define operations that the database will perform automatically for you instead of the operation the user intended. This lets you successfully circumvent operations that may not complete successfully or that might not be aware of other data items dependent on it. These include operations on views, and `CASCADE` operations on data.

INSTEAD OF Triggers

In Oracle, INSTEAD OF triggers provide a way to update views that cannot be updated directly by an SQL statement. This is most commonly found with views that do joins across several tables. INSTEAD OF triggers can be created for INSERT, UPDATE, and DELETE actions. The types of views that require an INSTEAD OF trigger are as follows:

- A view that uses set operators like UNION or INTERSECT
- A view that uses a DISTINCT operator in the SELECT statement
- A view that uses an aggregate function like SUM, MAX, or AVG
- A view that includes a GROUP BY, ORDER BY, MODEL, CONNECT BY, or START WITH clause
- A view that uses a collection expression in a SELECT list
- A view that uses a sub-query in a SELECT list
- A view that contains a sub-query marked WITH READ ONLY
- A view that joins multiple tables

In this example, you create a trigger that executes INSTEAD OF, an update to a view of several joined tables. You will have to modify the existing WEBCONTENT table for this example and add two more tables.

First, create the new tables, including one to hold author information and another to hold XSL templates that should be applied to the Web content.

```
create table WEBAUTHOR
(
  ID          NUMBER(8) not null,
  NAME        VARCHAR2(50) not null,
  DEPARTMENT VARCHAR2(20),
  EMAIL       VARCHAR2(100),
  PHONE       VARCHAR2(15),
  ARTICLECOUNT NUMBER(8) default 0
);

alter table WEBAUTHOR
  add constraint WEBAUTHORPK primary key (ID)
  using index;

create table WEBTEMPLATE
(
  ID           NUMBER(8) not null,
  NAME         VARCHAR2(20) not null,
  DESCRIPTION VARCHAR2(20),
  STYLESHEET  XMLTYPE not null
);

alter table WEBTEMPLATE
  add constraint WEBTEMPLATEPK primary key (ID)
  using index;
```

Next add a primary key to the WEBCONTENT table:

```
alter table WEBCONTENT
  add constraint WEBCONTENTPK primary key (ID)
  using index;
```

When you create constraints on a table, it is important to use meaningful names. Good naming practices will help you easily find problem constraints when troubleshooting.

Next, create the foreign keys to the new tables from WEBCONTENT:

```
alter table WEBCONTENT
  add constraint WEBCONTENTAUTHOR foreign key (AUTHORID)
  references WEBAUTHOR (ID);

alter table WEBCONTENT
  add constraint WEBCONTENTTEMPLATE foreign key (TEMPLATEID)
  references WEBTEMPLATE (ID);
create or replace view webcontentview as
select webcontent.id as contentID, webcontent.name, lastmodifiedby, content,
relatedcontentitem, approved, approvedby,
webcontent.authorid, webcontent.templateid, webauthor.name as authorname,
department, email, phone,
webtemplate.name as templatename, description, stylesheet
    from webauthor, webcontent, webtemplate
    where webcontent.authorid = webauthor.id
```

You should also run the webtablecontent.sql script provided on the book Web site to generate the content for this example. If you cannot access the Web site to get the SQL script, it is provided here:

```
DELETE FROM WEBCONTENT;
DELETE FROM WEBAUTHOR;
DELETE FROM WEBTEMPLATE;
COMMIT;

INSERT INTO WEBAUTHOR ( ID, NAME, DEPARTMENT, EMAIL, PHONE ) VALUES (
1, 'John Smith', 'Marketing', 'jsmith@someco.com', '222-222-2222');

INSERT INTO WEBAUTHOR ( ID, NAME, DEPARTMENT, EMAIL, PHONE ) VALUES (
2, 'Jane Doe', 'Sales', 'jdoe@someco.com', '222-222-3333');
COMMIT;

INSERT INTO WEBTEMPLATE ( ID, NAME, DESCRIPTION, STYLESHEET ) VALUES (
1, 'basic template', 'A basic template', XMLTYPE('<xsl:stylesheet version="1.0"
xmlns:xsl="http://www.w3.org/1999/XSL/Transform">
<xsl:template match="/">
<html>
<head><title>Search Engines</title></head>
<body bgcolor="white">
<font face = "arial">
<strong>
<xsl:value-of select="/webcontent/link" disable-output-escaping="yes"/>
</strong>
```

```
<br/>
<xsl:value-of select="/webcontent/bodytext" disable-output-escaping="yes"/>
</font>
</body
  </html>
</xsl:template>
</xsl:stylesheet>'));
COMMIT;

INSERT INTO WEBCONTENT ( ID, NAME, LASTMODIFIEDBY, CONTENT, RELATEDCONTENTITEM,
APPROVED,
APPROVEDBY, AUTHORID, TEMPLATEID ) VALUES (
22, 'test content', 'ORACLEBOOK', XMLTYPE('<webcontent>
<link>http://www.google.com</link>
<bodytext>Google is a great resource for searching the Internet.</bodytext>
</webcontent>')
, NULL, 0, NULL, 1, 1);

INSERT INTO WEBCONTENT ( ID, NAME, LASTMODIFIEDBY, CONTENT, RELATEDCONTENTITEM,
APPROVED,
APPROVEDBY, AUTHORID, TEMPLATEID ) VALUES (
23, 'test content 2', 'ORACLEBOOK', XMLTYPE('<webcontent>
<link>http://www.yahoo.com</link>
<bodytext>Yahoo is a great resource for searching the Internet.</bodytext>
</webcontent>')
, NULL, 0, NULL, 2, 1);
COMMIT;
```

Now try to update a couple of columns in the view you just created. If you issue an update statement against the `WEBCONTENTVIEW`, Oracle will complain that you can only update one underlying table at a time, as shown Figure 19-3. The way around this limitation is to create an `INSTEAD OF` trigger.

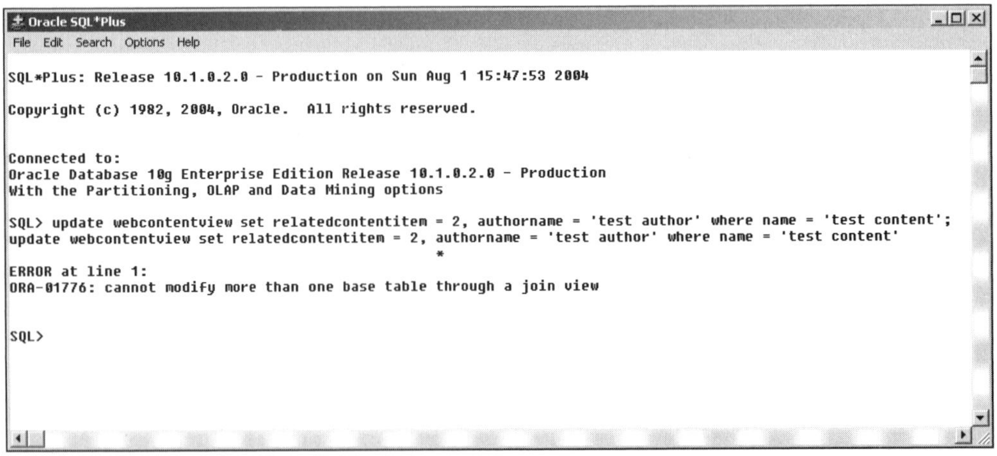

Figure 19-3: Error updating a view.

To update this view, you can create an `INSTEAD OF UPDATE` trigger on the `WEBCONTENTVIEW` view. This trigger will take the values in the new record, and update the relevant underlying tables. The trigger looks like this:

```
CREATE OR REPLACE TRIGGER webcontentview_update
INSTEAD OF UPDATE ON webcontentview

FOR EACH ROW

BEGIN

update webauthor set name = :new.authorname, department = :new.department, email =
:new.email, phone = :new.phone
where id = :new.authorID;

update webtemplate set name = :new.templatename, description = :new.description,
stylesheet = :new.stylesheet
where id = :new.templateid;

update webcontent set name = :new.name, content = :new.content, relatedcontentitem
= :new.relatedcontentitem,
approved = :new.approved where id = :new.contentid;

END webcontentview_update
```

Now when you do an update on the view, the trigger will be fired and the underlying tables will be updated (see Figure 19-4).

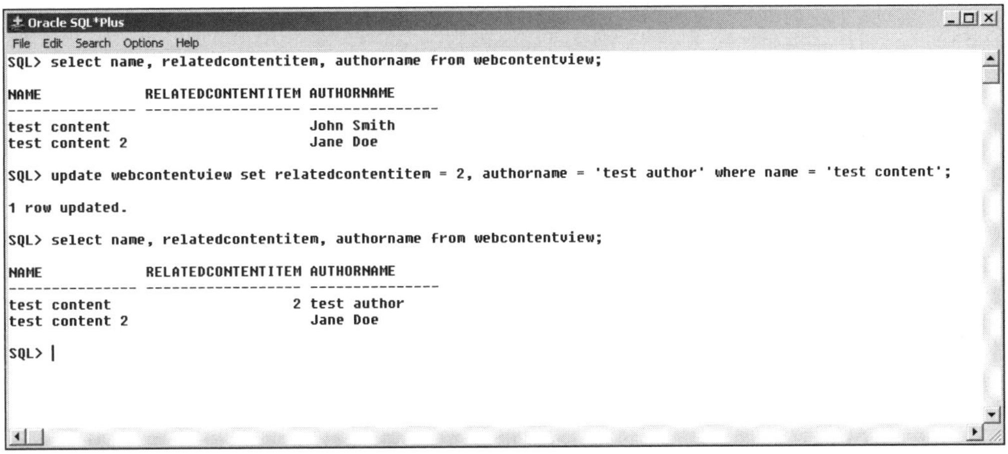

Figure 19-4: Updating a view using `INSTEAD OF`.

Triggers for Referential Integrity

Triggers can be used to enforce referential integrity on data tables in your schema. For example, when you delete an author from the WEBAUTHOR table, you may want to implement a CASCADE DELETE on the content that the author has written. This can easily be accomplished with a BEFORE DELETE trigger. The trigger for this operation is defined as:

```
create or replace trigger deleteAuthorContent
  before delete on webauthor
  for each row
begin

  delete from webcontent where authorid = :old.ID;

end deleteRelated;
```

The archiveContent trigger defined earlier will archive the content in the WEBCONTENTARCHIVE table before deleting it.

Triggers in Other Languages

Oracle supports procedures written in languages other than PL/SQL, like Java. You can write code in Java that performs the trigger actions instead of coding the trigger body in PL/SQL. While you cannot directly associate the Java code as the trigger, you can create a PL/SQL-based trigger and call the Java code as a procedure from the trigger body. For example, you can rewrite the trigger that updates LAST-MODIFIEDBY in Java. First, create the Java code to perform the triggering action. The filename for the class is webcontentTriggers.java. See Chapter 18, "Introduction to Java Database Programming," to see how to insert and register your java class with the database.

To compile the following example, make sure you include classes12.jar on your CLASSPATH. Classes12.jar can be found at $ORACLE_HOME/jdbc/lib.

```
import java.io.*
import java.sql.*
import oracle.sql.*
import oracle.core.lmx.*

public class webcontentTriggers
{
public static void updateAudit() Throws SQLException, CoreException
 {
    Connection con = JDBCConnection.defaultConnection();
    Statement s = con.CreateStatement();
    s.executeUpdate("update webcontent set lastmodifiedby = (select user from
dual)");
    s.close();
    return;
 }
}
```

Then create a PL/SQL procedure to call the Java code:

```
create or replace procedure updateWebContentUser()
IS language Java
name 'webcontentTriggers.updateAudit()';
```

Next, modify the PL/SQL trigger statement to call the Java code.

```
create or replace trigger contentupdate
  before update or insert on webcontent
  for each row

begin
Call updateWebContentUser();

end contentupdate;
```

Triggers and Mutating Tables

A mutating table is one that is in the process of being modified by an `INSERT`, `UPDATE`, or `DELETE` statement. Mutating tables are important to triggers because Oracle will prevent a trigger from operating on missing rows if the trigger is acting on its own table. If a session issues an `UPDATE` statement and the schema has a trigger that fires a row-level trigger operating on the table that the trigger is referencing, some of the data could have been changed by the original statement. Oracle will throw a runtime error when it tries to run the trigger on the table. Statement-level triggers are not affected by mutating tables.

Suppose you want to add a trigger to the database to automatically update the WEBAUTHORS table with the number of content items they have written. The trigger could take a count of the content items in the table with that author ID and update the WEBAUTHORS table with the number. The trigger to do that looks like the following:

```
create or replace trigger updateAuthorCount
  after update or insert on webcontent
  for each row
declare
authorcount NUMBER;

begin
select count(authorid) into authorcount from webcontent where authorid =
:new.authorid;
update webauthor set articlecount = authorcount where id = :new.authorid;
end ;
```

While this trigger will compile and look correct in the data dictionary, when you try to update the WEBCONTENT table, Oracle will throw the mutating table error (see Figure 19-5).

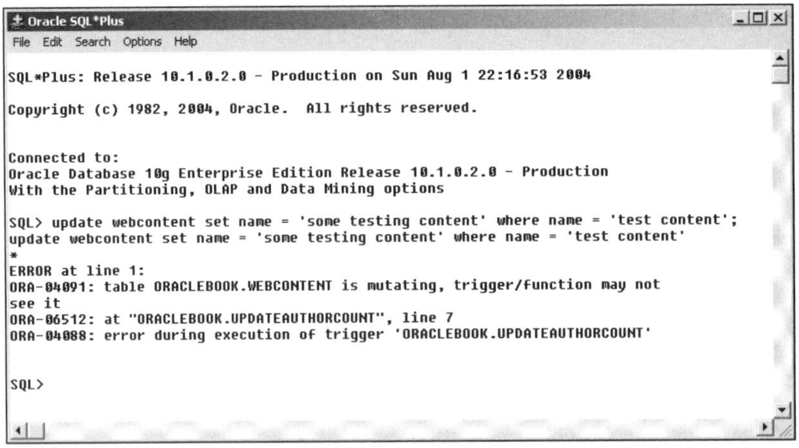

Figure 19-5: Mutating table error.

To solve the mutating table error, you should try to rewrite your trigger as a statement-level trigger, since they are not affected by data in flux. The preceding trigger can be rewritten as follows:

```
create or replace trigger updateAuthorCountNoMutate
  after update or insert on webcontent

declare
--Cursor to hold the author id
CURSOR authorIDList IS Select id from webauthor;

begin

FOR item in authorIDList LOOP
      update webauthor
      set articlecount = (Select count(authorid) from webcontent where authorid =
item.ID);
  END LOOP;

end ;
```

Make sure to disable the first trigger from firing, or else you will still get the mutating table error. This can be done with the statement:

```
ALTER TRIGGER UPDATEAUTHORCOUNT DISABLE;
```

Now when you issue an update statement, it should complete normally (see Figure 19-6).

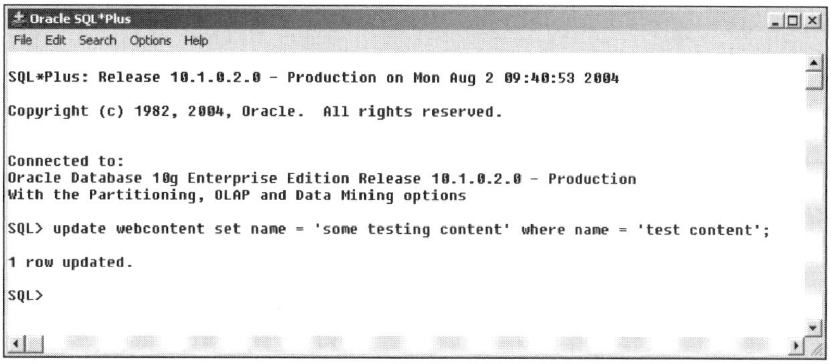

Figure 19-6: Mutating table error solved.

Removing Triggers

Sometimes you may want to stop triggers from firing when you are maintaining your database tables, or when you are developing new functionality. Detailed in this section are different ways you can disable triggers.

Deleting/Dropping Triggers

Just like tables and procedures, triggers can be deleted permanently from the database's data dictionary by using the `DROP` command. The syntax for dropping a trigger is as follows:

```
DROP TRIGGER triggerName;
```

Disabling Triggers

Sometimes you may want to temporarily disable triggers from firing without actually deleting them from the database. This may be because you want to work on a dependency of the trigger and want to keep it from firing, or because you are doing an intensive data load and don't want the overhead of the trigger to slow down the data load. This can be accomplished with the following command:

```
ALTER TRIGGER triggerName DISABLE;
```

To make the trigger active again, you can use this:

```
ALTER TRIGGER triggerName ENABLE;
```

You can also enable and disable all the triggers on a table with a single SQL statement:

```
ALTER TABLE TableName DISABLE ALL TRIGGERS;
ALTER TABLE TableName ENABLE ALL TRIGGERS;
```

Recompiling Triggers

When a trigger is created in the database, it is compiled and ready for execution. A compiled trigger has other dependencies in the database, and if any of these become invalid, the trigger will be marked invalid and will not execute. Sometimes you may need to manually recompile a trigger. This is accomplished by using the ALTER TRIGGER statement:

```
ALTER TRIGGER contentUpdate COMPILE;
```

Viewing Triggers in the Data Dictionary

You can view the currently saved triggers and their attributes by selecting them from Oracle's data dictionary views. There are three views defined in Oracle for triggers:

- USER_TRIGGERS
- ALL_TRIGGERS
- DBA_TRIGGERS

Figure 19-7 shows the fields you can access in any of trigger views listed.

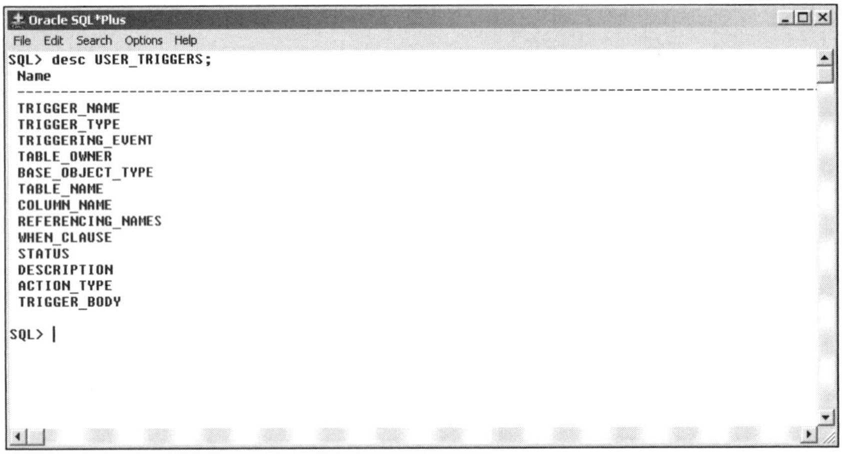

Figure 19-7: Fields for triggers.

For example, you can list some basic information about the triggers in your schema by issuing the following SQL statement:

```
select trigger_name, triggering_event, status from user_triggers;
```

This statement returns the trigger's name, the database event that fires the trigger, and whether the trigger is enabled or disabled. When run on the schema containing the tables and triggers you just created, the output will look like Figure 19-8.

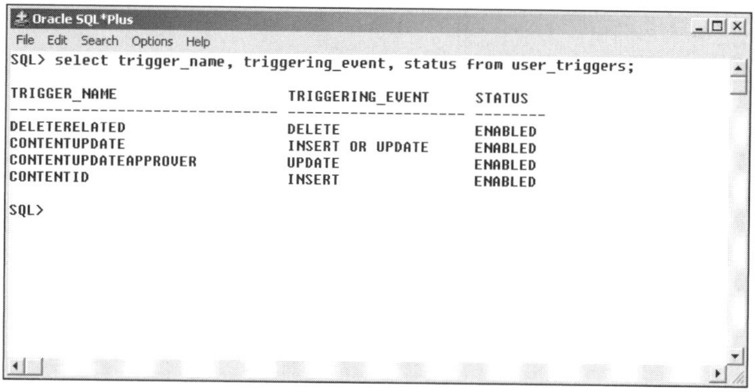

Figure 19-8: Selecting trigger information from the data dictionary.

Limitations of Triggers

Although triggers are an extremely flexible tool, there are a few restrictions on what you can do:

- A trigger body cannot be longer than 32K in length.
- Any `SELECT` statement executed in the trigger body must either be a `SELECT INTO` using bind variables or the `SELECT` statement defining a `CURSOR`.
- You cannot issue DDL statements inside a trigger body.
- You cannot use transaction keywords in a trigger body (`SAVEPOINT`, `COMMIT`, `ROLLBACK`). The trigger will execute and respect any enclosing transaction that it is a part of.
- `LONG` or `LONGRAW` data types can only be accessed in a trigger if their content can be converted to `VARCHAR2` or `CHAR` data.
- You cannot declare a `LONG` or `LONGRAW` variable inside a trigger body.
- `NEW` and `:PARENT` cannot access `LONG` or `LONGRAW` columns in a table.

Summary

In this chapter, you learned how to use triggers to effectively and automatically ensure database integrity. The chapter covered created, editing, and deleting triggers, as well as the different types of triggers you can create in Oracle. You have also seen how to create triggers in both PL/SQL and Java.

For standard database integrity checking, using simple foreign key relationships is a good practice, but sometimes you need more advanced functionality. Triggers are great to use for updating a value in a field of your table based on other data being inserted in the table, and for creating auto-number columns. Be careful how many triggers you create because they can affect database performance.

20

Regular Expressions and Expression Filter

The Oracle database has a proven capability to store and manage large data volumes effectively, from the perspective of backup, recovery, and operational excellence. As the size of the data repository increases (Oracle 10*g* is now capable of storing 8 exabytes, or 8,388,608 terabytes!), it is important to support more flexible and efficient ways to access and process the right set of content in a timely manner.

This chapter introduces two new features in Oracle 10*g*: regular expressions and the Expression Filter. Although their names sound similar, these features are quite different in their uses. They are grouped together in this chapter because they share a common goal: to programmatically process large sets of data more efficiently and effectively.

Regular expressions are a way to describe text patterns in order to process text programmatically. They are commonly used outside the database in command-line and operating system tools. This chapter introduces the basic syntax of regular expressions and how they might be applicable to database applications. It follows with a description of Oracle's support for regular expressions in the database, as well as some insight on the architecture and performance implications of using them.

Expression Filter supports a different paradigm of data processing to describe a user population's interest in expected data. Where a traditional application matches data against expressions in a `where` clause, Expression Filter enables the inverse situation by looking for expressions that match a particular data point. This is a unique way to process and route new data against large sets of existing data.

Both regular expressions and Expression Filter open up the possibilities to different classes of database processing that would be cumbersome to implement otherwise. Master these features and you will quickly find a use for them in an existing application or project.

Regular Expressions

Consider the task of processing a set of text data, either structured (for example, the contents of a large `varchar2` column) or unstructured (for example, an incoming XML stream over HTTP). In the context of database programming, following are some typical requirements for processing this text:

- Validating the content against a known set of data and optionally remove duplicates
- Matching the content against some search criteria and optionally performing text manipulation when a match occurs
- Formatting the content into a normalized form. For example, representing a telephone number as xxx-xxx-xxxx

All of these operations require a *pattern* to describe the desired content. Patterns are commonly used when you are working with text, to better organize or visualize the content. Following are some examples of familiar text patterns:

- An international phone number: +<country code>-<city code>-<phone number>
- A domestic phone number: (xxx) xxx-xxxx
- A Social Security number: xxx-xx-xxxx

Recognizing a pattern visually is one thing, but patterns must be defined programmatically in order be processed by a machine. A regular expression is a formula to describe complex patterns in text. Regular expressions open the door to powerful text processing in a standardized, repeatable manner without the need for extensive custom coding.

Consider the task of processing an input field from a Web form and validating that it is an e-mail address with the following characteristics:

- It is case-insensitive.
- Starts with a username containing letters, numbers, hyphens, and underscores.
- An @ sign follows the username.
- The host and domain name will consist of two or more groups of letters, numbers, hyphens, or underscores separated by a period (.).

Doing this programmatically (regardless of the programming language) would require a tangle of string manipulation code to match the stream of text.

This example only scratches the surface of text processing. With the increasing use of XML as an exchange medium, regular expressions are useful to validate, parse, and match against XML content. Life sciences and bio-informatics research are another example where regular expressions play an important role. Protein and DNA structures are represented as a long text string, and there are many combinations of these structures in a typical database. Drug discovery and research relies on looking for and matching specific protein and DNA data efficiently from very large databases of these structures.

The National Center for Biotechnology Information (`www.ncbi.nlm.nih.gov`) and the Protein Data Bank (`www.rcsb.org`) are examples of research organizations that host protein and DNA databases.

Regular Expression Concepts

Regular expressions originated in automata theory and formal language theory and as such have a daunting appearance at first. However, the underlying concepts are simple and powerful. It's the application of the concepts that takes some getting used to. So let's start with the concepts.

A regular expression pattern is expressed as a string comprising the following:

- ***Literal characters.*** The actual character to search for (e.g., the pattern `xyz` only matches an occurrence of "xyz")
- ***Meta-characters.*** Operators that specify algorithms to apply during the search (for example, the pattern `^xyz` will only match a line that starts with the string "xyz" and no other occurrences)

Common Meta-Characters

A summary of commonly used meta-characters is provided in the following table, together with some examples. For simpler referencing, the entries in the table have been classified into the role the meta-character plays in the pattern.

Meta-Character	Classification	Description	Example
`.`	Character range	Matches any single character	`.it` matches any three characters that end with "it", such as "ait", "bit", "cit", "Dit", "#it", "8it" . . .
`[]`	Character range	Specifies a range of characters. The engine will match exactly one of the characters.	`[xyz]` matches "x", "y", or "z", but not "a". `[a-z]` matches any lowercase letter. `gr[ea]y` matches either "grey" or "gray".
`[^]`	Character range	A match occurs for any character that is not included in the listed range.	`c[^a-z]t` matches "cAt", but not "cat".
`^`	Anchor	Matches a pattern that is at the beginning of a line.	`^hello` matches "hello, how are you", but not "I am saying hello".
`$`	Anchor	Matches a pattern that is at the end of a line.	`hello$` matches "I am saying hello", but not "hello, how are you".
`?`	Quantifier	Attempt to match the preceding expression zero or one time (i.e., it is optional).	`colou?r` matches both "color" and "colour".

Table continued on following page

<table>
<tr><th>Meta-Character</th><th>Classification</th><th>Description</th><th>Example</th></tr>
<tr><td>+</td><td>Quantifier</td><td>Looks for a pattern that occurs one or more times (i.e., at least once).</td><td>([a-k])+in matches "bin", "din", "fin", "kin". It does not match "in" or "sin".</td></tr>
<tr><td>*</td><td>Quantifier</td><td>Looks for a pattern that occurs zero or more times (i.e., it may or may not occur).</td><td>([a-k])*in matches "in", "bin", "din", "fin", "kin", but not "sin".</td></tr>
<tr><td>{m}</td><td>Interval</td><td>Look for a pattern to be repeated exactly m times.</td><td>(ab){2}yz matches "ababyz". It does not match "abyz" or "abababyz".</td></tr>
<tr><td>{m,}</td><td>Interval</td><td>Requires a pattern to repeat at least m times. Note:
{0,} is the same as *
{1,} is the same as +</td><td>(ab){2,}yz matches "ababyz", "abababyz", "ababababyz", and so on. It does not match "abyz".</td></tr>
<tr><td>{m.n}</td><td>Interval</td><td>Requires a pattern to repeat at least m times, but not more than n times.</td><td>(ab){2,3}yz matches "ababyz" and "abababyz". It does not match "abyz" or "ababababyz".</td></tr>
<tr><td>|</td><td>Operator</td><td>Matches a single regular expression out of several possible regular expressions.</td><td>I have a (fish|bird) matches "I have a fish" or "I have a bird".</td></tr>
<tr><td>\</td><td>Operator</td><td>The backslash operator is used to make a meta-character behave like a normal, literal character. This is also known as "escaping" a meta-character.</td><td>The pattern SQL*Plus does not match the literal string "SQL*Plus", but instead matches "SQLPlus", "SQLLPlus", "SQLLLPlus", and so on. This is because * is a meta-character that specifies a quantity (zero or more) of the preceding expression (L).
In this case the * should be escaped in the pattern, i.e., SQL*Plus, to achieve the desired effect.</td></tr>
</table>

Meta-Character	Classification	Description	Example
`()`	Subexpression	Treat the expression as a unit. The subexpression can be a string of literals or a complex expression containing operators. This allows you to apply an operator, e.g., a quantifier operator, to the entire group.	`Jan(uary)?` matches "Jan" and "January". It does not match "Janua", because the subexpression `uary` is treated as a single unit and must be present as a whole or not at all.
`\n`	Backreference	Stores the part of the string matched by the previous regular expression that was enclosed within brackets. The backreference counts subexpressions from left to right starting with the opening parenthesis of each preceding subexpression.	For a typical Web URL defined as `(http)://(www)([^/]+)(.*)(.html$)`, then:`\1` is the literal "http", `\2` is the literal "www", `\3` is the server name without the "www" prefix (e.g., oracle.com) `\4` is the relative URL to the file on the site, without the `.html` suffix. Backreferences are commonly used to find repeated occurrences of a pattern. For example `^(.*)\1$` matches any line consisting of two adjacent appearances of the same string, such as "sunsun", "moonmoon".
`[:class:]`	Character class	In English regular expressions, range expressions often indicate a character class. For example, `[a-z]` indicates any lowercase character. This is not portable in a multilingual environment because the first and last character of a given character class may not be the same in all languages. The POSIX standard uses the character class syntax to maintain portability in these cases.	If locale is set to Spanish, then `[[=n=]]`matches both "N" and "ñ" in the string "El Niño".

Table continued on following page

Meta-Character	Classification	Description	Example
`[.element.]`	Collating element	Collating defines how characters are ordered for purposes of sorting, merging, and comparing. A collating element is equal to one character in most cases (e.g., "a" in English) but may comprise two or more characters in some languages (e.g., "ch" in Spanish). When a regular expression refers to a range of values (e.g., `[a-z]`, it is based on a linguistic range, rather than a byte value range. Oracle implements these range expressions according to the linguistic definition based on the `NLS_SORT` parameter.	Collating elements can be used to define ranges in regular expressions. For example, the range `[a-z]` is relevant in English, but `[a-[.ch.]]` is relevant in Spanish. These expressions will evaluate to different matches depending on the `NLS_SORT` parameter.
`[=character=]`	Equivalence class	An equivalence class consists of a base letter and all of its a ccented versions.	`[=a=]` matches ä and â With an understanding of regular expression structure, you can now revisit the earlier requirement of validating an incoming text stream to ensure that it is a correct e-mail address.

```
^([-a-zA-Z0-9_]+)@(([-a-zA-Z0-9_]+[.])+[a-zA-Z]+)$
```

The above pattern represents the e-mail address in a single line of code! Furthermore, once defined, this pattern is now portable across different regular expression processors. Because the pattern is defined separately from the processor, it is easier to make ongoing changes to the "business logic" behind the valid-e-mail pattern, without having to reimplement any code. So for example, if the business rule changes to only accept e-mail addresses that end with a .gov, it is easily reflected by changing the expression to the following:

```
^([-a-zA-Z0-9_]+)@(([-a-zA-Z0-9_]+[.])+gov)$
```

Regular expressions optimize performance of text processing because they can be compiled once and matched repeatedly against many sources of data.

Guiding Principles

Recall that regular expressions are based on language theory. So there are many ways to represent a text pattern, just as there are many ways to articulate a sentence in a written language. The usage and implementation syntax of regular expressions is relatively easy, but the key to defining a correct text pattern is to understand the data, be aware of variations in that data, and choose a pattern representation that deals with the typical incoming data.

You should also consider the granularity of a pattern. A common mistake is to match too much by using quantifiers in a pattern — making it a greedy pattern. For example, if the intention is to match all words that start with "we" and end with "day", then at first glance the pattern `we.*day` looks appropriate. However, this pattern will also match the entire string "welcome to Jamaica. Hope you have a good day", which, of course, is more than a single word.

When formulating a pattern to match a sequence, it is best to approach the problem from two different perspectives:

- Keep looking in the text *until* you find a particular expression.
- Keep looking in the text *unless* you hit a particular expression.

These are subtly different, but a correct regular expression is usually the result of iteratively refining your expression based on the intersection of both of these perspectives.

> **There are many tutorials and syntax examples available on the Internet to further explain regular expressions. The rest of this chapter focuses on explaining Oracle's support for regular expressions within the database.**

Relevance to Database Applications

By now it should be clear that regular expressions unleash a lot of power to manipulate text data. The following are some scenarios that show the broad relevance of regular expressions in improving a database application. Each of the scenarios is addressed by a code example later in the chapter.

Presenting Data to a Client Application

Consider a requirement to format data from a database column for presentation to a client application — for example, a Social Security number that is stored as `char(9)` but must be represented as xxx-xx-xxxx. Today this processing is most likely happening outside of the database. Each application that requires the data would `select` the column and apply a format mask at the client side. This violates the good practice of encapsulating the underlying database structure because it is now difficult to change the storage structure in the database (e.g., to use an abstract data type) without breaking the applications.

Alternatively, applications tend to send back more data than necessary for client-side processing, because of limited pattern matching capability in databases. Regular expression can filter the set of rows to ensure that only the required subset of data is sent to the client, minimizing data transfer across the network.

Accepting Data from a Client Application

A database is only as good as the quality of the data it contains. Although it is possible to maintain data quality in application code outside of the database, this is typically not the best way, because it limits the rules to the application that defines them. A better approach is to define the quality rules (i.e., validation and integrity rules) together with the data in the database. This way, regardless of how the database is accessed or populated, the rules are always enforced.

Combining regular expressions with constraints in the database provides for a more expressive vocabulary to perform validation inside the database. It is no longer necessary to implement validation rules many times, in different applications — they can be represented as regular expressions and implemented once in the database.

Data Manipulation

Regular expressions can be used to search through large volumes of text and replace them in-place with alternative expressions. This kind of operation would traditionally require complex procedural code, or sending all data across the network to a client application for processing. Regular expression processing in the database reduces network traffic, improves performance and provides for tighter security in these cases.

There is a myriad of places where regular expression support will help your application. The next section describes how Oracle addresses these requirements in its support for regular expressions in the database.

Oracle Regular Expressions

Prior to Oracle Database 10*g*, an application developer had three options to process text data within a database application. None of these approaches, as described here, are efficient, intuitive, portable, or easily maintained over time.

- **Use SQL operators and procedural code.** The SQL engine supports `substr`, `instr`, and `replace` for basic text manipulation. The engine also supports wildcards (_ to match a single character, `%` to match zero or more characters) in conjunction with the `like` command for text manipulating with simple patterns. These constructs have limited use with complex patterns, because they lack the ability to specify quantifiers, intervals, and subexpressions within a pattern definition. Consider a simple query to search for the values "Chris" and "Christine". There is no unambiguous way to specify this pattern because `Chris%` will also match `Christina` and `Christian`. Anything beyond the simplest cases of pattern matching has to revert to hard-coding matching rules into a stored procedure, resulting in nonreusable code and an ongoing maintenance overhead.
- **Use a callout.** The Oracle database supports a callout from PL/SQL to an external application through the EXTPROC listener. A callout can be configured to use one of the many tools that support regular expressions, such as `awk` and `sed`. Callouts run outside of the database SGA and are costly at run time, since the (potentially large block of text) must be marshaled back and

forth between the database and external application. Not being native to the database also means the solution does not inherit the NLS support, performance, and high-availability features bundled with the database. While this is workable, it involves additional steps to deploy and maintain this configuration over time.

- **Use Oracle Java Virtual Machine.** Chapter 18, "Introduction to Java Database Programming," describes Oracle's Java architecture and native J2SE support within the database. So it is possible to load the Java implementation of a regular expression processor to run within the Oracle Java Virtual Machine (the Apache Jakarta project provides one such implementation at `http://jakarta.apache.org/regexp/index.html`). While this is the most desirable of the three options, it too would require additional configuration in each of the target databases that need regular expressions — an overhead that must be repeated for each database instance.

The Oracle Java Virtual Machine embedded in Release 10g is based on J2SE 1.4. This version of J2SE includes support for regular expressions through the javax.util.regex package. This version no longer requires a third-party regular expression processor such as the Apache Jakarta package referred to previously.

With the 10*g* Database release, Oracle supports regular expressions natively within the SQL engine. Oracle's implementation of regular expressions is based on the syntax and semantics defined by the POSIX standard — a widely used, portable flavor of regular expressions.

Regular expression support is implemented as a set of database functions to search and manipulate text data. These functions, `regexp_like`, `regexp_instr`, `regexp_substr`, and `regexp_replace`, are accessible from any environment where SQL or PL/SQL is used. They all have similar method signatures and are overloaded to support `char`, `nchar`, `varchar2`, `nvarchar2`, `clob`, and `nclob` data types as the input parameter.

REGEXP_LIKE

The `regexp_like` command returns a boolean indicating whether the pattern matched the given string or not. It does not provide details of how or where the match occurred within the string. The syntax for this command is as follows:

```
REGEXP_LIKE (src, pattern [, match_option])
Where:
  src: is the text to search within
  pattern: is the regular expression
  match_option: can include one or more of the following modifiers to change the
                default matching algorithm:
                'c' - case-sensitive matching (default);
                '' - case-insensitive matching;
                'n' - allow match-any-character operator;
                'm' - treat source string as multiple line.
```

This function is typically used in a `where` clause: for example, to look for all products that contain either "Standard Edition" or "Professional Edition" in their description, as shown Figure 20-1.

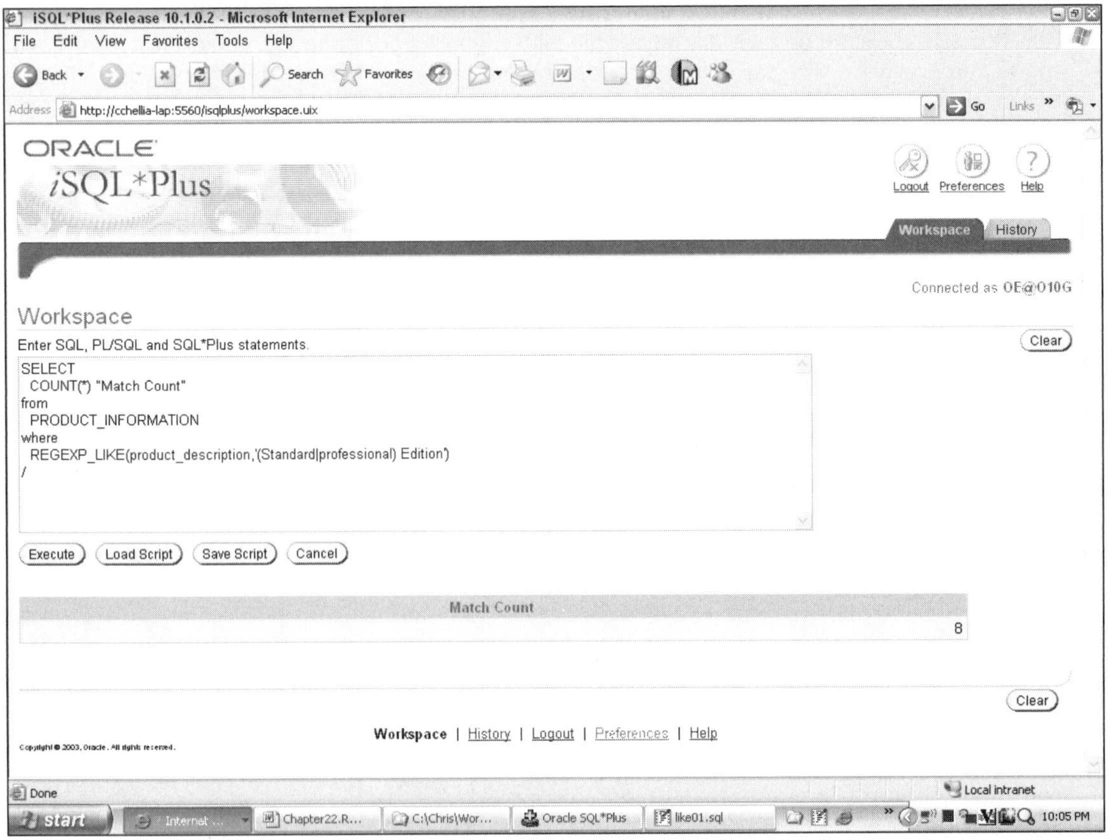

Figure 20-1: Using `regexp_like` in a `where` clause.

Note that "professional" is spelled with a lowercase p in the pattern; hence, not all potential matches are found. Figure 20-2 executes the same query but specifies a `match_option` for case insensitivity, and hence more rows are found.

REGEXP_INSTR

Like its `instr` counterpart, this function returns the character position of either the beginning or the end of the match for a pattern. The syntax for this command is as follows:

```
REGEXP_INSTR (src, pattern [, position [, occurrence [, return_option
            [,match_option]]]])
Where:
  src, pattern, match_option: are the same as shown for REGEXP_LIKE earlier
  position: the position in the string to start searching from (default = 1)
  occurrence: the occurrence to search for (default = 1)
  return_option: return the start position (0) or end position (1) of the match
```

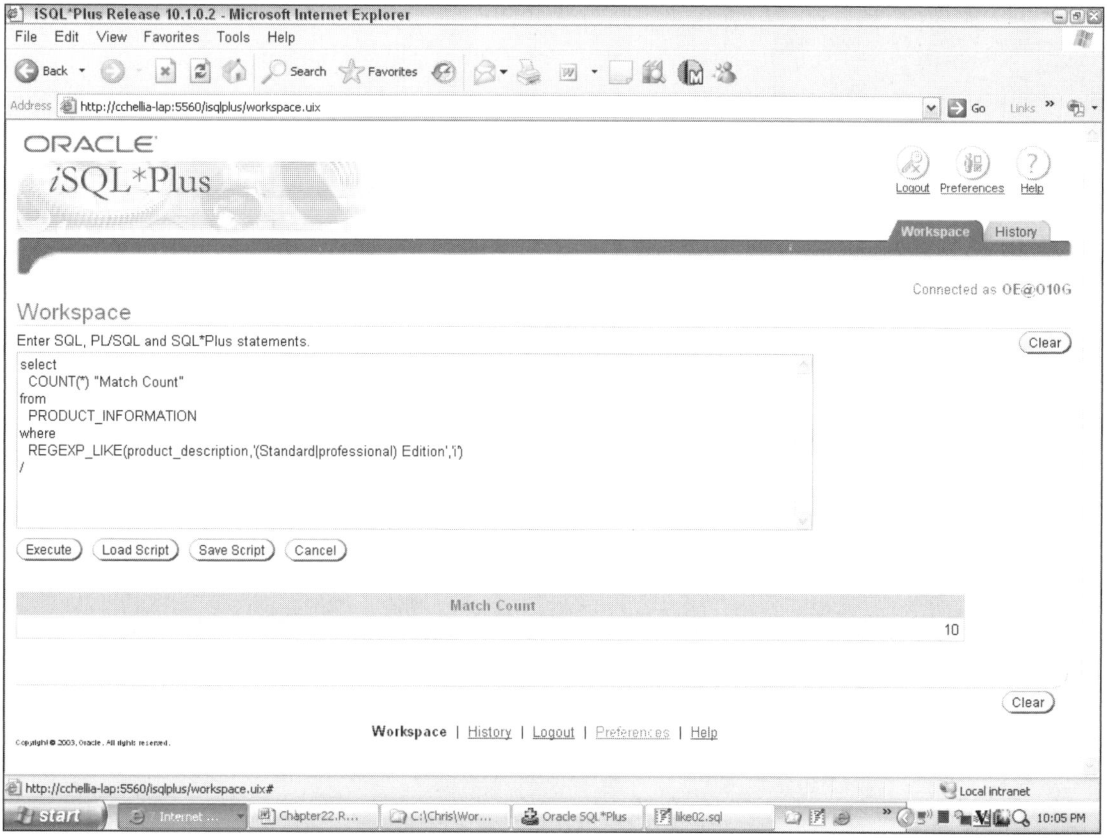

Figure 20-2: Using **`regexp_like`** with a **`match_option`**.

The example in Figure 20-3 shows a pattern that looks for one or more non-blank characters. It is used with `regexp_instr` to find the start position and the end position of the second occurrence of non-blank characters in the `product_name` column. This effectively gives you the start and end position of the second word of the product name. Combined with a `where` and `order by` clause, the result is a list of all products in which the second word is greater than nine characters long, ordered by the length of the second word.

Unlike `instr`, `regexp_instr` is only able to work from the start of a string and move forward, looking for the pattern. It is not able to start at the end of a string and work backwards to match the pattern.

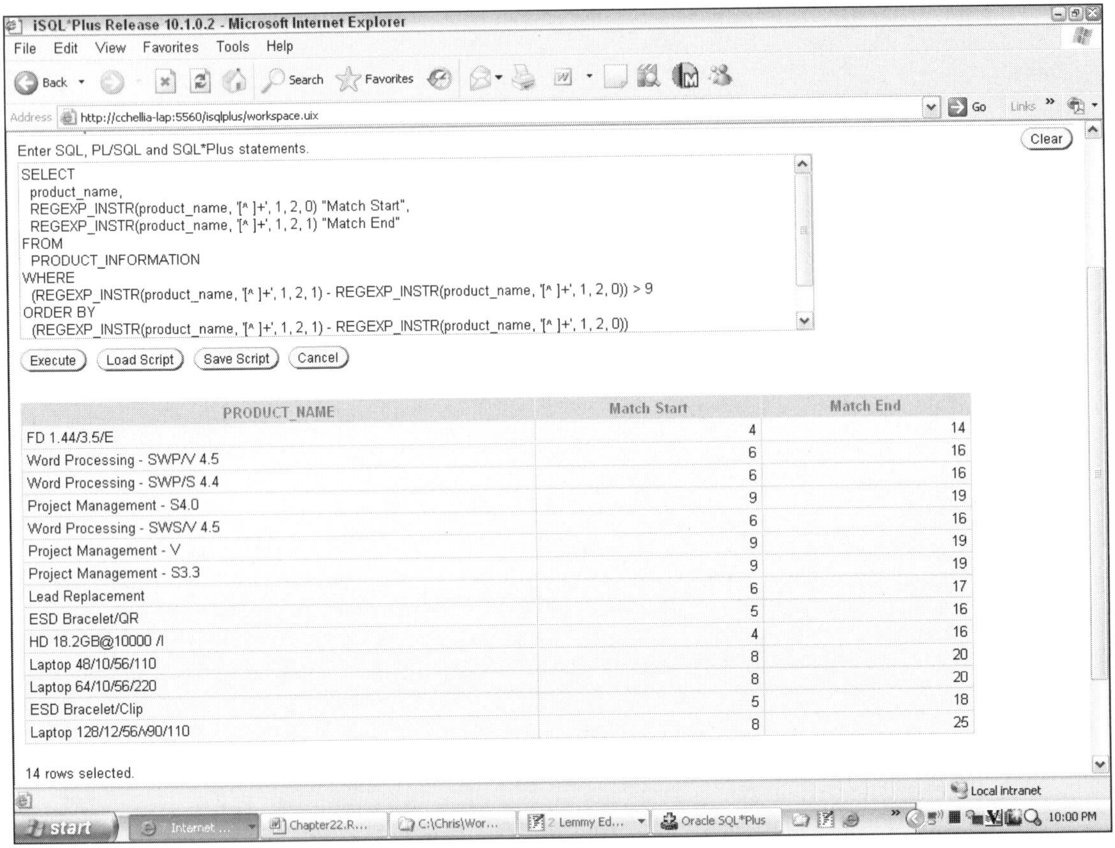

Figure 20-3: Using `regexp_instr` with `return_option`.

REGEXP_SUBSTR

This function extends the functionality of the `substr` function by searching for a regular expression in a string and returns the data that matches that pattern. It can be combined with a call to `regexp_instr` to return the position of the match as well.

The syntax for this command is as follows:

```
REGEXP_SUBSTR (src, pattern [, position [, occurrence [,match_option]]])
Where:
  src, pattern, match_option: are the same as shown for REGEXP_LIKE earlier
  position: the position in the string to start searching from (default = 1)
  occurrence: the occurrence to search for (default = 1)
```

The example in Figure 20-4 shows a pattern that looks for any character other than the `@` symbol. It uses this pattern in two calls to `REGEXP_SUBSTR` to return the data for the first and second occurrence of matches. This effectively returns everything before the `@` symbol (i.e., the e-mail ID) and everything after the `@` symbol (i.e., the e-mail domain).

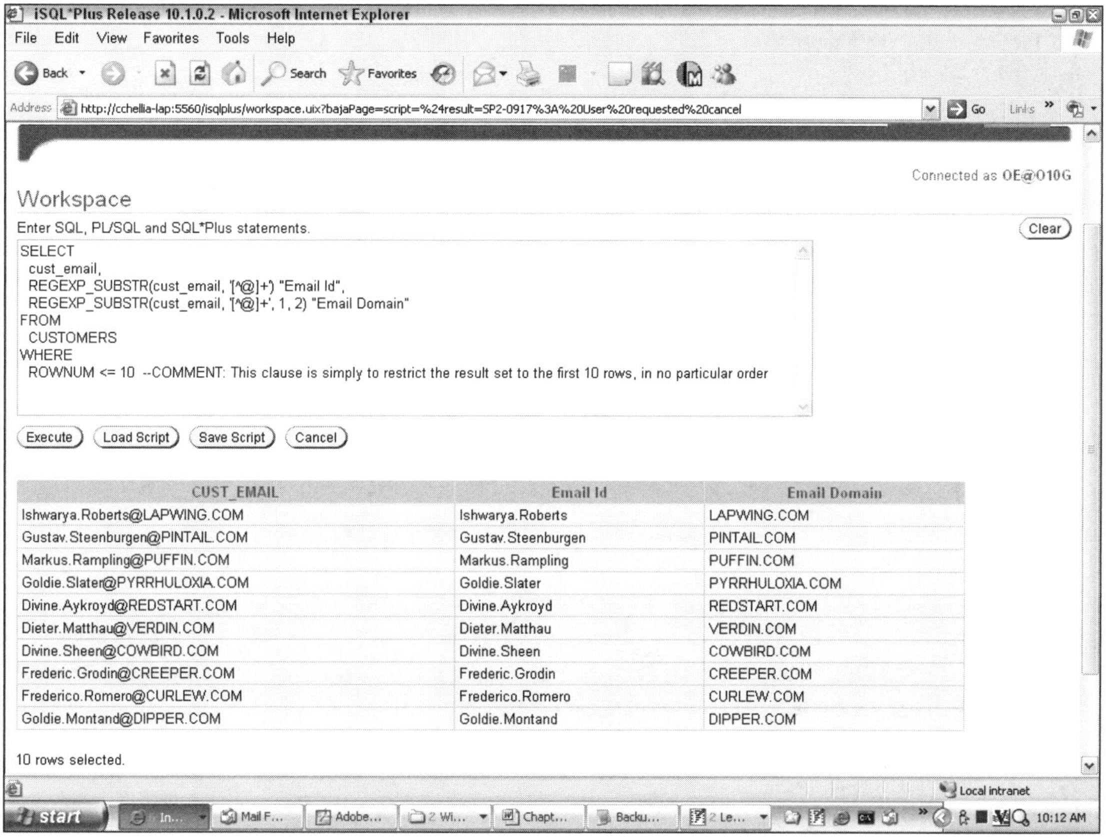

Figure 20-4: An example of `regexp_substr`.

Similar to Figure 20-3, another example of `regexp_substr` is shown in Figure 20-5, where a regular expression is used to pick out a positional word from the `product_description` column (in this case, it's the second word).

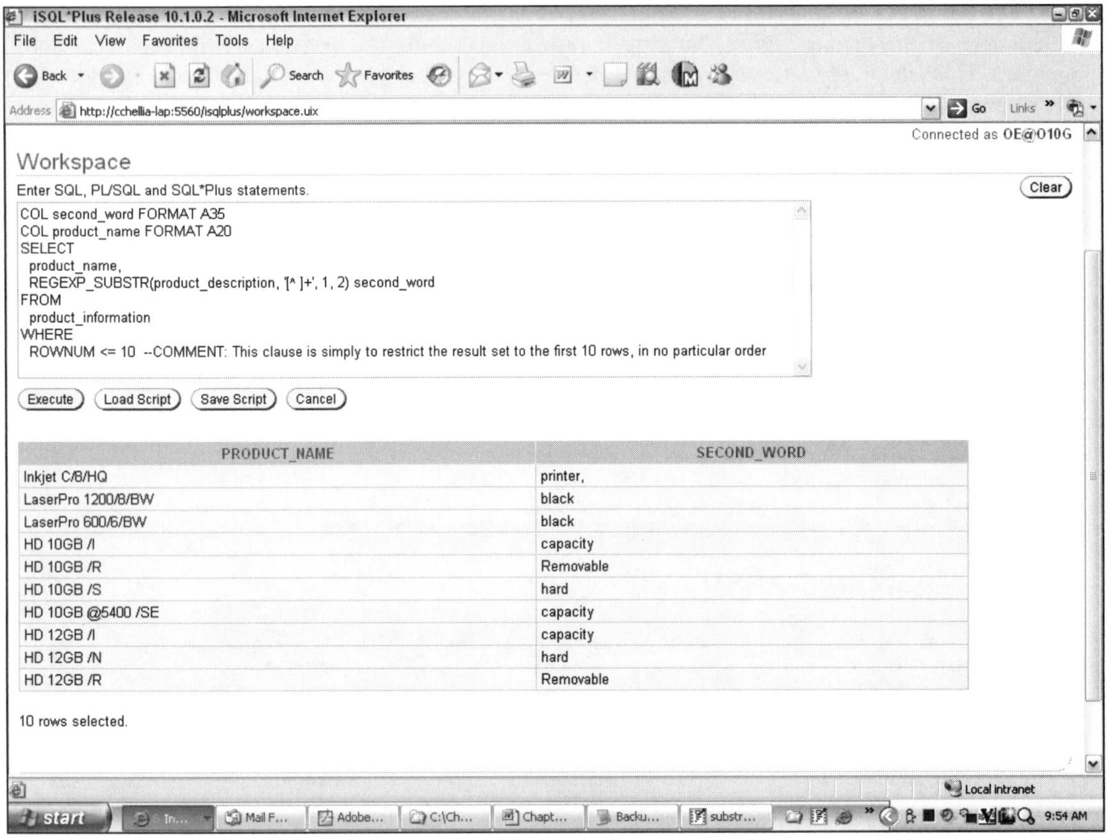

Figure 20-5: Using `regexp_substr` to pick out a positional word.

REGEXP_REPLACE

The power of regular expressions really becomes evident when a pattern match is coupled with a string to replace the match occurrence. `regexp_replace` returns the `src` string with every occurrence of the `pattern` replaced with the `replace` parameter. The `replace` parameter can contain up to 500 backreference instances in the form \n, where n is a number from 1 to 9. A backreference is an expression that was found in the original text and can be used to provide granular control over search and replace operations.

The syntax for this command is as follows:

```
REGEXP_REPLACE (src, pattern [, replace [, position [, occurrence
                [,match_option]]]])
Where:
  src, pattern, match_option: are the same as shown for REGEXP_LIKE earlier
  replace: the pattern to replace each match with (may include backreferences)
  position: the position in the string to start searching from (default = 1)
  occurrence: the occurrence to search for (default = 1)
```

Figure 20-6 uses data in the product_information table to illustrate this function. Assume that product catalogs have moved from a Web server (e.g., `http://www.supp-102094.com/cat/hw/p1797.html`) and are now stored on an FTP server as a .PDF (e.g.., `ftp://ftp.supp-102094.com/cat/hw/p1797.pdf`). This query uses `regexp-replace` to substitute `http` with `ftp` in the protocol, www with `ftp` in the server name, and `html` with `pdf` for the file type.

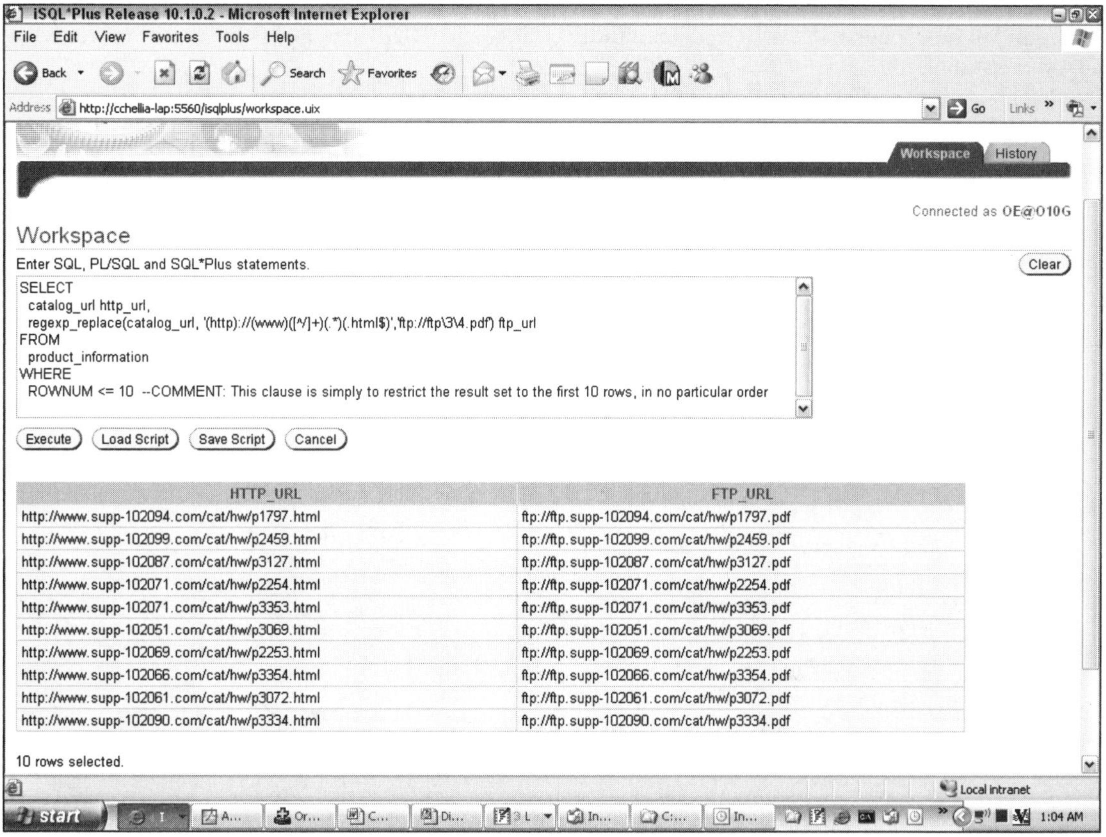

Figure 20-6: An example of using `regexp_replace`.

A variation of this SQL can be used in conjunction with `update` to modify all rows in the table accordingly.

```
UPDATE
  product_information
SET
  catalog_url = regexp_replace(catalog_url,
                              '(http)://(www)([^/]+)(.*)(.html$)',
                              'ftp://ftp\3\4.pdf') ;
```

Usage Scenarios

The introduction of regular expressions in the database provides some new and flexible options on how to design and architect an application. With this new capability it makes sense to delegate more processing from the client application or middle-tier closer to the actual data to leverage the scalability, security, and globalization features inherent to the database.

Regular expressions can be used in data definition language (DDL) statements to create indexes, views, and constraints.

Indexes

A typical table will have an index on columns that are frequently used. However, these indexes are not of much use to regular expressions, because they do not take into account the pattern being requested for a match. To illustrate, consider a table `t1` with column `c1` of `varchar2(2000)`, populated with data as shown in Figure 20-7. An index on column `c1` would create a b-tree based on the contents of each row, starting from the first character in the column (right-hand side of Figure 20-7).

```
CREATE INDEX t1_i1 ON t1 (c1);
```

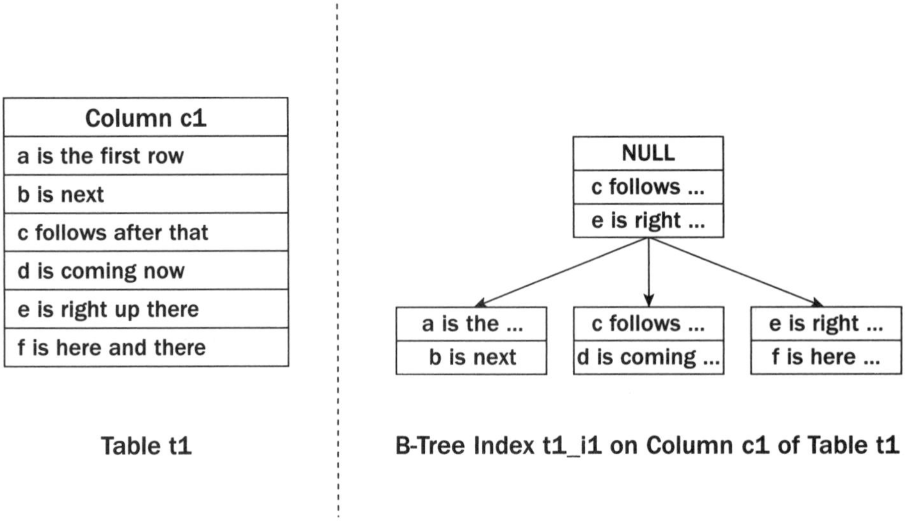

Figure 20-7: Example of a B-tree index.

If, for example, you were to search for the regular expression pattern "the", then this index is of no use because "the" occurs arbitrarily in the middle of the indexed column's contents. Figure 20-8 shows the `explain plan` the SQL engine will use to resolve the query, and it confirms that a full table scan is required. In fact the index will be of no use at all, except for simple patterns that are anchored to the start of the line — for example, '`^a is`'.

`explain plan` is a command used to show the execution plan the SQL engine will use to resolve a query. Understanding its output is useful for making informed decisions about database design.

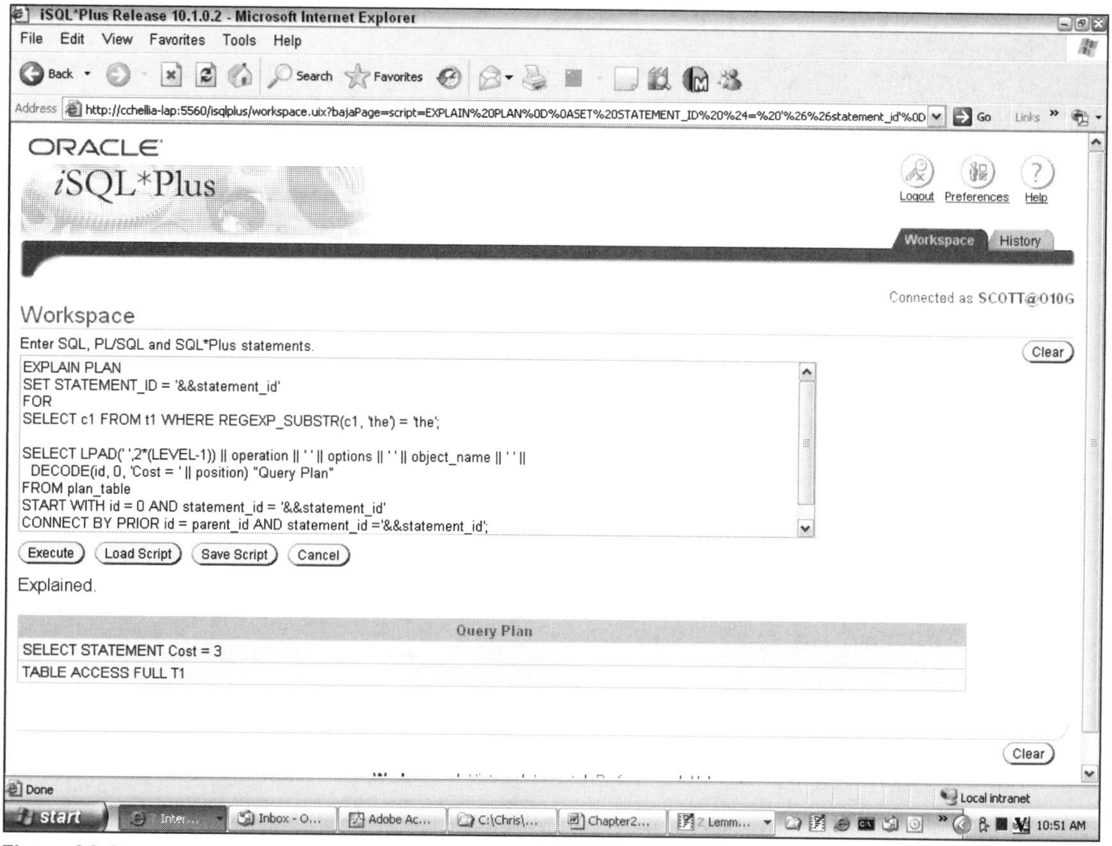

Figure 20-8: **`explain plan`** for a regular expression query using a simple index.

Don't let this bother you too much, because sometimes a full table scan is inevitable given the type of search — a regular expression is an arbitrary search of a column's contents, so there is no "perfect" index that covers all scenarios. However, if the search pattern is well known, then a function-based index can be used to avoid the full table scan. A function-based index is a b-tree index that is based on the result of applying a function on the column value, instead of just the column value. For this scenario, the command below creates a b-tree index using the value of `regexp_substr(c1, 'the')` instead of just `c1`.

```
CREATE INDEX t1_i1 ON t1 (REGEXP_SUBSTR(c1, 'the'));
```

This time, the `explain plan` shows that the query will use this index when resolving the regular expression and no longer requires a full table scan. Of course, this index will only be used for queries based on this pattern (see Figure 20-9). Extend this example with a more complex expression and you can see the power of providing indexed access for a complex text search.

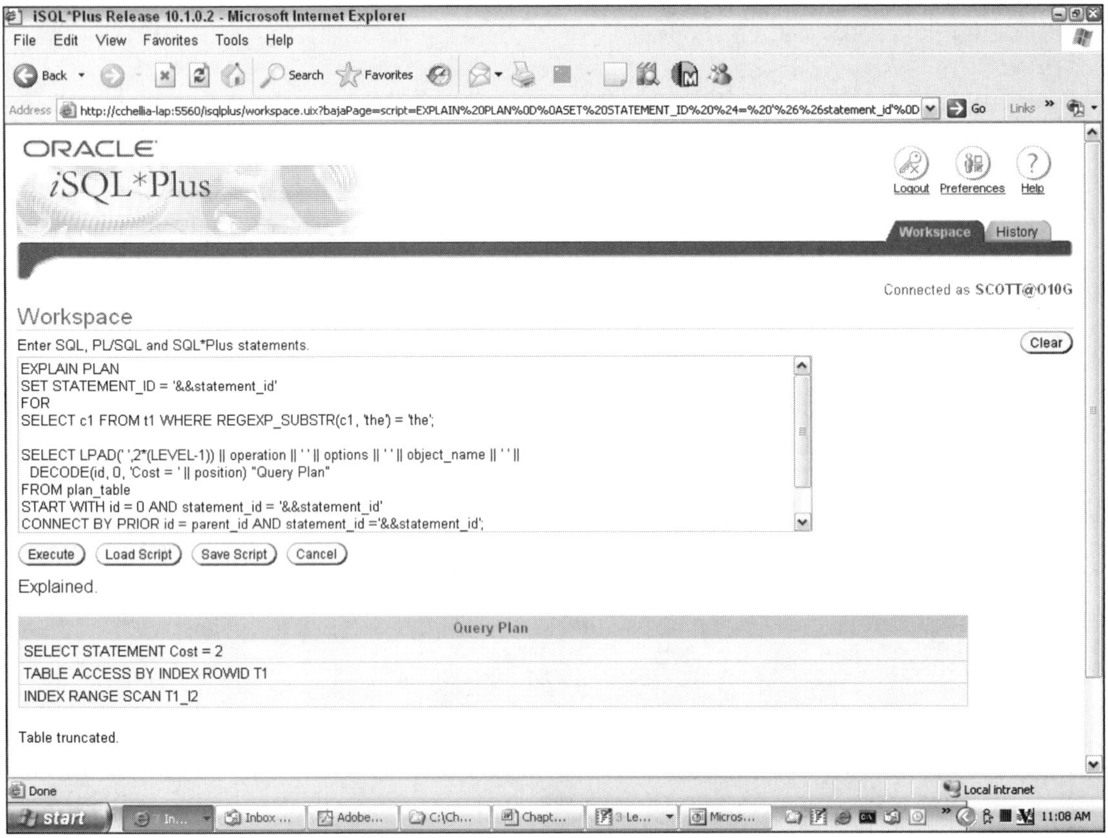

Figure 20-9: **`explain plan`** for a regular expression query using a function-based index.

Views

A view is typically used to format and subset a relational query so that only the right amount of information in the correct format is returned to the client application. Regular expressions can assist in both of these functions.

The following code creates a view to show the subset of products from the `product_information` table whose description contains the text "Standard Edition" or "'Professional Edition". A query against this view (see Figure 20-10) only shows the rows with the matching description.

```
CREATE OR REPLACE VIEW v1 AS
SELECT
  product_name,
  product_description
FROM
  product_information
WHERE
  REGEXP_LIKE(product_description,'(Standard|Professional) Edition')
```

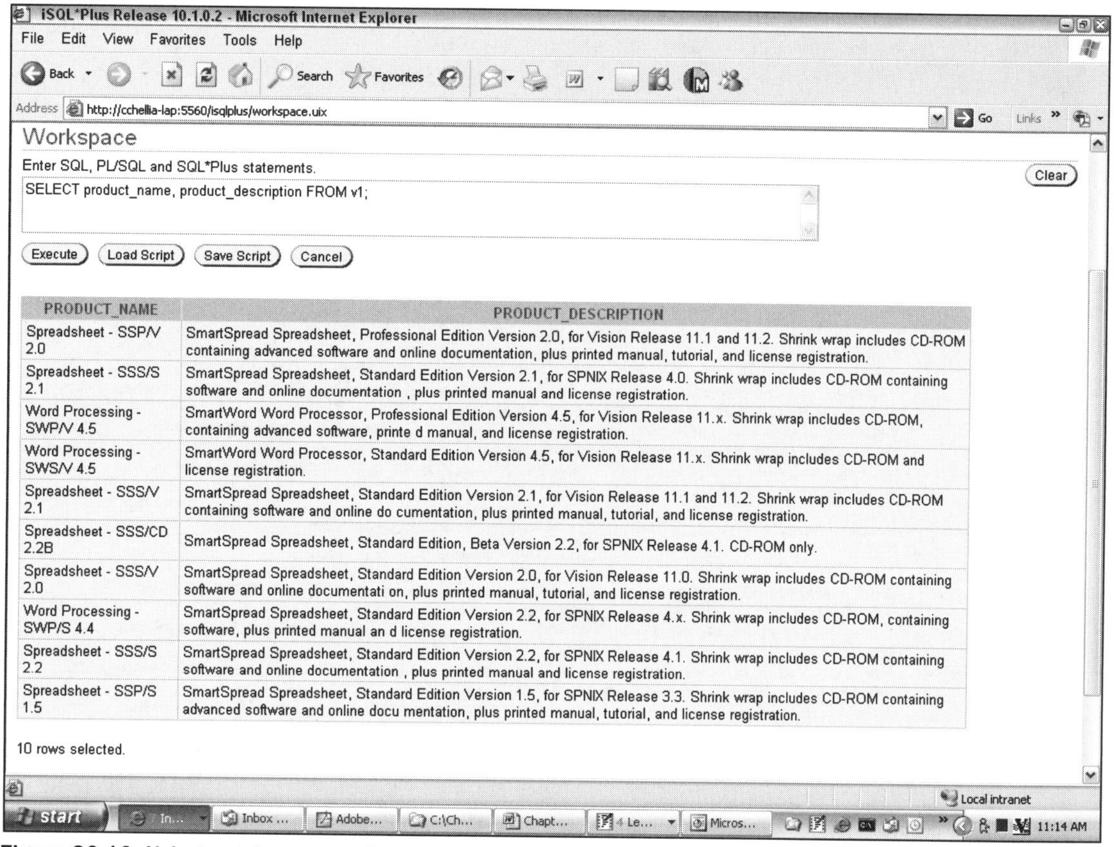

PRODUCT_NAME	PRODUCT_DESCRIPTION
Spreadsheet - SSP/V 2.0	SmartSpread Spreadsheet, Professional Edition Version 2.0, for Vision Release 11.1 and 11.2. Shrink wrap includes CD-ROM containing advanced software and online documentation, plus printed manual, tutorial, and license registration.
Spreadsheet - SSS/S 2.1	SmartSpread Spreadsheet, Standard Edition Version 2.1, for SPNIX Release 4.0. Shrink wrap includes CD-ROM containing software and online documentation , plus printed manual and license registration.
Word Processing - SWP/V 4.5	SmartWord Word Processor, Professional Edition Version 4.5, for Vision Release 11.x. Shrink wrap includes CD-ROM, containing advanced software, printe d manual, and license registration.
Word Processing - SWS/V 4.5	SmartWord Word Processor, Standard Edition Version 4.5, for Vision Release 11.x. Shrink wrap includes CD-ROM and license registration.
Spreadsheet - SSS/V 2.1	SmartSpread Spreadsheet, Standard Edition Version 2.1, for Vision Release 11.1 and 11.2. Shrink wrap includes CD-ROM containing software and online do cumentation, plus printed manual, tutorial, and license registration.
Spreadsheet - SSS/CD 2.2B	SmartSpread Spreadsheet, Standard Edition, Beta Version 2.2, for SPNIX Release 4.1. CD-ROM only.
Spreadsheet - SSS/V 2.0	SmartSpread Spreadsheet, Standard Edition Version 2.0, for Vision Release 11.0. Shrink wrap includes CD-ROM containing software and online documentati on, plus printed manual, tutorial, and license registration.
Word Processing - SWP/S 4.4	SmartSpread Spreadsheet, Standard Edition Version 2.2, for SPNIX Release 4.x. Shrink wrap includes CD-ROM, containing software, plus printed manual an d license registration.
Spreadsheet - SSS/S 2.2	SmartSpread Spreadsheet, Standard Edition Version 2.2, for SPNIX Release 4.1. Shrink wrap includes CD-ROM containing software and online documentation , plus printed manual and license registration.
Spreadsheet - SSP/S 1.5	SmartSpread Spreadsheet, Standard Edition Version 1.5, for SPNIX Release 3.3. Shrink wrap includes CD-ROM containing advanced software and online docu mentation, plus printed manual, tutorial, and license registration.

Figure 20-10: Using regular expressions to subset a view.

To format the result, the code following uses `regexp_replace`, and encloses the product version in bold markup (`<B>`, `<\B>`). Figure 20-11 shows the result.

```
CREATE OR REPLACE VIEW v2 AS
SELECT
  product_name,
  REGEXP_REPLACE(product_description, '(Standard|Professional) Edition',
'<B>\1<\B>') formatted_description
FROM
  product_information
WHERE
  REGEXP_LIKE(product_description,'(Standard|Professional) Edition')
```

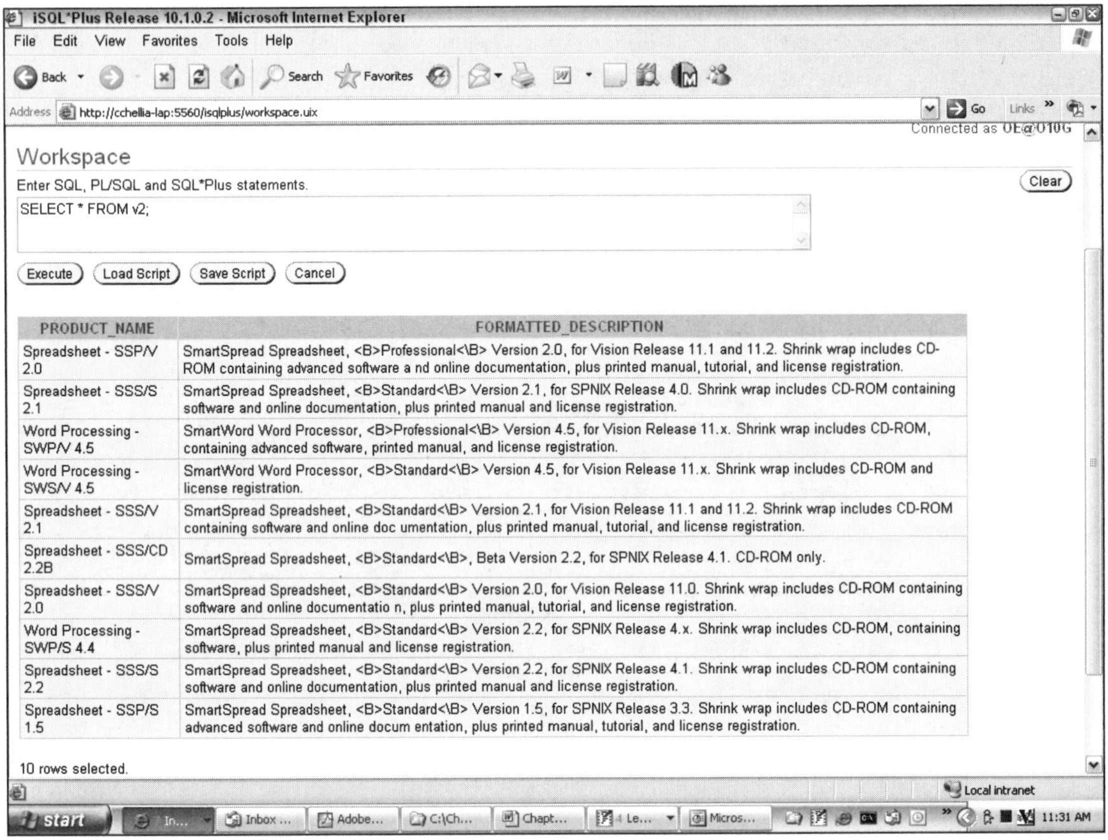

Figure 20-11: Formatting a view with **`regexp-replace`**.

Constraints

Regular expressions can be used with constraints to validate data entry. The example in Figure 20-12 shows a `check` constraint that enforces telephone numbers to be in the xxx-xxx-xxxx format. Any attempt to insert into this table with nonconforming telephone numbers will violate the constraint and be rejected.

Regular Expressions and NLS Support

Oracle adds an extra dimension to regular expressions because of the multilanguage support native in the database. Locale-sensitive applications that use regular expressions automatically leverage the native support for NLS within the database. This is important because regular expressions may behave differently depending on character set, language, territory, and sort order parameters. Native support in the database ensures application consistency and pattern portability across different locales.

A code sample of using regular expressions in conjunction with Oracle's NLS support is available at `www.oracle.com/technology/obe/obe10gdb/develop/regexp/regexp.htm`.

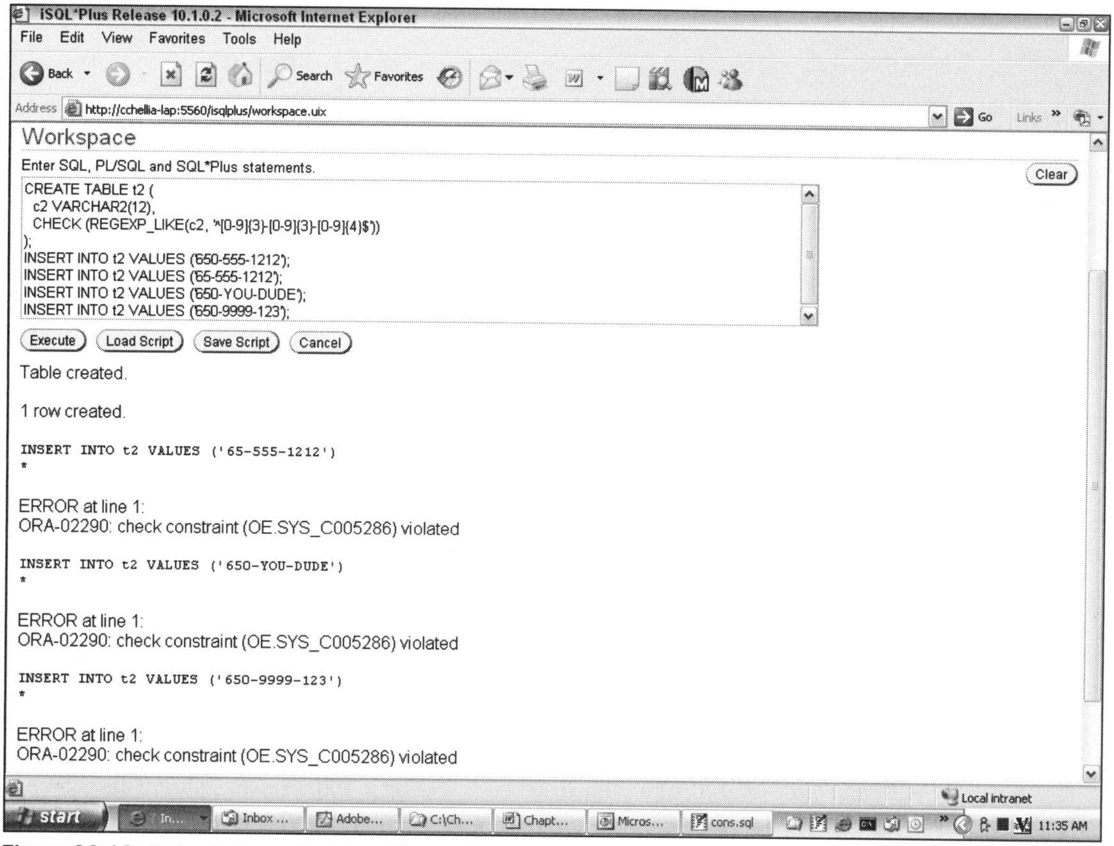

Figure 20-12: Enforcing constraints with regular expressions.

Architecture and Performance Considerations

This section briefly explains the architecture underlying regular expression support in the database. Understanding the architecture will provide a backdrop to better understand performance implications of using them in applications.

When a regular expression function is invoked, it is first necessary to parse, normalize, and then compile the expression. This occurs behind the scenes each time the function is invoked with a new pattern string. The result of the compilation is an internal finite state machine. All input data is then processed through the finite state machine to determine whether a match can be made or not. Once compiled for a pattern, the finite state machine is available for use repeatedly with new input data, without having to go through the (costly) compilation each time (see Figure 20-13).

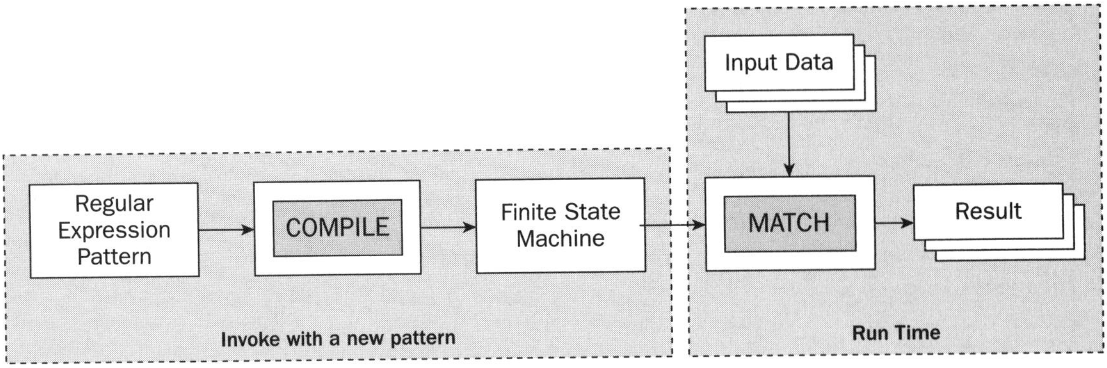

Figure 20-13: Regular expressions at run time.

Given the complexity to compile and match logic, regular expression functions (e.g., `regexp-substr`) can perform more slowly than their traditional counterparts (e.g., `substr`). There is no question that there is a cost to compile and match. As a guideline, if the expression is complex enough or if the pattern will be queried many times, then the economies of scale favor regular expression functions, because they are optimized and compiled. This is especially true if the alternative to using regular expressions requires many SQL conditions and predicates.

An exception to the previous guideline is the `regexp_like` function. This function only has to return the result of whether a match exists or not, without having to prove where it occurs. Its implementation is optimized based on this premise, and it can be considerably faster than the other functions.

Recall that a traditional index does not help much when resolving a regular expression. This is because a traditional index is a function of the data in the column. However, a regular expression match is a function of the data *and* the input pattern, which is unknown until run time (and there can be any number of these). If there are certain sets of patterns that are frequently evaluated, then a function-based index should be considered, as previously shown in Figure 20-9.

Ultimately, the runtime performance of a regular expression function is based on two interrelated factors: the complexity of the pattern and the input data it is being matched against. When defining a pattern, avoid excessive use of infinite quantifiers (`+`, `*`) and backreferences. When dealing with large sets of input data, these operators require significant memory buffers and CPU cycles to work through the pattern, leading to lower performance overall.

Expression Filter

Imagine a stock portfolio application that keeps track of statistical and financial information about the stock market. Subscribers to the application can maintain watch lists of interesting stocks and receive recommendations to buy or sell based on a set of criteria in their profile.

A typical relational implementation of this application would require a database table for the stock quotes and relevant data (see Figure 20-14). Presumably this table will receive updates many times in a typical trading day. As changes occur in the `stock` table, the application must iterate through each investor's profile and build a dynamic SQL query to see if the change matches the investment criteria of that investor as stated in their profile.

Stock

Symbol	PE	Price	Rating
ORCL	24.6	12.66	Strong Buy
SUNW	N/A	5.26	Hold
PSFT	N/A	21.23	Sell
BEAS	26.66	8.21	Sell

Figure 20-14: Example of stock table from stock portfolio application.

For example, at a point in time, Investor A may be interested in all stocks with a price earning (PE) ratio of less than 20 or price > 40. The data that matches this interest is resolved by the following SQL query:

```
SELECT
  symbol
FROM
  stock
WHERE pe <= 20
OR    price > 40
```

Investor B may be interested in all stocks where PE ratio is less than 10 and rating = "BUY", and data to match that interest is resolved by the following:

```
SELECT
  symbol
FROM
  stock
WHERE pe < 10
AND   UPPER(rating) = 'BUY'
```

While this is a typical implementation pattern, it quickly becomes unmanageable when real volumes of data are involved. Imagine that there can be many investors in the system and many factors that influence their interests. This contributes to a diverse range of interests in the system. For example, a user may be interested in ORCL if its price is between 10 and 12, but another only interested in the stock if its price is between 11 and 13. And, of course, the stock price is constantly changing on a regular trading day. In this dynamic environment, how would you proactively notify all investors any time their interest is satisfied, as soon as it happens? How could you predict the investors' reaction to a change for a particular stock, given that there are many combinations of expressions and possible value ranges?

This example briefly describes a class of applications where the interest is beyond just the existing data in the table, but any data that may become available in the future. For these types of applications, ideally the previous queries should be persisted and applied every time new data arrives or existing data is updated in the stock table. Examples of this usage model include publish/subscribe applications or applications that filter existing data for new interests, conditions, standards, or rules.

The Oracle Expression Filter feature in the database supports this type of database workload. With this support, the database can not only find data that match expressions but expressions that match a particular data point as well. Oracle Expression Filter allows developers to define, index, and evaluate expressions that describe interest in a piece of data. This feature allows expressions (or business rules) to be modified without changing the application. And because the expressions have been factored out, they can be indexed efficiently, making "match" queries faster overall.

The rest of this chapter explains the concepts and a concrete example of using Expression Filter for the example stock portfolio application and some other scenarios where they may be applicable.

Expression Filter Concepts

Variables that participate in an expression are known as *elementary attributes*. These attributes can be combined together with literals, functions (either standard database functions or user-defined functions), and table aliases to represent a simple condition, known as a *predicate*. Predicates are linked together by the logical operators `AND` and `OR` to form an *expression* that describes interest in some data. These expressions are in the same format as an SQL `where` clause and stored in an *expression data type* in the database. So for the stock portfolio application:

- `symbol`, `PE`, `price` and `rating` are examples of elementary attributes.
- `PE>'10'` and `UPPER(symbol)='ORCL'` are two examples of predicates.
- `(price < 15 AND UPPER(rating)='HIGH')` is an example of an expression.

Oracle 10*g* introduced an expression data type that can be used as a column of a user table. A user table can have more than one column of the expression data type. The collection of all data stored in an expression column of a table is known as an *expression set* (see Figure 20-15).

Relating this back to the stock portfolio application, you can now store an investor's interests as a set of predicates in an expression column in the table. This example creates a column called `interests` in the investor table.

```
CREATE TABLE investor (
  name            VARCHAR2(10),
  zipcode         NUMBER(5),
  phone           VARCHAR2(12),
  portfolioamount NUMBER,
  email           VARCHAR2(100),
  interests       VARCHAR2(2000)
)
/
```

Note that the `interests` column appears to be just a `varchar2` column in the table. This is because the expression data type is a *virtual* data type represented as a `varchar2`. There are two more steps necessary before this column can be used as an expression data type: (1) define an attribute set and (2) assign the attribute set to the table column.

Later you will populate the expression column with some sample interests and see the power of evaluating changes in stock information against the stored interests.

Define an Attribute Set

An *attribute set* is the meta data that describes the set of elementary attributes and functions used in an expression data type. This meta data is used at run time to validate contents of the expression set (see Figure 20-15).

The easiest way to create an attribute set is to group the elementary attributes into an Oracle object type and then invoke the `dbms_expfil.create_attribute_set` API to create an attribute set with the same name as the object type.

```
CREATE OR REPLACE TYPE PortfolioItem AS OBJECT (
  symbol          VARCHAR2(10),
  pe              NUMBER(5,2),
  price           NUMBER(5,2),
  rating          VARCHAR2(20)
)
/

EXEC DBMS_EXPFIL.CREATE_ATTRIBUTE_SET( attr_set => 'PortfolioItem',
                                       from_type => 'YES');
/
```

Alternatively, you can add individual elementary attributes to an attribute set using the `dbms_expfil_add_elementary_attribute` API.

By default, standard SQL functions (e.g., `upper`) are already implicitly defined in all attribute sets. But if you plan to use any user-defined functions in your expressions, they must be explicitly added to the attribute set using the `dbms_expfil_add_functions` API.

Linking back to the stock portfolio application, assume that the brokerage uses an analytical model to predict the probability of a company being acquired by another company — for example, in a takeover bid. They may make that analysis available to investors who in turn may use that information to decide whether or not to trade in a stock (i.e., their interest in the stock!). To enable use of this function in an Expression Filter it must first be registered in the attribute set.

```
-- In a real scenario this function would apply a more complex analytical model!
CREATE OR REPLACE FUNCTION probabilityOfBeingAcquired (symbol VARCHAR2)
  RETURN NUMBER IS
BEGIN
  RETURN 42; -- Returns 42 for all cases in this example!
END;
/

EXEC DBMS_EXPFIL.ADD_FUNCTIONS (attr_set => 'PortfolioItem',
                                funcs_name => 'probabilityOfBeingAcquired');
/
```

Assign an Attribute Set to a Table Column

Recall that the `interests` column in the investor table was defined as a `varchar2` column and as such it can contain any text, not just valid expressions. To enable the `varchar2` column as an expression data type, you must assign it to an attribute set, as shown here:

```
EXEC DBMS_EXPFIL.ASSIGN_ATTRIBUTE_SET( attr_set => 'PortfolioItem',
                                       expr_tab => 'investor',
                                       expr_col => 'interests');
```

`dbms_expfil.unassign_attribute_set` is the corresponding API to remove an attribute set from a column.

Assigning an attribute set to the `varchar2` column limits the scope of values it can now store. It is now limited to containing a valid expression (in SQL `where` clause format) that is made up of predicates and functions defined in the attribute set. All inserts or updates to this column are now validated against the meta data to ensure that it contains a valid expression.

This setup has effectively configured the `interests` column to be an expression data type. Figure 20-15 shows the relationship between the table column and the attribute set.

Investor

Name	Zipcode	Phone	Portfolio Amount	Email	Interests
Sarah	80126	720-555-1212	1000000	sgc@world.com	pe <= 20 OR price > 40
James	94065	650-555-1212	975000	ej@bigcar.com	UPPER(rating)="SELL" AND probabilityOfBeingAcquired > 40
					...

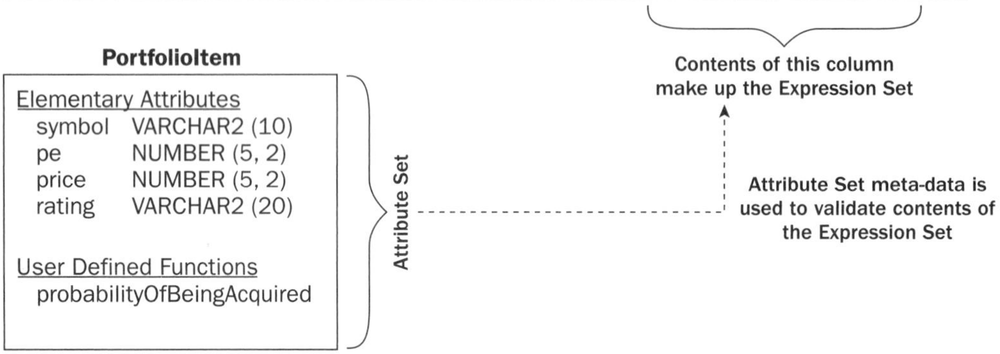

Figure 20-15: Relationship between expression set and attribute set.

Populate Expressions

Expressions are populated into the investor table using standard SQL to `insert`, `update`, or `delete`. The database will validate each expression to ensure it only contains the elementary attributes and functions specified in the corresponding attribute set, or else an error is raised. Expressions can also be loaded into a column of Expression data type using SQL*Loader.

Chapter 5 of the Oracle Database Application Developer's Guide — Expression Filter *details the full usage syntax of using Oracle utilities with Expressions.*

Some examples of populating expressions are shown here. In the first case, the investor Sarah is interested in stocks with PE <= 20 or anything where price > 40. The second case will fail, because the function name is spelt incorrectly and differs from what was specified in the attribute set. The third example rectifies the spelling error and sets up an interest for stock with a rating of SELL and a >40 percent probability of being acquired. The fourth example is interested in any stock less than $10 or with a STRONG BUY rating. And finally the fifth example shows an interest in ORCL stock with a PE < 10.

```
INSERT INTO
  investor
VALUES('Sarah', 80126, '720-555-1212', 1000000,
       'pe <= 20 OR price > 40');

-- We expect this row to fail, because of the incorrect function name.
-- Goes to show that expressions are being validated against registered metadata
INSERT INTO
  investor
VALUES('James', 94065, '650-555-1212', 975000,
       'UPPER(rating)=''SELL'' AND probabilityOfAcquitision > 40');

INSERT INTO
  investor
VALUES('James', 94065, '650-555-1212', 975000,
       'UPPER(rating)=''SELL'' AND probabilityOfBeingAcquired(symbol) > 40');

INSERT INTO
  investor
VALUES('Florence', 61640, '618-941-4126', 23000,
       'price<10 OR UPPER(rating)=''STRONG BUY''');

INSERT INTO
  investor
VALUES('Grace', 06155, '618-933-2637', 25006,
       'symbol=''ORCL'' AND pe < 10');
```

A real application would most likely present a GUI for an end user to graphically build his or her expressions, instead of using SQL `inserts` as shown. This GUI would be very similar to what is seen in query-by-example tools (e.g., Oracle Reports) which let you select a database column and apply a relational operator (e.g., >, <, `NOT`, =) on it. Except that you would build the expressions by selecting from items defined in the attribute set, rather than columns of a table.

Evaluate Incoming Data against the Expressions

To support expression data types, Oracle 10*g* introduced the SQL `evaluate` operator in the `where` clause. This operator takes in two parameters: name of the column storing the expressions (e.g., `investor.interests`), and the data item to evaluate it against (e.g., change in a stock's price). It returns `1` for all expressions that match the data item or `0` otherwise.

The incoming data item can be specified either as a `varchar2` with name-value pairs, or as an `AnyData` instance containing binary typed attributes. Both usages are shown in the examples to follow.

Figure 20-16 shows an incoming data item represented as name-value pairs. This query is looking for all investors interested in stock ticker ORCL and PE ratio = 18. The result has matched investor Sarah, who is interested in any stock where PE is <= 20 OR price > 40.

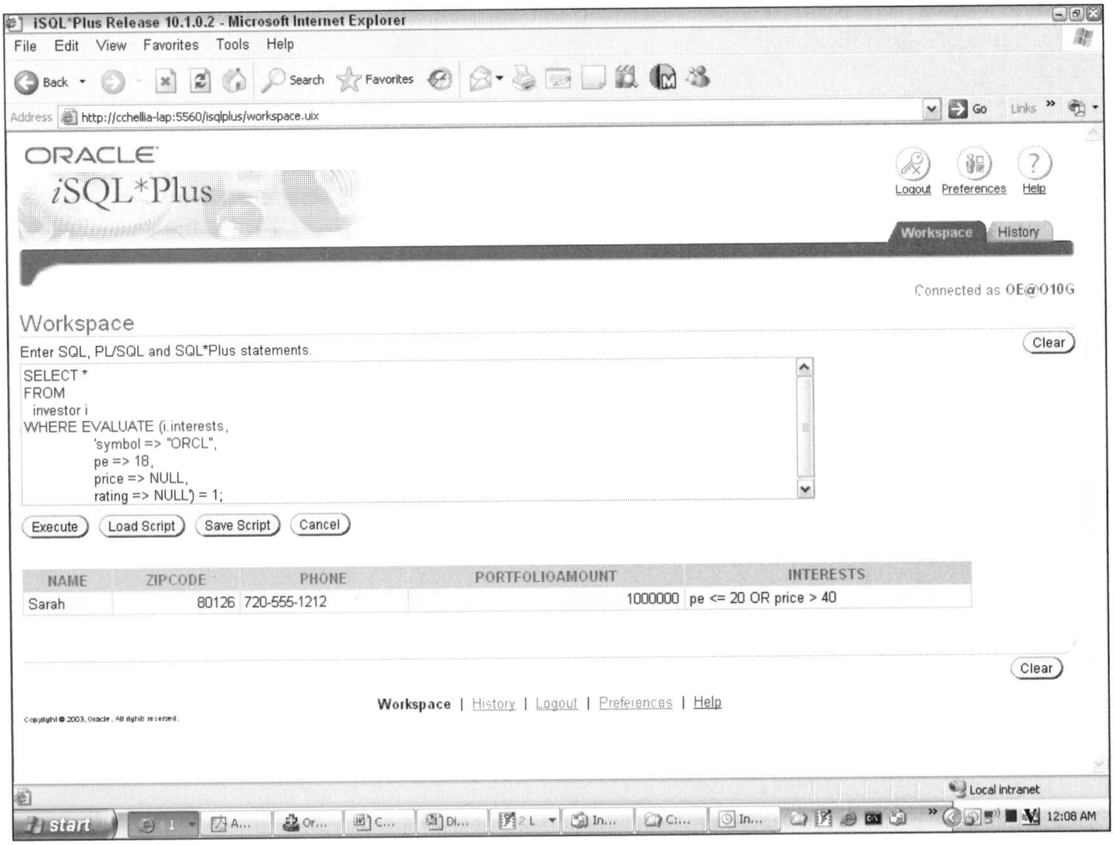

Figure 20-16: Example 1 of using `evaluate`.

The next example (see Figure 20-17) shows the incoming data as an instance of the `PortfolioItem` object type. It uses the `AnyData.convertObject` method to cast the instance into an `AnyData` instance and then passes it to the `evaluate` function. This time the query is looking for all investors interested in stock ticker ORCL with a PE ratio = 9. The result matches investor Sarah for the same reasons stated previously. It also matches investor Grace, who is specifically interested in ORCL stock when the PE ratio is < 10.

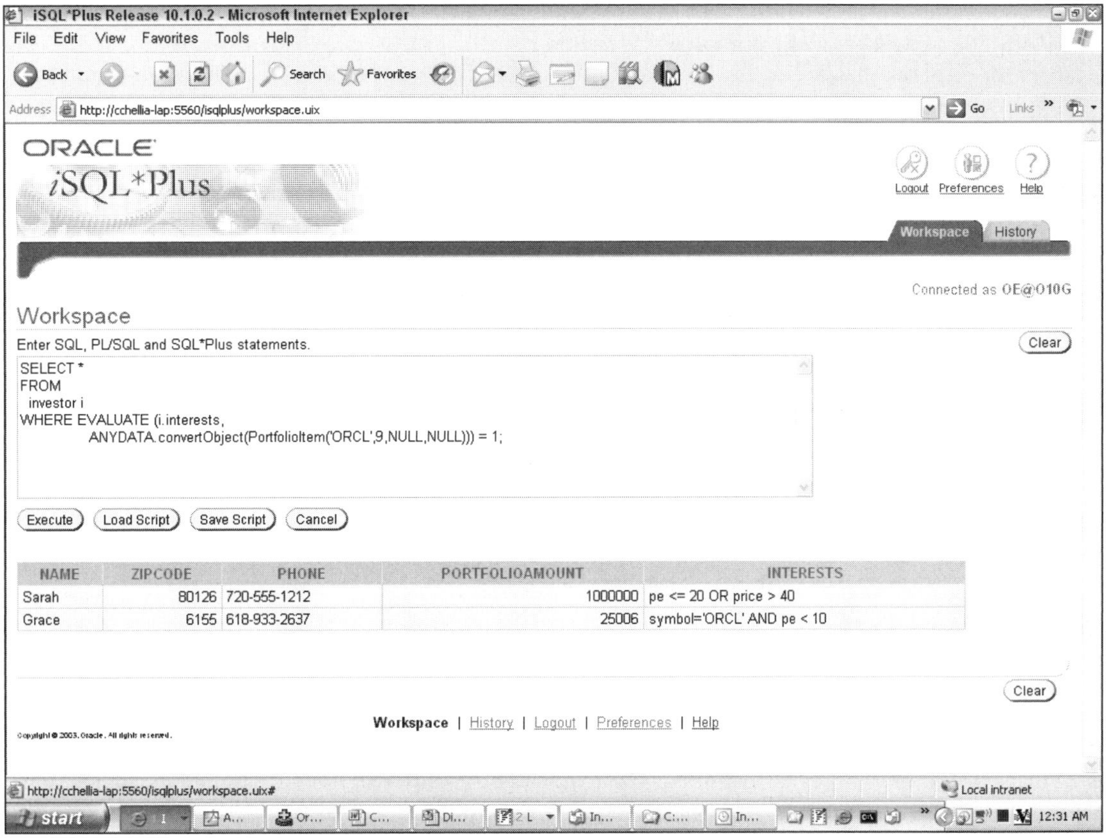

Figure 20-17: Example 2 of using `evaluate`.

To extend the example, the following code shows how the query from Figure 20-17 can be modified to directly notify the relevant investors by calling the `sendMail` function (from Chapter 18, "Introduction to Java Database Programming"). This code could also be attached to a trigger on the underlying stock table, so the process is completely automated in an elegant way.

```
SELECT sendMail('admin@your_brokerage.com',
                i.email, 'audit@your_brokerage.com',
                'Alert message from your_brokerage',
                'Hi ' || i.name || '. An event meets your investment criteria.')
FROM
  investor i
WHERE EVALUATE (i.interests,
                ANYDATA.convertObject(PortfolioItem('ORCL',9,NULL,NULL))) = 1;
```

Notice that Expression Filter has effectively decoupled the user's interests (subscriber) from the frequently changing stock data (publisher). Investors can change their profile at any time and it does not affect the application, because the previous SQL will always find the right set of investors that match the data at a given point in time. There is no need to change the SQL every time an investor changes their interests.

Indexing

With any relatively large expression set, there are bound to be common elements in their predicates. An Expression Filter index can be defined over an expression set to capitalize on this fact and speed up the `evaluate` operation.

An Expression Filter index normalizes the predicates by grouping them based on their left-hand sides and operators. Not all predicates are indexable, but where they are, Oracle maintains the index information in a set of persistent predicate tables (instead of the usual B-tree index). If an index exists, the query optimizer compares the cost of using the index versus alternate execution plans. The optimizer can also be forced to use the index if the `/*+ INDEX (your_index_name_here)*/` optimizer hint is specified.

If a column of expression data type is not indexed, then the `evaluate` operator builds and executes dynamic SQL for each expression stored in the column and executes it using the values passed in through the data item.

Relevance to Database Applications

Expression Filter is a good fit in applications where:

- There are a large number of incoming data items to be evaluated (e.g., frequent changes in stock price and statistic information during market hours)
- The incoming data is evaluated against many combinations of persistent queries containing conditional expressions (e.g., the profile or watch list of a large pool of investors)
- The conditional expression (SQL `where` clause) describes an interest in the incoming data items (e.g., Investor A is looking for a drop in PE ratio; Investor B is looking for a change in a stock's rating).
- The conditional expressions compare attributes with relational operators (`=`, `!=`, <, >, and so on).

There are many uses for Expression Filter in the database, in applications such as impact analysis (e.g., who would this change affect), demand analysis (e.g., what is the potential of this change), content based routing (e.g., where do I send this content), and publish/subscribe situations (e.g., who needs to know this information).

The stock portfolio application is one example of how this feature can help process a large volume of incoming data against an entity's interests by using a single `select` statement to `evaluate` matches. But imagine the power of Expression Filter in extending the scenario even further to support complex relationships between many entities — for example, if the portfolio application wanted to keep track of the category of investors (e.g. annual income, age group, etc.) attracted to a particular stock. In this case an Expression data type will be added to the stock table as well to manage the *m x n* relationship between the two. The possibilities are endless.

Expression Filter brings flexibility and an elegant solution to a certain set of problems. However, this comes at a price—at least in the short term. An Expression Filter index is not implemented natively in the Oracle Database 10g Release 1. As a result, a SELECT statement against this index can be up to 100% slower, due to the overhead in using the extensible indexing framework. DML statements also incur an overhead for Expression Filter maintenance. It is recommended to properly stress test an application using this feature prior to deploying it. Just like earlier database features (e.g., replication, partitioning), performance will improve as this capability becomes natively integrated into the database.

Summary

This chapter introduced two new ways to effectively access and process database content: regular expressions and Expression Filter. Regular expressions bring into the database support for powerful text matching and substitution capability through four new functions:

- `Regexp_like`
- `Regexp_instr`
- `Regexp_substr`
- `Regexp_replace`

Using these functions in conjunction with database constraints and views reduces the need for developers to write (messy) string manipulation code. Combined with a function-based index, regular expressions become very relevant today for applications that require fast and easily configurable pattern matching across large sets of text data.

Expression Filter extends the database to support a different class of applications such as personalization, impact analysis, content routing, and publish/subscribe. These types of applications match data against a set of persistent expressions in order to identify a match (contrary to the typical method of applying query expressions against a set of data). Oracle enables this feature through an expression data type and the SQL `evaluate` function.

21

Object Relational Interactions with Oracle

The Oracle database features strongly as a relational database management system (RDBMS), but what is sometimes overlooked is its strength and support of object-relational capabilities. In its traditional RDBMS role, the database focuses on efficient storage and management of data based on a scalar set of data types. The object-relational (OR) capability extends the relational model to provide persistence features that integrate extensible types and operations natively into the database.

This chapter first introduces the difference between object database management systems (ODBMSs) and relational database management systems. With that backdrop we introduce how an object-relational database (ORDBM) bridges the gap between the two technologies. We introduce Oracle's support for object types in the database and how it relates to Unified Modeling Language (UML) and the Java programming language.

Rather than recap the basic SQL syntax and access patterns for object types in the database, we refer you to the application walkthrough in Chapter 9 of the *Oracle Database Object Relational Developer's Guide — Object Relational Features*. Examples in this chapter extend the syntax shown in that guide and relate that application to the OE sample schema. We focus on showing some of the advanced capabilities such as the following:

- Programmatic access to oracle objects through Java
- Object views over existing relational data
- Declaring SQL types based on existing Java classes

The chapter also provides an overview of the JPublisher code generation tool.

Object Relational

Chapter 18, "Introduction to Java Database Programming," introduced the issue of impedance mismatch between an object-oriented (OO) programming language (Java) and using a relational database as a persistent store. To recap briefly, OO languages allow the definition of complex objects and promote encapsulation of business logic. Reuse and extensibility is natural in these languages through their support for inheritance and polymorphism (dynamic method dispatching and substitutability).

The *impedance mismatch* becomes apparent when trying to map these OO language properties to a RDBMS, which is *merely* capable of understanding two-dimensional structures (tables) of scalar data types (`number`, `char`, `date`). An RDBMS requires additional application services to handle persistence, query capability, concurrent access, security, and caching of objects as they are materialized from and stored into relational tables. These services are commonly referred to as *persistence services*.

Of course, the impedance mismatch is only an issue when you are mapping to a relational database. This section takes a step back to look at how pure object databases play in this space and how they compare to a relational database. With that backdrop, we introduce Oracle's object-relational capability, which bridges the gap between the two. Object-relational support gives developers the flexibility to build and deploy appropriate structures in the database for an application.

ODBMS and RDBMS and ORDBMS

An ODBMS doesn't have to deal with impedance mismatch and persistence services to map the OO language constructs to the database. This is because it natively stores instances of user-defined objects, instead of decomposing the objects down to rows and columns. An ODBMS *only* understands objects and provides *orthogonal* persistence, where a developer need not be aware that some objects are persistent and others are not. Persistence is completely transparent to the developer. The ODBMS solution is shown in Figure 21-1 (A).

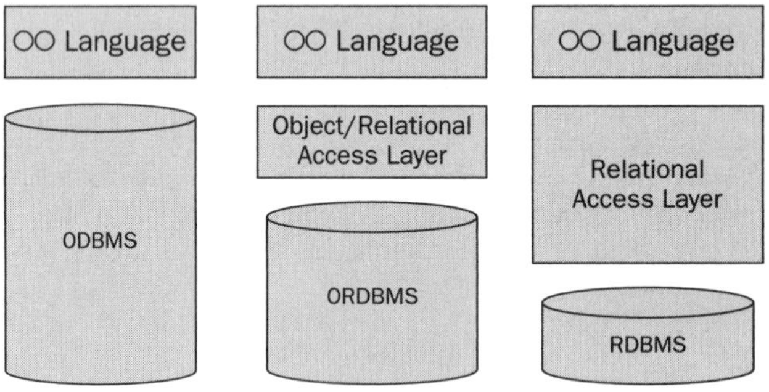

(A) **(B)** **(C)**

Figure 21-1: The ODBMS solution.

Clearly there are benefits here, since a developer enjoys the object-oriented programming model without having to deal with any persistence issues, implicitly or explicitly. Any modified objects are transparently flushed to the database as and when required.

There are a number of downsides associated with this approach and ODBMSs in general, primarily:

- There is a lack of standard tools for interoperating with ODBMS, such as standards for connectivity, online analytical processing, or reporting.
- Most ODBMS implementations are based on an in-memory object tree and are only scalable to the extent of maximum physical memory available on a machine.
- The long-term viability of pure ODBMS vendors is questionable, given that they have less than 2 percent of the global database market share, with a declining trend.
- Concurrent use and locking is an issue, especially with long-running transactions. This impedes the scalability of the system with a large user base.

Chapter 18 showed another (more commonly used) set of solutions based on using a persistence framework as an access layer over a RDBMS; see Figure 21-1 . Three variations of relational access layers were discussed to address persistence issues: pure JDBC, J2EE Entity Enterprise Java Beans (EJBs), and OracleAS TopLink. The benefits of using a persistence framework with an RDBMS include the following:

- It is a tried and tested platform, with good tools for monitoring and managing the system.
- It has a track record in performance and scalability to support a large user base.
- It has full and complete ACID support for short- and long-running transactions

However, object purists would claim that the downside of the RDBMS approach is that too much is lost in the relational access layer and that this layer detracts from the benefits gained by using an OO language.

The third approach, shown in Figure 21-1 (B), is the use of an ORDBMS to narrow the gap between a native object database and relational database. An ORDBMS provides an avenue to extend the scalar types in a database to define custom data types reflective of the business domain. Persistence is neither orthogonal nor transparent with this approach, but there is a smaller gap between the object-oriented language and underlying data — structures — hence, a simpler mapping layer.

With the advancements in JDBC 3.0 and SQL3, support for ORDBMS is becoming more mainstream and standardized. With this evolution, vendors such as Oracle have focused on making it simpler and more productive to use object-relational features. Oracle has a strong object-relational capability in the server and development tools such as JPublisher (discussed later) and OracleAS TopLink.

Introducing Oracle Objects

Oracle has provided native support for custom data types (referred to as *object types, SQL types*, or just *types*) since release 8.1.*x*. Object types in the database enable developers to better represent the data structures required for an application and simplify access to them. Object types minimize the object-relational impedance mismatch and hence reduce the need for a mapping layer between client-side objects and the database columns and tables that contain the data.

To illustrate, consider the pure relational implementation for the OE schema purchase order example. The data for this application is normalized across a number of different tables (`orders`, `order_items`, `product_information`, etc.). Each table consists of columns based on scalar data types (e.g., `date`, varchar2). Primary and foreign key constraints are created to provide identity and relationships between the tables. Business operations are then written in PL/SQL or as Java Stored Procedures against these tables. So there are plenty of schema objects—but it is not obvious how to visualize, track, and relate the relationships between these schema objects and the original business operations around a purchase order.

This section walks through an implementation of the purchase order example in an object-relational model. It shows the basic constructs and how to relate a UML class model into object-type definitions in the database. The constructs shown are an extension of the Purchase Order sample application from Chapter 9 of the *Oracle Database Object Relational Developer's Guide—Object Relational Features*, which is a part of the standard Oracle documentation set. Figure 21-2 depicts an object-oriented perspective of this application as a UML class diagram, the key classes being Customer, Stock (i.e., a catalog item) and Purchase Order (generated by Customer to purchase one or more Stock items).

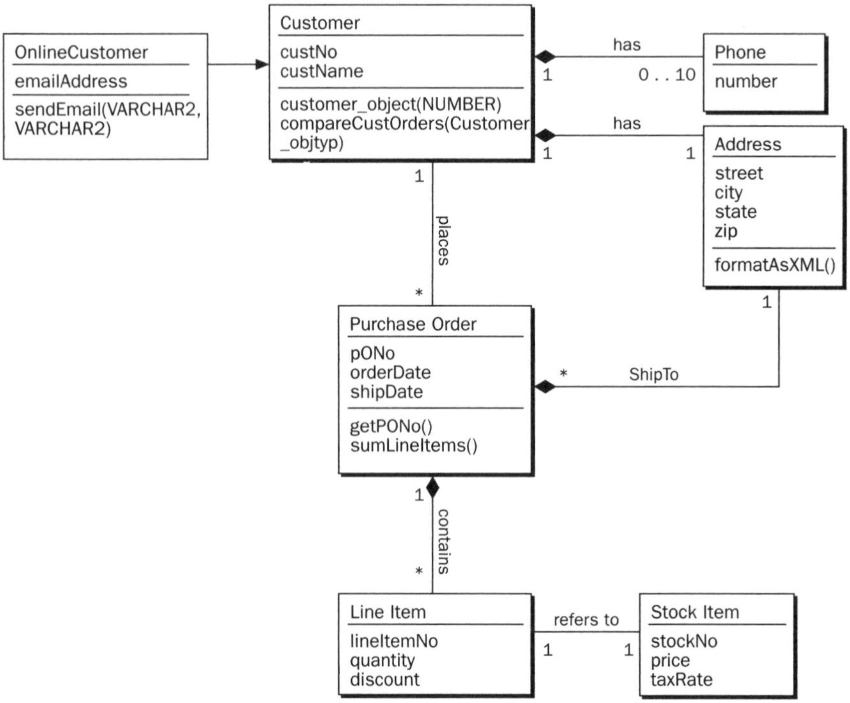

Figure 21-2: An object-oriented perspective as a UML class diagram.

Object Types

Object types (OT) are the building blocks for Oracle's support of OR features. Like a UML class definition, an object type is an SQL custom data type that encapsulates a concept or business entity. An object type groups the attributes, operations, and relationships relevant to a UML class into a single structure to better organize and access the data.

This section explains the four categories of Oracle object types: simple, reference, collection, and composite.

Simple Object Type

A simple object type consists of scalar data types. It is used to group a set of related attributes and methods to represent a *UML class*—for example, grouping the `Street`, `City`, `State`, and `Zip` attributes into an `Address_objtyp`, as shown in the following code. The declaration also shows how a method (a function in this case) can be associated with the object type. A more complete discussion on method declarations is provided later. The `StockItem_objtyp` is another example of grouping two scalar data types (`number`) into a simple object type.

```
CREATE OR REPLACE TYPE Address_objtyp AS OBJECT (
  Street          VARCHAR2(200),
  City            VARCHAR2(200),
  State           CHAR(2),
  Zip             VARCHAR2(20),
  MEMBER FUNCTION formatAsXML RETURN VARCHAR2
  );
/

CREATE OR REPLACE TYPE StockItem_objtyp AS OBJECT (
  StockNo     NUMBER,
  Price       NUMBER
  );
/
```

Reference Object Type

A `REF` is a logical pointer to represent relationships between class instances. It is an internal data type that is constructed from the object identifier (OID) of the referenced object. `REF`s model UML associations and can be based on singleton or collection object types described later in this section.

For example, consider the association between a line item and stock item. A stock item is typically defined once in a catalog, but many orders can be placed for that item. In a relational model, this will be represented with a `stock_id` foreign key in the `line items` table and requires a join to access the relevant stock information. The object-relational approach, more elegantly, uses a `REF` to represent this association:

```
CREATE OR REPLACE TYPE LineItem_objtyp AS OBJECT (
  LineItemNo    NUMBER,
  Stock_ref     REF StockItem_objtyp,
  Quantity      NUMBER,
  Discount      NUMBER
  );
/
```

`REF`s reduce the need for foreign key mapping between two classes by providing an easy forward navigation path between the objects. Associated objects are accessed by using dot notation to follow the `REF`s seamlessly, just as in the Java programming language. In the preceding example, given a `LineItem_objtyp` object instance, the price of the item is easily accessed with the following:

```
<instance_variable>.DEREF(stock_ref).price
```

Given that `REF`s are just pointers, it is possible for the object identified by a REF to become unavailable if it has been deleted or had permissions revoked. This is known as a *dangling* `REF`, and Oracle provides an SQL predicate (`is dangling`) to test for this condition. Dangling `REF`s can be avoided by declaring referential integrity constraints against object types.

Collection Object Type

An object type can include a collection of other objects within its definition. For example, a Purchase Order definition includes a set of Line Items associated with the Order (see Figure 21-2). Collections are used for UML associations that have a *cardinality* greater than 1 or *. Oracle supports two constructs to define collections — `varrays` and `nested tables`.

A `varray` is an ordered and bounded collection. It is useful for collections of fixed length (i.e., UML cardinality of 1..N), where the elements must be stored and accessed in the same order. For example, the following code creates a bounded array of 10 elements, each a `varchar2(25)`. `Varrays` are not limited to scalar data types. The `varchar2` in the example below may have been another custom object type.

```
CREATE OR REPLACE TYPE PhoneList_vartyp AS VARRAY(10) OF VARCHAR2(25);
/
```

A `nested table` is an unbounded and unsorted collection. It is useful for larger collections of unknown size (i.e., UML cardinality of 0..*). This example declares a `nested table` collection of the previously defined `LineItem_objtyp` object type.

```
CREATE OR REPLACE TYPE LineItemList_ntabtyp AS TABLE OF LineItem_objtyp;
/
```

`Varrays` are stored inline within a table structure. An SQL interaction with `varrays` will fetch the *whole* collection at once, which may have performance implications for the application. As such, `varrays` are more suited to smaller collections or usage patterns that iterate across the entire collection. Although the entire collection is fetched, individual elements can still be addressed using array offsets.

Conversely, SQL interactions with `nested tables` allow direct access to individual instances of objects within the collection. For example, an application can query and fetch a single instance of `LineItem_objtyp` without having to access the whole collection. `Nested table` collections are also stored in a separate underlying table, which provides the flexibility to define storage parameters specific to the type, volume, and access frequency of the data.

Composite Object Type

Composite object types are based on scalar *and* other data types. This is typically used to represent *UML aggregation* and *UML composition* associations to show the relationship between the parts that make up a whole. For example, consider that a car is made up of an engine and transmission, or as shown in the following, a `Customer_objtyp`, which contains an `Address_objtyp`, and a collection, namely, `PhoneList_vartyp`:

```
CREATE OR REPLACE TYPE Customer_objtyp AS OBJECT (
  CustNo           NUMBER,
  CustName         VARCHAR2(200),
  Address_obj      Address_objtyp,
  PhoneList_var    PhoneList_vartyp
) NOT FINAL;
/
```

The `NOT FINAL` keyword will be discussed later in this chapter.

And finally, the Purchase Order object type is an example of a composite object that includes the following:

- A REFerence to a customer
- A nested table of line items
- An address, which includes a varray of phone numbers

The type also declares two methods, which will be discussed in the following section.

```
CREATE OR REPLACE TYPE PurchaseOrder_objtyp AS OBJECT.
  PONo                    NUMBER,
  OrderDate               DATE,
  ShipDate                DATE,
  Cust_ref                REF Customer_objtyp,
  LineItemList_ntab       LineItemList_ntabtyp,
  ShipToAddr_obj          Address_objtyp,

  MAP MEMBER FUNCTION
    getPONo RETURN NUMBER,

  MEMBER FUNCTION
    sumLineItems RETURN NUMBER
  );
/
```

Object Type Methods

Methods are procedures or functions that are associated with an object type, to implement behavior specific for that type. They can be implemented in Java or PL/SQL in the database or any other language outside the database and accessed as external calls. Methods encapsulate the underlying data in an object by intuitively grouping business operations against the data, *together with* the data.

This section explains the four different types of methods that can be associated with an object type: member, constructor, comparison, and static methods.

Member Methods

Member methods are the preferred way to access an object instance's data or behavior against an object instance's data. Methods have access to an internal parameter named self that denotes the current instance. self is analogous to the this parameter that is implicitly available in all Java classes.

Consider the need to format customer addresses as XML in the Purchase Order application. A purely relational implementation might use a PL/SQL function to select the relevant columns from the table and insert tags accordingly to generate the output. This function might accept a customer_id parameter and query against the table to wrap the address attributes as XML:

```
CREATE OR REPLACE FUNCTION formatAsXML (customer_id NUMBER)
```

Alternatively, the function might accept each of the four attributes as a separate parameter and wrap them in XML:

```
--The following command has been split across two lines for clarity
CREATE OR REPLACE FUNCTION formatAsXML (Street VARCHAR2, City VARCHAR2,
                                        State VARCHAR2, Zip VARCHAR2)
```

Regardless of the approach, the function requires access privileges on the table. As the table evolves, the impact of the evolution is not clear because there is no logical tie between the table and the operations acting against it.

The object-relational approach associates operations *with* the type definition. An example was shown with the `formatAsXML` method declared within `Address_objtyp` earlier. This is more intuitive and provides for elegant queries — for example, this query prints the customer's address in XML format for all customers in `customer_objvw`:

```
SELECT c.address_obj.formatAsXML() FROM customer_objvw c;
```

There are better ways to generate XML from database queries, using Oracle's XML Development Kit and XML Database capabilities.

Constructor Methods

Like constructors in an object-oriented programming language, a constructor method returns a new, non-null instance of the object type. Oracle provides a default *attribute value constructor* for each object type. This is a constructor with the same name as the object type, and it accepts a value for each of the attributes defined. Following is an example of invoking the constructor in PL/SQL:

```
DECLARE
  newCustomer customer_objtyp := NULL;
BEGIN
  newCustomer := customer_objtyp(42,
                                 'Adams, Douglas',
                                 Address_objtyp('123 Handy Road',
                                                'Dandyville', 'CA', 94999),
                                 phonelist_vartyp('+1-650-555-1212',
                                                  '+61-8-9555-1212')
                                );
END;
/
```

The default constructor may be supplemented with one or more user-defined constructors to provide alternative ways to create instances of the object type, as in the following:

```
CREATE OR REPLACE TYPE Customer_objtyp AS OBJECT (

  ... some code snipped ...

  CONSTRUCTOR FUNCTION
    customer_objtyp(id IN NUMBER) RETURN SELF AS RESULT,

) NOT FINAL;
/
```

Using this definition, Figure 21-3 shows examples of how to invoke the custom constructor in PL/SQL and SQL respectively.

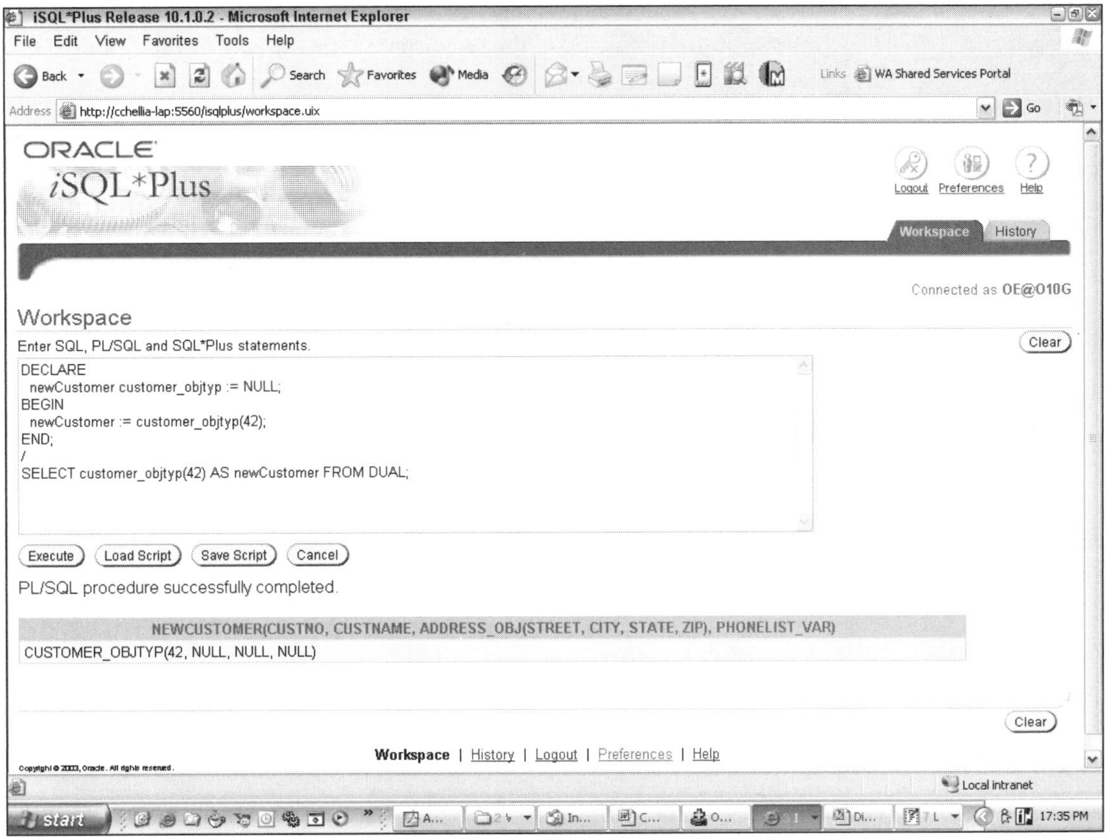

Figure 21-3: Invoking the custom constructor.

Although the default attribute value constructor is convenient, its signature will be subject to change as the object model changes. For example, if an attribute is added to an object type, then any code that invokes the default constructor must be modified to include the new attribute. It is a good practice to specify a custom constructor with the bare minimum number of attributes necessary for an object type, in order to minimize the impact of schema evolution (discussed later).

Comparison Methods

Scalar data types have a predefined order that is used when trying to compare or sort instances of them. For example, with a `date`, it is well known that 1-Feb-05 comes after 31-Jan-05. Object types, however, are made up of multiple attributes and data types and as such do not have an intrinsic basis to compare instances. Oracle supports two ways to define a basis for ordering (and hence sorting) object types — `map` methods and `order` methods.

An object type can only define one or the other but not both of these methods. Declaring either method enables object comparison (and hence sorting) in SQL statements. SQL involving comparisons (e.g., `object 1 <= object2`) or implicit sorts (e.g., `distinct`, `group by`, `order by`, `union`) are automatically rewritten by the SQL processor to invoke these functions. If neither method is defined, objects can only be compared for equality — that is, two instances of the same object type are only equal if values of all their corresponding attributes are equal.

A `map` method is a parameter-less member function prefixed with the `map` keyword. It returns a scalar data type. If defined, the method is automatically used to evaluate comparisons between instances. Object instances will be sorted based on the scalar data type it returns. `map` methods are usually based on the identity attribute of an object type — or, in relational-speak, the primary key attribute.

```
CREATE OR REPLACE TYPE PurchaseOrder_objtyp AS OBJECT (

  ... some code snipped ...

  MAP MEMBER FUNCTION
    getPONo RETURN NUMBER,

  );
/

CREATE OR REPLACE TYPE BODY PurchaseOrder_objtyp AS

  MAP MEMBER FUNCTION getPONo RETURN NUMBER IS
  BEGIN
    RETURN PONo;
  END getPONo;

  ... some code snipped ...

END;
/
```

In the Purchase Order example, the `getPONo` method is defined as the `map` method. So a query that compares two Purchase Order instances is implicitly rewritten to invoke the `map` method. For example, the expression `(PO1 > PO2)` is evaluated using `(PO1.getPONo() > PO2.getPONo())`.

An `order` method is a function that accepts a single parameter of another object of the same type. It returns a negative integer, zero, or a positive integer if the current object (`self`) is less than, equal to, or greater than the parameter passed in.

```
CREATE OR REPLACE TYPE Customer_objtyp AS OBJECT (

  ORDER MEMBER FUNCTION
    compareCustOrders(x IN Customer_objtyp) RETURN INTEGER

  ... some code snipped ...
) NOT FINAL;
/

CREATE OR REPLACE TYPE BODY customer_objtyp AS

  ORDER MEMBER FUNCTION compareCustOrders(x IN Customer_objtyp)
```

```
                                    RETURN INTEGER IS
    BEGIN
      RETURN SELF.CustNo - x.CustNo;
    END compareCustOrders;

    ... some code snipped ...

  END;
  /
```

`Order` methods should be used sparingly, as they are less efficient than `map`, especially when comparing large sets of data. They are invoked repeatedly and can only compare two objects at a time. However, they are useful when it is not easy to define the comparison semantics between objects — for example, with spatial objects, where the function may return the proximity to a certain well-defined spatial feature or location.

> **The Map and Order methods are the SQL object type equivalent of the java.util.Comparator interface in the Java programming language.**

Static Methods

Member, constructor, and comparison methods define behavior that applies to a *specific instance* of an object type. Those methods have access to the attribute and state of an object instance through the `self` parameter. `Static` methods do not have access to the `self` parameter. They are used to implement behavior applicable to the object type *as a whole* and not just a specific instance. `Static` methods are typically used to provide helper/utility functions, for example, to cast an object into another type. Static methods are also commonly used to implement the factory pattern for an object type, such as methods that control the lifecycle of an object (e.g. `createNewPurchaseOrder` or `deletePurchaseOrder`).

Inheritance Support

Inheritance and polymorphism are two important reasons for the popularity of OO programming languages. Although Oracle has supported object types in the database since release 8.0.*x*, support for inheritance (and hence polymorphism) was only added in later versions (release 9.*x* and above). This native support now makes it possible to map a nontrivial object model to object types in the database.

Like an inheritance hierarchy in the Java programming language, SQL inheritance allows object types to be declared in a hierarchy. An object type declared as `not final` is eligible to become a supertype (sometimes referred to as a *generalization*). New object types can then become subtypes (or a *specialization*) and inherit the attributes and methods from the supertype. Changes to attributes and methods in the supertype are automatically available to the subtypes. Like Java, Oracle only supports single inheritance, which means a subtype can inherit from only one supertype. Or in layman's terms, it means a *child* (subtype) can only have one *parent* (supertype), but a parent can have many children (subtypes), with no limit on the number of *generations*. Children automatically inherit all attributes and behavior of the parent unless they explicitly specify otherwise.

To better understand inheritance using the previous example, consider creating a specialized Customer type to represent online customers. This type will capture a customer's e-mail address, in addition to the attributes previously defined for a customer.

Notice the original definition of `Customer_objtyp` in the preceding code specified the `not final` keyword. With this declaration, a subtype (`OnlineCustomer_objtyp`) is created using the `under` keyword. There can be multiple levels in this hierarchy; so for example, further subtypes can be created `under OnlineCustomer_objtyp` to represent `DomesticOnlineCustomer_objtyp` and `InternationalOnlineCustomer_objtyp`. This subtype declares an attribute to store the customer's e-mail address and an additional method to send the customer an e-mail.

```
CREATE OR REPLACE TYPE OnlineCustomer_objtyp UNDER Customer_objtyp (
  EmailAddress     VARCHAR2(50),

  MEMBER FUNCTION
    sendEmail(subject IN VARCHAR2, msg IN VARCHAR2) RETURN VARCHAR2
)  NOT FINAL;
/
```

The preceding code invokes the `sendEmail` function, which was previously declared in Chapter 18, "Introduction to Java Database Programming." If this function is not present in the database, the command returns with an error message — "Warning: Type created with compilation errors".

The implementation body for a subtype is no different from a regular object type and has access to the `self` variable. In this case, the method calls a previously defined function (from Chapter 18, "Introduction to Java Database Programming") to send an e-mail to the customer.

```
CREATE OR REPLACE TYPE BODY OnlineCustomer_objtyp AS

  MEMBER FUNCTION sendEmail(subject IN VARCHAR2, msg IN VARCHAR2)
                  RETURN VARCHAR2 IS
  BEGIN
   RETURN sendMail('alert@database.com', SELF.EmailAddress, NULL, subject, msg);
  END sendEmail;

END;
/
```

All attributes and methods from the supertype are accessible directly from each instance of the subtype. Oracle creates a default *attribute value constructor* for the subtype that consists of all the supertype attributes followed by the subtype attributes. Figure 21-4 shows an example of invoking the attribute value constructor. It also shows an example of calling the new method defined in the subtype and, for completeness, how to call a method inherited from the supertype.

An object type or a method within an object type can be declared as `not instantiable`. In the case of an object type, this means no constructor is associated with it. In the case of a method, it means no implementation is associated with it — it's just a method signature. `not instantiable` is useful for defining classes and methods in an inheritance hierarchy. It is analogous to the `abstract` modifier in the Java programming and is used in the same context.

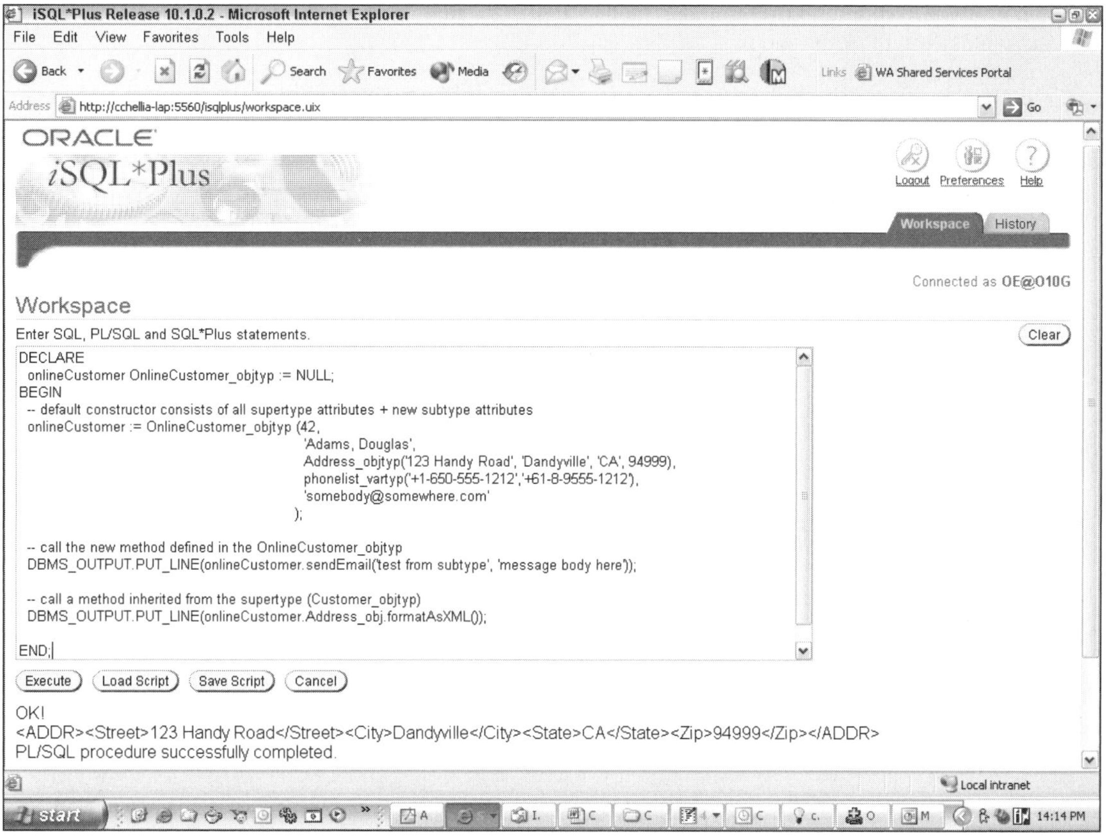

Figure 21-4: Invoking the attribute value constructor.

Schema Evolution

Change is inevitable, and as a result, schema evolution is an inevitable requirement. Changes to a business model can and usually will affect an application. In a relational model, the impact of the change can be minimized with well-defined SQL and underlying data management tools provided by the RDBMS (e.g., import/export, SQL*Loader, `create table as select`, etc.). There is added complexity when dealing with changes in an object model, which typically consists of composite types and references.

Oracle supports the following changes to an object type through the `alter type` command:

- Add and drop attributes to an object type.
- Add and drop methods to an object type.
- Increase the length, precision, or scale of a numeric attribute (e.g., `number`).
- Increase the length of a varying length character attribute (e.g., `char` or `varchar2`).
- Alter the `final` and `instantiable` status of an object type.
- Modify the limit and size of `varray`s and collection elements.

An `alter type` command first updates the internal data dictionary representation of the object type. This is usually a quick operation.

It will then propagate the change to dependent schema objects (e.g., subtypes and tables). There are two keywords to specify how and when this happens. The time for this operation to complete is dependent on the volume of data and type of change. The `cascade` keyword propagates changes to dependent schema objects. The default option associated with `cascade` is `including table data`, which converts the data to the new format simultaneously while propagating the change. The alternative is `not including table data`, in which case Oracle leaves the underlying data untouched. Even though the data is in the old structure, query results are always converted into the most current version prior to display. The conversion adds a performance overhead at run time.

The different versions of an object type as it evolves can be reconstructed by querying the `[ dba | all | user ]_type_versions` data dictionary view.

Mapping to UML Concepts

Oracle's object type support provides a rich ORDBMS interface to represent a UML class model as database structures. Developers benefit by reducing the complexity and maintenance effort to flatten classes down to scalar database types. Applications benefit by minimizing the runtime performance overhead to assemble relational structures into an object model.

The following table serves as a summary and quick reference of how Oracle ORDBMS features map to UML constructs or concepts

UML Concept	Oracle ORDBMS
Class	Object type.
Attribute	Attribute defined in an object type. Attributes can be scalar data types or previously defined object types.
Method	Method defined in an object type. Methods can be implemented in PL/SQL, Java, or external languages. Oracle supports the following methods: ❑ Member methods ❑ Constructor methods ❑ Comparison methods (`map`, `order`) ❑ Static methods
Cardinality	Bounded (`varray`) or unbounded (`nested table`) collections. Collections can be single level or multilevel (collections within collections).
Association (navigation)	`REF` as a pointer to an existing object.
Composition	Composite object types.
Aggregation	Composite object types or `REF` data types.
Inheritance	Object type inheritance through `final`, `not final`, `under`, and `instantiable` constructs.

Using Oracle Object Types

The previous section introduced how to define and create object types that map to an application's class model. This section looks at different ways to use these object types in an application, namely:

- Using an existing Java class definition as a persistent object type
- Using object-type definitions to create instances of objects in the database
- Using Java to interact with objects in the database

Existing Java Class as a Persistent Object Type

Support for SQLJ object type (sometimes called SQL Type of Language Java) was introduced in Oracle 9*i* Release 9.*x*. It is a way to define a custom type in the database that is based on an existing Java implementation. The Java class must implement either the JDBC standard interface (`java.sql. SQLData`) or the Oracle-specific `oracle.sql. ORAData` interface. These interfaces are discussed in more detail later in this chapter in the "Using Java to Interact with Database Objects" section.

Consider a Java application to manage a catalog or inventory. This application will most likely have a Java class to represent a `Product`. A trivial implementation of this class is shown here, with a single method to calculate the markup for a particular product. Note that the class implements `SQLData`, a JDBC 2.0 feature, to support Java interaction with an ORDBMS.

```
package ch21;

import java.sql.*;
import java.sql.*;
import oracle.jdbc.*;
import oracle.sql.STRUCT;
import oracle.jpub.runtime.MutableStruct;

public class Product implements SQLData
{
  public static final String _SQL_NAME = "OE.PRODUCT_OBJTYP";
  public static final int _SQL_TYPECODE = OracleTypes.STRUCT;

  public int productId;
  public String productName;
  public float listPrice ;
  public float minPrice ;

  public Product (int productId, String productName, float listPrice, float
minPrice)
  {
    setProductId (productId);
    setProductName (productName);
    setListPrice (listPrice);
    setMinPrice (minPrice);
  }

  public void readSQL(SQLInput stream, String type)
  throws SQLException
  {
    setProductId (stream.readInt());
    setProductName (stream.readString());
```

```
    setListPrice (stream.readFloat());
    setMinPrice (stream.readFloat());
  }

  public void writeSQL(SQLOutput stream)
  throws SQLException
  {
    stream.writeInt(getProductId());
    stream.writeString(getProductName());
    stream.writeFloat(getListPrice());
    stream.writeFloat(getMinPrice());
  }

  public String getSQLTypeName() throws SQLException
  {
    return _SQL_NAME;
  }

  /* accessor methods */
  public void setProductId (int productId) { this.productId = productId;}
  public void setProductName (String productName) {this.productName = productName;}
  public void setListPrice (float listPrice) {this.listPrice = listPrice;}
  public void setMinPrice (float minPrice) {this.minPrice = minPrice; }
  public int getProductId () {return productId;}
  public String getProductName () {return productName;}
  public float getListPrice () {return listPrice; }
  public float getMinPrice () {return minPrice;}

  // Business Operations (Methods)
  public float markup() {
    return ((minPrice > 0.0f) ? (listPrice / minPrice) : 0.0f);
  }

}
```

The following command loads the class into the database:

```
loadjava -user oe/oe -resolve ch21\Product.java
```

The next step is to declare the object type to SQL with a `create type` command. The type is defined as `using sqldata` because it implements the `SQLData` interface. Each attribute and method is optionally defined with the `external` keyword. Note that SQLJ object types will not have a type body, since the implementation is provided in the Java class.

```
CREATE OR REPLACE TYPE Product_objtyp AS OBJECT
EXTERNAL NAME 'ch21.Product' LANGUAGE JAVA
USING SQLDATA (

  productId NUMBER (9) EXTERNAL NAME 'productId',
  productName VARCHAR2 (80) EXTERNAL NAME 'productName',
  listPrice NUMBER EXTERNAL NAME 'listPrice',
  minPrice NUMBER EXTERNAL NAME 'minPrice',

  MEMBER FUNCTION markup RETURN NUMBER EXTERNAL NAME 'markup() return float'
);
/
```

The SQLJ object type is then available for use anywhere in place of a regular object type. In this example, it is used as the basis of an object view:

```
CREATE OR REPLACE VIEW Product_objvw
OF Product_objtyp
WITH OBJECT IDENTIFIER (productId)
AS SELECT
  pi.product_id,
  pi.product_name,
  pi.list_price,
  pi.min_price
FROM
  product_information pi
;
```

There is no longer an impedance mismatch, since the client object matches the server definition. Object instances are accessible both through Java and SQL. Figure 21-5 shows a query against the object view, invoking the method implemented in Java.

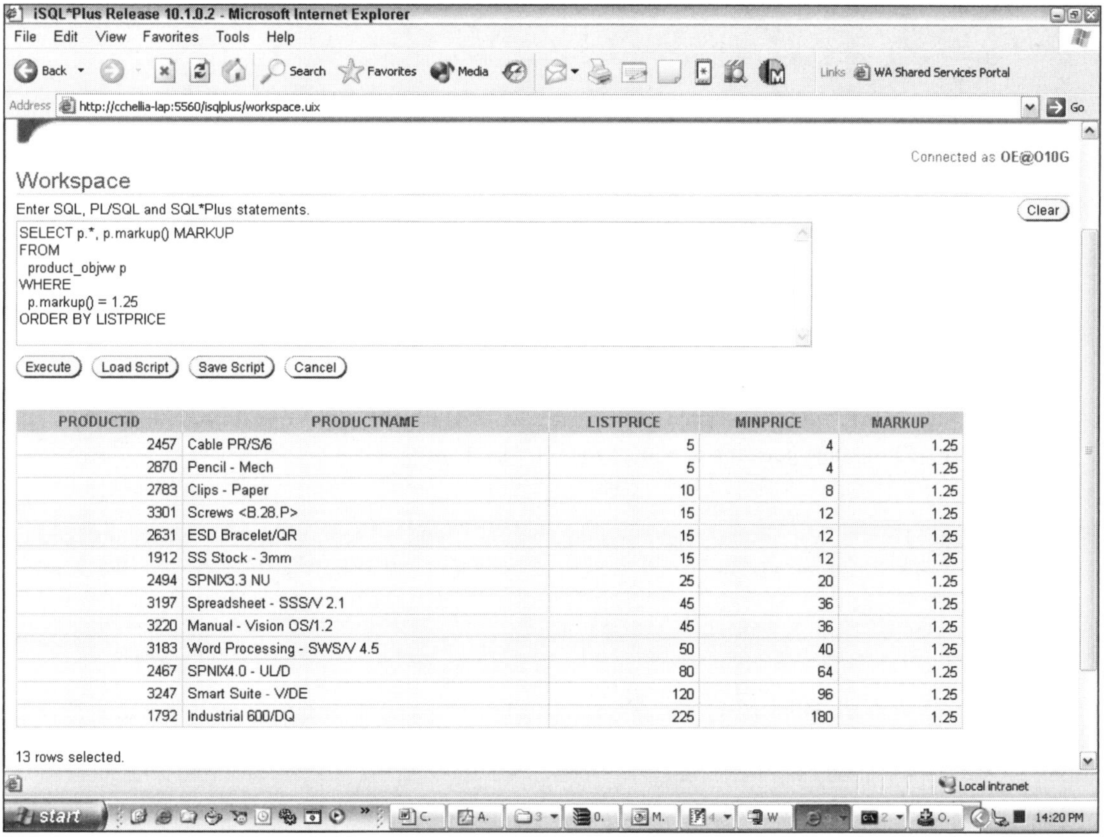

PRODUCTID	PRODUCTNAME	LISTPRICE	MINPRICE	MARKUP
2457	Cable PR/S/6	5	4	1.25
2870	Pencil - Mech	5	4	1.25
2783	Clips - Paper	10	8	1.25
3301	Screws <B.28.P>	15	12	1.25
2631	ESD Bracelet/QR	15	12	1.25
1912	SS Stock - 3mm	15	12	1.25
2494	SPNIX3.3 NU	25	20	1.25
3197	Spreadsheet - SSS/V 2.1	45	36	1.25
3220	Manual - Vision OS/1.2	45	36	1.25
3183	Word Processing - SWS/V 4.5	50	40	1.25
2467	SPNIX4.0 - UL/D	80	64	1.25
3247	Smart Suite - V/DE	120	96	1.25
1792	Industrial 600/DQ	225	180	1.25

Figure 21-5: Invoking the method implemented in Java.

Creating Instances of Object Types in the Database

The definition of an object type or SQLJ object type specifies a data structure template and associated behavior. It does not associate any storage, nor does it provide a way to create instances of the object in the database. This section walks through four usage patterns of how to realize object types, as summarized in Figure 21-6.

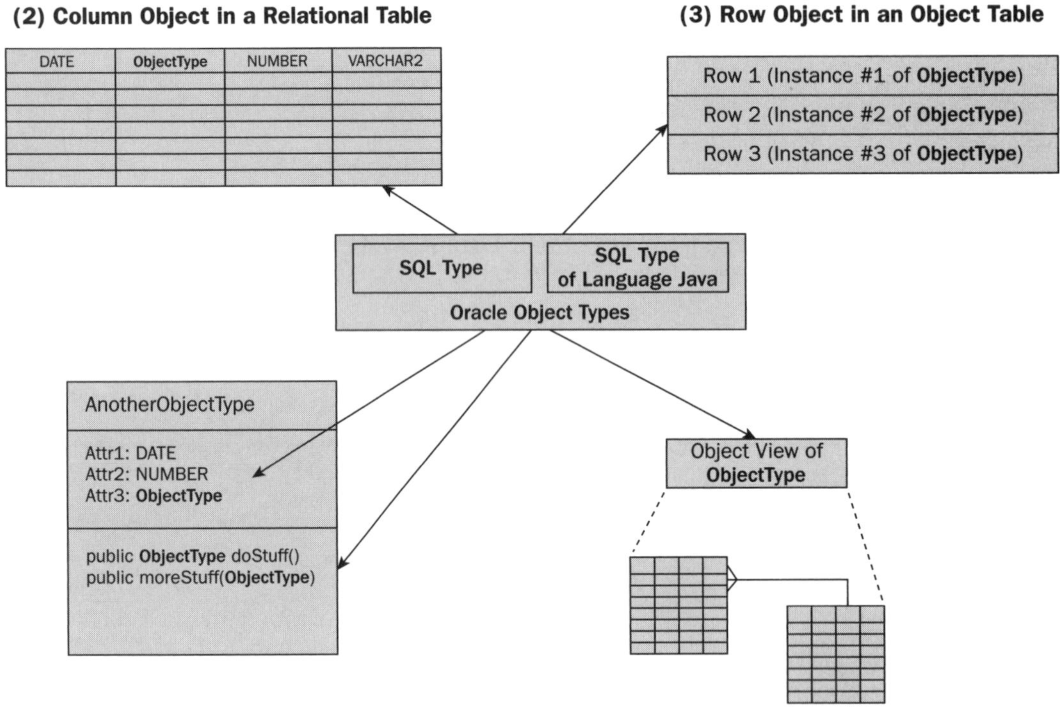

Figure 21-6: Four usage patterns of how to realize object types.

The first usage pattern was shown earlier, where an object type is used as part of a composite object. Object types can be used as attributes, method parameters, or function return values in other object types. Object types can be used as columns in a relational table. An instance is created in the column by invoking the constructor or by assigning a previously created instance to the column. Such instances have all the attributes and methods defined for its type and are referred to as *column objects*.

Figure 21-7 shows an example of using a column object. In the first `select` statement, the instance is retrieved as a whole, while the second `select` statement accesses each attribute within the instance as a column.

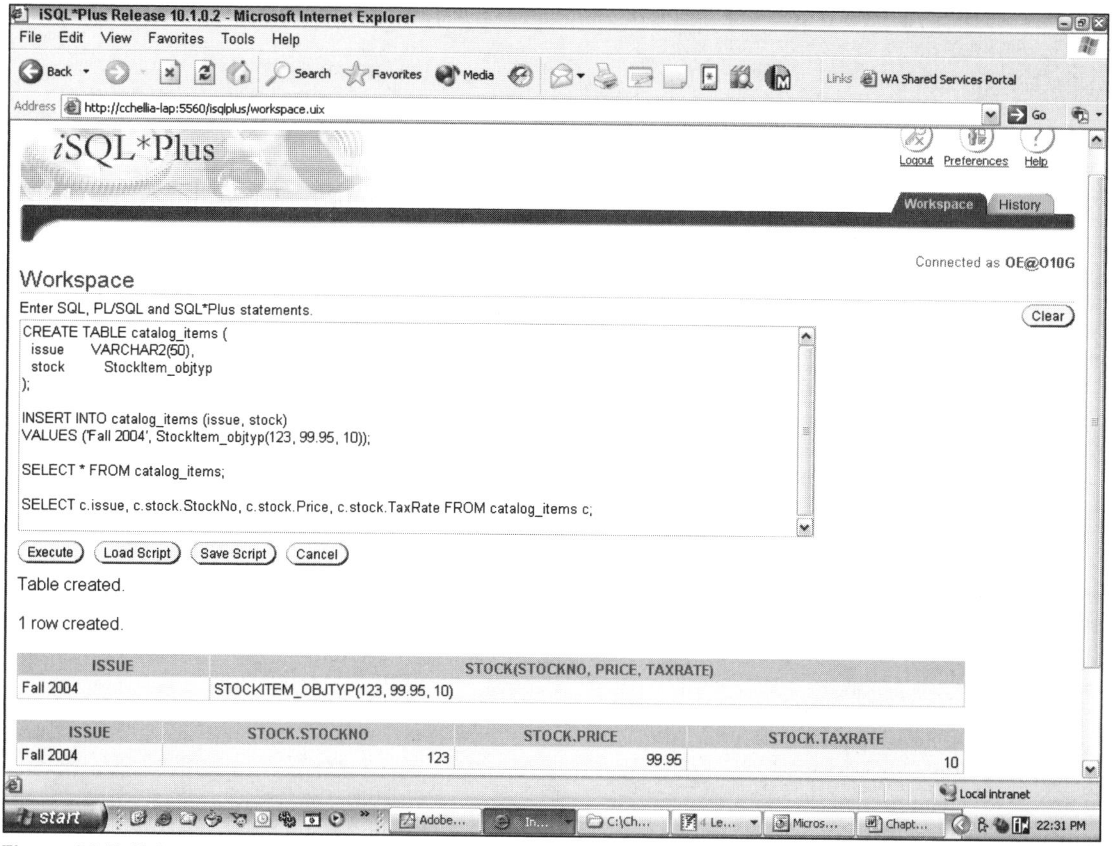

Figure 21-7: Using a column object.

Another approach uses an object (as opposed to a relational) table, which is based on a specific data type. Each row of that table contains an object instance of the specific data type. Such instances are referred to as *row objects*. Unlike column objects, row objects have a unique object identifier (OID) and hence can be the target of a `REF`. Figure 21-8 creates an object table (`stock_items`) and inserts an instance into the table. In the first `select` statement, the instance is retrieved as a set of attributes, while the second `select` statement uses the `value` function to access the instance as a complete object.

Figure 21-8: Inserting an instance into the table.

Object views create an abstraction over a set of existing relational tables. They materialize object data types from an underlying relational schema as row objects — that is, with an object identifier — and are capable of being `REF` targets. This provides the benefits of the ORDBMS without making changes to the underlying relational tables. An example of object views is shown later in this chapter.

Using Java to Interact with Database Objects

Support for object-relational structures was introduced in release 2.0 of the Java Database Connectivity (JDBC) API. The API provides two interfaces to materialize an SQL type as object instances in Java: `java.sql.Struct` (for weakly typed access) and `java.sql.SQLData` (for strongly typed access). Oracle supports both of these methods. Additionally, Oracle provides `oracle.sql.STRUCT` and `oracle.sql.ORAData` — both extensions to the specification that better leverage the native database features and provide performance improvements (see Figure 21-9).

A struct (`java.sql.Struct`) is the Java representation of an object type. It contains a value for each attribute of the SQL type it represents. Structs provide a loosely typed mapping of an SQL (object) type into Java. This means that each attribute of the SQL type is represented as an instance of `java.lang.Object`. It is up to the application developer to know the data type of the attribute, cast the value accordingly, and build an instance of the object based on the attributes. A struct maintains its data in native SQL format without the need for type conversions. They are best used in Java applications that manipulate objects natively in the database without having to convert and render the objects in a user interface (e.g., a command-line utility application).

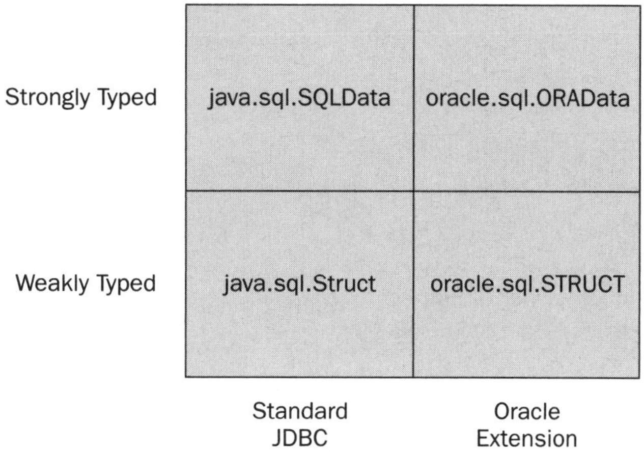

Figure 21-9: `oracle.sql.STRUCT` and `oracle.sql.ORAData`.

An alternative way to materialize SQL objects is to provide a class (commonly called a *custom Java class*) that implements the `SQLData` interface. In this case, the JDBC driver will stream the values from the database, instantiate an instance of this class, and populate it with the values — transparent to the developer. A typical implementation of a custom Java class for the `StockItem_Objtyp` is shown in the following. This class can be written manually as shown here or automatically generated by Oracle JPublisher (see the "Publishing Object Types" section later in the chapter).

```
package ch21.sqldata;

import java.sql.*;
import oracle.jdbc.*;
import oracle.sql.STRUCT;
import oracle.jpub.runtime.MutableStruct;

public class StockItem implements SQLData
{
  public static final String _SQL_NAME = "OE.STOCKITEM_OBJTYP";
  public static final int _SQL_TYPECODE = OracleTypes.STRUCT;

  public java.math.BigDecimal m_stockno;
  public java.math.BigDecimal m_price;
  public java.math.BigDecimal m_taxrate;

  /* constructor */
  public StockItem()
  {
  }

  public StockItem(java.math.BigDecimal stockno, java.math.BigDecimal price,
java.math.BigDecimal taxrate) throws SQLException
  {
    m_stockno = stockno;
```

```
      m_price = price;
      m_taxrate = taxrate;
    }

    public void readSQL(SQLInput stream, String type)
    throws SQLException
    {
        m_stockno = stream.readBigDecimal();
        m_price = stream.readBigDecimal();
        m_taxrate = stream.readBigDecimal();
    }

    public void writeSQL(SQLOutput stream)
    throws SQLException
    {
        stream.writeBigDecimal(m_stockno);
        stream.writeBigDecimal(m_price);
        stream.writeBigDecimal(m_taxrate);
    }

    public String getSQLTypeName() throws SQLException
    {
      return _SQL_NAME;
    }

}
```

When using a custom Java class, the developer must register a *type map* with the JDBC connection. A type map is an instance of `java.util.Map` that matches each SQL type with a custom Java class implementing `SQLData`. This enables the JDBC driver to instantiate the correct objects and associate them with the query results. Assuming a set of custom Java classes exist for each of the previously defined SQL types, the following code shows how to use these classes to read from the database. A custom Java class can also be used to update the database using a `PreparedStatement` or `CallableStatement`.

```
package ch21;

import java.util.*;
import java.sql.*;
import oracle.sql.*;
import oracle.jdbc.*;
import oracle.jdbc.pool.*;
import ch21.sqldata.*;

public class UsingSQLData {

public static void main (String[] args) {
  new UsingSQLData();
}

public UsingSQLData() {

try {

  // OracleDataSource implements java.sql.DataSource;
  OracleDataSource ods = new OracleDataSource();
```

```
        ods.setURL("jdbc:oracle:thin:@//cchellia-lap:1521/O10G");
        ods.setUser("oe");
        ods.setPassword("oe");

        // Get connection from DataSource
        Connection conn = ods.getConnection();
        conn.setAutoCommit(false);

        // Setup JDBC TypeMap
        Map map = conn.getTypeMap();
        try {
          if (null == map) map = new Hashtable();
          map.put("OE.CUSTOMER_OBJTYP", Class.forName("ch21.sqldata.Customer"));
          map.put("OE.ADDRESS_OBJTYP", Class.forName("ch21.sqldata.Address"));
          map.put("OE.STOCKITEM_OBJTYP",
Class.forName("ch21.sqldata.StockItem"));
          map.put("OE.LINEITEM_OBJTYP", Class.forName("ch21.sqldata.LineItem"));
          map.put("OE.PURCHASEORDER_OBJTYP",
            Class.forName("ch21.sqldata.PurchaseOrder"));
        } catch (Exception e) {
          e.printStackTrace();
        }
        conn.setTypeMap(map);

        Statement stmt = conn.createStatement();
        ResultSet rset = null;
        rset=stmt.executeQuery("SELECT VALUE(p) FROM po_objvw p WHERE p.PoNo
=2455");

        while (rset.next()) {
          PurchaseOrder po = (PurchaseOrder) rset.getObject(1);
          Ref custRef = po.getCustRef();
          Customer cust = (Customer) custRef.getObject();
          Address addr = po.getShiptoaddrObj();

          System.out.println("Customer: " + cust.getCustname() + ". Order Date:
" +
            po.getOrderdate());
          System.out.println("Address: " + addr.getStreet() + ", " +
addr.getCity() +
            ", " + addr.getState() + " " + addr.getZip());

          Array lines = po.getLineitemlistNtab();
          int noLines = ((oracle.sql.ARRAY) lines).length();
          Object[] line = (Object[]) lines.getArray();

          for (int i=0; i < noLines; i++) {
            LineItem li = (LineItem) line[i];
            Ref stockRef = li.getStockRef();
            StockItem stock = (StockItem) stockRef.getObject();
            System.out.println("\tLine item: " + li.getLineitemno() + ". Price:
" +
              stock.getPrice() + ". Qty: " + li.getQuantity());
          }
        }

        rset.close();
```

```
60.         stmt.close();
61.         conn.close();

62.         } catch (SQLException se) {
63.           se.printStackTrace();
64.         }
65.       }
66.    }
```

The previous code shows how to materialize the object instance from an object view into a Java class. Once the instance is materialized (line 40), you could use dot notation to traverse all the relationships. Output from running this application on the command line (`java ch21.UsingSQLData`) is shown here:

```
Customer: Pacino, Mammutti. Order Date: 1999-09-21 02:34:11.0
Address: 2120 Heights Dr, Eau Claire, WI 54701
        Line item: 2. Price: 299. Qty: 32
        Line item: 3. Price: 80. Qty: 54
        Line item: 1. Price: 500. Qty: 3
```

Using SQLData provides a stronger type mapping between the SQL object and custom Java class. For example, the `rset.getObject(1)` statement is cast directly into a `PurchaseOrder` object instead of reading and populating individual attributes of the `PurchaseOrder` object.

Oracle's extension to `SQLData`, `ORAData`, further simplifies access to the object types by providing convenience classes and methods to work with REFs and collections. If the custom class implements `ORAData`, then lines 39 to 58 in the preceding can be replaced with the following simpler code segment:

```
1.        while (rset.next()) {
2.          PurchaseOrder po = (PurchaseOrder) rset.getObject(1);
3.          Customer cust = po.getCustRef().getValue();
4.          Address addr = po.getShiptoaddrObj();

5.          System.out.println("Customer: " + cust.getCustname() + ". Order Date: "
+
6.            po.getOrderdate());
7.          System.out.println("Address: " + addr.getStreet() + ", " +
addr.getCity() +
8.            ", " + addr.getState() + " " + addr.getZip());

9.          LineItemList lines = po.getLineitemlistNtab();

10.         for (int i=0; i < lines.length(); i++) {
11.           LineItem li = lines.getElement(i);
12.           StockItem stock = li.getStockRef().getValue();
13.           System.out.println("\tLine item: " + li.getLineitemno() + ". Price: "
+
14.             stock.getPrice() + ". Qty: " + li.getQuantity());
15.         }
16.       }
```

Specifically, note how lines 41 to 42 in the original segment is replaced with line 3 to access REFs. Similarly, lines 48 to 52 can be replaced with lines 9 to 11 for easier access to collections.

Object Views on Relational Data

Object views project relational tables into a virtual object table of a specific data type. Each row in the view is an object instance with attributes, methods, and a unique identifier (OID). It is a way to realize the benefits of an OO programming paradigm and use Oracle's ORDBMS capability without converting existing data into object tables.

In this section, we map the object types created earlier for the Purchase Order application to the existing relational tables in the OE sample schema. This process will highlight some of the key benefits of using object views for this application, namely:

- The existing relational application is untouched and continues to work normally.
- The views can supplement the existing table data with dynamic columns materialized by functions (e.g., `calculate_discount()` shown later)
- With an object facade, the relational tables can benefit from simpler object binding with an OO language.
- The ability to query the data in new ways by following forward references (dot notation) instead of writing complex joins spanning many tables.
- Minimize network round-trips, because the views are synthesized within the server without having to transfer unnecessary data to the client.

The statement that follows creates an object view (`StockItem_objvw`) based on the `StockItem_objtyp` type. This type has attributes for `StockNo`, `Price`, and `TaxRate`. The first two attributes are mapped to the `product_id` and `list_price` columns from the `product_information` table. However, this table does not have a column for tax rate. In this example, the view invokes a function (`calculate_tax`) to calculate the tax rate based on the product's category. The instances materialized by this view are row objects and will have a unique object identifier based on the `StockNo`. Note that the `StockNo` attribute is mapped to the `product_id` column, the primary key on the table. It is typical for the object identifier attribute to be based on the primary key column.

```
CREATE OR REPLACE VIEW StockItem_objvw
OF StockItem_objtyp
WITH OBJECT IDENTIFIER (StockNo)
AS SELECT
  pi.product_id,
  pi.list_price,
  calculate_tax(pi.category_id)
FROM
  product_information pi
;
```

The code sample below maps the `customers` table to the `Customer_objvw` view. The instances materialized by this view are row objects and will have a unique object identifier based on the `CustNo` attribute. These instances can be the target or a `REF`.

The address columns from the `customers` table are grouped into an instance of `Address_objtyp`. Because the address instance is a column object, it does not have unique OID and cannot be the target of a `REF`. This is the intended behavior, since the address is represented as a composition in the UML object model (previously shown in Figure 21-2).

Note that the relational `customers` table has an embedded collection of phone numbers (`phone_list_typ`).

```
PHONE_LIST_TYP VARRAY(5) OF VARCHAR2(25)
```

However, the `customer_objtyp` requires an instance of `phonelist_vartyp`:

```
PHONELIST_VARTYP VARRAY(10) OF VARCHAR2(25)
```

The `cast` function is used to typecast the `phone_list_typ` collection into an instance of `phonelist_vartyp`.

```
CREATE OR REPLACE VIEW customer_objvw
OF customer_objtyp
WITH OBJECT IDENTIFIER (CustNo)
AS SELECT
  c.customer_id,
  c.cust_last_name || ', ' || c.cust_first_name,
  Address_objtyp (c.cust_address.street_address,
                  c.cust_address.city,
                  SUBSTR(c.cust_address.state_province,1,2),
                  c.cust_address.postal_code),
  CAST (c.phone_numbers AS OE.PHONELIST_VARTYP)
FROM
  customers c
;
```

The Purchase Order object view (`po_objvw`) is a more complex example and better explained with line numbers:

```
1.      CREATE OR REPLACE FUNCTION TS_TO_DATE(p_ts TIMESTAMP) RETURN DATE IS
2.      BEGIN
3.        return p_ts;
4.      END;

5.      CREATE OR REPLACE FUNCTION calculate_discount RETURN NUMBER IS
6.      BEGIN
7.        return 10;
8.      END calculate_discount;

9.      CREATE OR REPLACE VIEW po_objvw
10.     OF PurchaseOrder_objtyp
11.     WITH OBJECT IDENTIFIER (PoNo)
12.     AS SELECT
13.       o.order_id,
14.       TS_TO_DATE(o.order_date) OrderDate,
15.       TS_TO_DATE(o.order_date + 14) ShipDate,
16.       MAKE_REF(customer_objvw, o.customer_id) AS Cust_ref,
17.       CAST (
18.         MULTISET (
19.           SELECT
20.             oi.line_item_id,
21.             MAKE_REF(StockItem_objvw, oi.product_id),
22.             oi.quantity,
23.             calculate_discount()
24.           FROM
```

```
25.         order_items oi
26.       WHERE oi.order_id = o.order_id
27.     ) AS LineItemList_ntabtyp
28.   ) AS LineItemList_ntab,
29.   Address_objtyp (c.cust_address.street_address,
30.                   c.cust_address.city,
31.                   SUBSTR(c.cust_address.state_province,1,2),
32.                   c.cust_address.postal_code) AS ShipToAddr_obj
33. FROM
34.   orders o,
35.   customers c
36. WHERE c.customer_id = o.customer_id
37. ;
```

Lines 1 to 8 define wrapper functions to supplement or wrap columns from the OE relational schema. For example, there is no discount column in the existing tables, so this data has to be hard-coded or calculated by a function as shown in this case.

Line 11 defines the attribute that forms the unique object identifier for the view. The `PoNo` attribute maps to `orders.order_id` column, which is the primary key.

Line 14 wraps the `timestamp` from the column as a `date`. The function could optionally format the date as required.

Line 15 calculates a `ShipTo` date, since this information is not available in the relational schema. It assumes it to be `OrderDate` plus 14 days.

Line 16 uses the `make_ref` function to create a `ref` pointer to the customer associated with this order. The first parameter is an object table (or view, in this case) and the second is the unique identifier within that table or view. A similar reference is created in line 21.

Lines 19 to 26 are the typical query issued to list all the line items associated with a purchase order.

Lines 18 and 27 use `multiset` to specify that the output of the previous query is a collection of `LineItemList_ntabtyp` instances.

Lines 17 and 28 use the `cast` function to typecast the `multiset` of `LineItemList_ntabtyp` instances as a `LineItemList_ntab` nested table.

Lines 29 to 32 create an `Address_objtyp` column object.

This object view significantly simplifies queries for purchase order information. There is no need for joins, and queries can directly access the methods associated with the Purchase Order object. Figure 21-10 shows a query that lists the customer name, address, and order total for a range of purchase orders. This query accesses a single object view and traverses through the rest of the object structure using dot notation.

Figure 21-11 shows an example of listing the contents of the line items along with basic purchase order information. Note the use of the `table` function to make the nested collection appear like a regular database table.

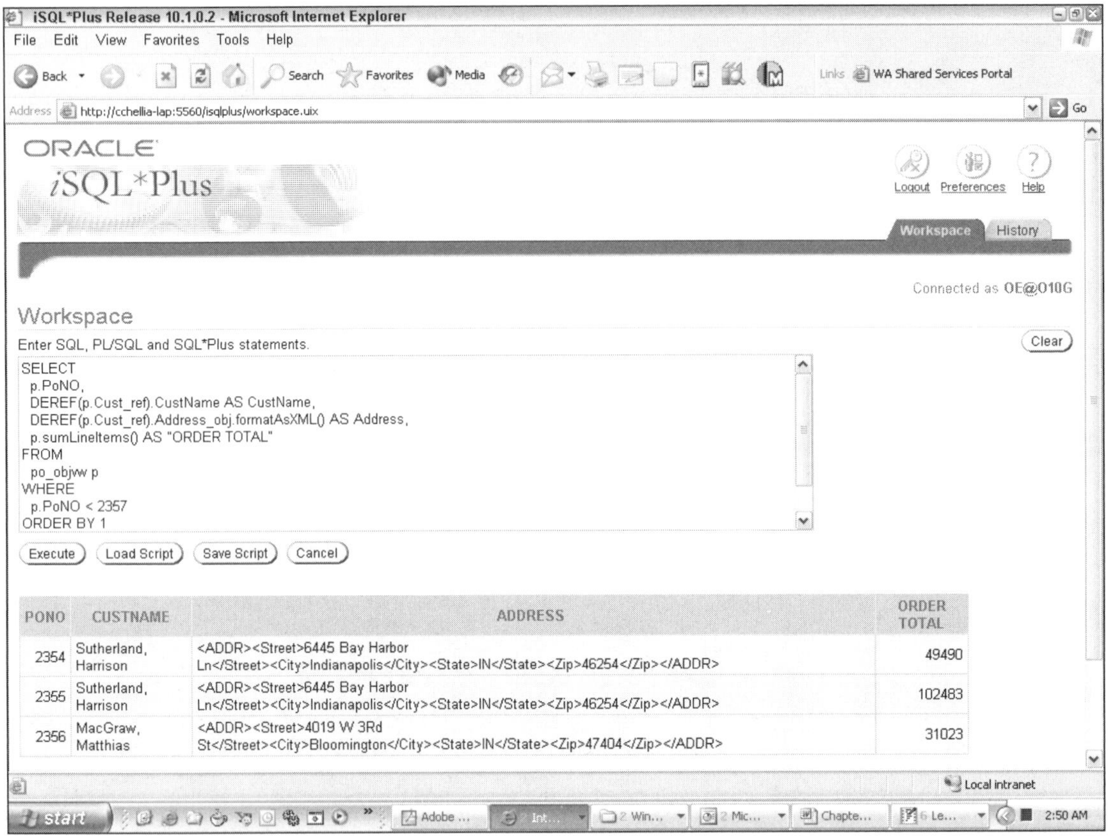

Figure 21-10: A query that lists the customer name, address, and order total for a range of purchase orders.

These examples show how queries are simplified with object views. It is also possible to update the underlying tables through the object views. However, for anything other than the most trivial object views, this requires an `instead of` trigger to procedurally update the underlying relational structures. `instead of` triggers can be implemented in PL/SQL or Java in the database.

Apart from querying and updating though a more natural, business-oriented interface, object views open the door for the relational structures to be accessed through OO languages, such as Java, as described in the "Publishing Object Types" section coming up in the chapter.

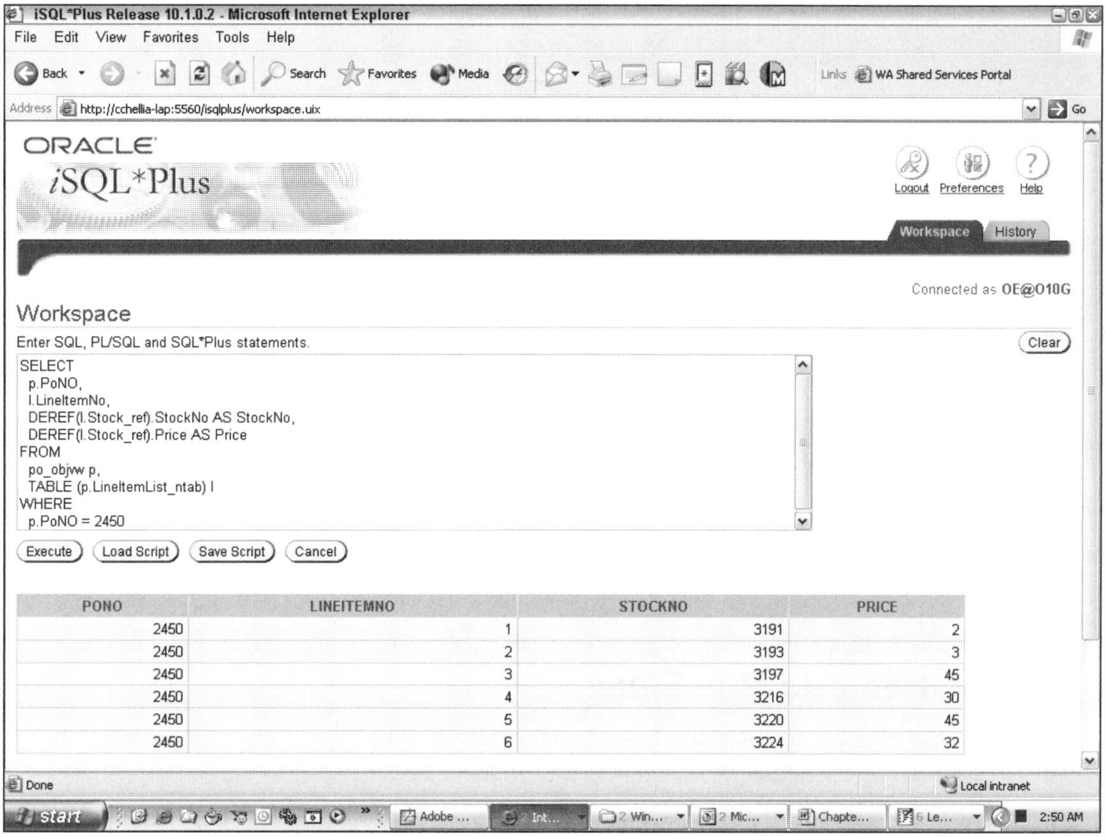

Figure 21-11: An example of listing the contents of the line items along with basic purchase order information.

Oracle JPublisher (JPub)

Oracle JPublisher (JPub) is a code generation utility to expose the object-relational and JVM capabilities of the Oracle database to application developers. Specifically, it provides support for publishing server-side Java, PL/SQL, and SQL (DML and object types) for access from outside the database — for example, from an application server or client application. In the 10*g* version, Oracle JPublisher also generates code to support Web service invocations from the database or into the database.

Figure 21-12 shows the key output capabilities of JPublisher. It generates code based on data dictionary definitions and a range of configuration options to tweak the output. Although a full discussion on JPublisher is outside the scope of this chapter, this section covers some of the key usage patterns, emphasizing the features related to the ORDBMS capabilities.

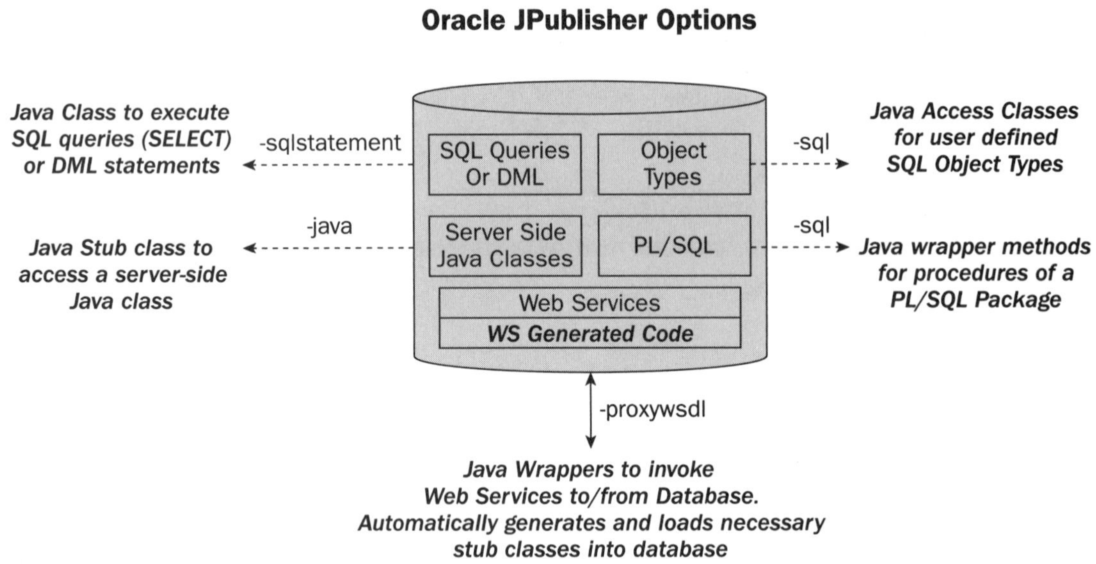

Figure 21-12: The key output capabilities of JPublisher.

Configuration and Run Time

The examples in this section were developed on Windows XP, JDK 1.4.2_03 against Oracle Database 10*g* Enterprise Edition 10.1.0.2 (Win32)

The `CLASSPATH` is an environment variable that points to the list of libraries, components, and other applications required by a Java application, such as JPub. At the very least, database applications must point to the JDBC driver implementation to connect to the server. The driver version must coincide with the version of JVM used by the application. It must also be compatible with the version of the database server. It is recommended to use the JDBC drivers that ship with the same version of the database, located in $OH/jdbc/lib. For the 1.4 JVM, the archive to include is ojdbc14.jar.

The following command configures the `CLASSPATH` requirements for JPub in a Win32 environment. Substitute `<OH>` for the database `ORACLE_HOME`.

```
SET PATH=<OH>\bin;%PATH%
@REM The command below should be on a single line.
@REM It has been split across two lines for clarity.
SET CLASSPATH=.;<OH>\jdbc\lib\ojdbc14.jar;<OH>\lib\xmlparserv2.jar;
<OH>\sqlj\lib\runtime12ee.jar;<OH>\sqlj\lib\translator.jar;%CLASSPATH
```

In a Unix/Linux bourne shell environment, the command is as follows:

```
PATH=<OH>/bin:$PATH
# The command below should be on a single line.
# It has been split across two lines for clarity.
CLASSPATH=.:<OH>/jdbc/lib/ojdbc14.jar:<OH>/lib/xmlparserv2.jar:
<OH>/sqlj/lib/runtime12ee.jar:<OH>/sqlj/lib/translator.jar:$CLASSPATH
```

JPub is fully accessible on the command line. However, in the interest of configuration management in development projects, it accepts input configuration files. A key file is the properties file, which stores the equivalent of the command-line options. For example, consider the following command, which shows the use of a small set of possible configuration parameters for JPub.

```
@REM The command below should be on a single line.
@REM It has been split across two lines for clarity.
Jpub -user=oe/oe -url=jdbc:oracle:thin:@cchellia-lap:1521:O10G
-case=mixed -dir=..\..\gen -package=ch21.oradata
```

This becomes error-prone with a large set of parameters. Instead, these options can be specified in a properties file (e.g., jpub.props).

```
jpub.user=oe/oe
jpub.url=jdbc:oracle:thin:@cchellia-lap:1521:O10G
jpub.case=mixed
jpub.dir=..\..\gen
jpub.package=ch21.oradata
jpub.usertypes=oracle
jpub.input=jpub.infile
```

The properties file is then passed as a parameter, and JPub processes its contents as if they were inserted in sequence on the command line.

```
jpub -props=jpub.props
```

The next step is to specify a list of SQL or PL/SQL entities or server-side Java classes to be published, together with any related information and instructions. Again, these can be specified on the command line with either a `-java` or `-sql` or `-sqlstatement` flag, but it is recommended to use an input file with the list. For example, contents of `jpub.infile` as specified in the preceding properties may specify the following:

```
SQL PhoneList_vartyp AS PhoneList
SQL StockItem_objtyp AS StockItem
```

This will generate Java access classes for the `StockItem_objtyp` and `PhoneList_vartyp` object types defined in the OE schema. The generated Java classes will be called `StockItem` and `PhoneList`, respectively.

Publishing SQL and DML Statements

The JPublisher `-sqlstatement` option publishes SQL queries (`select` statements) or DML statements (`insert`, `update`, or `delete` statements) as Java methods in a class. This is useful for exposing SQL as Web services. It is also a quick way to access SQL and DML from Java without writing the underlying JDBC code.

For example, consider using the Fast Lane Reader/Writer Java pattern, to directly access a database table and/or make updates. This provides a convenient approach to optimize the necessary SQL and publish with JPublisher.

Assuming the jpub.props file contains the following:

```
jpub.user=oe/oe
jpub.usertypes=jdbc
jpub.url=jdbc:oracle:thin:@cchellia-lap:1521:O10G
jpub.case=mixed
jpub.package=ch21.sqlstmt
jpub.dir=..\..\gen
jpub.sqlstatement.class=FastLaneProduct
jpub.sqlstatement.updateListPrice="UPDATE product_information SET
  list_price=:{listPrice NUMBER} WHERE product_id=:{productId NUMBER
```

then the command `jpub -props=jpub.props` generates a class called `ch21.sqlstmt.FastLaneProduct` with the following method:

```
public int updateListPrice (
  java.math.BigDecimal listprice,
  java.math.BigDecimal productid)
throws SQLException
```

A Java application can then create an instance of this class and quickly update the data without the developer having to write tedious JDBC code.

```
Connection conn = ods.getConnection();
...
FastLaneProduct flp = new FastLaneProduct(conn);
int returnCode = flp.updateListPrice(new BigDecimal(259), new BigDecimal(1726));
```

Publishing Java Stored Procedures

Chapter 18 described the process to deploy Java classes as Java Stored Procedures in the database. However, these procedures were only accessible to Java and JDBC after they were published with a call specification. This is not optimal and introduces some limitations on how Java Stored Procedures can be used, because:

- The call spec only permits Java types which have an SQL equivalent.
- Exceptions were poorly propagated between the Java and SQL layers.
- Performance degradation occurs at run time with the need to cast between Java data types and SQL data types

With JPublisher (`java` option), Oracle Database 10*g* supports native Java interface — a way for Java (or Web services) outside the database to directly invoke Java Stored Procedures in the database natively, *without* going through a call spec.

This feature is best illustrated with an example. Recall the `ch18.JavaMail` class that was deployed into the OE schema in Chapter 18. It was associated with a PL/SQL call spec to publish the Java method. Prior to Oracle Database 10*g*, the only way to access the stored procedure from Java was through a JDBC statement, accessing the PL/SQL wrapper. This is no longer necessary with Oracle Database 10*g*. The command

```
jpub -user=oe/oe -url=jdbc:oracle:thin:@cchellia-lap:1521:O10G -java=ch18.JavaMail
```

generates a Java class with a constructor that accepts a JDBC connection:

```
public JavaMail(java.sql.Connection conn) throws java.sql.SQLException
```

This class has a method that will natively invoke the stored procedure in the database using the Java reflection API.

```
// The code below should be on a single line.
// It has been split across two lines for clarity.
public java.lang.String sendMail(java.lang.String p0,java.lang.String
 p1,java.lang.String p2,java.lang.String p3,java.lang.String p4
```

Publishing Object Types

The JDBC `SQLData` interface and Oracle's extension to it (`ORAData`) were introduced in the "Using Java to Interact with Database Objects" section earlier in the chapter. Oracle's JPublisher can generate a custom Java class that implements either of these interfaces based on the type definitions in the data dictionary.

An input file (`jpub.infile`) is used to specify object types to publish. Using the `as` keyword, each type may include the name of the custom Java class that will be generated. An example is shown with the following `jpub.infile` and `jpub.properties` files. Note that `jpub.usertypes` is specified to be `jdbc` — this generates SQL Data-compliant classes.

```
jpub.infile

SQL PhoneList_vartyp AS PhoneList
SQL StockItem_objtyp AS StockItem
SQL LineItem_objtyp AS LineItem
SQL Address_objtyp AS Address
SQL Customer_objtyp AS Customer
SQL LineItemList_ntabtyp AS LineItemList
SQL PurchaseOrder_objtyp AS PurchaseOrder
```

```
jpub.props

jpub.user=oe/oe
jpub.url=jdbc:oracle:thin:@cchellia-lap:1521:O10G
jpub.input=jpub.infile
jpub.case=mixed
jpub.dir=..\..\gen
jpub.package=ch21.sqldata
jpub.usertypes=jdbc
```

Invoking `jpub -props=jpub.props` generates classes for `oe.stockitem_objtyp`, `oe.lineitem_objtyp`, `oe.address_objtyp`, `oe.customer_objtyp`, and `oe.purchaseorder_objtyp`. However, no helper classes are generated for the collection types.

```
jpub.infile:1.25: J2T-131, WARNING: When -usertypes=jdbc, nothing is generated for
collection types such as OE.PHONELIST_VARTYP
jpub.infile:6.29: J2T-131, WARNING: When -usertypes=jdbc, nothing is generated for
collection types such as OE.LINEITEMLIST_NTABTYP
```

With the usertypes parameter set to oracle, JPublisher generates 12 classes instead — one class for each of the seven entries from jpub.infile (including both the collections) and five REF helpers for each of the non-collection classes (e.g., AddressRef.java).

Support for Web Services

Oracle JPublisher with the proxywsdl flag generates code for Web services within the database. Refer to the *Oracle Database JPublisher User's Guide* for specifics on this support.

Summary

In this chapter, we first recapped the differences between using a relational and an object-relational approach to building the Purchase Order application, highlighting the benefits of the latter. Granted the relational model has a well-understood syntax and constructs to support this application. It would consist of a number of normalized tables, primary and foreign key constraints, and business operations implemented as Java Stored Procedures or PL/SQL functions/packages. Queries across the set of tables would use joins. DML operations would hit multiple tables and rely on referential integrity constraints to maintain data integrity across the tables.

The object-relational approach requires additional effort up front to define a set of object types that reflect the problem domain. These types would closely resemble the UML class diagram for the application. This effort is justified by numerous benefits such as the following:

- Better data encapsulation — access to the data through methods declared with the object types.
- Simpler, more intuitive SQL queries that match an application's use cases. instead of triggers and update methods can also simplify DML against these objects.
- A clear relationship between schema objects, making it easier to manage the impact of schema evolution.
- Tools to generate OO language bindings of database objects to Java or C++.
- Developer productivity and application performance productivity as a result of less impedance mismatch.

These benefits, together with the maturity of standards supporting object-relational interactions (e.g., JDBC, SQL3), are compelling reasons to embrace Oracle's object-relational capability. Oracle marries the traditional strengths of the relational database (backup, recovery, management, performance, transaction support, etc.) with the productivity of an OO language and complete interoperability between both paradigms.

22

Oracle XML DB

With version 10*g*, Oracle has fully incorporated XML into its architecture and created an ideal platform for modern development. XML has emerged over the past few years as the de facto standard for portable data storage. With its human-readable hierarchical structure, XML provides an attractive medium for a data repository, but its positive attributes also make XML much harder to manage. Since version 8*i*, Oracle has incorporated tools in the database to make working with XML much easier for developers. Oracle calls its core XML technology *XML DB*. After reading this chapter, you will have an understanding of the basic technologies included with XML DB and how and when to use them.

Examples in this section use the Order Entry sample schema included with Oracle. The schema name Oracle creates is OE. If you created the sample database when installing Oracle, you probably have the OE schema installed. If not, you can install it using the Database Configuration Assistant (dbca). Check the Oracle documentation for more information about installing the sample schemas.

Overview of the XML DB Repository

Oracle and other databases have traditionally been used to manage relational data stored in a table structure. While the relational model has been proven to be highly successful at managing strongly related data, it is less successful at managing hierarchical data that is loosely related. Relational data lends itself nicely to being stored in table structures with key relationships to connect it to other data. Hierarchical data like XML tends to be stored best in a hierarchical folder structure like a file system. Oracle combines both of these storage methods to give you the best of both worlds: an extremely powerful relational engine and a highly optimized hierarchical storage engine for XML data.

Oracle XML DB stores XML data in tables optimized for this purpose. Oracle makes use of a highly optimized foldering module to map relational structures to path-based structures, as well as special indexes on these tables to speed up path-based access. Oracle can access path-based resources with the same speed if not faster than the OS file system.

The repository also provides several ways of getting data in and out for use with applications. The Oracle XML DB repository allows for both SQL-based access and path-based access. SQL-based access is traditionally what developers think of when dealing with a database. You can query tables and views using either PL/SQL or Java to get data out of the repository. Path-based access is new, and it provides a very powerful and easy way to get data in and out of the repository using familiar file system–type syntax.

XML DB is tightly coupled with Oracle's foldering module, which generates and tracks path information for resources stored in the database, and Oracle's protocol servers, which provide access to the repository using standards-based protocols like WebDAV (Web-based Distributed Authoring and Versioning), HTTP (Hypertext Transfer Protocol), and FTP (File Transfer Protocol). It is possible to use standard business applications like Microsoft Office to update XML content in Oracle simply by writing to a virtual file system over one of these protocols.

Following is a summation of SQL-based access:

- ❑ Uses SQL for querying data
- ❑ Uses XMLType API for XML manipulation using PL/SQL, Java, or C

Following are characteristics of path-based access:

- ❑ Uses standard URIs to access data
- ❑ Can use SQL `RESOURCE_VIEW` and `PATH_VIEW` to access data
- ❑ Can use standard protocols like FTP, HTTP, and WebDAV to access content in the repository

Protocol-Based Access to XML in the Oracle Repository

One of the most powerful and useful new additions to Oracle is the ability to work with XML data stored in relational tables as if it is located on the file system. Oracle makes this possible by building popular protocols like FTP, HTTP, and WebDAV right into the database. To external applications like Web application servers, content management applications, and content creation tools, the Oracle XML repository can look like any other file system.

If you have XDB installed and configured (the sample database Oracle installs for you is already configured for XDB), you can access a schema via HTTP over port 8080. The following examples use the OE sample schema. You may have to log in to Enterprise Manager and enable the schema before you can log in.

To log in to the database, you simply go to `http://your_server_address:8080/`. Oracle will prompt you for a login and password. These would be the same as the login you would use to log in to the schema using SQL Plus. Once logged in, you should see something similar to Figure 22-1 in your Web browser.

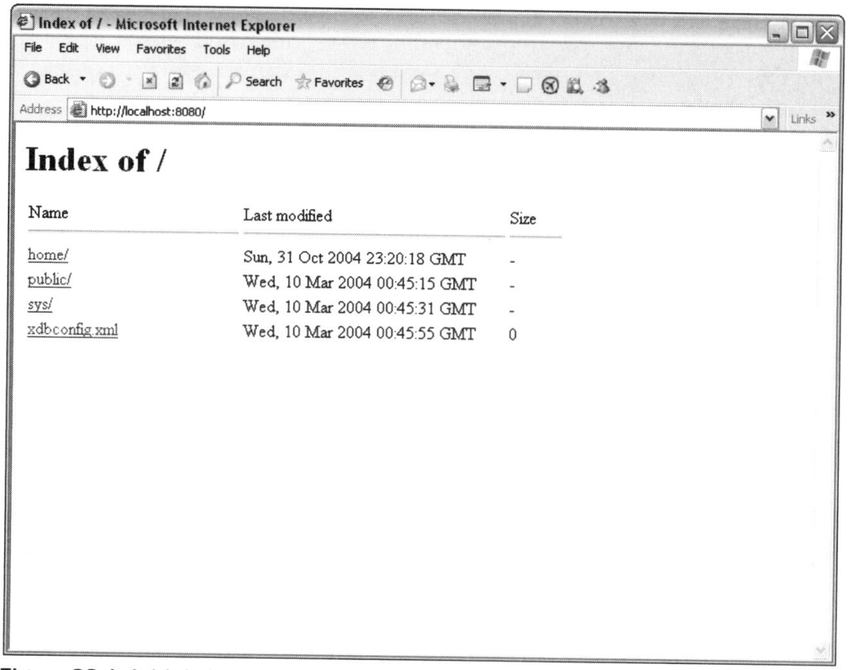

Figure 22-1: Initial view.

The home folder contains the XML data stored in Oracle. You can access XML data, XSL style sheets, and XML Schemas stored in the database schema here. In the root folder of each schema, there is a configuration file named xdbconfig.xml that controls how XML DB is configured for that schema. You can set options like server names and port numbers for FTP, WebDAV, and HTTP in this file. This file can be edited in the Java-based Enterprise Manager, or by connecting and downloading it via FTP or WebDAV.

Following is the code from the sample xdbconfig.xml file:

```
<xdbconfig xmlns="http://xmlns.oracle.com/xdb/xdbconfig.xsd"
                 xmlns:xsi="http://www.w3.org/2001/XMLSchema-instance"
                 xsi:schemaLocation="http://xmlns.oracle.com/xdb/xdbconfig.xsd
                                     http://xmlns.oracle.com/xdb/xdbconfig.xsd">
   <sysconfig>
      <acl-max-age>900</acl-max-age>
      <acl-cache-size>32</acl-cache-size>
      <invalid-pathname-chars>,</invalid-pathname-chars>
      <case-sensitive>true</case-sensitive>
      <call-timeout>300</call-timeout>
      <max-link-queue>65536</max-link-queue>
      <max-session-use>100</max-session-use>
      <persistent-sessions>false</persistent-sessions>
      <default-lock-timeout>3600</default-lock-timeout>
      <xdbcore-logfile-path>/sys/log/xdblog.xml</xdbcore-logfile-path>
      <xdbcore-log-level>0</xdbcore-log-level>
```

```
<resource-view-cache-size>1048576</resource-view-cache-size>

<protocolconfig>
    <common>
       <extension-mappings>
          <mime-mappings>
            <mime-mapping>
              <extension>au</extension>
              <mime-type>audio/basic</mime-type>
            </mime-mapping>
            <mime-mapping>
              <extension>avi</extension>
              <mime-type>video/x-msvideo</mime-type>
            </mime-mapping>
            <mime-mapping>
              <extension>bin</extension>
              <mime-type>application/octet-stream</mime-type>
            </mime-mapping>
          </mime-mappings>
          <lang-mappings>
            <lang-mapping>
              <extension>en</extension>
              <lang>english</lang>
            </lang-mapping>
          </lang-mappings>
          <charset-mappings>
          </charset-mappings>
          <encoding-mappings>
            <encoding-mapping>
              <extension>gzip</extension>
              <encoding>zip file</encoding>
            </encoding-mapping>
            <encoding-mapping>
              <extension>tar</extension>
              <encoding>tar file</encoding>
            </encoding-mapping>
          </encoding-mappings>
       </extension-mappings>
       <session-pool-size>50</session-pool-size>
       <session-timeout>6000</session-timeout>
    </common>
    <ftpconfig>
      <ftp-port>2100</ftp-port>
      <ftp-listener>local_listener</ftp-listener>
      <ftp-protocol>tcp</ftp-protocol>
      <logfile-path>/sys/log/ftplog.xml</logfile-path>
      <log-level>0</log-level>
      <session-timeout>6000</session-timeout>
      <buffer-size>8192</buffer-size>
    </ftpconfig>
    <httpconfig>
      <http-port>8080</http-port>
```

```
                <http-listener>local_listener</http-listener>
                <http-protocol>tcp</http-protocol>
                <max-http-headers>64</max-http-headers>
                <session-timeout>6000</session-timeout>
                <server-name>XDB HTTP Server</server-name>
                <max-header-size>16384</max-header-size>
                <max-request-body>2000000000</max-request-body>
                <logfile-path>/sys/log/httplog.xml</logfile-path>
                <log-level>0</log-level>
                <servlet-realm>Basic realm="XDB"</servlet-realm>
                <webappconfig>
                  <welcome-file-list>
                    <welcome-file>index.html</welcome-file>
                    <welcome-file>index.htm</welcome-file>
                  </welcome-file-list>
                  <error-pages>
                  </error-pages>
                  <servletconfig>
                    <servlet-mappings>
                      <servlet-mapping>
                        <servlet-pattern>/oradb/*</servlet-pattern>
                        <servlet-name>DBURIServlet</servlet-name>
                      </servlet-mapping>
                    </servlet-mappings>
                    <servlet-list>
                      <servlet>
                        <servlet-name>DBURIServlet</servlet-name>
                        <display-name>DBURI</display-name>
                        <servlet-language>C</servlet-language>
                        <description>Servlet for accessing DBURIs</description>
                        <security-role-ref>
                          <role-name>authenticatedUser</role-name>
                          <role-link>authenticatedUser</role-link>
                        </security-role-ref>
                      </servlet>
                    </servlet-list>
                  </servletconfig>
                </webappconfig>
              </httpconfig>
          </protocolconfig>
        <xdbcore-xobmem-bound>1024</xdbcore-xobmem-bound>
        <xdbcore-loadableunit-size>16</xdbcore-loadableunit-size>
      </sysconfig>
   </xdbconfig>
```

Navigating down into the home directory, you can get to the XML data stored in the schema, as shown in Figure 22-2.

Clicking on any of the XML documents returns the full content of the XML file, as shown in Figure 22-3. Access to these files is as fast as the OS file system, thanks to Oracle's ultra-optimized foldering code.

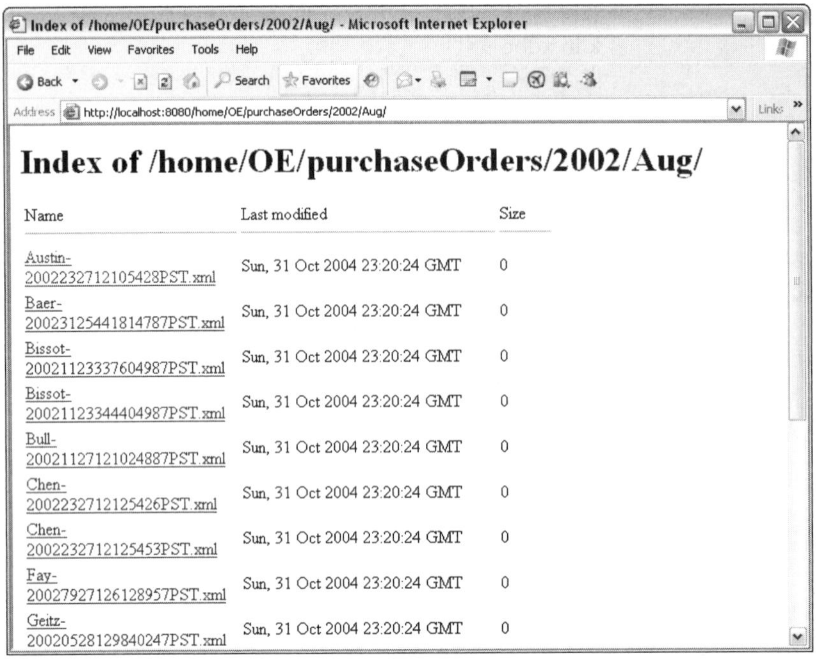

Figure 22-2: August purchase orders in the OE schema.

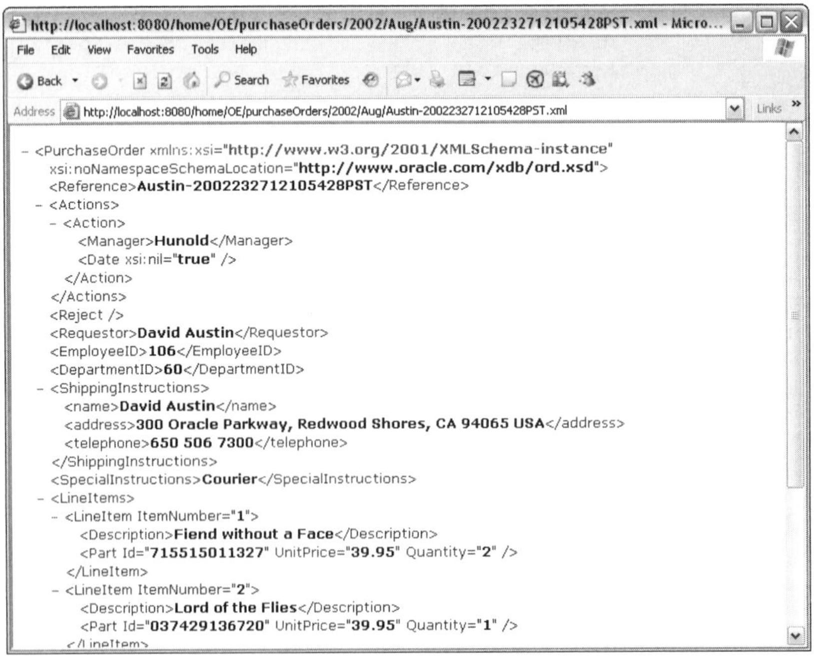

Figure 22-3: Full XML document.

You can also access the same data via FTP. You simply connect using your favorite FTP client and start reading and writing files. Look in xdbconfig.xml file under the ftpconfig section to find the FTP port Oracle is listening to. By default, the server sets up FTP on port 2100. Figure 22-4 shows a FTP connection using SmartFTP.

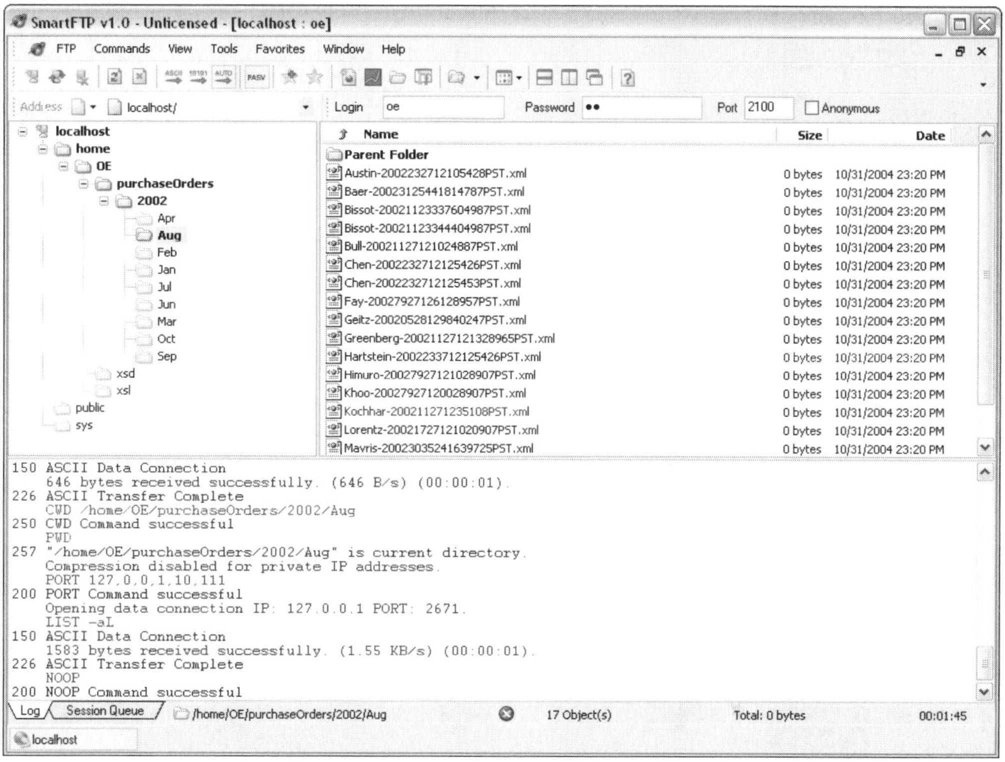

Figure 22-4: Connecting via FTP.

Finally, you can map a network drive to the Oracle WebDAV server to use the Oracle repository like a file system. The WebDAV protocol allows file system mounting over HTTP. It adds additional actions to regular HTTP like PUT that allow documents to be saved back to the server over HTTP. Applications can open and use Oracle data as if it were a local file. The easiest way to mount a WebDAV server on Windows is to use Web folders. To do this, open the My Network Places icon in Windows Explorer and click on the Add New Network Place icon. Once you complete the wizard, the WebDAV mount will be available in the My Network Places folder in Windows Explorer. Figure 22-5 shows the address page of the wizard where you would specify the Oracle server name and port for the WebDAV mount.

Once the Web folder is created, you can open XML files in Oracle just as if they were on the file system. For example, you can use MS Word to open and edit XML, as shown in Figures 22-6 and 22-7.

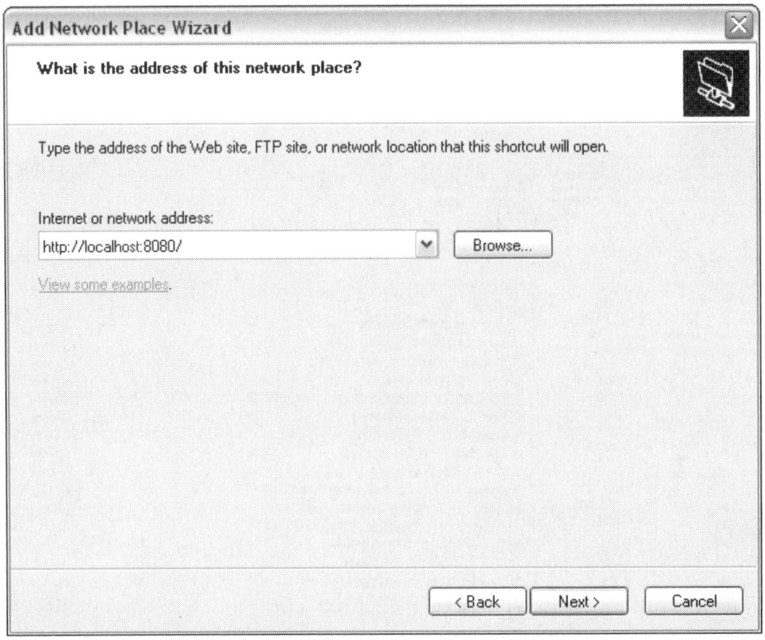

Figure 22-5: Adding a WebDAV mount.

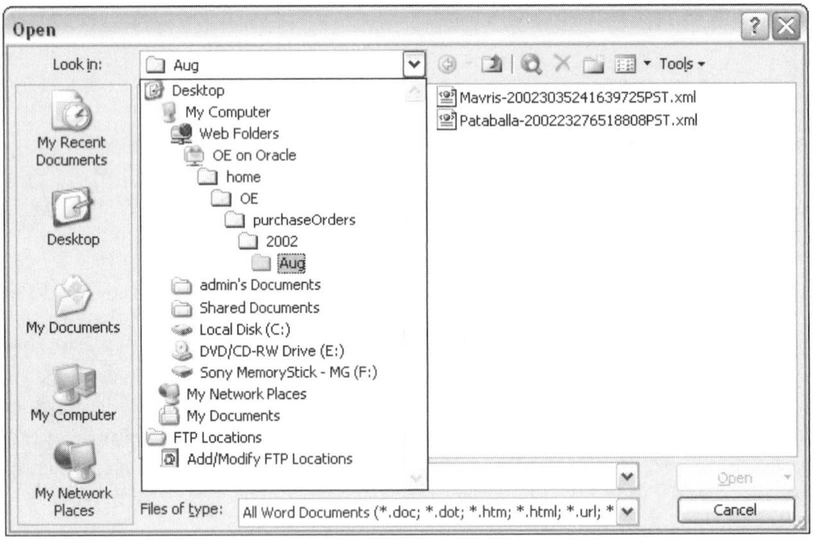

Figure 22-6: Opening XML from Word.

After editing an XML file, you can save it to the WebDAV folder using the normal save operation in the application you are in, and the data will be updated in Oracle automatically.

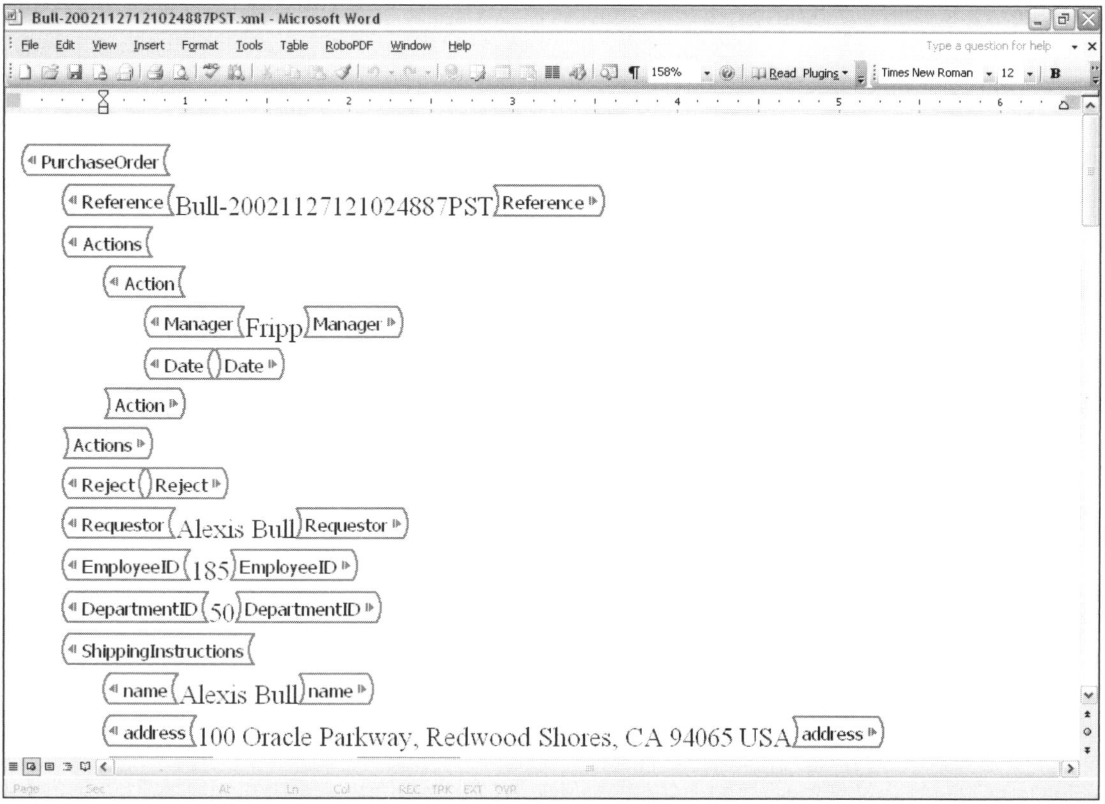

Figure 22-7: Editing XML in Word.

SQL-Based Access to XML Data in the Oracle Repository

Oracle's XML repository can also be queried using standard SQL. When you install XML DB, a special schema called `XDB` is created. All the meta data for managing the Oracle XML DB repository is stored in an XMLType table called `XDB$RESOURCE` in the `XDB` schema. This table contains records representing each file or folder in Oracle XML DB repository and can be queried using SQL. Unfortunately, this table is not directly accessible to developers. Instead, Oracle has provided two public views that provide access to the underlying table: `RESOURCE_VIEW` and `PATH_VIEW`. Using these two views, you can access any content stored in the repository.

```
SQL> desc RESOURCE_VIEW;
 Name                                      Null?    Type
 ----------------------------------------- -------- ----------------------------
 RES                                                SYS.XMLTYPE(XMLSchema "http:
                                                    //xmlns.oracle.com/xdb/XDBRe
                                                    source.xsd" Element "Resourc
                                                    e")
 ANY_PATH                                           VARCHAR2(4000)
 RESID                                              RAW(16)
```

Following is a description of the RESOURCE_VIEW fields:

- RES— An XMLType representing a resource in the Oracle XML repository
- ANY_PATH — A VARCHAR2 that specifies a path that can be used to access the resource
- RESID — A RAW that represents the resources object ID

You can see the fields provided in the PATH_VIEW view by issuing the following command.

```
SQL> desc PATH_VIEW;
 Name                                      Null?    Type
 ----------------------------------------- -------- ----------------------------
 PATH                                               VARCHAR2(1024)
 RES                                                SYS.XMLTYPE(XMLSchema "http:
                                                    //xmlns.oracle.com/xdb/XDBRe
                                                    source.xsd" Element "Resourc
                                                    e")
 LINK                                               SYS.XMLTYPE
 RESID                                              RAW(16)
```

Following is a description of PATH_VIEW fields:

- PATH — A VARCHAR2 representing a path name of a resource
- RES — An XMLType representing the resource referred by PATH
- LINK — An XMLType containing information about the link to the resource.
- RESID — A RAW object ID

The main difference between the two views is that RESOURCE_VIEW provides only one PATH to a resource, and PATH_VIEW returns all the paths to each resource. This is necessary because resources can have multiple paths. If you only need to store one path to each resource, then RESOURCE_VIEW would be the better choice to use, as it is faster in the database.

Additionally, Oracle provides two special functions for working with RESOURCE_VIEW and PATH_VIEW: under_path(resource_path) and equals_path. Using under_path allows you to limit the results of queries to return only rows that are under the specified path, and equals_path determines if a resource exists in a specific path. These functions return a 1 if true and a 0 if false.

The syntax for EQUALS_PATH is as follows:

```
EQUALS_PATH(resource_column, path)
```

where resource_column points to a resource column in the view, and path is a string specifying the path to search.

The syntax for UNDER_PATH is as follows:

```
UNDER_PATH(resource_column, [depth], pathname, [correlation])
```

where resource_column points to a resource column in the view, an optional depth parameter is used to control how deep to search, pathname is a varchar2 string specifying a path to search, and an optional correlation parameter can be specified to connect the function to a DEPTH or PATH operator.

For example, suppose you want to find out how many purchase orders are stored in OE schema for August 2002. You can use the RESOURCE_VIEW along with under_path to count the resources in that folder:

```
Select count(*) from resource_view where
under_path(RES,'/home/OE/purchaseOrders/2002/Aug') = 1
;

  COUNT(*)
----------
        17
```

There are two special operators you can use with under_path and exists_path called DEPTH and PATH. These can be used to report back the current DEPTH and PATH of the row in the result set. You pass them an integer argument to correlate them back to the calling statement. In the case of PATH, it returns the path specified without the base path.

Following is an example of how PATH and DEPTH can be used:

```
SELECT PATH(1), DEPTH(1) FROM resource_view
WHERE UNDER_PATH(res, '/home/OE/purchaseOrders/2002', 1) = 1;


PATH(1)                                    DEPTH(1)
-----------------------------------------  -------------------------------
Apr                                        1
Apr/Abel-20021127121040707PST.xml          2
Apr/Abel-20021127121040807PST.xml          2
...
Apr/Khoo-20027927125028907PST.xml          2
...
Aug                                        1
Aug/Austin-2002232712105428PST.xml         2
Aug/Baer-20023125441814787PST.xml          2
Aug/Bissot-20021123337604987PST.xml        2
Aug/Bissot-20021123344404987PST.xml        2
... etc.
```

The following example retrieves additional information about the link to a specific resource by using the EXTRACT package to reference different fields in the LINK and RES XMLType items in the PATH_VIEW:

```
SELECT path, extract(link, '/LINK/Name/text()').getstringval(),
             extract(res, '/Resource/DisplayName/text()').getstringval()
   FROM path_view
   WHERE path = '/home/OE/purchaseOrders/2002/Aug/Kochhar-20021127123510 8PST.xml';
```

You can use any XMLType function on `RES` to extract what you need. For example, to extract the contents of an XML document stored in the repository, you can use the following query:

```
select r.res.extract('/Resource/Contents/*')
from RESOURCE_VIEW r
where any_path = '/home/OE/purchaseOrders/2002/Aug/Kochhar-200211271235108PST.xml';
```

Using `getClobVal()` will return the entire contents of RES.

```
select r.res.getClobVal()
from RESOURCE_VIEW r
where any_path = '/home/OE/purchaseOrders/2002/Aug/Kochhar-200211271235108PST.xml';
```

You can use the views to retrieve resources via their resource ID:

```
select resid from resource_view
where extract(res, '/Resource/DisplayName/text()').getstringval() = 'Kochhar-
200211271235108PST.xml';

RESID
--------------------------------
B0ED7D6A22894F98B921EC3E9D917E49

select any_path from resource_view
where resid = 'B0ED7D6A22894F98B921EC3E9D917E49';

ANY_PATH
--------------------------------------------------------------------------------
/home/OE/purchaseOrders/2002/Aug/Kochhar-200211271235108PST.xml
```

You can insert new records into the views. To do so, you must specify an XML document or XMLType for the `RES` field that conforms to the `http://xmlns.oracle.com/xdb/XDBResource.xsd` XML Schema. For example:

```
INSERT INTO resource_view VALUES(sys.xmltype.createxml('
  <Resource xmlns="http://xmlns.oracle.com/xdb/XDBResource.xsd"
xmlns:xsi="http://www.w3.org/2001/XMLSchema-instance"
  xsi:schemaLocation="http://xmlns.oracle.com/xdb/XDBResource.xsd
http://xmlns.oracle.com/xdb/XDBResource.xsd">
  <Author>Test Guy</Author>
  <DisplayName>temporary_path</DisplayName>
  <Comment>I will be inserted then deleted promptly</Comment>
  <Language>en</Language>
  <CharacterSet>ASCII</CharacterSet>
  <ContentType>text/plain</ContentType>
  </Resource>'), '/home/OE/temporary_path', NULL);
```

Updates work the same way as inserts. You specify the `RES` document as follows:

```
UPDATE resource_view set res = sys.xmltype.createxml('
  <Resource xmlns="http://xmlns.oracle.com/xdb/XDBResource.xsd"
xmlns:xsi="http://www.w3.org/2001/XMLSchema-instance"
  xsi:schemaLocation="http://xmlns.oracle.com/xdb/XDBResource.xsd
http://xmlns.oracle.com/xdb/XDBResource.xsd">
```

```
    <Author>Test Guy</Author>
    <DisplayName>perm_path</DisplayName>
    <Comment>I will no longer be deleted</Comment>
    <Language>en</Language>
    <CharacterSet>ASCII</CharacterSet>
    <ContentType>text/plain</ContentType>
    </Resource>')
  where any_path = '/home/OE/temporary_path';
```

You can also delete from the views:

```
DELETE FROM resource_view WHERE any_path = '/home/OE/temporary_path';
```

If you delete a resource that has multiple paths from `resource_view`, all the paths will be deleted. If you delete it from `path_view`, only the specified path will be deleted.

Sometimes you may need to delete paths recursively. You can do so by using the `UNDER_PATH` function along with the `depth` operator:

```
DELETE FROM (SELECT 1 FROM resource_view
WHERE UNDER_PATH(res, '/home/OE/temporary_path ', 1) = 1
order by depth(1) desc
```

This would delete everything under /home/OE/temporary_path.

Enabling a New Schema for Use with XDB Repositories

By uploading XML Schemas to the database, you can enable a new schema you create. The easiest way to do this is through the Java-based Oracle Enterprise Manager Console that comes on the Oracle 10*g* client CD. See the XML Schema section and the example at the end of the chapter for details on how to do this. Once a schema has been uploaded, documents can be added to the server over WebDAV, FTP, or programmatically. You must also create repository folders and set permissions correctly for the users.

ACL-Based Security on Oracle XML Repositories

Oracle uses ACL-based (ACL stands for access control list) security to protect XML repository folders and content. Oracle comes with three preset ACLs. You can also define your own ACL file and upload it to the database or design a new ACL using Enterprise Manager. The ACLs that come with Oracle are as follows:

- `all_all_acl.xml`—Grants full access to the repository to everyone
- `all_owner_acl.xml`—Grants full access to the repository to the owner
- `ro_all_acl.xml`—Grants read-only access to the repository for all users

The easiest way to set ACLs is to use the Enterprise Manager Console application. Each resource in the repository has a Security tab where you can choose a new ACL file. ACL files can be created using the Grant Privileges On menu option available when you right-click on a repository resource. Figures 22-8 and 22-9 show how to set the ACL and the dialog box used to create an ACL list.

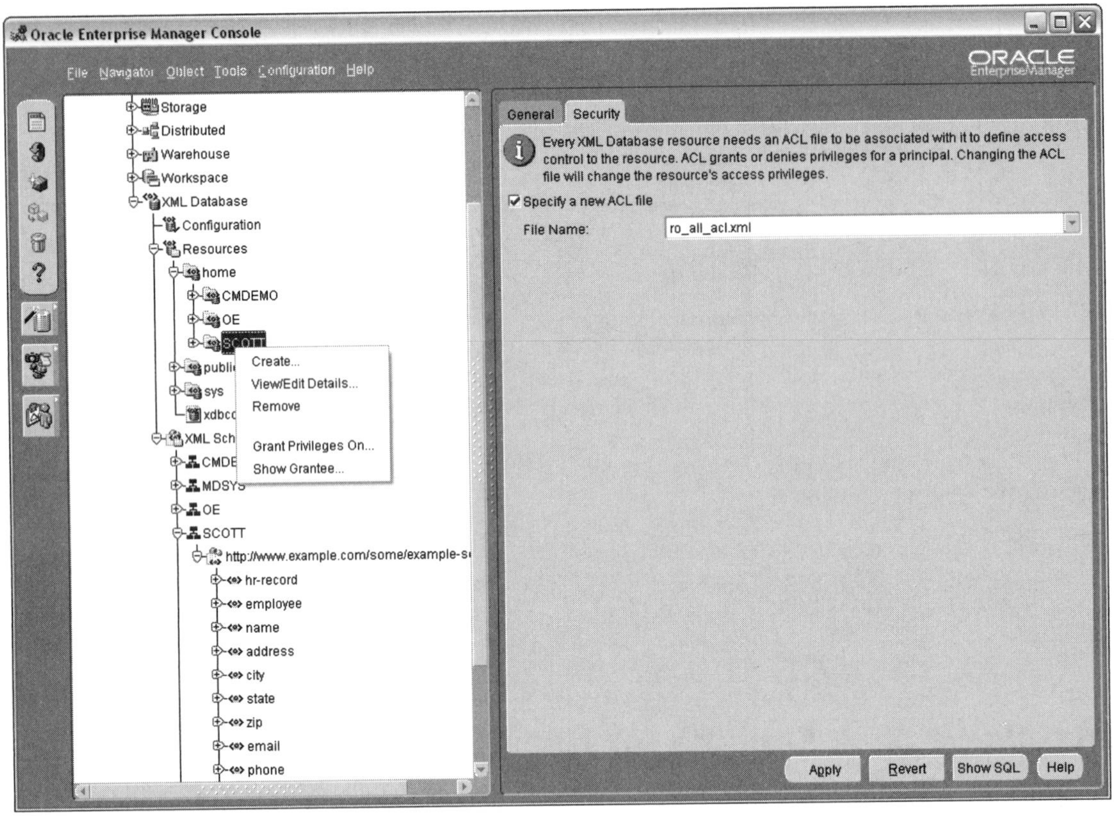

Figure 22-8: Changing the ACL.

Privileges available in Oracle are as follows:

- `read-properties` — Allows reading a resource's properties
- `read-contents` — Allows reading a resource's content
- `update` — Allows updating a resource's properties and contents
- `link` — Allows resources to be linked to a container
- `unlink` — Allows resources to be unlinked from a container
- `link-to` — Allows resource linking
- `unlink-from` — Allows resource unlinking
- `read-acl` — Allows reading of the ACL
- `write-acl-ref` — Allows changes to the resource ID
- `update-acl` — Allows updating the resource ACL

- `resolve` — Allows browsing of a container
- `dav:lock` — Allows locking using WebDAV
- `dav:unlock` — Allows unlocking a WebDAV lock

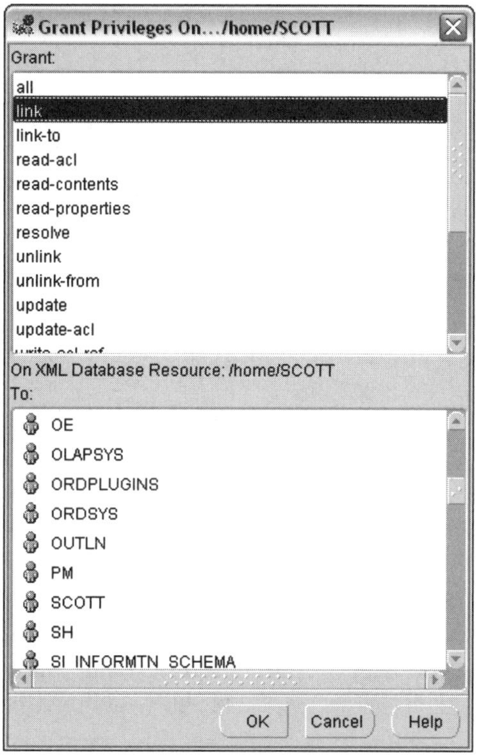

Figure 22-9: The Grant Privileges dialog box.

Grouped permissions in Oracle are as follows:

- `all` — Grants `dav:read`, `dav:write`, `dav:read-acl`, `dav:write-acl`, `dav:lock`, and `dav:unlock` privileges
- `dav:all` — Grants everything except `linkto`
- `dav:read` — Grants `read-properties`, `read-contents`, and `resolve` privileges
- `dav:write` — Grants update, link, unlink, unlink-from privileges
- `dav:read-acl` — Grants `read-acl` privileges
- `dav:write-acl` — Grants `write-acl-ref` and `update-acl` privileges

For more information on the syntax for creating ACL files, see the "Oracle XML DB Resource Security" chapter in the *Oracle XML DB Developer's Guide.*

XMLType

Before XMLType, life was hard for Oracle XML developers. To store XML in the database, you had to both parse the XML document in application code and insert the resultant data in a relational structure, or you could just stuff the whole XML document into a `CLOB` column and forget about it until your application requested the document. Fortunately, Oracle created a way for the database to manage XML natively.

XMLType is Oracle's new data type for storing XML data. The XMLType data type can be used just like any other data type in Oracle. You can use it as a column type in a table, in a variable in a PL/SQL script, or in a view declaration. An XMLType data type can contain any well-formed valid XML document. To maintain XML validity, XMLType columns and tables can be forced to conform to an XML Schema. Oracle can perform many operations on XMLType data using built-in functions, and it can query data within them using standard XPath expressions. The XMLType object has several member functions to process XML as well. Oracle can index XMLType data for fast searching and retrieval, as well as create SQL constraints on XML.

To give you maximum flexibility, XMLType columns can be stored either in a structured or unstructured fashion. XML data stored in an unstructured XMLType is stored as a `CLOB`. When stored in a structured XMLType, the XML data is parsed and stored in an optimized fashion by Oracle. XMLType uses the Oracle C XML parser internally so you get the benefit of the fastest possible parsing.

There are trade-offs in making a storage choice that will affect the performance of your application. You should choose unstructured storage when you know you will be retrieving and inserting an entire XML document and you don't want to do updates or searches on the individual elements of the document. Next, we'll look at the pros and cons of unstructured versus structured storage.

> **What happens if you make the wrong choice between structured and unstructured storage? Don't worry, you can use Oracle's EXPORT and IMPORT utilities to move your data out of the table, change the storage type, and put the data back.**

Following are the advantages of unstructured storage:

- Since the XML inserted is not parsed, unstructured storage is the fastest method of getting XML in and out of the database. XML documents are also stored exactly as they are inserted byte for byte, including white space.
- Any type of XML can be stored in an unstructured XMLType without having to conform to an XML Schema.

Following are the advantages of structured storage:

- XML documents are pre-parsed when inserted into the database. Oracle can validate the documents and ensure they conform to an XML Schema.
- Since the XML document is pre-parsed, Oracle can optimize most operations on the XML to be as efficient as possible. Sections or individual elements of the XML document can be updated in place using query rewrite without having to update the entire XML document. XPath statements also take advantage of query rewrite and run much faster under structured storage.
- Structured storage supports B-tree-, text-, and function-based indexes.
- SQL constraints are supported on XML data. You can use XML documents in foreign key relationships.

Following are disadvantages of unstructured storage:

- Any operations on the XML data are very expensive in terms of database processing as Oracle must convert the CLOB data to a DOM object to perform any kind of XPath or Oracle XML function.
- Any update to the XML document requires that the entire document is retrieved and written back to the database.
- You cannot use SQL integrity constraints in unstructured storage on an XML document, and only text and function-based indexes are supported.

Following are disadvantages of structured storage:

- XML documents are parsed before they are inserted into the database. This has a slight performance hit on the database when you are inserting and retrieving entire XML documents.
- You can only store documents that conform to an XML Schema in a structured XMLType. If you change the XML Schema definition, you could have to reload the XML documents already stored in the XMLType column or table.

Creating XMLType Columns and Tables

If you want to use non-schema-based unstructured storage, you simply create a table of XMLType objects, or an XMLType column in an existing table. To insert an XML document, you create a `DIRECTORY` object to store the base directory path of your XML files and then insert each one. If the column is not associated with an XML Schema, Oracle knows to store them as unstructured in a `CLOB` field. Creating structured storage XMLType tables and columns is slightly more complicated, as you need to create an XML Schema document to describe how the XML should be stored. See the "XML Schema" section later in the chapter for more details.

The following creates an XMLType column and inserts data:

```
DROP TABLE xmlExample;

CREATE TABLE xmlExample(
ID varchar2(32),
Name varchar2(20),
Data XMLType
);

CREATE DIRECTORY my_path AS '/path/to/xmlfiles/';

INSERT INTO xmlExample(ID, Name, Data)
       VALUES
       (sys_guid(),'my document',
         xmltype
         (
           bfilename('MY_PATH', 'mydocument.xml'),
           nls_charset_id('AL32UTF8')
         )
       );
```

If your XML document is small, you can also just insert it into the table as a string value.

```
INSERT INTO xmlExample(ID, name, data)
       VALUES
       (sys_guid(),'my document',
       '<root><tag>some data</tag><tag>some more data</tag></root>'
```

If you would like to create tables based on an existing XML Schema, you simply create the table and specify additional information about how to store the XML, the registered XML Schema you want to use, and the element within the XML document you want to store in the table or column. As you can see in the examples following, you can simply specify `STORE AS CLOB` to override Oracle's default structured method of storing schema-based content.

```
-- Create an XMLType table where the XML is stored as a CLOB
CREATE TABLE xmlExample OF XMLType
  XMLType STORE AS CLOB
  XMLSCHEMA "http://www.example.com/some/sampleschema.xsd"
  ELEMENT "root_XML_element";

-- Create a table where the XML is a column stored as a CLOB
CREATE TABLE xmlExample2 (id NUMBER, name VARCHAR2(20), doc XMLType)
  XMLType COLUMN doc
  STORE AS CLOB
  XMLSchema "http://www.example.com/some/sampleschema.xsd"
  ELEMENT "root_XML_element";

-- Create an XMLType table where the XML is stored as structured data
CREATE TABLE xmlExample3 OF XMLType
  XMLSCHEMA "http://www.example.com/some/sampleschema.xsd"
  ELEMENT "root_XML_element";

-- Create a table where the XML is a column stored as structured data
CREATE TABLE xmlExample4 (id NUMBER, name VARCHAR2(20), doc XMLType)
  XMLType COLUMN doc
  XMLSchema "http://www.example.com/some/sampleschema.xsd"
  ELEMENT "root_XML_element";
```

XML Views

If you would rather store your data in relational tables but still need to access your data as XML, you can create an XMLType view. This kind of view will return an XMLType data type that you can perform further processing on. This technique can be useful when you have legacy data that you want to XML-enable, or data that you need to share with another party that requires XML or is on another platform besides Oracle, and you need a common data format.

You can also go the other way as well. By using the XML functions in Oracle, you can create a relational view over XML, thereby exposing XML data to applications that can only access relational data.

Viewing Relational Data as XML

To create an XMLType view, you create a standard Oracle view and use the XML/SQL functions to generate XML from the relational data. The view returns an XMLType for each row returned from an SQL query on the view.

```
CREATE OR REPLACE VIEW custXML of XMLType with OBJECT ID
(EXTRACT(OBJECT_VALUE, '/CUSTOMER_ID').getnumberval())
AS
SELECT XMLFOREST(c.CUSTOMER_ID,
c.CUST_FIRST_NAME as "firstname",
c.CUST_LAST_NAME as "lastname",
SYS_XMLGEN(c.CUST_ADDRESS) as "address",
SYS_XMLGEN(c.PHONE_NUMBERS) as "phone",
c.CREDIT_LIMIT,
c.CUST_EMAIL,
c.DATE_OF_BIRTH,
c.MARITAL_STATUS,
c.GENDER,
c.INCOME_LEVEL)
FROM CUSTOMERS c
WHERE c.CREDIT_LIMIT = 2500;

SELECT * FROM custXML;

<CUSTOMER_ID>253</CUSTOMER_ID>
<firstname>Sally</firstname>
<lastname>Bogart</lastname>
<address>
  <CUST_ADDRESS>
   <STREET_ADDRESS>215 4Th Ave Se</STREET_ADDRESS>
    <POSTAL_CODE>52401</POSTAL_CODE>
    <CITY>Cedar Rapids</CITY>
    <STATE_PROVINCE>IA</STATE_PROVINCE>
    <COUNTRY_ID>US</COUNTRY_ID>
  </CUST_ADDRESS>
</address>
<phone>
  <PHONE_NUMBERS>
    <VARCHAR2>+1 319 123 4269</VARCHAR2>
  </PHONE_NUMBERS>
</phone>
<CREDIT_LIMIT>2500</CREDIT_LIMIT>
<CUST_EMAIL>Sally.Bogart@WILLET.COM</CUST_EMAIL>
<DATE_OF_BIRTH>1985-01-14</DATE_OF_BIRTH>
<MARITAL_STATUS>married</MARITAL_STATUS>
<GENDER>M</GENDER>
<INCOME_LEVEL>H: 150,000 - 169,999</INCOME_LEVEL>
... etc.
```

The XML data returned from the view can be further processed by Oracle's XSLT processor or any other XML tool.

Viewing XML Data as Relational Data

You can also create views to expose XML data stored in Oracle as relational data. This can be very handy for legacy applications that cannot process XML but still need access to the data. Just like creating a view from SQL to XML, you use the Oracle XML functions to extract the data. If you take this approach, you should ensure that your XML is stored in a structured XMLType for performance reasons.

```
CREATE OR REPLACE VIEW warehouse_to_sql
AS
SELECT WAREHOUSE_ID, WAREHOUSE_NAME,
extractvalue(warehouse_spec, '/Warehouse/Building') as buliding,
extractvalue(warehouse_spec, '/Warehouse/Area') as area,
extractvalue(warehouse_spec, '/Warehouse/Docks') as docks,
extractvalue(warehouse_spec, '/Warehouse/DockType') as dockType,
extractvalue(warehouse_spec, '/Warehouse/WaterAccess') as wateraccess,
extractvalue(warehouse_spec, '/Warehouse/RailAccess') as railaccess,
extractvalue(warehouse_spec, '/Warehouse/Parking') as parking,
extractvalue(warehouse_spec, '/Warehouse/VClearance') as clearance
FROM warehouses;


select WAREHOUSE_ID, WAREHOUSE_NAME, AREA, PARKING, CLEARANCE from
WAREHOUSE_TO_SQL;

WAREHOUSE_ID     WAREHOUSE_NAME       AREA     PARKING     CLEARANCE
 --------------- -------------------  -------  ----------  ------------
 1               Southlake, Texas     25000    Street      10 ft
 2               San Francisco        50000    Lot         12 ft
 3               New Jersey           85700    Street      11.5 ft
 4               Seattle, Washington  103000   Lot         15 ft
 5               Toronto              (null)   (null)      (null)
 6               Sydney               (null)   (null)      (null)
 7               Mexico City          (null)   (null)      (null)
 8               Beijing              (null)   (null)      (null)
 9               Bombay               (null)   (null)      (null)
```

XML Schema

XML Schema is a standard that was created by the World Wide Web Consortium (W3C) to be used as a way to detail the structure and data types of XML documents. XML Schema was created as the replacement for XML document type definitions (DTDs). XML Schema is dense enough to warrant its own book, so this section will concentrate mostly on the Oracle extensions to, and use of, the XML Schema. A great primer on XML Schema can be found on the W3C site at `http://www.w3.org/TR/xmlschema-0`

XML Schema is an integral technology in Oracle 10*g* XDB. Oracle uses XML Schema to validate XML files and XMLTypes, as meta data to control how XML documents are mapped to Oracle tables and structures, and to support the storage of XML as structured content in the database. When you load an XML Schema document into Oracle, the database creates the relevant object types and tables to hold data. Oracle-specific XML Schema annotations allow you to have fine-grain control over how the tables and types created to store decomposed XML are named and structured.

Attaching an XML Schema to an XMLType table or column allows that data to be stored as structured XML. Structured XML is decomposed into its parts and stored as object types and `VARRAY`s. An object type is created from each `complexType` found in the XML Schema, and `VARRAY`s are created for each element. Oracle maps the scalar data types defined in XML Schema to the scalar data types supported by standard SQL.

Oracle provides support for the following tasks through XML Schema:

- Registering W3C-compliant XML Schemas as either local to the database schema or global
- Validating XML documents against registered XML Schemas
- Generating an XML Schema from database object types
- Referencing another user's XML Schemas
- Name resolution between global and local names
- Generating database tables and database objects from an XML Schema during registration
- Creating XMLType tables, views and columns based on registered XML Schemas
- Storing XML into default tables when schema-based XML documents are inserted into the Oracle XDB repository

When you upload an XML Schema to Oracle, the database parses the XML Schema file and creates special tables and object types to store the elements of the file. The benefit is that Oracle can manage the data as efficiently as table-based relational data, but the end user or developer can still access the XML file as a whole without worrying about the storage details of each document that conforms to a registered XML Schema.

Another benefit is that you can use an XML Schema stored in Oracle to validate XMLTypes and XML documents. For example, Oracle will not let you insert an invalid XML document in the XDB repository if it is based on an XML Schema.

Creating an XML Schema Document

Oracle supports well-formed W3C-compliant XML Schema definitions and defines Oracle-specific annotations to the XML Schema to control how the schema is translated into tables and types in Oracle.

For this section, you will use the example.xml and example-schema.xsd files from the Web site. The XML file describes an example HR record that represents an employee and the XSD file is the XML Schema document that provides the schema for the HR record.

The following is from the example.xml file:

```
<?xml version="1.0"?>
<hr-record xmlns:xsi="http://www.w3.org/2001/XMLSchema-instance"
xsi:schemaLocation="http://www.example.com/some/example-schema.xsd">
<employee ID="1234">
<name>Joe Employee</name>
<address>55 Main St Apt. 4</address>
<city>Anytown</city>
<state>NY</state>
```

```
<zip>10011</zip>
<email>joe@company.com</email>
<phone>
    <phone_type>home</phone_type>
    <number>212-555-5555</number>
</phone>
<phone>
    <phone_type>work</phone_type>
    <number>212-555-4444</number>
</phone>
<hire_date>1999-12-12</hire_date>
<salary>100000</salary>
<manager_id>123</manager_id>
</employee>
</hr-record>
```

Now here is the code from the example-schema.xsd file:

```
<?xml version="1.0" encoding="UTF-8"?>
<xs:schema xmlns:xs="http://www.w3.org/2001/XMLSchema"
    xmlns:xdb="http://xmlns.oracle.com/xdb"
    elementFormDefault="qualified
  <xs:element name="hr-record">
    <xs:complexType>
      <xs:sequence>
        <xs:element ref="employee"/>
      </xs:sequence>
    </xs:complexType>
  </xs:element>
  <xs:element name="employee">
    <xs:complexType>
      <xs:sequence>
        <xs:element ref="name"/>
        <xs:element ref="address"/>
        <xs:element ref="city"/>
        <xs:element ref="state"/>
        <xs:element ref="zip"/>
        <xs:element ref="email"/>
        <xs:element maxOccurs="unbounded" ref="phone"/>
        <xs:element ref="hire_date"/>
        <xs:element ref="salary"/>
        <xs:element ref="manager_id"/>
      </xs:sequence>
      <xs:attribute name="ID" use="required" type="xs:integer"/>
    </xs:complexType>
  </xs:element>
  <xs:element name="name" type="xs:string"/>
  <xs:element name="address" type="xs:string"/>
  <xs:element name="city" type="xs:NCName"/>
  <xs:element name="state" type="xs:NCName"/>
  <xs:element name="zip" type="xs:integer"/>
  <xs:element name="email" type="xs:string"/>
  <xs:element name="phone">
    <xs:complexType>
```

```
        <xs:sequence>
          <xs:element ref="phone_type"/>
          <xs:element ref="number"/>
        </xs:sequence>
      </xs:complexType>
    </xs:element>
    <xs:element name="phone_type" type="phoneNumber_types"/>
    <xs:element name="number" type="USPhone"/>
    <xs:element name="hire_date" type="xs:date"/>
    <xs:element name="salary" type="salaryRange"/>
    <xs:element name="manager_id" type="xs:integer"/>

    <xs:simpleType name="salaryRange">
       <xs:restriction base="xs:integer">
         <xs:minInclusive value="10000"/>
         <xs:maxInclusive value="1000000"/>
       </xs:restriction>
    </xs:simpleType>

    <xs:simpleType name="phoneNumber_types">
       <xs:restriction base="xs:string">
         <xs:enumeration value="work"/>
         <xs:enumeration value="home"/>
         <xs:enumeration value="cell"/>
       </xs:restriction>
    </xs:simpleType>

    <xs:simpleType name="USPhone">
       <xs:restriction base="xs:string">
         <xs:pattern value="\d{3}-\d{3}-\d{4}"/>
       </xs:restriction>
  </xs:simpleType>

  </xs:schema>
```

The XML Schema describes a few types that require specific formatting for data, like `USPhone`, and require specific values, like the `phoneNumber_types`. This schema can be created in Oracle without change.

Uploading a Schema

Once you have created a new XML Schema, you can upload and register it a couple of different ways. You can use the PL/SQL API to upload the schema, or you can use Enterprise Manager Console to upload the schema. When you register an XML Schema, Oracle creates object types that represent the elements of the document, as well as XMLType tables to hold the global types specified in the schema.

The simplest way to do this is to use the Oracle Enterprise Manager Console. Launch the application, log in as `SYS`, and navigate to the XML Database/XML Schema section. Right-click here and choose Create. Fill in the schema URL, change the owner to `SCOTT`, and select the XSD file. Figure 22-10 shows the Create XML Schema dialog box in Enterprise Manager.

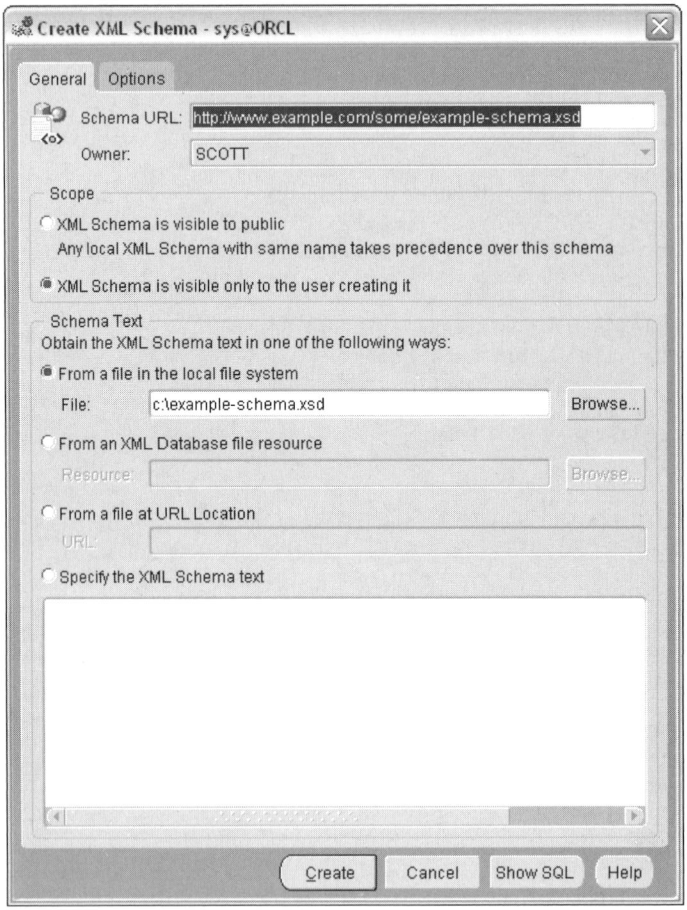

Figure 22-10: Creating a new XML Schema.

On the Options tab, you can choose to generate tables based on the schema, generate object types based on the XML Schema, generate JavaBeans, and create the schema regardless of errors. Figure 22-11 shows the options that are available to you.

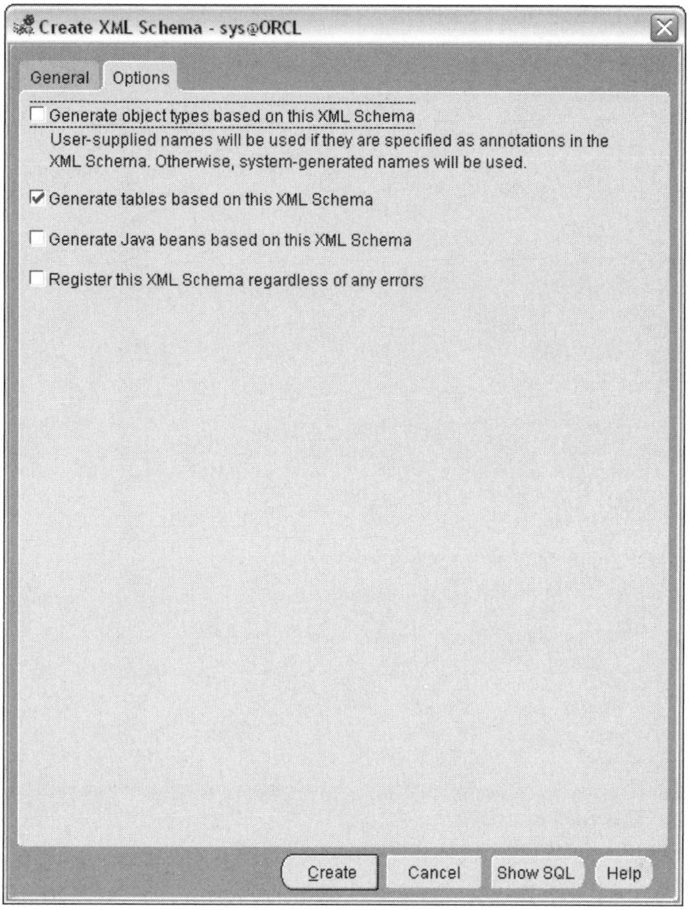

Figure 22-11: Setting XML Schema options.

Oracle will read the XML Schema and create the tables and types to store the content properly. You should see this in the expanded view of the schema similar to what is shown in Figure 22-12.

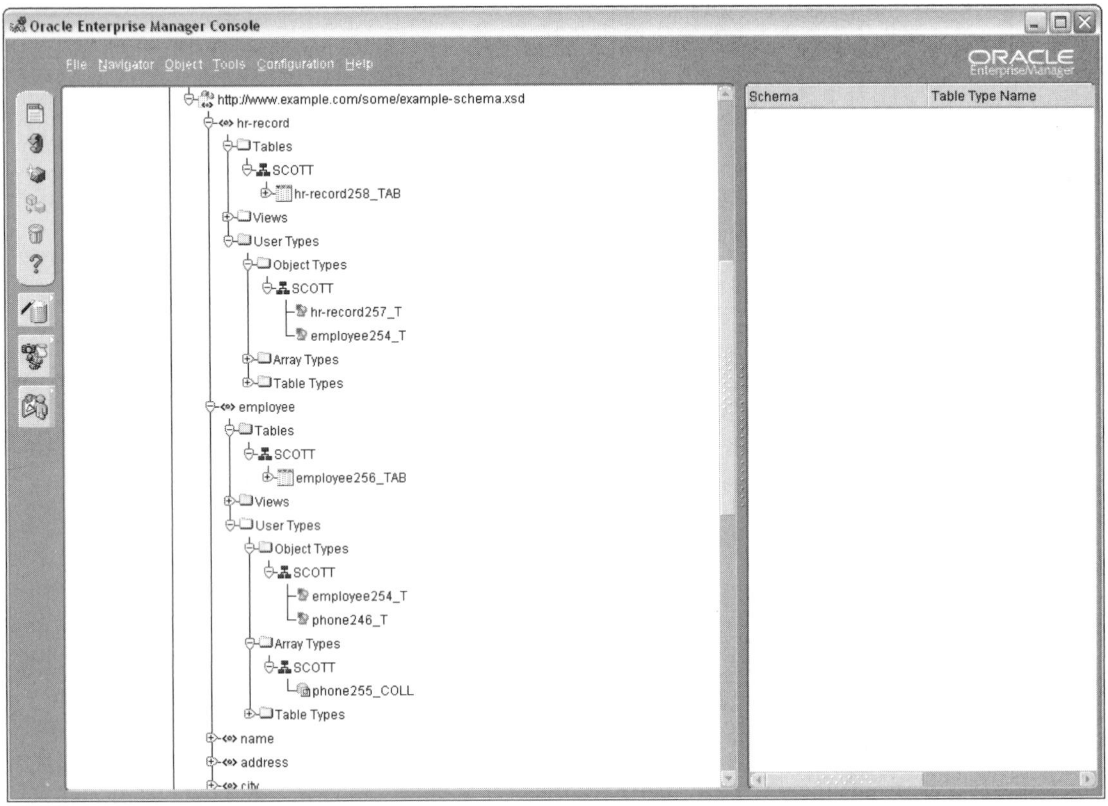

Figure 22-12: Oracle XML Schema objects.

Your XML Schema is now ready to be used for XML validation and XML storage. Once an XML Schema is uploaded in a user schema, documents can then be uploaded and accessed from the Oracle XML repository.

Uploading with PL/SQL

The `DBMS_XMLSCHEMA` package provides methods for adding and removing schemas:

- `registerSchema()` — Registers a schema with Oracle
- `deleteSchema()` — Deletes a previously defined schema

Following is an example using `registerSchema()`:

```
BEGIN
  CREATE DIRECTORY my_path AS '/path/to/xmlfiles/'
  DBMS_XMLSCHEMA.registerSchema(
    SCHEMAURL => 'http://www.example.com/schema/example/someSchema.xsd',
    SCHEMADOC => bfilename('my_path','someSchema.xsd'),
    CSID => nls_charset_id('AL32UTF8'));
END;
```

Valid options for `registerSchema` are as follows:

- `SCHEMAURL` — A URL that is the unique ID of the schema.
- `schemaDoc` — A valid XML Schema document.
- `local` — A boolean value determining if the schema is local or global:
    - Schemas are registered as local schemas by default under /sys/schemas/username/.
    - Global schemas are added under /sys/schemas/PUBLIC/, and you need write permissions to create one there.
- `genTypes` — A boolean value determining if the schema compiler should generate object types. The default value is `TRUE`.
- `genBean` — A boolean value determining if the schema compiler should generate Java Beans. The default value is `FALSE`.
- `genTables` — A boolean value determining if the schema compiler should generate default tables. The default value is `TRUE`.
- `force` — A boolean value determining if the schema compiler should complain about errors but create the schema anyway. The default value is `FALSE`.
- `owner` — States the name of the database user that owns the XML Schema object. By default, the user registering the schema is the owner.
- `Csid` — Specifies the char set of the input schema. If equal to 0, the schema encoding is determined by the MIME type.

To delete, you can issue the following command:

```
begin
dbms_xmlSchema.deleteSchema(' schemaurl=>
http://www.example.com/schema/example/someSchema.xsd',
delete_option=>DBMS_XMLSchema.Delete_Cascade_Force);
end;
```

The `delete_option` set in `deleteSchema` specifies how the delete should work. Valid constants in the `DBMS_XMLSCHEMA` package are as follows:

- `DBMS_XMLSCHEMA.DELETE_RESTRICT`
- `DBMS_XMLSCHEMA.DELETE_INVALIDATE`
- `DBMS_XMLSCHEMA.DELETE_CASCADE`
- `DBMS_XMLSCHEMA.DELETE_CASCADE_FORCE`

Oracle-Specific Annotations

Using XML Schema annotations, you can have fine-grained control of how the schema gets mapped during registration. Oracle will annotate the XML Schema for you automatically, as is evident by revisiting the schema you created previously. Pulling up the schema definition in Enterprise Manager looks like this:

```
<?xml version="1.0" encoding="WINDOWS-1252"?>
<xs:schema xmlns:xs="http://www.w3.org/2001/XMLSchema"
    elementFormDefault="qualified" xmlns:oraxdb="http://xmlns.oracle.com/xdb"
    oraxdb:flags="263" oraxdb:schemaURL="http://www.example.com/some/example-
    schema.xsd" oraxdb:schemaOwner="SCOTT" oraxdb:numProps="28">
  <xs:element name="hr-record" oraxdb:propNumber="2861" oraxdb:global="true"
      oraxdb:SQLName="hr-record" oraxdb:SQLType="hr-record257_T"
      oraxdb:SQLSchema="SCOTT" oraxdb:memType="258" oraxdb:defaultTable="hr-
      record258_TAB" oraxdb:defaultTableSchema="SCOTT">

    <xs:complexType oraxdb:SQLType="hr-record257_T" oraxdb:SQLSchema="SCOTT">
      <xs:sequence>
        <xs:element ref="employee" oraxdb:propNumber="2860" oraxdb:global="false"
            oraxdb:SQLName="employee" oraxdb:SQLType="employee254_T"
            oraxdb:SQLSchema="SCOTT" oraxdb:memType="258" oraxdb:SQLInline="true"
            oraxdb:MemInline="false" oraxdb:JavaInline="false"/>
      </xs:sequence>
    </xs:complexType>
  </xs:element>
  <xs:element name="employee" oraxdb:propNumber="2873" oraxdb:global="true"
      oraxdb:SQLName="employee" oraxdb:SQLType="employee254_T"
      oraxdb:SQLSchema="SCOTT" oraxdb:memType="258"
      oraxdb:defaultTable="employee256_TAB" oraxdb:defaultTableSchema="SCOTT">
    <xs:complexType oraxdb:SQLType="employee254_T" oraxdb:SQLSchema="SCOTT">
      <xs:sequence>
        <xs:element ref="name" oraxdb:propNumber="2863" oraxdb:global="false"
            oraxdb:SQLName="name" oraxdb:SQLType="VARCHAR2" oraxdb:memType="1"
            oraxdb:SQLInline="true" oraxdb:MemInline="false"
            oraxdb:JavaInline="false"/>
        <xs:element ref="address" oraxdb:propNumber="2864" oraxdb:global="false"
            oraxdb:SQLName="address" oraxdb:SQLType="VARCHAR2" oraxdb:memType="1"
            oraxdb:SQLInline="true" oraxdb:MemInline="false"
            oraxdb:JavaInline="false"/>
        <xs:element ref="city" oraxdb:propNumber="2865" oraxdb:global="false"
            oraxdb:SQLName="city" oraxdb:SQLType="VARCHAR2" oraxdb:memType="1"
            oraxdb:SQLInline="true" oraxdb:MemInline="false"
            oraxdb:JavaInline="false"/>
        <xs:element ref="state" oraxdb:propNumber="2866" oraxdb:global="false"
            oraxdb:SQLName="state" oraxdb:SQLType="VARCHAR2" oraxdb:memType="1"
            oraxdb:SQLInline="true" oraxdb:MemInline="false"
            oraxdb:JavaInline="false"/>
        <xs:element ref="zip" oraxdb:propNumber="2867" oraxdb:global="false"
            oraxdb:SQLName="zip" oraxdb:SQLType="NUMBER" oraxdb:memType="2"
            oraxdb:SQLInline="true" oraxdb:MemInline="false"
            oraxdb:JavaInline="false"/>
        <xs:element ref="email" oraxdb:propNumber="2868" oraxdb:global="false"
            oraxdb:SQLName="email" oraxdb:SQLType="VARCHAR2" oraxdb:memType="1"
            oraxdb:SQLInline="true" oraxdb:MemInline="false"
            oraxdb:JavaInline="false"/>
```

```
        <xs:element maxOccurs="unbounded" ref="phone" oraxdb:propNumber="2869"
            oraxdb:global="false" oraxdb:SQLName="phone"
            oraxdb:SQLType="phone246_T" oraxdb:SQLSchema="SCOTT"
            oraxdb:memType="258" oraxdb:SQLInline="true" oraxdb:MemInline="false"
            oraxdb:JavaInline="false" oraxdb:SQLCollType="phone255_COLL"
            oraxdb:SQLCollSchema="SCOTT"/>
        <xs:element ref="hire_date" oraxdb:propNumber="2870" oraxdb:global="false"
            oraxdb:SQLName="hire_date" oraxdb:SQLType="DATE" oraxdb:memType="12"
            oraxdb:SQLInline="true" oraxdb:MemInline="false"
            oraxdb:JavaInline="false"/>
        <xs:element ref="salary" oraxdb:propNumber="2871" oraxdb:global="false"
            oraxdb:SQLName="salary" oraxdb:SQLType="NUMBER" oraxdb:memType="2"
            oraxdb:SQLInline="true" oraxdb:MemInline="false"
            oraxdb:JavaInline="false"/>
        <xs:element ref="manager_id" oraxdb:propNumber="2872" oraxdb:global="false"
            oraxdb:SQLName="manager_id" oraxdb:SQLType="NUMBER" oraxdb:memType="2"
            oraxdb:SQLInline="true" oraxdb:MemInline="false"
            oraxdb:JavaInline="false"/>
      </xs:sequence>
      <xs:attribute name="ID" use="required" type="xs:integer"
          oraxdb:propNumber="2862" oraxdb:global="false" oraxdb:SQLName="ID"
          oraxdb:SQLType="NUMBER" oraxdb:memType="2"/>
    </xs:complexType>
  </xs:element>
  <xs:element name="name" type="xs:string" oraxdb:propNumber="2874"
      oraxdb:global="true" oraxdb:SQLName="name" oraxdb:SQLType="VARCHAR2"
      oraxdb:memType="1" oraxdb:defaultTable="name253_TAB"
      oraxdb:defaultTableSchema="SCOTT"/>
  <xs:element name="address" type="xs:string" oraxdb:propNumber="2875"
      oraxdb:global="true" oraxdb:SQLName="address" oraxdb:SQLType="VARCHAR2"
      oraxdb:memType="1" oraxdb:defaultTable="address252_TAB"
      oraxdb:defaultTableSchema="SCOTT"/>
  <xs:element name="city" type="xs:NCName" oraxdb:propNumber="2876"
      oraxdb:global="true" oraxdb:SQLName="city" oraxdb:SQLType="VARCHAR2"
      oraxdb:memType="1" oraxdb:defaultTable="city251_TAB"
      oraxdb:defaultTableSchema="SCOTT"/>
  <xs:element name="state" type="xs:NCName" oraxdb:propNumber="2877"
      oraxdb:global="true" oraxdb:SQLName="state" oraxdb:SQLType="VARCHAR2"
      oraxdb:memType="1" oraxdb:defaultTable="state250_TAB"
      oraxdb:defaultTableSchema="SCOTT"/>
  <xs:element name="zip" type="xs:integer" oraxdb:propNumber="2878"
      oraxdb:global="true" oraxdb:SQLName="zip" oraxdb:SQLType="NUMBER"
      oraxdb:memType="2" oraxdb:defaultTable="zip249_TAB"
      oraxdb:defaultTableSchema="SCOTT"/>
  <xs:element name="email" type="xs:string" oraxdb:propNumber="2879"
      oraxdb:global="true" oraxdb:SQLName="email" oraxdb:SQLType="VARCHAR2"
      oraxdb:memType="1" oraxdb:defaultTable="email248_TAB"
      oraxdb:defaultTableSchema="SCOTT"/>
  <xs:element name="phone" oraxdb:propNumber="2882" oraxdb:global="true"
      oraxdb:SQLName="phone" oraxdb:SQLType="phone246_T" oraxdb:SQLSchema="SCOTT"
      oraxdb:memType="258" oraxdb:defaultTable="phone247_TAB"
      oraxdb:defaultTableSchema="SCOTT">
    <xs:complexType oraxdb:SQLType="phone246_T" oraxdb:SQLSchema="SCOTT">
      <xs:sequence>
```

```
          <xs:element ref="phone_type" oraxdb:propNumber="2880" oraxdb:global="false"
              oraxdb:SQLName="phone_type" oraxdb:SQLType="XDB$ENUM_T"
              oraxdb:SQLSchema="XDB" oraxdb:memType="259" oraxdb:SQLInline="true"
              oraxdb:MemInline="false" oraxdb:JavaInline="false"/>
          <xs:element ref="number" oraxdb:propNumber="2881" oraxdb:global="false"
              oraxdb:SQLName="number" oraxdb:SQLType="VARCHAR2" oraxdb:memType="1"
              oraxdb:SQLInline="true" oraxdb:MemInline="false"
              oraxdb:JavaInline="false"/>
        </xs:sequence>
      </xs:complexType>
    </xs:element>
    <xs:element name="phone_type" type="phoneNumber_types" oraxdb:propNumber="2883"
        oraxdb:global="true" oraxdb:SQLName="phone_type" oraxdb:SQLType="XDB$ENUM_T"
        oraxdb:SQLSchema="XDB" oraxdb:memType="259"
        oraxdb:defaultTable="phone_type245_TAB" oraxdb:defaultTableSchema="SCOTT"/>
    <xs:element name="number" type="USPhone" oraxdb:propNumber="2884"
        oraxdb:global="true" oraxdb:SQLName="number" oraxdb:SQLType="VARCHAR2"
        oraxdb:memType="1" oraxdb:defaultTable="number244_TAB"
        oraxdb:defaultTableSchema="SCOTT"/>
    <xs:element name="hire_date" type="xs:date" oraxdb:propNumber="2885"
        oraxdb:global="true" oraxdb:SQLName="hire_date" oraxdb:SQLType="DATE"
        oraxdb:memType="12" oraxdb:defaultTable="hire_date243_TAB"
        oraxdb:defaultTableSchema="SCOTT"/>
    <xs:element name="salary" type="salaryRange" oraxdb:propNumber="2886"
        oraxdb:global="true" oraxdb:SQLName="salary" oraxdb:SQLType="NUMBER"
        oraxdb:memType="2" oraxdb:defaultTable="salary242_TAB"
        oraxdb:defaultTableSchema="SCOTT"/>
    <xs:element name="manager_id" type="xs:integer" oraxdb:propNumber="2887"
        oraxdb:global="true" oraxdb:SQLName="manager_id" oraxdb:SQLType="NUMBER"
        oraxdb:memType="2" oraxdb:defaultTable="manager_id241_TAB"
        oraxdb:defaultTableSchema="SCOTT"/>
    <xs:simpleType name="salaryRange">
      <xs:restriction base="xs:integer">
        <xs:minInclusive value="10000"/>
        <xs:maxInclusive value="1000000"/>
      </xs:restriction>
    </xs:simpleType>
    <xs:simpleType name="phoneNumber_types">
      <xs:restriction base="xs:string">
        <xs:enumeration value="work"/>
        <xs:enumeration value="home"/>
        <xs:enumeration value="cell"/>
      </xs:restriction>
    </xs:simpleType>
    <xs:simpleType name="USPhone">
      <xs:restriction base="xs:string">
        <xs:pattern value="\d{3}-\d{3}-\d{4}"/>
      </xs:restriction>
    </xs:simpleType>
  </xs:schema>
```

As you can see, Oracle provides annotations for controlling the names of generated objects, schema name, SQL data type mappings, and so on. All of these options can be specified when you create your schema if you don't want Oracle to do it for you.

XML Annotations

To specify Oracle XML annotations, you need to import the namespace into your XML Schema file. For example, the schema tag in the example schema file defines the namespace `oraxdb`:

```
<xs:schema xmlns:xs="http://www.w3.org/2001/XMLSchema"
    xmlns:oraxdb="http://xmlns.oracle.com/xdb
```

The annotations listed following all take the general form of `oraxdb:annotation = "value"`.

Annotations Specified in Elements

Listed in the text that follows are the Oracle-specific annotations you can include in elements of an XSD definition. They allow for fine-grained control over how Oracle generates the underlying storage for your objects.

SQLName

Its value specifies the name of the SQL object attribute created from an XML element. The default value is the element name.

SQLType

Its value specifies the name of the SQL type created from an XML element. The default value is the element name.

SQLCollType

Its value specifies the name of the SQL collection type created from an XML element with `maxOccurs > 1`. The default value is the element name.

SQLSchema

Its value can be any valid schema in the database, and it defaults to the user registering the schema. This annotation specifies the user that owns the type specified in SQLType.

SQLCollSchema

Its value can be any valid schema in the database, and it defaults to the user registering the schema. This annotation specifies the user that owns the type specified in SQLColType.

maintainOrder

Boolean value with a default value of `TRUE`. If `TRUE`, the collection is mapped to a `VARRAY`; otherwise, the collection is mapped to a `NESTED TABLE`.

SQLInline

Boolean value with a default value of `TRUE`. When the value is `TRUE`, this element will be stored inline as an embedded attribute; otherwise, a `REF` value is stored.

maintainDOM

Boolean value with a default value of TRUE. If TRUE, XML in this element retains DOM fidelity. The XML you get for output is guaranteed to be the same as what went in. If FALSE, Oracle can strip processing instructions and other items from the XML. The elements are not guaranteed to come out in the same order, either.

columnProps

Its value can be any valid column storage clause with a default value of NULL. Contains the column storage clause that will be inserted into the CREATE TABLE statement.

tableProp

Its value can be any valid table storage clause with a default value of NULL. The storage clause that will be appended to the default CREATE TABLE statement.

defaultTable

Its value can be any table name with a default value of the element's name. It contains the name of the table for XML storage.

Annotations Specified in Elements Declaring Global ComplexTypes

Listed in the following text are the Oracle-specific annotations that can be included in elements in an XSD definition that control how that element gets mapped to an SQLType.

SQLType

Its value can be a valid SQL type name, and the default value is generated from the element name. It specifies the SQL type name for an element.

SQLSchema

Its value can be any valid schema in the database, and defaults to the user registering the schema.

maintainDOM

A boolean value with a default value of TRUE. If TRUE, XML in this element retains DOM fidelity. The XML you get for output is guaranteed to be the same as what went in. If FALSE, Oracle can strip processing instructions and other items from the XML. The elements are not guaranteed to come out in the same order either.

Annotations Specified in XML Schema Declarations

Listed in the following text are Oracle-specific annotations you can specify in XML Schema declarations.

mapUnboundedStringToLob

A boolean value with a default value of FALSE. If TRUE, unbounded strings are mapped to CLOBs, and unbounded binary data gets mapped to BLOBs. If FALSE, unbounded strings are mapped to VARCHAR2(4000) and unbounded binary data gets mapped to RAW(2000).

StoreVarrayAsTable

A boolean value with a default value of `FALSE`. If `TRUE`, the `VARRAY` is stored as a table. If `FALSE`, the `VARRAY` is stored in a `LOB`.

SQL/XML and Query Rewrite

Oracle provides a powerful bridge between the XML and SQL worlds. By using XML DB, you can expose data stored in relational table as XML and also go the other way by treating XML as relational data. In the case of creating a Web site with dynamic content, the developer's tasks become much simpler, as the content can be stored in the database either as relational data or XML, and can be transformed to HTML or some other format by the XSLT processor within Oracle. Developers can shift time-intensive work from the application server layer of their application to the database.

Oracle accomplishes this feat by implementing the upcoming SQL/XML standard in the database. The SQL/XML standard describes how XML should be queried from any SQL statement, and how an SQL statement should create XML from relational data. Oracle makes heavy use of XPath to perform its XML queries from within an SQL statement.

SQL/XML defines some functions that can be used from within an SQL statement to access XML content:

- `existsNode(XMLType, XPath)` — This function checks if a node exists in an XML document by executing an XPath expression. The function takes an XPath expression as its input and returns a `0` or `1` depending on if the specified node exists.

```
SELECT EXISTSNODE(warehouse_spec, '/Warehouse/Building') as RESULT FROM WAREHOUSES
WHERE warehouse_id = 1;

    RESULT
----------
         1
```

- `extract(XMLType, XPath)` — This function returns nodes from an XML document that match the expression in the XPath argument. The function takes an XPath expression as an argument and returns either an XML document if one node is found or an XML fragment if more than one node is found.

```
SELECT EXTRACT(warehouse_spec, '/Warehouse/Building') as RESULT FROM WAREHOUSES
WHERE warehouse_id = 1;

RESULT
--------------------------------------------------------------------------------
<Building>Owned</Building>
```

- `extractValue(XMLType, XPath)` — This function returns the value of a node or attribute specified in the XPath expression argument. The XPath expression must evaluate to a single node or attribute and the value is returned as the appropriate SQL type.

```
SELECT EXTRACTVALUE(warehouse_spec, '/Warehouse/Building') as RESULT FROM
WAREHOUSES WHERE warehouse_id = 1;

RESULT
--------------------------------------------------------------------------------
Owned
```

- `updateXML(XMLType, XPath, Value)` — This function allows you to update portions of an XML document based on a set of XPath expressions.

```
UPDATE warehouses
SET warehouse_spec = UPDATEXML(warehouse_spec,
'/Warehouse/Building/text()','Leased')
WHERE warehouse_id = 1;
```

- `XMLSequence(XMLType, XPath)` — This function turns the high-level elements of an XML document into elements of a `VARRAY`.

```
SELECT XMLSEQUENCE(EXTRACT(warehouse_spec, '/Warehouse/*')) FROM warehouses
  WHERE warehouse_id = 1;

XMLSEQUENCE(EXTRACT(WAREHOUSE_SPEC,'/WAREHOUSE/*'))
--------------------------------------------------------------------------------
XMLSEQUENCETYPE(XMLTYPE(<Building>Owned</Building>
), XMLTYPE(<Area>25000</Area>
), XMLTYPE(<Docks>2</Docks>
), XMLTYPE(<DockType>Rear load</DockType>
), XMLTYPE(<WaterAccess>Y</WaterAccess>
), XMLTYPE(<RailAccess>N</RailAccess>
), XMLTYPE(<Parking>Street</Parking>
), XMLTYPE(<VClearance>10 ft</VClearance>
))
```

Oracle also provides SQL/XML functions to change relational data to XML:

- `xmlElement()` — Creates an element from a table column
- `xmlAttributes()` — Adds the value from a table column to an element
- `xmlForest()` — Creates a group of elements from table columns
- `xmlAgg()` — Aggregates a bunch of children elements under a parent
- `sys_xmlgen()` — Can generate XML from object types or columns

Using these functions, you can expose existing relational data as XML for new applications, data transport, or conversion. See Chapter 13, "Functions," for details on their exact syntax.

SQL to XML

The following example uses the SQL/XML functions to convert the relational data in the OE customers table to an XML document:

```
Select xmlElement(
"customer",
xmlAttributes(c.CUSTOMER_ID as "customerID"),
xmlForest(
c.CUST_FIRST_NAME as "firstname",
c.CUST_LAST_NAME as "lastname"
),
```

```
sys_xmlgen(c.CUST_ADDRESS) as "address",
sys_xmlgen(c.PHONE_NUMBERS) as "phone_numbers",
xmlForest(
c.CREDIT_LIMIT as "credit_limit",
c.CUST_EMAIL as "email",
c.DATE_OF_BIRTH as "dob",
c.MARITAL_STATUS as "status",
c.GENDER as "gender",
c.INCOME_LEVEL as "income"
)
) as XML
FROM customers c
WHERE c.credit_limit = 2500;
```

Following are the results of the previous SQL query:

```
XML
--------------------------------------------------------------------------------
<customer customerID="492"><firstname>Sally</firstname><lastname>Edwards</lastna
me><address><CUST_ADDRESS>
  <STREET_ADDRESS>1632 Splash St</STREET_ADDRESS>
  <POSTAL_CODE>361168</POSTAL_CODE>
  <CITY>Chandigarh</CITY>
  <STATE_PROVINCE>Har</STATE_PROVINCE>
  <COUNTRY_ID>IN</COUNTRY_ID>
</CUST_ADDRESS>
</address><phone_numbers><PHONE_NUMBERS>
  <VARCHAR2>+91 172 012 4861</VARCHAR2>
</PHONE_NUMBERS>
</phone_numbers><credit_limit>2500</credit_limit><email>Sally.Edwards@TURNSTONE.
COM</email><dob>1980-01-06</dob><status>married</status><gender>F</gender><incom
e>K: 250,000 - 299,999</income></customer>

<customer customerID="251"><firstname>Raul</firstname><lastname>Wilder</lastname
><address><CUST_ADDRESS>
  <STREET_ADDRESS>65 Cadillac Sq # 2701</STREET_ADDRESS>
  <POSTAL_CODE>48226</POSTAL_CODE>
  <CITY>Detroit</CITY>
  <STATE_PROVINCE>MI</STATE_PROVINCE>
  <COUNTRY_ID>US</COUNTRY_ID>
</CUST_ADDRESS>
</address><phone_numbers><PHONE_NUMBERS>
  <VARCHAR2>+1 313 123 4241</VARCHAR2>
</PHONE_NUMBERS>
</phone_numbers><credit_limit>2500</credit_limit><email>Raul.Wilder@STILT.COM</e
mail><dob>2045-12-15</dob><status>married</status><gender>M</gender><income>E: 9
0,000 - 109,999</income></customer>
... etc.
```

Notice that Oracle doesn't waste resources formatting the XML results to look good on screen. While this may be okay for application consumption of the XML file, you may want to print XML for human use. You can use the `EXTRACT()` function to pretty-print the XML, as it has internal formatting logic. This technique should be used sparingly, since it forces Oracle to create a DOM object representing the XML document — a very inefficient practice.

```
Select xmlElement(
"customer",
xmlAttributes(c.CUSTOMER_ID as "customerID"),
xmlForest(
c.CUST_FIRST_NAME as "firstname",
c.CUST_LAST_NAME as "lastname"
),
sys_xmlgen(c.CUST_ADDRESS) as "address",
sys_xmlgen(c.PHONE_NUMBERS) as "phone_numbers",
xmlForest(
c.CREDIT_LIMIT as "credit_limit",
c.CUST_EMAIL as "email",
c.DATE_OF_BIRTH as "dob",
c.MARITAL_STATUS as "status",
c.GENDER as "gender",
c.INCOME_LEVEL as "income"
)
).extract('/*') as XML
FROM customers c
WHERE c.credit_limit = 2500
```

would result in a formatted result:

```
XML
--------------------------------------------------------------------------------
<customer customerID="492">
  <firstname>Sally</firstname>
  <lastname>Edwards</lastname>
  <address>
    <CUST_ADDRESS>
      <STREET_ADDRESS>1632 Splash St</STREET_ADDRESS>
      <POSTAL_CODE>361168</POSTAL_CODE>
      <CITY>Chandigarh</CITY>
      <STATE_PROVINCE>Har</STATE_PROVINCE>
      <COUNTRY_ID>IN</COUNTRY_ID>
    </CUST_ADDRESS>
  </address>
  <phone_numbers>
    <PHONE_NUMBERS>
      <VARCHAR2>+91 172 012 4861</VARCHAR2>
    </PHONE_NUMBERS>
  </phone_numbers>
  <credit_limit>2500</credit_limit>
  <email>Sally.Edwards@TURNSTONE.COM</email>
  <dob>1980-01-06</dob>
  <status>married</status>
  <gender>F</gender>
  <income>K: 250,000 - 299,999</income>
</customer>
... etc.
```

Oracle optimizes the XPath operations on XML documents based on how they are stored. Unstructured documents are converted to a DOM model, and the XPath is applied using the DOM API. Structured documents make use of query rewriting to maximize performance. Understanding query rewriting will help you design an XML database application that will correctly meet your needs.

The Oracle query rewrite engine is tasked with converting XML XPath expressions into relational operations. This has several benefits. First, you can work in a familiar XML format without worrying how Oracle retrieves the data, but still receive the benefit of optimized access and fast querying. Second, once Oracle rewrites the query in SQL terms, it can pass it to the database optimizer, which then creates an optimized execution plan. By rewriting XPath queries in SQL, Oracle insulates the database optimizer from having to know about XPath and XML, and can use the same optimization logic as other SQL queries.

Transforming XML

One of the most common tasks developers face when working with XML is performing XSLT transformations. Oracle 10*g* provides a high-performance XSLT processor with XML DB for you to use to transform XML. Oracle implements its XSLT and XML parsers in C for speed, and has created a thin binding layer around the C code to provide access from Java and PL/SQL. The benefit for developers is access to a highly optimized and efficient transformation engine from any language the database supports.

There are essentially three ways to transform content in XML DB:

- Using the `XMLTransform()` function
- Using the `transform()` method of an XMLType
- Using the `DBMS_XSLPROCESSOR` PL/SQL API

The `XMLTransform()` and `XMLType.transform()` functions are essentially the same. They take XMLType data and a passed in XSLT style sheet and return the transformed result as a string.

The usage of XMLTransform is as follows:

```
XMLTransform(XMLType, XMLType)
```

where the first parameter is an XMLType containing the XML document you want to transform, and the second XMLType contains the XSL style sheet.

The transform method operates on the XML document XMLType itself, and therefore you only pass in the XSL style sheet.

```
XMLType.transform(Stylesheet)
```

For example, you can use XSL to format the XML you created earlier in the XML Schema example.

First, upload an XSL style sheet to the SCOTT repository you created earlier. Save it in a folder named XSL at the same level as the XML folder created earlier.

```
<?xml version="1.0" encoding="WINDOWS-1252"?>
<xsl:stylesheet version="1.0" xmlns:xsl="http://www.w3.org/1999/XSL/Transform"
                xmlns:xdb="http://xmlns.oracle.com/xdb"
                xmlns:xsi="http://www.w3.org/2001/XMLSchema-instance">

<xsl:template match="/hr-record/employee">

<html>
<body bgcolor="white">

<font size = "+1"><xsl:value-of select = "name"/></font><br/>
```

```
<xsl:value-of select = "address"/><br/>
<xsl:value-of select = "city"/>, <xsl:value-of select =
"state"/> <xsl:value-of select = "zip"/><br/>
<xsl:value-of select = "email"/><br/><br/>

<xsl:for-each select="phone">
 <xsl:value-of select = "phone_type"/>:  <xsl:value-of select = "number"/><br/>
</xsl:for-each>

<br/><br/>
Hired:  <xsl:value-of select = "hire_date"/><br/>
Salary:  <xsl:value-of select = "salary"/><br/>

</body>
</html>

</xsl:template>
</xsl:stylesheet>
```

Now you can issue a simple SQL query against the repository to see the transformed output:

```
select r.res.transform(
 (xdbUriType('/home/SCOTT/XSL/example.xsl').getXML())
)
from RESOURCE_VIEW r
where any_path = '/home/SCOTT/XML/example.xml';
```

A Content Management Example

The real power of Oracle's XML technology becomes obvious when you are building content management solutions. The ability to store content directly in the database greatly simplifies the process for managing content. Before this was possible, developers usually ended up writing XML to the file system on a server or network storage device and storing meta data about the file in a relational database.

In this example, you have been tasked with creating a small intranet Web site for your company to display information on the vendors your company does business with. The business users of your organization want a familiar, easy-to-use interface for editing content, and the technology group would like to use XML and Oracle as the back end.

To implement this system, you will use Microsoft's Vendor Information sample InfoPath template to create a user interface, publish the template in the Oracle repository using the Oracle Enterprise Manager, and then create a Java servlet that can access the Oracle repository to display the XML file as an HTML Web page on the company intranet.

Creating the Content Management Application Front End

Microsoft Office InfoPath is a new application launched by Microsoft with the release of Microsoft Office 2003. InfoPath provides an easy-to-use interface for end users to create, publish, edit, and share XML-based form solutions. InfoPath is available from Microsoft as a standalone product, and also comes bundled with Microsoft Office 2003 Professional Enterprise Edition. For more product information on Info Path, see `www.microsoft.com/office/infopath/prodinfo/default.mspx`. A trial version is available from Microsoft at `www.microsoft.com/office/infopath/prodinfo/trial.mspx`.

InfoPath generates standard XML files, utilizes XML Schemas to provide data integrity and validation, and uses XSLT for presentation. InfoPath provides a powerful development platform for XML forms developers on its own, but because of its ease of use, familiar Microsoft Office interface, and XML output, it can provide an ideal solution for writing the content entry forms for a content management application.

While the front end for this example uses Microsoft InfoPath, it is only because we feel that it provides an elegant solution. If you do not have or do not wish to purchase InfoPath, you can follow the example, skip the InfoPath section, and work with the output XML, XSD, and XSLT files using the XML tools of your choice.

Creating the InfoPath Form

The first step in creating the content management application is to create the InfoPath form. Instead of designing one from scratch, you will use the Vendor Information sample that comes with InfoPath.

If you would rather just work with the raw XML files, skip ahead to the next section that details how to set up Oracle XML DB. You can download and use the files from the book Web site to follow along. Figure 22-13 show the basic InfoPath interface when you launch the application.

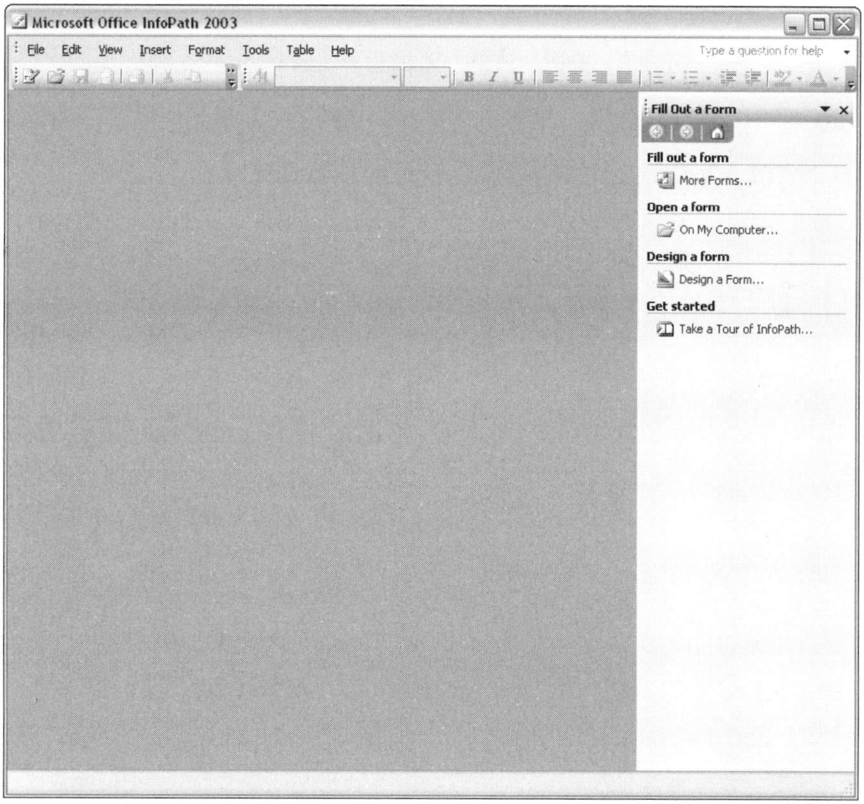

Figure 22-13: The InfoPath interface.

Next, open the Vendor Information sample by choosing File | Open | Sample Forms | Vendor Informationas shown in Figure 22-14.

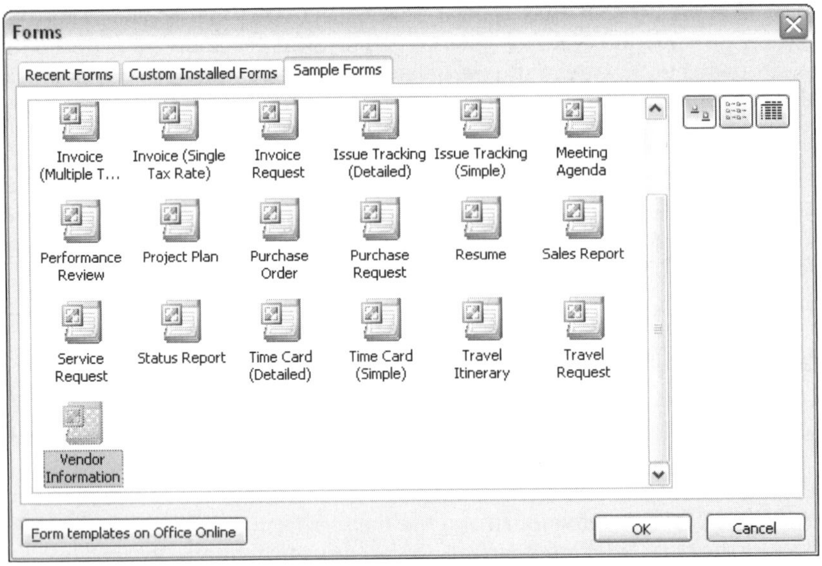

Figure 22-14: Open the Vendor Information template.

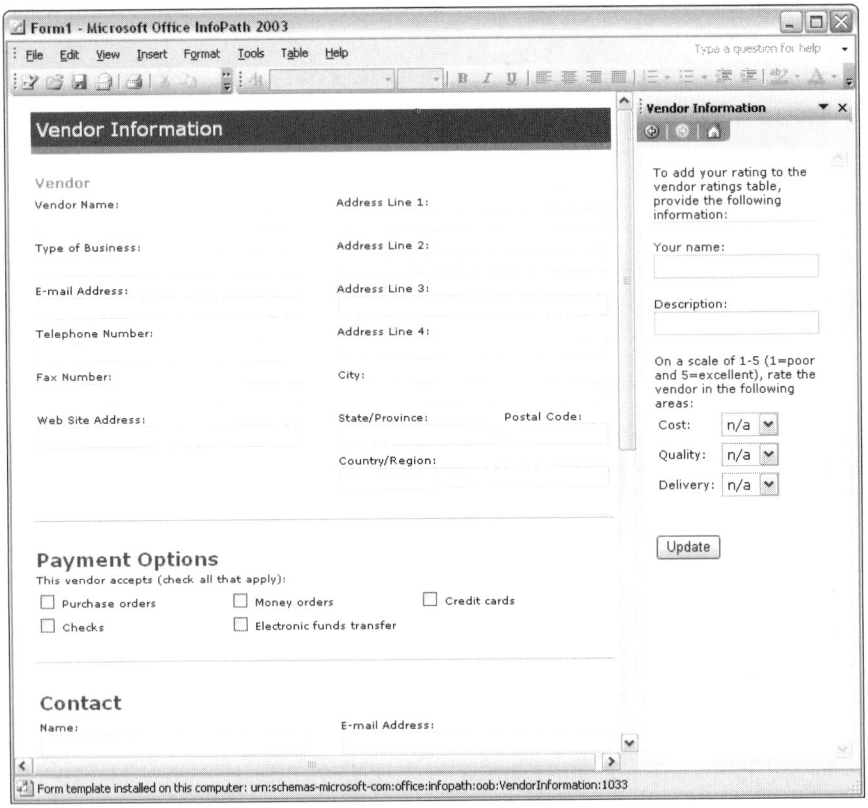

Figure 22-15: The Vendor Information form.

InfoPath provides a Microsoft Office–type environment for working with XML. InfoPath uses XML Schema and XSLT to render its XML file, but it adds other nice features like context-sensitive help wizards for content creation, and the ability to share and route XML forms. Figure 22-15 shows the Vendor Information form open with the ratings subform displayed on the right.

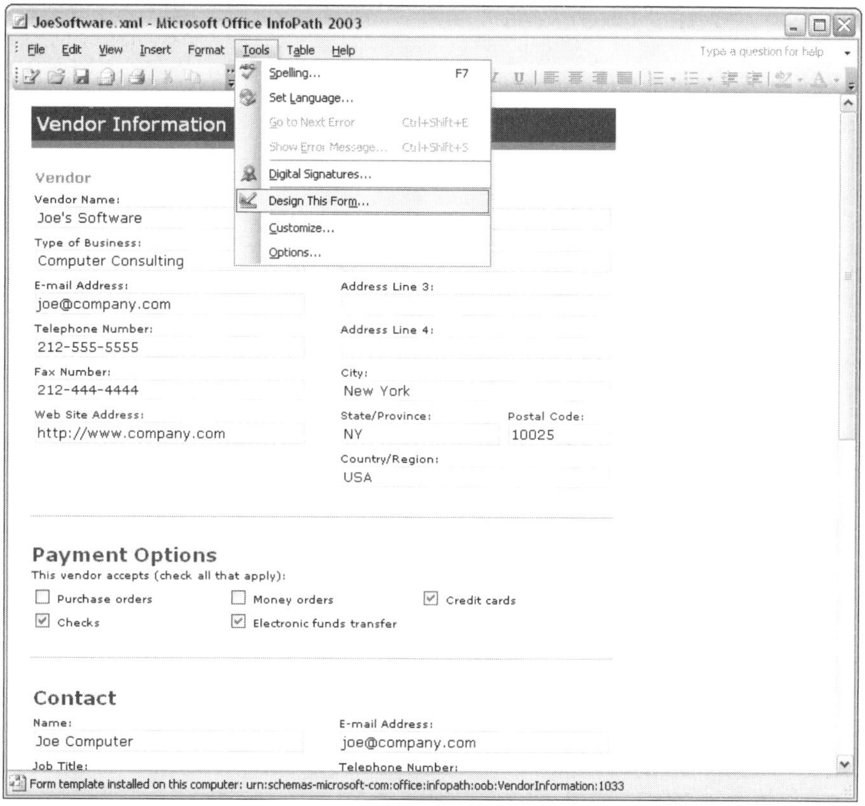

Figure 22-16: Exporting the InfoPath contents.

To store vendor information XML records in Oracle, you have to extract the standard files from the Vendor Information template. To the user, the form appears to be a single file, but it is really made up of a collection of files. You can get at those underlying files by switching into design mode and choosing Extract Form Files from the File menu. Choose a directory to save the embedded files to and click OK. Figures 22-16 and 22-17 illustrate the process.

Once InfoPath is done exporting files, you will have a bunch of XML and HTML files in the directory you specified InfoPath to write to. These control various aspects of the InfoPath form. For this example you will primarily be concerned with view_1.xsl, schema.xsd, and template.xml. A description of each file follows. You can download these files from the book Web site if you are following along without InfoPath. Figure 22-18 shows the list of exported files that make up an InfoPath form.

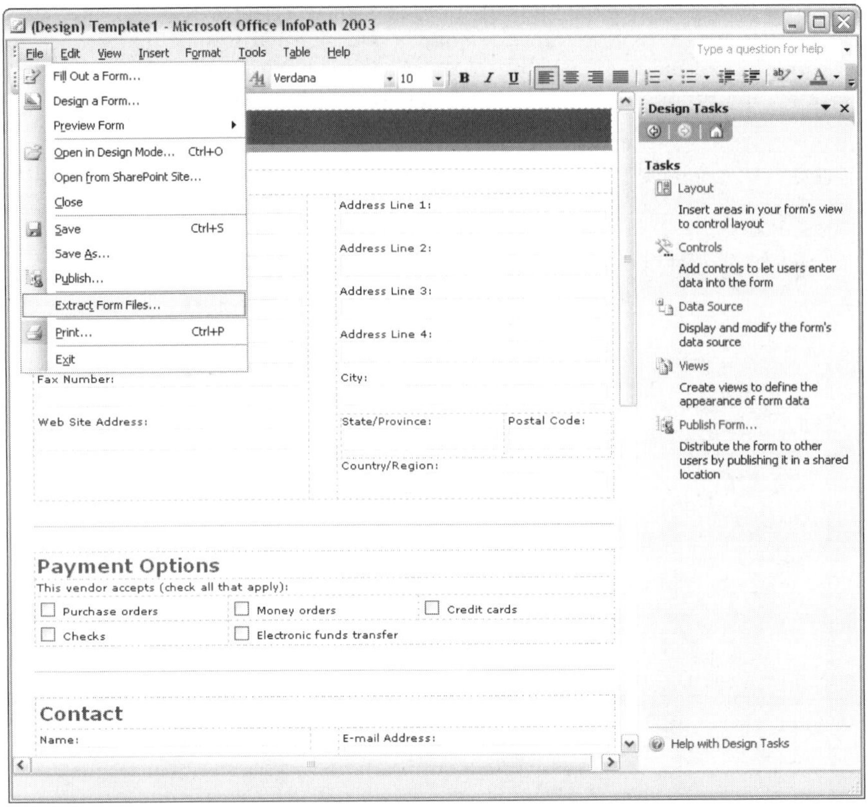

Figure 22-17: Extracting files from the Vendor Information template.

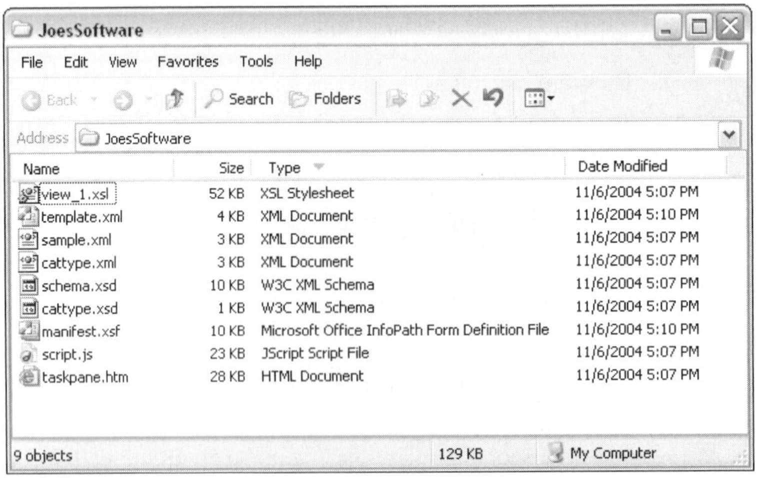

Figure 22-18: Files that make up the Vendor Information template.

- view_1.xsl — The default XSLT file for rendering the form
- template.xml — The template for XML output of the form
- sample.xml — Sample blank output of the XML output of the form
- cattype.xml — The XML file containing category listings for product information
- schema.xsd — The XML Schema definition for the Vendor Information template
- cattype.xsd — The XML Schema definition for the category listings data
- manifest.xsf — The InfoPath form definition
- script.js — JavaScript file containing dynamic script for the template
- taskpane.htm — The HTML and code for the dynamic sidebar

Creating a New Oracle Schema for Content

Now that the InfoPath form has been split into its separate files, you can create the Oracle schema that will hold the vendor information content. The first step is to log in to Oracle and create the new schema. You can accomplish this by logging in to SQLPlus as `SYS` and issuing the following commands:

```
Create user CMDEMO identified by CMDEMO;
Grant connect, resource to CMDEMO;
```

This creates a new database schema and user, as well as grants that user the ability to connect to and write programs for Oracle 10*g*.

The next step is to create the XML DB schema for the vendor information template. This will allow Oracle to manage the vendor information XML file as a path-based asset in the database. Since the application will be storing and retrieving the XML documents in their entirety, you can use simple LOB-based storage for the XML. Choosing LOB-based storage will instruct Oracle to create only a single table to store XML in.

To create an XML Schema for the vendor information XML template in the CMDEMO schema, you must perform the following steps:

1. Open Enterprise Manager and navigate to the XML Database/XML Schema section in the tree view on the left. Right-click on the section and choose Create. When the Create XML Schema dialog box comes up, enter the schema name, set the owner to CMDEMO, and choose From a File on the File System. Choose the schema.xsd file that was exported from the InfoPath file. Here you can also set the schema to be visible system-wide, or just to the user that is creating it. In this case, set the option to Visible to the Public. Figure 22-19 shows the Create XML Schema form in Enterprise Manager.

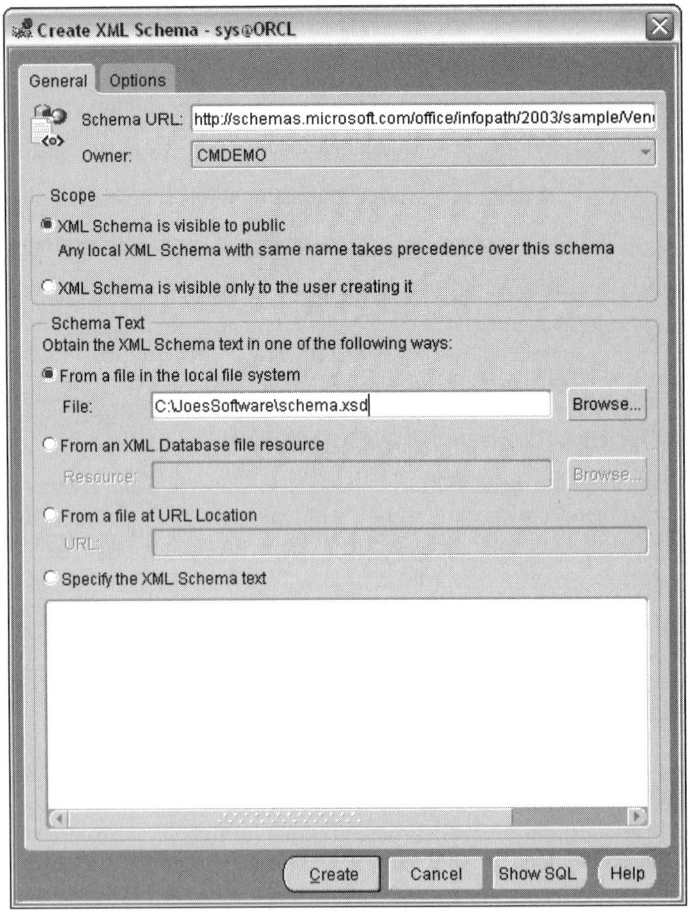

Figure 22-19: Creating a new XML Schema.

2. Next, you must tell Oracle that you want to use LOB storage for the XML documents. Choose the Options tab, and choose Generate Tables Based on This Schema. Uncheck Generate Object Types based on this XML Schema. Figure 22-20 shows the Options screen.

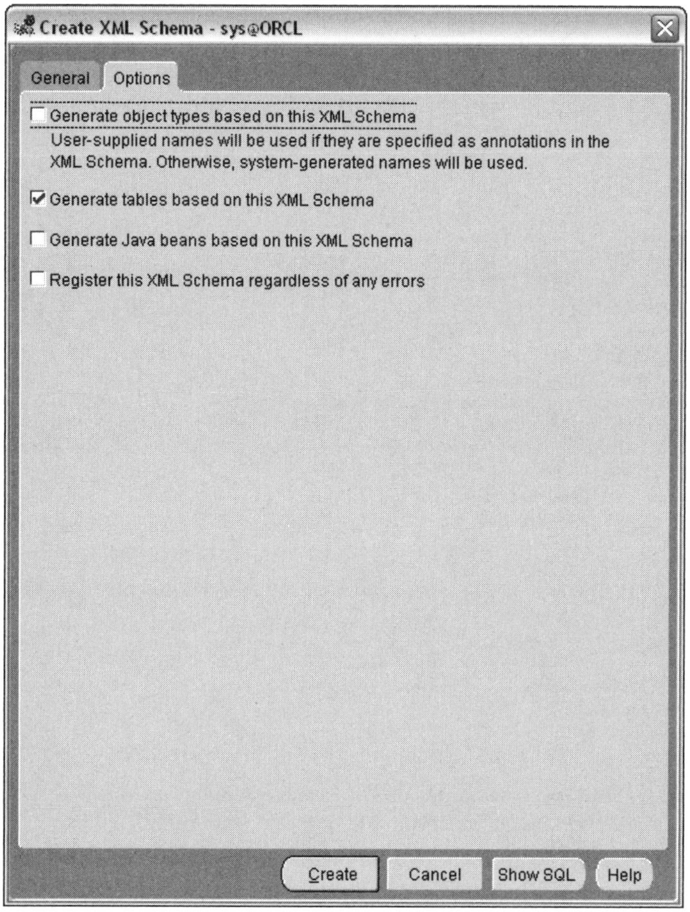

Figure 22-20: Setting XML Schema options.

3. Next, choose Create, and Oracle uploads, parses, and creates the XML Schema for you in the database. Oracle also creates a table in the schema to store your XML files, some indices, and a trigger to manage deleting and updating. Figure 22-21 shows the results of the schema creation.

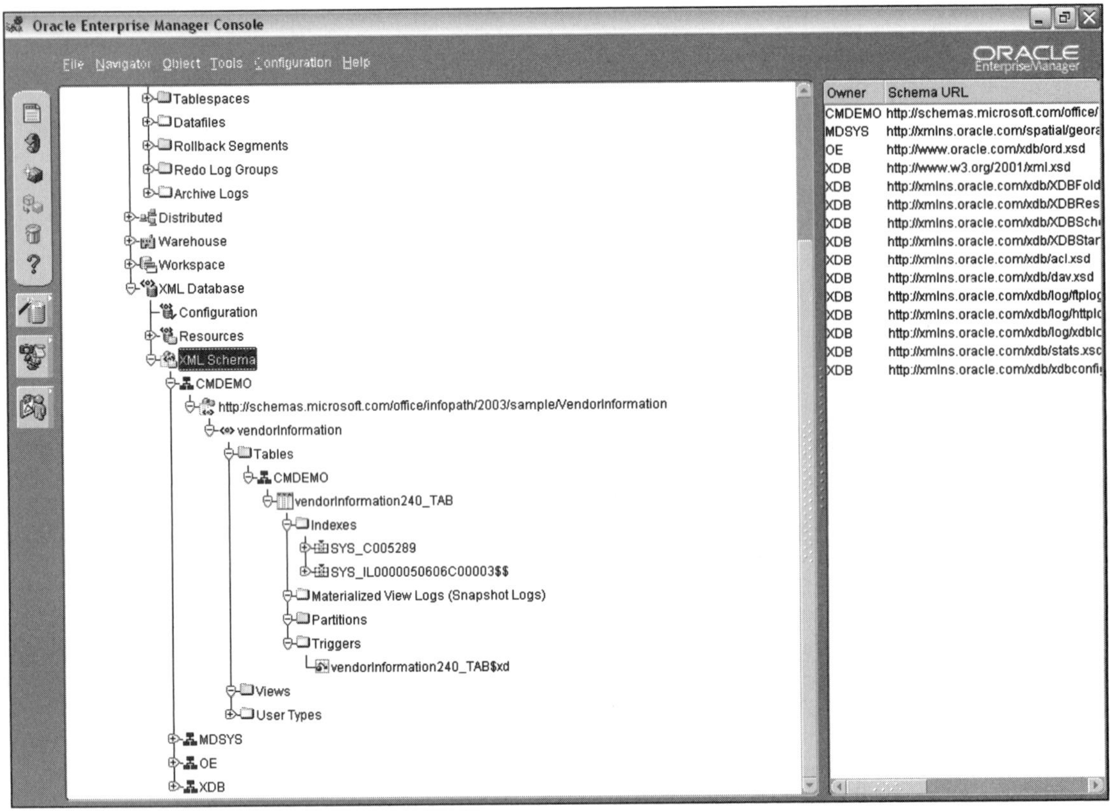

Figure 22-21: Oracle created objects from an XML Schema import.

4. After uploading the XML Schema, Oracle create a CMDEMO folder in the /home folder in the XML resources section. You should grant all permissions on it to the CMDEMO user. In a production system, more limited permissions should be used, but for development, grant all to CMDEMO. To do this, right-click, choose Grant Privileges and then choose Grant All to CMDEMO.

5. Once the permissions have been set, you can map the repository to your local machine as a Web folder, if you haven't done so already. In Windows, go to My Network Places and choose Add a New Network Place. Enter the HTTP address of your Oracle WebDAV server and save. Figure 22-22 shows the screen where you specify the WebDAV server address.

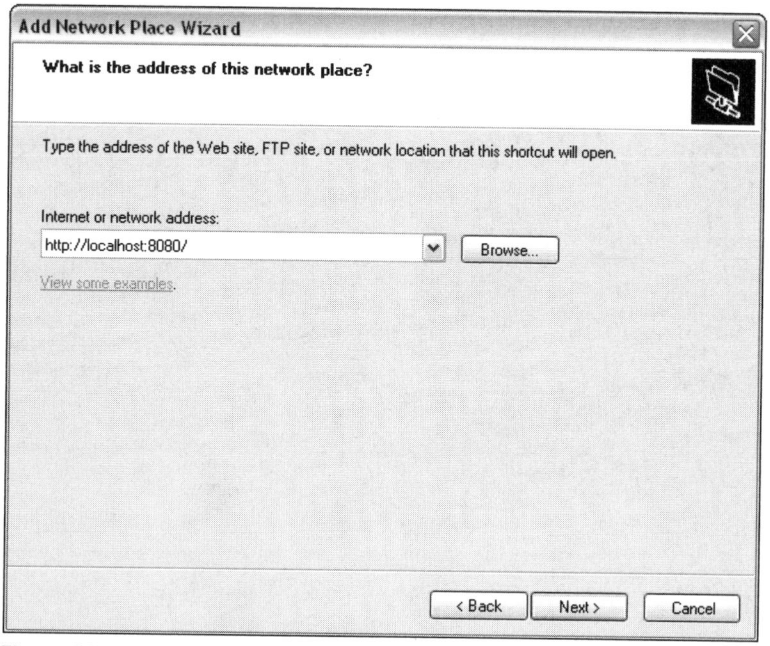

Figure 22-22: Adding a WebDAV Web folder.

6. After you have created the WebDAV folder, open it by logging in as `CMDEMO` and create two new folders in the repository under /home/CMDEMO. Name them `NYCVendors` and `XSL`, respectively.
7. The next step is to upload the XSL file created by InfoPath. This file contains many Microsoft-specific tags, so you may want to copy it and remove the extra information. In this case, the generated view_1.xsl file has been copied to Web_view.xsl and edited to remove the extra tags and the dynamic buttons. The Web_view.xsl file presents a read-only view of the data for presentation on the Web. Figure 22-23 shows the file uploaded through the WebDAV mount into the XSL directory.

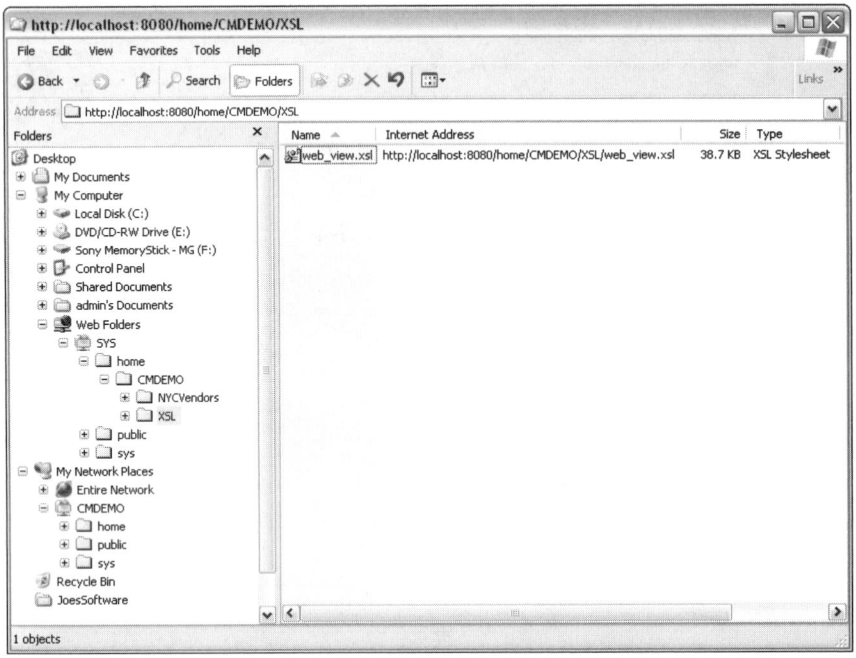

Figure 22-23: Uploading Web_view.xsl to the XSL folder in Oracle.

Creating Some Sample Content

Now that you have created the facility for Oracle to manage your XML data, its time to create some sample content and store it in the DB.

1. Open the Vendor Information template in InfoPath and fill out the form. Clicking on the buttons to add ratings or edit the products table demonstrates the dynamic sidebar feature of InfoPath. If you are not using InfoPath, you can open template.xml from the sample files with Microsoft Word or any other text editor and edit the template content. Figures 22-24 and 22-25 illustrate adding content using InfoPath and Word.

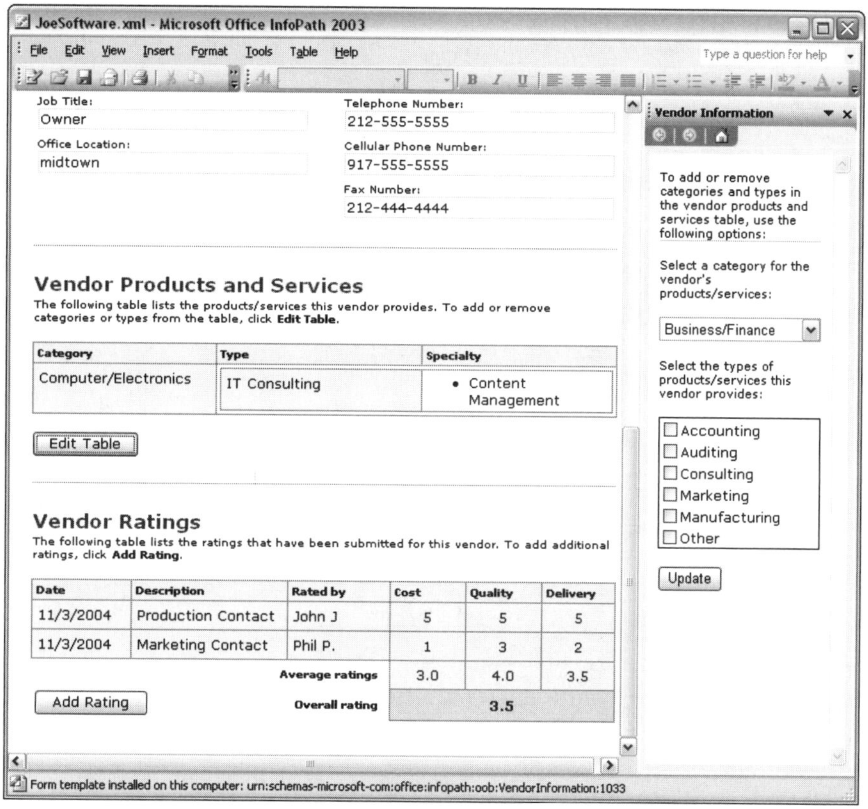
JoeSoftware.xml - Microsoft Office InfoPath 2003
File Edit View Insert Format Tools Table Help
Type a question for help
Job Title:
Owner
Office Location:
midtown
Telephone Number:
212-555-5555
Cellular Phone Number:
917-555-5555
Fax Number:
212-444-4444
Vendor Products and Services
The following table lists the products/services this vendor provides. To add or remove categories or types from the table, click Edit Table.
Category
Type
Specialty
Computer/Electronics
IT Consulting
Content Management
Edit Table
Vendor Ratings
The following table lists the ratings that have been submitted for this vendor. To add additional ratings, click Add Rating.
Date
Description
Rated by
Cost
Quality
Delivery
11/3/2004
Production Contact
John J
5
5
5
11/3/2004
Marketing Contact
Phil P.
1
3
2
Average ratings
3.0
4.0
3.5
Add Rating
Overall rating
3.5
Vendor Information
To add or remove categories and types in the vendor products and services table, use the following options:
Select a category for the vendor's products/services:
Business/Finance
Select the types of products/services this vendor provides:
Accounting
Auditing
Consulting
Marketing
Manufacturing
Other
Update
Form template installed on this computer: urn:schemas-microsoft-com:office:infopath:oob:VendorInformation:1033

Figure 22-24: Edit Vendor Information sidebar.

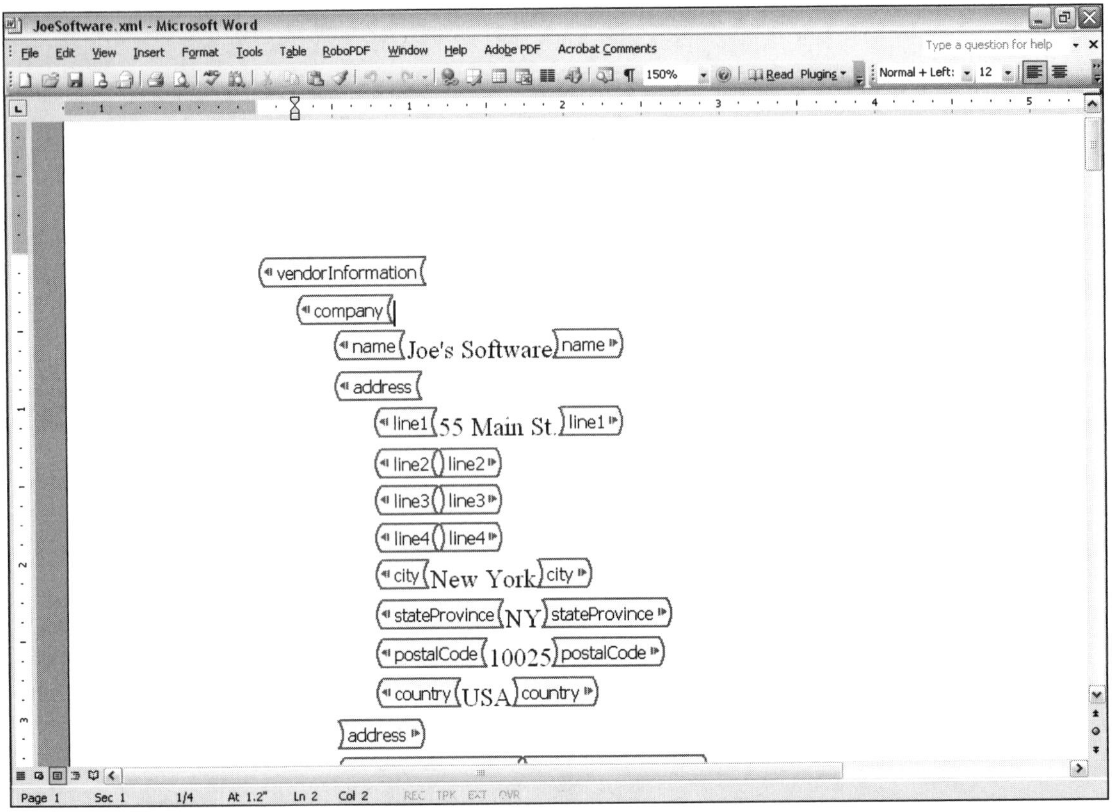

Figure 22-25: Editing content in Microsoft Word.

2. Once you have filled in the template, you should end up with something that looks like Figure 22-26 in InfoPath. Your results will look different if you are using a different editor.

3. Finally, you can save the file to Oracle using the WebDAV mount. When you save a file in InfoPath, only the XML data is output. Choose the save command from the file menu, navigate to your WebDAV mount point and then to /home/CMDEMO/NYCVendors. Save the file as JoeSoftware.xml. This process is the same no matter which program you are using to edit the XML file. Figure 22-27 shows the save dialog.

Vendor Information

Vendor

Vendor Name: Joe's Software	**Address Line 1:** 55 Main St.
Type of Business: Computer Consulting	**Address Line 2:**
E-mail Address: joe@company.com	**Address Line 3:**
Telephone Number: 212-555-5555	**Address Line 4:**
Fax Number: 212-444-4444	**City:** New York
Web Site Address: http://www.company.com	**State/Province:** NY **Postal Code:** 10025
	Country/Region: USA

Payment Options

This vendor accepts (check all that apply):

☐ Purchase orders ☐ Money orders ☑ Credit cards
☑ Checks ☑ Electronic funds transfer

Contact

Name: Joe Computer	**E-mail Address:** joe@company.com
Job Title: Owner	**Telephone Number:** 212-555-5555
Office Location: midtown	**Cellular Phone Number:** 917-555-5555
	Fax Number: 212-444-4444

Vendor Products and Services

The following table lists the products/services this vendor provides. To add or remove categories or types from the table, click **Edit Table**.

Category	Type	Specialty
Computer/Electronics	IT Consulting	• Content Management

Edit Table

Vendor Ratings

The following table lists the ratings that have been submitted for this vendor. To add additional ratings, click **Add Rating**.

Date	Description	Rated by	Cost	Quality	Delivery
11/3/2004	Production Contact	John J	5	5	5
11/3/2004	Marketing Contact	Phil P.	1	3	2
		Average ratings	3.0	4.0	3.5
Add Rating		Overall rating		3.5	

Figure 22-26: The completed Vendor Information form.

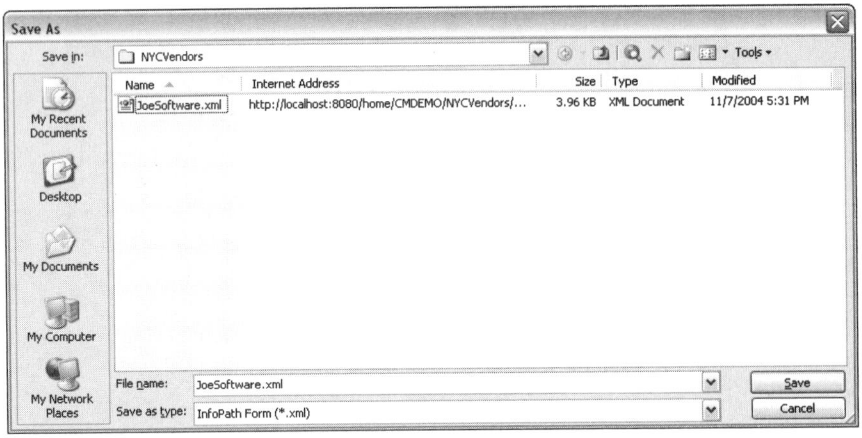

Figure 22-27: Saving the InfoPath XML output to Oracle.

Creating a Java Servlet to Display the Content as HTML

Now that you have created the content entry form, XSL file, and content database, you need a means for displaying the content to users of the intranet Web site. One way to do this is to create a Java servlet that can access the Oracle repository and render the XML content using XSLT. The example servlet following retrieves the XML and XSL files from Oracle using http, but you could also access the files from a WebDAV folder just as easily. The servlet takes two parameters on the URL string: a `c` parameter, which specifies the content XML file without the .xml extension, and a `t` parameter, which specifies the XSL template for the transformation, also without the .xsl file extension.

The following servlet is a very simple example. In a production system, you would want to implement more advanced features like an XSL cache to store frequently requested XSL style sheets, and an output cache to store the results of XSLT transformations. XSLT output could also be written to the file system, and only updated by the servlet when the modified date of the XSL or XML changes.

```
import java.io.*;
import java.net.*;
import javax.servlet.*;
import javax.servlet.http.*;
import javax.xml.transform.*;
import javax.xml.transform.stream.*;

public class xslProcessor extends HttpServlet{

 TransformerFactory tf = TransformerFactory.newInstance();

 String xmlURL = "http://localhost:8080/home/CMDEMO/NYCVendors/";
 String xslURL = "http://localhost:8080/home/CMDEMO/XSL

 public void doGet(HttpServletRequest req, HttpServletResponse res)
throws IOException, ServletException {

  URL content = new URL(xmlURL + req.getParameter("c") + ".xml");
  URL template = new URL(xslURL + req.getParameter("t") + ".xsl");

  String userPassword = "CMDEMO:CMDEMO";
```

```
String encoding = new sun.misc.BASE64Encoder().encode(userPassword.getBytes());

URLConnection uc1 = content.openConnection();
URLConnection uc2 = template.openConnection();

uc1.setRequestProperty ("Authorization", "Basic " + encoding);
uc2.setRequestProperty ("Authorization", "Basic " + encoding);

if( content != null && !content.equals("")
    && template != null && !template.equals("") ) {
 try {

  Transformer trans = tf.newTransformer(
    new StreamSource(uc2.getInputStream()) );
  trans.transform(new StreamSource(
    uc1.getInputStream()), new StreamResult( res.getOutputStream() ));

  } catch(Exception e){ e.printStackTrace(); }

} else {
  PrintWriter out = res.getWriter();
  out.println("please provide an xml file and xsl file using "
  + "the c and t parameters.<br>do not include the .xml or .xsl" );
}
}
}
```

Installing the Servlet in Apache Tomcat

You can install the xslProcessor servlet in any Web application in Tomcat by copying the servlet into the WEB-INF/classes directory and editing the Web.xml file to add references to this servlet. In this example, the servlet was installed in the Servlet-examples Web application that comes with Tomcat. The servlet was compiled and copied to WEB-INF/classes, and the following additions were made the Web.xml file to map the servlet to a request URL pattern:

```
<servlet>
<servlet-name>xslProcessor</servlet-name>
    <servlet-class>xslProcessor</servlet-class>
</servlet>

<servlet-mapping>
    <servlet-name>xslProcessor</servlet-name>
    <url-pattern>/servlet/xslProcessor</url-pattern
</servlet-mapping>
```

You may need to change the port Tomcat listens to by default if you are running other Web server software on your machine. Oracle's Web listener is configured to listen on port 8080 by default, the same port that Tomcat listens to by default. You can change the port in Tomcat's server.xml located in the conf directory.

Look for the following:

```
<!-- Define a non-SSL Coyote HTTP/1.1 Connector on port 8080 -->
    <Connector port="8080"
               maxThreads="150" minSpareThreads="25" maxSpareThreads="75"
               enableLookups="false" redirectPort="8443" acceptCount="100"
```

```
debug="0" connectionTimeout="20000"
disableUploadTimeout="true" />
```

and set the port to another number like 8081.

You can go to the Apache Tomcat documentation for more information about how to configure Tomcat and how to create and deploy Web applications. The documentation for version 5.5 can be found at `http://jakarta.apache.org/tomcat/tomcat-5.5-doc/index.html`.

After registering the servlet with Apache, you should be able to issue the address `http://localhost:8081/servlets-examples/servlet/xslProcessor?c=JoeSoftware&t=Web_view` and get the result shown in Figure 22-28.

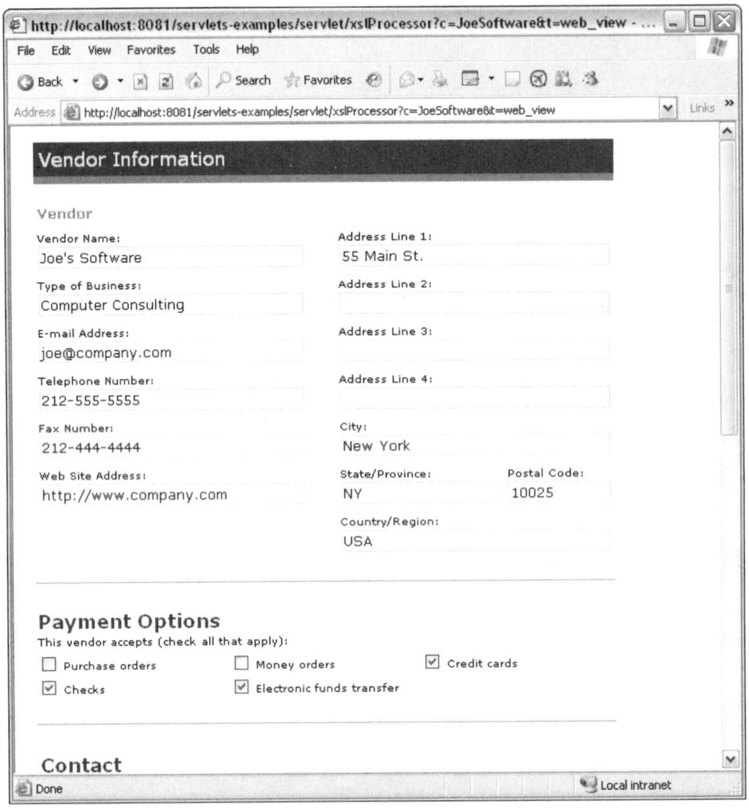

Figure 22-28: The rendered output in Internet Explorer using Apache Tomcat.

Oracle XML Outside the Database — Oracle XDK

Oracle also provides a rich set of tools for building XML applications outside of the database. Oracle has built upon many of the commonly available XML APIs and packaged them together for use in the Oracle Application Server or most J2EE-compliant application servers. In addition to the Java tools, many of the common tools and APIs are exposed in C and C++.

Listed following are the main components of the Oracle XDK and a brief overview of what you can do with them.

XML Parser

The Oracle XDK supplies a high-performance XML parser that supports both the DOM tree-based model and the SAX event-based parsing model. The XML parser supports namespaces and document validation using XML Schemas and DTDs. The XML parser is available for Java, C, C++, and PL/SQL.

XSLT Processor

Oracle supplies a high-performance XSLT processor that is used for XSL style sheet transformations. Oracle's XSLT processor implements the XSLT and XPath 1.0 standards, as well as a draft of the XSLT and XPath 2.0 standard. The XSLT processor is also SAX-based, which gives it a performance boost over DOM-based parsers, and is thread-safe as well. The XSLT processor is available for Java, C, C++, and PL/SQL.

XVM

XVM is a high-performance XSLT transformation engine that is a combination complier and virtual machine. XVM compiles XSL style sheets into a platform-independent byte code that can be executed on the Oracle style sheet virtual machine. The main benefit of using XVM is gaining additional speed by effectively separating compile time activities from runtime document processing. XVM is only available in C or C++.

XML Schema Processor

This component validates XML documents against XML Schemas and DTDs. The Schema processor supports XML Schema Part 0: Primer, XML Schema Part 1: Structures, XML Schema Part 2: Datatypes, and uses SAX parsing. The component is built on the Oracle XML parser and is available in Java, C, C++, and PL/SQL.

JAXP

JAXP provides a mechanism to seamlessly integrate multiple XML parsers in your application and easily switch between them. Applications built using JAXP can take advantage of the Oracle SAX and DOM XML parsers and the XSLT processor. JAXP is only available in Java.

JAXB Class Generator

JAXB, or Java Architecture for XML Binding, is a toolkit that builds a collection of Java classes from an XML Schema document. It hides the complexity of parsing and manipulating XML documents and provides a familiar object-based structure for accessing or creating their contents. The Oracle version implements version 1.0 of the JAXB specification with the following exceptions:

- Javadoc generation
- The List and Union features of XML Schema
- SimpleType mapping to TypeSafe Enum class and IsSet property modifier
- XML Schema component "any" and substitution groups
- Customization of XML Schema to override the default binding of XML Schema components
- On-demand validation of the content tree

JAXB is only available for Java.

XML Class Generator

XML Class Generator is similar to JAXB but is for use in C++. It creates C++ classes for each type found in a DTD or XML Schema.

XML SQL Utility (XSU)

The Oracle XML SQL Utility allows you to easily transform relational data stored in Oracle to XML, and automatically parse XML files and insert and update data-stored relational tables from them. The XML SQL Utility is available for Java and PL/SQL and can be accessed using a Java API, PL/SQL, or API, or by using a Java-based command-line application. Other capabilities of the XML SQL Utility include the following:

- Generating XML elements or attributes for row data
- Dynamically generating DTDs
- Creating XML documents as strings or DOM trees
- Generating XML xchemas from SQL queries

XSQL Servlet

The Oracle XSQL servlet is a J2EE servlet that can be integrated with a Web application server to provide dynamic translation of Oracle data to XML. When working with the XSQL servlet, you create XSQL files that contain special tags denoting SQL statements. When requested from the application server, the SQL gets executed and the results are returned in XML. You can optionally transform the results by associating an XSLT style sheet with the .xsql page.

XML Pipeline Definition Language

This component allows you to create an XML document that specifies a series of events or processing tasks to be applied to a given XML document. Pipeline tasks can be DOM or SAX parsing, or XSLT transformations. Oracle implements version 1.0 of the XML Pipeline Definition Language. This component is implemented in Java.

JavaBeans

Oracle provides most of the XDK functionality wrapped in JavaBeans. This allows JSP developers to take advantage of the XDK components in a Web application. The JavaBeans are available in Java and provide access to the following services:

- **DOMBuilder JavaBean.** Wraps the functionality of the XML parser
- **XSLTransformer JavaBean.** Wraps the functionality of the XSLT transformer
- **DBAccess JavaBean.** Can access CLOB tables that hold XML documents
- **XMLDiff JavaBean.** Compares two DOM trees and outputs the differences
- **XMLCompress JavaBean.** Wraps the XML Compressor
- **XML DBAccess JavaBean.** Extends DBAccess to support XMLType tables and columns
- **XSDValidator JavaBean.** Wraps the XML Schema Validator

Oracle SOAP Server

The Oracle SOAP Server exposes database services as Web services using the SOAP protocol. Oracle SOAP server can service requests over HTTP or HTTPS and implements SOAP 1.1. The SOAP server can only be programmed using Java, but should be compatible with standard SOAP clients written in any other language.

TransX Utility

The TransX Utility provides facilities for simplifying the loading of globalized strings into the database. It can be used as a Java command-line application or a Java-based API. The utility works with simple XML file formats, and automatically switches the `NLS_LANG` parameter based on the encoding specified in the translated XML file.

XML Compressor

The XML Compressor compresses XML documents to a binary byte stream to save memory. The XML compressor is an XDK-only technology and can operate on both DOM and SAX streams. The DOM and SAX streams are compatible and can be used to generate each other. Compressed XML documents can be saved to a BLOB field in the database for later retrieval. The XML Compressor component is only available in Java.

For more information and details about using the individual components of the Oracle XDK, refer to the *Oracle XML Developer's Kit Programmer's Guide* included with your Oracle 10*g* documentation.

Summary

Oracle 10*g* is a robust platform for creating XML-enabled applications. Oracle 10*g* gives you the ability to blur the distinction between XML and relational data, and provides high-performance querying capabilities on XML stored in the database. Oracle's XML repository provides a simple way to store and retrieve XML data for applications that are not specifically database-aware, and the repository module exposes several standard protocols for data access.

In this chapter you learned how to access and use the Oracle XML repository, learned how to create XML views over relational data, were introduced to Oracle's new XMLType data type, saw how to create an XML Schema definition, and learned how to transform XML data using Oracle's internal XSLT engine. Finally, the chapter provided an introduction to the technologies provided in the external XDK toolkit.

23

HTML-DB

Oracle Database 10*g* includes a complete development and deployment environment for developing applications without the use of any other programming tool. This environment is called HTML-DB, since both the developer and user interface to its applications is a basic browser.

The first section gives you a basic introduction to the use of this tool. Since HTML-DB is highly wizard-driven, you can probably learn it best by creating a simple application, which you will do in this chapter.

What Is HTML-DB?

Architecturally, HTML-DB is a collection of PL/SQL packages that make up the application. The packages that are the core of HTML-DB provide a declarative HTML development environment that prompts you for information about the specifics of your target application. Once you have supplied this information, the PL/SQL packages in HTML-DB generate another set of PL/SQL packages that can make up the application.

This simplified explanation of the architecture and implementation of HTML-DB skips over a great deal of the functionality offered by the tool. HTML-DB includes the ability to automatically create menus and navigational aids to pull together different parts of an application, as well as a complete HTML-based interface to SQL and database object maintenance for an Oracle database. In addition, you can use HTML-DB to quick-start application development by easily importing data from other sources, such as an Excel spreadsheet. You will learn more about these capabilities as you explore HTML-DB by creating an application in the course of this chapter.

If you are familiar with Oracle technology over the past several years, this description may sound a bit familiar. Didn't Oracle have another product that sounded quite a bit like HTML-DB?

Well, yes. The product originally known as WebDB was introduced with Oracle8*i* as part of the database. This tool used PL/SQL packages to create HTML-based applications. The development tool, like the deployment environment, was browser-based. WebDB became Oracle Portal, with an emphasis on creating a common interface to different applications, through portlets, as well as a way to collect information from different sources. Oracle Portal is now a part of Oracle Application Server.

Some of the key members of the original team that created WebDB are also part of the team that created HTML-DB. If you detect some similarities, it's probably more than a coincidence. But the emphasis in Oracle Portal has moved away from the creation of applications to the creation of unified access to a variety of different applications and data sources. Portal still has application development capabilities, but HTML-DB is aimed directly at the need to create HTML-based applications that access Oracle data. The biggest difference between HTML-DB and Oracle Portal is in the packaging — HTML-DB comes as a part of Oracle Database 10*g* and Portal comes with various bundles of Oracle Application Server.

The HTML-DB Environment

Before moving on to installing and using HTML-DB, you can look at the broad areas of functionality provided by the product by taking a brief tour of the overall HTML-DB environment.

> *The development interface to HTML-DB is steadily evolving, so, depending on when you read this chapter, the interface you see might be slightly different from the one shown in this chapter. The basic usage of the interface, however, is still essentially the same.*

Figure 23-1 shows the home page for an HTML-DB developer.

You can see the three broad areas of HTML-DB functionality on this page:

- Application development, which gives you the ability to create modules and assemble them into flows, or applications
- SQL Workshop, which acts as a browser-based interface to using all kinds of SQL against database objects, including SQL to create or modify database objects or system parameters
- Data Workshop, which helps you to load data to your Oracle database and unload data from your Oracle database in a number of common formats

You will be using some of the capabilities in two of these areas in this chapter when you build a simple sample application.

Please be aware that the remainder of this chapter takes you on a quick flyover of HTML-DB. This exercise will give you some idea of the way that HTML-DB works and how you can use some of its capabilities, so you can decide if this solution might be right for you. But entire books can be written on this topic — I know, I wrote a couple on its predecessors — so the depth and breadth of the product cannot be covered completely in a single chapter.

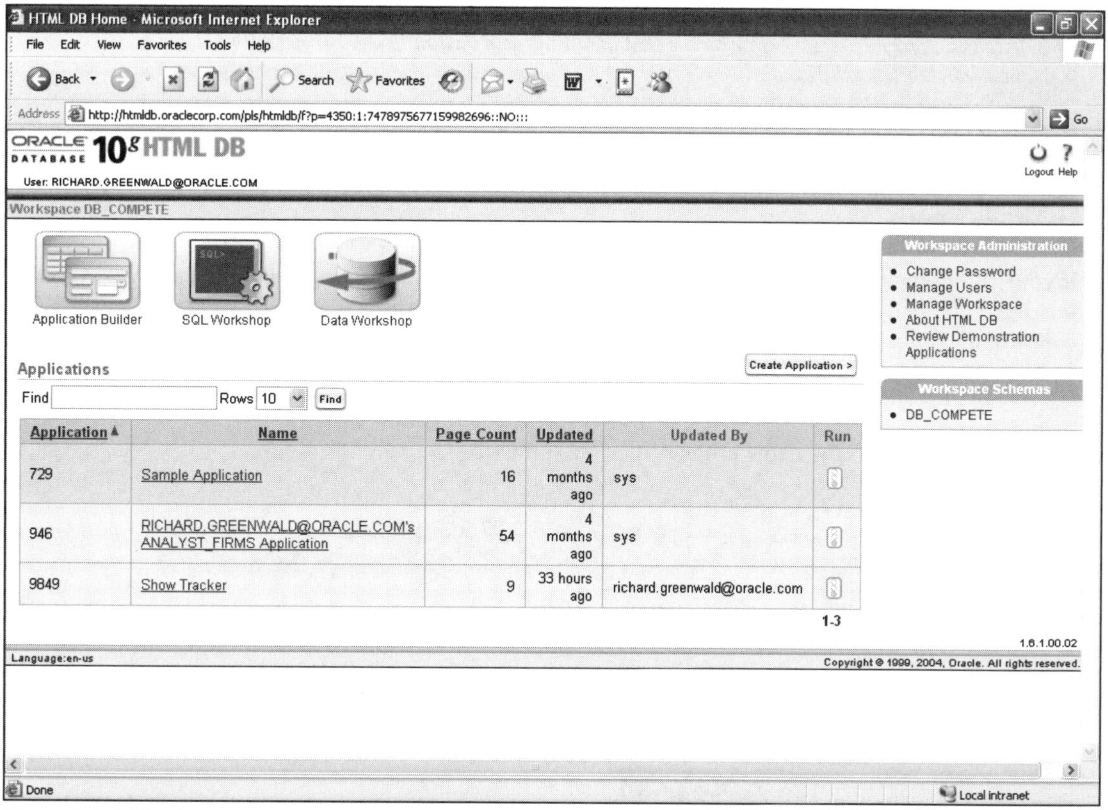

Figure 23-1: The home page for an HTML-DB developer.

Installing HTML-DB

HTML-DB is not installed with the single-disk installation process described in Chapter 7, "Installing Oracle," of this book. HTML-DB comes on the companion disk for Oracle Database 10*g*, which is a separate download from Oracle Technology Network (`http://otn.oracle.com`).

Installation of HTML-DB is essentially installation of the PL/SQL packages that are used to present the development environment and the user environment to their respective participants. In this installation process, we will assume that you have downloaded the appropriate ZIP file, decompressed it, and transferred it to a CD in drive D. This is to simulate installing from a CD, but you can also place the unpacked software on your hard drive.

The companion disk contains documentation, examples, and two software products, HTML-DB and the Oracle HTTP Server. For the purposes of this chapter, we will install both products, since both are required to use HTML-DB. You will also need Oracle XML DB in order to use HTML-DB, but this is normally installed with the default installation of Oracle Database 10*g*.

If you are not sure if you have the HTTP server installed, you can run the Oracle Universal Installer, as shown in Figure 23-2, and click on the Installed Products button to get a review of the currently installed Oracle modules.

Installing HTML-DB and the Oracle HTTP Server requires 80 MB of space on the system home drive and 535 MB of space in the target `ORACLE_HOME` directory. You will specify a different `ORACLE_HOME` directory as part of the installation process, since you cannot have HTML-DB in the same `ORACLE_HOME` as your Oracle Database 10*g*.

If your computer supports autorun, the page shown in Figure 23-2 should appear as soon as you insert the disk into the drive. If your computer does not support autorun, you can get to the same page by entering the following:

```
drive_name:\autorun\autorun.exe
```

where *`drive_name`* is the name of the drive containing the CD.

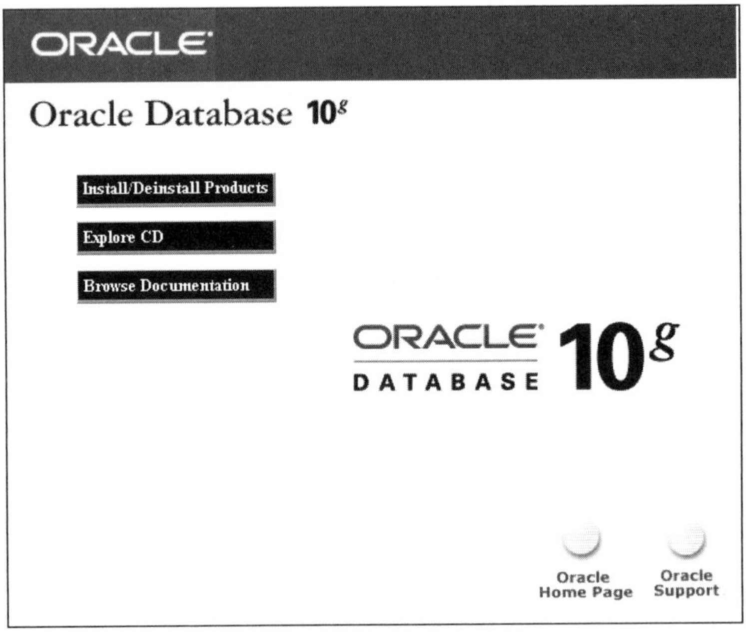

Figure 23-2: The initial installation page.

Clicking on Install/De-install Products starts up the Oracle Universal Installer, as shown in Figure 23-3.

On this page, click on the Next button to bring up the page shown in Figure 23-4.

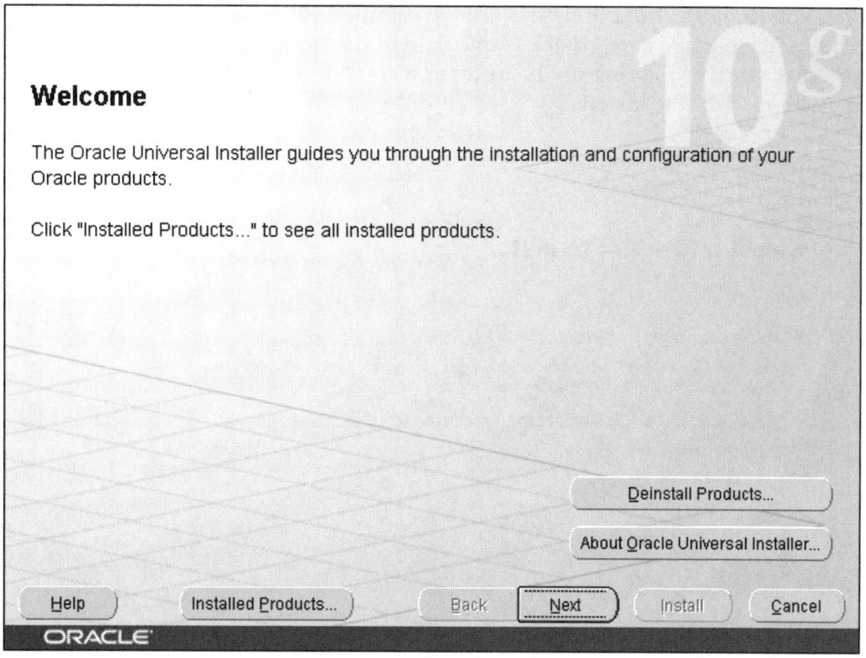

Figure 23-3: The Oracle Universal Installer.

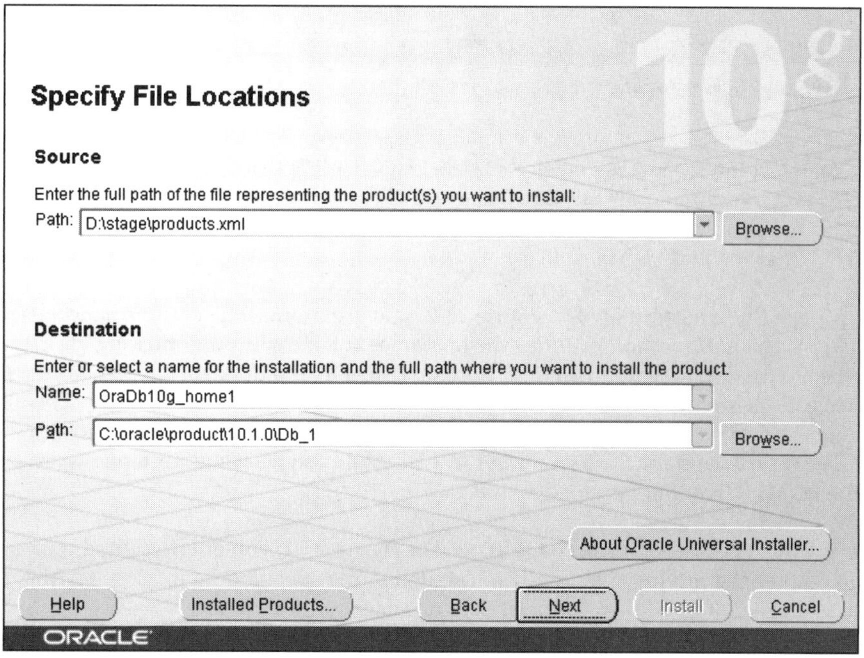

Figure 23-4: The second page in installation of HTML-DB.

At this point, you should use the Browse button to select a new directory to install the companion products, and change the name entered in the Name field in the Destination section. Once you do this, you can click on Next, which will bring up the next page. As shown in Figure 23-5, here you can select which type of products you want to install.

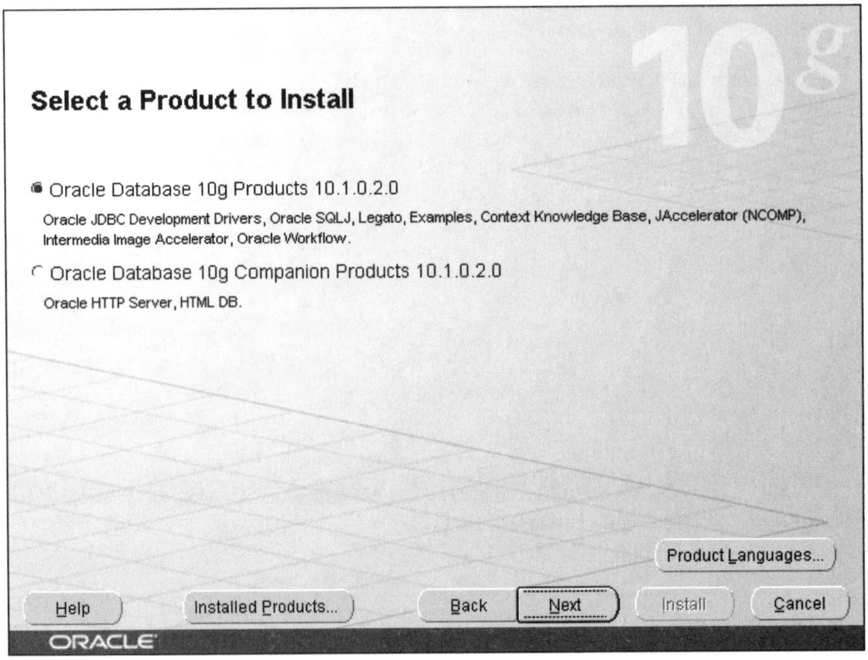

Figure 23-5: Selecting products to install.

On this page, select the second set, labeled Oracle Database 10*g* Companion Products, which will install both Oracle HTTP Server and HTML-DB. Once you click on the Next button, the page shown in Figure 23-6 appears. You should click on both the products shown on the page: the Apache Standalone, which is Oracle HTTP Server, and HTML-DB.

On the next page, shown completed in Figure 23-7, you are prompted for information used to configure the installation. This information includes the hostname for the computer hosting HTML-DB; the service name for the Oracle database that will be hosting HTML-DB; the password for the user `SYS`, which is needed to install the proper packages for HTML-DB; and the tablespace in which to install the packages. The port requested is the port for the Oracle listener, which is needed to properly install the HTML-DB packages. The default port for the listener is 1521. You will also be asked for a password that will be used for the HTML-DB administrator account.

After entering the information in the page shown in Figure 23-7, you are presented with a confirmation page, which shows the products that will be installed in the specified `ORACLE_HOME` directory. To start with the actual installation of the products, click on the Install button.

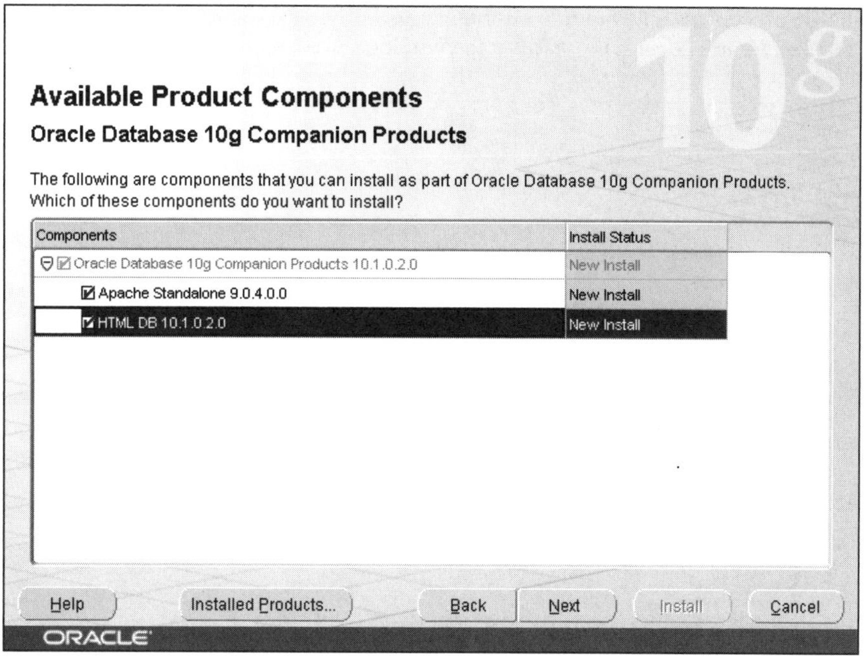

Figure 23-6: Selecting products to install.

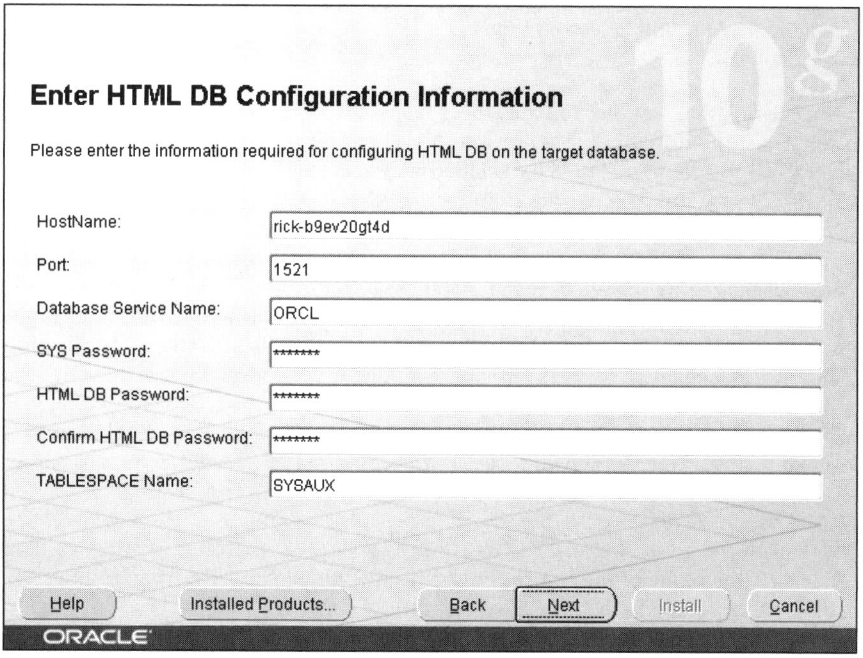

Figure 23-7: Configuration information for HTML-DB.

The installation process goes through two initial steps: copying the software files and running a setup program. As the files are copied, the status page will look like Figure 23-8.

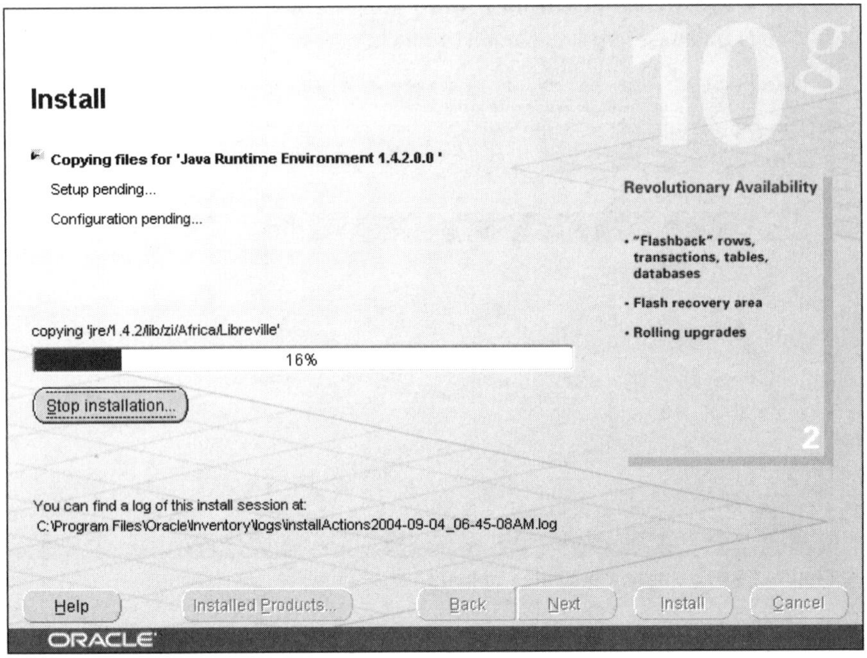

Figure 23-8: Status of copying files.

Once the Oracle Universal Installer finishes these tasks, it runs two Configuration Assistants. A Configuration Assistant is an automated process that handles the installation and configuration of the targeted products. In order to install HTML-DB, the Oracle HTTP Server is started, and then the HTML-DB Configuration Assistant runs, as shown in Figure 23-9.

This Configuration Assistant starts by installing the packages that form the core of the HTML-DB product. Once these packages are installed, the status messages for the HTML-DB Configuration Assistant indicate that it is creating a bunch of pages. These pages are the actual user-interface pages for the development environment. The HTML-DB development environment is actually an application generated by the core HTML-DB packages.

Once the Configuration Assistant has completed, it presents a success page, as shown in Figure 23-10. This page contains the URL you can use to access the Oracle HTTP Server, which is as follows:

```
http://hostname:7777
```

where `hostname` is the name of the computer hosting the Oracle HTTP Server, followed by the port number listed on the page (which is 7777, by default).

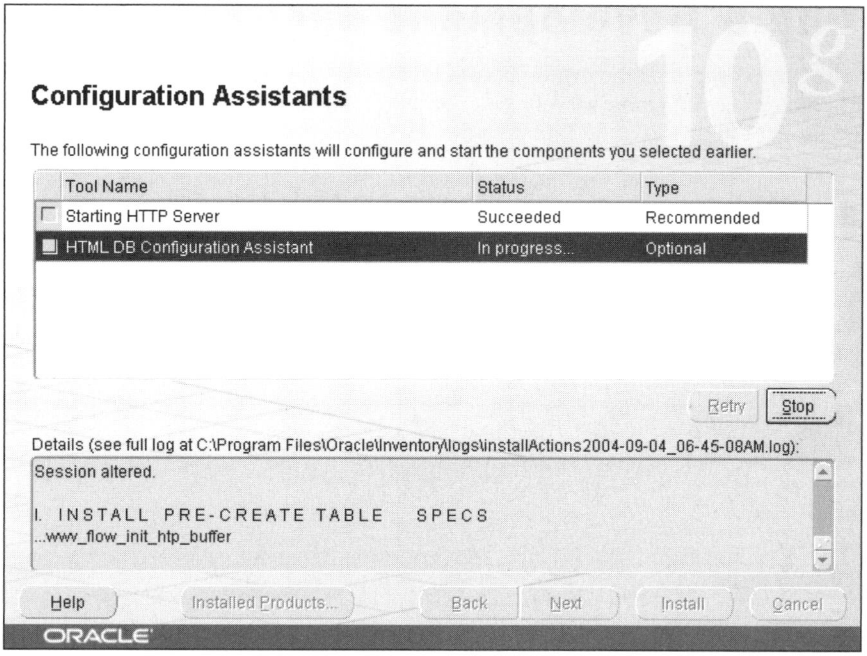

Figure 23-9: The Oracle HTML-DB Configuration Assistant at work.

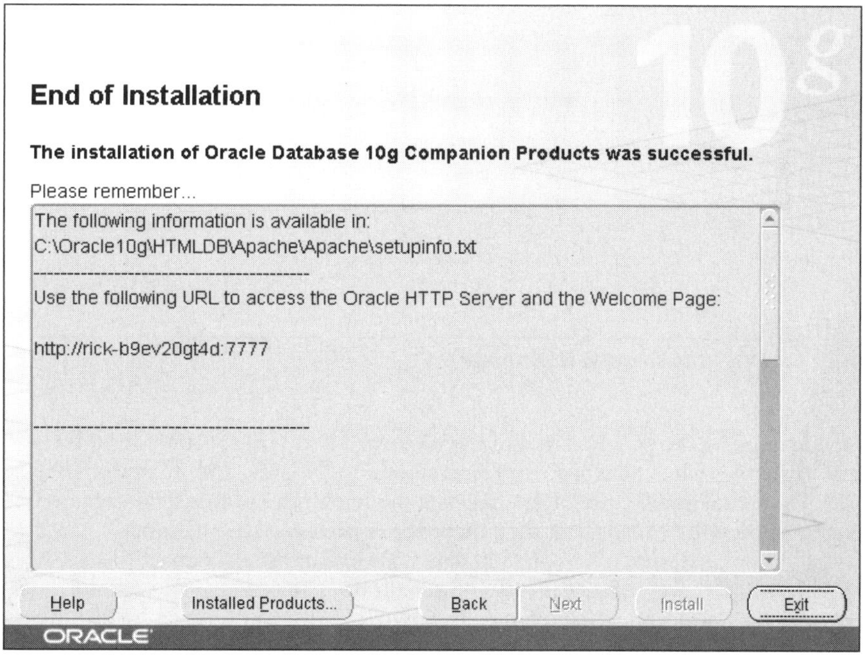

Figure 23-10: The completion of a successful installation of HTML-DB.

Preparing a Development Environment

Now that you have completed the installation of HTML-DB, the next step is to create a place for the modules of your application to reside — a place to hold the PL/SQL packages that will deliver your application interface to the user and interact with the Oracle database.

Creating a Workspace

The home for an application is called a workspace. You start creating a workspace by using the URL `http://hostname:port/pls/htmldb/htmldb_admin` to bring up the HTML-DB administration page. As before, `hostname` is the name of the computer hosting HTML-DB and `port` is the port number for the Oracle HTTP Server — 7777. The login page that appears is shown in Figure 23-11.

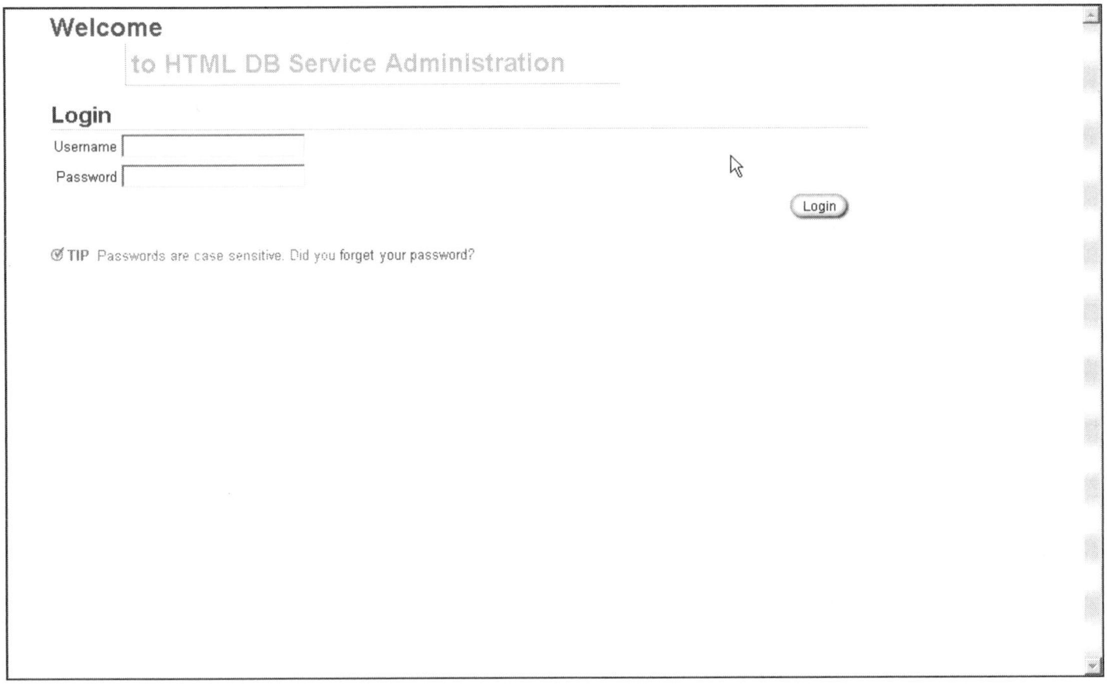

Figure 23-11: Logging in to create a workspace.

You have to log in using the user `ADMIN` and the password that you specified for this user in the installation process. The page that is returned from a successful login is the administration page, shown in Figure 23-12. The actual appearance of the pages in the remainder of this section may differ slightly from the version you will be using, but the functionality is essentially the same.

HTML-DB has multiple levels of security. An administrator can create workspaces for developers. Developers can create applications that have their own security controls. To create a workspace, click on the Create Workspace menu choice, which brings up the page shown in Figure 23-13.

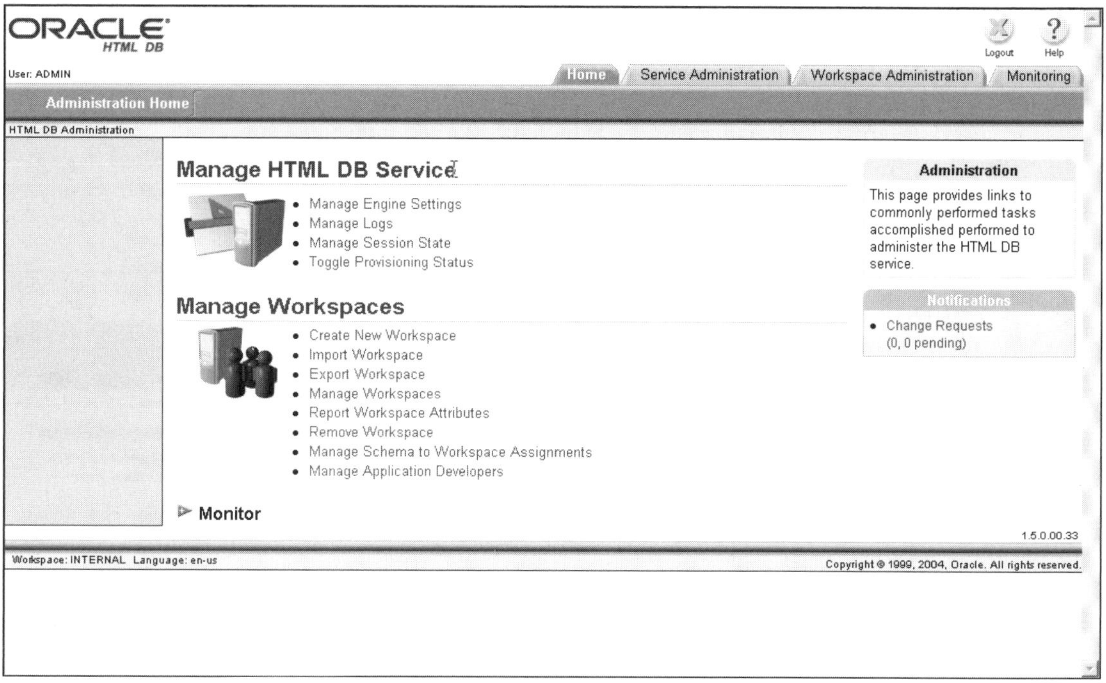

Figure 23-12: The HTML-DB administration page.

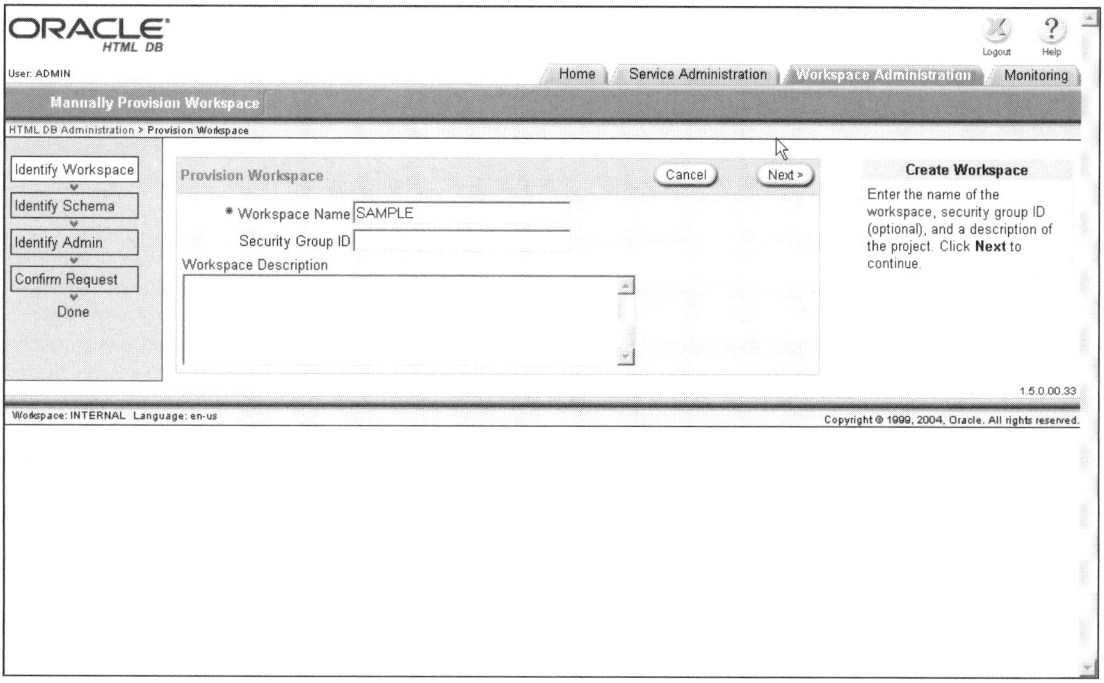

Figure 23-13: Creating a workspace.

For the purposes of this sample application, give the workspace the name of "Sample Workspace" and click on Next. You can see a list of the steps this process will require along the left-hand side of the page—an arrangement that is common across the HTML-DB development environment.

On the next page, shown in its completed state in Figure 23-14, you have to specify a schema to hold the workspace. A workspace is a subset of a schema, so you can group multiple workspaces in a single schema for both security and maintenance productivity. To keep this workspace separate from any existing schemas, you will choose to create a new workspace.

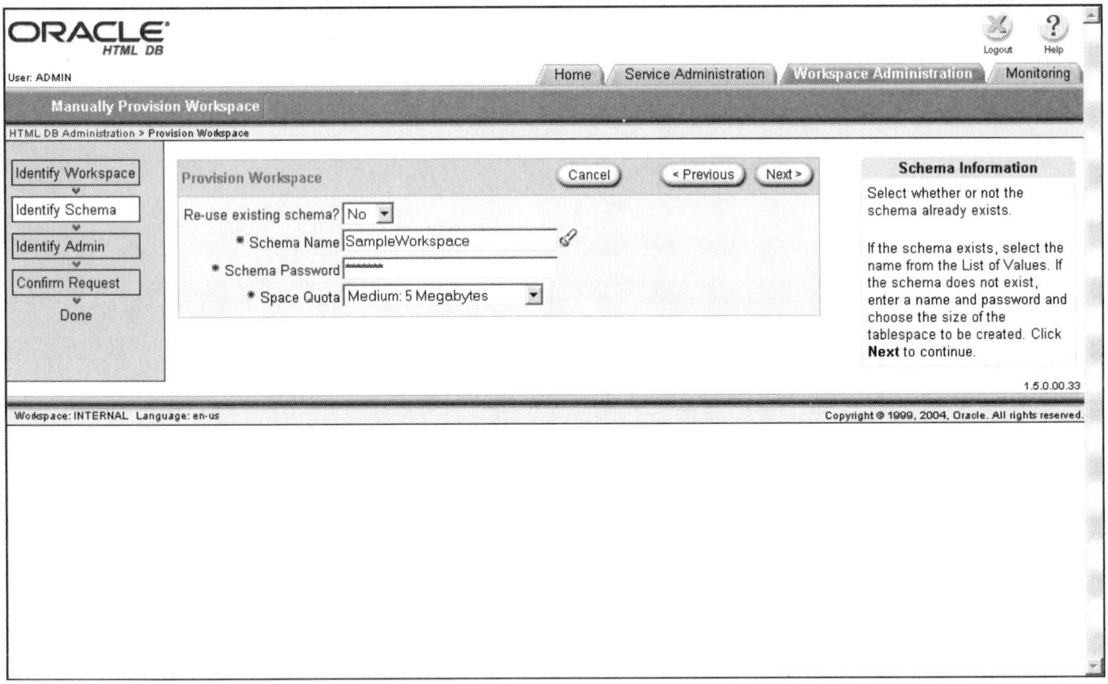

Figure 23-14: Choosing a schema for a workspace.

As shown in Figure 23-14, you should enter the schema name of `SampleWorkspace` for the workspace, give it a password, and select the size allotted for the workspace. Although you probably won't need that much space for this sample application alone, you should select Medium as the size. Keep in mind that this workspace, by default, only holds the PL/SQL packages generated for the workspace, not the data used for the application.

Once you have entered this information, click on Next again, which brings up a page to assign an administrator for the workspace. By default, the administrator for this workspace is the `ADMIN` user you are currently using. You could assign different administrators for different sets of workspaces for administrative flexibility. For this simple application, enter the password for the `ADMIN` user, enter an e-mail address for the administrator to receive requests for changes in the workspace, and click on Next.

The final page in this process, shown in Figure 23-15, reviews the information about the workspace you have entered and presents a Provision button to actually create and provision the workspace.

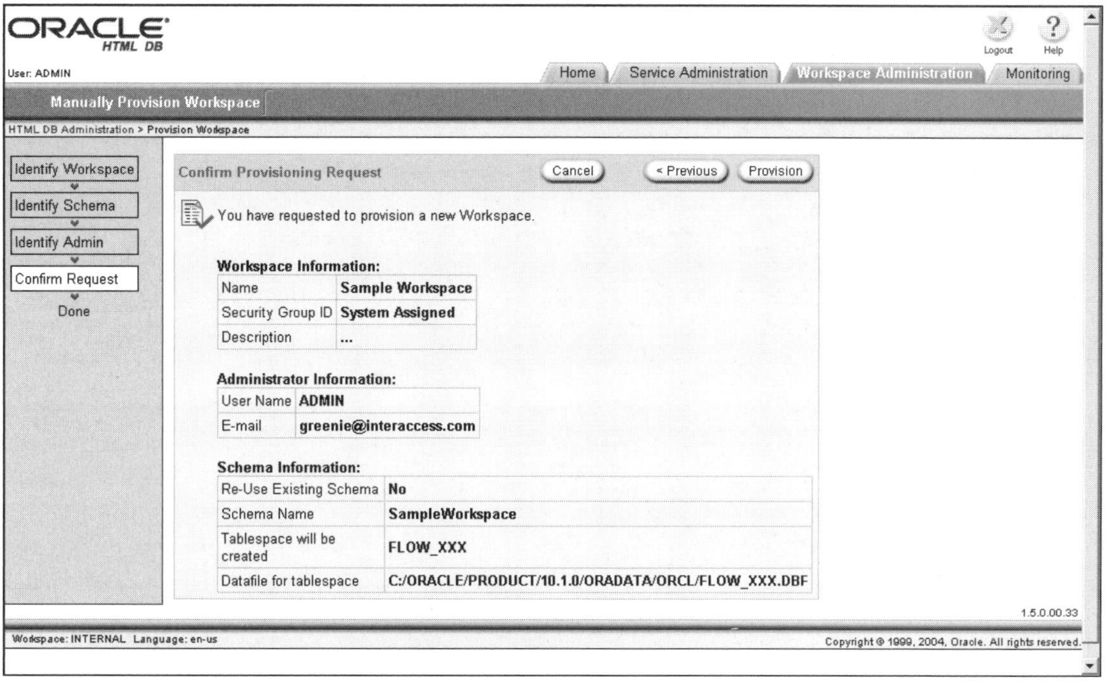

Figure 23-15: The final step in creating a workspace.

Creating the workspace brings up a success page, with the option to return to the administration page.

Creating an Application Developer

A workspace is a location to hold the results of application development. As an initial step to creating an application, you will also have to create an application developer from the administration page. You start by clicking on the Manage Application Developers page on the administration page, which was shown in Figure 23-12. Doing so brings up the page shown in Figure 23-16.

You could just use the `ADMIN` user to create an application in the SampleWorkspace workspace, but for any type of real development work, you would want to create at least one other developer identity to use the workspace. Start by clicking on the Create button, which brings up the page shown in Figure 23-17.

Figure 23-16: Managing application developers.

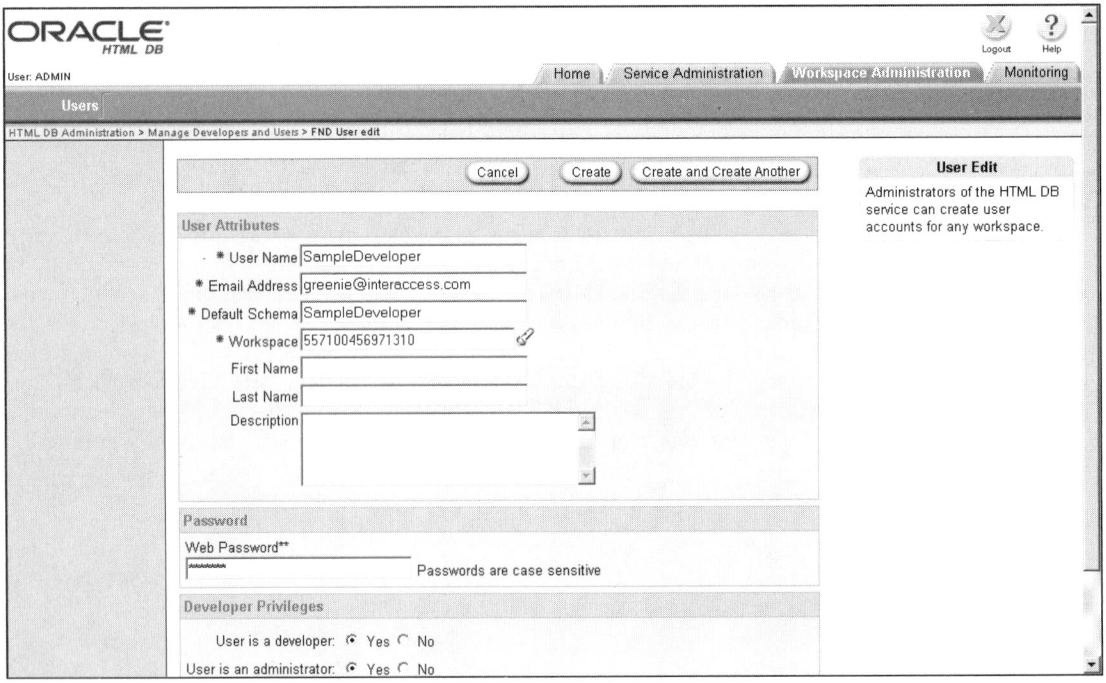

Figure 23-17: Creating a user.

The page shown in Figure 23-17 is already filled in with the name of `SampleDeveloper`, an e-mail address, a default schema for the user, and a workspace for the user. Notice that the workspace is an identifier. This value was placed into the field when you select the name of the workspace from the pop-up list, which is shown when you click on the little flashlight to the right of the field. You also have to assign a password for the user, which will be used to log in to the HTML-DB development environment.

Once you have successfully created a development user, you should log out as the ADMIN user and use the URL `http://host:7777/pls/htmldb/htmldb_login` to log back in to HTML-DB as the `SampleDeveloper` developer in the Sample Workspace workspace. (HTML-DB stores this information in capital letters, but logging in is not case-sensitive.)

Once you log in, you should see a page like the one shown earlier in Figure 23-1. After logging in, you are ready to begin work on this sample application.

Importing Data

Much of your development work will take the approach of designing and creating your database schemas and objects before you start to develop the applications that will use them. HTML-DB makes it possible to essentially skip this step by allowing you to import data directly from a number of sources. This feature means you can take an Excel spreadsheet and use it as the basis of your Oracle database table. The ability to quickly move data from Excel to an Oracle table is one of the nice features of HTML-DB, and one that you will use to jumpstart your application development.

The sample application you will create stems from a collection of music shows stored in an Excel spreadsheet. The amount of data in the spreadsheet has gradually grown beyond the ability of Excel to handle it well. In addition, moving to HTML-DB will allow the addition of more functionality for the use of this data, allowing the data to be stored and queried in more ways, and adding additional data that is logically related to existing data.

This type of relationship is meat and potatoes for a relational database, but quite a bit more complicated to use effectively in a spreadsheet. It would be much better to put the data into a relational database, like, say, Oracle, where it could be used as the basis of more flexible and powerful querying and enhancement. Once the data is in an Oracle database, extending the range of the data and its usefulness will be much easier.

One of the nice features of HTML-DB is the ability to import data from a spreadsheet. This easy process allows you to save the data you have already captured as a starting point. Although in this chapter you will be using this data to build an HTML-DB application, you could also use this functionality to simply transfer data to and from your Oracle database for any reason at all.

To start the import process, click on the Data Workshop icon on the home page, which brings up the home page for importing and exporting data, shown in Figure 23-18.

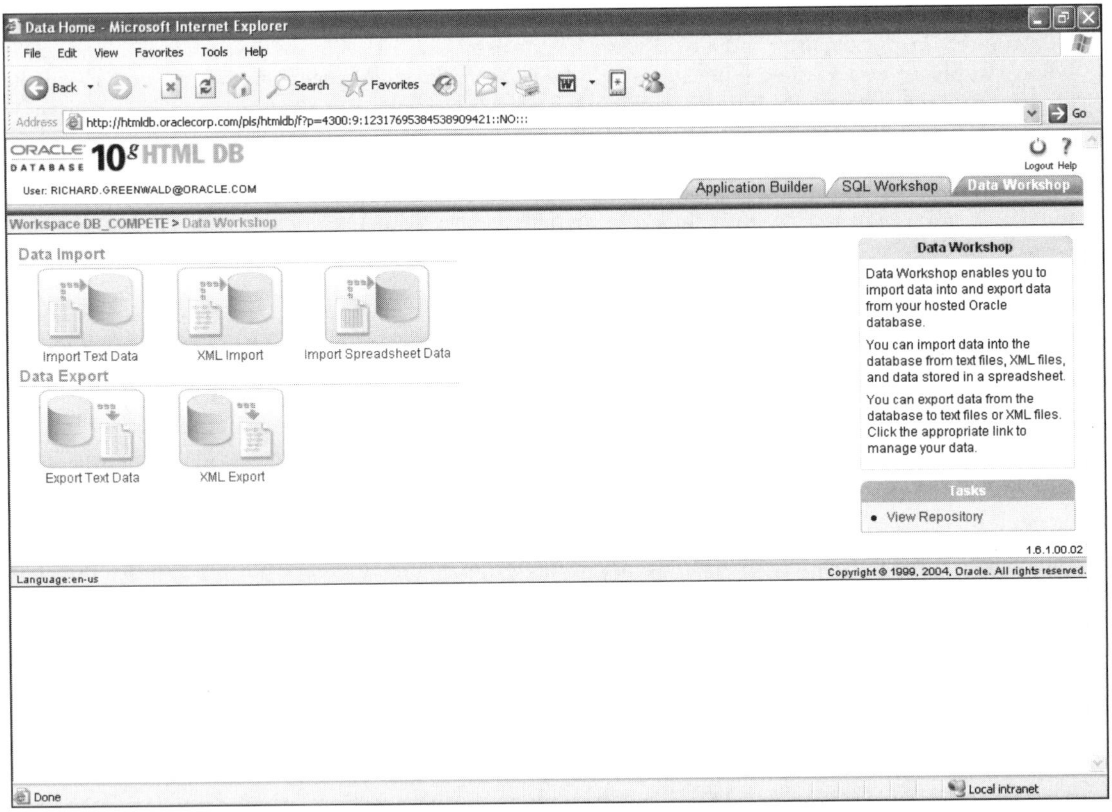

Figure 23-18: Data Workshop home page.

On this page, you can see that you can import or export data as text data, which is comma-separated data, or XML data. You can also import data from an Excel spreadsheet by cutting and pasting the data. Since the data already exists in a spreadsheet, you can click on the Import Spreadsheet Data icon on the page, which brings up the page shown in Figure 23-19.

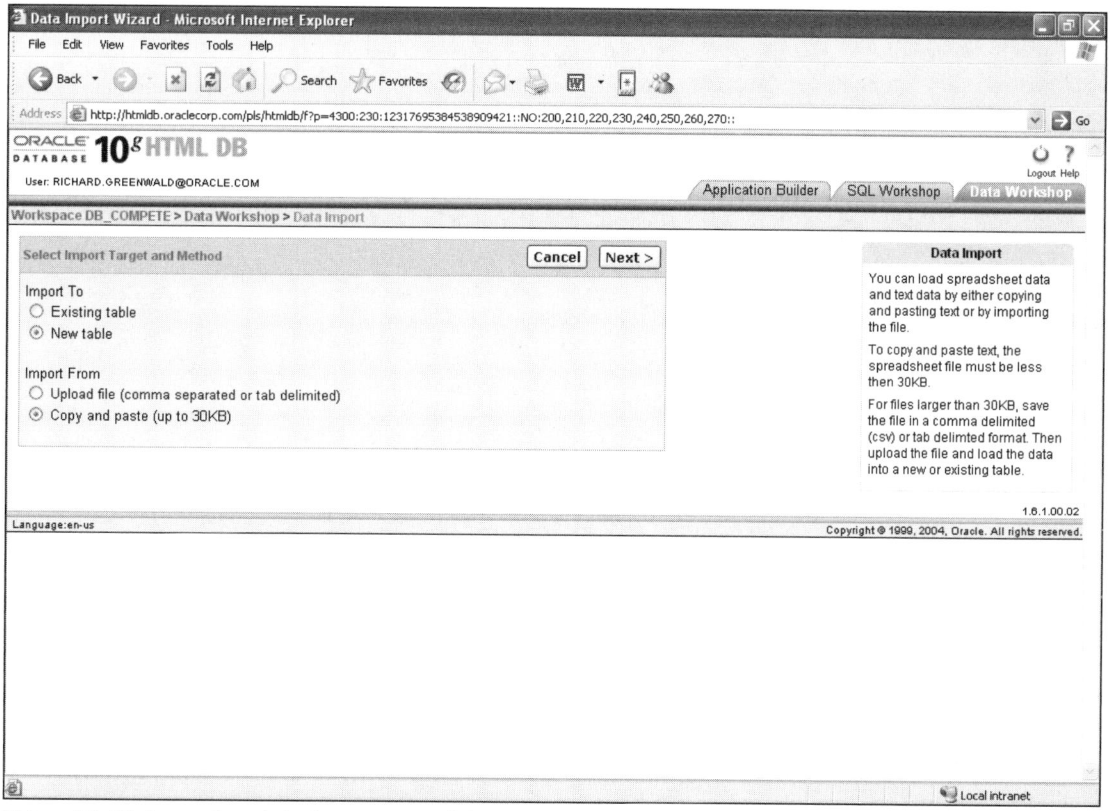

Figure 23-19: Importing data from a spreadsheet.

On this page, you can choose to upload data into an existing table or to load the data into a new table. You will want to choose to create a new table for this data, the default, and also leave the default choice to copy and paste the data. As noted on the page, there is a limit of 30 KB for data that will be copied and pasted during the import process.

Click on Next to bring up the page shown in its completed form in Figure 23-20. This page contains a field to paste data into, as well as a single check box that is used to indicate if the column names for the table should come from the first row of the data. As it happens, the spreadsheet that contains the data, included in the file `CH28_IMPORT_DATA.XLS`, does contain appropriate column headings, so you should leave this box checked. You will have the option to change these default column headings in the next page.

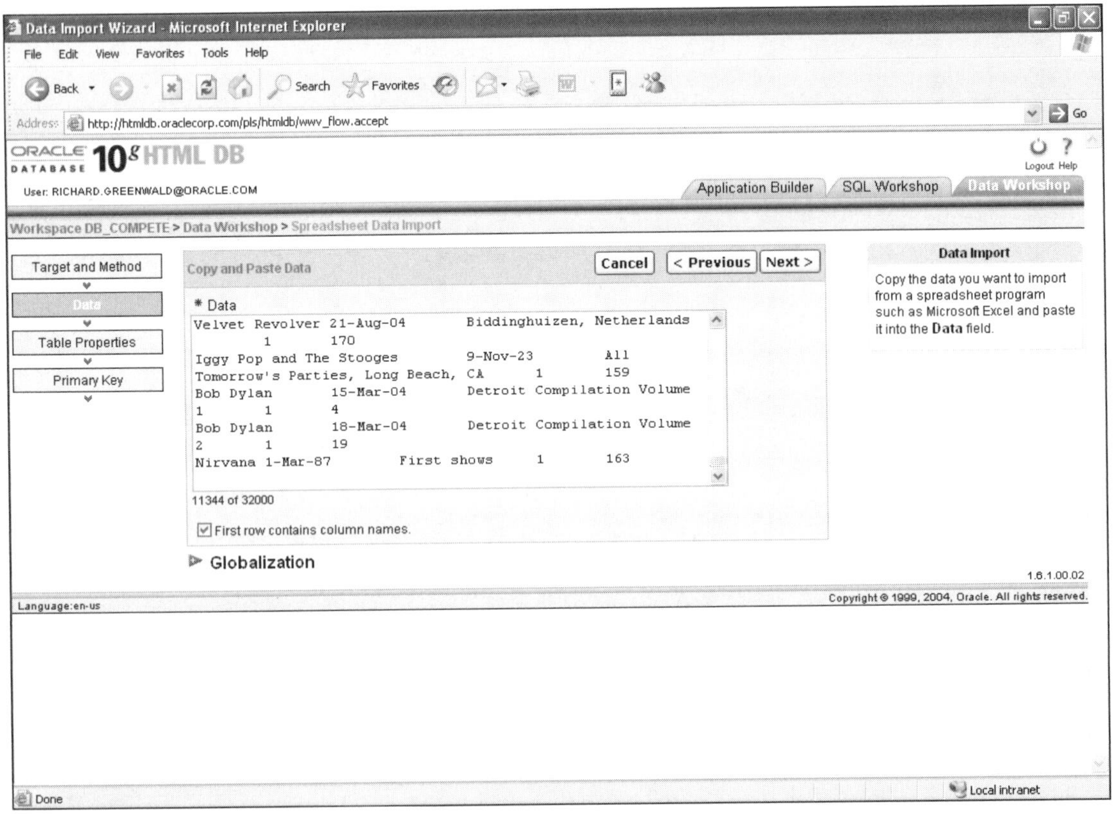

Figure 23-20: Importing data from a spreadsheet, step 2.

Open the `CH28_IMPORT_DATA.XLS` spreadsheet and copy all of the spreadsheet, then come back to this page and paste the data into the window. When you have completed this set of actions, click on Next.

The next page, shown completed in Figure 23-21, prompts you for the table name for the imported data and shows you the column names, data types, and a selection of data that will be imported into the designated table. You can see that the data that was in the first row of the spreadsheet has been taken as the default column names, and that HTML-DB Data Workshop has made some intelligent assumptions about the column sizes for the data. Although the column lengths may be a bit long at 255 characters, `VARCHAR2` data only stores the data entered, so the column lengths shouldn't matter that much. The import process also recognized that the date of the show should be a `DATE` column.

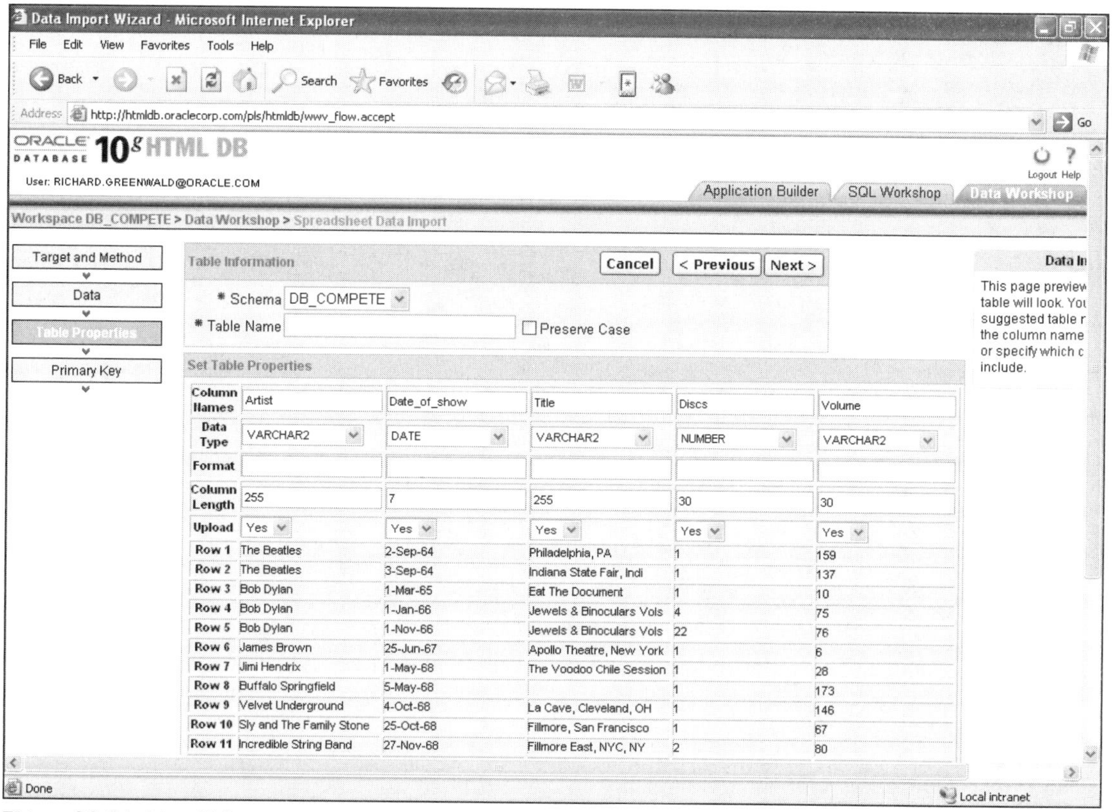

Figure 23-21: Identifying a target table.

You can also see that the `Volume` column has been assigned a data type of `VARCHAR2`, while the data shown looks like only numbers. The reason for this assignment is that later rows include multiple file logs, separated by commas, which the Data Workshop properly concludes cannot be stored as a single number.

Enter `Shows` as the table name and click on Next. On this page, shown in Figure 23-22, you can see that the Data Workshop Import Wizard is helping you to create a valid relational table. You don't have to have a unique primary key as part of a table definition, but having a unique primary key makes everything go more smoothly. HTML-DB knows this, so this page asks you if the imported data happens to already have a unique primary key. If it doesn't, the import process will assign a default ID number for each row, as well as either use an existing Oracle sequence object or create a new one to support the generation of this ID. You should accept the default choices on this page, which will cause the use of a generated ID column and create a sequence object to support it.

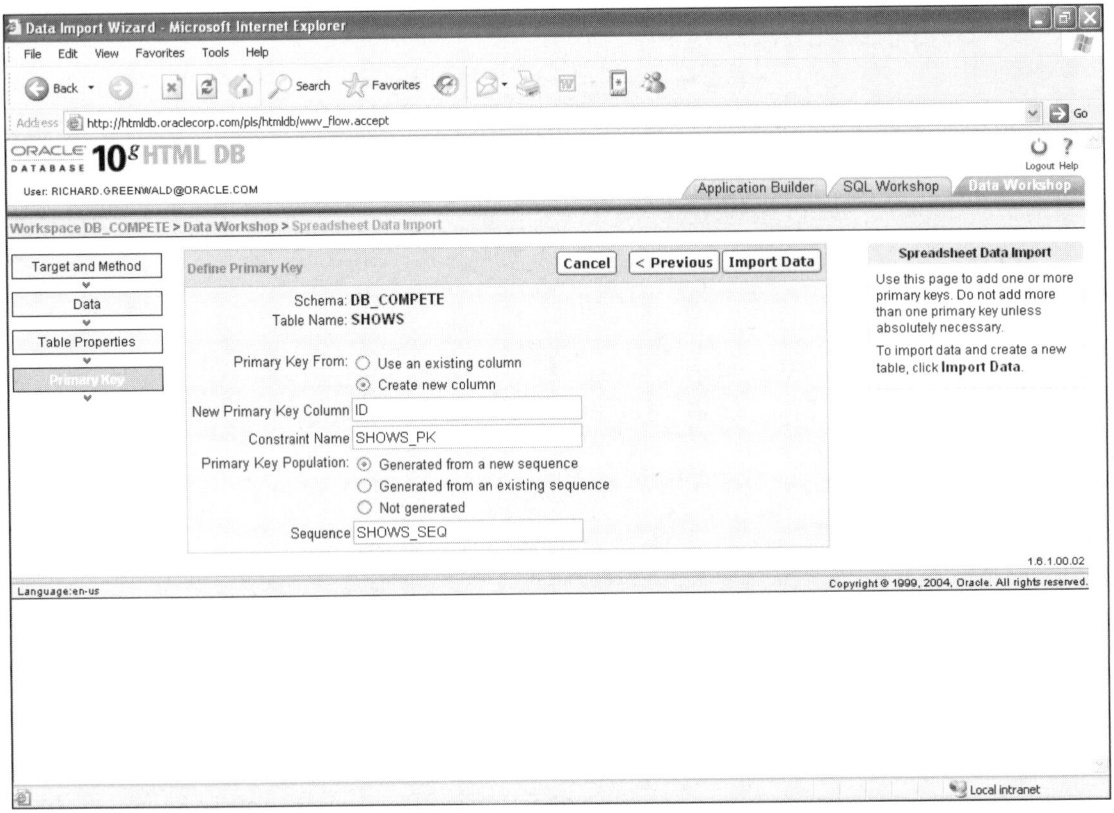

Figure 23-22: Identifying a unique primary key.

The page shown in Figure 23-23 is the last page in the import process. The final page in the import process shows that the process was a success, along with some statistics on how many rows were successfully imported and how many failed to be imported, which usually occurs because the data in the row did not meet the data type requirements. This page also lets you immediately delete the imported table (or others) by simply checking a box.

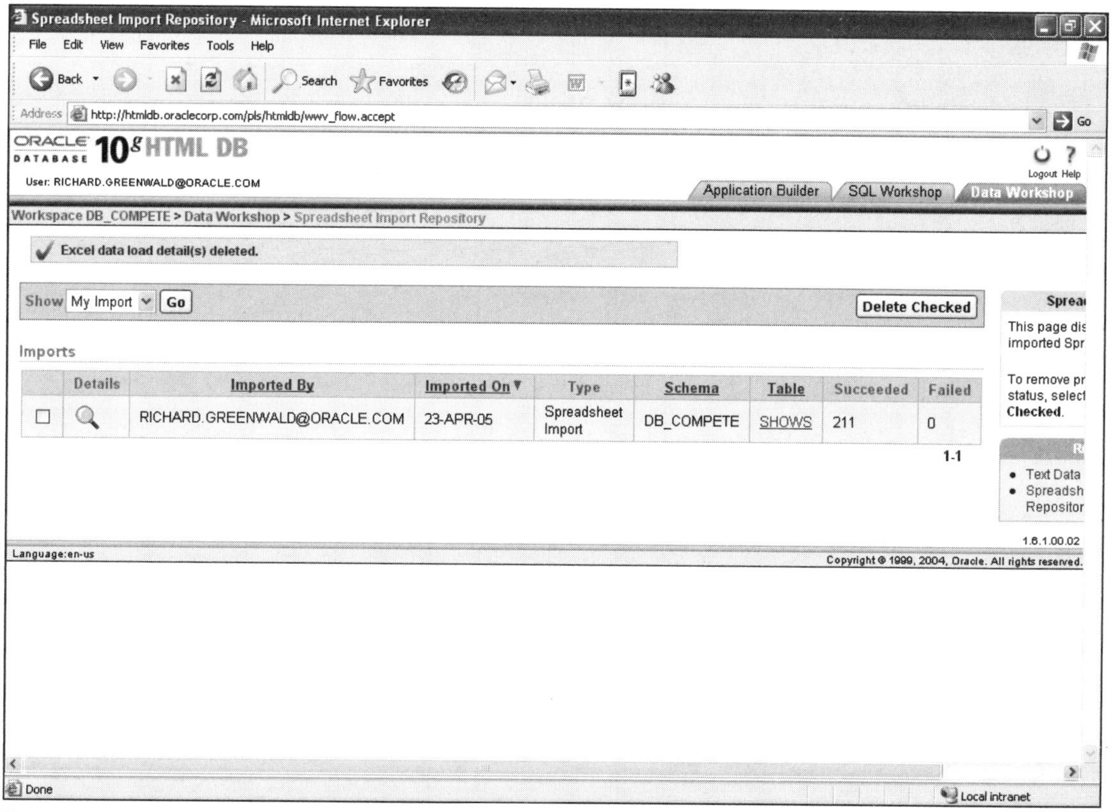

Figure 23-23: The results of the import process.

Creating an Application

One of the great virtues of a highly productive development environment is the ability to create application modules rapidly. HTML-DB delivers this advantage in a big way by making it possible to create an entire application system with just a handful of mouse clicks. Although this may sound too good to be true, the remainder of this section walks you through the creation of a simple application based on the data you just imported.

To start, return to the home page for HTML-DB, as shown in Figure 23-1. Once on this page, click on Application BuilderCreate Application icon, which brings up the page shown in Figure 23-24.

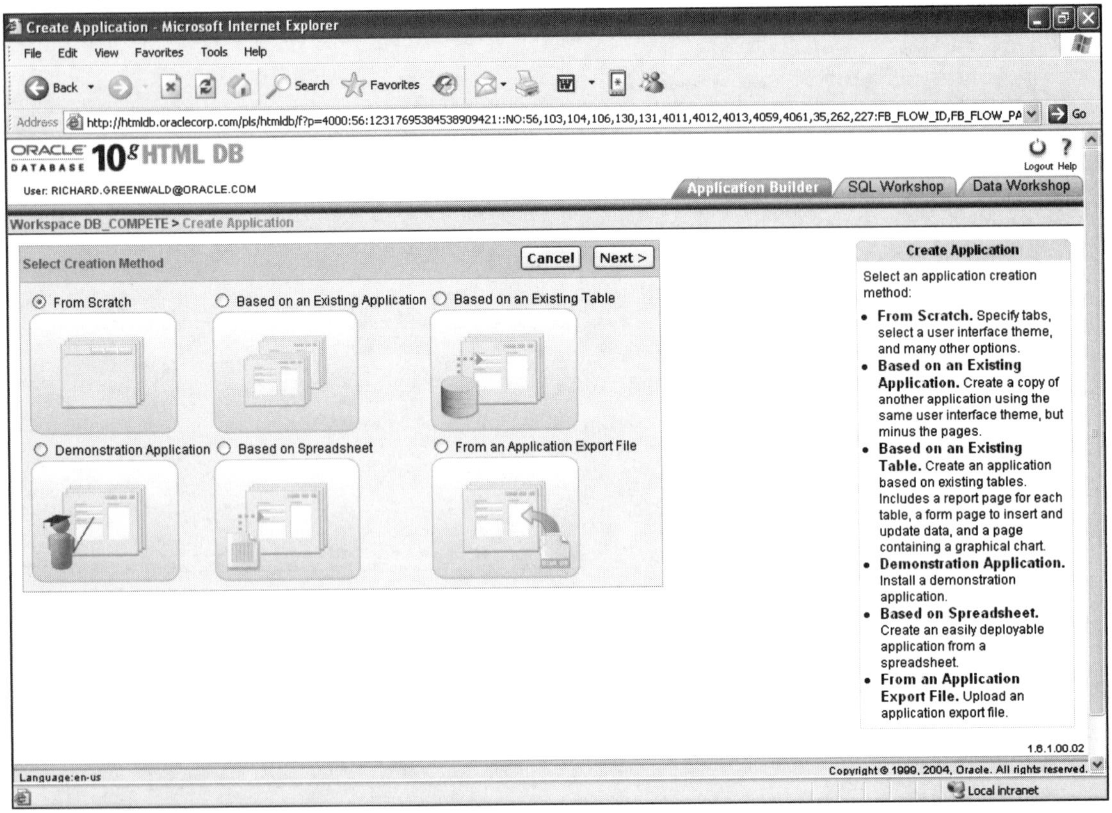

Figure 23-24: The Application Builder home page.

This page begins the process of building an application by allowing you to choose which wizard to use. You can create an application from scratch, or one that is based on another application, the demonstration application, data in a spreadsheet, or from an existing application that has been exported. Since you just imported the data you will need for your sample application, you want to select the choice on the right of the first row of icons, which lets you create an application based on a table. Click on this choice to move to the next page, which is shown in Figure 23-25.

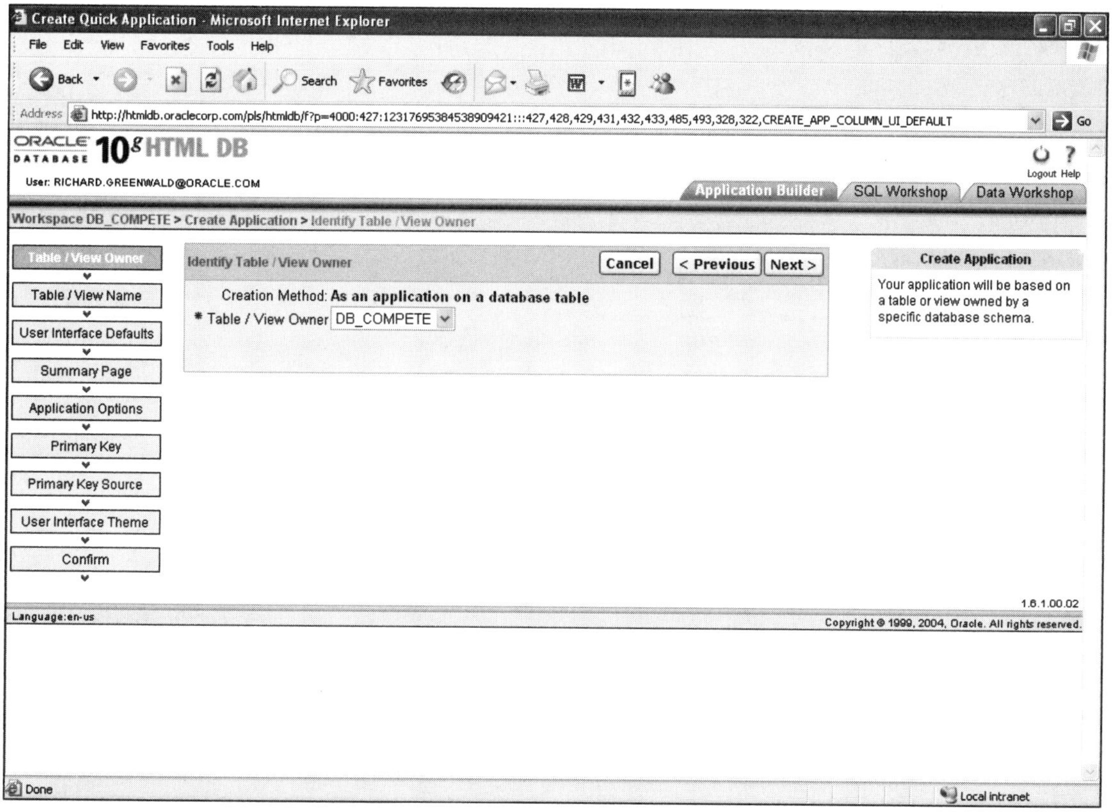

Figure 23-25: Starting to build an application based on a table.

On this page, you select the schema that will contain the table you will use. In this example, you can simply click on Next, which brings up the page shown in Figure 23-26.

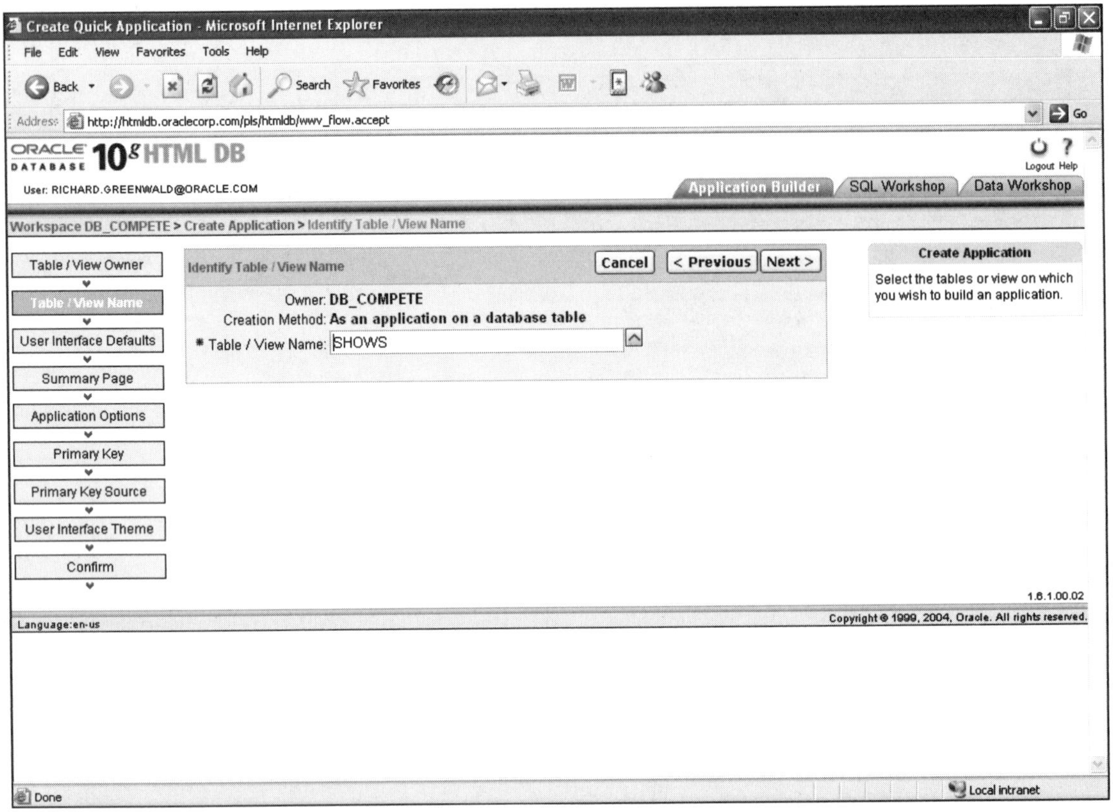

Figure 23-26: Selecting a table.

This page allows you to select a table on which to base your application. Clicking on the arrow to the right of the text entry box brings up a list of the tables in the previously selected schema. Select the `SHOWS` table from this list, which adds the name of the table into the text entry box, leaving it as shown in Figure 23-26. Once you have selected the proper table, click on Next, which brings up the page shown in Figure 23-27.

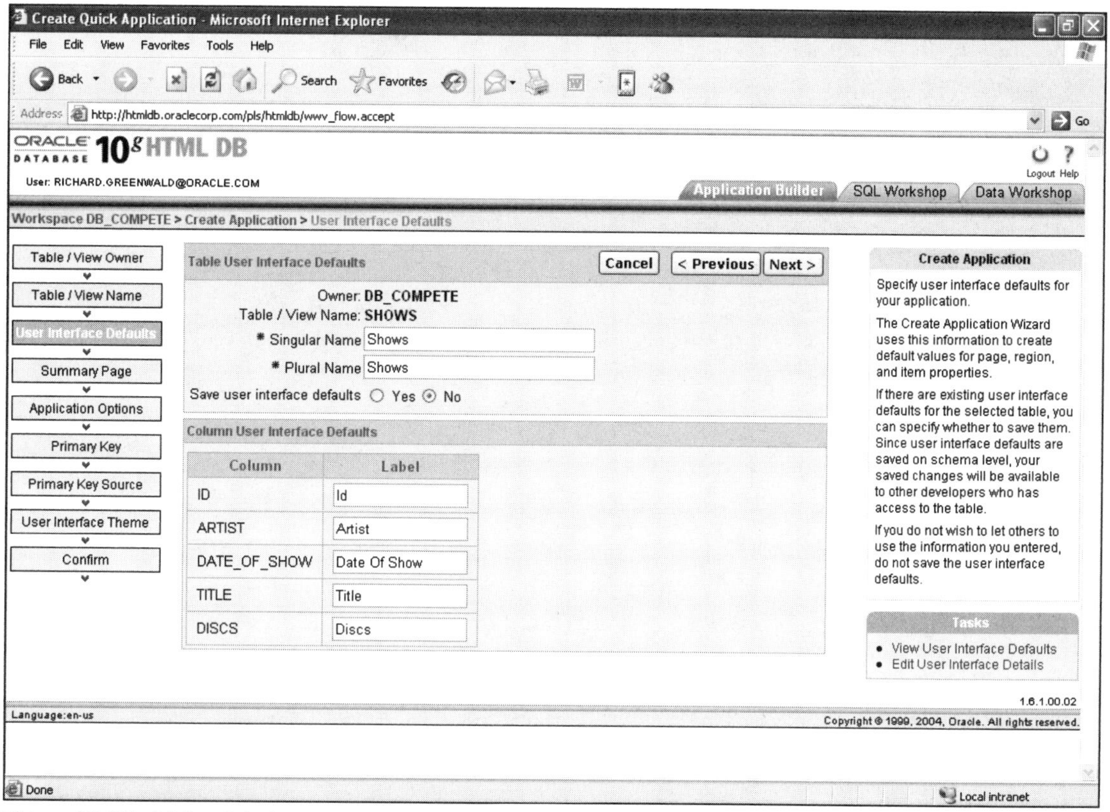

Figure 23-27: Adding labels.

This page enables you to change the default labels for any of the column names, as well as assign a name for the default form table, listed as the Singular Name, and the report regions, listed as the Plural Name. For this application, you can enter `Show` as the singular name and `Shows` as the plural name, as well as change the label for the ID column to `ID`. Once you have done this, click on Next, which brings up the page shown in Figure 23-28.

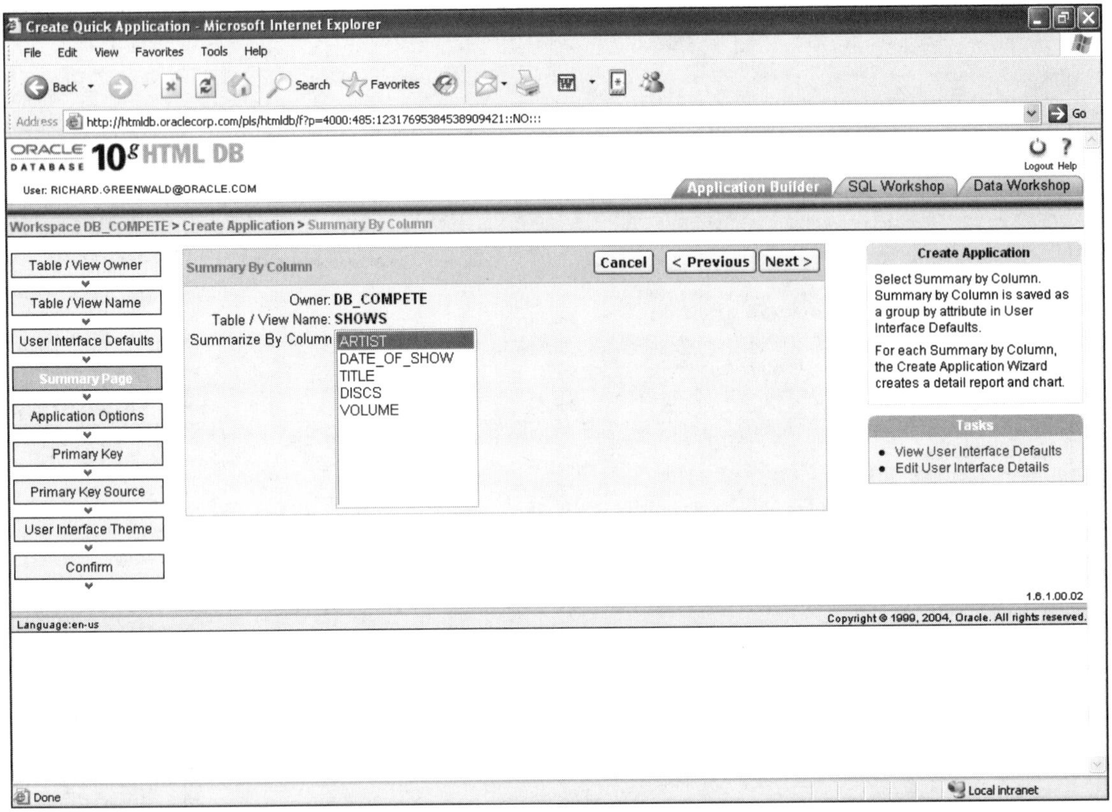

Figure 23-28: Selecting a column for summary information.

This page allows you to select a column you can use to group the data. To demonstrate one of the additional capabilities of this HTML-DB wizard, select the `ARTIST` column. This selection causes a few more pages to be added to the process of defining this application, and produces a nice result in the final product. Once you have selected the `ARTIST` column, click on Next.

The next page, shown in Figure 23-29, asks what sort of summary information you want. You don't really want to aggregate the number of disks, so don't select that numeric column You don't need an average, so uncheck that box below the list box. After these actions, click on Next to bring up the page shown in Figure 23-30.

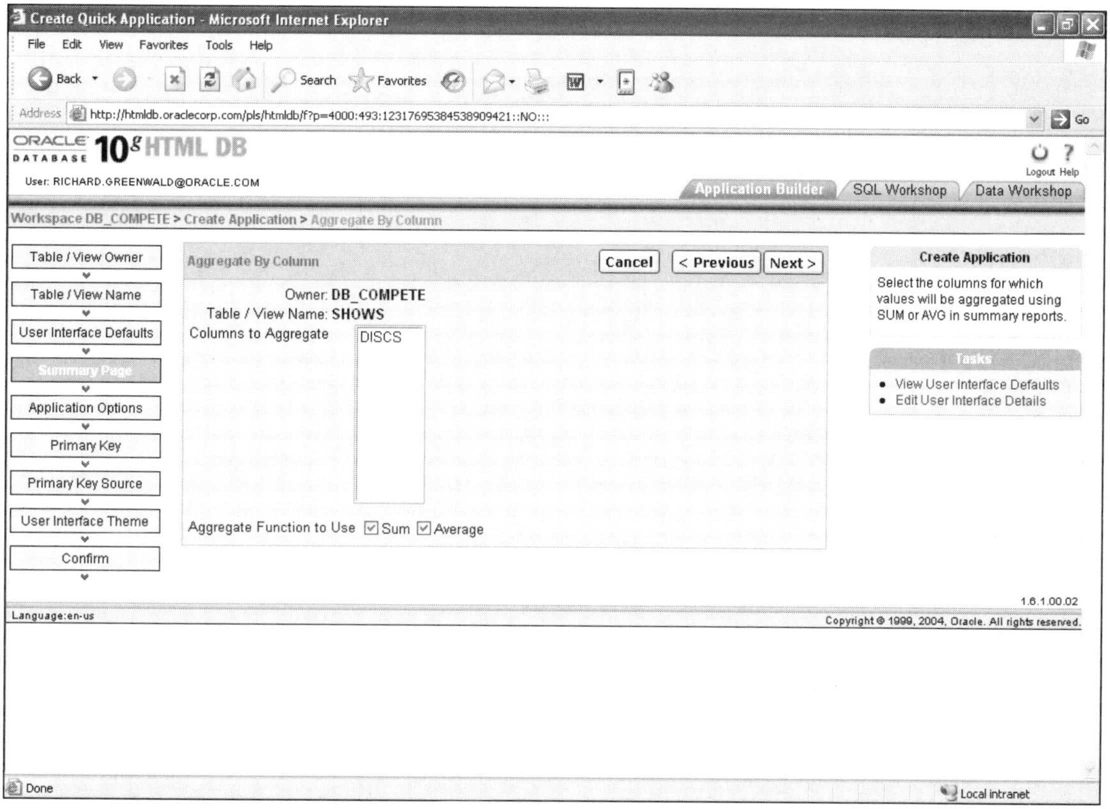

Figure 23-29: Selecting aggregates.

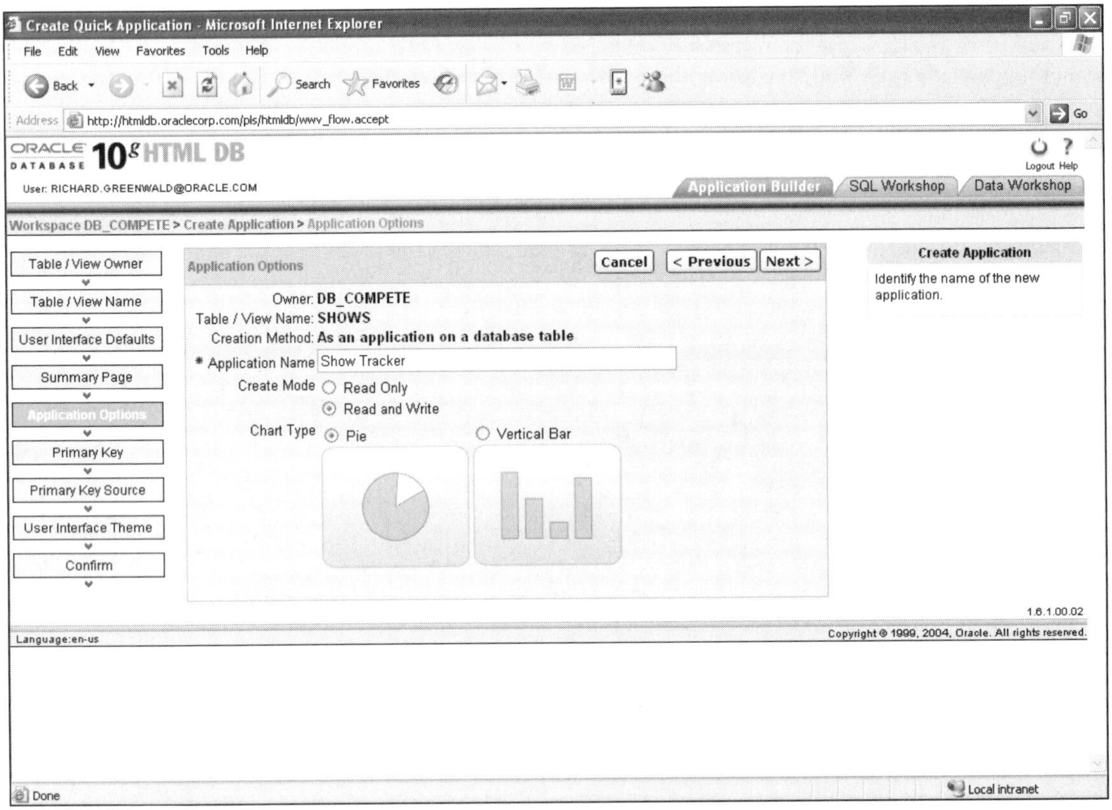

Figure 23-30: Specifying application information.

The next page in the wizard prompts you for a name for your application, as well as whether the application will allow users to update and add information and, since you specified an aggregate, what type of chart to use. In this example, you can change the name of the application to "Show Tracker" and click on Next, which brings up the page shown in Figure 23-31.

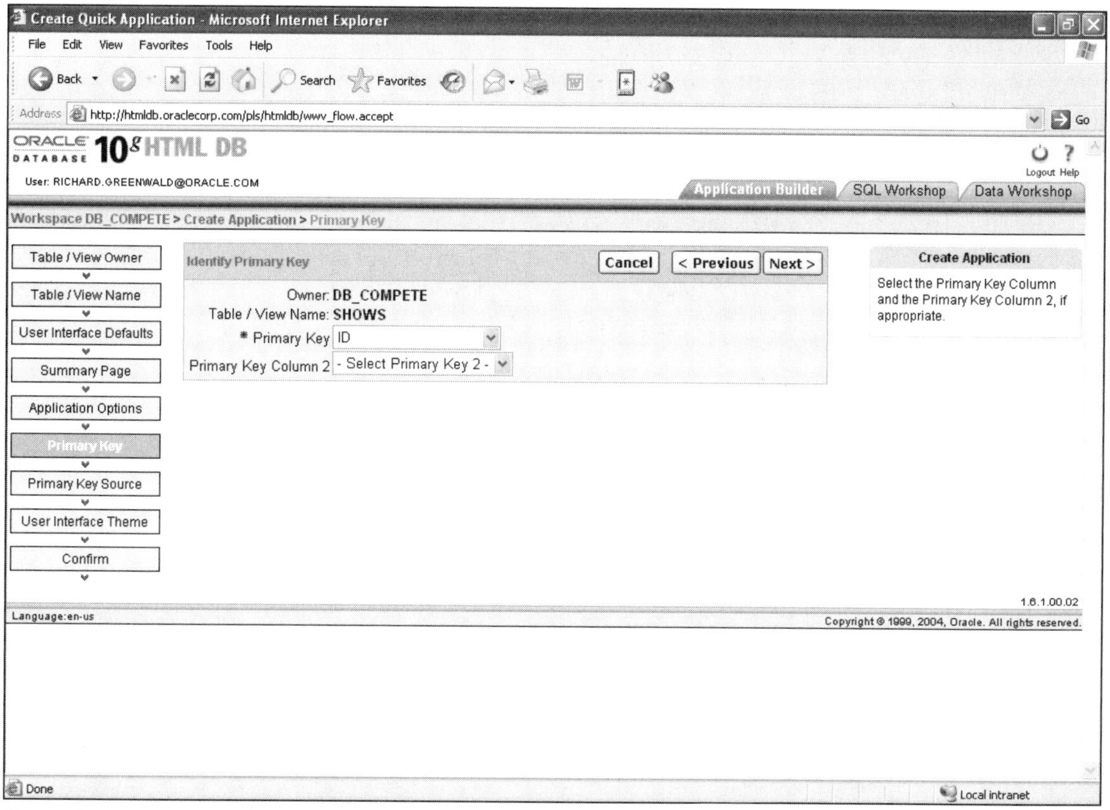

Figure 23-31: Selecting the primary key.

This page prompts you for a primary key, which is used to properly insert and update rows in the target table. You can accept the default, which is the ID column, and click on Next to bring up the page shown in Figure 23-32.

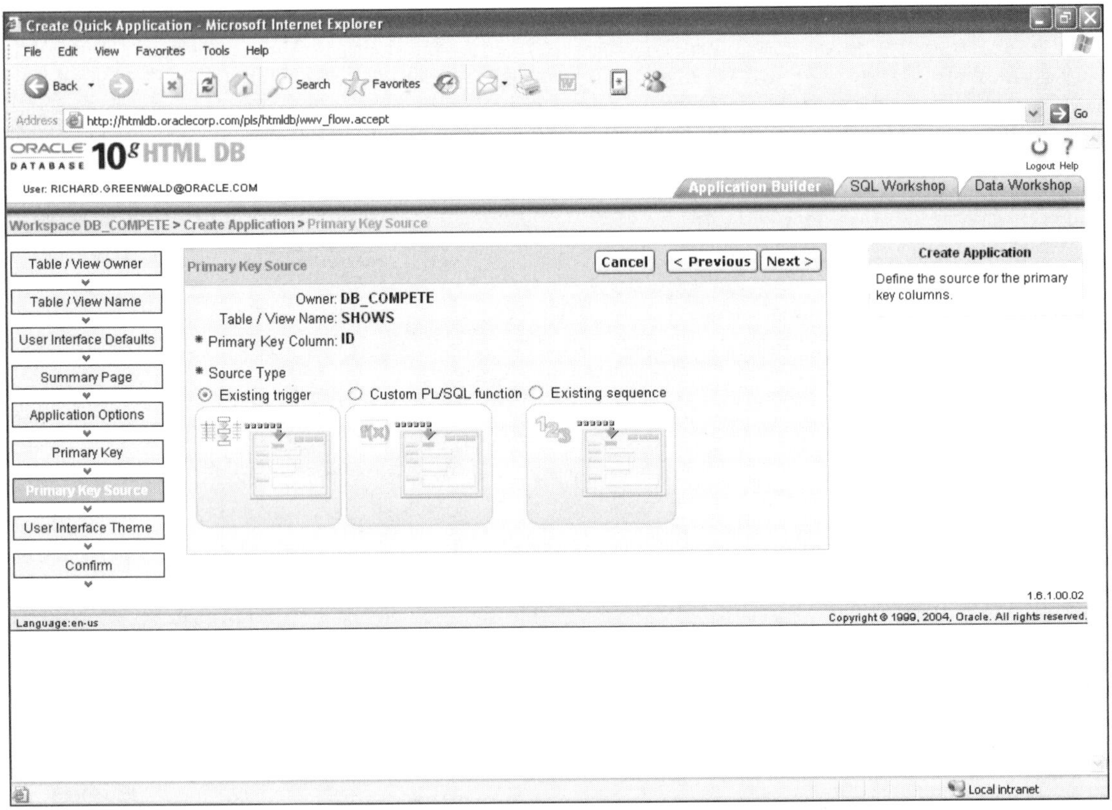

Figure 23-32: Selecting the source of a new primary key.

The next page asks you for the source of the primary key. This source will be used for creating a new primary key when you insert new rows into the table. You can select the rightmost option, `Existing sequence`, which causes a list box top to appear below the main choice icons. In this list box, select the `SHOWS_SEQ` number from the drop-down list that appears below the option choices once you select the sequence. This sequence was created as part of the import process for your Excel spreadsheet.

The next page, shown in Figure 23-33, lets you select a theme, which specifies the appearance of your application. Since the illustrations for this chapter will only be in black and white, Theme 7 will work nicely, but you could choose any theme that seems appropriate for the application.

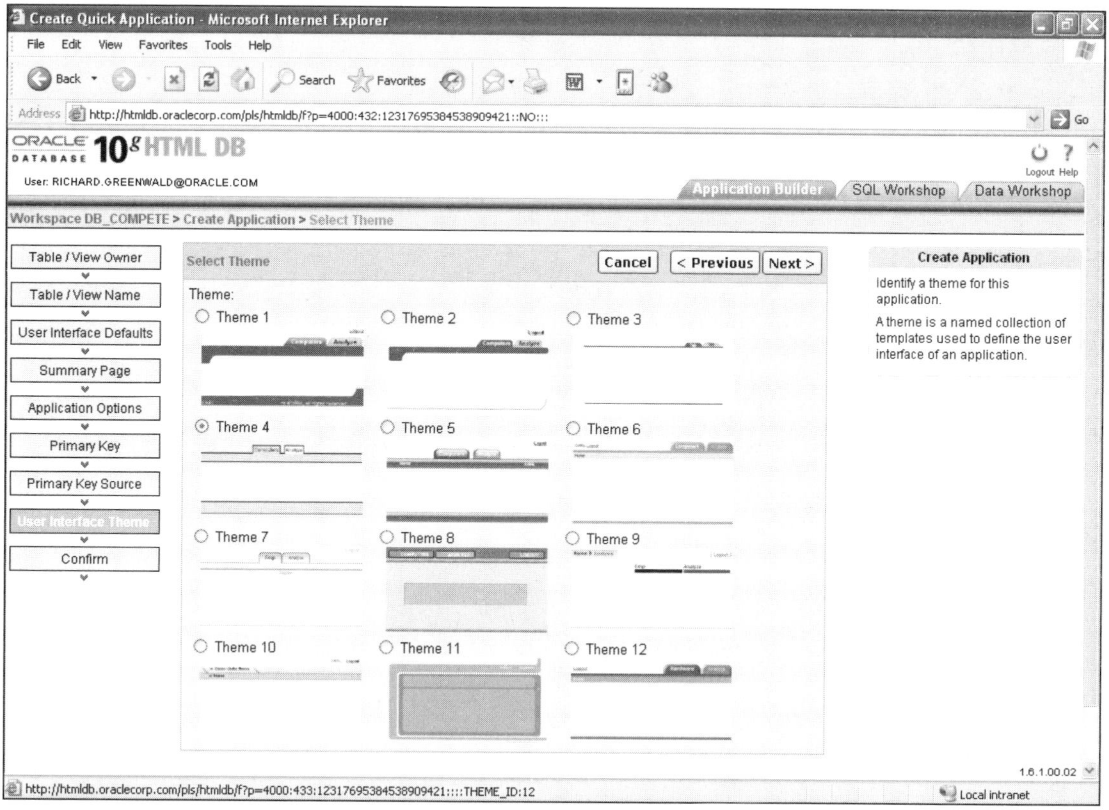

Figure 23-33: Selecting a theme.

HTML-DB also gives you the ability to create your own themes.

After selecting a theme, click on Next. The final page in the wizard confirms the owner, table name, application name, and theme, and it shows an illustration of the theme. Click on Create, and HTML-DB creates the entire application for you. When the application has been successfully generated, HTML-DB shows you the results screen shown in Figure 23-34.

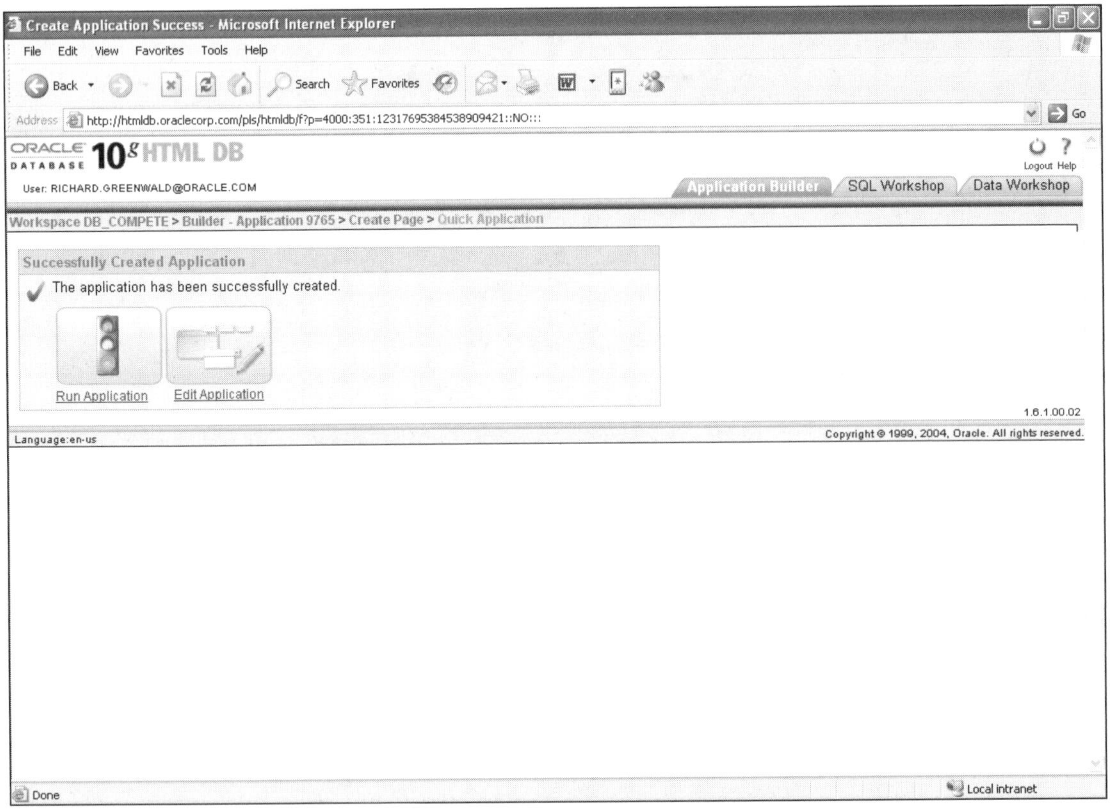

Figure 23-34: Success!

This development process was fairly easy, but the functionality included in the application is fairly sophisticated. The next section explores the fruits of your labor.

Functionality in Your HTML-DB Application

To run the application you just created, click on the Run Application icon shown on the success page that just appeared, which brings up the page shown in Figure 23-35.

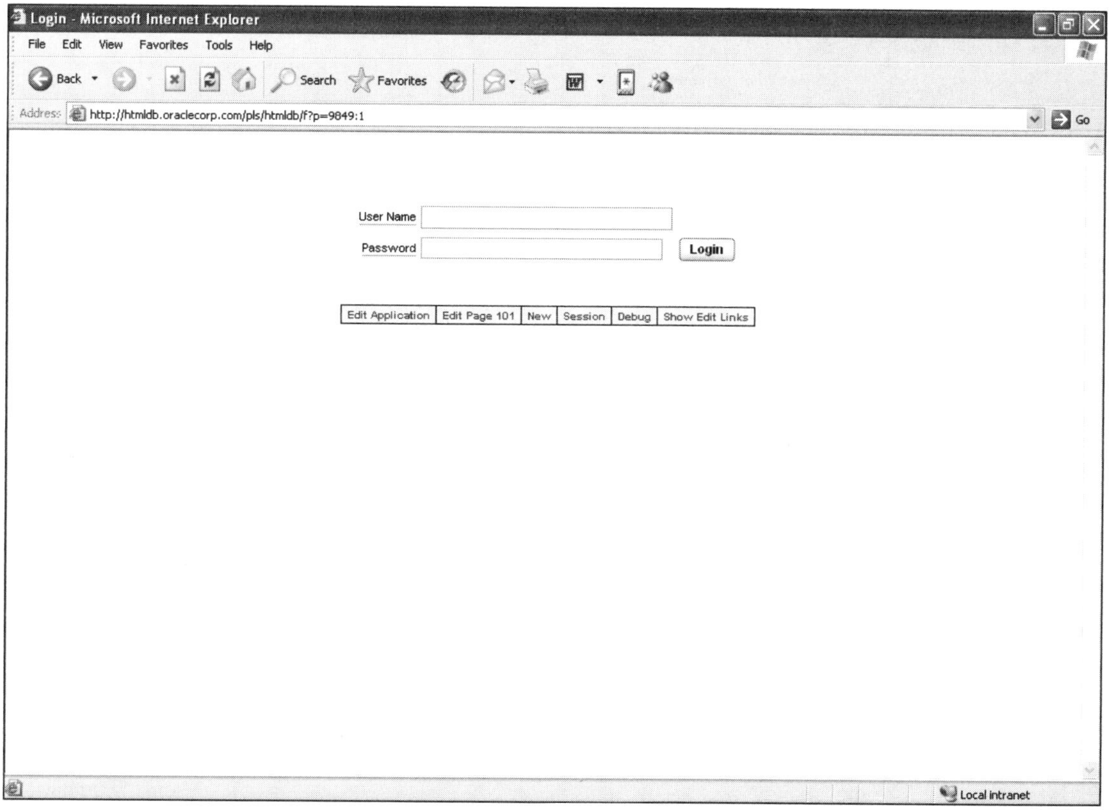

Figure 23-35: The login page.

This first page of the application prompts for a login username and password, which is part of the built-in security for your default application. You can also see a series of links at the bottom of the page, which give you quick access that allows you to edit the attributes of the application or page, view session or debug information or create a new object for the application There is also a link to show edit links for each object on the page. Clicking on this toggles icons on and off, which allows you to edit the attributes of each item on the page.

To see the rest of the application, log in with the password you assigned for the `ADMIN` user and click on the Login button, which brings up the page shown in Figure 23-36.

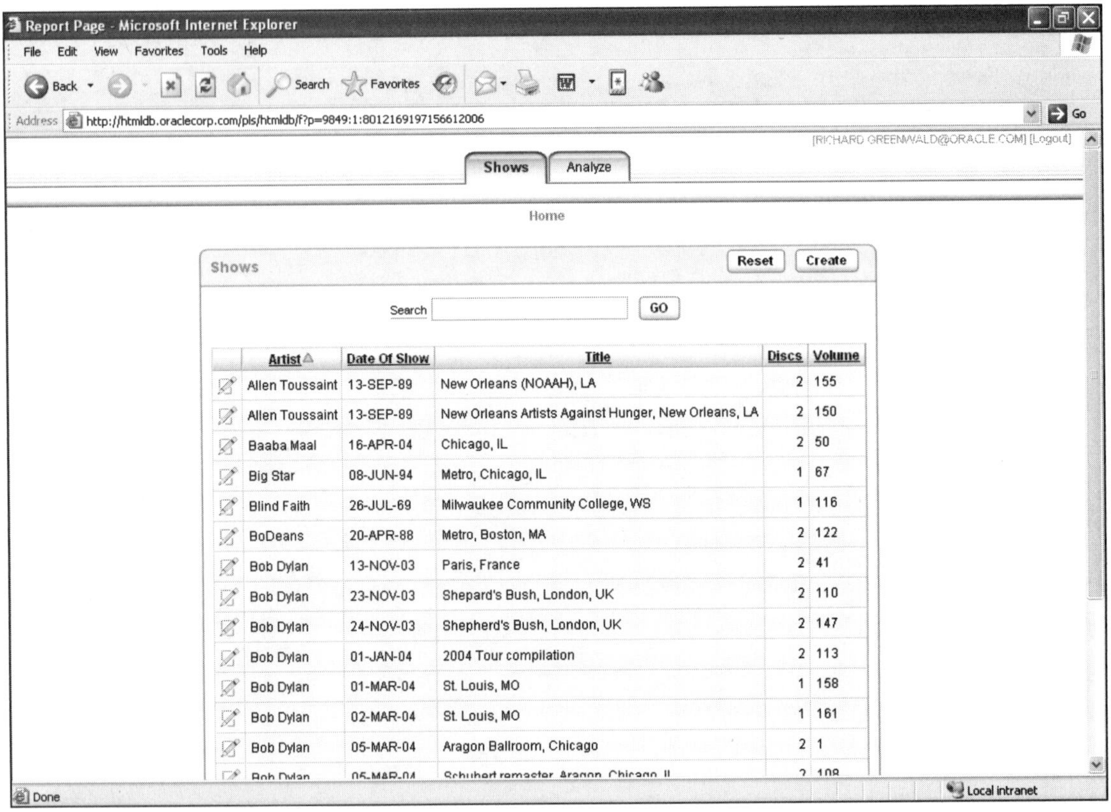

Figure 23-36: The home page for your application.

The default home page of the application is a report page, since you probably want to see a listing of your data right off the bat. The information on the page is presented in a clear way, with a lot of functionality built into it. The basic display shows the rows in the `SHOWS` table, sorted in ascending order on the value of the `Artist` column. You can change the sort order by simply clicking on the heading of a particular column. Initially, a click on the heading sorts the data in ascending order and displays an upward arrow icon to indicate that the column is being used for an ascending sort. Clicking on the column head again causes the sort to be redone in descending order and the arrow to be reversed.

To the left of each row is an edit icon. Clicking on the icon brings up an edit page, as shown in Figure 23-37. Once on this page, you can change the values for the row or delete the row, as well as abandon the edit. You can also use the Previous and Next buttons at the bottom of the page area to scroll through the rows, but keep in mind you will be scrolling through the rows based on the primary key of the rows. Since the value for this column was assigned to the rows in the order they were imported, scrolling on this page may not provide a really meaningful presentation of data with this particular table.

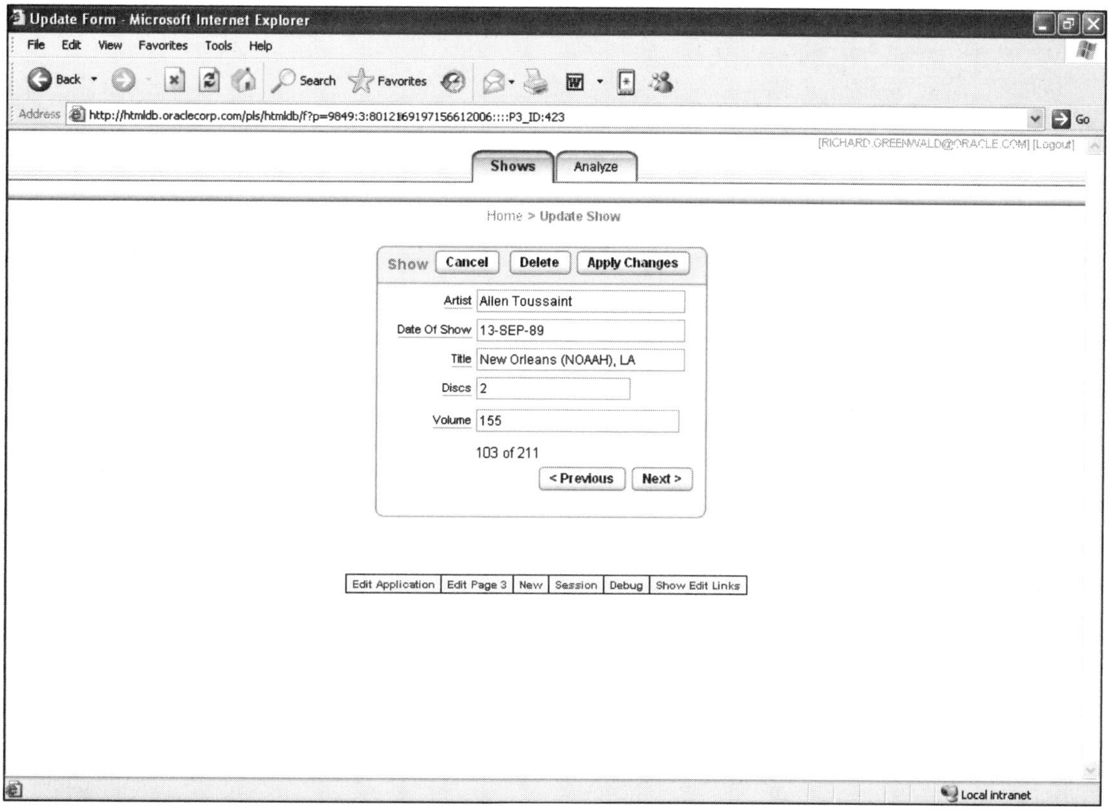

Figure 23-37: An edit page.

Don't worry if this type of capability seems like more than you want to give users. The security on the underlying table is always enforced, and you can edit the attributes of any particular page to remove or shape functionality by changing attributes. You will work with attributes a little more in the next section when you create a page by yourself. For now, just click on Cancel to return to the main reporting page.

At the top of this page, you can see a button labeled Create. Click on this to bring up the page shown in Figure 23-38. This page allows you to enter new information into the table. Although this page is fairly basic, you can create objects like a list of values to enforce referential integrity through the list of drop-down lists, as well as limiting value entry with radio buttons or check box objects.

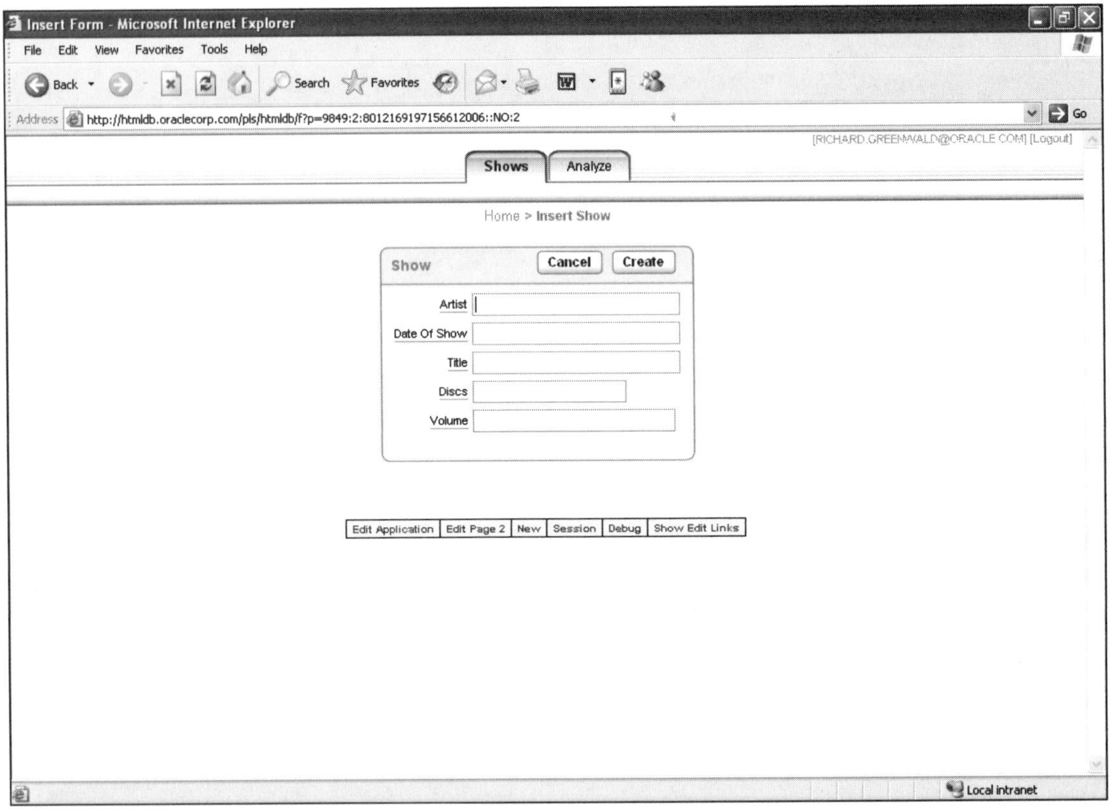

Figure 23-38: Adding a row to a table.

This page also helps you understand how to use tabs and bread crumbs to navigate through the application. If you look at the breadcrumb trail in the center of the upper part of the page, you can see a history of the navigation required to get to this page. You can click on Home to go to the home page for the application. You can also see that the tab labeled Shows is highlighted. Clicking on the tab will cause you to to return to the home page for that tab, which is also the home page for the application.

Another piece of built-in functionality in the main report page is the search capability. You can enter any text in the field labeled Search and click on the Search button. This action causes the HTML-DB application to retrieve all rows that contain the entered text in any column in the table. Figure 23-39 shows the result of a search on the text "London". HTML-DB returns the rows containing the text, with the text highlighted in red.

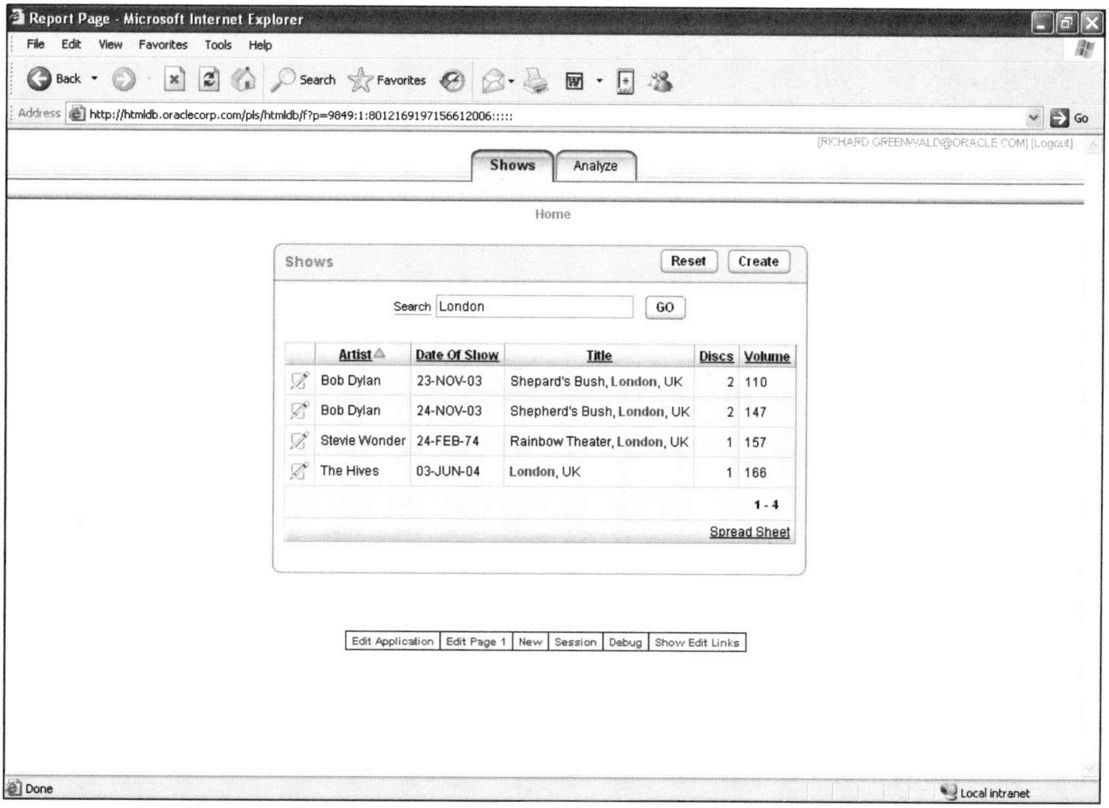

Figure 23-39: The result of a search operation.

The final piece of functionality in this default page comes from the little link labeled Spread Sheet. Clicking on this link prompts the user for a filename to use to save the data in a file. With this simple link and the search capability, you can easily find and extract data from a relational table into a comma-separated variable file.

To explore more the rest of this default application, click on the Home Analyze tab to return to the home page for this section of the application, which is shown in Figure 23-40.

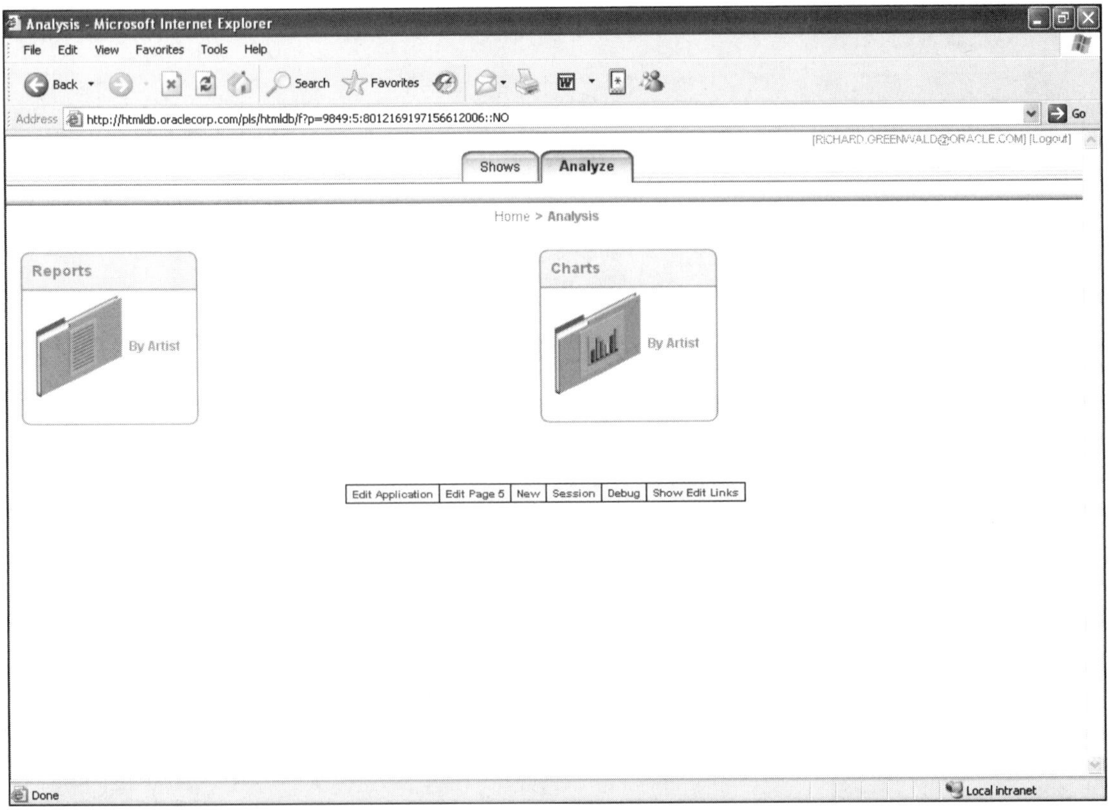

Figure 23-40: The home page for the Analyze tab.

This page has two options for displaying the results of the aggregation you specified in the wizard. The left choice shows a report of the total number of shows for each artist. Clicking on this link brings up a fairly boring view of all the artists who are only represented by one show. You could make this report a little more interesting by clicking on the column heading labeled `Count` to change the sort order and show the most popular artists.

The same information is represented in a more visually interesting chart, which is delivered by clicking on the right-hand menu choice on the page, which brings up the page shown in Figure 23-41.

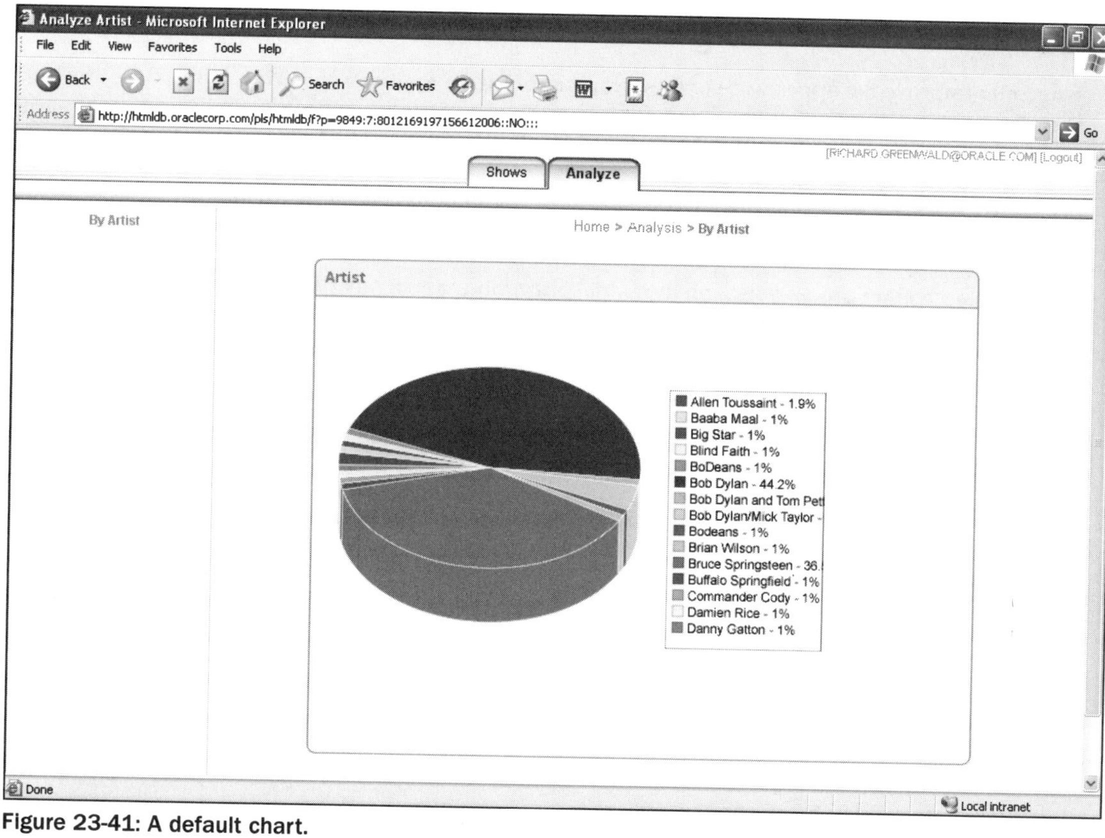

Figure 23-41: A default chart.

Well, maybe this page will appear The display of charts in an HTML-DB application is dependent on using an SVG Viewer, a free download from Adobe. If you do not have this plug-in installed, you will see a page similar to the one in Figure 23-41, but with a request to download the viewer and a link to the Adobe download site rather than the display of the chart.

Once you download the SVG Viewer, you will see the chart shown in Figure 23-41. It graphically displays the percentages of the shows of an artist out of the total number of shows.

You may notice that there does not appear to be a listing for all the artists represented in the underlying `SHOWS` table. By default, HTML-DB only includes the first 15 values for the summaries. These 15 artists are the first 15 unique values for artists, after the `SHOWS` table is sorted by artist. The table has to be sorted by the aggregate column in order to come up with the total count.

Adding a New Page

You could improve the appearance of the default application easily by changing some of the attributes of the various pages. But you will probably get a broader introduction to these attributes, as well as add more cool functionality to the application, by adding a new page.

Since the shows in the SHOWS table all contain a date, it might be interesting to look at the shows as if they were part of a calendar. HTML-DB helps you to create these calendar pages with another wizard.

To begin the creation process, click on the Edit Application link in any page that you run, or use the bread crumbs at the top of a development page to go back to the home page for the application. At the top of the listing of pages for the application, click on Create Page, which brings up the page shown in Figure 23-42.

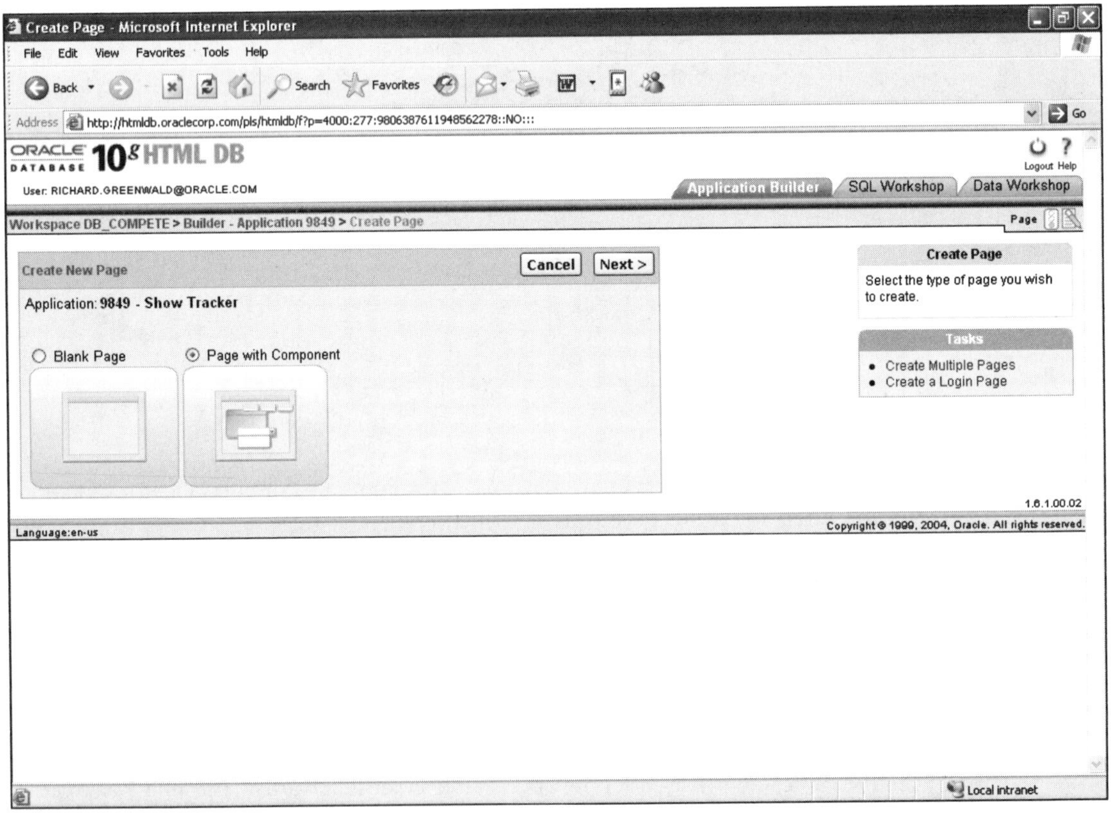

Figure 23-42: Creating a page.

The only two choices on this page are to create a blank page, which you will then fill in yourself, or to create a page with a component on it. Since a calendar is one of the choices for a component, select this icon and click on Next to bring up the next page, as shown in Figure 23-43.

In the development wizards, you can also just click on the appropriate icon, which is the equivalent of selecting the icon and clicking on Next.

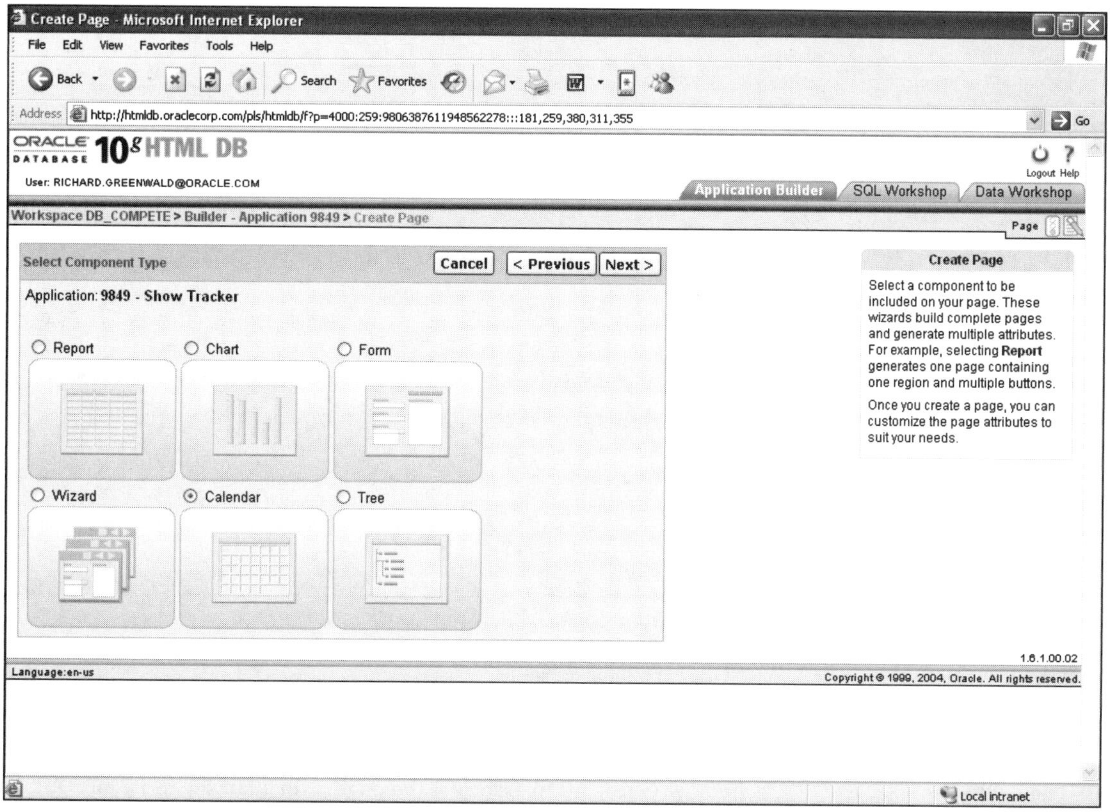

Figure 23-43: Selecting a component.

Select the Calendar component and click on Next. The page that comes up next gives you the choice between an SQL calendar or an easy calendar. The only difference between the two is that an SQL calendar allows you to write an SQL statement to deliver the appropriate date and display values. You might want to use this option if you had to manipulate data for either one of these options. Since the `SHOWS` table is set up with a proper date, you can use the Easy Calendar choice. Select this option and click on Next to bring up the page shown in Figure 23-44.

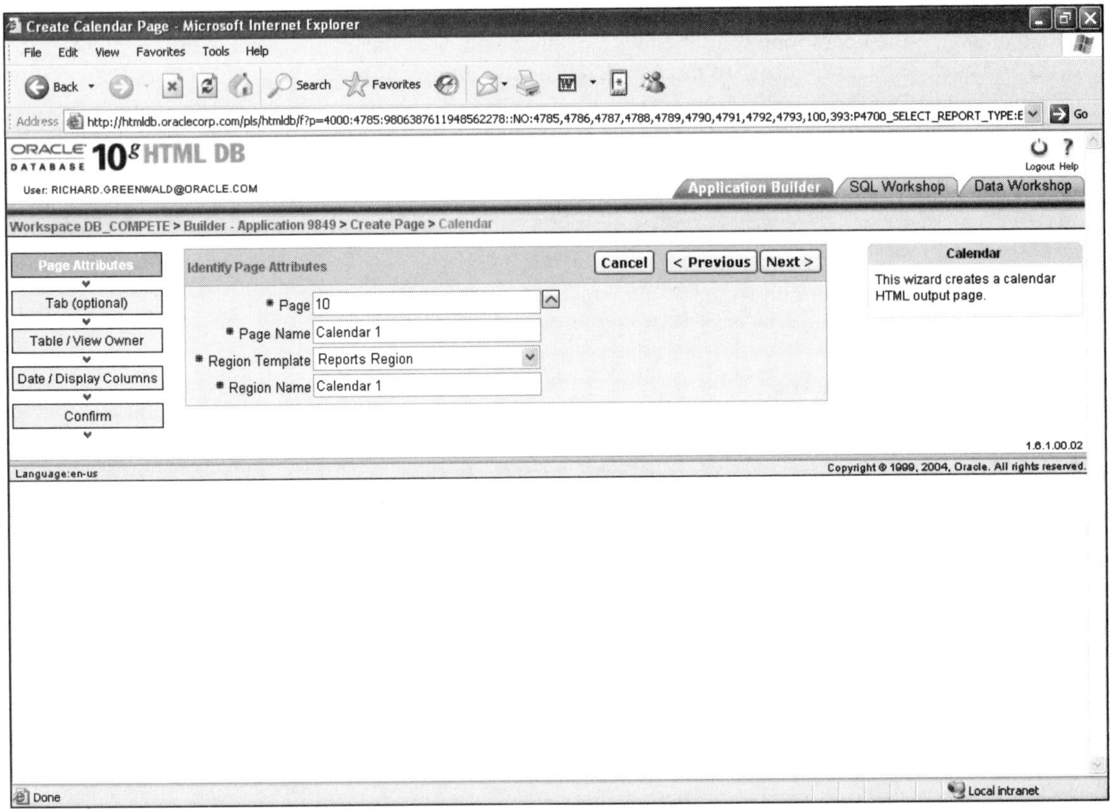

Figure 23-44: Page attributes for a calendar page.

Since this application will only have one calendar, you can change the name of the page and region to `Calendar`, and click on Next.

The next page asks you to specify how you want to associate the page with a tab set and a tab. A tab set is a group of tabs. Although this application only has one tab set, you could have two levels of tabs, with different tab sets. You don't have to assign a page to a tab, but you would have to create another method of navigation to the page, such as a link or menu choice. For the purpose of this application, you should select the second choice to use an existing tab set and add a new tab. Once you do, two list boxes will appear that ask you to select a tab set and give a name for a new tab. Select the only available tab set, the TS1 tab set, which already contains a tab for Shows and Analyze. Give the new tab the name of `Calendar` and click on Next.

The next page calls for you to select a table for the calendar component. Select the `SHOWS` table and click on Next to bring up the page shown in Figure 23-45.

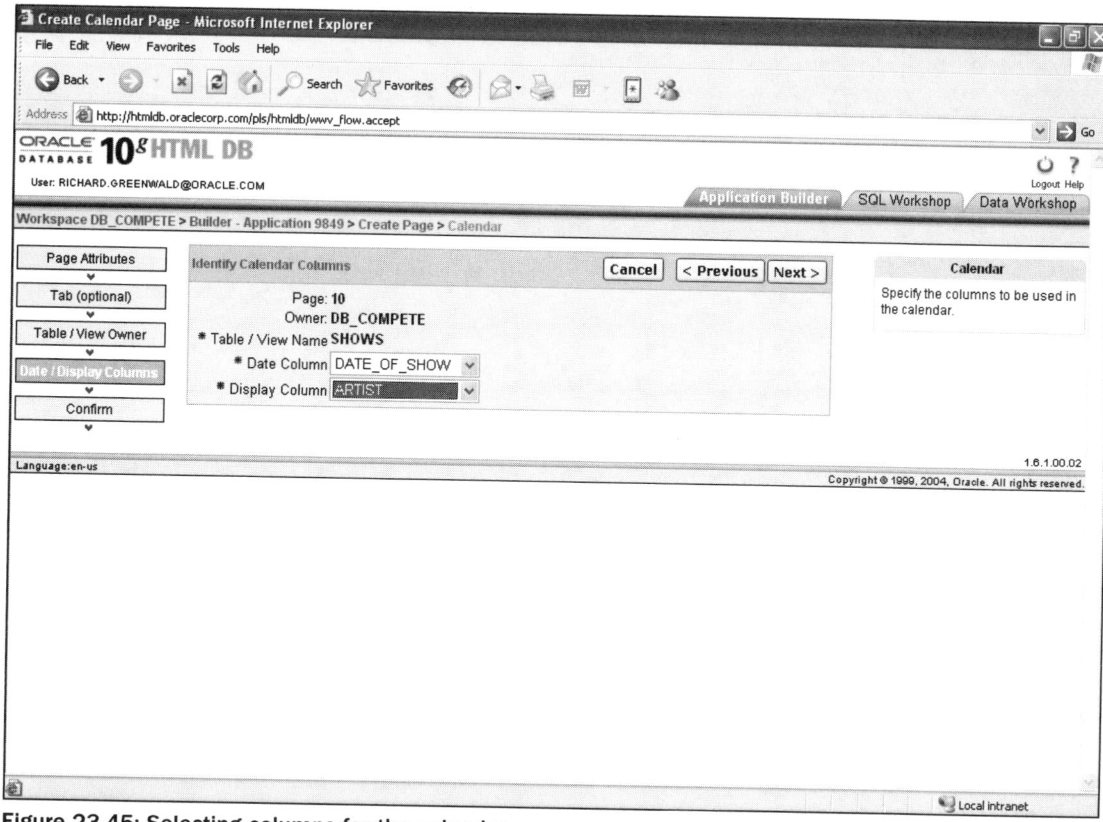

Figure 23-45: Selecting columns for the calendar.

This page prompts you for the most important information — what column contains the date and what column you want to display. Select the `DATE_OF_SHOW` column, which is the only one that appears, since it is the only date column in the table. Select the `ARTIST` column to display the name of the performer in the appropriate place on the calendar. Click on Next to finish your specification for the calendar component. Once you click on this button, you are presented with a page that summarizes the specifications you have made. Click on Finish to create the page, which brings up a success page.

On this page, click on the Run Page icon. You will first be asked to log in, and then our calendar will appear, complete with navigation push buttons that allow you to go to a previous or later month or to return to the current date. Use the Previous push button to go to June 2004, which is shown in Figure 23-46.

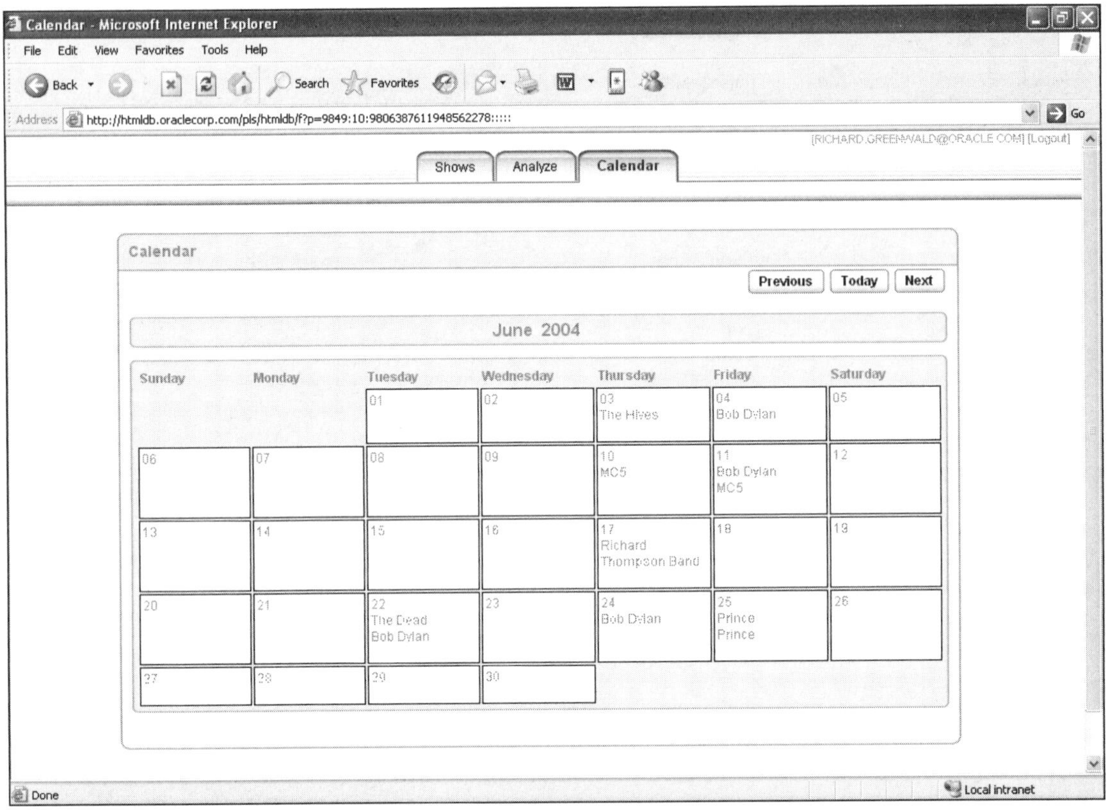

Figure 23-46: A month in your calendar.

If you felt it was somewhat cumbersome to move a month at a time, be aware that you could easily add push buttons to move a year at a time, or even add a data picker object to use the built-in functionality of that object to select a specific date and then move to it.

The calendar looks good, yes? But it cries out for a bit more functionality. It would be really useful if you could click on any of the shows listed and go to the update page for that show. Since that update page already exists, you can add this capability by modifying a few attributes of the page.

Modifying Page Attributes

To start the process, click on the Edit Page 10 link at the bottom of the page, although your page may have a different number. This action brings up the initial page attribute page shown in Figure 23-47.

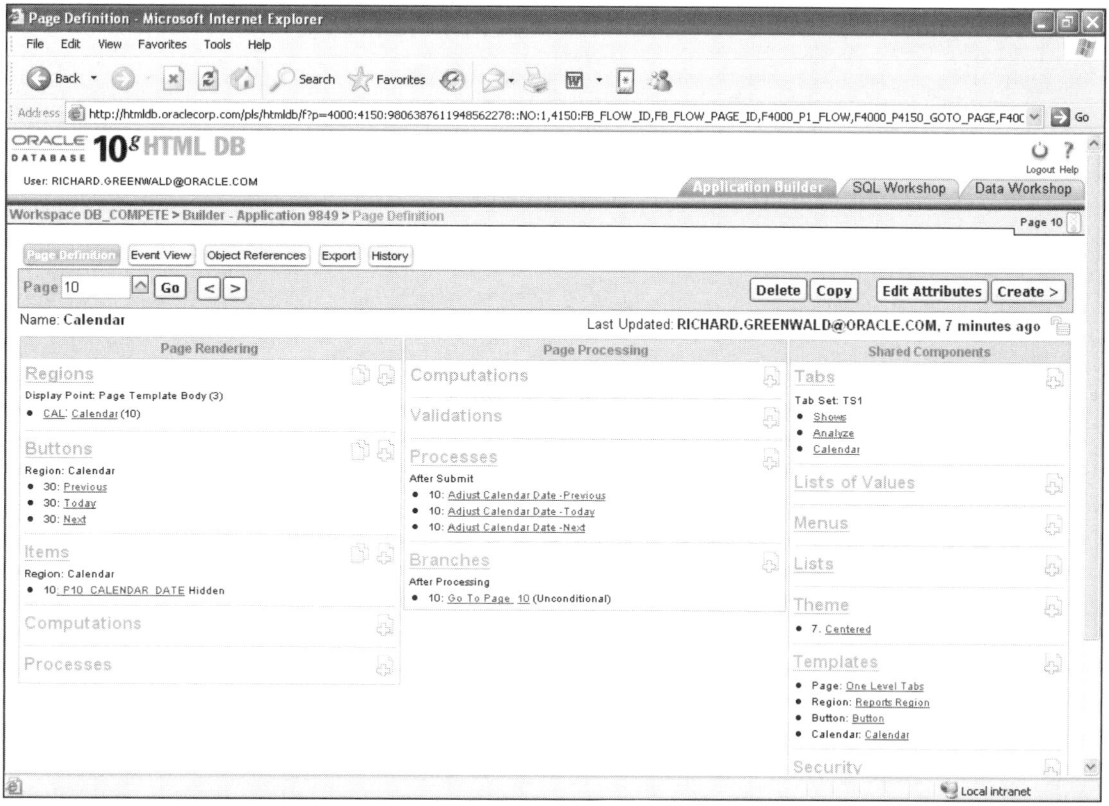

Figure 23-47: The initial page attribute page.

There are three basic areas of this page

- ❑ Page Rendering, which lists the objects on the page
- ❑ Page Processing, which lists the processes used in the page
- ❑ Shared components, which list the shared components that are part of the page

You can see that there are entries in many of these areas. It is beyond the scope of this chapter to describe all of the areas on this page. To make the desired modification, click on the Calendar entry in the Regions area, which is the upper left area on the page. The next page initially shows a tab with the Region Definition. Click on the tab to show the Calendar attributes. Once you bring up this tab, either click on the Column Link entry in the bread crumbs just below the heading or simply scroll down to the area shown in Figure 23-48.

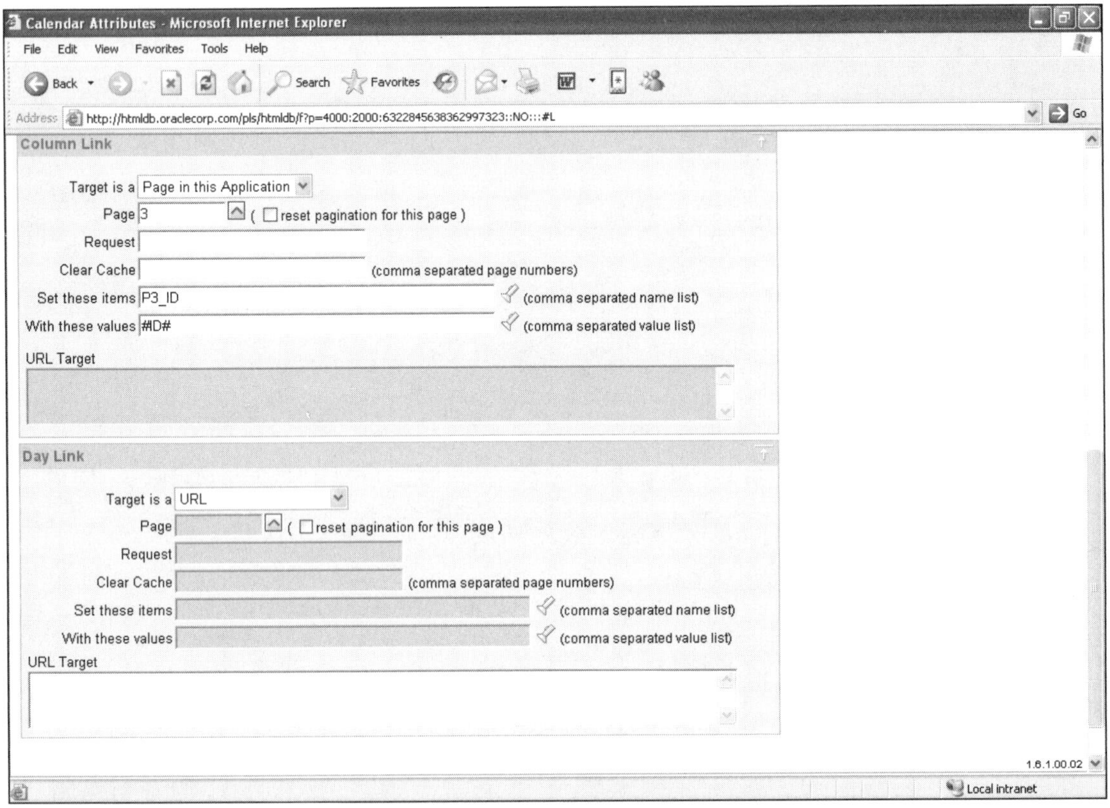

Figure 23-48: Adding a date link.

In this area, you have to fill in three pieces of information. The first is to select a page in the application to link to, which you can find by using the pop-up list that appears when you click on the up arrow to the right of the Page field. You should select the Update Form, which is Page 3.

The next step is to pass the information needed for the update page to properly display the right show. HTML-DB creates a data item for each column used in a page. By default, the item is given a name that follows the format of `Pnn_columnname`, where *nn* is the page number and *columnname* is the name of the column. Since the target page is Page 3 and the column name is ID, you should add the entry of P3_ID in the field labeled Set These Items. You want to pass the value of the ID column to the update page, so enter `#ID#` in the next field, labeled With These Values.

You could, of course, pass multiple values or link to something other than another page in the application.

You have done all that you have to do to add the desired functionality to the calendar. Scroll back up to the top of the page and click on the Apply Changes button. This action brings you back to the main page attributes page. On the far right of the main title bar for the page, next to the text with the page name, is a small icon of a traffic light. Click on this icon to run the page, as shown in Figure 23-49.

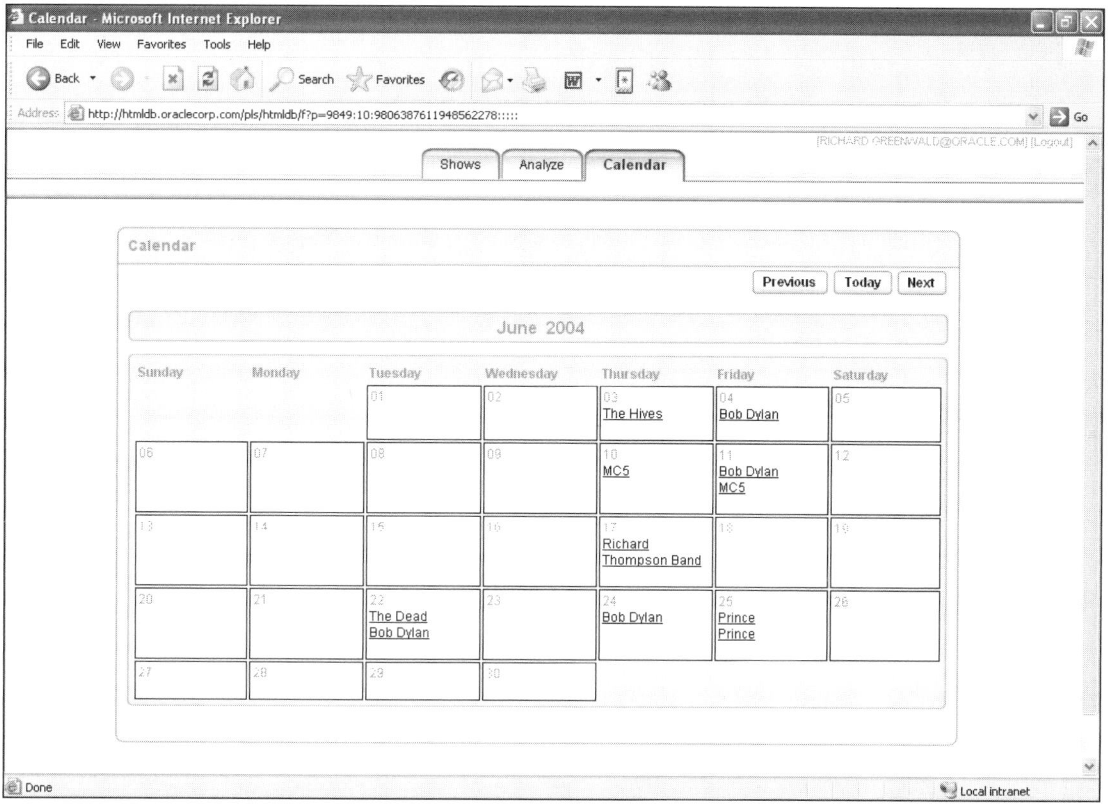

Figure 23-49: The new, improved calendar page.

This page has the same entries, but each entry is a link. You can click on any of the links to bring up the update page for that entry.

Running the Application

The only thing left for this application is to allow another user to access it from his or her browser. HTML-DB applications are accessed with the following URL code:

```
host:port/pls/htmldb/f?p=flow:port
```

where `host` is the name of the server hosting the HTML-DB packages, `port` is the port number for the Oracle HTTP Server (as mentioned, 7777 by default), `flow` is the number of the application (known as a flow in HTML-DB), and `page` is the page number within the application. If the hostname of your server was `RICKEG`, the application number was 104, and the starting page of the application was 1, the URL would look like this:

```
http://RICKEG:7777/pls/htmldb/f?p:103:1
```

If the initial page was a logon page, the user would have to log on before he or she could enter the application.

Is That All There Is?

There is a whole lot more in HTML-DB that space will not allow us to show you. For instance, HTML-DB provides a complete SQL interface to an Oracle database, as shown in Figure 23-50.

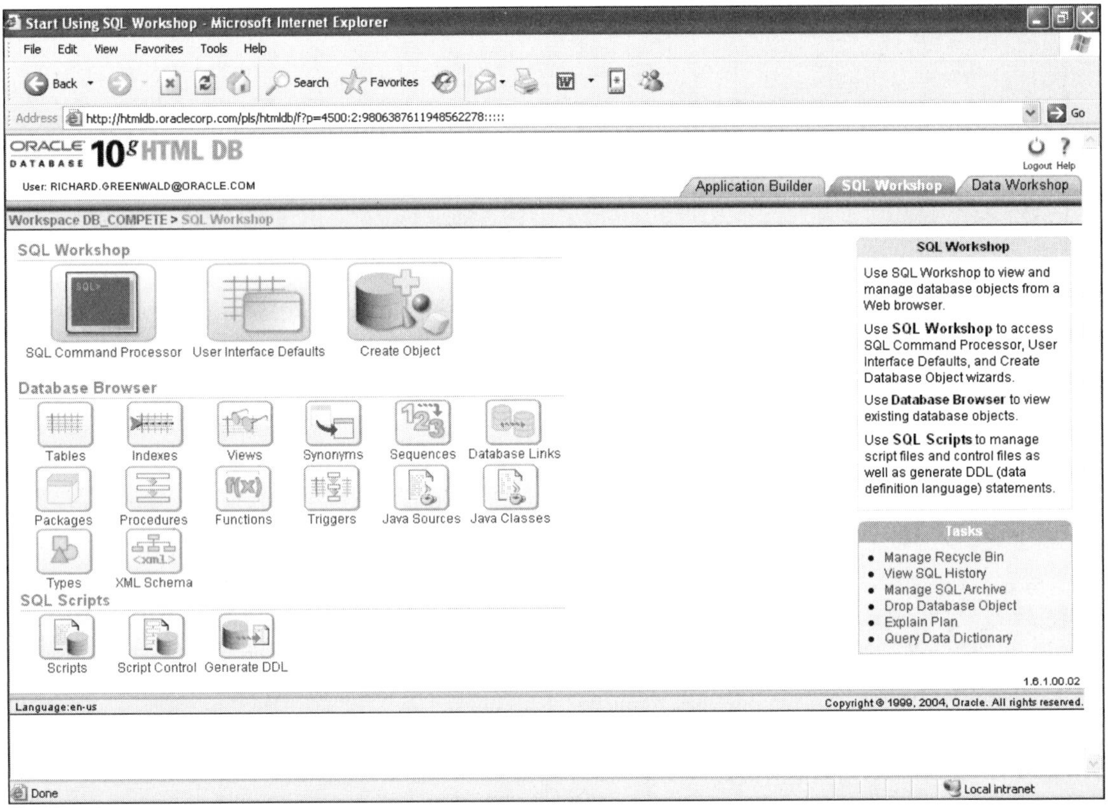

Figure 23-50: The SQL Workshop.

You can use the SQL Workshop to run SQL; create, view, and modify a wide variety of database objects; generate DDL for any particular object; or even create and run scripts.

There is also a lot more that you can do in HTML-DB applications, including creating pages that use automatically generated calendars to show time-related information, or tree structures to provide an easy way to drill down on data in multiple levels. But the page limitations of this book prevent these type of explorations.

The Next Step

You have seen a lot of functionality in just this brief tour of the HTML-DB environment. If you think that this type of application can address some of your users' needs, you should start working with HTML-DB to learn more about its capabilities. Although the documentation for the tool is somewhat sparse at this writing, the wizard-driven nature of the environment makes it easy to simply play around to discover what you need. There is also an active support forum at the Oracle Technology Network, `http://otn.oracle.com`.

You should also be aware that HTML-DB receives periodic updates outside of the normal upgrade cycle for the Oracle database. By the time you read this, a new release of HTML-DB should have a number of enhancements, including a more robust way to create applications automatically. You can keep track of all the latest news about HTML-DB at `www.oracle.com/technology/products/database/htmldb/index.html`.

Summary

HTML-DB is a tool you can use for creating HTML-based applications. You can generate a fairly substantial default application with just a handful of mouse clicks. You can use this default application as a starting point and then modify it or add your own custom reports, forms, and charts to it.

HTML-DB can also be used to create and manage database objects — you can even create a table directly from a spreadsheet in one process. Because HTML-DB builds HTML-based applications, the applications are truly cross-platform. And, since the HTML-DB development environment is also HTML-based, you can create applications from virtually any platform.

HTML-DB is a great addition to the database functionality of Oracle 10*g*.

24

High-Speed Data Movement

For many years, data warehouses have been populated using incremental "batch" loading techniques—at predefined times. For example, a load into the data warehouse of new and modified transactions within the last 24 hours from source systems might be scheduled at midnight. This approach is common especially where large data volumes are to be loaded and complex data transformations occur during the loading process. We'll discuss Oracle facilities for such data loading and transformations in Chapter 25, "Data Loading and Management." However, as business decision makers change their focus from long-term and strategic planning to short-term and tactical judgments, the need for more current near real-time data grows. The Oracle database provides a number of facilities for data movement that can enable rapid and very frequent loading for near real-time analysis. These facilities are the subject of this chapter. Specifically, we'll focus on the Oracle Database 10*g* Data Pump, and Streams.

At first blush, the discussion of data movement may seem a little out-of-bounds for a programmers' book. After all, data movement is usually more often a topic in guides for database administrators or for data warehousing architects. We provide this discussion here since programmers play an important role in the determination of data and loading requirements and the building of extraction, transformation, and loading (ETL) scripts. This chapter and the next attempt to briefly explain what is possible and what a programmer should know about these processes. We hope that these chapters enable you to make better choices when selecting deployment strategies that meet your business' needs while also better leveraging your current technology infrastructure.

The first topic in this chapter describes export and import, a procedure not typically thought of as high speed for data movement. For many years, Oracle provided an export/import facility. The performance of this facility was greatly improved in a new version that first appeared in Oracle Database 10*g* and is now sometimes called the *Data Pump*. We'll describe how the new export/import is used and the relative performance that might be expected compared to the previous export/import.

In some situations, movement of entire tablespaces makes sense for bulk movement of data. Oracle's Transportable Tablespaces provide this capability. They are sometimes leveraged in combination with Oracle partitioning to enable very fast addition of large incremental data loads to very large data warehouses. For the first time in Oracle Database 10*g*, Transportable Tablespaces can be moved from source databases to target databases on platforms that have different operating systems.

Where near real-time data is needed, a *trickle* feed (a data feed where a little bit of data is loaded on a nearly continuous basis) can be preferable to traditional batch feeds. Oracle provides a Streams facility that is based on Advanced Queues and log-based replication enabling such feeds from Oracle sources, or from other sources (through the use of a Messaging Gateway).

Finally, since setting up and managing data movement is most often a job for a DBA, we'll briefly describe Enterprise Manager's role in Export/Import and Streams setup and management for the benefit of our audience of programmers. For more detailed explanations, we suggest you or your DBA also consult the Oracle administration references.

Export/Import and the "Data Pump"

Export and import utilities have long provided a means to move existing Oracle database data and objects (such as tables in Oracle format) from one Oracle database to another. The export/import support of movement of objects includes the meta data needed to re-create the tables' indexes, constraints, grants, and other attributes. At one time, the export and import provided the only set of utilities, aside from writing code, for moving data among Oracle instances running on different operating systems. Today there are other additional utilities that help enable this process (Transportable Tables Spaces and Streams), as we'll discuss in this chapter.

While useful for their heterogeneous support, export and import were not known for their performance until the arrival of Oracle Database 10*g*. The Oracle Database 10*g* Data Pump version continues to support the old export/import format such that data and objects from previous Oracle database versions can be imported into the current version. But the Data Pump adds much higher performing export (`expdp`) and import (`impdp`) utilities that support a new format for data and objects exchange. The Data Pump's new export utility is about 60 percent faster in single stream than the old export. It can be used in conjunction with external tables (described in the next chapter) for high-speed database "unloads" to data files.

A command line example of using the `empdp` utility to create a dump file follows and would work with the sample schema and data provided in a standard Oracle Database 10g installation provided the bi user has proper privileges for exporting `sh` schema files:

```
expdp bi/bi TABLES=sh.supplementary_demographics DUMPFILE=d:\my_data\demotable.dmp
NOLOGFILE=Y
```

This command would export the table `supplementary_demographics` to the dump file `demotable.dmp` in the `d:\my_data` directory.

In addition to command line access, the Data Pump export facility can also be accessed through Oracle Enterprise Manager. Figure 24-1 shows the Enterprise Manager interface to the new Data Pump export.

The Data Pump import is about 15 to 20 times faster in single stream than the old import. From the command line, `impdp` has a similar syntax for the import of Data Pump dumpfiles to the previously described `empdp`. However, since the Data Pump uses an import format that is new and consistent with Oracle Database 10*g* exports and there are many pre-Oracle Database 10*g* export files being created and in use, Oracle Enterprise Manager must be capable of importing both current and previous export formats. Hence, the new Enterprise Manager import interface (see Figure 24-2) allows you to specify whether the import is an Oracle Database 10*g* version or a pre–Oracle Database 10*g* version.

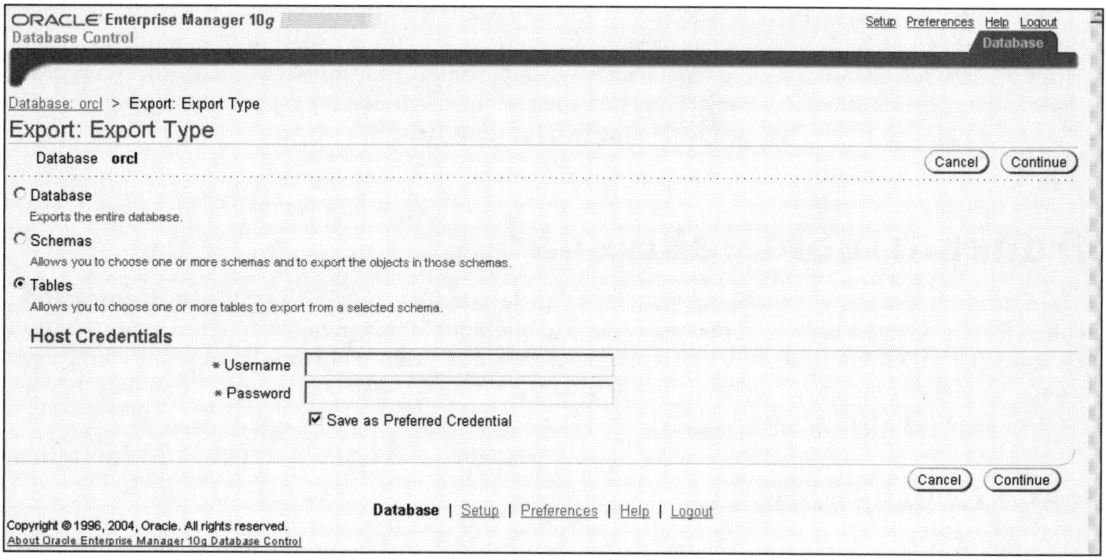

Figure 24-1: Oracle Enterprise Manager 10*g* Database Control Export interface.

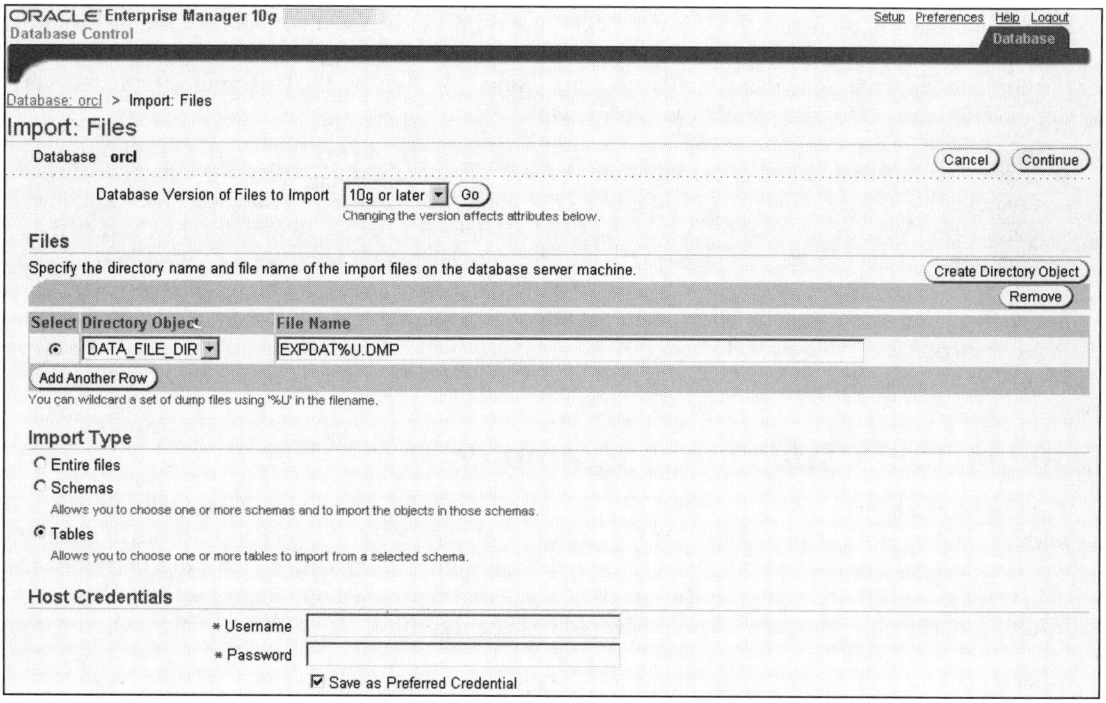

Figure 24-2: Oracle Enterprise Manager 10*g* Database Control Import interface.

Data Pump also features the ability to specify the number of threads for parallelization, restart export and import of jobs, detach and reattach from long-running jobs for monitoring from multiple locations, support network connections to remote instances, and estimate how much disk an export will consume before the export is attempted. Object types can be selectively chosen for export and import using the Enterprise Manager interfaces pictured in the two previous figures.

Transportable Tablespaces

Transportable Tablespaces enable movement of Oracle data files containing table data, indexes, and other Oracle database objects from one database to another without going through an export/import process. Therefore, Transportable Tablespaces can provide an extremely rapid means of moving bulk amounts of data from one database to another. Transportable Tablespaces do require that data dictionaries for the source and target tables are identical.

Usage Considerations

Transportable Tablespaces are often used in conjunction with Oracle's Partitioning Option for the database. The Partitioning Option enables the database to be split by a variety of supported partitioning schemes, including by continuous ranges of values and discrete lists of values. The benefit to the Partitioning Option is that new partitions can be added and loaded and indexes can be locally applied while the rest of the database is operational. It is this capability that is frequently used with Transportable Tablespaces as part of the high-speed load process. There are also backup advantages and some potential query performance advantages to using the Partitioning Option. As a result, the Partitioning Option is very popular for large-scale data warehouse deployment.

Transportable Tablespaces first appeared in the Oracle8*i* version of the database. The initial release had several restrictions, including the need for identical Oracle database versions on identical hardware/operating system platforms, with identical block sizes for Oracle database sources and targets. The Oracle9*i* database version removed the restriction for source/target common database block sizes. As of Oracle Database 10*g*, Transportable Tablespaces can be used between Oracle database sources and targets that reside on different hardware platforms running different operating systems. A sample of some of the platforms you can now move Transportable Tablespaces to from a 32-bit Windows platform include 64-bit HP-UX, IBM AIX, Sun Solaris, and Linux.

Transportable Tablespace Examples

The following example shows how you can assemble and move Transportable Tablespaces for single or multiple tablespaces and partitions (that are, of course, built on tablespaces). For purposes of illustration, we show moving a single partition, a `sales_q4_2001` partition, from a `sales` table to a partitioned target data warehouse. This example uses the sample schema that is part of a standard Oracle Database 10*g* installation. We'll first show the steps that would be used regardless of whether partitioning is involved.

The first step is to physically create a table to contain data to be transported:

```
CREATE tablespace example_tts datafile 'transport_sales.dbf' size 20m reuse
autoextend on;
```

You might also create the tablespace through Oracle Enterprise Manager Database Control (under the Administration tab).

In the next step, a Transportable Tablespace is defined and populated from a q4 partition on the source:

```
CREATE TABLE tts_sales_q4_2001
TABLESPACE example_tts
NOLOGGING
AS
SELECT prod_id, cust_id, time_id, channel_id, promo_id, quantity_sold, amount_sold
FROM sh.sales partition (sales_q4_2001);
```

Next, the tablespace to set to read-only (assuming you have proper privileges):

```
ALTER TABLESPACE example_tts READ ONLY;
```

Note that example_tts could contain multiple tables. Keep in mind that transport of tablespaces is allowed only for a complete self-contained set of tablespaces such that they don't have dependencies that extend to other tablespaces that are not included.

If source and target data dictionaries are not identical for tablespaces to be moved, the meta data describing objects in the Transportable Tablespace must be exported from the source. The syntax using Oracle's export utility would be similar to the following:

```
EXP TRANSPORT_TABLESPACE = y
TABLESPACES = example_tts
FILE = sales_q4.dmp
```

In this example, the file named sales_q4.dmp will contain the meta data. Next, the meta data is imported at the target using the import utility:

```
IMP TRANSPORT_TABLESPACE = y
DATAFILES = 'transport_sales.dbf'
TABLESPACES = example_tts
FILE = sales_q4.dmp
```

Data can then be inserted from the tts_sales_q4_2001 Transportable Tablespace created previously. In a practical implementation, you would probably create equivalent partitions in the target data warehouse to be populated. In this example, we have already created a sales_q4_2001 partition in the target database. We will insert the data into our target data warehouse partition using the following syntax:

```
INSERT /*+ APPEND */ into sales_q4_2001
SELECT * FROM tts_sales_q4_2001;
commit;
```

Since for a new partition at the destination, indexes and constraints should match those in other target partitions, you will likely need to create indexes and add constraints to multiple partition columns as part of this process, thus adding several steps to the process.

Next, let's compare this somewhat lengthy process that can be used regardless of the presence of partitions to one where we leverage the fact that each partition has its own tablespace. Because of this, the need to create a temporary copy can be eliminated. Instead, you can simply transport that tablespace to the target by setting the tablespace to read only and exchange the partition to a separate table (using ALTER TABLE and EXCHANGE PARTITION) while maintaining indexes and validation. In this example, we'll first add a new partition to the example schema. The syntax is as follows:

```
ALTER TABLE sh.sales ADD PARTITION sales_q1_2004
 VALUES LESS THAN (TO_DATE('01-APR-2004','dd-mon-yyyy'));
```

We would then create a table tts_sales_q1_2004 similar to the previously described example of creating tts_sales_q4_2001. Next, we would exchange partitions as follows:

```
ALTER TABLE sh.sales EXCHANGE PARTITION sales_q1_2004
 WITH TABLE tts_sales_q1_2004 INCLUDING INDEXES WITH VALIDATION;
```

This use of EXCHANGE PARTITION is very popular where large bulk data increments are moved from Oracle partitioned sources to Oracle partitioned targets.

Streams

Oracle Streams enable sharing of data and events between source databases and target databases/applications. Sources and targets involved need not be identical, since transformations can be processed at multiple points in a data streams process. Unlike the other data movement capabilities described in this chapter, Streams are usually thought of as continuous feeds, not as batch (bulk) feeds. The model for source to target deployment is commonly called *publish and subscribe*—where the publishers are the databases that are the sources of change and the subscribers are the defined destinations.

Oracle Streams leverage two database features, Advanced Queues and log-based replication, that are used in combination and are key to enabling "near real-time" or "trickle feed" deployments for data warehouses and other destinations. The Advanced Queues (AQ) capability has existed in the Oracle database since Oracle 8. AQ enables transportation of messages over queues among Oracle databases or using Oracle's Message Gateway to other queuing solutions such as IBM's MQSeries and TIBCO. The log-based replication feature was added to the Oracle database in the Oracle9*i* Release 2 version and is based on tracking of record changes in Oracle database logs. Coincidentally, Streams also became available in the Oracle9*i* Release 2 database. An additional component, the Oracle's Application Server, provides a middleware component for a Streams deployment.

Streams Phases and Processes

The Streams process can be described as having three phases: capture, staging, and consumption of data or structural changes. Events can include data manipulation language (DML) and/or data definition language (DDL) changes. Streams capture changes in messages at the source database that are enqueued as events, propagated from one queue to another, and dequeued and applied at a target database using the AQ functionality. Each Streams process has a rule set containing user-specified rules for capture and apply. Streams can be programmed to handle automatic conflict detection and resolution of any conflicts using custom or Oracle provided conflict resolution routines.

Transformations can be applied at various points along the way and might include changing column data types, renaming a column, or using PL/SQL functions. Keep in mind that since the purpose in using Streams is to create a continuous feed, you will probably not want these transformations to be overly complex or lengthy. For example, comparisons of names and addresses against a table of valid values for all of North America with subsequent cleanup is probably not advised! Complex transformations introduce latency (since they can take considerable time) and processing cycles. If you need to perform complex transformations to meet business requirements, a better solution might be manual or automated creation of more traditional ETL scripts for batch loading as described in the next chapter. If your business needs to analyze near real-time data, then you might focus your attention on ensuring cleaner source data through stricter data input standards during population of your transactions/source systems.

The log-based portion of the capture in Streams gathers information directly from Oracle redo logs creating logical change records (LCRs) that can be part of the events. Redo logs that are accessed can include archived redo logs and active redo logs.

After events are captured, they are placed in a staging area queue. AQ provides the engine to store messages in queues for retrieval and processing. Messaging can occur via synchronous communications (based on requests/replies) or asynchronous communications in a disconnected or deferred model. In synchronous communications, a subscriber (application or other staging area) evaluates the contents of the message including rules and, if matching the subscription, will consume the message or propagate it to the correct other staging area. Alternatively, events in staging areas might also be propagated using routing specifications.

When messages in the staging area are consumed by the apply engine, changes are applied to the target database or consumed by an application. A variety of apply mechanisms are supported, including a default apply for DML and DDL changes and user-supplied LCRs, horizontal subsetting where subsets of the entire data source are only valid at certain targets, user-defined apply procedures, and application explicit dequeues.

Most programmers' activity will probably center on creation and maintenance of the DML and DDL scripts for Streams AQ. Most often, these scripts are hand-coded. However, Oracle Warehouse Builder (OWB, described in chapter 25) is a code generator for ETL and does provide support for AQ. For example, AQ scripts can be deployed to OWB targets and then set up to be subscribers to appropriate sources.

Configuring and Monitoring Advanced Queues

Advanced Queues are most commonly scheduled and managed by database administrators. This strategy is appropriate in many organizations, since DBAs are usually responsible for overall performance of the systems involved. Most DBAs will use Oracle Enterprise Manager to create, start, stop, and drop queues; manage propagation schedules; add and remove subscribers; and create, modify, or remove transformations. Queue status can also be viewed using Enterprise Manager, including error reporting and statistics.

The setup of AQ is typically through the Oracle Workflow component of Oracle Application Server Control. Oracle Enterprise Manager Grid Control is often the starting point, since it provides access to all of the needed Oracle application servers and databases. Through Grid Control, with proper access rights, it is possible to log into an individual Application Server Control interface that is installed as part of each Application Server infrastructure.

To enable AQ data management and access, several database roles are provided as part of a standard Oracle installation. The roles include AQ_ADMINISTRATOR_ROLE, AQ_USER_ROLE, and GLOBAL_AQ_USER_ROLE. The DBA can assign AQ roles to users through Oracle Enterprise Manager. Figure 24-3 shows how one might determine if AQ roles are assigned for a specific user.

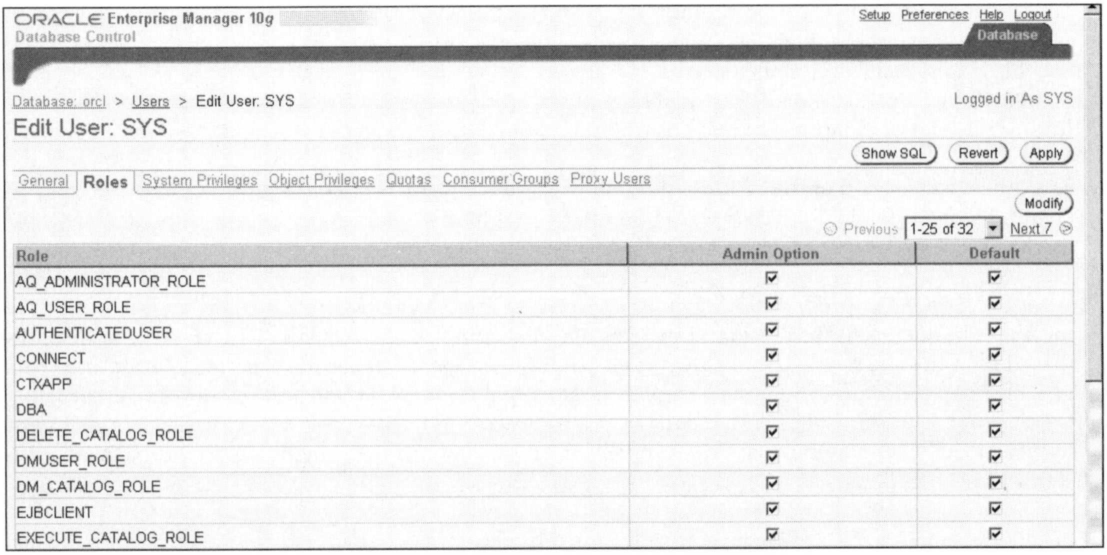

Figure 24-3: Oracle Enterprise Manager 10g Database Control interface to roles.

Two parameters must be set in the database initialization parameters: AQ_TM_PROCESSES (set to at least one to enable time monitoring processes that monitor delay events and notification mailers) and JOB_QUEUE_PROCESSES (set to 11 or more to handle propagation of Business Event System messages by Oracle Workflow). Figure 24-4 shows setting of the AQ_TM_PROCESSES through Enterprise Manager.

After the parameters and roles are set properly, queues can be created through the Application Server Control link to Oracle Workflow. The first step when using the Workflow for AQ setup is usually creating a database link (DBLINK) between source and destination and then testing the connection by the DBA or application server manager. Workflow is then used to set up the functional processes through which a message will proceed as part of a business event. Functions are defined in the order that they must occur, establishing prerequisites Once these flows are created, Workflow enables monitoring of business event agents, and setup and monitoring of propagation scheduling. Monitoring of multiple agents and configurations is possible by using the Enterprise Manager Grid Control Management System interface to the agents shown in Figure 24-5. Deployed agents can show details such as queue name, owner, type, and status (ready, waiting, processed, expired, or undeliverable) for monitoring purposes.

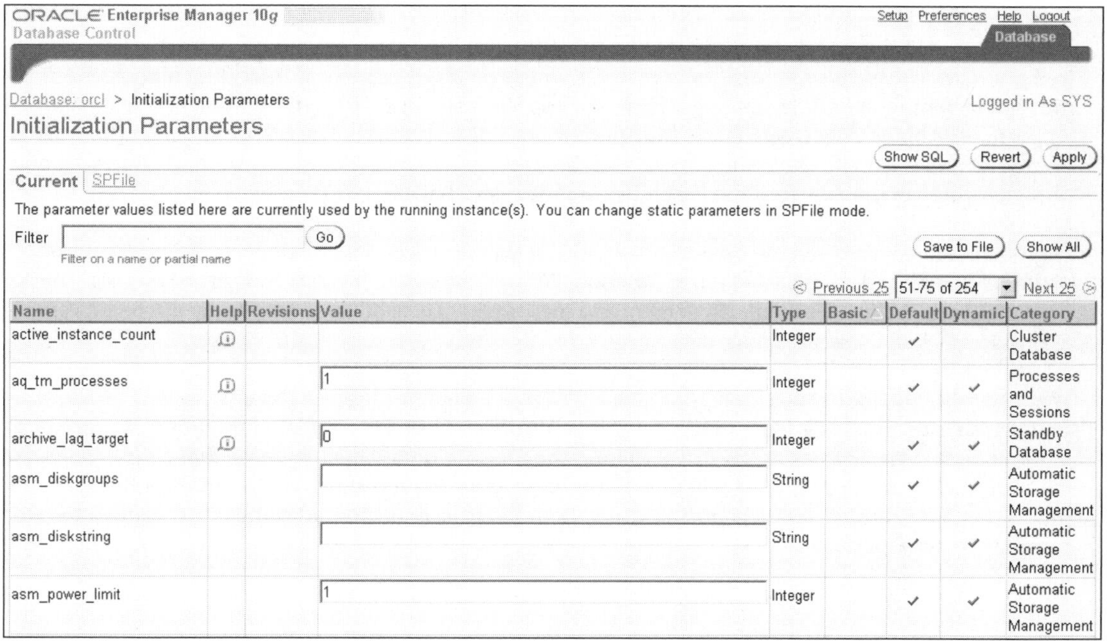

Figure 24-4: Setting `AQ_TM_PROCESSES` in Oracle Enterprise Manager 10g Database Control.

Figure 24-5: Oracle Enterprise Manager 10g Grid Control management of agents.

Summary

In this chapter, we covered several features in the Oracle database capable of providing high-speed data movement between multiple databases. Each of these features can enable business analysts to gain timely access to distributed data when data is transported to a single database. The usefulness and appropriateness of each feature is usually determined by similarities and differences between sources and targets, since each provides different functionality and capability to propagate changes.

High speeds in data transfer are particularly attainable where source data is relatively clean. The introduction of data cleansing and complicated transformations can add latency to the data movement process. The next chapter takes a closer look at data movement and management capabilities typically used where cleansing is a consideration. In those situations, data transfer and loading is generally a batch process.

What should you do if source data is not clean, there is a need for high-speed data movement, and transformations would be particularly complex? The best solution might be elimination of unclean data at the source. A typical way to do this is to limit the input of data values to those that can be validated at the source at the time of input. While this may add programming complexity to source online transaction processing applications, it also significantly reduces the time and programming effort needed to build complex transformations later.

25

Data Loading and Management

In Chapter 24, "High-Speed Data Movement," we covered the use of Streams, Transportable Tablespaces, and the new high-speed import/export mechanism in Oracle Database 10*g*. In this chapter, we'll discuss facilities more typically used in batch loading. As noted in the previous chapter, the scheduling and maintenance of loading processes are often managed by a database administrator. A database administrator and database architect are usually directly involved in the design of such loading scripts, since they must perform well and provide a true representation of the data that business analysts desire. This chapter provides an introduction into the capabilities that Oracle has in this area. You'll likely want to further consult data warehousing and database administration books on this topic.

Batch loads are typically used when very large data volumes are loaded and where data transformations are necessary and complex. Oracle includes SQL*Loader, External Tables, and other extraction, transformation, and loading (ETL) extensions to the database. We describe these capabilities and provide some example scripts in this chapter. Since ETL scripts are increasingly more likely to be created using ETL tools instead of through manual programming, we also describe how you can use Oracle's Warehouse Builder (OWB) tool to generate ETL scripts.

A classic approach to ETL includes processing each needed transformation separately with creation and loading of temporary staging tables at each step. This approach provides a means to easily determine where problems might occur in a series of ETL processes. The alternative approach, used where load times and available disk space are a concern, is to combine multiple transformations into a single SQL statement.

In this chapter, we describe many techniques for speed-up, including combining of transformations and leveraging ETL functionality that Oracle has introduced in the database. We discuss how minimizing steps and Oracle's features can enable parallel pipelined data transformations to occur.

Parallel pipelining is an important concept in speed-up. Parallel pipelining enables loading to begin while other data is still going through the transformation process. Leveraging pipelining and other features outlined here can make a dramatic improvement in reducing the time it takes to extract, transform, and load your data.

We'll also describe how partitions in Oracle's Partitioning Option can be leveraged to reduce these load windows, and we'll touch on the usage of Enterprise Manager for scheduling jobs and maintenance of partitions.

SQL*Loader

SQL*Loader enables loading data from flat files into an Oracle database. In legacy relational databases where ODBC is not supported, or where nonrelational databases are used, dumping the data into a flat file may provide the best means to make the data available for movement. Of course, you might have your own set of flat files containing data from spreadsheets or other sources that you also want to load into Oracle.

Higher-speed direct-path loading provided through SQL*Loader can be used where data transformations between source and target are limited to data type conversions and handling `NULL`s. Where more complex transformations are needed, you can write the transformations in SQL and use the slower conventional-path loader. For additional speed-up, SQL*Loader can be set up to load jobs in parallel, providing scalable performance gains by taking advantage of multiple CPUs that are common in the database server computer platforms of today.

Direct path loading does have some restrictions. Tables to be loaded cannot have any transactions pending and the tables cannot be clustered. When loading a single partition, a global index must not have been applied. Referential and check constraints must not be enabled on the table that the partition is a member of. Finally, enabled triggers are not allowed.

For purposes of illustration, assume you have a sales data file from October of 2003 that you want to load into the sales fact table that is defined in the `sh` schema provided as part of the Oracle Database 10*g* standard installation. The name of the flat source data file in our illustration will be `salesOct2003.dat`, with fields in this file delimited by semicolons (`;`). A control file would need to be created that could be called from SQL*Loader. You will name the control file `sh_sales_fact.ctl`. The control file is created containing syntax similar to the following:

```
LOAD DATA
INFILE salesOct2003.dat
APPEND

INTO TABLE sh.sales
FIELDS TERMINATED BY ";"
(PROD_ID, CUST_ID, TIME_ID, CHANNEL_ID, PROMO_ID,
 QUANTITY_SOLD, AMOUNT_SOLD)
```

The data could be direct-path loaded using the following command from a valid administrator account:

```
sqlldr admin/password control=sh_sales_fact.ctl direct=true
```

Alternatively, through Oracle Enterprise Manager (installed as part of a standard Oracle Database 10*g* installation), you could run the control file by selecting the Maintenance tab and then the Load Data from File link. This wizard-driven utility first asks you for the control filename (see Figure 25-1), the data filename (if not specified in the control file), the load method, and options governing row skipping, load termination, and indexes. The wizard then provides you with a summary of your selections. You can then choose to submit the job or schedule it.

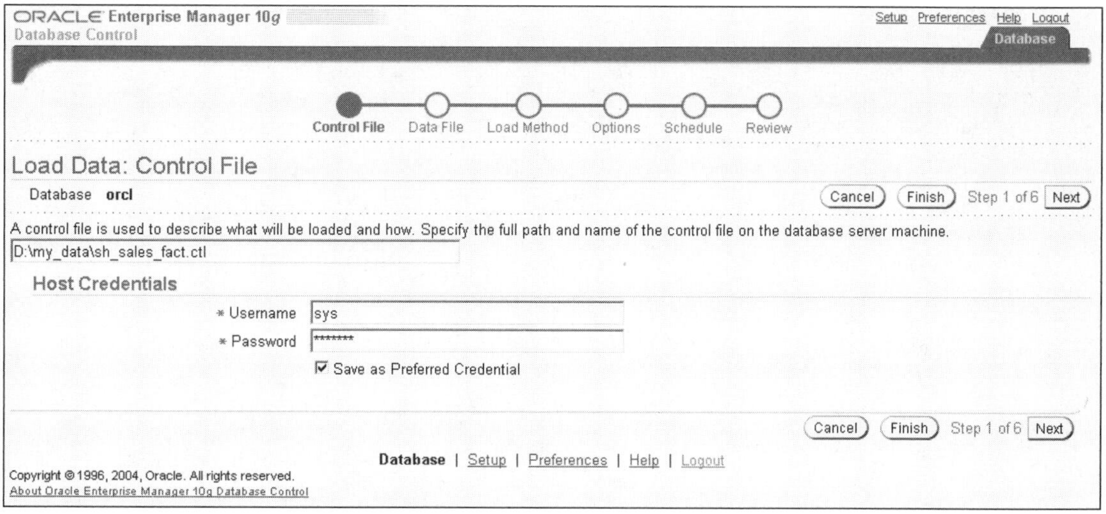

Figure 25-1: Oracle Enterprise Manager 10g Database Control interface to setting up and scheduling loads.

External Table Database Feature

Instead of first loading the data in the database and then applying SQL, external tables (first introduced as a database feature with Oracle9*i*) enable data in flat files to appear as if in a virtual database table for query and joining prior to data loading. SQL can be applied prior to loading to enable pipelining of the loading to occur during the transformation phase. Selecting from external tables is recommended as part of a loading process (using direct path insert as select into the database) when the external data source needs to be joined with a relational table and where transformations are complex. Prior to Oracle Database 10*g*, external tables must be read only. As of Oracle Database 10*g*, the external table feature can also be used for database unloads where data transfer is desired using the Data Pump described in the previous chapter.

Defining External Tables

An external table, such as the `sales_transactions_ext` table found in the sample `sh` schema provided as part of the Oracle Database 10*g* standard installation, is created using syntax similar to the following:

```
CREATE TABLE sh.sales_transactions_ext
(
prod_id NUMBER(6),
```

```
cust_id NUMBER,
time_id DATE,
channel_id NUMBER(2),
promo_id NUMBER(6),
quantity_sold NUMBER(3),
amount_sold NUMBER(10,2),
unit_cost NUMBER(10,2),
unit_price NUMBER(10,2)
)
ORGANIZATION external
(
TYPE oracle_loader
DEFAULT DIRECTORY data_file_dir
ACCESS PARAMETERS
(
RECORDS DELIMITED BY NEWLINE CHARACTERSET US7ASCII
BADFILE log_file_dir:'ext_1v3.bad'
LOGFILE log_file_dir:'ext_1v3.log'
FIELDS TERMINATED BY "|" LDRTRIM
)
location
(
'sale_1v3.dat'
)
)REJECT LIMIT UNLIMITED;
```

This script creates definitions that describe the external table representation of data fields to the database server. You might think of the external table definition as a view that allows you to run SQL against the external data without physically first loading it into the database. The definitions are used when needed during the SQL process.

In the above example, directories were preassigned as part of the Oracle Database 10*g* installation process. If you were to create these directories, you would use syntax similar to the following for data_file_dir:

```
CREATE DIRECTORY data_file_dir AS
'd:\oracle\product\10.1.0\DB_1\demo\schema\sales_history'
```

The actual name of the directory depends on where you installed the Oracle database on your system. You would use syntax similar to the following for log_file_dir:

```
CREATE DIRECTORY log_file_dir AS 'd:\oracle\product\10.1.0\DB_1\demo\schema\log'
```

Note that in Oracle9*i* and Oracle Database 10*g* Release 1, external tables cannot be temporary tables nor can you specify constraints on an external table. In addition, an external table cannot contain object type, varray, or LONG columns. As restrictions change with releases, you should also consult the Oracle SQL Reference documentation for the release you are using.

Loading from External Tables

Now that definitions have been set, you can use the `sales_transactions_ext` external table definitions from within your database to load data. For example, you might want to load data from your flat file source into your database target `costs` table by leveraging the `sales_transactions_ext` definitions as in the following script:

```
INSERT /*+ APPEND */ INTO sh.costs
(
time_id,
prod_id,
promo_id,
channel_id,
unit_cost,
unit_price
)
SELECT
time_id,
prod_id,

promo_id,
channel_id,

SUM (unit_cost),
SUM (unit_price)
FROM sh.sales_transactions_ext
GROUP BY time_id, prod_id, channel_id, promo_id;
```

Transformations

The data you wish to load from your source systems may not exist in the form you desire in your target database. For example, data fields may be of inconsistent lengths or types. You might also need to cleanse the data and remove invalid entries or combine duplicate entries. Transformations are often used for these purposes.

Transformations are typically written in SQL or PL/SQL, or by using table functions. SQL transformations include `CREATE TABLE AS SELECT` (for new tables) and `INSERT TABLE AS SELECT` (for existing tables and illustrated in the previous coding example). Oracle9*i* and newer database releases also feature `UPDATE`, `MERGE`, and multi-table insert SQL transformations.

`CREATE TABLE AS SELECT` and `INSERT TABLE AS SELECT` provide an efficient means for executing a query and storing the results of the query. Either can be used for data substitution, or you might choose to use `UPDATE` for data substitution. You would typically not select to use `UPDATE`, however, if a large number of rows were involved. `MERGE` provides better performance and simpler coding where a value may be updated in a row (if that row exists) or inserted (if it does not exist).

An example of how you might apply `MERGE` in combination with `UPDATE` follows:

```
MERGE INTO sh.sales
USING sh.sales_transactions_ext
ON (sales_transactions_ext.prod_id=sales.prod_id and
    sales_transactions_ext.time_id=sales.time_id and
    sales_transactions_ext.channel_id=sales.channel_id and
    sales_transactions_ext.promo_id=sales.promo_id and
```

```
    sales_transactions_ext.cust_id=sales.cust_id)
WHEN MATCHED THEN
UPDATE SET sales.quantity_sold=sales_transactions_ext.quantity_sold,
           sales.amount_sold=sales_transactions_ext.amount_sold
WHEN NOT MATCHED THEN
INSERT VALUES (sales_transactions_ext.prod_id, sales_transactions_ext.cust_id,
               sales_transactions_ext.time_id, sales_transactions_ext.channel_id,
               sales_transactions_ext.promo_id,
               sales_transactions_ext.quantity_sold,
               sales_transactions_ext.amount_sold);
```

In the previous example, when the `id` fields match, an `UPDATE` occurs. If the `id` fields don't match, a new record is to be inserted via an `INSERT`.

Multi-table insert enables insertion of data into one or more tables depending on the business transformation rules that are applied. Multi-table inserts can be unconditional, conditional `ALL` for all values, or conditional `FIRST` for values given a higher priority. Conditional and unconditional inserts can be combined (depending on business rules) in the same statement.

Using simple PL/SQL, transformation of data occurs row by row. Prior to Oracle9*i*, intermediate staging tables (with their overhead and performance implications) were generally used where multiple transformations occurred. Oracle added Table Functions in Oracle9*i* to enable pipelined and parallel execution of transformations. Table Functions can return multiple rows, use cursors (a set of rows) as input, allow subqueries to pass multiple rows as results to the functions, and return result sets incrementally.

Change Data Capture

Often you want to extract data that has changed in the source system. Many companies have sought an easy method to enable this capability. Solutions generally have included the use of timestamps in source data, partitions identified by time, analysis of tables in their before and after states, and dumping of updated values immediately to staging areas for propagation to downstream systems. For example, materialized views use triggering within the Oracle database for Change Data Capture and leverage materialized views logs to keep track of changes.

Oracle introduced Change Data Capture in Oracle9*i*, but because of numerous changes, you'll probably want to investigate this capability beginning with Oracle Database 10*g* targets. Both source and target tables can exist in versions of the Oracle Database 10*g*. (Oracle9*i* Release 2 source Change Data Capture is also supported with Oracle Database 10*g* targets provided those targets are at Oracle Database 10*g* Release 2 or later.) Change Data Capture can operate in synchronous mode, where changed data is captured with each SQL statement performing a data manipulation language (DML) operation such as an `INSERT`, `UPDATE`, or `DELETE`. Change Data Capture can also be used in an asynchronous fashion (in the Enterprise Edition of the Database) after commits occur. Asynchronous Change Data Capture leverages the data that is sent to Oracle redo logs and Oracle's Streams (described in Chapter 24, "High-Speed Data Movement").

Change Data Capture uses a publish and subscribe model. Database administrators generally set up and manage the infrastructure serving as publisher. The DBAs define source databases and a staging database (including a change table, change sets — that is, logical grouping of changed data — and change source). DBAs give access to subscribers needing the changed data that is present in the change tables.

Partitioning and the Speed of ETL

Oracle's Partitioning Option, available in the Oracle Enterprise Edition of the database, is frequently implemented in large-scale data warehouses for improving manageability and availability. For example, the Partitioning Option enables partitions to be taken offline for maintenance while the rest of the database remains available. As a result, range partitioning (based on date) is common, though other partitioning schemes are sometimes used such as list partitioning based on a discrete set of values, or a composite of range-hash or range-list.

ETL efficiency and performance is often closely related to how the partitioning scheme is laid out, especially for large fact tables. Where range partitioning is used, a common approach is to partition using the same time unit as the frequency of load. For example, when daily loads are required, matching daily partitions are set up. Since partitions can be merged, they are often merged into less granular partitions later. A merger of hourly partitions into a monthly partition might take place at the end of each month.

A typical high-speed loading process starts with the creation of new partitions for the fact table in the data warehouse. Often a set of these partitions are created in anticipation of future loads. Outside of the data warehouse a table is created that exactly matches an empty partition and is loaded with data. Indexing and constraints are applied, and when ready, an `EXCHANGE PARTITION` is used to populate the data warehouse's empty partition.

Other alternatives exist. As an example, you might also use Transportable Tablespaces (discussed in Chapter 24) in situations where the original source system is also Oracle and tablespace definitions in source and target are identical.

Many companies seek to save on disk storage volume and the associated costs for their data warehouses by compressing data using Oracle's table compression feature. Keep in mind that loading data and compressing it during the process can double the load times. As a result, where partitioning is implemented, compression is sometimes applied only to older partitions that are no longer updated. Newer and changing partitions remain uncompressed. As partitions age and are no longer updated, they are then compressed as well.

Range partitioning enables maintenance of rolling windows where data remains online for fixed time periods (such as for the most recent 24 quarters). Using relatively simple syntax, you can add or delete partitions. In the sample `sh` schema provided as part of the Oracle Database 10*g* standard installation, the sales fact table is partitioned by quarters. If you were to add a new quarter partition, `SALES_Q1_2004`, and want to rid yourself of the oldest partition, `SALES_Q1_1998`, you can remove the oldest partition by simply using the following:

```
ALTER TABLE sh.sales DROP PARTITION sales_q1_1998
```

Figure 25-2 illustrates the rolling window process just described:

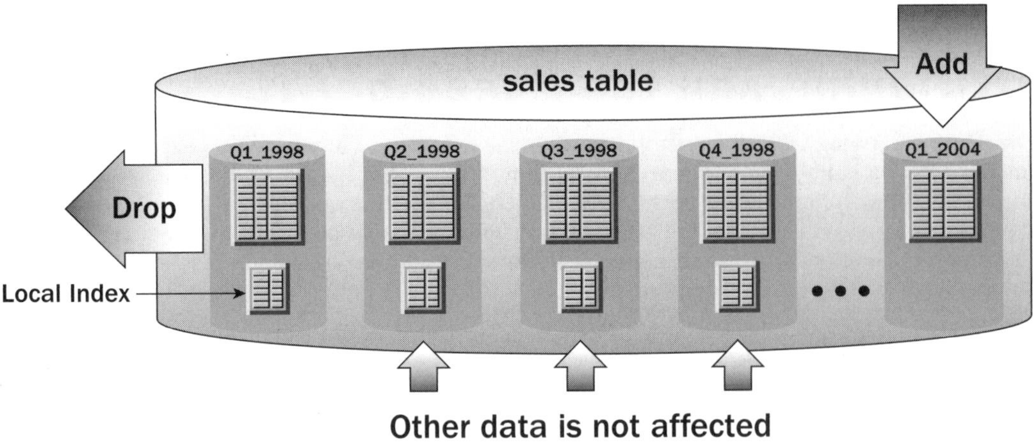

Figure 25-2: Rolling window illustration using Oracle Partitioning Option.

Of course, rather than using commands to add or delete partitions, you can also manage them through Enterprise Manager. Figure 25-3 shows some of the partitions in the sample `sh.sales` table as seen in Enterprise Manager. You'll see the buttons in this figure specifically for adding and deleting partitions.

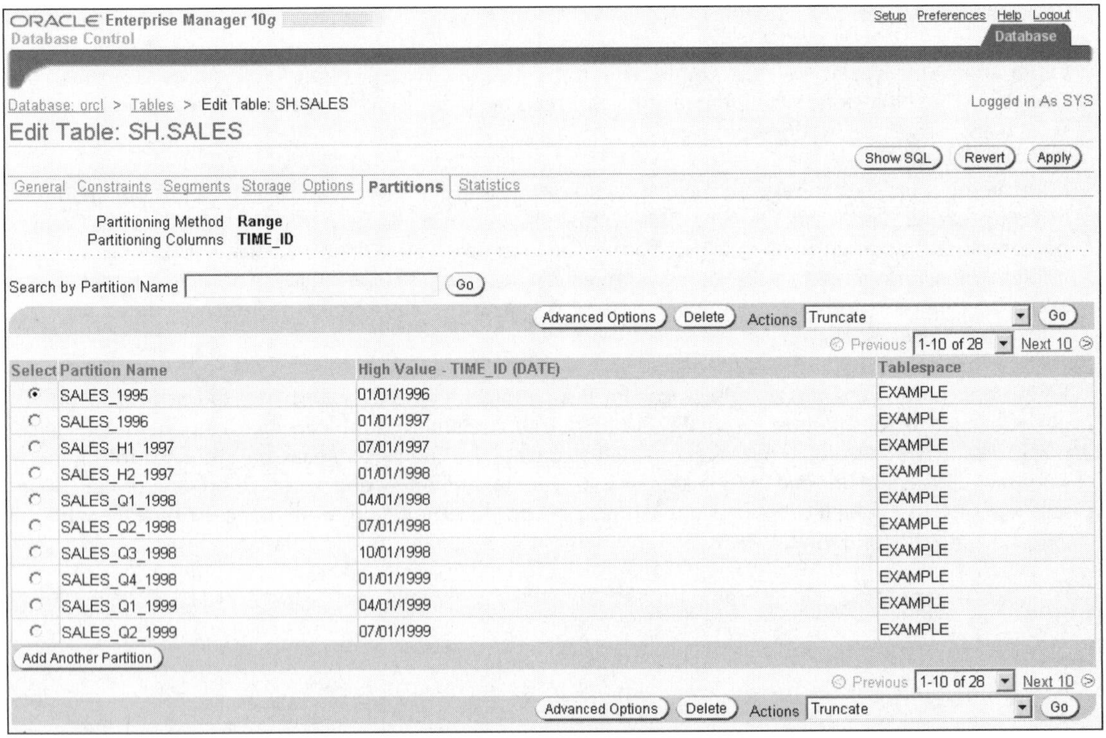

Figure 25-3: Partitions interface through Oracle Enterprise Manager 10g Database Control.

In Chapter 26, "Business Intelligence Query," we'll describe the usefulness of materialized views in providing summary levels in the database enabling faster queries. As materialized views often need refreshing immediately or shortly after detailed tables are refreshed, partitioning of tables containing data at a detailed level can be helpful. Such partitioning enables parallel DML to occur during the materialized views refresh. As of Oracle9*i* , Partition Change Tracking (PCT) is also enabled for fast refresh when detailed tables are partitioned.

Oracle Warehouse Builder

Thus far, we have described rapid data movement and loading functionality in the Oracle database through manual creation of scripts. An increasingly common way of creating the needed ETL scripts is through the usage of tools. Oracle offers Oracle Warehouse Builder (OWB) as part of its Development Suite precisely for this purpose. For example, you can use OWB to generate ETL scripts in PL/SQL for populating a data warehouse or operational data store from a relational source. OWB can also generate SQL*Loader files for loading data from flat files. In addition, you can use OWB to design the target data warehouse, data mart, or operational data store tables. These designs can include star schema, third normal form, or variations. Table creation scripts for these targets can also be generated by OWB. OWB's meta data repository of source, target, and mapping information includes a browser interface for viewing meta data reports, data lineage diagrams, and impact analysis. A Runtime Audit Browser is deployed to the targets and provides HTML-based access to results information about loadings.

Typical Build and Deploy Steps Using OWB

Typical steps when using OWB often occur as follows:

1. Design the target tables or import meta data that describes the target tables. These designs sometimes include dimensions, levels, hierarchies, attributes, and facts.
2. Import the meta data describing the source(s) to be used.
3. Build mappings from source table columns to target table columns using OWB's graphical drag-and-drop interface, including transformations, joins, filters, and other operations.
4. Design any process flows where there are dependencies between ETL jobs.
5. Validate the design including source to target mappings.
6. Generate the ETL scripts.
7. Instantiate (transfer) the ETL scripts to the target system.
8. Register ETL jobs with a job scheduler, most commonly using Oracle Enterprise Manager.
9. Run the job(s) that populate the target.
10. Review the results of the load using the Runtime Audit Browser on the target.

If you use OWB to design your target tables, you would also generate the table creation scripts in OWB, transfer those scripts to your target system, and run the scripts creating the tables prior to step 7.

For SAP applications programmers who are building data warehouses, an alternative exists to generating PL/SQL scripts for ETL to data stored in underlying source relational database tables. Instead, you can set up a remote function call (RFC) connection to your SAP source. Then you can use OWB to list functional areas within SAP (such as financial) and list source tables associated with the functional area. You can then select the source tables you want included in your maps and use OWB to generate SAP ABAP code for your ETL.

An Example Using OWB

Figure 25-4 shows a typical mapping created using OWB. In this example, we have mapped appropriate flat file columns to target table columns. We also generated a product identifier (`product_id`) for the target table, since none was provided in the flat file source.

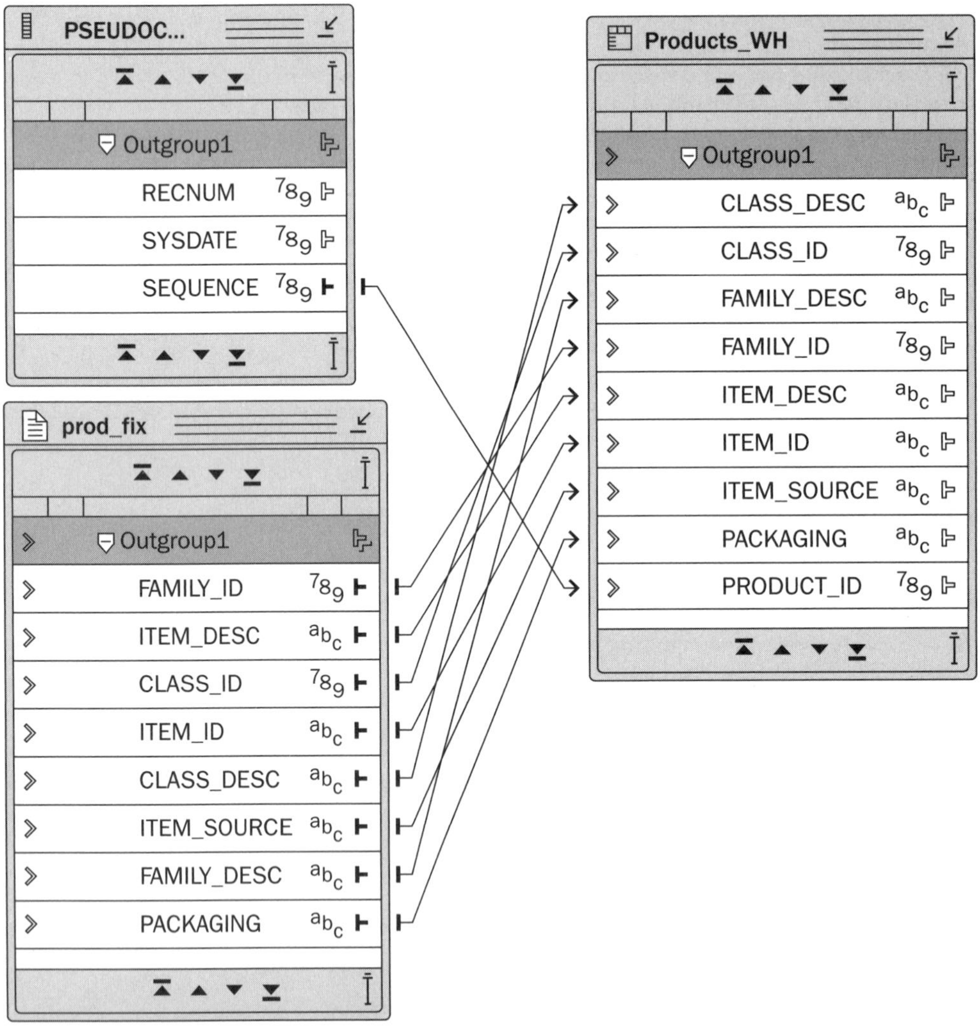

Figure 25-4: Typical mapping in Oracle Warehouse Builder.

In most situations, you'll add other operators to the ETL process, including joins, transformations, filters, and others. OWB includes a family of transformations based on functionality provided in the Oracle database. These global transformations include administration functions, character functions, conversion functions, date functions, numeric functions, OLAP functions, XML functions, and others. You can supplement this library by defining your own transformations using PL/SQL and build custom transformation libraries that can be shared. Recent editions of OWB also include a name and address operator that can be used in the cleansing of names and addresses in your data. The operator compares your data to data in non-Oracle-supplied name and address libraries available for OWB.

In the example, you next validate the mapping. A typical validation output screen is shown in Figure 25-5. There are some nonfatal warnings indicated, but the mapping is valid.

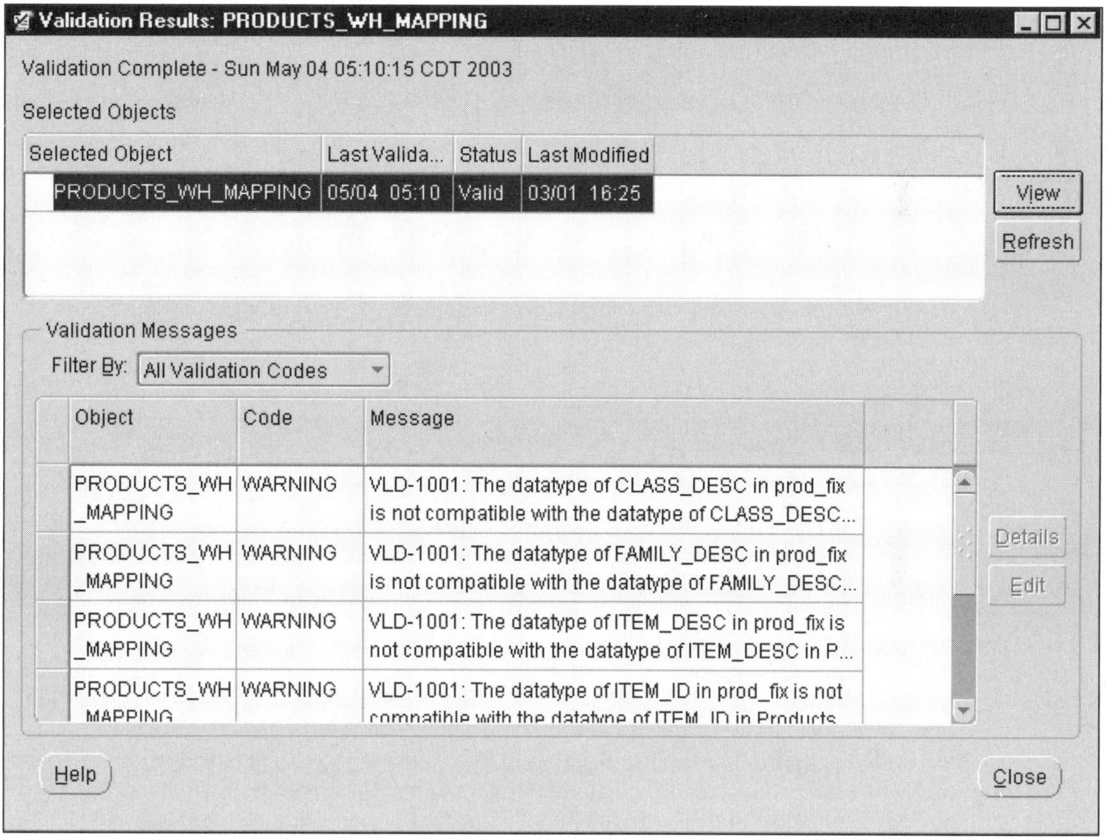

Figure 25-5: Validation results in Oracle Warehouse Builder.

Assuming you are happy with these results, you are ready to generate the code. As the source is a flat file, an SQL*Loader file is generated for us by OWB. Figure 25-6 shows what such an SQL*Loader file might look like.

Code Viewer: PRODUCTS_WH_MAPPING [0 error(s), 6 warning(s)]

Code Edit Search View

```
OPTIONS ( DIRECT=TRUE,PARALLEL=FALSE, ERRORS=50, BINDSIZE=50000, ROWS=200, READSIZE=65536)
LOAD DATA
  CHARACTERSET WE8MSWIN1252
  INFILE 'E:\my_data\owb_source\prod.fix' "STR 'X'ODOA''"
  READBUFFERS 4
  INTO TABLE "PRODUCTS_WH"
  APPEND

  FIELDS


  (
  "FAMILY_ID" POSITION (97:99) INTEGER EXTERNAL ,
"ITEM_DESC" POSITION (32:66) CHAR ,
"CLASS_ID" POSITION (120:122) INTEGER EXTERNAL ,
"ITEM_ID" POSITION (1:11) CHAR ,
"CLASS_DESC" POSITION (123:142) CHAR ,
"ITEM_SOURCE" POSITION (67:96) CHAR ,
"FAMILY_DESC" POSITION (100:119) CHAR ,
"PACKAGING" POSITION (12:31) CHAR ,
"PRODUCT_ID" SEQUENCE
  )
```

Line 1 Column 1 | Read Only | Windows: CR/LF

Figure 25-6: SQL*Loader file generated by Oracle Warehouse Builder.

As mentioned earlier, OWB will generate PL/SQL files where the mapping includes relational sources. Oracle sources are accessed through a database link, while non-Oracle relational sources are typically attached through an ODBC connection. When PL/SQL code is generated, you can select to have it generated as set based, row based, row based (for target only), set based with failover to row based, and set based with failover to row based (for target only). You would likely want to use row-based ETL where you believe source data is not very clean and set-based where you wish to maximize load performance. Figure 25-7 shows some of the typical PL/SQL generated for a set-based loading process.

As you could see in the figures showing generation of SQL*Loader and PL/SQL scripts, these scripts are similar to what you would write manually. You might want to edit these scripts outside of OWB. However, keep in mind that if you do so, such changes will not show up if you need to regenerate scripts later. Such regeneration can be necessary because of changes in source systems or in the target warehouse. You would need to manually edit the scripts again to provide the same changes. Where multiple parties are working with OWB and modifying the same ETL scripts, you should consider carefully whether it is worthwhile to edit scripts outside of the tool.

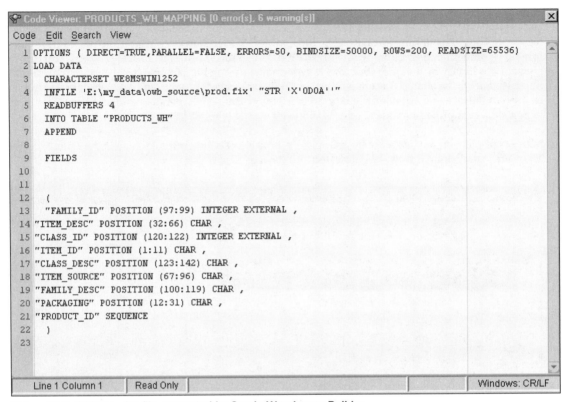

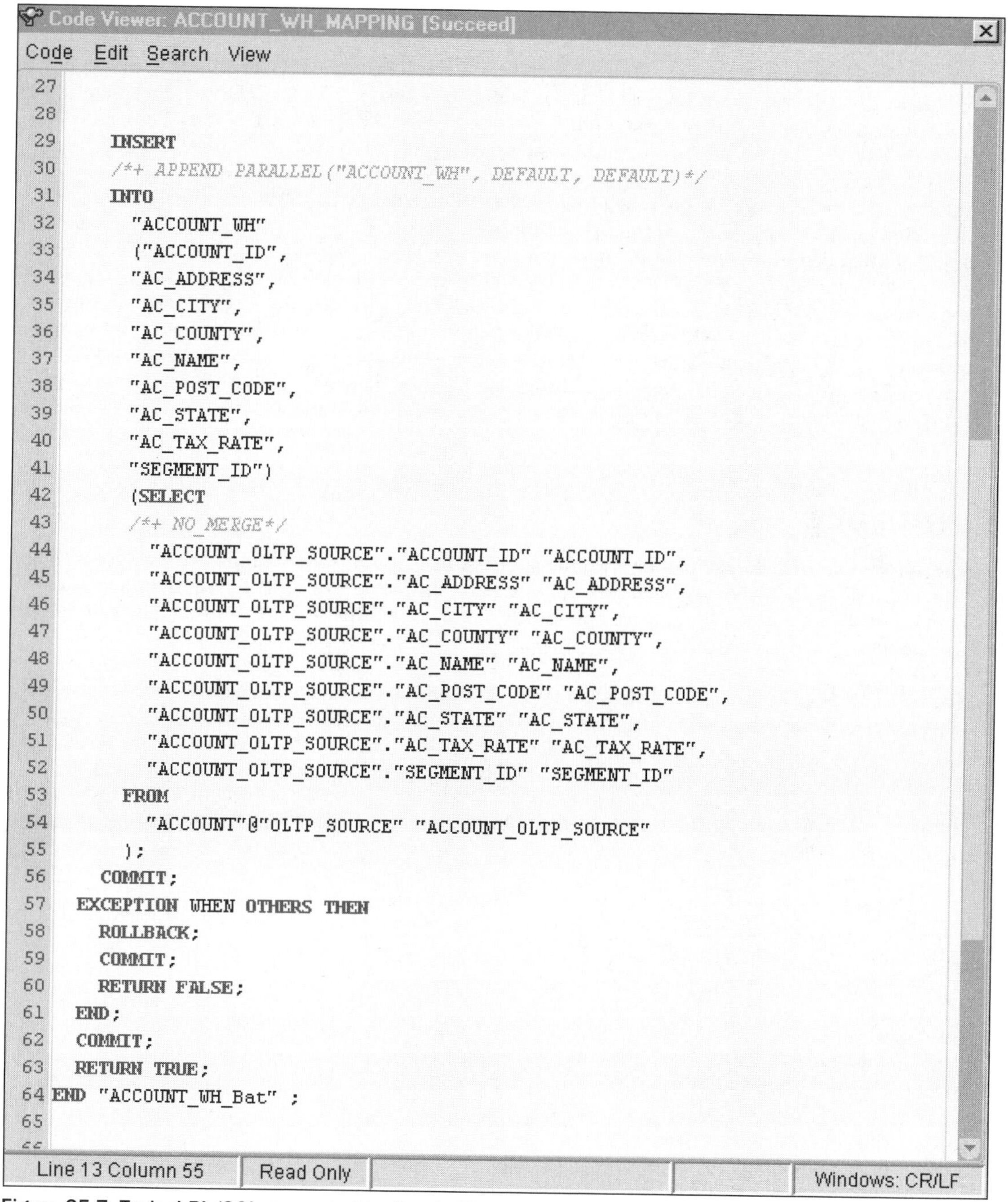

Code Viewer: ACCOUNT_WH_MAPPING [Succeed]
Code Edit Search View
INSERT
/*+ APPEND PARALLEL("ACCOUNT_WH", DEFAULT, DEFAULT)*/
INTO
"ACCOUNT_WH"
("ACCOUNT_ID",
"AC_ADDRESS",
"AC_CITY",
"AC_COUNTY",
"AC_NAME",
"AC_POST_CODE",
"AC_STATE",
"AC_TAX_RATE",
"SEGMENT_ID")
(SELECT
/*+ NO_MERGE*/
"ACCOUNT_OLTP_SOURCE"."ACCOUNT_ID" "ACCOUNT_ID",
"ACCOUNT_OLTP_SOURCE"."AC_ADDRESS" "AC_ADDRESS",
"ACCOUNT_OLTP_SOURCE"."AC_CITY" "AC_CITY",
"ACCOUNT_OLTP_SOURCE"."AC_COUNTY" "AC_COUNTY",
"ACCOUNT_OLTP_SOURCE"."AC_NAME" "AC_NAME",
"ACCOUNT_OLTP_SOURCE"."AC_POST_CODE" "AC_POST_CODE",
"ACCOUNT_OLTP_SOURCE"."AC_STATE" "AC_STATE",
"ACCOUNT_OLTP_SOURCE"."AC_TAX_RATE" "AC_TAX_RATE",
"ACCOUNT_OLTP_SOURCE"."SEGMENT_ID" "SEGMENT_ID"
FROM
"ACCOUNT"@"OLTP_SOURCE" "ACCOUNT_OLTP_SOURCE"
);
COMMIT;
EXCEPTION WHEN OTHERS THEN
ROLLBACK;
COMMIT;
RETURN FALSE;
END;
COMMIT;
RETURN TRUE;
END "ACCOUNT_WH_Bat" ;
Line 13 Column 55
Read Only
Windows: CR/LF

Figure 25-7: Typical PL/SQL generated by Oracle Warehouse Builder.

Nonrelational Targets

OWB is designed to fully leverage Oracle relational database features. However, OWB also supports flat files as targets. More recently, OWB also added support for the Oracle OLAP Option that enables multidimensional cubes to be stored within the Oracle relational database. The OLAP Option is described in more detail in Chapter 27, "Business Intelligence Analysis."

OWB is used to construct the Analytic Workspace (AW) needed by the OLAP Option. The meta data definition for targets is abstracted from the implementation, so the programmer can define a dimension once, and that definition can be implemented for both a relational schema and the multidimensional AW. As with relational targets, OWB is then used to create mappings from source to target tables. Unlike the Analytic Workspace Manager (AWM) in Oracle Database 10*g*, the maps in OWB can, of course, include transformations. AWM would be used instead if you just need to build simple maps from relational tables in the data warehouse to OLAP cubes and then generate the loading code. OWB includes built-in OLAP DML functions such as allocation, aggregation, forecasting, numeric and time series functions, and financial functions. You can also create custom calculations.

Summary

This chapter described data loading and management features in Oracle commonly used in loading Oracle databases. We also described Oracle Warehouse Builder, a tool available for building maps between database and flat file sources and Oracle and flat file targets. We illustrated the ability of OWB to automate creation of extraction, transformation, and loading scripts.

These loading utilities are sometimes used for initial loading of online transaction processing systems but are more commonly used in consolidating and cleansing data to be loaded in operational data stores and data warehouses. The introduction of these utilities has had a tremendous impact in reducing the amount of custom programming needed and increasing speed and flexibility in deployment.

Once the data is loaded in a usable form, you'll be ready to query it and analyze it. That is the subject of the next two chapters.

26

Business Intelligence Query

Business intelligence can be defined as the retrieval and manipulation of data needed to produce information required for business decisions. The retrieval method is through queries. Many such queries are demonstrated in the SQL examples provided in this book. In this chapter, we describe how leveraging certain database features and designs enables business intelligence queries to perform optimally. The goals for design of such systems are often different from online transaction processing (OLTP) systems, where extremely efficient updating is the primary goal. In OLTP systems, a great deal of design work is spent ensuring that data is only stored once in a third normal form (3NF). While such designs are great for transactions-oriented systems and operational data stores where reporting requirements are usually known well in advance, such designs may not be appropriate when data is primarily historical and for business analysts who have questions of a more ad hoc nature.

Ad hoc queries often form the basis of gathering the data needed for business intelligence. Business-oriented questions may be formulated such that a large transaction (fact) table surrounded by multiple dimensions or lookup tables provides an ideal schema for ease of understanding and optimization. This is called a star schema and is described in this chapter. We also provide examples of queries that leverage this schema.

Another common business requirement is the need to drill to different levels of detail in a hierarchy. Oracle provides this summary level capability through materialized views. This chapter describes what materialized views are, how you determine where they are needed, and how you create and maintain them.

Advanced Oracle features for business intelligence make use of the cost-based optimizer. As optimization techniques could be either rules-based or cost-based prior to Oracle Database 10*g*, remember to use the cost-based optimizer if using an older release of the database. As of Oracle Database 10*g*, the cost-based optimizer is the only optimizer officially supported. In addition, much of the business intelligence functionality described here is only available in the Enterprise Edition of the database. Since Oracle features in the various editions can differ in different versions of the database, if you are running an edition other than Enterprise Edition, you should consult the Oracle documentation regarding supported features.

The focus of providing SQL examples in this chapter is relevant even though many business analysts seeking business intelligence often use tools such as Business Objects, Cognos, Hyperion's Brio, MicroStrategy, Oracle Discoverer, and others instead of manually writing SQL. It is important to remember that these business intelligence tools commonly access the Oracle database by generating SQL. In fact, they usually provide the ability to see the SQL generated by the tool. Knowledge of how this SQL works and leverages the database can be extremely useful to both programmers and analysts.

Thus far, we haven't discussed the manipulation of data in our business intelligence definition. In this book, we'll focus that discussion around the analytics, OLAP, and data mining capabilities in Oracle. That material is covered in the next chapter (Chapter 27, "Business Intelligence Analysis").

Performance management and tuning (optimization) is discussed in Chapter 28. However, maintaining levels of performance proactively while handling business intelligence queries of widely differing complexities is worth a mention now. This topic includes proper database design (touched upon here), as well as optimal SQL and parallelization. Oracle can also be configured to prevent the popularly phrased "query from hell" even when all is not optimal. So, we'll briefly touch on using the Database Resource Manager to do exactly that at the close of this chapter.

Schema for Business Intelligence

A variety of schema can be used in business intelligence applications. A 3NF is sometimes used where standard reports are common and there are relatively few ad hoc queries that could introduce an extremely large number of joins. Where 3NF is used and ad hoc queries take place, a common practice is to improve performance by leveraging partition-wise joins through the introduction of composite range-list partitioning. When both tables in the join are equi-partitioned on their join keys, much larger table joins can be broken into a smaller joins involving pairs of relatively smaller partitions.

To illustrate a partition-wise join, we'll use two partitioned tables, sales and costs, from the `sh` schema provided as part of the Oracle Database 10*g* standard installation. Both are partitioned on `time_id` into quarterly (and other) partitions. In this query, we are interested in the channels that sold items where the unit price was $600 greater than unit cost in the first quarter of 1998.

```
SELECT costs.channel_id, costs.unit_price, costs.unit_cost
FROM sh.sales, sh.costs
WHERE sales.channel_id = costs.channel_id
     AND sales.time_id BETWEEN TO_DATE ('01-JAN-1998', 'DD-MON-YY')
              AND TO_DATE ('01-APR-1998', 'DD-MON-YY')
     AND (costs.unit_price - costs.unit_cost) > 600
     GROUP BY costs.channel_id, costs.unit_price, costs.unit_cost;
```

This query joins data that is only in the SALES_Q1_1998 partition of each table. The results returned are shown in Figure 26-1 (as viewed in *i*SQL*Plus).

Larger numbers of joins are common in business intelligence queries, often leveraging common lookup tables or dimensions. A star schema frequently provides a more optimal and understandable solution than 3NF. The star schema consists of a single fact table surrounded by multiple dimensions and linked by a foreign key relationship. Figure 26-2 illustrates a star schema that is part of the `sh` schema provided in an Oracle Database 10*g* standard installation. This schema consists of the sales transaction or fact table surrounded by dimensions for time, channels, customers, products, and promotions. Foreign keys in the sales fact table point to the primary keys in each of the dimensions. This schema easily enables queries such as "How many products were sold by my channels during a specific promotion in the past three months?"

CHANNEL_ID	UNIT_PRICE	UNIT_COST
2	1572.7	969.4
2	1753.2	1145.65
3	1572.7	957.04
3	1753.2	1131.05
3	1782.72	1181.01
4	1550.99	943.74
4	1702.99	1102.43
4	1726.83	1124.02
4	1753.2	1115.33
4	1753.2	1136.52
4	1753.2	1137.64

11 rows selected.

Figure 26-1: Output from partition-wise join in example.

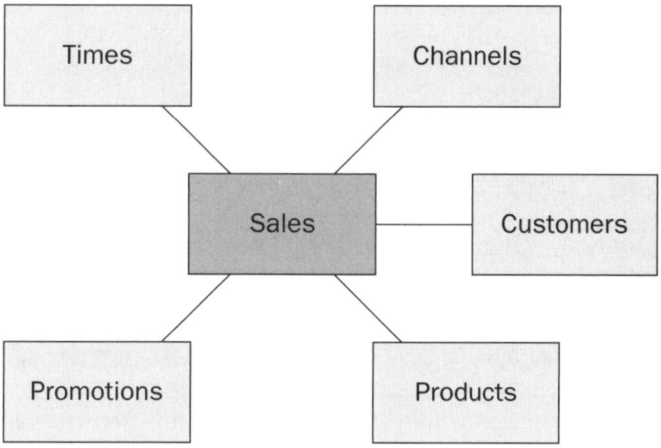

Figure 26-2: Star schema example illustration.

For such queries, the best optimization will occur using the cost-based optimizer when the `STAR_TRANSFORMATION_ENABLED` initialization parameter is set to be `TRUE`. Note that this initialization parameter is not always set this way in some Oracle database installations, so you or your DBA should check this initialization parameter. If this parameter is not set to `TRUE`, your results will not agree with the subsequent example in this section. This initialization parameter can be checked and reset using Oracle Enterprise Manager 10*g* Database Control's administration interface.

Oracle recommends that bitmap indexes be created on the foreign keys from the fact table, matching columns in dimension tables to further improve performance. (Whereas a regular index stores a list of `rowids` for each key and corresponding rows, a bitmap index replaces the list of `rowids` with a bitmap indicating whether the key value is present. Since bitmaps are ideal to speed joins in where clause scenarios, applying them to the foreign keys in a star schema can greatly improve performance of typical star queries.) Using the sample schema example, you might wish to create a bitmap index for the sales fact table that matches the foreign key to the promotions table. (The Oracle-provided sample schema actually comes with the bitmap indexes already created.) The command would typically be executed by your DBA or someone with similar adequate privileges and would look like this:

```
CREATE BITMAP INDEX sales_promo_bix
ON sh.sales (promo_id)
LOCAL;
```

We specified `LOCAL` since only local bitmap indexes are permitted on partitioned tables.

A variation of the star schema is the snowflake schema. A snowflake schema has columns in dimension tables that are mapped to other tables. Since such a schema introduces more foreign key joins that can negatively impact performance, Oracle generally recommends avoiding the use of such schemas unless necessary.

Let's examine a typical star query. In this example, using the `sh` schema, we wish to understand what channels are selling the large deals (amount sold greater than 1,000) to customers in California with relatively low credit (less than 7,000) in August of 1998. The query would be formulated as follows:

```
SELECT channels.channel_desc, times.calendar_month_desc, sales.promo_id,
sales.amount_sold
FROM sh.channels, sh.customers, sh.times, sh.sales
WHERE sales.time_id = times.time_id
AND sales.cust_id = customers.cust_id
AND sales.channel_id = channels.channel_id
AND customers.cust_credit_limit < 7000
AND customers.cust_state_province = 'CA'
AND times.calendar_month_desc = '1998-08'
AND sales.amount_sold > 1000
GROUP BY sales.promo_id, channels.channel_desc, times.calendar_month_desc,
sales.amount_sold;
```

The results of the query are shown in Figure 26-3 (as viewed using *i*SQL*Plus).

To understand how your optimizer handled the query against this star schema, you would generate an Explain Plan for this query. You can generate an explain plan by adding the following line just before the `SELECT` statement:

```
EXPLAIN PLAN FOR
```

Then you would add the following line of code after the query statement:

```
SELECT plan_table_output FROM
table(dbms_xplan.display('plan_table',null,'serial'));
```

Note that if you are using SQL*Plus for this example, you would need to have set autotrace on.

The Explain Plan as shown in *i*SQL*Plus appears in the following two figures (as it is produced on two pages). These figures (Figures 26-4 and 26-5) illustrate how the query might be solved. Oracle will initially use the bitmap indexes on the foreign keys to retrieve needed rows from the fact table, combine individual bitmaps into a single bitmap, and then retrieve the relevant rows of data from the fact table creating a result set. This retrieval is sometimes called the *star transformation step*—transformation of the star into a subquery representation. In the second stage, the results set is joined to dimension tables.

CHANNEL_DESC	CALENDAR_MONTH_DESC	PROMO_ID	AMOUNT_SOLD
Internet	1998-08	350	1052.99
Internet	1998-08	350	1067.73
Internet	1998-08	350	1108.99
Partners	1998-08	350	1067.73
Partners	1998-08	350	1108.99
Partners	1998-08	350	1463.19
Partners	1998-08	350	1638.5
Partners	1998-08	350	1726.83
Direct Sales	1998-08	350	1013.99
Direct Sales	1998-08	350	1108.99
Direct Sales	1998-08	350	1205.99
Direct Sales	1998-08	350	1222.87
Direct Sales	1998-08	350	1239.99
Direct Sales	1998-08	350	1244.33
Direct Sales	1998-08	350	1257.35
Direct Sales	1998-08	350	1495.99
Direct Sales	1998-08	350	1501.23
Direct Sales	1998-08	350	1516.93
Direct Sales	1998-08	350	1655.65
Direct Sales	1998-08	350	1708.95

20 rows selected.

Figure 26-3: Results from example star query.

PLAN_TABLE_OUTPUT
Plan hash value: 2643881527

	Id	Operation	Name	Rows	Bytes	Cost (%CPU)	Time	Pstart	Pstop	

	0	SELECT STATEMENT		1	54	386 (2)	00:00:05			
	1	SORT GROUP BY		1	54	386 (2)	00:00:05			
	* 2	HASH JOIN		1	54	385 (2)	00:00:05			
	* 3	HASH JOIN		1	41	382 (2)	00:00:05			
	4	PARTITION RANGE ITERATOR		19	467	366 (1)	00:00:05	KEY	KEY	
	* 5	TABLE ACCESS BY LOCAL INDEX ROWID	SALES	19	467	366 (1)	00:00:05	KEY	KEY	
	6	BITMAP CONVERSION TO ROWIDS								
	7	BITMAP AND								
	8	BITMAP MERGE								
	9	BITMAP KEY ITERATION								
	10	BUFFER SORT								
	* 11	TABLE ACCESS FULL	TIMES	30	480	15 (0)	00:00:01			
	* 12	BITMAP INDEX RANGE SCAN	SALES_TIME_BIX					KEY	KEY	
	13	BITMAP MERGE								
	14	BITMAP KEY ITERATION								
	15	BUFFER SORT								
	* 16	TABLE ACCESS FULL	CUSTOMERS	156	3120	331 (2)	00:00:04			
	* 17	BITMAP INDEX RANGE SCAN	SALES_CUST_BIX					KEY	KEY	
	* 18	TABLE ACCESS FULL	TIMES	30	480	15 (0)	00:00:01			

Figure 26-4: Explain plan output of parallel bitmap star join example (first page).

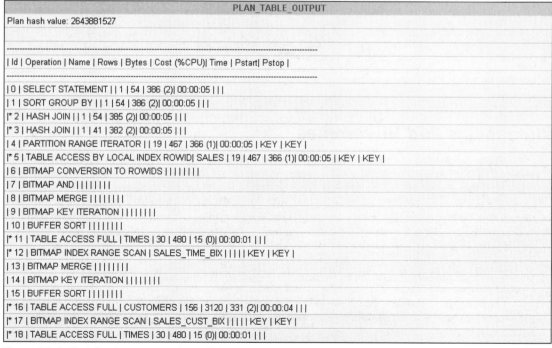

```
PLAN_TABLE_OUTPUT
| 19 | TABLE ACCESS FULL | CHANNELS | 5 | 65 | 3 (0)| 00:00:01 | | |
-------------------------------------------------------------------------------------------------------------------

Predicate Information (identified by operation id):
---------------------------------------------------

2 - access("SALES"."CHANNEL_ID"="CHANNELS"."CHANNEL_ID")
3 - access("SALES"."TIME_ID"="TIMES"."TIME_ID")
5 - filter("SALES"."AMOUNT_SOLD">1000)
11 - filter("TIMES"."CALENDAR_MONTH_DESC"='1998-08')
12 - access("SALES"."TIME_ID"="TIMES"."TIME_ID")
16 - filter("CUSTOMERS"."CUST_STATE_PROVINCE"='CA' AND "CUSTOMERS"."CUST_CREDIT_LIMIT"<7000)
17 - access("SALES"."CUST_ID"="CUSTOMERS"."CUST_ID")
18 - filter("TIMES"."CALENDAR_MONTH_DESC"='1998-08')

38 rows selected.
```

Figure 26-5: Explain plain output of parallel bitmap star join example (second page).

You can also create a bitmap join index if you have DBA privileges to join two or more tables and enable faster star transformations. Bitmap join indexes are only allowed to dimension table columns that are primary keys (and are enabled) or have unique constraints. Using the sample `sh` schema from the standard Oracle Database 10*g* installation, we'll first create a unique constraint for the `cust_src_id` column in the `customers` table:

```
ALTER TABLE sh.customers ADD CONSTRAINT cust_src_id_unique
UNIQUE (cust_src_id) DISABLE VALIDATE;
```

We'll then create a bitmap join index from the sales table to this `cust_src_id` column using the following code:

```
CREATE BITMAP INDEX sales_cust_src_id_bjix
ON sh.sales(sh.customers.cust_src_id)
FROM sh.sales, sh.customers
WHERE sh.sales.cust_id= sh.customers.cust_src_id
LOCAL;
```

Dimensions and Hierarchies

Dimensions are created in order to enable easy lookup of key parameters in a query. Most queries have some element of time as a dimension (for example, "show me the sales total for the first quarter"), but other common dimensions (depending on your business) might include products, customers, employees, projects, locations, and others. More often than not, you will want to have dimensions that contain hierarchies ranging from macro levels to sublevels. For example, in a time dimension, at a macro level, you might be dealing with years. However, you might want the ability to do lookups easily by quarters, months, days, or hours.

Oracle enables you to define specific tables as dimension object types. Dimensions can be created using a `CREATE DIMENSION` command or using Oracle Enterprise Manager, Oracle's database management tool that is automatically installed with Oracle Database 10*g*. The creation process can include naming of the dimension and defining levels, hierarchies, and attributes. These tasks usually require the privileges that a DBA would have been assigned.

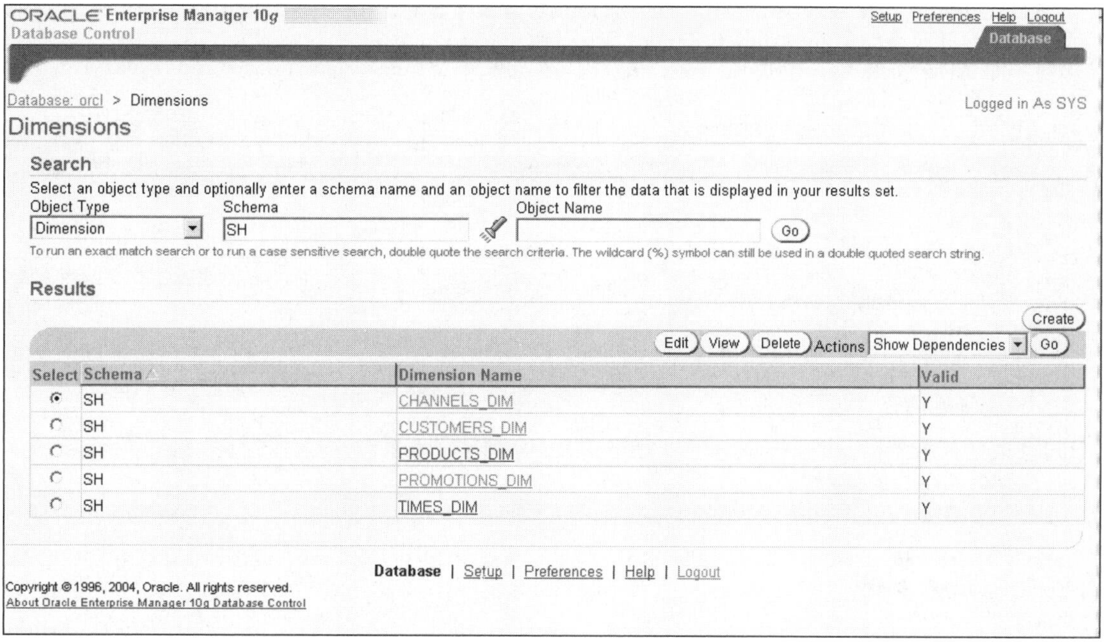

Figure 26-6: Dimensions in the example schema viewed through Oracle Enterprise Manager.

These dimensions typically contain multiple levels. By selecting the time dimension and viewing the levels, you can see the definitions shown in Figure 26-7.

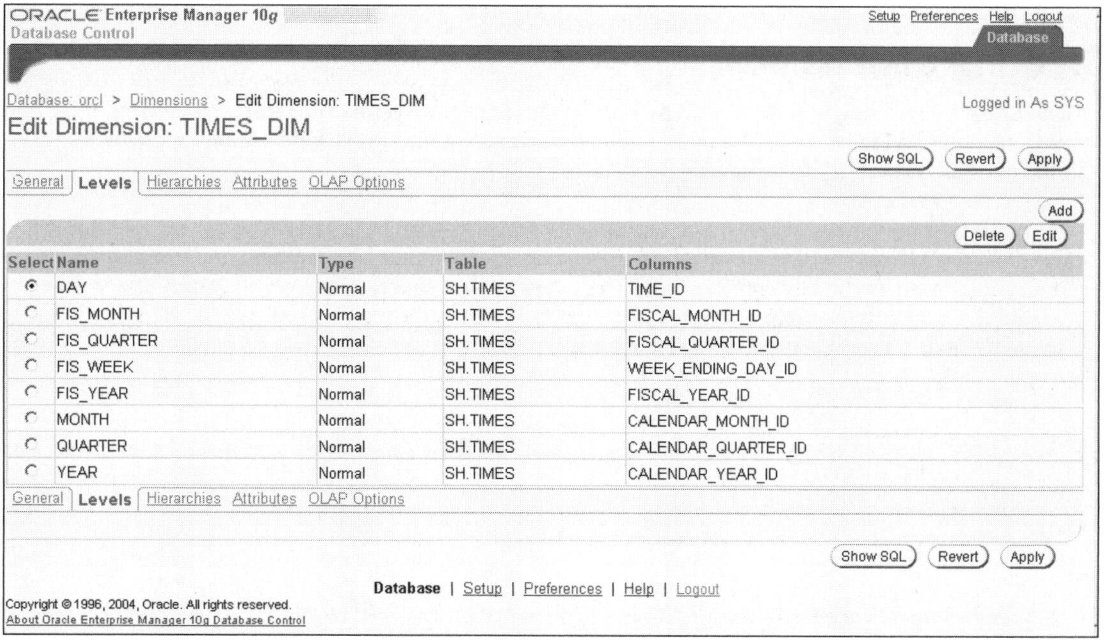

Figure 26-7: Levels in the example time dimension viewed through Oracle Enterprise Manager.

Hierarchies define the way in which the levels roll up to each other. Dimensions in Oracle can have multiple hierarchies. The sample time dimension has two hierarchies. Figure 26-8 shows the `FIS_ROLLUP`, in which day rolls up to week, week rolls up to month, month rolls up to quarter, and quarter rolls up to year.

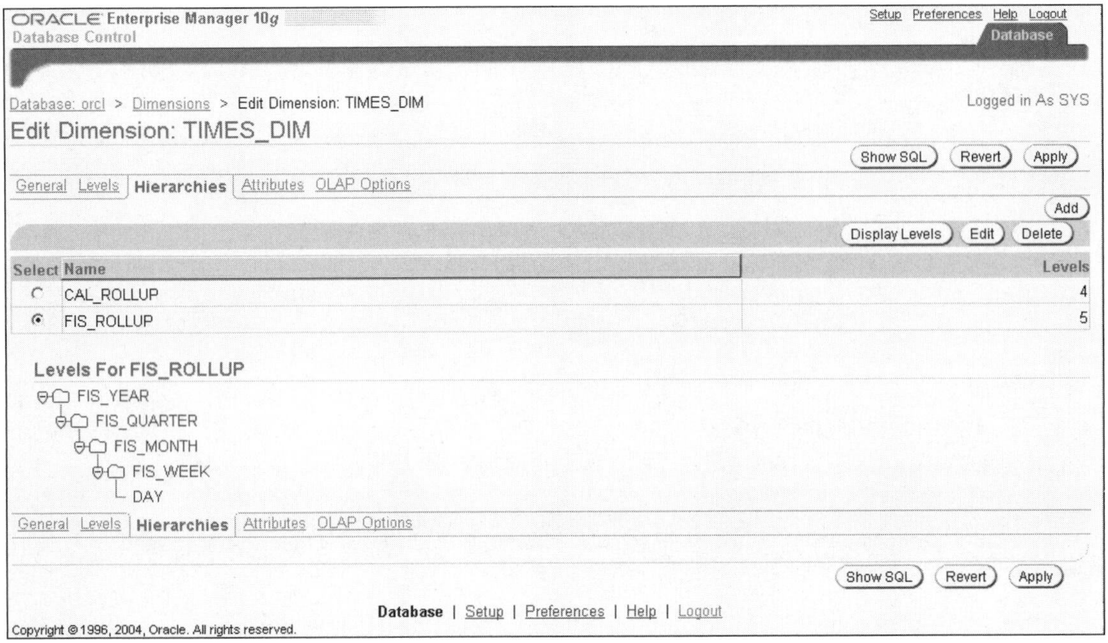

Figure 26-8: A hierarchy in the example time dimension viewed through Enterprise Manager.

Creating Dimensions

The Enterprise Manager interface can be used in creating dimensions. You start by selecting the Create button shown in Figure 26-6. Then you name your dimension, create levels, create hierarchies, and name attributes as needed in the subsequent interfaces.

As mentioned previously, you can also use `CREATE DIMENSION` in SQL*Plus to create a dimension table. As in Enterprise Manager, you name the dimension, create levels, create hierarchies, and name attributes, but you would do so by directly entering SQL. The following is a simple example using definitions from the `warehouses` table in the sample `oe` schema provided as part of the Oracle Database 10*g* standard installation. The code creates a `warehouses` dimension table.

```
CREATE DIMENSION oe.warehouses_dim
 LEVEL warehouseIS (warehouses.warehouse_id)
 LEVEL location IS (warehouses.location_id)
HIERARCHY location_rollup
 (warehouse     CHILD OF
 location)

ATTRIBUTE warehouse DETERMINES
(warehouses.warehouse_name);
```

Dimensions may be altered in Enterprise Manager using the Edit action (see Figure 26-6 for the location of the button) or by using the `ALTER DIMENSION` syntax. For example, you could drop the hierarchy definition from the previous example with this command:

```
ALTER DIMENSION oe.warehouses_dim DROP HIERARCHY location_rollup;
```

As always, see the Oracle SQL Reference documentation for a complete list of syntax options.

Summary Tables and Materialized Views

Business analysts often pose queries that require summarizations of detailed data. For example, a senior sales manager might simply want to see total sales in a geographic location for the quarter without drilling to see the details of individual transactions. Such levels of interest are common in many companies. For years the solution to improving performance for such queries was to create a smaller summary table that held sums of the detailed transactions. Queries would be manually redirected to those tables, or summary reports would be created that directly accessed those tables.

Oracle added the capability of creating summary tables for fact and dimension tables as materialized views beginning in Oracle 8*i*. Materialized views actually exist as tables (hence, "materialized"). They can be refreshed automatically when detailed tables are loaded using a fast (incremental) refresh, provided a materialized view log exists for the detailed tables, or using a complete refresh. A force refresh will perform an incremental refresh of the materialized view if possible, and a complete refresh if not. You can also defer the refresh by selecting `NEVER` as the refresh parameter.

The greatest benefit of using materialized views is that Oracle's cost-based optimizer recognizes their existence and will automatically redirect queries to the right summary level for optimum performance. This means that SQL need not be aware of the existence of materialized views and any common business intelligence ad hoc query tool that generates SQL can leverage them. In fact, it is advised not to write SQL mapped to specific materialized views if your organization is likely to remove summary tables that are not frequently used or deemed unnecessary. For query rewrite to occur, the `QUERY_REWRITE_ENABLED` initialization parameter must be set to `TRUE`.

Materialized views are of three types. They can contain aggregate functions such as `SUM`, `COUNT(n)`, `COUNT(*)`, `AVG`, `VARIANCE`, `STDDEV`, `MIN`, and `MAX`. (These functions are described in more detail in the next chapter.) Materialized views can also contain only joins with no aggregates. Where you need multiple views of joins or joins with aggregates, nested materialized views can have definitions based on other materialized views or can reference other relations in the database.

If you performed the Oracle Database 10*g* standard installation, you already have some sample materialized views tables in the `sh` schema. To view these from Enterprise Manager, under the Administration tab you can choose to view materialized views. Enter `sh` as the schema name and press Go on the Materialized Views page to see a list. An example is the `CAL_MONTH_SALES_MV` materialized view. Enterprise Manager will provide you with information about the last analyze date, refresh state, compile state and definition, and the materialized view query, as shown in Figure 26-9.

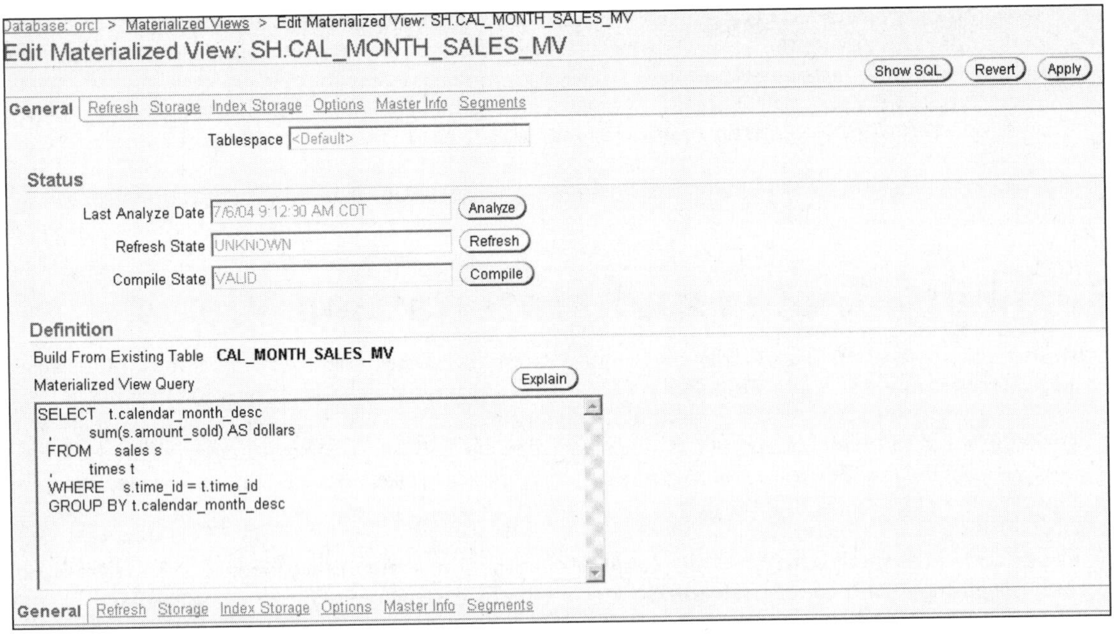

Figure 26-9: Materialized view described in Oracle Enterprise Manager.

You can also use the Explain feature in Figure 26-9 for the query to determine what materialized views capabilities are enabled, including whether it is fast-refreshable, the types of query rewrite you can perform, and what partition change tracking (PCT) refresh is possible, as shown in Figure 26-10:

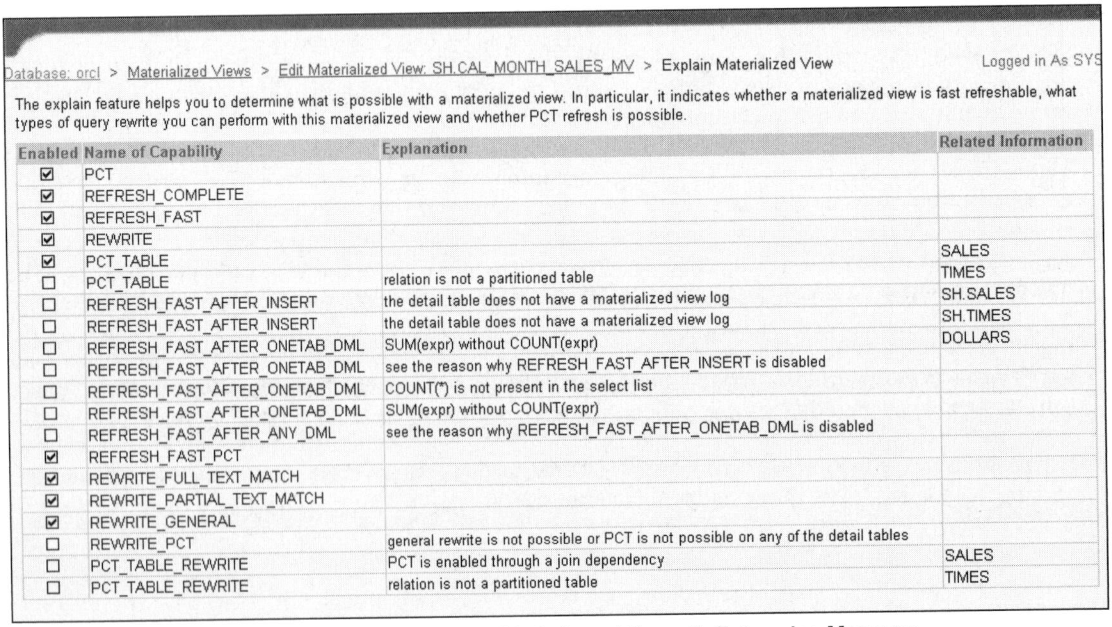

Enabled	Name of Capability	Explanation	Related Information
☑	PCT		
☑	REFRESH_COMPLETE		
☑	REFRESH_FAST		
☑	REWRITE		
☑	PCT_TABLE		SALES
☐	PCT_TABLE	relation is not a partitioned table	TIMES
☐	REFRESH_FAST_AFTER_INSERT	the detail table does not have a materialized view log	SH.SALES
☐	REFRESH_FAST_AFTER_INSERT	the detail table does not have a materialized view log	SH.TIMES
☐	REFRESH_FAST_AFTER_ONETAB_DML	SUM(expr) without COUNT(expr)	DOLLARS
☐	REFRESH_FAST_AFTER_ONETAB_DML	see the reason why REFRESH_FAST_AFTER_INSERT is disabled	
☐	REFRESH_FAST_AFTER_ONETAB_DML	COUNT(*) is not present in the select list	
☐	REFRESH_FAST_AFTER_ONETAB_DML	SUM(expr) without COUNT(expr)	
☐	REFRESH_FAST_AFTER_ANY_DML	see the reason why REFRESH_FAST_AFTER_ONETAB_DML is disabled	
☑	REFRESH_FAST_PCT		
☑	REWRITE_FULL_TEXT_MATCH		
☑	REWRITE_PARTIAL_TEXT_MATCH		
☑	REWRITE_GENERAL		
☐	REWRITE_PCT	general rewrite is not possible or PCT is not possible on any of the detail tables	
☐	PCT_TABLE_REWRITE	PCT is enabled through a join dependency	SALES
☐	PCT_TABLE_REWRITE	relation is not a partitioned table	TIMES

Figure 26-10: Materialized view capabilities enabled viewed through Enterprise Manager.

Using the SQL Access Advisor (Summary Advisor)

Oracle provides a summary advisor useful in determining the need and potential usefulness of new materialized views while also analyzing the usefulness of those already implemented. When using Oracle Enterprise Manager 10*g*, you'll find the Summary Advisor (as it was known prior to Oracle Database 10*g*) in Advisor Central and now named the SQL Access Advisor. Figure 26-11 shows the initial page of the SQL Access Advisor, where you define the workload source to be used for the analysis. You can analyze the need for materialized views (and also indexes through this interface) based on recent SQL activity (selected from the cache), an imported workload from a repository you own, or a hypothetical workload based on schemas and tables.

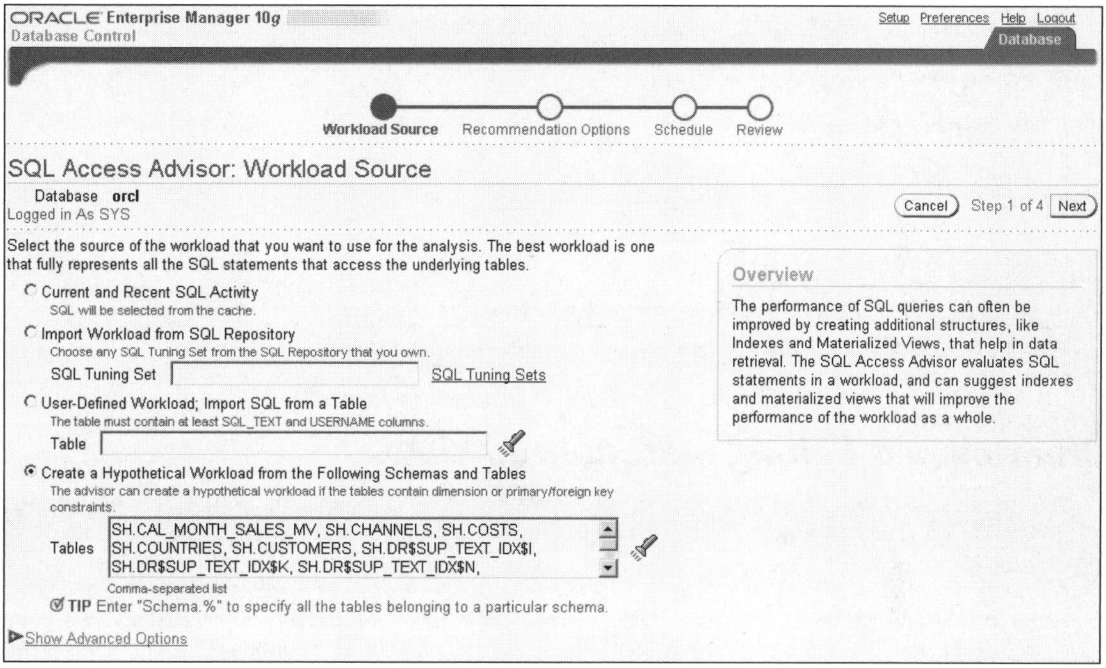

Figure 26-11: SQL Access Advisor in Oracle Enterprise Manager.

Next, you'll be asked whether you want recommendations regarding materialized views or indexes, or both. The analysis can be limited and faster, or more comprehensive. The running of the Advisor is then scheduled. To get things started immediately or to schedule running the Advisor at a specific time and date, choose the Standard scheduling option. After scheduling and reviewing a summary of your selections thus far, you'll be ready to submit the job. When the job is complete, a new Automatic Database Diagnostic Monitor (ADDM) advisory appears in Advisor Central for your review. Figure 26-12 shows a typical recommendation page from within an ADDM advisory suggesting creation of a materialized view.

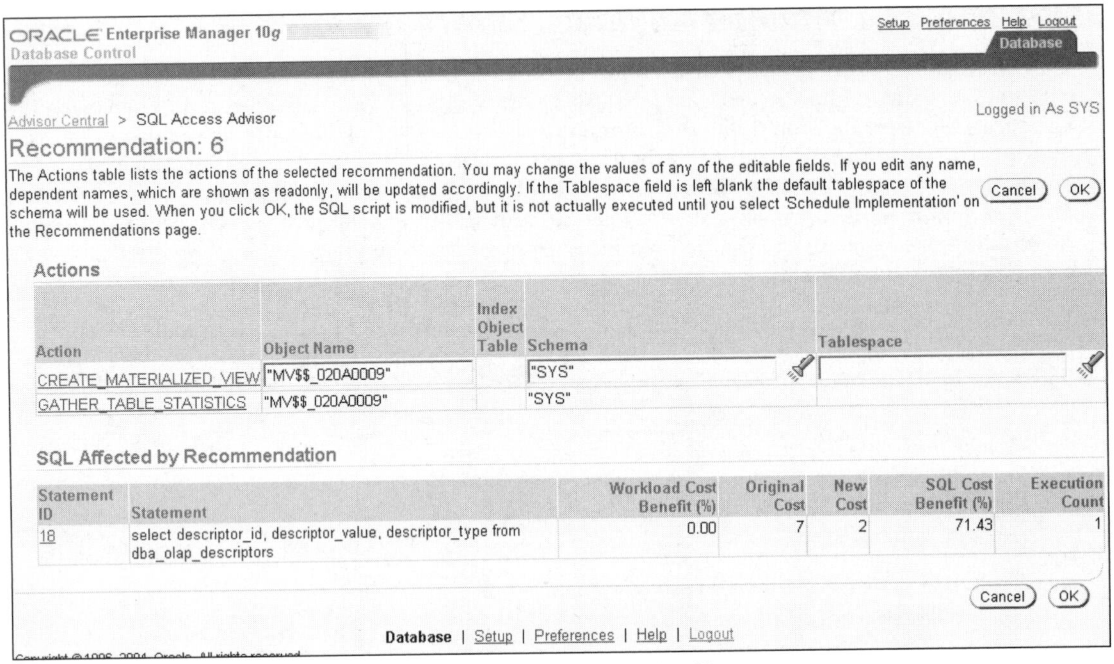

Figure 26-12: SQL Access Advisor recommendations in Enterprise Manager.

Creating and Editing Materialized Views

You can create a materialized view by selecting such a recommendation via the SQL Access Advisor within Enterprise Manager (see Figure 26-12). After selecting this action, you then schedule the materialized view creation.

Alternatively, you can use the `CREATE MATERIALIZED VIEW` statement to create materialized views. For example, you might want to create a materialized view in anticipation of future workload demand that is not yet indicated in current workload analysis. The following provides a typical example of the syntax used:

```
CREATE MATERIALIZED VIEW sh.cust_sales_mv
BUILD IMMEDIATE
USING INDEX
REFRESH FORCE
ENABLE QUERY REWRITE
AS
SELECT customers.cust_id,
       SUM(amount_sold) AS sales_in_dollars
FROM sh.sales, sh.customers
WHERE sales.cust_id= customers.cust_id
GROUP BY customers.cust_id;
```

In this example, we chose to `BUILD IMMEDIATE`, which populates the materialized view with data after it is created. Alternatively, we could have specified `BUILD DEFERRED` and delayed data population to a later time. Our refresh is a `REFRESH FORCE`, though we could have, of course, specified other refresh options. If unspecified, the defaults would have been `ON DEMAND` and `FORCE`.

Figure 26-13 shows an Explain of this materialized view.

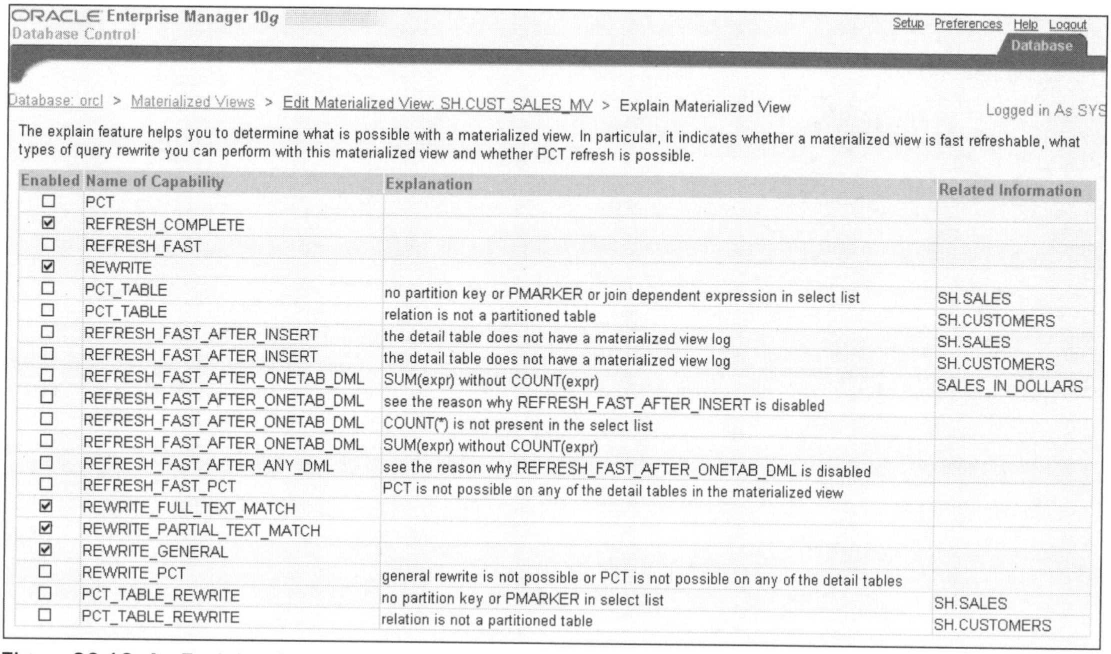
ORACLE Enterprise Manager 10g
Database Control
Setup Preferences Help Logout
Database
Database: orcl > Materialized Views > Edit Materialized View: SH.CUST_SALES_MV > Explain Materialized View
Logged in As SYS
The explain feature helps you to determine what is possible with a materialized view. In particular, it indicates whether a materialized view is fast refreshable, what types of query rewrite you can perform with this materialized view and whether PCT refresh is possible.

Enabled	Name of Capability	Explanation	Related Information
☐	PCT		
☑	REFRESH_COMPLETE		
☐	REFRESH_FAST		
☑	REWRITE		
☐	PCT_TABLE	no partition key or PMARKER or join dependent expression in select list	SH.SALES
☐	PCT_TABLE	relation is not a partitioned table	SH.CUSTOMERS
☐	REFRESH_FAST_AFTER_INSERT	the detail table does not have a materialized view log	SH.SALES
☐	REFRESH_FAST_AFTER_INSERT	the detail table does not have a materialized view log	SH.CUSTOMERS
☐	REFRESH_FAST_AFTER_ONETAB_DML	SUM(expr) without COUNT(expr)	SALES_IN_DOLLARS
☐	REFRESH_FAST_AFTER_ONETAB_DML	see the reason why REFRESH_FAST_AFTER_INSERT is disabled	
☐	REFRESH_FAST_AFTER_ONETAB_DML	COUNT(*) is not present in the select list	
☐	REFRESH_FAST_AFTER_ONETAB_DML	SUM(expr) without COUNT(expr)	
☐	REFRESH_FAST_AFTER_ANY_DML	see the reason why REFRESH_FAST_AFTER_ONETAB_DML is disabled	
☐	REFRESH_FAST_PCT	PCT is not possible on any of the detail tables in the materialized view	
☑	REWRITE_FULL_TEXT_MATCH		
☑	REWRITE_PARTIAL_TEXT_MATCH		
☑	REWRITE_GENERAL		
☐	REWRITE_PCT	general rewrite is not possible or PCT is not possible on any of the detail tables	
☐	PCT_TABLE_REWRITE	no partition key or PMARKER in select list	SH.SALES
☐	PCT_TABLE_REWRITE	relation is not a partitioned table	SH.CUSTOMERS

Figure 26-13: An Explain of a materialized view in Oracle Enterprise Manager.

To ensure performance and the right results from materialized views, Oracle recommends that dimensions either be denormalized or joins between tables in a normalized/partly normalized dimension be guaranteed as unique. Dimensional hierarchical integrity must also be ensured. Compiling your materialized views will ensure that they are in a valid state. Enterprise Manager provides the compile status of your materialized views, as well as a Compile button to aid in doing this (see Figure 26-9).

After you have created a materialized view, you may need to edit it. You can do this through Enterprise Manager by selecting the materialized view or by using the `ALTER MATERIALIZED VIEW` statement. For example, you can change the refresh option (`FAST`, `FORCE`, `COMPLETE`, `NEVER`), refresh mode (`ON COMMIT` or `ON DEMAND`), recompile the materialized view, enable or disable it for query rewrite, or make it considered as `fresh`.

Of course, you can also delete materialized views using Enterprise Manager or using the `DROP MATERIALIZED VIEW` statement.

Aggregation through SQL: Rollup and Cube

As aggregation can provide much-needed business intelligence information and can be invaluable in ad hoc queries, Oracle includes `ROLLUP` and `CUBE` extensions to SQL that are used with the `GROUP BY` clause. `ROLLUP` is used to compute aggregations at multiple levels. `CUBE` is used to generate cross-tabulations in a single query.

Let's first look at how ROLLUP can be used. In this example, aggregates are to be computed for the first three months of 1998 for all product categories using data in the sh schema that is part of the Oracle Database 10*g* standard installation. The query to generate this result is as follows:

```
SELECT times.calendar_month_desc month,
       products.prod_category AS product_category,
       SUM(sales.amount_sold) AS sales_in_dollars
FROM sh.sales, sh.products, sh.times, sh.customers
WHERE sales.time_id = times.time_id
  AND sales.prod_id = products.prod_id
  AND sales.cust_id = customers.cust_id
  AND times.calendar_month_desc in ('1998-01', '1998-02', '1998-03')
  AND customers.cust_state_province in ('CA')
GROUP BY ROLLUP (times.calendar_month_desc, products.prod_category);
```

Figure 26-14 shows the result of this query. Rollup figures for each month appear on the monthly lines where PRODUCT_CATEGORY is blank. The total of all sales for the three months appears on the last line.

MONTH	PRODUCT_CATEGORY	SALES_IN_DOLLARS
1998-01	Photo	19010.39
1998-01	Hardware	41608.29
1998-01	Electronics	9938.18
1998-01	Software/Other	25716.36
1998-01	Peripherals and Accessories	53110.18
1998-01		149383.4
1998-02	Photo	32042.33
1998-02	Hardware	69180.67
1998-02	Electronics	12579.07
1998-02	Software/Other	28900.14
1998-02	Peripherals and Accessories	71116.63
1998-02		213818.84
1998-03	Photo	9740.58
1998-03	Hardware	22879.33
1998-03	Electronics	6523.47
1998-03	Software/Other	17048.78
1998-03	Peripherals and Accessories	49675.76
1998-03		105867.92
		469070.16

19 rows selected.

Figure 26-14: Output of example query using rollup in Oracle.

A query leveraging CUBE to generate a cross-tabulation is illustrated in the next example. This example uses the same tables and three months of data and a similar query but instead uses GROUP BY CUBE:

```
SELECT times.calendar_month_desc month,
       products.prod_category AS product_category,
       SUM(sales.amount_sold) AS sales_in_dollars
FROM sh.sales, sh.products, sh.times, sh.customers
WHERE sales.time_id = times.time_id
  AND sales.prod_id = products.prod_id
  AND sales.cust_id = customers.cust_id
```

```
    AND times.calendar_month_desc in ('1998-01', '1998-02', '1998-03')
    AND customers.cust_state_province in ('CA')
  GROUP BY CUBE (times.calendar_month_desc, products.prod_category);
```

The results are shown in the following figure. The three-month total of all products appears on the top line, followed by the three-month totals for each product category. Monthly totals then follow (see Figure 26-15).

MONTH	PRODUCT_CATEGORY	SALES_IN_DOLLARS
		469070.16
	Photo	60793.3
	Hardware	133668.29
	Electronics	29040.72
	Software/Other	71665.28
	Peripherals and Accessories	173902.57
1998-01		149383.4
1998-01	Photo	19010.39
1998-01	Hardware	41608.29
1998-01	Electronics	9938.18
1998-01	Software/Other	25716.36
1998-01	Peripherals and Accessories	53110.18
1998-02		213818.84
1998-02	Photo	32042.33
1998-02	Hardware	69180.67
1998-02	Electronics	12579.07
1998-02	Software/Other	28900.14
1998-02	Peripherals and Accessories	71116.63
1998-03		105867.92
1998-03	Photo	9740.58
1998-03	Hardware	22879.33
1998-03	Electronics	6523.47
1998-03	Software/Other	17048.78
1998-03	Peripherals and Accessories	49675.76

24 rows selected.

Figure 26-15: Output of example query using `cube` **function in Oracle.**

Proactive Management of Complex Query Workloads

Business intelligence queries often range from the very simple and predictable to the very complex and ad hoc. For many, managing these mixed workloads for optimal performance is usually reactive, occurring after a performance problem is identified. Tuning and diagnostics tools typically aid in identifying the exact nature of the problem and the potential solution. We briefly introduced the use of the Automatic Database Diagnostic Monitor to analyze usage of materialized views in this chapter.

A DBA can also proactively manage a complex business intelligence query environment. Oracle's facility for doing this is the Database Resource Manager first introduced in Oracle*8i* to set levels of service and allocate percentages of CPU time and degree of parallelism. For example, a DBA might allocate higher

CPU percentages and levels of service for generating simple reports in time to meet service level agreements (SLAs) while allocating lower percentages to groups that submit ad hoc queries during the time the reports are being generated. The Oracle9*i* Database Resource Manager and newer versions also include the ability to enable proactive query governing, automatic queuing of queries, and dynamic reprioritization of queries to other resource groups. Queries submitted that are determined through cost-based optimizer statistics to be long-running and resource-intensive and that exceed predefined limits can be automatically aborted or run at a lower and less obtrusive priority level.

The Database Resource Manager is accessible through Enterprise Manager under the Administration tab. The Resource Manager section includes several facilities. The Resource Manager Consumer Groups interface enables defining what database-defined roles are assigned to each consumer group. The Resource Consumer Group Mapping interface enables members to be assigned based on Oracle username, operating system username, client program name, client machine name, service name, module name, or module name and action.

Consumer groups are allocated resources based on levels they are assigned using the Resource Plans interface. Multiple plans can be prepared for potential activation. Figure 26-16 illustrates assigning of CPU percentages at multiple levels in a sample `SYSTEM_PLAN`. Other values that can be set through Resource Plans for these groups include maximum degree of parallelism, maximum number of sessions and timeout, maximum undo space, maximum estimated execution time, group to switch to after a certain execution time, and maximum idle times.

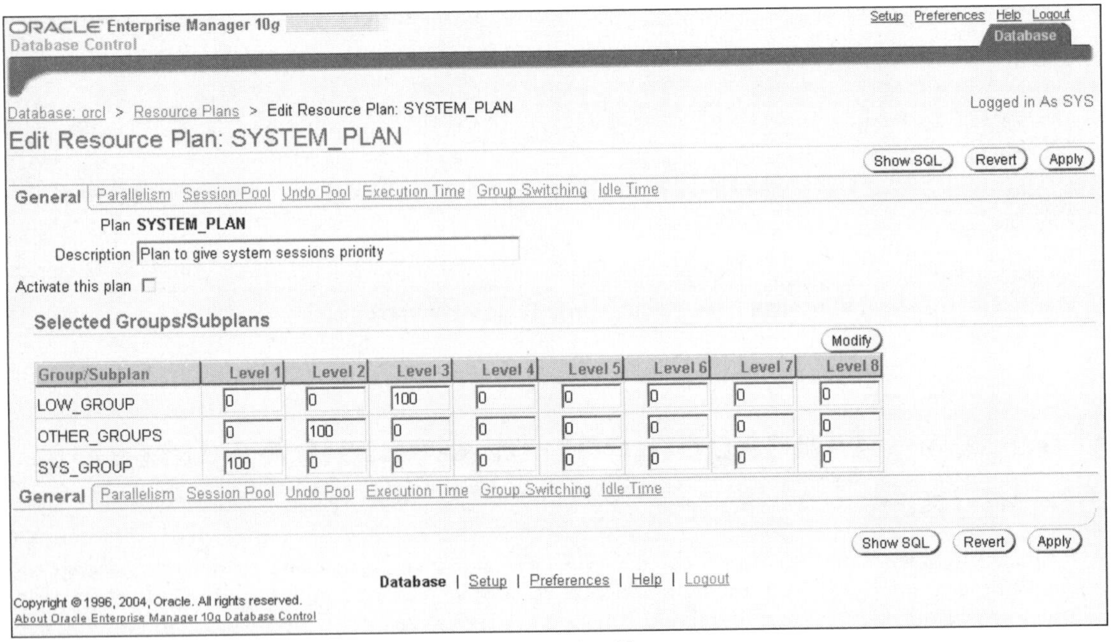

Figure 26-16: Resource Plan interface in Oracle Enterprise Manager.

Once you have defined your resource plan, you'll be ready to activate and monitor it. A Resource Monitors interface provides this capability. DBAs can view statistics for each consumer group, including active sessions, sessions waiting, requests, CPU wait times, CPU waits, consumed CPU times, and yields. Statistics can be updated manually or every 30 seconds.

Summary

This chapter covered basic queries and the underlying schema typically used for business intelligence solutions. We described the use of partition-wise joins and bitmap indexes, dimensions and hierarchies, summary tables and materialized views, and aggregation through SQL. We also described some of the proactive query management capabilities in Oracle.

For an operational data store (ODS) or enterprise data warehouse design, a third normal form may be desired. The creation of summary levels and star schema is often foreign to database designers more familiar with OLTP systems. However, as business analysts begin to submit their own ad hoc queries, including star schema and summaries can simplify access. Many Oracle-based data warehouses that are part enterprise data warehouse and part data mart are designed today using a hybrid schema that includes third normal form for detailed data and summary levels and star schema where needed.

Such data stores are often used for more sophisticated analysis than simple queries. For example, analytics and analytical processing, statistical analysis, forecasting and trend analysis, and data mining are sometimes required to provide needed business intelligence. The next chapter describes these techniques and provides examples.

27

Business Intelligence Analysis

As business intelligence can be defined as the retrieval and manipulation of data needed to produce information required for business decisions, data analysis often plays a critical role. This analysis of data increasingly occurs in the database and leverages analysis functions provided by the database. Until recently, most business analysts extracted data out of the database into spreadsheets, client/server business intelligence tools on the desktop, and special online analytical processing (OLAP) servers. The growth of browser-based deployment strategies created the desire to perform more analysis where the data is — in the database. As a result, a growing amount of analysis now uses extensions to SQL and Java APIs provided in Oracle. Many popular business intelligence tools, such as Oracle Discoverer, Business Objects, and Cognos, provide support for the extended SQL and the APIs.

This chapter describes the use of standard database analytic capabilities and also describes some of the optional components of the Oracle database: the OLAP Option and Data Mining Option. These solutions provide a range of analysis sophistication, from simple mathematical functions to trending and forecasting to the application of sophisticated algorithms and mathematical models used in making predictions. Note that some of these examples are date specific and that Oracle periodically revises the sample data set to make the data appear more current or more interesting. If your query runs but the results vary, chances are that this is due to such changes in the data set. Simply changing the year you query to one that is relevant to your data set will yield results. We'll begin by examining the simpler techniques possible using analytic SQL extensions in Oracle's database.

SQL Analytics and Statistics

Oracle's family of SQL analytic functions was first introduced in Oracle9*i*. The two releases of Oracle9*i* focused on providing the library of analytic functions defined in the 1999 ANSI SQL extensions. Oracle Database 10*g* adds many more types of analytics and statistics beyond those in the standard. Some of the commonly used functions include ranking and percentiles, cumulative and moving aggregate windows, reporting, lag/lead analysis, first/last analysis in an ordered group, linear regression and other statistics, inverse percentile, and hypothetical rank and distribution.

A multistep processing flow is defined when programs are written to use these functions. First, joins, `WHERE`, `GROUP BY`, and `HAVING` clauses are performed. The `GROUP BY` is used to create analytic partitions in order to divide query results into groups of rows. (Note: These analytic partitions are not be confused with Oracle's table partitions.) In the next step of the process, analytic functions are applied to the results set. When a query has an `ORDER BY` clause at the end, that processing then occurs.

In the following sections, we provide examples showing usage of many of these functions in SQL statements and expected results using the sample schema (`sh` and `oe`) and data that are part of the standard installation of an Oracle Database 10*g* release. This chapter serves as an introduction to these functions. Additional examples of these and other analytic functions are provided in the *Oracle Data Warehousing Guide*, part of the standard database documentation set provided by Oracle.

Ranking and Percentiles

Ranking functions sort values from smallest to largest (or vice versa) and provide a numeric indication of where a value falls on the list of values. The default for ranking is ascending order (the smallest value ranked first, followed by the second smallest, the third smallest, and so on) though you can also specify rank in descending order. Simple ranking (the `RANK` function) handles ties by giving equal values the same rank and then giving the next value a ranking based on where it falls on the list (so if two values are tied for fifth, the next value would be ranked seventh). Alternatively, you could use Oracle's `DENSE_RANK`, which would instead rank the next value sixth if a tie occurs in the fifth ranking. Null values are considered larger than any other value, though you can override this for either ascending or descending order by specifying a `NULLS FIRST` or `NULLS LAST` clause.

Let's look at some examples. You might want to see a ranking of the products you have in inventory from fewest to most. The following syntax would enable you rank the `quantity_on_hand` using the ranking function:

```
SELECT product_id,
     TO_CHAR (quantity_on_hand, '9,999,999') QUANTITY,
     RANK() OVER (ORDER BY quantity_on_hand) AS quantity_rank
FROM oe.toronto_inventory;
```

The highest ranked results (lowest quantity in inventory) reported using Oracle's sample data set would appear as in Figure 27-1 in *i*SQL*Plus, showing the product ID, quantity, and quantity rank.

PRODUCT_ID	QUANTITY	QUANTITY_RANK
2416	42	1
2417	42	1
2422	42	1
2423	43	4
1940	44	5
1733	46	6
1734	46	6

Figure 27-1: Output of a ranking in the default ascending order.

Note that this query returns the entire results set. For purposes of brevity, we are only showing a portion of the results here and in some of the other examples that follow. Of course, you can also formulate the query such that only the top N ranks are returned by enclosing the `RANK` function in a subquery and specifying a filter condition outside of the subquery (e.g., `WHERE quantity_rank <= N`).

If you would want to rank the product quantities you have in inventory (`quantity_on_hand`) from most to fewest, you would use a similar syntax, but you would additionally specify descending (`DESC`) order:

```
SELECT product_id,
     TO_CHAR (quantity_on_hand, '9,999,999') QUANTITY,
     RANK() OVER (ORDER BY quantity_on_hand DESC) AS quantity_rank
FROM oe.toronto_inventory;
```

This query produces the results shown in Figure 27-2 you are when using the Oracle Database 10*g* release sample schema and data set.

PRODUCT_ID	QUANTITY	QUANTITY_RANK
3300	237	1
3301	237	1
3501	220	3
3502	216	4
3503	216	4

Figure 27-2: Output of a ranking in descending order.

Of course, you might want to handle ties in rankings differently. For example, you might want a denser ranking such that if a tie occurs ranking two values as rank N, the next unique value would have a ranking value of N+1 (instead of N+2). The following example uses the `DENSE_RANK` function to create such a ranking. As in the previous example, descending order for `quantity_on_hand is specified`:

```
SELECT product_id,
     TO_CHAR (quantity_on_hand, '9,999,999') QUANTITY,
     DENSE_RANK() OVER (ORDER BY quantity_on_hand DESC) AS quantity_rank
FROM oe.toronto_inventory;
```

Since two items were tied for first, the third most stocked item now appears second in ranking in the output shown in Figure 27-3 (instead of third as it appeared in Figure 27-2).

PRODUCT_ID	QUANTITY	QUANTITY_RANK
3300	237	1
3301	237	1
3501	220	2
3502	216	3
3503	216	3

Figure 27-3: Output of a dense ranking in descending order.

The `CUME_DIST` or cumulative distribution function computes position of a value relative to a set of values, also sometimes known as the inverse of a percentile. The numerator of the calculation is the row count for a given value, and the denominator is the size of the set (total number of rows for all values). The following example shows the default ascending ranking (though, as before, descending could be specified):

```
SELECT product_id,
     TO_CHAR (quantity_on_hand, '9,999,999') QUANTITY,
     CUME_DIST() OVER (ORDER BY quantity_on_hand) AS quantity_cume_dist
FROM oe.toronto_inventory;
```

The highest ranked quantity would have the lowest cumulative distribution value, as illustrated in Figure 27-4.

PRODUCT_ID	QUANTITY	QUANTITY_CUME_DIST
2416	42	.026315789
2417	42	.026315789
2422	42	.026315789
2423	43	.035087719
1940	44	.043859649
1733	46	.061403509

Figure 27-4: Output of a cumulative distribution.

If you simply want to report the row number of each ranking, you can do so by using the `ROW_NUMBER` function.

The inverse of the `CUME_DIST` function — that is, finding what value computes to a certain percentile — was formerly quite difficult. Oracle now features the `PERCENTILE_CONT` function (for use where values are continuous) and the `PERCENTILE_DISC` function (for use where values are discrete) to perform this computation.

`PERCENT_RANK` is similar to `CUME_DIST` but computes using rank less 1 as the value in the numerator and size of the set less 1 in the denominator. Therefore, the top ranked item(s) will always have a percent rank of 0. The following SQL is used in this example:

```
SELECT product_id,
     TO_CHAR (quantity_on_hand, '9,999,999') QUANTITY,
     PERCENT_RANK() OVER (ORDER BY quantity_on_hand) AS quantity_percent_rank
FROM oe.toronto_inventory;
```

The highest ranked `quantity_on_hand` results and their percent rank appear as shown in Figure 27-5.

PRODUCT_ID	QUANTITY	QUANTITY_PERCENT_RANK
2416	42	0
2417	42	0
2422	42	0
2423	43	.026548673
1940	44	.03539823
[illegible]	[illegible]	[illegible]

Figure 27-5: Output of a percentile ranking.

Where data needs to be grouped into buckets for analysis (sometimes used as a precursor to data mining), the `NTILE` function is useful. The number of buckets is specified, and each row is assigned into a bucket. In the following example, the product and `quantity_on_hand` data is broken up into 100 buckets:

```
SELECT product_id,
     TO_CHAR (quantity_on_hand, '9,999,999') QUANTITY,
     NTILE(100) OVER (ORDER BY quantity_on_hand) AS quantity_ntile_100
FROM oe.toronto_inventory;
```

The products and their associated highest ranked quantities are assigned to the buckets as shown in Figure 27-6.

PRODUCT_ID	QUANTITY	QUANTITY_NTILE_100
2416	42	1
2417	42	1
2422	42	2
2423	43	2
1940	44	3
1733	46	3
1734	46	4
1737	47	4
1738	47	5

Figure 27-6: Output of `NTILE` function assigning buckets.

These are relatively simple examples of ranking. Ranking can also be used on multiple expressions and within groups (using partitions) and per cube and rollup. A hypothetical ranking function is provided for determining where an imaginary value would rank if it occurred. Hypothetical ranking and distribution are covered in the "Linear Regression and Other Advanced Functions" section of this chapter.

Windows Functions for Cumulative and Moving Aggregates

Oracle provides a set of cumulative and moving aggregate windows functions including cumulative and moving sum (`SUM`), moving average (`AVG`), moving maximum (`MAX`), moving minimum (`MIN`), row count (`COUNT`), standard deviation (`STDDEV`), and variance (`VARIANCE`). In addition, Oracle provides `FIRST_VALUE` and `LAST VALUE` functions used in returning the first and last values in a window (and very useful when used with extremely large data sets).

This section begins with an example using `SUM`. This example shows cumulative sales to customers in the year 2001 by using quarterly data in the Oracle Database 10*g* release sample schema and data set:

```
SELECT customers.cust_id, times.calendar_quarter_desc,
    TO_CHAR (SUM(amount_sold), '99,999,999') AS Quarter_Sales,
    TO_CHAR (SUM(SUM(amount_sold))
    OVER (PARTITION BY customers.cust_id
        ORDER BY customers.cust_id, times.calendar_quarter_desc
        ROWS UNBOUNDED PRECEDING), '99,999,999') AS Cum_Sales
    FROM sh.sales, sh.times, sh.customers
   WHERE sales.time_id = times.time_id AND sales.cust_id = customers.cust_id AND
times.calendar_year=2001
GROUP BY customers.cust_id, times.calendar_quarter_desc
ORDER BY customers.cust_id, times.calendar_quarter_desc;
```

In this example, the data is partitioned by customer ID (`cust_id`). Prior to running this query, you'll want to check to see if your data set aligns with this query since Oracle periodically changes the sample data set. For example, you could get a different answer from the preceding query or no rows returned at all if you have no data from 2001. For an early release of Oracle Database 10*g*, cumulative sales for each customer appear in the table shown in Figure 27-7, adjacent to each customer's quarterly sales results.

CUST_ID	CALENDAR_QUARTER_DESC	QUARTER_SALES	CUM_SALES
2	2001-01	6,018	6,018
2	2001-02	7,355	13,373
2	2001-03	4,195	17,568
6	2001-02	7,213	7,213
6	2001-03	8,093	15,307
7	2001-02	6,828	6,828
9	2001-01	6,409	6,409
9	2001-04	7,098	13,507
14	2001-03	1,499	1,499
17	2001-03	5,960	5,960
17	2001-04	4,544	10,504
19	2001-02	166	166
19	2001-03	201	367
22	2001-01	3,069	3,069
23	2001-01	25	25
23	2001-02	12,698	12,723
23	2001-04	1,980	14,702
27	2001-04	7,254	7,254

Figure 27-7: Output of a cumulative sum showing cumulative sales for each customer.

Now, let's compute the moving average of sales for two months for a specific customer. Moving averages can be useful in the smoothing of data for purposes of discovering trends and minimizing peaks and valleys. Prior to formulating the query, you looked at Oracle's data set. Customer 2 looked interesting, as in the year 1998, the customer consistently bought the goods offered. (Note that, once again, you'll want to confirm that you have data in your sample set that aligns with this example.) Now you'll look at both the monthly sales data and the two-month moving average (average of current and preceding month) for customer 2 using this query:

```
SELECT customers.cust_id, times.calendar_month_desc,
    TO_CHAR (SUM(amount_sold), '99,999,999') AS Monthly_Sales,
    TO_CHAR (AVG(SUM(amount_sold))
    OVER (ORDER BY customers.cust_id, times.calendar_month_desc
        ROWS 1 PRECEDING), '99,999,999') AS Moving_2_Month_Avg
    FROM sh.sales, sh.times, sh.customers
   WHERE sales.time_id = times.time_id AND sales.cust_id = customers.cust_id AND
times.calendar_year=1998 AND customers.cust_id IN (2)
GROUP BY customers.cust_id, times.calendar_month_desc
ORDER BY customers.cust_id, times.calendar_month_desc;
```

Note the use of AVG in formulating the previous query, as a moving average is computed. The month in 1998, monthly sales, and two-month moving average appear in the results as shown in Figure 27-8 for a version of the data that comes with Oracle Database 10*g*.

CUST_ID	CALENDAR_MONTH_DESC	MONTHLY_SALES	MOVING_2_MONTH_AVG
2	1998-01	5,219	5,219
2	1998-03	8,728	6,973
2	1998-04	300	4,514
2	1998-05	9,193	4,747
2	1998-06	410	4,802
2	1998-07	536	473
2	1998-08	1,809	1,172
2	1998-09	8,281	5,045
2	1998-10	3,070	5,675
2	1998-11	10,269	6,669
2	1998-12	136	5,203

11 rows selected.

Figure 27-8: Output of a moving average computation.

In addition to computing a moving average using previous data, you can center your aggregate function around a current row. This example we computes a centered 15-day average (e.g., current date and plus/minus seven days) for a specific customer (11) in 1998:

```
SELECT sales.cust_id,  times.time_id,
    TO_CHAR (SUM(amount_sold), '99,999,999') AS Daily_Sales,
    TO_CHAR (AVG(SUM(amount_sold))
    OVER (PARTITION BY sales.cust_id
    ORDER by times.time_id
    RANGE BETWEEN INTERVAL '7' DAY PRECEDING AND
    INTERVAL '7' DAY FOLLOWING), '99,999,999')
    AS Centered_15_Day_Avg
    FROM sh.sales, sh.times
    WHERE sales.time_id = times.time_id
    AND times.calendar_year=1998
    AND sales.cust_id IN (11)
GROUP BY sales.cust_id, times.time_id
ORDER BY sales.cust_id, times.time_id;
```

Provided the version of your data set contains values that align with the example (e.g., 1998), the results of this query showing dates of sales activity, sales, and centered 15-day average sales for customer 11 appear in Figure 27-9.

As noted previously, other statistical analysis functions are available for use. Window aggregates can also be analyzed for duplicates, applied with physical offsets, and varied for rows based on specified conditions.

CUST_ID	TIME_ID	DAILY_SALES	CENTERED_15_DAY_AVG
11	18-JAN-98	251	135
11	22-JAN-98	19	100
11	27-JAN-98	30	25
11	13-FEB-98	395	224
11	15-FEB-98	215	224
11	19-FEB-98	62	224
11	16-MAR-98	127	141
11	18-MAR-98	273	141
11	22-MAR-98	23	141
11	31-MAR-98	27	27
11	15-APR-98	136	765
11	17-APR-98	602	765
11	21-APR-98	1,556	765
11	29-APR-98	166	166
11	16-MAY-98	176	120
11	18-MAY-98	162	120
11	22-MAY-98	23	120
11	15-JUN-98	140	848
11	21-JUN-98	1,556	848
11	29-JUN-98	261	261
11	16-JUL-98	367	213
11	18-JUL-98	250	213
11	22-JUL-98	22	213
11	16-AUG-98	150	164

Figure 27-9: Output of a centered average computation.

Lag/Lead Analysis

Lag and lead functions are used in comparing a value at a point in time versus previous values and subsequent values. Such computations are popular in financial analysis (such as for investigating changes in stock prices over a period of time). The following is a sales example in which the query produces lag and lead indicators for sales over a 15-day defined period in 2001:

```
SELECT sales.time_id,
    TO_CHAR (SUM(amount_sold), '99,999,999') AS Daily_Sales,
    TO_CHAR (LAG(SUM(amount_sold),1)
    OVER (ORDER BY sales.time_id), '99,999,999') AS Lag_Indicator,
    TO_CHAR (LEAD(SUM(amount_sold),1)
    OVER (ORDER BY sales.time_id), '99,999,999') AS Lead_indicator
    FROM sh.sales
    WHERE
    sales.time_id>=TO_DATE ('01-JAN-2001') AND
    sales.time_id<=TO_DATE ('15-JAN-2001')
GROUP BY sales.time_id;
```

Provided the version of your sample data set is in alignment with this query, the results of this query using an Oracle Database 10*g* release sample schema and data set would appear as in Figure 27-10.

TIME_ID	DAILY_SALES	LAG_INDICATOR	LEAD_INDICATOR
01-JAN-01	27,841		21,523
02-JAN-01	21,523	27,841	49,547
03-JAN-01	49,547	21,523	41,494
04-JAN-01	41,494	49,547	28,001
05-JAN-01	28,001	41,494	26,480
06-JAN-01	26,480	28,001	56,536
07-JAN-01	56,536	26,480	31,978
08-JAN-01	31,978	56,536	34,764
09-JAN-01	34,764	31,978	117,817
10-JAN-01	117,817	34,764	23,242
11-JAN-01	23,242	117,817	25,692
12-JAN-01	25,692	23,242	37,225
13-JAN-01	37,225	25,692	48,667
14-JAN-01	48,667	37,225	21,217
15-JAN-01	21,217	48,667	

15 rows selected.

Figure 27-10: Output showing lag and lead indicators.

First/Last Analysis

First and last analysis functions are useful in applying an aggregate over a set of rows that rank first or last, such as comparisons with minimum or maximum values. These types of comparisons are popular where products are sold. For example, you might want to understand your highest minimum price list price in each product category and the highest minimum price you sell products for in each of those categories. The following query provides that answer using the Oracle Database 10*g* release sample data and schema order entry product table:

```
SELECT products.category_id,
    MAX (list_price)
    KEEP (DENSE_RANK LAST ORDER BY (min_price)) AS List_Price_of_Highest_Min,
    MAX (min_price) AS Highest_Minimum_Price
FROM oe.products
GROUP BY category_id;
```

The results of this query are as shown in Figure 27-11.

CATEGORY_ID	LIST_PRICE_OF_HIGHEST_MIN	HIGHEST_MINIMUM_PRICE
11	1023	909
12	699	568
13		731
14	699	560
15	48	355
16	78	63
17	333	270
19	3219	2606
21	50	44
22	65	54
24	1500	1303
25	555	448
29	222	195
31	3980	3347
32	300	246
33	125	111
39	112	99

17 rows selected.

Figure 27-11: Output of a highest minimum comparison.

Linear Regression and Other Advanced Functions

Oracle provides other advanced functions useful in analysis including linear regression , hypothetical ranking, a width bucket function, and a new advanced package of statistical functions in Oracle Database 10*g*. Linear regression functions enable the fitting of an ordinary-least-squares regression line to a set of paired numbers. The following functions are provided:

`REGR_COUNT`	Number of non-null number pairs used to fit a regression line
`REGR_AVGX`	Average of independent variables for a regression line
`REGR_AVGY`	Average of dependent variables for a regression line
`REGR_SLOPE`	Slope of a regression line
`REGR_INTERCEPT`	Y-intercept of the regression line
`REGR_R2`	R-squared or coefficient of determination

Diagnostic statistics computational functions are also provided for regression analysis including `REGR_SXX`, `REGR_SYY`, and `REGR_SXY`. The following query demonstrates usage of some of these functions and produces a regression count and average of independent variables (`REGR_AVGX`), and it computes the Y-intercept of a regression line using the Oracle Database 10*g* release sample schema and data set:

```
SELECT order_items.product_id,
REGR_COUNT(inventories.quantity_on_hand, order_items.unit_price) Count,
REGR_AVGX (inventories.quantity_on_hand, order_items.unit_price) Avg_Unit_Price,
REGR_INTERCEPT (inventories.quantity_on_hand, order_items.unit_price) Intercept
FROM oe.inventories, oe.order_items
```

```
WHERE inventories.product_id = order_items.product_id
        AND inventories.product_id IN (1797, 1820)
GROUP BY order_items.product_id;
```

The results of this query are as shown in Figure 27-12, as viewed in *i*SQL*Plus.

PRODUCT_ID	COUNT	AVG_UNIT_PRICE	INTERCEPT
1797	9	327.2	18.6666667
1820	15	51.6666667	75

Figure 27-12: Output of regression values.

A common application of ranking and distribution in sales activities is to determine how important a deal really is. For example, if you sold a deal of a certain size, where would it rank in your deals? The hypothetical ranking function first appeared in Oracle9*i* Release 2 to answer such questions. In this example, you determine the hypothetical rank, hypothetical percent rank, and hypothetical cumulative distribution of a deal that is $65,000. The following query uses the sample orders entry orders table:

```
SELECT order_mode,
     RANK (65000) WITHIN GROUP
     (ORDER BY orders.order_total DESC) AS Hypothetical_Rank,
     TO_CHAR (PERCENT_RANK (65000) WITHIN GROUP
            (ORDER BY orders.order_total), '9.999') AS Hypoth_Pct_Rank,
     TO_CHAR (CUME_DIST (65000) WITHIN GROUP
            (ORDER BY orders.order_total), '9.999') AS Hypoth_Cume_Dist
      FROM oe.orders
WHERE order_mode = 'direct'
GROUP BY order_mode;
```

The results of this query show where the sales revenue figure would rank among "direct" orders (see Figure 27-13).

ORDER_MODE	HYPOTHETICAL_RANK	HYPOTH_PCT_RANK	HYPOTH_CUME_DIST
direct	10	.877	.878

Figure 27-13: Output of hypothetical ranking.

Earlier, we described the `NTILE` function for putting rankings into buckets. For numeric or date/datetime types, a `WIDTH_BUCKET` function can be used to generate equi-width histograms and return bucket numbers assigned after the expression is evaluated.

Oracle Database 10*g* release added several additional capabilities especially useful in advanced analysis. The PL/SQL package `DBMS_FREQUENT_ITEMSETS` enables counting how often multiple events occur together (useful in market basket analysis). The `DBMS_STAT_FUNCS` package provides a new statistical package of functions, including descriptive statistics, hypothesis testing in parametric tests, cross-tab statistics, hypothesis testing for nonparametric tests, and nonparametric correlation.

Descriptive statistics functions in `DBMS_STAT_FUNCS` include `MEDIAN` and `STATS_MODE`. Hypothesis testing in parametric tests functions include `STATS_T_TEST_ONE` (single sample), `STATS_T_TEST_PAIRED` (paired samples), `STATS_T_TEST_INDEP` (pool variances), `STATS_T_TEST_INDEPU` (unpooled variances), `STATS_F_TEST`, and STATS_ONE_WAY_ANOVA. The cross-tab statistics function is STATS_CROSSTAB and can return values such as observed value of chi-squared, significance of observed chi-squared, degree of freedom for chi-squared, Cramer's V statistic Phi coefficient, the contingency coefficient, and Cohen's Kappa. Hypothesis testing for nonparametric tests functions include STATS_WSR_TEST (Binomial Test or Wilcoxon Signed Ranks Test), STATS_MW_TEST (Mann-Whitney Test), and the STATS_KS_Test (Kolmogorov-Smirnov Test). Nonparametric correlation functions include CORR_S (Spearman's Rho coefficient) and CORR_K (Kendall's Tau-b coefficient).

Finally, Oracle also includes support for user-defined aggregate functions written in languages such as PL/SQL, Java, and C; simple and searched CASE expressions; and data densification in reporting (for joins using PARTITION BY).

OLAP

Online analytical processing is the usage of multidimensional data (fact-based transactional data surrounded by dimensions or lookup tables) for applications that include forecasting and trend analysis. OLAP deployment has taken two forms in the past. Relational online analytical processing (ROLAP) leverages data stored in a relational star schema, a fact table with foreign key relationships to dimensions. This approach is described in Chapter 26, "Business Intelligence Query," where we discuss Oracle's star schema and materialized views (providing multiple levels). The second approach is called multidimensional online analytical processing (MOLAP).

A MOLAP engine is a separate database engine with facts and dimensions prejoined in what is referenced as a "cube." Oracle previously provided such a solution in the Express product. Beginning with Oracle9*i*, Oracle began imbedding MOLAP functionality in the relational database as an "OLAP Option." The cubes are stored as objects within the relational database. An advantage of this deployment approach is that the same DBA can manage MOLAP and relational data using the same underlying database administration capabilities. An even more significant advantage is that drill-through from OLAP cubes into detailed relational data can appear seamless to business analysts. For example, tools such as Business Objects and Cognos ReportNet use SQL to drill from the levels in MOLAP cubes into the relational data. Oracle provides a Java API to OLAP, enabling more advanced manipulation of the MOLAP cube. Oracle's Discoverer tool and spreadsheet add-in feature (OracleBI) access the OLAP Option via this API. Both Discoverer and the spreadsheet add-in provide a wizard for generating and modifying queries. Figure 27-14 shows the query editor as it appears when using the spreadsheet add-in. For custom building of Java-based applications, Oracle offers a Java development tool, JDeveloper, with Business Intelligence Java Beans (BI Beans).

Building an Oracle OLAP cube is a multistep process. At this writing, sample cubes and cube data are not provided in the sample schema installed with Oracle Database 10*g*. However, Oracle does document the building of a sample schema in the *Oracle OLAP Applications Developer's Guide* provided in the standard Oracle documentation set. SQL scripts are listed in the documentation for defining users and tablespaces, building a "Globalx" star schema, and defining an OLAP catalog for meta data. OLAP cubes reside in their own analytic workspace, so the meta data setup includes definitions of dimensions, measures, facts, and the cubes themselves. Two types of meta data need be created: CWM1 for management and CWM2 to define the analytic workspace.

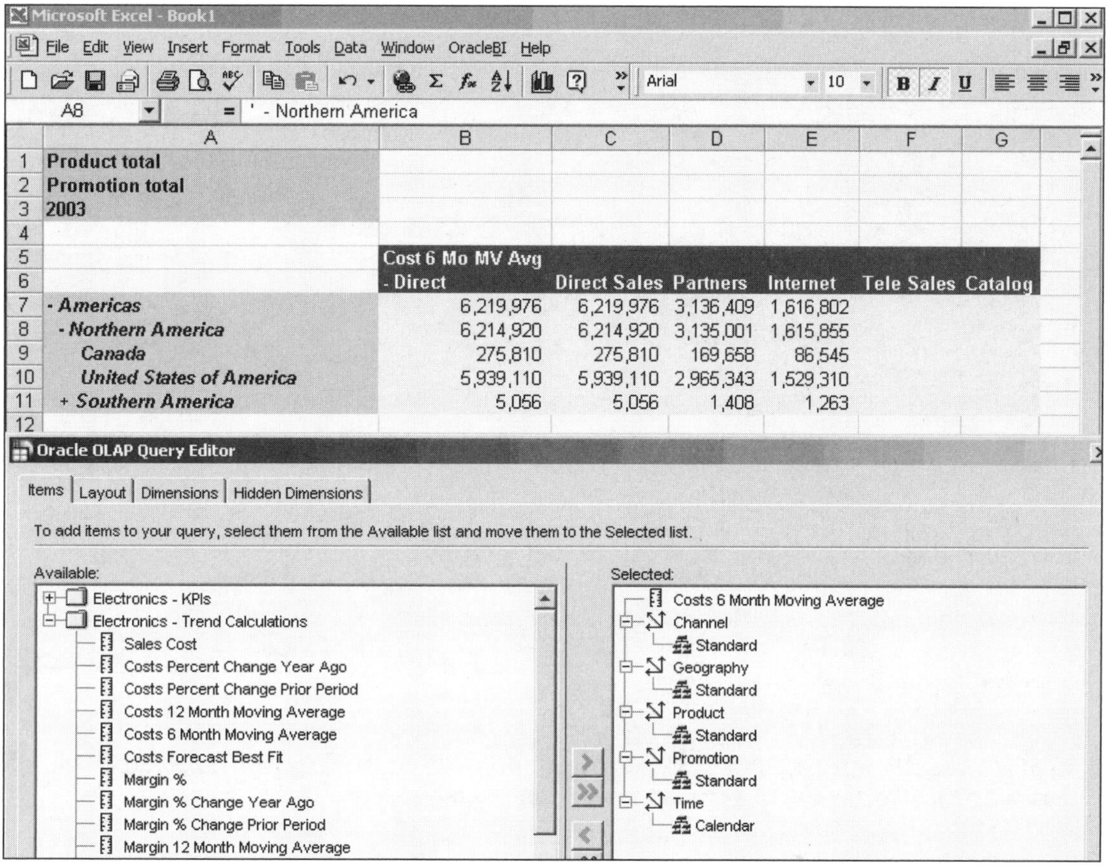

Figure 27-14: Oracle Spreadsheet add-in with OLAP Query Editor.

From a practical standpoint, when you develop OLAP solutions, you will probably create cubes using the capabilities provided in Oracle Warehouse Builder (OWB) or the Analytic Workspace Manager (AWM). OWB is part of Oracle's Development Suite and is primarily known as an extraction, transformation, and loading (ETL) tool for data warehousing. It also serves as a meta data repository and design tool and supports building of the analytic workspaces and meta data for OLAP. Figure 27-15 shows a cube as represented in OWB.

You can also use AWM for creating and maintaining the meta data that defines an OLAP cube. Figure 27-16 shows a mapping in AWM from a relational table into an analytic workspace.

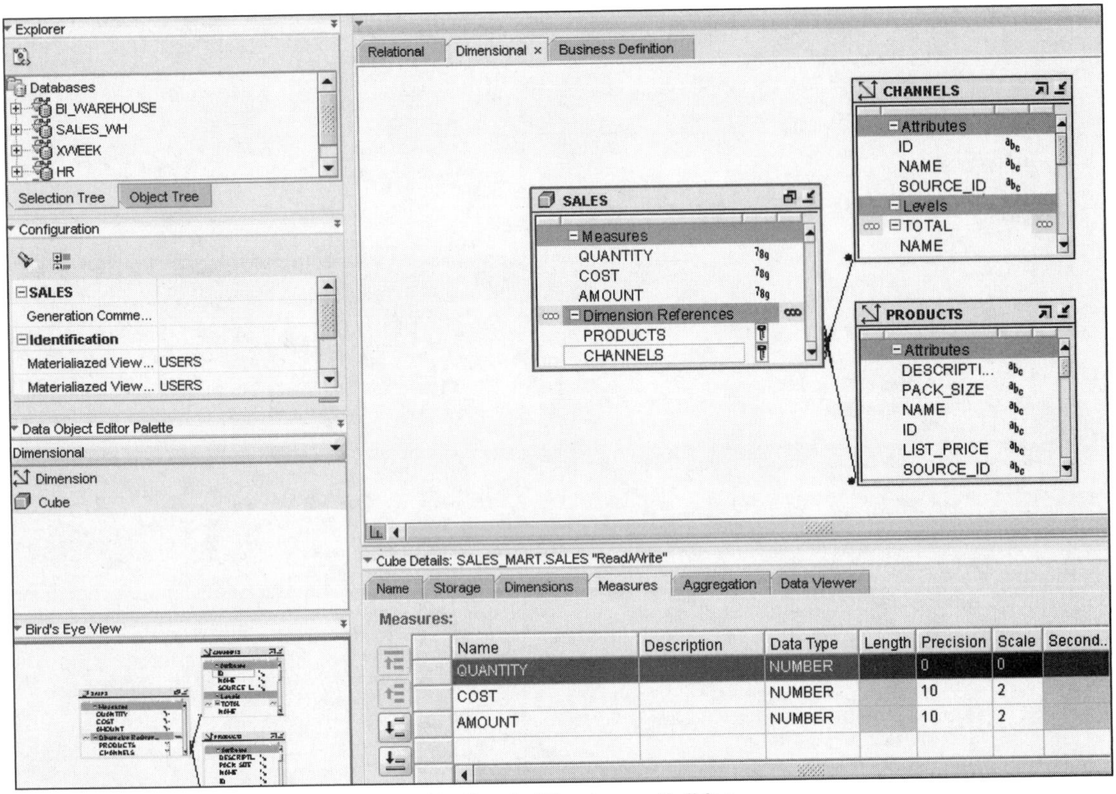

Figure 27-15: OLAP Cube as represented in Oracle Warehouse Builder.

Enterprise Manager is used for defining the meta data used for cube management. Figure 27-17 shows a cube creation screen in Oracle Enterprise Manager.

Once deployed, business analysts using business intelligence tools and applications cannot usually tell if they are accessing data stored in OLAP cubes or relational tables. When these tools provide access to the data via SQL, the hierarchies linking OLAP cube levels to relational levels are defined by data modelers via meta data level descriptions stored in the tools. Tools that leverage the Java APIs, such as Oracle's Discoverer, automatically open a Java API interface when accessing the data stored in the OLAP Option.

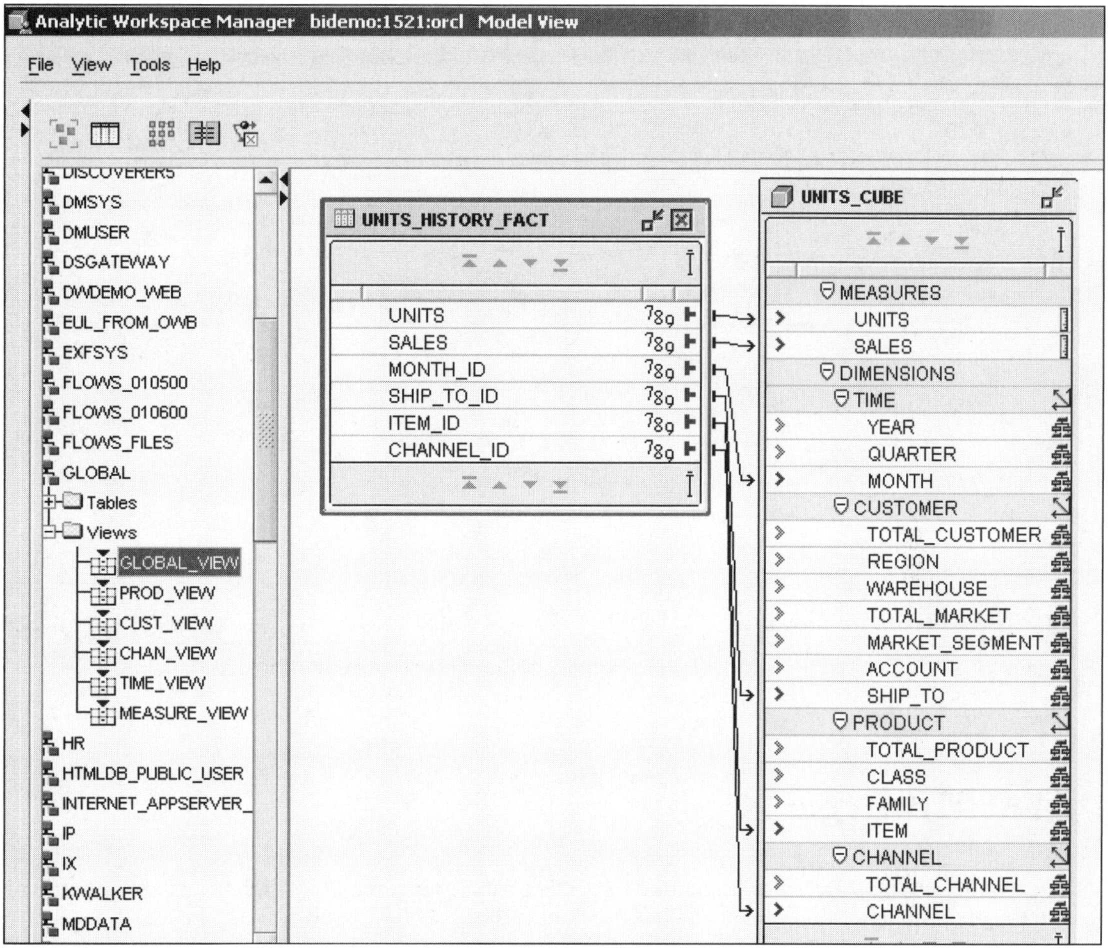

Figure 27-16: AWM mapping from relational fact table to OLAP cube.

As OLAP applications can be custom-built using the Java API, JDeveloper provides a set of reusable components to provide consistency in development (the BI Beans). The API is documented in the *Oracle OLAP Application Developer's Guide* and the *Oracle OLAP Developer's Guide to the API*, provided in the standard Oracle documentation set. Class libraries are provided in an OLAP API JAR file. You'll also need certain Oracle JDBC JAR files for deployment. Both are provided as part of the Oracle Database installation. JDeveloper provides the JDK version 1.2 that is also needed.

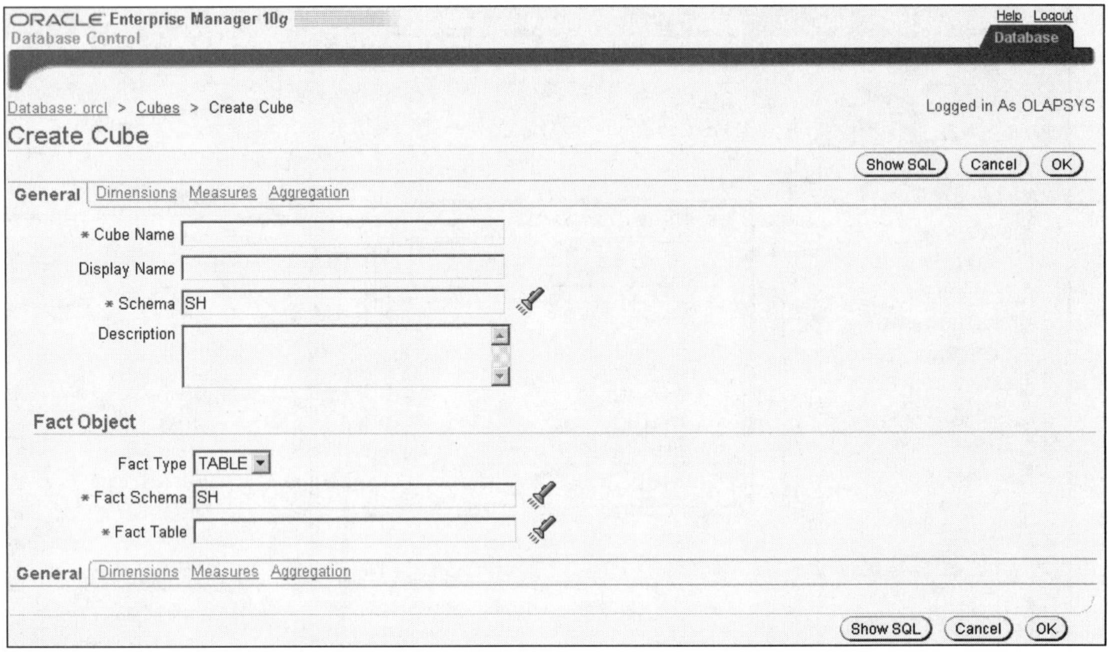

Figure 27-17: Cube creation interface in Enterprise Manager Database Control.

Data Mining

Data mining is a technique generally used in very difficult analysis problems where a very large number of variables and data are present and understanding future outcome has a high return on investment. It is typically used to solve problems in areas such as fraud detection, product failure prediction, and customer churn analysis.

Similar to OLAP, data mining is in transition from primarily being deployed on standalone database engines to leveraging embedded technology in multipurpose data warehouses. Oracle's Data Mining Option for the database provides a set of algorithms that can be accessed via SQL or via a Java API for data mining. Tools from SPSS (Clementine) and InforSense support access to the Oracle data mining algorithms. As of Oracle Database 10*g*, Oracle offers a data mining development tool named Data Miner (replacing the previous DM4J that was based on Oracle's JDeveloper).

Oracle enables deployment of data mining for a variety of applications Classification algorithms (Support Vector Machines, or SVM; Naïve Bayes; and Adaptive Bayes Network) can be used to predict discrete outcomes in binary or multiclass situations, such as which product is likely to fail or performance levels that a new employee might attain. Regression algorithms (SVM) are used where continuous values are predicted, such as the likely number of sales for a new product. Association Rules can find related items and are popularly used in market-basket analysis. The data sets can also be segmented using clustering algorithms (Enhanced K-Means, O-Cluster), and relative attribute importance can be determined using

Minimum Descriptive Length (MDL). Feature extraction (Non-negative Matrix Factorization, or NMF) can be used to describe data in a much smaller feature set. Finally, text mining is supported using SVM, NMF, Association Rules, or K-Means.

An emerging standard for data mining is the Data Mining's Group Model Predictive Markup Language (PMML). Oracle supports PMML for Naïve Bayes and Association Rules models.

Oracle provides data mining programming examples as part of the installation of the Oracle Database 10*g* in the `$ORACLE_HOME/dm/demo/sample` directory. This directory includes examples written in Java and PL/SQL. These code samples demonstrate attribute importance using an MDL-based algorithm; Association Rules using the Apriori algorithm; classification using the Adaptive Bayes Network algorithm, the Naïve Bayes algorithm, and the SVM algorithm; feature extraction using the NMF algorithm; regression using the SVM algorithm, and text extraction and classification using NMF and SVM. Some of the scripts are designed to use the sample sales data and `sh` schema installed with Oracle Database 10*g*.

Setting up data mining is often an involved process. Having a closer look at the examples will give you some insight into this process. For example, running the `svmc_sh.sql` script in *i*SQL*Plus demonstrates classification using the Support Vector Machine algorithm. The steps in the script are typical data mining procedures:

1. Setup of training data
2. Creation of a settings table
3. Model building
4. Model testing
5. Test data preparation
6. Populating a cost matrix
7. Applying test data to the model
8. Computing a confusion matrix
9. Applying the model to a full data set

When you run the sample script, the result you'll see is the SVM complexity factor, convergence tolerance value, and kernel function shown in Figure 27-18.

SETTING_NAME	SETTING_VALUE
ALGO_NAME	ALGO_SUPPORT_VECTOR_MACHINES
SVMS_COMPLEXITY_FACTOR	.19459740583167701
SVMS_CONV_TOLERANCE	.001
SVMS_KERNEL_FUNCTION	SVMS_LINEAR

```
Display MODEL SIGNATURE
PL/SQL procedure successfully completed.
```

Figure 27-18: Support Vector Machine output using the Data Mining Option.

Summary

This chapter provided examples using the embedded analysis features within the Oracle database. These examples included some of the analytics and statistical functions, and usage of the OLAP and Data Mining Options. The examples demonstrating analytics and statistics can be reproduced using the sample schema that is included in a standard Oracle Database 10*g* installation. A sample OLAP Option schema is described in the standard Oracle documentation referenced in this chapter and is worth investigation if you wish to learn more about using the OLAP Option. The Data Mining Option examples discussed here are provided in a subdirectory built during the Oracle Database 10*g* installation.

The usage of analytics and statistics is becoming common practice for many business analysts. The OLAP Option is used by a smaller number of business analysts interested in performing trend analysis and forecasting. They might also use this option where high-speed manipulation of multidimensional cubes is desired. A very small number of analysts might use data mining to select the best algorithm to predict outcomes where a large number of variables exist.

Though this concludes the section of the book focused primarily on business intelligence and data warehousing, performance of queries and optimization are closely related topics. The next chapter discusses optimization.

28

Optimization

If you have been reading this book in the order the chapters have been presented, you have covered a lot of ground, from the basics of the Oracle database to more advanced development topics. But this book is not completely finished, just as your job is not finished once you successfully finish the creation of an application. After development comes deployment, and one of the key indicators of a successful deployment is an application that performs well.

Performance, of course, means different things to different interest groups. Your performance may be judged by how well you meet deadlines in the creation of your application or module. A database administrator may judge performance by how much CPU or memory is used by an Oracle instance. But to your constituency of users, performance is primarily determined by a judgment of response time, or how quickly data is returned from the Oracle database, compared to their expectation of that response time.

Of course, response time is based on many factors, such as the amount of available resources on the Oracle server and the network and the design of the database and the application. But you should still strive for the best performance available in your environment, performance that is based on the properly optimized retrieval of requested information.

What Is Optimization?

The outcome just described comes as the result of the work of the Oracle optimizer. This part of the Oracle database is responsible for discovering the best way to retrieve information requested by a user. To understand the need for an optimizer, you need to step back and remind yourself of one of the key premises of relational databases.

One of the primary benefits seen for relational technology was the ability to separate the physical access of data, which is done by the database, with the logical request for data, specified through an SQL statement. An SQL statement does not have to specify how to retrieve data — just what data was desired.

We have already discussed how the Oracle database can make a choice between retrieving data directly from the data blocks of the table, or use an index to direct the query to the relevant data. Take this simple situation and compound it with a table with many indexes, or a query that requests data from multiple tables, and add in additional requirements, such as the need to select data, sort data or group data, and calculate aggregate values, and you can see that an Oracle database may face a wide number of access choices.

The purpose of the optimizer is to sort through these choices and come up with the best plan of attack for data retrieval, which is known as the execution plan. A clever optimizer takes into account the presence of indexes, the relative speed of various access methods, and the resources available to the database server, as well as the specific access directives in the query. Oracle 10*g* Database has a clever optimizer that is based on the cost of these various access choices. Prior to Oracle 10*g*, the database allowed you to choose another type of optimizer, a rule-based optimizer, which predated the cost-based optimizer. The following section explains the different types of optimizers, since many of you may be using earlier versions of the Oracle database, and so may still be able to use the rule-based optimizer.

The Oracle Optimizer

The Oracle database has had an optimizer for a very long time. Initially, the Oracle database used a rule-based optimizer. This optimizer made its decisions about execution plans based on a series of rules, which were evaluated in a fixed order. The rules made perfect sense and were the result of many years of working with the Oracle database and its users.

However, the rule-based optimizer suffered from some faults, too. First, the set of rules used were finite, and in that sense, somewhat limited in the complexity they could encompass. As the complexity of the Oracle database grew with the introduction of new features, such as materialized views and function-based indexes, the rule-based optimizer was not enhanced to take advantage of them.

The rule-based optimizer had another basic flaw. Sometimes a choice between two different steps in an execution plan would end up in a tie — the rule-based optimizer could not determine which choice was more efficient. In these situations, the tie was resolved by looking at the order of the tables in the SQL query. The result of this form of tie-breaking meant that the same logical query could generate two different execution plans, based on the order of tables in the statement. This outcome flies in the face of relational theory, which requires that an SQL statement should be independent of the order of entities, when a simple re-ordering of the table could result in different execution plans and different performance. Besides, this anomaly meant that you, the developer, would have to be aware of things like the composition of the database in order to properly write your SQL. You certainly don't need that!

In version 7, Oracle introduced the cost-based optimizer. The cost-based optimizer can be considered to consist of shades of gray in contrast to the black-and-white decision-making process of the rule-based optimizer. With the cost-based optimizer, the Oracle database is able to consider resource usage, or cost, when it made decisions about which steps to use in an execution plan.

You saw the cost-based optimizer at work in one of the examples in Chapter 10 on indexes. The Oracle database determined that retrieving a small number of rows would be optimally executed by using an index, while retrieving more rows would be faster by directly accessing the data blocks of the table.

Initially, some Oracle users did not use the cost-based optimizers, based on the suspicion that it would not work as well as the rule-based optimizer. In the early versions of the cost-based optimizer, this suspicion was sometimes based on evidence. In the years since its introduction, the quality of the decisions made by the cost-based optimizer has improved, and new features of the Oracle database, such as bitmap and function-based indexes, have been taken into account by the cost-based optimizer, but not the rule-based optimizer.

In earlier books, we would have advised you to embrace the cost-based optimizer because of its advanced sophistication. With the release of Oracle 10*g*, we can merely state that the rule-based optimizer is no longer officially supported. The remainder of this chapter will exclusively concentrate on the cost-based optimizer, referred to simply as the optimizer from here on.

Optimizer Modes

At the start of this chapter, we stated that performance, from a user's point of view, was primarily determined by their expectation of response from an application. Although this definition is accurate for interactive use of systems, some IT tasks are mainly run in batch, where there is no direct user interaction. These types of tasks have a different view of performance, since a batch job doesn't need to waste cycles interacting with humans, but instead can concentrate on completing the entire job as rapidly as possible.

Because of this different requirement, the Oracle optimizer has two basic modes of operation. In one mode, identified by the keyword `FIRST_ROWS`, the goal of the optimizer is to get the first information back to the requestor as fast as possible. In the other mode, `ALL_ROWS`, the goal of the optimizer is to complete all the work for the request as fast as possible.

You can understand the effect of these two modes on optimizer choices with the simple matter of sorted data. Assume that an SQL query comes into the optimizer with an `ORDER BY` clause, and there is an index with the data already sorted in that order. If the optimizer is in `FIRST_ROWS` mode, the index will be more likely to be used, since the index already has the information in the desired sort order. Because of this pre-sorting, as soon as the first set of rows is retrieved from the Oracle database, the rows can be sent back to the requestor.

On the other hand, if the optimizer is in `ALL_ROWS` mode, it may be more efficient for Oracle to get all the rows directly from the data blocks in the table and then sort them. Although neither of these approaches will absolutely be chosen, depending on a host of other factors, the specified mode will help the Oracle optimizer to make the best selection.

Desupported Optimizer Modes

Prior to Oracle 10*g*, there were two other optimizer mode settings, `CHOOSE` and `RULE`. The `RULE` optimizer mode required the use of the rule-based optimizer, while the `CHOOSE` optimizer mode allowed Oracle to choose whether to use the rule-based optimizer or the cost-based optimizer.

Since the rule-based optimizer is no longer supported, these additional optimizer modes are also no longer supported.

Setting Optimizer Modes

You can set the optimizer mode for either the entire Oracle instance or a session. To set the optimizer mode for the instance, set the `OPTIMIZER_MODE` initialization parameter to the desired mode. To set the optimizer mode for a session, issue the following command at any time during the session:

```
ALTER SESSION SET OPTIMZER_MODE = mode
```

where *mode* is one of the keywords for an optimizer mode.

The keyword for the `ALL_ROWS` mode is `ALL_ROWS`. There are four different options for the `FIRST_ROWS` mode: `FIRST_ROWS_1`, `FIRST_ROWS_10`, `FIRST_ROWS_100`, and `FIRST_ROWS_1000`. The trailing number indicates the number of rows that should be used to estimate the best response time. The Oracle optimizer may take a slightly different approach to rapid return of one row, as opposed to rapid return of 100 or 1,000 rows.

Statistics

As Roger Angell, the brilliant baseball writer, once said, "Statistics are the fruit of love." For the Oracle optimizer, statistics are more than this — they form the basis for the entire decision-making process.

The cost-based optimizer understands how an Oracle database works and also understands the composition of your particular database instance. This latter understanding is granted through the use of statistics.

Statistics and Cost

It is one thing for the optimizer to know that a particular table has a particular index that contains a particular set of data. But there are times when the actual composition of the data in that index can make a difference.

To understand, assume that there are two indexes on a table, `INDEX_A` and `INDEX_B`. The Oracle optimizer is presented with a query to retrieve data from the table. The query contains selection criteria for data in both indexes. Which index should be used?

The optimal way to proceed with an execution plan is to first use an index that can rapidly eliminate the largest number of rows from the result set, which will leave a smaller set of rows to process in the next step of the selection process. The index that will provide the greater selectivity is one with a higher cardinality, a higher number of distinct values in the index.

The Oracle optimizer makes this determination by looking at the statistics for the various indexes. These statistics allow the optimizer to increase its palette of cost analysis by taking into account the actual content of the database objects that might be used in the execution plan.

You can direct Oracle to collect statistics based on an entire database object or to take a sampling of the contents of the object, to save on the overhead of statistics collection, as described in the following section.

Types of Statistics

The example cited in the previous section was somewhat crude, with the optimizer only determining how many values were in a particular index. In fact, the Oracle database collects many different statistics. You can gather statistics for a table, index, schema, or for the entire database.

For columns, statistics include the following:

- Number of distinct values for the column
- Average length of the column

For indexes, statistics include the following:

- Number of rows in the index
- Number of distinct values in the index
- Height of the index
- Number of leaf blocks in the index
- Average number of leaf blocks visited per distinct value in the index
- Average number of data (table) blocks visited per distinct value in the index
- Clustering factor, which was described in Chapter 10 on indexes

For tables, statistics include the following:

- Number of rows in the table
- Average row length of the table
- Total number of blocks the table uses

For both tables and indexes, Oracle keeps statistics on the average number of blocks in the buffer cache and the hit ratio for object if the statistics are gathered automatically, or explicitly gathers system statistics. The optimizer uses these statistics to estimate the cost of I/O for queries, based on the need to fetch data blocks from disk rather than from the buffer cache.

In addition to these data-based statistics, Oracle 10*g* Database also collects some system statistics. These statistics are used to describe the hardware capabilities of the particular server being used. The system statistics that are collected at system startup concern CPU speed, I/O seek time, and I/O transfer speed. Other system statistics that can be collected after the database instance has been running concern aspects like maximum I/O throughput, single data block and multiblock read time, and average multiblock read count. You can also set these statistics manually.

Finally, the Oracle optimizer also takes into account some other distribution factors, such as the cluster factor, which helps the optimizer to understand how efficiently data blocks can be retrieved once their index entries have been found (and was described in Chapter 10 on indexes), and data skew, which can be addressed through the use of histograms, which are described later in this chapter.

You can see that the Oracle optimizer has a pretty comprehensive view of the composition of the data in the database with these varied statistics and information derived from them.

You should keep in mind that the Oracle optimizer is only as effective as the accuracy of its statistics. If the optimizer is seeing a statistical picture of a table or index that is no longer accurate or was never accurate to begin with because of estimation, the optimizer cannot be expected to necessarily make the proper optimization choice.

Collecting Statistics

Not all of these statistics are used for every optimization task, but any of them could be used at any time. You instruct the Oracle database to collect statistics with the package `DBMS_STATS`, which comes built-in with the Oracle database. Although the collection of statistics is typically the job of a database administrator, the following example will give you a basic idea of how to use the `DBMS_STATS` package to collect statistics.

To collect statistics for the `SH` schema in the database, you could use the procedure in the `DBMS_STATS` package `GATHER_SCHEMA_STATS`, with no additional options, by entering the following syntax in *i*SQL*Plus, included as `CH28_GATHER_SCHEMA_STATS_NORM.SQL`.

```
EXEC DBMS_STATS.GATHER_SCHEMA_STATS( ownname => 'SH');
```

This version of the procedure would gather statistics by using an internal estimate of the sampling size. Typically, you would collect statistics at non-peak times so as to not impose undue overhead on your system. Once you're sure the overall composition of your database settles in, you may be able to limit the time required for statistics collection by limiting the scope of collection, such as only collecting on volatile tables. You can also add parameters to the `GATHER_DATABASE_STATS` call to only collect statistics on objects whose statistics are stale, or old; objects without statistics; or to let Oracle determine which objects need new statistics.

The Oracle 10*g* Database has made statistics collection easier by allowing you or the database administrator to automatically collect statistics, which will free you from the burden of having to either manually run statistics collection or set up a job to accomplish this task. By default, Oracle 10*g* automatically collects database statistics during the maintenance window, which, by default, is between 10 P.M. and 6 A.M. on weekdays and all day on weekends. The automatic collection of statistics is accomplished with a job run by the database scheduler, so you could emulate this option by explicitly defining your own job.

Keep in mind that gathering new statistics on data composition will automatically cause the Oracle optimizer to reoptimize queries and disregard any shared query execution plans in memory.

Statistics and Change

If you are the worrisome type (or, some might contend, the realistic type), you may have found a cause for concern in the preceding description of how easy it is to collect statistics. The cause of concern comes from the possibility that updated statistics could result in a different execution plan for an SQL statement, one that might not perform as well as a previous plan. Your users are happy with a particular expectation of performance, then someone updates statistics, and as a result things go to heck in a handbasket.

While we believe in the efficacy of the Oracle optimizer, this concern is certainly logically valid. The scenario described is not all that common, since many objects in the database retain the same basic statistical values and ratios over time. For instance, the size of indexes and tables does not typically increase dramatically in a short span of time. Additional statistical considerations like the cardinality of index values, the height of the index, the average lengths of columns and tables, and the clustering factor for an index typically do not change rapidly, once a database has achieved a certain size. In addition, many statistics are not called into play for each and every optimization. If you are doing sorting and a range-based selection based on a particular value in an index, the index will frequently be used because it provides these functions automatically.

Still, there may be times when you want to prevent statistics from being collected and potentially upsetting the established performance levels in the database. The Oracle database gives you a few options to avoid this outcome.

First, you could just refrain from collecting statistics, maintaining a particular view of the database entities forever. This approach will work, but it also prevents any improvement in performance that could come from better execution plans, based on the different constitution of the database, by the Oracle optimizer.

Second, you can lock statistics for a table or a schema with a procedure in the `DBMS_STATS` package. Once you lock statistics for an entity, the statistics do not change until they have been unlocked.

Oracle also allows you to save a set of statistics before you update them. You could take this approach to save the statistics, update the statistics to reflect the current composition of the database, and then, in the event of a performance problem, simply reload the earlier statistics.

The final option is to use *stored outlines*, which are described later in this chapter. A stored outline is a static copy of an execution plan, which circumvents the involvement of the optimizer in the retrieval process.

We feel that we should inform you of these various options, but we believe that you should always start by letting the Oracle optimizer do its thing to the best of its ability, and this includes using the most up-to-date view of statistics.

Production and Test Environments

As soon as you roll out a single application based on your Oracle database, you will probably establish two environments: one for your production applications and another for new development and maintenance of existing production applications. In most cases, the development environment will at least contain less data than your full-blown production environment.

Since the Oracle optimizer relies on a statistical portrait of the database and its contents to create execution plans, how can you properly test optimization for a production application in a test environment? Oracle allows you to export statistics from one database instance and then import them to another instance. With this method, you can ensure that the optimizer in your test instance will think that it has the same composition as your production instance. You export and import statistics with procedures from the built-in `DBMS_STATS` package.

Histograms

There is one more type of information that can be used to supplement the basic statistics used by the optimizer. This information is called a histogram.

A *histogram* provides a more in-depth look at the composition of a table or index. Most statistics provide insight into how many different values are contained in a data object. But a value can represent a single row or a large percentage of rows in the database.

Consider the following set of data. A table has a column called STATUS, and there is an index on this column. There are 10 different numeric codes for this column, but one of these values, "7," which stands for the status of "Complete," is in 60 percent of the rows in the table, as shown in a scaled-down version in Figure 28-1.

1	2	3	4	5	6	7	7	7	7	7	7	7	7	7	7	7	7	7	7	7	7	7	7	8	8	8	9	9	10

Figure 28-1: An unbalanced data distribution.

The Oracle database, by default, will assume that each of the 10 values is equally represented, so that any particular value will be present in 10 percent of the rows in the table. This information might cause the Oracle optimizer to use the index to retrieve data when there is a selection criterion on the STATUS column.

But if the selection criterion asks for rows with a value for the column equal to 7 the execution plan will access 60 percent of the rows in the index, which would not be the most optimal way of getting at the data. If 60 percent of the rows were being accessed, it would be much faster for Oracle to just retrieve the data directly from the table and avoid the extra I/O caused by accessing the index.

For scenarios like this, a histogram provides a view of the actual composition of the index or table. You can use one of the procedures in the DBMS_STATS package to create a histogram for a column, either explicitly or automatically, based on the data skew the procedure finds in the column, as described in the next section.

Keep in mind that skewed data values would be one reason why you would not want to use bind variables in an SQL statement, a practice we highly recommended in Chapter 2 on SQL execution.

Working with Histograms

Of course, you may not be completely aware of what indexes or columns are affected by data skew. By default, the DBMS_STATS procedures collect information on data distribution and create histograms where appropriate. If you want to limit the calculation of statistics for columns that display signs of skew, you can run the GATHER_* procedures with the SKEWONLY keyword to limit collection to the appropriate entities, with syntax like this:

```
EXEC DBMS_STATS.GATHER_DATABASE_STATS( method_opt => 'SKEWONLY')
```

The Oracle optimizer is aware of any histograms that exist and will use the information in them in calculating an optimal access method.

To show how the optimizer uses histograms, you can look at the PROD_ID in the SALES table in the SH schema. To first see evidence that the values in the column are skewed, you can run the following SQL statement (CH28_HISTO_EVID.SQL):

```
SELECT PROD_ID, COUNT(*) FROM SH.SALES WHERE PROD_ID = 30 OR PROD_ID = 136;
```

The results are shown in Figure 28-2.

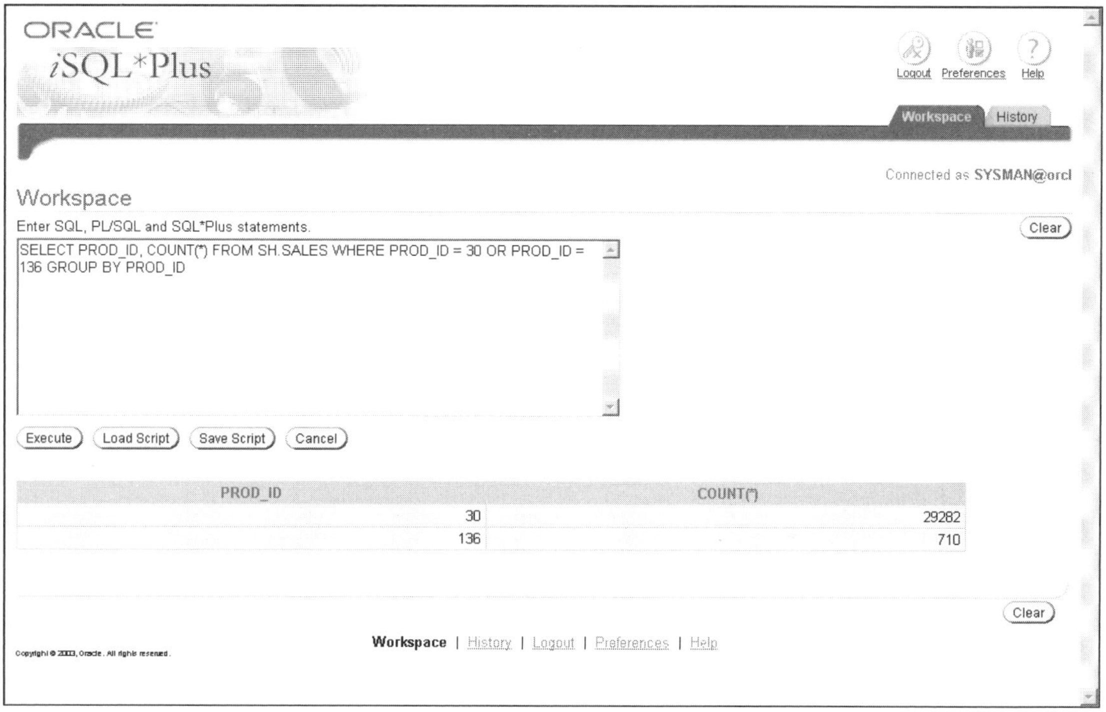

Figure 28-2: Evidence of data skew.

You can see that there are many more values for the PROD_ID of 30 than there are for the PROD_ID of 136.

To see how the optimizer uses this information, you can run the same query twice, with a different selection criterion, and look at the execution plan to see how the optimizer made different choices.

First, run the following SQL statement, which is included as CH28_PROD_ID_30.SQL:

```
SELECT CHANNEL_ID, COUNT(*) FROM SH.SALES WHERE PROD_ID = 30 GROUP BY CHANNEL_ID
```

From the results of this query, you can see that the Oracle optimizer has selected a full table scan as the beginning of the optimal execution plan, as shown in Figure 28-3.

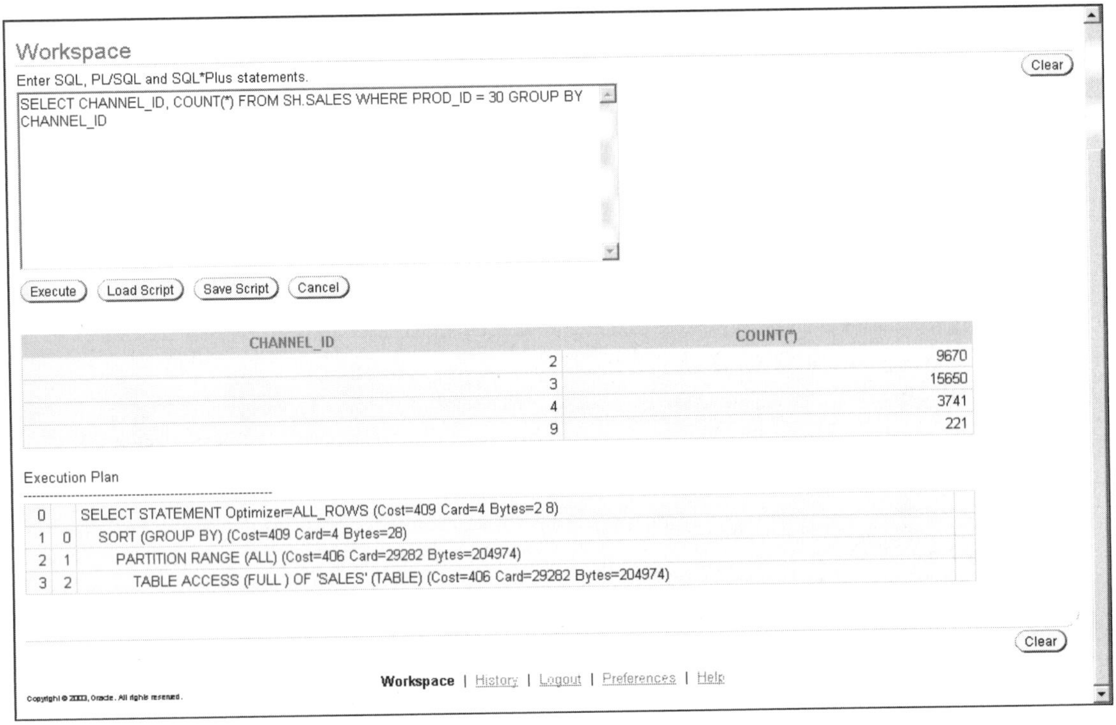

Figure 28-3: SQL query using table scan.

Now, run the SQL script `CH28_PROD_ID_136.SQL`, shown here:

```
SELECT CHANNEL_ID, COUNT(*) FROM SH.SALES WHERE PROD_ID = 136 GROUP BY CHANNEL_ID
```

which is almost exactly like the preceding query, except that the selection criterion now calls for those rows where `PROD_ID` equals 136, with many fewer qualifying rows. The result is shown in Figure 28-4.

The Oracle optimizer was aware of the lower number of rows that would be returned with this second query and therefore used the index.

Keep in mind that histograms cannot be used if you were to have a bind variable in the SQL, such as:

```
SELECT CHANNEL_ID, COUNT(*) FROM SH.SALES WHERE PROD_ID = :n_prod_id GROUP BY
CHANNEL_ID
```

since the Oracle optimizer would not necessarily be able to tell how many rows the value for the bind variable would produce. If you have a bind variable, the Oracle database cannot normally determine if the specific value used is skewed or not. In some cases, the Oracle database is smart enough to get around this limitation with something called bind variable peeking. As the name implies, this operation allows the Oracle optimizer to look at the actual value in a bind variable as it is being parsed the first time, so that information on the data distribution can be used. However, this peeking only takes place on the first parse of an SQL statement. After the statement has been parsed and is stored in the shared SQL area, subsequent executions of the statement will merely retrieve the parsed version without bothering to look at the value in the bind variable. For this reason, if you have an SQL statement that would be affected by data skew, you should avoid using bind variables for those data values.

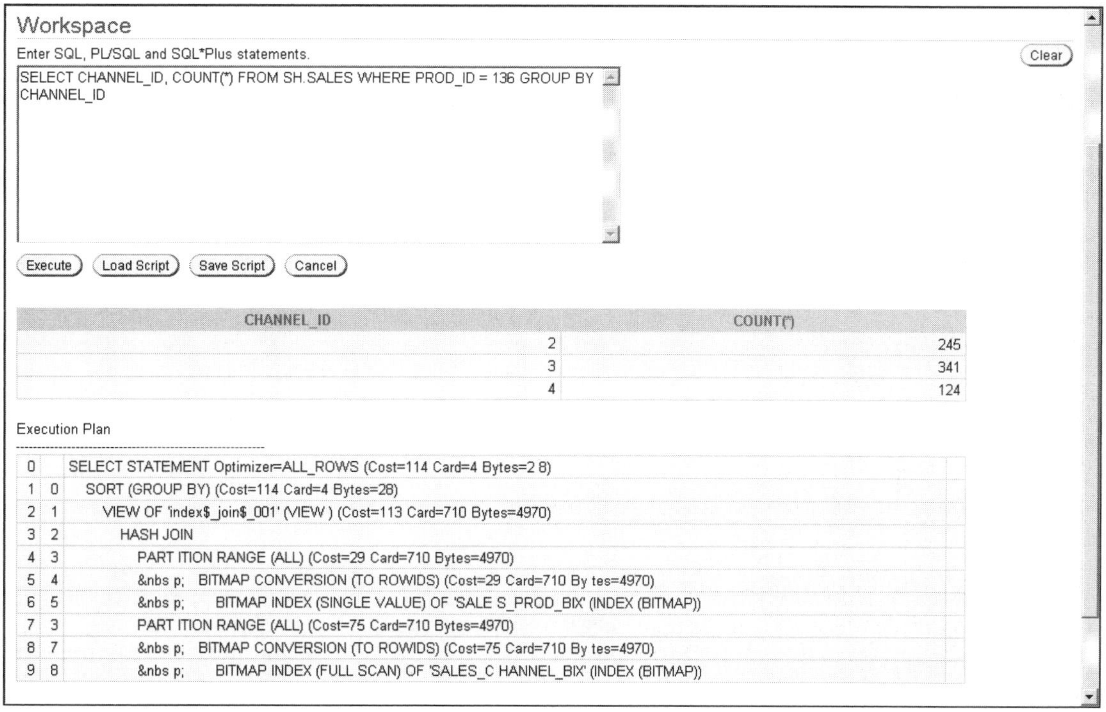

Figure 28-4: SQL query using index.

Execution Plans

The end result of the optimization process is the creation of an execution plan. You have already seen execution plans earlier in this book, as in the listings included in Chapter 10 on indexes. This section will take a closer look at the steps that make up an execution plan.

The Execution Plan

From the view of the application or user, the Oracle database responds to a query by returning data — one simple step. But this illusion is, in part, due to the power of SQL, which can specify a relatively complex request with a small set of verbs and operators. The reality is that this easy-to-describe result — the return of data — is the result of a series of discrete steps.

The execution plan is a roadmap that describes the steps that Oracle plans to take to satisfy a request for data. Each step in the plan includes the target of the step, the type of access or data interaction the step will involve, and the estimated cost of the step in computer resources. The execution plan will let you understand exactly how the Oracle optimizer plans to get the rows requested by a query.

Before starting to look at execution plans, you need to understand the different types of data operations that can be part of the execution plan.

Data Operations

There are three basic categories of data interaction that can be part of an execution plan: data access, which describes how Oracle will actually retrieve data; join operations, which describe how Oracle will join together data that has been retrieved; and a variety of other operations, such as sorting, aggregation, and windowing, which act on intermediate results retrieved by earlier operations.

Data Access

All queries are asking for data, so every execution plan includes one or more steps that retrieve data from the Oracle database. There are two basic ways that Oracle can get data: by accessing the data blocks in a table directly or by using an index to retrieve data or pointers to table-resident data. In addition, there are specific ways that Oracle accesses data in clustered or hash clustered tables.

Table Access

Table access operations retrieve data from the data blocks that make up the table. There are several ways to get at this data:

- `Full table scan`—This operation scans the entire table. Although it may sound like the slowest way to access data, the Oracle database can read data directly from the table very rapidly, so this type of access can be faster than using an index, as shown in Chapter 10 on indexes. One of the reasons this type of access can be faster is the ability to read multiple blocks with a single I/O. You can shape this capability with the initialization parameter `DB_MULTI_BLOCK_READ`, which specifies how many blocks to read with an I/O. Reading multiple blocks with a single I/O does have a downside, in that larger reads fill up memory caches faster, which can impact overall performance, so you should test your performance as you adjust this parameter.
- `PARTITION`—This operation performs one or more access operations for each partition needed in the query. The Oracle optimizer knows to, in appropriate circumstances, eliminate accessing some partitions. For instance, if you have a partition based on the value of `EMP_NO`, and the query includes a range selection on the `EMP_NO` column, the Oracle optimizer knows what partition(s) it should use.
- `ROWID`—The `ROWID` for a row is the fastest way for Oracle to access to the row, as the identifier includes information Oracle can use to go directly to the block that contains the row. Indexes include a `ROWID` for the row represented by an index entry, so this type of access typically follows an index access.
- `CLUSTER` access—This type of operation accesses rows in a cluster table, described in Chapter 10 on indexes.
- `Hash access`—This type of operation accesses rows in a hash cluster table, described in Chapter 10 on indexes.

Index Access

Index access operations retrieve data from an index, which is frequently followed by access data in the table.

- INDEX — There are a number of different types of index access operations:
  - UNIQUE SCAN — Uses the index to retrieve a single ROWID from the index.
  - RANGE SCAN — Uses the index to return the ROWIDs for a range of index values. This operation, by default, returns ROWIDs for the values in ascending order, but it can also return ranges in descending order.
  - FULL SCAN — Performs a full scan on an index, similar to a full scan on a table.
  - FAST FULL SCAN — Performs a full index can with multiblock reads, similar to a full table scan.
  - SKIP SCAN — Used in a specific case of an index with multiple columns. If a query uses the later columns in the index without using the leading columns, Oracle can skip some index blocks if the leading columns contain the same value. For example, if an index contained COL_A, COL_B, and COL_C, and a query used a selection criterion of COL_C = 100, an index skip scan would look for the first value of COL_A and COL_B and see if there was a value for COL_C that equaled 100. If this entry was not found, Oracle could skip index blocks where the values for COL_A and COL_B were identical, since the database knew that there would be no more possible candidates for selection in those rows.
- BITMAP — This operation uses a bitmap index for access.
- PARTITION — This operation is similar to the PARTITION operation for tables; it iterates over a number of index partitions.

Joins

Whenever a query calls for two or more tables, Oracle has to find some way to join the tables together. Joins work by taking a row from one table, called the driver table, and checking the value of the join key with another table. The Oracle optimizer will try and pick the driver table that will produce the smallest number of rows, to reduce the overhead of subsequent join comparisons.

This section covers access methods that are typically used to create data sets from more than one source, although some, like UNION, are not technically referred to as a join.

- NESTED LOOP — A nested loop walks through the values from one set of data and compares them to values in another set of data. The inner loop does the comparison with the second set of data.
- SORT-MERGE — This operation takes two sets of data, both sorted on the join key, and joins them together.
- HASH — The optimizer builds a hash table on the join key of the smaller table, which it keeps in memory, then scans the larger table and uses the hash table to find matching values. Typically used in data warehouse scenarios.
- UNION — This operation joins two sets of data together and eliminates duplicate rows.

Sorting and Other Operations

There are a number of other access steps that may be listed in an execution plan. Following are the more popular options:

- `SORT`—This operation returns rows in sorted order. If the rows are already in sorted order, based on retrieval through an index, this step is not necessary. There are several varieties of `SORT` access:
    - `UNIQUE`—Uses a sort operation to eliminate duplicate rows
    - `JOIN`—Sorts rows prior to performing a merge-join operation
    - `ORDER BY`—Sorts rows based on an `ORDER BY` clause
    - `GROUP BY`—Sorts rows based on a `GROUP BY` clause
    - `AGGREGATE`—Retrieves a single row as a result of applying a group function to a set of rows
- `AND-EQUAL`—This operation takes in multiple sets of `ROWID`s and returns the intersection of the values while eliminating duplicates.
- `CONCATENATION`—This operation is like a `UNION`, except that it can accept more than two sets of rows.
- `COUNT`—This operation returns a count of the number of rows in a particular set.
- `FILTER`—This operation goes through a set of rows and eliminates some, based on some condition. In viewing an execution plan, this type of access is usually not indicated as a separate step but identified with some type of footnote.
- `FIRST ROW`—This operation returns the first row requested by a query.
- `INTERSECTION`—This operation takes two sets of rows and returns the intersection between them while eliminating duplicate rows.
- `INLIST ITERATOR`—This operation indicates that the next subtask in the execution plan is performed for the next value in an `IN` list from the query.
- `MINUS`—This operation takes two sets of rows and returns those rows in the first set that are not in the second set, while eliminating duplicate rows.
- `VIEW`—This operation executes the query that defines a view and returns the rows.

Execution Statistics

Earlier in this chapter, we discussed the statistics that are collected for use by the Oracle optimizer. The process of executing a query or any other SQL data manipulation statement, such as `INSERT`, `UPDATE`, or `DELETE`, also generates statistics that can help you to understand what sort of activity the Oracle database had to perform to obtain the results. The execution statistics give you a more complete understanding of the resources used by Oracle in executing a query, so they can be used as part of your overall performance comparisons.

These statistics can be shown with some of the tools used for viewing execution plans, so you should understand their meaning before we go on to discuss how to see execution plans. This section provides a very high level overview of the meaning of these statistics; for a more complete understanding of the full-scale implications of these statistics, refer to a book on tuning Oracle.

Overall Execution Statistics

There are three basic phases where resources are used in executing queries. Figure 28-5 shows a sample listing of statistics for an SQL statement, which shows the categories this section and the next section will discuss.

```
SELECT customer_id, o.order_id,  oi.product_id, sum(quantity_on_hand)
    FROM oe.orders o, oe.order_items oi, oe.inventories i
    WHERE o.order_id = oi.order_id AND oi.product_id = i.product_id
        AND customer_ID < 103
    GROUP BY customer_id, o.order_id, oi.product_id

call     count       cpu    elapsed       disk      query    current        rows
------- ------  -------- ---------- ---------- ---------- ----------  ----------
Parse        1      0.03       0.03          0          3          0           0
Execute      1      0.00       0.00          0          0          0           0
Fetch        3      0.01       0.08         14         16          0          24
------- ------  -------- ---------- ---------- ---------- ----------  ----------
total        5      0.04       0.12         14         19          0          24

Misses in library cache during parse: 1
Optimizer mode: ALL_ROWS
Parsing user id: 54

Rows     Row Source Operation
-------  ---------------------------------------------------
     24  SORT GROUP BY (cr=16 pr=14 pw=0 time=88427 us)
    126   HASH JOIN  (cr=16 pr=14 pw=0 time=87904 us)
     48    HASH JOIN  (cr=9 pr=8 pw=0 time=32574 us)
      8     TABLE ACCESS BY INDEX ROWID ORDERS (cr=2 pr=2 pw=0 time=25395 us)
      8      INDEX RANGE SCAN ORD_CUSTOMER_IX (cr=1 pr=1 pw=0 time=21082
us)(object id 49838)
    665     INDEX FAST FULL SCAN ORDER_ITEMS_UK (cr=7 pr=6 pw=0 time=6464
us)(object id 49832)|
   1112    TABLE ACCESS FULL INVENTORIES (cr=7 pr=6 pw=0 time=54048 us)
```

Figure 28-5: A sample statistics listing output from the TKPROF program.

The first phase is the parse phase, where Oracle checks the syntax of an SQL statement and the optimizer creates the execution plan. If an SQL statement is being parsed for the first time, this phase will consume some resources, but if Oracle is able to retrieve an SQL statement from the shared SQL pool, this phase uses virtually no resources.

The second phase is the execute phase, where Oracle actually executes the statement. All SQL statements use resources to execute, whether they are queries or write statements. If the required data is cached in the library cache of the shared pool, the resources used will be minimal.

The third phase is the fetch phase, which details the resources used to retrieve rows that will be returned to the requestor.

Each of these phases has a number of broad statistics categories associated with it:

- **CPU.** Lists the CPU time spent on the phase.
- **Elapsed.** Lists the overall time spent on the phase. An elapsed time that is significantly longer than the CPU time can indicate that Oracle is waiting for resources.

- **Disk.** Indicates the number of I/O operations performed for the phase. This figure can be different from the number of blocks returned, since Oracle may be performing multiblock reads.
- **Query.** Represents the number of block buffers retrieved from the buffer cache as part of a consistent read operation.
- **Current.** Represents the number of block buffers used in the buffer cache to create a "current image view" of a block to take part in a write operation.
- **Rows.** Indicates the number of rows used by the SQL statement, typically only relevant in the fetch phase of a query or the execute phrase of an `INSERT`, `UPDATE`, or `DELETE` operation.

Detailed Statistics

After the overall statistics are displayed, Oracle shows a list of more detailed statistics that relate to the overall SQL statement. These statistics reveal a great deal about exactly how Oracle is using resources to satisfy the statement. These statistics include the following:

- **Recursive calls.** SQL calls that are made on behalf of the SQL statement submitted, such as calls to the data dictionary or to PL/SQL code for user-defined functions.
- **Db block gets.** Retrievals of data base blocks from disk, required for write operations that require the most current version of data.
- **Consistent gets.** Retrievals of database blocks from the buffer cache. Each row read requires a consistent get.
- **Physical reads.** I/O operations required to fetch data blocks from disk.
- **SQL*Net statistics.** The number of bytes received and sent to the client.
- **Sort statistics.** The number of sort operations done in memory and that required disk to perform.
- **Redo size.** Indicates the amount of redo buffer space this SQL statement required. Redo buffers are used to protect data integrity against database failures. Redo is only required for write operations.

The next section shows what some of these statistics mean when gathered against an SQL query running against an Oracle database in a production environment.

Execution Plan and Statistics — An Example

The best way to get a basic understanding of execution plans and statistics is to walk through an actual example. For this example, you will use a somewhat complex query that is included as `CH28_COMPLEX_QUERY.SQL` and shown in Figure 28-6.

*The screenshots in this section will use iSQL*Plus, although there are several ways to get this information which are described in the next section.*

The query used is as follows:

```
SELECT o.customer_id, o.order_id,  oi.product_id, SUM(quantity_on_hand)
     FROM oe.orders o, oe.order_items oi, oe.inventories i
     WHERE o.order_id = oi.order_id AND oi.product_id = i.product_id
```

```
        AND customer_ID < 103
    GROUP BY o.customer_id, o.order_id, oi.product_id;
```

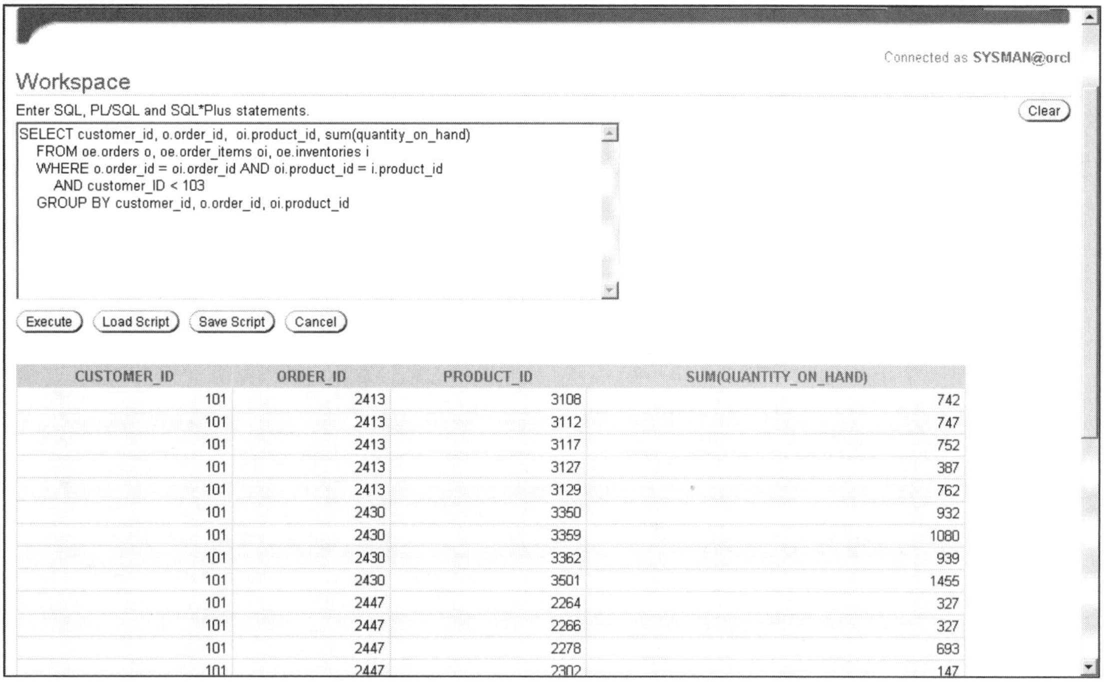

Figure 28-6: A complex query and results.

This query joins three tables, groups the result and computes an aggregate value, and imposes a range selection criterion. The query returns 24 rows; however, we are more interested in how the query works rather than the results, so the rest of the screen shots in this chapter will not show the returned rows.

The execution plan for the query is shown in Figure 28-7.

The first thing to understand about the execution plan is the meaning of the two columns of numbers on the left-hand side of the plan. The numbers in the farthest left column are simply line numbers for identification. The next set of numbers, which are echoed by the indentations in the step descriptions, are more interesting. These numbers represent the reverse order of the execution of the steps. Some steps, as you can see, are executed simultaneously.

You can also see that each step has three numbers following it: cost, which is a number used by the Oracle optimizer to denote the relative cost of the step; card, which is short for cardinality, or the selectivity of the step; and bytes, which is a tally of the overall number of bytes used in the step.

For a better understanding of how these steps are executed, refer to Figure 28-8, which shows the steps laid out in the order they are run.

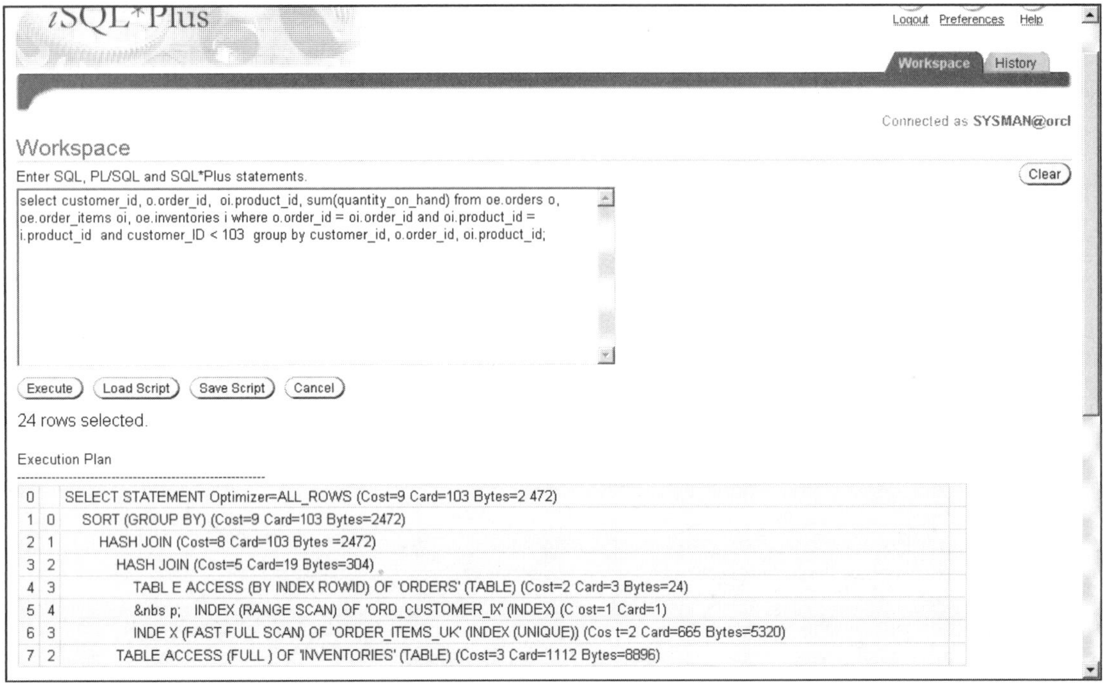

Figure 28-7: Execution plan for a complex query.

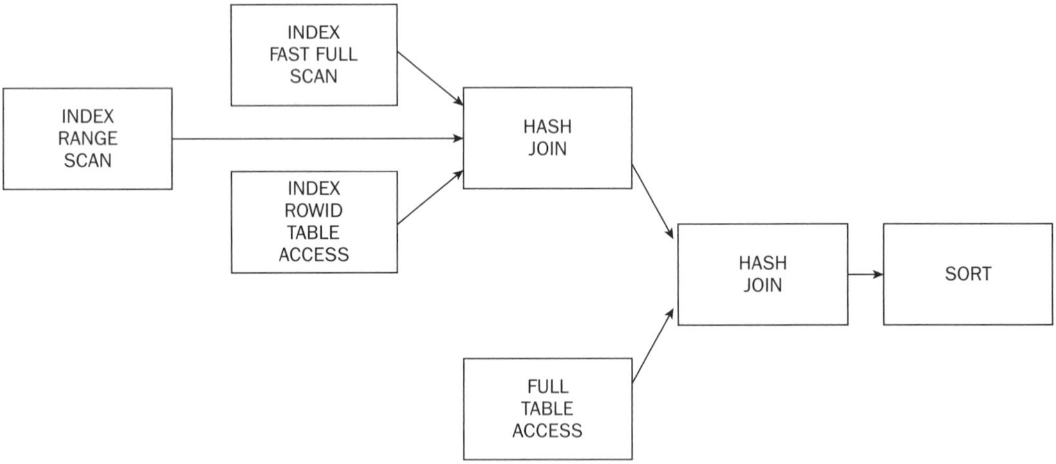

Figure 28-8: Execution plan steps in order.

In this figure, you can see that the first step taken is an index range scan to select the customers whose `CUSTOMER_ID` is less than 103. Oracle started with this step since it would produce the smallest number of rows, making it the best choice to drive the rest of the joins and the query.

Once this step is complete, Oracle accesses the data in the actual table with the ROWIDs from the previous step, and also does a fast full scan of the index for the ORDER_ITEMS table to prepare for the join in the next step.

The Oracle optimizer has decided to use a hash join to connect the ORDERS table and the ORDER_ITEMS table in the next step. At the same time that this step is taking place, Oracle does a full table scan to get the necessary data from the INVENTORIES table. Once this information has been obtained, Oracle does another hash join to link the two intermediate result sets, then sorts the data. This final action brings you to the 0 level of the execution steps, when Oracle passes the results back to the user.

The display of the execution plan gives you an exact understanding of the steps taken by Oracle to deliver query results. If you are having performance issues, you should start by looking at the execution plan to see if Oracle is taking any inefficient steps, such as doing a full table scan and discarding most of the rows as a result of some criteria.

> *Understanding the execution plan is only a prerequisite to taking any sort of action. As we strongly suggest in the section on hints, you should also understand why Oracle has made the optimization choices has made before you try and fix the situation.*

The next step in any investigation is usually to see how the query is using the resources described previously. Performance problems stem from a lack of resources, and the Oracle database has a lot of ways of saving resources, so what looks like an inappropriate optimizer choice may turn out to be a correct one.

To begin understanding some of the ways that Oracle uses resources, you can start by running the script CH28_FIRST_TIME_COMPLEX_QUERY.SQL. This script turns on the appropriate reporting, turns off the display of the results, and, importantly, clears both the data buffers and the stored SQL cache. In a real production environment, of course, this query would normally run in this virgin state once, taking advantage of these caches on subsequent runs, but the purpose of this step is to help you understand the impact of those advantages.

The results of running this script are shown in Figure 28-9.

A couple of the statistics jump out at you right away. First, there are what seem to be a whole lot of recursive SQL calls. Remember, though, that Oracle is doing a lot of work under the covers in the parsing phase of SQL execution. The database has to check the validity of column names, get column lengths, understand the available indexes, and so forth. Each of these questions is easily answered with an SQL query to the data dictionary. The performance of the database does not really suffer that much, despite all this activity, because Oracle knows how often the data dictionary is used and provides rapid access to it.

The second interesting statistic is that there are both physical reads and consistent gets, which are logical reads. The physical reads are necessary because there is no data in the data buffers, and some physical I/O is required to fetch the necessary blocks from disk. The number of consistent gets is significant higher than the number of physical reads, because each physical read gets multiple blocks of data and some data blocks are logically read more than once.

To understand how Oracle would work in a production environment, run the script called CH28_SECOND_TIME_COMPLEX_QUERY.SQL next. This script does not clear out the data buffers or SQL cache, so you can see how Oracle uses them to reduce resource usage. The results of this run are shown in Figure 28-10.

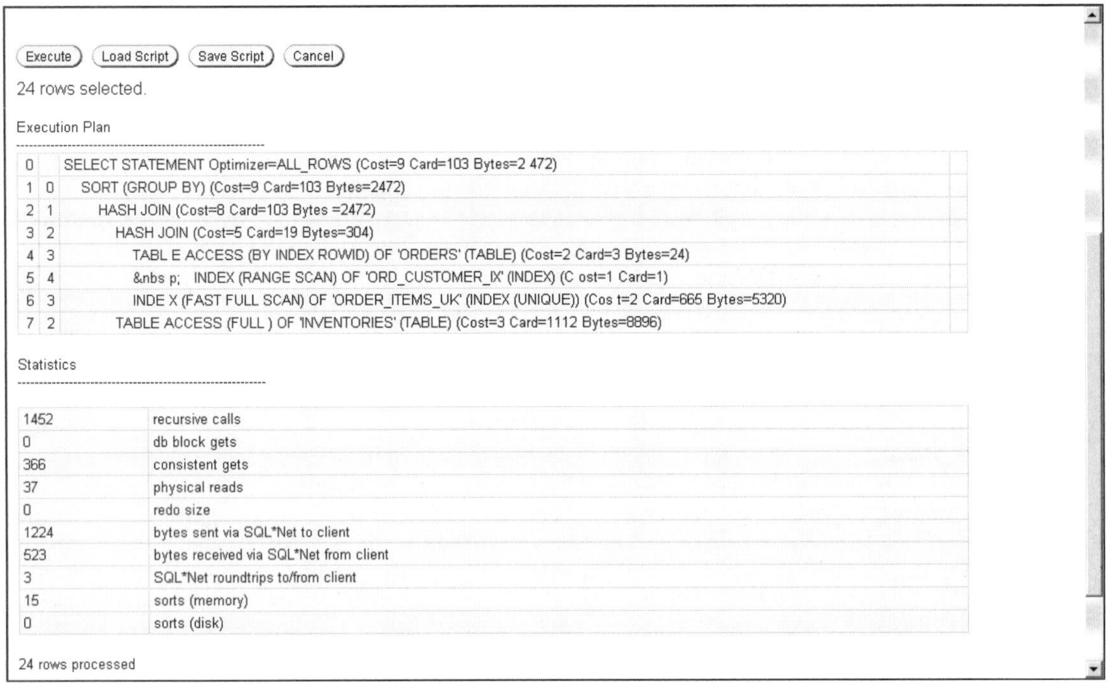

Execute | Load Script | Save Script | Cancel

24 rows selected.

Execution Plan

0		SELECT STATEMENT Optimizer=ALL_ROWS (Cost=9 Card=103 Bytes=2 472)
1	0	SORT (GROUP BY) (Cost=9 Card=103 Bytes=2472)
2	1	HASH JOIN (Cost=8 Card=103 Bytes =2472)
3	2	HASH JOIN (Cost=5 Card=19 Bytes=304)
4	3	TABL E ACCESS (BY INDEX ROWID) OF 'ORDERS' (TABLE) (Cost=2 Card=3 Bytes=24)
5	4	&nbs p; INDEX (RANGE SCAN) OF 'ORD_CUSTOMER_IX' (INDEX) (C ost=1 Card=1)
6	3	INDE X (FAST FULL SCAN) OF 'ORDER_ITEMS_UK' (INDEX (UNIQUE)) (Cos t=2 Card=665 Bytes=5320)
7	2	TABLE ACCESS (FULL) OF 'INVENTORIES' (TABLE) (Cost=3 Card=1112 Bytes=8896)

Statistics

1452	recursive calls
0	db block gets
366	consistent gets
37	physical reads
0	redo size
1224	bytes sent via SQL*Net to client
523	bytes received via SQL*Net from client
3	SQL*Net roundtrips to/from client
15	sorts (memory)
0	sorts (disk)

24 rows processed

Figure 28-9: Performance statistics for the first run of a query.

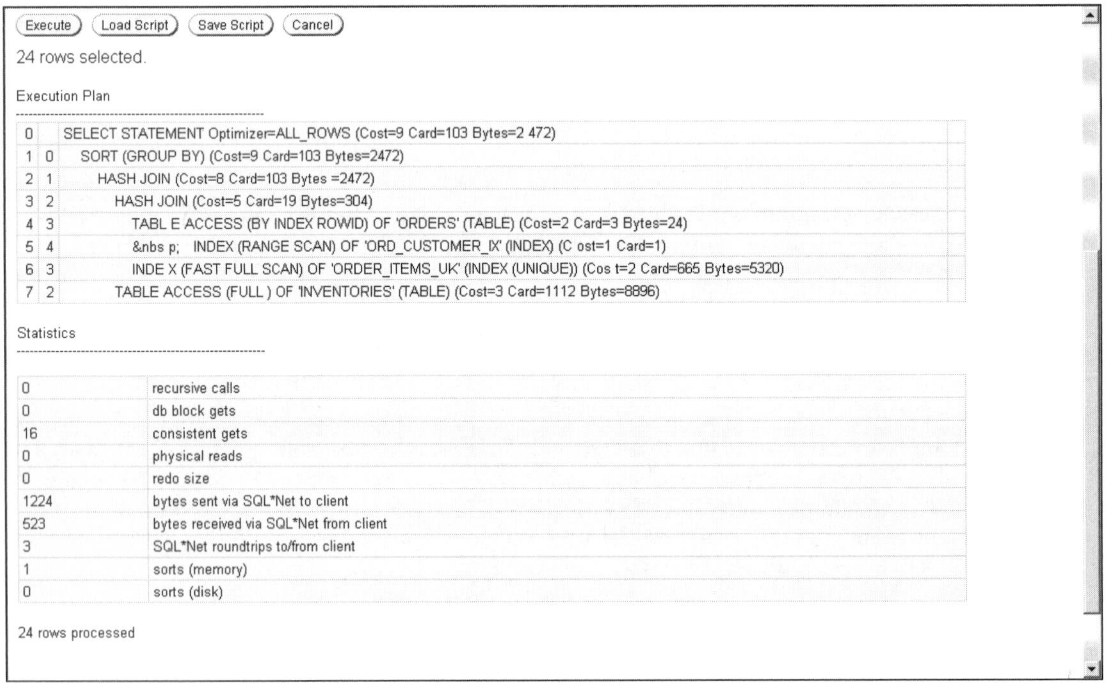

Execute | Load Script | Save Script | Cancel

24 rows selected.

Execution Plan

0		SELECT STATEMENT Optimizer=ALL_ROWS (Cost=9 Card=103 Bytes=2 472)
1	0	SORT (GROUP BY) (Cost=9 Card=103 Bytes=2472)
2	1	HASH JOIN (Cost=8 Card=103 Bytes =2472)
3	2	HASH JOIN (Cost=5 Card=19 Bytes=304)
4	3	TABL E ACCESS (BY INDEX ROWID) OF 'ORDERS' (TABLE) (Cost=2 Card=3 Bytes=24)
5	4	&nbs p; INDEX (RANGE SCAN) OF 'ORD_CUSTOMER_IX' (INDEX) (C ost=1 Card=1)
6	3	INDE X (FAST FULL SCAN) OF 'ORDER_ITEMS_UK' (INDEX (UNIQUE)) (Cos t=2 Card=665 Bytes=5320)
7	2	TABLE ACCESS (FULL) OF 'INVENTORIES' (TABLE) (Cost=3 Card=1112 Bytes=8896)

Statistics

0	recursive calls
0	db block gets
16	consistent gets
0	physical reads
0	redo size
1224	bytes sent via SQL*Net to client
523	bytes received via SQL*Net from client
3	SQL*Net roundtrips to/from client
1	sorts (memory)
0	sorts (disk)

24 rows processed

Figure 28-10: Performance statistics for the first run of a query.

In this run, you can see that there are no physical reads at all, since the data buffers still contain all the data that is needed for the query. You can also see that there are no recursive SQL calls, because this time, the query used a saved execution plan, so there was no need to query the data dictionary for validation. Even the number of sorts has been reduced, since some of them were probably associated with the recursive SQL statements spawned by the initial execution.

This little exercise has illuminated the way that the Oracle database optimizes its use of computer resources. The mere reduction of resource utilization is not necessarily the solution to performance problems, but by cleverly optimizing some of its most common operations, Oracle can not only deliver good performance but also scale well as users are added to the system.

You did not see all of the statistics that were discussed in the previous section in this example because the tool we were using to examine the statistics, *i*SQL*Plus, did not report on all of them. The next section discusses different tools that can be used to get information about optimization and resource utilization, which can deliver slightly different sets of available statistics.

Viewing Execution Plans and Statistics

In theory, a proper relational database should return the right data in the most efficient way. Oracle probably does as good a job at this as any database on the market. But no product (or author, or person) is ever perfect. Because of this, you will sometimes want to take a peek at the information Oracle uses to guide its retrieval of data.

Over the years, Oracle has offered a number of tools you can use to help to understand the statistics and execution plan for SQL statements. This section covers these assorted tools.

AUTOTRACE

In the previous section, you saw execution plans and statistics displayed in *i*SQL*Plus. To get this information, you had to use the autotrace capability of the tool.

`AUTOTRACE`, as its name implies, turns on automatic tracing of SQL statements as well as enabling the display of information after an SQL statement has executed. The syntax for enabling this capability in *i*SQL*Plus is as follows:

```
SET AUTOTRACE [ON/OFF/TRACE] option;
```

The keyword `ON` by itself turns on the display of both execution plan and statistics. The keyword `OFF` by itself turns off all display. The keyword `TRACE` by itself shows both execution plan and statistics without showing the results of the actual SQL statement.

The *option* can be `EXPLAIN`, which shows you the `EXPLAIN PLAN` for a query, or `STATISTICS`, which shows you the statistics for the query. To use `AUTOTRACE`, you must have a table called `PLAN_TABLE` set up in your schema, as explained in the next section on `EXPLAIN PLAN`.

Once you set `AUTOTRACE` on for an *i*SQL*Plus session, it remains on until you terminate the session or explicitly turn it off.

EXPLAIN PLAN

The EXPLAIN PLAN functionality is the basis for the AUTOTRACE functionality — it is used to tell the Oracle optimizer to store the results of its optimization, the execution plan. The syntax for EXPLAIN PLAN is fairly straightforward:

```
EXPLAIN PLAN FOR SQL_statement
```

where *SQL_statement* is the SQL statement that will create the execution plan. When you use this syntax, Oracle will store the information describing the steps of the execution plan in a table called PLAN_TABLE in the user's schema. This table must exist before using EXPLAIN PLAN. Oracle comes with a script called UTLXPLAN.SQL that can be used to create this table.

The actual name of the script for creating the table may vary a bit between different operating system platforms. You can use the clause INTO schema.table before the FOR SQL_statement clause to direct the output to a PLAN_TABLE in a different schema.

By default, the SQL statement is simply given an identification number, which is stored in the PLAN_ID column of the PLAN_TABLE. You can add the clause SET STATEMENT_ID = statement_id , between the EXPLAIN PLAN keywords and the FOR keyword, where statement_id is a quoted identifier, to give a more meaningful name to the plan steps for the statement, which is stored in the STATEMENT_ID column of the PLAN_TABLE.

Running the statement simply stores the information in the PLAN_TABLE. To get the information out of the PLAN_TABLE, you have to run an SQL statement against it. Figure 28-11 shows some of the results of a simple query against the PLAN_TABLE after running EXPLAIN PLAN on the complex SQL statement we have been using.

As you can see, this information is not as clearly presented as the presentation that results from using AUTOTRACE in *i*SQL*Plus. You can use the following SQL statement, included for a statement whose STATEMENT_ID is "Complex query" as CH28_PLAN_TABLE_QUERY.SQL, against the PLAN_TABLE to make the execution plan easier to understand:

```
SELECT depth, operation, options,
object_name, position
    FROM plan_table
    START WITH id = 0 AND statement_id = statement_id
    CONNECT BY PRIOR id = parent_id AND
    statement_id = statement_id;
```

Figure 28-12 shows the result.

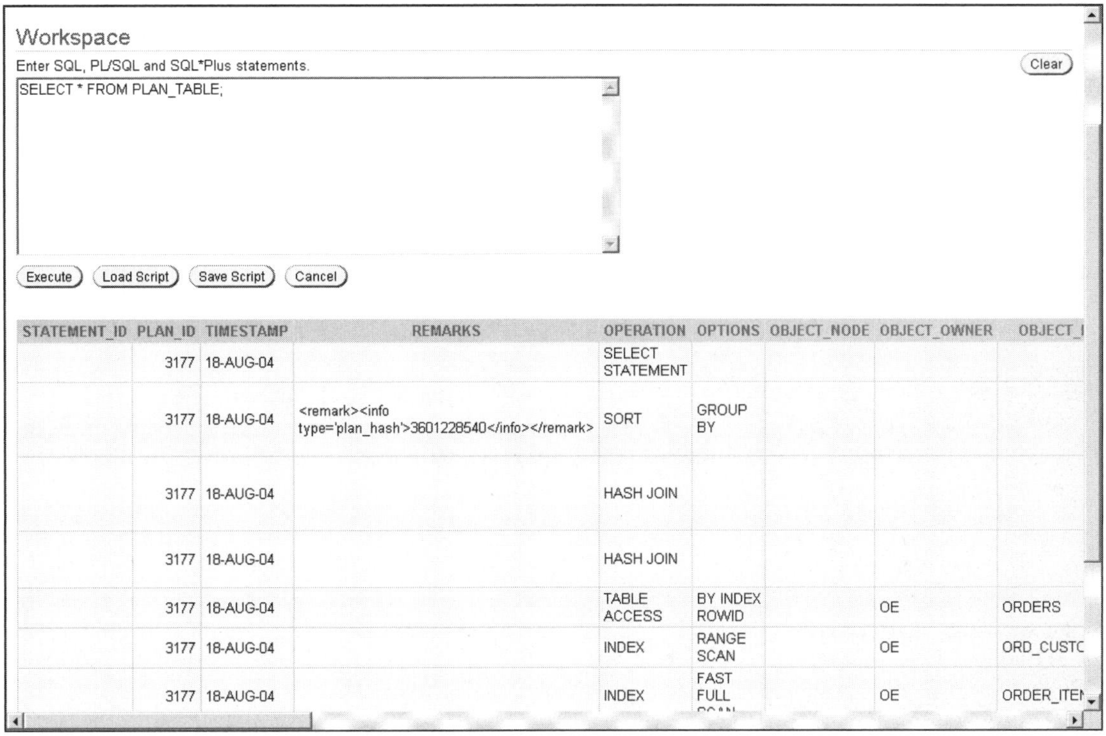

Workspace

Enter SQL, PL/SQL and SQL*Plus statements.

Clear

```
SELECT * FROM PLAN_TABLE;
```

Execute | Load Script | Save Script | Cancel

STATEMENT_ID	PLAN_ID	TIMESTAMP	REMARKS	OPERATION	OPTIONS	OBJECT_NODE	OBJECT_OWNER	OBJECT_I
	3177	18-AUG-04		SELECT STATEMENT				
	3177	18-AUG-04	<remark><info type='plan_hash'>3601228540</info></remark>	SORT	GROUP BY			
	3177	18-AUG-04		HASH JOIN				
	3177	18-AUG-04		HASH JOIN				
	3177	18-AUG-04		TABLE ACCESS	BY INDEX ROWID		OE	ORDERS
	3177	18-AUG-04		INDEX	RANGE SCAN		OE	ORD_CUSTC
	3177	18-AUG-04		INDEX	FAST FULL		OE	ORDER_ITEM

Figure 28-11: The contents of the **`PLAN_TABLE`**.

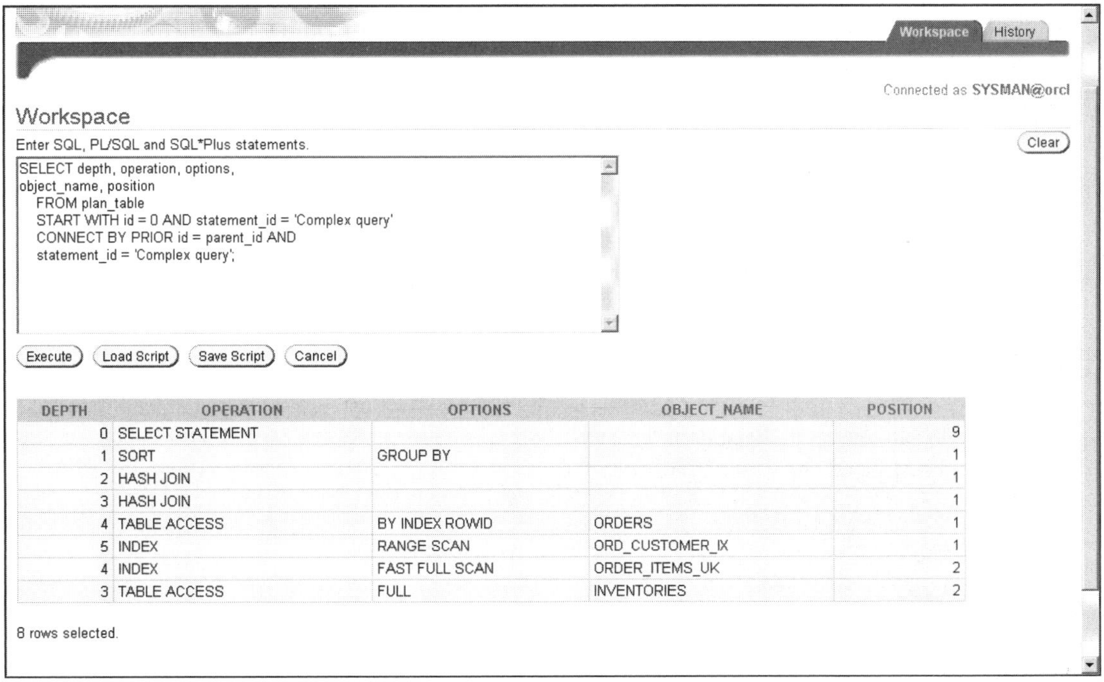

Workspace | History

Connected as SYSMAN@orcl

Workspace

Enter SQL, PL/SQL and SQL*Plus statements.

Clear

```
SELECT depth, operation, options,
object_name, position
  FROM plan_table
  START WITH id = 0 AND statement_id = 'Complex query'
  CONNECT BY PRIOR id = parent_id AND
  statement_id = 'Complex query';
```

Execute | Load Script | Save Script | Cancel

DEPTH	OPERATION	OPTIONS	OBJECT_NAME	POSITION
0	SELECT STATEMENT			9
1	SORT	GROUP BY		1
2	HASH JOIN			1
3	HASH JOIN			1
4	TABLE ACCESS	BY INDEX ROWID	ORDERS	1
5	INDEX	RANGE SCAN	ORD_CUSTOMER_IX	1
4	INDEX	FAST FULL SCAN	ORDER_ITEMS_UK	2
3	TABLE ACCESS	FULL	INVENTORIES	2

8 rows selected.

Figure 28-12: Selected information from the **`PLAN_TABLE`**.

The results shown in Figure 28-12 look a bit like the results from AUTOTRACE, but not quite as clear. But one potential advantage of using EXPLAIN PLAN and the preceding SQL statement is that you can do it in character-mode SQL*Plus.

SQL Trace and TKPROF

The optimization information you have seen so far has given you a look at the execution plan generated by the Oracle optimizer and some statistics on the resources used by the query. Earlier, you saw more a more complete display of execution statistics, which also included information broken down into the different phases of SQL execution — parse, execute, and fetch. The way to get these breakdowns is using SQL Trace and TKPROF.

SQL Trace

SQL Trace is a utility that traces the flow of SQL statements through Oracle. You can enable the SQL Trace facility and turn it on by setting the initialization parameter SQL_TRACE to TRUE, using the command-line syntax of

```
ALTER SESSION SET SQL_TRACE = TRUE;
```

or using the DBMS_SESSION.SET_SQL_TRACE procedure. Typically, you would enable SQL Trace at the session level, since it does add a bit of overhead. To stop the recording of the trace file, you enter the following:

```
ALTER SESSION SET SQL_TRACE = FALSE;
```

TKPROF

TKPROF is a tool for formatting and aggregating the text information collected in an SQL trace file. TKPROF is a command-line utility that will generate text output into a text file that aggregates the huge volume of statistics collected by SQL Trace so that you can understand it at a higher level.

The basic syntax for using TKPROF is as follows:

```
TKPROF trace_file output_file;
```

where *trace_file* is the file generated by SQL Trace and *output_file* is the destination of the report generated by TKPROF. TKPROF has additional parameters that can cause the SQL statements to be sorted in order of amounts of different operations, limit the number of SQL statements shown in the output file, or create an SQL script for inserting the results of TKPROF into a table in the database.

If your SQL Trace session involves data from dozens or hundreds of SQL statements, it is important that the aggregated output from TKPROF be sorted so that the "worst" SQL statements are displayed first. Since the ultimate goal of tuning (as stated in the beginning of the chapter) is reducing response time, output from TKPROF can be sorted according to the elapsed time of the SQL statement using the phrase sort=prsela,exeela,fchela. The phrase prsela represents the elapsed time spent parsing the SQL, the phrase exeela represents the elapsed time spent executing the SQL, and the phrase fchela represents the elapsed time spent fetching rows for the SQL. The comma-separated list of phrases causes TKPROF to aggregate the values for all three statistics before sorting output, ensuring that the SQL statement that consumed the most elapsed time overall is shown first.

Using SQL Trace and TKPROF

To illustrate how to use these tools, you can create an SQL Trace file for the execution of the complex SQL statement we have been using. In these two examples, we ran the `CH_33_CLEAR.SQL` script to clear out the SQL and data buffers before starting SQL Trace and running the complex query in the `CH28_COMPLEX_QUERY.SQL` script twice, although you can get the same effect by simply entering the code that follows as soon as you open up your *i*SQL*Plus session.

To start SQL Trace, use the following code in your *i*SQL*Plus window, which is included as `CH28_START_TRACE.SQL`:

```
ALTER SESSION SET TRACEFILE_IDENTIFIER = 'sample_query';
ALTER SESSION SET SQL_TRACE = TRUE;
```

You set the `TRACEFILE_IDENTIFIER` parameter to a specific name to make it easier to identify the trace file for this particular tracing session. SQL Trace will include the identifier in the name of the trace file, which you will need to run `TKPROF`.

Once you have turned on SQL Trace, run the `CH28_COMPLEX_QUERY.SQL` script twice, and then turn SQL Trace off by entering the following:

```
ALTER SESSION SET SQL_TRACE = FALSE;
```

Once you have finished collecting the trace file, you can run `TKPROF` against it by entering the following code at the command prompt:

```
TKPROF trace_file c:\tkprof_sample.txt SYS=NO AGGREGATE=NO
```

where *`trace_file`* is the name of the trace file generated. When we ran this example, our trace file was `c:\oracle\product\10.1.0\admin\orcl\udump\orcl_ora_6036_sample_query.trc`. Trace files are typically stored in the udump directory, specified by the initialization parameter `USER_DUMP_DEST`. You use the `SYS=NO` flag to tell `TKPROF` to exclude all recursive SQL done to support an SQL statement, so you don't see all the calls to the data dictionary that are done. The `AGGREGATE=NO` flag prevents `TKPROF` from giving aggregate totals for an SQL statement. This aggregation can be useful in some contexts, but since you want to see the separate executions of the same statement, you should turn it off. This output from `TKPROF` is included as `CH28_TKPROF_SAMPLE.TXT`.

To see the usefulness of using SQL Trace, look at the section of the `TKPROF` output file that covers the first execution of the SQL statement:

```
SELECT customer_id, o.order_id,  oi.product_id, sum(quantity_on_hand)
    FROM oe.orders o, oe.order_items oi, oe.inventories i
    WHERE o.order_id = oi.order_id AND oi.product_id = i.product_id
        AND customer_ID < 103
    GROUP BY customer_id, o.order_id, oi.product_id

call     count       cpu    elapsed       disk      query    current        rows
------- ------  -------- ---------- ---------- ---------- ----------  ----------
Parse        1      0.03       0.03          0          3          0           0
Execute      1      0.00       0.00          0          0          0           0
Fetch        3      0.01       0.08         14         16          0          24
------- ------  -------- ---------- ---------- ---------- ----------  ----------
```

```
total        5      0.04      0.12        14         19          0          24

Misses in library cache during parse: 1
Optimizer mode: ALL_ROWS
Parsing user id: 54

Rows     Row Source Operation
-------  ---------------------------------------------------
     24  SORT GROUP BY (cr=16 pr=14 pw=0 time=88427 us)
    126   HASH JOIN  (cr=16 pr=14 pw=0 time=87904 us)
     48    HASH JOIN  (cr=9 pr=8 pw=0 time=32574 us)
      8     TABLE ACCESS BY INDEX ROWID ORDERS (cr=2 pr=2 pw=0 time=25395 us)
      8      INDEX RANGE SCAN ORD_CUSTOMER_IX (cr=1 pr=1 pw=0 time=21082 us)(object
id 49838)
    665     INDEX FAST FULL SCAN ORDER_ITEMS_UK (cr=7 pr=6 pw=0 time=6464
us)(object id 49832)
   1112    TABLE ACCESS FULL INVENTORIES (cr=7 pr=6 pw=0 time=54048 us)
```

The bottom of this section shows you the now familiar execution plan, although this version also includes a count of the rows that were used in each step of the plan. The earlier statistics display the resources used in each phase of the processing of the SQL statement. For the purposes of this exercise, it is interesting to compare that set of statistics with the statistics of the second run of the same query, as shown in the following:

```
SELECT customer_id, o.order_id,  oi.product_id, sum(quantity_on_hand)
    FROM oe.orders o, oe.order_items oi, oe.inventories i
    WHERE o.order_id = oi.order_id AND oi.product_id = i.product_id
        AND customer_ID < 103
    GROUP BY customer_id, o.order_id, oi.product_id

call     count       cpu    elapsed       disk      query    current        rows
------- ------  -------- ---------- ---------- ---------- ----------  ----------
Parse        1      0.00       0.00          0          0          0           0
Execute      1      0.00       0.00          0          0          0           0
Fetch        3      0.01       0.00          0         16          0          24
------- ------  -------- ---------- ---------- ---------- ----------  ----------
total        5      0.01       0.00          0         16          0          24

Misses in library cache during parse: 0
Optimizer mode: ALL_ROWS
Parsing user id: 54
```

The count of each phase is the same, but the CPU time is greatly reduced. The elapsed time is reduced even more dramatically. And this quick comparison highlights the fact that this run of the query did not have to go to disk at all, which accounts for a significant part of the performance gain in elapsed time.

The sharp-eyed reader may have concluded that the Oracle database actually produces CPU resources, since the CPU time for the fetch step is .01, while the elapsed time is .00. The difference comes from the different ways that Oracle tracks elapsed and CPU time.

Even this brief introduction to the wonders of TKPROF has hopefully shown you that there is a wealth of information that comes from its use. Keep in mind that you can run TKPROF against the same trace file over and over again, to highlight different parts of the trace.

Enterprise Manager

Enterprise Manager is the main management tool used for Oracle software. Enterprise Manager allows you to look at the resources used by any particular SQL statement, as well as quickly find SQL statements that are using the most resources.

When you look at an SQL statement in Enterprise Manager, you can click down to another level to see the execution plan, as shown in Figure 28-13.

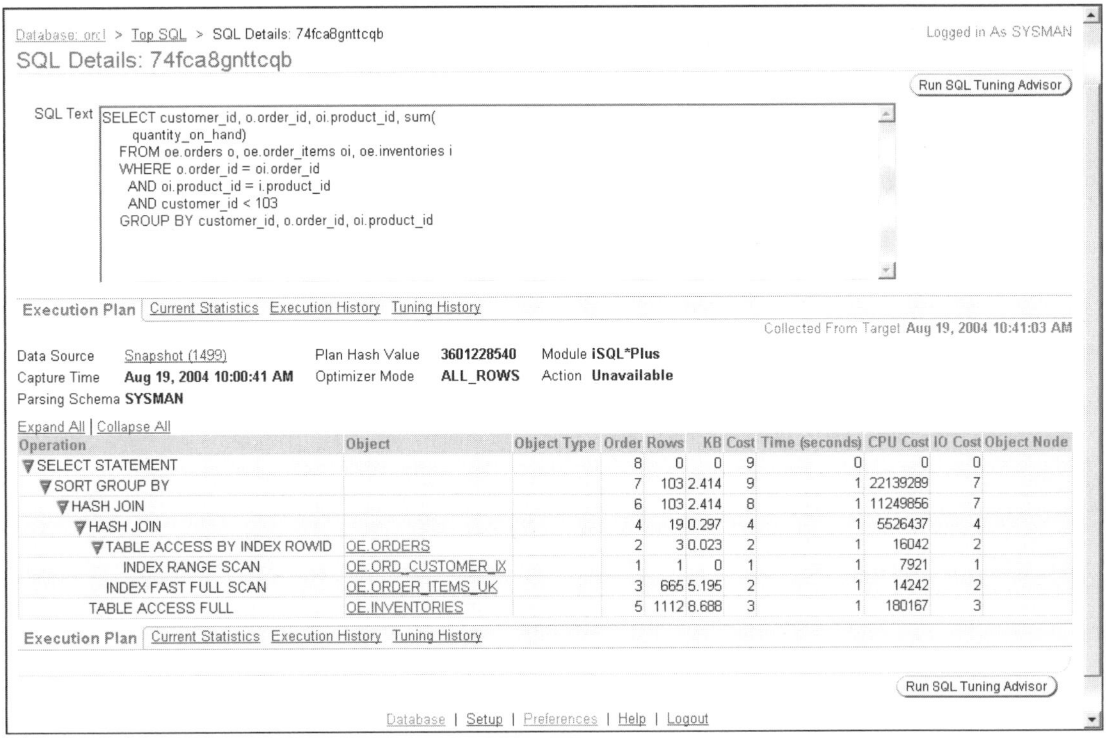

Database: orcl > Top SQL > SQL Details: 74fca8gnttcqb   Logged in As SYSMAN

SQL Details: 74fca8gnttcqb

Run SQL Tuning Advisor

SQL Text
```
SELECT customer_id, o.order_id, oi.product_id, sum(
      quantity_on_hand)
   FROM oe.orders o, oe.order_items oi, oe.inventories i
   WHERE o.order_id = oi.order_id
     AND oi.product_id = i.product_id
     AND customer_id < 103
   GROUP BY customer_id, o.order_id, oi.product_id
```

Execution Plan | Current Statistics | Execution History | Tuning History

Collected From Target Aug 19, 2004 10:41:03 AM

Data Source Snapshot (1499)   Plan Hash Value **3601228540**   Module **iSQL*Plus**
Capture Time **Aug 19, 2004 10:00:41 AM**   Optimizer Mode **ALL_ROWS**   Action **Unavailable**
Parsing Schema **SYSMAN**

Expand All | Collapse All

Operation	Object	Object Type	Order	Rows	KB	Cost	Time (seconds)	CPU Cost	IO Cost	Object Node
▼SELECT STATEMENT			8	0	0	9	0	0	0	
▼SORT GROUP BY			7	103	2.414	9	1	22139289	7	
▼HASH JOIN			6	103	2.414	8	1	11249856	7	
▼HASH JOIN			4	19	0.297	4	1	5526437	4	
▼TABLE ACCESS BY INDEX ROWID	OE.ORDERS		2	3	0.023	2	1	16042	2	
INDEX RANGE SCAN	OE.ORD_CUSTOMER_IX		1	1	0	1	1	7921	1	
INDEX FAST FULL SCAN	OE.ORDER_ITEMS_UK		3	665	5.195	2	1	14242	2	
TABLE ACCESS FULL	OE.INVENTORIES		5	1112	8.688	3	1	180167	3	

Execution Plan | Current Statistics | Execution History | Tuning History

Run SQL Tuning Advisor

Database | Setup | Preferences | Help | Logout

Figure 28-13: An execution plan in EM.

The display of information is a little different than you have seen in *i*SQL*Plus. For instance, each level in the plan is preceded by a blue arrow, which you can use to expand and contract the level. In addition, there is a lot of additional information close at hand, as you can see by the links at the bottom of the page.

V$SQL_PLAN and V$SQL_PLAN_STATISTICS

The data dictionary views `V$SQL_PLAN` and `V$SQL_PLAN_STATISTICS` are used to hold the actual execution plan and the actual statistics for the execution as performed by Oracle. These views are dynamic and only hold statistics for statements that are being held in the cursor cache for potential reuse. The `V$SQL_PLAN` view holds the planned execution steps, and the `V$SQL_PLAN_STATISTICS` hold the statistics based on the actual execution of a query, rather than the estimate based on statistics used `in EXPLAIN PLAN` and stored in `V$SQL_PLAN`.

Since the V$SQL_PLAN_STATISTICS view comes from the results of an SQL query, the view is the historical authority on what Oracle did. You can use standard SQL to retrieve information from the view if you have questions as to what Oracle actually did with a query.

Hints

We have emphasized several times that we believe that the Oracle optimizer, left to pursue its goals with the proper statistics, will deliver the optimal execution plan for almost all queries. There are rare exceptions where this may not be the case. For these rare occurrences, Oracle lets you use a hint, which can override the normal verdict of the optimizer in ways small and large.

A hint directs the optimizer to use a certain form of access for a particular step of the execution plan. For instance, if you add a hint to specify a full table scan for one of the tables in a query, the Oracle optimizer will take the suggestion for that particular table but use its own judgment (in the light of the forced execution step) for other parts of the plan.

Syntax of a Hint

To add a hint to an SQL statement, you use the following syntax:

```
KEYWORD /*+ hint */ rest_of_statement
```

Or:

```
KEYWORD --+ hint
rest_of_statement
```

where KEYWORD is the first word of the SQL statement — SELECT, INSERT, UPDATE, or DELETE — hint is the actual syntax of the hint, which depends on the hint and its parameters (detailed in the next section), and *rest_of_statement* is the remainder of the SQL statement. You can have more than one hint on an SQL statement, with each hint being separated by a space within the hint delimiters.

As you can see, the hint syntax is a lot like the syntax for a comment. In fact, if you don't use the correct syntax for the hint, the Oracle database will just ignore the hint altogether, thinking that it is just a comment. Oracle will not return an error in this case, since a comment can be anything, so you should always make sure you test a statement with a hint by looking at the execution plan to make sure that the hint was actually used by the Oracle optimizer.

Available Hints

Hints come in several varieties — optimizer mode hints, access path hints, join hints, query transformation hints, and parallel operations hints. The following tables summarize the hints in each category and supply the syntax for the particular hint.

Optimizer Mode Hints

The following hints control the operation of the optimizer itself.

Hint	Description	Syntax
FIRST_ROWS(*n*)	Tells the optimizer to create an execution plan that will return the first *n* rows as rapidly as possible. Appropriate to optimize interactive response. Cannot be used for all queries, such as those with an aggregate clause, which will require all rows to be collected before any can be returned.	/*+ FIRST_ROWS(*n*) */
ALL_ROWS	Tells the optimizer to create an execution plan that will return all rows as quickly as possible. More appropriate for batch operations.	/*+ ALL_ROWS */
CPU_COSTING	Causes the optimizer to take into account the cost in CPU cycles for operations. On by default.	/*+ CPU_COSTING */
NO_CPU_COSTING	Instructs optimizer to ignore CPU costs when calculating optimal execution plan.	/*+ NO_CPU_COSTING */
CHOOSE	Allowed optimizer to choose between rule-based optimizer and cost-based optimizer. Not supported in Oracle 10*g*.	/*+ CHOOSE */
RULE	Forced use of rule-based optimizer. Not supported in Oracle 10*g*.	/*+ RULE */

Access Path Hints

These hints force the optimizer to use a specific type of access for a table or view. These hints, by themselves, only specify access to a single table or view, so the optimizer may not use the hint if the access type indicated by the hint is not appropriate for the table or view when that object is accessed in the optimization process. The index_spec parameter, described for the INDEX hint, is used in many of these access path hints.

Hint	Description	Syntax
FULL	Suggests a full table scan on the specified table. We have found that the table must have an alias, and the alias is used in hint.	/*+ FULL(*table*) */
CLUSTER	Suggests a cluster scan on the specified table.	/*+ CLUSTER(*table*) */
HASH	Suggests a hash scan on the specified table.	/*+ HASH(*table*) */
INDEX	Suggests that the optimizer perform an index scan on the specified index or indexes. The *index_spec* is in the form of *table index* for each index in the spec. If the *index_spec* parameter contains one index, the optimizer does an index scan on that index. If the *index_spec* contains more than one index, the optimizer estimates the cost on each named index and does an index scan on the least expensive index. If there is no *index_spec*, the optimizer chooses the lowest cost index scan.	/*+ INDEX(*index_spec*) */

Table continued on following page

Hint	Description	Syntax
NO_INDEX	Disallows use of indexes specified in *index_spec*. If no indexes are specified, disallows use of all indexes on the table.	/*+ NO_INDEX (*index_spec*) */
INDEX_ASC / INDEX_DESC	Similar to INDEX hint. Normally, indexes are stored in ascending order, in which case the INDEX_ASC hint is exactly like the INDEX hint.	/*+ INDEX_ASC (*index_spec*) */ /*+ INDEX_DESC (*index_spec*) */
INDEX_COMBINE	Suggests use of combined bitmap indexes.	/*+ INDEX_COMBINE (*index_spec*) */
INDEX_JOIN	Suggests use of an index join for the statement.	/*+ INDEX_JOIN (*index_spec*) */
INDEX_FFS / NO_INDEX_FFS	Suggests or disallows a fast full index scan on an index. A fast full index scan is similar to a table scan, but on an index.	/*+ INDEX_FFS (*index_spec*) */ /*+ NO_INDEX_FFS (*index_spec*) */
INDEX_SS*	Series of hints that suggest the use of an index skip scan. The different hints are similar to the matching INDEX* hints.	/*+ INDEX_SS (*index_spec*) */
		/*+ INDEX_SS_ASC (*index_spec*) */
		/*+ INDEX_SS_DESC (*index_spec*) */
		/*+ NO_INDEX_SS (*index_spec*) */

Join Hints

There are actually two categories of join hints: hints pertaining to the order that joins are done in, which covers the LEADING and ORDERED hints, and hints on how join operations are accomplished. All of these hints are covered in the following table. When required, the *table_spec* parameter is a list of table aliases, separated by spaces.

Hint	Description	Syntax
LEADING	Specifies the order in which tables should be joined by the list of tables in *table_spec*.	/*+ LEADING(*table_spec)*
ORDERED	Specifies that tables should be joined in the order they are listed in the query.	/*+ ORDERED */
USE_NL	Forces the use of a nested loop for the join, with the first table alias in *table_spec* driving the loop.	/*+ USE_NL(*table_spec*) */

Hint	Description	Syntax
NO_ USE_NL	Suggests the use of hash join or sort merge for table join between two tables listed in *table_spec*. Oracle may not be able to accomplish join without a nested loop, which will cause hint to be ignored.	/*+ NO_USE_NL (*table_spec*) */
USE_NL_WITH_ INDEX	Similar to USE_NL, except that USE_NL will force a table scan of the inner table in the join.	/*+ USE_NL_WITH_ INDEX(*table_spec*) */
USE_MERGE / NO_ USE_MERGE	Specifies or disallows join to be done with a merge join.	/*+ USE_MERGE (*table_spec*)*/ /*+ NO_USE_MERGE (*table_spec*)*/
		USE_HASH /
NO_ USE_HASH	Causes join to be done with a hash join.	/*+ USE_HASH (*table_spec*)*/ /*+ NO_USE_HASH (*table_spec*)*/

Query Transformation Hints

The Oracle optimizer can do a number of magical tricks known collectively as query transformations. Query transformations let Oracle rewrite submitted SQL in order to take advantage of certain Oracle features, such as materialized views, to improve performance.

Hint	Description	Syntax
USE_CONCAT	Forces optimizer to transform compound `OR` conditions in `WHERE` clause to a set of separate queries with a `UNION ALL` to join them. Normally, this only happens if the cost of the transformation would be less.	/*+ USE_CONCAT */
NO_EXPAND	Prevents concatenation, described in previous hint, for compound `OR`s or `IN` clauses.	/*+ NO_EXPAND */
REWRITE	Forces rewrite of query to use materialized views, described in Chapter 26 on business intelligence query. If there is a *view_spec*, forces use of one of the listed views; without a *view_spec*, uses most appropriate materialized view.	/*+ REWRITE (*view_spec*) */
NO_REWITE	Disables query rewrite for query.	/*+ NO_REWRITE */
MERGE / NO_ MERGE	Instructs optimizer to merge a view into the overall query or to prevent this type of merge.	/*+ MERGE(*view_spec*) */ /*+ NO_MERGE (*view_spec*) */

Table continued on following page

Hint	Description	Syntax
STAR_ TRANSFOR-MATION / NO_ STAR_TRANSFOR-MATION	Instructs optimizer to either perform a star transformation, which, in a star schema, transforms the SQL WHERE clause into subqueries, or to disallow this transformation.	/*+ STAR_TRANSFOR MATION */
		/*+ NO_STAR_TRANS FORMATION */
FACT / NO_FACT	Used in the context of the star transformation to indicate that the table that is the object (table) of the hint either is or is not the fact table.	/*+ FACT (*table*) */
		/*+ NO_FACT (*table*) */
UNNEST / NO_ UNNEST	Forces optimization where a subquery is added into the main SQL statement or disallows it.	/*+ UNNEST */
		/*+ NO_UNNEST */
NO_QUERY_ TRANSFORMATION	Disallows use of any query transformations.	/*+ NO_QUERY_ TRANS FORMATION */

Parallel Operations Hints

Parallel operations, which were covered in Chapter 2 can also be directed with the following set of hints.

Hint	Description	Syntax
PARALLEL	Specifies the number of servers (*num_servers*) used for a particular table (*table*). The *table* parameter can be DEFAULT, which will cause the initial default value to be used.	/*+ PARALLEL (*table num_servers*) */
NO_PARALLEL	Disallows parallel execution on *table*.	/*+ NO_PARALLEL (*table*)
PARALLEL_INDEX	Specifies the number of servers (*num_servers*) used for a particular index (*index*). The *index* parameter can be DEFAULT, which will cause the initial default value to be used.	/*+ PARALLEL (*index num_servers*) */
NO_PARALLEL_ INDEX	Disallows parallel execution on *index*.	/*+ NO_PARALLEL (*index*) */
PQ_DISTRIBUTE	Specifies how rows from joined tables should be distributed over parallel servers..	For syntax information, refer to the Oracle documentation

Now Don't Use Them

Since hints are a valid piece of Oracle syntax, we feel a duty to explain their use to you, the Oracle developer. Having done that in the previous sections, we now feel that we should do our best to dissuade you from using them in the overwhelming majority of situations.

We have a few reasons for this effort:

- As mentioned earlier, Oracle does not return errors if a hint is incorrect. One of the results of this is merely inconvenient — you don't know if a hint is having the desired effect without testing. But another aspect of this behavior is more insidious. If you were to have a hint on a particular index, and the name of that index changed, the hint would no longer work, but Oracle would not let you know.
- Hints can be hard to locate in your SQL code, so it can be hard to estimate the impact of database changes on SQL that contain hints. For this reason and the previous one, you should carefully document your hints. Without this careful documentation, you could end up having to isolate and diagnose a performance problem caused by a hint that is no longer valid because of a changed object name.
- Over time, your database can change in structure and composition. If these changes could affect the way an SQL statement is optimized, a hint would prevent the improvement from taking place.
- The Oracle optimizer is improved with each new release, so any problem that your hint was designed to avoid may disappear. Each new release of the optimizer can take into account new features of the Oracle database that might end up improving the performance of your SQL even more, improvements that will be ignored when you use a hint to direct the optimizer.
- If you want to use a hint to stabilize performance, there are better ways to reach this goal. You can stabilize the way that an SQL query is executed by either not updating statistics, as described in the preceding item, or by using stored outlines, as described in the next section. By stabilizing your statistics, you can still test new releases for performance improvements by storing your statistics, updating them, and then restoring the old statistics if appropriate.

So when can you use hints appropriately? Only when you have explicitly performed the following three steps:

- You have determined the exact SQL statement that is causing a performance problem.
- You have tested the performance of the SQL statement in a production environment to establish a baseline performance.
- You understand why the Oracle optimizer made its choice. This step is frequently skipped, as developers blame what they think is an incorrect optimizer choice on a faulty decision process in the optimizer or a bug. Although we are sure that the readers of this volume are among the most brilliant developers in the world, the Oracle optimizer is the product of decades of work by some very smart people. If you don't understand why the optimizer made its decision, you may still have some things to learn about the Oracle database and its optimizer. Don't skip this step in the interest of "efficiency" — this step is where you will deepen your knowledge of Oracle in a way that will pay off many times over down the road.
- You test the SQL statement with the hint in a production environment to ensure that the hint actually does result in better performance.

Once you have completed these four steps, you have performed the proper due diligence for the use of the hint. Only after completing these steps should you deploy the newly hinted SQL into your production application.

Stored Outlines

Earlier in this chapter, we mentioned a feature in the Oracle database called a stored outline. A stored outline is a stored execution plan. When a particular SQL query has a stored outline, Oracle will simply use that execution plan, rather than going through the optimization process. In this way, a stored outline ensures that the execution plan will never change — a certainty referred to as *plan stability*.

Stored outlines are a set of hints that are used to guide the optimizer. As noted in the preceding section on hints, a few hints will not be used at all times. But hints protect an SQL query from changing because of changed statistics or runtime environment.

This feature contains both the virtues and the failings of stored outlines. A stored outline is a static entity, which can help to ensure consistent levels of performance. However, a stored outline cannot change in response to the changing composition of the database or runtime environment. If you choose to use a stored outline, you may be forgoing the option of an execution plan that will actually be better than the stored plan, because of changing conditions.

As with hints, you should carefully consider the pros and cons of using stored outlines before you jump at the reduced execution time they can produce. As with the collection of new statistics, you should consider testing in a real-world deployment scenario both with and without stored outlines to see if they will provide any actual performance benefits.

Creating Stored Outlines

You can create stored outlines in one of three ways. The first and broadest way is to set the initialization parameter `CREATE_STORED_OUTLINES` to `TRUE`. This setting causes the creation of stored outlines for every SQL statement while it is set.

The second method is to use the `CREATE OUTLINE` statement. The syntax for this statement is as follows:

```
CREATE OR REPLACE outline_name ON sql_statement
```

The `OR REPLACE` keyword is optional, but it must be used to update an existing outline. Additional keywords, as explained in the Oracle documentation, allow you to specify that an outline is public or private, is copied from an existing outline, has a specific name (`outline_name` in the syntax example) or uses the name generated by Oracle, or is assigned an outline to a category for easier comprehension.

You can also use procedures in the `DBMS_OUTLN` package to create and manage stored outlines. This package has procedures that let you create outlines, drop outlines, work with category outlines, and update outlines.

In order to create outlines, the current schema must have CREATE ANY OUTLINE privilege. To use the DBMS_OUTLN package, you must have the EXECUTE_CATALOG_ROLE privilege.

Using Stored Outlines

The USE_STORED_OUTLINES initialization parameter is used to tell Oracle to use any stored outlines. The syntax for the parameter is as follows:

```
USE_STORED_OUTLINES = TRUS/category_name/FALSE
```

Setting the parameter to TRUE enables the use of all categories, while using a *category_name* with the parameter only enables the use of stored outlines in that particular category. Setting the parameter to FALSE disables the use of stored outlines.

A similar parameter, USE_PRIVATE_OUTLINES, enables the use of outlines that exist in the current session only.

You can also use the ALTER OUTLINE SQL statement to enable or disable individual outlines, as well as perform different maintenance operations, such as rebuilding or renaming an outline or changing the category of an outline.

Editing Stored Outlines

You can also edit a stored outline. Enterprise Manager comes with an outline editor that allows you to change the hints associated with an outline in your own session. Once you are done editing a private copy of the outline, you can copy it from your private outline to the public outline — of course, after testing it thoroughly.

Of course, changing a stored outline carries with it some of the same downsides as using hints, in that you are forcing the Oracle database to optimize a query in a particular manner, regardless of the current Oracle environment. We strongly urge you to come to a complete understanding of your queries, through both contemplation and testing, as a preliminary step to the use of stored outline.

Summary

The subject of Oracle database performance is broad and deep. Many brilliant people have spent their whole working careers on this topic, creating thousands of pages of information — and they are still not done. This chapter was not meant to be a comprehensive guide to performance tuning for Oracle, but just an introduction to the concepts, data, and tools that will allow you to analyze the performance of your applications' data access.

Oracle has an advanced, cost-based optimizer, which uses statistics about both the data in the database and the database environment to select optimal access paths. You can set the optimizer mode to let Oracle know the type of access your application will require. These optimizer modes help to shape the outcome of the optimization process.

The results of the Oracle optimizer's work can be viewed through an execution plan, which lists the steps used to retrieve data. You can see this plan, as well as statistics reflecting the low-level operations performed in executing a query, with configuration switches in *i*SQL*Plus or with the use of Enterprise Manager, as well as other tools and data sources.

This chapter covered an explanation of optimizer hints, which guide the decisions made by the optimizer. The chapter listed available hints, but, more importantly, advises you not to use hints except as a last resort. The chapter closed with a discussion of stored outlines, used by Oracle to avoid the use of the optimizer redundantly.

We hope that you have gained some valuable knowledge in your reading of this book, and wish you the best of luck in all your endeavors, both Oracle-related and in the even more important parts of your life.

Index

Symbols and Numerics

A

D

E

F

I

K

L

M

N

O

P

S

V

W

Y